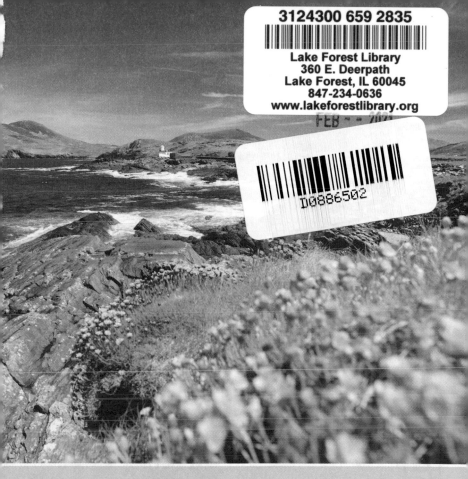

# THE ROUGH GUIDE TO
# IRELAND

This thirteenth edition updated by
**Norm Longley**

ROUGH
GUIDES

# Contents

**A NOTE TO READERS**

At Rough Guides, we always strive to bring you the most up-to-date information. This book was produced during a period of continuing uncertainty caused by the Covid-19 pandemic, so please note that content is more subject to change than usual. We recommend checking the latest restrictions and official guidance

ST. COLMAN'S CATHEDRAL AND COLOURED HOUSES IN COBH

# Introduction to
# **Ireland**

Over the past three decades, Ireland has transformed itself with quiet determination. Gone – or certainly on its way out – is the image of a conservative, introspective, dourly rural nation, while the infamous unrest and violence of the Troubles has, mercifully, faded away. An outward-looking Ireland has stepped forward, energized by rejuvenated cities, where the fresh ideas introduced by immigrants and returnees during the Celtic Tiger years of the 1990s are maturing nicely. Of course, it's not called the Emerald Isle for nothing and Ireland's physical appeal endures clear and true as a jewel – but it's by no means a blanket of green. From the Burren's grey limestone pavement and the black peat bogs of the Midlands (where some of the prehistoric gold ornaments on show in Dublin's National Museum were dug up) to Connemara's gold- and purple-tinged mountains, Ireland's smouldering – even unnerving – good looks can send a shiver down your spine. And when the sun is shining the sky throbs bluer than anywhere else on earth – or so the Irish would have you believe.

While Dublin, Belfast and the other cities are cranking up the cosmopolitan – from hipster coffee shops to edgy, internationally relevant arts scenes – their on-message worldliness is not the be all and end all: **traditional culture** is cherished by even the most city-slicking of the Irish. Moreover, as Northern Irish historian J. C. Beckett (1912–96) noted, his homeland "has no natural focal point, no great crossing-place of routes, no centre from which influence spreads naturally." The lay of the land and the **road network** lend themselves to a democratic exploration, with each part of the country fair game, and you're unlikely to feel swallowed up by the cities' gravitational pull. In **rural areas**, switch modes to walking boots or two wheels

THE ROCKY SHORE AT DUNAFF IN COUNTY DONEGAL

(motorized or otherwise) and you'll be in no great hurry to return to the urban sprawl, however vibrant.

In some areas **public transport** coverage fades to black, and you have no choice but to feel your way – the perfect opportunity to get to grips with Ireland's rich textures. The **west coast** is famous for its long beaches and windswept cliffs with views of the western islands; the drama of the landscape here is awe-inspiring, not least to the surfers who flock to Donegal and Galway. In the **east**, outside Dublin, the crumpled granite of the Wicklow Hills sits in stark contrast to the lush central plain just a few kilometres away. Cross the border into **Northern Ireland** and it is a short journey through rolling hills – known locally as drumlins – to the spectacular coast road that leads to the geological wonder of the **Giant's Causeway**.

Scattered across these landscapes is an abundance of **historic sites**. The very earliest of these include enigmatic prehistoric tombs, stone circles and hill forts. It is possible to trace the history of successive waves of immigration, whether Christian pilgrims, Viking raiders or Norman settlers, through the stone churches, distinctive **round towers** and high crosses strewn across the landscape. Ireland's **monasteries** were important centres of Christian learning during the Middle Ages, and the monks' elaborate craftsmanship is preserved in surviving illuminated manuscripts, such as the *Book of Kells*, held at Dublin's Trinity College. Doughty **castles** and tower houses record the twelfth-century Anglo-Norman invasion, while numerous **stately homes** from the

eighteenth and nineteenth centuries attest to the wealth and political power of the Protestant Ascendancy both north and south. A remarkable aspect of Ireland's landscape is the tendency for physical features to have **sacred associations** – few counties do not shelter a pile of stones called "Diarmuid and Gráinne's Bed", where the star-crossed lovers are said to have slept together on their flight from the great warrior Fionn Mac Cumhaill.

Inseparable from Ireland's history is its cultural heritage, a happy coming together of millennia and myriad influences from home and abroad. Here you have the richest store of **mythological traditions** in northern Europe, folkloric associations at every turn and world-famous literature and poetry. But there are a couple of elements you'll likely encounter in vivid form on a daily basis – particularly if you're a pub-goer. First you have **traditional music**, with its ballads and *sean-nós* ("old-style" Irish-language singing) recounting tales of love, history and humour. Then there's the *craic*, the talking therapy of Ireland's pubs, a combination of unlikely yarns, surreal comedy and plain old chatter and gossip. **Dublin**, which has long enjoyed a reputation as a culturally rich city, remains the epicentre of artistic activity. The Republic's capital is justifiably proud of its literary tradition, which takes in (among countless other luminaries) Oscar Wilde, Flann O'Brien and James Joyce, whose famously complex and experimental *Finnegans Wake* is – besides its many other triumphs – a worthy encapsulation of the sheer weightiness of Irish culture.

Ireland is rightly renowned for the **welcome** extended to visitors, and the tourist sector is, unsurprisingly, at the centre of its plans for lasting economic recovery. Northern Ireland and Belfast, in particular, have taken full advantage of the sudden influx of visitors previously deterred by the Troubles. What they will encounter is an Ireland where, finally, the past is significant for its **cultural riches** rather than the shadow it casts – and where the future is all about that big blue sky.

# Where to go

**Dublin** is the Republic's main entry-point, a confident capital whose raw, modern energy is complemented by rich cultural traditions, and which boasts outstanding **medieval monuments** and the richly varied exhibits of the **National Gallery** and **National Museum**. South of the city, the desolate **Wicklow Mountains** offer a breathtaking contrast to city life.

If you arrive on the **west coast** at Shannon Airport in County Clare, Ireland's most spectacular landscapes are within easy reach. **Clare**'s coastline rises to a head at the vertiginous **Cliffs of Moher**, while inland lies **the Burren**, a barren limestone plateau at odds with the lush greenery characteristic of much of Ireland. To Clare's south, Limerick's **Hunt Museum** houses one of Ireland's most diverse and fascinating collections. The **Wild Atlantic Way**, meanwhile, is a scenic west coast driving route launched in 2014 that encourages exploration on this side of the island.

**County Kerry**, south of Limerick, features dazzling scenery, an intoxicating brew of seascapes, looming mountains and sparkling lakes. Though the craggy coastline traversed by the **Ring of Kerry** is a major tourist attraction, it's still relatively easy to find seclusion. In County Galway, to Clare's north, lies enthralling **Connemara**, untamed bogland set between sprawling beaches and a muddle of quartz-gleaming mountains; in contrast, university cities such as **Galway** and **Limerick** provide year-round festivals and

## THE BEST PUBS FOR TRADITIONAL MUSIC

If the Irish didn't invent the **pub**, they've certainly espoused its cause with great vigour. Indeed, alongside the local church and the betting shop (for men), the pub retains a pivotal place in Irish society. It's the place where stories are narrated, deals and pacts are made, jokes are told and traditional music is heard. During the 1990s, the "Irish pub" concept (albeit with "authentic" period decor manufactured in Dublin) spread to far-flung points of the globe. Yet experiencing the real thing on its home turf to a live soundtrack of **traditional music** is still an unbeatable experience. With a pint of the black stuff in hand, here are some of the best, entirely authentic pubs to get you started on a lifelong love affair with *bodhráns*, tin whistles, pipes and fiddles:

- **Buckley's** Killarney (see page 276)
- **De Barra's** Clonakilty (see page 249)
- **The Five Points Whiskey & Alehouse** Belfast (see page 475)
- **O'Donoghue's** Dublin (see page 104)
- **Reel Inn** Donegal Town (see page 423)
- **Seán Og's** Tralee (see page 298)
- **Tigh Coili** Galway City (see page 343)

buzzing nightlife. Further north, **Donegal** offers a dramatic mix of rugged peninsulas and mountains, glistening beaches and magical lakes.

Dotted around the west coast are numerous **islands**, providing a glimpse of the harsh way of life endured by remote Irish-speaking communities. The **Arans** are the most famous – windswept expanses of limestone supporting extraordinary prehistoric sites – but the savagely beautiful landscape of the **Blasket Islands**, off Kerry's coast, is equally worthy of exploration. **Achill Island**, the largest and accessible by bridge, is home to five spectacular blue flag beaches.

On Ireland's southern coast, **Cork**'s shoreline is punctuated by secluded estuaries, rolling headlands and historic harbours, while **Cork city** itself is the region's hub, with a vibrant cultural scene and nightlife. Nearby, the pretty seaside town of **Cobh** (previously called Queenstown) is renowned as the departure point for over 2.5 million Irish immigrants bound for North America after the Great Famine, and as a port of call for the ill-fated RMS *Titanic* in 1912. To Cork's east, **Waterford city** houses the wondrous Viking and medieval collections of Waterford Treasures, while, in Ireland's southeastern corner, **Wexford**'s seashore features broad estuaries teeming with bird life and expansive dune-backed beaches.

THE RUINS OF HORE ABBEY IN TIPPERARY

Inland, the Republic's scenery is less enchanting, its **Midland** counties characterized by fertile if somewhat drab agricultural land, as well as broad expanses of **peat bog**, home to endangered species of rare plants. However, there is gentle appeal in Ireland's great watercourse, the **Shannon**, with its succession of vast loughs, and the quaint river valleys of the southeast.

Numerous **historic** and **archeological sites** provide fine alternative attractions. The prehistoric tomb at Meath's **Newgrange** and the fortress of **Dun Aengus** on Inishmore are utterly mesmerizing; County Cork features many **stone circles**; and there's a multitude of **tombs** and **ring forts** across the west coast counties. Stunning early **Christian monuments** abound, too, including those located on **Skellig Michael** and the **Rock of Cashel** and atmospheric sites at **Clonmacnois**, **Glendalough** and **Monasterboice**. Of more recent origin, the Anglo-Irish nobility's planned **estates**, developed during the eighteenth and nineteenth centuries around impressive Neoclassical mansions, are visible across Ireland.

Much of **Northern Ireland's** countryside is intensely beautiful and unspoiled. To the north are the green **Glens of Antrim** and a coastline as scenic as anywhere in Ireland, with, as its centrepiece, the bizarre basalt geometry of the **Giant's Causeway**. The **Antrim Coast Road**, meanwhile, is one of Ireland's most scenic drives. In the southeast, **Down** offers the contrasting beauties of serene **Strangford Lough** and the brooding presence of the **Mourne Mountains**, while, to the west, **Fermanagh** has the peerless lake scenery of **Lough Erne**, a fabulous place for watersports, fishing and exploring island monastic remains. Evidence of the Plantation is also provided by planned towns and various grand **mansions**, often set in sprawling, landscaped grounds.

To get to grips with the North's history, a visit to its **cities** is essential, not least for their tremendous museums: **Belfast**, with its ship-building past and grand public buildings, built on the profits of industry; **Derry**, which grew around the well-preserved walls of its medieval antecedent; and the cathedral town of **Armagh** where St Patrick established Christianity in Ireland.

# When to go

Whenever you visit Ireland it's wise to come prepared for wet and/or windy conditions, especially along the west coast, which faces the Atlantic, the source of much of Ireland and Britain's weather. On average (see page 45), it **rains** around 150 days a year along the east and southeast coasts, and up to as many as 225 days a year in parts of the west and southwest. April is the driest time across most of the island, while December and January are the wettest. Whatever the case, the weather is very changeable and you'll often find a soggy morning rapidly replaced by brilliant sunshine in the afternoon. Most years also see long periods of gorgeous weather, though predicting their occurrence is often well nigh impossible. Generally, the **sunniest months** (see page 45) are April, May and June, while July and August are the warmest with temperatures sometimes reaching as high as 25°C. Overall, the southeast gets the best of the sunshine.

# Author picks

Our authors scoured every inch of the Emerald Isle to bring you these hand-picked gems, from the best of Dublin's pubs to the glories of taking to two wheels in Co. Mayo.

**Ticking off Dublin's pubs** In Joyce's *Ulysses*, Leopold Bloom queried whether it would be possible to cross Dublin without passing a pub – and with more than seven hundred dotted around the city, it would be a mean feat indeed. A cliché it may be, but there's something very special about a perfect pint of Guinness in a Dublin pub – *The Palace Bar* (see page 102) offers you this and gorgeous interiors to boot.

**Twitching on Rathlin Island** Hop on board the Rathlin ferry from Ballycastle (see page 491) for the short crossing to Northern Ireland's only inhabited island. It's home to a colony of seals and an RSPB nature reserve attracting guillemots, puffins, razorbills and the red-billed chough.

**Live like royalty in Ashford Castle** The former home of the Guinness family, this 800-year-old castle (see page 370) is the definition of luxury. The majestic lakeside setting amid 350 acres of ancient woodland is a world away from the usual tourist hubbub.

**Bag a bargain in Belfast** From snazzy boutique clothes shops to quirky independent bookstores, many a pleasant afternoon can be spent indulging in some retail therapy in resurgent Belfast (see page 478).

**Cycle the Great Western Greenway** Opened in 2011, this glorious 42km route (see page 374), along a former railway track in Mayo, is the longest off-road walking and cycling trail in Ireland. Broken down into three easy-to-manage sections, it's a favourite with families: Achill to Mulranny (13km), Mulranny to Newport (18km) and Newport to Westport (11km).

Our author recommendations don't end here. We've flagged up our favourite places – a perfectly sited hotel, an atmospheric café, a special restaurant – throughout the Guide, highlighted with the ★ symbol.

RATHLIN ISLAND

CYCLING THE GREAT WESTERN GREENWAY

# 25

# things not to miss

It's not possible to see everything that Ireland has to offer in one trip – and we don't suggest you try. What follows, in no particular order, is a selective and subjective taste of the country's highlights: from geological wonders and ancient ruins to activities and experiences both on land and at sea. All highlights are colour-coded by chapter and have a page reference to take you straight into the Guide, where you can find out more.

1

### 1 WILD ATLANTIC WAY
See page 26
This coastal drive covers 2500km from Donegal to Cork and takes in some of the most rugged and awe-inspiring scenery in Europe.

### 2 TRINITY COLLEGE, DUBLIN
See page 62
Wonder at the ninth-century *Book of Kells*, housed in the Old Library, before wandering through the city-centre campus, taking in the best of Dublin's architecture.

### 3 TITANIC BELFAST
See page 461
Taking pride of place in the heart of Belfast's newly developed Titanic Quarter, this interactive museum takes visitors on a fascinating journey through the city's maritime heritage and the story of the ill-fated RMS *Titanic*.

### 4 TRADITIONAL MUSIC
See page 588
Often loud, often raucous and always fun, traditional Irish music can be heard in many pubs and at dedicated festivals such as the Willie Clancy Festival in Miltown Malbay every July.

### 5 SURFING AT TULLAN STRAND AND ROSSNOWLAGH BEACH
See page 418
Thunderous waves roll in at Ireland's surfing capital, attracting fans from around the globe.

6

7

8

### 6 BRÚ NA BÓINNE
See page 139
This extraordinary ritual landscape is simply one of the world's most important prehistoric sites.

### 7 GARNISH ISLAND
See page 261
Sail across from Glengarriff Pier, past the basking seals, to discover these magical, otherworldly gardens.

### 8 BANTRY HOUSE
See page 258
A magnificent setting for some lavish artworks, among formal gardens overlooking Bantry Bay.

### 9 SKELLIG MICHAEL
See page 281
A remarkable and inspiring early Christian hermitage clinging to a mountain summit on a wild, bleak island.

### 10 THE ROCK OF CASHEL
See page 221
Rising high above the Golden Vale, the Rock features an entrancing group of early ecclesiastical remains.

### 11 KILMAINHAM GAOL
See page 86

A grim encounter with the Spartan conditions experienced by those deemed enemies of the state, with superb displays on Irish political history and the gaol's restoration.

### 12 THE BURREN
See page 326

A barren expanse of cracked limestone terraces stretching towards the Atlantic, peppered with a multitude of fascinating megalithic remains.

### 13 GLENDALOUGH
See page 121

Often referred to as "the valley of the two lakes", this wonderfully remote and beautiful mountain valley also shelters an atmospheric monastery.

### 14 KINSALE
See page 243

Imposing forts and some of Ireland's finest cuisine – particularly during October's annual Gourmet Festival – in a glorious bayside setting.

### 15 BUNRATTY CASTLE & FOLK PARK
See page 315

Unashamedly touristy, this superbly restored medieval castle sits at one end of a fully replicated nineteenth-century Irish village. One of the best family days out in the country.

13

14

15

16

17

### 16 KILLARNEY NATIONAL PARK
See page 269
The grandeur of the lakes and mountains has been drawing visitors to Killarney for over three centuries.

### 17 HORN HEAD
See page 439
Possibly the most magnificent of County Donegal's numerous rugged peninsulas, with plenty of exhilarating cliff-top walks, guillemots, gulls and puffins.

### 18 THE GOBBINS CLIFF PATH
See page 486
One of the most hair-raising walks in Europe, this guided 2.5 hour walk crosses spectacular bridges, climbs jagged rock staircases, and follows a narrow path along a breathtaking cliff-face.

### 19 THE GIANT'S CAUSEWAY
See page 493
Marvel at the eerie but entirely natural basalt formation of the Causeway and discover the myths and legends that surround it in the award-winning visitor centre.

### 20 DERRY'S CITY WALLS
See page 502
A visit to Derry is incomplete without a stroll around the ramparts of the only completely walled city in Ireland.

18

19

20

21

22

23

www.galwayoysterfest.com

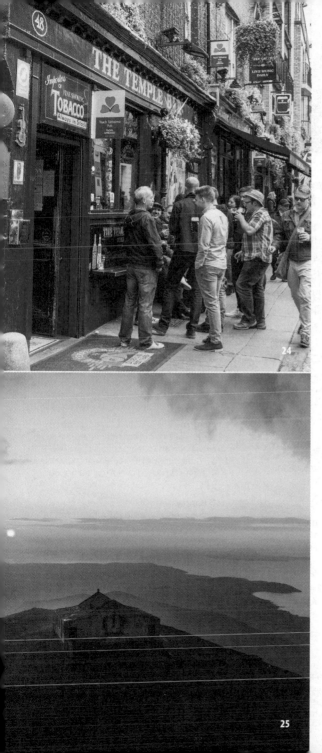

### 21 KYLEMORE ABBEY, CONNEMARA
See page 367
One of Connemara's most historic sites, the spectacular Kylemore Abbey comes with a beautifully restored walled garden and Neogothic church.

### 22 DUN AENGUS
See page 353
The spectacular cliff-edge "Fort of Aonghas" is the Iron Age capital of the Aran Islands.

### 23 GALWAY BAY OYSTERS
See page 337
Galway lays claim to Ireland's finest oysters – try your hand at a shucking competition during the Galway International Oyster and Seafood Festival every September.

### 24 DUBLIN PUBS
See page 101
Feel the heartbeat of the city's social life, with over seven hundred venues to choose from, fuelled by perfect pints of Guinness and healthy doses of *craic*.

### 25 CROAGH PATRICK
See page 373
It's a steep two-hour climb, but the fine views across Clew Bay, and the mountain's religious and historical resonance, make it all worthwhile.

# Itineraries

Ireland is compact but it packs an awful lot in. Five days on the Wild Atlantic Way guarantees a host of unforgettable vistas, while a few days in the southwest will introduce foodies to a feast of local delicacies. The coastline around the Giant's Causeway in the North is simply one of the world's great road trips – at 120 miles (190km) it can easily be driven in a day, though you're bound to want to slow down and savour the ride.

## A SOUTHWEST FOODIE TRIP

Allow three to four days to cover these 140km, sampling some of the finest produce the island has to offer, from seafood to superb cheeses.

❶ **Kinsale** The southwest's culinary honeypot boasts a beautiful harbour setting. For seafood lovers, the pick of the crop is the *Fishy Fishy Café and Restaurant*, serving up the freshest catch from the morning's haul. See page 243

❷ **Clonakilty** Heading west, you'll come to the source of the famous Clonakilty Black Pudding, sold at traditional butcher's Twomey's. Enjoy fine local produce for dinner at the *Inchydoney Island Lodge and Spa*, which overlooks the beach just outside of town. See page 247

❸ **Baltimore** Further southwest lies the small harbour village of Baltimore where the award-winning *Rolf's* makes a perfect leisurely lunch stop – it serves delicious local and organic lunches during the summer months. See page 252

❹ **Schull** Continue onto Schull where the Ferguson family produce their excellent Gubbeen cheese and meats. They sell at various local markets, including the Sunday morning Schull Market (Easter to Sept). See page 255

❺ **Durrus** The beautiful village of Durrus has an excellent option for dinner. In the evening head to the fabulous *Blairscove House & Restaurant*, with its impressive choice of Irish meats cooked over a roaring fire. See page 257

❻ **Bantry** Finish off your gastronomic gallivanting with a trip to Bantry Market, one of West Cork's largest. Located in the main square, it runs every Friday morning from 9.30am–1pm. See page 257

## CAUSEWAY COASTAL ROUTE

The distances are short but the views are immense on this spectacular road trip.

❶ **Carrickfergus** From Belfast, head north on the M2 to Carrickfergus, home to a twelfth-

---

**Create your own itinerary with Rough Guides**. Whether you're after adventure or a family-friendly holiday, we have a trip for you, with all the activities you enjoy doing and the sights you want to see. All our trips are devised by local experts who get the most out of the destination. Visit **www.roughguides.com/trips** to chat with one of our travel agents.

century Anglo-Norman castle, complete with cannons, portcullis and ramparts. See page 482

**❷ The Glens of Antrim** A drive through the Glens of Antrim guarantees waterfalls, forests, glacier-gouged valleys and the pretty villages of Carnlough, Cushendall and Cushendun – *Game of Thrones* fans might recognize some of the location backdrops en route. See page 486

**❸ Rathlin Island** Explore the market town of Ballycastle before hopping on the ferry to craggy Rathlin Island, which offers fantastic birdwatching and nature walks. Get some rest at the *Manor House*, a charming, National Trust-owned B&B. See page 491

**❹ The Giant's Causeway** Channel your inner Indiana Jones at Carrick-a-rede rope bridge before continuing on to the Causeway, with its world-famous rock formations. See page 493

**❺ Bushmills** Continue along the coastline to Bushmills for a tour (and a dram) at its famed whiskey distillery before booking in to the cosy *Bushmills Inn*. See page 495

**❻ Portstewart** Explore ruined Dunluce Castle (believed to have been the inspiration for Cair

Paravel in C. S. Lewis' *The Chronicles of Narnia*) then continue, via the classic seaside town of Portrush, to picturesque Portstewart, with its 3km stretch of golden sand. See page 497

**❼ Roe Valley Country Park** Sample Roe Valley Country Park's riverside walks, ending your trip at the Green Lane Museum. See page 499

## IRELAND'S ANCIENT EAST

Become immersed in Ireland's fascinating history, from ancient burial sites to Norman castles and Viking towns.

**❶ Greystones** Forty minutes south of Dublin, this picturesque seaside village is full of great places to eat and boutique shops. See page 115

**❷ Powerscourt Estate** Explore the most fabulous garden in Ireland on the grounds of a lavish eighteenth-century mansion. See page 118

**❸ St Kevin's Way** Follow the path of medieval pilgrims on this 29km trail that ends in the stunning monastic settlement of Glendalough. See page 122

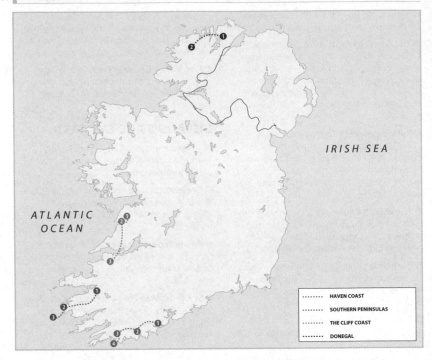

**❹ St Canice's Cathedral** Just over an hour south of Wicklow, Kilkenny city is a rambler's dream, full of winding medieval streets and historical distractions. At its heart is the magnificent St Canice's cathedral and round tower. See page 185

**❺ Dunbrody Famine Ship** On the way to Waterford it's worth the detour to visit this incredible reproduction of an 1840s emigrant vessel. With a guided tour, costumed performers, and fine exhibitions, it provides a unique insight into the lives of the many Irish forced to leave the country during the Famine. See page 200

**❻ Viking Waterford** Ireland's oldest city, Waterford recently celebrated its 1100th anniversary. Take a walk through the old city ("the Viking Triangle") and soak up the history. See page 204

## THE WILD ATLANTIC WAY

At over 2500km, the Wild Atlantic Way is the world's longest defined coastal touring route. Stretching the length of the rugged Atlantic

coast, from the Southern Peninsulas to the Northern Headlands, it's an unforgettable way to explore the west of Ireland. Although it's possible to travel the route by bus (and even bike), it's more relaxing to rent a car and enjoy it at your own pace. With so many tempting detours and unmissable sights, it can be a daunting task even choosing where to begin. These itineraries pick out some of the highlights on the route, starting in Cork and winding all the way up to Malin Head – the country's most northerly point. For more routes, interactive maps and a host of other resources visit ⓦ wildatlanticway.com.

## THE HAVEN COAST

### Day one

Starting in the handsome heritage town of Kinsale (see page 243), head south to the Old Head of Kinsale – a remarkable little peninsula with great views looking back on the town and the surrounding countryside. Continue west along the R600 to the pleasant town of Clonakilty (see page 247) to spend the night.

**Day two**

After sampling some of the famous Clonakilty black pudding, pay a visit to Inchydoney Beach (see page 247). Just south of the town, it was recently voted best beach in Ireland – quite an achievement considering the competition. Get back on the winding road and enjoy the beautiful scenery of the Haven Coast, stopping for lunch in Rosscarbery. From there it's a short trip to the Drombeg Stone Circle (see page 248), an ancient circle of seventeen large standing stones, believed to be over 2000 years old. Continue on to Skibbereen (see page 250), home to a fantastic heritage centre with a Great Famine commemoration exhibition.

**Day three**

From Skibbereen it's a twenty-minute drive to Baltimore (see page 252), an idyllic village and the perfect place to do a spot of whale-watching. Humpback whales, basking sharks, and Risso's dolphins can all be seen here. Finish the day with a fantastic meal in *Rolf's* restaurant and a few pints with the locals.

## SOUTHERN PENINSULAS

**Day one**

Starting in Killorglin (home of the Puck Festival; see page 275), it should take just under an hour to reach Cahersiveen (see page 278), a small town overlooking Valentia Harbour. From the town it's worth the fairly steep walk to the summit of Beentee Mountain to enjoy the panoramic views. Next visit Valencia Island (see page 280), a place of enduring traditional Irish culture. End the day in Portmagee (see page 279), a town of great pubs and even better seafood.

**Day two**

A visit to Skellig Michael (see page 281) is a must (although increased popularity due to the *Star Wars* film means advance booking is essential). A UNESCO World Heritage site, the island is home to a 1300-year-old monastic site, reached by a precarious ascent up an ancient stone stairway.

## THE CLIFF COAST

**Day one**

Spend the morning exploring the utterly unique and otherworldly landscape of the Burren (see page 326), calling into the Burren Nature Sanctuary in Kinvara. From there it's an hour's drive to the charming little village of Doolin (see page 324). Either head to the impressive Doolin Cave or catch one of the many trad sessions in the local pubs. Next it's a short drive to one of the highlights of the whole Wild Atlantic Way – the Cliffs of Moher (see page 325). Whether experienced on a clear day or in blustery rain, these magnificent cliffs are truly a sight to behold. It's then a fifteen-minute drive to Lahinch (see page 324), a lively town full of surfers and great places to eat and drink.

**Day two**

Leaving Lahinch, head for the Loop Head peninsula (see page 322), just over an hour away. The drive itself is stunning but be sure to climb the famous Loop Head lighthouse and take in the magnificent views that stretch from Kerry back up to the Cliffs of Moher. Finish the day in John. B Keane's in Listowel (see page 298), where you can learn the fine art of pulling the perfect pint of Guinness.

## DONEGAL

**Day one**

From Buncrana (see page 446) it's a 25-minute drive to the ancient site of Grianán Ailigh (see page 446). This stone fort sits majestically on the Inishowen Peninsula, and the panoramic views are breathtaking. Afterwards continue up to Malin Head (see page 449), the most northerly point in Ireland. Enjoy a blustery walk around Banba's Crown before heading back to Buncrana for the night.

**Day two**

Everything that makes the Wild Atlantic Way so special is distilled in this drive around Donegal's Northern Headlands – stunning vistas, great food and drink, and a palpable connection to the past. Starting again in Buncrana, this time head for the village of Rathmullan (see page 441), from where the Flight of the Earls took place in 1607. Push onward to Fanad Head (see page 441), stopping along the way to enjoy some incredible beaches and coastal viewpoints. Pop into *The Singing Pub* (see page 440) for lunch before heading to the gorgeously picturesque Glenveagh National Park & Castle (see page 436).

DUBLIN'S MODERN TAKE ON THE TRADITIONAL GEORGIAN DOOR

# Basics

# Getting there

**Dublin is the Republic of Ireland's main point of arrival, Belfast that of the North, while Shannon, near Limerick city in Co. Clare, is the major airport giving direct access to the west coast.** There's an ever-changing route map of flights between Britain and Ireland – book early to get the best price. Train–ferry and bus–ferry combinations are kinder to the environment and generally cheaper, though of course they take longer. For those bringing their own car, there's a wide range of ferry routes from southwest Scotland, northwest England and Wales to Northern Ireland, Dublin and Wexford. North American visitors can fly direct to Shannon, Dublin or Belfast, but those from South Africa, Australia and New Zealand have to travel via Britain, Europe or the Gulf. If you're thinking of booking an organized tour, there are plenty of interesting options based in Ireland that have an online presence.

## Flights from Britain

It's never been easier or cheaper to fly from Britain to Ireland. There are dozens of **routes** available, with new destinations regularly appearing and unsuccessful routes being phased out. With so much competition, **prices** can be ridiculously cheap, especially if you book online. The secret is to book as early as possible: the biggest carrier, Ryanair, for example, offers fares of under £20 one-way if booked well in advance, but these can rise to over £150 one-way if left till the last minute. Flight time between London, for example, and any airport in Ireland is between one hour and one hour thirty minutes.

## Flights from the US and Canada

**From the US and Canada**, Aer Lingus, the national airline of the Republic, offers the widest choice of routes, including nonstop flights from Boston, Chicago, New York, Orlando, San Francisco, Toronto and Washington to Dublin, and from Boston and New York to Shannon. If booked well in advance, their low-season fares from New York (JFK) to Dublin start at around US$600 return (including taxes), from San Francisco around US$950 and Can$660 from Toronto. In high season fares rise to US$1070 from New York, US$1400 from San Francisco, Can$1110 from Toronto. Flying time to Dublin, for example, is around six hours thirty minutes from New York and Toronto and ten hours fifteen minutes from San Francisco.

## Flights from Australia, New Zealand and South Africa

Travel from Australia, New Zealand and South Africa is generally via London, or one of the other European or Gulf cities such as Frankfurt or Abu Dhabi which have nonstop flights to Ireland. From Australia and New Zealand, it takes over twenty-four hours to reach Ireland, from South Africa at least thirteen hours. **Fares** (including taxes) to Dublin from Sydney start at around A$1500, from Auckland around NZ$1750, and from Johannesburg around R6000.

## Ferries

Ferry **routes** to Ireland are detailed below, along with the length of each voyage; Ⓦaferry.com will give you an overview of what's currently available and allow you to compare prices. High-speed catamarans (which also take cars) operate on some of these routes (see page 30), though some don't run in the winter and in bad weather they're more likely to be cancelled than regular ferries.

**Prices** vary hugely according to the time of year, and even the day and hour you travel. Most ferry companies have peak seasons of July and August and may charge higher fares around public holidays; generally, it's cheaper to travel midweek, and to book online and in advance. As an example of prices, Stena Line's single fares for a car and driver from Holyhead to Dublin Port cost from around

---

## A BETTER KIND OF TRAVEL

At Rough Guides we are passionately committed to travel. We believe it helps us understand the world we live in and the people we share it with – and of course tourism is vital to many developing economies. But the scale of modern tourism has also damaged some places irreparably, and climate change is accelerated by most forms of transport, especially flying. We encourage all our authors to consider the carbon footprint of the journeys they make in the course of researching our guides.

£80 off-peak (Tues & Wed) to around £160 at peak times (weekends); additional passengers cost £30 per adult, while foot passengers are charged £35 per adult, plus £10 per bicycle.

## Trains

Combined train and boat journeys from Britain generally use one of three **routes** across the Irish Sea: Cairnryan to Belfast, Holyhead to Dublin or Fishguard to Rosslare. Journey times are generally quicker than by coach: London to Dublin, for example, takes around eight hours, Glasgow to Belfast as little as four hours fifty minutes.

Ticket prices are **calculated** partly on a zonal basis, but also depend on which boat you take and whether you book in advance. For Dublin, they range from £38 single from Manchester, for example, including the cost of a boat from Holyhead, while from London they start at £47; add around £18 one-way if you're continuing by train to Cork, for example. Online, you can **book** train–boat tickets through Raileasy or Irish Ferries. Otherwise, you can book tickets in person at most railway stations in Britain, including through-tickets to other places in Ireland.

## Buses

The main bus services to Ireland are provided by National Express and Bus Éireann, under the brand name **Eurolines**, crossing the Irish Sea via Cairnryan, Holyhead and Pembroke. They can be cheaper than travelling by train if booked well in advance, but take far longer. The daily through-service from London to Dublin, for example, takes around twelve hours thirty minutes and **costs** £69 for a standard return. Direct coaches also run between other major cities in Britain and Ireland; a standard return ticket from London to Cork can cost £48, for example. Cheap advance offers, known as "funfares", can be accessed online, and reductions are also available for anyone under 26 or over 59. Tickets can be **booked** at any National Express agent, by phoning ☎08717 818178, or online at ⓦ eurolines.co.uk.

### AIRLINES

#### FROM BRITAIN
**Aer Lingus** ⓦ aerlingus.com
**British Airways** ⓦ britishairways.com
**Cityjet** ⓦ cityjet.com
**easyJet** ⓦ easyjet.com
**Jet2.com** ⓦ jet2.com
**Ryanair** ⓦ ryanair.com

#### FROM THE US AND CANADA
**Aer Lingus** ⓦ aerlingus.com
**Air Canada** ⓦ aircanada.com
**Air Transat** ⓦ airtransat.com
**American Airlines** ⓦ americanairlines.com
**Delta** ⓦ delta.com
**Lufthansa** ⓦ lufthansa.com
**United** ⓦ united.com

#### FROM AUSTRALIA, NEW ZEALAND AND SOUTH AFRICA
**Air New Zealand** ⓦ airnewzealand.com
**British Airways** ⓦ britishairways.com
**Emirates** ⓦ emirates.com
**Etihad Airways** ⓦ etihad.com
**Lufthansa** ⓦ lufthansa.com
**Qantas** ⓦ qantas.com
**Singapore Airlines** ⓦ singaporeair.com
**South African Airways** ⓦ flysaa.com

### FERRY AND CATAMARAN CONTACTS

**Irish Ferries** ☎08717 300 400, ⓦ irishferries.com. Holyhead to Dublin Port (3hr 25min, catamaran 1hr 50min); and Pembroke to Rosslare (4hr).
**P&O** ☎01304 448888, ⓦ poferries.com. Cairnryan to Larne (2hr); Liverpool to Dublin (8hr 30min).
**Stena Line** ☎08447 70 70 70, ⓦ stenaline.co.uk. Fishguard to Rosslare (3hr 30min); Liverpool to Belfast (8hr); Holyhead to Dublin Port (3hr 15min); and Cairnryan to Belfast (2hr 15min).

### RAIL CONTACTS

**The Man in Seat 61** ⓦ seat61.com
**Raileasy** ⓦ raileasy.co.uk

### AGENTS AND OPERATORS

**Bunk Campers** Northern Ireland ☎028 9081 3057, ⓦ bunkcampers.com. Campervan rental in Belfast and Dublin.
**Extreme Ireland** Republic of Ireland ☎01 907 3265, ⓦ extremeireland.ie. Hiking and adventure multi- and one-day tours all around Ireland; activities include kayaking, horseriding, mountain-climbing and cycling.
**Go Visit Ireland** Republic of Ireland ☎066 976 2094, ⓦ govisitireland.com. Small-group, customized and self-guided walking, cycling and hike-and-bike tours mostly on the west coast, as well as horseriding and kayaking.
**Ireland Walk Hike Bike** Republic of Ireland ☎087 250 2434, ⓦ irelandwalkhikebike.com. Kerry based outfit offering a wide range of guided and self-guided walking holidays in the region, as well as self-guided cycling holidays.
**Irish Boat Rental Association** Republic of Ireland ⓦ boatholidaysireland.com. Umbrella association of companies who rent out cruisers for holidays on the Shannon. See ⓦ iwai.ie or ⓦ waterwaysireland.org for fuller listings across the country.
**Irish Cycling Safaris** and **Irish Ways** Republic of Ireland ☎01

260 0749, Ⓦ cyclingsafaris.com and Ⓦ irishways.com. Long-established and well-regarded companies, based at University College Dublin, offering guided and self-led cycling and walking tours all over the country, with accommodation and luggage transfer covered.

**Irish Horse-Drawn Caravans Federation**

Ⓦ irishhorsedrawncaravans.com. Companies in Wicklow, Laois and Mayo offering horse-drawn caravan holidays, driving and sleeping in traditional, wooden covered wagons.

# Getting around

It's easy to travel between the Republic's larger towns and cities by public transport. However, it's common for small towns and villages to have just one or two bus services per week, often geared towards market days. Transport in Northern Ireland is equally sparse in rural areas, with just a few train lines across the region, though the bus network is pretty comprehensive. Renting a car is perhaps the easiest way to explore rural and remote areas across Ireland, though traffic has become increasingly heavy on major routes. Picturesque areas are particularly enjoyable on a bike, though you may need to bring your own as rental outlets have dried up in rural areas. If you want to travel quickly from Dublin or Belfast to outlying areas, it's also worth considering the internal flights available.

## By rail

Train services in the **Republic** are operated by Iarnród Éireann (Irish Rail; Ⓦ irishrail.ie). Prices are usually higher than taking a coach, though journeys are often much quicker – for example, the train from Dublin to Killarney can take at least two and a half hours less than the bus. Most of the lines fan out from Dublin towards the southern and western coasts, but there are few links between them, and some counties (such as Donegal and Cavan) have no rail links at all.

**Tickets** come in a variety of formats – single, day return, open return, family day and open returns, and student tickets. However, bear in mind that a standard single is much more than half the cost of an open return ticket – for example, a standard single from Dublin to Killarney is €68.55, a return €89.75. Tickets booked online in advance for specific trains are generally much cheaper – as little as €24 for a Dublin–Killarney single; if you miss your train, you can pay an extra €10 at the ticket office to get on a later service, if seats are available.

The only line operating **between the Republic and the North** is the Dublin–Belfast Enterprise service. The **North**'s rail service is operated by Translink (Ⓦ translink.co.uk) and restricted to just a few lines running out of Belfast. Services are generally efficient and the rolling stock has been recently updated. Fares are pretty reasonable – for example, travelling from Belfast to Derry costs £13 single and £19.50 day return – and often comparable with bus services.

You can also **transport bikes** on trains (see page 33).

### Rail and bus passes

Although rail passes for travel within the Republic represent reasonably good value, a combined bus and rail pass, such as the Irish Explorer, is probably more useful owing to the limitations of the rail network. Passes are available at all major train and bus stations.

The Trekker ticket (€110) allows unlimited travel over the Republic's rail network for four consecutive days. The **Irish Explorer** pass (€160) covers five days' rail travel out of fifteen consecutive days, though you can extend this to cover both rail travel and bus travel on Bus Éireann services for eight days out of fifteen days (€245).

For travellers just visiting Dublin, it can be worthwhile investing in a Leap Visitor Card, which offers unlimited travel on bus, DART, and Luas services. A one-day pass costs €10, three days costs €19.50, and seven days €40.

Bus Éireann offers an **Open Road** pass for travel on buses within the Republic, which can be purchased online (Ⓦ buseireann.ie). Three days' travel out of six, for example, costs €60, with the option to extend it for €16.50 per day.

In the North, Translink's Rambler ticket (£9.50) provides unlimited travel around the bus network after 9.15am on Sundays and during school holidays (including July and August). Families can take advantage of a variety of day passes for trains and/ or buses.

If your visit to Ireland is just part of a grander European trip, it's well worth investigating the range of different passes on offer, such as InterRail (Ⓦ inter-rail.eu) and Eurail (Ⓦ eurail.com).

## By bus

**Bus Éireann** (Ⓦ buseireann.ie) runs express coach and slower local services throughout the Republic. Ticket prices are generally far more reasonable than trains and you can often snap up cheap deals, especially between Dublin and Cork. Timetables and fares (including special deals) for the major routes can be found on the website. The majority of buses show destinations in both Irish and English, but some in rural areas may only display the former.

A vast number of **private bus companies** also operate in the Republic, running services on major routes, as well as areas not covered by the Bus Éireann network (especially Co. Donegal). The names, contact details and routes of these companies are listed in the Guide, where applicable. These can sometimes be cheaper and quicker than Bus Éireann, but are usually very busy at weekends, when advance booking is advisable.

In **Northern Ireland**, Metro (Belfast city buses), **Ulsterbus** (local buses) and **Goldline** (long-distance), all part of Translink (see page 31), run a pretty comprehensive network of regular and reliable services across Northern Ireland.

You can **transport bikes** on buses (see page 33).

# By car and motorcycle

Travelling by **car** or **motorbike** is the ideal way to explore at your leisure, especially in remote areas. You might be tempted to take on the Wild Atlantic Way, a signposted route around the west coast all the way from west Cork to Donegal (see page 26) – and if you enjoy that, you could keep going along the Causeway Coastal Route, which runs from Derry to Belfast for over 300km, mostly along the N2. If you bring your own vehicle, it's essential to carry its registration document and certificate of **insurance** – and make sure that your existing policy covers you for driving in Ireland. Whether bringing your own vehicle or renting one on arrival, you'll need to be in possession of a valid **driving licence** (and should carry it with you – a photocopy is insufficient). A driving licence from any EU country is treated like an Irish licence, while all other visitors are allowed to drive on a valid non-EU licence for a stay of up to 12 months.

In the Republic, unleaded **petrol** costs around €1.40 a litre; the equivalent price in Northern Ireland is about £1.25.

## Rules of the road

The fundamental rule of the road in Ireland, both North and South, is to **drive on the left**. Wearing **seat belts** is compulsory for drivers and passengers, as is the wearing of helmets for motorcyclists and their pillion riders. The Republic's **speed limits** are 50–60km/h in built-up areas (though in some parts of inner-city Dublin it's 30km/h), 80km/h on rural roads (denoted by the letter "R" on maps and signposts), 100km/h on national roads (denoted by an "N", and a green colour scheme on signposts) and 120km/h on motorways ("M" roads, with a blue colour scheme on signposts). Maximum speeds in Northern Ireland are 20–40mph in built-up areas, 70mph on motorways and 60mph on most other main roads. Minor rural roads in the Republic are generally poor in quality, often potholed and sometimes rutted – a situation notably different from the North where the overwhelming majority of roads, of all categories, are well maintained. **Signposts** in the Republic generally provide place names in both Irish and English, though in the Gaeltacht (Irish-speaking areas) you'll only encounter signposts in Irish. Virtually all signposts in the Republic provide distance information in kilometres; in the North distances are given in miles.

## Parking

Throughout Ireland many town centres require payment for on-street **parking**, either using ticket machines or a disc or card parking scheme (discs or cards can be purchased in adjacent shops). If you don't display a ticket or disc you may end up with a parking fine or, particularly in Dublin, Cork and Galway, your car being clamped or towed away.

## Car rental

Outlets of multinational **car rental companies**, such as Avis and Hertz, can be found at airports, in the cities and in some tourist towns. Rental charges are fairly high – expect to pay around €35/£30 per day plus insurance – though prices are often much cheaper in the Republic than in the North, with the best offers garnered if you book well in advance, especially via the internet. Sometimes smaller local firms can undercut the big names.

In most cases, you'll need to be 23 or over (though some companies may accept younger drivers with a price hike) and able to produce a full and valid driving licence, with no endorsements incurred during the previous two years. Considering the nature of Ireland's roads, it's always advisable to pay for extra collision damage waiver (CDW). The daily rate for this from the car-rental companies is usually at least €10/£7, or you can buy it more cheaply in advance from specialist insurance agencies (such as ⓦ icarhireinsurance.com), but it guarantees that you won't be liable for a hefty bill if you suffer an accident or any other damage. If you're planning to cross the border, ensure that your rental agreement provides full insurance; in some cases, you may need to pay extra.

Booking a car prior to your journey saves time when you arrive in Ireland and provides the chance to shop around on the web for the best deals. We've listed the main brokers and agencies below.

## CAR-RENTAL AGENCIES

**Argus** Ⓦ arguscarhire.com
**Auto Europe** Ⓦ autoeurope.com
**Avis** Ⓦ avis.com
**Budget** Ⓦ budget.com
**Car Rental Ireland** Ⓦ carrentalireland.com
**Dan Dooley** Ⓦ dan-dooley.ie
**Europcar** Ⓦ europcar.com
**Great Island** Ⓦ greatislandcarrentals.com
**Hertz** Ⓦ hertz.com
**Holiday Autos** Ⓦ holidayautos.co.uk
**Nova** Ⓦ novacarhire.com
**Thrifty** Ⓦ thrifty.com

## By bike

Apart from some steep ascents, occasional poor road surfaces and an unpredictable climate, Ireland provides ideal territory for **cycling**, one of the most enjoyable ways to explore the country's often stunning scenery. The tourist board's website, Ⓦ ireland.com, details waymarked **trails across the island** (see page 42), as well as specialist cycling-tour operators.

If you plan to **bring your own bike**, note that some airlines will transport bicycles for free as long as you keep within your weight allowance, but it's always worth checking with them well in advance.

Across the island, minor roads in rural areas are generally quiet, but major roads are well worth avoiding due to heavy traffic. Bikes are easy to **transport** over long distances by train, but less so by bus. In the Republic, the cost of taking a bike on a mainline train is €6 (free on Dublin–Belfast trains) and is most easily booked online. On DART and commuter services you can take bikes with you for free but only **at off-peak hours**. Folding bicycles incur no charge and can be carried on any service.

Bus companies will generally allow bikes to be carried for a fee, as long as there is room in the luggage compartment. In the Republic, prices vary according to the company but can come to over €10 for a long journey. Folding bicycles can be brought at no extra cost. In the **North** carrying a bike is free on Ulsterbus and Goldline services and on the trains, but is only permitted on the latter at off-peak hours.

### Bike rental

Thanks to a rise in insurance premiums, far fewer places in the Republic now **rent out** bikes – though **Dublin** now has a city bike scheme (see page 93) – and there are still just a small number of outlets in

the North, meaning that it's always wise to book your wheels well ahead. Rental rates are generally around €20 per day, €120 per week, with an extra charge of €5 per day or €20 per week for hiring panniers, though a helmet is usually included free. A deposit of anything from €100 to €200 is also required. When collecting your bike, check that its brakes and tyres are in good condition, and make sure that it comes equipped with a pump and repair kit. If you're planning on cycling in upland areas it makes sense to rent a bike with at least sixteen gears and preferably 24.

## By air

The quickest way to reach outlying areas is to take a scheduled flight to one of the **regional airports** dotted around the country. Aer Lingus operates the largest network. Prices can be as little as €40 one-way, if booked online well in advance, and much time can be gained; for instance, the flight from Dublin to Donegal takes only an hour, compared with at least four hours on the bus.

## DOMESTIC AIRLINES

**Aer Lingus** Ⓦ aerlingus.com
**Ryanair** Ⓦ ryanair.com

# Accommodation

**You'll find accommodation to suit most budgets across Ireland, from swish city hotels and luxurious converted castles to historic country houses and B&Bs. There are also plenty of hostels, varying hugely in quality and atmosphere, but all providing a bed and usually a kitchen; lots offer much more. Finally, there are well-run campsites and, for the hardy, the chance to pitch a tent in a farmer's field or on common land.**

You'll need to book your accommodation well in advance over **St Patrick's Day**, **Easter**, summer **public holidays** (see page 47), and during all of **July** and **August**. Accommodation is at a premium in Dublin throughout the year, especially at weekends, and may be booked out in places such as the **Aran Islands**, **Belfast**, **Cork**, **Derry**, **Dingle**, **Galway city**, **Kilkenny** and **Killarney**, and during major festivals elsewhere (see page 38). Be aware that during busy periods or popular events (concerts, rugby matches, and so on) prices can be hiked to eye-wateringly exorbitant rates. Many establishments close over the Christmas period.

## ACCOMMODATION PRICES

Throughout this book, for hotels, guesthouses and B&Bs, we've noted how much you can expect to pay for a **double room in high season**. Unless otherwise indicated, breakfast is included, but do check this at the time of booking. For **hostels**, we've given a per-adult price for dorms in high season and, where appropriate, a per-room price for double or twin rooms. For **campsites**, we've noted the price for two adults and a tent in high season.

Some establishments provide **single rooms**, but, in most cases, single travellers will occupy a double room. In hotels, there may be no discount on the room price at all for single occupation. You're more likely to get a good deal at traditional B&Bs, where the single rate may be around 25 percent higher than the cost of a double per person.

### ACCOMMODATION CONTACTS

**Adams & Butler** ⓦ adamsandbutler.com. A selection of mostly rural and historic houses and castles across Ireland for luxury self-catering.

**B&B Ireland** ⓦ bandbireland.com. The major B&B association in the Republic (plus a few members in the North), with over a thousand tourist-board-approved members and booking available on its website.

**Good Food Ireland** ⓦ goodfoodireland.ie. This network of high-quality food purveyors includes a large number of good hotels where the emphasis is on cuisine.

**Hidden Ireland** ⓦ hiddenireland.com. Over thirty B&Bs in private homes, mainly in the Republic, most of which are selected for their historic nature or architectural merit, as well as a similar number of self-catering properties.

**Ireland's Blue Book** ⓦ irelands-blue-book.ie. Upmarket country-house hotels and B&Bs, as well as restaurants, both North and South.

**Irish Farmhouse Holidays** ⓦ irishfarmholidays.com. More than 300 farmhouse B&Bs, some in exquisite rural locations.

**Irish Hotels Federation** ⓦ irelandhotels.com. Covering numerous hotels and guesthouses across Ireland, with a comprehensive listing, direct booking and special offers available on the website.

**Irish Self Catering Federation** ⓦ letsgoselfcatering.ie. Tourist-board-approved site, a good starting point for finding your preferred holiday home.

**Northern Ireland Hotels Federation** ⓦ nihf.co.uk. Smaller than its equivalent in the Republic, but still offering an extensive range of around a hundred hotels and guesthouses.

### B&Bs and guesthouses

The overwhelming majority of **B&Bs** and **guesthouses** across Ireland are welcoming family homes and provide clean and cosy rooms, usually with en-suite facilities. Most B&Bs in the Republic, and virtually all in Northern Ireland, are registered with the official tourist board, but many other places open their doors during local festivals or high season. Registration is usually a guarantee of well-maintained standards and good service, though non-registered places are not necessarily of lower quality. Most B&Bs and guesthouses serve mammoth **breakfasts** (see page 37).

## Hotels

In most areas **hotels** are usually the most expensive option, particularly in cities such as Dublin, Galway and Belfast which provide high-end "boutique" accommodation as well as the big chains such as Sheraton and Radisson. Offering more character are Ireland's country houses, mansions and castles, offering sumptuous rooms in astonishingly scenic locations. Aimed at weekend breakers, these often also provide spa facilities and gourmet restaurants.

Away from the main tourist areas, it's still possible to find real bargains. Most hotels in the Republic offer reductions mid-week, but in the North, especially in Belfast or Derry, you're far more likely to get a good deal at the weekend. Budget chains Jury's Inn, Premier Inn and Travelodge also have a growing presence in the major cities and can offer very competitive deals if booked in advance.

## Hostels

Well-run, good-quality **hostels** can be found across all of Ireland, often in lovely, off-the-beaten-track locations. Meals, bike rental and other facilities are also sometimes provided, as detailed within the Guide. Booking ahead is advisable, especially in Dublin and Galway at all times, and elsewhere during high season or local festivals.

### Independent hostels

There are dozens of **independently run hostels** across Ireland, many belonging to the Holiday Hostels of Ireland association (IHH; ⓦ hostels-ireland.com) or the Independent Hostel Owners organization (IHO; ⓦ independenthostelsireland.com). All IHH hostels are approved by either Fáilte Ireland or the NITB (see page 48), meaning that their facilities meet certain standards. Some IHO hostels are also approved, but those that aren't usually provide equivalent facilities. Most hostels offer dorms of varying sizes, as well as smaller private and family rooms, and are open year-round.

The character of independent hostels varies enormously, from the serene and bucolic to the urban and noisy. Though most hostels are efficiently run, there's generally a relaxed atmosphere, often with no curfews. In the most popular tourist areas, however, they can be crammed to the rafters at busy times. The vast majority provide free bedding, but some may charge a fee for a sheet sleeper, and many will charge for a towel. In high season expect to pay €20–30 for a dorm bed in Dublin, and around €15–25 elsewhere; in Northern Ireland you'll usually pay £10–20.

### An Óige and HINI hostels

The Republic's Youth Hostel Association, **An Óige** (centralized booking on ☎01 830 4555, or at Ⓦanoige.ie; annual membership €25, under-25s €15, family €45), has 24 hostels concentrated mainly in popular tourist spots. Most offer smaller dorms or private rooms, usually with very good facilities, especially in some of the urban hostels. Rates are around €12–25 per night depending on season and room. **Hostelling International Northern Ireland** (HINI; ☎028 9032 4733, Ⓦhini.org.uk; annual membership £15, under-25s £10, family £30, one-adult family £15) has just four hostels, most of which are recently built or refurbished. Prices are around £10–20 per night.

Membership of either organization or the umbrella **Hostelling International** (HI) is not needed to stay in an An Óige or HINI hostel, but it does give you ten percent off accommodation at most hostels, as well as providing numerous **discounts**, ranging from travel to entry to attractions. So, if you're planning to use the An Óige/HINI network a lot, it's worth joining your own country's HI-affiliated association in advance.

### HOSTELLING INTERNATIONAL AFFILIATED ASSOCIATIONS

**Hostelling International Canada** Ⓦ hihostels.ca
**Hostelling International South Africa** Ⓦ hihostels.com
**Hostelling International USA** Ⓦ hiusa.org
**Hostelling Scotland** Ⓦ hostellingscotland.org.uk
**YHA Australia** Ⓦ yha.com.au
**YHA New Zealand** Ⓦ yha.co.nz
**Youth Hostel Association** England and Wales Ⓦ yha.org.uk

### Camping

The website of the **Irish Caravan and Camping Council** (Ⓦcamping-ireland.ie) gives details of around a hundred sites all over Ireland. The price of a night's stay at a campsite depends on the area's popularity, facilities and tent size. Usually it will cost around €20/£16 for two adults to pitch a tent in high season. Some hostels also allow camping on their land for around €5–10/£4–8 per person per night, with use of a kitchen and showers.

**Camping rough** is possible in many parts of Ireland, though the likelihood of rain coupled with the lack of proper facilities may prove a deterrent. Some of the terrain in Ireland's windy west, often boggy or rocky, may make pitching a tent difficult too. Off the beaten track, many farmers in the Republic will allow camping in one of their fields, usually for a few euros. It's permissible to camp in some state forests in the North, but not in the Republic.

# Food and drink

**Few visitors come to Ireland just for the food (though plenty come to drink). However, the quality and choice on offer have improved markedly in the last twenty years. A new generation of small-scale artisan producers has emerged, be they cheese-makers, organic farmers, fish-smokers or bakers, and the best Irish chefs seek out this local produce to re-create and adapt traditional dishes using global techniques. It's well worth looking out for Good Food Ireland signs (or checking out Ⓦgoodfoodireland.ie), a network of high-quality restaurants, cafés, hotels, producers and cookery schools,**

---

### TRADITIONAL DISHES

**Bacon and cabbage** Shoulder of pork boiled with cabbage.
**Boxty** Potato pancakes.
**Carrageen** Edible seaweed, used to make a blancmange-like dessert.
**Champ** Northern Irish version of colcannon, with spring onions.
**Colcannon** Mashed potato mixed with cabbage and often leeks.
**Crubeen** Boiled pig's trotters.
**Drisheen** Sausage of sheep and beef blood with oatmeal and pepper.
**Fadge** Northern fried potato bread.
**Soda bread** Bread baked with bicarbonate of soda, buttermilk and flour.

## TOP FIVE CHEESES

**Ardrahan** From Kanturk, Co. Cork, with powerful, complex flavours of milk and mustard.

**Desmond** Piquant, long-matured, Swiss-style cheese from Co. Cork; also Gabriel, a hard, aromatic and full-bodied Gruyère-like cheese from the same makers.

**Durrus** Semi-soft, washed-rind, raw milk cheese from west Cork.

**Kilshanny** Type of Gouda, sweet, hard and milky, made in Lahinch, Co. Clare; sometimes flavoured with garlic, cumin or nettles.

**Wicklow Bán** Hand-crafted on a family farm in Wicklow, this is a mild and creamy Brie.

**who are committed to using local, seasonal, artisan ingredients wherever possible.**

## Food

Irish meat is internationally renowned, especially Aberdeen Angus beef and lamb from the west coast, the latter appearing in **Irish stew**, a classic broth with potatoes, onions and carrots. Variants to look out for include Achill lamb, what the French call *pré-salé*: as the animals graze on seaside meadows, the meat is naturally salty and a little sweet; and air-dried Connemara lamb from Oughterard, a little like Italian Parma ham. Beef, pork and lamb of course crop up in excellent sausages, which may be accompanied for breakfast by **black pudding**, a sausage of pig's blood, and **white pudding**, made from pig's offal and cereals (butchers in Clonakilty specialize in these puddings).

### Seafood

Fresh **fish** and **seafood** such as prawns, lobsters, crabs and mussels, particularly from the west coast, Dublin Bay and Carlingford Lough, Dundrum Bay and Strangford Lough in the North, are also generally excellent. Among Ireland's many seafood festivals, the most famous are at Clarinbridge and nearby Galway city celebrating Galway Bay's **oysters**. These large, silky European flat oysters are some of the best in the world, having matured for about three years in anticipation of a season that runs from September until April. Ireland is also home to dozens of excellent **smokehouses**, which smoke not only delicately flavoured, satiny salmon, but also mussels, eels, bacon and chicken.

### Cheese

**Cheese-making** in Ireland entirely died out during the eighteenth century, partly because of the plantations and the rise of the international butter trade. However, legend has it that Irish monks had exported the secrets of cheese-making to Europe in the sixth century, while many kinds of Irish cheese are recorded in early texts – notably the twelfth-century *Aislinge Meic Conglinne*, a brilliantly satirical tale about a king possessed by a demon of gluttony, and an underfed monk who tries to tempt the demon out with a vision of a foodie's paradise. Since the 1970s, cheese-making has blossomed once again, especially in Munster, often handmade by farmers.

## Drink

Dark, creamy **stout** has long been Ireland's most popular drink. It's always granted two minutes' settling time halfway through pouring and you should let it settle again once it's fully poured. Brewed in Dublin, Guinness is the market leader, but Beamish and Murphy's from Cork are also worth trying, as are microbrewery-produced stouts and beers.

The other indigenous tipple is **whiskey** (from *uisce beatha*, "water of life"). Apart from an inexplicable change in spelling, the main differences with Scotch whisky is that the Irish versions generally don't have the smoky, peaty flavour found in many Scotches, as the malt is dried in smokeless kilns rather than over peat fires; they are often smoother too, being triple-distilled whereas Scotch only goes round twice. The main brands are Jameson's, Power's, Paddy's – all three of which are now distilled in Midleton, Co. Cork – and Bushmills, made in Co.

## SPECIALITY DRINKS

**Black and Tan** Stout and ale.

**Black velvet** Stout and champagne.

**Hot port** Winter warmer, made with port, hot water, lemon and cloves.

**Hot whiskey** As above, with whiskey instead of port.

**Irish coffee** Invented in Foynes, Co. Limerick, in the 1940s to warm up miserable transatlantic flying-boat passengers; whiskey, coffee, sugar and cream.

**Poteen** (poitín, "little pot") Subject of many a song, a powerful, usually illicitly distilled whiskey that varies enormously in quality – some being fit only to strip paint.

## CRAFT BEER IN IRELAND

Not too long ago, the letters IPA (India Pale Ale – a hoppy, cloudy beer with a more bitter taste than larger) stood for little outside of a small conclave of hipsters. Now, with in excess of one hundred micro-breweries now operating in Ireland, the nascent craft beer industry shows no signs of slowing down. With most pubs and off-licences stocking a daunting selection of these beers, it can be hard to know where to start. Here are five of the best:

**Black Donkey Sheep Stealer** Traditionally brewed Irish farmhouse ale with a crisp finish.
**Blacks of Kinsale Black IPA** A suitably Irish twist on an IPA, with a nice malty taste of stout.
**Brú Dubh Irish Craft Stout** A traditional dry stout brewed with chocolate malt and magnum hops.
**Franciscan Well Rebel Red** A medium-bodied Irish red ale.
**Kinnegar Brewing Scraggy Bay** An India Pale Ale with a deliciously hoppy bite.

Antrim and the preferred drop in the North. A notable newcomer to the scene is Teeling Whiskey, a Dublin-based independent distillery producing some superb single malts.

## Restaurants

The widest array of **restaurants** is concentrated in the big cities – where, alongside Dublin and Belfast, Cork has a particularly vibrant scene – and in gourmet hotspots such as Kilkenny, Kinsale, Kenmare and Dingle, but good places can be found all over the country, sometimes in quite unexpected locales, as detailed throughout the Guide. Off the beaten track, it's usually worth phoning ahead, as opening hours can be erratic and, in winter, some establishments in tourist areas close down entirely. There's no getting away from the fact that dining out in Ireland is expensive, particularly when you factor in the high price of wine, but many fine restaurants offer cheaper, simpler menus at lunch time, and plenty also lay on good-value **early-bird menus** in the evening – two or three courses for a set price, usually available until 7 or 7.30pm, though often not at weekends. Found in small towns across the country, though sometimes takeaway only, the most widespread ethnic restaurants are Chinese, Indian and Italian, followed by Thai; reflecting recent immigration patterns, you'll find Eastern European delis in many large towns and restaurants.

## Pubs and cafés

Most **pubs** across the country will be able to rustle you up a simple sandwich or toastie and a cup of tea or coffee, and many offer a substantial **lunch**. This is often based around a carvery, serving slices of roast meat, potatoes and veg, as well as sandwiches and salads – which regularly feature crab and other seafood in coastal areas – and hot staples such as Irish stew and soups. An increasing number of Irish pubs now also serve meals in the evening. Similar fare is also available in traditional daytime **cafés**, alongside cakes and scones, which are now augmented in some towns by deli-cafés, offering a more interesting array of food.

## Markets

Virtually every sizeable town now hosts a **farmers' market**, often on a Saturday. The best markets – colourful, vibrant affairs that are worth a visit in their own right – are the permanent English Market in Cork city; the Temple Bar Food Market in Dublin, the Galway city market and the Midleton market in east Cork, all on Saturdays; and St George's Market in Belfast, on Fridays and Saturdays. For a full list of farmers' markets around the country, go to the Irish Food Board's website, ⓦ bordbia.ie/irish-food-markets, and, for the north, ⓦ discovernorthernireland.com/things-to-do/shopping/best-markets.

## THE FULL IRISH

Big **breakfasts** are an Irish tradition and are generally available at old-style cafés, often all day long; however, visitors are most likely to come across them at their hotel or B&B, where they're invariably included in the price. The "full Irish" or "Ulster fry" typically consists of bacon, sausage, eggs and tomatoes, sometimes stretching to mushrooms, black pudding and white pudding, though many hotels and B&Bs now offer less hearty alternatives such as smoked salmon and fruit salad.

# The media

**Both the Republic and the North have a wide range of daily and weekly newspapers, the latter often county-based in their coverage. The choices for Ireland-based TV are more limited both sides of the border, but there's an abundance of local radio stations, together with several national stations in the Republic.**

## Newspapers and magazines

The Republic's most popular middlebrow **newspapers** are the *Irish Times* and the more populist *Irish Independent*. Though generally liberal, if sometimes tinged by old-fashioned Ascendancy attitudes, the *Times* offers comprehensive news coverage of events both at home and abroad and often excellent features (⦿irishtimes.com). The *Independent* (⦿independent. ie) has a more right-of-centre outlook, while the *Irish Examiner* (⦿irishexaminer.com) has a Munster-based focus and generally less analytical coverage of news. British newspapers are commonly available in Dublin and other cities and some produce Irish editions.

Every county has at least one weekly newspaper, often conservative and usually crammed with local stories of little interest to outsiders. However, some, such as the *Kerryman*, the *Kilkenny People* and the *Donegal Democrat*, often provide good coverage of local events and very readable features. To delve deeper into the seamy world of Irish politics, turn to the monthly *Village* (⦿villagemagazine.ie) or the satirical fortnightly **magazine** *Phoenix* (⦿thephoenix.ie).

The **North**'s three morning dailies are the Nationalist *Irish News* (⦿irishnews.com), the Unionist *News Letter* (⦿newsletter.co.uk) and the *Belfast Telegraph* (⦿belfasttelegraph.co.uk). The widest circulation belongs to the *Irish News*. All UK national papers are also available in the North.

## Television and radio

In the **Republic**, the three main **TV channels** are operated by the state-sponsored Radio Telefís Éireann (RTÉ; ⦿rte.ie). As well as imported shows, the main news and current affairs channel, RTÉ 1, also features the popular home-grown Dublin-based soap, *Fair City*, and Friday's *Late Late Show*, a long-standing chat and entertainment institution. RTÉ 2 is a little more bubbly, with a smattering of locally produced programmes, though still swamped by imported tat and overburdened by sporting events. Some of the most innovative viewing is provided by the Irish-language channel TG4 (which provides English subtitles; ⦿tg4.ie), including excellent traditional-music shows and often incisive features on the culture of Irish-speaking areas. In most of the Republic, the four major British terrestrial TV channels are available on cable or satellite.

RTÉ also operates four **radio stations**, three of which are English-language: the mainstream RTÉ Radio 1 (FM 88–89), whose morning shows are largely devoted to current affairs and chat; RTÉ 2FM (FM 90–92), which is more music- and youth-oriented; and Lyric FM (FM 96–99), which mixes popular classics with jazz and occasionally inspiring world-music shows. Raidió na Gaeltachta (FM 93) is the national Irish-language station, with broadcasts including traditional music.

**Northern Ireland** receives television and radio programmes from the BBC (⦿bbc.co.uk) and has a limited, if often keenly followed, number of locally produced current-affairs productions. On BBC Radio Ulster (FM 92.4–95.4), *Talkback* (Mon–Fri noon–1.30pm) offers lively discussions on the North's political situation. The BBC's main commercial rival, Ulster Television (⦿u.tv), relies on the standard ITV diet of soaps and drama. In most parts of the North you can also watch or listen to RTÉ programmes.

# Festivals and events

**Ireland has a plethora of annual festivals, ranging from small local affairs to major international occasions and significant events in the sporting calendar. For more on the big events in Belfast, Cork, Derry, Dublin, Galway and Kilkenny, see the appropriate chapter sections or boxes.**

### JANUARY

**Temple Bar Tradfest** ⦿ tradfest.ie. Sprawling music festival focusing on traditional and folk music. Venues range from intimate pubs to Dublin Castle and St. Patrick's Cathedral.

### FEBRUARY–APRIL

**Tedfest** ⦿ tedfest.org. A long weekend of wackiness in the Aran Islands at the end of February, celebrating the characters and storylines of the hugely popular sitcom *Father Ted*.
**St Patrick's Day** March 17; ⦿ stpatricksday.ie. Almost every Irish town and village commemorates the national patron saint's day, though the most significant celebration is the week-long festival held in Dublin.

**Irish Grand National** ⓦ fairyhouse.ie. The biggest event of the National Hunt horseracing season takes place at Fairyhouse, Co. Meath, on Easter Monday.

## MAY

**North West 200** ⓦ northwest200.org. Major international motorcycle road-racing event held in Portstewart, Co. Derry, in the middle of the month.

**Fleadh Nua** ⓦ fleadhnua.com. One of the country's biggest traditional music festivals, held in Ennis, Co. Clare, over a week in late May.

## JUNE

**Writers' Week** ⓦ writersweek.ie. Ireland's biggest literary festival, five days of workshops and events in Listowel, Co. Kerry, over the bank holiday weekend at the beginning of June.

**Forbidden Fruit** ⓦ forbiddenfruit.ie. One of the best music festivals of the year, set in the gorgeous grounds of Dublin's Irish Museum of Modern Art for three days at the beginning of the month.

**The Cat Laughs** ⓦ thecatlaughs.com. Four-day comedy festival featuring an array of renowned and lesser-known acts, staged in Kilkenny in early June.

**Bloomsday** ⓦ bloomsdayfestival.ie. A week of Dublin-based James Joyce-related events leading up to June 16, the day on which his masterwork *Ulysses* is set.

**Irish Derby** ⓦ curragh.ie. The major event in the Irish flat-racing season, held at the Curragh, Co. Kildare, in late June or early July.

**Dublin Pride** ⓦ dublinpride.ie. Over a week of festivities celebrating diversity culminate in a carnival-style parade through the city centre – one of the biggest parties of the year.

**Body and Soul** ⓦ bodyandsoul.ie. This boutique music festival takes place in Ballinlough Castle, Co. Westmeath on the Summer Solstice weekend. As well as a top-tier line-up, expect comedy, holistic therapies, a midnight masquerade ball, and plenty of great food.

## JULY

**Willie Clancy Summer School** ⓦ scoilsamhraidhwillieclancy. com. Hugely popular, week-long traditional music event with a host of pub sessions and several concerts, hosted in Miltown Malbay, Co. Clare, at the beginning of July.

**Orange Order Parades** July 12. Unionists and Loyalists commemorate the Battle of the Boyne and close down much of Northern Ireland in the process.

**Galway International Arts Festival** ⓦ giaf.ie. Massive festival of music, drama and general revelry over a fortnight from the middle of the month.

**Mary from Dungloe** ⓦ maryfromdungloe.ie. Ten days of entertainment in Co. Donegal, often featuring Daniel O'Donnell and culminating in a beauty contest (where one of the prizes is sometimes a date with the man himself); runs from late July.

**Yeats International Summer School** ⓦ yeatssociety.com. Sligo-based late-July to August literary festival focusing on the life of the poet.

**Galway Races** ⓦ galwayraces.com. The west of Ireland's biggest horse-racing event, long celebrated in the song of the same name; held over a week at the end of the month.

## AUGUST

**Kilkenny Arts Festival** ⓦ kilkennyarts.ie. All manner of musical and literary events, recitals and exhibitions staged in the city over ten days in mid-August.

**GAZE** ⓦ gaze.ie. LGBTQ film festival celebrating diversity and activism, now in its 25th year. Screenings in various Dublin locations for five days at the beginning of August.

**Puck Fair** ⓦ puckfair.ie. Three days of mayhem in Killorglin, Co. Kerry, culminating in the crowning of a goat as King Puck; takes place in the middle of the month.

**Rose of Tralee International Festival** ⓦ roseoftralee.ie. Tremendously popular event, focused on a beauty contest, but offering an enormous range of other entertainment; late August.

**Fleadh Cheoil na hÉireann** ⓦ comhaltas.ie. Competitive traditional-music festival, drawing hundreds of participants and big crowds – different towns bid for the mid- to late-August event each year.

**Ould Lammas Fair** More than four hundred years old, Ballycastle's traditional market fair remains a huge draw, featuring livestock sales, and bucket-loads of music, dancing and entertainment on the last Monday and Tuesday of the month.

## SEPTEMBER

**Electric Picnic** ⓦ electricpicnic.ie. Hugely popular rock and dance festival held at Stradbally Hall, Laois, over the first weekend.

**All-Ireland Senior Hurling and Football Finals** ⓦ gaa.ie. The zenith of the sporting year for Gaelic games, with the hurling on the first or second Sunday and the football on the third or fourth Sunday, in Dublin's Croke Park.

**Lisdoonvarna Matchmaking Festival** ⓦ matchmakerireland.com. A month-long date-athon which attracts hopeful suitors from all over the world, and there's plenty of traditional entertainment too.

**Dublin Fringe Festival** ⓦ fringefest.com. Lively programme of theatre, dance, performance arts and comedy, featuring hundreds of events spread over more than a fortnight.

**Dublin Theatre Festival** ⓦ dublintheatrefestival.ie. Ireland's most prestigious drama festival, commencing late in the month and running for more than a fortnight.

**Culture Night** ⓦ culturenight.ie. An all-island event where arts and cultural organisations open late into the night for talks, tours, performances and other events, all for free.

**Galway Oyster Festival** ⓦ galwayoysterfest.com. Boisterous four-day festival to kick off the annual oyster season.

## OCTOBER

**Wexford Opera Festival** ⓦ wexfordopera.com. Prestigious and massively popular international festival lasting for a fortnight commencing in mid-October.

**Belfast International Arts Festival** ⓦ belfastinternationalarts festival.com. Major arts festival, running for two weeks from the middle of the month.

**Cork Jazz Festival** ⓦ guinnessjazzfestival.com. Ninety venues and four days of jazz in all its forms at the end of the month.
**Metropolis** ⓦ metropolisfestival.ie. An indoor music festival in the Royal Dublin Society with a heavy emphasis on the visual, from stunning set designs to unexpected installations.
**Derry Halloween Carnival** ⓦ derryhalloween.com. Street theatre, music and mayhem, especially during the fireworks display on October 31.

### NOVEMBER

**Cork Film Festival** ⓦ corkfilmfest.org. Established in 1956 and still going strong with a broad-ranging programme of big-budget and international cinema staged early in the month or in late Oct.
**Dublin Book Festival** ⓦ dublinbookfestival.com. A four-day celebration of Irish authors and publishers, with readings, workshops, walking tours and plenty of other literary events.

### DECEMBER

**Wren Boys.** On St Stephen's Day (December 26), it was traditional for men and children carrying the corpse of a wren to go around the neighbourhood knocking on doors, asking for money to bury the bird while singing songs and telling jokes – the money, of course, would be spent on a party. The tradition can still be found in a few places, such as Dublin's Sandymount and Dingle in Co. Kerry.
**New Year's Festival Dublin** ⓦ nyfdublin.com. Three days of festivities including concerts, street parties and fireworks.

# Culture and etiquette

**Ireland likes to describe itself as the land of Cead Míle Fáilte ("a hundred thousand welcomes"), which you'll often see inscribed on pubs, and that's essentially true for most visitors. In terms of general etiquette, wherever you go, you'll encounter the standard Irish greeting – an enquiry about your health ("How are you?" sometimes just abbreviated to "About you?" in parts of the North) – and it's reasonable to return the compliment. Also, if someone buys you a pint in a pub, then an even-handed gesture is to pay for the next round.**

## Children

**Children** are very well received, though few places, including cafés, hotels and many key attractions, are actually designed with them in mind. Baby supplies are readily available and most B&Bs and hotels welcome children, and an increasing number have cots. It's usually fine to take a child into a pub during the daytime, though definitely not so legally in the Republic after 9pm.

## Women

Irish women's economic and social status has much improved over the last couple of decades, with the Republic even outranking Germany and the Netherlands in terms of gender equality.

In terms of the travel experience, **female visitors** are unlikely to encounter problems. However, as with anywhere, if you're travelling alone or to an unfamiliar area, it's worth adopting a cautionary attitude, particularly when enjoying pubs and nightlife. In the rare case of experiencing a serious personal assault, contact either a rape crisis centre (see page 44) or the Tourist Assistance Service (see page 44), as local police forces are unlikely to be experienced in these situations.

## Racism

With over seventeen percent of the Irish population born abroad, and the number of people with dual Irish nationality double what it was in 2011, Ireland continues to grow ever more diverse. That being said, it's still possible that foreign visitors could encounter **racist attitudes** at some point in their travels.

The situation differs in Northern Ireland where, following the vote to leave the EU, incidents of racial violence are on the rise. However, these are highly localised, and tourists, of whatever culture, are very rarely the victims of assaults.

Ireland also has its own recognized ethnic minority, the **Travellers** (widely known by a range of insulting epithets), against whom discrimination remains widespread, both North and South.

## LGBTQ Ireland

Ireland's attitude towards the LGBTQ community has come a long way in a remarkably short period of time. A country traditionally seen as culturally conservative, it is now one of the most inclusive and welcoming countries to visit.

Being the first country in the world to approve same-sex marriage by popular vote in 2015 wasn't just a huge step towards equal rights, it was recognition of how Irish society has changed. And it's not just the big cities, either – a closer look at the referendum results show that rural areas voted overwhelmingly to pass the bill.

This, coupled with Ireland's first gay Taoiseach being appointed in June 2017 with barely an eyelid batted, points to a far wider acceptance of the LGBTQ community than ever before. This isn't to say, however, that homophobic attitudes don't exist. While visitors are unlikely to encounter any trouble, if support is needed, contact Ⓦlgbt.ie.

## Alcohol

The pub has long been at the centre of Irish society and the ready availability of alcohol has played a major part in the development of the national psyche and as a Muse to some of the country's greatest writers (O'Brien, Kavanagh, Behan) and actors (Richard Harris and Peter O'Toole).

Consumption is gradually falling but the Irish are still among Europe's heaviest drinkers, imbibing as a whole on average some twenty percent more than their continental European neighbours, and that's despite the government's heavy excise duties on drink. According to Alcohol Action Ireland, more than half of the population have harmful drinking patterns (40 percent of women and 70 percent of men) and binge-drinking, especially among the 18–25 age group, is a significant problem. By contrast, thanks to movements such as the Pioneer Total Abstinence Association, around a fifth of the Irish population are teetotal.

# Sports

**Hurling and Gaelic football are among the fastest and most physical sports in the world, and well worth catching on your travels, whether on TV or, preferably, live. Rugby and soccer are also widely followed, while going to the races is a great day out, with less of the snobbery sometimes found in Britain. Golf is also hugely popular north and south of the border.**

## Hurling and Gaelic football

Both Gaelic football and hurling, Ireland's two main indigenous sports, are played at a rollicking pace on huge pitches, 140m long and 80m wide, between teams of fifteen; goalposts are H-shaped, with three points awarded for a goal, when the ball goes under the crossbar into the net, and a point when it goes over the crossbar. Over two thousand clubs in villages and parishes all over Ireland vie for the privilege of reaching the club finals, held on St Patrick's Day at 80,000-seater Croke Park in Dublin, one of the largest stadiums in Europe (see page 87), while the more popular and prestigious intercounty seasons begin with provincial games in the early summer, reaching their climax in the All-Ireland County Finals in September, also at Croke Park. Details of all fixtures for hurling and Gaelic football can be obtained from the Gaelic Athletic Association (Ⓦgaa.ie).

**Hurling** is played with a leather *slíothar*, similar in size to a hockey ball, and a hurley (or *camán*), a broad stick made of ash that is curved outwards at the end. The *slíothar* is belted prodigious distances, caught and carried on the flattened end of the player's hurley. It's a highly skilled game of constant movement and aggression that does not permit a defensive, reactive style of play. Cork, Kilkenny and Tipperary are the most successful counties, though Limerick, Galway and Waterford have emerged in the modern era. No county from the North has ever won an All-Ireland Final, though the sport is very popular in the Glens of Antrim and parts of the Ards Peninsula in Co. Down. **Camogie**, the women's version of hurling, is becoming increasingly popular, and is also well worth watching. Dublin has won the most camogie All-Irelands, though they haven't prevailed since 1984 and the most successful team in the modern era has been Cork.

**Gaelic football** has similarities with both rugby and association football, but its closest relation is Australian Rules Football; indeed every autumn, Australia play Ireland in a hurly-burly series of "international rules" matches that are known for their frequent brawling. The round Gaelic ball, which is slightly smaller than a soccer ball, can be both kicked and caught. However, running with the ball is only permitted if a player keeps control by tapping it from foot to hand or by bouncing it, and throwing is not allowed – the ball must be "hand-passed", volleyball-style. Whereas hurling's strongholds are in the southern counties of the island, footballing prowess is more widely spread – Kerry is the most successful county, though Dublin have been the dominant force in recent years.

## Rugby union and soccer

**Rugby union** and **soccer** are very popular in Ireland and tickets for international matches, especially for rugby, can be hard to come by. The Republic's home soccer matches (Ⓦfai.ie) and Ireland's rugby matches (Ⓦirishrugby.ie) are played at Dublin's Aviva Stadium (formerly Lansdowne Road). Northern Ireland's soccer matches (Ⓦirishfa.com) are played at Windsor Park, Belfast (see page 478). For the international rugby team, which is a joint Republic–Northern Ireland side, the main event of the year is the Six Nations Championship, a series of international games played in February and March against England, France, Wales, Scotland and Italy. You're more likely to get tickets, however, for matches featuring the four provinces, Munster (which includes Irish rugby's natural heartland, Limerick), Leinster, Connacht and, in Northern Ireland, Ulster, who all complete in the Pro 14 League (Ⓦpro14.rugby) with teams from Scotland, Wales, Italy and South Africa.

Soccer is played semi-professionally in both the North and the Republic, organized into the Danske Bank Premiership and the Airtricity Premier Division respectively. Both international teams field most of their players from the English leagues; Manchester United and Liverpool are the most popular clubs among Irish fans. Glasgow Celtic are also popular both north and south, Rangers in the north, with support following Catholic and Protestant divisions, respectively.

## Racing

Going to the **races** is a hugely popular and enjoyable day out in Ireland. A good place to get a sense of the Irish passion for horses is the National Stud in Kildare (see page 127), while for details of all meetings, go to Horse Racing Ireland's website Ⓦgoracing.ie. The Irish Grand National is run at Fairyhouse in Co. Meath on Easter Monday (see page 105), followed in April by the five-day Irish National Hunt Festival at Punchestown in Co. Kildare (see page 128); at the Curragh, the classic flat-racecourse in Kildare (see page 128), the Irish 1000 Guineas and 2000 Guineas are held in May, the Irish Derby in late June or early July, the Irish Oaks in July and the Irish St Leger in September. Dublin's racecourse (see page 128) plus notable local meetings, such as those at Galway, Killarney, Listowel, Sligo and Downpatrick, are described in the Guide. One local oddity worth mentioning is the meeting at Laytown in Co. Meath, the last remaining beach racing under Jockey Club rules, held once a year when the tides are at their lowest (Ⓦlaytownstrandraces.ie).

# Outdoor activities

**Despite the weather, Ireland is a great place for getting out and about. Cycling is one of the best ways to appreciate the quiet pleasures of the Irish countryside, while walkers can take advantage of generally free access across much of the countryside and a number of waymarked trails. With over 120 sailing and yacht clubs, plenty of lakes, rivers and sheltered coastline to explore and some great beaches for surfers, there are many opportunities for watersports enthusiasts, too.**

## Cycling

Signposted **cycling trails** in the Republic include the Beara Way (see page 259) and the Sheep's Head Cycling Route (see page 256) in Cork, and the Kerry Way (see page 277). On- and off-road routes are detailed on Ⓦsportireland.ie, but trails in the North are better documented and promoted: for detailed information on the many routes here, the best places to start are Ⓦcycleni.com and Ⓦsustrans.org.uk. They include the Kingfisher Trail (see page 559), which also stretches into Leitrim and Cavan. Other cross-border routes include the 326km North West Trail, mainly on quiet country roads through Donegal, Tyrone, Fermanagh, Leitrim and Sligo. Getting around the country by bike is a great option (see page 33).

## Fishing

There are plenty of opportunities for sea **angling** and dozens of rivers and lakes for fly- and game-fishing. For information, the best places to start are Angling Ireland's website, Ⓦfishinginireland.info, and the tourist-board site, Ⓦireland.com. Great Fishing Houses of Ireland (Ⓦirelandflyfishing.com) covers a dozen or so specialist hotels and B&Bs.

### A NOTE ON ACCESS

Unlike the North, the Republic has no public "rights of way", but there is a tradition of relatively free access to privately owned countryside. In recent years, the growing numbers and occasional carelessness of walkers, as well as insurance worries, have led some farmers to bar access to their land, and, in response, the government has begun to pay farmers who maintain popular walks across their land under the National Walks Scheme. In general, the majority of landowners do not object to walkers crossing their property. For detailed advice on **access**, including a Good Practice Guide, have a look at Ⓦmountaineering.ie or and Ⓦleavenotraceireland.org.

## BIRDWATCHING

With a wide variety of migrating flocks, including a large number of rare species, visiting its shores, Ireland is a great place for **birdwatching**; Wexford Wildfowl Reserve (see page 194), where thousands of Greenland white-fronted geese and pale-bellied brent geese spend the winter, Cape Clear (see page 253), famous for spotting rare migratory birds in October, and the wetlands at Castle Espie (see page 526) are especially fruitful hunting grounds. The best general contacts are ⓦ irishbirding.com, Birdwatch Ireland in the Republic (ⓦ birdwatchireland. ie) and, in the North, the Royal Society for the Protection of Birds (ⓦ rspb.org.uk).

## Golf

**Golf**, which was probably first brought to Ireland by the Ulster Scots, attracts huge numbers of visitors every year; the Golfing Union of Ireland, based in Kildare (ⓦ golfnet.ie), provides details of over four hundred clubs, north and south, with online booking.

## Horseriding

**Horseriding**, whether over the hills or along the beaches, is also a popular pastime, for both novices and experienced riders, who also have the option of multi-day trails rides. Stables in popular locations are listed throughout the Guide, including Killarney and Clifden. The Association of Irish Riding Establishments (ⓦ aire.ie) maintains standards among riding centres in the Republic and the North and publishes details on its website (ⓦ discovernorthernireland.com).

## Walking and mountain climbing

There are dozens of waymarked long-distance **walking trails** in the Republic, ranging from routes through or around mountain ranges, such as the Wicklow Way (see page 119), the Táin Way (see page 151), the Slieve Bloom Way (see page 176) and the Western Way (see page 360), to walks around entire peninsulas, like the Sheep's Head Way (see page 256), the Beara Way (see page 259), the Kerry Way (see page 277) and the Dingle Way (see page 297). The Ulster Way (see page 567) in the North, the oldest and longest waymarked walking trail in Ireland, is a 625-mile circuit of the whole province, taking in the Giant's Causeway, the Sperrins and the Mournes; it's now divided into link sections, which can be skipped by taking public transport, and quality sections. For information on these trails in the Republic, go to ⓦ sportireland.ie, which also has details of hundreds of looped day walks; in the Guide, we list the very useful websites on the Wicklow, Kerry and Dingle Ways, which include details of walker-friendly accommodation. In the North, ⓦ walkni.com has comprehensive information on all aspects of walking. Some councils and local tourist offices have produced helpful map guides for the main routes too, but you should always get hold of the relevant Ordnance Survey map and carry a compass.

Other **walking highlights** include the ascents of Croagh Patrick in Co. Mayo (see page 373) and of Carrauntoohil, for more experienced walkers, in Co. Kerry (see page 277), the easily accessible Bray–Greystones walks in Co. Wicklow (see page 115) and just about anywhere in Connemara (see page 360), notably the excellent Diamond Hill trail in the national park; not to mention walks in the Wicklow (see page 119) and Killarney (see page 269) national parks.

Mountaineering Ireland, an organization that covers hill-walking and rambling, as well as climbing, maintains a compendious website (ⓦ mountaineering. ie). Particularly useful walking guidebooks are listed in Contexts, see page 610. Some guided walking tour operators are detailed on page 30, while more complete lists are available on ⓦ ireland.com.

If you need help in a real emergency on the mountains, call ❶ 999 or ❶ 112 and ask for **mountain rescue** (ⓦ mountainrescue.ie).

## Watersports

### Sailing

Ireland's many **sailing** clubs include the Royal Cork Yacht Club, established in Cobh in 1720, which is thought to be the oldest in the world. Dozens of regattas, such as Calves Week in Schull, and traditional boat festivals, such as the Wooden Boat Festival in Baltimore and Cruinniú na mBád in Kinvarra, are held every year. The most popular areas for sailing are the relatively sheltered waters of the east coast, especially in Dublin Bay; Cork Harbour and west Cork; Lough Swilly on the north coast of Donegal; Strangford Lough in Co. Down; and some of the larger lakes, such as Lough Derg in Co. Clare. Popular sailing clubs are listed in the Guide; for further information contact the Irish Sailing Association (ⓦ sailing.ie).

## Canoeing and kayaking

Inland waterways and sheltered coasts – notably in west Cork (see page 250), Dingle (see page 291) and Waterford (see page 212) – offer **canoeing** and **kayaking** opportunities, ranging from day-trips and touring to rough- and white-water racing. We've detailed rental and guided trip providers in the Guide; Canoeing Ireland's website covers courses and clubs in the South (Ⓦcanoe.ie), while the North has a comprehensive website, Ⓦcanoeni.com, that includes canoe trails for multi-day touring. Another useful website is Ⓦiska.ie.

## Surfing, wind-surfing and kite-surfing

There are some superb beaches for **surfing** (Ⓦirish-surfing.ie) and its spin-offs, **wind-surfing** (Ⓦwind-surfing.ie) and **kite-surfing** (Ⓦiksa.ie). For kite- and wind-surfing, some of the best spots are: Rosslare, Co. Wexford; Tramore, Co. Waterford; Castlegregory, Kerry; Rusheen Bay, Co. Galway; Keel Strand, Achill and Elly Bay, Belmullet, in Mayo; Lough Allen, Leitrim; and Rossnowlagh, Co. Donegal. Surfers head for: Garrettstown and Inchydoney, Co. Cork; Inch and Brandon Bay, Kerry; Lahinch, Clare; Easkey, Mullaghmore and Strandhill, Co. Sligo; Bundoran and Rossnowlagh, Co. Donegal; Portrush, Antrim; and Tramore, Co. Waterford.

## Scuba diving

Right in the path of the warm North Atlantic Drift current, Ireland offers some of the best **scuba diving** in Europe, notably off the rocky west coast. We've listed dive centres throughout the Guide, and you can get further information from Diving Ireland (Ⓦdiving.ie) and Ⓦukdiving.co.uk.

# Travel essentials

## Costs

Though it's still possible to get a main **meal** in cafés and pubs for around €10, a three-course restaurant dinner will usually cost at least €30, with a bottle of wine setting you back around €20, though some offer "early bird" menus and midweek set menus at reduced rates. The price of a pint in a pub is around €4–5, significantly higher in some city-centre clubs.

The cheapest **accommodation** is a hostel dorm bed, which will cost around €12–20, rising to as much as €30 at peak periods in Dublin. Alternatively, it's also possible to get a decent bed and breakfast from around €35 per person sharing or €45 in Dublin. So, even if you count the cents, you're likely to spend a daily minimum of around €35, and more than double this if you're eating out and staying in a B&B.

The main change in the **North** over the last two decades has been the fall in the value of the pound against the euro. This has meant that while quoted prices are roughly the same as their euro equivalents in the Republic, they are comparatively cheaper.

## Crime and personal safety

**Crime** in Ireland is largely an urban affair and generally at a low level compared with other European countries. However, thieves do target popular tourist spots, so don't leave anything of value visible in your car and take care of your bags while visiting bars and restaurants. It's sensible to seek advice from your accommodation provider about safety in the local area and take as much care as you would anywhere else.

Crimes against individuals are relatively rare, except in certain inner-city areas, and seldom involve tourists. The **Republic**'s police force is An Garda Síochána (☎112 or ☎999 for emergencies, Ⓦgarda.ie), more commonly referred to as the guards or **Gardaí**, whom you'll find generally helpful when it comes to reporting a crime. The Irish Tourist Assistance Service (☎01 666 9354, Ⓦitas.ie) offers support to tourist crime victims. Rape crisis support is available from the Dublin Rape Crisis Centre (☎1800 778888, Ⓦdrcc.ie), which can also direct you to similar agencies across Ireland.

Away from the sectarian hotspots, crime in **Northern Ireland** is very low. In the unlikely event that your person or property is targeted, contact the Police Service of Northern Ireland (☎999 for emergencies, Ⓦpsni.police.uk). The presence of the British army has diminished almost to invisibility, though it is just possible you might encounter police or army security checks on the rare occasion of a major incident.

## Discount cards

For all attractions in the Guide, we've given the adult entry price. The majority of sites offer reduced rates for children (under-5s usually get in free), students (for which you'll need ID such as an International Student Identity Card, Ⓦisic.org) and senior citizens.

An annual **Heritage Card** (€40, senior citizens €30, children/students €10, family €90; Ⓦheritageireland. ie) is worth considering if you're planning to visit many historic sites and monuments in the Republic. It provides unlimited entry to attractions run by the Office of Public Works (sites are detailed throughout the Guide) and is mostly easily purchased at the first OPW site that you visit.

## CLIMATE

Average maximum and minimum daily temperatures (°C/°F) and monthly rainfall (mm)

|  | Feb | Apr | Jun | Aug | Oct | Dec |
|---|---|---|---|---|---|---|
| **BELFAST** | | | | | | |
| Max/min (°C) | 7/5 | 10/6 | 15/11 | 17/12 | 11/8 | 7/5 |
| Max/min (°F) | 45/41 | 50/43 | 59/52 | 63/54 | 52/46 | 45/41 |
| Rainfall (mm) | 77 | 66 | 72 | 101 | 106 | 106 |
| **CORK** | | | | | | |
| Max/min (°C) | 9/3 | 13/5 | 19/10 | 20/12 | 14/7 | 9/3 |
| Max/min (°F) | 48/37 | 55/41 | 66/50 | 68/54 | 57/45 | 48/37 |
| Rainfall (mm) | 79 | 57 | 57 | 71 | 99 | 122 |
| **DUBLIN** | | | | | | |
| Max/min (°C) | 8/2 | 13/4 | 18/9 | 19/11 | 14/6 | 8/3 |
| Max/min (°F) | 46/36 | 55/39 | 64/48 | 66/52 | 57/43 | 46/37 |
| Rainfall (mm) | 55 | 45 | 57 | 74 | 70 | 74 |
| **LIMERICK** | | | | | | |
| Max/min (°C) | 8/3 | 13/6 | 18/11 | 20/13 | 14/7 | 8/4 |
| Max/min (°F) | 46/37 | 55/43 | 64/52 | 68/55 | 57/45 | 46/40 |
| Rainfall (mm) | 72 | 58 | 64 | 84 | 96 | 106 |

Members of **An Óige/YHA/HINI** (see page 35) also receive discounts on entry to certain sites. A number of historic buildings and sites in the North are operated by the **National Trust**. Membership (£72; under-26s £36, family £126, one-adult family £78; Ⓦ nationaltrust.org.uk) provides free and unlimited entry to these and all National Trust–run sites in Britain too. More than eighty sites across Ireland are members of the independent **Heritage Island** organization (Ⓦ heritageisland.com) whose booklet (€6.99) provides discounted admission prices or other special offers.

## Electricity

The standard **electricity** supply is 220V AC in the Republic and 240V AC in the North. Most sockets require three-pin plugs. To operate North American appliances you'll need to bring or buy a transformer and an adapter; only the latter is needed for equipment made in Australia or New Zealand.

## Entry requirements

UK nationals do not need a passport to enter the Republic, but it's a good idea to carry one – and note that airlines generally require official **photo ID** on flights between Britain and Ireland. Under current EU regulations, British passport holders are entitled to stay in the Republic for as long as they like.

Travellers from the US, Canada, Australia, New Zealand and South Africa can enter the **Republic** for up to three months with just a passport. For further information on immigration and visas, contact the Irish Naturalization and Immigration Service, 13–14 Burgh Quay, Dublin (☎ 1890 551500, Ⓦ inis.gov.ie). A full list of Irish consulates and embassies is available on the Department of Foreign Affairs website, Ⓦ dfa.ie.

US, Canadian, Australian, South African and New Zealand citizens can enter **Northern Ireland** for up to six months with just a passport. Full details of British diplomatic representatives overseas are available on the Foreign Office's website, Ⓦ gov. uk. For further information on immigration and visas, go to Ⓦ gov.uk/government/organisations/ uk-visas-and-immigration.

The **border** between Northern Ireland and the Republic has no passport or immigration controls, and remains an open border following the UK's departure from the EU.

Note that visa regulations are subject to frequent changes, and at the time of writing, border controls were much more stringent than usual due to the Covid-19 pandemic, so it's always wise to contact the nearest embassy or high commission before you travel.

## ROUGH GUIDES TRAVEL INSURANCE

Rough Guides has teamed up with WorldNomads.com to offer great travel insurance deals. Policies are available to residents of over 150 countries, with cover for a wide range of adventure sports, 24hr emergency assistance, high levels of medical and evacuation cover and a stream of travel safety information. Roughguides.com users can take advantage of their policies online 24/7, from anywhere in the world – even if you're already travelling. And since plans often change when you're on the road, you can extend your policy and even claim online. Roughguides.com users who buy travel insurance with WorldNomads.com can also leave a positive footprint and donate to a community development project. For more information, go to ⓦroughguides.com/travel-insurance.

### IRISH EMBASSIES ABROAD

**Australia** 20 Arkana St, Yarralumla, Canberra, ACT 2600 ☎ 02 6214 0000, ⓦ dfa.ie/irish-embassy/australia.
**Canada** 130 Albert St, Suite 1105, Ottawa, ON K1P 5G4 ☎ 613 233 6281, ⓦ dfa.ie/irish-embassy/canada.
**New Zealand** Handled by the embassy in Australia.
**South Africa** 2nd Floor, Parkdev Building, Brooklyn Bridge Office Park, 570 Fehrsen St, Brooklyn 0181, Pretoria ☎ 012 452 1000, ⓦ dfa.ie/irish-embassy/south-africa.
**UK** 17 Grosvenor Place, London SW1X 7HR ☎ 020 7235 2171, ⓦ dfa.ie/irish-embassy/great-britain.
**US** 2234 Massachusetts Ave NW, Washington, DC 20008 ☎ 202 462 3939, ⓦ dfa.ie/irish-embassy/usa.

### BRITISH EMBASSIES AND HIGH COMMISSIONS ABROAD

**Australia** Commonwealth Ave, Yarralumla, ACT 2600 ☎ 02 6270 6666.
**Canada** 80 Elgin St, Ottawa, ON K1P 5K7 ☎ 613 237 1530.
**New Zealand** 44 Hill St, Wellington 6011 ☎ 04 924 2888.
**South Africa** 255 Hill Street, Arcadia 0028, Pretoria ☎ 012 421 7500.
**US** 3100 Massachusetts Ave NW, Washington, DC 20008 ☎ 202 588 6500.

## Emergencies

Across Ireland, in the case of an **emergency** call either ☎ 999 or ☎ 112.

## Health and insurance

Visitors from the UK are entitled to **medical treatment** in the Republic under a reciprocal agreement between the two countries. This will give access only to state-provided medical treatment in the Republic, which covers emergency hospital treatment but not all GPs' surgeries – check that the doctor you're planning to use is registered with the local Health Board Panel. Citizens of some other countries also enjoy reciprocal agreements – in Australia, for example, Medicare has such an arrangement with Ireland and Britain.

None of these arrangements covers all the medical costs you may incur or repatriation, so it's advisable for all travellers to take out some form of **travel insurance**. Most travel insurance policies exclude so-called dangerous sports unless an extra premium is paid; in Ireland this could mean, for example, horseriding, scuba diving, wind-surfing, mountaineering and kayaking.

Ireland, like the rest of the world, was hit by the Covid-19 pandemic. Check ⓦ www.gov.ie for the latest updates and requirements regarding the pandemic such as mask-wearing.

## Internet

Nearly all hotels, hostels and B&Bs in Ireland, as well as many restaurants, pubs and cafés, now offer free wi-fi. Otherwise, some B&Bs, hotels and hostels will let you access the internet on their computer. Where internet cafés do exist, expect to pay around €4/£4 per hour.

## Mail

In the **Republic**, post is handled by An Post (the national postal service; ⓦ anpost.com); allow two days (or more) for a letter to reach Britain, for example. Small letters and postcards to any destination overseas cost €1.10. Main post offices are usually open Monday to Friday 9am to 5.30pm, Saturday 9am to 1pm (in cities sometimes until 5.30pm on Saturday). From **the North** with the Royal Mail (ⓦ royalmail.com), postcards and the smallest letters cost 97p to airmail abroad. Main post offices are generally open Monday to Friday 9am–5.30pm, Saturday 9am to 12.30pm.

## Maps

The **maps** in this guide will provide you with sufficient detail to navigate your way around cities, towns and counties. For more detail, there's the Ordnance Survey of Ireland's (ⓦosi.ie) four *Holiday* maps at 1:250,000 scale (€8.26), dividing the country into quadrants, and its *Official Road Atlas of Ireland* (1:210,000; €10.40), produced in conjunction with the Ordnance Survey of Northern Ireland, is extremely useful if you're driving.

The majority of tourist offices will provide free local maps, but, if you're planning on walking or exploring a locality fully, then the OSI's *Discovery* 1:50,000 scale series of maps (€8.45 each) is the best bet for the Republic. The Ordnance Survey of Northern Ireland (ⓦosni.gov.uk) produces a similar *Discoverer* series (£6.70).

If you're walking or cycling, the OSI/OSNI also produce special-interest 1:25,000-scale maps covering areas such as the Aran Islands, Killarney National Park, Lough Erne, Macgillycuddy's Reeks, and the Mourne and Sperrin mountain ranges. All of these maps can be purchased via the internet.

## Money and cards

The **currency** of the Republic is the euro (€), divided into 100 cents (c). Northern Ireland's currency is the pound sterling (£), though notes are printed by various local banks and are different from those found in Britain; however, standard British banknotes can still be used in Northern Ireland.

**Exchange rates** fluctuate, but, at the time of writing, £1 sterling was equivalent to around €1.15 and US$1.40, €1 was worth £0.88 and US$1.20. The best exchange rates are provided by banks, though it's easiest to use an ATM, for which your own bank or credit card company may charge a fixed-rate or percentile fee. Unless you're absolutely stuck, avoid changing money in hotels, where the rates are often very poor. In areas around the border between the Republic and the North many businesses accept both currencies.

### Credit and debit cards

The handiest means of obtaining cash is to use a **debit or credit card**. ATMs are very common throughout Ireland except in remote rural areas (where you're likeliest to find one in a supermarket), with most accepting Visa/Plus, MasterCard and Cirrus/Maestro. Major credit cards, such as Visa/Plus and MasterCard, and all cards bearing the Eurocard symbol, are widely accepted, though in rural areas you'll find that they're not accepted by some B&Bs.

## Opening hours and public holidays

**Shops and businesses** across Ireland usually open 9am to 5.30pm, Monday to Saturday, though newsa-

gents and petrol stations (many of which also have grocery stores) are often open earlier and later. Most large towns generally have a day when all shops open late (until 8pm or 9pm), usually Thursdays, and some also open on Sundays from around noon (1pm in Northern Ireland) until 6pm. Lunch-time closing still applies in some smaller towns, where also some businesses (except pubs) close for a half-day midweek. In rural areas opening times are far more variable.

Banks in the Republic are generally open from Monday to Friday between 10am and 4pm, and until 5pm one day a week, usually Wednesday or Thursday, sometimes closing for lunch in remoter areas. In the North, they open Monday to Friday 9.30am to 4.30pm, with some opening for longer hours and on Saturdays, though others may close for lunch. Post offices are also closed on Sunday (see page 46).

Throughout Ireland **cafés** tend to open in the daytime, Monday to Saturday. **Restaurants** usually open for lunch and again for dinner every day, though, away from the major towns and popular tourist areas, many may be closed at lunch times or all day on certain days of the week (especially out of season).

The law in the Republic states that **pubs are allowed to open** Monday to Thursday 10.30am–11.30pm, Friday and Saturday 10.30am–12.30am, Sunday 12.30–11pm. In the North the hours are Monday to Saturday 11.30am–11pm and Sunday 12.30–10pm. Some pubs apply for late licences, usually at weekends, while across Ireland **clubs** have variable opening days, though the majority are open from

| PUBLIC HOLIDAYS | | |
|---|---|---|
| **Holiday** | **Republic** | **N Ireland** |
| New Year's Day | √ | √ |
| St Patrick's Day – March 17 | √ | √ |
| Good Friday | √ | √ |
| Easter Monday | √ | √ |
| May – first Mon | √ | √ |
| May – last Mon | × | √ |
| June – first Mon | √ | × |
| Orange Day – July 12 | × | √ |
| Aug – first Mon | √ | × |
| Aug – last Mon | × | √ |
| Oct – last Mon | √ | × |
| Christmas Day | √ | √ |
| St Stephen's Day/ Boxing Day – Dec 26 | √ | √ |

Thursday to Sunday and hours tend to be from around 10pm to 2am (or later in the major cities). Note that in the Republic all pubs and clubs are closed on Good Friday and Christmas Day.

On **public holidays**, away from the cities, most businesses will be closed, apart from pubs, newsagents, some supermarkets, grocers and petrol stations. If St Patrick's Day, Orange Day, Christmas Day or St Stephen's Day falls at the weekend, then a substitute holiday is taken at the beginning of the following week.

## Phones

The international **dialling code** for the Republic is +353, and for Northern Ireland, as part of the UK, it's +44. If you're calling the North from the Republic, however, knock off the 028 area code and instead dial 048 followed by the eight-digit subscriber number.

### Mobile phones

Roaming charges for mobile phones within the EU were abolished in 2017, meaning that UK travellers can use their mobiles throughout the Republic at no extra cost, a situation that looks unlikely to change despite the UK's exit from the EU – that said, check with your network provider for data allowance and charges. Travellers from other parts of the world will need to check whether their phone is multi-band GSM, and will probably also want to find out from their provider what the roaming charges are. The cheapest way to get round roaming charges is to get hold of a UK or Irish pay-as-you-go SIM card to insert in your phone, which will give you a local number and eliminate charges for receiving calls. Vodafone in the Republic (Ⓦvodafone.ie), for example, are currently offering a €30 thirty-day package (plus €10 for a SIM card), which includes 100 minutes of international calls and 8GB of data, as well as free calls and texts to any network.

## Smoking

Smoking is illegal in all public buildings and places of employment across Ireland. Some hotels, but increasingly few B&Bs, have bedrooms available for smokers. Many pubs in cities and large towns have outdoor areas allocated for smokers, some covered and heated.

## Time

Ireland is on **GMT**, eight hours ahead of US Pacific Standard Time and five hours ahead of Eastern Standard Time. Clocks are advanced one hour at the end of March and back again at the end of October.

## Tipping

Though discretionary, **tipping** restaurant staff or taxi drivers is the expected reward for satisfactory service; ten to fifteen percent of your tab will suffice.

## Toilets

**Public toilets** are usually only found in the big towns in the Republic (especially in shopping malls), though in the North are much more common and generally well maintained. Toilet doors often bear the indicator *Fir* (men) and *Mná* (women).

## Tourist information

The Irish tourist development agency, **Fáilte Ireland** (Ⓦdiscoverireland.ie), as well as the **Northern Ireland Tourist Board** (NITB; Ⓦdiscovernorthernireland.com) both provide a wealth of area-specific information on their websites. Abroad, the two boards combine as **Tourism Ireland**, with their main point of contact for the public at Ⓦireland.com. There are also plenty of local and regional tourism websites, and we have listed the best of these in the relevant sections of the Guide.

Both Fáilte Ireland and the NITB provide an extensive network of **tourist offices**, covering every city, many major towns and almost all the popular tourist areas. Additionally, some local councils provide their own offices. Tourist offices offer plenty of information on local attractions and can book accommodation. Bear in mind, though, that the opening hours of tourist offices are especially volatile, depending on budgets and staffing levels and varying from year to year and often from month to month.

## Travellers with disabilities

**Travellers with disabilities** should glean as much information as possible before travelling since facilities in Ireland are generally poor – the best place to start looking is on the joint tourist board website, Ⓦireland.com/en-us/about-ireland/once-you-are-here/accessibility. For example, older buildings, including most B&Bs, may lack lifts and their entrances may not have been converted to allow easy wheelchair access.

All new buildings and many hotels, however, now have wheelchair access. Go to Ⓦaccessibleireland.

com for island-wide listings of hotels with disabled facilities, as well as visitor attractions.

The main **transport** companies (see page 31) have considerably improved their facilities for travellers with disabilities, with, for example, low-floor buses in many cities and kneeling coaches on some long-distance routes. Drivers with disabilities travelling with their cars from Britain can usually obtain reduced rates for ferry travel, depending on the time of year. Motability Ireland near Dublin (☎01 835 9173, ⓦ motabilityireland.com) offer vehicle rental all over Ireland.

# Dublin

HA'PENNY BRIDGE

**1**

# Dublin

Set beside the shores of curving Dublin Bay, Ireland's capital city, Dublin, is a vibrant, dynamic place, which despite its size remains utterly beguiling and an essential part of any visit to the country. Much of Dublin's centre has been redeveloped over the last few decades, so alongside the city's historic buildings – its cathedrals and churches, Georgian squares and town houses, castles, monuments and pubs – you'll discover grand new hotels and shopping centres, stunning new street architecture and a state-of-the-art tramway system.

More than a quarter of the Republic of Ireland's population of four and a half million lives within the Greater Dublin area. Most Dubliners are intensely proud of their city, its heritage and powerful literary culture, and can at times exhibit a certain snobbishness towards those living in Ireland's rural backwaters (often termed "culchies"). Locals are noted for their often caustic brand of humour, but there is also a warmth in their welcome – it's easy to find yourself drawn into conversation or debates in bars and cafés (or, if you smoke, outside them). Dubliners are also increasingly style-conscious; where once the city looked inwards for inspiration, today it glances both east and west, to Europe and America, catching new trends and bringing a decidedly Irish slant to bear upon them.

Most of Dublin's attractions are contained within a relatively compact area, spreading either side of the many-bridged **River Liffey**, which divides the city between its **northside** and **southside**. These have very distinct characters, defined over the city's historical development: stereotypically, the south is viewed in terms of its gentility while the north is seen as brash and working class, home of the true Dub accent. Certainly, the southside is regarded as more fashionable and fashion-conscious, thanks to its **Grafton Street** shopping area and the rejuvenated **Temple Bar** arts quarter, yet the north possesses Ireland's two most renowned theatres and its own increasingly lively nightlife. On either side of the river it's easy to escape the city's bustle, to relax or picnic in one of the squares or green spaces; or visitors can head to the shoreline for seaside strolls and blustery cliff-top walks.

West of the centre is the green expanse of **Phoenix Park**, while across the river to the south lies the grim memorial of **Kilmainham Gaol** and, to the east, is the more

---

### A DECADE OF CENTENARIES

The decade between **1912 and 1922** was one of the most eventful in Irish history. The passing of Home Rule, the beginning of World War One, the growth of militant Ulster Unionism, the Easter Rising of 1916, the War of Independence and Civil War, as well as the rise of the labour and suffrage movements, were among the many momentous events which radically reshaped the political and social fabric of Ireland and its relationship with Britain during that period.

The programme **A Decade of Centenaries** (ⓦdecadeofcentenaries.com) began in 2012 to mark the 100th anniversary of these events at a local and national level, with exhibitions, public discussions and other commemorative initiatives. The programme focuses on the everyday experience of ordinary people, as well as the leaders and key actors.

The biggest event held so far has been "Ireland 2016" (ⓦireland.ie), a year-long programme remembering those who fought and died in the 1916 Rising, and reflecting on the legacy of that period. Commemorations are planned to continue until 2023, a century after the creation of the Irish Free State. See the website for events and listings.

TRINITY COLLEGE

# Highlights

**❶ Trinity College** Admire the illuminated *Book of Kells* and the magnificent Long Room, or just enjoy the architecture. See page 62

**❷ The National Museum – Archaeology** Prehistoric gold and Christian treasures are the highlights of this collection. See page 65

**❸ The National Gallery** A graceful showcase, especially for Irish art and the vibrant Yeats collection. See page 66

**❹ The Chester Beatty Library** An elegant, world-renowned display of manuscripts, prints and objets d'art. See page 72

**❺ Dublin Spire** The 121m pin-like monument is also called the Monument of Light for the way it

catches the sun. See page 78

**❻ Bloomsday** Don a straw hat and join the festivities in celebration of Joyce's *Ulysses*. See page 81

**❼ Kilmainham Gaol** Tour the city's most historically significant prison and visit the museum for insights into Republican history. See page 86

**❽ Croke Park** Catch an inter-county hurling or football match at the stadium home of Gaelic games. See page 87

**❾ The Cobblestone** A magnet for traditional music fans and an atmospheric pub to boot. See page 104

**HIGHLIGHTS ARE MARKED ON THE MAP ON PAGE 56**

# DUBLIN

Liverpool  Holyhead

Baily Lighthouse

Nose of Howth

Cliff Walk

Cliff Walk

Howth

Sutton

Howth Junction

*Dublin Bay*

James Joyce Tower and Museum

Dalkey Island

Killiney Bay

Killiney

Dún Laoghaire

Bray & Greystones

Dalkey

Dalkey & Killiney Hills

Sandycove & Glasthule

DART

Bull Island

RAHENY

Monkstown

N11

Blackrock

Wicklow

Dublin Port

SANDYMOUNT

DART

STILLORGAN

FOXROCK

ARTANE

N11

Leopardstown Racecourse

The Casino

Clontarf

Docklands

RINGSEND

DONNYBROOK

M50

SANDYFORD

MARINO

Tara Street

Pearse

BALLSBRIDGE

DUNDRUM

National Botanic Gardens

Connolly

RATHFARNHAM

Airport, Drogheda, Marino & Malahide

M1

DART

RATHMINES

Monaghan

Glasnevin Cemetery

N2

Heuston

CRUMLIN

FINGLAS

N4

KILMAINHAM

N3

Phoenix Park

BLANCHARDS-TOWN

Cavan

Royal Canal

M50

River Liffey

Grand Canal

Sligo

N7

M50

CLONDALKIN

TALLAGHT

Carnac Valley Tourist Caravan and Camping Park & Limerick

0    2
kilometres

N

obviously appealing **Guinness Brewery and Storehouse**. In the city's **suburbs**, the attractions of the northside have a definite edge over those to the south of the river: most compelling are the national **cemetery at Glasnevin**; the splendid stadium home of the Gaelic Athletic Association, **Croke Park**, which contains a fine museum; and the architectural wonders of the **Casino at Marino**. For a scenic breather from the city, take the southerly branch of the DART to panoramic **Dalkey and Killiney Hills**.

## Brief history

Dublin's origins date back to ninth-century **Viking** times when the Norsemen saw the strategic potential of Dublin Bay and established a trading post on the Liffey's southern bank. They adopted the location's Irish name, Dubh Linn ("dark pool"), for their new home, soon amalgamating with an Irish settlement on the northern bank called Baile Atha Cliath ("place of the hurdle ford"), which remains the Irish name for the city.

The twelfth century saw Dublin conquered by the **Anglo-Normans** when Dermot MacMurrough, the deposed King of Leinster, sought help from Henry II to regain his crown. In return for Dermot's fealty, Henry sent Strongbow (see page 571) and a contingent of Welsh knights to restore MacMurrough's power. Strongbow conquered Dublin in the process and, concerned at this threat to his authority, Henry came over to Ireland to assert control, establishing Dublin as the focus for British sway over Ireland. This became the centre of the **"English Pale"** (from the Latin *palum*, meaning originally a "stake", though later a "defined territory"), ruling over the areas of Anglo-Norman settlement in Ireland; since Irish resistance to conquest was so strong in other parts of the country, the pejorative phrase "beyond the pale" evolved as a means of signifying (at least in English terms) a lack of civilized behaviour.

Only a few buildings have survived from before the seventeenth century, mainly in the area encompassing Dublin Castle and the two cathedrals, and much of the city's layout is **Georgian**. During this period, Dublin's Anglo-Irish nobility and its increasingly wealthy mercantile class used their money (often, in the aristocracy's case, derived from confiscated land granted as a reward for services to the Crown) to showcase their wealth in the form of grandiose houses, public buildings and wide thoroughfares. Wealthy members of the elite revelled in their new-found opulence, filling their houses with works by the latest artists and craftsmen, and seeking to enhance their own cachet by patronizing the arts; Handel conducted the first performance of his *Messiah* in the city, for example. Increasing political freedom resulted in demands for self-government, inspired by the American and French revolutions. The legislative independence achieved during "Grattan's Parliament" in 1782 was to be short-lived, however, and the failure of the **1798 Rebellion** (see page 574), led largely by members of the Protestant Anglo-Irish Ascendancy, inevitably led to the 1801 **Act of Union** and the removal of Dublin's independent powers.

With Ireland now governed by a British vice-regent, Dublin sank into a period of **economic decline**, brought about by its inability to compete with Britain's flourishing industries. The city remained the focus of agitation for self-rule, and by the end of the nineteenth century had also become the centre for efforts to form a sense of Irish national consciousness via the foundation of the **Gaelic League** in 1893. This sought to revive both the Irish language and traditional culture, and set the scene for the **Celtic literary revival**, led by W.B. Yeats and Lady Gregory, who established the Abbey Theatre in 1904. The political struggle for independence remained a live issue and events came to a head with the **Easter Rising** of 1916 (see page 78). The city's streets saw violence again during the **civil war**, which followed the establishment of the Irish Free State in 1921.

Austerity and much **emigration** followed Independence and it was not until the 1950s that Dublin began to emerge from its colonial past. The city's infrastructure was ravaged by ill-conceived redevelopment in the 1960s which saw the demolition of many Georgian edifices, as well as the creation of poorly planned "sink" estates to replace dilapidated tenements. A couple of decades later city planners began to address

1

the issue of inner-city depopulation, constructing apartment blocks to house Dublin's wealthy middle classes. The most obvious evidence of reinvigoration in the city centre is the Temple Bar area, though the original intention to develop a Parisian-style quarter of *ateliers* and arts centres soon fell foul of the moneygrubbers, and the area is now home to a plethora of kitsch tourist bars and fast-food chains. East of the centre, reconstruction continues in the city's docklands.

## CENTRAL DUBLIN

**■ ACCOMMODATION**

| | |
|---|---|
| Ashling Hotel | 6 |
| Belvedere Hotel | 3 |
| Clifden Guesthouse | 2 |
| Hilton Garden Inn | 5 |
| Maldron Hotel | 4 |
| Marian Guest House | 1 |

**■ DRINKING & NIGHTLIFE**

PUBS & BARS

| | |
|---|---|
| The Bernard Shaw | 2 |
| Frank Ryan & Son | 6 |
| Hill 16 | 3 |
| Kavanagh's (aka The Gravediggers) | 1 |
| Ryan's | 5 |

TRADITIONAL MUSIC PUBS

| | |
|---|---|
| The Brazen Head | 9 |
| The Cobblestone | 4 |
| Hughes' Bar | 7 |
| O'Shea's Merchant | 10 |

DJ BARS & LIVE MUSIC

| | |
|---|---|
| 3Arena | 8 |
| Vicar Street | 11 |

**● EATING**

| | |
|---|---|
| Chapter One | 2 |
| Eatyard | 1 |
| The Fumbally | 5 |
| Urbanity | 4 |
| Wuff | 3 |

**D** DART Station
**L** LUAS Stop

0 — 200 metres

The so-called Celtic Tiger years of the late 1990s and early 2000s saw the wealth of the city grow exponentially, as a property boom drove the demolition of derelict or vacant buildings to make way for new apartments and offices.

Another legacy of the boom was the arrival of **migrants**, particularly from Africa and Eastern Europe, which, together with the city's longer-standing Chinese community, saw Dublin gradually inch towards multiculturalism.

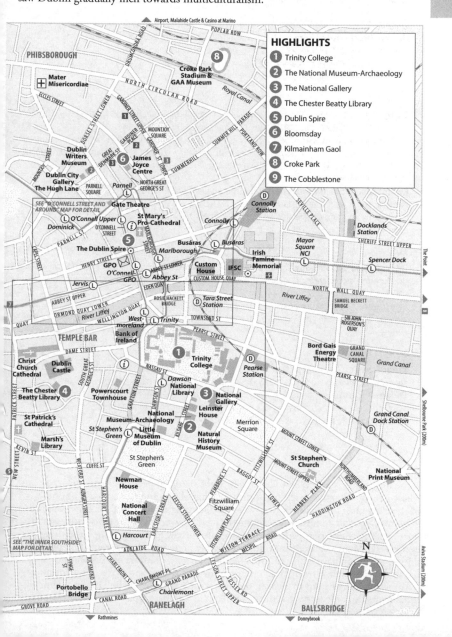

### HIGHLIGHTS

1. Trinity College
2. The National Museum-Archaeology
3. The National Gallery
4. The Chester Beatty Library
5. Dublin Spire
6. Bloomsday
7. Kilmainham Gaol
8. Croke Park
9. The Cobblestone

**1**

## FESTIVALS AND EVENTS

### JANUARY

**Temple Bar Tradfest** ☎01 677 2397, ⓦtradfest.ie. Five days and nights of traditional music pub sessions, concerts, instrument workshops and more in the heart of the city.

### FEBRUARY

**Dublin International Film Festival** ☎01 687 7974, ⓦdiff.ie. Held at cinemas and other venues across the city centre for eleven days at the end of February/beginning of March. While screening the latest in new Irish cinema, the festival also has a decidedly international flavour and its hundred or so films include special themes and retrospectives.

### MARCH

**Easter Rising** Commemorations take place on Easter Sunday, featuring speeches and a march from the General Post Office to Glasnevin Cemetery.

**St Patrick's Festival** ☎01 676 3205, ⓦstpatricksfestival.ie. Running for five days on and around St Patrick's Day (March 17), this city-wide festival includes a parade, light shows, concerts, funfair, films, exhibitions and a *céilí mór*, in which thousands of locals and visitors fill the streets in a traditional danceathon.

**Mountains to Sea dlr Book Festival** ⓦmountainstosea.ie. Celebrating the county's literary heritage, this is held over the last weekend in March at The Pavilion Theatre, Dún Laoghaire, with readings by well-known Irish and international poets, master classes, exhibitions and children's events.

### MAY

**International Dublin Gay Theatre Festival** ⓦgaytheatre.ie. A fortnight of LGBTQ-focused drama, comedy, cabaret and musical theatre with international and Irish casts taking place at a variety of city-centre locations.

**International Literature Festival** ☎01 415 1295, ⓦilfdublin.com. Major Irish and international writers and poets take part in six days of readings, discussions and other events around the city centre.

### JUNE

**Bloomsday** ⓦbloomsdayfestival.ie. The James Joyce Centre organizes a week of events in mid-June, culminating in Bloomsday itself (June 16), the day on which Joyce's *Ulysses* is set.

**Dublin Pride** ⓦdublinpride.ie. A week of celebration by the city's LGBTQ communities, featuring all manner of events, culminating in a vibrant and entertaining street parade.

**Dalkey Book Festival** ⓦdalkeybookfestival.org. Described by Salman Rushdie as "the best little festival in the world", this literary festival attracts world-renowned writers to its picturesque south Dublin setting every year.

The financial crisis of 2008 called a halt to the dizzying pace of development. Many new buildings were left half-finished, while shops and office blocks on some of the city's most prestigious streets were without tenants for years at a time. But the downturn has had an upside; cheaper rents have allowed more creative businesses to open, with new galleries, performing spaces and places to eat popping up seemingly every week. Many of the city's overpriced, overly pretentious restaurants that prevailed during the boom have withered, clearing the way for a plethora of excellent new cafés, restaurants and bars offering much more innovative dishes and better value for money.

As the economy begins to recover, the cranes are returning to the Dublin skyline. Its inhabitants can only hope that the city's planners and developers have learned from the mistakes of the past.

1

**Forbidden Fruit** ⓦforbiddenfruit.ie. Taking place in the grounds of the Royal Hospital Kilmainham over the June bank holiday weekend, this is the city's premier annual music gathering, featuring top draw bands such as Elbow and the Flaming Lips.

**JULY**
**Vodafone Comedy Festival** ⓦvodafonecomedy.com. A stellar line-up of mostly Irish comedians in the stunning surrounds of the Iveagh Gardens over four days.

**AUGUST**
**Dublin Horse Show** ⓦdublinhorseshow.com. Five-day festival of equestrian events in early August at the RDS arena in Ballsbridge, featuring major international showjumpers participating in the Nations' Cup.
**Dublin Viking Festival** ☏01 222 2242, ⓦdublinia.ie. The last weekend in August sees a re-created Viking village established off Wood Quay, which features plenty of wandering inhabitants and the chance to watch re-enacted combats.

**SEPTEMBER/OCTOBER**
**Gaze LGBTQ Film Festival** ⓦgaze.ie. A strong bill of Irish and international LGBTQ films screened over five days towards the end of September at the Irish Film Institute (see page 70).
**Culture Night** ⓦculturenight.ie. Hundreds of arts and cultural organizations around the city open their doors until late for one Friday in mid-September, with free events, tours, talks and performances.
**All-Ireland Senior Hurling and Gaelic Football finals** Two of Ireland's major sporting events are staged at Croke Park (see page 87) in September: the hurling final on the first or second Sunday and the football final on the third or fourth Sunday.
**Dublin Fringe Festival** ⓦfringefest.com. Ireland's biggest performing arts festival takes place over more than two weeks from mid-September featuring music, dance, street theatre, comedy and children's events.
**Dublin Theatre Festival** ☏01 677 8899, ⓦdublintheatrefestival.ie. A major celebration of theatre, held during the last few days of September and the first two weeks in October, this includes performances of new and classic drama at various city-centre venues.
**Dublin City Marathon** ☏01 623 2250, ⓦkbcdublinmarathon.ie. Featuring ten thousand entrants, the race takes place on the last Monday in October and involves a roughly circular course starting from Fitzwilliam Street Upper, heads north across O'Connell Bridge, and takes in Phoenix Park and some southern suburbs before the finish at Merrion Square North.

**DECEMBER**
**NYF Dublin** ⓦnyfdublin.com. Four days of festivities to ring in the New Year, with a "procession of light" through the city centre culminating in a big countdown concert on College Green.

# The Southside

The southside is home to one of Dublin's most important historic sights, **Trinity College**, whose main draw for visitors is the glorious *Book of Kells*. The area also boasts stylish Georgian streets, which lie to the east of College Green and Grafton Street, and are where you'll find the compelling displays of the **National Gallery** and the **National Museum**. On the west side of Trinity begins **Temple Bar**, which somehow manages to remain the city's hub for both carousing and art, overlooked sternly by **Dublin Castle**, British headquarters in Ireland until 1921 and now home to the glorious collections of the **Chester Beatty Library**. Dublin's two iconic cathedrals, **Christ Church** and **St Patrick's**, stand to the west of here.

**INNER SOUTHSIDE**

SEE "TEMPLE BAR" MAP

**SHOPPING**

| | |
|---|---|
| Avoca | 2 |
| Books Upstairs | 1 |
| Brown Thomas | 5 |
| Celtic Whiskey Shop | 13 |
| George's Street Arcade | 7 |
| Hodges Figgis | 6 |
| Irish Design Shop | 3 |
| Kilkenny | 8 |
| Powerscourt Townhouse Centre | 9 |
| The R.A.G.E and The Record Spot | 11 |
| Sheridan's Cheesemongers | 12 |
| Ulysses Rare Books | 10 |
| Walton's | 4 |

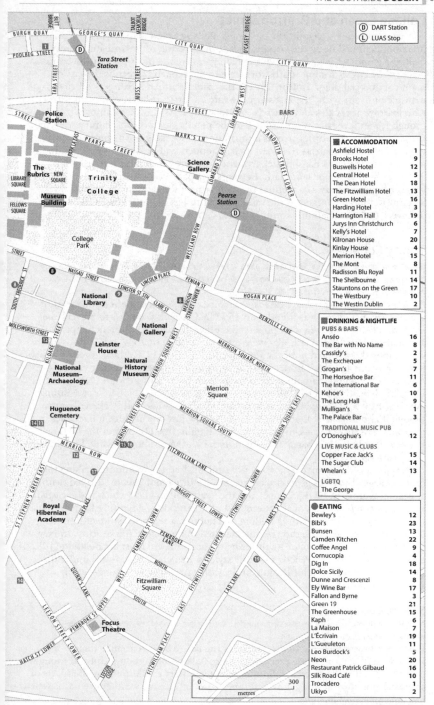

**D** DART Station
**L** LUAS Stop

■ **ACCOMMODATION**

| | |
|---|---|
| Ashfield Hostel | 1 |
| Brooks Hotel | 9 |
| Buswells Hotel | 12 |
| Central Hotel | 5 |
| The Dean Hotel | 18 |
| The Fitzwilliam Hotel | 13 |
| Green Hotel | 16 |
| Harding Hotel | 3 |
| Harrington Hall | 19 |
| Jurys Inn Christchurch | 6 |
| Kelly's Hotel | 7 |
| Kilronan House | 20 |
| Kinlay House | 4 |
| Merrion Hotel | 15 |
| The Mont | 8 |
| Radisson Blu Royal | 11 |
| The Shelbourne | 14 |
| Stauntons on the Green | 17 |
| The Westbury | 10 |
| The Westin Dublin | 2 |

■ **DRINKING & NIGHTLIFE**

**PUBS & BARS**

| | |
|---|---|
| Anséo | 16 |
| The Bar with No Name | 8 |
| Cassidy's | 2 |
| The Exchequer | 5 |
| Grogan's | 7 |
| The Horseshoe Bar | 11 |
| The International Bar | 6 |
| Kehoe's | 10 |
| The Long Hall | 9 |
| Mulligan's | 1 |
| The Palace Bar | 3 |

**TRADITIONAL MUSIC PUB**

| | |
|---|---|
| O'Donoghue's | 12 |

**LIVE MUSIC & CLUBS**

| | |
|---|---|
| Copper Face Jack's | 15 |
| The Sugar Club | 14 |
| Whelan's | 13 |

**LGBTQ**

| | |
|---|---|
| The George | 4 |

● **EATING**

| | |
|---|---|
| Bewley's | 12 |
| Bibi's | 23 |
| Bunsen | 13 |
| Camden Kitchen | 22 |
| Coffee Angel | 9 |
| Cornucopia | 4 |
| Dig In | 18 |
| Dolce Sicily | 14 |
| Dunne and Crescenzi | 8 |
| Ely Wine Bar | 17 |
| Fallon and Byrne | 3 |
| Green 19 | 21 |
| The Greenhouse | 15 |
| Kaph | 6 |
| La Maison | 7 |
| L'Écrivain | 19 |
| L'Gueuleton | 11 |
| Leo Burdock's | 5 |
| Neon | 20 |
| Restaurant Patrick Guilbaud | 16 |
| Silk Road Café | 10 |
| Trocadero | 1 |
| Ukiyo | 2 |

**1**

# College Green and Grafton Street

Formerly open fields beyond the city walls, **College Green** is today just a road junction, hemmed in by the curving facade of the Bank of Ireland and Trinity College's grandiose west front, whose main gates are the most popular meeting place in the city. Running south from here to St Stephen's Green is the city's main commercial drag, **Grafton Street**. This pedestrianized street gets off to an inauspicious start with "the tart with the cart", a kitsch bronze, complete with wheelbarrow of cockles and mussels, of **Molly Malone**, who was immortalized – though it's unlikely she ever existed – in the popular nineteenth-century song. For people-watchers, Grafton Street is a must, noted especially for its buskers, who range from string quartets to street poets. Shoppers will be drawn here, too, in particular to the city's flagship department store, **Brown Thomas** (see page 107). The street's other major landmark, **Bewley's** (see page 98), was founded by the Quaker Bewley family as a teetotal bulwark against the demon drink, and owes its beautiful mosaic facade to the mania for all things Egyptian that followed the discovery of Tutankhamun's tomb in 1922.

## Trinity College

College Green • Tours (30min) mid-May to Sept 14 every 20min 10.15am–3.40pm; see website for schedule during the rest of the year • Free campus access to visitors; tours €3, or €16 including admission to the Old Library – if there are any queues there, this combination ticket will allow you to jump them • ☎ 01 896 1000, ⓦ tcd.ie

An imposing and surprisingly extensive architectural set piece right at the heart of the city, **Trinity College** was founded in 1592 by Queen Elizabeth I to prevent the Irish from being "infected with popery and other ill qualities" at French, Spanish and Italian universities. Catholics were duly admitted until 1637, when restrictions were imposed that lasted until the Catholic Relief Act of 1793; the Catholic Church, however, banned its flock from studying here until 1970 because of the college's Anglican orientation. Famous alumni range from politicians Edward Carson and Douglas Hyde, through to philosopher George Berkeley and Nobel Prize-winning physicist Ernest Walton, and to writers such as Swift, Wilde and Beckett. Trinity, though it also calls itself Dublin University, is now just one of three universities in the capital: its main rival, University College Dublin (UCD), part of the National University of Ireland, is based at Belfield in the southern suburbs; while Dublin City University is in Glasnevin.

From just inside the main gates, Trinity students lead thirty-minute **walking tours** of the college. The gates give onto eighteenth-century **Front Square**, flanked, with appealing symmetry, by the Chapel and the Examination Hall, which is the elegant, stuccoed setting for occasional concerts. On the east side of adjoining Library Square is the college's oldest surviving building, the **Rubrics**, a red-brick student dormitory dating from around 1701, though much altered in the nineteenth century. In New Square beyond, the School of Engineering occupies the old **Museum Building** (1852), designed in extravagant Venetian Gothic style by Benjamin Woodward under the influence of his friend, John Ruskin, and awash with decorative stone-carving of animals and floral patterns.

### Science Gallery

Pearse St • Tues–Fri noon–8pm, Sat & Sun noon–5pm; closed for 2 weeks over Christmas and New Year • Free • ☎ 01 896 4091, ⓦ dublin.sciencegallery.com

In the northeastern corner of the college at the Pearse Street entrance (handy for Pearse DART Station) is the excellent **Science Gallery**. Both thoughtful and thought-provoking, it hosts high-tech and interactive temporary exhibitions on all aspects of science, from how the body uses fat to the causes of extreme weather events, as well as interesting one-off lectures.

**1**

## Douglas Hyde Gallery

Entrance on Nassau St • Wed, Fri & Sat noon–6pm, Thurs noon–7pm • Free • ☎ 01 896 1116, ⓦ douglashydegallery.com

In Fellows' Square on the south side of Library Square, the modern Arts Block is home to the **Douglas Hyde Gallery**, one of Ireland's most important galleries of modern art. Temporary exhibitions focus on Irish and international artists whose work is not yet well known, or has been previously overlooked. Gallery 2 regularly hosts exhibitions of ethnographic and craft artefacts.

## The Old Library and the Book of Kells

Fellows' Square • May–Sept Mon–Sat 8.30am–5pm, Sun 9.30am–5pm; Oct–April Mon–Sat 9.30am–5pm, Sun noon–4.30pm; closed for 10 days over Christmas and New Year • €16 • ☎ 01 896 2320, ⓦ tcd.ie/library

Trinity's most compelling tourist attraction is the **Book of Kells**, kept in the eighteenth-century **Old Library**. On the library's ground floor, beautiful pages are displayed not just from the *Book of Kells* (around 800 AD), but from other works such as the *Book of Armagh* (early ninth century) and the *Book of Mulling* (late eighth century). The books themselves are preceded by a fascinating exhibition, **Turning Darkness into Light**, which sets Irish illuminated manuscripts in context – ranging from ogham (the earlier, Celtic writing system of lines carved on standing stones) to Ethiopian books of devotions.

### Brief history

Pre-eminent for the scale, variety and colour of its decoration, the *Book of Kells* probably originated at the monastery on Iona off the west coast of Scotland, which had been founded around 561 by the great Irish scholar, bard and ruler St Colmcille (St Columba in English). After a Viking raid in 806 the Columbines moved to the monastery of Kells in County Meath, which in its turn was raided four times between 920 and 1019. Although they looted the book's *cumdach* or metal shrine cover, the pagan Norsemen did not value the book itself, however, and despite spending some time buried underground and losing thirty folios, it survived at Kells up to the seventeenth century when it was taken to Dublin for safekeeping during the Cromwellian Wars. The 340 calfskin folios of the *Book of Kells* contain the four New Testament Gospels along with preliminary texts, all in Latin. It's thought that three artists created the book's lavish decoration, which shows Pictish, Germanic and Mediterranean, as well as Celtic, influences. Not only are there full-page illustrations of Christ and the Virgin and Child, but an elaborate decorative scheme of animals and spiral, roundel and interlace patterns is employed throughout the text, on the initials at the beginning of each Gospel and on full-length "carpet pages".

### The Long Room

Upstairs is the library's magnificent **Long Room**, built by Thomas Burgh between 1712 and 1732 and enlarged, with a barrel-vaulted ceiling, in 1860. As a copyright library, Trinity has had the right to claim a free copy of all British and Irish publications since 1801; of its current stock of four million titles, 200,000 of the oldest are stored in the Long Room's oak bookcases. Besides interesting temporary exhibitions of books and prints from the library's collection, the Long Room also displays a gnarled fifteenth-century harp, the oldest to survive from Ireland, and a rare original printing of the 1916 Proclamation of the Irish Republic, made on Easter Sunday in Dublin's Liberty Hall.

# The Bank of Ireland

College Green • House of Lords: Mon, Tues & Fri 10am–3.45pm, Wed 10.30am–3.45pm; Thurs 10am–4.45pm; guided tours Tues 10.30am, 11.30am & 12.30pm • Entry and tours free • ☎ 01 677 6801

The Neoclassical granite **Bank of Ireland**, opposite Trinity on College Green, was constructed in 1729 by Sir Edward Pearce – himself an MP – as the **House of Parliament**. An Irish parliament had existed in one limited form or another since the

**1**

thirteenth century, but achieved its greatest success here in 1782, when "Grattan's Parliament" (so named after the prime mover behind the constitutional reform) was granted legislative independence from the British Parliament. Catholics were still barred from sitting, but many signs of Irish sovereignty were established during this period, including the founding of the Bank of Ireland itself. Around this time, the Lords deemed it necessary to build themselves a separate entrance on Westmoreland Street, designed in 1785 by James Gandon in the Corinthian style in order to distinguish it from the Ionic colonnade of what is still the main entrance. After the Rebellion of 1798, however, the Irish House was persuaded and bribed to vote itself out of existence, and with the 1801 Act of Union Ireland became part of the United Kingdom, governed from Westminster. The Bank of Ireland bought the building for £40,000 in 1802, and the Commons chamber was demolished to remove a highly charged symbol of independence.

### House of Lords
The barrel-vaulted **House of Lords** was also meant to be knocked down, but survives to this day to host high-level state functions and as the main attraction for visitors, especially during its interesting, weekly guided tours. Here you'll find one or two exhibits such as the Lord Chancellor's richly embroidered purse, used to carry the Great Seal of Ireland, and tapestries showing William of Orange's victories over James II and his Catholic supporters, the *Siege of Derry* and the *Battle of the Boyne*. The richly stuccoed **Cash Hall** – an elegant spot to do any banking chores you may have – used to be the Parliament's Hall of Requests, where constituents would petition their representatives.

## Powerscourt Townhouse
59 South William St • Mon–Fri 10am–6pm, Sat 9am–6pm, Sun noon–6pm • ☎ 01 679 4144, ⓦ powerscourtcentre.ie

The **Powerscourt Townhouse**, once the eighteenth-century Palladian mansion of Lord Powerscourt (see page 118), is now home to a stylish shopping centre. The house's main door leads straight onto the trompe l'oeil stone floor of the entrance hall and, beyond, the central mahogany staircase, with its flighty rococo plasterwork and what are thought to be the most elaborately carved balusters in Ireland. The café-bar in the atrium is notable for its location – bathed in light on sunny days – in what was once the mansion's inner courtyard.

## Leinster House (Oireachtas)
Kildare St • Entrance by guided tour only, Mon & Fri 10.30am & 2.30pm • Free • ☎ 01 618 3271, ⓦ oireachtas.ie

Ireland's political and cultural establishments have their power bases in the tight confines of Kildare Street and Merrion Square. Kildare Street is dominated by the imposing **Leinster House**, the city's largest eighteenth-century mansion, designed by one of Ireland's greatest architects Richard Castle (1690–1751). Built on open fields in1745 for the Earl of Kildare James FitzGerald, the town house started a trend among the gentry and wealthy, who eschewed traditionally fashionable parts of the city to build new homes in the surrounding area. Originally called Kildare House, it was renamed when the earl became Duke of Leinster in 1766. Dublin's largest Georgian-style district grew up around Leinster House, and still survives today.

After the formation of the Irish Free State in 1922, the building was acquired by the newly formed government. It has since been home to the Irish parliament, the Oireachtas (pronounced something like "or-ruck-tas"), which is divided into Dáil Eireann (House of Representatives) and Seannad Eireann (the Senate). Portraits of two of the leading members of the first Dáil, Cathal Brugha and Michael Collins, hang opposite each other in the entrance hall, alongside paintings of past Irish presidents and an original copy of the 1916 Proclamation.

# Natural History Museum

Merrion St • Tues–Sat 10am–5pm, Sun & Mon 1–5pm • Free • ☎ 01 677 7444, ⓦ museum.ie

The charmingly unreconstructed displays of the **Natural History Museum** have been impressing visitors since the "Dead Zoo" first opened its doors to the public in 1857. Recent conservation work has improved access and provided new learning opportunities – including a discovery zone where visitors can handle taxidermy and open drawers to see what is lurking inside – but overall, the exhibition style and furnishings have changed little in 150 years.

The ground floor is dedicated to native Irish species, and includes the skeleton of an 11,000-year-old deer alongside a variety of mammals, birds and fish. The upper floors feature animals from around the world, laid out in the nineteenth century by taxonomic group, which aimed to demonstrate the evolution of animal life.

# The National Museum – Archaeology

Kildare St • Tues–Sat 10am–5pm, Sun & Mon 1–5pm • Free • ☎ 01 677 7444, ⓦ museum.ie

The **National Museum – Archaeology** is a must-see for visitors to Dublin. Undoubtedly the stars of the show here are a stunning hoard of prehistoric gold and a thousand years' worth of ornate ecclesiastical treasures, but the whole collection builds up a fascinating and accessible story of Irish archaeology and history. The shop in the beautiful entrance rotunda sells a range of high-quality crafts inspired by works in the museum, and there's a small café.

**Prehistoric gold**, much of it discovered during peat-cutting, takes pride of place on the ground floor of the main hall. From the Earlier Bronze Age (c.2500–1500 BC) come *lunulae*, thin sheets of gold formed into crescent-moon collars. After around 1200 BC, when new sources of the metal were apparently found, goldsmiths could be more extravagant, fashioning chunky torcs, such as the spectacular Gleninsheen Collar and the Tumna Hoard of nine large gold balls, which are perforated, suggesting that when joined together they formed a huge necklace. Further prehistoric material is arrayed around the walls of the main hall, including the 15m-long Lurgan Logboat, dating from around 2500 BC, which was unearthed in a Galway bog in 1902.

The adjacent **Treasury** holds most of the museum's better-known ecclesiastical exhibits, notably the ornate eighth-century Ardagh Chalice, the Tara Brooch, decorated with beautiful knot designs, and the Cross of Cong, created to enshrine a fragment of the True Cross given to the King of Connacht by the Pope in 1123. Also on the ground floor is **Kingship and Sacrifice**, showcasing the leathery bodies of four Iron Age noblemen that were preserved and discovered in various bogs around Ireland.

Upstairs, **Viking-age Ireland** (c.800–1150) features models of a house and the layout of Dublin's Fishamble Street, while **Medieval Ireland** (1150–1550) moves on to cover the first English colonists, their withdrawal to the fortified area around Dublin known as "the Pale" after 1300, and the hybrid culture that developed all the while – you can listen to recordings of poetry written in Ireland in Middle Irish, Middle English and Norman French. Unmissable here is a host of strange, ornate portable **shrines**, made to hold holy relics or texts, including examples for all three of Ireland's patron saints: the Shrine of St Patrick's Tooth, the Shrine of St Brigid's Shoe (see page 126) and the Shrine of the Cathach, containing a manuscript written by St Colmcille (St Columba), legendary bard, scholar, ruler and evangelizer of Scotland.

# The National Library

Kildare St • Mon–Wed 9.30am–7.45pm, Thurs & Fri 9.30am–4.45pm, Sat 9.30am–12.45pm; Genealogy Room Mon–Wed 9.30am–5pm, Thurs–Fri 9.30am–4.45pm, Sat 9.30am–12.45pm • Free • ☎ 01 603 0200, ⓦ nli.ie

The **National Library** was opened on Kildare Street in 1890, shortly after the National Museum, whose design it mirrors across the courtyard of Leinster House. Besides prestigious public talks and readings, its main draws are its long-term temporary exhibitions on subjects such as W.B. Yeats and Seamus Heaney, which are mounted in a beautiful, high-tech space on the lower ground floor. Visitors are also allowed up to the hushed domed **Reading Room** on the first floor, decorated with ornate bookcases and an incongruously playful frieze of cherubs. It is in the office here that Stephen Dedalus engages the librarians – who appear under their real names – in literary talk in the "Scylla and Charybdis" episode of *Ulysses*. In the **Genealogy Room**, library staff can give advice to anyone researching their family history on how to access the records here and elsewhere in Dublin, as well as in Belfast.

## The National Gallery

Merrion Square West • Mon–Sat 9.15am–5.30pm, Thurs 9.15am–8.30pm, Sun 11am–5.30pm, public hols 10am–5.30pm; guided tours Sat 12.30pm, Sun 11.30am & 1.30pm • Entry and tours free • ☏ 01 661 5133, ⓦ nationalgallery.ie

The **National Gallery** hosts a fine collection of Western European art dating from the Middle Ages to the twentieth century, most of which is held within the gallery's two oldest, but newly modernised, buildings – namely the Milltown and Dargan wings.

A significant portion of the permanent exhibition is given over to **Irish art** from the seventeenth century onwards. The highlight is the collection of paintings by Jack B. Yeats (1871–1957), younger brother of the writer W.B. Yeats, which traces the artist's development from an unsentimental illustrator of everyday scenes to an expressive painter in abstract, unmixed colours. Other works include early twentieth-century portraits by William Orpen (1878–1931) and John Lavery (1856–1941), as well as more modern Irish landscapes by Gerard Dillon (1916–71).

Watercolours by **Turner** are exhibited every January, when the light is low enough for these delicate works. Highlights of the European collection include *Kitchen Maid with the Supper at Emmaus*, the earliest known picture by **Velázquez** (1599–1660); **Vermeer**'s *Woman Writing a Letter with her Maid*, one of only 35 accepted works by the artist, with his characteristic use of white light from the window accentuating the woman's heated emotions; and **Caravaggio**'s dynamic *The Taking of Christ*, in which the artist portrayed himself as a passive spectator on the right of the picture, holding a lamp.

## Merrion Square

Begun in 1762, **Merrion Square** represents Georgian town planning at its grandest. Its long, graceful terraces of red-brown brick sport elaborate doors, knockers and fanlights, as well as wrought-iron balconies (added in the early nineteenth century) and tall windows on the first floor, where the main reception rooms would have been; the north side of the square was built first and displays the widest variety of design.

The broad, manicured lawns of the square's gardens themselves are a joy, quieter than St Stephen's Green, and especially agreeable for picnics on fine days. Revolutionary politician Michael Collins is commemorated with a bronze bust on the gardens' south side, near a slightly hapless stone bust of Henry Grattan (see page 574), while writer, artist and mystic George Russell ("AE") stands gravely near the southwest corner and his former home at no. 74. But the square's most remarkable and controversial statue is at the northwest corner, where **Oscar Wilde** reclines on a rock facing his childhood home at no. 1 (now the American College Dublin), in a wry, languid pose. In front of him, a male torso and his wife Constance, pregnant with their second child, stand on plinths inscribed with Wildean witticisms: "This suspense is terrible. I hope it will last", "I drink to keep body and soul apart." Nearby on the railings around the square's gardens, dozens of artists hang their paintings for sale every Sunday.

The Merrion Square South terrace has the greatest concentration of famous former residents, giving a vivid sense of the history of the place: politician Daniel O'Connell bought no. 58 in 1809; the Nobel Prize-winning Austrian physicist, Erwin

Schrödinger, occupied no. 65; Gothic novelist Joseph Sheridan Le Fanu died at no. 70, which is now the Arts Council; and W.B. Yeats lived at no. 82 from 1922 to 1928. At no. 39 stood the British Embassy, which was burnt down by a crowd protesting against the Bloody Sunday massacre in Derry in 1972.

## The National Print Museum

Haddington Rd • Mon–Fri 9am–5pm, Sat & Sun 2–5pm; guided tours 11.30am and 2.30pm • Free • ☎ 01 660 3770, ⓦ nationalprintmuseum.ie

Housed in the former chapel of Beggar's Bush barracks, the **National Print Museum** traces the history of print in Ireland, telling surprisingly affecting tale through video, rare documents, demonstrations and workshops. The ground floor is filled with original and mint-condition printing presses, still in use today, while the mezzanine level displays temporary exhibitions and a fascinating hidden library. A specialist reference library requiring an appointment to explore, it houses an extraordinary collection of books, pamphlets, journals and periodicals relating to printmaking, typography, paper-making and associated crafts.

## St Stephen's Green

As well as being a major landmark and transport hub for buses, taxis and the LUAS, **St Stephen's Green** is central Dublin's largest and most varied park, whose statuary provides a poignant history lesson in stone, wood and bronze. The Green preserves its distinctive Victorian character with a small lake, bandstand, arboretum and well-tended flower displays. It was originally open common land, a notoriously dirty and dangerous spot and the site of public hangings until the eighteenth century. In 1880, however, it was turned into a public park with funding from the brewer Lord Ardilaun (Arthur Guinness), who now boasts the grandest of the Green's many statues, seated at his leisure on the far western side. Over at the northeast corner, a row of huge granite monoliths – nicknamed "Tonehenge" – has been erected in honour of eighteenth-century nationalist **Wolfe Tone**, behind which stands a moving commemoration of the **Great Famine**. Meanwhile, on the west side of the central flower display, a tiny plaque inlaid in a wooden park bench commemorates the so-called "fallen women" – mostly unmarried mothers or abused girls – who were forced to live and work in severe conditions in Ireland's **Magdalen laundries**; the last of them, in Dublin, wasn't closed down until 1996. From the Green's northwest corner, by the top of Grafton Street, you can hire a **horse and carriage**, either as a grandiose taxi or for a tour of the sights, which will typically set you back €40–50 for thirty minutes.

The main sightseeing draws in the area date from the Georgian period: the splendid stuccowork of **Newman House** and the elegant streets and squares to the east of the Green, as well as the excellent **Little Museum of Dublin**.

Termed in the eighteenth century "Beau Walk", **St Stephen's Green North** is still the most fashionable side of the square. The **Shelbourne Hotel** here claims to have been "the best address in Dublin" since its establishment in 1824 (see page 96). Beyond the hotel at the start of Merrion Row, the tiny, tree-shaded **Huguenot Cemetery** was opened in 1693 for Protestant refugees fleeing religious persecution in France. A large plaque inside the gates gives a roll call of Huguenot Dubliners, among whom the most famous have been writers Dion Boucicault and Sheridan Le Fanu.

### Newman House and the Museum of Literature Ireland

85–86 St Stephen's Green South • Tues-Sun 10.30am–6pm, Thurs till 7.30pm • €10 • ☎ 01 477 9811, ⓦ moli.ie

**Newman House** boasts probably the finest Georgian interiors in Dublin, noted especially for their decorative plasterwork. The place is named after John Henry Newman, the famous British convert from Anglicanism, who was invited to found

**1**

## GEORGE BERNARD SHAW

Born in Dublin in 1856, **George Bernard Shaw** grew up among a Protestant family fallen on hard times. His father was an unsuccessful grain merchant and alcoholic – prompting Shaw to become a lifelong abstainer – and there was no money to pay for his education. At 15 he started work as a junior clerk for a land agency, but five years later went to London to join his mother who had moved there to further the musical career of one of his sisters. Reliant on what little income his mother earned as a music teacher, Shaw set about educating himself by spending his afternoons in the reading room of the British Museum. He hoped to become a novelist, but following the rejection of no fewer than five novels, turned his hand to journalism instead, contributing music and drama criticism to London newspapers.

Shaw was a devout socialist, joining the Fabian Society in 1884, writing pamphlets and gaining a reputation as a natural orator. He espoused numerous causes, including electoral reform, vegetarianism and the abolition of private property. His **theatrical career** began in the 1890s when, influenced by Ibsen, he began to compose plays focusing on social and moral matters, rather than the romantic and personal subjects which then dominated British theatre.

In 1898 he married the heiress Charlotte Payne-Townshend and the same year saw the production of his first successful play, *Candida*. A stream of equally lauded comedy-dramas followed – including *The Devil's Disciple, Arms and the Man, Major Barbara* and *Pygmalion* – though he later turned to more serious drama, such as *Heartbreak House* and *Saint Joan*. Simultaneously, he maintained an active career as a **critic**, journalist and essayist, his often bitterly ironic wit ("England and America are two countries separated by a common language") becoming legendary. In 1925 he was awarded the **Nobel Prize for Literature**, but initially rejected the honour before relenting and giving his prize money to a newly established Anglo-Swedish Literary Foundation.

Shaw's attitude to Ireland was ever ambivalent – he once commented "I am a typical Irishman; my family came from Yorkshire" – and, though he remained interested in Irish affairs and became a personal friend of Michael Collins, his brand of democratic socialism would have been antipathetic to the austere Catholic and anti-British state that emerged post-independence. Shaw died in 1950 at Ayot St Lawrence, Hertfordshire.

A plaque outside 33 Synge St marks Shaw's birthplace, which, although closed to the public at the time of writing, plans to reopen as a home for writers in residence..

the Catholic University of Ireland here in 1854 as an alternative to Anglican Trinity College and the recently established "godless" Queen's Colleges in Belfast, Cork and Galway. James Joyce and Éamon de Valera were educated at what became University College Dublin (UCD), which now occupies a large campus in the southern suburbs.

Newman House actually comprises two houses: **No. 85** is a Palladian mansion built by Richard Castle in 1738 and adorned with superb Baroque stuccowork by the Swiss Lafranchini brothers, notably in the ground-floor **Apollo Room**, where the god himself appears majestically over the fireplace, attended by the nine muses on the surrounding walls. The much larger **no. 86**, with flowing rococo plasterwork by Robert West, the notable Dublin-born imitator of the Lafranchinis, was added in 1765. The English poet **Gerard Manley Hopkins** lived here when Professor of Classics at the university in 1884 (after five wretched years in Dublin, he died of typhoid and was buried in an unmarked grave in Glasnevin Cemetery), while Joyce studied here between 1899 and 1902. While it is Joyce's work that forms the centrepiece of the **Museum of Literature Ireland**, it combines artefacts, installations and immersive audio-visual displays to dazzling effectto The rotating exhibitions celebrating contemporary Irish literature are first class, are there are engaging workshops for teens and children too.

## Little Museum of Dublin

15 St Stephen's Green North • Daily 9.30am–5pm • Guided tour on the hour every hour • €10 • ☎ 01 661 1000, ⓦ littlemuseum.ie

Crammed into two floors of a Georgian house, the **Little Museum of Dublin** displays more than five thousand artefacts and curios telling the social history of twentieth-century Dublin. Beginning with a photograph of Queen Victoria arriving in Dún Laoghaire in 1900, the exhibition traces the transformation of the city over a hundred years, using newspaper clippings, old photographs, children's toys, ticket stubs, posters, letters and other bric-a-brac on loan from the people of Dublin since the museum opened in 2011.

Temporary exhibitions cover subjects ranging from Irish emigration to America and the challenges of tenement living in 1913, to the early days of U2 and Dublin street style through the decades. Regular lectures are held on Dublin-themed topics, spanning literature, art, history, music and more.

Visitors looking to meet Dubliners and learn more about the city first-hand over a free drink can sign up online for the museum's excellent "City of a Thousand Welcomes" greeting service, which matches local volunteers with tourists.

## Fitzwilliam Square

The area to the east of St Stephen's Green is the best in the city for a Georgian architectural tour, where an aimless wander will reveal plenty of wrought-iron balconies and much-photographed doorways sporting elegant knockers and fanlights. At its centre lie the still-private lawns of the small but well-preserved **Fitzwilliam Square** (1825), where, at no. 42, W.B. Yeats lived from 1928 to 1932. His brother, the painter Jack B., had a house and studio round the corner at no. 18 Fitzwilliam Place, which together with its continuation Fitzwilliam Street forms a – now much-interrupted – kilometre-long terrace of Georgian houses, marching off towards the magnificent backdrop of the Wicklow Mountains.

## Royal Hibernian Academy

15 Ely Place • Mon, Tue & Thurs–Sat 11am–5pm, Wed 11am–8pm, Sun noon–5pm • Free • ☎ 01 661 2558, ⓦ rhagallery.ie

The **Royal Hibernian Academy** is one of the country's leading contemporary art venues. Hosting major temporary shows by Irish and international artists, its well-designed viewing spaces are also home to the RHA Annual Exhibition, usually from May to July.

## Temple Bar

Sandwiched between the busy thoroughfare of Dame Street and the Liffey, **Temple Bar** is marketed, with a fair dose of artistic licence, as Dublin's "Left Bank" (inconveniently, it's on the right bank as you face downstream). Its transformation into the city's main cultural and entertainment district came about after a 1960s plan for a new central bus terminal here was abandoned after much procrastination. Instead, the area's narrow cobbled streets and old warehouses, by now occupied by short-lease studios, workshops and boutiques, began to be sensitively redeveloped as an artistic quarter in the 1980s, and is now home to numerous **galleries** and **arts centres** (see page 70). It also shelters a huge number of hotels, restaurants, pubs and clubs, engendering a notoriously raucous nightlife scene that attracts more outsiders than Dubliners.

Most people enter Temple Bar from Dame Street, past the unusual and highly controversial 1970s **Central Bank**, whose floors are suspended from the roof by external cables. The main access from the north side is the cast-iron **Ha'penny Bridge**, Dublin's oldest and most renowned pedestrian river crossing, with great views of the river along the quays in both directions. It began life in 1816 as the Wellington Bridge but soon acquired its nickname thanks to a halfpenny toll, which was levied until 1919.

1

| ■ ACCOMMODATION | | ● EATING | | ■ DRINKING & NIGHTLIFE | | | | ● SHOPPING | |
|---|---|---|---|---|---|---|---|---|---|
| The Clarence | 4 | Avoca Café | 5 | CLUBS & LIVE MUSIC | | PUBS & BARS | | Claddagh Records | 2 |
| The Morgan | 2 | Chez Max | 4 | Button Factory | 3 | The Porterhouse | 2 | Cow's Lane Market | 3 |
| Oliver St John Gogarty's | 3 | Irish Film Institute Café Bar | 1 | Four Dame Lane | 5 | The Stag's Head | 6 | Temple Bar Food | |
| Temple Bar Hotel | 1 | Queen of Tarts | 2/3 | Olympia Theatre | 4 | | | Market | 1 |
| | | | | Workman's Club | 1 | | | | |

The central **Temple Bar Square** is a popular spot for people-watching, with several open-air cafés. It hosts a small book market on Saturdays and Sundays (11am–6pm), while the nearby **Meeting House Square** has an excellent food market (see page 107) on Saturdays (10am–4.30pm). The Designer Mart on Cow's Lane every Saturday (10am–5pm) showcases Irish handmade craft and design.

At the bottom of Parliament Street are the **Sunlight Chambers**, whose curious facade merits a short detour. Built in the early twentieth century in the style of an Italian

### TEMPLE BAR GALLERIES AND ART CENTRES

Temple Bar boasts more **galleries** and **arts centres** than you can shake a paintbrush at – even the helpful **information centre/Temple Bar Cultural Trust** on Essex Street East (Mon–Fri 9am–5.30pm, Sat 10am–5.30pm plus March–Oct Sun noon–3pm; ☎01 677 2255, ⊛templebar.ie) houses a small exhibition space for independent, "no-grants" artists. Below are some of the highlights.

**The Ark** 11A Eustace St ☎01 670 7788, ⊛ark.ie. Europe's first custom-built cultural centre for children, hosting plays, exhibitions, workshops, festivals, concerts and multimedia programmes for 2–12-year-olds.

**Gallery of Photography** Meeting House Square ☎01 671 4654, ⊛galleryofphotography.ie. Stages some great (free) shows of contemporary photographs from Ireland and around the world in smart, well-lit rooms above a good photographic bookshop. Mon & Sun 1–6pm, Tues–Sat 11am–6pm.

**Irish Film Institute** 6 Eustace St ⊛ifi.ie. An eighteenth-century Quaker meeting house (see page 105), which has been converted into an art-house cinema, with a fashionable bar-restaurant (see page 99).

**National Photographic Archive** Meeting House Square ☎01 603 0374, ⊛nli.ie. Mounts a series of often fascinating temporary exhibitions, mostly on Irish historical subjects, from the 5.2 million photographs in the National Library's collection. Free. Mon–Sat 10am–4.45pm.

**Project Arts Centre** 39 East Essex St ☎01 881 9613, ⊛projectartcentre.ie. One of Dublin's most renowned contemporary performance art spaces, hosting theatre, dance, film and music shows (see page 105).

**Temple Bar Gallery and Studios** 5–9 Temple Bar ☎01 671 0073, ⊛templebargallery.com. This publicly funded gallery, purpose-built in the 1990s with thirty artists' studios attached, exhibits cutting-edge Irish and international artists working in a wide range of media. Wed–Sat 11am–6pm.

**CYCLING IN DUBLIN**

Dublin is a long way behind other bike-friendly cities, but things are improving. Almost every road has a **cycle lane**, but some are so poorly designed that traffic often blocks the lane entirely. Whether in a designated lane or not, cyclists should take extreme care and remain vigilant, particularly for cars taking left-hand turns across the cycleway.

Although cycling in the city centre can be a congested and unpleasant affair, there are plenty of enjoyable routes further out. A cycle to **Howth** from the city centre takes just over an hour, and for the most part it's a beautifully scenic coastal ride. Starting at O'Connell Bridge, head east along the north side of the Liffey, through the IFSC and north through the East Wall to Clontarf. From there it's a straight and flat cycle lane for 10km into Howth.

For a shorter ride head to the **Poolbeg Lighthouse**, the perennially popular Sunday walking spot for Dubliners. A 4km-long long stone pier jutting out into the middle of Dublin Bay, it's usually a windy and cobweb-clearing walk with panoramic views of the city's coastline. The most enjoyable route is straight down the Grand Canal, through Bath Avenue, taking the first exit on the Sean Moore Road roundabout. It'll take just over half an hour, but be warned – towards the end, the route passes through a fairly unattractive industrial wasteland by the Dublin docks.

You'll find plenty more routes, maps, and safety tips on ⓦ dublincycling.com

Renaissance palace by the Sunlight soap company, the Chambers' exterior sports colourful ceramic friezes on the theme of hygiene; underneath the soot you can make out farmers and builders getting their clothes dirty on the upper tier, and women washing them below.

# Dublin Castle

On a ridge above the Liffey, where previously the Vikings had established themselves, the Anglo-Norman invaders rebuilt Dublin in the thirteenth century around the doughty **Dublin Castle**. The main element of the walled city became the seat of British power in Ireland for seven hundred years, successfully withstanding all attempts to take it by force. It did, however, succumb to a major fire in 1684 and was rebuilt during the eighteenth century as a complex of residential and administrative buildings over two quadrangles, giving a sedate collegiate appearance. The outline of the medieval castle is traced by the **Upper Yard**; above its original main gate, the Cork Hill State Entrance, stands a statue of *Justice*, wearing no blindfold and turning her back on the city – a fitting symbol of British rule, locals reckon. Visitors are free to walk around the courtyards, now home to police and tax offices, before visiting the **State Apartments** or the world-class collection of books and objets d'art from around the globe in the **Chester Beatty Library**.

## The State Apartments

Daily 9.45am–5.45pm (last admission 5.15pm; sometimes closed for state occasions so check ahead); frequent guided tours (1hr 10min) run daily and include the State Apartments, Viking Excavation and Chapel Royal • €8 (€12 with guided tour); Heritage Card • ⓣ 01 645 8813, ⓦ dublincastle.ie

**The State Apartments** were built as the residence of the English viceroy and are entered from the Upper Yard. Inside the apartments, the Grand Staircase leads up to the east wing of bedrooms and drawing rooms, refurbished to their eighteenth- and nineteenth-century style after a major fire in 1941. The brass chandelier in the Throne Room, with its shamrock, rose and thistle emblems, commemorates the 1801 Act of Union, while the Picture Gallery beyond is lined with viceroys, including – hiding ignominiously behind the door – the First Marquis of Cornwallis, who not only lost the American colonies, but also faced rebellions as viceroy, first of India, then of Ireland (1798). St Patrick's Hall, formerly a ballroom that hosted investitures of the Knights of St Patrick, is now used for the inaugurations and funerals of Irish presidents. Its overblown, late eighteenth-century ceiling paintings show St Patrick converting the Irish, Henry II receiving the submission of the Irish chieftains, and George III's coronation.

Public access also includes the **Chapel Royal** in the Lower Yard, an ornate Gothic Revival gem, and the excavations of the **Undercroft**, which have revealed the base of the gunpowder tower of the medieval castle and steps leading down to the moat (fed by the old River Poddle on its way down to the Liffey), as well as part of the original Viking ramparts.

## The Chester Beatty Library

Mon, Tues, Thurs & Fri 9.45am–5.30pm, Wed 9.45am–8pm, Sat 9.45am–5.30pm, Sun noon–5.30pm; Nov–Feb closed Mon; guided tours Wed 1pm, Sat 2pm, Sun 3pm • Entry and tours free • ☎ 01 407 0750, ⓦ chesterbeatty.ie

To the south of the Chapel Royal lies the pretty **castle garden**; now adorned with a swirling motif taken from the passage grave at Newgrange, it marks the site of the "black pool" (*dubh linn*) from which the city derives its name. Overlooking the garden from the renovated eighteenth-century Clock Tower Building, the **Chester Beatty Library** preserves a dazzling collection of books, manuscripts, prints and objets d'art from around the world. Superlatives come thick and fast here: as well as one of the finest **Islamic collections** in existence, containing some of the earliest manuscripts from the ninth and tenth centuries, the library holds important biblical papyri, including the earliest surviving examples in any language of Mark's and Luke's Gospels, St Paul's Letters and the Book of Revelation. Elegantly displayed in high-tech galleries, the artefacts are used to tell the story of religious and artistic traditions across the world with great ingenuity. It's well worth timing your visit to coincide with lunch at the excellent *Silk Road Café* (see page 99).

The collection was painstakingly put together by the remarkable **Sir Alfred Chester Beatty**, an American mining magnate who moved himself and his works to Dublin in the early 1950s, after cutting a deal with the Irish government on import taxes and estate duties. In 1957 he was made the first honorary citizen of Ireland, and, when he died in 1968, he bequeathed his collection to the state and was given a state funeral.

It makes sense to start with the second-floor gallery, which covers "Sacred Traditions", while the first floor deals with "the Arts of the Book" (alongside a space for fascinating temporary exhibitions), with each divided into Western, Islamic and Eastern sections; exhibits range from sixteenth-century biblical engravings by Albrecht Dürer to books carved in jade for the Chinese emperors, and from gorgeously illustrated collections of Persian poetry to serene Burmese statues of the Buddha.

## City Hall

2 Dame St • Mon–Sat 10am–5pm • Free • ☎ 01 222 2222, ⓦ dublincity.ie

In front of the castle stands the gleamingly restored rotunda of **City Hall**, where creamy Portland-stone columns, interspersed with statues of notables, including Daniel O'Connell (the city's first Catholic Lord Mayor), are bathed in wonderful natural light from the dome. The sumptuous Neoclassical building was constructed between 1769 and 1779 as the Royal Exchange, but fell into disuse after the Act of Union of 1801 passed governance of Ireland back to London; Dublin Corporation bought it in 1851, and it's still the venue for city council meetings. Arts and crafts murals under the dome trace Dublin's history, while the colourful floor mosaic shows the civic coat of arms, three castles topped by flames, which apparently represent the zeal of the citizens to defend Dublin – reinforced by the city motto *Obedientia Civium Urbis Felicitas* ("Happy the City whose Citizens Obey"). The basement houses an oft-overlooked exhibition tracing Dublin's civic history from 441AD (see page 73).

## THE STORY OF THE CAPITAL

The vaults beneath City Hall now shelter ***The Story of the Capital** (Mon–Sat 10am–5.15pm, Sun 2–5pm; last admission 1hr before closing; €4), a fascinating multimedia journey through Dublin's history and politics – with occasional hints of self-promotion for the exhibition's sponsors, the city council. The story is told through exhaustive display panels, slick interactive databases and a series of videos, complemented by an entertaining audio-guide narrated by Irish actress Sinead Cusack with snippets from leading historians. There are few exhibits as such, though a notable exception is the intricate city seal and its safe, which was instituted after the seal was stolen in 1305 and required the presence of all six keyholders.

# Christ Church Cathedral

Christchurch Place • April–Sept Mon–Sat 9.30am–7pm, Sun 12.30–2.30pm & 4.30–7pm; March & Oct Mon–Sat 9.30am–6pm, Sun 12.30–2.30pm & 4.30–6pm; Nov–Feb Mon–Sat 9.30am–5pm, Sun 12.30–2.30pm • €8, joint ticket with Dublinia €18 • ☎ 01 677 8099, ⓦ christchurchcathedral.ie

Occupying the highest point of the old city, **Christ Church Cathedral** sits above Wood Quay, the location of a Viking settlement of more than two hundred houses over which the Dublin Corporation controversially built its Civic Offices in the early 1980s.

The Gothic cathedral is now hemmed in by buildings and traffic, but inside you'll find some fascinating remnants from its long history as the seat of the (now Anglican) Archbishop of Dublin and Glendalough. From as early as the seventh century, there may have been a small Celtic church on these grounds, and in about 1030, the recently converted Viking king of Dublin, Sitric Silkenbeard, built a wooden cathedral here. This in turn was replaced by the Normans, who between 1186 and 1240 erected a magnificent stone structure to mark their accession to power. Of this, the crypt (which is Dublin's oldest functioning structure), two transepts (which retain many original Romanesque carvings) and the remarkable **leaning north wall** can still be seen. The weight of the original vaulted stone ceiling caused the roof to collapse in 1562, bringing down the south wall and pulling the north side of the nave half a metre out of the perpendicular. In the 1870s, distiller Henry Roe lavished the equivalent of €30 million on the heavy-handed restoration you can see today, and bankrupted himself.

### Tomb of Strongbow

Near the main entrance at the southwest corner you'll come across the strange **tomb of Strongbow**, the Norman leader who captured Dublin in 1170 and was buried here six years later. The original, around which the landlords of Dublin had gathered to collect rents, was destroyed by the sixteenth-century roof collapse, and had to be replaced with a fourteenth-century effigy of one of the earls of Drogheda so that business could proceed as usual. The small half-figure alongside is probably a fragment of the original tomb, though legend maintains that it's an effigy of Strongbow's son, hacked in two by his own father for cowardice in battle.

## DUBLIN AND THE MESSIAH

Opposite the cathedral on Fishamble Street once stood **Neal's Music Hall**, where **Handel** conducted the combined choirs of Christ Church and St Patrick's cathedrals in the first performance of his *Messiah* in 1742. As the takings were going to charity, ladies were requested not to wear hoops in their crinolines, to get more bums on seats. Jonathan Swift exclaimed, "Oh, a German, a genius, a prodigy." In a private garden on the site, the composer's reward is a statue of himself conducting in the nude, perched on a set of organ pipes. Every April 13, on the anniversary of the first performance, Our Lady's Choral Society gives a sing-along performance of excerpts from the *Messiah* here.

**1**

## The chapels

The chapels off the choir show the Anglo-Normans celebrating their dual nationality. To the left stands the **Chapel of St Edmund**, the ninth-century king of East Anglia who was martyred by the Vikings, while on the right is the **Chapel of St Laud**, the sixth-century bishop of Coutances in Normandy. The floor tiles here are original – those in the rest of the cathedral are 1870s replicas – while on the wall there's an iron cage with some of the bars removed, which used to contain the embalmed heart of twelfth-century St Laurence O'Toole, Dublin's only canonized archbishop, before it was stolen in 2012.

## The crypt

If you descend the stairs by the south transept, you'll reach the **crypt**, the least changed remnant of the twelfth-century cathedral; formerly a storehouse for the trade in alcohol and tobacco, it's one of the largest crypts in Britain and Ireland, extending under the entire cathedral for 55m. Here you'll find the **Treasures of Christ Church** exhibition, which includes an interesting twenty-minute audiovisual on the history of the cathedral, as well as a miscellany of manuscripts and church silverware, and a mummified cat and rat, which were frozen in hot pursuit in an organ pipe in the 1860s. Look out also for a ropey tabernacle and pair of candlesticks made for James II on his flight from England in 1689, when, for three months only, Latin Mass was again celebrated at Christ Church (the existing cathedral paraphernalia was hidden by quick-thinking Anglican officials under a bishop's coffin). In extravagant contrast is a chunky silver-gilt plate, around 1m wide, presented by King William III in thanksgiving for his victory at the Battle of the Boyne in 1690.

# Dublinia

St Michael's Hill • Daily: March–Sept 10am–6.30pm; Oct–Feb 10am–5.30pm • €12, children €7, family ticket €30; joint ticket with Christ Church Cathedral €18 • ⊕ 01 679 4611, ⓦ dublinia.ie

Located at the crossroads of the medieval city, and housed in the former Synod Hall of the Church of Ireland, **Dublinia** provides a lively, hands-on portrait of Viking and medieval Dublin that's especially good fun for kids. Themes such as the plague and the medieval fair are explored via walk-through tableaux of streets and houses, sound effects and lots of fun interactive displays. An archaeology room explores how the city's past has been unearthed, with a re-created excavation site and lab where visitors can examine medieval bugs under a microscope.

On the second floor, in the Great Hall, where the Anglican bishops met until 1982, the focus is on the Vikings, with all manner of objects excavated from nearby Wood Quay on display; in addition, there's a near-life-size ship, audiovisuals on the sagas and the chance to try on slave chains  Before crossing the graceful, much-photographed bridge over to Christ Church Cathedral, it's worth climbing **St Michael's Tower**, a remnant of the seventeenth-century Church of St Michael and All Angels, for fine views over the city.

# St Audoen's

Corn Market (near High St) • April–Oct daily 9.30am–5.30pm, last admission 4.45pm • Free • ⊕ 01 677 0088, ⓦ heritageireland.ie

Just to the west of Dublinia, on the corner of Bridge Street, stand two churches dedicated to St Audoen (in French, St-Ouen, seventh-century bishop of Rouen and the patron saint of Normandy). The monumental but largely uninteresting nineteenth-century Catholic version overshadows its neighbour, **Protestant St Audoen's**, which was built around 1190 and is now an intriguing tourist site. There are still services every Sunday at 10.15am – the church has been continuously used for worship for over eight centuries, longer than any other in Dublin.

The most fascinating aspect of a visit is seeing the physical evidence of how the church's fortunes waxed and waned over the centuries. As it prospered through close association with the city's guilds, St Audoen's expanded in stages around its original single-naved church, including the addition, in 1431, of **St Anne's Guild Chapel**, making a two-aisled nave. The latter is now the main exhibition area, with informative displays on the parish and the guilds.

Until the Reformation, St Audoen's was the most prestigious parish church among Dublin's leading families. Afterwards, however, many members of the all-important Guild of St Anne refused to become Protestant and the congregation declined. By the nineteenth century St Audoen's had retreated to its original single nave, by the simple expediency of removing the roofs from the other parts of the church and letting them rot. You can now poke around the open-air **chancel** and **Portlester Chapel**, where, before the building was declared a national monument, locals would hang their washing out to dry.

Behind the Protestant church, steps descend to thirteenth-century **St Audoen's Arch**, the only remaining gate in the **Norman city walls** – a dramatic, though heavily restored, remnant stretching for 200m along Cook Street, 7m high and tipped with battlements.

## St Patrick's Cathedral

Patrick St • March–Oct Mon–Fri 9.30am–5pm, Sat 9am–6pm, Sun 9am–10.30am, 12.30–2.30pm & 4.30–6pm; Nov–Feb Mon–Fri 9.30am–5pm, Sat 9am–5pm, Sun 9–10.30am & 12.30–2.30pm • €8 • ☎ 01 453 9472, ⓦ stpatrickscathedral.ie

The history of **St Patrick's Cathedral** is remarkably similar to that of its fellow Anglican rival Christ Church up the road. It was built between 1220 and 1270 in Gothic style, but its roof collapsed in 1544, leading to a decline that included its use as a stable by Cromwell's army in 1649. Its Victorian restoration, however, by Sir Benjamin Guinness in the 1860s, was more sensitive than at Christ Church, and it has a more appealing, lived-in feel, thanks largely to its clutter of quirky funerary monuments. Dublin has

---

### JONATHAN SWIFT

*"Here is laid the body of Jonathan Swift…where fierce indignation can no longer rend the heart. Go, traveller, and imitate if you can this earnest and dedicated champion of liberty."*

Swift's epitaph in St Patrick's Cathedral, penned by himself and translated here from the Latin, conveys not only his appetite for political satire and campaigning, but also perhaps a certain prescience about the longevity of his fame. Born in Dublin in 1667 and educated at Trinity College, Swift went to England in 1689 to work as secretary to the retired diplomat Sir William Temple. Here he met Esther Johnson, nicknamed **Stella**, the daughter of Temple's housekeeper, who became his close companion – whether platonic or sexual, no one knows – until her death in 1728. Swift was ordained in the Church of Ireland in 1695, and wrote his first major work, **A Tale of a Tub**, anonymously in 1704, satirizing the official churches and the unscrupulous "modern" writers of his day. Sent to London to lobby the government for the relief of church taxes, from 1710 he was at the centre of England's political and literary life, a friend of Tory ministers as well as of Alexander Pope and John Gay. When the Tories fell from power, however, instead of the English bishopric he had hoped for, he was made Dean of St Patrick's, in 1713. Here he turned his caustic wit on Irish injustices, writing a series of pamphlets in the 1720s and 1730s including **A Modest Proposal**, one of the most admired works of irony in the English language, which suggests that the Irish poor sell off their children to the rich as "a most delicious, nourishing and wholesome food". At this time, too, he wrote his most famous work, the gloriously imaginative satirical novel, **Gulliver's Travels** (1726). Swift's later years were blighted by a progressive mental illness, and when he died, in 1745, he left his estate to build St Patrick's on James's Street, the first psychiatric hospital in Ireland.

**1**

two Church of Ireland cathedrals because, in the 1190s, Archbishop John Comyn left the clergy of Christ Church and built his own palace and church here outside the city walls, and therefore beyond the jurisdiction of the city provosts.

To the right of the entrance in the harmoniously proportioned nave are diverse memorials to **Jonathan Swift**, the cathedral's dean for 32 years (see page 75), including his and his long-term partner Stella's graves, his pulpit and table, and a cast of his skull – both his and Stella's bodies were dug up by Victorian phrenologists, studying the skulls of the famous. The **Door of Reconciliation** by the north transept recalls a quarrel between the earls of Kildare and Ormond in 1492. Ormond fled and sought sanctuary in the cathedral's chapterhouse, but Kildare, eager to make peace, cut a hole in the door and stretched his arm through to shake Ormond's hand – so giving us the phrase "chancing your arm". Nearby in the north aisle of the choir, a simple black slab commemorates **Duke Frederick Schomberg**, who advised William of Orange to come to Ireland in 1686 but had the misfortune to be slain at the ensuing Battle of the Boyne. His family didn't bother to erect a memorial for him, so it was left to Dean Swift to do the honours here in 1731; in Swift's words, "The renown of his valour had greater power among strangers than had the ties of blood among his kith and kin."

In the northwest corner of the nave you'll find a slab carved with a Celtic cross that once marked the site of a well next to the cathedral, where **St Patrick** baptized converts in the fifth century. Back near the entrance, you can't miss the extravagant **Boyle monument**, which Richard Boyle, Earl of Cork, erected in 1632 in memory of his wife Katherine who had borne him fifteen children, including the famous chemist Robert Boyle (shown in the bottom-centre niche). Viceroy Wentworth, objecting to being forced to kneel before a Corkman, had the monument moved here from beside the altar, but Boyle exacted revenge in later years by engineering Wentworth's execution.

## Marsh's Library

St Patrick's Close • Mon & Wed–Fri 9.30am–5pm, Sat 10am–5pm; closed for 10 days over Christmas and New Year • €3 • ☎ 01 454 3511, ⓦ marshlibrary.ie

Behind St Patrick's Cathedral lies the oldest public library in Ireland, **Marsh's Library**, which has remained delightfully untouched since it was built by Sir William Robinson, the architect of Kilmainham Hospital, in 1701, and still functions as a research and conservation library. Its founder, Archbishop Narcissus Marsh, was particularly interested in science, mathematics and music, and oversaw the first translation of the Old Testament into Irish. His books form one of the library's four main collections, totalling 25,000 works, relating to the sixteenth, seventeenth and early eighteenth centuries. They're housed in beautiful rows of dark-oak bookcases, each with a carved and lettered gable (for cataloguing purposes) topped by a bishop's mitre, and three screened alcoves, or "cages", where readers were locked in with rare books. The library mounts regular exhibitions from its collections on subjects such as astronomy, and displays a death mask of its former governor, Jonathan Swift, as well as a cast of his companion Stella's skull.

# The Northside

Running due north from O'Connell Bridge, broader than it is long, to Parnell Square, **O'Connell Street** is the main artery of Dublin's northside. This bustling thoroughfare was originally laid out in the fashion of the grand Parisian boulevards, but poor redevelopment since the damage caused by the 1916 Rising means there are few vestiges of its former grandeur.

Nowadays, the street is lined with fast-food outlets and ugly modern shop frontages, but the historic **GPO** remains a central focal point, opposite which soars the remarkable stainless-steel **Dublin Spire**. A number of other important monuments also remain, mostly positioned in the street's broad central reservation. Just north of O'Connell Bridge, you'll encounter first the imposing figure of the politician **Daniel O'Connell**, "The Liberator", who played a major role in nineteenth-century political campaigns to secure independence. The winged figures by his side represent O'Connell's bravery, patriotism, fidelity and eloquence, while the smaller female figure nearby symbolizes Ireland unchained. At the Abbey Street junction is a statue of the trade unionist **Jim Larkin**, who led the workers of Dublin in the 1913 Lockout, caught in the act of addressing a crowd.

At the very top of O'Connell Street stands an imposing statue of **Charles Stewart Parnell**, the leading late nineteenth-century advocate of Irish Home Rule. The plinth records his famous declaration:

*No man has a right to fix the boundary to the march of a nation. No man has a right to say to his country, "Thus far shalt thou go and no further."*

The streets around represent a consumer's paradise and, particularly on Liffey Street Lower and in the burgeoning **Italian quarter** centred on Bloom Lane (the result of a local developer's fascination with all things Tuscan), you'll find plenty of stylish bars and cafés. Notable cultural landmarks east of O'Connell Street include the **Abbey Theatre**, centre of the twentieth-century revival in Irish theatre, and, along The Quays, the opulent eighteenth-century **Custom House**.

**Parnell Square**, at the top of O'Connell Street, might lack the allure of its southside Georgian equivalents, but it still has a certain grace. The Square's north side hosts one of Dublin's premier galleries, the **Hugh Lane**, as well as the **Dublin Writers Museum**, an excellent place to learn about the city's literary history, while nearby is a centre devoted to the works of the acclaimed writer **James Joyce**.

To the west lie the **Old Jameson Distillery**, in the historic **Smithfield** area, and **Collins Barracks**, home to the National Museum's collection of decorative arts.

| ■ ACCOMMODATION | | ● SHOPPING | |
| --- | --- | --- | --- |
| Abbey Court | 9 | Chapters Bookstore | 1 |
| Abraham House | 2 | Moore St Market | 2 |
| Academy Plaza Hotel | 1 | The Winding Stair | 3 |
| Beresford Hotel | 8 | | |
| Globetrotters | 5 | | |
| The Gresham Hotel | 3 | | |
| Isaacs Hostel | 7 | | |
| Jacob's Inn | 4 | | |
| The Morrison | 11 | | |
| Sky Backpackers | 10 | | |
| The Townhouse | 6 | | |

| ● EATING | | | | ■ DRINKING AND NIGHTLIFE | | | | | | |
| --- | --- | --- | --- | --- | --- | --- | --- | --- | --- | --- |
| Brother Hubbard | 3 | Soup Dragon | 7 | **PUBS & BARS** | | **DJ BARS, LIVE MUSIC & CLUBS** | | | **LGBTQ** | |
| Caffè Cagliostro | 4 | The Winding Stair | 6 | The Flowing Tide | 1 | The Academy | 2 | | Pantibar | 5 |
| The Gresham Hotel | 1 | The Woollen Mills | 5 | The Lotts | 3 | The Grand Social | 4 | | | |
| Musashi | 2 | | | Sin É | 6 | | | | | |

**1**

# Dublin Spire

O'Connell St, near junction with Earl St North

The northside's most remarkable landmark marks the spot where Nelson's Pillar stood until it was blown up by Republicans in 1966. Known colloquially as "The Stiletto in the Ghetto", "The Nail in the Pale", or more simply "The Spike", the astonishing **Dublin Spire** is easily the tallest structure in the city – a 120m-high stainless-steel needle, surmounted by an illuminated beacon. Three metres wide at its base, it tapers to a mere 15cm at its summit. In the early morning or at dusk its surface takes on an ethereal blue colour, while at night it seems to loom ominously over the city. What the ghost of **James Joyce**, whose adjacent and somewhat rakish statue stands just down Earl Street North, would make of it is open to question.

# The General Post Office

O'Connell St Lower • **GPO** Mon–Sat 8.30am–6pm • Free • **Museum** Mon–Sat 10am–5pm • €15 • ☎ 01 705 7000, ⊕ gpowitnesshistory.ie

Just to the left of the Spire stands one of O'Connell Street's few remaining buildings of major historical importance: the **General Post Office**, whose significance lies in its role as the **rebels' headquarters** during the Easter Rising of 1916. The building was constructed in 1818 but only its Ionic portico survived the fighting – and still bears the marks of gunfire. Following restoration, the GPO reopened in 1929 and inside its marble halls you'll find Oliver Sheppard's intricately wrought bronze statue *The Death of Cúchulainn*, representing a key moment in the Irish legend *Táin Bó Cúailnge* (see page 152).

## THE EASTER RISING

The initial impact of some historical events often runs counter to their long-term effects, and such was the case with the **Easter Rising** of 1916. Truth be told, this inherently idealistic rebellion was a bungled affair from start to finish, and it was only the repressive response of the British Army, whose political overlords were unsurprisingly sidetracked by the seemingly more pressing affairs taking place in the fields of Flanders, that gave the event its pivotal role in attaining Ireland's independence.

The Rising was organized by the **Irish Republican Brotherhood** (IRB), a Republican grouping founded in 1858, led by educationalist and Gaelic cultural revivalist **Patrick Pearse**, with the support of the Irish Citizen Army's Dublin Brigade under socialist and trades union activist **James Connolly**. Impelled by the continuing failure of democratic means to achieve the goal of independence, they concocted a plan to take over by force, aided by the much larger **Irish Volunteers**, a Nationalist corps founded in 1913, and using arms acquired from Germany. The armaments were, however, intercepted by the British, and though the Volunteers' leader withdrew his support, the Rising still went ahead.

On the morning of Easter Monday, the rebels took control of a number of key buildings in the city centre and further afield (see page 578). They made the **General Post Office** on O'Connell Street their base, and it was from here that Pearse emerged to make his Proclamation of the Irish Republic. The British response was initially guarded, but a full-scale battle soon ensued, destroying much of the surrounding area and heavily damaging rebel-held buildings elsewhere in the city.

It took five days for the rebellion to be suppressed and its leaders captured. Dubliners decried the uprising at its outset, dismayed by the devastation ravaged upon their city by the fighting. Had the British simply imprisoned the IRB's leaders, it's extremely unlikely later political developments would have occurred as quickly as they did, but the draconian decision was made to **execute** all of them (with the exception of Éamon de Valera, who had US citizenship). In the process, the British created national martyrs, transforming the situation irrevocably and ultimately leading to a bitter war of independence.

1

The building, which still functions as Dublin's largest post office, now houses a state-of-the-art permanent exhibition called **GPO Witness History**, focusing on the 1916 rising. Refreshingly, it explores both sides of the conflict, as well as its causes and aftermath. Using slick touchscreens, audiovisual booths and many previously unseen artefacts it is one of the finest and most informative approaches to the subject in the city.

## The Abbey Theatre

26–27 Lower Abbey St • Tours Mon, Wed & Fri 4pm, Sat 11am • €10 • ☎ 01 887 2200, ⓦ abbeytheatre.ie

Just east of O'Connell Street's southern end stands the **Abbey Theatre**, focal point for Ireland's twentieth-century cultural revival. It first opened its doors in December 1904 to present three plays, two by the poet and dramatist W.B. Yeats and the other by his patron Lady Gregory. The theatre's company turned professional in 1906 and Yeats and Gregory, along with J.M. Synge, became its first directors. The staging of Synge's own tragicomic *Playboy of the Western World*, with its frank language and suggestion that Irish peasants would condone a murder, provoked riots on its opening night, while later, in 1926, Seán O'Casey's *The Plough and the Stars* incited bitter outrage, the audience regarding its view of the Easter Rising as derisive not least because the theatre had begun to receive state funding the previous year.

The original Abbey burnt to the ground in 1951 and its more modern, outwardly grim replacement opened in 1966. Informative guided tours – a must for anyone interested in the link between Ireland's culture and politics – take in both back- and front-stage areas and recount key moments in the Abbey's history. Its programme continues to include a range of drama, blending revivals of Irish classics with works by established writers such as Brian Friel and younger dramatists, while the much smaller Peacock Theatre in the basement is devoted to new experimental works. During the first years of the twenty-first century the theatre suffered disastrous financial mismanagement and was bailed out in 2006 by the largest grant ever awarded by the Arts Council of Ireland.

Backstage **tours** offer an insight into the history and behind-the-scenes work of the theatre; they take place while plays are running on the Abbey stage.

## The Custom House

Custom House Quay, north bank of River Liffey • Visitor centre Daily 10am–4.30pm

Opened in 1791, the imposing **Custom House** is one of several notable Dublin landmarks designed by the English architect James Gandon (others include the Four Courts and O'Connell Bridge). The Custom House cost the then unearthly sum of £500,000 sterling to construct, owing to its bulk and the intricacy of Gandon's architectural detail – and because it was constructed on a submerged mudflat which required covering by a layer of solid pine planks. Such cost proved even more extravagant when the Act of Union transferred customs and excise to London in 1800. The building's grandiose Neoclassical exterior, more than 100m long, features heads sculpted by Gandon's contemporary Edward Smyth, with cattle heads symbolizing Ireland's beef trade and the others representing Ireland's rivers (including the Liffey above the main entrance). Its 35m-high-dome was based upon Christopher Wren's Greenwich Hospital.

After 1801, the Custom House became the administrative centre for the city's work on public hygiene and Poor Law relief, the latter demonstrated by an enormous Famine pot. The building suffered a major fire in 1833 and was completely gutted in 1921 after being set alight by the IRA. Subsequently restored, though with significant changes to its internal structure and facade, it housed various government departments and some of its more illustrious employees, including Brian O'Nolan, better known as the comic novelist Flann O'Brien, and the songwriter Percy French. You can learn more about the building's illustrious history in the new **visitor centre**, which is due to open in late 2021.

**1**

## The Irish Famine Memorial

To the east of the Custom House, and set between the looming presence of the International Financial Services Centre and the Liffey, is the **Irish Famine Memorial**. These six life-sized bronze figures were designed and cast by the Dublin sculptor Rowan Gillespie to mark the 150th anniversary of the worst year of the Great Famine (see page 575). That these stark, beseeching figures are staring eastwards towards Britain is not coincidental.

## Dublin City Gallery – The Hugh Lane

Parnell Square North • Tues–Thurs 9.45am–6pm, Fri 9.45am–5pm, Sat 10am–5pm, Sun 11am–5pm; tours Sun 2pm • Entry and tours free, but €2 donation suggested • ☎ 01 222 5550, ⊕ hughlane.ie

The elegant, Georgian, stone-clad Charlemont House, with its curved outer and inner walls and Neoclassical interior, has provided a permanent home for the **Dublin City Gallery – The Hugh Lane** since 1933. Sir Hugh, a nephew of Lady Gregory (see page 346), wanted Dublin to house a major gallery of Irish and international art. He amassed a considerable collection by persuading native artists to contribute their work and purchasing many other paintings himself, particularly from the French Impressionist school and Italy.

The gallery holds around half of the Lane collection (the rest is in London's National Gallery) and only a fraction is on display here at any one time, though you're likely to see works by Renoir, Monet and Degas, as well as Pissarro and the Irish painters Jack B. Yeats, Roderic O'Connor and Louis le Brocquy, and there are also stained-glass pieces by Evie Hone and Harry Clarke. The gallery usually hosts temporary exhibitions of more modern artworks.

Part of the gallery is devoted to a re-creation of Dublin-born painter **Francis Bacon's studio**, transported from its original location at Reece Mews in South Kensington, London, where the artist lived and worked for the last thirty years of his life. After his death in 1992, his studio was donated to the gallery by his heir, John Edwards, and reconstructed here with astonishing precision – more than seven thousand individual items were catalogued and placed here with verisimilitude in the reconstruction. The studio can only be viewed through the window glass, but among the apparent debris are an old Bush record player, empty champagne boxes and huge tins of the type of matt vinyl favoured by Bacon, the fumes of which exacerbated his asthma. The surrounding rooms hold displays of memorabilia, such as photographs and correspondence, as well as large canvases from the painter's last years.

The gallery runs guided **tours** of the exhibits, a programme of **lectures and films** related to its current shows (various times; €5) and very popular classical-music **concerts** (Sun noon; free).

## Dublin Writers Museum

18 Parnell Square • Mon–Sat 9.45am–5pm, Sun & public hols 11am–5pm • €8 • ☎ 01 872 2077

The **Dublin Writers Museum** highlights Ireland's literary history, featuring not just giants such as Wilde, Shaw, Joyce and Beckett, but also lesser-known figures like Sheridan Le Fanu and Oliver St John Gogarty. The ground floor contains a plethora of displays on particular writers or literary schools, and it is well worth picking up the free and entertaining audio-guide to receive background information on the authors. The hall downstairs, hung with modern paintings of writers, leads to an outdoor Zen garden where you can contemplate works you've purchased in the museum's bookshop.

On the first floor is the Gallery of Writers, an elegant salon with plasterwork by Michael Stapleton, which features James Joyce's piano and more paintings, of which the most impressive is John B. Yeats's portrait of George Moore. Beside this is the Gorham Library, which features numerous rare editions.

The museum's basement houses one of the northside's best restaurants, *Chapter One* (see page 101).

## BLOOMSDAY

Perhaps no other writer has so encapsulated the life, lore and mores of his native city as **James Joyce** so successfully achieved in his remarkable novels, most notably **Ulysses** (1922). So precise are the author's descriptions of the locales visited by the book's protagonists on the date of the book's setting, June 16, that it is possible literally to follow in their footsteps. This annual pilgrimage undertaken by Joycean aficionados across the city has become known as Bloomsday. Though you can undertake to cover the **Bloomsday** route independently (a *Ulysses* map is available from the Visit Dublin Centre on Suffolk St), guided walks are organized by the James Joyce Centre. There are plenty of other associated events, including re-creations by actors of some of the book's central passages and concerts devoted to music referenced in the novel.

Strangely, for someone who documented his native city's life with such pride, Joyce came to loathe Dublin, once describing the place in a letter as a "city of failure, of rancour and of unhappiness", and concluding "I long to be out of it." Though his early works, such as the short-story collection **Dubliners** and the semi-autobiographical novel **A Portrait of the Artist as a Young Man**, draw heavily upon his upbringing, Catholic education and Dublin experiences, by the time of the latter's publication in 1916, Joyce had long abandoned Ireland. Not long after meeting a Connemara-born chambermaid, Nora Barnacle, in June 1904, the pair eloped to Europe. Other than two brief visits to Ireland, Joyce spent the rest of his life in exile living in cities across Europe – in Pola (now Pula) in Istria, Trieste, Zurich and, notably, Paris, where *Ulysses* was published in 1922 and where he finally wed Nora in 1931. Joyce's only subsequent published work was the convoluted **Finnegans Wake** (1939). When he died in 1941, *Ulysses* was still unavailable in Ireland (though it never officially fell foul of Ireland's censorship laws, booksellers were loath to stock copies), and was not published in the country until the 1960s.

# The James Joyce Centre

35 North Great George's St • Oct–March Tues–Sat 10am–5pm, Sun noon–5pm; April–Sept Mon–Sat 10am–5pm, Sun noon–5pm • €5 • ☎ 01 878 8547, ⓦ jamesjoyce.ie

Occupying a grand eighteenth-century town house restored in the 1980s, the **James Joyce Centre** celebrates the work of perhaps Ireland's most imaginative yet most complex writer. Joyce spent part of his life living in the inner northside, and drew upon his experiences in the creation of his characters and the settings for his works. The building features decorative stucco mouldings by Michael Stapleton. The ground floor houses a small shop full of Joyceiana, such as books and prints, and an airy courtyard which includes the actual period door of 7 Eccles St, the fictional home of Leopold and Molly Bloom, two of the main protagonists in *Ulysses*, as well as a somewhat enigmatic, modernist Joyce-inspired sculpture of a cow.

The building's upper floors house a re-creation of the tiny room occupied by Joyce in Trieste, featuring various books, pianola music-rolls and a splendid collection of hats, as well as photographs of people and places associated with *Ulysses*, and touchscreen consoles tracing the development of the novel's plot and its variety of characters. Three short documentary films on the writer's life can also be viewed. The centre's **walking tour** (April–Sept Tues, Thurs & Sat 11am & 2pm; Oct–March Sat 11am; €10; 1hr), which begins here, is well worth taking if you want to learn more about Joycean connections with the surrounding area.

# Smithfield

The area christened **Smithfield Village** by developers is more an ongoing process of urban renewal than an identifiable community, but at its centre lies the city's largest civic open space, cobbled **Smithfield**. Surrounded by rising blocks of executive

**1,**

flats, shops and restaurants, Smithfield still manages to host one of the city's major sights – the 300-year-old **Dublin Horse Fair**, which takes place twice a year and draws a number of traders and other horse-lovers from the city and outlying rural areas.

## The National Museum – Decorative Arts and History

Benburb St • Tues–Sat 10am–5pm, Sun 2–5pm • Free • ☎ 01 677 7444, ⓦ museum.ie

The **National Museum – Decorative Arts and History** is housed in the eighteenth-century **Collins Barracks**, which surrounds Europe's largest regimental drilling square. The buildings set around this quadrangle contain a wonderful series of galleries devoted to the fine arts of Ireland and selected works from abroad. Unquestionably, the best of these is **Curator's Choice**, on the first floor of the west block, which is selected by museum curators from all over Ireland. Among its draws are a medieval oak carving of St Molaise; the extravagant cabinet presented by Oliver Cromwell to his daughter Bridget in 1652; and the remarkable fourteenth-century Chinese porcelain Fonthill Vase. The **Out of Storage** section is another highlight, bringing together everything from decorative glassware to a seventeenth-century suit of Samurai armour. There are also displays on Celtic art, coinage, silverware, period furniture, costumes and scientific instruments, and there are usually plenty of temporary exhibits. The third floor boasts a permanent exhibition on Eileen Gray, widely regarded as one of the most influential designers and architects of the twentieth century.

On the ground floor is a chain of thematically interconnected galleries, **Soldiers and Chiefs**, devoted to almost five hundred years of Irish **military history**. Apart from an array of helmets and weaponry, there's the remarkable Stokes tapestry, created by one Stephen of that ilk, a British soldier who devoted his spare time to the depiction of contemporary garrison life and was honoured to have his work shown to Queen Victoria on a royal visit to Ireland in 1849.

## Croppy's Acre

**Croppy's Acre**, on Benburb Street, marks the location where many of those executed for their part in the 1798 Rebellion are buried ("croppy" being a derogatory term for the rebels on account of many of them sporting closely cropped hair in the style of some French revolutionaries, an act in itself considered seditious) – a Wicklow-granite monument marks the precise location of their graves. The park is also home to Éamonn O'Doherty's *Anna Livia* sculpture, a bronze embodiment of her namesake the River Liffey.

## The Four Courts

Inn's Quay • Mon–Fri 10am–4pm • ☎ 01 888 6000, ⓦ courts.ie

The imposing riverside structure of the **Four Courts**, fronted by Corinthian columns and surmounted by an impressive dome, has seen many a legal hearing since it first opened its doors in 1802. Like the Custom House (see page 79), it was designed by James Gandon, and took some sixteen years to complete at a cost of £200,000 sterling. The Four Courts was seized by Republicans opposed to the Anglo-Irish Treaty in 1921, and heavily bombarded by Free State forces during the subsequent Civil War using, ironically, howitzers borrowed from the British. However, before the siege came to its inevitable end, the rebels accidentally set off explosives inside the building, destroying the Public Records Office and innumerable irreplaceable historic documents in the process. After rebuilding, the Four Courts reopened in 1931 and nowadays houses the **High Court of Justice** and, following the construction of the new Criminal Court of Justice on Parkgate Street, now only hears civil cases.

## St Michan's Church

Church St • March–Oct Mon–Fri 10am–12.45pm & 2–4.45pm, Sat 10am–12.45pm; Nov–Feb Mon–Fri 12.30–3.30pm, Sat 10am–12.45pm • €5 • ☎ 01 872 4154, ⓦ cathedralgroupdublin.ie

Constructed in 1095 by the Vikings in honour of a Danish bishop, **St Michan's Church** was substantially rebuilt some six hundred years later. Next to the church organ, reputedly once played by Handel, is the unusual Penitents' Pew, in which parishioners knelt facing the congregation to confess their errant ways. It is the church's **vaults**, however, that hold the most fascination. Guided **tours** descend an almost sheer staircase to view the contents of tiny crypts, which contain a dozen **bodies**, some dating back more than seven hundred years. These have been mummified by a process that involves two factors: the vaults' limestone walls, which absorb the air's natural moisture, and the methane produced by vegetation decaying below the floor. One of the mummies is believed to have been a Crusader, another a nun, and a third, which lacks a hand, may have been a repentant thief. Another crypt contains John and Henry Sheares, executed for their role in the 1798 Rebellion, as well as the death mask of one of its leaders, Wolfe Tone. Two other rebels, Oliver Bond and the Reverend William Jackson, are buried in the church's graveyard, and some reckon an unmarked grave to the rear houses the body of Robert Emmet, leader of the 1803 rising.

## Jameson Distillery

Bow St • Mon–Thurs & Sun 10am–5.30pm, Fri & Sat 10am–7pm • €25 • ☎ 01 807 2355, ⓦ jamesonwhiskey.com

The buildings of the **Old Jameson Distillery**, where John Jameson set up his whiskey company, have long been turned over to a touristy but popular shrine to "the hard stuff". Forty-minute long guided **tours** whirl visitors through the process itself, from milling and mashing to the essential distillation element; while the separation of water from alcohol only occurs once in bourbon and twice in Scotch, the production of *uisce beatha* (Irish for "water of life", anglicized to "whiskey") involves a three-stage process. The tour ends with a tasting.

# West of the centre

Unless you're a keen walker, you'll want to take a bus or LUAS tram to reach some of the city's western attractions. Highlights on the north side of the river include the vast grounds of **Phoenix Park**, with the dazzling interiors of **Farmleigh** mansion lying just beyond. Across the Liffey, the area west of the old city is dominated by the mammoth Guinness Brewery, whose wares are celebrated by the **Guinness Storehouse**. Further west lies the suburb of **Kilmainham**, home to the impressive **Irish Museum of Modern Art** and the forbidding **Kilmainham Gaol**, where the leaders of the 1916 Easter Rising were executed.

## Phoenix Park

Main gates at Parkgate St and Castleknock Gate • Open access 24hr • ☎ 01 821 3021, ⓦ phoenixpark.ie • Buses #25 and 26 stop near the main entrance; catch them at Merrion Square, Nassau St or Merchant's Quay

The undulating landscape of **Phoenix Park** – Europe's largest urban walled park – sprawls across some 1750 acres. Originally intended as a deer park for Charles II (a small herd still ranges across its fields), the park takes its name from Phoenix House, the original residence of the British viceroys, whose title derived from the Irish *fionn uisce* ("clear water"). The park is bisected by Chesterfield Avenue and a few side roads open to traffic, but most of it is open space, sparsely dotted with trees, shrubs and wild flowers, with a few areas of woodland and hawthorn. It's an ideal place to escape the city's bustle, a popular venue for sports, and offers plenty of spots for a picnic.

**1**

By the park's Parkgate Street entrance lies the **People's Garden**, a pleasant area of formal flowerbeds and hedges. The nearby **Wellington Monument** took some 44 years to complete before it was finally unveiled in 1861. The obelisk – at some 60m – is the tallest of its kind in the British Isles – features bas-reliefs, using bronze from cannons captured at Waterloo, which depict scenes from the successful military campaigns of the "Iron Duke". West from here, alongside Military Road, is the derelict **Magazine Fort**, built on the site originally occupied by Phoenix House. The only way to visit the fort is on a guided tour every Sunday between April and September, with tickets (free) available on the day from the Visitor Centre on a first come first served basis. Otherwise, it's an easy climb up the hill to take a trip around its walls and to take in some fine views.

## Dublin Zoo

Off Chesterfield Ave • Daily 9.30am–6pm; Oct–Feb closes at dusk; last admission 1hr before closing • €20, children under 16 €14.50, children under 3 free, family €56 • ☎ 01 474 8900, ⊛ dublinzoo.ie

Heading northwest from the People's Garden along Chesterfield Avenue will bring you to **Dublin Zoo**, spread over sixty acres, which focuses today on raising species threatened by extinction, such as Asian elephants, Amur tigers and waldrapp ibis. The zoo is themed around different habitats, among them the African Savannah, which has giraffes, hippos and southern white rhinos, the Orangutan Forest, Wolves in the Woods, and the Gorilla Rainforest, home to a charismatic troop of western lowland gorillas. There is also a city farm for younger children.

## Áras an Uachtaráin

Off Chesterfield Ave, north of the zoo • Sat 10.30am–3.30pm • Free guided tours; tickets from Phoenix Park Visitor Centre only on the day • ☎ 01 617 1000, ⊛ president.ie

The impressive Palladian **Áras an Uachtaráin**, pronounced "arus an ucterawn", was the home of Britain's viceroys from the 1780s until Ireland's independence, and since 1938 it has been the official residence of the President of Ireland. Tours start from the Phoenix Park Visitor Centre (minibus transport provided) and whisk you through a section of the grandly decorated house, including the State Reception Rooms and the Presidential Office.

## Phoenix Monument and Ashtown Castle

At the park's centre on Chesterfield Avenue rises the **Phoenix Monument**, dating from 1747, which more resembles an eagle or falcon than the phoenix it supposedly represents. To its southwest, by the US Ambassador's Residence, is the 30m-high stainless-steel **Papal Cross**, bearing testament to the spot where the late Pope John Paul II celebrated Mass in September 1979 before a congregation of around 1.25 million people.

Northwest of the Monument is the **Phoenix Park Visitor Centre** (daily 9.30am–6pm; ☎ 01 677 0095), which recounts the history of the park through the ages, focusing on its flora and fauna. Adjacent is **Ashtown Castle**, an early seventeenth-century tower house whose existence was only uncovered when the former residence of the Papal Nuncio, which had been constructed around it, was demolished in 1978. Tickets for daily tours of the castle can be obtained from the visitor centre.

## Farmleigh

White's Rd • Grounds: April–Sept 10am–9pm, Oct–March 10am–6pm; House: daily 10am–5.30pm (last tour 4.30pm) • €8 • ☎ 01 815 5914, ⊛ farmleigh.ie • Take the #37 bus from either Suffolk St or the Quays and get off at the Castleknock Gate of Phoenix Park; upon entering the park take the path to your right, and you'll reach Farmleigh in 15min

White's Gate on the park's northwestern fringe provides access to one of the most splendid buildings in the city, **Farmleigh**. Constructed in 1752 for the Trench family, the building was later purchased by Edward Cecil Guinness, the first Earl of Iveagh, as a rustic residence offering easy access to his brewery. Extensions were made in the

1880s, and the Guinness family remained in residence until 1992. Farmleigh was then purchased by the Irish government for use as a state guesthouse (which means tours may not be available if a visiting delegation is in residence). Tours begin in the **dining room**, whose unusual decorations include statues of Bacchus either side of the fireplace and a clock inlaid in its centre. The hall features Waterford-crystal chandeliers and a pair of debtors' chairs in which the paupers' legs would be trapped until they agreed to pay their debts, while the **library** contains four thousand items on loan from the Iveagh Collection, including a first edition of *Ulysses* and books dating back to the twelfth century. The **Blue Room**, which is dedicated to Ireland's Nobel Prize winners, has another strange fireplace – this one situated below a window. However, the real treat is the **ballroom** whose Irish oak floor was constructed of wood originally intended for Guinness barrels; the doors here, fringed with delicate linen portières, lead you out to a massive, plant-stocked conservatory. Behind the house there's a tea room in the stable block and an extremely pleasant walled garden.

Farmleigh hosts a number of free **cultural events** from July to September, ranging from ballet and brass bands in the gardens to indoor concerts in the ballroom; tickets are limited and only available via the house's website.

## The Guinness Storehouse

St James's Gate • Daily: July & Aug 9am–8pm; Sept–June 9.30am–7pm; last entry 2hr before closing • €18 • ☏ 01 408 4800, ⓦ guinness-storehouse.com • Bus #123 (from O'Connell St or Dame St) stops outside the brewery

South of the Liffey, much of James Street, west of the old city, is centred around the colossal complex of the **Guinness Brewery**. Founded by Arthur Guinness in 1759, the Guinness Brewery initially manufactured ale, but in the 1770s started making porter, a drink so named because of its popularity with the porters of London's markets. Arthur's new brew, whose distinctive black colouring derived from the addition of roasted barley to the brewing process, found such favour that by 1796 it was being exported to London, and three years later ale production ceased altogether. From that point, Guinness and his successors never looked back and, at its peak in the middle of the twentieth century, their brewery produced some 2,500,000 pints of their now eponymous product a day.

Although it is possible to experience the brewery itself on a high-end tour, most people content themselves with a visit to the seven-storey **Guinness Storehouse**, signposted from Crane Street, a high-tech temple to the black stuff. Its self-guided tour kicks off with the brewing process – a whirl of water (not from the Liffey, despite the myth) and a reek of barley, hops and malt – before progressing to the storage and transportation areas. A huge barrel dominates the section on the lost art of coopering, and nearby there's an engine from the brewery's old railway system. The remainder of the tour consists of an array of marketing memorabilia, supported by plenty of facts and figures about the Guinness empire, and there's a gallery on John Gilroy, an esteemed painter who designed many of the company's advertisements. Right at the top of the tower is the *Gravity Bar*, where you can savour your complimentary pint of perhaps the best Guinness in Dublin while absorbing the superb panorama of the city and the countryside beyond.

## The Irish Museum of Modern Art

Royal Hospital, Military Rd, Kilmainham • Tues–Fri 11.30am–5.30pm, Sat 10am–5.30pm, Sun & public hols noon–5.30pm; guided tours of the exhibitions Wed 1.15pm, Sat & Sun 2.30pm • Entry and tours free • ☏ 01 612 9900, ⓦ imma.ie • Take the Luas Red Line to Heuston Station, which is a 5min walk from the museum; alternatively, the #90 goes frequently to Heuston Station from Connolly Station

Based on Les Invalides in Paris, the **Royal Hospital** in Kilmainham was built between 1680 and 1684 to house war pensioners. Part of the building now houses the **Irish Museum of Modern Art** (IMMA), which has a justifiable reputation for its imaginative exhibitions, covering selections from both its own permanent collection of 3500 works

1

and loaned pieces. All shows are temporary and range from retrospectives of major international artists to new works by modern Irish painters and sculptors. Some of IMMA's most exciting exhibitions draw upon the museum's Outsider Art collection – works, largely paintings, by unschooled artists that explore the psyche – as well as the Madden Arnholz collection of Old Master prints, drawing upon the works of Goya, Rembrandt and Hogarth. The permanent "Old Man's House" exhibition recounts the history of the Royal Hospital site, from its days as an ancient burial ground and Viking settlement to the present day.

## Kilmainham Gaol

Inchicore Rd, Kilmainham • Daily: April & May 9am–6pm; June–Aug 9am–6.30pm; Sept 9.30am–6pm; Oct–March 9.30am–5.30pm; guided tours every 45min until 1hr 15min before closing • €9 (€8 online); Heritage Card • ☎ 01 453 5984, ⓦ kilmainhamgaolmuseum.ie • Buses #69 and #79 from Aston Quay, and #13 and #40 from either O'Connell St or College Green all stop at or near Kilmainham Gaol; ask the bus driver to let you off at the nearest stop

Beside **Bully's Acre**, one of the city's oldest cemeteries, lies **Kilmainham Gaol**, which holds an iconic position in the history of Ireland's struggle for independence and came to symbolize both Irish political martyrdom and British oppression. Opened in 1796, it became the place of incarceration for captured revolutionaries, including the leaders of the 1916 Easter Rising, who were also executed here. Even after the War of Independence, Republicans continued to be imprisoned here, though it closed in July 1924 after the release of its last inmate, Éamon de Valera – later to become Ireland's Taoiseach and president. **Tours** of the gaol provide a chilling impression of the prisoners' living conditions and spartan regime. Its single cells ensured that they were forced into solitary contemplation, and since the building was constructed on top of limestone, their health was often sorely affected by damp and severe cold in winter. Before embarking on the tour, it's well worth visiting the **exhibition galleries**. The ground-floor display includes a mock-up of a cell and an early mug-shot camera, and there's a small side gallery showing paintings by Civil War internees and a huge self-portrait of Constance Gore-Booth (see page 397), who was better known as the Countess Markiewicz, posing as the Good Shepherd. The upstairs gallery provides an enthralling account of the struggle for independence with numerous mementos, old cinematic footage of Michael Collins and the letter ordering the release of Charles Stewart Parnell.

# The northern suburbs

You'll want fine weather for a trip north to the beautiful **Botanic Gardens** and the adjacent **Glasnevin Cemetery**, which has been the final resting place for major figures in Irish history since 1832. To the east lie **Croke Park**, a major sports arena and home to the innovative **GAA Museum**, the exquisite Georgian **Casino at Marino** and, at the end of the DART line, **Howth**, an attractive seaside village with a fine **cliff walk** (see page 88).

## The National Botanic Gardens

Botanic Rd; entrance on Glasnevin Hill, off Botanic Rd • March to mid-Oct Mon–Fri 10am–5pm, Sat & Sun 10am–6pm; mid-Oct to Feb daily 10am–4.30pm; guided tours Sun noon & 2.30pm • Entry and tours free • ☎ 01 857 0909, ⓦ botanicgardens.ie • From the centre, catch bus #13 from Merrion Square or O'Connell St, or #19 from South Great George's St or O'Connell St

The **National Botanic Gardens** on the south bank of the River Tolka in Glasnevin are a great place to wander on a fine day, although their magnificent Victorian wrought-iron glasshouses offer diversion and shelter whatever the weather. Laid out between 1795 and 1825 with a grant from the Irish parliament, the gardens were, in 1844, the

1

first in the world to germinate orchids from seed successfully, and, in August of the following year, the first to notice the potato blight that brought on the Great Famine. Nowadays, a total of around twenty thousand species and cultivated varieties flourish here, including an internationally important collection of cycads, primitive fern-like trees. Highlights include the rose garden, collections of heather and rhododendrons, the Chinese shrubbery and the arboretum.

## Glasnevin Cemetery

Finglas Rd (with pedestrian entrance through the original Prospect Square Gate) • Daily 10am–5pm; guided tours (1hr 30min) daily 11.30am, 1pm & 3.30pm • Museum only €4.50, museum and O'Connell's Tower €9.50, museum, tower and tour €22 • ☎ 01 830 1133, ⓦ glasnevintrust.ie • Served by buses #40 and #40A/B/C from Parnell St

Founded as a burial place for Catholics by the nationalist political leader Daniel O'Connell in 1832, **Glasnevin Cemetery** is now the national cemetery, open to all denominations and groaning with Celtic crosses, harps and other patriotic emblems marking the graves of more than 1.5 million people. It's well worth timing your visit to coincide with one of the fascinating guided **tours**, which includes access to the renovated crypt of O'Connell, who is also commemorated near the entrance by a 50m-high round **tower**; having survived a Loyalist bomb in 1971, the newly renovated tower has an exhibition recalling O'Connell's life, but in any case is well worth the 222-step climb to the top for terrific views across the cemetery grounds. In addition, a small **museum** has interactive exhibits telling the story of hundreds of the most famous people buried in the cemetery – many of them gathered around the tower.

Among them you'll find the graves of Countess Markiewicz (see page 397); Éamon de Valera, prime minister, president and architect of modern Ireland, and his old rival Michael Collins, the most charismatic leader of the successful independence struggle; while from the arts, there's Gerard Manley Hopkins's unmarked grave in the Jesuit plot (see page 68); W.B. Yeats's muse Maud Gonne MacBride; writer, drinker and Republican Brendan Behan; and Alfred Chester Beatty (see page 72). To the right of the tower is the Republican plot, with a memorial to hunger strikers, from Thomas Ashe who died in 1917 to Bobby Sands in 1981, and in front of the tower lie the recent graves of 18-year-old Kevin Barry and eight other Volunteers who were hanged by the British during the War of Independence; originally buried in Mountjoy Prison, their bodies were moved here with the full honours of a state funeral in October 2001. For refreshment after your visit, exit via the pedestrian gate at Prospect Square beside *Kavanagh's (*aka *The Gravediggers)*, a particularly atmospheric old pub (see page 103).

## Croke Park and the GAA Museum

Cusack Stand, St Joseph's Avenue • **GAA Museum** June–Aug Mon–Sat 9.30am–6pm, Sun 9.30am–5pm; Sept–May Mon–Sat 9.30am–5pm, Sun 10.30am–5pm • €8 • **Stadium tour** 4–8 daily, see website for details; note there are no tours on match days • €14, including entry to the museum • **Skyline tour** 2–6 daily, see website for details • €21 including entrance to the museum • ☎ 01 819 2323, ⓦ crokepark.ie • Croke Park is served by numerous bus routes: from the city centre, the #1, #11, #13, #16, #33, #41 and #44 all stop within a 5min walk of the stadium; alternatively, it's a 15min walk from Connelly train station

Home of the **Gaelic Athletic Association** (GAA), **Croke Park** is a magnificent, much redeveloped and now very modern stadium whose capacity of 82,000-plus puts it among the largest in Europe. Situated under the Cusack Stand is one of Dublin's finest museums, the **GAA Museum**, whose creatively designed exhibits provide an enthralling account of not only the sports of hurling and Gaelic football, but also lesser-known games such as camogie (the women's version of hurling) and handball. Historical and political contexts are explored in a thoroughly engaging manner – since its foundation in 1884 the GAA has always been irrevocably linked with Irish Nationalism. Thus the museum does not shirk from recounting key politically sensitive events such as the first Bloody Sunday, when British troops fired on the crowd attending a match in 1920,

1

---

### THE HOWTH CLIFF WALK

Clinging to the slopes of a rocky peninsula and overlooking an animated fishing harbour, the village of **Howth** (rhymes with "both"), at the end of the DART line, is a good place to escape the rigours of the city centre when the weather is good, with some appealing quayside restaurants and pubs. By far the best way to appreciate the location is to do the **Cliff Walk** around the peninsula, taking in great views south over the city to the Wicklow Mountains and north to the Boyne Valley. The footpath runs for some 8km clockwise from the village round to the west-facing side of the peninsula, followed by a 3km walk by the sea along Strand Road and Greenfield Road to Sutton DART station; allow at least three hours in total. (Bus #31B, serving Sutton and Eden Quay in the city centre in one direction, Howth village or The Summit in the other, runs roughly parallel but well above the path for much of the way, along Carrickbrack Road, so you can bail out of the walk if you feel like it.)

You first head east out of Howth village along Balscadden Road to the **Nose of Howth**, before the path turns south, crossing the slopes above the cliffs, which are covered in colourful gorse and bell heather in season; for refreshment on this stretch, the area known as **The Summit**, just inland of the path, has a pub and a café. The southeast point is marked by the **Baily Lighthouse**, which, until March 1997, was the last manned lighthouse on Ireland's coastline. The path along the south-facing coast of the peninsula is the most spectacular part of the walk, providing close-up views of cliffs, secluded beaches and rocky islands.

---

killing twelve people in the process. On a lighter note, upstairs you can have a go at whacking a hurling ball or test your balance and reaction time via various simulations.

Taking the **stadium tour** is highly recommended, not just to view this remarkable arena first hand, but to learn more about key events in its history – including, not least, the momentous decision in 2005 to suspend the GAA's constitution to allow professional Rugby Union and Association Football international matches to take place in the stadium. Previously, only previously only games of Irish origin, played by amateurs, could be staged at what is now called the Aviva Stadium (formerly called Lansdowne Road). Visitors with no aversion to heights can take a skyline tour around a walkway 44m above the ground, for panoramic views of the city and its key landmarks.

## Malahide Castle and Gardens

Back Rd, Malahide • Can be visited by guided tour only: tours (45min) leave hourly 9.30am–4.30pm • Castle €14, includes gardens and butterfly house; gardens and butterfly house €7.50 • ☎ 01 816 9538, ⓦ malahidecastleandgardens.ie • Dart trains get here in 30min from the city centre (check ⓦ irishrail.ie for times), or take bus #32 or #42 (45min) from Connolly Station

Set in 250 acres of parkland in a pretty seaside town, **Malahide Castle** was home to the Talbot family for more than eight hundred years, until the last surviving member of the family died in 1973. The core building dates from 1185, making it one of the oldest castles in Ireland. Later additions such as the circular corner turrets, built after a fire in 1782, give it a fairy-tale appearance.

Guided **tours** take in the castle's principal rooms – the Great Hall and Oak Room are the most impressive – featuring an extensive collection of eighteenth-century furniture and Irish artworks – while an interactive exhibition in the visitor centre explores the fascinating history of the Talbot Family. The ornamental walled **gardens**, covering about 22 acres, are also worth exploring; they were largely created by the last Talbot to live in the castle, Lord Milo Talbot, an enthusiastic plant collector who is also believed to have been a Soviet spy. The gardens are also home to the Republic's only **butterfly house**, where you can have fun trying to identify more than twenty colourful species.

# South Dublin coast

**1**

A ride on a DART train south along the coast, as well as giving access to **Sandycove**'s James Joyce Museum and the charming historic neighbourhood of **Dalkey**, is a scenic attraction in itself, displaying the great sweep of Dublin Bay before dramatically skirting **Dalkey and Killiney hills** and arrowing off towards Bray and Greystones (see page 115).

## The James Joyce Tower and Museum

Sandycove Point • Daily 10am–6pm, closes at 4pm Nov–March; last admission 1hr before closing • Free • ☎ 01 280 9265, ⊛ joycetower.ie • To get here, catch the DART to Sandycove & Glasthule station, from where it's a 10min walk down Islington Ave then east along the seafront

The diverting **James Joyce Museum** in Sandycove is housed inside an impressive **Martello tower**, one of fifteen such towers erected along the coast between Dublin and Bray in 1804–06 against the threat of invasion by Napoleon. Built with 2.5m-thick granite circular walls and an armoured door 4m off the ground as the only entrance, the towers never fired a shot. Joyce stayed here for just a week, in September 1904, a month before he left the country for Italy with Nora Barnacle. At the time, his host, the writer and wit Oliver St John Gogarty, was renting the tower from the War Office for £8 a year as digs during his medical studies. Joyce immortalized the tower as the setting for the opening chapter of his masterpiece, *Ulysses* – and Gogarty as "stately, plump Buck Mulligan" – and it's now the focus for readings and celebrations every year on June 16, Bloomsday (see page 81).

Opened in 1962 by Sylvia Beach, who first published *Ulysses* in Paris in 1922, the museum displays Joyce's guitar, waistcoat and walking stick, as well as one of two official death masks (the other is in Zurich where he died in 1941). There are also copious letters, photos, and rare and first editions, notably one of *Ulysses* beautifully illustrated by Matisse. On the first floor, Gogarty's living quarters in the former guardroom have been re-created as Joyce described them, and you can climb up to the gun platform on the roof for panoramic views of Dublin Bay.

## Dalkey

Around the coast from Sandycove, **Dalkey** (pronounced "Dawky") is a pretty seaside suburb set against the tree-clad slopes of Dalkey Hill. In medieval times, it prospered as a fortified settlement and the main port of Dublin, until the dredging of the River Liffey in the sixteenth century took away its business. Nowadays, with the building of the railway, Dalkey's characterful old houses and villas are much sought-after by well-to-do commuters, as well as celebrities seeking privacy.

### Dalkey Castle and Heritage Centre

Castle St • Mon & Wed–Fri 10am–6pm, Sat, Sun & public hols 11am–6pm; Living History theatre tours every 30min: Mon–Fri 10.15am–4.30pm; Sat, Sun & public hols 11.15am–4.30pm • €9 • ☎ 01 285 8366, ⊛ dalkeycastle.com

Dalkey's main street boasts two fortified warehouses from the town's medieval heyday. Goat Castle – now known as **Dalkey Castle** – across the road from Archibold's Castle, serves as an attractive and well-designed **Heritage Centre**. The detailed exhibition, with panels written by playwright and local resident Hugh Leonard, covers the town's history, especially its transport systems and literary associations, the latter including an exhibit on Joyce, who set the second chapter of *Ulysses* in Dalkey. The castle interior is impressive in itself, and fine views are to be had from the battlements. The entry price includes Living History theatre tours in which suitably attired actors recount the lives and times of a selection of Dalkey's medieval residents.

The Heritage Centre regularly organizes interesting guided **historical walks** in the town (June–Aug Wed & Fri at noon; €7), and can also arrange guided literary tours (for groups of six or more) to settings in the work of James Joyce, George Bernard

1

## DALKEY AND KILLINEY HILLS

A walk up adjoining **Dalkey and Killiney hills**, before descending to Killiney DART station, offers panoramic views of the city and its environs, and can all be done in an hour and a half from Dalkey DART station if you walk at a moderate pace. From Dalkey, head southeast on Sorrento Road, and then either take the easier route to the right up Knocknacree and Torca roads, or continue along cliffside Vico Road, from where steps and a path ascend steeply. On Torca Road, Shaw fans might want to track down privately owned **Torca Cottage**, where George Bernard Shaw lived for several years as a boy and where he occasionally returned to write in later years. On the way to Dalkey Hill's summit, with its crenellated former telegraph station and fine views over Dublin Bay, you'll pass Dalkey quarry, which provided the granite blocks for the massive piers of Dún Laoghaire harbour below.

From here, follow the partly wooded ridge up to Killiney Hill, where a stone obelisk, built to provide work during the severe winter of 1741, enjoys even more glorious views, north to Howth and south to Killiney Bay and the Wicklow Mountains. From the obelisk, you can quickly descend to the park gate on Killiney Hill Road; from here it's a fifteen-minute walk down Victoria Road and Vico Road through the leafy and exclusive borough of Killiney, to the DART station by the beach.

Shaw, Flann O'Brien, Hugh Leonard and Maeve Binchy. The Centre also participates in Bloomsday (see page 81), re-enacting the Dalkey schoolroom scene in *Ulysses* and staging a special Joycean evening of entertainment.

### Dalkey Island

If you want to take a trip out to tiny **Dalkey Island**, some 300m offshore, then your best bet is to pay a visit to Coliemore Harbour, down Coliemore Road from the southern end of the town, and negotiate a trip with one of the local fishermen (high season only). Once a Viking base, the island features the ruins of a seventh-century church, a Martello tower and gun battery from Napoleonic times, a herd of semi-wild goats, and views of seals and a variety of seabird species.

### ARRIVAL AND DEPARTURE

Dublin's train and bus stations are centrally located while efficient local transport makes the city centre easily accessible from the airport and ferry terminals.

#### BY PLANE

#### DUBLIN AIRPORT

The airport (☏01 874 1111, ⊛dublinairport.com) is 11km north of the centre. The arrivals hall in both terminals (T1 and T2) has several ATMs and a number of car rental outlets, while T1 also has a bureau de change (daily 7am–4pm).

#### GETTING TO THE CENTRE

Buses to the centre depart from outside the arrivals exit; the journey takes 30min–1hr depending upon the service and time of day.

**By Airlink bus** The most direct buses are the Airlink bus #747 (every 10–15min Mon–Sat 5.45am–11.30pm, every 15–20min Sun 7am–11.30pm; €7 single, €12 return), which runs to Heuston railway station via O'Connell St and Busáras, the central bus station; and #757 (every 30min

Mon–Sat 5am–11.55pm, Sun 7.25am–11.45pm; same prices), which runs to Charlotte Way (Camden Street) via Merrion Square.

**By city bus** The slower but cheaper option (€3.30) is to take one of the regular Dublin Bus services such as the #16 to O'Connell St and College Green (every 15min Mon–Sat 6am–11.30pm, Sun 8am–10.40pm), or #41 to Abbey St Lower, just off O'Connell St (every 20–30min Mon–Sat 4am–11.50pm, every 30min Sun 4am–11.35pm).

**By Aircoach** Aircoach (⊛aircoach.ie) operates three services: from Dublin Airport to Stillorgan and Leopardstown via the city centre (every 15–30min daily 24hr); to Greystones via Ballsbridge (hourly); and to Dalkey via Sandymount and Dún Laoghaire (hourly). Tickets cost €6–15 single and €10–21 return, depending on how far you're going.

**By taxi** The taxi rank is outside the arrivals exit; a metered cab to the centre should cost between €25–30.

#### BY TRAIN

Information on train services and timetables is available on

🚉 01 836 6222, 🌐 irishrail.ie. Services listed are for Mon–Sat; extra services may run on Mon and/or Fri, but fewer on Sun.

**Dublin Connolly** Services from Belfast, Sligo and Rosslare terminate at Connolly Station, a 15min walk east of O'Connell St and connected to the centre by regular buses and LUAS trams – it's also on the DART line.

Destinations Belfast (8 daily; 2hr 10min); Boyle (6–8 daily; 2hr 30min); Carrick-on-Shannon (6–8 daily; 2hr 10min); Drogheda (33 daily; 30min–1hr); Enniscorthy (3–5 daily; 2hr–2hr 15min); Newry (8 daily; 1hr 15min); Rosslare Harbour (Rosslare Europort; 3–6 daily; 3hr); Sligo (6–11 daily; 3hr 5min); Wexford (3–5 daily; 2hr 35min); Wicklow (4–6 daily; 1hr 10min).

**Dublin Heuston** Heuston Station, 3km west of the centre, serves trains from Cork, Galway, Kerry, Kilkenny, Limerick, Mayo and Waterford, and is connected to the centre by LUAS and buses #90 and #92. Luggage can be left at the nearby Tipperary House B&B (🚉 01 679 5317; €5/24hr).

Destinations Athlone (11 daily; 1hr 35min); Castlebar (3 daily; 3hr 10min–3hr 20min); Cork (12–15 daily; 2hr 50min); Galway (9–11 daily; 2hr 40min); Kildare (20–30 daily; 40min); Kilkenny (6 daily; 1hr 45min); Killarney (7 daily, most with a change at Mallow; 3hr 30min); Limerick (13–15 daily, most with a change at Limerick Junction; 2hr 15min–2hr 30min); Tralee (7 daily, most with a change at Mallow; 4hr); Waterford (6 daily; 2hr 25min); Westport (43 daily; 3hr 35min).

**Tara Street and Pearse** Two other southside stations, Tara Street and Pearse, serve DART and suburban railways. Note that some commuter trains from Co. Meath terminate at the Docklands Station, some 3km east of the centre.

## BY BUS

Note that most express services to Northern Ireland and Counties Donegal and Sligo also call at Dublin Airport. Additionally, the Wexford/Rosslare Harbour service begins at the airport, picking up at Busáras en route.

**Busáras** Dublin's central bus station is on Store St behind the Custom House, some 10min walk east of O'Connell St. It serves Bus Éireann express coaches from all parts of Ireland

(North and South) as well as the Airlink service and coaches from Britain. City buses run into the centre along Talbot St, a block to the north, while there are LUAS Red Line (see page 92) stops outside the bus station's northern exit or to the west on Abbey St Lower. Alternatively, a taxi can usually be hailed on Beresford Place just south of Busáras. There are left-luggage lockers in the station's basement (€6–10 depending on size).

Destinations Athlone (hourly; 2hr 5min); Belfast (20 daily; 2hr 30min–2hr 55min); Boyle (5–7 daily; 3hr–3hr 20min); Cahir (6 daily; 3hr 5min); Carrick-on-Shannon (5–7 daily; 2hr 45min–3hr); Carrick-on-Suir (6 daily; 3hr); Cashel (6 daily; 2hr 50min); Cavan (10–11 daily; 1hr 50min–2hr 10min); Cork (6 daily; 4hr 25min); Derry (11 daily; 4hr); Donegal town (11 daily; 3hr 45min); Drogheda (most services operate out of the Talbot St depot, but buses after 9pm leave from Busáras; hourly; 1hr 25min); Enniscorthy (hourly; 2hr 25min); Enniskillen (11 daily; 2hr 20min); Galway (15 daily; 3hr 30min); Kildare (mostly from Connolly LUAS stop; 13–15 daily; 1hr 30min); Kilkenny (7 daily; 2hr–2hr 30min); Killarney (5 daily, change at Limerick; 6hr 10min); Limerick (hourly; 3hr 40min); Letterkenny (9–10 daily; 4hr); Monaghan (20–21 daily; 1hr 55min); Newry (hourly; 1hr 35min); Omagh (19–21 daily; 2hr 55min); Rosslare Harbour (18 daily; 3hr 20min); Sligo (7 daily; 3hr 35min–4hr); Tralee (6 daily, change at Limerick; 6hr 10min); Waterford (13 daily; 3hr–3hr 30min); Westport (4 daily; 5hr–5hr 30min); Wexford (hourly; 2hr 50min); Wicklow (from Busáras or George's Quay; every 30min–1hr; 1hr–1hr 30min).

### BY FERRY

**Dublin Port** All services arrive at Dublin Port, 3km east of the centre. Dublin Bus service #53 runs from Talbot St (near Busáras station) to the port (hourly; €3 single), while Morton's Coaches operate a bus transfer service to the port (€4.50 single, €6 return), departing from Westmoreland St at 7am, 12.30pm, 2pm & 7pm.

**Ferry companies** Irish Ferries 🚉 0818 300400, 🌐 irishferries.com; P & O 🚉 01 407 3434, 🌐 poferries.com; Stena Line 🚉 01 204 7799, 🌐 stenaline.ie.

## GETTING AROUND

The best way to get to know Dublin is **on foot**; however, to visit the city's outlying attractions you'll need to make use of the efficient and comprehensive **public transport** network. The easiest (and cheapest) way to pay for journeys is with a pre-paid **Leap Card** (see page 92), which covers all types of public transport in the city.

### BY BUS

Dublin Bus (🌐 dublinbus.ie) operates a network of 136 routes covering just about everywhere in the city and extending far beyond its boundaries into Dublin County, as well as to Kildare, Meath and Wicklow.

**Information** Most of its bus stops display printed timetables and a basic route map, while many now have digital displays with real-time information on when the next bus is due to arrive. See 🌐 dublinbus.ie for more ticket and route details, or download the excellent Dublin Bus app, which allows you to plan your route and search timetables by address. A free guide to the services, timetables and excellent free visitors' map are available from the company's offices at 59 O'Connell St Upper (Mon–Fri 9am–5.30pm; 🚉 01 873 4222).

**Fares** All bus fares are exact-change only; regular ticket prices range from €2.15 for a short ride to €3.30 for the

**1**

longest journeys (child fares €1–1.40) within the suburban area. If you don't have the exact fare and pay more than required, you'll receive a refund voucher from the bus driver; this and your bus ticket should be presented at the Dublin Bus office (see page 91) to obtain a refund.

**Timetables** Most services operate around 6.30am–11.30pm on weekdays, starting later and finishing earlier on Sundays. Special Nitelink buses run in the small hours on a limited number of routes (Sat & Sun midnight–4am; every 30min–1hr; €6.60); these buses run from D'Olier St and Westmoreland St, and have the suffix "N" (e.g. 46N).

### BY TRAM

LUAS (w luas.ie) – the Irish for "speed" – currently operates two overground tramway routes, which are much quicker than buses and avoid traffic congestion. Trams run every 5–15min (Mon–Fri 5.30am–12.30am, Sat 6.30am–12.30am, Sun 7am–11.30pm).

**Fares** Singles cost €2.10–3.30 and returns €3.70–5.70 (children €1–1.30 and €1.90–2.40 respectively). Tickets can be bought from machines at the tramway stops.

**The Green Line** This north–south line commences at Broombridge, then heads through the city centre and down to the southeastern suburbs of Sandyford and Brides Glen.

**The Red Line** This east–west line runs from The Point in Docklands, joining a small branch from Connolly Station at Busáras, before heading along Abbey St to Collins Barracks and crossing the river at Heuston Station then heading southwest to the suburbs of Tallaght and Saggart.

### BY TRAIN

**DART services** The trains of the Dublin Area Rapid Transit system or DART (Mon–Sat 6.20am–midnight, Sun 9.20am–11.40pm; w irishrail.ie) link Howth and Malahide to the north of the city with Bray and Greystones to the south via places such as Blackrock, Dún Laoghaire and Dalkey. It's certainly the quickest option for visiting some of the outlying attractions. Single fares cost €2.20–4.45, with returns at €3.95–8.10 (children's fares €1.15–1.75 and €1.90–3.05), though buying a Leap Card (see page 92) is a cheaper option.

**Iarnród Éireann services** The suburban train services operated by Iarnród Éireann (w irishrail.ie) utilize the same tracks as the DART, but stop at fewer stations (Connolly, Tara St and Pearse in the centre, the new Docklands station just east of the centre, Blackrock, Dún Laoghaire and Bray to the south and Howth Junction to the north). The Northern Commuter line from Pearse Station via Tara St and Connolly is the quickest means of making day-trips to Malahide and to Drogheda for Brú na Boinne.

### BY TAXI

Dublin's taxis vary in size from saloon cars to people carriers; they all have an illuminated box on the roof displaying the driver's taxi licence number. The basic rate is currently €4 for the initial charge (ie just getting into the taxi), then around €1.30/km thereafter, though rates are higher between 8pm and 8am Mon–Sat and all day Sun and public holidays. There are also extra charges for additional passengers, usually €1 each.

---

## TRAVEL PASSES

To save the hassle of buying individual tickets for each journey, the easiest solution is a pre-paid **Leap Card** (w leapcard.ie), available for one day (€10), three days (€19.50) or seven days (€40). Cards are valid for travel on all Dublin Bus services (including Airlink but excluding Nitelink), LUAS and DART services within the short-hop zone (the entire DART network and suburban rail services as far as Balbriggan to the north, Maynooth and Celbridge to the west and Kilcoole to the south), and can be purchased in most newsagents. The electronic card must be validated at the beginning and end of your journey by touching it against the machines on board the bus or at LUAS and DART stations, until you hear the tone.

A bewildering range of **travel passes** is available from the Dublin Bus office (see page 91), newsagents and other shops displaying the Dublin Bus sign, and from DART and suburban railway stations. A three-day Freedom Card for tourists (adult €39.50, child €14) includes travel to and from the airport on the Airlink service (so is best bought at the airport's travel information desk), all Dublin bus services (except Nitelink) and the company's hop-on-and-off city tour (see page 94).

One-day passes for the LUAS service cost €7.30 for adults and €3 for children, and a seven-day pass is €28 (€10 for children) when purchased from station machines. A combined one-day bus and LUAS pass is €10.

The price of most DART railway/suburban rail passes depends on the starting and finishing points of your journey. A one-day pass is €12.15 for adults or €20 for a family of two adults and two children.

**Taxi ranks** Ranks include those at the northwest corner of St Stephen's Green, next to the Bank of Ireland on College Green, outside the *Westin Hotel* on Westmoreland St, in front of the *Gresham Hotel* on O'Connell St or on the western branch of Parnell St.

**Companies and apps** Smartphone users can download the excellent Free Now app (free), which allows you to order an approved taxi driver to collect you from your current location within minutes. Alternatively, Lynk Taxis (☎01 820 2020) and Dublin Taxi 24/7 (☎01 492 2233) are reliable options. Most companies can supply a wheelchair-accessible taxi if booked an hour or more in advance.

### BY CAR

Note that during Dublin's "rush-hour" period (weekdays 7–10am and 4–7pm) traffic is very congested; some areas, such as The Quays and Dame St, are best avoided at all times.

**Car rental** Rental companies include Avis (airport ☎01 605 7500 and 39 Old Kilmainham Rd ☎01 605 7501, ⒲ avis.com); Budget (airport ☎01 844 5150 and 151 Drumcondra Rd ☎01 837 9611, ⒲ budget.ie); Hertz (airport ☎01 844 5466 and 151 South Circular Rd ☎01 709 3060, ⒲ hertz.ie); Irish Car Rentals (airport ☎01 814 4013812 2820 and Park Lane, Spencer Dock ☎01 648 5900670 7890, ⒲ irishcarrentals.com).

**Parking** A good southside option is the Royal College of Surgeons multistorey off the west side of St Stephen's Green (open 24hr, €4/hr or €10 overnight). On-street spaces are hard to find, but Merrion Square and Fitzwilliam Square are often good bets.

### BY BIKE

Dublinbikes (⒲ dublinbikes.ie) offers a three-day ticket which costs €5 (credit/debit card required) and can be purchased from fourteen of the city's fifty bike stations, of which the most central are at St Stephen's Green East and West, Merrion Square West, Dame St, High St, the Custom House, Jervis St and Parnell Square North. You're provided with a personal ID number and a PIN of your own choosing and can then use your ticket to unlock a bike from the stands. The first 30min of any ride are free (as long as the bike is returned to a stand within that period); after that it's €0.50/1hr, rising to €6.50/4hr. Bikes come with automatic lights and a lock, but helmets are not provided. Note that €150 will be debited from your card if the bike is stolen or not returned within 24hr. Visitors can also rent a range of bikes by the day from Phoenix Park Bikes, just inside the Parkgate St entrance to Phoenix Park (☎087 379 9946, ⒲ phoenixparkbikes.com; €10/3hr, €15/day). Biking.ie (⒲ biking.ie) rents good-quality mountain bikes (Ticknock; ☎01 206 3919; €45/day), as well as offering mountain-biking lessons and tours of Dublin and Wicklow (2hr 30min, €50).

## INFORMATION AND TOURIST PASSES

**Visit Dublin Centre** The main tourist office (Mon–Sat 9am–5.30pm, Sun & public hols 10.30am–3pm; ☎1850 230 330, ⒲ visitdublin.com) is at 25 Suffolk St, a short distance west of the Grafton St junction with Nassau St; as well as providing information and making accommodation reservations (€5 per booking), there are also desks for currency exchange and the purchase of tickets for events. Discover Ireland has an office at 14 O'Connell St Upper (Mon–Sat 9am–5pm).

**Listings information** The national daily *Irish Times* and the local daily *Evening Herald* are useful sources of information, notably for cinema and theatre listings, and the former also produces a weekly Friday listings supplement, *The Ticket*. Free listings magazines include *Totally Dublin* (⒲ totallydublin.ie) and *Le Cool* (⒲ dublin.lecool.com), while listings websites ⒲ dublintown.ie and ⒲ entertainment.ie are also useful. The O'Connell St Lower branch of Eason's stocks just about every magazine published in Ireland, along with all Irish and UK daily and Sunday newspapers.

**Dublin Pass** Available at any Tourist Information Office or online at ⒲ dublinpass.ie, the Dublin Pass provides free entry to over thirty of Dublin's top visitor attractions, as well as a Hop on Hop off bus tour and special offers on theatre tickets, restaurants and shops. It is available for one, two, three or five days, costing between €69 and €139 for an adult and between €36 and €80 for a child (aged 5–15). It's well worth checking just how many attractions you'll be able to visit when judging whether this represents a good deal.

**Heritage Card** A Heritage Card (€40) gives free entry to attractions across the city – and the whole of the Republic (see page 44) – run by the Heritage Service (☎01 647 6592, ⒲ heritageireland.ie). Dublin attractions include: Áras an Uachtaráin, the Casino at Marino, Farmleigh, Kilmainham Gaol, Dublin Castle, National Botanic Gardens, Phoenix Park Visitor Centre, Royal Hospital Kilmainham, St Audoen's, St Stephen's Green and Croppy's Acre. Cards are available from Heritage Service sites or tourist offices, and are valid for one year.

**Heritage Island** The €8.90 Heritage Island brochure (☎01 236 6890, ⒲ heritageisland.com) offers a range of discounted admission prices, usually two visitors for the price of one or a percentage reduction, across the whole of Ireland (see page 45). Dublin attractions offering discounts include Christ Church Cathedral, City Hall, Dalkey Castle, Dublin Zoo, Dublinia, the GAA Museum, the Guinness Storehouse, the Jameson Distillery and St Patrick's Cathedral. It can be purchased ahead of time online with free shipping worldwide.

1

## TOURS

One of the easiest ways of seeing Dublin's attractions is a guided **city tour**, and there are plenty available – whether by open-top bus, on foot, along the river, or on a land and water tour. Adult prices are provided below, though most tour operators offer discounts for children, students and senior citizens.

### OPEN-TOP BUS TOURS

If time is short a convenient way of seeing the sights is to take a ride on a hop-on-and-off open-top bus tour. Commentary is provided either by the driver (some of whom also readily break into fitting songs), an on-board guide or a pre-recorded tape. All tickets offer a range of discounts to the city's attractions. All the tours follow roughly the same route, covering Parnell Square, Trinity College, St Stephen's Green, Dublin Castle, the cathedrals, the Guinness Storehouse, Kilmainham, Phoenix Park and Collins Barracks; some tours go to Glasnevin Cemetery. The full circular tour lasts around 1hr 30min, depending on traffic congestion, and tickets are valid for 24hr from the time of first use.

**Dublin Bus** ☎ 01 873 4222, ⊛ dodublin.ie. Dublin bus offer two hop-on-hop-off tours: the Original Tour, leaving from outside the main Dublin Bus office at 59 O'Connell St (daily every 15min 9am–5pm); and the Docklands Tour, starting at Parnell Square North (daily hourly 9.30am–3.30pm) Tickets cost €22 and can be purchased from the Dublin Bus office (see page 91), from the driver and from tourist information centres. The company also operates a Ghostbus Tour (Mon–Thurs 8pm, Fri & Sat 8pm & 9pm; €28; not suitable for under-14s; 2hr) visiting the city's spookier spots.

**Big Bus Dublin** ☎ 01 685 4045, ⊛ loveireland.com. This company also operates a hop-on-hop-off City Sightseeing Tour (daily every 15min 9am–5pm; €22), departing from 13 Upper O'Connell St. Tickets can be purchased from the driver and some hotels.

### RIVER CRUISES

**Dublin Discovered** ☎ 01 473 0000, ⊛ dublindiscovered.ie. A waterborne trip along the River Liffey. Sailings depart from Bachelors Walk (daily: March–Nov 11.30am, 12.30pm, 2.15pm & 3.15pm; April–Oct 10.30am, 11.30am, 12.30pm, 2.15pm, 3.15pm & 4.15pm). The 45min tour includes guided commentary and costs €15.

### WALKING AND CYCLING TOURS

Several general and specialist walking tours are available, covering all manner of subjects from the city's history, and its physical and social fabric, to literature and music, all led by informative and entertaining guides.

**The 1916 Rebellion tour** ☎ 086 858 3847, ⊛ 1916rising.com. A tour that describes the events that lead to the Easter Rising, the Rebellion itself and its aftermath. Begins inside the *International Bar*, 23 Wicklow St (March–Oct Mon–Sat 11.30am, Sun 1pm; 2hr; €15).

**Dublin Literary Pub Crawl** ☎ 087 263 0270, ⊛ dublinpubcrawl.com. Starts upstairs at *The Duke* on Duke St and involves actors performing extracts from major works in a number of pubs with literary connections (April–Oct daily 7.30pm; Nov–March Thurs–Sun 7.30pm; 2hr 15min; €15).

**Fab Food Trails** ☎ 01 497 1245, ⊛ fabfoodtrails.ie. For those keen to enjoy the local delicacies on offer, this guided saunter around the city's range of food outlets, with a decided leaning towards the artisan, will prove agreeably satiating (10am Sat all through the year and also Fri in summer; 2hr 30min; €65); starting points vary – call for details and to book.

**Hidden Dublin Tours** ☎ 01 709 3999, ⊛ hiddendublintours.com. Concentrating on the more salacious aspects of the city's history, this company offers a variety of tours (daily; 1hr 30min–2hr; €19–25), including a Haunted History tour, a "Northside Ghost Walk" and various other themed walks.

**Historical Tours** ☎ 087 688 9412, ⊛ historicaltours.ie. A tour run by Trinity history graduates covering Dublin's development and major events, which starts from Trinity College's front gate (April & Oct daily 11am; May–Sept daily 11am & 3pm; Nov–March Fri–Sun 11am; 2hr; €14).

**Pat Liddy's Walking Tours** ☎ 01 832 9406, ⊛ walkingtours.ie. This renowned local historian offers a number of highly informative two-hour walking tours, including Best of Dublin, and Highlights and Hidden Corners (€15), as well as customized private tours; tours offered in French, German and Irish too.

**See Dublin by Bike** ☎ 087 695 5976, ⊛ seedublinbybike.ie. The Taste of Dublin (2hr 30min, €30) is a whistle-stop tour of Dublin's major sights, which also takes in trendy Camden St, the fruit market, Grand Canal and the Docklands. The tour departs from the multistorey car park on Drury St at 10am daily. Specialist tours – U2's Dublin and A Literary Tour – are also available for groups.

**Traditional Irish Music Pub Crawl** ☎ 01 475 3313, ⊛ discoverdublin.ie/events/musical-pub-crawl. Two musicians guide you on a tour of half a dozen pubs, performing songs and music while recounting Ireland's musical history. Tours begin upstairs at *Oliver St John Gogarty's*, Fleet St (daily 7.30pm; 2hr 30min; €16).

## ACCOMMODATION                    SEE MAPS PAGES 56, 60, 70 AND 77

Dublin offers plenty of **accommodation** to choose from for all budgets, with the northside and suburbs offering the best value. Hotels in the city centre tend to be expensive, though many offer discounts midweek or outside high season (especially via internet bookings), while B&Bs usually provide a very welcoming and comfortable alternative. If money is tight and you want to be near the action, hostels are the best option and almost all have private rooms. **Booking** in advance is always highly advisable, and is essential around major festivals such as St Patrick's Day, in July and August, and on weekends all year round, especially when major concerts or sporting events are taking place. There is one campsite on Dublin's outskirts.

## HOTELS AND B&BS

Many of the city's top-range hotels are located around St Stephen's Green, though the northside also has some chic options. Temple Bar is the most central, but as the location of choice for hen and stag parties it can be very noisy at night. Dublin has a staggering number of B&Bs and you'll find economically priced options on the northside's Gardiner St or in the pleasant southside suburbs of Ballsbridge, Donnybrook and Rathmines, which are all within easy reach of the centre. All rooms listed provide en-suite bathrooms and wi-fi unless stated otherwise.

### TEMPLE BAR

**The Clarence** 6–8 Wellington Quay ☎01 407 0800, ⓦtheclarence.ie. Owned by U2, this former bolthole for priests and lawyers up from the country has been transformed into an informal luxury hotel. All 45 rooms come with a state-of-the-art multimedia system, and some have balconies overlooking the Liffey. The building also contains the *Cleaver East* restaurant in the former ballroom and the swish *Octagon Bar*. €190

**Harding Hotel** Copper Alley, Fishamble St ☎01 679 6500, ⓦhardinghotel.ie. Massively popular due to its budget-conscious high-season room rate and spacious twins, doubles, triples and family accommodation, the *Harding* also includes the atmospheric *Darkey Kelly's* bar (taking its name from an eighteenth-century Copper Alley brothel-keeper), which supplies good food and a regular programme of live entertainment. €140

**The Morgan** 10 Fleet St ☎01 643 7000, ⓦthemorgan. com. Sheer bliss in terms of the quality of its accommodation, the *Morgan* offers crisply designed rooms of varying size, though none is anything less than extremely comfortable. €160

**Temple Bar Hotel** 13–17 Fleet St ☎01 677 3333, ⓦtemplebarhotel.com. From its bright and airy lobby to its attractive, modern en-suite bedrooms, the *Temple Bar* has a high reputation for service and good value, though some of its front-facing rooms can suffer from late-night street noise. The hotel's bar is a popular spot and there's reduced-rate secure car parking nearby. €180

### THE INNER SOUTHSIDE

**Brooks Hotel** Drury St ☎01 670 4000, ⓦbrookshotel. ie. Compact, four-star boutique hotel, on a quiet road that's handy for Temple Bar and Grafton St, with bright and airy bedrooms, a small gym and sauna, the well-regarded Francesca's restaurant and a cracking whiskey bar. €240

**Buswells Hotel** 23–27 Molesworth St ☎01 614 6500, ⓦbuswells.ie. Popular with politicians thanks to its proximity to Leinster House, *Buswells* offers pleasantly designed en-suite rooms in a converted Georgian town house. Ornate plasterwork and fireplaces testify to those origins and the hotel also has the smart Trumans restaurant, its own bar and secure overnight parking. €210

**Central Hotel** 1–5 Exchequer St ☎01 679 7302, ⓦcentralhoteldublin.com. This centrally located place has been in business since 1887, making it one of the city's oldest hotels. Rooms are well equipped and reasonably well soundproofed, though some can feel a little cramped. The first-floor *Library Bar* is a popular spot for everything from morning coffee to pre-dinner drinks. €170

**The Dean Hotel** 33 Harcourt St ☎01 607 8110, ⓦthe dean.ie. A modern boutique hotel just a stone's throw from Stephen's Green. The plush bedrooms have a stylish industrial decor and come kitted out with record players, fully stocked smeg fridges and Nespresso machines, as well as seriously comfortable beds. The rooftop bar terrace offers great views of the city. Noise can be a problem on weekends. €199

**The Fitzwilliam Hotel** St Stephen's Green ☎01 478 7000, ⓦfitzwilliamhoteldublin.com. With an expansive foyer and luxurious, colourful rooms designed by Sir Terence Conran, the *Fitzwilliam* offers deluxe accommodation in a marvellous central location. Room rates vary considerably depending on size and facilities (though all include a CD player and fresh flowers supplied daily); there's also a beauty salon, roof garden, bars, secure parking and restaurant. €300

**Green Hotel** 1–5 Harcourt St ☎01 607 3600, ⓦthe greenhotel.ie. Swish, classy, yet thoroughly modernist, this hotel occupies a spot overlooking the southwestern corner of the Green. As well as its lively bar and economically priced bistro, fitness centre and libraries, the hotel provides 68 spacious double rooms equipped with fridges and power showers and a number of even more luxurious suites. Doubles €210

**Harrington Hall** 70 Harcourt St ☎01 475 3497, ⓦharringtonhall.com. Occupying elegant Georgian premises south of St Stephen's Green, this guesthouse has 29 thoughtfully furnished and generously sized rooms, complete with secondary glazing and ceiling fans. Substantial discounts available in low season. Free parking. €179

**Jurys Inn Christchurch** Christchurch Place ☎01 454 0000, ⓦjurysinn.com. Bang opposite the cathedral (though don't compare the relative architectural merits), *Jurys* is a chain hotel that offers consistent, no-frills comfort. Rooms are both restful and functional and there is a restaurant, café and bar on site. €199

★ **Kelly's Hotel** 36 Great George's St South ☎01 648 0010, ⓦkellysdublin.com. This southside stalwart has been rejuvenated by the owners of *L'Gueuleton* (see page

100), with 16 rooms spread over three narrow floors (note that there's no lift); doubles are fashionably, but not uncomfortably, minimalist; the executive rooms offer more space, while the penthouse suite (€300) sleeps four people. The resident's only Candle Bar is a great spot to round off the evening Over 18s only. **€139**

**Kilronan House** 70 Adelaide Rd ☎01 475 5266, ⓦkilronanhouse.com. It's hard to top the welcome at this fine Georgian town house, which features elegant decoration including Waterford crystal chandeliers, orthopedic mattresses in all its rooms and free parking. The one economy room has a bathroom outside the room. Economy room **€90**; en-suite rooms **€149**

★ **Merrion Hotel** Merrion St Upper ☎01 603 0600, ⓦmerrionhotel.com. The Duke of Wellington's dismissal of his Irish connections, "being born in a stable doesn't make one a horse", rings even hollower now that his birthplace at no. 24 Merrion St Upper is part of this very civilized luxury hotel. Four eighteenth-century town houses have been elegantly redecorated in Georgian style and hung with a superb collection of Irish art, overlooking a private landscaped garden. The hotel is also home to a fancy spa, the two-star Michelin restaurant Patrick Gilbaud (see page 100), and the infinitely less formal *Cellar Restaurant*. **€370**

**The Mont** Merrion St Lower ☎01 607 3800, ⓦthemonthotel.ie. Just off Merrion Square, this three-star hotel housed in a former bank has cool, colourfully furnished rooms all providing a high degree of comfort at excellent prices, as well as an attractive location. You can refuel well in either the Speranza restaurant or the funky Sin Bin Bar. **€160**

**Radisson Blu Royal** Golden Lane ☎01 898 2900, ⓦradissonhotels.com. A spruce, modernist hotel tucked away off Aungier St with elegant and well-accoutred rooms and suites and its own brasserie, fitness club and secure parking. **€289**

★ **The Shelbourne** 27 St Stephen's Green ☎01 663 4500, ⓦtheshelbourne.com.com. The grande dame of Dublin hotels is today looking better than ever, from the gilded lobby and grand staircase to some 265 immaculately prepared rooms. The hotel's raft of eating and drinking options include the *Horseshoe Bar* (see page 102) and the Lord Mayor's Lounge, where you can tuck into traditional afternoon tea, accompanied by views of the Green and the tinkling of a piano. There's a fitness room and a luxurious spa and pool. **€359**

**Stauntons on the Green** 83 St Stephen's Green ☎01 478 2300, ⓦstauntonsonthegreen.ie. Set in an unbeatable location on the south side of the Green with its own private gardens, this luxurious guesthouse has a good mix of singles, doubles (including some very cosy ones), triple and family rooms, which offer both comfort and style befitting this Georgian building. All the rooms overlook either the Green or Iveagh Gardens. **€159**

**The Westbury** Harry St, off Grafton St ☎01 679 1122, ⓦdoylecollection.com. The glossy lobby of this luxurious five-star hotel is an indicator of the treats that lie in store. Its bedrooms are not so much furnished as designed to pamper, and the range of facilities on offer includes a fitness centre, a svelte bar specializing in champagne cocktails, and underground parking. **€310**

**The Westin Dublin** Westmoreland St ☎01 645 1000, ⓦmarriott.com. Hiding behind the facade of the old Allied Irish Bank building just north of Trinity College, the *Westin* is a marvellously luxurious establishment. Its 191 elegantly equipped bedrooms feature a blend of mahogany furniture and sensitive colour design while bathrooms are finished in gleaming Italian marble. The bar is housed in the former bank's vaults, and the lounge has a stunning glass roof. Breakfast not included. **€380**

### THE NORTHSIDE

**Academy Plaza Hotel** 10–14 Findlater Place, Cathal Brugha St ☎01 878 0666, ⓦacademyplazahotel.ie. Tucked away behind O'Connell St, this well-appointed hotel sports simply furnished en-suite rooms – including triples and quads – as well as a fine range of breakfasts and a friendly bar. **€159**

**Ashling Hotel** 10–13 Parkgate St ☎01 677 2324, ⓦashlinghotel.ie. Conveniently set near Heuston Station, this modern four-star hotel's luxuriously furnished rooms provide all essential amenities and plenty of space, as well as a pleasant bar and excellent breakfasts; secure parking is available. Rates exclude breakfast. **€180**

**Belvedere Hotel** Great Denmark St ☎01 873 7700, ⓦbelvederehoteldublin.com. The *Belvedere's* Georgian exterior encompasses a very amenable modern hotel. Rooms are attractively furnished, bright and airy, and most are wheelchair-accessible. Big discounts available during off-season, with rates as low as €89. **€189**

**Beresford Hotel** 21 Store St ☎01 813 4700, ⓦberesfordhotelifsc.com. Though its setting opposite Busáras isn't exactly auspicious, the *Beresford's* attractive modern interior, friendly staff and one hundred well-accoutred bedrooms more than compensate. As well as a fitness room, the hotel has an attached Italian restaurant and a cosmopolitan café-bar. Breakfast not included. **€159**

**Clifden Guesthouse** 32 Gardiner Place ☎01 874 5611, ⓦclifdenhouse.com. One of the northside's most reliable options, this comfortable Georgian house is well maintained by very friendly hosts. Fifteen pleasant en-suite rooms include doubles as well as a triple and a family room. Off-street parking is available. **€159**

**The Gresham Hotel** 23 O'Connell St Upper ☎01 874 6881, ⓦriu.com. The *Gresham* isn't just a splendidly equipped four-star hotel, it is also one of Dublin's landmarks, a place where you don't have to be a guest to enjoy afternoon tea in the opulent surroundings of its lobby or sample the meals in its restaurant. Rooms are pleasantly furnished and spacious while the individually designed penthouse suites, including ones devoted to artist Marc Lamb, architect (and designer of the Spire) Ian Ritchie, and actors Liz Taylor and Richard Burton, offer differing views of the city. Rooms facing O'Connell St can be noisy. €165

**Hilton Garden Inn** Custom House Quay ⊕01 854 1500, ⊛hilton.com. This sparkling hotel boasts a fabulous riverside location with staggering views of Dublin's developing docklands from rooms on the upper storeys. Immaculate rooms aside, facilities include a restaurant/bar and pantry. €160

**Maldron Hotel** Smithfield Village ⊕01 485 0900, ⊛maldronhotelsmithfield.com. A great addition to the Smithfield area, this new-build hotel provides excellently equipped and furnished rooms, tastefully decorated using primary colours, and has a remarkably good-value restaurant. There's secure overnight parking nearby and it's handily placed for music sessions at *The Cobblestone* (see page 103). Excellent midweek rates. €189

**Marian Guest House** 21 Gardiner St Upper ⊕01 874 4129. Immensely popular due to its budget prices and warm welcome, the *Marian* offers clean and comfortable en-suite and standard rooms, plus a filling breakfast. Most have shared bathrooms but some en suites are available. There's off-street parking, and buses #16 and #41 stop around the corner on Dorset St Upper. €100

**The Morrison** Ormond Quay Lower ⊕01 887 2400, ⊛morrisonhotel.ie. Shiny surfaces and clean lines dominate at this swish temple of minimalism; while natural tones prevail in the lobby and ultra-cool bar, the luxurious rooms are dazzlingly white with shocks of vibrant pinks and purples. The sleek Morrison Grill and flashy Quay 14 cocktail bar are the hotel's very commendable dining/drinking options. €290

**The Townhouse** 47–48 Gardiner St Lower ⊕01 878 8808, ⊛dirl.com. This superbly converted Georgian house remains an oasis of calm in one of the city's busiest streets. Elegant twins, doubles, triples and a family room are thoughtfully decorated and include sizeable en-suite facilities (though the cheapest rooms have shared bathrooms). A buffet breakfast is served in an elegant dining room with a balcony, and there are secure off-street parking spaces. €130

## HOSTELS

Dublin has numerous hostels, the majority of which offer both dormitory accommodation (€12–25/person, depending on the season) and private rooms, usually sleeping between two and four people (€25–60/person). Most rooms are en suite and the standard of private rooms is often as good as at B&Bs. Several Dublin hostels belong to the IHH, though a few are members of the IHO (see page 34) – all those listed below are affiliated to IHH unless stated otherwise. Many hostels offer free breakfast and provide internet access.

### THE SOUTHSIDE

**Ashfield Hostel** 19–20 D'Olier St ⊕01 679 7734, ⊛ashfieldhostel.com. One of the centre's most popular choices provides over 130 beds in a variety of bright and spacious rooms, all with en-suite facilities. Dorms come in a variety of sizes, from four to eighteen-bed, as well as comfortable doubles. Free breakfast and walking tours. Dorms €16, doubles €72

**Kinlay House** 2–12 Lord Edward St ⊕01 679 6644, ⊛kinlaydublin.ie. A very lively and busy hostel near Christ Church Cathedral, *Kinlay House* offers good-value private rooms as well as both small six-bed and much bigger 24-bed dorms. There's a large kitchen as well as a café, common room with pool table, and tablets for internet access. Dorms €18, doubles €33

**Oliver St John Gogarty's** 18–21 Anglesea St ⊕01 671 1822, ⊛gogartys.ie. This well-equipped hostel above a popular tourist pub in the centre of Temple Bar has more than 130 beds in a range of accommodation, including standard and en-suite twins and up to eight- and ten-bed dorms. Kitchen and laundry facilities are available. Dorms €12, doubles €35

### THE NORTHSIDE

**Abbey Court** 29 Bachelors Walk ⊕01 878 0800, ⊛abbey-court.com. Right next to O'Connell Bridge, this upmarket, well-designed hostel provides en-suite twins/doubles and dorms ranging from four to thirty-four beds. Very security conscious, access is via keycards and there are lockers in every room. There's also a café, kitchen, two TV lounges, a conservatory and a barbecue area. Dorms €18, doubles €80

**Abraham House** 82–83 Gardiner St Lower ⊕01 855 0600, ⊛abrahamshostel.com. One of the larger northside hostels, *Abraham House* has both a friendly staff and atmosphere. En-suite rooms range from private singles, doubles and triples, to dorms ranging in size from four to sixteen-beds. There's a good kitchen and lockers. Dorms €15, doubles €80

★ **Globetrotters** 46 Gardiner St Lower ⊕01 873 5893, ⊛globetrottersdublin.com. This 94-bed hostel offers six- to twelve-bed dorms, equipped with some of the most comfortable bunks in Dublin. All are en suite, there's a good kitchen, and a full Irish breakfast is included in the price, which can be eaten in the Japanese garden out back. €18

**Isaacs Hostel** 2–5 Frenchman's Lane ⊕01 855 6215, ⊛isaacs.ie. Efficiently run and very welcoming, Dublin's oldest independent hostel is still one of its best and consists of four- to sixteen-bed dorms and some cosy twin-bedded private rooms. Although none is en suite, the shared bathrooms are well equipped with hairdryers and straighteners; facilities include a high-quality kitchen, a

1

café, sauna, games room and reading room.. The hostel also runs free walking tours and pizza nights. Dorms €14, twins €60, triples €85,

★ **Jacobs Inn** 21–28 Talbot Place ☎01 855 5660, ⓦjacobsinn.com. Dublin's largest hostel, which nevertheless remains one of the most convivial, with a ground-floor kitchen and dining room, a first-floor common room with pool table and large-screen TV, a rooftop terrace with great views and a daily walking tour. Accommodation is en suite and well equipped, ranging from large private rooms with TVs to twelve-bed dorms. Dorms €16, doubles €80

**Sky Backpackers** 2–4 Litton Lane ☎01 872 8389, ⓦskybackpackers.dublinhotelsweb.com. Housed in a former recording studio in a quiet side street off Bachelors Walk, this recently refurbished small hostel offers eight- and ten-bed en-suite dorms as well as comfortable private rooms. There's a sizeable kitchen, and they also run free daily walking tours. Dorms €17, doubles €88

## CAMPING
**Camac Valley Tourist Caravan & Camping Park** Corkagh Regional Park, Naas Rd, Clondalkin ☎01 464 0644, ⓦcamacvalley.com. The only campsite within easy reach of the city centre lies 8km southwest of Dublin. This well-equipped, family-oriented site offers excellent facilities, including kitchen, laundry and shop, as well as fine views of the surrounding countryside. Take bus #69 from Aston Quay, or it's a 5min drive from the Red Cow LUAS station. €20

## EATING                         SEE MAPS PAGES 56, 60, 70 AND 77

It's fair to say that no one used to come to Dublin just for the cuisine, but the last decade or so has seen a complete transformation in the city's culinary fortunes. Aside from fantastic modern Irish cooking – the city now boasts five Michelin-starred restaurants – it's now possible to sample a wide variety of cuisines, from Lebanese to Nepalese. Many restaurants offer lunchtime or **early-bird** (typically before 7pm) **set menus** of two or three courses, sometimes for as little as half the cost of their regular evening meals. Some cafés and restaurants also provide good-value **weekend brunch**. In addition, plenty of pubs (see page 101) dish up decent, reasonably priced, hearty food, with more ambitious menus available at gastropubs such as *The Exchequer* (see page 102).

### CAFÉS AND QUICK MEALS
Dublin has long had a thriving café scene, but it is only recently that Dubliners have got serious about coffee. A string of artisan coffee shops has popped up all over the city, where internationally acclaimed baristas take pride in selling you the perfect brew. While Irish breakfast tea is a perennial favourite, most cafés also offer a selection of herbal blends. As well as cafés, we've listed below other good spots for a quick, tasty, inexpensive meal. For a splurge with a difference, "Art Tea" at the *Merrion Hotel* (see page 96) is a lot of fun: delicious afternoon tea in the drawing rooms, with cakes that creatively reflect the surrounding paintings from the hotel's excellent collection of nineteenth- and twentieth-century, mostly Irish, art (€55).

### THE SOUTHSIDE
★ **Avoca Café** 11 Suffolk St ☎01 677 4215, ⓦavoca. com. The bright, buzzy, modern Irish café on the top floor of this department store (see page 106) dishes up everything from a full Irish breakfast (€13.50) to organic falafel (€15.60) as well as an array of cakes, all beautifully presented and courteously served in a bright dining room with vintage furniture. The food hall and deli in the basement offers salads and sandwiches to take away (from €4.50). Mon–Fri 9.30am–4.30pm, Sat 9.30am–5pm, Sun 11am–5pm.

**Bewley's** 78 Grafton ☎01 672 7720, ⓦbewleys.com. Iconic café serving a range of delicious breakfasts, cakes and light meals served up in a gorgeous interior spread over several floors. The window tables overlooking the street are especially sought after, and don't miss the six beautiful stained-glass windows by Harry Clarke at the back of the ground floor. Mon–Wed 8am–10pm, Thurs–Sat 8am–11pm, Sun 9am–10pm.

**Bibi's** Emorville Ave ☎01 454 7421, ⓦbibis.ie. A genuinely special place to have brunch, *Bibi's* is the not-so-secret neighbourhood café that people from all over Dublin flock to on weekends. A converted house and former dress shop on a red-bricked terrace, it serves a small but perfect menu. The butternut squash eggs with chilli butter (€10) are a must. Try and get there on a weekday when it's less hectic, and enjoy the warm light and great coffee. Mon & Wed–Fri 9am–4.30pm, Sat 9am–5pm, Sun 10am–5pm.

**Bunsen** 3 South Anne St ☎01 652 1022, ⓦbunsen.ie. With a menu so small it fits on a business card, Bunsen does one thing, and it does it well: burgers. No fuss classic old-school burgers (from €7.95) cooked to perfection. Grab a soda or a shake while you're at it. Mon & Tues noon–9pm, Wed & Thurs noon–9.30pm, Fri & Sat noon–10.30pm, Sun 1–9.30pm.

**Coffee Angel** 15 Leinster St ☎01 664 0000, ⓦcoffeeangel.com. There are numerous outlets of this coffee chain throughout the city, all serving superior coffee and snacks. Mon–Fri 7.30am–5pm, Sat 9am–6pm, Sun 10am–5pm.

**Cornucopia** 19–21 Wicklow St ☎01 677 7583, ⓦcornucopia.ie. Friendly, vegetarian, buffet café serving an excellent range of breakfasts, salads, soups and main courses, as well as cakes, breads, juices and organic wine. Mon–Sat 8.30am–10pm, Sun noon–10pm.

**TOP 5 TAKEAWAY COFFEES**
**The Bernard Shaw** See page 102
**Brother Hubbard** See below
**Coffee Angel** See page 98
**Kaph** See below
**Urbanity** See below

**Dolce Sicily** 43 Dawson St ☎086 840 7360, ⓦdolce sicily.ie. Tucked away in the basement of a wonderfully colourful Georgian town house, *Dolce Sicily* is the perfect place to recharge your batteries and indulge your sweet tooth. Choose from a veritable smorgasbord of treats from a famous Sicilian Cannolo (€5) to a moreish Ricotta and Nutella Tart (€6). Also serves sandwiches and wine. Mon–Wed 7.30am–9.30pm, Thurs & Fri 7.30am–10pm, Sat 9am–10pm, Sun 9.30am–9.30pm.

★ **Dunne and Crescenzi** 14–16 South Frederick St ☎01 675 9892, ⓦdunneandcrescenzi.com. A cosy, popular Italian café-restaurant and wine bar, with croissants and spot-on coffee, all manner of Italian sandwiches and excellent plates of antipasti, as well as salads, pastas (from €13.50) and daily special main courses. Bookings taken only for dinner. Mon–Sat 10.30am–10/11pm, Sun 10.30am–9pm.

★ **The Fumbally** Fumbally Lane ☎01 529 8732, ⓦthefumbally.ie. One of the best brunch spots in Dublin, serving excellent coffee, falafel wraps with purple slaw (€6), and gorgeous "green eggs" with avocado and fried chorizo (€7.50), in a cavernous empty retail space filled with mismatched vintage furniture. Tues, Thurs & Fri 8am–5pm, Wed 8am–5pm & 7–9.30pm, Sat 10am–5pm.

**Irish Film Institute Café Bar** 6 Eustace St ☎01 679 5744, ⓦifi.ie. Great for an inexpensive lunch or dinner, whether sitting in the smart bar or the echoing atrium. Simple meals range from lamb flatbreads (€7.25) and burgers to fish cakes and goat's cheese salad, with lots of vegetarian options. Mon–Thurs noon–11.30pm, Fri & Sat noon–12.30am, Sun noon–11pm.

**Kaph** 31 Drury St ☎01 613 9030, ⓦkaph.ie. Superb coffee in an ultra-cool setting. Try one of their home-made cakes (€3) for the perfect mid-morning energy boost. Great music, too. Mon–Sat 8am–7pm, Sun 11am–6pm.

**Leo Burdock's** 2 Werburgh St ☎01 454 0306, ⓦleo burdock.com. Dublin's most famous fish-and-chipper (takeaway only, but the garden of Christ Church Cathedral is just over the road) is all gleaming surfaces and friendly service. The multi-award-winning menu now stretches to lemon sole goujons (€6.99), but otherwise there are no surprises. Mon–Thurs & Sun 11.30pm–midnight, Fri & Sat 11.30am–1am.

**Queen of Tarts** Cork Hill and Cow's Lane ☎01 670 7499, ⓦqueenoftarts.ie. The former location is the cosy, original branch of this patisserie-cum-café, while the latter around the corner provides more elbow room and outdoor tables on the pedestrianized alley. Both offer veggie and meaty fry-ups (€13) and granola for breakfast; savoury tarts (€13) and a few other hot dishes, salads and all sorts of sandwiches (€9.50) for lunch; and yummy cakes baked on the premises to keep you going between mealtimes. Mon–Thurs 8am–7pm, Fri 8am–8pm, Sat 8.30am–8pm, Sun 9am–7pm.

**Silk Road Café** Chester Beatty Library, Dublin Castle ☎01 407 0770, ⓦsilkroadkitchen.ie. Stylish and good-value museum café, spilling over into the library's sky-lit atrium. Mostly Middle Eastern food: Lebanese chicken (€11.95), falafel, spinach and feta filo pie and very good salads, as well as great coffee and titbits such as Turkish delight and baklava. Mon–Fri 10am–4.45pm, Sat 11am–4.45pm, Sun 1–4.45pm; closed Mon Oct–May.

**THE NORTHSIDE**

**Brother Hubbard** 153 Capel St ☎01 441 1112, ⓦbrotherhubbard.ie. Nestled in the middle of vibrant Capel St, *Brother Hubbard* is a very busy little café serving serious food. Go for the grilled halloumi sandwich (€10.95) or the three salad plate (€10.95). Make sure to save room for their divine brownies. Mon 8am–4.30pm, Tues–Fri 8am–10pm, Sat 9am–10pm, Sun 9am–4.30pm.

**Caffè Cagliostro** Blooms Lane ☎01 888 0860, ⓦwallace winebars.ie. A tiny Italian café serving excellent espresso and pastries (from €2.50), with newspapers for perusal and a sunny outdoor terrace. Mon–Thurs 7am–6.30pm, Fri 7am–10pm, Sat 8.30am–6.30pm, Sun 10am–6pm.

**Eatyard** Cross Guns Bridge, Glasnevin St ☎01 906 0218, ⓦthe-eatyard.com. A cool food market that attracts a lot of hungover 30-somethings on Saturday and Sunday afternoons. Plenty of stalls serving a wide selection of grub, from Taiwan street food to Venezuelan vegan wraps. Thurs–Sun noon–10pm.

**The Gresham Hotel** 23 O'Connell St Upper ☎01 874 6881. Enjoy afternoon tea (€35/person, daily 2–6pm) in the opulent surroundings of this grand hotel's lobby. Booking essential. Daily 7.30am–10.30pm.

**Soup Dragon** 168 Capel St ☎01 872 3277, ⓦsoup dragon.com. A small and inexpensive lunchtime favourite serving the most delicious soups and stews in the city. Everything from the bread to the chowder is made on site. Soups start at €5.30. Mon–Fri 8am–4pm.

**Urbanity** 11 Coke Lane ☎01 874 7288, ⓦurbanity.ie. Tucked away at the bottom of Smithfield, this trendy café has a simple philosophy: everything must be made from scratch, from the almond butter to the pickles. Even the coffee beans are roasted on site, with predictably aromatic results. Lunch ranges from mint and wild garlic grilled halloumi (€12.50) to a 15hr slow roast Asian-style pork belly (€14). Mon–Fri 8am–4pm, Sat & Sun 10am–4pm.

★ **The Woollen Mills** 42 Lower Ormond Quay ☎01 828 0835, ⓦthewoollenmills.com. A sister restaurant to the

**1**

*Winding Stair*, this "eating house" in an old haberdashery sprawls over four floors, with huge windows and a roof terrace opening out over the Ha'penny Bridge. The food is fresh, local and seasonal, and caters for all types of eaters at all times of the day: grab a good takeaway coffee and a bun from their on-site bakery for breakfast, a salad box for lunch, or lounge over a supper feast of roasted Wicklow lamb with smoked violet garlic puree (€27) and a craft beer at night. Mon–Thurs noon–9pm, Fri & Sat noon–10pm, Sun noon–7pm.

**Wuff** 23 Benburb St ☏01 633 7959, ⓦwuffrestaurant. ie. A lively neighbourhood bistro in the heart of Smithfield, serving up the likes of veggie chorizo benedict (€13.50) for breakfast, pulled jackfruit sandwiches (€13.95) and salads for lunch, and heartier dishes like golden beer-battered fish with twice-cooked chips (€16) for dinner. Mon–Wed 8am–4pm, Thurs & Fri 8am–9.30pm, Sat 10am–9.30pm, Sun 10am–4pm.

## RESTAURANTS

The majority of Dublin's restaurants are on the south side of the river in the city centre. An abundance of excellent new places to eat have opened up around the George's St/South William St area, stretching up Camden St as far as Portobello. Eating out in Temple Bar tends to be overpriced and underwhelming. It's worth booking ahead, especially in the evenings.

### THE SOUTHSIDE

**Camden Kitchen** 3A Camden Market ☏01 476 0125, ⓦcamdenkitchen.ie. Housed in the historic Camden Market building on a residential Georgian street in Portobello, the top-class chefs combine a passion for local and wild Irish produce with inspiration from their travels abroad to create dishes such as organic Irish salmon with seaweed and capers, and warm potato and shallot (€15). The set lunch (three courses €23.50) and early-bird menu (€33) offer the best value. Tues 5.30pm–10pm, Wed–Fri noon–2.30pm & 5.30–10pm, Sat 5.30–10pm.

**Chez Max** 1 Palace St ☏01 633 7215, ⓦchezmax. ie. Archetypal French bistro at the gate of Dublin Castle, offering a wide-ranging evening menu of classic dishes, supplemented by specialities from the owner's home region in southwest France; expect the likes of beef bourguignon and duck confit alongside cold meat and cheese platters, sweet and savoury crêpes and delicious French breakfasts. Mon–Fri 8am–midnight, Sat & Sun noon–midnight.

**Dig In** 19 Camden St ☏478 9626, ⓦdigin.ie. Despite its slightly pretentious claim to be an Art Diner – though to be fair there's some fantastic wallbound artwork on display – this place certainly delivers in terms of its food offer, from small plates (salt beef tacos) to salads and mains such as a tasty chicken pot pie. Daily noon–midnight.

**Ely Wine Bar** 22 Ely Place ☏01 676 8986, ⓦelywinebar.

ie. Popular, congenial and reasonably- priced wine bar that offers snacks and main meals like pan-fried guinea fowl with barley and bacon (€24), to accompany around eighty wines by the glass. Carefully sourced, mostly organic Irish ingredients, including fresh beef and pork from their own farm in the Burren. Mon–Fri noon–late, Sat 5pm–late.

**Fallon and Byrne** 11–17 Exchequer St ☏01 472 1010, ⓦfallonandbyrne.com. Foodie heaven in a converted telephone exchange: a smart grocery store and deli (for lunch to eat in or take away) on the ground floor; a seductive, Parisian-style brasserie upstairs, offering everything from burgers to superb seared sea bream with squid terrine and smoked almond oil (€26); and a wine bar and shop in the basement, serving cheaper food. Daily noon–3pm & 5.30–9pm (Wed & Thurs till 10pm, Fri & Sat till 11pm).

★ **The Greenhouse** 21 Dawson St ☏01 676 7015, ⓦthegreenhouserestaurant.ie. Currently one of just three, two-Michelin starred restaurants in the whole of Ireland, The Greenhouse remains the standard bearer for Irish cuisine. Head chef Mickael Valjanen conjures up magical dishes like turbot with violin courgette and green tomato emulsion, and while the ambience here is measured, it's far from stuffy. Nor is it outrageously expensive, with tasting menus from €75. Tues–Sat 5.30–9.30pm, plus Thurs–Sat noon–2pm.

**La Maison** 15 Castlemarket ☏01 672 7258, ⓦlamaisondublin.com. The outdoor tables at this quaint French restaurant on the pedestrianized Castlemarket are the most in demand even in winter when heaters and blankets keep diners warm while they enjoy bowls of *moules frites* (€14.50). The giant 32oz *cote de boeuf* for two people (€59) is especially recommended. Daily noon–11pm.

★ **L'Écrivain** 109 Lower Baggot St ☏01 661 1919, ⓦlecrivain.com. This one Michelin-starred restaurant, housed in three beautifully converted Georgian coachhouses, offers inspired cooking of multi-faceted but harmonious dishes such as poached lobster with grapes, chervil, peach and cucumber. All menus change seasonally. The eight-course tasting menu (€90) is a real treat. Mon–Thurs & Sat 6.30–10pm, Fri 12.30–3.30pm & 6.30–10pm.

**L'Gueuleton** 2 Fade St ☏087 939 3608, ⓦlgueuleton.com. Great French bistro food such as wild Wicklow venison with pomme fondant and cavolo nero (€27) from an open kitchen at reasonable prices, accompanied by good-value French wine. Daily 12.30–3.30pm & 5.30–10pm.

**Neon** 17 Camden St ☏01 405 2222, ⓦneon17.ie. This trendy, always-buzzing Asian street-food restaurant offers an array of fiery Thai curries (€13.60), Vietnamese soups (from €7) and stir-fries. Enjoy over a beer or glass of wine at the rustic communal tables, before pouring your own whipped ice-cream cone for dessert. Daily noon–10pm.

**Restaurant Patrick Gilbaud** Merrion Hotel, Merrion St Upper ☏01 676 4192, ⓦrestaurantpatrickgilbaud.ie. The second of the city's two-Michelin starred restaurants,

1

## TOP 5 CHEAP EATS

**Avoca Café** See page 98
**Bunsen** See page 98
**Dunne & Crescenzi** See page 99
**The Fumbally** See page 99
**Neon** See page 100

this is as exceptional – and as formal – as you'd expect. A la carte menus (€98–160) may feature anything from ravioli of blue lobster with lobster coconut cream and toasted almond to caramelised veal sweetbread with tamarind and date, all prepared with infinite class. The three-course lunch at €65 is probably better value. Tues–Sat 12.30–2.30pm & 7–10pm.

**Trocadero** 4 St Andrew's St ☎ 01 677 5545, ⍟ trocadero. ie. A welcoming haven, done out with plush booths, signed photos of showbiz visitors and yards of red velvet. Excellent though predictable food, whether a la carte or on the good-value pre-theatre set menu (vacate the table by 7.30pm; €28 for three courses). Mon–Fri 5–10pm, Sat 4.30–10pm, Sun 3–10pm.

**Ukiyo** 7–9 Exchequer St ☎ 01 633 4071, ⍟ ukiyobar. com. Chic Korean and Japanese bar-restaurant, serving bento boxes (€10) and mains like slow cooked pork with cauliflower kimchi (€18), with a novel take on the Dublin snug: karaoke booths in the basement for €30/hr. Mon–Sat noon–2.30am, Sun noon–1.30am.

### THE NORTHSIDE

**★ Chapter One** 18–19 Parnell Square North ☎ 01 873 2266, ⍟ chapteronerestaurant.com. Housed in the cellars of the Dublin Writers Museum, this Michelin-starred culinary gem specializes in modern Irish food, inspired by the Irish landscape, seasons and new Irish artisan producers. A signature dish from the tasting menu is pig's tail stuffed with Fingal Ferguson's bacon, lobster, basil puree and mustard fruits. The restaurant offers a pre-theatre menu (5–7pm, €50 for three courses), otherwise expect to pay around €70 plus wine. Wed & Thurs 5–10pm, Fri & Sat 12.30–2pm & 7.30–10pm.

**Musashi** 15 Capel St ☎ 01 532 8068, ⍟ musashidublin. com. Decent Japanese restaurants in Dublin are few and far between, but *Musashi* is up there with the best. Serving mostly sushi, the menu is just varied enough to cater for those uninterested in fish. Try the pork gyoza – as close to perfection as a dumpling can get. Mon–Thurs & Sun noon–10pm, Fri & Sat noon–11pm.

**The Winding Stair** 40 Ormond Quay Lower ☎ 01 872 7320, ⍟ winding-stair.com. Set above the bookshop of the same name (see page 106), with its views across the Liffey (ask for a seat by the window), this is one of the most enjoyable northside spots for lunch (three-course set menu €26.95). Evenings feature a pre-theatre dinner (€30.95) or a la carte (around €45 for three courses); all menus (which change daily) feature traditional Irish cooking with a modern twist using local and seasonal produce. Daily noon–10.30pm.

### THE SUBURBS

**★ Caviston's** 59 Glasthule Rd, Sandycove ☎ 01 280 9245, ⍟ cavistons.com. Near Sandycove and Glasthule DART station, this restaurant works to a basic but hugely successful formula – the day's freshest fish and seafood cooked simply. Booking is essential and there are a few outside tables in summer. There are three lunch sittings (Tues–Sat noon, 1.30pm & 3pm) and evening sittings Thurs, Fri and Sat (6pm & 8.15pm). Three courses will set you back around €40 plus wine, but the two-course set menu is a steal at €21. Tues–Wed noon–3.20pm, Thurs–Sat noon–3.20pm & 6–9pm.

## DRINKING
## SEE MAPS PAGES 56, 60, 70 AND 77

Dubliners boast that their city possesses the finest **pubs** in the world. They're probably right too, but with over seven hundred watering holes to choose from, forming the backbone of the capital's social life, there's no harm in checking out their assertion. Along the way, you'll also be able to test out competing claims about the hometown drink, **Guinness**: that it tastes better here is not open to doubt, but locals argue about exactly which pub pours the best drop (is the travel-shy liquid better at *Ryan's*, just across the river from the brewery, than downstream at *Mulligan's*?). In general, the stout is best in the characterful and sociable historic pubs, many of which retain their cut-glass screens, ornate woodcarving and cosy snugs, often with a private hatch to the bar. Alongside the more traditional pubs, a plethora of cosmopolitan **bars** has sprung up, be they cavernous microbreweries serving craft beers, studenty DJ bars or chic designer cocktail lounges. Pubs operate strict trading hours, and most close at 11.30pm Sunday to Thursday and 12.30am on Friday and Saturday. Bars and nightclubs with late licences are noted in the reviews below. Traditional music pubs (see page 103) are great for a drink in their own right. Dublin also has a number of LGBTQ bars (see page 105) as well as some highly entertaining pub tours (see page 94).

### TEMPLE BAR AND THE SOUTHSIDE

**Anséo** 18 Camden St ☎ 01 475 1321. Unpretentious, easy-going venue with plenty of velour banquettes to chill out on. DJs at weekends, comedy night on Wed and occasional live music. Mon–Thurs noon–11.30pm, Fri noon–12.30am, Sat 10–12.30am, Sun 10am–11pm.

**The Bar with No Name** 3 Fade St ☎ 087 122 1064, ⍟ noname.bar. With no formal name or a sign outside it can

1

be easy to miss this place – it's on the first floor, entered to the left of *L'Gueuleton* (from whose kitchen weekend brunch is served). Lovely, big outdoor terrace, cool soundtrack and a loft feel, with bare floorboards, and modern art on the walls. Try one of their famous mojitos and soak up the vibes. Mon–Wed 12.30–11.30pm, Thurs 12.30pm–1am, Fri & Sat 12.30pm–2am, Sun noon–11pm.

**Cassidy's** 27 Westmoreland St ☎ 01 670 8604. With its graffitied walls, mismatched furniture and a spectacular array of craft beers on draught or by bottle, this refurbished hipster hangout also serves pizza and plays consistently great music. Mon–Thurs & Sun 4pm–12am, Fri & Sat 4pm–1am.

★ **The Exchequer** 3 Exchequer St ☎ 01 670 6787, ⓦ theexchequer.ie. Sleek, modern gastropub where you can plonk yourself on a bar stool, a sofa or at a restaurant table. The cuisine ranges from Asian (Chaing Mai spiced hotdog) to seafood (sea bream with a radish, peanut and snow pea salad), while the weekend roast (with vegetarian option) is an absolute belter. Wed–Fri 1–11pm, Sat & Sun noon–11pm.

**Grogan's** 15 South William St ☎ 01 677 9320, ⓦ grogans pub.ie. Lively, eccentric traditional pub, popular with budding writers and artists. One of the most popular spots in the city on a sunny day, the outdoor seating area quickly fills, with punters taking their drinks to the street outside. On a more typically drizzly day, sit inside and order one of their famous cheese toasties while admiring the original artwork on the walls. Mon–Thurs 10.30am–11.30pm, Fri & Sat 10.30am–12.30am, Sun 12.30–11pm.

**The Horseshoe Bar** Shelbourne Hotel, 27 St Stephen's Green ☎ 01 663 4500. In this luxury hotel, the *Horseshoe's* deep-red leather banquettes and white marble counter maintain a cosy pub feel. The recent cleaning of the cautionary, satirical prints by Hogarth above the bar has not deterred the city's politicos and journos, who still gather here to swap tall tales and set the world to rights. Tues & Wed 3.30–11.30pm, Thurs 3.30pm–12.30am, Fri & Sat noon–1.30am, Sun 11am–11pm.

**The International Bar** 23 Wicklow St ☎ 01 677 9250, ⓦ international-bar.com. Old-fashioned pub decorated with stained glass and ornate woodcarving that heaves congenially at weekends. Nightly comedy shows including improv on Mon, plus jazz on Tues and Thurs, and poetry and music on Wed. Mon–Wed 11am–11.30pm, Thurs–Sat 11am–12.30am, Sun 11am–11pm.

**Kehoe's** 9 South Anne St ☎ 01 677 8312, ⓦ kehoes dublin.ie. This meeting place used to double up as a grocery and is now a watering hole full of character, with cosy snugs and a low mahogany bar. Frequently rated among the city's best pubs. Mon–Thurs & Sun 10am–11pm, Fri & Sat 10am–1am.

**The Long Hall** 51 South Great George's St ☎ 01 475 1590. Old-time classic, sporting ornate plasterwork, mirrors and dark-wood panelling, a suitably long bar, friendly staff

and a good pint of Guinness. Mon–Thurs noon–11.30pm, Fri & Sat noon–12.30am, Sun 12.30–11pm.

**Mulligan's** 8 Poolbeg St ☎ 01 677 5582, ⓦ mulligans. ie. A little off the beaten track, this large no-nonsense pub pours an excellent pint and remains a favoured watering hole for workers at the nearby *Irish Times*. Mon–Thurs 11am–11.30pm, Fri & Sat 11am–12.30am, Sun 12.30–11pm.

★ **The Palace Bar** 21 Fleet St ☎ 01 671 7388, ⓦ the palacebardublin.com. Relaxing, sociable, 200-year-old pub, former haunt of writers Behan, Kavanagh and Flann O'Brien, now famed both for the quality of its pint and for its handsome decor. Also does lunchtime soup and sandwiches. The overflow bar upstairs hosts sessions of traditional music on Wed, Thurs & Sun. Mon–Thurs 10.30am–11.30pm, Fri & Sat 10.30am–12.30am, Sun 12.30–11.30pm.

**The Porterhouse** 16 Parliament St ☎ 01 679 8847, ⓦ porterhousebrewco.ie. Rambling microbrewery-bar, where for €5 you can sample three different stouts, lagers or ales. Live music every night, including traditional sessions on Sun, and good food. Mon–Wed 11.30am–midnight, Thurs 11.30am–1am, Fri & Sat 11.30am–2am, Sun noon–midnight.

★ **The Stag's Head** 1 Dame Court ☎ 01 679 3687, ⓦ stagshead.ie. Pretty Victorian bar, all dark woods and stuffed, tiled and stained-glass stags, that attracts a hugely varied crowd. Decent pub grub during the day (Mon–Sat) and a good live music session most Sundays from around 7–8pm. The upstairs bar hosts regular gigs, comedy and storytelling events. Mon–Thurs & Sun 10am–11pm, Fri & Sat 10am–1am.

## THE NORTHSIDE

★ **The Bernard Shaw** Cross Guns Bridge, Glasnevin ☎ 01 906 0218, ⓦ thebernardshaw.com. Following its relocation from the southside to the northside, this long established bar, café and creative space remains one of the city's most popular boozers, not least thanks to the colourful outdoor space with its gallery and murals; in addition there's the Big Blue Bus serving excellent pizzas, and cheap mojitos (two for €10), and the neighbouring Eatyard food market with vendors from all over. Thurs–Sun noon–midnight.

**The Flowing Tide** 9 Abbey St Lower ☎ 01 874 4108. Long connected with the Abbey Theatre opposite, this pub features tasteful stained-glass windows, a mural celebrating the theatre's history and a horseshoe-shaped bar. Mon–Thurs 10.30am–11.30pm, Fri & Sat 10.30am–12.30am, Sun 12.30–11pm.

**Frank Ryan & Son** 5 Queen St ☎ 01 872 5204, ⓦ frank ryans.com. Definitely a place for respite from the city's hurly-burly, this sociable, old-fashioned bar is cosiness incarnate. The friendly staff serve a grand pint of stout. Mon–Thurs 4–11.30pm, Fri & Sat 4pm–12.30am, Sun 6–11pm.

**Hill 16** 16 Gardiner St Middle ☎ 01 874 4239. Named after Croke Park's most popular stand, the bar is a magnet for GAA devotees, particularly those who follow the fortunes of Dublin's Gaelic football team. Mon–Thurs 10.30am–11.30pm, Fri & Sat 10.30am–12.30am, Sun 12.30–11pm.

**Kavanagh's (aka The Gravediggers)** Prospect Square, Glasnevin ☎01 830 7978. One of the city's finest old pubs, located just outside the old entrance to Glasnevin Cemetery, where it has consoled mourners (and changed little) since 1833. It's best reached from the present-day entrance by retracing your steps along Finglas Rd and taking the first small lane on the left along the cemetery walls. Mon–Thurs 10.30am–11.30pm, Fri & Sat 10.30am–midnight, Sun 12.30–11pm.

**The Lotts** 9 Liffey St Lower ☎01 872 7669, ⓦthelottscafebar.com. It's often standing-room-only at this friendly corner bar, with a snug which lays claim to being the northside's smallest. It offers a tasty selection of Mediterranean-inspired meals in its fashionable café-bar next door. Mon–Thurs 10.30am–11.30pm, Fri & Sat 10.30am–12.30am, Sun 12.30–11pm.

★ **Ryan's** 28 Parkgate St ☎01 677 6097, ⓦfxbuckley. ie. The longtime challenger to the reputation of *Mulligan's* (see page 102) for serving the best pint of Guinness in the city, based on its proximity to the brewery just across the river, serves bar meals plus steaks and seafood in its upstairs restaurant. Mon–Thurs noon–10pm, Fri & Sat noon–11pm, Sun 12.30–9pm.

**Sin É** 14–15 Ormond Quay Upper ☎01 555 4036. This candlelit bar appeals to a lively cosmopolitan crowd because of its wide selection of brews and eclectic choice of nightly musical entertainment (sometimes live gigs, but mostly DJs). Mon–Wed 12.30pm–1am, Thurs 12.30pm–2am, Fri & Sat 12.30pm–3am, Sun 12.30pm–12.30am.

## LIVE MUSIC

SEE MAPS PAGES 56, 60, 70 AND 77

Dublin's **music scene** is thriving but ever-changing, so it's always wise to check **listings** on ⓦdublintown.ie.ie, or in *The Ticket* (see page 93), or the fortnightly rock-and-style magazine *Hot Press*. Ticket prices are dependent on the venue's size and the performers' status, usually costing €8–30, although major gigs can be as much as €100. There are also a number of **open-air events** during the summer, including one-off gigs by major acts at places such as Croke Park and Marlay Park in Rathfarnham. **Traditional music** is flourishing in the city with a number of pubs offering sessions, usually commencing at around 9.30pm. Listings of these can be found at ⓦdublinsessions.ie, or ask for advice in Claddagh Records (see page 106).

### LIVE MUSIC VENUES

**3Arena** Dame St ☎01 819 8888, ⓦ3arena.ie. Once a railway depot, the cavernous 3Arena, 1.5km east of O'Connell Bridge, is Ireland's largest dedicated music venue with a capacity of thirteen thousand. Unsurprisingly, it hosts major international names with high prices to boot. The venue is served by the LUAS red line Docklands branch.

**The Academy** 57 Abbey St Middle ☎01 877 9999, ⓦtheacademydublin.com. The latest occupant of these premises offers a variety of largely alt/indie gigs. Fri and Sat are huge club nights in its Main Room, Green Room and Academy 2 sections. Mon–Fri 11pm–2.30am, Sat 10.30pm–2.30am, Sun 11pm–1am (doors open earlier for gigs).

**Button Factory** Curved St ☎01 670 9202, ⓦbuttonfactory.ie. A remarkably left-field venue with a more than eclectic booking policy covering everything from traditional music to alt/indie bands via modern jazz and tribute groups. The place transforms itself into a late club (until 3am Fri–Sun) at weekends – with a wide variety of differently themed events. Opening hours vary.

**Olympia Theatre** 72 Dame St ☎01 679 3323, ⓦolympia.ie. This old, intimate and much-esteemed venue continues to stage a variety of musical events, featuring major Irish names as well as international stars.

**The Sugar Club** 8 Leeson St Lower ☎01 678 7188, ⓦthesugarclub.com. A lush and plush southside venue, just off St Stephen's Green, *The Sugar Club* hosts a diverse and often far from mainstream variety of entertainment (bands, torch-singers, comedy, cabaret) – some divine, others dreadful, but the atmosphere is often very much on the button. Opening hours vary.

**Vicar Street** 58–59 Thomas St West ☎01 454 5533, ⓦvicarstreet.com. Arguably the city's premier small live music venue, this three-hundred-seater has an estimable programme that includes live music, comedy and other events, and features major names.

**Whelan's** 25 Wexford St ☎01 478 0766, ⓦwhelanslive. com. *Whelan's* has remained one of the city's most successful live venues over the last two decades, thanks to an extensive programme of the old and the new – a blend of traditional music, renowned folk acts, emerging talent and occasional one-off performances by major names. As well as live music they also host some great club nights, like the ever-popular Indie and Alternative Dance Party (Thurs 10.30pm). Mon–Sat 5pm–3am, Sun 5pm–2am.

### TRADITIONAL MUSIC PUBS

**The Brazen Head** 20 Bridge St Lower ☎01 679 5186, ⓦbrazenhead.com. Established in 1189 and laying claim to the title of Ireland's oldest pub, *The Brazen Head's* many rooms feature all manner of music-related memorabilia on the walls and ramble round a large courtyard. Traditional musicians play every night at 9.30pm (as well as Sun 3.30–6.30pm), though the quality of the sessions can be extremely variable. Mon–Thurs 10.30am–midnight, Fri & Sat 10.30am–12.30am, Sun 12.30–midnight.

★ **The Cobblestone** 77 King St North ☎01 872 1799,

1

Ⓦcobblestonepub.ie. Arguably the best traditional-music venue in Dublin, this dark, cosy, wooden-floored bar is also a fine place to sample the hoppy products of the nearby Dublin Brewing Company. High-quality sessions take place nightly from around 9pm (from 7pm on Thurs), and on Sun afternoons, while the *Back Room* hosts a variety of gigs. Even during the day there's likely to be a group of musicians having a session by the front door. Mon–Thurs 4–11.30pm, Fri 4pm–12.30am, Sat 1.30pm–12.30am, Sun 1.30–11pm.

**Hughes' Bar** 19 Chancery St Ⓣ01 872 6540. Tucked away behind the Four Courts, *Hughes' Bar* attracts the cream of the city's traditional musicians to its nightly sessions (10pm until closing time). Fri can draw a large crowd, so arrive early to grab a seat. Mon–Thurs 7am–11.30pm, Fri & Sat 7am–12.30am, Sun 7–11pm.

**O'Donoghue's** 15 Merrion Row Ⓣ01 660 7194, Ⓦodonoghues.ie. The centre of the folk and traditional music revival that began in the late 1950s, forever associated with ground-breaking balladeers The Dubliners. Nightly sessions (from about 9.30pm) draw a considerable crowd of tourists, while the large heated courtyard is more of a draw for locals. Mon–Thurs 10am–midnight, Fri & Sat 10am–1am, Sun 11am–midnight.

**O'Shea's Merchant** 12 Bridge St Lower Ⓣ01 679 3797, Ⓦosheasmerchant.com. Opposite the more famous *Brazen Head*, the *Merchant* nurtures the atmosphere of a homely, good-natured country pub in the centre of the city, providing sanctuary for "culchies" from any county, but especially Kerrymen. Traditional sessions are hosted every night in high season from around 10pm, including set dancing on Mon & Wed, and it's a good place to watch a GAA game. Mon–Thurs 10.30am–11.30am, Fri & Sat 10.30am–12.30am, Sun 12.30–11pm.

## NIGHTLIFE
SEE MAPS PAGES 60, 70 AND 77

It is best to check the latest listings in the *Event Guide* or *Hot Press* (see page 103), as Dublin's **club scene** is volatile. Clubs can be found in most areas of the city centre and prices vary considerably, depending on the venue, night of the week and whether a "name" DJ is spinning the turntables – the venues listed below often have free entry, but can charge up to €20 on certain nights.

**Copper Face Jacks** 29–30 Harcourt St Ⓣ01 425 5300, Ⓦcopperfacejacks.ie. The most popular of several similar late-night venues along Harcourt St, and notorious for its pop tunes and groups of single lads and lasses looking for a good time. Daily 10pm–2.30am.

**Four Dame Lane** 4 Dame Lane Ⓣ01 679 0291, Ⓦ4dame lane.ie. Announced by burning braziers, this bar-club probably has the stylistic edge over its bare-brickwork-and-wood rivals. The tunes are good too, encompassing anything from techno to soul, with a DJ Thurs–Sun in the ground-floor bar, Fri and Sat in the upstairs Loft room. Mon & Tues 4pm–midnight, Wed–Sat 4pm–2.30am, Sun 4pm–1am.

**The Grand Social** 35 Lower Liffey St Ⓣ01 677 1224, Ⓦthegrandsocial.ie. On the northside of the Ha'penny Bridge, in-house and guest DJs spin funky disco, indie, classic rock and electro at the weekends. There's a popular jazz club every Mon night, and the indoor Ha'penny Flea Market on a Sat afternoon. Mon–Wed 4.30–11.30pm, Thurs 4pm–2.30am, Fri 3pm–2.30am, Sat noon–2.30am, Sun 3–11pm.

**Workman's Club** 10 Wellington Quay Ⓣ01 670 6692, Ⓦtheworkmansclub.com. A maze of interconnecting rooms in a red-brick building fronting the River Liffey houses dance floors, venues for live music and poetry readings, themed bars and a rooftop terrace. The bar on the ground floor serves American-style barbecues (until 9pm), accompanied by craft beers and cocktails. Daily 5pm–3am.

## ARTS AND CULTURE

Drama played a pivotal role in Ireland's twentieth-century cultural revival and Dublin's theatres continue to act as a crucible for innovation, alongside staging a range of Irish classics. Highlights include the **Dublin Theatre Festival** (late Sept to mid-Oct; Ⓦdublintheatrefestival.com) and the **Dublin Fringe Festival** (mid-Sept; Ⓦfringefest. com). Ticket prices vary; as a rule, you should expect to pay €10–20 per ticket for fringe shows, €20–40 for mainstream. Advance bookings can be made at the venues or through Ticketmaster (Ⓣ081 871 9300, Ⓦticketmaster.ie). If you're budget-conscious, it's worth enquiring about low-cost previews and occasional cut-price Monday and Tuesday night shows, while students (with ID) and senior citizens can sometimes find good concessionary rates. All **cinemas** operate a policy of cheap seats (around €5–7) daily before 5pm (6.30pm in some cases); standard prices are €9–12. Student discounts are often available.

**The Abbey Theatre** Abbey St Lower Ⓣ01 878 7222, Ⓦabbeytheatre.ie. The National Theatre of Ireland (see page 79) tends to show international and Irish classics plus new offerings by contemporary playwrights.

**Bord Gáis Energy Theatre** Grand Canal Square Ⓣ01 677 7999, Ⓦbordgaisenergytheatre.ie. Two-thousand-seater in the Docklands, mostly offering light entertainment and musicals.

**Gaiety Theatre** South King St Ⓣ0818 719388, Ⓦgaiety theatre.ie. Known as "The Grand Old Lady of South King Street" the Gaiety specialises in operatic and musical productions, with dramatic shows from time to time.

**Gate Theatre** 1 Cavendish Row, Parnell Square Ⓣ01 874 4045, Ⓦgatetheatre.ie. Founded in the 1920s in an eighteenth-century building leased from the Rotunda

Hospital, the Gate has a reputation for staging adventurous experimental drama as well as established classics in its small, elegant auditorium, and gave an early boost to the acting careers of James Mason and Orson Welles.

**Irish Film Institute** 6 Eustace St ☎ 01 679 3477, ⓦifi. ie. The focus for Irish cineastes provides a broad programme of international and new Irish films in a beautifully converted Quaker meeting house. It is the hub of the International Film Festival in Feb (ⓦdiff.com), as well as numerous other fantastic events like Horrorthon (Oct) and the French Film Festival (Nov). They often show films using Ireland's only 70mm projector, and there's an excellent film-related bookshop beside the bar and café-restaurant (see page 99).

**Light House Cinema** Smithfield ☎ 01 872 8006, ⓦlighthousecinema.ie. A little away from the centre, this four-screen cinema is acclaimed for its imaginative programming and hosts the Dublin LGBTQ Film Festival (ⓦgaze.ie) at the end of September.

**New Theatre** 43 Essex St East ☎ 01 670 3361, ⓦthe newtheatre.com. This theatre stages a variety of classic, rarely performed and new drama. Continually supporting new writers, it's a great place to see vibrant, emerging talent.

**Project Arts Centre** 39 Essex St East ☎ 01 881 9613, ⓦprojectartscentre.ie. Renowned for its experimental and often controversial Irish and international theatre, this flagship of the contemporary art scene also hosts dance, film, music and performance art.

## SPORTS

Dublin and its surrounds offer plenty of scope to exploit the national obsessions of football (Gaelic and regular), hurling, rugby and horse and greyhound racing. If they can't attend a match or a meet, Dubliners are always keen to indulge in a second national pastime, gambling.

**Soccer** The Republic's national team plays most of its home games at the Aviva Stadium (☎ 01 238 2300, ⓦ aviva stadium.ie). The Aviva Stadium is on Lansdowne Rd, which is situated to the southeast of the centre, and is easily accessible via the adjacent DART station. The city currently has five teams playing in the professional League of Ireland: Bohemians (ⓦbohemianfc.com); St Patrick's Athletic (ⓦst patsfc.com); Shamrock Rovers (ⓦshamrockrovers.ie); Shelbourne (ⓦshelbournefc.ie); and UCD (ⓦucdsoccer. com). Standards are about the equivalent of the English Football League's Second Division. Most games take place on Fri nights and tickets generally cost around €12–15.

**Gaelic football and hurling** Most of the season's major games are played at Croke Park (see page 87); more info is available at ☎ 01 836 3222, ⓦgaa.ie. In football, the All-Ireland Final occurs on the third or fourth Sun in Sept and has been won by Dublin on 29 occasions (a record beaten only by Kerry). The Dubs have a poor record at hurling, so the crowd at the All-Ireland Final on the first or second Sun in Sept mainly consists of out-of-towners. You'll be hard pushed to get tickets for either of the finals, but you're quite likely to get in for a semi-final at "Croker" – expect to pay

around €35 to stand, and sing, on the famous Hill 16, €50 to sit in the stands and less for earlier rounds.

**Greyhound racing** The city has one dog-racing venue: Shelbourne Park (Tues, Fri & Sat) in Ringsend, in Docklands, east of the centre. Entry is around €10 and details of events can be found at ⓦigb.ie.

**Horse racing** Dublin's nearest large racecourse is Leopardstown (☎ 01 289 0500, ⓦleopardstown.com), in the southern suburb of Foxrock (LUAS to Sandyford station then a 15min walk). Races are held at weekends at various points of the year and on Thurs evenings during June and July, but the main events are the four-day Christmas Festival starting on St Stephen's Day (Dec 26), and the Hennessy Cognac Gold Cup in Feb. The Irish Grand National is held on Easter Mon at Fairyhouse (☎ 01 825 6167, ⓦfairyhouse.ie) in Ratoath, 24km northwest of Dublin, followed in April by the Irish National Hunt Festival at Punchestown (see page 128), 40km southwest of Dublin. Flat-racing classics are held at the Curragh, nearly 50km southwest of the capital (see page 128). Bus Éireann lays on race-day transport to Fairyhouse.

**Rugby** Ireland's home games are played at the Aviva Stadium (☎ 01 238 2300, ⓦavivastadium.ie). The provincial rugby side Leinster (ⓦleinsterrugby.ie) plays its own home games at the RDS in Ballsbridge, southeast of the centre. For big match days, particularly during the Six Nations in February, most pubs with a decent screen will be packed to the rafters.

## LGBTQ DUBLIN

**SEE MAPS PAGES 60 AND 77**

As attitudes to homosexuality in Dublin have become increasingly liberal over the last two decades, so the capital's **LGBTQ** community has grown in confidence, and a small but vibrant scene has established a niche in the city's social life. The latest **information** on LGBTQ events and venues in Dublin is provided by *Outhouse*, 105 Capel St (☎ 01 873 4999, ⓦouthouse.ie), a resource centre for LGBTQ people with a café (Mon–Fri 1–9.30pm, Sat 1–5.30pm) and a small library. The free magazine *GCN* (*Gay Community News*

ⓦgcn.ie) has detailed listings of upcoming events and can be found in the LGBTQ-friendly Books Upstairs, College Green, or in clubs and bars; ⓦgaire.com has useful local information, message boards and online chat.

**The George** 89 South Great George's St ☎ 01 478 2983, ⓦthegeorge.ie. Ireland's longest-established LGBTQ bar still draws huge crowds at weekends. There are two distinct sections: a lushly decorated main venue on two floors, and a quieter, more traditional pub with an older clientele to the right. Entertainment includes karaoke, game shows, DJs and Sunday-night jazz followed by bingo with drag queen Shirley Temple-Bar. Mon 2–11.30pm, Tues–Fri 2pm–2.30am, Sat noon–2.30am, Sun 12.30pm–1.30am.

**Pantibar** 7–8 Capel St ☎01 874 0710. Owned by Irish LGBTQ icon, drag queen Pandora "Panti" Bliss, this lush bar provides all manner of entertainment from Monday's "Make and Do with Panti" (an alternative take on domestic crafts and games) to various themed nights in the basement, including "Panticlub" (Thurs–Sat). Apartments are available to rent on the upper floors. Mon, Wed & Sun 5–11.30pm, Tues 5pm–2am, Thurs & Fri 5pm–2.30am.

## SHOPPING

SEE MAPS PAGES 60, 70 AND 77

The southside is the most fruitful hunting ground for shoppers, offering Irish and global designer clothes around **Grafton St**, and more alternative boutiques in the George's St **Arcade** and **Temple Bar**. Also south of the river, you'll find an attractive and eclectic range of artisan products gathered from around the country, from cheeses and whiskey to ceramics. Despite a revamp, Dublin's most extensive shopping boulevard, **O'Connell St**, is likely to hold little of interest for the visiting consumer, though the raucous Moore St market, off Henry St, is always entertaining.

### ARTS, CRAFTS AND FASHIONS

**Avoca** 11 Suffolk St ☎01 677 4215, ⊛avoca.com. Highly successful small department store, stocking its own clothing ranges for women and children, jewellery, beautiful rugs and throws woven at the original mill in Avoca, Co. Wicklow, plus deli goods. Mon–Wed & Sat 9.30am–6pm, Thurs & Fri 9.30am–7pm, Sun 11am–6pm.

**Irish Design Shop** 41 Drury St ☎01 679 8871, ⊛irish designshop.com. Tiny shop run by two Irish jewellers, selling a range of Irish woodcraft, textiles, prints and pottery. Mon–Sat 10am–6pm, Sun 1–5pm.

**Kilkenny** 6 Nassau St ☎01 677 7066, ⊛kilkennyshop. com. A varied collection of fine Irish crafts: Newbridge silver cutlery and jewellery; Jerpoint glassware; extensive ranges of ceramics; and women's clothes and accessories by contemporary designers. Mon–Wed, Fri & Sat 8.30am–7pm, Thurs 8.30am–9pm, Sun 10am–6pm.

**Powerscourt Townhouse Centre** South 59 William St ☎01 6794144, ⊛powerscourtcentre.ie. On the second floor of the building (see page 64), the Design Centre stocks established Irish designers of women's fashion, such as Philip Treacy and John Rocha, as well as diverse international names. The Loft Market opposite is a cutting-edge showcase for young local designers of clothes and jewellery. Mon–Fri 10am–6pm, Sat 9am–6pm, Sun noon–6pm.

### BOOKS AND MUSIC

**Books Upstairs** 17 D'Olier St ☎01 677 8566, ⊛books upstairs.ie. An excellent independent bookstore operating since 1978 with a fine selection of Irish books, as well as literary and intellectual journals. Mon–Fri 10am–7pm, Sat 10am–6pm, Sun 2–6pm.

**Chapters Bookstore** Ivy Exchange, Parnell St ☎01 879 2700, ⊛chapters.ie. Claiming to be Dublin's largest bookshop, its ground floor features a massive range of fiction and fact, including impressive sections on Irish literature and history. Upstairs is devoted to the secondhand section which also includes bargain-priced CDs and DVDs. Mon–Wed, Fri & Sat 9.30am–6.30pm, Thurs 9.30am–8pm, Sun noon–6.30pm.

**Claddagh Records** 2 Cecilia St, Temple Bar ☎01 677 0262, ⊛claddaghrecords.com. Unquestionably the finest traditional and folk music emporium in Dublin, with helpful and knowledgeable staff. Mon–Fri 10.30am–5.30pm, Sat noon–5.30pm.

**Hodges Figgis** 56–58 Dawson St ☎01 677 4754. A Dublin institution since the eighteenth century, behind an ornate facade, including a huge range of books on and from Ireland on the ground floor. A joy to simply browse and lose track of time. Mon–Wed & Fri 9am–7pm, Thurs 9am–8pm, Sat 9am–6pm, Sun noon–6pm.

**The R.A.G.E and The Record Spot** 8 Crow St. ☎01 598 6372, ⊛therage.ie. This is really two shops in one: upstairs sells retro games and consoles, while the basement has a stock of over ten thousand secondhand records and various vinyl-related merchandise. Mon–Sat 11am–7pm, Sun noon–6pm.

**Ulysses Rare Books** 10 Duke St ☎01 671 8676, ⊛rare books.ie. A delightful little antiquarian bookshop, this is the place to come for first editions and other rare books by Irish writers, specializing in twentieth-century literature. Mon–Sat 9.30am–5.45pm.

**Walton's** Blanchardstown Retail Park ☎01 960 3232, ⊛waltons.ie. Dublin's leading music shop sells traditional Irish instruments, as well as teaching aids, sheet music and recordings. The attached music school (☎01 478 1884, ⊛newschool.ie) offers 1hr or 2hr crash courses for beginners in the tin whistle and the *bodhrán*. Mon–Sat 9am–6pm, Sun noon–6pm.

**The Winding Stair** 40 Ormond Quay Lower ☎01 872 6576, ⊛winding-stair.com. One of the city's oldest bookshops, stocking a selection of titles you might not find in larger stores. It has a small secondhand section, which is especially good on Irish literature and biography. Upstairs is one of the northside's finest restaurants (see page 101). Mon & Fri 10am–6pm, Tues–Thurs & Sat 10am–7pm, Sun noon–6pm.

### DEPARTMENT STORES AND MARKETS

**Brown Thomas** 88–95 Grafton St ☎01 605 6666, ⊛brownthomas.com. The city's flagship department store is sophisticated and pricey, featuring a long roll call of Irish and international designer labels. Mon, Wed & Fri 9.30am–8pm, Tues 10am–8pm, Thurs 9.30am–9pm, Sat 9am–8pm, Sun 11am–7pm.

**Cow's Lane Market** Off Essex St West. On a pedestrianized alley in Temple Bar stalls concentrate on contemporary women's clothes, bags and jewellery, generally sold by the designers themselves. Sat 10am–5pm; closed Jan & Feb.

**George's Street Arcade** Between South Great George's St and Drury St ⓦ georgesstreetarcade.ie. Laidback indoor market, which claims to be Europe's oldest, offering secondhand books and records, vintage and street clothing, jewellery, cafés and speciality foods. Mon–Wed, Fri & Sat 9am–6pm, Thurs 9am–8pm, Sun 11am–6pm.

**Moore St Market** Moore St. This lively street market is a longstanding Dublin institution and much reflects the city's changing ethnicity. The traditional butchers, fishmongers and greengrocers are still present, though you're bound to see price tags in Cantonese too, and there are also a number of Afro-Caribbean stalls and shops. Daily around 10am–dusk.

## FOOD AND DRINK

**Celtic Whiskey Shop** 27–28 Dawson St ⓣ 01 675 9744, ⓦ celticwhiskeyshop.com. Probably the best selection of Irish whiskeys anywhere, including rare examples from distilleries that have now closed down. The well-informed staff always have bottles open to taste and will ship around the world. Mon–Sat 10.30am–6.30pm, Sun 12.30–6pm.

**Sheridan's Cheesemongers** 11 South Anne St ⓣ 01 679 3143, ⓦ sheridanscheesemongers.com. Fantastic, pungent array of cheeses, mostly by Irish artisan producers, plus cold meats and other deli goods, sold by knowledgeable staff. Mon–Wed & Fri 10am–6pm, Thurs 10.30am–6.30pm, Sat 9.30am–6pm, Sun noon–6pm.

**Temple Bar Food Market** Meeting House Square. A magnet for Dublin's foodies, but also one of your best bets to grab Sat lunch, with stalls selling crêpes, Mexican food, olives, sushi, breads, cakes, cheeses, and a West Clare oyster bar. Mon–Wed 10am–6pm, Thurs 10.30am–6.30pm, Fri 10am–6pm, Sat 9.30am–6pm, Sun noon–6pm.

## DIRECTORY

**Dentist** For dental emergencies contact the Dublin Dental School and Hospital, Lincoln Place ⓣ 01 612 7200, ⓦ dental hospital.ie.

**Embassies** Australia, 47–49 St Stepehen's Green ⓣ 01 664 5300; Canada, 7–8 Wilton Terrace ⓣ 01 234 4000; South Africa, Alexandra House, Earlsfort Centre, Earlsfort Terrace ⓣ 01 661 5553; UK, 29 Merrion Rd ⓣ 01 205 3700; US, 42 Elgin Rd ⓣ 01 668 8777.

**Hospitals** Those with accident and emergency departments include: Beaumont Hospital, Beaumont Rd ⓣ 01 809 3000; Mater Misericordiae, Eccles St ⓣ 01 803 2000; St James's, James St ⓣ 01 410 3000; and St Vincent's, Elm Park ⓣ 01 221 4000. In emergencies dial ⓣ 999 or ⓣ 112 for an ambulance.

**Lost property** Dublin Bus ⓣ 01 703 1321; Bus Éireann ⓣ 01 836 6111; Connolly Station ⓣ 01 703 2358; Heuston Station ⓣ 01 703 3299; airport ⓣ 01 814 5555.

**Police** The main police station (Garda Síochána) is at 1–6 Pearse Street (ⓣ 01 666 9000). The Irish Tourist Assistance Service (ⓣ 01 666 9354, ⓦ itas.ie) offers support to tourist victims of crime.

**Post offices** General Post Office, O'Connell St Lower (Mon–Sat 8.30am–6pm; ⓣ 01 705 7600); 19 St Andrew's St (Mon–Fri 9am–6pm, Sat 9am–1pm; ⓣ 01 705 8256); 31–36 Ormond Quay Upper (Mon–Fri 9am–5.30pm; ⓣ 01 804 4359); 16 Merrion Row (Mon–Fri 9am–1pm & 2.15–5.30pm; ⓣ 01 676 5961). Many newsagents sell postage stamps.

# Around Dublin: Wicklow, Kildare and Meath

WALKERS IN WICKLOW MOUNTAINS NATIONAL PARK

# Around Dublin: Wicklow, Kildare and Meath

**2**

The counties of Wicklow, Kildare and Meath equate roughly with the Pale, the fortified area around Dublin to which the English colonists retreated after 1300. The colonists coined the expression "beyond the pale" and implanted the language, customs and government of lowland England in these "obedient shires", leaving today's visitors a rich architectural legacy of castles, abbeys and, from a later period, stately homes. Wicklow, Kildare and Meath are much sought-after by modern-day settlers, too: unable to afford Dublin's property prices, thousands of the capital's workers have set up home in these commuter counties in the last twenty years.

This chapter sweeps clockwise, starting from the Wicklow coast south of Dublin and pulling up just short of Drogheda in County Louth to the north. If you have your own transport, this would make a very satisfying loop around the capital through diverse terrains, from the expansive, sandy beaches and spectacular granite mountains of County Wicklow (Cill Mhantáin; ⓦvisitwicklow.ie), through the grassy, horse-rearing heath of the Curragh and the Bog of Allen in Kildare (Cill Dara; ⓦintokildare. ie), to the lush, undulating farmland of Meath (An Mhí; ⓦmeath.ie). The **highlights** detailed opposite would form a sound basic itinerary. If you have more time to spare, in County Wicklow, add in Parnell's home, **Avondale House**, designed by James Wyatt and surrounded by forested parkland; the Neoclassical marvels of **Russborough**; the atmospheric seat of the Celtic High Kings, the **Hill of Tara**; and the impressive **Battle of the Boyne Visitor Centre** in Meath.

It wouldn't be possible to cover this same arc by **public transport**, which tends to run radially in and out of Dublin. Most of the places described in this chapter, however, are accessible on a day-trip from the capital by bus or train, with organized **tours** also available in many cases. If you're **driving**, you'll generally be travelling in the opposite

---

### IRELAND'S ANCIENT EAST

Ireland's **Ancient East** is the east coast's answer to the Wild Atlantic Way (see page 26), although it's admittedly a more difficult sell. Whereas the Wild Atlantic Way is a clearly defined touring route, Ireland's Ancient East is a more vague proposition, geographically speaking. Stretching from the northeast to Cork Harbour, into the midlands and everywhere in between, its sheer scale can be a bit off-putting, and it's hard to know where to begin. That said, the official **website** (ⓦirelandsancienteast.com) is an excellent and comprehensive resource that's worth taking the time to explore. Full of **maps**, in-depth **itineraries** and featured attractions, it should be the first step in planning a road trip. Designed as a way to encourage people to explore areas outside of the capital, the focus is very much on history, from **Neolithic tombs** and **ringforts** to **Norman castles** and **famine workhouses**. Featured routes include Through the Gardens of the East (two days, 114km) from Carlow to Wicklow, Round Towers and Castles (two days, 297km) from Meath to Offaly, and Myths and Secrets of Ancient Lands (three days, 274km) from Meath to Louth via Cavan.

If driving isn't an option, Bus Éireann offer an "Open Road" tourist pass for €60. This allows for three days of unlimited travel out of six consecutive days, with the possibility of topping up for €16.50 for each additional day. Further details and tailored itineraries can be found at ⓦbuseireann.ie/openroadticket.

POWERSCOURT HOUSE AND GARDENS

# Highlights

❶ **Walking in the Wicklow Mountains** Wild and desolate terrain, traversed by the Wicklow Way, within easy reach of Dublin. See page 118

❷ **Powerscourt** Beautiful ornamental gardens and the highest waterfall in Ireland. See page 118

❸ **Glendalough** Hidden deep in this remote valley lies one of the best-preserved and most charismatic monastic sites in the country. See page 121

❹ **The National Stud, Kildare town** Learn all about one of Ireland's major industries at the national horse-breeding centre and enjoy the quirky gardens. See page 127

❺ **Castletown** Just west of Dublin, a Palladian mansion of unrestrained extravagance. See page 129

❻ **Trim** A historic town boasting the largest Anglo-Norman castle in Ireland and other fine medieval remains. See page 131

❼ **Loughcrew Cairns** These Neolithic mounds are slightly less impressive than Brú na Bóinne, but more scenic and far less touristy. See page 135

❽ **Brú na Bóinne** Don't miss the extraordinary prehistoric passage graves of Newgrange and Knowth. See page 139

**HIGHLIGHTS ARE MARKED ON THE MAP ON PAGE 112**

N

0   kilometres   10

Brittas Bay

Wicklow Head

Wicklow

Rathnew

Ashford

Mount Usher Gardens

Glenealy

VALE OF AVOCA

Avondale House

Meeting of the Waters

Avoca

Macreddin

Woodenbridge

Arklow

Wexford

WEXFORD

M11

N11

N11

Greystones

Bray

Kilruddery House

Enniskerry

Great Sugar Loaf (503m)

Powerscourt

Knockree

Luggala (595m)

Roundwood

Glenmacnass Waterfall

Laragh

Glendalough

Derrybawn (474m)

Rathdrum

M11

Glencree

Sally Gap

Lough Tay

St Kevin's Way

Glenmalure

Lugnaquilla (924m)

Moyne

Aughrim

Wicklow Way

Tinahely

Shillelagh

Clonegall

N80

N18

Blessington

Blessington Lakes

WICKLOW MOUNTAINS

WICKLOW

Naas

Punchestown

Russborough House

THE CURRAGH

Donard

Glen of Imaal

Hollywood

Baltinglass

Tullow

CARLOW

N80

M9

N7

Newbridge

Curragh Racecourse

National Stud

Kildare

KILDARE

N9

Castledermot

Carlow

N80

M9

Rathangan

Monasterevin

N7

Athy

River Barrow

N80

Waterford

N9

ORFALY

Portarlington

Vicarstown

LAOIS

N80

N8

Portlaoise

N7

Limerick

Abbeyleix

Cork

M8

N80

**HIGHLIGHTS**

1   Walking in the Wicklow Mountains
2   Powerscourt
3   Glendalough
4   The National Stud, Kildare town
5   Castletown
6   Trim
7   Loughcrew Cairns
8   Brú na Bóinne

2

---

## TOURS FROM DUBLIN

Organized **tours** are especially useful if you want to take in more than one sight in a day; those which include Newgrange (see page 139) guarantee a place on the guided tour of the passage grave. It's best to book in advance, either directly or through a tourist office or your hotel. All admission charges are usually included in the price, though not lunch.

**Gray Line** ☎ 01 685 4045, ⓦ loveireland.com. Runs an excursion to Newgrange and the Hill of Tara (April–Oct Mon, Tues, Fri & Sat 8.45am; €37) from the O'Connell St tourist office. Also a Wicklow Mountains Tour, including the Guinness Lakes, Glendalough and Avoca from the tourist centre at 14 O'Connell St Upper (9.15am; from €33).

**Mary Gibbons Tours** ☎ 086 355 1355, ⓦ new grangetours.com. Takes in Newgrange, the Hill of Tara and the Boyne Valley, picking up at the *Mespil Hotel* on Mespil Rd, then stopping at Leeson St, the *Shelbourne Hotel* on St Stephen's Green, and the A.I.B bank on O'Connell St (Mon–Fri 8.50am, Sat & Sun 7.30am; €45).

**The Wild Wicklow Tour** ☎ 01 280 1899, ⓦ wild wicklow.ie. Explores Glendalough and heads off the beaten track into the mountains (€33), departing from outside the *Shelbourne Hotel*, St Stephen's Green (daily 8.50am), calling at the *Hotel Riu Plaza The Gresham* (daily 9.10am) and several other pick-up points en route.

---

direction from Dublin's rush-hour traffic jams, but be sure to avoid Friday afternoons coming out of the capital and Sunday or bank holiday evenings returning, which are particularly bad.

# The Wicklow coast

County Wicklow's main draw is without doubt the stunning scenery of the inland mountains, but the **coast** can offer some very attractive beaches, notably at **Brittas Bay**, south of Wicklow town, and is easily accessible from Dublin. The N11 runs the length of the county roughly parallel to the sea, while by **train**, the DART service runs as far as Bray and Greystones, and the scenic main line to Rathdrum, Enniscorthy, Wexford and Rosslare stops at Bray, Greystones and Wicklow town. Keen to maintain its independence from Dublin, **Bray** is a lively, sometimes rowdy, resort and commuter town, which offers an expansive beach and the finest walk along this coast, across Bray Head to the village of **Greystones**. Halfway down the county's seaboard, **Wicklow** town enjoys a fine setting and a good choice of upmarket places to stay – if you have your own transport, this would make a good base for exploring the mountains. County Wicklow is known as the "garden of Ireland" and the local tourist board provides full details of gardens that can be visited, concentrated in the coastal strip (ⓦ visitwicklow.ie).

## Bray and around

Just south of the border with County Dublin, the formerly genteel Victorian resort of **BRAY** draws a great influx of day-tripping city-dwellers down the DART line on summer weekends, when the amusement arcades and fast-food outlets along the seafront go into overdrive. The attractive sand and shingle beach, however, dramatically set against the knobbly promontory of **Bray Head**, is long enough to soak up the crowds, and the enterprising town lays on a diverse roster of **festivals** to broaden its appeal, including the prestigious Bray Jazz Festival over the bank holiday weekend in early May (ⓦ brayjazz. com) and the Bray Air Display at the end of July (ⓦ brayairdisplay.com).

### National Sea Life Centre

Strand Rd • Daily 10am–5pm • €14.50, children €9.50 (discounts if booked online); Heritage Island • ☎ 01 286 6939, ⓦ visitsealife.com/bray

Bray's main attraction, especially popular with children, is the **National Sea Life Centre** on the seafront. Run by fishy enthusiasts, the aquarium lays on plenty of activities for kids, as well as informative display boards that'll keep adults interested. Inevitably, the more exotic, far-flung creatures provide the big thrills, notably the blacktips in the reef shark tank and "probably the largest shoal of piranhas in Ireland".

## Killruddery House and Gardens

Just south of the town • **Gardens** April & Oct Sat & Sun 9.30am–6pm; May–Sept daily 9.30am–6pm • €8.50 • **House** Guided tours July–Sept daily 1–4pm • €15.50 (includes gardens); Heritage Island • ☎ 01 286 3405, ⓦ killruddery.com • 20min walk from the southern end of the seafront or bus from Bray DART station (Dublin Bus #84 or #184, or Finnegan's – ⓦ finnegan-bray.ie)

Used as a film and TV location on many occasions, including for *My Left Foot* and *The Tudors*, the **Killruddery** estate is most notable for its **gardens**. Designed in the seventeenth century in early French formal style, and added to in the nineteenth, they're the oldest gardens in Ireland, featuring extensive walks flanked by hornbeam, beech and lime hedges, a café and an eighteenth-century "sylvan theatre" framed by a high bay hedge and terraced banks. The 200m-long twin ponds, once stocked with fish for the table, were designed as "water mirrors" in front of the main **house**. The latter, built in the 1820s in Tudor Revival style, is still home to the Brabazon family (the earls of Meath), and boasts some fine plasterwork ceilings. When the house is open, you can get into the **Orangery**, which was erected in the 1850s after the fashion of London's Crystal Palace, and restored in 2000 – so styling itself "Ireland's Millennium Dome". Killruddery hosts an imaginative roster of **activities**, as well as a farmers' market every Saturday (10am–4pm).

## Greystones

Just south of Bray, and easily accessible on the DART line, the idyllic seaside village of **Greystones** makes a lovely day-trip from Dublin, particularly on a sunny day. Originally a small fishing hamlet, it became a popular Victorian holiday destination, and it's easy to see why. Much of it has remained the same since then – from the gently sloping main street to the leafy avenues lined with elegant houses and pretty churches. It's now a rather more upmarket settlement of boutique shops and excellent restaurants, but it still manages to retain much of its old-world charm. Watched over by the Sugarloaf Mountain, Greystones is set between the curving expanse of its **south beach** (from which the village takes its name) and the recently redeveloped **marina** and smaller north beach. Exiting the train station, the main street is to the right, while the south beach lies to the left.

### ARRIVAL AND INFORMATION BRAY AND AROUND

**By train** Bray is served by frequent DART trains from Dublin (Mon–Fri roughly every 10–15min, Sun hourly; 40min), with around every third train continuing to Greystones (Mon–Fri every 30min, Sat hourly, slightly less frequent on Sun; 50min).

---

## A WALK OVER BRAY HEAD TO GREYSTONES

There's an excellent two- to three-hour **walk** from Bray seafront south across Bray Head to **Greystones**, a beautiful seaside village at the end of the DART line with several pubs serving food. The start of the trail is at the south end of the promenade, a five-minute walk from Bray DART station. You can follow the comparatively flat **cliff path** that runs above the rail tracks for most of the way giving close-up views of rocky coves and slate pinnacles, lashed by magnificent waves on windy days, as well as possible sightings of kestrels, peregrine falcons, dolphins, whales and basking sharks. Alternatively, if you have more time, take on the steep climb over the top of **Bray Head** for great views of Killiney Bay and the cone-shaped hills inland known as Little Sugar Loaf and Great Sugar Loaf, with a distant backdrop of the Wicklow Mountains. The latter route ascends rapidly from the end of Bray seafront through pine woods and over gorse slopes to a large cross, 200m above sea level, which was erected to mark the Holy Year of 1950; from here a track winds across the ridge below the 240m summit of Bray Head, before you turn sharp left down to join the cliff path which will bring you into Greystones.

**Tourist office** Bray's tourist office is in the town council building in the Civic Centre on Main St, a 10min walk inland from the DART station (Tues–Fri 10am–1pm & 2–4.30pm; ☎ 01 286 7128, ⊚ bray.ie).

## ACCOMMODATION AND EATING

**The Happy Pear** Church Rd, Greystones ☎ 01 287 3655, ⊚ thehappypear.ie. Starting out as a small fruit and veg shop, *The Happy Pear* has now become a Greystones institution, thanks to its well stocked shop and adjoining café serving organic vegetarian fare – much of it grown on their own farm (wraps from €6, mains from €7.50). Mon–Fri 8.30am–5pm, Sat & Sun Sun 8am–5pm.

**The Martello Hotel** 47 Strand Rd, Bray ☎ 01 286 8000, ⊚ themartello.ie. Ideally located right on the seafront, *The Martello* provides 25 contemporaneously furnished en-suite rooms, as well as nineteen self-catering apartments. There's a nightclub attached so it can get noisy on weekends. Ask for a quiet room when booking. Doubles €102, apartments €120

# Wicklow and around

**WICKLOW**, 27km south of Bray, is a modest, easy-going county town, though change is under way now that it's within the ever-expanding range of Dublin commuters, as evidenced by new boutiques and galleries, and the closure of several old pubs. Transport connections are less favourable for tourists than workers, however, as there are no buses from here into the heart of the Wicklow Mountains just to the west, but if you have a car, you could base yourself at one of several fine country hotels near the town for upland jaunts.

Built around a small port that busies itself with fishing, timber and yachts, the town is enlivened by its unusual setting: the River Vartry broadens into a lough here before flowing into the Irish Sea, cutting off a narrow strip of land, **the Murrough**, that's rich in bird life, notably wintering swans and geese. On a small rise above the harbour's south pier stand the meagre ruins of twelfth-century **Black Castle**, which affords fine views of the coast, north to the Sugarloaf Mountains and south to Wicklow Head. Wicklow hosts a lively three-day arts festival in May.

## Wicklow's Historic Gaol

Kilmantin Hill • Daily: Feb–Nov 10.30am–4.30pm, Dec & Jan 11am–3.30pm • €9.50 (includes tour) • ☎ 0404 61599, ⊚ wicklowshistoricgaol.com

The town's major tourist attraction is **Wicklow's Historic Gaol**, dating from 1702, just up Kilmantin Hill from Market Square; after holding numerous members of Sinn Féin from 1918, the gaol finally closed for good in 1924 before it was later repurposed as a storehouse for the council. The interactive tour builds up a lively and imaginative picture of life in the prison, focusing on the transportation of almost fifty thousand Irish convicts to Australia and fleshed out by sections on the 1798 Rebellion and the Great Famine. On the last Friday evening of the month, the gaol also runs adults-only ghost tours.

---

### WICKLOW FILM DRIVES

From classics like *Barry Lyndon*, *My Left Foot* and *Michael Collins* to blockbusters such as *Braveheart* and *King Arthur*, Wicklow has provided the stunning backdrop to an incredibly varied selection of **films**, earning the county the soubriquet of "Hollywood of Europe". You can explore these cinematic vistas on one of the three officially designated **driving routes**. The **Braveheart Drive** (80km) starts, aptly enough, in Hollywood. A looping tour of the west Wicklow mountains, it takes in the Sally Gap, Blessington Lakes, and the spectacular Glenmacnass Waterfall. The **Excalibur Drive** (68km), starts and finishes in the village of Roundwood, and showcases some vastly contrasting scenery – bogland, mountain peaks, picturesque farms and the opulent Powerscourt Estate. Finally the **Michael Collins Drive** (72km) stretches from Wicklow town to one of the finest beaches on the east coast – Brittas Bay. For more information, see ⊚ visitwicklow.ie.

## Mount Usher Gardens

5km northwest of Wicklow, on the N11 just south of Ashford · Daily 10am–5.30pm (Oct–Feb till 5pm) last admission 4.30pm · €8 · ☏ 0404 49672, ⓦ mountushergardens.ie · Bus #133 from Dublin

Designed by Dubliner Edward Walpole in 1868, in the Robinsonian style made famous by the eponymous gardener, **Mount Usher Gardens** shelter a plethora of rare trees, shrubs and flowers, including dazzling rhododendrons, azaleas and maples, and the finest eucalyptus specimens in Europe, all growing in an informal style in the woodlands and meadows. Running through the gardens is the River Vartry, broken up here by a remarkable series of nineteenth-century weirs, watercourses and miniature suspension bridges.

## Silver Strand and Brittas Bay

Any bus on the inland N11 to Arklow will put you off at Jack White's Crossroads, from where it's a 30min walk to Brittas Bay

Running south from Wicklow, off the R750 towards Arklow, is a series of fine, sandy beaches, beginning at **Silver Strand**, a lovely, sheltered spot just 5km from town. Backed by rolling dunes, **Brittas Bay**'s 3km strand, around 8km further on, is especially attractive and popular with weekending Dubliners, offering surfing and stand-up paddleboarding (ⓦ brittasbaysurfschool.com), while there's also kiteboarding on the beach.

### ARRIVAL AND INFORMATION                                  WICKLOW AND AROUND

**By train** Wicklow's train station is a 15min walk northwest of the centre, off the Rathnew (Dublin) road.
Destinations Dublin Connolly (3–5 daily via Greystones, Bray, Tara St and Pearse; 1hr 10min); Rosslare Europort (3–4 daily via Rathdrum, Enniscorthy and Wexford; 1hr 45min).
**By bus** Buses stop either on Summer Hill, just east of Market Square, or on Marlton Rd behind the *Grand Hotel*, just west of the centre.

Destinations Avoca (1–2 daily via Glenealy, Meeting of the Waters and Rathdrum; 35min); Dublin (airport, via several city-centre drop-off points; at least hourly; 1hr 50min); Enniscorthy (9 daily; 1hr 25min); Wexford (9 daily; 1hr 50min).
**By taxi** Wicklow Cabs, Main St (☏ 0404 66888).
**Tourist office** Rialto House, Fitzwilliam Square (Mon–Fri 9.20am–5.15pm; ☏ 0404 69117, ⓦ visitwicklow.ie).

### ACCOMMODATION

★ **Ballyknocken House** Glenealy, 8km southwest of town just off the Rathdrum road ☏ 0404 44627, ⓦ bally knocken.ie. Charming, creeper-clad 1850s farmhouse furnished with antiques, which serves superb breakfasts, using home-grown fruit and home-made bread and cakes. Also on offer are cookery courses with celebrity chef Catherine Fulvio and a range of walking programmes, while excellent Italian-influenced four-course set dinners are available at weekends if pre-arranged. €130
★ **Hunter's Hotel** About 3km from Wicklow on the R761 north of Rathnew ☏ 0404 40106, ⓦ hunters.

ie. Ireland's oldest coaching inn, dating from the early eighteenth century, is very comfortable yet unpretentious and welcoming, with an excellent restaurant; most bedrooms overlook the glorious two-acre gardens on the banks of the River Vartry, where afternoon tea is served in fine weather. Half-board packages available. €170
**Tinakilly** Just over 1km out of town on the Rathnew road ☏ 0404 69274, ⓦ tinakilly.ie. Grand Victorian mansion, covered in creepers and set in huge, mature landscaped gardens that run down to the sea; some rooms have four-poster or half-tester beds. €130

### EATING AND DRINKING

**Bridge Tavern** Bridge St ☏ 0404 64760, ⓦ bridgetavern. ie. Founded in 1759 on the site of an earlier shebeen, this venerable tavern is looking as good as ever, thanks to lots of seductive leather and dark wood filling the spacious, well-lit bars, and a flower-strewn riverside courtyard – here you can enjoy dishes like pan seared rib eye, and Moroccan lamb tagine. Mon–Thurs noon–11.30pm, Fri & Sat noon–12.30am, Sun noon–11pm.
**Halpin's Bridge Café** Bridge St ☏ 0404 32677, ⓦ halpinscafe.com. Friendly and well-kept café, where

you can read their newspapers to a background of mellow jazz, while tucking into a range of toasties and wraps (€6–7) as well as home-made soups, gourmet sandwiches, salads, cakes and speciality teas and coffees. Mon–Sat 8.30am–5pm, Sun 10am–5pm.
**Phil Healy's** Fitzwilliam Square ☏ 0404 67380, ⓦ phils ofwicklowtown.ie. Congenial, wood-panelled pub with lots of craft beers in bottles and on tap, a creative food menu and traditional sessions on Wed. Mon–Thurs 4–11.30pm, Fri 2pm–12.30am, Sat noon–12.30am, Sun noon–11pm.

**2**

# The Wicklow Mountains

If your time in Ireland is limited, it's well worth considering a stay in Dublin followed by a few days high up in the fresh air and magnificent scenery of the **Wicklow Mountains**. So close to the capital that they're often called the Dublin Mountains – by Dubliners, at any rate – they only rise to 924m at their highest point, Lugnaquillia, but form the largest area of continuous upland in Ireland. This granite mass is wild, desolate and sparsely populated at its centre, and, despite the influx of outdoorsy city-dwellers at weekends, never feels crowded. The range has been heavily glaciated to form attractive valleys, lakes and corries, while an extensive covering of peat supports purple heather and yellow gorse in abundance. To protect this huge natural playground on Dublin's doorstep, part of the massif has been designated as a national park, and walkers are signposted onto the **Wicklow Way**, a managed, long-distance trail that bisects the mountains from north to south. Wicklow Tourism's website (ⓦvisitwicklow. ie/wicklow-walks) covers all manner of **hiking** across the county, with route maps and descriptions. One of the most popular (and satisfying) walks is to the top of the **Sugarloaf Mountain**, which, looming Vesuvius-like over the Wicklow and Dublin skyline, is the most recognisable mountain in the area. The climb is a gentle one, taking about an hour, and the views from the summit are simply stunning. To reach the starting point, take the N11 south to Kilmacanogue, go over the bridge and take the first left – the car park is the next left under the arch.

## Powerscourt

1km southwest of Enniskerry • **Gardens** Daily 9.30am–5.30pm; closes at dusk in winter • €11.50 (includes audio-guide); Heritage Island • **Waterfall** Daily: Jan, Feb, Nov & Dec 10.30am–4pm; March, April, Sept & Oct 9.30am–5.30pm; May–Aug 9.30am–7pm; closed 2 weeks prior to Christmas • €6.50 • ☎ 01 204 6000, ⓦ powerscourt.com

In the northeastern foothills of the Wicklow Mountains, just outside the village of **Enniskerry**, lies the massive **Powerscourt Estate**, where, given fine weather, you could easily pass a whole day. Although the estate is now something of an all-round leisure complex, with two golf courses, a garden centre, craft shops, distillery and a luxury hotel, the central attraction remains the **formal gardens**, whose spectacular design matches their superb setting facing Great Sugar Loaf Mountain.

In the late twelfth century, a castle was built on this strategic site by the Anglo-Norman le Poer (Power) family, from whom it takes its name. However, what you see today dates from the early eighteenth century, when Richard Castle designed one of the largest Palladian mansions in Ireland here, flanked by terraced gardens that were further developed in the nineteenth century. The **house** remains impressive from a distance, but most of its interior was destroyed by a fire in 1974 (on the eve of a party to celebrate major refurbishment) and it now shelters an exhibition of dolls' houses and toys.

### The gardens

The terraced **Italian Gardens** slope gracefully down from the back of the house. The uppermost terrace, with its winged figures of Fame and Victory flanking Apollo and Diana, was designed in 1843 by the gout-ridden Daniel Robertson, who used to be wheeled about the site in a barrow, cradling a bottle of sherry – the last of the sherry apparently meant the end of the day's work. A grand staircase leads down to a spirited pair of zinc winged horses guarding the **Triton Lake**, whose central statue of the sea god (based on Bernini's fountain in the Piazza Barberini in Rome) fires a jet of water 30m skywards.

On the east side of the terraces are the curious **Pepper Pot Tower** (accurately modelled on the pepper pot from the eighth Viscount Powerscourt's dinner set), surrounded by fine North American conifers, and a colourful **Japanese Garden** of maples, azaleas and fortune palms, laid out on reclaimed bogland. To the west of the Italian Gardens lies the **walled garden**, with its rose beds, herbaceous borders and fine ceremonial

**2**

## THE WICKLOW WAY

The Republic's oldest designated long-distance walk, opened in 1982, the **Wicklow Way** runs the length of the Wicklow Mountains from Dublin's southern suburbs, taking in wild uplands and picturesque valleys, as well as long, boring stretches of conifer plantation. The trail cuts across the Glencree valley, passes Lough Tay and continues to Glendalough, before entering Glenmalure and skirting Lugnaquillia, the highest Wicklow peak; the walk finishes after 130km at Clonegall on the Wexford–Carlow border. The whole route is waymarked with yellow signs and can be walked in five to six days, though some people take as many as ten.

The Way begins at Marlay Park in Dublin's southern suburbs – take the #16 bus from O'Connell Street to get there. Its highlight – if you lack the time or inclination to complete the whole Way – is probably the 29km section from **Knockree to Glendalough**, which passes the Powerscourt waterfall and can be covered in one very long day – or preferably two, with a short detour to overnight at Roundwood.

Finding **accommodation** is not usually a problem, and some B&Bs will collect you from, or deliver you to, parts of the route, or ferry your bags to your next resting place, if given prior notice; there's now also a dedicated and usually cheaper luggage transfer service (☎ 086 269 8659, ⓦ wicklowwaybaggage.com), who also offer taxi transfers to the Way from Dublin Airport. Three An Óige hostels line the route – at Knockree (see page 120), Glendalough (see page 123) and Glenmalure (see page 123). Accommodation in Roundwood, Laragh/Glendalough and Glenmalure is detailed in the text. An excellent **website** (ⓦ wicklowway.com) gives full details of other accommodation along the route, as well as trail descriptions, maps and other useful advice.

Ordnance Survey **maps** nos. 56 and 62 cover almost the whole route at 1:50,000, with nos. 50 and 61 picking up the extremities. EastWest Mapping (ⓦ eastwestmapping.ie) also produce *The Wicklow Way Map Guide*, a booklet of 1:50,000 maps with accompanying text, as well as digital mapping of the region.

If you want to leave the practicalities to someone else, there are **guided walking tours** on and around the Wicklow Way by outfits such as Irish Ways (see page 30), Hilltop Treks (☎ 087 784 9599, ⓦ hilltoptreks.com) and Footfalls (☎ 0404 45152, ⓦ walkinghikingireland.com).

entrances: the Chorus Gate, decorated with beautiful golden trumpeters, and the Bamberg Gate, which originally belonged to Bamberg cathedral in Bavaria and features remarkable perspective arches as part of its gilded ironwork design.

### The waterfall

The estate's final attraction, **Powerscourt Waterfall**, is Ireland's highest at 120m. The falls leap and bound diagonally down a rock face to replenish the waters of the River Dargle in the valley below. It's 6km further down the road from the main gate, but well signposted.

### ARRIVAL AND DEPARTURE                                            POWERSCOURT

**By bus** Enniskerry is accessible from Dublin on the #44 bus from O'Connell St, D'Olier St or Merrion Square (hourly; 1hr), or the DART train to Bray followed by the #185 bus (frequent; 30min), which sometimes continues to the main gate of Powerscourt Estate.

### ACCOMMODATION AND EATING

**Avoca Terrace Café** Powerscourt House, ☎ 01 902 2110. Excellent, self-service café, run by Avoca (see page 124), offering dishes such as lemon tart (€6.25) and smoked Wicklow trout salad (€13.95), and a terrace that provides sumptuous views of the garden. Daily 9.30am–5pm.

**Ferndale** Enniskerry ☎ 01 286 3518, ⓦ ferndalehouse. com. You'll probably want to push on further into the mountains for somewhere to stay, but Enniskerry does have this good B&B on the village square, an attractive, all-en-suite place, furnished in period style, in an early Victorian house set in pretty gardens. €90

## Glencree and around

To the west of Powerscourt, beyond Knockree, the village of **GLENCREE** lies at the head of its eponymous valley and on the old **military road** from Dublin south into the mountains. To flush out insurgents from the 1798 Rebellion, some of whom evaded capture in Wicklow until 1803, the authorities in Dublin were obliged to build this road right along the backbone of the range. In the village, there's a **cemetery** for German airmen who died in Ireland during the two world wars. Nearby, just south of the cemetery, is the **Glencree Centre for Peace & Reconciliation** (Mon–Fri 9.30am–5pm, Sat & Sun 9.30am–5.30pm; ☎01 282 9711, ⊚glencree. ie), created to support people affected by the conflict in the North, fittingly occupies a former British army barracks, built to guard the military road. It houses a café with an outdoor terrace and a visitor centre that displays diverse temporary exhibitions.

### South into the mountains

South of Glencree, the military road (R115) climbs past the dramatic twin tarns of Lough Bray Lower and Upper (accessible by boggy paths opposite a car park) and then through ever wilder terrain towards one of the Wicklow Mountains' two main passes, the **Sally Gap**. From here the military road continues south through superb countryside, passing the beautiful **Glenmacnass Waterfall**, down to Laragh and Glendalough. If you fancy stretching your legs along the way, pull in at the car park 2.5km south of Sally Gap, cross the road and follow the rough, boggy path for 45 minutes or so to the prominent summit of **Luggala**, or Fancy Mountain; from here, you'll be rewarded with precipitous views straight down to Lough Tay and a panorama to the south and west of Lough Dan and the major Wicklow peaks.

### Lough Tay

The R759 heading southeast of Sally Gap winds its way down to Sraghmore, 3km north of Roundwood, passing impressive **Lough Tay**, where scree slopes tumble headlong into the water from the summit of Luggala. You can walk from one of the car parks above Lough Tay north up the Wicklow Way for about fifteen minutes to the memorial to J.B. Malone (one of the pioneers of Irish hill-walking and of the Way itself) for the finest view of the ensemble, and on to the top of White Hill in another twenty minutes for further scenic delights.

| ACCOMMODATION | GLENCREE AND AROUND |
|---|---|
| **Knockree Youth Hostel** 7km southwest of Enniskerry ☎01 276 7981, ⊚anoige.ie. Lying on the Wicklow Way, this ultra-modern "five-star" hostel is bright, colourful and well-equipped; most rooms have en-suite bathrooms, and there are fine views of the lush valley of Glencree and Great | Sugar Loaf. Breakfast available. Several times a day, the #185 from Bray DART station continues from Enniskerry to Shop River, about a 40min walk north of the hostel. Dorms **€20**, doubles **€65** |

## Roundwood

From Dublin, you can reach Glendalough on the old military road (R115), but the quicker route is along the N11 and R755 through **ROUNDWOOD**, which is accessible on the St Kevin's bus service (see page 123). This attractive village claims to be the highest in Ireland, at 220m above sea level, and enjoys a gentle setting on the eastern flank of the Wicklow range by the **Vartry Reservoir** – a good spot for an easy, flat, evening stroll. With a decent range of food and accommodation, Roundwood is a popular stop for hikers on the Wicklow Way, which is just 2.5km away. Wedged between the R759 and the R755 a little north of the village, **Ballinastoe Forest** is crisscrossed with mountain-biking trails, with bike rental, mountain-biking lessons and tours available (☎083 434 6992, ⊚biking.ie).

**Riverbank** Dublin Rd, north of the village centre ☎01 281 8117, ✉riverbank1@eircom.net. Family home with a lovely garden, bright, pine-floored and furnished en-suite bedrooms, and a drying room. Offers luggage transfer, transport to/from the trail for walkers, and packed lunches. Good rates for singles. Closed Nov–Feb. €70

**Roundwood Caravan & Camping Park** North end of the village ☎01 281 8163, ⓦdublinwicklowcamping. com. Large, smart, well-equipped campsite with a shop,

laundry service and campers' kitchen. Closed mid-Sept to April. €26

★**The Roundwood Inn** Main St ☎01 281 8107. Roundwood's best place to drink is this cosy, seventeenth-century hunting lodge. It also serves great bar meals, ranging from local seafood to delicious Irish stew (€12.25), as well as dishes such as roast leg of Wicklow lamb (€17.50) in its more formal, weekend restaurant. Bar menu daily noon–8.45pm; restaurant Fri & Sat dinner 7.30–9pm, Sun lunch 1–2pm.

# Glendalough and Laragh

Visitor Centre and monastic site daily: mid-March to mid-Oct 9.30am–6pm; mid-Oct to mid-March 9.30am–5pm; last admission 45min before closing • Visitor Centre €5; monastic site free; Heritage Card • ☎0404 45325, ⓦheritageireland.ie and ⓦglendalough.ie

A deep glaciated valley in the heart of the Wicklow Mountains, **GLENDALOUGH** ("valley of the two lakes") provides a delightfully atmospheric location for some of the best-preserved monastic sites in Ireland. Despite the coach parties, enough of the valley's tranquillity remains for you to understand what drew monks and pilgrims here in the first place.

The Glendalough Visitor Centre, its adjacent car park and the main monastic site are on the eastern side of the **Lower Lake**, while further west up the valley is the larger and more impressive **Upper Lake**, with its wooded cliffs and dramatic waterfall as well as more ruins, the national park information point and another car park. On the main road in, about 2km east of the visitor centre, lies the small village of **LARAGH**, which has most of the area's amenities, notably accommodation (though no ATM – the nearest is in Roundwood or Rathdrum); the Green Road from the south end of Laragh will allow you to walk along the south bank of the river to the Glendalough Visitor Centre and beyond, away from the traffic on the main road.

### Brief history

The monastery at Glendalough was established in the sixth century by **St Kevin** (Caoimhín), who retreated to the valley to pray in solitude. His piety attracted many followers to the site, especially after his death in 618, and the monastic community here came to rival Clonmacnois (see page 172) for its learning. It was raided by the Vikings at least four times between the eighth and eleventh centuries, then by the English in the fourteenth, and was finally dissolved during the Reformation. Pilgrimages continued, however, as the pope declared that seven visits to Glendalough would earn the same indulgence as one to Rome, but the pilgrims' abstemious devotions on St Kevin's Day (June 3) were often followed by drink and debauchery, and in 1862 a local priest banned the gatherings.

### The Lower Lake

The **visitor centre** features photographic displays and a film on Glendalough's place within Ireland's monastic heritage as well as a model of how the monastery is thought to have looked at the height of its activity.

Once you've entered the **monastic site**, through a double stone archway that was once surmounted by a tower, you'll come to its largest structure, the roofless but impressive **Cathedral of SS Peter and Paul**, begun in the early ninth century. Among the tombs outside stands **St Kevin's Cross**, one of the best remaining relics from the period, consisting of a granite monolith decorated with an eighth-century carving of a Celtic cross over a wheel; unusually, the quadrants of the cross have not been cut through, which suggests that it was left unfinished. Above the doorway of the nearby twelfth-century **Priests' House**, which may have been the site of Kevin's tomb-shrine, are faint

2

## WALKS AND ACTIVITIES AROUND GLENDALOUGH

The **Wicklow Mountains National Park Information Office** (May–Sept daily 10am–5.30pm; Feb–April & Oct Sat & Sun 10am–5.30pm; Jan, Nov & Dec Sat & Sun 10am–4pm; plus extra days during school holidays; ☎0404 45425, ⦿wicklowmountainsnationalpark.ie), at the eastern end of Glendalough's Upper Lake, has details of local walking routes and conditions and sells a series of leaflets on the national park, including *The Walking Trails of Glendalough* (also available from the visitor centre), which covers waymarked routes taking anything from 45 minutes to four hours. A map of the walking trails can be downloaded from the website, while a couple of good hikes in the area are also covered by Joss Lynam's *Easy Walks near Dublin*. The visitor centre contains an exhibition on the park's **wildlife**, which includes deer, red squirrels, hen harriers, red grouse and lots of birds of prey, and runs free guided nature walks, such as bat walks in summer and rut walks to observe deer in the autumn.

**St Kevin's Way** follows what was the main pilgrim path to Glendalough in medieval times. Waymarked with yellow pilgrim symbols, the 29km trail runs eastwards along country tracks and quiet roads from Hollywood, near the N81 south of Blessington, climbing to the **Wicklow Gap**, before following the descent of the Glendasan River for 7km to the Glendalough Visitor Centre. *St Kevin's Way*, a booklet by Peter Harbison and Joss Lynam, covers the route with comprehensive 1:50,000 maps and text.

The easiest to follow and most satisfying short **hike** is on the south side of Glendalough valley, where it's possible to climb 474m **Derrybawn** in around an hour, for spectacular views. Follow the Wicklow Way south from the national park information point past the Poulanass Waterfall, before eventually peeling left off the waymarked forest track up a narrow path, which climbs steeply to the edge of the forest and then straight up to Derrybawn's ridge and summit cairn.

For **horseriding**, try Glendalough House, about 3km north of Laragh in Annamoe (☎0404 45116, ⦿glendaloughhouse.ie).

---

carvings of figures believed to depict the saint and two (later) abbots. Downhill from here stands the two-storey, eleventh-century **St Kevin's Church**, whose steeply pitched roof and bell turret so resemble a chimney that the building is also known as "St Kevin's Kitchen", although it was almost certainly an oratory. Glendalough's **Round Tower** rises to over 30m, its conical roof having been restored in 1876. Such tapering stone towers are found only in Ireland and probably had multiple functions, as belfries, watchtowers, treasuries and places of refuge from danger – the entrance is usually well above ground level, accessible by a ladder that could be removed if necessary. To the south of St Kevin's Church, a footbridge crosses the river to the **Deerstone**, so called after a legend that claims that a tame doe squirted milk into the hollowed-out stone to feed the twin orphaned babies of one of Kevin's followers. In fact, it's a bullaun, one of many all over Ireland, a stone believed to have magical powers that was used for grinding medicines.

### The Upper Lake

You can drive to the **Upper Lake** car park along the north side of the valley, but it's more enjoyable to walk from the Deerstone along the signposted **Green Road** (part of the Wicklow Way), a scenic track that skirts the south side of the Lower Lake. After twenty minutes or so, this will bring you to the Upper Lake and the tiny, ruined, late tenth-century, Romanesque **Reefert Church**, whose small cemetery is thought to contain the graves of local chieftains (its name means "royal burial ground" in Irish). From here a path runs up to **St Kevin's Cell**, a typically Celtic, corbel-roofed "beehive" hut on a promontory overlooking the lake. Further up the cliff, **St Kevin's Bed** is a small cave that may have been a Bronze Age tomb, into which the saint reputedly moved to avoid the allures of an admirer called Caitlín; he's supposed to have offered the final resistance to her advances by chucking the poor woman into the lake. On the opposite side of the lake, a trail runs along the north shore and on up the valley, passing nineteenth-century zinc and lead mines.

## ARRIVAL AND DEPARTURE                                    GLENDALOUGH AND LARAGH

**By bus** St Kevin's bus service (☎01 281 8119, ⬤glenda loughbus.com) runs daily (at 11.30am) from Stephen's Green North in Dublin, via Bray and Roundwood, to Laragh and Glendalough Visitor Centre. Another option is to take a minibus from Rathdrum (see page 124).

## ACCOMMODATION

**Glendalough Hermitage Centre** St Kevin's Parish Church, just west of Laragh ☎087 935 6696, ⬤glenda loughhermitage.ie. This spiritual retreat on the north side of the road to Glendalough offers pilgrims of all faiths comfortable stone hermitages in a tranquil, gorse-strewn garden. Self-catering; restaurants and shops are a 5min walk away. Two-night minimum stay. **€80/night**

**Glendalough Hotel** Glendalough ☎0404 45135, ⬤glendaloughhotel.com. Bright, family-run Victorian hotel right by the visitor centre offering great views from many of the colourful, en-suite bedrooms, some of which have balconies; good-value half-board deals available. Very good rates for singles. **€110**

**Glendalough International Hostel** Glendalough, on the road to the Upper Lake ☎0404 45342, ⬤anoige. ie. Large, comfortable, recently refurbished, all-en-suite

hostel, offering breakfast and packed lunches, a well-equipped kitchen, drying room and laundry facilities. Dorms **€18**, doubles **€60**

**Lynham's Hotel** Laragh ☎0404 45345, ⬤lynhamsof laragh.ie. Airy, spacious, modern hotel overlooking the Glenmacnass River at the heart of the village, behind a popular bar with open fires in winter and outside tables by the river in summer; half-board deals offered. Bar, restaurant and lounge – all commendable – round things off nicely. **€140**

**Riversdale House** Wicklow Gap road, just over 1km northwest of the Glendalough Visitor Centre ☎0404 45858, ⬤glendalough.eu.com. Hospitable, well-run B&B in a tranquil location with great views. The en-suite rooms are simply and tastefully furnished, and breakfast is taken in the picturesque sun room overlooking the Glendasan River. Packed lunches available for walkers. **€90**

## EATING

**Glendalough Green Café** Laragh ☎0404 45151. Attractive, welcoming deli-café with outdoor tables on the green, dishing up tasty home-made soups (€5.25), home-baked breads and cakes (€3.75), salads, speciality teas and coffees. Daily 8.30am–5.30pm.

**The Wicklow Heather** Glendalough road, Laragh ☎0404 45157, ⬤wicklowheather.ie. Just off the green in Laragh, this is a cosy restaurant with a whiskey bar and attractive patio tables. It serves everything from breakfast and morning coffee to upmarket dinners featuring, for example, roast Barbary duck breast (€22), as well as Wicklow lamb and Irish salmon. Daily 8.30am–9.30pm (Sat till 10pm).

# Glenmalure

Arrowing down from the northwest around the Avonbeg River, **Glenmalure** is the next valley south of Glendalough, overshadowed to the southwest by Wicklow's highest peak, wild and lonely **Lugnaquillia** (924m). Besides the river, this peaceful, enclosed glen has room only for a thin strip of emerald fields and a narrow, gorse-flanked road between its steep slopes of scree and forestry. For drivers and cyclists, the military road offers a scenic route there, branching off the R755 just south of Laragh and continuing southwest; walkers can follow the Wicklow Way out of Glendalough, skirting Derrybawn Mountain and 657m Mullacor before descending into the valley. At the point where the military road hits the glen stands a ruined barracks, used in the suppression of the 1798 Rebellion.

## ARRIVAL AND ACCOMMODATION                                         GLENMALURE

**By bus** Minibuses run to Glenmalure from Rathdrum (see page 124).

★ **Glenmalure Lodge** ☎0404 46188, ⬤glenmalure lodge.ie. Quaint and welcoming 200-year-old coaching inn in a beautiful spot on the Wicklow Way, near the military road, offering comfortable, en-suite B&B, decent food and a cosy bar with a turf fire and outdoor tables; luggage transfer and packed lunches can be arranged for walkers. **€100**

**Glenmalure Youth Hostel** ☎01 830 4555, ⬤anoige. ie. Northwest of *Glenmalure Lodge*, the valley road ends at a car park and footbridge over the river, where a track runs over and up to this hostel. It's very basic (no electricity or running water), but has a gas-powered kitchen and a log fire, and holds interest as the house formerly owned by playwright J.M. Synge and by W.B. Yeats's muse, Maud Gonne McBride. Open daily June–Aug and Saturdays Sept–May. **€15**

## Rathdrum and around

In the lush foothills at the southeastern edge of the Wicklow Mountains, the main settlement is peaceful **RATHDRUM**, its long main street and pretty village green perched high above the Avonmore River. A few kilometres downstream, the quaint village of Avoca still trades on its role as the location for the now-defunct BBC-TV series *Ballykissangel*. Venturing further afield, you might well be tempted to stay or eat at the excellent *Brook Lodge and Wells Spa* (see page 125) to the west of Avoca at **Macreddin**, a village which fell into decline in the late nineteenth century but has recently been beautifully redeveloped by the enterprising hoteliers.

### Avondale House

2km south of Rathdrum village • April, May, Sept & Oct Tues–Sun 11am–4pm; June–Aug daily 11am–5pm • €7; open access to grounds, though parking on-site costs €5 (coins only); Heritage Island • ☎ 0404 46111, ⊕ coillte.ie

Small but beautifully proportioned **Avondale House** – completed in 1779 – is the birthplace and home of **Charles Stewart Parnell**, the nineteenth-century campaigner for home rule who was dubbed "the uncrowned king of Ireland". Over the main door in the hall hangs a poignant banner, representing the arms of Ireland's four provinces in pastel colours; given to Parnell in the 1880s, when home rule seemed a racing certainty, it was vainly intended for display in the future Irish House of Commons. The beautiful, bright dining room nearby is adorned with delicate, foliate stuccowork in Wedgwood style by the Lafranchini brothers (who also decorated Dublin's Newman House). Upstairs, the highlight is the **master bedroom** where Parnell was born, with a bay of large windows overlooking the grounds. Extensive renovation of the house – which is due for completion some time in 2022 – will include an exhibition on the Parnell's. A simultaneous redevelopment of the estate, which stretches over five hundred acres and is owned by the Irish Forestry Board, Coillte, will feature a new visitor centre with café and restaurant; otherwise, there are several **trails** (20min–3hr), through the forested parkland, which boasts rare tree species and fine views of the Avonmore River.

### Avoca

Set in the beautiful, thickly wooded **Vale of Avoca,** 10km south of Rathdrum on the R752, **AVOCA**'s most notable feature is its famous eighteenth-century **mill** – original home of the now-nationwide Avoca shops – where you can watch the weavers at work on a mill tour (daily: summer 9am–6pm; winter 9.30am–5.30pm; free; ☎ 0402 35105 ⊕ avoca.com). You can eat at the excellent **café** here and, of course, there's a shop selling the fruits of the looms as well as the other good-quality gifts the Avoca chain is known for.

### ARRIVAL AND INFORMATION — RATHDRUM AND AROUND

**By train** Rathdrum's train station is down by the river, a 10min walk from Main St.

Destinations Dublin Connolly (3–5 daily via Wicklow, Greystones and Bray; 1hr 20min); Rosslare Europort (3–4 daily via Enniscorthy and Wexford; 1hr 30min).

**By bus** Rathdrum (20min) and Avoca (35min) are served by one or two buses daily from Wicklow.

**By minibus** Roughly connecting with services to and from Dublin, there's a minibus/taxi to Glendalough and Glenmalure, via Laragh, from the train station and the market square, which would allow you, for example, to walk the Wicklow Way from Glendalough to Glenmalure (€8 single, €14 return based on three people travelling; advance booking required on ☎ 087 817 6630, ⊕ wicklowwaybus.com).

**Tourist office** There's a small tourist office in Rathdrum's market square (Mon–Fri 9.30am–5pm; ☎ 0404 46262), and another in Avoca's old courthouse (Mon–Fri 9am–5pm; ☎ 0402 35022).

### ACCOMMODATION AND EATING

#### RATHDRUM

**Bates** 3 Market St ☎ 0404 29988, ⊕ batesrestaurant. com. In a cosy, grey-stone cottage just off the market square, *Bates* is a top-quality, moderately priced restaurant with friendly service, serving dishes such as Wicklow venison loin with butternut squash purée and thyme jus. Three-course early bird menu €25. Wed–Thurs 6–8.30pm, Fri & Sat 5.30–9.30pm, Sun 12.30–8pm.

**Hidden Valley Resort** ☎ 086 727 2872, ⓦ hiddenvalley. ie. Down by the river, with its own lake, this camping and caravan park has a campers' kitchen and a laundry room, as well as various self-catering lodges. Also on offer are kayak rental, swimming, aqua park, laser tag, a rock wall and lots of other activities. Closed late Sept to mid-March. Camping **€33**, lodges **€80**

**Jacob's Well** Main St ☎ 0404 46282, ⓦ jacobswell rathdrum.com. Well-equipped, comfortable B&B with cheery en-suite bedrooms, great showers and a sitting room with a turf fire. It's in a separate building from the welcoming and popular pub, which offers well prepared, hearty lunch and dinner, and good Guinness. **€80**

**MACREDDIN**

★ **Brook Lodge and Wells Spa** 12km southwest of Rathdrum ☎ 0402 36444, ⓦ brooklodge.com. Located in a secluded valley, this luxurious, modern country-house-style hotel boasts a lovely spa, swimming pool, two excellent restaurants, a pub with its own microbrewery, plus free bicycles and an equestrian centre. **€160**

2

# Russborough House

3km south of Blessington village • Visit by guided tour (hourly: March–Sept daily 10am–5pm; phone ahead to check Oct–Feb hours) • House €12; maze €3; family ticket €30, including the maze; bird of prey centre €9; Heritage Island • ☎ 045 865239, ⓦ russborough.ie

Standing on the western edge of the Wicklow Mountains, **Russborough House** is a lavish Palladian country house designed by Richard Castle for Joseph Leeson, later Lord Russborough and the Earl of Milltown, whose family had made their money in the brewing trade. Castle died before the project was completed, leaving Francis Bindon to oversee the fulfilment of his grand design. Completed in 1751, the Wicklow-granite building's 200m frontage, with its curving colonnaded wings, is the longest of its kind in Ireland.

Known for its outstanding **art collection** – much of which has been donated to the National Gallery for safekeeping – the house also boasts a sumptuous **interior**, featuring Baroque plasterwork ceilings by the Lafranchini brothers, notably in the saloon, depicting the four seasons, and in the music room, where the ingenious geometrical design seems to add height to the room. Further beautiful stuccowork, representing hunting and garlands, adorns the cantilevered main staircase, which was ornately carved out of dark Cuban mahogany by Irish craftsmen in the eighteenth century. Other highlights include the Italian-marble fireplace in the dining room depicting Bacchus and vines, and a series of French clocks dating back as far as the fifteenth century, which are still wound every Tuesday. The **grounds** contain a **maze** and about 4km of trails, which will take you past a walled garden, and there's also a **bird of prey centre** where you can handle several owl species.

## ARRIVAL AND DEPARTURE                    RUSSBOROUGH HOUSE

**By bus** Blessington is about 1hr 40min from central Dublin on the #65 bus from Poolbeg St or South Great George's St (10–14 daily). Some of these services (4–6 daily) continue southwest of Blessington, towards Ballymore Eustace: ask

---

**PILFERED PAINTINGS AT RUSSBOROUGH**

Renowned for its **art collection**, Russborough House has been **burgled** on no fewer than four occasions, though almost all of the stolen paintings have subsequently been recovered. The first burglary was in 1974, when nineteen paintings were stolen by Englishwoman Rose Dugdale in order to raise funds for the IRA. The house was again broken into in 1986, by "The General", aka Martin Cahill, one of Dublin's most notorious criminals (this episode featured prominently in John Boorman's 1998 film *The General*). Russborough was burgled again in 2001, possibly by an associate of Cahill's, when a Gainsborough portrait was stolen for the third time, along with a work by Bellotto. Both were recovered in September 2002, only days before a fourth break-in, which netted five pictures including two by Rubens – all of which have been returned to the house, and subsequently sent to the National Gallery. Replicas of the paintings remain in the house.

the bus driver to let you off at the Russborough stop, which will leave you at the end of the road leading to the house, a 15min walk away; otherwise you can walk to Russborough along the Blessington Greenway Walk, which runs through woodland along the shores of Blessington Lake from the Avon Rí Activity Centre at the south end of Blessington, which should take approximately 1hr (see ⓦ visitwicklow.ie).

## EATING

★ **Grangecon** Kilbride Rd, just off Blessington's main street ⓣ 045 857892, ⓦ grangeconcafe.blogspot.com. Excellent café-restaurant in the old schoolhouse, which sources the very best, mostly organic and seasonal ingredients from the top local suppliers and makes everything in-house, from soda bread to lemon curd for their tarts. Great sandwiches (around €8) and shepherd's pie, and scrummy home-made lemonade. Tues–Sat 9am–4pm.

# County Kildare

In contrast to the harsh landscape of the Wicklow Mountains to the east, **County Kildare** is prosperous farming country, which was gladly seized and fortified by the English as part of the medieval Pale. Rich pasture for cattle and horses in the north of the county gives way to fertile ploughland in the south, the **Bog of Allen** in the northwest providing the only unproductive blot on the landscape. The county's main attractions for visitors are neatly concentrated in two areas. Servicing the bloodstock farms on **the Curragh**'s lush heathland, **Kildare town** is generally a low-key affair, where you can explore the monastery and church founded by St Brigid in the fifth century, and see what all the equine fuss is about at the fascinating **National Stud**. To the north of town, you can trace the development of the Bog of Allen at the nature centre in **Lullymore**. Meanwhile, up on the county's northern edge lies one of Ireland's finest stately homes, **Castletown**.

## Kildare town

In **KILDARE**'s quiet moments, of which there are many, you are keenly aware that the pre-eminent local business all takes place outside of town, for **the Curragh**, which stretches east from the town to the River Liffey, is Ireland's horse-racing centre. The underlying limestone of this huge plain, the largest area of semi-natural grassland in Europe, is good for a horse's bone formation, and the grass is said to be especially sweet. Consequently, the Curragh is home not only to a famous racecourse, but also to dozens of stud farms and stables, engaged in the multimillion-euro pursuit of breeding and training racehorses, one of the country's biggest sources of income – as vividly illustrated at the **National Stud**.

### St Brigid's Cathedral

Market Square • May–Sept Mon–Sat 10am–1pm & 2–5pm, Sun 2–5pm; tower closed in heavy rain • Cathedral €2 suggested donation; tower €4 • ⓣ 045 521 229, ⓦ kildare.ie

Kildare is arrayed around a triangular main square, which retains its central, nineteenth-century Market House and is overlooked by the huge Church of Ireland **Cathedral of St Brigid**. In the late fifth century, **St Brigid** is said to have founded a religious house here on a major pagan site, which became an important monastic centre of art, learning and culture – the *Book of Kildare*, for example, produced here in the seventh century but now lost, was, according to twelfth-century scholar Giraldus Cambrensis, dictated by an angel and as magnificent as the *Book of Kells*. Brigid herself, who may well have originated as the Celtic goddess Brigantia, is Ireland's second most important saint after Patrick, with many holy wells that are thought to cure sterility dedicated to her. Known also for her healing, farming and negotiating skills, Brigid has seen a recent revival of interest as an icon of feminine spirituality and an alternative to the patriarchal institutions of the Church.

The present cathedral was originally constructed in the thirteenth century, but the north transept and choir were destroyed during the 1641 Rebellion, and the building was largely reconstructed in the nineteenth century. Its twelfth-century **round tower**, the second highest in Ireland at 33m, is surmounted by mid-eighteenth-century battlements that replaced the original roof, and affords a fine panorama from the top. On the north side of the church is the restored **fire temple** – Brigid had cannily preserved the pagan cult of fire, and a fire is still lit here every year on **St Brigid's Day**, Feb 1 (ⓦsolasbhride.ie/feile-bride), formerly the pagan festival of spring.

**2**

## The National Stud

Tully, 2km south of central Kildare • Mid-Feb to early Dec daily 9am–6pm; 35min guided tours 10.30am, noon, 2pm & 4pm • €14, children €8; tours free; Heritage Island • ☎ 045 521617, ⓦ irishnationalstud.ie • Served by shuttle buses from Kildare town, as well as buses from Dublin's Connolly LUAS stop (Mon–Fri at 9.30am, returning at 3.45pm; Sat at 9.30am & 1.30pm, returning at 11.20am & 3.50pm; Sun at 10am & noon, returning at 3.05pm & 5.35pm)

The **National Stud** shows the highly evolved business of horse breeding in action. Here, you can look round the stables themselves and stroll through two attractive on-site **gardens**. It's worth timing your visit to coincide with one of the entertaining **guided tours**.

The stud farm was established here, by the mineral-rich River Tully, in 1900 by Colonel William Hall Walker, of the famous Scotch whisky family. Hall Walker's methods were highly successful, though eccentric: each newborn foal's horoscope was read, and those on whom the stars didn't shine were immediately sold, regardless of their lineage or physical characteristics. In 1915, the colonel presented the farm to the

---

### THE GRAND AND ROYAL CANALS

County Kildare is traversed by the **Royal and Grand canals**, which run from Dublin to the River Shannon. Reminders of Ireland's mercantile confidence in the eighteenth century, before the disenfranchisement of the Act of Union, they were built to service the mills, distilleries and breweries of a minor industrial revolution. Passenger boats on both canals were soon eclipsed by the railways and stopped running around 1850, but freight services continued until as late as 1960.

Completed in stages between 1779 and 1805, the **Grand Canal** heads out from south Dublin to Robertstown in County Kildare, where it splits into two branches. The 50km southern branch (aka the Barrow Line), completed in 1791, meets the River Barrow at Athy in the south of the county, allowing passage as far south as Waterford; the main waterway runs west via Tullamore in County Offaly to Shannon Harbour, a total of 114km from Dublin.

The **Royal Canal**, a rival northern route opened between 1796 and 1816, was never quite as successful, though it managed to reach a peak tonnage of 112,000 in 1847. It runs along the northern border of County Kildare, before heading northwest to Mullingar and joining the Shannon, 144km from north Dublin, at Cloondara in County Longford.

The canals are flanked by a series of pleasantly undeveloped – and easy-to-follow – **trails**, the Royal Canal Way, the Grand Canal Way and the Barrow Way; for more information and descriptions of the routes see ⓦ sportireland.ie. Even better, rent a **barge** and hit the waterways for a few days of leisurely cruising – operating the old but ingenious locks, quietly drifting under ancient bridges and through intensely green and lush landscapes is a memorable and relaxing experience. Jennifer's Travels (☎086 342 5546, ⓦjenniferztravels. com) has a large, beautiful four-birth barge specifically built for holiday travel, complete with kitchen, shower and peat burning stove. Pick-up is in Monasterevin, about 45 minutes from Dublin (rates are variable; call for quotes).

Another option is to go with Canalways Ireland (☎045 524 646, ⓦcanalways.ie). They have a larger selection of barges, with a two- to four-berth costing €1295 for one week in high season. Their Grand Canal route starts in Rathangan, Co. Kildare, and ends in either Shannon Harbour, Offaly, or Lucan, Dublin. A transfer from Dublin Airport can be arranged for €65 per person.

**2**

## HORSE RACING IN KILDARE

Two of Ireland's major racecourses, where you're practically guaranteed a fun, boisterous day out, are just a short trot from Kildare. The major Irish flat-racing classics are held at the **Curragh Racecourse**, about 5km east of town (☎ 045 441205, ⓦ curragh.ie): the Irish 1000 Guineas and 2000 Guineas in May, the Irish Derby in late June or early July, the Irish Oaks in July and the Irish St Leger in September. You can take special **bus** services to get to the Curragh from Dublin on race days (ⓦ dublincoach.ie), and there are free shuttle buses to the course from Kildare town for passengers on Dublin Coach's other services (see page 128) and from Kildare **train station** (ⓦ irishrail.ie).

About 20km east, just south of the town of Naas, **Punchestown Racecourse** (☎ 045 897704, ⓦ punchestown.com) hosts the five-day Irish National Hunt Festival in April, a more rural affair that attracts a lot of farmers. Have a look at their website for details of special buses from Dublin and Naas (which is on the train line from Connolly Station) during the festival.

British government – who promptly made him Lord Wavertree – on condition that it became the British National Stud. It was finally transferred to the Irish government in 1944 at an agreed valuation.

Within the attractive grounds, there are various yards, paddocks and stallion boxes, as well as a café. But the highlight of the tour has to be the **horses** themselves. They include fallabellas from Argentina, the smallest horses in the world (above pony height), as well as top stallions who command up to €70,000 for what's quaintly called a live cover and who jet as far afield as Australia to mate with local mares. From February until July, you should be able to see mares and their young foals in the paddocks. Don't pass up the opportunity to visit the stud's **horse museum**, whose prize exhibit is the skeleton of Arkle, one of racing's greatest steeplechasers, who died in 1970.

### The gardens

The grounds of the National Stud contain two beautiful gardens (included in the admission price). The beautiful and playful **Japanese Garden** was created by Colonel Hall Walker and two Japanese gardeners on a reclaimed bog between 1906 and 1910. A product of the Edwardian obsession with the Orient, it symbolizes the life of man from oblivion to eternity. Over miniature hills and waterfalls, past colourful flowers and trees, it follows from birth to death a delightful numbered trail, which yields a choice between bachelorhood and marriage, as well as a few false leads along the way.

Close by, the recently created **St Fiachra's Garden** – named after the Irish monk who became the patron saint of gardeners – is perhaps a little less compelling. It comes across as a stylishly enhanced arboretum, encompassing a lake in which has been placed a group of 5000-year-old bog-oak trunks, branchless and blackened, suggesting not only death but also longevity.

| ARRIVAL AND INFORMATION | KILDARE TOWN |
| --- | --- |

**By bus** As well as the Bus Éireann services to Dublin (mostly Custom House Quay, via O'Connell Bridge; Mon–Sat roughly hourly, Sun roughly every 2hr; 1hr 30min), which stop on Kildare's main square, private buses include Dublin Coach (ⓦ dublincoach.ie) to Dublin, Dublin Airport, Limerick and Ennis; and J.J.Kavanagh (ⓦ jjkavanagh.ie) to Dublin, Dublin Airport, Limerick and Shannon Airport.

**By train** The train station is a 10min walk north of the main square; there are frequent services to Dublin Heuston (20–30 daily; 40min).

**Tourist office** The tourist office (Mon–Fri 9.30am–1pm & 2–5pm, Sat 10am–2.30pm; ☎ 045 530672; ⓦ kildare heritage.com) and its heritage centre are in the eighteenth-century Market House in the centre of the main square.

### ACCOMMODATION AND EATING

**Harte's** The Square ☎ 045 533557, ⓦ harteskildare.ie. A nineteenth-century pub exterior with pretty hanging baskets conceals this lively gastropub, which presents some bold and successful menu choices such as smoked trout on sourdough, and bacon loin with a honey and mustard glaze and duck fat roasties. They've also a fine selection of craft beers from their very own Dew Drop brewhouse. The three-course Sunday lunch €29.95 is a steal. Tues–Thurs noon–3.45pm & 5–9pm, Fri & Sat noon–3.45pm & 5–9.45pm, Sun 12.30–8.30pm.

★ **JJ Mahon's** Just off the square on Claregate St ☎ 045 521316. Smartly kept, traditional pub done out in cosy dark woods and green leather. Walls cluttered with knickknacks and framed historical ephemera give it a nice old-world feel, and there's always a warm atmosphere. Mon–Thurs 10.30am–11.30pm, Fri & Sat 10.30am–12.30am, Sun 12.30–11pm.

**Lord Edward** The Square ☎ 045 522232, ⓦsilken thomas.com. Behind – and owned by – the *Silken Thomas* pub, the *Lord Edward* offers comfortable en-suite rooms in an eighteenth-century lodge that's been smartly converted using a lot of polished wood and earth tones. Breakfast is not included in the price, but is available at the pub; half-board packages also available. **€90**

**Silken Thomas** The Square ☎ 045 522232, ⓦsilken thomas.com. The town's major hospitality complex, with several bars, including *Lil's* pub, the *Squires* sports bar and *Flanagan's Lounge*, which offer tempting breakfasts, lunches and dinners (most dishes €10–15), and a smart, modern and popular evening restaurant, *Chapter 16*, where main courses such as chicken breast with black pudding croquettes cost €15–20. Mon–Thurs 8am–11.30pm, Fri & Sat 8am–12.30am, Sun 9am–11pm.

# The Bog of Allen

To the north of Kildare town lies the great **Bog of Allen**, Ireland's most famous peatland. Actually a complex of bogs that once covered two thousand square kilometres between the rivers Liffey, Barrow, Shannon and Boyne, it's now much diminished by drainage and stripping.

## Bog of Allen Nature Centre

Lullymore, 16km north of Kildare town • Mon–Fri 9am–5pm, last admission 4pm, plus weekend openings for special events May–Sept; closed public hols • €5 donation requested • ☎ 045 860133, ⓦ ipcc.ie

The best place to get a handle on the bog is in **Lullymore**, a tranquil parish and former monastic settlement on the road to nowhere 16km north of Kildare, which sits on an island of mineral soil, surrounded by peat. Here you'll find the **Bog of Allen Nature Centre**, run by the Irish Peatland Conservation Council, a charity whose aim is to ensure the conservation of a representative sample of Irish bogs. Informative exhibits at the centre, which is housed in the farm buildings of nineteenth-century Lullymore Lodge, trace the development of bogs, as well as their significance as habitats for rare animals and plants. The latter include species such as sundews, butterworts and pitcher plants, which have developed the capacity to eat insects, as the peat they grow on is deficient in nutrients; a greenhouse in the centre's back garden displays carnivorous plants from Ireland and around the world, and their various methods of drugging, gluing or otherwise catching the poor critters. Next to the centre, a 100m boardwalk has been built over Lodge Bog, a small raised bog that's home to around 150 species of plants, including carnivorous round-leaved sundews, as well as mountain hares, foxes and over seventy species of butterflies and moths.

# Castletown

Celbridge, 18km west of Dublin • March–Oct daily 10am–6pm, last admission 5pm; Nov to mid-Dec Wed–Sun 10am–5.30pm; 1hr guided tours daily at 11am & 3pm • €8; Heritage Card & Heritage Island • ☎ 01 628 8252, ⓦ castletown.ie • Dublin Bus #67, mostly from Connolly LUAS stop; coming by car on the M4 take Exit 6, signposted for Castletown (access by car is through the gates off Barnhall Rd; the gates at Main St Celbridge are for pedestrians and cyclists only)

The oldest and largest Palladian country house in Ireland, **Castletown** is also one of the very finest. Its plain, grey but elegant facade, built in the style of a sixteenth-century Italian town palace, conceals a wealth of beautiful and fascinating interior detail. The nicest approach to the house is on foot through its extensive parkland, along a beautiful avenue of lime trees that begins at the northern end of Celbridge's high street.

The house was built for William Conolly, son of a Donegal publican who, as legal adviser to William III, became the wealthiest man in Ireland from dealing in forfeited

**2**

## BOGS

**Bogs** once covered around one-sixth of Ireland's surface, a higher proportion than any other European country apart from Finland. They began to form around nine thousand years ago after the last Ice Age, when retreating glaciers and ice sheets left central Ireland covered by myriad shallow lakes. Gradually the partly decomposed remnants of mosses, pondweeds, water lilies and reeds built up on many of the lake beds as layers of peat, reducing the area of open water and eventually forming **fens**.

Between 7500 and 1500 years ago, further changes occurred to most of Ireland's fens. As the fen peat became so thick that it filled up the lakes, its surface was colonized by sphagnum moss which, able to hold twenty times its own weight in water, accelerated the accumulation of peat. Thus, huge, sponge-like domes of water were formed above the level of the surrounding land, known as **raised bogs**, which have an average peat depth of 9–12m. Around 4000 years ago, a different kind of bog began to develop in areas of very high rainfall, either along the west coast or in the mountains. These **blanket bogs** carpet the land surface with a layer of black peat, 2–6m thick.

It's not surprising that, as such a prominent part of the environment, bogs occupy a significant place in Irish **folk history**, as evidenced by the many songs, poems and stories associated with the annual harvesting of the turf. They are also **habitats** of great ecological value, sheltering many rare and protected species of plant and animal. And, as well as being important to biologists and climatologists, bogs have produced some of the most spectacular finds of Irish **archaeology**. The slow rate of organic decomposition that allowed the bogs to form in the first place has also preserved thousands of remarkable artefacts from the Neolithic period to the Middle Ages. These include ornaments and weapons, some of which were deliberately left in sacred bog pools as votive offerings during the Bronze Age; surprisingly intact human bodies, a few of which are now on display at Dublin's National Museum (see page 65); elaborate wooden roads from the Bronze and Iron Ages, such as the Corlea Trackway (see page 169); and indeed, whole settlements that were engulfed by peat, as at Céide Fields (see page 381).

The bogs of Ireland, however, are under grave threat. Man has **exploited** the peatlands on a small scale for many centuries. Marl, the chalky soil found beneath the peat, is a lime-rich fertilizer; the peat itself has always been cut and dried for use as fuel; and the overlying mat of vegetation on the bog surface was once used as roof insulation. However, in the twentieth century, exploitation dramatically accelerated. Bord na Móna (the Irish Turf Board) introduced large-scale, mechanized extraction schemes, especially from raised bogs, producing fuel for power stations and domestic use, as well as horticultural peat. There have been further losses to forestry programmes and agricultural intensification, to the extent that only twenty percent or so of the original peatlands, around one-thirtieth of Ireland's landmass, remains intact.

For more information on bogs, go to the Irish Peatland Conservation Council's excellent website at ⓦipcc.ie.

---

estates after the Battle of the Boyne. Though construction began in 1722, under first the Italian architect Alessandro Galilei and then his acquaintance, Edward Lovett Pearce, the interior was still unfinished at the time of Conolly's death seven years later. A second phase of work began in 1758, when great-nephew Tom Conolly married the 15-year-old Lady Louisa Lennox, who set about altering and redecorating the house to restrained, Neoclassical designs by Sir William Chambers, the architect of the Casino at Marino, Dublin.

Although you're free to explore the house and gardens at your leisure, the engaging guided tour is worth a look. It begins by the **Grand Staircase**, its cantilevered Portland-stone steps and solid brass banisters weighing at least ten tons. Rococo stuccowork by the Swiss-Italian Lafranchini brothers, depicting Tom Conolly in high relief and personifications of the four seasons, swirls extravagantly over the walls here, but in such a huge, white space manages to appear delicate and restrained. The ground-floor **Brown Study** is the only room to retain its original, rich pine panelling and narrow oak doors from the 1720s, and features a portrait of William III, donated to William Conolly by the king himself. On the same floor lies perhaps the most ostentatious display of wealth and fashion at Castletown: over six years, at huge cost and with painstaking effort, Lady Louisa had the walls of the **Print Room** papered with black-and-white prints from London and Paris, portraying everything from biblical scenes to famous actors of the day, complemented by decorative borders of swags, chains and masks; it must have looked fantastic in its original state, on a background of bright yellow paint.

The highlight upstairs is the **Long Gallery**, which was decorated by Lady Louisa with busts of Greek and Roman philosophers and murals of Classical scenes of love and tragedy, in the style of the recently rediscovered Pompeii. From the gallery's windows you can make out the **Conolly Folly**, some 3km north, an arcane, 50m-high edifice consisting of an obelisk perched shakily on top of a cascade of arches. Attributed to Richard Castle, it was built in 1740 as a monument to Speaker Conolly by his widow, and as a Famine relief scheme.

# County Meath

The rich limestone lowlands of **County Meath**, bisected by the River Boyne and supporting ample cattle pasturage, have always attracted settlers and invaders. The valley's Neolithic people somehow found the resources and manpower to construct the huge, ornately decorated passage graves of **Newgrange**, **Knowth** and **Dowth**, part of the extraordinary landscape of ritual sites known as **Brú na Bóinne**, which is today one of the country's most famous and best organized visitor attractions. In contrast, the **Loughcrew Cairns**, a similarly extensive grouping of burial mounds in the far northwest corner of the county beyond the small market town of Kells, have failed to garner present-day resources for excavation and tourist development, leaving you to explore this mysterious, hilltop landscape unaided and usually in solitude. The **Hill of Tara** started out as a Stone Age cemetery, too, but evolved into one of Ireland's most important symbolic sites, the seat of the High Kings of the early Christian period. Meath also caught the eye of the Anglo-Norman invaders, who heavily fortified and held several parliaments at **Trim**, where you can visit the mighty castle and several other well-preserved medieval remnants. Meath's other noteworthy sights are on either side of Brú na Bóinne in the northeast of the county: to the west, **Slane's** historic castle and monastery, which enjoy a picturesque setting on a steep, wooded hillside above the River Boyne; and to the east, the site of one of the most significant battles in Ireland's history, the **Battle of the Boyne**, now commemorated by a high-tech visitor centre.

## Trim and around

Fifty kilometres northwest of Dublin, **TRIM** is one of the most attractive towns within striking distance of the capital. Its imposing Anglo-Norman castle overlooks the curving, tree-flanked River Boyne and some picturesque ruins across on the north bank, while verdant meadows run downriver to the extensive remains of two medieval churches and a fine bridge. Trim is also the easiest jumping-off point for the Cistercian abbey of **Bective**, set in lush countryside to the northeast.

### Trim Castle

Castle St • Mid-March to Sept daily 10am–6pm; Oct & Feb to mid-March daily 9.30am–5pm; Nov–Jan daily 9am–5pm; 45min guided tours of the keep every hour on the hour; due to their popularity in summer, it's best to arrive as early in the day as possible; last admission and tour 1hr before closing • €5 for admission to the castle grounds plus guided tour, €2 castle grounds only; Heritage Card • ☎ 046 943 8619, ⓦ heritageireland.ie

The town's outstanding centrepiece is **Trim Castle**, which is intact enough to have been used as a location for Mel Gibson's 1995 film *Braveheart*. In 1172, Henry II, fearing that the adventurer Strongbow might try to establish his own Anglo-Norman kingdom in Ireland, granted the lordship of Meath to Hugh de Lacy, who along with his son Walter gradually built the most impressive castle in Ireland, the "keystone of the Pale", at this important ford over the Boyne. It's well worth taking one of the illuminating guided **tours** of the keep, and leaving yourself enough time to poke around the enclosure's assorted towers, ruined buildings and mighty curtain wall.

The cruciform floor plan of the **keep** was a unique experiment in military architecture – the design increased possible angles of attack and thus was not emulated elsewhere. However, with walls up to 5m thick and over 20m high, which have survived to this day, the keep was obviously stout enough. The tour inside reveals a chapel, the former Great Hall, a bedroom with an early walk-in wardrobe and spectacular views of the town from the battlements.

The fording of the Boyne was defended by the castle's strongest tower, the **Magdalen Tower**, at the northern tip of the curtain wall, but during a period of greater stability and prosperity in the late thirteenth century, this was converted into private apartments, and a new **Great Hall** was built alongside. On the right-hand side of the hall, look out for a passage cut through the bedrock from the river gate, which allowed stores brought by boat from Drogheda on the coast to be delivered directly to the cellar.

### Talbot's Castle

Across the river from Trim Castle • No public access

Crossing the river by the footbridge under the castle walls, you can see the only surviving remnant of the fourteenth-century outer walls, the arched **Sheep Gate**. Nearby stands **Talbot's Castle** (privately owned), a beautiful manor house built in 1415 by Sir John Talbot, the Lord Lieutenant of Ireland. In the eighteenth century, Jonathan Swift (see page 75), who was rector of nearby Laracor, bought the building and turned it into a Latin school, whose most famous alumnus was Arthur Wellesley, later the Duke of Wellington and MP for Trim. The house had been constructed on the site of an Augustinian abbey, St Mary's, which in turn had been built over one of the first monasteries in Ireland, dating from the fifth century. All that remains of St Mary's is the **Yellow Steeple**, a huge, half-ruined belfry that's so named because it glows in the evening sunlight.

### Newtowntrim Cathedral

1.5km east of the town centre on Lackanash Rd, accessible off the Dublin road or by footpath along the north bank of the Boyne • Open access 24hr • ☎ 046 943 8053, ⓦ discoverboynevalley.ie

The beautiful remains of thirteenth-century **Newtowntrim (SS Peter & Paul) Cathedral** stand in riverside meadows. The priory of Newtowntrim was founded here under the protective gaze of Trim Castle in 1202 by Simon de Rochfort, Bishop of Meath, and was soon elevated to become the seat of his diocese, with the construction of the largest and most sophisticated Gothic cathedral in Ireland. Substantial parts of the nave and chancel can still be seen, alongside a ruined refectory.

### The priory and St Peter's Bridge

Just across the river from Newtowntrim Cathedral is another fine ruin, the **Priory of St John the Baptist**, also founded by Simon de Rochfort in the early thirteenth century. It was used as a hospital and guesthouse (with its own brewery) by the *Fratres Cruciferi*, the Crutched (or Cross-bearing) Friars, Augustinian monks who had attended the Crusaders. Between the cathedral and the priory, the Boyne is spanned by the wonderful Norman **St Peter's Bridge**, which is reckoned to be the second-oldest bridge in the country.

## Bective Abbey

8km northeast of Trim • Open access 24hr • ☎ 041 988 0300, ⓦ discoverboynevalley.ie • From Trim, take the Navan road, look out for a signposted right turn and then it's just over 1km on the left

In a beautiful setting by an old arched bridge on the west bank of the River Boyne, the ruins of **Bective Abbey** are a fine example of Cistercian architecture. Founded as a satellite of Mellifont (see page 150) in 1147, the abbey soon rose to prominence, its abbot holding a peer's seat in the Irish Parliament. The place was rebuilt in the thirteenth century, though only one wall of the nave remains from this phase. The majority of the extant building dates from the fifteenth century or later, remaining so remarkably intact because it was converted into a mansion house after Henry VIII's dissolution of the abbey in 1536. The sturdy and imposing fifteenth-century **tower** at the entrance is especially well preserved, and the south and west ranges of the **cloister** remain partly roofed – keep your eyes peeled for a carving of a monk near the southwest corner.

2

### ARRIVAL AND INFORMATION

### TRIM AND AROUND

**By bus** Buses from Drogheda (4–9 daily via Slane; 1hr 10min) and Dublin (7–21 daily; 1hr) stop by the Lidl superstore, on the ring road around the east of the compact town centre, though one or two also stop near the castle.

**Tourist office** Next to the castle, the helpful visitor centre (Mon–Thurs 10am–5pm, Fri 10am–4.30pm; ☎ 046 943 7227, ⓦ discoverboynevalley.ie) houses a medieval armoury exhibition.

### ACCOMMODATION AND EATING

**Crannmór** 1.5km north of town on the Dunderry road ☎ 046 943 1635, ⓦ crannmor.com. Welcoming B&B, popular with fishermen, in a creeper-clad Georgian country house set amid fine gardens and paddocks. Very good rates for singles. Closed Dec–Feb. €75

**Franzini O'Brien's** Opposite the castle ☎ 046 943 1002, ⓦ franzinis.com. Solid all-rounder of a restaurant with a bright, informal air, set in a peerless location right opposite the castle entrance. The global menu includes prawn tempura, chicken ruskini and beef teriyaki noodles. Early-bird €22.95-for-two-courses deal available all evening midweek. Tues–Fri 5–10pm, Sat 5–9.30pm, Sun 2–8.30pm.

**James Griffin's** High St, across the river from the castle ☎ 046 943 1295, ⓦ jamesgriffinpub.ie. *Griffin's* is a gnarly, hundred-year-old pub with bare stone walls, that

offers a wide selection of Irish whiskies and craft beers, and hosts traditional music sessions on Thurs, acoustic sessions Fri & Sat. Mon–Fri 3–11.30pm, Sat 1pm–12.30am, Sun 1–11pm.

**Trim Castle Hotel** ☎ 046 948 3000, ⓦ trimcastlehotel. com. Bright, spruce, four-star hotel right opposite the castle, sympathetically designed in a tasteful, contemporary style. Lots of special offers on their website, including midweek room-only and weekend breaks with dinner. €150

**The Welcome All Café** Inside the tourist office. A popular, keenly priced, family-run café, offering home-baked scones with jam and cream (€2.30) and great combos such as leek and potato soup with a sandwich (€6) and lasagne with tea or coffee (€8.50). Mon–Fri 9.30am–5.30pm, Sat & Sun noon–5.30pm.

# Hill of Tara

Archaeological site open access; visitor centre mid-May to mid-Sept daily 10am–6pm, last admission 5pm • €5, including a guided tour of the site; Heritage Card • ☎ 046 902 5903, ⓦ heritageireland.ie and ⓦ hilloftara.org

Perhaps more than anywhere else in Ireland, the **Hill of Tara** is loaded with both historical and mythical significance. It's best known as the seat of the High Kings of Ireland in the early centuries after Christ, but had been a major ritual site since the late Stone Age, giving it plenty of time to accrue prehistoric legends. The aura of this long, grass-covered hill, covered with mostly circular mounds and ditches, is unmistakable, and the views of the surrounding countryside are magnificent.

In the **visitor centre**, an impressive twenty-minute film provides the historical and mythological background and shows some stunning views of the hill from the air. The centre occupies a nineteenth-century church, adorned with beautiful painted windows showing the Pentecost and the Apostles. Executed by Evie Hone in 1935, they commemorate the 1500th anniversary of St Patrick's mission to bring Christianity to Ireland.

**TARA: HISTORY AND MYTH**

It's likely that people started using the **Hill of Tara** in the Neolithic period (c.3500 BC) as a place for burials and for ritual gatherings, with no resident population. Around sixty monuments, mostly barrows, have been discovered on the hill, the latest probably dating to the late Iron Age (c.400 AD). So much for the archaeology, but mythology, literature and propaganda have imbued Tara with a far greater significance, as the ritual seat of kings – who did not have to be based here, but derived their authority from association with this revered place.

The earliest Irish sagas portray the hill as the home of the master-of-all-trades **Lug**, the greatest of the Celtic gods and the divine manifestation of Tara's kingship, and the goddess **Medb** (Maeve), who could also legitimize a king, sometimes by getting him drunk and sleeping with him – if she couldn't find a suitable candidate, Medb would rule herself. Of these legendary kings, the greatest were **Cormac Mac Airt** and **Conaire Mór**, semi-divine embodiments of peace, prosperity and righteousness. On somewhat firmer ground, seventh-century historical texts tell of recent struggles between the dynasties of Leinster, Northern Ireland and the **Uí Néills** (pronounced "Ee-nails"; based in the northwest and the midlands) for the kingship of Tara. The Uí Néills came out on top, but while the title *rí Temrach* (king of Tara) would have given them special status over the other kings, territorial control over the whole island was not a possibility until the ninth century, when the island became less politically fragmented. In the eleventh century, however, geopolitical reality bit, and Tara lost out to the big city, Dublin.

Tara's significance continues into modern times: during the **1798 Rebellion** some of the United Irishmen made a dramatic last stand on the hill, while in 1843 Daniel O'Connell harnessed the symbolic pull of the site to stage his biggest "monster meeting" here, attended by up to a million people, as part of his campaign to repeal the Union with England.

### The Rath of the Synods

Hard up against the wall of the church's graveyard, the first of the mounds you come to is the 83m-wide ring fort known as the **Rath of the Synods**, the reputed location of ecclesiastical synods in the sixth century. It's the untidiest of Tara's mounds: not only has it been partly destroyed by the church graveyard, but between 1899 and 1902 members of a cult, the British Israelites, dug up the rath, believing they would find the Ark of the Covenant. It's a particular shame that they kept no record of their efforts as this site went through many functions over the centuries: from early Bronze Age barrow, through palisaded ceremonial building, back to cemetery, and finally to ring fort. A Roman seal and lock have been found from this last phase, evidence of contact with the Roman world (probably Britain) in the fourth and fifth centuries AD.

### The Mound of the Hostages

The next tumulus to the south is the earliest on the site, the so-called **Mound of the Hostages**. It takes its name from the primitive medieval peacekeeping practice of exchanging hostages with neighbouring kingdoms, who were supposedly imprisoned within the mound by Cormac Mac Airt. Built around 3000 BC, it's actually a Neolithic tomb with a 4m-long passage that was reputed to have given entry to the other world. Access is no longer possible, but you can admire the typical concentric circles and zigzag patterns carved on one of the portal stones. No fewer than two hundred cremated late Neolithic burials were found here, to which were added around forty from the Bronze Age, some cremated, some inhumed, the latter including a high-ranking teenage boy wearing a necklace of jet, amber, bronze and exotic faïence beads.

### The Forrad, Cormac's Residence and around

A 1km-long circular bank, the **Royal Enclosure**, surrounds the Mound of the Hostages, and two larger, conjoined earthworks: the **Forrad**, a Bronze Age burial complex, and **Cormac's Residence**, an Iron Age ring fort to the east. In the centre of the Forrad is the **Stone of Destiny** (the *lia fáil*), a phallic standing stone used in the coronation of the High Kings. Tradition states that the royal candidate had to drive his chariot wheel against the stone, and the gods, if they approved, would screech out his name. To the south of the Royal Enclosure lie the crescent-shaped remains of the **Enclosure of King Laoghaire** (see page 138), who is said to be buried here standing upright and dressed in his armour, facing his enemies, the Leinstermen.

### The Banqueting Hall

To the north of the church, the so-called **Banqueting Hall** is actually two low banks of earth running parallel for over 200m. Though traditionally held to have been an enormous hall into which thousands of men from all over Ireland would have collected on ritual occasions, this was in fact probably Tara's ceremonial entrance avenue, aligned with the Mound of the Hostages and flanked by tombs and temples.

### Gráinne's Fort

West of this avenue stands **Gráinne's Fort**, a burial mound surrounded by a circular ditch and bank. Like many ancient sites throughout Ireland, it has become associated with the tale of "The Pursuit of Diarmuid and Gráinne": the daughter of Cormac Mac Airt, Gráinne is betrothed to the king's elderly commander, Fionn Mac Cumhaill, but falls in love with one of his young warriors, Diarmuid, and elopes with him from Tara, with Fionn and his warriors in hot pursuit.

---

**ARRIVAL AND ACCOMMODATION**                               **HILL OF TARA**

**By bus** Dublin–Navan buses from Busáras will drop you at Tara Cross, about 1km from the site (every 30min; 1hr).

**Bellinter House** Bellinter, 5km northwest of Hill of Tara, off the M3 ☎ 046 903 0900, ⓦ bellinterhouse. com. This Georgian manor house set in extensive grounds overlooking the River Boyne has been converted into a stylish hotel. A bolthole for the Dublin media crowd, it offers plenty of retro chic and quirky features in its redesign, an outdoor hot tub, seaweed baths and other spa treatments, as well as wellies to borrow. In the vaulted cellar, there's an excellent restaurant, a branch of Dublin's *Eden*, that uses local, seasonal ingredients whenever possible. **€140**

---

## The Loughcrew Cairns and Oldcastle

Sited on a row of four hills at the far northwestern tip of County Meath, the **Loughcrew Cairns** consist of more than thirty chambered mounds and over a hundred curiously carved stones. Local folklore has bestowed on the hills a colourful name, **Sliabh Na Caillighe** (as now marked on Ordnance Survey maps, meaning "Mountain of the Sorceress"), and foundation legend: the said witch, believing she would become mistress of all Ireland if she leapt from hill to hill carrying an apron full of rocks, performed the mighty jumps, shedding handfuls of stones on each peak, but fell at the last, breaking her neck (a cairn at the bottom of the easternmost hill is traditionally known as the witch's grave). The true story of the cairns' construction is only slightly less amazing: archaeologists believe that between approximately 3500 and 3300 BC, Neolithic people travelled considerable distances to build these communal tombs, each of which may have taken anything from four to thirty years to complete. The alignment of the passage tombs and the elaborate carvings on their stone slabs display an association with sun worship, and it's obvious that this high-status ritual site was meant to be visible from afar. In reverse, the cairns afford a magnificent panorama over quiet lakes and gently undulating farmland, encompassing up to sixteen counties on a clear day.

**2**

Though on a smaller scale, the Loughcrew Cairns are contemporary with the more famous burial sites at Brú na Bóinne, but, having never been comprehensively excavated, provide quite a different experience for the modern-day visitor. If you're going to visit both complexes, it makes sense to take the guided tours of the reconstructed mounds of Newgrange and Knowth first, before letting your imagination run wild on the unspoilt ritual landscape at Loughcrew. The cairns lie around 5km southeast of **Oldcastle**, a thriving village that sports several galleries and boutiques. While you're in this area, it's also well worth visiting the attractive **Loughcrew Gardens**.

## Cairn T

Carnbane East hill · Late May to early Sept daily 10am–6pm, last admission 5.15pm; outside official opening hours, you can pick up the key and a torch from the café at Loughcrew Gardens (€50 or passport as deposit) · Free · Coming by car, turn off the N3 at the town of Kells and follow the Oldcastle road for about 15km, before forking left towards Loughcrew Gardens; after 3km a right turn leads to the car park beneath the summit of Carnbane East after about 1km, from where it's a steep, 10min walk up to Cairn T

The majority of the Loughcrew tombs are located on top of two hills, Carnbane East and Carnbane West, though unfortunately the latter is private land and currently inaccessible to visitors; **Cairn T** is the focus of the summit of **Carnbane East**, and probably of the whole complex – most of the tombs on the other hills face towards it. The cairn's 113m circumference is reinforced by large kerbstones, behind which originally ran the thick layer of white quartz (as at Brú na Bóinne) that gave the hill its name: *carn bán* is Irish for "white cairn". On the north side is one of the largest kerbstones, known as the "Hag's Chair", where the witch of legend sat smoking her pipe (local lore adds that any wish you make while sitting here will come true). You can make out faint traces of carved Neolithic whorls on this stone, as well as a prominent cross, which strongly suggests that Masses (officially forbidden under the penal laws) were held in secret here during the eighteenth century.

The cairn's low, 5m-long **passage**, aligned with the rising sun on the equinox days in March and September (just south of east), leads into a roughly circular chamber with three side recesses. Once your eyes become accustomed to the gloom, you'll start seeing wonderful, mysterious carvings – chevrons, whorls, waves, petals – on the large stones all around you. These incisions are especially ornate in the back recess, where a prominent sun pattern may have been specifically designed to catch the first rays of the equinox sun along the passage.

## Loughcrew Gardens

Loughcrew, Oldcastle · Mid-March to Oct Mon–Fri 9.30am–5.30pm, Sat & Sun 11am–5.30pm; Nov to mid-March Mon–Fri on request, Sat & Sun 11am–4pm · €7 · ☎ 049 854 1356, ⓦ loughcrew.com

Signposted on the southwestern side of Carnbane East, the **Loughcrew Gardens** are most famous for their impressive seventeenth-century avenue of grotesquely fluted **yew trees**. They also encompass nineteenth-century lawns, herbaceous borders, ponds and a grotto, as well as signposted woodland walks, fairy trail for kids, a café and the family church of St Oliver Plunkett (see page 147), now roofless. The oldest part of the church was formerly a tower house, the seat of the Plunketts until the 1652 Act of Settlement, when Cromwell's surveyor, Sir William Petty, installed his brother-in-law, William Naper, at Loughcrew.

| INFORMATION AND ACCOMMODATION | LOUGHCREW CAIRNS AND OLDCASTLE |
|---|---|

**Tourist information** *Kraft Kaffee*, a craft shop, café and official tourist information point on Millbrook Rd, Oldcastle (Tues, Wed & Fri 10am–5pm, Sat 10am–4pm; ☎ 049 854 2645, ✉ kraftkaffee@gmail.com).

**The Fincourt** Oliver Plunkett St, Oldcastle ☎ 049 854 1153, ⓦ fincourt.com. This traditional inn provides a warm welcome and seven smart, comfortable and well-equipped en-suite rooms and a self-catering apartment (€120). The pub itself has bar food, an open fire and a quiet beer garden at the back. **€90**

# Kells

A town of unique historical and cultural significance, **KELLS** is a twenty-minute drive from the Hill of Tara on the M3. Once a major monastic site, the town is best known for **Kells Abbey**, a former monastery from which the *Book of Kells* takes its name. Although not created here, the book was safely kept in the monastery for hundreds of years, roughly from the ninth century to the sixteenth century. Today the monastic site includes a 27m **round tower**, **St Colmcilles church** and four stunning **high crosses**. Nearby on Church Lane is a tenth-century oratory known as St Colmcilles house, which is thought to have housed the saint's relics. A fifth high cross dating from the ninth century, known as the "market cross", can be found in front of the old courthouse at the east end of town. All of these sites are in the centre of Kells and a short walk from each other.

## INFORMATION AND ACCOMMODATION                                              KELLS

**Tourist office** Housed in the civic offices on Headfort Place, the welcoming tourist office has a copy of the *Book of Kells* on display (Tues–Fri 9am–5pm, Sat 9am–4pm, closed for lunch 1.30–2pm; ☎ 046 924 7508, ✉ kellscourthouse@discoverboynevalley.ie).

**The Headfort Arms Hotel** Headfort Place, Kells ☎ 046 924 0063, ⓦ headfortarms.ie. In business for almost two hundred years, this luxury hotel is the perfect base to explore the Boyne Valley. The 45 bedrooms are a comforting mix of old and new decor and ambience, each with orthopaedic beds and excellent showers. The attached *Vanilla Pod* restaurant is the best in town. Restaurant Mon–Sat 5–11pm, Sun 12.30–9.30pm. €99

# Slane

Fifty kilometres north of Dublin, the village of **SLANE** enjoys a handsome setting on a south-facing slope above the leafy River Boyne, with the junction of the N2 and the N51 between Drogheda and Navan forming a prominent crossroads at the centre of the village.

## Slane Castle

Main entrance 1km west of the village centre • Guided tours usually early June to late Aug daily 11am–5pm (but sometimes closes for events so check ahead) • Castle €14, distillery €14, combined house and distillery tour €27 • ☎ 041 988 4477, ⓦ slanecastle.ie and ⓦ slaneirishwhiskey.com

The village grew up around **Slane Castle**, whose estate extends westwards from the large Gothic gate by the bridge over the River Boyne. The main entrance for visitors, however, is now round the back of the castle, about 1km west of the village crossroads. The era's finest architects – Gandon, Wyatt and Johnston – constructed the castle, with its mock battlements and turrets, from 1785 onwards, while Capability Brown designed the grounds. A devastating fire struck in 1991, however, and it took until 2001 for the castle to open again, with its interior redesigned in largely contemporary style as a venue for conferences and society weddings. Consequently, the guided tour smacks a little of *Hello* magazine, though there are one or two points of architectural interest remaining, notably the lofty ballroom, with its ornate fan vaulting and an original carved wooden chandelier, which was built by Thomas Hopper for George IV's 1821 visit to his mistress, Lady Conyngham. The present Conyngham, Henry, Lord Mountcharles, is a friend of rock band U2, who lived here while recording *The Unforgettable Fire* in 1984, and mounts huge concerts in the grounds most summers. New to the site is the **Slane Whiskey Distillery**, housed in the old stables building; tours take in the barley room, cooperage, production area and warehouse before concluding with a tasting.

## The Hill of Slane

Around 1km north of the village centre • Open access 24hr

From the main crossroads in the village, it's a fifteen-minute walk north and west up to the **Hill of Slane**, which affords views over rolling farmland to the Irish Sea at Drogheda

2

and the Wicklow Mountains. Here, in 433, according to tradition, **St Patrick** lit the Paschal (Easter) Fire for the first time in Ireland, signalling the arrival of Christianity. In this he challenged the pagan *Bealtaine* fire on the Hill of Tara, 15km to the south, lit by the High King, Laoghaire, to celebrate the arrival of summer. Laoghaire was soon won over, however, and although the king did not take on the new religion himself, he allowed his subjects to be converted. These included St Earc, who became Patrick's great friend and follower, and established a **monastery** here on the hill, which eventually evolved into a Franciscan house. Today you can see the extensive remains of its sixteenth-century church and fine bell tower, along with an associated college built around an open quadrangle.

## Francis Ledwidge Museum

1km east of the village centre on the N51 towards Drogheda • Summer daily 10am–5pm; phone for winter hours • €3 • ☎ 041 982 4544, Ⓦ francisledwidge.com

The **Francis Ledwidge Museum** is housed in a simple farm labourer's cottage which, in 1887, was the birthplace of the poet Francis Ledwidge, whose work derived inspiration from the beautiful landscape around his home here, as well as from the history and myth of County Meath. The small museum includes re-creations of the kitchen and the poet's bedroom, some fascinating display boards and a pretty, shady garden out the back. Although a member of the Irish Volunteers, Ledwidge, like 150,000 other Irishmen, joined the British Army in World War I to protect the rights of small nations, to try to secure Home Rule after the end of the war and to fight "an enemy common to our civilization", as he put it. He survived the horrors of Gallipoli in 1915 – the year in which his only volume of poems, *Songs of the Fields*, was published – but was killed by a stray shell at the Third Battle of Ypres in 1917. Inscribed on a plaque by the cottage's front door are the lines written by Ledwidge about his poet friend, Thomas MacDonagh, who was executed by the British for his part in the 1916 Easter Rising:

*He shall not hear the bittern cry*
*In the wild sky, where he is lain,*
*Nor voices of the sweeter birds*
*Above the wailing of the rain.*

## ARRIVAL AND DEPARTURE

SLANE

**By bus** Slane is served by buses from/to Drogheda (7–14 daily; 30min); Dublin (about 20 daily; 1hr); Monaghan (about 20 daily; 1hr); and Trim (4–9 daily; 45min).

## ACCOMMODATION AND EATING

**Conyngham Arms Hotel** Main St ☎ 041 988 4444, Ⓦ conynghamarms.ie. Conveniently located just west of the main crossroads in the centre of the village, this eighteenth-century coaching inn has sixteen individually styled rooms with ornate beds, some four-poster, and nice touches such as blackout curtains, bathrobes, local handmade toiletries and Nespresso machines. Attached is a popular country kitchen restaurant serving excellent food all day. Good weekday rates. **€89**

**George's Patisserie and Deli** 51 Chapel St ☎ 041 982 4493, Ⓦ georgespatisserie.com. Lovely little bakery-café just north of the crossroads on the N2, serving sublime strawberry tarts and chocolate Sachertorte (€3.95), as well as soup (€4.95) and sandwiches (€5.50) on various home-made artisanal breads. Daily 9am–4pm, closed Tues.

**Slane Farm Hostel** Harlinstown House, just over 2km west of the village beyond the castle ☎ 041 988 4985, Ⓦ slanefarmhostel.ie. Comfortable, attractive, en-suite budget accommodation can be found in the converted coach house and stables of this working farm; the hostel also offers a well-equipped kitchen, laundry facilities, camping and self-catering cottages. Camping **€24**, dorms **€22**, doubles **€70**

**Tankardstown** Hotel Rathkenny, 5km north of Slane ☎ 041 982 4621, Ⓦ tankardstown.ie. An elegant eighteenth-century manor house, this upmarket hotel includes an orangery, a fine restaurant, Brabazon, and a central courtyard of cottage suites, which include sitting rooms and kitchens and either one or two bedrooms – ideal for families. Doubles **€260**, cottage suites **€220**

# Brú na Bóinne

8km east of Slane • Visitor centre daily: Feb–April & Oct 9.30am–5.30pm; May & second half of Sept 9am–6.30pm; June to mid-Sept 9am–7pm; Nov–Jan 9am–5pm; last admission 45min before closing; Knowth closed mid-Oct to Easter • Visitor centre €5; joint ticket with Newgrange & Knowth €18 • ☎ 041 988 0300, ⓦ heritageireland.ie; Heritage Card • The last minibuses to Newgrange and to Knowth depart 1hr 45min before closing; for full transport details see page 140

To the east of Slane, between a U-bend in the River Boyne and the N51 to the north, **Brú na Bóinne** (the "palace of the Boyne") encompasses the spectacular 5000-year-old **passage graves** of **Newgrange**, **Knowth** and **Dowth**, high round tumuli raised over stone passages and burial chambers. Entry is funnelled through the impressive **visitor centre** on the south side of the river, which provides detailed information on the significance of the sites, their construction and artwork, and the Neolithic society that created them, as well as housing a **tourist information desk** and café. A footbridge crosses from the centre to the north side of the river, where the compulsory minibuses shuttle you to Newgrange and Knowth, which have both been comprehensively excavated and reconstructed, for **guided tours**. The passage tomb at Dowth, which has been badly damaged by road-builders and cack-handed nineteenth-century archaeologists, is closed to visitors.

Brú na Bóinne is one of Ireland's foremost attractions, and the **numbers** visiting each site daily are strictly limited. Booking by phone isn't possible, so it's advisable to arrive as early in the day as you can and book your places on the minibuses, which have timed departures. There's no point in arriving late in the day, as it takes at least three hours to see Newgrange, Knowth and the visitor centre.

## Newgrange

**Newgrange** is unquestionably the most striking of the Brú na Bóinne mounds, not least because its facade of white quartz stones and round granite boulders has been reassembled. The quartz originally came from Wicklow, the granite from the Mourne and Carlingford areas, exemplifying the mind-boggling levels of resources and organization lavished on this project, by these farmers who used nothing but simple tools of wood and stone. It has been estimated that the tumulus, which is over 75m in diameter, weighs 200,000 tons in total and would have taken around forty years to build. It was the final resting place of a high-status family within the Neolithic community – the cremated remains and grave goods of at least five people were recovered from the burial chamber during excavation – but seems also to have had a wider purpose as a ritual site or gathering place.

The **entrance stone** is one of the finest examples of the art of the tomb-builders, who carved spectacular but enigmatic spirals, chevrons, lozenges and other geometric designs onto many of the large stones around the mound and up the 19m passage. The tomb's pivotal feature, however, is a **roof-box** above the entrance whose slit was perfectly positioned to receive the first rays of the rising sun on the day of the **winter solstice** (December 21); the light first peeps into the cruciform burial chamber itself before spreading its rays along the length of the passage. The engaging guided tour provides an electrically powered simulation in the burial chamber, while tickets for the real thing are decided by lottery each year. To prehistoric farmers, this solstice marked the start of a new year, promising rebirth for their crops and perhaps new life for the spirits of the dead.

It seems probable that by around 2000 BC, in the Late Neolithic or Early Bronze Age, the mound had collapsed and fallen into disuse, but it still provided a powerful focal point for ritual. During this era, a huge religious enclosure known as the **pit circle** was constructed here, consisting of a double circle of wooden posts, within which animals were cremated and buried in pits. To this was added a circle of around 35 **standing stones**, which may have had an astronomical function; about a dozen of them remain upright.

## Knowth

It's well worth signing up for the lively guided tour of **Knowth** too, which provides some telling contrasts with the more famous Newgrange – not least in interpretation: the archaeologist in charge of this site, for example, thought the white quartz stones discovered around the main passage entrance were to reflect the sun, so left them as a shimmering carpet on the ground. The Knowth mound is pierced by two passages, each around twice the length of the Newgrange tunnel, aligned roughly with sunrise and sunset on the equinox days in March and September and leading to back-to-back burial chambers. Unfortunately, it's no longer possible to follow the passages themselves, but the tour takes you inside the mound to look along the eastern tunnel, and you can also climb on top of the mound for views of the Hill of Slane and the Wicklow Mountains.

Knowth is even richer in **Neolithic art** than Newgrange, with about 250 decorated stones discovered here – over half of all known Irish passage-tomb art. The mound is surrounded by over 120 huge kerbstones, one of which supports a carved pattern of crescents and lines that may represent the equinox; elsewhere, patterns of circular and serpentine incisions have been interpreted as local maps, showing the River Boyne and the burial mounds. Hard by the main mound, you can poke around eighteen smaller or **satellite mounds**, at least two of which were built before the main tomb. The Knowth mound attracted habitation in various eras right up until the sixteenth century AD, and your guide will show you several **souterrains**, underground tunnels that were dug in the early Christian period for hiding, escape and possibly food preservation.

### ARRIVAL AND DEPARTURE

BRÚ NA BÓINNE

**By bus** Take Bus Éireann service #100 from Dublin to Drogheda (which is also served by trains from Pearse, Tara Street or Connolly stations), and then the #163 bus to the visitor centre, which connects with the #100 twice a day (Mon–Sat).

**By car** If you have your own transport, follow signs, either from the south side of the bridge in Slane or from the M1 motorway to the southwest of Drogheda, to the visitor centre, which is 2km west of Donore village.

### ACCOMMODATION

**Newgrange Lodge** Just east of the Brú na Bóinne Visitor Centre ☏ 041 988 2478, ⓦ newgrangelodge. com (An Óige & IHO). Occupying a substantially rebuilt farmhouse, *Newgrange Lodge* offers a wide range of attractive and comfortable en-suite budget accommodation with under-floor heating, and extensive communal areas including a well-equipped kitchen and a barbecue area. Dorms €21, doubles €69

**Rossnaree** 2km west of the visitor centre on the Slane road ☏ 041 982 0975, ⓦ rossnaree.ie. This Italianate Victorian country house offers four luxurious, individually styled rooms, as well as art courses and fly-fishing on the estate. Sumptuous breakfasts feature eggs from their own hens, seasonal vegetables from the walled garden, freshly squeezed orange juice and home-made muesli. €150

# The Battle of the Boyne Visitor Centre

Oldbridge, 3km north of Donore Village • Daily May–Sept 10am–4.30pm; Oct–April 9am–4pm • €5; Heritage Card • ☏ 041 980 9950, ⓥ battleoftheboyne.ie • Bus Éireann service #100 from Dublin to Drogheda (which is also served by trains from Pearse, Tara Street or Connolly stations), and then the #163 bus to the visitor centre, which connects with the #100 twice a day (Mon–Sat); can also be reached from Brú na Bóinne by car making for Donore, then heading north for 3km to the river, or from the Drogheda–Slane road (N51) by crossing the Obelisk Bridge

On July 1, 1690 (July 11, 1690 according to our modern, Gregorian calendar, though it's celebrated by Northern Protestants on July 12, after some convoluted mathematical interpretation following the eighteenth-century change to the Gregorian calendar), William III met his father-in-law, the deposed King James II, at the **Battle of the Boyne**, the largest ever set-piece battle on Irish or British soil. At stake were the English throne, now held by the Protestant William with support from the pope and the Catholic king of Spain, and the dominance of Europe by the French, who backed the Catholic James. At the head of an army of 36,000 English, Dutch, Protestant Irish, French Huguenots and Danes, William took up position on the north side of the river just west of Drogheda, while on the opposite bank, James commanded 24,000 men, mostly Irish irregulars, but including seven thousand well-armed French soldiers. To counter William's flanking movement, upriver and around the Knowth mound, James was drawn into sending most of his force westward, which allowed the main Williamite army to cross the river to Oldbridge and put the Jacobite centre to flight. The Irish and French regrouped to carry on fighting for another year, notably at Aughrim and Limerick, but James kept running, via Dublin and Kinsale, to France, never to return.

Oldbridge House, a fine 1740s limestone mansion on the south bank of the River Boyne, houses the **visitor centre**, commemorating the battle and the 1500 men who died. It houses an impressive exhibition, delicately worded but marshalling telling quotes from participants in the battle, and an audiovisual, which puts the blame on the French. Overlooking the walled garden, there's an attractive pavilion café with outdoor tables. Admission is free to the surrounding parkland, which features display boards and five signposted battlefield walks of up to fifty minutes, and on summer Sundays and bank-holiday Mondays you can watch a musketeer and a cavalryman giving hourly "living history" displays on the front lawn.

# Louth, Monaghan and Cavan

CLOUGHOUGHTER CASTLE

# Louth, Monaghan and Cavan

Louth, Monaghan and Cavan all share a border with Northern Ireland and, as throughout the North, still bear many signs of the Plantation in the form of grand country estates (known simply as "big houses") and planned towns. Louth is Ireland's smallest county and the most northerly in the Leinster province, and much of its activity is focused on the historic town of Drogheda, set on the banks of the Boyne, whose fertile valley also boasts major religious sites at Monasterboice and Mellifont.

In Lough's northeast the **Cooley Peninsula** provides somewhat dramatic relief from the county's otherwise drab coastline and played an active role in the greatest of Irish mythological epics, the *Táin Bó Cúailnge* (Cattle Raid of Cooley; see page 152).

The topography of **Monaghan** and **Cavan**, both in Ulster, is markedly different. Monaghan's landscape is characterized by eruptions of small hills, known as drumlins, and its sense of life is encapsulated in the writing of Patrick Kavanagh from **Inniskeen**. Monaghan's few towns offer little of interest, though the busy **county town** itself is attractively laid out and features a few buildings of note, plus one of the region's best festivals. To the southeast, the hilltop market town of **Clones** is a former ecclesiastical centre and also strongly associated with Irish lace-making. To Monaghan town's north lies **Glaslough**, an estate village set around the grandiose **Castle Leslie**.

In contrast, much of Cavan is defined by its waterways and small lakes, offering a multitude of choices for anglers. The **Shannon–Erne Waterway** offers the most readily navigable route through the lakes, for which **Belturbet** provides a good starting point. Away from the major roads that pierce both Monaghan and Cavan, the countryside has an unhurried charm, though it's easy to get lost when navigating its tangled grid of lanes without a map or compass. **Cavan** town itself is agreeable enough, but offers little to warrant more than a passing visit. The county's west provides some stark and rugged landscapes, ideally explored via the **Cavan Way**, which passes through **Cavan Burren**, a stunning limestone plateau scattered with prehistoric monuments.

Most of the attractions in Louth (which has rail links to Dublin and Belfast) and Monaghan are easily accessible by **public transport**, but bus services in Cavan are somewhat less frequent.

## Drogheda and around

**DROGHEDA** (pronounced "droch – as in loch – edda") was once two separate Viking settlements, huddled together on either side of the River Boyne. These developed into twin towns during the Anglo-Norman period, whose intermittent rivalry was quashed by a royal charter uniting the pair in 1412. The town incurred the most infamous onslaught of Cromwell's Irish campaign of 1649 when its defending garrison and many inhabitants were massacred by the Lord Protector's army.

Drogheda's attractions lie both sides of the **River Boyne**. The walled town, which developed in the late medieval period, became one of Ireland's most important religious and political centres – the parliament would occasionally convene in Drogheda – and a few remnants from this time are still visible. Later constructions by the town's Protestant middle classes, such as the **Tholsel** and **courthouse**, reflect a burgeoning confidence enhanced by Drogheda's growing importance as a manufacturing town, thriving on the export of linen, shoes and alcohol. Its old **docks**, which were once the focus for the numerous trades that developed here during the eighteenth and

# Highlights

**❶ Drogheda** One of Ireland's liveliest towns, rich in antiquities and with an array of atmospheric pubs. See page 144

**❷ Monasterboice** Ecclesiastical relics here include Ireland's tallest round tower and also two of the most splendid high crosses in the whole of the country. See page 150

**❸ The Cooley Peninsula** Closely associated with the Irish epic saga, the *Táin Bó Cúailnge*, Cooley's mountains offer tremendous views of Carlingford Lough, while Carlingford itself has some terrific restaurants. See page 151

**❹ Inniskeen** The birthplace of one of the country's greatest poets, Patrick Kavanagh, celebrates its scion through an excellent and informative resource centre. See page 156

**❺ The Lakes of Cavan** Known collectively as Lough Oughter and linked by an extraordinary complex of atmospheric waterways, this is perfect walking territory. See page 158

**❻ Cavan Burren** This magnificent prehistoric landscape is replete with archaeological and geological treasures, as well as providing splendid views of the surrounding countryside. See page 159

HIGHLIGHTS ARE MARKED ON THE MAP ON PAGE 146

# LOUTH, MONAGHAN AND CAVAN

## HIGHLIGHTS

1 Drogheda
2 Monasterboice
3 The Cooley Peninsula
4 Inniskeen
5 The Lakes of Cavan
6 Cavan Burren

N

Belfast

IRISH SEA

DOWN

MOURNE MOUNTAINS

Greencastle
Carlingford Lough
Rostrevor
Warrenpoint
Omeath
Carlingford
Cooley Peninsula
Dundalk Bay
Dunany Point
Clogher Head
Newry
A2
IV

ARMAGH

Armagh
A28
A3

Crossmaglen
N53
Dundalk
M1
N52
N52
RJ32

**3** Carlingford

**1** Drogheda
**2** Monasterboice
Mellifont Abbey
Collon
Slane
N2

LOUTH

Ardee
N2

**4** Inniskeen
N2
Carrickmacross
RJ78
RJ80
RJ81
Lough Muckno

MEATH

Kells
N3
Navan
M3

N12
Monaghan
N2
N54

MONAGHAN

Glaslough
N2
A28

Clones
RJ89
RJ83
R180
R192
R165
R188
RJ95

CAVAN

Cavan
N3
Ballyjamesduff
R154
Lough Sheelin
N55

FERMANAGH

Enniskillen
M
Ulster Way
Upper Lough Erne

Belturbet
Milltown
Ballyconnell
Killeshandra
Lough Oughter
**5** KILLYKEEN FOREST PARK
R199

Bawnboy
R200

Belcoo
Lough Macnean
**6** Blacklion
Cavan Way
Dowra
Lough Allen

LEITRIM

Ballinamore
Shannon–Erne Waterway
Carrick-on-Shannon

LONGFORD

Lough Gowna
Edgeworthstown
N4
Longford
N5
Dromod

WESTMEATH

ROSCOMMON

Lough Boderg

Sligo

0   15
kilometres

nineteenth centuries, are now being regenerated with vitality, while the town itself sports some prominent sights. Drogheda also plays host to one of Ireland's most colourful events, the **Irish Maritime Festival** (ⓦmaritimefestival.ie) in June, the highlight of which is a magnificent flotilla of Tall Ships sailing down the Boyne.

To the north of Drogheda lie the remains of the monasteries of **Monasterboice** and **Mellifont**, two of Ireland's most significant ecclesiastical sites, the former including a superb high cross and the latter providing ample evidence of its erstwhile power and importance.

## Tholsel, St Laurence Gate and Magdalene Tower

Positioned at the junction of West Street and Shop Street is the eighteenth-century **Tholsel**, the former town hall, a solid limestone building topped by a domed tower which features a four-faced clock; it now houses the tourist office (see page 149). A short distance east from here is **St Laurence Gate**, one of the few vestiges of the town's medieval walls. This imposing barbican, with its two tall rounded towers, once housed a portcullis protecting the tollgate just within; unfortunately, it's not open to visitors. Another dominant structure lies a little to the northwest of St Laurence Gate, in the shape of the two-storey **Magdalene Tower**, the erstwhile belfry and only remnant of a large Dominican friary founded here around 1224 by the Archbishop of Armagh, Lucas de Netterville.

## The Highlanes Gallery

36 Laurence St • Wed–Sat 10.30am–4.30pm • Free • ☎ 041 980 3311, ⓦ highlanes.ie

Housed in a former Franciscan church a few paces down from St Laurence Gate, the enlightening **Highlanes Gallery** features works from the municipal collection (dating from the seventeenth century) as well as a rolling programme of temporary exhibitions, taking in everything from sculpture and installations to children's art. In an unusual aside, you'll also find here the sword and mace presented to Drogheda by William of Orange shortly after the Battle of the Boyne.

## St Peter's Church (Church of Ireland)

St Peter's Place, Peter St

**St Peter's Church** (Church of Ireland) is a graceful mid eighteenth-century edifice whose porch and spire were added by the renowned Irish architect Francis Johnston in 1793. The church replaced the original thirteenth-century structure whose stone steeple was blown down by a violent storm in 1548 and subsequently refurbished with a wooden replacement. During the massacre that followed the 1649 siege of the town, many people sought sanctuary in the steeple but perished when Cromwell's troops set it ablaze.

## St Peter's Church (Roman Catholic)

West St

The town's other **St Peter's Church** (Roman Catholic) is a solidly neo-Gothic late nineteenth-century structure topped by an elegant spire and accessed via a sweeping stone stairway. Its interior is equally impressive, featuring stout granite pillars and walls of Bath stone, and just off its left-hand aisle is a small shrine devoted to **Oliver Plunkett**, Archbishop of Armagh and Primate of All Ireland from 1670. Towards the end of that decade, at a time of widespread anti-Catholic feeling in England, Titus Oates, a former Anglican clergyman and convicted perjurer who had earlier converted to Catholicism, hatched a fabricated claim (which became known as the Popish Plot) that the pope was preparing to invade the country and had installed Plunkett as one of the main organizers of the papal army. Plunkett was arrested and put on trial in Dundalk, but, when the jury failed to convict him, was moved first to Dublin and then to Newgate prison in London. Found guilty of treason on July 1, 1681, he was hanged, drawn and quartered, and his remains were thrown onto a fire, but his head and other parts of his body were rescued. The head finally arrived back in Ireland around 1722, following a circuitous route via Rome, and is now contained in a silver-ornamented box within the shrine – grisly indeed. The other parts of Plunkett's body on view (essentially a few bones) weren't returned until after his canonization in 1975 – here too is the door of his cell from Newgate prison.

## Millmount Hill

Rising high above the south bank of the Boyne is **Millmount Hill**. The hill features strongly in Irish mythology, supposedly being the burial place of the Celtic poet Amergin, while its strategic value was quickly recognized by the Anglo-Normans who constructed a motte here in the late twelfth century. Subsequently, a **castle** was erected – which in later years provided the fiercest resistance to Cromwell during the 1649 siege.

### Martello Tower

Mon–Sat 10am–5.30pm, Sun 2–5pm • €6 with Drogheda Museum • ☎ 041 983 3097, ⓦ droghedamuseum.ie

In 1808 the old fortifications were replaced by the barracks and **Martello tower** which stand here today. The tower was severely damaged by shelling during the 1922 Civil War, though it has since been restored. Inside, there's an impressive display of weaponry, but a better reason to visit is for the unhindered **views** of the town.

## Drogheda Museum Millmount

Barrack St • Mon–Sat 10am–5.30pm, Sun & public hols 2–5pm • €6 with Martello Tower • ☎ 041 983 3097, ⓦ droghedamuseum.ie

The barracks square houses the **Drogheda Museum Millmount**, featuring a somewhat random, though occasionally stimulating, assemblage of local artefacts. The highlight is the Banners room, where you'll find a splendid collection of banners, many over two hundred years old and which represent the various crafts and trades that operated hereabouts in the late eighteenth and early nineteenth centuries; three guild banners (representing weavers, carpenters and shoemakers) stand out – these are supposedly the only remaining ones in Ireland. Elsewhere, Drogheda's manufacturing history considers, among other things, the town's erstwhile role as a major producer of alcoholic beverages, when there were once no fewer than fourteen breweries and sixteen distilleries.

### ARRIVAL AND DEPARTURE

DROGHEDA

**By train** The train station (☎ 041 983 8749) is half a mile southeast of town, just off Dublin Rd.

Destinations Belfast (7 daily; 1hr 40min); Dublin (Mon–Sat every 20–30min, Sun hourly; 30min–1hr); Newry (7 daily; 40min).

**By bus** The bus station (☎ 041 983 5023) is on Donore Rd, just south of the river.

Destinations Matthews: Dublin (Mon–Sat hourly, Sun 10; 1hr).

Bus Éireann: Collon for Mellifont (Mon–Sat hourly; 15min); Donore for Newgrange (Mon–Sat 2 daily; 10min); Navan (Mon–Sat 8 daily, Sun 4; 30–55min).

### INFORMATION AND TOURS

**Tourist office** Inside the Tholsel on West St (Mon–Fri 9.30am–5.30pm, plus Sat March–Sept; ☎ 041 987 2843, ⓦ drogheda.ie).

**Bike rental** Useful for getting to either Monasterboice or Mellifont Abbey, bikes can be rented from Quay Cycles at 11a North Quay (☎ 041 983 4526; €15/day).

**Walking tours** Guided tours of the town are organized through the Drogheda Museum Millmount, but only for groups of eight or more (1hr 30min; €5; ☎ 041 983 3097).

### ACCOMMODATION

SEE MAP PAGE 148

**The D** Scotch Hall, Marsh Rd ☎ 041 987 7700, ⓦ thed hotel.com. Very style-conscious riverside establishment providing swish rooms of handsome proportions – some with balcony – alongside a convivial waterside bar and restaurant. Plenty of off-season and early-booking bargains on offer. €110

**Scholars Townhouse Hotel** King St ☎ 041 983 5410, ⓦ scholarshotel.com. The handsome redbrick frontage of this renovated former Christian Brothers residence conceals sixteen modestly sized rooms; many of the original features have been retained, including the oak panelling, stained-glass windows and high-coved ceilings, lending substantial charm to the place. Faultless hospitality too. €113

**Spoon and the Stars** 13 St Mary's Terrace ☎ 041 987 3333, ⓦ spoonandthestars.com. Cheerful and relaxed independent hostel on the main N1 road with eight- and ten-bed dorms, as well as a handful of doubles, some with bathrooms. There's also a comfy lounge (with Sky TV and a games console), a little terrace garden, a self-catering kitchen and laundry facilities. Bus #101 from Dublin stops right outside. Breakfast included. Dorms €22, doubles €60

**Westcourt Hotel** 29 West St ☎ 041 983 0965, ⓦ westcourt.ie. The most central of the town's hotels, this comfortable establishment offers variously configured rooms furnished with attractive mahogany beds with deep mattresses and tastefully upholstered chairs. €99

### EATING

SEE MAP PAGE 148

★ **Ariosa** 1 Laurence St ☎ 01 801 0962, ⓦ ariosacoffee. com. This tiny little coffee house across from the Tholsel does the meanest caffeine shot in town; grab a newspaper and a bar stool, and savour a freshly roasted cuppa with a pastry. Mon–Sat 8am–5pm, Sun 10am–5pm.

**Goodwins** Scotch Hall, Marsh Rd ☎ 041 987 7700, ⓦ the dhotel.com. The D hotel's upmarket steakhouse offers more cuts (€26–32) than you can shake a frying pan at, as well as other meaty treats like Leinster lamb rack and roast pork tenderloin – but for a real nosh-up try the bottomless brunch (Sat & Sun noon–3pm; €29.95). Tues–Sat 5–10pm.

**Relish** Highlanes Gallery, 36 Laurence St ☎ 041 980 3295, ⓦ relishcafe.ie. Refreshingly bright, conservatory-style café-deli offering gut-busting breakfasts, light bites (chowder, paninis, sausage rolls) and mains (€12) such as fish cakes with gratin potato and salad – gourmet cakes and superb coffee too. Mon–Wed 9am–7pm, Thurs–Sun 9am–9pm.

★ **Scholars Townhouse Restaurant** King St ☎ 041 983 5410, ⓦ scholarshotel.com. Little has changed, ambience-wise, in this hotel's high-class restaurant over the years, as the oak-panelled walls, painted ceiling (depicting the Battle of the Boyne) and antique-filled cabinets testify. The food,

3

however, is a thoroughly modern affair, so expect the likes of ham hock terrine and pecan crumble, and confit belly pork with black apple butter and hash brown. The three-course lunch menu is terrific value (€29). Daily 5.30–10pm.

## DRINKING
SEE MAP PAGE 148

★ **Clarke's Bar** 19 Peter St ☎ 041 983 6724, ⓦ clarkes ofdrogheda.com. Don't let the tatty exterior fool you: this former grocer's shop, all dark and woody with some very cosy snugs, is a fabulous boozer with bags of charm and plenty of chatter. Regular events too. Mon–Thurs 1–11.30pm, Fri & Sat noon–12.30am, Sun 12.30–11pm.

**Sarsfields** 128 Cord Rd ☎ 041 983 8032. Another inviting old bar, though a bit more low-key than the others in town. Still, some terrific evenings of music await, featuring anything from modern bluegrass to singer-songwriters. Daily 11am–midnight.

# Monasterboice

6km north of Drogheda • Dawn to dusk • Free • Take the Drogheda–Dundalk bus (hourly; 20min) and ask to be set down at the Monasterboice Inn, from where it's an easy 15min signposted walk

**Monasterboice** has an idyllic rural setting and the remains of its monastic settlement – founded in either the eighth or ninth century – include not only one of Ireland's finest **high crosses**, dating from the tenth century, but one of the best-preserved **round towers** in the country too. The two ruined **churches** within the enclosure, which date from the thirteenth century, probably had little connection with the, by then, defunct monastery.

### The crosses

The stocky **St Muiredach's Cross**, just inside the churchyard, manifests an elaborate series of carved panels depicting a variety of biblical events, loosely arranged in supposed chronological order. The base of its **east face** begins in the Garden of Eden, before moving upwards to the stories of Cain and Abel, David and Goliath, Moses bringing water to the Israelites and the Magi bearing gifts for the newborn Christ. Above these, the cross's carved wheel depicts the Last Judgement and the risen multitudes pleading for entry into Heaven. The **west face** depicts events during the later life of Christ, ranging from his arrest at Gethsemane to the Ascension, though the hub of the cross's wheel shows Moses with the Ten Commandments.

The taller **West Cross**, unfortunately chipped at its top, features another array of biblical scenes, though erosion makes most of them indecipherable. Certainly, its **east face** features David and the lion, and the **west** includes the Resurrection, but much of the remainder is difficult to discern. Adjacent to the West Cross is what's reckoned to be the tallest **round tower** in Ireland, standing at some 30m high, though it has long since lost its conical cap and cannot be entered for safety reasons.

# Mellifont Abbey

R168, 10km northwest of Drogheda • May–Sept daily 10am–6pm • €5; Heritage Card • ☎ 041 982 6103, ⓦ mellifontabbey.ie • The infrequent Drogheda–Collon bus stops at Monleek Cross, from where it's a 3km walk

Founded in 1142 by St Malachy, **Mellifont Abbey** was the first and subsequently most important Cistercian foundation in Ireland, eventually heading an affiliation of more than twenty monasteries. Set in a tranquil spot by the River Mattock, Mellifont must once have been a hugely impressive complex, though its scant ruins leave much to the imagination. After the Reformation the abbey passed into the hands of Edward Moore, who converted its buildings into a fortified residence. Here, in 1603, the great Irish chieftain **Hugh O'Neill** was besieged by Lord Mountjoy until starvation forced his surrender. During the Battle of the Boyne, William of Orange based himself at Mellifont, after which the property was abandoned and fell ultimately into dilapidation. It eventually passed into the hands of the Office of Public Works in the late twentieth century.

## The site

Before touring the remains, take in the small exhibition in the **visitor centre** by the entrance, which details the foundation's history and provides a scale model of the abbey's layout. Entrance to the site is via the church's **north transept**, which features the remains of two stone *piscinae* – sinks for cleaning sacred serving vessels. As the church was built on sloping ground the broad nave has an uncommon feature, a crypt constructed to ensure it remained level. Next to the **south transept** stood the chapterhouse, whose floor features medieval glazed tiles, though some of these have been brought here from other parts of the abbey.

The tallest and finest remnant of the abbey stands in its expansive cloister garth, a remarkable, octagonal arched **lavabo**, with fountains and basins where the monks would wash. Behind the lavabo, the southern ruins included both the calefactory (or warming house), the only heated room in the entire complex, and the refectory. The remaining ruins rarely rise above knee height, and you'll need to consult the various display-boards or buy the visitors' guide to interpret them.

# The Cooley Peninsula

The **Cooley Peninsula** is Louth's most hyped tourist destination, and while it's true that the mountains and surrounding rich verdure offer great walking territory and many a stunning seascape, the countryside lacks the raw, rugged and often downright exhilarating feel of the Mournes (see page 535) over the other side of **Carlingford Lough**. That said, there's still plenty here to delight, even if **Carlingford** village itself has somewhat meretriciously cashed in on its waterside location.

If you start from Dundalk, look out for signs to the *Ballymascanlon Hotel*, a kilometre or so after the R173 turn-off from the N1. A footpath from the hotel's car park runs beside the golf course to the **Proleek Dolmen**, a regular photographic feature in tourist brochures. Perched on the points of three triangular stones, its massive capstone weighs a remarkable 46 tons and, having inspected the scene, you'll probably spend the rest of the day wondering about the ingenuity of prehistoric hoisting engineers.

## Carlingford

Set a short distance back from the lough's southern shore, the trim and charming former fishing village of **CARLINGFORD** is by far the best base for exploring the peninsula. Its tight and tortuous streets reflect its medieval origins and house a host of places where you can eat, drink and sleep; indeed the village has quite a reputation – surprisingly, perhaps – for being a bit of a party place at weekends, so be prepared for big crowds and

---

### WALKS ON THE COOLEY PENINSULA

The varied terrain of the Cooley Peninsula offers a range of opportunities for **walking**, whether in the hills (often with sumptuous views across the lough to the Mournes), by the shore or along lush valleys. The longest waymarked walk is the 40km **Táin Way**, which takes a circular route around Slieve Foye (587m), up to the west above Carlingford village. Count on two days to complete this – you'll need proper walking equipment and clothing, adequate supplies of food and drink and the Ordnance Survey of Ireland Discovery map #36. A fabulous coastal path is the 7km-long **Carlingford–Omeath Greenway**, which tracks the old Dundalk, Newry and Greenore railway and is open to both walkers and cyclists. Otherwise, there are plenty of other walks that are easily accessible from Carlingford village; the useful **Cooley Walks pamphlet**, available for €4.50 from the tourist office in Carlingford outlines ten scenic walks in the area, ranging from one to four hours in duration.

## TÁIN BÓ CÚAILNGE (THE CATTLE RAID OF COOLEY)

The location of many an Irish legend is still immediately identifiable thanks to a wealth of extant place names, and perhaps no more so than in the case of the **Táin Bó Cúailnge**. Set around 500 BC, many of the events in perhaps the greatest of the Celtic epics clearly take place in the mountains of the Cooley Peninsula. The villainess of the tale is **Medb**, the great Queen of Connacht, who so envies her husband Aillil's White Bull (Finnbenach) that she determines to capture the Brown Bull of Cooley (Donn Cúailnge). Drawing Aillil into her campaign, she begins a war against the east of Ireland, targeting Ulster in particular. All the Ulster men are rendered immobile by a curse except the tale's hero, **Cúchullain**, who is left to confront Medb's armies single-handedly. Much of the plot concerns his feats and victories, often achieved in bloodthirsty fashion, and the text is also brought to life by vivid topographical detail. The first known written version of the saga was included in the twelfth-century **Book of the Dun Cow**, and Thomas Kinsella's twentieth-century English translation encapsulates much of the vivacity of the Irish-language version (see page 608).

no little noise. Moreover, this is not a place for the light of purse or pocket: prices here are significantly higher than elsewhere in the county or across the water in Down.

Carlingford's name is Old Norse in origin, deriving from "Kerlingfjörthr" (the fjord of the hag-shaped rock), and indicating that this was once a Viking settlement. Standing sentinel by the lough shore is the roofless ruin of **King John's Castle**, so-named after the English king who supposedly stopped in the village for two days in 1210 during the war with the Irish Knights. The village itself contains some impressive later buildings, not least the **Tholsel**, the sole surviving town gate from the fifteenth century, albeit heavily modified in the nineteenth century. Further along, and dating from the same period, stands the **Mint**, a fortified town house where coins were minted from the mid-fifteenth century onwards. Just beyond here you arrive in the market square (as central a point as any in the village) and the substantial ruins of **Taaffes Castle**, another superb medieval remnant, which was most likely a trading depot for the merchant classes.

### ARRIVAL AND DEPARTURE

### CARLINGFORD

**By bus** Buses serving Dundalk (Mon–Sat 7 daily; 55min) and Newry (Mon–Sat 4 daily; 25min) stop outside the old Station House on the waterfront.

**By ferry** The Carlingford car ferry (passengers €1.50, cars €7; ☏086 415 0585, ⓦcarlingfordferry.com) makes the 15min crossing across Carlingford Lough from Greenore,

6km south of Carlingford, to Greencastle, just outside Rostrevor in County Down, thus saving a 40min drive around the coastline; from Greenore, ferries depart on the half hour (Mon–Sat 7.30am–8.30pm, Sun 9.30am–8.30pm), and from Greencastle they depart on the hour (Mon–Sat 7am–8pm, Sun 9am–8pm).

### INFORMATION AND ACTIVITIES

**Tourist office** The tourist office (April–Sept daily 9.30am–5.30pm; Oct–March Mon–Fri same times; ☏042 941 9692, ⓦcarlingford.ie) occupies the restored railway station house on the waterfront. At 2pm on weekends during the summer they offer guided walks of the town (€6); meet in the car park in front of the tourist office.

**Bike rental** On Yer Bike at Carlingford Marina (☏087 992

1559, ⓦonyerbike.ie; €20/day).

**Activities** Carlingford Adventure on Tholsel St (☏042 937 3100, ⓦcarlingfordadventure.com) offers a range of activities, including rock climbing, kayaking, paddle-boarding and ziplining on the Skypark, Ireland's highest zipwire, located just outside the village.

### ACCOMMODATION

**The Bay Tree** 3 Newry St ☏042 938 3848, ⓦbaytree. ie. The *Bay Tree*'s seven rooms offer a high level of comfort, each one vaguely themed on Celtic history. The colour combinations of grey, beige and mauve are tasteful enough, while the smart furnishings include sturdy wooden

bedsteads and wood-framed mirrors. **€89**

★ **Ghan House** Just below the Heritage Centre ☏042 937 3682, ⓦghanhouse.com. Sitting pretty behind a high-walled garden, *Ghan House* is a beautifully kept eighteenth-century building with twelve exquisitely furnished rooms

bursting with antiques and family heirlooms – eight of these are garden rooms, all with mountain views. There is also an exceptionally good restaurant. €105
**Mourneview** Belmont, 2km south of Carlingford ☎ 042 937 3551, ⓦ mourneviewcarlingford.com. A welcome antidote to the hustle and bustle of the village itself, this charmingly run B&B sits in perfect rural isolation with delightful mountain views from its six neat rooms. €90

### EATING AND DRINKING

**The Bay Tree** 3 Newry St ☎ 042 938 3848, ⓦ baytree.ie. Almost on a par with *Ghan House*, the *Bay Tree*'s sparkling restaurant offers a thoughtfully crafted menu with fish to the fore – the Carlingford Oysters three ways (€10) is the perfect starter – though there's plenty more besides, such as pork belly with creamed cabbage and black pudding bon bon (€24). Wed–Sat 6–9pm, Sun 1–7.30pm.

★ **Ghan House** Just below the Heritage Centre ☎ 042 937 3682, ⓦ ghanhouse.com. The undoubted culinary star in Carlingford is *Ghan House*, which serves modern Irish cuisine over a variety of fixed menus – including a four-course restaurant menu (€55) and a six-course midweek tasting menu (Tues–Thurs 6–7.30pm; €45) – plus a three-course Sunday lunch (€33). Dishes might include treacle-cured salmon with saffron ice cream, followed by Mourne mountain lamb with artichoke and pearl barley, with ingredients from their own herb and vegetable gardens. Top class. Daily 6–9.30pm.

**PJ O'Hares** Tholsel St ☎ 042 937 3106, ⓦ pjohares carlingford.ie. The liveliest of the village's many pubs (and that's saying something), *PJ*'s is a rambling, old-fashioned grocery-cum-pub with a warren of bars frequented by a good-natured crowd; live music or DJs at least four nights a week. Daily 11am–11.30pm, Fri & Sat until midnight.

**Ruby Ellens** Newry St ☎ 042 937 3385, ⓦ rubyellens. com. An absolute gem of a tea house, from the floral-patterned cushions and fresh flowers on the tables to an outstanding range of thirst-quenching brews, served in exquisite china teacups, and assorted lip-smacking cakes. At just €14.95, afternoon tea is a good punt. Daily 9am–6pm.

# Monaghan town

All the elements of post-Plantation urban planning are well to the fore in **MONAGHAN TOWN**, which derived its prosperity from the linen industry and was long the base of a British garrison. The hub of the town plan is the **Diamond**, in whose centre stands the Rossmore monument, a flamboyant nineteenth-century drinking fountain. A short distance west is **Church Square**, dominated by an impressive obelisk commemorating a garrison member who died at the Battle of Inkerman, and is surrounded by stately, early nineteenth-century buildings, including a Neoclassical courthouse, a very fetching Regency Gothic church and an appropriately sturdy bank. Just downhill from here on Market Street is the late eighteenth-century **Market House**, a charming, arched limestone edifice whose exterior is embellished with exquisite carvings of oak apples and leaves; now home to the tourist office, it also hosts occasional arts and literary events. If you're in the region at the beginning of September, the rocking **Harvest Blues Festival** (ⓦ harvestblues.ie) is well worth checking out.

## Monaghan County Museum

1–2 Hill St • Mon–Fri 11am–5pm, Sat noon–5pm • Free • ☎ 047 82928, ⓦ monaghan.ie/museum

To gain some understanding of the area's development, make tracks for the wonderful **Monaghan County Museum**, just behind the Market House. A hugely rich and varied collection begins with some superb archaeological finds, notably the remarkably well-preserved Lisdrumturk cauldron, made from beautifully riveted bronze sheets. The most exceptional exhibit, however, is the fourteenth-century **Cross of Clogher**, a glorious, finely worked oak cross encased in bronze and adorned with bosses and panels, the uppermost of which depicts the Crucifixion. There's also comprehensive coverage of the county's various crafts and industries – many now sadly defunct – most notably **lace**, which was especially prominent in nearby Clones (see page 155).

### ARRIVAL AND INFORMATION                    MONAGHAN TOWN

**By bus** Monaghan's bus station (☎ 047 82377) is on North Rd, a 5min walk north of Church Square.

Destinations Bus Éireann: Cavan (Mon–Fri 7 daily, Sat & Sun 4–5 daily; 55min); Clones (Mon–Fri 4 daily, Sat 2;

30min); Letterkenny (8 daily; 1hr 50min).

Ulsterbus: Armagh (Mon–Sat 10 daily, Sun 4; 30–45min); Belfast (Mon–Sat 2 daily; 1hr 45min); Omagh (3 daily; 55min).

**Tourist office** The seasonal tourist office is located in the Market House on Market St (June–Sept Mon–Fri 10am–

1pm & 2–5pm, Sat 1–5pm; ☏ 047 81122, ⊛ monaghan tourism.com). At 11am every Saturday between April and September, there are free 1hr 30min guided walking tours of the town, departing from the *Westenra Arms Hotel* on the Diamond.

### ACCOMMODATION AND EATING

**Andy's** 12 Market St ☏ 047 82277, ⊛ andysrestaurant. ie. If you like chicken, then this is the place to come: their garlic chicken with sweet sherry, or chicken fillet with tangy mushrooms and onion sauce (€17.95) – which has been on the menu for the best part of 40 years – are just two options. Tues–Fri 4–9.30pm, Sat 2–9.30pm, Sun 11.30am–8.30pm.

**Coffee Break with Barbara** 14 Church Square Yard ☏ 047 72799. Secreted away in a tiny courtyard next to the courthouse, this happy little café serves the tastiest coffee in town, while carbon filament bulbs, chipboard tables and corner sofas make for a cosy ambience. Mon–Fri 8.30am–

5pm, Sat 9am–5pm.

**Grove Lodge** Old Armagh Rd ☏ 047 84677, ⊛ grove lodge-bnb.com. Large and modern family home a 10min walk southeast of the centre, with three pleasant en-suite rooms: two doubles and one family. **€70**

**The Hillgrove Hotel** Old Armagh Rd, half a mile east of town ☏ 047 81288, ⊛ hillgrovehotel.com. Fortunately, the gaudily designed reception area doesn't extend to the rooms, which are far more tasteful, as well as being spacious and well furnished. There's an outstanding spa facility for guest use too. **€99**

# County Monaghan

What few other sites Monaghan does have, besides Monaghan town, are dispersed around and about the county. In the north and west respectively, **Glaslough** and **Clones** both merit brief visits, while fans of Patrick Kavanagh can acquaint themselves with his work in **Inniskeen**, to the southeast.

## Glaslough

Eleven kilometres northeast of Monaghan lies the somewhat otherworldly estate village of **GLASLOUGH**, dominated by a lengthy Famine wall (see page 575) which surrounds the estate of **Castle Leslie**. The Leslie family can reputedly trace back its origins to Attila the Hun and arrived in Ireland in 1633 in the shape of John Leslie who had been appointed Bishop of Raphoe. A colourful character, Leslie became known as the "fighting bishop", thanks to his victory as leader of an army over Cromwell at the Battle of Raphoe. When Charles II was restored to the throne, Leslie received £2000 as a reward for loyalty and used the sum to purchase Glaslough Castle and its demesne in 1665. His descendants have remained in occupation ever since and have included some equally intriguing figures. John Leslie's son Charles was charged with high treason for arguing a little too strenuously against the penal laws, but escaped and fled to France. Subsequently pardoned by George I, he returned to Glaslough where his children often entertained **Jonathan Swift**, who was not always complimentary about them in return:

*Here I am In Castle Leslie*
*With Rows And Rows Of Books Upon The Shelves*
*Written By The Leslies*
*All About Themselves.*

The current and very grand castle was built in the late nineteenth century and the family became connected by marriage to the Churchills – both Randolph and Winston stayed here. Later owners included Desmond Leslie, a former RAF pilot who authored *Flying Saucers Have Landed*, a supposedly factual account of the first alien contact with humans. His daughter now runs the castle. Even if you're not staying here, you're free to wander around the estate, which has one of the finest **equestrian centres** in the country (€40 for a 1hr hack or €50 for a 45min lesson); you can also boat, fish and kayak on the lake.

## ACCOMMODATION AND EATING
**GLASLOUGH**

★ **Castle Leslie** ☎ 047 88100, ⓦ castleleslie.com. Often patronized by the rich and famous, *Castle Leslie* is an utterly majestic – though thoroughly unpretentious – place to stay. In the castle itself, accommodation consists of a range of sumptuously decorated and themed rooms, some defined by colour and others by historical reference (the Mediterranean room with its stone bed is brilliant), while *The Lodge*, which backs on to the stables, offers more contemporary rooms, though still imbued with spades of charm. *The Lodge* also accommodates the refined *Snaffles* restaurant, which offers an evening menu (€68) starring the likes of glazed pork cheek with spiced squash purée, and roast fillet of halibut with Portavogie prawns and comté cheese foam, and the buzzy *Conor's Bar*, where a three-course menu costs a very reasonable €30. You could also stop by for afternoon tea (€25). Snaffles restaurant daily 6–9.30pm; Conor's Bar daily 11am–9pm. Lodge €150, castle €180

# Clones

**3**

Near the border with Fermanagh, the town of **CLONES** (pronounced "clo-nez") lies 20km southwest of Monaghan town, overlooking drumlin country from its hilltop perch. Being right on the border, Clones was hit hard during the Troubles, and today feels a little neglected, though it does merit a brief stop if passing through. It's also the location for one of the country's best small **film festivals** (ⓦ clonesfilmfestival.com), held at the end of October. Points of interest in the town include a ninth-century **round tower** – originally five storeys high – and a richly carved **high cross**, which stands in the Diamond, somewhat overshadowed by the sombre shape of **St Tiernach's Church** (Church of Ireland). The cross's front panels depict scriptural scenes, such as the Garden of Eden, while the reverse is devoted to scenes from Christ's life.

## Cassandra Hand Centre
Ball Alley Lane • Mon–Fri 10.30am–3.30pm • Free • ☎ 047 52997, ⓦ cassandrahandcentre.com

A five-minute walk south of the Diamond, the **Cassandra Hand Centre** is named after the founder of Clones Lace, whose profits went into the construction of a school here in 1859; the building functioned as such up until the beginning of World War I. Its main role these days is as a genealogy centre, but it's worth popping in to view the mock-up classroom and the exhibition on local folk who made good – perhaps the most notable of these is the boxer Barry McGuigan, World Featherweight champion in 1985.

---

### CLONES LACE

The area around Clones has a strong tradition of **lace-making**, a generally home-based industry which, at its peak in the 1850s, saw more than 1500 workers supplying markets as far afield as Paris, Rome and New York. Passed on from mother to daughter, the lace-making craft was introduced to Clones by the wife of the local Church of Ireland rector, Cassandra Hands, as a means of supplying income in the desperate post-Famine times. Rather than following the time-consuming Venetian needlework style, Clones women opted for a crochet hook as a means of expediency, and began producing work embellished by the flora of their local environs, often characterized by the multi-twirled **Clones knot**. Clones lace was embroidered into blouses and dresses, but its own elaborate style was gradually replaced by simpler designs. Nevertheless, it remains an important local tradition and, in 1989, a co-operative was established to reinvigorate the craft. There are still several lace-makers in the area and some of their work is on display at the **Ulster Canal Stores** (see page 156), where you can also purchase some of their wares.

## Ulster Canal Stores

Cara St • Tues–Sat 9.30am–5.30pm • Free • ☎ 047 52125, ⓦ ulstercanalstoresvisitorcentre.ie

Heading further out of town on the road towards Cavan, you'll pass the **Ulster Canal Stores**, which once served as the distribution centre for wares arriving in Clones by water. Trade on the canal, which connected Belfast to Lough Erne, peaked in the 1890s, but competition from the railways led to the canal's demise, and it eventually closed in 1931. Nowadays it functions as a visitor centre with a fabulous **museum** dedicated to Clones lace alongside the history of the town; there's a welcoming little café here too.

### ARRIVAL AND INFORMATION CLONES

**By bus** Bus Éireann: Armagh (Mon–Sat 3 daily, Sun 1; 1hr); Cavan town (Mon–Sat 3 daily, Sun 1; 30min); Monaghan town (Mon–Sat 2 daily, Sun 1; 25min). Ulsterbus: Enniskillen (Mon–Sat 4–6 daily, Sun 1; 50min).

**Tourist information** The helpful Ulster Canal Stores can furnish you with any information you might need; they also offer free guided tours of the town at 11am every Sat between May and October.

### ACCOMMODATION AND EATING

**Adamson Bar** Analore St ☎ 047 81789, ⓦ briana damsons.ie. The pick of Clones' drinking dens by virtue of its traditional music sessions on Fridays and Saturdays. Daily 11am–11pm.

**Creighton Hotel** Fermanagh St ☎ 047 51055, ⓦ creightonhotel.ie. The only hotel in town is this spruce nineteenth-century building at the bottom of the street, with tip-top, though really rather overpriced, rooms. Its restaurant and bar are easily the best places to eat in town. **€100**

**Cuil Darach** Fermanagh St ☎ 047 52147, ⓦ cuildarach. com. B&B above a pub/restaurant, with standard pine-furnished rooms; the restaurant itself offers a menu of attractively sauced chicken and steak dishes (mains from around €10), though it's more fun to eat in the bar. **€80**

# Inniskeen

Best accessed from Dundalk, a dozen kilometres east, the village of **INNISKEEN** was the birthplace of the influential poet and writer **Patrick Kavanagh**, born on a local farm in 1904 (see page 600). The village itself is pretty enough, with plenty of reminders of its ancient past, such as the superb tenth-century round tower and twelfth-century Norman lookout post.

## Patrick Kavanagh Centre

St Mary's Church • Mon–Fri 10am–4.30pm, Sat 11am–4.30pm • €10 • ☎ 042 937 8560, ⓦ patrickkavanaghcentre.com

At the heart of the village stands St Mary's Church, whose annexe houses the revamped **Patrick Kavanagh Centre**, which has stacks of memorabilia related to the poet, including photographs, manuscripts and his death mask, as well as a specially commissioned series of twelve paintings based upon his epic and extraordinarily emotive poem *The Great Hunger*. The centre stages several weekends devoted to poetry and writing, plus an annual weekend in late September celebrating Kavanagh's life and work. His grave, along with that of his wife, can be found in the church cemetery. Otherwise, devotees of the poet can follow a town trail highlighting all the prominent Kavanagh landmarks.

### ARRIVAL AND DEPARTURE INNISKEEN

**By bus** Iniskeen is a 20min bus ride from Dundalk on the Dundalk–Carrickmacross service.

### ACCOMMODATION AND EATING

**Gleneven House** 100m or so towards Dundalk from the Kavanagh Centre ☎ 042 937 8294, ⓦ gleneven.com. The only accommodation in the village is provided by this handsome Georgian house, which has a mix of comfy en-suite and standard rooms. **€70**

**Raglan Road Tea Room** Next to St Mary's Church ☎ 087 212 8868. If you're in need of refreshment, head to this sweet little café for a coffee with cake, a simple breakfast, or a light lunch (around €6–8), surrounded by books and bric-a-brac. Mon–Sat 9.30am–4.30pm.

# Cavan town and around

Nowadays a busy market town, **CAVAN** was once the seat of the O'Reilly clan who built a Franciscan abbey here in 1300, although this succumbed to a fire in 1451. Later, the town itself was razed to the ground in 1576 by a female member of the clan and subsequently rebuilt. Much of what you see today dates from the nineteenth and twentieth centuries and all that remains of the reconstructed abbey is its eighteenth-century **bell tower**, on Abbey Street, standing next to the grave of Owen Roe O'Neill. In truth there's next to nothing to see in Cavan itself, but it does possess a clutch of decent places to sleep and eat, and makes an ideal base from which to explore the county's western reaches.

## ARRIVAL AND INFORMATION — CAVAN TOWN AND AROUND

**By bus** The bus station (☎ 049 433 1353) is at the southern end of Farnham St.

Destinations Bus Éireann: Belturbet (8 daily; 20min); Clones (Mon–Fri 3 daily, Sun 1; 30min); Donegal town (8 daily; 2hr); Dublin (hourly; 2hr); Kells (hourly; 1hr); Monaghan town (Mon–Fri hourly, Sat & Sun 3–4 daily; 55min); Navan (8 daily; 1hr 15min).

Ulsterbus: Clones (Mon–Sat 2 daily; 30min); Monaghan town (Mon–Sat 2 daily; 55min).

**Tourist office and bike rental** The tourist office (April–Sept Mon–Fri 9am–5pm; ☎ 049 433 1942, ⊚ thisiscavan. ie) is 300m northeast of the bus station in the Johnston Library and Farnham Centre, itself part of the county council building. Bikes can be rented from here too.

## ACCOMMODATION AND EATING

**Black Horse Inn** 1 Church St ☎ 049 436 8396, ⊚ the blackhorseinn.ie. A long wooden bar with neon lighting and beer barrels for tables presages the inn's modern restaurant, where you can sample hearty dishes like grilled chicken with a pepper and Jack Daniels sauce (€18.50). Daily 11.30am–11.30pm, Fri & Sat till midnight; food served noon–3pm & 6–10pm.

**Chapter 1** 12 Main St ☎ 049 437 3488, ⊚ chapter1. ie. Old-school decor and a convivial atmosphere contrive to make this place a massive hit, but it's the freshly made New York-style bagels (£6.50) that really pull in the punters; the superb café sessions every other Thursday evening feature live performances. Mon–Sat 8.30am–6pm, Sun 11am–6pm.

**Cherville B&B** Drumalee, a 15min walk southeast of the town centre ☎ 049 437 2855. Super friendly guesthouse with four rooms decorated in deep red, vivid pink and jet black colours, alongside, for example, the occasional zebra print furnishing; a generous tray of sweet and savoury snacks and a cracking breakfast tops it off. **€80**

**Farnham Estate Hotel** 3km southeast of town on the Dublin road ☎ 049 437 7700, ⊚ farnhamestate. ie. Set within the grounds of a vast country estate, this super-luxurious spa hotel is as swish as you'd expect, with rooms in both the Great House itself and in a modern wing. If you fancy a bite to eat, eschew the restaurant and make a beeline for the terrific *Wine Goose Cellar Bar*. **€130**

# Ballyjamesduff

**BALLYJAMESDUFF** is a pleasant, small crossroads town, 15km southeast of Cavan town along back lanes or a little further via the N3. James Duff himself, the Earl of Fife, was an early Plantation landlord of the area, and one of his descendants, Sir James Duff, commanded English troops during the suppression of the 1798 Rebellion – making the more sombre Irish version of his name, "Black Séamus", rather appropriate to local ears.

## Cavan County Museum

Virginia Rd • Tues–Sat 10am–5pm; June–Sept also Sun 2–5.30pm • €6 • ☎ 049 854 4070, ⊚ cavanmuseum.ie

Housed in a former convent, the **Cavan County Museum** has an impressive collection covering all aspects of the county's history. Major items on display include the Killycluggin Stone, dating from 200 BC and decorated in classic Celtic La Tène artwork, and replicas of Celtic stone idols dating from the second century BC to the second century AD, as well as the impressive 1100-year-old Lough Errol **dugout boat**. One room explores the Great Famine with some moving exhibits, including shoes from a famine graveyard, as well as items removed from a famine workhouse near Enniskillen. On a lighter note, also represented here is the painter, poet and songwriter Percy French who worked in the county for a spell as an inspector of drains – one of his more famous comic songs is *Come Back Paddy Reilly to Ballyjamesduff*.

Outside, there's the fun **Trench Experience**, an enormous 350m-long ditch designed to evoke conditions in the trenches during World War I. Complete with barbed wire and mock battlefield – and some clever sound and visual effects – it's impressively authentic. Some 659 men from Cavan perished in the Great War.

# West Cavan

To the west of Cavan town lies the assortment of various-sized lakes that forms the system known as **Lough Oughter**, through which the River Erne contrives to manage a pathway to Upper Lough Erne (see page 565). Roads are few and landmarks limited to the occasional small hill, while the rush-fringed lakes lure many anglers. The land gradually assumes dominance over water west of the hillside town of **Belturbet**, beyond which the inhospitable and bleak strip doglegs between counties Fermanagh and Leitrim, becoming ever craggier as it rises through wild, boggy hills. At the county's northwestern tip, the **Cavan Way** terminates at the tiny border village of **Blacklion**.

## Belturbet and around

One of the most pleasant bases for exploring the lough is **BELTURBET**, some 18km north of Cavan town, a hillside village rising steeply from the River Erne. Very popular with anglers, the village is also a base from which to explore the **Shannon–Erne Waterway**; Aghinver Boats (☎049 952 4775; ⦿abcboats.com) down at the marina rents out three- and six-seater boats for the day (€70–100) between March and October.

### Drumlane Church
1.5km south of Miltown on the R201 from Belturbet

Apart from the delights of lough-side walks, the major source of interest around the lakes is **Drumlane Church**, which enjoys a picturesque setting between two lakes. St Mogue, a pupil of Wales's patron St David, founded a monastery here in the sixth century, while the medieval church is part of an abbey founded here by monks from Kells in County Meath. Now ruined and roofless, the church's west doorway has carved heads of possibly ecclesiastical figures or monarchs, which probably date from the fifteenth century. Nearby, an eleventh-century **round tower** features now barely distinguishable carvings of birds, thought to be a cock and a hen and believed to bear some relevance to the Resurrection.

### ARRIVAL AND DEPARTURE                                    BELTURBET

**By bus** Bus Éireann services depart from outside the post office on The Diamond to Cavan town (7 daily; 20min) and Enniskillen (7 daily; 35min).

### ACCOMMODATION AND EATING

**Church View** 8 Church St ☎049 952 2358, ⦿churchviewguesthouse.com. Located just behind the library, off the main road, this friendly B&B is popular with local fishermen; the seven en-suite rooms are complemented by a guest lounge with complimentary refreshments. **€70**

**The Seven Horseshoes** 12 Main St ☎049 952 2166, ⦿thesevenhorseshoes.com. One of the county's oldest hostelries holds a handful of functional rooms. Better is the warming, brick- and wood-panelled bar, easily the most appealing spot in the village for a bite to eat (it's strong on seafood and steaks) or a pint. Mon–Thurs 10.30am–11.30pm, Fri & Sat 10.30am–12.30am, Sun 12.30–11pm; food served 12.30–4pm & 6–9pm. **€80**

# The Cavan Way and Blacklion

The county's northwestern reaches provide superb walking terrain, best accessed via the signposted 26km **Cavan Way**, which runs through jagged landscapes from Dowra in County Leitrim (see page 404) to the small border village of **Blacklion** where it joins the **Ulster Way**. The hills above Blacklion command dramatic views across Lough Macnean east to Fermanagh's lakelands and west to the mountains of Sligo and Leitrim. About halfway along the route is the **Shannon Pot**, the source of Ireland's longest river but a mere trickle here.

## Cavan Burren Park

3km south of Blacklion • Dawn to dusk • Free • ☎ 049 952 6121, ⓦ cavanburrenpark.ie

Spectacularly sited on the slopes of the Cuilcagh Mountain is the **Cavan Burren Park**, a remarkable limestone plateau where megalithic tombs, cist graves and ancient stone huts comprise a fantastic trove of prehistoric treasures; many examples of rock art have also been identified here. Just beyond the car park, an open-air **visitor centre** outlines the many fascinating features of Cavan Burren, and is the starting point for four short, looped **walks** through the park, ranging from 1.3km to 3km.

### ARRIVAL AND INFORMATION

### THE CAVAN WAY AND BLACKLION

**By bus** Blacklion is served by buses from/to Enniskillen (Mon–Sat 4 daily, Sun 2; 30min) and Sligo (Mon–Sat 4 daily, Sun 2; 1hr).

**Tourist information** Housed inside the Market House building, Blacklion's tourist office (Mon–Fri 9am–5pm, Sat 9am–4pm; ☎ 071 985 3941, ⓦ blackliontouristoffice.com) has stacks of great info on the Cavan Way and Cavan Burren.

### ACCOMMODATION AND EATING

**Keepers Arms** Bridge St, Bawnboy ☎ 049 952 3318, ⓦ keepersarms.com. Located in the village of Bawnboy, on the main road up towards Blacklion, this terrific little inn has nine tidy rooms above a friendly bar. €80

★ **Macnean House** Main St, Blacklion ☎ 071 985 3022, ⓦ nevenmaguire.com. *Macnean House* is run by one of Ireland's best-known chefs, Neven Maguire, whose modern Irish cooking is up there with the finest in the country. Expect scintillating combinations like seared partridge breast with toasted brioche and a game and foie gras terrine, and buttermilk *panna cotta* with poached raspberries. Not cheap, but worth every penny; €98 for the tasting menu and €45 for the Sunday lunch menu. Wed–Sat sittings at 6pm & 9.30pm, Sun lunch sittings at 12.30pm & 3.30pm plus 7–8.30pm.

3

# The Midlands: Westmeath, Longford, Offaly and Laois

CLONMACNOIS

# The Midlands: Westmeath, Longford, Offaly and Laois

Obeying the siren call of the west coast, most foreign tourists, and indeed Irish holiday-makers, put their foot down to motor through the Midlands as quickly as possible. It's true that you're unlikely to want to make a comprehensive tour of the area, but if you fancy a stopover off the main radial routes out of Dublin, there are some compelling sights, and a surprisingly varied landscape, to discover.

The dairy farms of **County Westmeath** (Iarmhí) are interspersed with large, glassy lakes, including Lough Ennell to the south of **Mullingar**, the county town, on whose shores **Belvedere House** is well worth a short detour off the N4. Among the county's more northerly lakes nestle the quirky gardens of **Tullynally Castle** and the pastoral charms of the **Fore Valley**, where you can poke around medieval monastic remains and be entertained by their wondrous legends. The N4 ploughs on through **County Longford** (An Longfort), mostly rich grasslands but blending into Northern Ireland's drumlin country in its northern third. In the south of the county, the **Corlea Trackway Visitor Centre** gives a fascinating glimpse of a prestigious but ill-fated Iron Age road-building project.

The **River Shannon** and its seasonal floodplain delineates most of the Midlands' western border, running down through **Athlone**, a major junction town whose **castle** has been give an excellent, high-tech redevelopment. Just south of here, the major ecclesiastical site of **Clonmacnois** enjoys a dreamy setting above the river's meanders and meadows. Follow the river downstream and you'll come to the neat village of **Shannonbridge**, and once you cross the bridge you'll be in the neighbouring province of Connaught.

Elsewhere, **County Offaly** (Uíbh Fháilí) is known for its bogs, but the charming town of **Birr**, with its imposing castle and Georgian terraces, makes the best base in the Midlands. To its east rises the attractive bulge of **Slieve Bloom**, with a thick topping of blanket bog, beyond which **County Laois** (pronounced "leash") is mostly lush grazing and cereal land.

### Brief history

These counties were mostly beyond the Pale, the enclave around Dublin that the Anglo-Normans retreated to in the fourteenth and fifteenth centuries, and indeed Offaly is named after the *Uí Failí* (O'Connor Faly), Irish chieftains who would attack the Pale and then retreat to their strongholds deep in the boglands. In the sixteenth century, however, this region was fairly comprehensively planted, when land was confiscated from native Irish owners and given to loyal English landlords. In 1541, Westmeath was split off from County Meath, and in 1556 Offaly and Laois were created as "King's County" and "Queen's County", respectively, with the latter's main town named Maryborough (now Portlaoise) after the current monarch. Bypassed by the Industrial Revolution, many of the planned estate-towns that were attached to these landholdings remain to this day, along with the vestiges of a slow, steady rural style of living.

# Mullingar and around

Set in lush cattle-country, **MULLINGAR**, the county town of Westmeath, holds little of interest for visitors, except as a base for visiting **Belvedere House**, a Georgian mansion in a lovely setting on Lough Ennell, or the historically important **Hill of Usineach**.

SEAN'S BAR

# Highlights

❶ **Belvedere House** A beautifully restored Georgian hunting lodge, set in attractive gardens, overlooking Lough Ennell. See page 164

❷ **The Hill of Uisneach** This important prehistoric site is considered by historians to be the symbolic centre of the country. See page 165

❸ **The Fore Valley** Explore the rich ecclesiastical history of this remote, green valley or suspend your disbelief in appreciation of its Seven Wonders. See page 166

❹ **Sean's Bar** Soak up the atmosphere at this ancient and inviting pub in Athlone. See page 171

❺ **Clonmacnois** The Midlands' pre-eminent historical site, a prestigious complex of churches and ornate high crosses overlooking the River Shannon. See page 172

❻ **Birr Castle** Wander around the huge and varied grounds and immerse yourself in the scientific exploits of the talented Parsons family at the Historic Science Centre. See page 174

**HIGHLIGHTS ARE MARKED ON THE MAP ON PAGE 164**

## Belvedere House

5km south of Mullingar on the N52 • House daily: March–Oct 9.30am–5pm; Nov–Feb 9.30am–4pm; gardens daily: March & Oct 9.30am–6pm; April & Sept 9.30am–7pm; May–Aug 9.30am–8pm; Nov–Feb 9.30am–4.30pm; last admission 1hr before closing • €8; or €4 with an Athlone Castle ticket (see page 168); Heritage Island • ☎ 044 933 8960, ⓦ belvedere-house.ie

Set in abundant gardens on the eastern shore of Lough Ennell, **Belvedere House** was built in the 1740s by Richard Castle as a hunting lodge for Robert Rochfort, later the first Earl of Belvedere, the so-called "Wicked Earl", whose main pastime seems to have been making life hell for his wife and brothers. In 1743 he falsely accused his wife Mary of having an affair with his brother Arthur and imprisoned her for the next 31 years at their nearby main residence, Gaulstown. It was only when the Earl died that she was released by their son, whom she no longer recognized. Meanwhile, the Earl had successfully pressed charges of adultery against Arthur, who, unable to pay the damages of £20,000, lived out his days in debtors' prison.

The **house** itself, which commands beautiful views of the lake, has been painstakingly restored and authentically refurbished by Westmeath County Council.

It holds some gorgeous fireplaces of carved Irish oak with Italian marble insets, but is most notable for the exquisite craftsmanship of its **rococo ceilings**, the work of a French stuccodore, Barthelemij Cramillion. Look out especially for the vivid depictions of the Four Winds, a fire-breathing dragon and a horn of plenty in the dining room, while the library, intended for night-time use, features sleeping cherubs wrapped in a blanket of clouds, a crescent moon and stars, and on the cornice a swirl of flowers with their heads closed.

A feud between Robert Rochfort and his other brother George was behind one of the gardens' main sights, the **Jealous Wall**. When George commissioned Richard Castle in the 1750s to build Tudenham House, a much larger mansion than Belvedere, just 1km away, the Earl of Belvedere spent £10,000 building this huge Gothic folly, three storeys high and nearly 60m long, just to block the view. The extensive woodlands and lawns make for a pleasant stroll: the 45-minute **Earl's Trail**, for example, will take you along the lakeshore and back, past a restored ice-house and follies known as the Octagonal Gazebo and the Gothic Arch.

## The Hill of Uisneach

Near the village of Loughnavalley, 9km miles southwest of Mullingar • Access is by guided tour (2hr, 3km; must be booked in advance); May–Sept daily at 1pm; €15 • ☏ 087 718 9550, ⓦ uisneach.ie

The unprepossessing **Hill of Uisneach** is the ancient seat of the Kings of Meath and a prehistoric meeting place of renown. Its most famous feature is "**The Catstone**", a 6m-high limestone boulder that from certain angles resembles the shape of a cat about to pounce. Sitting at the centre of a low earthen ridge, the stone is known in Irish as *Ail na Mireann*, which translates as the "stone of divisions" – it marks the point where the five ancient provinces of Ireland met, and was considered the symbolic centre of the country. There are now four provinces in Ireland: Ulster, Munster, Leinster and Connaught, but in ancient times there was a **fifth province**, known as **Mide** (now Co. Meath). Celtic mythology recounts that this fifth province could also refer to the magical "otherworld", and the Catstone was regarded as a gateway to it. For these and other reasons, the Hill of Uisneach has played a significant role in the Irish imagination.

Although Uisneach is only 182m at its highest point, on a clear day hills in twenty counties are visible from the summit, with all-encompassing views of the Irish Midlands. You're also surrounded by traces of the past, including a **ring fort** in a figure of eight, **Lough Lugh**, named after the Sun God Lugh, and **St. Patrick's Bed**, a megalithic tomb. The hill is marked by several stretches of lazy-beds where potatoes were grown, and the ruins of small farms abandoned in the exodus from the land during the hard times of the mid-nineteenth century. The tour is along an uneven walking path with a gentle incline to the summit.

### ARRIVAL AND INFORMATION

**By train** Trains on the Dublin–Sligo line stop at the station on the southwest side of the centre.
Destinations Dublin Connolly (6–9 daily; 1hr 15min); Sligo (6–7 daily; 1hr 50min).
**By bus** Most buses call at Castle St right in the heart of town, though some stop only at the train station.

### MULLINGAR AND AROUND

Destinations Athlone (up to 4 daily; 1hr); Dublin (10–21 daily; 1hr 30min); Sligo (5–6 daily; 2hr 20min).
**Tourist information** Market House, around the corner from the Castle St bus stop, on the main Pearse St (Mon–Fri 9.30am–5.10pm; ☏ 044 934 8650).

### ACCOMMODATION

**Greville Arms** Pearse St ☏ 044 934 8563, ⓦ greville armshotel.ie. Bang in the centre of town, this welcoming and refurbished old coaching inn is mentioned in James Joyce's *Ulysses* and boasts a small first-floor museum of local life. The 38 bedrooms are either contemporary and colourful, or plush and traditional with swagged curtains, gilt mirrors and padded headboards on the beds. Good rates for singles. **€90**

**Lough Ennell Caravan Park** 5km south of town off the N52, just beyond Belvedere House ☎ 044 934 8101, ⓦ caravanparksireland.com. Quiet, sheltered and well-equipped lakeside campsite. Surrounded by mature beech, birch, ash, chestnut and oak trees, it comes with a campers' kitchen, laundry, playground, minimart, restaurant and takeaway. Closed Nov–March. **€20**

**Lough Owel Lodge** Culleenmore, 3km north of town off the N4 ☎ 044 934 8714, ⓦ loughowellodge.com. The pick of the B&Bs around Mullingar, a friendly spot on an organic working farm a short stroll from the eponymous lake. The en-suite bedrooms (some with four-poster or half-tester beds) and lounges are large and attractive, and the breakfast is excellent. Family room; very good rates for singles. Closed Nov–March. **€85**

### EATING AND DRINKING

**Dominik's** 37 Dominick St ☎ 044 939 6696, ⓦ dominik srestaurant.ie. Smart and friendly contemporary restaurant that rustles up crowd-pleasing courses such as beef carpaccio with rocket and lemon, and rack of lamb with potato, a two-course main menu costing €21. Tues–Sat 5–10pm, Sun 1–9pm.

**Ilia Café** 28 Oliver Plunkett St ☎ 044 934 7354, ⓦ ilia mullingar.com. Relaxing daytime café where the tasty menu ranges from soups, salads, omelettes, bagels and simple main courses or curries, steaks and chicken wraps (under €11), to cakes and pastries, alongside herbal tea, filtered coffee and freshly squeezed orange juice. Mon–Sat 9am–6pm.

**Oscar's** 21 Oliver Plunkett St ☎ 044 934 4909, ⓦ oscars mullingar.com. Lively and unpretentious restaurant directly opposite *Ilia Café* that's well known locally for its reasonably priced pasta and pizza (around €15), as well as steaks and seafood (around €20–25). Mon–Thurs 6–9.30pm, Fri & Sat 6–10pm, Sun 12.30–2.15pm & 6–8.30pm.

# Castlepollard and around

The far north of Westmeath shelters two compelling and whimsical attractions, the gardens of Tullynally Castle and the Seven Wonders of the Fore Valley, near **Castlepollard**, a pretty eighteenth- and nineteenth-century village laid out around a large triangular green.

## Tullynally Castle

Just over 1km northwest of Castlepollard on the Granard road • Gardens and tea rooms April–Sept Thurs–Sun 11am–5pm • €8 • ☎ 044 966 1856, ⓦ tullynallycastle.ie

**Tullynally Castle** has been the seat of the Anglo-Irish Pakenhams, later Earls of Longford, since the seventeenth century. Remodelled as a rambling Gothic Revival castle to the designs of Francis Johnston in the early 1800s, it remains the family home, open only to pre-booked group visits (minimum twenty people) and for occasional concerts. During summer, the extensive **gardens**, and the Catoca tea rooms – cream teas a speciality – are open to casual visitors. Terraced lawns around the castle overlook parkland, laid out by the first Earl of Longford in 1760. From here winding paths lead through the woodland to lakes, a walled garden with a 200-year-old yew avenue and a limestone grotto, as well as a Chinese garden with a scarlet pagoda and a Tibetan garden of waterfalls and streams.

## The Fore Valley

To the east of Castlepollard off the R195 Oldcastle road, the **Fore Valley** is a charming, bucolic spot, sheltered between two ranges of low, green hills and dotted with some impressive Christian ruins. Around 630, St Fechin founded a monastery here, which had grown into a community of three hundred monks by the time he died in 665. Over the centuries since, various sites in the valley have become associated with Fechin's miraculous powers, known as the **Seven Wonders of Fore**, which, while far from jaw-dropping, do add some fun and interest to an exploration of the locale. All are within walking distance of the village of **Fore** at the heart of the valley.

## The Seven Wonders

To the west of the village, on the south side of the road, stands **St Fechin's Church**, now roofless, the oldest remaining building in the valley, dating probably from the tenth century. The first wonder lies over its main entrance, a massive lintel inscribed with a small cross-in-circle: the **stone raised by St Fechin's prayers**. Up the slope and across from the church, you'll find the **Anchorite's Cell**, a fifteenth-century tower to which the mausoleum chapel of the Greville-Nugent family was added in the nineteenth century (ask for the key behind the bar at the *Seven Wonders* pub in the village, which opens at around 12.30pm). Practising an extreme form of asceticism that was popular in the early and high Middle Ages, anchorites would stay in the tower, meditating and praying alone, with food brought to them by local people, until they died. Inside the chapel, an inscription commemorates the last hermit of Fore, and probably of all Ireland, Patrick Beglin, whose body is "hidden in this hollow heap of stones" – the second wonder, the **anchorite in a stone**. Like the other hermits, Beglin had vowed to remain in the cell until he died: in 1616, he fell trying to climb out, and broke his neck – thus enacting his promise.

Back down the slope and across the road you'll see the **water that will not boil**, a holy well known to cure headaches and toothaches, where in the nineteenth century rites were performed on St Fechin's Day (January 20). In the spring stands a dead ash tree, gaily festooned with sweet wrappers, stockings, knickers and coins (which caused the copper poisoning that killed the tree) – the fourth wonder, the **wood that will not burn**. Nearby, a stream that runs underground from Lough Lene to the south resurfaces at the ruined St Fechin's Mill – the **mill without a race**.

A couple of hundred metres across the marshy valley floor rise the substantial but compact remains of **Fore Priory** – the **monastery built on a bog**. It was erected in the early thirteenth century, one of very few in Ireland to follow the rule of St Benedict, the fifth-century Italian ascetic. Attached to the central cloister, of which several Gothic arches remain, you'll find the church to the north, the chapterhouse to the east, with the dormitory above, and the refectory to the south. A little away from the main buildings, up a small slope, there's a circular, thirteenth-century columbarium, where the monks kept doves, an efficient source of meat in the Middle Ages.

The seventh wonder is a little removed from the others to the south of the village – ask for directions at the coffee shop. A short woodland walk will bring you down to the attractive shore of Lough Lene, which is dotted with small, green islands. A stream flows out of the lake, apparently in the wrong direction, passing under an overgrown arched bridge, before disappearing into a sinkhole (to emerge at St Fechin's Mill) – the **water that flows uphill**.

**4**

### ARRIVAL AND INFORMATION

### CASTLEPOLLARD AND AROUND

**By bus** The daily bus service to Castlepollard from Dublin (1–2 daily; 2hr 20min) via Trim (supplemented by a weekly Mullingar–Castlepollard bus on Thurs; 30min) might work out for a visit to Tullynally, but the Fore Valley is too long a walk from Castlepollard. The local Salmon bus company (☎ 086 830 2657, ⌨ ourcounty.ie/listings/salmon-bus-hire) operates a return service from Castlepollard to Fore on Tues (roughly 30min).

**By car** With your own transport, Castlepollard is easily approached from Mullingar on the R394, or from the

Loughcrew Cairns near Oldcastle, just across the border in County Meath (see page 131).

**Tourist information** The *Abbey Café* in Fore (June–Sept daily noon–6pm; Oct–May Sat & Sun 11am–6pm; ☎ 044 966 1780, ⌨ foreabbeycoffeeshop@gmail.com) hosts a 20min audiovisual on the monastery (€3), sells local guidebooks, arranges guided tours and provides tourist information on the area. A 3km looped walk, St Fechin's Way (also known as the Nancy-Nelly Walk after two women who lived on the path) starts from the coffee shop.

### ACCOMMODATION

**Hounslow House** Fore, about 1km from the village and well signposted ☎ 044 966 1144, ⌨ hounslowhouse. com. Accommodation in single, double, triple and family

rooms is available at this large 200-year-old farmhouse set in extensive grounds with fine views of the valley. **€70**

# Athlone and around

Straddling the Shannon at its midpoint, **ATHLONE** is the bustling capital of the Midlands and an important road and rail junction on the Westmeath–Roscommon frontier. It probably derives its name from the *Táin Bó Cúailnge*, in which the remains of the white bull of Connacht, the Findbennach, after its defeat by Ulster's brown bull, are scattered throughout Ireland; its loins came to rest here at *Áth Luain*, the "Ford of the Loins". A bridge was first built over this ford in 1120 by Turlough O'Connor, king of Connacht, which the Anglo-Normans replaced with a stone bridge in 1210; they were also responsible for the mighty **castle**. Today, the town supports an important college, the Athlone Institute of Technology, as well as various civil-service offices and high-tech firms, but its main function for tourists is as a jumping-off point for the monastic site of **Clonmacnois** (see page 172), a 25-minute drive south of Athlone. Fewer visitors know about the **Corlea Trackway Visitor Centre**, 20km northeast, but the evocative, 2000-year-old wooden road preserved here is also well worth a visit if you have your own transport. Over the bank holiday weekend at the beginning of June, the **Oliver Goldsmith International Literary Festival** is held in nearby Ballymahon and Abbeyshrule (ⓦ olivergoldsmithfestival.com). Athlone hosts a lively farmers' market every Saturday morning, held on Market Place by the castle.

## Athlone Castle

Town centre, by the west side of the main bridge over the River Shannon • June–Aug Mon–Sat 9.30am–6pm; Sun 10.30am–6pm; March–May & Sept–Oct Tues–Sat 10am–5.30pm, Sun 11am–5pm; Nov–Feb Wed–Sat 10.30am–5pm, Sun 11.30am–5pm; last admission 1hr before closing • €9, or €4 with Belvedere House ticket (see page 164), €6 with Viking Tours ticket (see page 172); Heritage Island • ⓣ 090 644 2130, ⓦ athlonecastle.ie

**Athlone Castle** still casts a formidable shadow over the town, having weathered some bloody fighting during the Cromwellian Wars and the War of the Kings of the seventeenth century. The imposing, grey, thirteenth-century fortifications have been

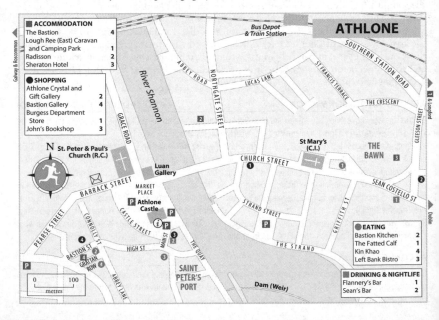

## ATHLONE'S WORLD-FAMOUS OPERA SINGER

One of the best-known **tenors** of his generation, **John Count McCormack** was born in Athlone in 1884, the son of working-class parents employed at the Athlone Woollen Mills. McCormack went on to sing at the Metropolitan Opera House in New York opposite Dame Nellie Melba, and in total made more than six hundred recordings, as well as the popular Hollywood film *Song O' My Heart* (1930). His records sold in their millions, making him one of the bestselling artists Ireland has ever produced. Towards the end of his life he broadcast on the radio with Bing Crosby.

A magnificent bronze **sculpture** of McCormack now forms the centrepiece of a newly designated square beside Athlone Civic Centre. Designed by the Irish artist, Rory Breslin, the sculpture stands on a plinth and marks the starting point of a self-guided **walking trail** covering twelve stops, including the house in which McCormack was born, his old school and Athlone Castle. The castle houses a permanent exhibition displaying programmes from his time with the Dublin Amateur Operatic Society, his Papal Chain, as well as a montage of photographs and HMV recordings, including his much-loved song, *I Hear You Calling Me*.

stylishly converted to house the lively and fascinating exhibitions of the **Athlone Castle Visitor Centre**. As well as some beautiful, early Christian, carved stone slabs, the centre houses impressive audiovisuals and interactive games, focusing on the vicious Sieges of Athlone during the War of the Kings. After the Battle of the Boyne, William III's army took control of eastern and southern Ireland, while the Jacobites attempted to defend the west along the line of the Shannon. In July 1690, Athlone Castle did its job, forcing the Williamites to retreat after a week; they returned with some serious artillery in June of 1691, however, and after building a pontoon over the river and reducing much of the castle to rubble, they took it from the Jacobites, who lost over 1200 men. Within two weeks of taking Athlone, William's men won the Battle of Aughrim, near Galway, and soon after the war was ended with the Treaty of Limerick.

Aside from the noise of the sieges, warring cries and drumbeats, a different type of sensory sensation marks the end of the tour, as the lyrical voice of **John Count McCormack** serenades visitors through loudspeakers in a new permanent first-floor exhibition celebrating the life of the famous Athlone-born tenor (see box).

## The Luan Gallery

Opposite the castle on the west bank of the Shannon • Tues–Sat 11am–5pm, Sun noon–5pm • Free • ✆ 090 644 2154, ⓦ athloneartsandtourism.ie

It's well worth checking out the exhibitions, workshops and events at the **Luan Gallery**, a lovely contemporary art gallery. The building was constructed in 1897 as Father Mathew [sic] Hall (named after the anti-alcohol campaigner), a temperance hall for entertainments to promote sobriety among the employees of Athlone Woollen Mills. The addition of a beautiful extension has created bright, airy exhibition spaces that afford great views of the river.

## Corlea Trackway Visitor Centre

2 Carton Rd, Keenagh, 20km northeast of Athlone • Easter–Sept daily 10am–6pm; guided tours every hour, on the hour, last tour 5pm • Free • ✆ 090 433 322386, ⓦ heritageireland.ie

It's a little tricky to get to the fascinating **Corlea Trackway Visitor Centre**, which is actually across the county border in Longford and signposted along a minor road off the R392, 20km northeast of Athlone, but its isolation in the midst of a desolate

## CYCLING AND WALKING ROUTES AROUND ATHLONE

Many regions of Ireland have repurposed old railway lines as cycling or walking routes, and the Midlands has joined the trend with the **Old Rail Trail Greenway**, which opened in 2017. Following a converted stretch of the former Midlands Great Western Railway, this 40km cycle and walking trail is a delightful rural route from Athlone to Mullingar. Generally flat and with a smooth sealed surface, it runs under historic stone arch bridges and is suitable for all ages and all types of bikes. For more information see ⓦ weastmeathcoco.ie.

For those who prefer to stroll around Athlone, the **Shannon Banks Nature Trail Walk** runs along the grassy verges or the promenade of the River Shannon as part of a 5km town trail. You can start on either a green or brown route from the quay wall at the castle and follow signs pointing to tree species such as sycamore, horse chestnut and red oak. Pick up a walking leaflet at the tourist office.

bog only adds to the appeal of the place. In 1984, Bord na Móna (the Peat Board) discovered a buried *togher*, an early Iron Age trackway, while milling turf here in Corlea raised bog. Dated to 148 BC, the trackway was made of split oak planks up to 4m in length that were meant to float on the bog surface, one of the most substantial and sophisticated of many such prehistoric roads found in Europe. However, the builders knew more about woodworking than the properties of the bog, because within ten years the heavy planks had sunk into the peat – which preserved them perfectly for the next two thousand years. The road connected dry land to the east with an island in the bog to the west, but it's clear that such a prestigious construction was intended for more than just the movement of animals by farmers: it may have been part of a ceremonial highway from the Hill of Uisneach, the ritual "centre of Ireland" that marked the division of the five ancient provinces, between Mullingar and Athlone, to the royal site of Rathcroghan in Roscommon (see page 410), via the narrow crossing of the Shannon at Lanesborough.

Excellent **guided tours** begin with the 18m of trackway that's preserved under cover in the visitor centre. Another 80m has been left outside under the turf, but the guides, as well as delving into the extraordinary ecology of the bog, will take you to the wooden walkway built over it, which gives a good idea of what the trackway would have looked like, undulating over the peaty tussocks.

### ARRIVAL AND INFORMATION
ATHLONE AND AROUND

**By train** The train station is on the north side of the centre on Southern Station Rd.
Destinations Dublin Heuston (12–15 daily; 1hr 40min–2hr); Galway (6–10 daily; 1hr 10min); Westport (4–5 daily; 2hr).
**By bus** The Bus Éireann station is at the train station; Citylink's most convenient stop is at AIT on Dublin Rd to the east of the centre.
Destinations Bus Éireann: Birr (2–3 daily; 50min); Dublin (most via the airport; hourly; 1hr 40min–2hr 20min); Galway (roughly hourly; 1hr 30min); Kilkenny (1–2 daily;

2hr 50min); Limerick (2–3 daily; 2hr 10min); Mullingar (up to 4 daily; 1hr); Waterford (1–2 daily; 4hr); Westport (4 daily; 2hr 45min–3hr); Ireland West Airport Knock (4 daily; 2hr 10min).
Citylink (ⓦ citylink.ie): Dublin and airport (7 daily; 2hr); Galway (7 daily; 1hr 40min).
**Tourist office** Inside the castle (mid-March to mid-May & mid-Sept to Oct Mon–Fri 9.20am–1pm & 1.30–5/6pm; mid-May to mid-Sept daily 9.20am–5/6pm; ☎ 090 649 4630).

### ACCOMMODATION
SEE MAP PAGE 168

**The Bastion** 2 Bastion St ☎ 090 649 4954, ⓦ the bastion.net. The pick of the town's guesthouses and a colourful, relaxing and funky bolthole. The decor of polished wooden floors, white walls and crisp white linens is splashed with colour from modern artworks and Peruvian wall hangings; some bedrooms share bathrooms. Breakfast

(not included) is taken in the neighbouring *Bastion Kitchen*. **€70**
**Lough Ree (East) Caravan and Camping Park** 3km north of Athlone on the N55 in Ballykeeran ☎ 090 647 8561, ⓦ loughreeeast.wixsite.com. Peaceful, spacious and well-equipped lakeside campsite with a campers'

kitchen, a recreation room and a 500m stretch of the Breensford trout river. Closed Oct–March. €20

**Radisson** Northgate St ☎090 644 2600, ⑩radisson hotels.com. This central hotel enjoys a peerless setting on the east bank of the Shannon overlooking the castle – have a sundowner at the heated riverside terrace bar to make the most of it – and offers smart, well-designed rooms with either an urban or soothing marine theme, a swimming pool and leisure club. €195

**Sheraton Hotel** Gleeson St ☎090 645 1000, ⑩marriott. com. Rooms range from classic and deluxe to spacious suites at the top of the distinctive twelve-storey tower, where floor to ceiling windows offer spectacular views across the River Shannon. All rooms are fitted out with marble bathrooms; nice perks include late check out, complimentary parking and free newspapers. Check the website for special deals. €190

## EATING
SEE MAP PAGE 168

**Bastion Kitchen** 1 Bastion St ☎090 649 8369, ⑩bastionkitchen.online. Small, popular and friendly health-food shop and café that serves soup with sourdough (€5), wraps and salads (€8), plus terrific home-baked cakes and scones, and sausage baps with tomato and onion relish for breakfast. Mon–Fri 8am–6pm, Sat 10am–5pm, Sun noon–5pm.

★ **The Fatted Calf** Church St ☎090 643 3371, ⑩the fattedcalf.ie. With its comfortable and elegant chairs made of cowhide leather, walls spruced with Danish artwork and a first-class menu, *The Fatted Calf* in a shiny new building has helped turn Athlone into a foodie enclave. Both the lunch and dinner menus may have suckling pork belly, farmhouse chicken or fillet of Irish seatrout among their dishes (€20–24); ingredients are local and seasonally sourced, and the merits of grass-fed beef can be savoured. Artisan cheeses and home-made chutney leave a long afterglow. Wed–Sat 5–9pm (plus Sat 12.30–3pm), Sun 2–8pm.

★ **Kin Khao** 1 Abbey Lane ☎090 649 8805, ⑩kinkhao thai.ie. Set in a cute yellow-and-red cottage, this is one of Ireland's best Thai restaurants. It offers tasty versions of all the classic Thai dishes, as well as delicious specialities such as *hor mok gai* (chicken curry soufflé; €18.50). Offers two-course lunches for €10, and early-bird deals (two courses for €22) until 7.30pm Mon–Thurs & Sun, 7pm Fri & Sat. Mon, Tues & Sat 5.30–11pm, Wed–Fri 12.30–2.30pm & 5.30–11pm, Sun 1.30–11pm.

**Left Bank Bistro** Fry Place ☎090 649 4446, ⑩left bankbistro.com. Stylish, laidback restaurant serving up plenty of seafood, some Asian-influenced dishes and more classic fare like rump of Roscommon lamb with garlic confit and rosemary jus. Prices for individual dishes are high, but you can ease the pain by opting for the two-course menu (€24.50; available all evening Tues–Fri and 5–6pm Saturdays); lunch, which consists of varied sandwiches, salads and hot dishes such as spicy buffalo wings or goats cheese crostini, is cheaper again. Tues–Sat 10.30am–9.30pm.

## DRINKING
SEE MAP PAGE 168

**Flannery's Bar** 4 Sean Costello St ☎086 831 3160. Monday night is blues night in this small but lively bar frequented by in-the-know Athloners. The music is top-notch and if you get talking to locals you'll hear many tall Midland tales – although don't believe all of them. Mon–Thurs & Sun 6–11.30pm, Fri & Sat 6pm–12.30am.

★ **Sean's Bar** 13 Main St, near the castle ☎090 649 2358, ⑩seansbar.ie. Another claimant to the title of Ireland's oldest pub, serving a house beer, AD 900, a pale ale brewed in Carlow. It's appealingly old-fashioned and sociable, with open fires, sawdust on the floor, live music most nights (including a traditional session Sat early evening) and a huge beer garden at the back stretching down towards the river. Mon–Thurs 10.30am–11.30pm, Fri & Sat 10.30–12.30am, Sun 12.30–11pm.

## SHOPPING
SEE MAP PAGE 168

**Athlone Crystal and Gift Gallery** St Mary's Square ☎090 647 7775. Based in a restored Victorian house in the centre of town, the gallery showcases a range of Irish-designed glassware, vases and crystal bowls, plus jewellery and other gifts. Mon–Sat 10am–5.30pm.

**Bastion Gallery** 6 Bastion St ☎086 843 7802 ⑩the bastiongallery.com. The owner makes exquisite hand-crafted jewellery such as pendants and earrings based on Ogham, the first written form of Gaelic. You'll also find quilts, scarves, toys, postcards and books, as well as unusual gifts. Thurs–Sat 12.30–6pm.

**Burgess Department Store** 1–7 Church St ☎090 647 2005 ⑩burgessofathlone.ie. Founded in 1839, Ireland's longest established department store occupies a substantial corner site. It stocks a large selection of fashions from well-known brand names to labels exclusive to Athlone, plus giftware, household furnishings and the like. Mon–Sat 9.30am–6pm.

**John's Bookshop** 9 Main St ☎090 649 4151 ⑩johns bookshop.com. A great place to while away an hour browsing secondhand and antiquarian books, as well as inscribed first editions. You'll come across rare books about the Shannon, fiction and poetry by Athlone authors such as John Broderick, and new and old travel books on Ireland. Tues–Sat 10.30am–6pm.

4

---

**BOAT TRIPS TO LOUGH REE AND CLONMACNOIS**

Viking Tours (☎086 262 1136, ⓦvikingtoursireland.ie; twenty-five percent discounts with Athlone Castle tickets) runs **boat trips on the Shannon** (March–Oct), which involve sailing in a partly open 20m wooden boat that's been made up to look like a **longboat**, with Viking costumes for kids to dress up in. Every day, the boat heads north around the islands of **Lough Ree** (1hr 15min; €15), which include Hare Island, site of a Viking encampment that has yielded considerable amounts of Viking treasure. Less often, it sails south on the scenic approach to **Clonmacnois** (€20, including return by bus to Athlone; 1hr 30min), allowing you 1hr 30min to look around the site, before a bus (30min) takes you back to Athlone. Departures are from the west bank of the river below the castle, where the latest schedule of trips is always posted – or consult their website.

---

# Clonmacnois

6km north of Shannonbridge • Daily: mid-March to May, Sept & Oct 10am–6pm; June–Aug 9am–6.30pm; Nov to mid-March 10am–5.30pm; last admission 45min before closing • €8; Heritage Card • ☎090 967 4195 • ⓦheritageireland.ie

The substantial remains of **Clonmacnois**, pre-Norman Ireland's most important Christian site, enjoy an idyllic location on the grassy banks of the gently meandering Shannon, 6km upstream from Shannonbridge. Here the river descends at a shallow gradient through flat land that floods extensively in winter, but in spring the receding flow leaves beautiful, nutrient-rich water meadows, some of the last of their type in Europe. The **Shannon Callows**, as they are known, become the summer home of rare wildflowers, grazing cattle, lapwings, curlews and redshanks.

### Brief history

The monastery was founded as a satellite of St Enda's house on Inishmore (see page 352) in around 548 by **St Kieran (Ciarán)**, who with the help of Diarmuid of the Uí Néills, the first Christian High King of Ireland, erected a wooden church here. Kieran brought with him a dun cow, whose hide later became Clonmacnois' major relic – anyone who died lying on it would be spared the torments of Hell – and who was commemorated in the *Lebor na hUidre* (Book of the Dun Cow), the oldest surviving manuscript written wholly in Irish. Perfectly sited at the junction of the Slí Mhor, the main road from Dublin Bay to Galway Bay, and the major north–south artery, the Shannon, the monastery grew in influence as various provincial kings endowed it with churches and high crosses. With a large lay population, Clonmacnois resembled a small town, where craftsmen and scholars produced illuminated manuscripts, croziers and other remarkable artefacts, many of which can be seen in the National Museum in Dublin. However, between the eighth and twelfth centuries the site was plundered over forty times by Vikings, Anglo-Normans and Irish enemies, and church reforms in the thirteenth century greatly reduced its influence. In 1552, Athlone's English garrison reduced it to ruins, though, as the burial place of Kieran, it has persisted to this day as a place of pilgrimage, focused on the saint's day on September 9.

### The visitor centre and high crosses

Clonmacnois' three magnificent **high crosses** have been moved into the excellent **visitor centre** to prevent further damage by the weather. The finest is the **Cross of the Scriptures**, a pictorial sermon showing the Crucifixion, Christ in the Tomb and the Last Judgement. It was erected in the early tenth century by Abbot Colman and Flann, the High King of Ireland, who may be depicted together (with Flann holding a pole) in the bottom scene on the shaft's east face. Standing 4m high, the cross is carved from a single piece of sandstone and may originally have been coloured. The other two crosses are about a century older and much simpler, the **South Cross** featuring the Crucifixion surrounded by rich interlacing, spirals and bosses, while the **North Cross** is carved with abstract Celtic ornaments, humans and animals.

## The site

Most of Clonmacnois' nine churches are structurally intact apart from their roofs, the largest being the **cathedral** straight in front of the visitor centre. It was built in 909 by Abbot Colman and King Flann, but its most beautiful feature now is the fifteenth-century north doorway, featuring decorative Gothic carving surmounted by Sts Dominic, Patrick and Francis. The last High King of Ireland, Rory O'Connor, was buried by the altar here in 1198. Several smaller churches encircle the cathedral, notably **Temple Ciarán**, the burial place of St Kieran, dating from the early tenth century.

In the western corner of the compound rises a fine **round tower**, erected in 1124 by Abbot O'Malone and Turlough O'Connor of Connacht, High King of Ireland and father of Rory. There's another round tower attached to the nave of **Temple Finghin**, which is Romanesque in style and thought to date from 1160–70.

In a peaceful, leafy glade about 500m away from the main site and signposted from the east side of the compound, the **Nun's Church** is the place to escape to if a fleet of tour coaches descends. Founded by Queen Devorguilla, who retired here as a penitent in 1170, it boasts a fine Romanesque doorway and chancel arch carved with geometrical patterns.

The site's tranquillity is often broken by coach tours in summer so, if you can, time your visit for late afternoon, when you might be lucky enough to catch the birds singing as the sun sets over the river.

**4**

### ARRIVAL AND DEPARTURE

### CLONMACNOIS

**By car, bike or boat** There's no public transport to Clonmacnois from Athlone, 21km away, but the trip is perfectly manageable in a day by renting a bike or a car or by taking a boat tour down the Shannon (see page 172).

### ACCOMMODATION AND EATING

**Kajon House** Under 2km southwest on the Shannonbridge road **☎** 090 967 4191. If you want to stay near the site, head for *Kajon House*, a friendly, comfortable B&B with en-suite rooms, in a bright, modern, pine-furnished house. You'll be offered tea and home-made scones when you arrive, and there are pancakes for breakfast, and evening meals on offer. Closed Nov–Feb. **€70**

**Lukers** By the bridge in Shannonbridge **☎** 090 967 4995, **⊕** lukersbar.com. Formerly a one-pub room dating from the 1750s, this popular establishment now also incorporates a bright stylish restaurant with a veranda looking on to the River Shannon. Steaks, burgers and fish form the basis of the lunch and evening menus and you'll also find light bites such as Galway Bay seafood and potato chowder (€6.50). After your meal look into the old bar for an aperitif. Daily 12.30–8.30pm; bar Mon–Thurs 11.30am–11.30pm, Fri & Sat 11.30am–12.30am, Sun 12.30–11pm.

# Birr

Around 45km south of Athlone at the confluence of the Camcor and Little Brosna rivers, **BIRR** is the Midlands' most attractive town, planned around the estate of Birr Castle, the home of the Parsons family, later the Earls of Rosse. Around central Emmet Square – formerly Duke's Square, though the unpopular statue of the Duke of Cumberland, victor over the Jacobites at the Battle of Culloden in 1746, is long gone from the central pillar – you'll find several broad Georgian terraces, graced with fanlights and other fine architectural details, notably St John's Mall to the east and Oxmantown Mall to the north off Emmet Street. Running south from Emmet Square, O'Connell Street, which becomes Main Street, heads down to Market Square.

Birr is not yet on the country's main tourist trail but supports some appealing places to stay and eat, making it an excellent base from which to explore the Shannon, Clonmacnois and Slieve Bloom. The town comes to life in early August during its **Vintage Week and Arts Festival** (Ⓦbirrvintageweek.com), when shop assistants, bar staff and townspeople deck themselves out in historic regalia, and there's a varied programme of street theatre, music, and art exhibitions. In October, the five-day **Offline Film Festival** (Ⓦofflinefilmfestival.com) features screenings, workshops and a short-film competition.

### Brief history

A monastery was first founded here in the sixth century, later becoming famous for the *Mac Regol Gospels* (now in the Bodleian Library, Oxford), an illuminated manuscript named after the early ninth-century abbot and bishop. Birr was settled by the Anglo-Normans, who built a castle here in 1208, later becoming the site of an O'Carroll stronghold between the fourteenth and seventeenth centuries. In the 1619 plantation of their territory (known as Ely O'Carroll), however, Sir Laurence Parsons was given Birr, which became known as Parsonstown. A descendant of his set about reconstructing the town in the 1740s in Neoclassical style, a development which continued in stages until as late as the 1830s.

## Birr Castle

Town centre, to the west of Emmet Square • Grounds & Historic Science Centre daily: mid-March to Oct 9am–6pm; Nov to mid-March 10am–4pm; castle May–Aug Mon–Sat at 10am, 11am & 1pm by advance booking through the website (no under-12s, no photography) • €9 • ☏ 057 912 0336, Ⓦbirrcastle.com

Birr's forbidding Gothic **castle** can only be visited on a guided tour during the summer months, but otherwise there's plenty of interest in the **Historic Science Centre** in the coach houses, which also shelter a pleasant summertime café, and in the varied grounds. In the nineteenth century, the Parsons family gained an international reputation as scientists and inventors. The third Earl of Rosse, William Parsons, devoted himself to astronomy, and in 1845 built the huge **Rosse Telescope**, with a 72-inch reflector, which remained the largest in the world until 1917. It was fully reconstructed in the 1990s, along with the massive, elaborate housing of walls, tracks, pulleys and counterweights needed to manoeuvre it, and can be seen in the garden. The fourth Earl, Laurence, and his mother, Mary, a friend of Fox Talbot's, were eminent photographers, while Laurence's brother, Sir Charles Parsons, was carving himself a varied and colourful career, which included building a small flying machine and a helicopter in the 1890s and spending 25 years unsuccessfully trying to make artificial diamonds. He'll be best remembered, however, as the inventor of the steam turbine and for his exploits at the 1897 Spithead Naval Review, celebrating Queen Victoria's Diamond Jubilee when, frustrated at the Royal Navy's foot-dragging, he gatecrashed in the *Turbinia*, the first steam-turbine ship, racing through the fleet at the unheard-of speed of 34 knots. Within a few years the technology was adopted by navies and passenger liners around the world. All of this is set in historical and global context in the Science Centre, with plenty of astrolabes, cameras and other instruments, and some lively audiovisuals.

You could easily spend a couple of hours strolling around the beautiful **castle grounds**, especially if you buy the booklet on its fifty most significant trees or let your kids loose on the treehouse adventure area. Beyond the wildflower meadows, which are left to grow tall until July every year, lie a nineteenth-century lake, a fernery and fountain, and the oldest wrought-iron suspension bridge in Ireland, dating from 1820. The walled gardens feature the tallest box hedges in the world, which are over three hundred years old, as well as intricate parterres and paths canopied with hornbeams in the formal, seventeenth-century-style Millennium Garden.

## BARACK OBAMA PLAZA

He may no longer be US president, but **Barack Obama**'s name still gets top billing at a visitor centre in an unlikely setting: a motorway service station near **Moneygall** in Co. Offaly, where his ancestors came from. The village was thrust into the spotlight in 2011 when Obama paid a presidential visit to find out about his great-great-great grandfather who emigrated from the village in 1851 in search of a better life. His visit is recalled in a first-floor exhibition "From Moneygall to the White House" and in a short film at Junction 23 off the M7 Dublin–Limerick motorway. It's part of an interpretative display on Irish emigration at **Barack Obama Plaza** (☎0505 45810, ⊛barackobamaplaza.ie) telling the fascinating story of the Irish in America and how they prospered. In Moneygall itself (which has a population of just 298) you can discover more about his connection to the area In Ollie Hayes' bar (☎0505 45230) on the main street, where Obama enjoyed a drink. The bar features a gallery of photographs of his visit, alongside a large cardboard cut-out figure of him, and the owner will tell you about the day the president dropped in on a small Irish town. Traditional music nights, with occasional set dancing, are held on Fridays.

## ARRIVAL AND DEPARTURE — BIRR

**By bus** Buses stop on Emmet Square.
Destinations Bus Éireann: Athlone (2–3 daily; 50min); Limerick (2–3 daily; 1hr 20min).

Kearns Transport (⊛kearnstransport.com): Dublin (2–6 daily; 2hr); Galway (via Portumna and Loughrea; Fri–Sun 1–2 daily; 2hr).

## ACCOMMODATION

**County Arms Hotel** Roscrea Rd ☎057 912 0791, ⊛countyarmshotel.com. Well-appointed rooms with queen-size beds are decorated to a high standard, while the Georgian suites come with king-size beds. Facilities include two restaurants, a pool, Jacuzzi, sauna and steam room, or you can take a stroll around the nine acres of garden. **€120**

**Dooly's Hotel** Emmet Square ☎057 912 0032, ⊛doolyshotel.com. The town's social hub, a welcoming Georgian coaching inn, with a chequered history; it was here in 1809 that the Galway Hunt partied a little too hard after a day in the field and managed to burn the hotel down, thus gaining a new name, the Galway Blazers. The bedrooms, some of which are on the small side, don't quite match the period elegance of the public rooms. **€130**

**The Stables** Oxmantown Mall ☎057 912 0263, ⊛thestablesbirr.com. Fan-lit nineteenth-century town house that's been fetchingly refurbished in a plush style, with chandeliers and gilt mirrors in the five spacious bedrooms. There's an open fire in its cosy lounge, and tea rooms in a courtyard seating. **€79**

**Townsend House** 1 Townsend St ☎057 912 1276, ⊛townsendhouse-guesthouse.com. On a busy street to the north of Emmet Square, this central, welcoming guesthouse provides en-suite rooms and wonderful breakfasts, in an airy, high-ceilinged Georgian house that's tastefully furnished with antiques. It also has a restaurant in the courtyard serving a tapas menu, with the likes of cod goujons and sticky sesame chicken. **€100**

## EATING AND DRINKING

**The Chestnut** Green St, between Emmet Square and the castle ☎087 220 8524, ⊛thechestnut.ie. Welcoming nineteenth-century bar, stylishly outfitted with dark wood and leather seats, and backed by a large beer garden, which hosts trad music on Thursdays and acoustic on Fridays, sometimes in the garden. Wed–Thurs 7–11.30pm, Fri 5pm–11.30am, Sat & Sun 3–11.30pm.

**Craughwell's** 1-3 Castle St, off the west side of Market Square ☎057 912 1839. Very sociable and cosy pub, with a good pint of Guinness and traditional music at weekends. Mon–Thurs 7–11.30pm, Fri & Sat 7pm–12.30am, Sun 1–11pm.

★ **Emma's** 31 Main St ☎057 912 5678. This mellow café with comfy banquettes prepares delicious panini and soup

(€8), as well as speciality teas and coffees, and a tempting array of freshly baked cakes, scones and gluten-free options. Mon–Sat 8.30am–6pm, Sun 10.30am–6pm.

**The Emmet** Dooly's Hotel, Emmet Square. The hotel's main restaurant is a formal, luxurious affair, serving dishes such as goat's cheese bon bons, and grilled sea bass with lemon and caper cream (€18). Mon–Sat 6–9pm, Sun 12.30–3pm & 6–9pm.

**Spinners** Castle St ☎057 912 3779, ⊛spinnersbirr.com. A family-run restaurant with a relaxing courtyard, warm atmosphere and a commitment to fresh organic food. Starters may include potted cashel blue cheese with apple chutney (€8); main courses such as baked brill with creamed leeks (€18.50), Bo bristle beer battered fish

4

(€14.50), or cauliflower and chickpea curry (€14) come with a flourish. A more casual dining bar serves lunches of quiche, burgers and sandwiches. Restaurant Fri & Sat 6–9pm, Sun 12.30–3.30pm; bar Wed–Thurs 5–9pm, Fri & Sat 12.30–9pm, Sun 12.30–7pm.

**The Thatch** Crinkill, on Military Rd, which runs east off the N62, about 2km south of Birr ☎057 912 0682, ⓦ thethatchcrinkill.com. This thatched white cottage conceals an equally appealing interior of exposed brick and stone, pine furniture, log fires and candlelight. The pub is most famous among locals for its food, such as rack of pork (€19) or steak and smoked hake (€21), while early birds can sample Clew Bay crab meat with a lime olive oil and balsamic dressing for starts and mains such as lamb tomahawk with scallion mash (€21) or penne pasta with mushrooms or tomatoes (€14.50). Food served Tues, 4–7.30pm, Wed & Thurs 4–9pm, Fri & Sat 12.30–9pm, Sun 12.30–7.30pm.

## ENTERTAINMENT

**Birr Theatre and Arts Centre** Oxmantown Mall ☎057 912 2911, ⓦ birrtheatre.com. Located on a fine Georgian street, the town's main creative hub hosts a varied programme of drama, music and artistic events throughout the year.

# Slieve Bloom

To the east of Birr, straddling the Offaly–Laois border, rises **Slieve Bloom**, the "mountain of Bladhma", named for an ancient Connacht warrior who sought refuge here. Although it extends only for about 20km across and down, the massif provides welcome relief from the flatness of the Midlands and a refuge for wildlife including bog plants such as the insect-eating sundew, and birds including skylarks, kestrels and the rare peregrine falcon. The waymarked 77km **Slieve Bloom Way** describes a heavily indented circuit of most of the range, before passing underneath the highest point – Arderin (527m), which means, rather hopefully, the "height of Ireland". But it is a sleepy landscape of bucolic laneways and gentle walking. Six short signposted loop walks created with sympathetic underfoot conditions are detailed on the useful website, ⓦ slievebloom.ie, while the Ordnance Survey of Ireland **map** #54 covers the whole of Slieve Bloom. For something more organized, there are **walking festivals** over the bank-holiday weekend in early May and over a weekend in July, as well as **guided walks** at least every Sunday (€5 per person).

The best base on the Offaly side of the mountains, within walking distance of the Slieve Bloom Way, is the charming village of **Kinnitty**, which huddles around a couple of pubs and a triangular green that's traversed by a tiny stream.

## INFORMATION AND ACCOMMODATION · SLIEVE BLOOM

**Tourist information** See ⓦ slievebloom.ie for information on guided walks, local accommodation and more.

**Ardmore House** Kinnitty ☎057 913 7009, ⓦ kinnitty. com. This nineteenth-century stone house with a lovely garden and a fine view of the mountain offers attractive en-suite B&B accommodation, home-baking and turf fires, and is especially accommodating to walkers, with its drying room and details on local routes. Self-catering cottage also available. **€90**

**Roundwood House** Mountrath, about 20km southeast of Kinnitty on the R440 ☎057 873 2120, ⓦ roundwood house.com. On the Laois side of the range, this handsome, three-storey Palladian villa set in extensive wooded gardens offers welcoming, traditional country-house accommodation. You can stay either in the spacious main house or the earlier, more compact Yellow House. On a wet day, Frank's Library, on the evolution of civilisation, is worth spending time in. Serves communal dinners at €60 for four-courses. Self-catering also available. **€180**

4

# Kilkenny, Carlow and Wexford

HOOK LIGHTHOUSE

# Kilkenny, Carlow and Wexford

Ireland's southeast is largely flat and has the country's best climate. The geography helps explain why it's a hotbed of hurling, the more expansive of Ireland's traditional sports: Kilkenny, in particular, is mad about the game. The county's attractions centre on its namesake city, which offers many historical sites, fine pubs and restaurants. To the south lie the evocative monasteries and trim waterside villages of the verdant Nore valley, and to the east, across the River Barrow, is County Carlow and its gentle green landscapes. County Wexford has much allure around the genial county town itself, with its thriving music scene. Meanwhile, the county's southwestern corner features ruined abbeys and a sweeping arboretum, running between the bleak wonders of the Hook Peninsula and the historic river port of New Ross.

Thanks to its strategic position just across St George's Channel from south Wales, Ireland's southeast has borne the brunt of the country's colonization. The **Vikings** founded an early settlement here, which grew into Wexford town, while the **Anglo-Normans** quickly exploited the area's economic potential and greatly altered its physiognomy. They developed Kilkenny and Wexford towns and built castles across the two counties, while also transforming uncultivated areas into productive farmland. However, control was not always easily maintained. The MacMurrough-Kavanagh Irish dynasty, based in the north of County Wexford, continually frustrated English attempts to control the region, and full conquest only occurred when **Cromwell** arrived in the mid-1600s. Even after this, County Wexford witnessed some of the most bitter fighting during the 1798 Rebellion, before the insurgents were decisively defeated at Enniscorthy.

## Kilkenny city and around

Unquestionably Ireland's most atmospheric medieval city, **KILKENNY** straddles the broad River Nore, doglegging past its striking **castle**. Downhill from here lies a compact grid of narrow streets, dating back to the city's origins, though little of its former gated walls remains. The main street wends its way from the castle, past **Rothe House and Gardens**, impressive evidence of the city's Tudor wealth, to Kilkenny's other main landmark, the well-preserved, medieval **St Canice's Cathedral** with its climbable round tower. North of the city the major attraction is the strange calcite formations of **Dunmore Cave**.

### Brief history

The first known settlement at Kilkenny is believed to have been a sixth-century monastic community founded by St Canice (*Cill Chainnigh* means "the church of Canice"). After the arrival of the **Anglo-Normans**, Strongbow erected a motte and bailey fort overlooking the Nore in 1172, which was later replaced with a stone structure by his son-in-law, William Marshall. The latter also built a city wall and towers and forced the local population to live outside its boundaries in an area still known as "Irishtown" today. Subsequently, the city's ownership passed through various hands, before James Butler, the third Earl of Ormonde, purchased the demesne in 1391.

Following the 1641 Rebellion, Kilkenny became the focus for the **Catholic Confederation**, an unlikely alliance of royalists loyal to Charles I and Irish landowners

WOODSTOCK GARDENS & ARBORETUM

# Highlights

**❶ Kilkenny city** Vibrant and historic, Kilkenny preserves its medieval framework, centred upon its imposing castle, and has several exciting festivals to boot. See page 180

**❷ Jerpoint Abbey** Atmospheric twelfth-century ruins, featuring a wonderful colonnaded cloister and fascinating carvings. See page 188

**❸ Inistioge** Gorgeous riverside village overlooked by the rejuvenated Woodstock Estate. See page 189

**❹ Wexford** Lively town that retains much of its medieval layout and is renowned for its opera festival. See page 191

**❺ Curracloe Beach** Seven miles of soft white sands that were the setting for the movies *Saving Private Ryan* and *Brooklyn*. See page 195

**❻ National 1798 Centre** Enniscorthy's enthralling multimedia account of the 1798 Rebellion. See page 196

**❼ Hook Head Lighthouse** The oldest operating lighthouse in the world sits at the tip of a wild strip of land. See page 198

**❽ Dunbrody Famine Ship** This replica "coffin ship" brings alive the hardship that emigrants to the New World had to endure. See page 200

**HIGHLIGHTS ARE MARKED ON THE MAP ON PAGE 182**

**5**

dispossessed by the Plantation. This established a parliament in Kilkenny, aimed at attaining Irish self-government and, in the process, restoring the rights of Catholics. However, its powers were short-lived, and, after Cromwell's arrival in 1650, the city's prosperity began to wane.

Nonetheless, nowadays Kilkenny still possesses an undoubted grandeur, largely untarnished by inappropriate modern building developments and, thanks to its castle and numerous other sights, as well as a lively nightlife and cultural scene, has become an integral part of the Irish tourist trail.

## Kilkenny Castle

The Parade, in the heart of town • **Castle** Daily: April–Sept 9am–5.30pm; Oct–March 9.30am–5pm; Nov–Jan admission by guided tour only • €8; Heritage Card • ☎ 056 770 4100, ⓦ kilkennycastle.ie

**KILKENNY, CARLOW AND WEXFORD**

**HIGHLIGHTS**

1. Kilkenny City
2. Jerpoint Abbey
3. Inistioge
4. Wexford
5. Curracloe Beach
6. National 1798 Centre
7. Hook Head Lighthouse
8. Dunbrody Famine Ship

Sitting strong above the Nore, Kilkenny's stately **castle** was built in the early thirteenth century by William Marshall, Earl of Pembroke, and purchased in 1391 by James Butler, third Earl of Ormonde. His descendants, surviving siege by Cromwell in 1650, subsequently built the grand entrance gateway later that century and developed the broad parklands that still extend to the southeast of the castle. Further work began around 1826, enhancing the castle's medieval exterior while adapting its interior in contemporary country-house style. The Butlers remained in residence until 1935, when a decline in the family's fortunes led to their departure and the auction of the castle's contents. The building fell into disrepair, until it was acquired by the Irish state in 1969.

Inside the castle, you'll be able to see the impressive hall, whose chequered floor is tiled with black **Kilkenny marble** (actually a polished limestone, but prevalent enough in the hills around Kilkenny to have given it the nickname "Marble City"), as well as a library, drawing room and nineteenth-century-style bedrooms. En route you'll pass a portrait of the first Duke of Ormonde, which, for a period in its life, hung in the gents' toilet of a restaurant in New York – a far-flung result of the 1935 auction. The castle's crowning glory is its extraordinarily long gallery, which occupies almost the entire length of the River Wing, replete with twin fireplaces and marble carvings of key moments in the history of the Butler dynasty. Its 1825 hammer-beam roof, punctuated by curving columns bearing the heads of various mythical beasts, is decorated by whimsical Pre-Raphaelite daubs.

**5**

## Kilkenny Design Centre and National Design & Craft Gallery

The Parade, opposite the castle entrance · **Kilkenny Design Centre** Daily 9am–6pm · ☎ 056 772 2118, ⓦ kilkennydesign.com · **National Craft Gallery** Wed–Sat 11am–5pm, Sun noon–5pm · Free · ☎ 056 779 6147, ⓦ ndcg.ie

The converted eighteenth-century coach house and stables of Kilkenny Castle house the **Kilkenny Design Centre**, which retails a broad range of premium Irish crafts, and has a recommended upstairs restaurant (see page 186) and a pleasant ground-floor café. Behind the shop, you'll find the attractive, airy premises of the **National Design & Craft Gallery**, which mounts a varied programme of exhibitions by Irish and international craftspeople, ranging from stained glass to quilts. Beyond the gallery, you can visit several small craft workshops in the courtyard and the beautiful walled gardens that back onto *Butler House* (see page 186).

## High Street and Parliament Street

Heading down the Parade from the castle and across the junction to the High Street leads past the **Tholsel**, the city's erstwhile financial exchange and, subsequently, town hall, constructed in 1761. The High Street blends seamlessly into Parliament Street, both replete with shops and cafés, intriguing alleys and offshoots.

## Medieval Mile Museum

2 St Mary's Lane, High St · Daily: April–Oct 8am–6pm; Nov–March 11am–4.30pm · €7 · ☎ 056 781 7022, ⓦ medievalmilemuseum.ie

Kilkenny's magnificent thirteenth-century St Mary's Church has been brilliantly repurposed into the **Medieval Mile Museum**, with more than eight hundred years of local history at its heart. Exhibits are displayed in a modern and interactive space, with a focus on the monastic founding of Kilkenny, plus the wealthy merchants who attended St Mary's between 1200 and 1650. Treasures include replica Ossary High Crosses, the *Liber Primus* (a medieval town book) and elaborate stone tombs.

## Rothe House and Garden

Parliament St · April–Oct Tues–Sun 11am–6pm · €7.50 · ☎ 056 772 2893, ⓦ rothehouse.com

A complex of three dwellings linked by courtyards, **Rothe House** is the finest remnant of the city's Tudor prosperity. It was built for a wealthy Kilkenny merchant and his twelve children between 1594 and 1610, and is now, fittingly, home to the Kilkenny Archaeological Society and offers a genealogical service. Look out for two huge Kilkenny marble fireplaces on the first floor and the second floor's impressive king-post roof, made of Irish oak beams. Behind the house, two walled gardens – one for vegetables and herbs, the other a still immature orchard – have been restored to their early seventeenth-century state, stretching back to a rebuilt section of the city wall.

---

### KILKENNY FESTIVALS

The major event in the city's packed cultural calendar is the ten-day **Kilkenny Arts Festival** (ⓦ kilkennyarts.ie) in August, featuring all manner of music, as well as drama, film, various exhibitions and literary goings-on. **Kilkenny Tradfest** (ⓦ kilkennytradfest.com) brings four days of traditional music, dance and workshops around St Patrick's Day in March, while the four-day **Kilkenny Roots Festival** (ⓦ kilkennyroots.com), over the bank holiday weekend at the start of May, spotlights American country and roots music. The bank holiday weekend in early June, meanwhile, hosts the marvellous four-day comedy festival, **The Cat Laughs** (ⓦ thecatlaughs.com), and the bank holiday weekend in late October sees an imaginative four-day festival of food, **Savour Kilkenny** (ⓦ savourkilkenny.com).

## Black Abbey

Just before Parliament Street becomes Irishtown, on Abbey Street, stands the **Holy Trinity Church**, more commonly known as the **Black Abbey**, thanks to the colour of the habits of its founders, the Dominicans. Dating from 1225, the abbey was suppressed during the Reformation and fell into disrepair. Now fully restored, and again a Dominican establishment, it houses some fine carvings and a glorious fifteen-panel rosary stained-glass window.

## St Canice's Cathedral & Round Tower

Coach Rd, north along Parliament St • **Cathedral** Mon–Sat 9am–5.30pm, Sun 1–5.30pm • €4 • **Tower** Same hours as cathedral, access weather permitting (no under-12s) • €3, joint ticket with cathedral €6 • ☎ 056 776 4971, ⓦ stcanicescathedral.ie

Kilkenny's Church of Ireland cathedral, thirteenth-century **St Canice's**, looms above Irishtown. Though its spire collapsed in 1332, the rest of this grand Gothic structure remains true to its date of origin. The magnificently carved interior contains many splendid sixteenth- and seventeenth-century tombstones, often cut from black Kilkenny marble, including some remarkable effigies of the Butler family. In the churchyard stands a graceful ninth-century **Round Tower**, the only vestige of St Canice's monastic settlement, whose 30m summit affords a superb vista of the city spread out below.

## Butler Gallery

John's Quay • Tues–Sat 10am–5pm (Thurs till 8pm), Sun 11am–5pm • Free • ☎ 056 776 1106, ⓦ butlergallery.ie

Occupying the nineteenth-century home of Joseph Evans, the Butler Gallery's permanent collection is among the finest in Ireland. Works date from the 1830s to the present and feature the likes of Paul Henry, Louis le Brocquy and Patrick Scott, though just as important is the entire gallery devoted to local-born artist Tony O'Malley (1913–2003) and his wife Jane. Self-taught, O'Malley is best known for his abstract and colourful landscape motifs, a body of work heavily influenced by his time living in St Ives, Cornwall, between 1960 and 1990.

## Dunmore Cave

10km north of Kilkenny, off the N78 • March to mid-June & mid-Sept to Oct daily from 9.30am, last tour 4pm; mid-June to mid-Sept daily from 9.30am, last tour 5pm; Nov to mid-March Wed–Sun from 9.30am, last tour 3pm • €5; Heritage Card • ☎ 056 776 7726, ⓦ heritageireland.ie

Formed in a limestone outcrop of the Castlecomer plateau, **Dunmore Cave**'s series of chambers features numerous beautiful calcite creations – curtains and crystals, stalactites and stalagmites; the most remarkable of the last stands some 4.5m high. The cave is referenced in the *Annals of the Four Masters* (see page 421), which recounts that the Vikings massacred a thousand people here in 928, a tale partially substantiated in 1967 when excavations uncovered the skeletons of more than forty women and children, and a Viking coin.

### ARRIVAL AND DEPARTURE                        KILKENNY CITY

**By train** The train station is off Dublin Rd, from where it's a 10min walk along John St to the city centre.

Destinations Dublin (4–6 daily; 1hr 30min); Thomastown (4–7 daily; 10min); Waterford (4–7 daily; 35min).

**By bus** Bus Éireann services leave from the train station and most also stop on Ormonde Rd in the centre; J.J. Kavanagh's stop on Ormonde Rd; Kilbride's New Ross buses stop on Ormonde Rd and the Parade, while their Graiguenamanagh buses stop at MacDonagh Junction, a shopping centre next

to the train station, and the Parade; and Dublin Coach M9 Express stops at Ormonde Rd and MacDonagh Junction.

Destinations Bus Éireann: Athlone (Mon–Sat 2 daily, Sun 1; 3hr); Inistioge (1 Thurs; 35min); New Ross (1 Thurs; 1hr 15min); Thomastown (Mon–Sat 2 daily, Sun 1; 30min); Waterford (Mon–Sat 2 daily, Sun 1; 1hr).

J.J. Kavanagh (ⓦ jjkavanagh.ie): Dublin and airport (6 daily; 2–3hr).

Kilbride (ⓦ kilbridecoaches.com): Graiguenamanagh

**5**

(Mon–Sat 2 daily; 55min); Inistioge (Mon–Sat 2 daily; 45min); New Ross (Mon–Sat 2 daily; 1hr 15min); Thomastown (Mon–Sat 2 daily; 30min).
Dublin Coach (@ dublincoach.ie): Dublin (9 daily; 1hr 45min).

## INFORMATION AND TOURS

**Tourist office** In the Shee Alms House, one of very few Tudor almshouses remaining in Ireland, on Rose Inn St (Mon–Sat 9am–5pm; ☎ 056 775 1500, @ visitkilkenny.ie). Pick up a "Craft Trail" leaflet here (or go to @ madeinkilkenny. ie or @ trailkilkenny.ie).

**Walking tours** Pat Tynan's 1hr10min walking tours of the medieval city (mid-March to Oct Mon–Sat 11am & 2pm; €12; ☎ 087 265 1745, @ kilkennywalkingtours.ie) depart from the tourist office.

**Cycling tours** Kilkenny Cycling Tours, 16 John St (☎ 086 895 4961, @ kilkennycyclingtours.com), provides tours of city (€25 for two hours) and county, as well as bicycle rental (€20/day).

**Kayaking tours** Go with the Flow (☎ 056 7801 299, @ gowiththeflow.ie) offers guided and self-guided kayaking and canoeing trips on rivers Nore and Barrow.

## ACCOMMODATION                                            SEE MAP PAGE 183

★ **Butler House** 16 Patrick St ☎ 056 772 2828, @ butler.ie. This expansive former dower house of Kilkenny Castle was decorously refurbished in the 1970s by Kilkenny Design Centre (in whose café breakfast is served; see page 186). Its spacious rooms marry Georgian refinement and modern furnishings and facilities to stunning effect, and some overlook the beautiful garden and castle. €135

**Celtic House** 18 Michael St ☎ 056 776 2249, @ celtic-house-bandb.com. Welcoming, well-maintained, modern town house B&B, adorned with the artist owner Angela's landscapes, and set in a quiet, fairly central location. Its four rooms are colourful, airy and en suite. €85

**Kilkenny Hibernian Hotel** 1 Ormonde St ☎ 056 777 1888, @ kilkennyhibernianhotel.com. Once a bank and later the HQ of a food company, this lovingly restored Victorian building features a variety of lavish accommodation furnished with red carpets and lots of polished wood, above two popular bars and a bar-restaurant. Good-value half-board deals. €90

**Kilkenny House Hotel** Freshford Rd ☎ 056 777 0711, @ kilkennyhousehotel.ie. A 20min walk from the centre, this two-storey hotel features large, bright, well-appointed rooms. A real bargain from Mon to Thurs and Sun, and a likely fallback at weekends, though prices almost triple on Sat. €59

**Kilkenny Tourist Hostel** 35 Parliament St (IHH) ☎ 056 776 3541, @ kilkennyhostel.ie. Large and well-run hostel in a very central Georgian town house, featuring spacious dorms, a few private rooms, a well-equipped kitchen, a turf fire in the sitting room and laundry facilities. Front dorms can suffer from street noise at weekends. Dorms €18, doubles €44

★ **Rosquil House** Castlecomer Rd ☎ 056 772 1419, @ rosquilhouse.com. An elegant and welcoming upmarket guesthouse, a 10min walk from the centre, with spacious, stylish and well-equipped rooms, an attractive sitting room and fine breakfasts. Self-catering mews also available. €90

**Zuni** 26 Patrick St ☎ 056 772 3999, @ zuni.ie. Located above the restaurant of the same name in a converted century-old theatre, with thirteen luxurious contemporary bedrooms featuring a minimalist decor of creams, whites and dark wood. Half-board deals available. €90

### CAMPSITE

**Treegrove Caravan & Camping Park** Danville House, 1.5km southeast of town on the R700 ☎ 086 830 8845, @ treegrovecamping.com. This popular, well-equipped site comes with a campers' kitchen, laundry and bike rental – it's a nice walk or bike ride into town along a tree-lined riverside path. They've also got pods sleeping two. Closed mid-Nov to Feb. €18, pods €70

## EATING                                                    SEE MAP PAGE 183

**Anocht** The Parade ☎ 056 772 2118, @ anocht restaurant.ie. On weekend evenings, Kilkenny Design Centre's upstairs café turns into a classy restaurant, *Anocht* (meaning "Tonight"), serving dishes such as duck breast with celeriac and tea soaked prunes. Take your pick from a set menu (€40) or a two-course early bird menu (€24.50), the latter served all night on Thursdays. Thurs–Sat & bank hol Sun 5.30pm–late.

**Aroi** Friary St ☎ 056 770 3644, @ aroi.eu. Affordable Asian food – marketed as street food, but portions are large – in a laidback but classy setting. The lunchtime special (€10) includes any main (try the Khao Pad Beef), plus gelato for dessert. Mon–Wed & Sun noon–9.30pm, Thurs–Sat noon–10.30pm.

**Cakeface Patisserie** 16 Irishtown ☎ 056 773 79971, @ cakeface.ie. Bright, welcoming café, using local ingredients from named sources wherever possible, with a pleasant, unobtrusive retro style. There's proper coffee and hot chocolate, plus gourmet sandwiches (around €8), and of course, cakes and desserts (try the "passionate tart", €4.50). Mon–Sat 10am–6pm, Sun 10am–5pm.

**Campagne** 5 The Arches, Gas House Lane ☎ 056 777 2858, @ campagne.ie. A Michelin starred restaurant since 2013, *Campagne* offers elegant and confident modern French cooking using local produce, served in olive-green booths decorated with colourful paintings of country life;

expect the likes of seared scallops with braised cabbage and morteau sausage. Keep your bank manager happy by coming for the lunch and early-bird set menu (€40 for three courses). Wed & Thurs 5.30–9pm, Fri 5–9.30pm, Sat 12.30–2.30pm & 5–9.30pm, Sun 12.30–3pm.

**The Gourmet Store** 56 High St ☎056 777 1727, ⓦgourmetstorekilkenny.ie. Deli supplying wonderful multi-layered sandwiches (all €4), salads and cakes to take away or eat in their small café, as well as stocking a vast assortment of culinary delights. Mon–Sat 8am–4pm.

**La Rivista** 22 Parliament St ☎056 777 1666, ⓦla rivista.ie. Hospitable Italian restaurant in a well-lit, high-ceilinged, modern space, dishing up moderately priced pizzas, tasty pasta and a varied selection of main courses, all in large portions. Good-value early bird menu, offering two courses for €21.95 Monday to Friday. Mon–Sat 5–10pm, Sun noon–9pm.

**Rinuccini** 1 The Parade ☎056 776 1575, ⓦrinuccini. com. Authentic Italian-run restaurant where classily prepared traditional dishes such as *suprema di pollo ai*

*funghi* (chicken with mushroom cream sauce; €24) are served with some élan; early-evening set menu nightly €25.50. Mon–Fri noon–2.30pm & 5–10pm, Sat noon–3pm & 5–10pm, Sun noon–9pm.

★ **Royal Spice** 2 Watergate ☎056 778 6010, ⓦroyal spice.ie. One of Ireland's best Indian restaurants, a stylish, modern affair that uses fresh local produce such as trout wherever possible. Less familiar dishes include a delicious lasuni prawn curry (€16.60) and there's a wide choice of vegetarian and vegan dishes, either as sides or mains. Three courses for €21.95 for early birds (5–9pm, Sat till 7pm). Mon, Wed & Thurs 5–10pm, Fri & Sat 5–11pm, Sun 4–9.30pm.

**Zuni** 26 Patrick St ☎056 772 3999, ⓦzuni.ie. Very fine and stylish modern Irish dishes with Mediterranean and Asian influences, such as sesame-seed-coated tuna with avocado and wasabi purée, served in a contemporary café-restaurant that used to be a theatre. On the pricey side (most mains €20–25), but there are early bird and tapas menus every evening and a cheaper, simpler lunch menu. Mon–Sat 12.30–2.30pm & 6–9.30pm, Sun 6–9pm.

## DRINKING AND NIGHTLIFE                                    SEE MAP PAGE 183

There are loads of great bars in town, many with traditional music sessions. Weekends, however, can get a bit too rowdy for some tastes, as Kilkenny is a popular venue for Irish stag and hen parties.

**Bridie's Bar and General Store** 72 John St ☎056 776 5133, ⓦlangtons.ie/bridies. Langtons owns some of the classiest bars in town, and *Bridie's*, with its traditional Irish shopfront, is a jewel in their crown. While not exactly authentic, the gleaming decor, friendly bar staff and enclosed garden will win you over. Mon–Thurs 9am–11.30pm, Fri 9am–12.30am, Sat 9am–2am, Sun 9am–11pm.

★ **Hole in the Wall** 17 High St ☎087 807 5650, ⓦhole inthewall.ie. Hard to categorize but impossible to ignore: Ireland's oldest-surviving town house, dating back to 1582, has been lovingly restored by a local cardiologist, who hosts regular musical evenings, including Singspiele, narrative shows on historical subjects enhanced with music, poetry and visuals. It's worth popping in to admire the architecture, even if it's just for a daytime coffee in the summer or an evening drink in the tiny tavern. Daily 1–11.30pm.

**John Cleere's** 28 Parliament St ☎056 776 2573, ⓦcleeres.com. The city's longest-running traditional music session is here on Mon, as well as an open session on Wed, and other music throughout the week in the

bar's theatre, which also hosts comedy and drama. Daily noon–12.30am.

**Kyteler's Inn** 27 St Kieran's St ☎056 772 1064, ⓦkytelersinn.com. This medieval inn's spooky reputation is linked to erstwhile resident Alice Kyteler who was accused of witchcraft in 1324. The bar has open fireplaces, solid oak beams and plenty of nooks and crannies, and offers traditional music at weekends in winter, nightly in summer – including free give-it-a-go *bodhrán* lessons (Mon & Tues at 6.30pm). Mon–Thurs 11am–11.30pm, Fri & Sat 11am–2am, Sun 11am–11.30pm.

**The Left Bank** The Parade ☎056 775 0016, ⓦleftbank. ie. This hulking, granite, Neoclassical edifice on Kilkenny's main corner, a former Bank of Ireland branch, has been reborn as a popular good-time bar, with regular live bands and DJs on Sat. The interior has been fitted out with huge carved mirrors, leather armchairs and ornate fireplaces and screens, while smokers are pampered with a covered, heated backyard with its own outdoor bar. Daily noon–1am.

**Tynan's** 2 John's Bridge ☎087 915 7121. You'll get a great pint of Guinness at this 300-year-old riverside pub, which is furnished with leather banquettes and a lovely carved-wood horseshoe-shaped bar, topped with marble. Mon–Thurs 10.30am–11.30pm, Fri & Sat 10.30–12.30am, Sun 11.30am–11pm.

## ENTERTAINMENT AND SPORT

**Nowlan Park** O'Loughlin Rd ☎056 776 5122, ⓦkilkennygaa.ie. The main stadium in hurling-mad Kilkenny currently holds 27,500 spectators, though there are plans to increase capacity. Match tickets only cost around €15.

**Watergate Theatre** Parliament St ☎056 776 1674, ⓦwatergatetheatre.ie. The leading venue in Kilkenny for the performing arts, the Watergate Theatre offers a varied programme of drama, classical and contemporary music, dance and comedy.

**5**

# Southern Kilkenny

Some of the county's finest spots lie towards its southern extremity, countryside defined by the lush valleys of the rivers **Barrow** and **Nore**. Near the Nore are major ecclesiastical remains at **Kells** and **Jerpoint Abbey**, while above the beguiling village of **Inistioge** you can explore the extensive gardens and arboretum of the Woodstock Demesne.

## Kells Priory

14km south of Kilkenny on the R697 • Open access • Enquire on-site about free tours (summer only)

The medieval village of **Kells** is a petite and picturesque settlement straddling a tributary of the Nore, the King's River. A short stroll east from the village centre along the Stonyford road stands one of the country's most atmospheric ruins, **Kells Priory**, set by the river. This Augustinian foundation was established in 1193 and had a turbulent history, being sacked in both 1252 and 1327, before dissolution in the 1540s. Most of its remains date from the fourteenth and fifteenth centuries, and inside the still-standing curtain wall, with its gatehouse and towers (earning it the local nickname "Seven Castles"), are a church and chapel and several domestic buildings.

## Jerpoint Abbey

2.5km southwest of Thomastown on the R448 • Daily: early March to Sept 9am–5.30pm; Oct & Nov 9am–5pm; Dec–Feb 9.30am–4pm • €5; Heritage Card • ☎ 056 772 4623, �🌐 heritageireland.ie

The major tourist sight in the south of the county is **Jerpoint Abbey**, which lies 20km south of Kilkenny city. Originally founded as a Benedictine house in 1158, the abbey was colonized by Cistercians some twenty years later. The oldest remains are the twelfth-century Romanesque church, but the rest, set around a beautifully colonnaded fifteenth-century cloister, follows the characteristic Cistercian design. The abbey features a number of thirteenth- to sixteenth-century tomb sculptures in the transept chapels and some intriguing carvings on the cloister arcade, including the "little man of Jerpoint" whose stomach-crossed hands and open-mouthed expression suggest either mirth or dyspepsia.

### ACCOMMODATION                         JERPOINT ABBEY

**Abbey House** ☎ 056 772 4166, �🌐 abbeyhousejerpoint. com. Top-notch, all-en-suite B&B opposite the abbey, in a restored, creeper-clad eighteenth-century mill house on the River Arrigle, with freshly squeezed orange juice and local rainbow trout for breakfast. **€90**

## Thomastown

The jumping-off point for Jerpoint Abbey, **THOMASTOWN**, 2.5km to the northeast, is a pleasant riverside town on the Dublin–Waterford train line. A walled town of some note in medieval times, Thomastown now maintains scant sense of its own antiquity, other than its old **bridge** across the Nore and the ruined thirteenth-century church of **St Mary's** at the top of the main street, Market Street.

### ARRIVAL AND DEPARTURE                    THOMASTOWN

**By train** Destinations Dublin (4–6 daily; 1hr 45min); Kilkenny (4–7 daily; 10min); Waterford (4–7 daily; 20min).
**By bus** Destinations Bus Éireann to: Athlone (1–2 daily; 3hr 20min); Dublin & Dublin Airport (7 daily; 2hr–2hr 25min); Inistioge (1 Thurs; 5min); Kilkenny (1–2 daily; 30min); New Ross (1 Thurs; 50min); Waterford (10–11 daily; 30–40min).
Kilbride (�🌐 kilbridecoaches.com) to: Inistioge (Mon–Sat 2 daily; 10min); Kilkenny (Mon–Sat 2 daily; 30min); New Ross (Mon–Sat 2 daily; 30min).

## EATING AND DRINKING

**Barrows Keep** Marsh's St ☎ 056 772 4728, ⓦ barrows keep.com Upmarket restaurant with a great outdoor space and wine selection serving organic, farm-to-table fare. The menu changes regularly, offering seasonal starters such as beetroot tartare; Irish sausage and gnocci (€9), and a selection of mains such as wild halibut (€26) or short ribs (€23) or mushroom and celeriac (€21). Take-away pizza is available mid-week. Wed–Fri 5.30–10pm, Sat 12.30–2.30pm & 5.30–10pm. Sun 1–6.30pm in summer.

★ **Blackberry Café** Market St ☎ 086 775 5303, ⓦ the blackberrycafe.ie. Excellent, central, daytime café, which uses locally sourced ingredients where possible to rustle up sandwiches, soups, quiches, salads and daily specials, as well as home-baked cakes and good coffees. Mon–Fri 9.30am–5.30pm, Sat 10am–5.30pm plus Sun noon–4pm in summer.

**The Hub** Market St ☎ 083 103 6533, ⓦ thehubthomas town.wixsite.com. Once you've had a thick slice of home-made cake (from €3.50), proper coffee or a freshly made milkshake (€3.75) in the quirky café, browse the indoor market with its range of local crafts, cards and secondhand books. Daily 8am–6pm.

# Inistioge

Eight kilometres down the Nore from Thomastown is the quaint village of **INISTIOGE** (pronounced "Inisteeg"), set around a tree-lined green, an old church and a narrow-arched stone bridge over the river. Unsurprisingly, the attractive location, with its rolling hills rising above the village, has drawn film-makers, and both *Circle of Friends* and *Widows' Peak* were shot here in the 1990s.

## Woodstock Gardens

2km south of Inistioge • Daily: April–Sept 9am–7.30pm; Oct–March 9am–4pm • Car park €5 • ☎ 056 779 4441, ⓦ woodstock.ie

The steep lane rising from Inistioge's village green leads to **Woodstock Gardens**. When its owners left Ireland during the War of Independence, the estate's Georgian mansion was taken over by the Black and Tans and, like many similarly tarnished dwellings, was burnt down after independence in 1922. However, since 1999 the county council have been restoring the Victorian **gardens**, and you can enjoy walks lined by firs and monkey puzzles, an arboretum, rose gardens, rockeries and breath-taking views of the Nore valley, as well as a summertime tea room in a cast-iron conservatory.

## ARRIVAL AND DEPARTURE INISTIOGE

**By bus** The first bus from Kilkenny arrives at 12.03pm, and the last bus returns at 2.25pm, so there isn't enough time to explore Woodstock in one day using public transport.

Destinations Kilbride (ⓦ kilbridecoaches.com) to: Kilkenny (Mon–Sat 2 daily; 40min); New Ross (Mon–Sat 2 daily; 20min); Thomastown (Mon–Sat 2 daily; 10min).

## ACCOMMODATION AND EATING

**Woodstock Arms** Village green ☎ 056 775 8440, ⓦ woodstockarms.ie. The village's main provider of hospitality is the *Woodstock Arms*, a pleasant, family-run pub with tables out on the green, offering well-appointed en-suite rooms, with good rates for singles. €85

---

### WALKS IN CARLOW AND SOUTHERN KILKENNY

Several worthwhile waymarked **trails** cross Carlow and southern Kilkenny. The **South Leinster Way** runs for 100km from Kildavin in County Carlow, via 800m Mount Leinster in the Blackstairs Mountains, to Carrick-on-Suir (see page 217) in Tipperary. The most attractive part is between Borris – in Carlow, where the path intersects the **Barrow Way** – and Mullinavat, especially the 16km from Graiguenamanagh to Inistioge. The southernmost section of the Barrow Way, a pretty 8km riverside path, is the most pleasant way to get from Graiguenamanagh to St Mullins (see page 191), and there are trails from **Kilkenny to Bennettsbridge** (12km) and from **Thomastown to Inistioge** (11km) along the Nore – for information on these, as well as on other walking routes, go to ⓦ trailkilkenny.ie or ⓦ irishtrails.ie, which feature downloadable maps.

## 5 Carlow

The county of **Carlow** has little in the way of major sights, but **Carlow Town** warrants a visit for its contemporary arts centre, VISUAL, and its local history museum, and if you have your own transport there are a couple of worthwhile attractions nearby. Carlow is at its prettiest to the west, along the River Barrow, which for much of its length forms the boundary with Kilkenny – the village of **St Mullins** has a lovely riverside towpath that's the perfect spot for a stroll.

### Carlow Town and around

For centuries, **Carlow Town**, 35 miles northeast of Wexford, was an Anglo-Norman stronghold at the edge of an otherwise fiercely Gaelic county. Today, the only thing to suggest the busy town's former frontier status is the remains of a once proud Norman **castle**, which lie beside the river at the west end of town. A far more modern attraction is the €18 million development of the **VISUAL Centre for Contemporary Art**. Southeast of Carlow Town, in charming Clonegal, **Huntington Castle and Gardens** and the nearby **Altamont gardens** warrant half a day of exploration.

#### VISUAL Centre for Contemporary Art

Old Dublin Rd; pedestrian entrance off College St, beside the cathedral • Tues–Sun 11am–5.30pm • Free • ☎ 059 917 2400, ⓦ visualcarlow.ie

In a vast, industrial-inspired glass and concrete space, **VISUAL** offers a varied programme of contemporary arts with a local and international focus – check online for events and workshops. Attached is the 320-seat George Bernard Shaw Theatre (named for the playwright, whose mother was from Carlow).

#### Carlow County Museum

College St • Jan–May & Sept–Dec Mon–Sat 10am–4.30pm; June–Aug Mon–Sat 10am–5pm • Free • ☎ 059 913 1554, ⓦ carlowcountymuseumblog.wordpress.com

Over three floors, the county **museum** displays eclectic artefacts that relate to local historic characters and events. Highlights include a 7m hand-carved wooden pulpit from Carlow Cathedral and a pipe that belonged to Captain Myles Keogh, who was killed in the Battle of Little Big Horn in 1876.

#### Altamont Gardens

Between Tullow and Bunclody, 23km southeast of Carlow Town • Daily: Jan & Dec 9am–4pm; Feb & Nov 9am–4.30pm; March & Oct 9am–5pm; April–Sept 9am–6.30pm • Free; parking €2 • ☎ 059 915 9444, ⓦ heritageireland.ie

Pathways meander the lawns, woodlands and riverbanks of pretty **Altamont Gardens**. Managed by the OPW since 1999, around 1500 different trees and shrubs are tended to, as well as 150 types of roses. The man-made lake is the romantic centrepiece, covered with waterlilies and crossed by a stone bridge. Note that some of the paths close in adverse weather as pathways are slippery.

#### Huntington Castle and Gardens

Clonegal, 30km southeast of Carlow • **House**: Visit by tour only, May–Sept hourly 2–5pm • €10 (includes gardens) • **Gardens**: May–Sept 11am–5pm • €6 • ☎ 053 937 7160, ⓦ huntingtoncastle.com

Built in 1625 on the strategically important Wexford–Dublin route, **Huntington Castle and Gardens** has been considerably altered since its early days as a granite keep. It's been a family home for generations – the first in Ireland to have electricity – and the extensive grounds include a 500-year-old Yew walk. There's also a tea room and adventure playground on-site.

## INFORMATION

**Tourist office** College St (Jan–May & Sept–Dec Mon–Fri 9.30am–5pm, Sat 10am–4.30; June–Aug Mon–Fri 9.30am–5pm, Sat 10am–5pm & Sun 2–4.30pm; ☎059

## CARLOW TOWN AND AROUND

913 0411; ⓦ carlowtourism.com). Map of 1hr self-guided historic walking tour is available.

## ACCOMMODATION AND EATING

### CARLOW TOWN

**Barrowville Town House** Kilkenny Rd ☎059 914 3324, ⓦ barrowville.com. An elegant regency building a short walk from the town centre. Bedrooms have an English country cottage feel, plus there's a drawing room and garden to relax in. Breakfast is served in the conservatory and there's parking out front. **€80**

**Lennons** VISUAL, Old Dublin Rd ☎059 917 9245, ⓦ lennons.ie. Stylish, award-winning bistro café on the lower ground floor of VISUAL. Produce is locally sourced and there are plenty of veggie options (warm goat's cheese and spiced pear salad; €13.50); they also have a coffee

kiosk on Potato Market in the town centre. Mon–Wed 10.30am–5pm, Thurs–Sat 10.30am–5pm & 6–9.30pm, Sun noon–4pm.

### CLONEGAL

**Huntington Castle** ☎053 937 7160, ⓦ huntington castle.com. Immaculately decorated period rooms in a seventeenth-century castle, with views over the formal lawns or the ruins of an early Cistercian Abbey. Full Irish breakfast is served in a beautiful Victorian kitchen; there's a tearoom in a renovated out building, and an award-winning bistro within walking distance in the village. **€180**

## St Mullins

A picturesque village on the Barrow Way walking route (see page 189), **St Mullins** is appealingly arranged at the bottom of a valley around a village green. Opposite the green is a perfectly dome-shaped castle earthwork and just behind are the remains of a monastery founded by St Moling in 696, consisting of the remnants of a medieval church and a round tower's stump. Beyond this, the road slopes down to a Barrow-side café.

### EATING

### ST MULLINS

**The Mullicháin Café** The Quay ☎051 424440, ⓦ the mullichaincafe.ie. In an eighteenth-century grain storehouse, with plenty of outdoor seating by the water. Simple menu, with soups, salads, paninis, wraps and pizzas

(€12–14), along with speciality tea, coffee and home-made cakes (try the lemon drizzle, €4.50). Feb Sat & Sun 11am–6pm, March–Oct Tues–Sun 11am–6pm.

# Wexford town

**WEXFORD** is a happy-go-lucky kind of town with plenty of scope for enjoying music in its **pubs**, but it has its serious side too, not least in the shape of its internationally renowned **opera festival**. There are few sights to see in the town itself – more is on offer in the surrounding area (see page 194) – but the appeal of the place lies in its atmosphere and setting: its long, narrow medieval lanes huddle for shelter inland of the exposed quays, which line the southern shore of the wide Slaney estuary, with the railway line to Rosslare dividing the main road from the promenade and a busy little marina. The town's main street is lined with shops, bars and cafés, with the **Bull Ring** at its heart.

The town began life as a Viking base for incursions and trading, before becoming an early Anglo-Norman conquest in 1169. Wexford later housed an English garrison whose loyalty to the Crown resulted in vicious fighting against Cromwell's army in 1649. It also played a significant role in the 1798 Rebellion, which was finally quelled at Enniscorthy (see page 196). Wexford's lengthy quays pay testimony to its re-emergence as a prosperous trading centre in the nineteenth century, though gradual silting of the harbour's entrance and the development of Rosslare Harbour led to its demise as a competitive port.

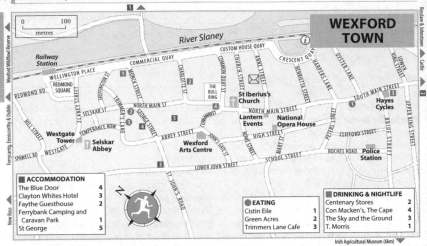

5

**WEXFORD TOWN**

| ■ ACCOMMODATION | |
| --- | --- |
| The Blue Door | 4 |
| Clayton Whites Hotel | 3 |
| Faythe Guesthouse | 2 |
| Ferrybank Camping and Caravan Park | 1 |
| St George | 5 |

| ● EATING | |
| --- | --- |
| Cistin Eile | 1 |
| Green Acres | 2 |
| Trimmers Lane Cafe | 3 |

| ■ DRINKING & NIGHTLIFE | |
| --- | --- |
| Centenary Stores | 2 |
| Con Macken's, The Cape | 4 |
| The Sky and the Ground | 3 |
| T. Morris | 1 |

## Westgate Tower and Selskar Abbey

1 Temperance Row • Guided 45min tours (Tower and Abbey) March–Oct Mon–Sat 3pm • €3 • ☎ 086 107 9497, ⓦ wexfordwalkingtours.net

Wexford's walls once had five gates, but the only survivor is the **Westgate Tower**, completed in 1300. The adjacent **Selskar Abbey** was founded by Alexander de la Roche who left Ireland to fight in the Crusades, but returned to discover that his fiancée, incorrectly advised of his death, had become a nun. He also took holy orders, becoming an Augustinian, and established Selskar in the early twelfth century. After the murder of Thomas Becket in 1170, Henry II came to Selskar Abbey to do penance. The abbey must have survived Dissolution since Cromwell's troops took the trouble to destroy it when they captured the town. Alongside its remains stand a fourteenth-century tower house and a nineteenth-century church, while part of the old town wall can be seen running along one side of the graveyard.

## The Bull Ring

On North Main Street, the **Bull Ring** derives its name from the time when bull-baiting, a once popular form of entertainment, took place here – the bull's hide, apparently, was given to the mayor, the meat to the poor. It later became a rallying-point for politicians – Charles Parnell, James Connolly, Éamon de Valera and Michael Collins all addressed the crowd here. The bronze monument of a 1798 Pikeman that stands in the square was sculpted by Oliver Sheppard, also responsible for *The Death of Cúchulainn* housed in the GPO in Dublin. On Fridays and Saturdays, the Bull Ring hosts an interesting **market** (Fri & Sat 9am–5pm), peddling everything from artisan foods to antiques, and handmade clothes to soaps.

## St Iberius's Church

31 North Main St • Mon–Sat 10am–4pm • ☎ 053 914 0652

A little further along Main Street from the Bull Ring is Anglican **St Iberius's Church**, named after Ibar, the contemporary of St Patrick who Christianized Wexford. It dates back to the late seventeenth century but was much remodelled in 1760 and features a fine Georgian interior, possibly designed by John Roberts (see page 207). The church's unusual gallery was installed to accommodate troops stationed in the town, and its broader-than-long shape was an ingenious answer to the problem of the site's proximity to the city wall. The church hosts regular classical-music concerts (ⓦ musicforwexford.ie).

**5**

## ARRIVAL AND DEPARTURE
WEXFORD TOWN

**By train** O'Hanrahan train station, which has left-luggage facilities, is on Redmond Square at the north end of the quays.
Destinations Dublin (3–4 daily; 2hr 35min); Enniscorthy (3–4 daily; 20min); Rosslare (3–4 daily; 20min); Rosslare Europort (3–4 daily; 25min).
**By bus** Buses stop on Redmond Square, close to O'Hanrahan station.

Destinations Bus Éireann: Dublin and airport (roughly hourly; 2hr–2hr 45min); Enniscorthy (roughly hourly; 20min); New Ross (5–8 Mon–Fri; 40min); Rosslare Europort (5–7 daily; 30min); Waterford (5–8 daily; 1hr).
Wexford Bus (ⓦwexfordbus.com): Dublin and airport (9–12 daily; 2hr 30min); Enniscorthy (9–12 daily; 30min), Waterford (7 daily; 1hr).

## INFORMATION

**Tourist office** Crescent Quay (Mon–Sat 9am–5.30pm; ☎053 912 3111, ⓦvisitwexford.ie).
**Walking tours** Hour-long tours of the town (March–Oct Mon–Sat 11am; €5; ⓦwexfordwalkingtours.net) pick up

from the tourist office.
**Bike rental** Hayes, 108 South Main St (☎053 912 2462, ⓦhayescycles.com) rent bikes for €20/day.

## ACCOMMODATION
SEE MAP PAGE 192

Book a few months in advance for rooms during the Opera Festival (see page 194).
**The Blue Door** 18 Lower George St ☎053 912 1047, ⓦbluedoor.ie. Welcoming, very central Georgian town house hung with pot plants, where the rooms are bright, attractive and comfortable and the breakfasts, served in the cheery front room, are tasty and generous. **€70**
**Clayton Whites Hotel** Abbey St ☎053 912 2311, ⓦclaytonwhiteshotel.com. There's been a hotel on this site since the eighteenth century, and today's version is a lavish affair offering airy, contemporary rooms, in addition to a 20m pool, kids pool, spa with Jacuzzi and sauna, and gym. The Terrace restaurant, overlooking the grand courtyard, and Library Bar, round things off nicely. **€80**
**Faythe Guesthouse** The Faythe ☎053 912 2249, ⓦfaytheguesthouse.com. A fine Victorian house in a

quiet part of town just southeast of the centre, whose pretty grounds include the remaining wall of an old castle, offering very agreeable rooms and a splendid lounge with an open fire. **€80**
**Ferrybank Camping and Caravan Park** ☎053 918 5256, ⓦwexfordswimmingpool.ie. Scenic, breezy seafront camping just across the bridge from the quays, with the public swimming pool, gym, sauna and steam room on site (discounted admission for campers), as well as a campers' kitchen, laundry, recreation room and playground. Motorhome **€25**, tent pitch **€14.50**
**St George** George St ☎053 914 3474, ⓦstgeorgeguesthouse.com. Welcoming, remodelled Georgian townhouse set around a courtyard with bright, comfortable, en-suite rooms and plenty of local advice. Reductions without breakfast or for stays of two nights or more; very good single rates. **€70**

## EATING
SEE MAP PAGE 192

★ **Cistin Eile** 80 South Main St ☎053 912 1616. Far from being just "another kitchen" as its Irish name might suggest, this informal restaurant is an exceptional place, serving imaginative modern Irish food with a rustic bent, in dishes such as Wicklow venison salad, spiced apple, red wine and rosehip (three courses €35). At lunchtime, you can feast on the market fish dish of the day for €13. Mon & Tues noon–3pm, Wed–Sat noon–3pm & 6–9pm.
**Green Acres** Selskar St ☎053 912 2975, ⓦgreenacres.ie. A handsome redbrick house with a modern glass

extension. Inside you'll find a well-stocked deli and wine shop, a first-floor art gallery and a bistro serving creative fare such as wild Wicklow game pie with braised kale and pickled cranberries (€29.50). Daily 9.30am–10pm.
**Trimmers Lane Cafe** 7 Trimmer's Lane ☎053 919 8956, ⓦtrimmerslanecafe.ie. Delightful café with outdoor seating on a broad pedestrianized street. A mouth-watering array of home-made cakes and pastries, in addition to salads, sandwiches and flatbreads, and some fab pasta dishes such as watercress and almond pesto (€11). Mon–Sat 9am–4pm.

## DRINKING AND NIGHTLIFE
SEE MAP PAGE 192

**Centenary Stores** Charlotte St ☎053 912 4424, ⓦthe stores.ie. The *Stores* are most famous among Wexford's youth as a weekend nightclub, but the original pub, at the heart of this entertainment complex in two 1850s town houses, is still a very congenial spot, with its dark wood floor and panelling, and a pleasant, south-facing outdoor area. Also serves inexpensive daytime food and hosts a traditional session Sunday lunchtime. Mon–Wed

10.30am–11.30pm, Thurs–Sat 10.30am–2am, Sun 12.30pm–1am.
**Con Macken's, The Cape** The Bull Ring. The undertaking side of the business, as claimed by the sign, has long gone, and this popular meeting place is very much a place to catch up with local news and watch the world pass by. Mon–Thurs 10.30am–11.30pm, Fri & Sat 10.30am–12.30am, Sun 1–11pm.

> ### WEXFORD FESTIVALS
>
> The biggest event in Wexford's cultural calendar is undoubtedly the prestigious **Wexford Opera Festival** (W wexfordopera.com) held over two weeks in late October, which draws not only performers and companies from around the world, but international audiences too, attracted by its distinctive programme of rarely performed works – tickets (booking opens in May or June) and accommodation need to be reserved months in advance. The main performances are supplemented by a variety of concerts and talks; by a broad-based **fringe festival** (W wexfordfringe.ie), featuring art exhibitions, drama, comedy and more music; and by an old-fashioned fairground and two **spiegeltents** on the Quays, which host cabaret, comedy and contemporary music (W wexfordspiegeltent.com).

**The Sky and the Ground** 112 South Main St 053 912 1273. This dark and woody bar, with a large beer garden at the back, is an atmospheric place for a pint, staging regular live music, including Candlelight Sessions on Tues, which feature everything from acoustic soloists to roots/Americana bands. Mon–Thurs 2–11.30pm, Fri & Sat 2pm–12.30am, Sun 2–11pm.

**T. Morris** Monck St 086 842 0498. Friendly, gnarly old bar, fitted with bare wooden floors, old grocers' drawers and signs to give a relaxed, sprawling, anything-goes air. It has one of Ireland's cutest beer gardens, decorated with fairy lights, bamboo and roses, and hosts traditional music on Wednesday nights. Mon–Thurs 4–11.30pm, Fri 4pm–12.30am, Sat noon–12.30am, Sun 3–11pm.

### ENTERTAINMENT

**National Opera House** High St 053 912 2144, W nationaloperahouse.ie. Ireland's only acoustically purpose-built opera house is home to the acclaimed Wexford Opera Festival, as well as hosting drama, dance, comedy and music throughout the year. There's also a panoramic rooftop café.

**Wexford Arts Centre** Cornmarket 053 912 3764, W wexfordartscentre.ie. Music, theatre, dance, comedy and art exhibitions are just some of the offerings that are laid on by the Wexford Arts Centre, which is located in the eighteenth-century market house.

# Around Wexford town

To Wexford's north lies Ireland's premier wildfowl sanctuary, **Wexford Wildfowl Reserve**, beyond which the coastline is punctuated by some lovely sandy beaches: 10km from town, past Curracloe, lies the powder-soft, dune-backed **Curracloe Beach**, a continuous seven-mile stretch that morphs into **Ballinesker Beach**; and further up the coast near Kilmuckridge is a broad beach popular with families, **Morriscastle**, known as "the golden mile".

To the west of Wexford is the impressive **Irish National Heritage Park**, while to the south runs rather bland countryside, though the ornate gardens of **Johnstown Castle** and the **Irish Agricultural Museum** are well worth visiting. The small seaside resort of **Rosslare** has a splendid beach, much enjoyed by families in summer, while **Rosslare Europort** is a major point of entry into Ireland. West along the south coast is the traditional fishing village of **Kilmore Quay**, with its thatched cottages, whitewashed walls, sandy beach and seasonal boat trips out to the bird sanctuary on the **Saltee Islands** (contact Declan Bates 053 912 9684). A little further out of the county town's orbit, energetic **Enniscorthy** is best known for its associations with the 1798 Rebellion, which is commemorated in an excellent museum.

## Wexford Wildfowl Reserve

North side of the Slaney estuary • Daily 9am–5pm • Free • 076 100 2660, W wexfordwildfowlreserve.ie • From Wexford, head 3km up the R741 Gorey road, then turn right for 2km

The fascinating **Wexford Wildfowl Reserve** occupies a charming patch of reclaimed land, 2m below sea level, known as the North Slobs (from Irish *slab*, meaning "mud, mire or a soft-fleshed person"), a maze of channels, reed beds, grazing lands and tillage. Between early October and mid-April, this peculiarly rich habitat is home to thousands of ducks, geese and swans, while in spring and autumn large numbers of birds on migration stop to feed here. Of particular importance in the former category are the ten thousand or so Greenland white-fronted geese, about a third of the world's population, which winter on the reserve after nesting in Greenland, as well as the two thousand pale-bellied brent geese, which arrive in mid-December after breeding in Canada. Year-round inhabitants include 42 wader species, mute swans and a healthy population of Irish hares. The reserve is home to various hides, and a well-run **visitor centre**, which houses an observation tower and an engaging little exhibition.

## Curracloe Beach and Raven Nature Reserve

Accessed via Curracloe village, 9km northeast of Wexford • Free guided walks daily at noon, 2pm and 4pm, contact ☎ 053 919 6313

**Curracloe Beach**, which deputized for Omaha Beach as the site of the D-Day landings in Steven Spielberg's World War II epic *Saving Private Ryan*, is a wide empty bay that stretches for miles. Extending south is **Raven Nature Reserve**, an expanse of dunes and pine forest that runs down to Raven Point at the mouth of the estuary.

## Irish National Heritage Park

4km west of Wexford off the N11 Dublin road at Ferrycarrig • Daily: May–Aug 9.30am–6.30pm, last admission 5pm; Sept–April 9.30am–5.30pm, last admission 3pm • €11 • ☎ 053 912 0733, ⊛ irishheritage.ie

The carefully researched **Irish National Heritage Park** will plug the gaps in your imagination, with sixteen full-scale reconstructions of the sites and buildings that configure Ireland's known history, right through from Mesolithic times. A tour around the park, either with a costumed guide or by yourself with an audio-guide, takes you past, and sometimes into, all manner of dwellings and ritual sites, including a crannog and Viking boatyard, while the undoubted centrepiece is an impressive facsimile of a twelfth-century castle (built over the ruins of a castle of that era). The park also has a falconry centre, visitor centre, playground and restaurant.

## Johnstown Castle and the Irish Agricultural Museum

6km south of Wexford • Daily: March–June, Sept & Oct 9am–5pm; July & Aug 9am–6pm; Nov–Feb 9am–4pm • **Museum and gardens** €9, **castle** €4 **(pre-booked only)** • ☎ 053 918 4671, ⊛ johnstowncastle.ie • Wexford Bus services to Kilmore Quay and to Rosslare from Redmond Square both pass within walking distance of the agricultural museum (⊛ wexfordbus.com)

It's well worth taking a trip from Wexford town to **Johnstown Castle**, a nineteenth-century Gothic Revival mansion. Now refurbished, it's possible to have a guided tour of the castle – the highlight of which is the remarkable 86-metre long servant's tunnel – though more appealing are the extensive grounds, featuring an abundance of trees and plants, outdoors and in hothouses, as well as ornamental lakes, rich woodland, a sunken Italian garden and a ruined medieval tower house. The estate's old farm buildings are now home to the **Irish Agricultural Museum**, which explores rural history via displays, artefacts, a wealth of furniture and machinery, and re-created workshops and kitchens. There's also a specific display on the Famine, recounting its impact, the search for a cure for potato blight, and the massive changes in rural Ireland that ensued. The grounds also incorporate a visitor centre with café, and a woodland play area.

## Rosslare and Rosslare Europort

Some 11km southeast of Wexford town, with a train station on the Rosslare Europort line, is **ROSSLARE** (aka Rosslare Strand), a single-street village with a massive and popular sandy beach and a superb **place to stay**, *Kelly's* (see page 196). A little further

**5**

---

### ENNISCORTHY FESTIVALS

The town's two principal festivals are the **Rockin Food Festival** (⊕ rockinfoodfestival.ie) over the August Bank Holiday weekend and which incorporates a huge food, drinks and craft market alongside all manner of rock'n'roll performances; and June's **Strawberry Festival** (⊕ strawberryfest.ie), whose festivities include loads of entertainments, a three-day literary festival and punnet-loads of Wexford's famous strawberries – which you'll see for sale at roadside stalls in and around the county at this time of year.

---

southeast along the coast, **ROSSLARE EUROPORT** (⊕ rosslareeuroport.ie) is a major ferry terminal surrounded by hotels and B&Bs, serving arrivals from Wales, France and Spain. Should you arrive by car, there's no reason to linger, and if you come on foot there are train and bus connections to various parts of Ireland.

#### ARRIVAL AND DEPARTURE

**By ferry** The terminal hosts a bureau de change, a Budget car rental outlet (☎ 053 913 3318, ⊕ budget.ie) and offices of the ferry companies (see page 30): Irish Ferries (for Pembroke; ⊕ irishferries.com) and Stena Line (for Fishguard; ⊕ stenaline.ie).

**By train** There are stations both at the Europort and in Rosslare village.

Destinations Dublin (3–4 daily; 3hr); Enniscorthy (3–4 daily; 45min); Rosslare (3–4 daily; 5min); Wexford (3–4 daily; 25min).

#### ROSSLARE AND ROSSLARE EUROPORT

**By bus** Buses stop at the port and the village. For Dublin, on any day except Thursday, change at Wexford.

Destinations Rosslare Europort to: Dublin (Thurs; 3hr 25min); New Ross (5–6 daily; 1hr 5min); Waterford (5–6 daily; 1hr 30min); Wexford (5–7 daily; 25min).

Rosslare to: New Ross (Mon–Sat 2 daily 1hr 40min); Rosslare Europort (5–6 daily; 5min); Waterford (5–6 daily; 1hr 20min); Wexford (Bus Éireann 5–6 daily, Wexford Bus 2–3 Mon–Sat; 20–40min).

#### ACCOMMODATION AND EATING

**Hotel Rosslare** Cliff Rd ☎ 053 913 3110, ⊕ hotel rosslare.ie. Surveying the harbour from a cliff-top position, this hotel provides furnished, spacious rooms in an unobtrusive contemporary style, some with balconies with great views – and it's very convenient for the ferry. **€80**

★ **Kelly's Resort** Coast Rd, 8min walk from Rosslare Strand train station ☎ 053 913 2114, ⊕ kellys.ie. Family-

run *Kelly's* sits in lovely Mediterranean gardens right by the 8km strand and offers the highest standards of service. There's a spa with thermal, seawater and seaweed treatments, as well as a host of activities for adults and kids. Its walls – including those in its two excellent restaurants – are adorned with one of the finest private collections of modern Irish art. All manner of packages available. Closed Dec & Jan. **€87**

## Enniscorthy

Around 24km north of Wexford, the busy town of **ENNISCORTHY** straddles the River Slaney, its main streets, such as Castle Hill, rising steeply from the west bank towards Market Square.

### National 1798 Centre

Parnell Rd (10min walk from Market Square, heading down Rafter St) • March–Oct Mon–Fri 9.30am–5pm, Sat & Sun 11am–5pm; last admission 1hr before closing • €7, €10 joint ticket with Enniscorthy Castle • ☎ 053 923 7596, ⊕ 1798centre.ie

The **National 1798 Centre** is a high-tech sound-and-vision fest, capturing the excitement of events prior to the Rebellion, the rising itself and its aftermath, all cogently set within broader intellectual and political contexts that brought about American independence and the French Revolution. An audiovisual features an enthralling debate between actors playing the roles of the Dublin-born Whig politician and philosopher Edmund Burke and Thomas Paine, the English radical and American revolutionary whose *Rights of Man* (1792) was a direct riposte to Burke's more conservative *Reflections on the Revolution in France* (1790). It was on the gorse-covered **Vinegar Hill**, opposite on the Slaney's eastern bank, that the rebels of 1798 met their bloody demise at the hands of British forces.

## Enniscorthy Castle

Castle Hill • Mon–Fri 9.30am–5pm, Sat & Sun noon–5pm • €6, joint ticket with 1798 Centre €10 • ☎ 053 923 4699,
Ⓦ enniscorthycastle.ie

Though it's a proper castle in the heart of town, with turrets, round towers and crenellations in the traditional style of Norman stone fortresses, **Enniscorthy Castle** has spent most of its 800-year existence as a private residence. Now completely renovated, it numbers among its exhibitions a first floor that's been re-created as it might have been when it was last inhabited, in the early twentieth century. Other engaging and thoughtful displays cover 1950s Ireland and the movie *Brooklyn* (scenes were filmed in Enniscorthy), as well as pioneering modernist furniture designer, Eileen Gray, who was born at nearby Brownswood House. Staff will escort you to the crenellated roof for fantastic views of the town, the river, Vinegar Hill with its ruined windmill and, to the west, the Blackstairs Mountains.

## St Aidan's Cathedral

Cathedral St • Daily 8.30am–6pm • Free • ☎ 053 923 5777, Ⓦ staidanscathedral.ie

Just west of Market Square along Main Street, **St Aidan's Cathedral** is an imposing Gothic Revival edifice, designed in the mid-nineteenth century by Augustus Pugin, who is responsible for the interior of the Palace of Westminster. As well as impressively high pointed arches, the cathedral features an oak carved pulpit and beautiful stained-glass windows depicting saints and bishops.

### ARRIVAL AND INFORMATION                                    ENNISCORTHY

**By train** The train station is on the east side of the river, just off Templeshannon, which leads north from Enniscorthy Bridge.
Destinations Dublin (3–4 daily; 2hr 15min); Rosslare Europort (3–4 daily; 50min); Wexford (3–4 daily; 25min).
**By bus** Buses set down outside the Bus Stop Shop on Templeshannon. For New Ross, Rosslare Europort and Waterford, change at Wexford.

Destinations Bus Éireann: Dublin and airport (roughly hourly; 2hr 25–3hr); Wexford (roughly hourly; 20min). Wexford Bus (Ⓦ wexfordbus.com): Dublin and airport (roughly hourly; 2hr 25min–3hr); Wexford (roughly hourly; 30min).
**Tourist office** Enniscorthy Castle is the official information point (☎ 053 923 4699).

### ACCOMMODATION

**Monart** 3km west of Enniscorthy ☎ 053 923 8999, Ⓦ monart.ie. Incredible destination hotel-spa in a converted eighteenth-century mill with vast landscaped gardens. It's five-star and far from cheap, although access to the thermal spa and classes is unrestricted for guests, and rates for singles

are considerably reduced. €260
**Riverside Park** The Promenade ☎ 053 923 7800, Ⓦ riversideparkhotel.com. Top-notch hotel near the 1798 Centre, with modern, attractive rooms, many of which overlook the river, and its own indoor pool, gym and sauna. €98

### EATING AND DRINKING

Enniscorthy hosts a lively **farmers' market** every Sat morning on Abbey Square.
**The Antique Tavern** 14 Slaney St, down towards the quays from Market Square ☎ 053 923 3428. Great spot for an atmospheric pint, a half-timbered, eighteenth-century pub with a wealth of local photos and memorabilia on its walls and a covered upstairs balcony for absorbing views of the river and Vinegar Hill. Roughly Mon–Thurs 5–11.30pm, Fri & Sat 5pm–12.30am, Sun 5–11pm.
**The Bailey** On the quays near Cottontree Café ☎ 053 923 0353, Ⓦ thebailey.ie. Converted into a café-bar from a nineteenth-century malt warehouse and decorated in plush Victorian style, *The Bailey* offers good food (all-day breakfast €11.95) and regular live gigs. Mon–Thurs 9am–

11.30pm (food till 9pm), Fri & Sat 9am–12.30am (food till 9.30pm), Sun noon–11.30pm (food till 8.30pm).
**Via Veneto** 58 Weafer St ☎ 053 923 6929, Ⓦ viaveneto.ie. A cosy, white-tablecloth restaurant offering authentic Italian main courses, including plenty of fresh fish, and much cheaper pizzas and pastas. Wed & Thurs 5.30–9.30pm, Fri & Sat 5.30–10pm, Sun 5–9pm.
**The Wilds** 23 Weafer St ☎ 053 923 7799, Ⓦ thewilds.ie. A bright, light-filled café and deli attached to a superb craft shop. Make a beeline here for breakfast (full-Irish €11.95), brunch (avocado and poached eggs on sourdough toast, roasted tomatoes and organic leaves €10) or lunch (selection of salads, gourmet sandwiches and burgers around €10). Tues–Fri 9am–5pm, Sat 10am–5pm, Sun 10am–4pm.

**5**

# Hook Peninsula and the Barrow estuary

The sightseeing highlight of Wexford's southwestern corner is the atmospheric ruin of **Tintern Abbey**, at the neck of the blustery **Hook Peninsula**, which is punctuated with sandy beaches and a fascinating medieval lighthouse. Circumnavigating Hook Head brings you to the pleasant little beach resort of **Duncannon** and nearby **Ballyhack**, whence car ferries cross the Barrow estuary to Passage East in County Waterford. This ferry service is 20km south of the first road crossing of the Barrow, at the busy town of **New Ross**, and is certainly worth taking if you're short of time, but that way you'd miss out on a tight cluster of attractions on the east bank of the river, notably the glorious remains of **Dunbrody Abbey**, the **John F. Kennedy Arboretum**, and the charming **Ros Tapestry** and vivid **Dunbrody Famine Ship** at New Ross.

## Tintern Abbey and Colclough Walled Garden

30km southwest of Wexford, off the R374 • **Abbey** Mid-May to late Sept daily 10am–5pm • €5; Heritage Card • ☎ 051 562650, ⓦ heritageireland.ie • **Walled garden** Daily: April–Sept 10am–6pm; Oct–March 10am–4pm • €5 • ☎ 083 3064 159, ⓦ colcloughwalledgarden.com

On the broad neck of the Hook Peninsula lie the dramatic ruins of **Tintern Abbey**. This early thirteenth-century Cistercian foundation was constructed by William Marshall, Earl of Pembroke, to give thanks for being saved from drowning at sea, and was populated by monks from its better-known namesake in Monmouthshire, Wales. After dissolution in 1536, the abbey was granted to one of Henry VIII's officers, Anthony Colclough, who much modified the buildings, while subsequent additions, including the battlemented walls, were made by his descendants, who lived here until the 1960s. Of the original cruciform church, the tower, chancel, cloister walls and south transept chapels are extant. Beyond the abbey, verdant woodland trails lead to the restored **Colclough Walled Garden** (pronounced "coke-lee"), which is traversed by a stream crossed by five small bridges.

## Hook Head

**Hook Head** itself is entirely exposed to the elements, serene in good weather – though very dangerous for swimming – and excitingly wild in a storm. The rocky shoreline has a wealth of fossils and it's a popular location for birdwatchers, who visit to spot migrations, as well as whale- and dolphin-watchers.

### Hook Lighthouse

Accessed by guided tour (every 30min); daily: July & Aug 9.30am–7pm; Sept–June 10am–5pm • €10 • ☎ 051 397055, ⓦ hookheritage.ie

The oldest operational lighthouse in the world, **Hook Lighthouse** was built by William Marshall in the early thirteenth century to guide ships safely into the Barrow estuary on their way to his thriving port of New Ross, replacing an earlier

---

### ACROSS THE ESTUARY TO WATERFORD: BALLYHACK

If you're heading for County Waterford, then the Passage East Car Ferry (☎ 051 382480, ⓦ passageferry.ie) from **Ballyhack**, 1km northwest of Arthurstown, is a boon, saving time and mileage with a five-minute crossing. Ferries operate a continuous service (June–Aug Mon–Sat 7am–9pm, Sun 9.30am–9pm; Sept–May Mon–Sat 7am–8pm, Sun 9.30am–8pm; car €8 single, €12 return; cyclist €2 single, €3 return). While waiting for the ferry, you might be tempted by a visit to **Ballyhack Castle**, a fifteenth-century tower house in the village built by the Knights Hospitallers of St John (May–Aug Sat–Wed 9.30am–5pm; free; ⓦ heritageireland.ie).

**5**

beacon. Apart from a short period during the 1600s, it has functioned ever since and became fully automated in 1996. Guided tours lead to the lighthouse's top, some 36m high, and recount its history, paying note to the monks who were the first light-keepers here; there's also a café and bakery. Check out their events roster on the website.

## Duncannon and around

**DUNCANNON** is a small, friendly village with a lovely beach protected from the elements by a rocky coastline at its southern extremity. On the beach, you can take **kitesurfing** and **stand-up paddleboarding lessons**, and in August there's a four-day **International Sand-Sculpting Festival**, in which a host of competitors produce astonishing, but sadly temporary, artworks, followed by a two-day **kitesurfing festival**.

### Duncannon Fort

Accessed by guided tour: April–Oct daily 11.30am, 12.45pm, 2.30pm & 3.45pm • €6 • ☎ 051 389530, ⓦ duncannonfort.ie

Looming above the village from its lofty promontory is **Duncannon Fort**, constructed in 1586, on the site of a Celtic fort and a Norman castle, as a bulwark against Spanish invasion. Much remodelled since then, the fort was burnt down by the IRA in 1922. Informative, forty-five minute tours of the fort include the ramparts, which have stunning views of the Barrow estuary and down to Hook Head.

### ARRIVAL AND INFORMATION
### DUNCANNON AND AROUND

**By bus** Destinations New Ross (Mon–Sat 3 daily; 35min); Waterford (Mon–Sat 3 daily; 1hr).

**Tourist office** By the post office (Mon–Fri 9.30am–5.30pm, plus June–Aug Sat & Sun 11am–4pm; ☎ 051 389530, ⓦ hookpeninsula.com).

**Hooked Kite Surfing** From €50 for a 1hr 30min lesson (☎ 087 675 5567, ⓦ hookedkitesurfing.ie).

### ACCOMMODATION AND EATING

**Dunbrody House** Just before Arthurstown, 3km north of Duncannon ☎ 051 389600, ⓦ dunbrodyhouse.com. Sumptuous 1830s mansion set in glorious parklands. As well as a luxurious spa, the hotel houses one of Ireland's foremost cookery schools so it's unsurprising that the restaurant here is exceedingly good, if pricey; a cheaper menu is offered in the seafood bar. **€135**

**Glendine House** On the east side of Arthurstown, 3km north of Duncannon ☎ 051 389500, ⓦ glendinehouse. com. With fine views of the estuary, this welcoming late Georgian country house in expansive grounds offers luxurious, upmarket B&B. Good rates for singles; self-catering cottage also available. **€98**

**The Moorings B&B** By the fort and beach in Duncannon ☎ 087 992 9138, ⓦ mooringsbnbwexford.com. Bright, modern, pine-floored and furnished house with comfortable, well-kept en-suite rooms and an attractive garden. Breakfast is served at a time that suits you. **€80**

★ **Roche's** By the beach in Duncannon ☎ 051 389188, ⓦ rochesbar.ie. *Roche's* features a cosy, old-fashioned front bar – home to traditional sessions on Fri – and larger spaces beyond, including a beer garden. The food here has a definite Asian bent, with the likes of Asian prawns with basmati rice, and vegetable satay in peanut sauce, among the dishes. Mon–Thurs 11am–11.30pm, Fri & Sat 11am–12.30am, Sun 12.30–11pm.

## Dunbrody Abbey

5km north of Arthurstown on the R733 • May to Sept daily 11am–5.30pm • Abbey €4; maze €7 (includes fee for pitch and putt course) • ☎ 086 275 9149, ⓦ dunbrodyabbey.com

Overlooking the Barrow estuary are the ruins of **Dunbrody Abbey**, a Cistercian monastery founded in 1170 by Hervé de Montmorency, on the instructions of his nephew, the Anglo-Norman invader, Strongbow. Its magnificent remains centre on a 60m-long early Gothic church, whose most notable features are the elegant west doorway and east window. Following Dissolution, the abbey passed into the hands of the Etchingham family whose descendants added the tower and nearby buildings and

**5**

own the land to this day. On site there's also a tea room, pitch and putt course, and a full-sized maze, which utilizes 1500 yew trees.

## John F. Kennedy Arboretum and Kennedy Homestead

8km north of Dunbrody Abbey on the R733 • **Arboretum** Daily: April & Sept 10am–6.30pm; May–Aug 9am–8pm; Oct–March 10am–5pm; last admission 45min before closing • €5; Heritage Card • ☎ 051 388171, ⓦ heritageireland.ie • **Homestead** Daily 9.30am–5.30pm • €8 • ☎ 051 388264, ⓦ kennedyhomestead.ie

The horticultural connection continues at the **John F. Kennedy Arboretum**, funded by Irish-Americans in memory of the former US president, who returned to visit his ancestors' homeland in 1963. The arboretum houses an astonishing assortment of more than 4500 trees and shrubs from the world's temperate regions, as well as a summertime tea room (May–Sept). Its grounds sweep upwards along the slopes of Slieve Coillte, whose 270m summit provides panoramic views of the surrounding countryside. JFK's great-grandfather, Patrick, was born a little to the northwest in Dunganstown, where the **Kennedy Homestead** describes his emigration to the US, fleeing the Famine in 1848, and traces the family's subsequent history.

## New Ross

**NEW ROSS** squats beside the River Barrow, its quayside marred by poor redevelopment and heavy traffic, but there's still life in the old place, especially in the lanes behind the frontage. The river provided access to the upstream countryside of Wexford and Kilkenny, and the town's importance beyond being a local embarkation point is emphasized by the quayside presence of the **Dunbrody Famine Ship**.

### Dunbrody Famine Ship

The Quay • Daily: April–Sept 9am–6pm; Oct–March 9am–5pm • €11; Heritage Island • ☎ 051 425239, ⓦ dunbrody.com

The **Dunbrody Famine Ship** tries to convey what life must have been like on a nineteenth-century "coffin ship". It's a faithful reconstruction, fully seaworthy, of the kind of three-masted barque that carried Irish emigrants to North America from ports such as New Ross, usually in appalling conditions – with death rates among the passengers commonly reaching twenty percent. Guided tours, complete with costumed actors playing passengers, take you around the ship. In the visitor centre, which houses a café, you can access a database of emigrants to the US and Canada between 1846 and 1851, the main Famine years when over a million people left Ireland.

### Ros Tapestry

The Quay, opposite the Kennedy sculpture • Mon–Sat 10am–5pm, Sun 11am–3pm • €9; Heritage Island • ⓦ rostapestry.ie

It's well worth visiting the enchanting **Ros Tapestry**, a hugely ambitious and fruitful community project. Depicting scenes from the Norman history of New Ross and the locality, such as the founding of Tintern Abbey (see page 198), in 2m-wide panels, the tapestry has been hand-stitched by a hundred volunteers in various towns around Wexford and Kilkenny since 1999. There's a self-guided audio-tour to explain not only the historical detail but also the variety of pictorial styles in the vividly colourful works.

---

**ARRIVAL AND INFORMATION**                                             **NEW ROSS**

**By bus** Buses stop on the quayside.
Destinations Bus Éireann: Dublin (4 daily; 3hr 10min); Enniscorthy (1 Weds; 1hr 30min); Kilkenny (1 Thurs; 1hr 15min); Rosslare Europort (5–6 daily; 1hr 5min); Waterford (9–10 daily; 20–40min); Wexford (5–8 daily; 40min).

Kilbride (ⓦ kilbridecoaches.com): Kilkenny (Mon–Sat 2 daily; 1hr 15min).
**Tourist office** At the Dunbrody Famine Ship (same hours; ☎ 051 425239; ⓦ visitnewross.ie).

**ACCOMMODATION AND EATING**

**Ann McDonalds Cafe** 8 Mary St ☎051 425391, ⓦann mcdonaldscafe.com. Popular local spot a 5min uphill stroll from the quayside. Friendly service and delicious home-cooked food, using plenty of local produce: sandwiches, soups and light bites from €4.95 and more substantial mains, including home-made lasagne (€9.95). Mon–Sat 8.30–9pm, Sun 9.30am–8pm.

**In a Nutshell** 8 South St ☎051 422777, ⓦinanutshell store.ie. Your best bet for eating out, parallel to and one block east of the quayside, an excellent daytime café and health-food deli serving everything from juices and smoothies to sandwiches (around €7), meat, seafood and cheese platters, and daily-special hot dishes. Mon–Sat 9am–6pm.

**MacMurrough Farm Cottages** 3km northeast of town ☎051 421383, ⓦmacmurrough.com. This welcoming working farm rents out lovely, comfortable, well-equipped self-catering cottages with central heating and stoves, one with a piano, at very good rates by the night or week. €60

# Waterford and Tipperary

CYCLISTS ON THE WATERFORD GREENWAY

# Waterford and Tipperary

The attractions of County Waterford (Port Láirge, or the Déise) are gaining more attention since the designation of the Copper Coast Geopark and Waterford Greenway – alternative itineraries between Waterford City in the east and the blossoming harbour town of Dungarvan in the west. Home to almost half the county's population, including a sizeable mob of students, Waterford City supports a lively nightlife and festival scene, and three fine museums displaying the Waterford Treasures. The county's coastline takes in several sandy beaches, not least at Dunmore East and the "holy city" of Ardmore, containing enthralling relics associated with St Declan, while its northern fringe is dominated by the lonesome and boggy Comeragh and Knockmealdown mountains, the latter running down to the ancient ecclesiastical centre of Lismore, in the heart of the gorgeous Blackwater valley.

In contrast to squat, coastal Waterford, **Tipperary** (Tiobraid Árann) is the wealthiest of Ireland's inland counties, deriving its prosperity from the flat and fertile plain known as the **Golden Vale**, which provides rich pickings for dairy farmers and horse-breeders. It's also one of the largest counties, stretching over 100km from top to toe. Most of Tipp's attractions lie in its southern reaches, including the historic towns of **Carrick-on-Suir**, home to one of Ireland's most graceful mansions, and **Cahir**, with its imposing thirteenth-century castle and ornamental nineteenth-century baronial villa. But by far the county's most breathtaking lure is the **Rock of Cashel**, a magnificent isolated outcrop rising from the Golden Vale and crowned by impressive Christian buildings spanning various periods. This southern part of the county is traversed by the **Tipperary Heritage Way**, an easy 56km waymarked trail that runs down the Suir valley from Cashel to Cahir and Ardfinnan, finishing at The Vee, in the Knockmealdown Mountains near the Waterford border.

### GETTING AROUND                                              CO. WATERFORD

If you're driving or cycling between Waterford and Wexford, note that the most southerly road crossing of the River Barrow is up at New Ross, it's worth considering the **ferry** between **Passage East**, 12km east of Waterford city, and Ballyhack (see page 198).

# Waterford city

In many ways **WATERFORD** is Ireland's least discovered city, often bypassed by tourists heading from Rosslare for the more hyped destinations of Cork and Kerry further west. Even the hardiest defender of this dockland city's reputation would be hard-pressed to mount a campaign centred upon Waterford's immediate allures. Though neat wooded hillsides figure north of Rice Bridge, the vista mainly encompasses ugly industrial development, with cranes and a refinery dominating the skyline and the unappealing quays of the River Suir offering barely a hint of the vibrant city lying behind.

But Waterford is one of those places where scraping the surface reveals numerous delights. Behind those ugly quays lies a complex of narrow lanes, first formed in medieval times, and many grand examples of Georgian town planning in the shape of sturdy town houses and elegant municipal and ecclesiastical buildings.

WATERFORD TREASURES, MEDIEVAL MUSEUM

# Highlights

**❶ Waterford Treasures** The city's history is brought evocatively to life in three museums of locally found discoveries from Viking and later times. See page 206

**❷ Waterford Greenway** A scenic 46km cycling and walking trail between Waterford and Dungarvan that follows a disused railway line. See page 211

**❸ Dungarvan** Clustered around its broad bay, this attractive town has plenty to enthral, including some great places to eat. See page 211

**❹ Ardmore** A delightful village with potent reminders of Ireland's monastic past, as well as a grand beach and exhilarating cliff-top walks. See page 213

**❺ Cahir Castle** One of the country's best-preserved Anglo-Norman strongholds. See page 218

**❻ The Rock of Cashel** Stunning medieval religious site, set high above the surrounding countryside. See page 221

**❼ The Glen of Aherlow** River valley in a beautiful setting, dwarfed by the adjacent Galtee Mountains. See page 220

HIGHLIGHTS ARE MARKED ON THE MAP ON PAGE 206

**6**

**Waterford Treasures**, the city corporation's historical collections dating right back to the Viking period, is split across three museums: Reginald's Tower, the Medieval Museum and the Bishop's Palace. While this does dilute their impact, each of the sites has considerable architectural interest in its own right. Along with the **Waterford Crystal** shop and factory, the three museums form the core of what's been branded, somewhat strangely, the "Viking Triangle", a wedge between The Mall and the quays that shelters some other fine buildings, including **Christ Church Cathedral**, in a complex of tiny, sometimes tortuous, lanes. To the west of here, opposite the clock tower, Barronstrand Street leads south from the quays to the main shopping streets, passing **Holy Trinity Cathedral**, and thence, via a couple of name changes, to John Street, whose bars, pubs and clubs form the nightlife focus.

## Brief history

Waterford's origins are integrally linked to the River Suir. The **Vikings** built a settlement here in the early tenth century to provide shelter for their longboats and to exploit the trading opportunities offered by the river, which along with the Barrow and the Nore provided easy access to the southeast's fertile farmland. The Viking settlement prospered and controlled much of this part of Ireland, exacting a tribute from the Celts called Airgead Sróine (Nose Money) since the punishment for welshers was to have their noses cut off.

Later, the course of both local and national history was much impacted by Strongbow's assault on the city in 1170, caused by **Dermot MacMurrough**'s attempts to gain sway over Ireland (see page 571). The success of the Anglo-Norman earl's bloody offensive not only led to his marriage to MacMurrough's daughter but brought his liege lord, **Henry II**, scurrying to Ireland the following year to assume control of the country's conquest. Henry granted a charter providing royal protection to the city, and his descendant, King John, increased its size by adding new walls and towers.

Though much affected by the Black Death and frequent incursions by both Irish and Anglo-Norman neighbours, Waterford continued to flourish as a **port**, reliant on trade in wool, hides and wine. Cromwell was repelled in 1649, but a year later

**HIGHLIGHTS**

1. Waterford Treasures
2. Waterford Greenway
3. Dungarvan
4. Ardmore
5. Cahir Castle
6. The Rock of Cashel
7. The Glen of Aherlow

**WATERFORD AND TIPPERARY**

Ireton's troops took control and expelled many of the Catholic merchants. Protestant domination of the city's trade was reinforced by William of Orange's accession. The eighteenth century witnessed major architectural developments, mostly designed by locally born John Roberts. Shipbuilding prospered during the nineteenth century, the city becoming second only to Belfast in terms of tonnage constructed, and many Waterford-built vessels transported the city's famous **crystal**, first manufactured here in 1783. However, Waterford suffered economically during the second half of the twentieth century and the beginning of this century, witnessing factory closures and the virtual end of shipbuilding here.

**6**

## Reginald's Tower

Parade Quay • Jan to mid-March Wed–Sun 9.30am–5pm; mid-March to Dec daily 9.30am–5.30pm • €5; Heritage Card • ☎ 0761 102501, ⓦ waterfordtreasures.com

Waterford's city walls were once punctuated by seventeen towers, of which six still survive. By far the most impressive of these is **Reginald's Tower**, which stands at the corner of The Mall and the quays on the site of a Viking wooden tower and was possibly named after Ragnall, the founder of the city in 914. Dating from the late twelfth century, this circular, three-storey tower has 3m-thick walls. For a time it was a mint (the display on coinage here includes a tiny part of an Iraqi silver coin from 742 bearing a quotation from the Koran, "There is no god but Allah"), later becoming an arsenal before being used as a jail from around 1819. The tower now displays some of Waterford Treasures' Viking collection, including a meticulously carved bird-bone flute, a gaming board and a famously beautiful kite brooch.

## Medieval Museum

Cathedral Square • Mon–Fri 10am–5pm, Sat 10.30am–5pm, Sun 11am–5pm • €10, or €15 with the Bishop's Palace; Heritage Island • ☎ 0761 102501, ⓦ waterfordtreasures.com

The second of the Waterford Treasures museums is the **Medieval Museum**, whose impressive exhibits include the **Great Charter Roll** of 1373, which includes a colourful image of the walled town of Waterford, and the **Edward IV sword**, a mighty piece of silver weaponry presented to the Mayor of Waterford in 1462. Wedged between the Christ Church Cathedral and the Theatre Royal, its lovely curving facade of honey-coloured limestone is thoroughly modern, but it cleverly incorporates two medieval structures: the Choristers' Hall, the lower chamber of the cathedral deanery dating from the 1270s; and the fifteenth-century Mayor's Wine Vault, given to the cathedral by James Rice, whose graphic tomb can still be seen in the church (see page 208).

## The Bishop's Palace

The Mall • Mon–Fri 10am–5pm, Sat 10.30am–5pm, Sun 11am–5pm • €10, or €15 with the Medieval Museum; Heritage Island • ☎ 0761 102 501, ⓦ waterfordtreasures.com

Next door to the Medieval Museum, it's hard to miss the **Bishop's Palace**, faced with forbidding, dark-grey Leinster limestone and fronted by the outdoor tables of its popular café. It was designed in the Palladian style in 1743 by Richard Castle, but completed after his death in 1750 by "Honest" **John Roberts**, designer of many of the city's finest Georgian buildings. The ground and first floors have been refurnished in Georgian style, though the exhibits here are perhaps less compelling than in the other two Waterford Treasures museums. The highlights are three Rococo gilt mirrors carved in Dublin in the eighteenth century with lively Chinese dragons, and the oldest surviving piece of Waterford crystal, a wide-lipped 1789 decanter.

6

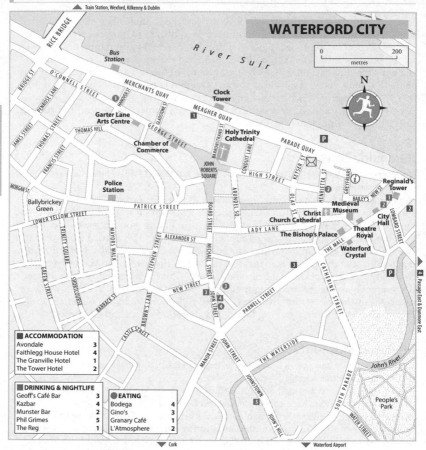

## Christ Church Cathedral

Cathedral Square • Easter–Sept Mon–Fri 10am–5pm, Sat 10am–4pm; Oct–Easter Mon–Sat 12.30–2.30pm; services on Sun 8.30am and 10am • Donation requested • ☎ 051 858958, ⓦ christchurchwaterford.com

After completing the Bishop's Palace, John Roberts designed the adjacent Church of Ireland **Christ Church Cathedral**, which took almost a quarter of a century to complete once work began in 1773. This stately Neoclassical edifice, which sometimes hosts classical music concerts, stands on the site of an eleventh-century Viking church, utilizing the base of the previous building. It features an ornate stuccowork ceiling and a fine "Arts and Crafts" window, added in the 1930s, by the stained-glass artist A.E. Child, as well as the somewhat grisly tomb of James Rice, a fifteenth-century mayor of Waterford, which graphically depicts his decaying corpse fed upon by worms and a toad. Just up from here on The Mall is another Roberts design, the squat **City Hall**.

## Waterford Crystal

The Mall • March Mon–Sat 9am–3.15pm, Sun 9.30am–3.15pm; April–Oct Mon–Sat 9am–4.15pm, Sun 9.30am–4.15pm; Nov–Feb Mon–Fri 9.30am–3.15pm • €16; Heritage Island • ☎ 051 317000, ⓦ waterfordvisitorcentre.com

**Waterford Crystal** was founded in 1783 but moved into this gleaming new shop and factory on The Mall in 2010. Tours of the factory, which now produces 45,000 pieces a year, will show you the making of the beech and pearwood moulds that only last a week, and crystal being cut with diamond-tipped wheels. However, the highlight has to be the heat and noise of the blowing room with its 1300°c furnace, where the red-hot molten crystal is shaped with supreme skill.

## Holy Trinity Cathedral

Barronstrand St • Daily 9am–evening Mass (see online for times) • Free • ☎ 051 875 166, ⓦ waterford-cathedral.com

John Roberts was the architect of the many-windowed **Chamber of Commerce** on George Street, but his prime ecclesiastical design is the Catholic **Holy Trinity Cathedral** on Barronstrand Street. This dates from 1793, but was much revised in the following century, resulting in today's flamboyant building. Its heavily ornate interior features a Baroque oak pulpit dwarfed by a soaring baldachin, all set beneath an impressively high-vaulted ceiling and ten Waterford crystal chandeliers.

### ARRIVAL AND DEPARTURE                                          WATERFORD CITY

**By train** Plunkett train station is just north of the river on Dock Rd.
Destinations Dublin (4–7 daily; 1hr 50min–2hr 15min); Kilkenny (4–6 daily; 35min).
**By bus** Bus Éireann services use the bus station on Merchants Quay on the south bank, while J.J Kavanagh's (ⓦ jjkavanagh. ie) terminate by the Bank of Ireland on Parnell St.
Destinations Bus Éireann: Cahir (8 daily; 1hr 15min);

Carrick-on-Suir (8 daily; 30min); Cork (hourly; 2hr 15min); Dublin and airport (hourly; 2hr 15min–3hr); Kilkenny (1–2 daily; 1hr); Killarney (hourly; 4hr 5min); Limerick (8 daily; 1hr 50min); New Ross (9–10 daily; 20–40min); Rosslare Europort (5–6 daily; 1hr 25min); Tralee (hourly; 4hr 45min); Wexford (5–8 daily; 1hr); Youghal (hourly; 1hr 25min).
J.J. Kavanagh's: Dublin and airport (7 daily; 2hr 20min–3hr 30min).

### INFORMATION AND TOURS

**Tourist office** 120 Parade Quay (Mon–Sat 9am–5pm; ☎ 051 875823, ⓦ visitwaterford.com). Ask here about the city pass, which gives admission to the three Waterford Treasures museums and Waterford Crystal for €20.

**Walking tours** An entertaining and informative 1hr tour of the city convenes at the tourist office (Mid-March to mid-Oct daily 11.45am & 1.45pm; €7; ☎ 051 873711, ⓦ jackswalkingtours.com).

### ACCOMMODATION                                              SEE MAP PAGE 208

**Avondale** 2 Parnell St ☎ 051 854689, ⓦ avondale guestaccommodation.com. Spruce accommodation in a sympathetically converted Georgian building, centrally located on the busy continuation of The Mall and very handy for the main sights. Breakfast not included. €80
**Faithlegg House Hotel** Faithlegg, 10km southeast of the centre, towards the mouth of the River Suir ☎ 051 382000, ⓦ faithlegg.com. Though it extends to a large modern annexe, this hotel has at its core an attractive late eighteenth-century mansion, where its best rooms come in traditional country-house style, with lofty ceilings, four-posters and huge sash windows. There's also a good restaurant, a spa, a large

swimming pool with kids' pool, and golf course. €120
**The Granville Hotel** Meagher Quay ☎ 051 305555, ⓦ granvillehotel.ie. This smart riverfront establishment has housed many a famous guest over the years; Daniel O'Connell and Charles Parnell both stayed here. Thoughtfully designed throughout, with large, comfortable and well-equipped rooms and good service. €108
**The Tower Hotel** The Mall ☎ 051 862300, ⓦ towerhotel waterford.com. Big and block-like, a prominent landmark near the river and opposite Reginald Tower, this well-equipped, 134-room hotel has generously proportioned bedrooms, a gym and a good-sized pool. €100

### EATING                                                      SEE MAP PAGE 208

**Bodega** 54 John St ☎ 051 844177, ⓦ bodegawaterford. com. This bistro and wine bar is an attractive, informal setting for dishes such as lobster croquettes with charred lime mayo, and slow-roasted organic pork belly with black pudding crumb and celeriac remoulade (€22). Thurs–Sat 4.30–10pm, Sun 3–9pm.
**Gino's** 62 John St ☎ 051 879513. Bright, neat branch of the long-running Cork institution, a no-frills restaurant

dishing up pizzas (around €10), salads, wine, beer and ice cream. Mon–Thurs 5–9pm, Fri 5–10pm, Sat 12.30–10pm, Sun 1.30–10pm.
**Granary Café** O'Connell St ☎ 051 854428, ⓦ granary cafe.ie. At the back of the airy eighteenth-century granary that used to host Waterford Treasures, this self-service café with a community feel offers a great selection of breakfasts, including espresso coffees, sandwiches from €4, quiches,

6

6

---

**WATERFORD FESTIVALS**

Waterford's festivals include **Spraoi** (ⓦspraoi.com) during the bank holiday weekend in early August, which showcases street performances and world music. There's a **food festival** over a September weekend (ⓦwaterfordharvestfestival.ie), while over ten days in October, **Imagine** (ⓦimagineartsfestival.com) encompasses music, visual arts, dance, comedy, theatre and the John Dwyer Trad Weekend.

---

pies and a daily special main course with two salads (€9.50). Mon–Sat 8am–5pm.

★ **L'Atmosphere** 19 Henrietta St ☎051 858426, ⓦrestaurant-latmosphere.com. Authentic, informal bistro with a good reputation for its unfussy, classic French dishes such as cassoulet of duck confit and Toulouse sausage. Two-course early bird menu (5–7pm) is just €18. Mon–Fri 12.30–2.30pm & 5.30pm–late, Sat & Sun 5.30pm–late.

## DRINKING AND NIGHTLIFE
SEE MAP PAGE 208

As well as some characterful pubs – some of which also serve decent food – there's a clutch of lively DJ bars and clubs around the junction of Parnell and John streets, an area being developed as the Apple Market (ⓦfacebook.com/theapplemarket.ie). Note that the city is not generally a good place to catch traditional music.

**Geoff's Café Bar** Apple Market, 8–9 John St. Behind its striking facade of astroturf and electric blue window, there are lots of dark, cosy corners in this huge traditional bar, and an attractive beer garden outside. Also serves excellent food. Mon–Thurs 11.30am–11.30pm, Fri & Sat 11.30am–12.30am, Sun 1–11pm.

**Kazbar** Apple Market, 57 John St ☎051 843730, ⓦkazbarwaterford.ie. Louche, vaguely Egyptian decor, a roof terrace and several tables outside for watching the world pass by at this busy late night watering hole, which serves good cocktails, shows major sporting events, has live music most nights, and DJs on Friday and Saturday evenings. Mon–Sat 10.30am–late, Sun 12.30pm–late.

**Munster Bar** Bailey's New St ☎051 874656, ⓦthemunsterbar.com. Down a narrow lane in the old quarter (also accessible from The Mall), this atmospheric 200-year-old pub is known particularly for its food, using local ingredients in dishes such as seafood pie, and hosts traditional sessions on Sun in summer. In good weather, enjoy the outdoor tables in the shadow of Greyfriars, a medieval Franciscan friary. Mon–Thurs 10.30am–11.30pm, Fri & Sat 10.30am–12.30am, Sun 12.30–11pm.

**Phil Grimes** 61 Johnstown ☎051 875759. Friendly, old-style bar with a small beer garden, live music in its upstairs venue and craft beers from the local Metalman and Dungarvan breweries. Mon–Thurs 4–11.30pm, Fri & Sat 4pm–12.30am, Sun 4–11pm.

★ **The Reg** 2 The Mall ☎051 583000, ⓦthereg.ie. Right next to Reginald's Tower, the sprawling premises include a much-coveted, heated roof garden overlooking the tower and the river, and a whiskey bar with leather sofas. The service is very good, the excellent food comes in generous portions, accompanied by craft beers on draught, and there are traditional sessions on weeknights, plus live bands and DJs at the weekend. Mon–Wed noon–11.30pm, Thurs noon–1.30am, Fri & Sat noon–2am, Sun noon–1.30am.

## ENTERTAINMENT

**Garter Lane Arts Centre** O'Connell St ☎051 855038, ⓦgarterlane.ie. Set in an eighteenth-century building, the city's most interesting arts venue hosts performances of music, dance, comedy and theatre, as well as exhibiting artworks and showing independent films.

# Waterford's coast

Waterford's coastline lacks the wildness of the shoreline further east, but there are still glorious, enticing beaches – especially at **Dunmore East**, **Stradbally** and **Ardmore** – and plenty of balmy cliff-top walks, not least at Ardmore, which is also a major ecclesiastical site. Among the larger towns here, it's best to give the kiss-me-quick resort of Tramore a wide berth (though it has a vast sandy beach and is popular with surfers); more picturesque is **Dungarvan**, which enjoys a peaceful bayside setting and offers some fine places to stay, eat and listen to traditional music. Between these two, the UNESCO **Copper Coast** is an unspoilt landscape with a fascinating geological history.

# Dunmore East

**DUNMORE EAST**, 16km southeast of Waterford, is a picturesque getaway for the city's wealthier denizens. The village is actually split in two, with the sheltered eastern part set neatly around a small, sandy beach backed by sandstone cliffs, while the much busier western half is built above and around a marina, and one of Ireland's busiest fishing harbours. There's a **food festival** over a weekend in late June, while in late August, the village comes to life for the four-day **Bluegrass Festival**. 10km inland on the Suir Estuary, **Woodstown Beach** is a popular outing – the gorgeous stretch of sand is backed by dunes and woods.

**6**

## ARRIVAL AND INFORMATION | DUNMORE EAST

**By bus** Suirway buses (ⓦsuirway.com) from/to Waterford (Merchants Quay; summer 8–10 daily, winter 7 Mon–Sat; 30min) stop opposite the *Bay Café*.

**Tourist information** See ⓦdiscoverdunmore.com.

## ACCOMMODATION AND EATING

**Bay Café** Dock Rd ☎087 674 3572. Inexpensive daytime café with a few outside tables above the harbour. Stuffs plenty of seafood in its sandwiches (including its famous open crab sandwich; €10.95), main courses and chowder. Daily 9am–5pm.

**Strand Inn** 7 Wellington Terrace ☎051 383174, ⓦthe strandinn.com. Life in the east village is focused around this popular eighteenth-century inn, where most bedrooms have balconies overlooking the sea, enjoying views out towards the Hook Head lighthouse; they have a fresh, modern style, with white bedding and splashes of colour, perhaps from pastel cushions or a sympathetic modern painting. Downstairs, the excellent restaurant (and the bar menu) specializes in fresh seafood, in dishes such as spicy and hot devilled crab "au gratin" (€24.50), with plentiful outdoor tables overlooking the beach. Bar food 12.30–9pm; restaurant breakfast & lunch only. **€110**

# Dungarvan and around

Attractive, bustling **DUNGARVAN** is splendidly situated on a large bay where the waters of the River Colligan broaden as they reach the sea, and where St Garvan founded a monastery in the seventh century. The handsome, early nineteenth-century streets of its town centre gather themselves around the main Grattan Square on the west side of the river. Unlike many of its fellow resorts, it remains largely unscathed by the blight of chain-store similitude. It plays host to the three-day **West Waterford Festival of Food** in April (ⓦwestwaterfordfestivaloffood.com); otherwise, its fine restaurants and pubs are supplemented by a **farmers' market** of food and crafts every Thursday morning in Grattan Square.

## Dungarvan Castle

Castle St • Late May to late Sept • Frequent guided tours daily 10am–6pm • Free • ☎058 48144, ⓦheritageireland.ie

The town's main attraction is **Dungarvan Castle**, squatting proudly at the eastern end of Davitt's Quay, also known as King John's Castle, as the king's constable, Thomas Fitz Anthony, lived here. Built in 1185 as an Anglo-Norman command base, it consists

---

### THE WATERFORD GREENWAY

Fifty years after the last train rolled along the Waterford–Dungarvan line, the disused railway reopened as the **Waterford Greenway**, for **walking** and **cycling**. The 46km off-road trail meanders through countryside from Waterford's quayside along the River Suir, across historic bridges and viaducts, through the atmospheric Ballyvoyle Tunnel and eventually to the coast and Dungarvan. There are short sections that can be tackled (access with parking is available) and plenty of stops for refreshments. **Bike hire** is available in Dungarvan, Kilmacthomas and Waterford City (from €25) and comes with a free shuttle bus option. Visit ⓦvisitwaterfordgreenway.com and ⓦwaterfordgreenwaybikehire.com.

**6**

**WATERFORD WATERSPORTS**

The best way to experience Waterford's coastline is from the sea on a **kayak**, **canoe** or **SUP** (stand-up paddleboard). Guided tours take in the area's caves, islands and coves and are often blessed with sightings of **whales** and **dolphins**. Ocean swell and decent breaks attract surfers to this coastline too, particularly around Tramore and Bunmahon.

**TOUR OPERATORS**

**Ardmore Adventures** ☎ 083 374 3889, ⊛ ardmorea dventures.ie. Offers watersports such as kayaking, snorkelling and surfing, as well as rock-climbing and abseiling on seacliffs. From €45/half-day.

**Bunmahon Surf School** ☎ 087 6398 210, ⊛ bunma honsurfschool.com. Small groups and beginners' boards at this friendly local surf school at the main entrance to the Bunmahon beach. All equipment is provided (including gloves and hats in winter). €35/2hr group lesson; €40 for SUP; rentals available too.

**Dunmore East Adventure Centre** ☎ 051 383783, ⊛ dunmoreadventure.com. This outfit down by the harbour offers kayaking, SUP, sailing, abseiling and climbing (with indoor and outdoor climbing walls). From €40/2hr, wetsuit and equipment provided.

of a shell keep with a curtain wall. Inside are eighteenth-century barracks, occupied by the IRA during the Civil War and burnt down when they abandoned the site. Subsequently, these were restored to become the local Garda station and now contain displays and an audiovisual on the castle's history.

## Waterford County Museum

St Augustine St • Mon–Fri 10am–5pm, plus some Saturdays in summer • Free • ☎ 058 45960, ⊛ waterfordmuseum.ie

Five minutes' walk west along Main Street from the castle will bring you to the spruce **Waterford County Museum** in the old town hall, which is run by enthusiastic volunteers and houses well-organized exhibits and display boards on local history. From their website, you can download a town trail app, with an audio-tour, map and lots of old photos.

## An Rinn (Ring Peninsula)

Nestled to the west of Dungarvan Bay is the picturesque headland of **An Rinn**, home to a vibrant Gaeltacht (Gaelic speaking) community. Explore the narrow country lanes and tiny fishing harbours, beaches and coves and enjoy spectacular views on a two hour hike out to Helvick Head from *Mooney's* pub in the village of Ring.

### ARRIVAL AND INFORMATION

**By bus** Buses stop on Davitt's Quay near the bridge at the top of the bay.

Destinations Cork (hourly; 1hr 25min); Lismore (3–7 Mon–Sat, plus 3 Sun in summer; 30min); Waterford (hourly;

### DUNGARVAN AND AROUND

50min); Youghal (hourly; 35min).

**Tourist office** 51 Main St (Mon–Fri 9.30am–5pm, Sat 10am–5pm; ☎ 058 41741, ⊛ dungarvantourism.com).

### ACCOMMODATION AND EATING

**Gourmet House** 3 Gratton Sq ☎ 058 40044, ⊛ facebook. com/www.gourmethouse.ie. Tiny coffeehouse with a fabulous selection of home-made cakes, scones and quiche, plus breakfast (from €5.50 for scrambled eggs on sourdough toast), late night "pop-up pizza" some weekend evenings (from €11; see Facebook for dates and book ahead) and beer and wine "anytime". Mon, Tues & Thurs 9am–5.30pm, Wed 9am–6.30pm, Fri & Sat 9am–6pm, Sun 10.30–5pm.

**The Local** 10 Grattan Square ☎ 058 41845, ⊛ thelocal. ie. A cosy bar run by a famous *uilleann* piper, with traditional music sessions at weekends, plus a winter concert series that has featured big names such as Liam Clancy and Liam O'Flynn. Terrific food too. Mon–Thurs noon–11.30pm, Fri & Sat noon–12.30am, Sun 12.30–11pm.

**The Moorings** Davitt's Quay ☎ 058 41461, ⊛ the moorings.ie. With waterfront tables on the quay and a large beer garden at the back, *The Moorings* is a lovely, old, nautical-themed pub serving good food. Dishes like Cajun chicken fillet burgers, and chilli beef with nachos (€14.95) go well with craft ales from the local Dungarvan Brewing

Company. Mon–Thurs 1–11.30pm, Fri & Sat noon–2am, Sun noon–11pm. **€90**

★ **The Tannery** 10 Quay St, near the castle ☎058 45420, ⓦtannery.ie. Excellent modern Irish restaurant in a stylishly converted leather warehouse, owned by TV chef Paul Flynn, who also offers cookery courses. Local, seasonal ingredients are used wherever possible in dishes such as crab *crème brûlée*, and duck breast with potato terrine and salt baked celeriac; the three-course menu will set you back €60, but the early bird menu is a bargain at €36.50 (5.30–7.30pm, to 6.30pm Sat). Tapas and simple mains are available (Tues–Sat evenings) in the downstairs wine bar, and there are very smart and tasteful bedrooms in two nineteenth-century town houses around the corner (breakfast is served in a cosy corner of the restaurant). Wed–Sat 5.30–9pm, Sun 12.30–3.30pm. **€110**

## The Copper Coast

The R675 traverses verdant countryside along the cliff-girt littoral between Dungarvan in the west and Tramore in the east that's been christened the **Copper Coast**, after the rich deposits that were extensively mined in the nineteenth century. Because of the area's geological heritage, it's been designated a UNESCO Geopark, with a **visitor centre** at **Bunmahon**, 24km east of Dungarvan. Bunmahon's appealing **beach** supports a surf school (see page 212) and is backed by dunes and a caravan park, while scenic **Stradbally**, 8km west on a minor road off the R675, has several fabulous beaches nearby, the choicest being the sheltered, sandy **Stradbally Cove**, a little way west of the village. Seven kilometres further along the coast towards Dungarvan lies **Clonea Strand**, an expansive sandy beach, full of day-trippers in summer.

There are no buses along this stretch of coast, but the roads can be explored by **bicycle**; the first 10km from Dungarvan are off-road, along the Waterford Greenway (see page 211).

### INFORMATION                                    THE COPPER COAST

**Copper Coast Visitor Centre** Knockmahon, Bunmahon (March–Oct daily 11am–5pm; ☎051 292828, ⓦcopper coastgeopark.com). The volunteer-led visitor centre is set in a deconsecrated 200-year-old Monksland Church; they provide detailed information on self-guided walks, including a short boardwalk trail over Fenor Bog, 12km east of Bunmahon. See the website for their varied menu of events, including seminars and guided tours, or to download walks (some of which have podcasts).

## Ardmore

The seaside village of **ARDMORE**, 20km southwest of Dungarvan, is an enchanting place, rich in religious history and relics, mainly associated with St Declan who established a monastery here some thirty years before St Patrick came to Ireland. His saint's day is still celebrated in the village with a **pattern festival** of music, theatre, walks and street entertainment in late July. There's a 1km-long sandy **beach** at the foot of the village, hemmed in by long, grassy headlands and flanked on its southern side by **St Declan's Stone**. According to legend, the saint's luggage was miraculously transported by this boulder when he travelled from Wales. Heading up the hill towards the southern headland leads past **St Declan's Well**, where the saint apparently conducted baptisms in the early fifth century, and where he later retired to a small cell for greater seclusion; on the site of the latter, a now-ruined church was built, probably in the twelfth century. From here there's an easy 4km **cliff walk**, with stunning views, around the headland, which will bring you back to the top of Main Street.

### St Declan's Cathedral

Above the town (and near the end of the cliff walk), on the site of Declan's original monastery, stands the ruins of a roofless but solid-looking twelfth-century Romanesque **cathedral** and a willowy, conically capped, 30m **round tower** of the same period. The cathedral contains two carved ogham stones, one of which is the longest in Ireland,

6

while its west outer wall features an arcade from a previous building, embellished with remarkable carvings of biblical scenes: in the lower row, you can make out Adam and Eve, the Adoration of the Magi and the Judgement of Solomon; at the right end of the upper row, look out for the scales held by the Archangel Michael, in the Last Judgement. In a corner of the graveyard is **St Declan's Oratory**, which possibly dates from the eighth century. The pit in the floor, once covered with a flagstone, is where he was supposedly buried, but pilgrims have scooped out the earth from the grave as it's believed to protect against disease.

### ARRIVAL AND ACTIVITIES ARDMORE

**By bus** As well as the direct service between Ardmore and Cork below, there are hourly buses from Waterford and Dungarvan to Youghal and Cork that pass along the N25, about 5km from Ardmore.
Destinations Cork (1–3 daily; 1hr 35min); Youghal (1–3 daily; 20min).

### ACCOMMODATION

★ **Cliff House** On the southern headland ☎ 024 87800, ⓦ cliffhousehotel.ie. Welcoming and hugely impressive hotel in an ingeniously striking but unobtrusive modern building, blending in homely touches and maritime features in a very Irish contemporary aesthetic. It makes the very most of its water's-edge location: all rooms have glorious views of the bay (many from their private balconies), as do the bar and restaurant, the spa, the outdoor Jacuzzi and even the 15m indoor pool. €235

**Round Tower** College Rd ☎ 024 94494, ⓦ round towerhotel.ie. This traditional family-run hotel offers ten restful and recently refurbished en-suite rooms, a bar and restaurant in a century-old former convent, with an attractive garden which hosts live music on Sun evenings in summer. €120

### EATING

**The Ardmore Gallery and Tearoom** Main St ☎ 024 94863, ⓦ ardmoregalleryandtearoom.ie. Good-value cakes, soup and sandwiches either in the bright gallery, which displays works by local artists, or out in the garden. April–Sept daily 9.30am–6.30pm; Oct–March Sat & Sun 1–5pm.

**The House** Cliff House, on the southern headland ☎ 024 87800, ⓦ cliffhousehotel.ie. "McGrath's Black Angus Beef: Garden Spinach, Potato, Kilbeggan Whiskey, Beef Tea"... the menu entries at this superb Michelin-starred restaurant run on like a Joycean stream of consciousness. There's plenty of imagination, too, in the complex but supremely skilful combinations of unusual ingredients, and in their intricate, almost sculptural, platings. If you're not up to the Ulyssean epic of the tasting menu (€115, plus wine), remember that the same kitchen turns out fantastic dishes such as pan-fried hake with potato gratin and salsa verde (€23.50) for the bar (daily from 12.30pm), which also shares the same broad deck and superb bay views. Tues–Sat 6.30–10pm.

**White Horses Restaurant** Main St ☎ 024 94040. Homely café-restaurant with a back garden run by three sisters, serving everything from afternoon tea and cakes, through lunches such as deep-fried plaice with tartare sauce, to interesting evening dishes such as crispy duckling with caramelized orange and kumquat sauce (main courses in evening from €20). May–Sept Tues–Sun 11am–late; Oct–Dec & mid-Feb to April Fri 6pm–late, Sat 11am–11pm, Sun 12.30–4.30pm.

# Northern Waterford

The northern stretch of the county, along the border with Tipperary, is studded with two modest but pretty mountain ranges, the **Comeraghs** and the **Knockmealdowns**, neither of which rises higher than 800m. **Ballymacarbry**, 25km north of Dungarvan on the R671 towards Clonmel, is the best jumping-off point for the Comeraghs, while historic **Lismore**, 25km west of Dungarvan in the beautiful Blackwater valley, provides easy access to the Knockmealdowns.

## The Comeragh Mountains

The best approach to the bleak moorland of the **Comeragh Mountains**, with its smattering of bogs, heather and upland lakes and its healthy ration of National

Looped Walks (Ⓦirishtrails.ie), is along the Nire valley. Now flanked by the signposted Comeragh Scenic Drive, the Nire descends westwards from beneath Knockaunapeebra (789m), the range's highest point, to waterside **Ballymacarbry**. There are three-day walking festivals in the Comeraghs in July (Ⓦcomeraghswild.com) and October (Ⓦnirevalley.com).

| ACCOMMODATION AND EATING | THE COMERAGH MOUNTAINS |
|---|---|
| **Ballymacarbry Hostel** Right on the R671 ☎052 618 5483, Ⓦballymacarbry.com. Large, 25-bed en-suite dorms, as well as a gym, sauna, kitchen and dining room, are available in the village's spacious and handily located community centre. **€20** | dairy farm, as well as excellent breakfasts and evening meals. A triple (€150) and family room (€170) also available. **€120** |
| **Glasha Farmhouse** Just northwest of Ballymacarbry, signposted 1km westward off the R672 ☎052 613 6108, Ⓦglashafarmhouse.com. Bright, tasteful rooms, some with Jacuzzi baths, an attractive garden and a conservatory on a | ★ **Hanora's Cottage** About 5km from Ballymacarbry up the Comeragh Scenic Drive ☎052 613 6134, Ⓦhanorascottage.com. This welcoming, adults-only guesthouse provides Jacuzzis in all the large, scenic rooms, a breakfast feast and splendid dinners in the restaurant; an ideal base for hiking in the mountains, *Hanora's* also offers a guided walking service, maps and packed lunches. **€110** |

**6**

# Lismore

Set amid rolling countryside on the south side of the River Blackwater lies the sleepy town of **LISMORE**, once a major religious centre. St Carthagh founded a thriving **monastery** here in 636 that became a great centre of learning and retained both religious and political importance for several centuries, despite periodic raids by the Vikings and later the Anglo-Normans. Every Sunday, Lismore hosts a farmers' and craft market in the lane leading up to the castle, plus in June there's an opera festival (Ⓦblackwatervalleyoperafestival.com) and Immrama, a festival of travel writing (Ⓦlismore-immrama.com).

## St Carthagh's Cathedral

6 Leycester St • April–Sept 9am–6pm; Oct–March 9am–4pm • Free; self-guided tour booklet €2 • ☎026 626 0200, Ⓦcashel.anglican.org

On the site of its medieval cathedral, wrecked by Edmund Fitzgibbon around 1600, stands the Church of Ireland **St Carthagh's Cathedral**, constructed some thirty years later – to get here head east up Main Street and turn left down North Mall. Much of its appearance derives from remodelling in the early 1800s, including the addition of its tower and spire, and it remains a charming building, set in a tree-lined cobblestone courtyard. Just inside the front door is a lovely stained-glass window by the Pre-Raphaelite Edward Burne-Jones, depicting two virtues: Justice and Humility. A Romanesque arch in the nave might possibly date from the original cathedral and leads to the imposing McGrath tomb which features carvings of the twelve Apostles, the Crucifixion and the martyr St Catherine. Stones set into the back wall, including a particularly stalwart bishop, date from the ninth to eleventh centuries.

## Lismore Castle Gardens and Gallery

Castle Ave • Easter to mid-Oct daily 10.30am–5.30pm; last admission 4.30pm • €8.50 • ☎058 54061; gardens Ⓦlismorecastlegardens.com, gallery, Ⓦlismorecastlearts.ie

Despite the cathedral's attractions it is the extravagant and graceful **Lismore Castle**, its fairy-tale turrets magnificently set above the River Blackwater, that overshadows the town. The Irish home of the Dukes of Devonshire was designed by Joseph Paxton (also responsible for the Crystal Palace for London's Great Exhibition of 1851) in the mid-nineteenth century, taking as its starting point the remains of a castle built by Prince John in 1185. Though the bulk of the castle cannot be visited, its huge **gardens**, set within the seventeenth-century outer defensive walls, present numerous exterior views from different aspects. The gardens consist of a host of magnolias, camellias and rhododendrons in season, as well as wildflower meadows and a yew-tree avenue where Edmund Spenser is believed to have written *The Faerie Queen*. Modern sculptures dot the gardens, and the formerly derelict west wing of the castle has been transformed into a **gallery** that hosts some excellent exhibitions of international contemporary visual art.

### The Heritage Centre

The Old Courthouse, Main St • Mon–Fri 9am–5.30pm, plus April–Oct Sat 10am–5pm & Sun noon–5pm • €5; Heritage Island • ☎ 058 54975, ⓦ discoverlismore.com

Lismore's fascinating history comes to life at the **Heritage Centre**, whose galleries recount the stories of some of the town's famous figures, including the chemist Robert Boyle who was born in the castle in 1627; and there's an entertaining 25-minute audiovisual, *The Lismore Experience*.

### ARRIVAL AND INFORMATION
LISMORE

**By bus** Change at Dungarvan Dungarvan (3–7 Mon–Sat, plus 3 Sun in summer; 30min) for a bus to Waterford.

**Tourist office** In the Heritage Centre. Walking tours of the town depart twice daily in summer (€5).

### ACCOMMODATION

**Ballyrafter Country House Hotel** About 1km northeast of the centre, just off the N72 ☎ 058 54002, ⓦ ballyrafterhouse.com. Swish and spacious traditional country house hotel set in broad, lawned grounds, built by the Duke of Devonshire in the early 1800s for his estate manager, with a snug bar, a restaurant with views of Lismore Castle and open fires; salmon fishing is a speciality

here. €100

**Pine Tree House** Ballyanchor ☎ 058 53282, ⓔ pinetree house@eircom.net. Modern house with en-suite double, twin and triple rooms, set in a large, attractive garden on Lismore's western outskirts, well signposted from the centre. €70

### EATING AND DRINKING

**The Classroom Bar** Main St ☎ 058 53842. Friendly, old-fashioned bar that serves a great pint of Guinness and hosts a long-running traditional music session every Thurs from about 10pm. Mon–Thurs 10.30am–11.30pm, Fri & Sat 10.30am–12.30am, Sun noon–11pm.

**The Summerhouse Café** Main St ☎ 058 54148. This

café is a well established highlight on Main St, serving up tasty, simple breakfasts (€9.95 for a full Irish with tea or coffee) and lunches (sandwiches from €5.50), as well as great espresso coffees. The bakery out back is where they produce the delicious cakes and pastries. Tues–Sat 10am–5pm.

## The Knockmealdown Mountains

North from Lismore the R668 to Cahir undulates upwards through a lovely river valley, garnished with a mass of woody greenery, before heading into the mountains. To the east, after 10km, rises **Knockmealdown** itself (793m), whose name translates aptly as "bare brown mountain", while a little further up the road lies the spectacular viewpoint known as **The Vee**. At this popular beauty spot, famous for its magnificent display of **rhododendrons** in late May and early June, the valley sides offer a perfectly chevron-shaped scene of the fields of Tipperary laid out far below, a panoply of greens, browns and yellows. The **Tipperary Heritage Way** north to Cashel begins here at The Vee, while the 70km **East Munster Way** starts down at Clogheen (see page 219) and heads east from The Vee to Carrick-on-Suir, via the northern foothills of the Knockmealdowns and the Comeraghs.

## The lower Suir valley

Rising in the Devilsbit Mountains in the north of Tipperary, the **River Suir**, Ireland's second-longest river after the Shannon, runs down the length of the county before abruptly turning east in the face of the Knockmealdown Mountains.

Along the way it nourishes countless dairy cattle and three significant towns along the southern border with Waterford. While Clonmel holds little of interest for visitors, nearby **Cahir** is a compelling destination, with its mighty castle and the whimsical Swiss Cottage, and **Carrick-on-Suir** is the site of a rare and well-preserved Elizabethan manor house. Feeding into the Suir to the northwest of Cahir, the luscious **Glen of Aherlow** is one of the county's prettiest spots and a fine base for exploring the scenic Galtee (or Galty) Mountains. Tucked away on the south side of the range are the fantastic stalactites and stalagmites of **Mitchelstown Cave**, while the attractive villages of **Clogheen** and **Ardfinnan** lie to the east of here in the lee of the Knockmealdowns.

**6**

# Carrick-on-Suir

In the far southeastern corner of County Tipperary lies the market town of **CARRICK-ON-SUIR**, famous as the birthplace of the Clancy Brothers, who are celebrated in a four-day festival over the June bank-holiday weekend that features street entertainment, art exhibitions and, of course, music (⊚clancybrothersfestival.org).

## Ormond Castle

Castle St • June–Oct frequent guided tours daily 10am–6pm • €5 • ☎ 051 640 787, ⊚ heritageireland.ie

The town's main point of interest is multi-gabled **Ormond Castle**, Ireland's only surviving Elizabethan manor house, which is situated at the far eastern end of Castle Street, a continuation of Main Street. Erected in the 1560s by Thomas ("Black Tom") Butler, tenth Earl of Ormonde, for an (unrealized) visit by his cousin, Elizabeth I, the recently restored house contains numerous tributes to her, most notably in the elaborate series of panels in the long gallery. Also displayed is a fine collection of royal charters, including one of 1661 granting the title Duke of Ormonde to Tom's descendant James.

### ARRIVAL AND INFORMATION

CARRICK-ON-SUIR

**By train** The train station is behind Greenside, the town park on the northeast side of the centre.

Destinations Cahir (Mon–Sat 2 daily; 40min); Limerick (Mon–Sat 2 daily; 1hr 15min); Waterford (Mon–Sat 2 daily; 25min).

**By bus** Buses stop at Greenside.

Destinations Cahir (8–10 daily; 40min); Limerick (8–10 daily; 1hr 55min); Waterford (8–10 daily; 40min).

**Tourist office** The tourist office and small heritage centre are in a converted church just off the north side of Main St (Mon–Fri 10am–4pm; ☎ 051 640200, ⊚ carrickonsuir.net).

### ACCOMMODATION AND EATING

**The Carraig** Main St ☎ 051 641455, ⊚ carraighotel. com. This smartly refurbished eighteenth-century hotel is the focal point of the town's hospitality, offering very reasonably priced rooms that have been tastefully updated in subdued colours. Downstairs, fine gastro pub fare is served in the bar (weeknight specials €14) and restaurant (mains such as Comeragh lamb with chive mash and shallots €22). Good-value half-board packages. Bar food daily 3–9pm; restaurant daily 8–10am & 12.30–2pm; Fri–Sun evenings only. __€89__

# Cahir

With a name that means "fort", the dominant feature of **CAHIR** is not surprisingly its castle, one of Ireland's largest and best preserved, surrounded by the waters of the River Suir at the western entrance to the town. The castle was a power base of the influential Butlers, the Earls of Ormonde, who were known as the Fitzwalters when they first came to Ireland with Prince John in 1185 and were granted a huge swathe of land in Munster. However, Theobald Fitzwalter was soon after made Chief Butler of Ireland, entitling him to a tenth of all incoming wine cargoes, and changed his family name to "Butler".

## Cahir Castle

Castle St • Daily: March to mid-June & Sept to mid-Oct 9.30am–5.30pm; mid-June to Aug 9am–6.30pm; mid-Oct to Feb 9.30am–4.30pm • €5; Heritage Card • ☎ 052 744 1011, ⓦ heritageireland.ie

The Butlers built their stronghold in the thirteenth century, though much, including the restored outer walls, dates from more recent times. It managed to survive a siege and bombardment by the Earl of Essex in 1599, as well as the invasions of Cromwell and William of Orange. However, after Cromwell's victory in 1650, the Butlers moved out and the castle fell slowly into disrepair, until it was given new life in the mid-nineteenth century by Richard Butler, the second Earl of Glengall, who impoverished himself in the process. The castle's entrance leads to the cramped middle ward, overshadowed by the thirteenth-century keep whose chambers feature various displays, including a model of the 1599 siege. To the left of here, a gateway, surmounted by defensive viewpoints on each side, leads to the more expansive outer ward. In the inner ward, parts of the larger of the two towers derive from the thirteenth and fifteenth centuries, though the banqueting hall was redesigned by William Tinsley in 1840 for use as the Butlers' private chapel.

## The Swiss Cottage

Ardfinnan Rd, 2km south off R670 • Guided 40min tours early April to late Oct daily 10am–6pm, last admission 5.15pm (maximum 12 people, so you may have a wait during the busy summer months) • €5; Heritage Card • ☎ 052 7441 144, ⓦ heritageireland.ie

Besides its castle, Cahir's other major attraction is the **Swiss Cottage**, a thirty-minute riverside stroll through parkland south from the town. Designed by John Nash, architect of the Royal Pavilion at Brighton, this lavish, thatched *cottage orné* on the castle demesne was constructed in the early 1800s for Richard Butler, the first Earl of Glengall, though his precise reason remains unclear. A contemporary scurrilous theory held that it was to enjoy clandestine liaisons with his mistress, but there is evidence that it was used occasionally as a residence and for entertaining guests. It has now been thoroughly restored using appropriate timbers and period decor. Entertaining **guided tours** start from the basement kitchen and visit the elegant salon, whose interior is decorated with one of the first commercially manufactured Parisian wallpapers, and music room, and ascend via a spiral staircase to the grand master bedroom with its commanding views of the countryside.

### ARRIVAL AND INFORMATION

### CAHIR

**By train** Cahir's train station is off Church St, a 5min walk northeast of the castle.
Destinations Carrick-on-Suir (2 Mon–Sat; 40min); Waterford (2 Mon–Sat; 1hr 5min).

**By bus** Buses stop opposite the castle outside the tourist office.
Destinations Carrick-on-Suir (8–10 daily; 40min); Cashel (6

daily; 20min); Cork (6 daily; 1hr 20min); Dublin and airport (6 daily; 2hr 25min–2hr 55min); Limerick (8–10 daily; 1hr 10min); Waterford (8–10 daily; 1hr 20min).

**Tourist office** In the castle car park (Easter to early Oct Tues–Sat 9.30am–1pm & 1.45–5.30pm; hours may be reduced from Sept; ☎ 052 744 1453, ⓦ visitcahir.ie).

### ACCOMMODATION

**Apple Farm** Moorstown, 6km east of Cahir on the main N24 road towards Clonmel ☎ 052 744 1459, ⓦ theapple farm.com. Ecofriendly camping and caravan site on this working fruit farm (Ireland's most famous fruit farm – you get a bottle of their apple juice on check in). The campers' kitchen and bathrooms are in a large barn. Playground, games room, tennis court and laundry facilities on-site, electric pitch €2.50 extra. Closed Oct–April. Price per person (tents free) €9

**Cahir House Hotel** The Square ☎ 052 744 3000,

ⓦ cahirhousehotel.ie. Built as a townhouse for the Butlers in 1770, this Georgian mansion provides comfy, colourful rooms and a small spa, in addition to a well-regarded bistro. Good room-only and single rates. €105

**Tinsley House** The Square ☎ 052 744 1947, ⓦ tinsley house.com. Just uphill from the castle on the town's main square, this B&B in a nineteenth-century town house offers en-suite bedrooms attractively furnished with antiques and decorated in bright pastel colours. €80

## EATING

**Galileo** Church St ☎052 744 5689, ⍟galileocafe.com. Just off The Square, this café-restaurant is surrounded by crafts shops in an attractively converted granary and offers pizza (from around €12), pasta and salads alongside more sophisticated mains like smoked salmon with cherry vine tomatoes and fresh dill. Mon–Sat noon–10pm, Sun 1–9pm.

**River House** 1 Castle St ☎052 744 1951, ⍟riverhouse. ie. Bright, modern, self-service café opposite the tourist office, with an outdoor terrace overlooking the castle and the river. Dishes up full breakfasts (€8), soups, all kinds of sandwiches, quiches and uncomplicated hot lunches, cakes, fresh juices and smoothies. Mon–Fri 8.30am–5pm, Sat & Sun 8.30am–6pm.

# Ardfinnan and Clogheen

Two villages to the south of Cahir offer great places to stay and ready access to the east–west ridge of the Knockmealdown Mountains beyond (see page 216). Nine kilometres from Cahir on the banks of the Suir lies the pretty village of **ARDFINNAN**, which is traversed by the 56km Tipperary Heritage Way from Cashel, via Cahir, to the panoramic vantage point called The Vee. Nine kilometres southwest of Ardfinnan is **CLOGHEEN**, from where it's a short but steep trip up the R668 Lismore road to The Vee and into the mountains.

## ARRIVAL AND INFORMATION          ARDFINNAN AND CLOGHEEN

**By bus** The #245 runs between Clonmel and Cork and calls at both Ardfinnan and Clogheen (10min apart).

Destinations Clonmel (1–2 daily; 20–30min); Cork (1–2 daily; 1hr 30min–1hr 40min).

## ACCOMMODATION AND EATING

### ARDFINNAN

★ **Kilmaneen** 5km south of Ardfinnan on the Newcastle road (signposted from the Hill Bar in the village centre) ☎052 613 6231, ⍟kilmaneen.com. This staggeringly good B&B, set in a 200-year-old farmhouse and extensive gardens, not only has cosy rooms and serves delicious breakfasts, but provides the perfect starting point for walks in the surrounding countryside and offers courses in everything from cooking to beekeeping. They'll even do a packed lunch for €7. Very good rates for singles; self-catering also available. **€90**

### CLOGHEEN

**Ballyboy House** 2.5km from Clogheen along the R665 Ardfinnan Rd ☎052 746 5297. Gorgeous seventeenth-century farmhouse, surrounded by lovely, diverse gardens and extensive woodland that's accessible on trails. Four-

posters and other antique furniture adorn the en-suite bedrooms, and breakfasts include home-baked bread; other meals can be provided by prior arrangement. Very good rates for singles; self-catering cottage available. **€70**

**The Old Convent** On the Vee road, just south of the centre ☎052 746 5565, ⍟theoldconvent.ie. An elegantly converted nunnery that styles itself a "gourmet hideaway", offering much-fêted, eight-course tasting menus in its restaurant (€75; non-residents welcome). Adults only. Mid-May to mid-Sept Thurs, Fri, Sat & Sun; mid-Sept to early Jan & mid-Feb to mid-May weekends only; closed Christmas. **€175**

**Parson's Green** Off the Ardfinnan road, just north of town ☎052 746 5290, ⍟parsonsgreen.ie. Spacious holiday park with campers' kitchens, laundry, café, playgrounds, pet farms and lots of other activities for kids. Closed Nov to mid-March. **€22.50**

# Mitchelstown Cave

Ballyporeen, 7km west of Clogheen • Guided tours: Jan & Dec Sat & Sun 10am–4pm; Feb–April & Nov daily 10am–4pm; May–Aug daily 10am–4.45pm; Sept & Oct 10am–4.30pm • €10 • ☎052 7467246, ⍟mitchelstowncave.com • From Clogheen, follow the signs up the northern route from the central crossroads; alternatively, it's easily accessed via the M8 west of Cahir

The convoluted system of grottoes at **Mitchelstown Cave** was discovered in 1833. Guided tours convey visitors through only a small section of the 3km of underground cavities, but these reveal some stunning calcite formations, such as "The Pillars of Hercules" and the frankly weird 9m-high "Tower of Babel", produced by the constant dripping of water on limestone over several eons.

## The Glen of Aherlow

To Cahir's northwest lies the lush and resplendent **Glen of Aherlow**, spreading some 18km from **Bansha** in the east to **Galbally** in the west, just across the border in County Limerick. Lying beneath the northern facade of the Galtee Mountains, the glen is a marvellous place to drive or cycle around and the scenic circular route is well worth taking. The best vantage point for spectacular views is by the entrance to the Glen of Aherlow Nature Park, 1.5km north of the junction of the R663 and R664, which is the trailhead for five National Looped Walks (ⓦirishtrails.ie). From the wooded ridge of Slievenamuck, the glen lies spread out below, light reflecting from the river, and the mountains looming beyond. The signposted **Ballyhoura Way** runs through the Glen to Galbally, on its 80km journey from the train station at Limerick Junction via the Ballyhoura Mountains to St John's Bridge in north Cork. For information on **walking** (including leaflets with directions and maps, which are also downloadable at ⓦaherlow. com) and the diverse festivals in the area, contact the tourist office, while for details of local group walks throughout the year, go to ⓦgalteewalkingclub.ie.

### INFORMATION

### THE GLEN OF AHERLOW

**Tourist information** At the back of the *Coach Road* pub is a small tourist office (Mon–Fri 9am–5pm, plus June–Sept Sat 10am–4pm; ☏ 062 56331, ⓦaherlow.com).

### ACCOMMODATION

All of the establishments listed are near the R663/R664 junction.

**Aherlow House Hotel** ☏ 062 56153, ⓦaherlowhouse.ie. This former hunting lodge has bright, spacious rooms, a top draw restaurant and an inviting bar with log fire; traditional afternoon tea (€18.95) is served in the Parlour Room. Self-catering lodges also available. **€89**

**Ballinacourty House** ☏ 062 56000, ⓦballinacourty house.com. These converted eighteenth-century stables house pleasant en-suite rooms around a lovely cobbled courtyard dotted with flowerbeds; there's also a popular, reasonably priced restaurant here. Self-catering cottages also available. Restaurant Wed–Sun evenings, plus Sun lunch time. **€70**

**Ballinacourty House Caravan and Camping Park** ☏ 062 56559, ⓦcamping.ie. Campsite in the grounds of *Ballinacourty House*, with a campers' kitchen, TV room, laundry, playground, tennis court and minigolf. Closed Oct–March. **€18**

# Cashel

Though it has some other noteworthy sights, the town of **CASHEL** – the name derives from the Irish *caiseal*, meaning "stone fort" – is utterly overshadowed by the stunning **Rock of Cashel**, an outcrop that rears out of the surrounding fertile plain, the Golden Vale. Surmounted by important ecclesiastical remains, the Rock is a hotspot on the tourist trail, so is best visited in the early morning before the hordes arrive or in the late

---

### THE RISE OF THE ROCK

According to legend, the **Rock of Cashel** first rose to political prominence in the fourth or fifth century AD, when a major fortress was established by the descendants of Eógan Mór who went on to found a dynasty of kings-cum-bishops reigning over this part of Munster. The Eóganacht were ousted from Cashel in 978 by the Dál Cais line from Killaloe in County Clare, Brian Boru becoming the overlord of Cashel, and subsequently achieving dominance over Ireland in 1002. His descendant, Murtagh, granted the Rock to the Church in 1101 and, some fifty years later, when the papacy established four archbishoprics in Ireland, one of which was at Cashel, an early medieval **cathedral** was built here. By then, however, the Eóganacht had regained control under Cormac Mac Cárthaigh, who built the adjoining **Cormac's Chapel**, finished in 1134. The whole site was sacked by Cromwell's forces in 1647, but was still used by the Church of Ireland until 1749 when cathedral status was granted to St John's Church on John Street.

afternoon when the coaches have departed. Cashel's annual **festival** (ⓦcashelartsfest.com) offers a variety of cultural events over ten days at the end of September.

## The Rock of Cashel

Just north of the town centre • Daily: Jan to mid-March & mid-Oct to Dec 9am–4.30pm; mid-March to early June & mid-Sept to mid-Oct 9am–5.30pm; early June to mid-Sept 9am–7pm; last admission 45min before closing; free 45min guided tours, call ☎ 062 61437 for times • €8; Heritage Card • ☎ 062 61347, ⓦ heritageireland.ie

Viewed from afar, the **Rock of Cashel** is a captivating sight, a freak and solitary lump of limestone, reflecting the light in diverse ways throughout the day and topped by a collection of walls, towers, turrets and crenellations of *Gormenghast* proportions. It might seem heretical to suggest so, but this vista is actually the best thing about the Rock, since, despite its staggering location and much-trumpeted billing, when you get there the site is actually far less atmospheric than other notable ecclesiastical complexes, not least Kells Priory (see page 188) and Quin Abbey (see page 316). Nonetheless, despite the swarms of coach-borne tourists, there's plenty to see and much to marvel at.

### The Hall of the Vicars Choral

Once inside, the Rock's first sight is the fifteenth-century **Hall of the Vicars Choral**, which used to house the choir charged with singing at the cathedral's services. Its upper floor features a minstrels' gallery as well as a fine eighteenth-century Flemish tapestry showing Solomon receiving the Queen of Sheba, while the lower houses the original twelfth-century **St Patrick's Cross** (the one outside – on the cross's original spot – is a replica). Badly worn, it bears a carving of Christ on one side and the saint on the other, and is unusual in not having a ring around the cross head. Directly opposite the Hall of the Vicars Choral is **Cormac's Chapel**, perhaps the most atmospheric of Ireland's

Romanesque churches; its appealing south facade of brown sandstone, decorated with the typical blind arcades of the period, stands in warm contrast to the grey limestone used elsewhere on the Rock and in most Irish churches.

### The cathedral and round tower

Constructed on the site of the earlier establishment between 1230 and 1270, the huge Gothic **cathedral** is typically Anglo-Norman in form, with pointed arches and loftily set lancet windows. It also features some smaller quatrefoil casements, as well as a nave unusually shorter than the choir, caused by the construction of a **tower** on the west side, built for the archbishops' accommodation and refuge during the fifteenth or sixteenth century. Abutting the cathedral's north transept, the **Round Tower** is the Rock's earliest building, dating from the beginning of the twelfth century. It's nearly 30m high but cannot be climbed, so you'll have to make do with the fine views of the lush countryside around the Rock from ground level.

## Brú Ború Cultural Centre

Rock Lane, near the castle · **Sounds of History** Mon–Fri 9am–5pm, Sat 10am–4pm · €5 · **Traditional music shows** (1hr 30min) late June to late Aug Tues–Sat 9pm, followed by a traditional session · €20 · ☎ 062 61122, ⓦ bruboru.ie

In the eastern shadow of the Rock, beyond the car park, is the **Brú Ború Cultural Centre**, which offers a genealogical service for South Tipperary. It houses a craft shop and the entertaining **Sounds of History** multimedia exhibition, which races through the development of Irish cultural history, focusing particularly on St Patrick, Brian Boru, and traditional-music song and dance. In summer the centre's theatre hosts shows staged by the renowned Brú Ború performance group and Comhaltas Ceoltóirí Éireann, the national organization for the promotion of Irish music.

## Hore Abbey and Bishop's Walk

Just downhill from the Rock's entrance, paths lead west and south. The former leads some of the way towards **Hore Abbey**, a thirteenth-century Cistercian monastery, probably built by those working on the Rock's cathedral. Set in open fields, the ruins themselves are impressive and afford an excellent unobstructed view of the Rock. The southerly **Bishop's Walk** path back to town via the grounds of Cashel Palace Hotel, which was designed in 1730 by Sir Edward Lovett Pearce, architect of Dublin's House of Parliament.

## The Heritage Centre

In the market house, Main St · March–Oct daily 9.30am–5.30pm; Nov–Feb Mon–Fri 9.30am–5.30pm · Free · ☎ 062 61333, ⓦ cashel.ie

Also in the town centre, look in on the **Heritage Centre** attached to the tourist office, which is home to a scale model of Cashel as it looked in 1640 (accompanied by an audio commentary on the history of the town), as well as the original charters granted to the town in the seventeenth century by Charles II and James II.

### ARRIVAL AND INFORMATION
CASHEL

**By bus** Buses stop near the market house on Main St. Listed services are run by Bus Éireann.

Destinations Cahir (6 daily; 20min); Cork (6 daily; 1hr 40min); Dublin and airport (6 daily; 2hr 5min–2hr 35min).

**Tourist office** In the market house, Main St (March–Oct daily 9.30am–5.30pm, Nov–Feb Mon–Fri 9.30am–5.30pm; ☎ 062 61333, ⓦ cashel.ie). A town audio-guide is downloadable from the website; enquire about borrowing a tablet.

### ACCOMMODATION
SEE MAP PAGE 221

Despite the Rock's popularity you should have no problems finding **accommodation**, with plenty of B&B options in town and many more in the surrounding countryside, especially on the Dualla road.

**Cashel Holiday Hostel** 6 John St (IHH An Óige) ☎ 062 62330, ⓦ cashelhostel.com. Appealing, central hostel in a Georgian town house, with a well-equipped kitchen and sociable dining area, a cosy sitting room, laundry facilities and a barbecue area. Dorms €20, twins €50

**Cashel Palace Hotel** Main St ☎062 62002, ⓦcashel palacehotel.ie. A long-awaited renovation has seen the venerable *Palace Hotel* returned to something like it former glory. Now under the prestigious Relais and Chateaux banner, the 42 rooms are as sumptuous as you'd expect, and are complemented by a gorgeous spa complex overlooking the gardens and several first rate dining possibilities, among them the *Bishop's Buttery Restaurant* and *Guinness Bar*. €150

**Cashel Town B&B** 5 John St ☎062 62330, ⓦcashel bandb.com. Under the same management as *Cashel*

*Holiday Hostel* next door, with a wide variety of cheery, colourful standard and en-suite bedrooms (€10 extra for private bathroom), and home-made bread for breakfast, which is not included in the rates. Self-catering apartments available. €55

**O'Brien's Cashel Lodge and Camping Park** Dundrum Road, about 1km from the main tourist office on the northwest side of town near Hore Abbey ☎062 61003, ⓦcashel-lodge.com. In a bucolic setting looking up towards the Rock, this well-run en-suite B&B with a self-catering kitchen is situated in an attractively renovated 200-year-old outhouse on a working farm. Camping, with shower blocks and a kitchen, also available. Camping €20, doubles €85

## EATING
SEE MAP PAGE 221

**The Bakehouse** 6 Main St, opposite the tourist office ☎062 61680. A bakery with pavement tables and an upstairs self-service coffee shop serving cakes, pies, salads and sandwiches, such as tuna melt panini (€6). Mon–Sat 8am–5.30pm, Sun 9am–5.30pm.

**Café Hans** Moor Lane ☎062 63660. A slimmed-down, more informal and more economically priced version of its adjacent sibling, serving salads, sandwiches and dishes such as Toulouse sausage with tarragon and onion gravy (€12), as well as great desserts. No bookings, cash only. Tues–Sat noon–5.30pm.

**Chez Hans** Moor Lane ☎062 61177, ⓦchezhans.net. Cashel's finest restaurant, in a beautiful nineteenth-century building that was once a church lecture hall. The food is exceptional, employing locally sourced meat and wild

Irish fish (crispy skinned Dingle hake with braised fennel and sauce verge; €26), and prices are more manageable if you come for the weekday menu (Tues–Thurs 6–10pm, Fri 6–7pm; €30 for two courses). Tues–Sat 6–10pm, Sun 12.30–3.30pm & 5.30–8pm.

★ **Mikey Ryan's Bar and Kitchen** 76 Main St ☎062 62007, ⓦmikeyryans.ie. Outstanding gastro-pub with a menu that champions local artisan farmers, distillers and brewers. The two-course Sunday lunch (€26.50) is divine and desserts might include sticky toffee pudding or a vegan chocolate mousse (€7). Owned by a thoroughbred stud owner, look out for the garden horse-box bar. Mon–Sat 10.30am–late, Sun noon–late. Food served 10.30am–3pm & 6–9.30pm.

## DRINKING
SEE MAP PAGE 221

**Brian Boru** 49 Main St ☎062 63381. Vast, stylish but unpretentious bar, which offers decent pub grub and hosts DJs and/or bands at weekends and a nightclub on Sat. Mon–Thurs 10.30am–11.30pm, Fri 10.30am–12.30am, Sat 10.30am–2am, Sun 12.30–11pm.

**Donoghue's Pub** 81 Main St ☎086 405 5491. Tucked behind the heritage centre, this little pub has a big atmosphere. Sports on screen, a pool table, great beers and cocktails, and occasional live music. Mon–Fri 6pm–late, Sat & Sun noon–late.

# Cork

COLOURFUL HOUSES IN COBH

# Cork

Cork is far and away Ireland's largest county, though nearly all visitors simply ignore its massive hinterland of dairy farms, dotted with low mountains and evergreen plantations. The coast's the thing, and in an east–west spread of over 170km it unfurls an astonishing diversity. Based around an island near the mouth of the River Lee, Cork city, the capital of the self-styled "rebel county", is renowned for its independent spirit, and packs a good cultural and social punch in its compact, vibrant centre. With its excellent restaurants, cafés and specialist food market, the city also sets a high culinary tone, which much of the rest of the county keeps up.

**7**

Further reminders of a prosperous seafaring past can be seen around Cork city in the ports of **Cobh**, **Youghal** and especially **Kinsale**, each of which has reinvented itself in its own singular way as a low-key, pleasurable resort. To the west of the city as far as **Skibbereen**, the coastline, though it meanders wildly through inlets and hidden coves, remains largely gentle and green, with a good smattering of sandy beaches and a balminess that has attracted incomers and holiday-homers from the rest of Ireland and Europe. Facing each other across the shelter of Roaring Water Bay, the good-time ports of **Baltimore** and **Schull** are popular with a cosmopolitan, watersports crowd, but the offshore islands of **Sherkin** and **Clear** presage wild country ahead. **Mizen Head** is the first of Cork's and Kerry's five highly irregular, southwesterly fingers of folded rock, which afford spectacular views of each other and the Atlantic horizon. The next, narrow **Sheep's Head**, is perhaps the most charming, where – especially if you slow down to walking pace – you'll feel as if you're getting to know every square kilometre of gorse, granite and pasture and just about every inhabitant. Shared between Cork and Kerry, the **Beara Peninsula** is especially dramatic, epitomized by gorgeous **Glengarriff**'s backdrop of dark, bare rock, stunning seascape and lonely mountain passes.

## GETTING AROUND                                                                                CORK

**By bus** Regional services operated by Bus Éireann will get you around most of the county and you can find timetables on their website (ⓦ buseireann.ie). Check timetables carefully (and use the journey planner), as services tend to be weekly or monthly rather than daily.

**By train** The only regional train services are from Cork City, east to Cobh and Midleton, and west to Killarney, via Mallow.

**By bike/on foot** The elaborate landscape of west Cork is great country for walking or cycling, both of which pursuits are served by waymarked routes on the Sheep's Head and the Beara. Bikes can be rented in the main towns and often through rural accommodation.

# Cork city

The Republic's second city, **CORK** (Corcaigh, "marshy place") is strongly characterized by its geography. The centre sits tight on a kilometre-wide island, much of which was reclaimed from marshes, in the middle of the River Lee, while the enclosing hills seem to turn this traditionally self-sufficient city in on itself. Given this layout and its history, it comes as no surprise that Corkonians have a reputation in Ireland for independence of spirit, not to say chippiness. Indeed, in many ways, Cork sees itself not in second place but as a rival to Dublin. It produces its own national newspaper, *The Irish Examiner*, brews Murphy's and Beamish, its own versions of the national drink, stout (though now under the aegis of the Dutch brewer, Heineken), and supports a vigorous artistic, intellectual and cultural life of its own. Even its social divisions match Dublin's:

THE ENGLISH MARKET

# Highlights

**❶ The English Market** Cork styles itself as the Food Capital of Ireland, and the best producers can be found here in Cork City's bustling covered market. See page 237

**❷ Kinsale** A pretty harbour, impressive forts and some of the best restaurants in Ireland. See page 243

**❸ Drombeg** One of the country's finest Bronze Age stone circles, in a bucolic setting with views of the sea. See page 248

**❹ Clear Island** Hop on the ferry for varied bird-watching and pleasant walking. See page 253

**❺ Mizen Head** The view from Ireland's most southwesterly point – accessed by a suspension

bridge across a gorge – is nothing short of stunning. See page 255

**❻ The Sheep's Head Way** The shortest and easiest major walking route in southwestern Ireland, around a wild and lonely peninsula. See page 256

**❼ Bantry House and Gardens** Sumptuous art treasures in a beautiful spot overlooking Bantry Bay. See page 258

**❽ Beara Peninsula and Healy Pass** The peninsula's loop road meanders between crashing ocean and craggy mountains; the hairpin bends of Healy Pass are unforgettable. See page 259

**HIGHLIGHTS ARE MARKED ON THE MAP ON PAGE 228**

here too the south side of the river is generally more affluent, while the north side has more public housing and a stronger working-class identification.

In colonial times, Cork also maintained its own strong links with London, through its role as a major **port**, proof of which can still be seen all around town. The main drag, curving St Patrick's Street, was originally a waterway lined with quays, while you can still spot eighteenth-century moorings on Grand Parade. Though contemporary Cork doesn't make the most of its long riverfront, much of which is now lined by major roads, the channels of the Lee, spanned by more than twenty bridges, break up the cityscape and pleasantly disorientate. At the start of the twenty-first century, Grand Parade and St Patrick's Street were revamped with huge criss-crossing streetlights to represent the masts of ships. The harbour area has Ireland's largest concentration of chemical factories, fortunately downstream of the centre, while the city's other main modern industry, computers, is linked to the prestigious university, to the west of the centre. All of this has spawned a widespread commuter belt, but the compact island is still the place for the many excellent restaurants, lively pubs and artistic venues.

The best of the city's sightseeing options are the **Crawford Art Gallery**, with its fine collection of eighteenth- to twentieth-century art, **Cork City Gaol**, which vividly evokes life in a nineteenth-century prison, and the hi-tech cosmological displays of **Blackrock Castle Observatory**. In truth, however, none of Cork's sights are absolute must-sees, though it's a pleasant place to stroll around on a fine day. The city centre is essentially the eastern part of the island ("the flat of the city"), with its quaysides, bridges, old warehouses and the narrow alleys of the medieval heart, plus a segment to the north of the River Lee that has MacCurtain Street as its central thoroughfare.

## Brief history

In the seventh century, **St Finbarr** established a monastery at Cork, on the site of today's cathedral, to the southwest of the modern centre. Three centuries later, the Vikings created a separate settlement, an island in the River Lee's marshes, which was taken over in the twelfth century by the Anglo-Normans. They strengthened the defences of the

---

### BLARNEY

*Blarney, Blarney, what he says he does not mean. It is the usual Blarney.*

So spoke Queen Elizabeth I, and a legend and its accompanying tourist phenomenon were born. Though supposedly loyal to the queen, the **Lord of Blarney**, Cormac MacCarthy, had been stalling her emissary, Sir George Carew, who had been sent to restore English control of Munster, sidetracking him with wine, women and words. MacCarthy, it was said, could talk "the noose off his head", and over the centuries blarney came to mean "flattering, untrustworthy or loquacious talk associated with…Irish people" (*The Encyclopedia of Ireland*). This story of the word's origin, however, may itself be blarney…

At some stage in the nineteenth century, with the beginnings of mass tourism to the southwest of Ireland, it became popular to kiss the **Blarney Stone**, part of the machicolations of **Blarney Castle**, a fine fifteenth-century tower house, set in attractive grounds, in the village of the same name, 8km northwest of Cork. The stone stands over a 26m drop, and planting a smacker on it is meant to grant "the gift of the gab". If you're really feeling that tongue-tied, buses run to Blarney from Parnell Place bus station (Mon–Sat every 30min, Sun hourly; 20–30min), and the castle is open year-round (March, April & Oct daily 9–6pm; May & Sept Mon–Sat 9am–6.30pm, Sun 9am–6pm; June–Aug Mon–Sat 9am–7pm, Sun 9am–6pm; Nov–Feb daily 9am–5pm; last admission 30min before closing; €16; Heritage Island; Ⓦ blarneycastle.ie). Legions of the verbally challenged queue up in summer, when it's best to turn up early in the morning or late in the afternoon.

# CORK CITY

M8 to Dublin, N25 to Youghal & Waterford

Blackrock Castle Observatory

■ ACCOMMODATION

| | |
|---|---|
| Auburn House | 4 |
| Blarney Caravan and Camping Park | 1 |
| The Blarney Stone | 9 |
| Brú Bar & Hostel | 6 |
| Garnish House | 10 |
| Hayfield Manor | 13 |
| Isaac's | 5 |
| Jurys Inn | 8 |
| Kinlay House | 2 |
| Metropole Hotel | 7 |
| River Lee Hotel | 11 |
| Shandon Bells | 12 |
| Shelia's Hostel | 3 |

● EATING

| | |
|---|---|
| Café Paradiso | 7 |
| The Crawford Art Gallery Café | 2 |
| The Electric | 9 |
| Farmgate Café | 5 |
| Isaac's | 1 |
| Market Lane | 8 |
| Nash 19 | 3 |
| Orso | 6 |
| The Quay Co-op | 10 |
| The Sandwich Stall | 4 |

■ DRINKING & NIGHTLIFE

| | |
|---|---|
| An Spailpín Fánach | 11 |
| Arthur Mayne's | 8 |
| Chambers | 9 |
| Charlie's | 10 |
| The Corner House | 2 |
| Crane Lane Theatre | 7 |
| Franciscan Well | 3 |
| The Long Valley | 6 |
| Old Town Whiskey Bar at Bodega | 5 |
| Rising Sons Brewery | 4 |
| Sin É | 1 |

● SHOPPING

| | |
|---|---|
| English Market | 3 |
| Mother Jones Flea Market | 1 |
| Plugd Records | 2 |

Airport, Passage West, Ringaskiddy & Kinsale

S1 — Limerick & Blaney

Cork City Gaol

Fitzgerald Park & Cork Public Museum

University

Killarney & N22

central part of the island with the construction of vast city walls, leaving the west and east ends to the swamp and later developing suburbs on the slopes to the north and south. The fortifications were largely destroyed, however, in the successful **Williamite siege** of 1690, and became redundant when the marshes were reclaimed soon after. The next century witnessed great wealth, through the trade in butter and pickled meat and the development of the port for provisioning westbound sailing ships. Brewing and distilling plants were established, which persist to this day, along with glass, silver and lace industries, but the Act of Union and the introduction of steamships brought stagnation in the nineteenth century. At the start of the last century, Cork took an active part in the **War of Independence** and the **Civil War**, and suffered as a consequence. In 1920, the Royal Irish Constabulary murdered the Lord Mayor, Tomás MacCurtain, and as a reprisal for an ambush, the Black and Tans burnt much of the city centre to the ground in 1921. MacCurtain's successor as mayor, Terence MacSwiney, was incarcerated and went on hunger strike, which after 74 days led to his death on October 24, 1920.

## The centre

Three roughly east–west arteries define Cork's commercial centre, bracketed to the west by the wide boulevard of **Grand Parade**: the crescent of **St Patrick's Street** (aka Patrick Street), bustling with major chainstores; **Oliver Plunkett Street**, home to more traditional shops and pubs; and the city's grand financial and legal hub, **South Mall**. On the north side of Patrick Street, restaurants line the pedestrianized alleys of the old French quarter around **Paul Street**, though the main culinary venue is undoubtedly the covered **English Market** (see page 237), a joy for the senses that's well worth wandering through. Just south of the centre, on the way to St Finbarre's Cathedral (see box), is the seventeenth-century **Elizabeth's Fort** on Barrack St (Tues–Sat 10am–5pm, Sun noon–5pm; plus Mon May–Sept; free; ☎021 4975947, ⓦelizabethfort.ie), which functioned as a Garda station until 2013. These days, you're free to wander the star-shaped fort (there are some great city views from the walkway along the walls), or join the daily free historical tour at 1pm.

### The Crawford Art Gallery

Emmet Place • Mon–Sat 10am–5pm, Sun 11am–4pm • Free • ☎ 021 480 5042, ⓦ crawfordartgallery.ie

The city's major set-piece sight is the **Crawford Art Gallery**. Its main focus is its interesting temporary exhibitions of Irish and international art in a striking modern extension, but it also has an excellent café (see page 235) and a permanent collection of Irish and British art from the eighteenth century onwards that's worth a quick mosey. The lion's share of the collection is housed on the first floor, where you'll have to wade

---

#### NEO-GOTHIC CORK

For those with a taste for it – and with shoe leather to spare – there's plenty of **neo-Gothic church architecture** to see in Cork, mostly along the river banks. The highlight is William Burges's **St Finbarre's Cathedral** on Proby's Quay (Mon–Sat 9.30am–5.30pm, plus April–Nov Sun 12.30–5pm; €6; ⓦcorkcathedral.webs.com), consecrated in 1870, whose three soaring, French Gothic spires are visible all over the city. The well-lit interior, which is elaborately decorated with red Cork marble, stained glass and Italianate mosaics, also impresses with its lofty proportions. Leading nineteenth-century practitioners Augustus Pugin and George Pain also worked in Cork. The **Church of SS Peter and Paul**, just off St Patrick's Street in the centre, was designed by Pugin and sports some fine woodcarving. Pain was the architect of **Holy Trinity Church** on Father Mathew Quay, with its handsome lantern spire, which was built in the 1830s and 1840s by booze-busting Father Theobald Mathew, who persuaded three million people to take the "total abstinence pledge", as well as of **St Patrick's Church** out to the northeast on Lower Glanmire Road.

through some sentimentally cloying nineteenth- and twentieth-century works. Look out, however, for a fascinating *View of Cork*, painted in about 1740 by John Butts: you can pick out the waterway that is now Patrick Street, the 1724 Custom House (with a Union Jack in the courtyard), which is now the gallery you're visiting. There are also some fine representative works by Limerick-born Seán Keating (1889–1977), many of whose academic realist paintings have achieved iconic status. Though obviously posed in a studio, his *Men of the South* (1924) achieves the restrained grandeur of a classical frieze, depicting a grim-faced IRA column waiting to ambush British soldiers. Keep an eye out also for a piercing portrait of actor Fiona Shaw by Victoria Russell on the staircase to the first floor and – on the second floor – pencil and watercolour studies by Harry Clarke (1881–1931) for his Keats-inspired stained glass window "The Eve of St Agnes".

## West of the centre

The west end of the island narrows around a residential area, which is home to hospitals and university buildings as well as a couple of interesting small museums. North of these, to the west of Shandon in the posh suburb of Sunday's Well, is the forbidding red sandstone of **Cork City Gaol**.

### Glucksman Gallery

University College Cork, 1km from Grand Parade off the south side of Western Rd • Tues–Sat 10am–5pm, Sun 2–5pm • Free • ☎ 021 490 1844, ⓦ glucksman.org

In the northeast corner of the university's main campus, it's well worth checking out the **Glucksman Gallery**. This striking building of wood, glass, limestone and steel, which was shortlisted for the 2005 RIBA prize, hosts rotating exhibitions of contemporary art, as well as free guided tours, talks, concerts and a restaurant.

### Cork Public Museum

5min walk from the Glucksman Gallery off the north side of Western Rd • Tues–Fri 10am–4pm, Sat 11am–4pm, plus May–Sept Sun 2–4pm • Free • ☎ 021 427 0679, ⓦ corkcity.ie

Facing the leafy north channel of the River Lee, sits **Fitzgerald Park**, where you'll find the **Cork Public Museum**, a celebration of Cork and Corkonians – including sports personalities Sonia O'Sullivan and Roy Keane, both of whom have donated shirts. The museum traces the city's history through interesting documents and memorabilia, with a particular concentration on the period from the Great Famine to The Emergency, as World War II was known in Ireland. Some beautiful examples of Cork silver and glassware are on display, alongside archaeological finds from the Neolithic era onwards and engaging temporary exhibitions on subjects such as prehistoric gold.

### Cork City Gaol

Convent Ave, Sunday's Well • Daily: Jan–March & Oct–Dec 10am–4pm; April–Sept 9.30am–5pm • €10, audio-tour €2, guided group tours and evening tours €10 (book in advance) • ☎ 021 430 5022, ⓦ corkcitygaol.com • 15min walk across the river from Fitzgerald Park (signposted from the nearby footbridge)

Skilfully designed for its punishing purpose in 1818 by the Pain brothers, George and James, the **Cork City Gaol** operated until 1923 when Republican prisoners – among them Countess Markiewicz (see page 397) and short story writer Frank O'Connor – were released after the Civil War. A lively and informative audio-tour guides you round the well-preserved cells, where the individual stories of real-life prisoners are recounted. An audiovisual courtroom drama finishes the tour evocatively, projected onto the walls of one of the gaol's imposing drum galleries.

From the late 1920s until the early 1950s, the top floor of the gaol was home to the studios of Radio Éireann (now RTÉ), which have now been replaced by the **Radio Museum**. There's lots of interesting material on the pioneers of radio here, a re-creation of the old studio, a large collection of early radios, and a "juke box" of archival recordings.

# Shandon and north of the centre

To the north of the centre, **Shandon**'s narrow residential streets and alleys tumble down the slope towards the River Lee. At the centre of this area stands cobbled O'Connell Square, home to the round and tubby former **butter market**.

## Butter Museum

O'Connell Square • March–Oct daily 10am–5pm; Nov–Feb Sat & Sun 11am–3pm • €4 • ☎ 021 430 0600, ⓦ thebuttermuseum.com

The fascinating story of the dairy trade and its major impact on the development of the city is told in the **Butter Museum**, opposite the old butter market. The museum begins with dairy culture in early Ireland, as illustrated by a keg of bog butter: on remote grazing lands, milk was churned into butter on the spot and preserved in the bogs for later use; to this day, such kegs are often turned over by peat-cutters, who'll swear the butter is still edible. In the eighteenth century, thanks to its fertile hinterland and its site on the largest natural harbour in the northern hemisphere, Cork became the main provisioning port in the Atlantic for both the British Navy and trade convoys, with most Cork butter ending up in the West Indies. In the following century, the city managed to ride out the agricultural collapse caused by the Napoleonic Wars and the Famine, by gearing the butter trade to the English market through rigorous controls – the butter-market building you see outside was where barrels were washed and weighed, to avoid underhand practices by farmers.

## St Anne's Shandon

Church St • Jan, Feb, Nov & Dec Mon–Sat 11am–3pm, Sun 11.30am–3pm; March–May & Oct Mon–Sat 10am–4pm, Sun 11.30am–4pm; June–Sept Mon–Sat 10am–5pm, Sun 11.30am–4.30pm • Church free; tower and bells €5 • ☎ 021 450 5906, ⓦ shandonbells.ie

**St Anne's Shandon** is a graceful, early eighteenth-century Anglican church, built partly of white limestone, partly of puce sandstone – a combination that is said to have inspired the red-and-white "rebel" flag of County Cork. Its steeple, the city's most famous landmark, is flanked by four huge, notoriously unreliable clocks – earning the nickname "the four-faced liar" – and topped by a giant golden salmon as a weather vane. It's possible to climb the 132 steps of the tower for matchless views of the city and to ring the bells.

# Blackrock Castle Observatory

2km east of centre on south bank of River Lee • Daily 10am–5pm, last admission 4pm; tower and dungeon tours Mon–Fri on application, Sat & Sun 1.30pm & 3.30pm • €6.50; children €4.50; family €18 • ☎ 021 435 7917, ⓦ bco.ie • City bus #202 towards Mahon from bus station will put you off at the pier in Blackrock village, leaving an easy 10min walk to the castle

Originally built in the sixteenth century, **Blackrock Castle Observatory** is now home to two dynamic and imaginative exhibitions: **Cosmos at the Castle**, beautifully produced, large-screen audiovisuals containing up to three hours of material that you can explore interactively in as much depth as you choose, not just on cosmology, but on life, the universe and everything; and **Journeys of Exploration**, a similarly stimulating interactive experience that recalls the history of the castle and surrounding area. The programme of visiting exhibitions is well regarded, and there's also a very good café-restaurant here.

## ARRIVAL AND DEPARTURE                                    CORK CITY

**By plane** Travelling by plane, you'll arrive at Cork Airport (ⓦ corkairport.com), which lies 7km south of the centre, off the Kinsale road and has ATMs and a bureau de change. From here, Bus Éireann's #226/226A bus runs, in one direction, to the bus station on Parnell Place and Kent train station (Mon–Sat every 30min, Sun hourly; 30min), and, in the other direction, to Kinsale (hourly; 30min). If you want a quick getaway, Citylink operates through-coaches from Cork

Airport to Limerick and Galway.

**By train** Cork Kent station is 1km northeast of the city centre on the Lower Glanmire Rd.

Destinations Cobh (Mon–Sat at least hourly, 11 on Sun; 25min); Dublin Heuston (hourly; 2hr 40min); Fota (Mon–Sat at least hourly, 11 on Sun; 13min); Killarney (6–9 daily, often with a change at Mallow; 1hr 30min–2hr); Midleton (Mon–Sat at least hourly, 9 on Sun; 25min); Tralee (6–9 daily, often with a change at Mallow; 2hr–2hr 30min).

**By bus** The Bus Éireann station is on Parnell Place alongside Merchant's Quay. Harrington's and O'Donoghue's private buses to Castletownbere (see page 261) stop nearby on Parnell Place, while Aircoach and Citylink buses use St Patrick's Quay on the north side of the river, the latter starting from Cork Airport 30min earlier. Most city buses stop on the central St Patrick's Street.

Destinations Bus Éireann: Adrigole (Mon, Sat & Sun; 3hr); Baltimore (1–2 daily; 2hr); Bantry (4–6 daily; 1hr 50min); Cahir (6 daily; 1hr 20min); Cashel (6 daily; 1hr 40min); Castletownbere (4 weekly; 3hr); Clonakilty (7–8 daily; 1hr 10min); Dublin and airport (6 daily; 3hr 45min–4hr 10min); Ennis (hourly; 3hr); Galway (hourly; 4hr 20min); Glengarriff (2–3 daily; 2hr 10min); Goleen (1–2 daily; 2hr 45min); Killarney (hourly; 1hr 30min); Kinsale (from Kent train station, via the bus station and the airport; hourly; 1hr); Limerick (hourly; 1hr 45min); Midleton (frequent; 30min); Schull (1–2 daily; 2hr 20min); Shannon Airport (hourly; 2hr 30min); Skibbereen (5–7 daily; 1hr 45min); Tralee (hourly; 2hr 15min); Waterford (hourly; 2hr 15min); Youghal (hourly; 50min).

Aircoach (ⓦ aircoach.ie): Dublin and airport (hourly; 3hr–3hr 20min).

Citylink (ⓦ citylink.ie): Galway (5 daily; 3hr); Limerick (5 daily; 1hr 30min).

Dublin Coach (ⓦ dublincoach.ie): Kilkenny (8 daily; 2hr 35min).

**By car** If you're arriving by car, note that parking on the street requires a disc, which can be picked up from convenience stores. There's a useful multistorey car park on Coal Quay beside the Opera House.

## GETTING AROUND

**Bike rental** Cycle Scene, 396 Blarney St (€15/day; ☏ 021 430 1183, ⓦ cyclescene.ie).

**Car rental** Most of the big multinationals such as Budget (☏ 021 431 4000, ⓦ budget.ie) are represented at Cork Airport. There are few local outfits, but they include friendly and amenable Great Island Car Rentals, who are centrally placed at 47 MacCurtain St (☏ 021 481 1609, ⓦ greatislandcarrentals.com) and can deliver to the airport.

**Taxis** There are ranks on Patrick St. Companies include Cork Taxi Co-op (☏ 021 427 2222, ⓦ corktaxi.ie).

## INFORMATION AND TOURS

**Tourist office** 125 St Patrick's St (Mon–Sat 9am–5pm; ☏ 021 425 5100, ⓦ purecork.ie).

**Walking tours** Two-hour tours of the city pick up at the tourist office (May–Oct Mon & Tues 11am, Wed noon, Thurs–Sat 11am; €12; ☏ 087 700 4981, ⓦ corkcitywalk.eu).

**Bus tours** Cronin's operates a hop-on, hop-off tour in an open-top double-decker (every 45min; 1hr 15min; buy tickets on board or at the tourist office; €15, valid for two consecutive days; ☏ 021 430 9090, ⓦ corkcitytour.com), departing from opposite the tourist office and passing the train station, the public museum and the Glucksman Gallery, St Anne's Shandon and Cork City Gaol.

**Boat tours** Atlantic Sea Kayaking runs kayaking trips (April–Sept; from €60/person; ☏ 0282 1058, ⓦ atlantic seakayaking.com) around the city by river or out into the harbour.

## ACCOMMODATION SEE MAP PAGE 230

Cork's **hotels** range from no-frills to luxurious, and there are scores of **B&Bs** and more upmarket **guesthouses**, which are mostly concentrated near the university along Western Road (city bus #208 from St Patrick's St or #205 from Kent train station and St Patrick's St), and at the opposite end of town on the busy Lower Glanmire Rd, near the train station. A variety of **hostels** can be found mostly on the north bank of the River Lee; for summer accommodation in halls try ⓦ studentvillage.ie or ⓦ uccsummerbeds.com. Beds are in short supply during the city's many festivals (see page 237), when early booking is advisable.

### HOTELS

★ **Hayfield Manor** Perrott Ave, College Rd ☏ 021 484 5900, ⓦ hayfieldmanor.ie. Giving a taste of the countryside among the terraces of the southwestern suburbs, 500m west of St Finbarr's Cathedral, this five-star 1920s manor house has been decorated in a fresh, modern, rural style and much extended. Service is attentive and congenial, while facilities include an imposing pool, an outdoor Jacuzzi in the pretty garden, a spa, a conservatory bistro and an excellent modern Irish restaurant, *Orchids*. **€229**

**Isaac's** 48 MacCurtain St ☏ 021 450 0011, ⓦ hotelisaacs cork.com. Good-value, well-run hotel in a former furniture warehouse with an attractive courtyard and waterfall behind its grand, Victorian, redbrick facade, and smart, colourful, well-equipped bedrooms. Serviced apartments also available. **€190**

**Jurys Inn** Anderson's Quay ☏ 021 494 3000, ⓦ jurysinns. com. Bright, smart accommodation in a large, efficiently run, welcoming hotel. Central but in a slightly quieter location towards the east end of the "island". **€115**

**Metropole Hotel** MacCurtain St ☏ 021 464 3700, ⓦ themetropolehotel.ie. A landmark building in a central location by the bus station, this completely revamped hotel now looks better than ever, with beautifully appointed rooms complemented by a welter of eating and drinking possibilities, including the glam Prosecco Lounge and the

MET café. Great welcome by reception staff and use of the fitness centre and its 20m pool is included. **€149**
**River Lee Hotel** Western Rd ☎ 021 425 2700, ⓦ doyle collection.com. Pleasing modern hotel decorated with pale stone and grainy wood, a 10min walk west of the centre overlooking the leafy university campus. The rooms are large and well designed with comfortable beds and their own music system. The bistro and bar feature broad terraces on the river, and there's an attached leisure club with pool, gym and spa. **€174**

## GUESTHOUSES AND B&BS

**Auburn House** 3 Garfield Terrace, Wellington Rd ☎ 021 450 8555, ⓦ auburnguesthouse.com. Well-maintained, en-suite B&B in a central but peaceful spot north of the river, with fine breakfasts, including vegetarian, and parking facilities. Good rates for singles. **€90**
**The Blarney Stone** 1 Carriglee Terrace, Western Rd ☎ 021 427 0083, ⓦ blarneystoneguesthouse.com. Gleaming white nineteenth-century guesthouse opposite the university, lavishly furnished with Waterford Crystal chandeliers, antique fireplaces and swag curtains, offering a diverse breakfast menu that caters for various dietary requirements, and off-street parking. **€119**
**Garnish House** Western Rd ☎ 021 427 5111, ⓦ garnish. ie. Victorian guesthouse of a high standard opposite the university, where you'll get a warm welcome and a delicious breakfast from a diverse menu that stretches to eggs Benedict with smoked salmon; some rooms have a Jacuzzi. Self-catering is also available, as is off-street parking. **€109**
**Shandon Bells** 44 Western Rd ☎ 086 022 0280 , ⓦ shandonbellscork.ie. Very helpful and informative owners at this B&B 15min from the centre, overlooking

the southern channel of the river near the university. Bright, colourful, en-suite rooms, a varied breakfast menu and a waterside patio for fair weather. Off-street parking available. **€80**

## HOSTELS

★ **Brú Bar & Hostel** 57 MacCurtain St (IHH & IHO) ☎ 021 455 9667, ⓦ bruhostel.com. The city's most central hostel, a welcoming, rambling former hotel above a sociable backpackers' bar, which live music nightly. The clean, basic, high-ceilinged rooms (four- or six-bed dorms, plus one private room that sleeps three at €50); all have private bathrooms (most are en suite), and there's a kitchen and dining and TV room (lots of DVDs to borrow). Prices include a simple breakfast. Dorms from **€17**
**Kinlay House** Bob and Joan's Walk, Shandon (IHH) ☎ 021 450 8966, ⓦ kinlayhousecork.ie. Large, well-run, partly en-suite hostel, on a quiet lane next to St Anne's Church, with singles, doubles and twins alongside dorms; laundry facilities and kitchen. Price includes a light breakfast. Dorms **€20**, doubles **€56**
**Sheila's Hostel** 4 Belgrave Place, Wellington Rd (IHH & IHO) ☎ 021 450 5562, ⓦ sheilashostel.ie. Cork's biggest hostel, efficiently run and welcoming, with a good kitchen, laundry facilities, a cinema room and a sauna. Dorms **€18**, doubles **€50**

## CAMPSITE

**Blarney Caravan and Camping Park** Stone-view, 3km north of Blarney ☎ 021 451 6519, ⓦ blarneycaravanpark. com. The nearest campsite, about 10km northwest of the city centre, with campers' kitchen, laundry, shop, play area and an 18-hole pitch'n'putt. Closed late Oct to March. **€22**

## EATING                                             SEE MAP PAGE 230

Eating out is one of the great pleasures of Cork – the city's chefs place a high premium on sourcing the best of local, artisanal ingredients, which they creatively put to good use. The best place to get a feel for Cork's culinary enthusiasm is the **English Market** (see page 237).
**Café Paradiso** 16 Lancaster Quay, Western Rd ☎ 021 427 7939, ⓦ paradiso.restaurant. Popular, unpretentious restaurant serving excellent and innovative Mediterranean-influenced vegetarian and vegan cuisine. The three-course dinner menu costs €48, but there are cheaper early-bird (till 6.45pm) menus. Stylish accommodation also available for diners. Tues–Sat 5.30–10pm.
**The Crawford Gallery Café** Emmet Place ☎ 021 427 4415, ⓦ crawfordgallerycafe.com. Classy and affordable café-restaurant in a gorgeous ground-floor room of the gallery (see page 231). You can lunch on the likes of leek and cheddar cheese tart (£14) and, after a short spin round the gallery, you might well find yourself tempted back for tea and cake. Mon–Fri 9am–4pm, Sat 8.30am–4pm.

**The Electric** 41 South Mall ☎ 021 422 2990, ⓦ electric cork.ie. Behind the Art Deco exterior of a former bank, this innovative bar-restaurant shelters a lovely light-filled restaurant upstairs (steaks are a speciality; rib eye €26), as well as a white-tiled fish bar (no reservations) overlooking the river, which rustles up dishes such as tiger prawn cassoulet (€12). The downstairs bar serves food all day, alongside craft beer and cocktails, and has tempting tables on a riverside boardwalk. Restaurant daily noon–3pm & 5–10pm; fish bar Wed–Sat 5–10pm; bar food daily 10am–10pm.
★ **Farmgate Café** English Market, Princes St ☎ 021 463 2771, ⓦ farmgate.ie. Superb café-restaurant overlooking the market's bustling stalls. Places a strong emphasis on local ingredients and food products: daily specials depend on what's fresh from the butcher and fishmonger. Cooked breakfasts to order (from €7.50), great cakes and desserts and excellent lunches, which feature salads and savoury tarts, as well as many classic dishes such as tripe and onion with dritheen (€11). The dining room has table service

**7**

7

(mains around €10; booking essential if you want to come around 1pm), or there's self-service (with a cheaper menu that includes sandwiches). Mon–Sat 8.30am–5pm; breakfast 8.30–11am; lunch noon–3.30pm.

★ **Isaac's** 48 MacCurtain St ☎ 021 450 3805, ⓦ isaacs restaurant.ie. Popular, informal and welcoming restaurant in an eighteenth-century warehouse with bare stone walls, candles and a buzzy atmosphere. The short, global menu, supplemented by daily specials, ranges from Indian lamb curry to roast chicken (mains €16–19). There's plenty of choice for veggies and some great comfort desserts like pear and rhubarb crumble. Set menu €23 for two courses Mon & Tues 5.45–9.30pm, Wed–Sat 5.45–7pm. Mon–Sat 12.30–2.30pm & 5.30–9.30pm, Sun 6–9pm.

**Market Lane** 5 Oliver Plunkett St ☎ 021 427 4710, ⓦ marketlane.ie. Crisp bistro decor featuring lots of polished wood, an open kitchen and a long bar in a bright corner location provides the setting for bargain €12 lunches of soup, a half-sandwich, a chocolate pot and coffee (Mon–Fri). Later in the day you can tuck into tasty fare such as lamb and stout puff pastry pie, perhaps taking advantage of their early bird (Mon–Thurs 5–7pm, Sun 1–7pm; €25 for three courses). Mon–Wed noon–9.30pm, Thurs noon–10pm, Fri & Sat noon–10.30pm, Sun 1–9.30pm.

**Nash 19** 19 Princes St ☎ 021 427 0880, ⓦ nash19.com. Bright, efficient daytime café serving delicious, high-quality

cuisine – including a tapas style shared plate of meats and cheese (€24), soups (€5.50), a warm salad of the day (from €10.50) and hot and cold breakfasts at reasonable prices; various dietary requirements catered for. Tues–Sat 9am–6pm.

**Orso** 8 Pembroke St ☎ 021 243 8000, ⓦ orso.ie. Head for this small, mellow café for great breakfasts, superb espressos and mostly Middle Eastern mains at lunch, such as flatbread with three cheeses, fresh mint and pine nuts (with salad, €10.50). Dinners are more complex and the cakes – like their popcorn, chocolate and malteser bar – serious. No bookings. Mon 8.30am–6pm, Tues–Sat 8.30am–10/10.30pm.

**The Quay Co-op** 24 Sullivan's Quay ☎ 021 431 7026, ⓦ quaycoop.com. Self-service, partly organic workers' cooperative café above a health-food store, serving tasty, substantial and cheap vegetarian and vegan meals (and catering for many other dietary requirements), great salads (from €6.95) and soups (€3.90), plus a selection of desserts. There's a more basic "coffee dock" on the ground floor. Mon–Sat 11am–9pm, Sun noon–9pm.

**The Sandwich Stall** English Market, Grand Parade ⓦ facebook.com/thesandwichstall. Cute corner stall in the market selling gourmet sandwiches (from €6), hot soups (€3) and channa masala (€5.50 with all the trimmings). You can perch at the bar and wash your lunch down with a strong coffee. Mon–Sat 9am–4pm.

## DRINKING AND NIGHTLIFE

SEE MAP PAGE 230

The city boasts dozens of great **bars**, specializing in characterful and unreconstructed old **pubs**. These would generally be worth seeking out for their atmosphere alone, but a high proportion of them also host **music**, traditional or otherwise. For general **information** on the arts, nightlife and entertainment, consult the free monthly leaflet, *Whazon* (ⓦ whazon.com), which can be picked up in cafés and arts venues. Plugd Records (see page 237) is a good place for info on the gig and club scenes.

**An Spailpín Fánach** 28 South Main St ☎ 021 427 7949. Rambling, rustic and unpretentious, the "Migrant Worker" was established opposite the now defunct Beamish and Crawford Brewery in the eighteenth century, and hosts traditional music most nights. Mon–Thurs 5–11.30pm, Fri 12.30pm–12.30am, Sat 3pm–12.30am, Sun 5–11pm.

**Arthur Mayne's** 7 Pembroke St ☎ 021 427 9449, ⓦ cork heritagepubs.com. Atmospheric, not to say creepy, conversion of an ancient pharmacy with dozens of old apothecary items left on the shelves, beyond which cellar-like cubicles connect with the Crane Lane Theatre bar. If you can peel your eyes away from the decor for a minute, you'll find an excellent menu of well-kept wines by the glass, as well as meat and cheese plates, sandwiches and weekend brunch. Mon–Thurs 10am–2am, Fri & Sat 10am–2.30am, Sun 11am–2am.

**Chambers** Washington St ☎ 021 465 8100, ⓦ facebook.

com/chamberscork. The city's main LGBTQ bar and club, with DJs every night and regular events; €5 admission Fri & Sat after 11pm. Wed–Sun 4pm–2am.

**Charlie's** 2 Union Quay ☎ 021 431 8342, ⓦ charliesbar cork.com. Dimly lit, grungy pub with an early licence and frequent live music, mostly blues but including traditional session on Sun afternoon. Mon–Sat 7am–late, Sun 12.30pm–late.

★ **The Corner House** 7 Coburg St ☎ 021 450 0655, ⓦ thecornerhouse.ie. Welcoming pub, similar in feel to *Sin É* next door, though more spacious and airy. Great local bands from 6pm on Saturdays, Bluegrass most Sunday evenings, traditional music Mon, Wed, Thurs and every second Fri. Call them or check the website for details. Mon–Thurs 3.30–11.30pm, Fri & Sat 3.30pm–midnight, Sun 3.30–11pm.

**Crane Lane Theatre** Phoenix St ☎ 021 427 8487, ⓦ cranelanetheatre.ie. Cosy, vibrant theatre bar, offering a wide range of craft beers, though much of the action happens under the hanging plants in the big, heated courtyard out front. Live bands – anything from folk and blues to jazz and country – and/or DJs every night. Mon–Fri 2pm–2am, Sat & Sun noon–2am.

**Franciscan Well** 14b North Mall ☎ 021 439 3434, ⓦ franciscanwellbrewery.com. On the site of a medieval monastery whose well was known for its curative properties, this microbrewery-bar knocks out great stout, lager, ale and wheat beer, which can be enjoyed out the back in the sunny/heated beer-yard. Also offers pizzas from a wood-fired oven (daily 1–10pm) and brewery tours (Sun–Thurs 2pm, 4pm & 6pm), while diverse events include a Wednesday night storyteller. Mon–Thurs 1–11.30pm, Fri & Sat 1pm–12.30am, Sun 1–11pm.

**The Long Valley** 10 Winthrop St ☎021 427 2144, ⓦthe longvalleybar.ie. Fine traditional bar, sporting a large snug at the front and decorated with plants, old views of Cork and a mishmash of wooden furniture, some of it rescued from a cruise-liner. Famous for its tasty doorstep sandwiches (from €4.50) at lunchtime. Poetry, stories and acoustic music on Mon nights from 9.30pm (ⓦobheal.ie). Mon–Thurs 11am/noon–11.30pm, Fri & Sat 11am/noon–12.30am, Sun roughly noon–11pm.

**Old Town Whiskey Bar at Bodega** 44–45 Cornmarket St ☎021 427 3756, ⓦoldtownwhiskeybar.com. Barn-like all-rounder in a former covered food market on the redeveloped Cornmarket. The decor is chandeliers, arched colonnades and a lofty bar and the food's especially good here, including meat and cheese plates and brunches. Late on Fri & Sat nights, it turns into one of Cork's most popular clubs. Mon–Thurs 10am–11.30pm, Fri & Sat 10am–2.30am, Sun 10am–11pm.

**Rising Sons Brewery** Cornmarket St ☎021 241 4764, ⓦrisingsonsbrewery.com. Award-winning small-batch microbrewery opposite Bodega offering daily tours and tastings (€10 including two beers), quality bar food and a projector showing sports events. Mon–Thurs noon–11.30pm, Fri & Sat noon–12.30am, Sun 11.30am–11pm.

**Sin É** 8 Coburg St ☎021 450 2266, ⓦcorkheritagepubs. com. Cosy, candlelit pub, hung with all sorts of bric-a-brac and memorabilia and offering a wide range of beers. Frequent, varied live music, including traditional at 6.30pm every night (5.30pm on Sundays). The name means "That's It" because there used to be a funeral parlour next door. Mon–Thurs 12.30–11.30pm, Fri & Sat 12.30pm–12.30am, Sun 12.30–11pm.

## ENTERTAINMENT

**Cork Opera House** Emmet Place ☎021 427 0022, ⓦcorkoperahouse.ie. The city's main performance venue, hosting high-quality drama, dance, opera, comedy and concerts of all hues, with more eclectic shows in the attached Half Moon Theatre.

**Everyman** MacCurtain St ☎021 450 1673, ⓦeveryman cork.com. Cork's oldest traditional theatre, dating back to the late nineteenth century, offers a varied menu of drama, dance, opera, music and comedy.

**Triskel Christchurch** Tobin St ☎021 427 2022, ⓦtriskel artscentre.ie. The main contemporary arts centre is actually two integrated buildings – Christchurch, a fine, early Georgian Protestant church, deconsecrated and beautifully renovated, where arthouse films, interesting gigs and art exhibitions are put on; and its original home on Tobin St, which includes an art gallery and a café, *Scrypt Café-Bar*.

## SHOPPING SEE MAP PAGE 230

**English Market** Accessed either from Princes St or Grand Parade ⓦcorkcity.ie. A Victorian covered market with the city's best fishmongers, greengrocers and butchers – stocking the local delicacies of tripe and *drisheen*, a type of black pudding – and all manner of pungent specialist stalls where you could build a great picnic (perhaps for eating in the small Bishop Lucey Park, on the other side of Grand Parade): cheeses, cold meats and smoked fish, olives, salads and deli goods, bread, cakes, and even wine and chocolates. Mon–Sat 8am–6pm.

**Mother Jones Flea market** York St, near the corner of MacCurtain St ☎085 175 1554. Purveys vintage clothes, antiques and books. Fri–Sun 11am–6/7pm.

**Plugd Records** Upstairs at The Roundy, 1 Castle St ☎085 823 6966, ⓦplugdrecords.com. This legendary record store not only has a prodigious stock of vinyl, but also sells publications and limited prints, and hosts in-store gigs. Wed–Sat 11am–6pm.

---

## CORK FESTIVALS

Cork city hosts plenty of lively festivals, of which the largest and most prestigious are the **midsummer festival**, a wide-ranging celebration of the arts in late June (ⓦcorkmidsummer. com), the **jazz festival** in October (ⓦguinnessjazzfestival.com) and the **film festival** in November, with a particular focus on short films (ⓦcorkfilmfest.org). There's also an international **choral festival** in late April or early May (ⓦcorkchoral.ie), the Cork **LGBTQ Pride** festival in July/August (ⓦcorkpride.com) and **an early-music festival** in October, shared between the city and East Cork (ⓦeastcorkearlymusic.ie). The biggest festival in County Cork is held in September and revolves around food; **A Taste of West Cork** (ⓦatasteofwestcork.com) is hosted by a number of towns, and you'll find food markets, cookery demonstrations, tastings and special events in Skibbereen, Clonakilty, Bantry and elsewhere.

## DIRECTORY

**Exchange** The main banks are on and around St Patrick's St, and there are bureaux de change at the big hotels.

**Gaelic football and hurling** Cork is one of the few counties that's strong on both Gaelic games, and Páirc Uí Chaoimh, 2km east of the centre off Centre Park Rd, is one of the country's major stadiums (though you might have more luck getting tickets for the smaller Pairc Ui Rinn, also 2km east, but on Boreenmanna Rd); for fixtures, consult ⓦ gaacork.ie or The *Irish Examiner*.

**Pharmacy** Phelan's Late Night Pharmacy, 9 Patrick St ☏ 021 427 2511.

**Police** The main police station is on Anglesea St ☏ 021 452 2000.

# East Cork

East Cork occupies a blind spot in the eyes of many visitors, their focus set on the more spectacular coastline to the west, but several interesting places are worth considering, all of them served by public transport. A suburban train service makes possible an excellent, varied day-trip across the Lee estuary to **Fota Island**, with its sensitively restored Neoclassical hunting lodge and wildlife park, and on to the attractive harbour town of **Cobh** on Great Island. Further east lies **Midleton**, the traditional home of Jameson whiskey and a culinary hub. In an expansive setting at the mouth of the River Blackwater, the historic, easy-going resort of **Youghal**, some 40km east of Cork, marks the border with County Waterford.

## Fota House, Arboretum & Gardens

Carrigtwohill, Fota Island • **House** March–Oct daily 10am–5pm • Free; guided tours (daily 12.30pm, 2pm & 3.30pm) €8 • **Victorian Gardens** March–Sept Mon–Fri 10.30am–3pm, Sun 2–5pm • Free; guided tours (noon) €5 • **Arboretum** April–Oct 9am–6pm; Nov–March 9am–5pm • Free • Car parking €3 • ☏ 021 481 5543, ⓦ fotahouse.com

If you travel from the mainland by road, you're hardly aware that **Fota** is an island in Cork Harbour. Its main attraction is **Fota House, Arboretum & Gardens**, built in the 1740s as a hunting lodge for the Barry family, whose main seat had by then moved from nearby Barryscourt Castle to Castlelyons near Fermoy. In the early nineteenth century, the house was substantially redeveloped and extended in elegant Neoclassical style, and now lies a ten-minute walk from Fota train station. Excellent guided tours reveal plenty of telling details, with the highlights being the **entrance hall**, a beautifully symmetrical space divided by striking ochre columns of *scagliola* (imitation marble), and the ceiling of the **drawing room**, with its plasterwork doves, musical instruments, hunting implements and delicately painted cherubs and floral motifs. The tour also goes below stairs to the **servants' quarters**, which include an impressive octagonal game-larder and such features as gaps at the top of the windows of the butler's servery – added so that food smells would tantalize the poor servants rather than the house guests. For visitors, there's a nice little café in the long gallery and billiard room, plus it's well worth touring the **gardens** at the rear of the house where the Victorian "Frameyard" – a complex of glasshouses – has been restored to its former glory.

Much of the estate's formal gardens and its internationally significant **arboretum**, laid out in the mid-nineteenth century, are under the care of the Office of Public Works, with free access. At its best in April and May, the arboretum hosts a wide range of exotic trees and shrubs, with many rare examples, including some magnificent Lebanese cedars, a Victorian fernery and a lush, almost tropical, lake.

## Fota Wildlife Park

Carrigtwohill, Fota Island • Daily 10am–6pm; last admission 4.30pm • €16.90, children €11.50, family ticket from €49.50, car parking €3 • ☏ 021 481 2678, ⓦ fotawildlife.ie

In the former estate of Fota House, **Fota Wildlife Park** is renowned for its success in breeding cheetahs, which, along with monkeys, giraffes, bison and many other species, wander about in seventy acres of open countryside. There's also a tropical house, featuring snakes, lizards and turtles, while events include the daily cheetah run and other animal feeding times, as well as weekend wildlife talks.

## Cobh

On the southern coast of Great Island, with extensive views of Cork Harbour, **COBH** (pronounced "cove") makes a great escape from the city on a fine day. This historic and unpretentious resort, clinging onto a steep, south-facing slope, sports a stony beach, a promenade with a bandstand and gaily painted rows of Victorian hotels and houses. Ireland's – and possibly the world's – first **yacht club** was founded in Cobh in 1720 and although the Italianate building now houses the Sirius Arts Centre (⊛siriusartscentre.ie), the port's cruise-liner tradition continues. Each year, dozens of huge cruise ships dock at this fine natural harbour, said to be the second-largest in the world (by navigable area) after Sydney; Cobh was a port of call for the *Sirius*, the first steamship to cross the Atlantic, in 1838, and for the *Titanic* on her disastrous maiden voyage in 1912, while many of the victims of the sinking of the *Lusitania* in 1915 (see page 244) were buried in the Old Church Cemetery, 2km north of Cobh. The port was also a major supply depot during the American and Napoleonic wars, and became Ireland's main point of emigration after the Great Famine.

### Cobh Heritage Centre: the Queenstown Story

Seafront • Wed–Sun 10am–4pm (last admission 3pm) • €11; Heritage Island • ☎ 021 481 3591, ⊛ cobhheritage.com

Cobh's long and often tragic seafaring history is vividly detailed at the **Queenstown Story**, a multimedia heritage centre (which also offers a genealogical service) with a pleasant café in the former Victorian train station on the seafront (the town was renamed Queenstown after a visit by Queen Victoria in 1849, but its old name was restored after Independence).

### The Titanic Experience

White Star Line Building, 20 Casement Square • Daily: April–Sept 9am–6pm; Oct–March 10am–5.30pm; last tour 45min before closing • €10 • ☎ 021 481 4412, ⊛ titanicexperiencecobh.ie

Cobh was the last port of call for the *Titanic*, with the final 123 passengers boarding here on April 11, 1912. The White Star Line ticket office where they assembled, backed by its now-ruinous wooden pier, has been turned into a visitor attraction, a short way east of the tourist office along the seafront. Amid re-creations of third- and first-class cabins, it's revealed that while first had a heated swimming pool, the seven hundred third-class passengers had to share two baths. There are some interesting audiovisuals, including footage of the wreck, discovered in 1985, as well as games and interactive quizzes.

---

### COBH TOURS AND WATERSPORTS

Although the Royal Cork Yacht Club has moved across the harbour to Crosshaven, messing about in **boats** is still a strong feature of life in the town. Sail Cork, which is based 5km out at East Ferry Marina at the eastern end of Great Island (☎ 021 481 1237, ⊛ sailcork.com), runs **sailing and kayaking courses**, and there's a people's regatta in August. Contact Cork Harbour Boat Hire (☎ 086 074 7926, ⊛ corkharbourboathire.com; boat from €60/hr) if you fancy being skipper for an hour or two (though there's always a safety boat to guide you). For landlubbers, the engaging and enterprising Michael Martin (☎ 021 481 5211, ⊛ titanic.ie) organizes hour-long *Titanic*-themed **walking tours**, starting from the *Commodore Hotel* (daily 11am, plus 2pm in summer; €15–21; Oct–March pre-booking essential).

## Spike Island

Cork Harbour, reached from Kennedy Pier • Accessible only by ferry Feb, March & Nov Sat, Sun & school hols; April–Sept daily, sailing times vary, see website • €22, includes ferry and 1hr guided tour • ☎ 021 237 3455, ⓦ spikeislandcork.ie

At various points in history, **Spike Island** has been a monastery, a fortress, a home and the largest prison in the British Isles – earning it the moniker "Ireland's Alcatraz". Your visit lasts around three hours and includes a guided tour of the parade ground, buildings and bastions of star-shaped Fort Mitchel, prison cells (the modern-day prison only closed in 2004) and the 1950s punishment block; you are then free to wander the island or visit the on-site café.

## Cobh Museum

Scots Church, High Rd • April–Oct Mon–Sat 11am–1pm & 2–5pm, Sun 2.30–5pm • €4 • ☎ 021 481 4240, ⓦ cobhmuseum.com

If your appetite for salty tales and memorabilia hasn't been sated, get along to the **Cobh Museum**, housed in a nineteenth-century Presbyterian church on the west side of the town centre, on the hillside above the railway station. The interior is crowded with engaging exhibits, much of which is focused on the sinking of Lusitania and Cobh's Naval history.

## St Colman's Cathedral

5 Cathedral Terrace • Mon–Fri 8am–7pm, Sat & Sun 10am–7pm • Donation welcome • ☎ 021 481 3222, ⓦ cobhcathedralparish.ie

Looming above the town is the massive neo Gothic **St Colman's Cathedral**, which was consecrated in 1919 and has a 49-bell carillon – the largest in Europe. The views from up here are worth the steep walk and in summer (May–Sept Sun 4.30pm) you can enjoy carillon recitals (viewed from inside the cathedral on closed-circuit television – there's no public access to the bell tower).

### ARRIVAL AND DEPARTURE                                           COBH

**By train** The station is towards the western end of the seafront, serving frequent trains from/to Cork (Mon–Sat at least hourly, 11 on Sun; 25min).

**By ferry** Cross River Ferries run between Glenbrook near Passage West, on the mainland southeast of Cork city, and Carrigaloe, a few kilometres north of Cobh on Great Island (daily 6.30am–9.30pm, every 10min or so; 5min; car €6 single, €8 return; pedestrian/cyclist €1.50 single, €2 return; ☎ 021 481 1485, ⓦ crossriverferries.ie).

### GETTING AROUND AND INFORMATION

**Car rental** Great Island (see page 234) has a car rental base at Rushbrooke, just north of Cobh, and meets disembarking passengers at the cruise-ship terminal.

**Tourist office** Cobh's helpful tourist office is in Market House, Casement Sq (Mon–Fri 9am–5.30pm, Sat & Sun 10.30am–4.30pm; ☎ 021 481 3612, ⓦ visitcobh.com).

### ACCOMMODATION

**Bella Vista** Spy Hill ☎ 021 481 2450, ⓦ bellavistahotel. ie. The large en-suite rooms at this hotel have more character than the modern exterior might suggest, and the views across the cathedral and harbour are what's important here (not to mention the friendly staff). Self-catering suites also available. Rooms €95, suites €105

**Waters Edge** Yacht Club Quay ☎ 021 481 5566, ⓦ watersedgehotel.ie. Between the heritage centre and Sirius Arts Centre stands this tastefully decorated hotel, where many of the bright, spacious bedrooms – as well as the fine restaurant – have seafront verandas. €138

### EATING AND DRINKING

**Rob Roy** Pearse Square ☎ 021 481 1055. This friendly locals' pub with tables out on the square offers craft beers and a clever sampler tray of three stouts (Guinness up against the local Murphy's and Beamish). There are traditional sessions on Thurs and early evening Sun, and live music, usually traditional or blues, on Sat. Roughly Mon–Thurs noon–11.30pm, Fri & Sat noon–12.30am, Sun noon–11pm.

**Sliced** 14 Parnell Place ☎ 021 235 5545, ⓦ sliced.ie. Sprightly restaurant doling out cracking wood-fired pizzas (from €13.50) in addition to pasta, hot baps (cajun, beef brisket), salads and desserts. Daily noon–11pm.

# Midleton

The busy market town of **MIDLETON** is arrayed round a broad, lively main street, which is bypassed to the south by the N25, so makes a pleasant stopover, just 18km east of Cork (plenty of commuters make use of the local train line). Midleton has created a strong culinary reputation for itself and in early September hosts a **food festival** (@ feastcork.ie).

## The Jameson Experience

Off the south end of Main St • Daily: 10am–4.45pm (tours at 11am, 1pm, 2.30pm & 4.15pm) • €23; Heritage Island • ☎ 021 461 3594, @ jamesonwhiskey.com • Shuttle bus from St Patrick's Quay, Cork; call for details

The town's main visitor activity is **The Jameson Experience** at the **Old Distillery**. Whiskey is no longer made in this partly eighteenth-century distillery, but you'll be shown around the carefully restored machinery – including the largest pot still in the world, with a capacity of 32,000 gallons – in the atmospheric old buildings, and you'll get a taste of the "water of life" (*uisce beatha*) at the end.

### ARRIVAL AND INFORMATION

### MIDLETON

**7**

**By train** Cork (Mon–Sat at least hourly, 9 on Sun; 25min).
**By bus** Cork (frequent; 30min), Youghal (hourly; 30min).
**Tourist office** At the distillery entrance (summer only,

irregular hours, but usually Mon–Fri 10am–1pm & 2–5pm; ☎ 021 461 3702).

### ACCOMMODATION

**An Stór Townhouse** Drury's Lane (IHH) ☎ 021 463 3106, @ anstortownhouse.com. In a converted wool store off the east side of Main St, this comfortable, welcoming town house has twin, double, triple and quad rooms, as well as a self-catering kitchen/dining room and plenty of local information at hand. Breakfast is included, but €5 extra for a full Irish. Doubles **€70**, quads **€140**

★**Ballymaloe House** Around 10km southeast of Midleton, off the R629 Cloyne–Ballycotton road ☎ 021 465 2531, @ ballymaloe.ie. Attached to the famous restaurant, accommodation in this delightful, vine-covered, originally fifteenth-century manor house and adjacent courtyard mixes country-house style with contemporary art. There's a summertime outdoor pool, five-hole golf course, croquet and a tennis court, plus bicycles for guests' use and walks around the extensive grounds, farm and the garden of Ballymaloe's nearby cookery school. Attached to

the house is a seventeenth-century grain store that's been converted into a venue for music, theatre and events such as a festival of books and food in May. Various packages available; very good single rates. **€250**

**Castlemartyr Resort** 10km east of Midleton on the N25 ☎ 021 421 9000, @ castlemartyrresort.ie. Opulent hotel – think electronic curtains and traditional afternoon teas – in an eighteenth-century manor house, flanked by a striking modern extension and the ruins of the original medieval castle that was once owned by Sir Walter Raleigh. There's a luxurious ESPA spa, two excellent restaurants: *The Bell Tower*, using the best of local, seasonal ingredients, and the more casual evening-only *Twelve Ten: The Grill*. Bikes are available for guests to explore the 200-acre estate, which was landscaped by Capability Brown but now encompasses an eighteen-hole golf course. **€185**

### EATING AND DRINKING

Midleton hosts one of the country's best **farmers' markets** (Sat 9am–1pm), offering everything from cheese, smoked fish and meats to breads, cakes and chocolate.

★**Ballymaloe House** Around 10km southeast of Midleton, off the R629 Cloyne–Ballycotton road ☎ 021 465 2531, @ ballymaloe.ie. This stalwart on Ireland's fine dining scene offers exceptional modern dishes using local ingredients, such as poached wild salmon with samphire in tomato and basil sauce, with some nice traditional touches – you'll be asked if you want second helpings and you choose your dessert from a groaning trolley. Five-course set dinner menu €80. Closed Jan. Daily: breakfast 8–10.30am; lunch 1–2pm; dinner 6.30–9.30pm.

★**Farmgate Restaurant & Store** Coolbawn, off the west side of Main St ☎ 021 463 2771, @ farmgate.ie. Big sister to *Farmgate Café* (see page 235) in Cork, a bustling café-restaurant where they prepare local ingredients carefully and simply, at reasonable prices. For lunch (noon–3.30pm) most main dishes are €10–15; for dinner, a little more expensive. Their own bakery and deli out front sells fresh artisanal produce. Tues & Wed 9am–5pm, Thurs–Sat 9am–5pm & 6.30–9.30pm (last orders).

**Finín's** 75 Main St ☎ 021 463 1878, @ finins.ie. Don't be fooled by the traditional pub frontage here – it's more restaurant than bar, decorated with colourful modern paintings, where you can choose between light dishes such

7

as delicious chicken-liver pâté on toast (€9) and fancier meals like fillet steak in wine, cream and mushroom sauce (€24). Simple three-course menu €29. Tues–Sat noon–9pm.

**JJ Coppinger** 55 Main St ☎021 463 4914, ⚲jj coppingers.ie. Main Street's most stylish bar is all exposed brick and downlighting. They stock over a hundred whiskeys – tastings from €14/person – and get packed out on live music nights (Thurs, Sat & Sun). Mon–Thurs 9am–11pm, Fri & Sat 9am–12.30am.

**O'Donovan's** Opposite the distillery on Main St ☎021 463 1255. Formal white-tablecloth restaurant offering excellent dishes such as duck confit with chorizo and black-eyed peas, a warm welcome and a good-value early-bird menu (three courses for €27.50). Tues–Fri 5–9pm, Sat 6–9pm.

# Youghal

**YOUGHAL** (pronounced "yawl") enjoys a lush, picturesque setting on the west bank of the River Blackwater's estuary, the border with County Waterford. It was one of Ireland's leading ports in the medieval era, with a scattering of ancient buildings to show for it – as well as a **historical festival** in late September (⚲youghalcelebrateshistory.com), when field trips, concerts and other entertainments accompany an international historical conference. It later became a centre for the carpet industry, but today is popular with holidaying Irish families, who take their leisure on the long sandy **beach** to the southwest.

## Main Street

Youghal's long, gently curving **Main Street** is lined with tall, colourfully painted nineteenth-century buildings, interspersed with a few more historic structures. Bridging the south end of the street, the most obvious of these is the Georgian **clock tower**, which stands on the site of a medieval gate. It's a huge but well-proportioned sandstone affair that once served as a prison (tours available through the tourist office; €9.50; ⚲youghalclockgate.ie).

Further north on Main Street, you'll find the **Red House**, a typically steep-roofed Dutch-style home built around 1710, and, opposite, a restored tower house, **Tynte's Castle**, from the fifteenth century.

## Collegiate Church of St Mary's

Church St · April–Sept 10am–5pm, Oct–March 10am–4pm · ☎024 91014, ⚲youghal.cloyne.anglican.org

Turning left off Main Street, at the seventeenth-century almshouses near the Red House, will bring you to Youghal's main historic site, the Anglican **Collegiate Church of St Mary's**. On the site of the fifth-century monastic settlement of St Declan of Ardmore, it's one of the oldest functioning churches in Ireland, built in about 1250. On its north side stands an unusual fortified bell tower, dating probably from the fifteenth century, while inside, the squat Gothic nave boasts impressive oak roof trusses. Almost bursting out of the south transept, an extravagant, multicoloured monument commemorates Richard Boyle, the seventeenth-century Earl of Cork who did much to develop Youghal, along with his two wives and children, including the chemist Robert. Beyond the church lie the pretty gardens of The College (founded 1464) and the well-preserved thirteenth-century **landward town walls**, which provide great views of the bay.

### ARRIVAL AND DEPARTURE                                                    YOUGHAL

**By bus** Buses from Cork Cork (hourly; 50min) and Midleton (hourly; 25min) stop at the north end of Main St.

### INFORMATION AND TOURS

**Tourist information** The tourist office and the attached heritage centre, which recounts the port's history since the ninth century, are on Market Square, between Main St and the harbour, near the clock tower (summer daily 9am–5pm; winter Mon–Fri 9am–3pm; heritage centre free; ☎024 20170, ⚲youghal.ie).

**Boat tours** In summer, Blackwater Cruises (☎087 988 9076, ⚲blackwatercruises.com) runs 1hr 30min trips (€20) up the beautiful Blackwater River, lined with castles, country houses and ruined abbeys, from the jetty near the tourist office.

**Walking tours** Interesting tours of the town depart from the tourist office (July & Aug Mon–Fri 11am & 3pm; at other times, book through the tourist office; 1hr 30min; €7).

## ACCOMMODATION

As well as the **accommodation** below, there are also dozens of B&Bs, many of them out on the Cork road near the beach.

★ **Aherne's** 163 North Main St ☎ 024 92424, ⍟ ahernes. net. Superb small hotel in the centre of town, with spacious bedrooms around a courtyard; the rooms are a little dated, but tastefully decorated with antique furniture, and breakfasts are great. Half-board packages and self-catering apartments also available, as well as a private carpark. €120

**Avonmore House** South Abbey ☎ 024 92617, ⍟ avonmorehouse.com. Bright, colourful, en-suite rooms in an elegant, centrally located Georgian mansion, a short way south of the tourist office, with home-baked soda bread and kippers or pancakes for breakfast. Very good rates for singles. €105

**Clonvilla** Clonpriest, around 7km southwest of town near the beach, on the R633 towards Ballymacoda, about 4km off the N25 ☎ 024 98288, ⍟ clonvillayoughal. weebly.com. This caravan and camping park offers a campers' kitchen, laundry facilities and a playground, as well as inexpensive B&B. Closed Nov–Feb. Camping €20, B&B €75

**Roseville** New Catherine St ☎ 021 201 9637, ⍟ roseville youghal.com. Located right in the town centre, north from the tourist office, this is an attractive, detached, period house with a large garden and room-service breakfast. Closed mid-Dec to mid-Jan. €120

## EATING AND DRINKING

★ **Aherne's** 163 North Main St ☎ 024 92424, ⍟ ahernes.net. The excellent restaurant here uses local, seasonal ingredients wherever possible but is known especially for its fresh seafood such as chargrilled monkfish with a smoked salmon risotto and basil pesto; three-course menu €40. You can also choose from the all-day menu, including sandwiches, by the open fire in the very congenial bar (two courses for €30). Wed–Sun: bar food noon–8.30pm, restaurant 6.30–9.30pm.

**Moby Dick's** Market Square, opposite the tourist office ☎ 024 92756. One for movie buffs: for the filming of *Moby Dick* with Gregory Peck in 1954, John Huston transformed Youghal's waterfront into New Bedford, Massachusetts, and the pub where he planned each day's filming is now hung with signed photos of the shoot. Mon–Thurs 10.30am–11.30pm, Fri & Sat 10.30am–12.30am, Sun noon–11pm.

**The Nook (Treacy's)** 20 North Main St, by the turn-off for St Mary's Church ☎ 024 92225, ⍟ findthenook.ie. Relaxing and cosy, traditional, hundred-year-old pub with a spruce black-and-white café at the front and a beer garden at the back, which is very popular for its varied lunches (Mon–Fri). Traditional music Wed, Thurs & Fri in summer. Mon–Thurs 10.30am–11.30pm, Fri & Sat 10.30am–12.30am, Sun noon–11pm.

**Priory Coffee** 56 North Main St ☎ 085 252 5906, ⍟ priory coffee.com. A branch of the well regarded, Cork-based coffee chain. As well as gourmet coffee, there are pastries (from €2.50), nutri bites (€2), toasties and salad boxes (around €8) to choose from, plus they've just opened a fish and chip restaurant upstairs. Daily 8am–6pm (brunch from 10am).

★ **Sage** North Main St, just north of the clock tower ☎ 024 85844, ⍟ facebook.co/sagecafeyoughal. Comfort food café-restaurant, where everything is home-made and locally sourced whenever possible. There are soups, salads, sandwiches and quiches (all €5.50–12), or you could round things off with a fantastic rhubarb tart, among a mouthwatering display of cakes and desserts. Mon–Sat 10am–6pm.

## ENTERTAINMENT

**Comhaltas** Brú na Sí, Blackwater Heights, on the west side of town ☎ 087 793 4504, ⍟ comhaltas.ie. In summer, the local branch of this non-profit organization for the promotion of Irish traditional music puts on a stage show of song, dance and storytelling. July & Aug Mon & Thurs evenings.

# Kinsale and around

**KINSALE**, 25km south of Cork city and the first (or last) stop on the Wild Atlantic Way (see page 26), enjoys a glorious setting at the head of a sheltered harbour around the mouth of the Bandon River. Two imposing **forts** and a fine **tower-house** remain as evidence of its former importance as a trading port, and Kinsale has built on its cosmopolitan links to become the **culinary capital** of the southwest. Add in plenty of opportunities for watersports on the fine local beaches at **Garrettstown** and **Garrylucas**, and a number of congenial pubs, and you have a very appealing, upscale resort town.

**7**

Bandon ▲

**KINSALE**

0 ........ 50
metres

| ■ ACCOMMODATION | |
|---|---|
| Blindgate House | 6 |
| Dempsey's Hostel | 1 |
| Garrettstown House |  |
| Holiday Park | 5 |
| Old Bank House | 2 |
| Pier House | 4 |
| The White House | 3 |

| ● EATING | | | ■ DRINKING AND NIGHTLIFE | |
|---|---|---|---|---|
| Bastion | 3 | | The Greyhound | 3 |
| Bulman | 1 | | Jim Edward's | 4 |
| Dino's | 2 | | The Spaniard | 1 |
| Fishy Fishy | 5 | | Tap Tavern | 5 |
| Max's | 4 | | The White House | 2 |

## Brief history

St Multose founded a monastery at Kinsale in the sixth century, and by the tenth the Vikings had established a trading post. After the Anglo-Normans walled the town in the thirteenth century, it really began to take off, flourishing on trade, fishing and shipbuilding in its excellent deep harbour, which became an important rendezvous and provisioning point for the British Navy. The **Battle of Kinsale** in 1601 was a major turning point in Irish history, leading to the "Flight of the Earls" to the Continent six years later which saw the end of the old Gaelic aristocracy: Philip III of Spain had sent forces to Kinsale to support the Irish chieftains, but communications were poor and Chief Hugh O'Neill, more accustomed to guerrilla warfare, was defeated by Elizabeth I's army in a pitched battle.

In 1689 **James II** landed here in his attempt to claim back the throne, only to flee ignominiously from this same port a year later, after defeat at the Battle of the Boyne. His supporters fought on, however, burning the town and holing up in James Fort and Charles Fort. After a series of decisive attacks by the Duke of Marlborough, they surrendered on favourable terms and were allowed to go to Limerick for the final battle under Patrick Sarsfield (see page 304).

During World War I, in May 1915, a German submarine torpedoed the passenger liner *Lusitania* off the Old Head of Kinsale, as it was sailing from New York to England. Twelve hundred of the passengers and crew were lost, and the sinking was a major factor in the USA's eventual entry into the war.

## Kinsale Regional Museum

Market Place • April–Oct Wed–Sat 10.30am–1.30pm • Free • ☎ 021 477 7930

The **Kinsale Regional Museum** is immediately recognizable in the warren of lanes at the centre of town by its Dutch-style triple gables, which were added in 1706 to the market house of 1600. Upstairs, the courtroom where the inquest into the loss of the *Lusitania* took place has been left partly as it was, augmented, poignantly, by an almost pristine deckchair from the wreck, as well as a medal produced in Germany to celebrate the sinking. Otherwise, the museum is a dusty collection of tools, maps and any old rope, dotted with a few curiosities such as the shoes of the eight-foot three-inch Kinsale Giant, who made a fortune on the English stage in the eighteenth century as a novelty act.

## Desmond Castle

Cork St • Easter–Oct daily 10am–6pm, last admission 5pm • €5; Heritage Card • ☏ 021 477 4855, ⓦ heritageireland.ie

A fine example of an urban tower house, **Desmond Castle** was built around 1500 as a town residence and customs house by the Earl of Desmond, who had recently been given control of the wine trade from France, Spain and Portugal to Bristol by King Henry VII. The architectural highlight is the façade, pierced by ogival windows, including unusual corner pairs on the first floor, and stamped with the Desmond coat of arms surmounted by Henry VII's royal standard. Interesting displays inside trace the building's chequered, often grim history – including stints as a jail and workhouse – as well as local connections with the global wine trade. Many of the "Wild Geese" – Irishmen who fled the country in the sixteenth to eighteenth centuries, especially after the Battle of Kinsale and the Battle of the Boyne – went on to have successful second careers in viticulture, notably Richard Hennessy of Cork who settled in Cognac in the 1740s, and the Lynches of Galway, producers of the famous claret, Château Lynch-Bages. Note, though, that the castle is currently closed pending extensive renovation works, and is not expected to reopen until 2022.

## James Fort

2km southwest of Kinsale, cross the bridge over the River Bandon, turn left and continue for another 1km • Open access

On the west side of the harbour, Kinsale spreads south for a couple of kilometres to the broad mouth of the Bandon River. On a long spit of land between the river and the outer harbour, **James Fort** is a great place for a picnic, with fine views that stretch from the town around to the open sea. Built in 1602–4 on the site of a walled fortification that was easily captured by the English from the Spanish forces at the Battle of Kinsale, it's a five-sided fort whose walls are now fetchingly overgrown with ferns and brambles. The new fort, however, proved equally vulnerable when, in 1649, a well-placed gun on the higher ground to the west led to its surrender to the Cromwellians, and in the 1680s, the building of Charles Fort finally rendered James Fort obsolete. On the southeast-facing side of the narrow peninsula, there's a small and pleasant sandy **beach** (signposted).

## Charles Fort

3km southeast of Kinsale, beyond the village of Summercove • Mid-March to Oct daily 10am–6pm; Nov to mid-March 10am–5pm (closed for a week over Christmas); last admission 1hr before closing • €5; Heritage Card • ☏ 021 477 2263, ⓦ heritageireland.ie

Kinsale's most compelling sight, the formidable **Charles Fort**, lies on the east side of the harbour. On a fine day, the best way to get there is to **walk**, skirting round Scilly village and then following the lower, shoreline road, with refreshment available at *The Spaniard* and *The Bulman* (see page 247). It's also possible to extend the walk along the scrub-covered slopes out to the point at the end of the outer harbour (2hr return from the fort at an easy pace).

> ### KINSALE FESTIVALS
>
> Kinsale hosts a varied and prestigious weekend **arts festival** in July (ⓦ facebook.com/kinsaleartsweekend); a weekend **gourmet festival** in mid-October (ⓦ kinsalerestaurants.com); and a **fringe jazz festival** to coincide with the main jazz festival in Cork over the bank holiday weekend in late October.

Begun in 1678, Charles Fort stands on the site of Anglo-Norman Ringcurran Castle, which had been destroyed on Cromwell's orders in 1656. **Sir William Robinson**, architect of the Royal Hospital, Kilmainham (see page 85), adapted the classic, star-shaped design of the great French military engineer Vauban, but his advice to build extra fortifications at the top of the hill was not followed – though the fort was almost impregnable from the sea, the Duke of Marlborough was easily able to unseat the Jacobites by attacking on land in 1690. Most of the buildings on the twelve-acre site were damaged during the Irish Civil War in 1922, but the eerie roofless shells are substantial enough to give a ready impression of what life in the fort must have been like for its garrison of four hundred, and you can flesh out the picture by sampling the fascinating displays and audiovisuals in the rebuilt Barracks Stores. The former ordnance sheds opposite now house a café.

## ARRIVAL AND INFORMATION
### KINSALE AND AROUND

**By bus** Buses stop on Pier Rd, right at the heart of Kinsale; there's a direct bus hourly from Cork (50min), via Cork Airport (see page 233).

**Tourist information** The friendly, well-informed tourist office, which has plenty of useful free literature on the town, is on Pier Rd (Jan–May, Nov & Dec Tues–Sat 9.15am–5pm, closing for lunch; June–Oct daily 9am–5pm; ☏ 021 477 3481, ⓦ kinsale.ie).

## TOURS AND ACTIVITIES

**Bike rental** Mylie Murphy, 8 Pearse St (☏ 021 477 2703, emyliemurphyshop@hotmail.com). From €15/day.

**Cruises** The tourist office has the times of cruises past the two forts to the outer harbour and the Bandon River on the *Spirit of Kinsale* (roughly March–Oct; €14; ☏ 086 250 5456, ⓦ kinsaleharbourcruises.com).

**Horseriding** For horseriding, contact Kinsale Equestrian Centre, 2km northwest of the centre off the Bandon road (☏ 086 853 0894, ⓦ kinsale-equestrian.ie).

**Walking tours** From the tourist office, Dermot Ryan (daily 10.30am; 1hr; €5; ☏ 086 826 7656, ⓦ kinsaleheritage.com) and Don and Barry (March–Oct daily 11.15am, plus 9.15am May–Sept; 1hr; €8; ☏ 087 250 0731, ⓦ historicstrollkinsale.

com) run engaging historical walking tours, while evening ghost tours meet at the *Tap Tavern* on Guardwell (April–Sept Sun–Fri 9pm; 1hr; €10; ☏ 087 948 0910).

**Watersports** Oysterhaven Activity Centre (☏ 021 477 0738, ⓦ oysterhaven.com), 5km east of Kinsale on Oysterhaven Bay, has sailing, windsurfing and kayaking, while Ocean Addicts (☏ 087 790 3211, ⓦ oceanaddicts.ie) does diving and snorkelling. At long, sandy Garrettstown Beach, 12km southwest of town, H2O does sea kayaking trips and courses (☏ 087 393 1633, ⓦ h2oseakayaking.com), while Kinsale Surf Adventures (☏ 083 107 5757, ⓦ kinsalesurfschool.com) and GTown Surf School (☏ 087 876 8549, ⓦ surfgtown.com) offer surfing and stand-up paddleboarding.

## ACCOMMODATION
### SEE MAP PAGE 244

There are dozens of **B&Bs** and a particularly good selection of upmarket **guesthouses** in Kinsale, as well as a **hostel**. Booking is advisable in high summer and during festivals.

### KINSALE

**Blindgate House** Blindgate ☏ 021 477 7858, ⓦ blindgatehouse.com. Bright, stylish and welcoming guesthouse a 5min walk west of the town centre up the hill. Decorated with natural fabrics and contemporary furniture, and offering great breakfasts and a quiet garden to relax in. Closed Dec–March. €130

**Dempsey's Hostel** Eastern Rd ☏ 021 477 2124, ⓦ dempseyhostel.com (IHH). Basic hostel with a pleasant conservatory and garden on the main Cork road, about 1km from the centre; basic camping facilities. Dorms €17, doubles €46

**Old Bank House** 11 Pearse St ☏ 021 477 4075, ⓦ oldbankhousekinsale.com. Very comfortable and luxurious Georgian town house in a central location, with its own

bakery-café and deli. Many of the well-equipped rooms overlook the harbour, and there's plenty of choice for an excellent breakfast. Very good single rates. €130

★ **Pier House** Pier Rd ☏ 021 477 4169, ⓦ pierhousekinsale.com. A charming haven in a pretty garden right in the centre of town, with a bright, contemporary-rustic look enlivened with modern art. Most of the well-equipped rooms have sleigh beds and terraces or balconies, some with views of the harbour, and breakfast includes such delights as crêpes with fresh fruit. Closed Dec–Jan. €100

**The White House** Pearse St ☏ 021 477 2125, ⓦ white-house-kinsale.ie. Not the place if you're after peace and quiet, but if you want to be in the heart of the action above a fantastic pub, this stylish guesthouse with large en-suite rooms is great choice. €105

### AROUND KINSALE

**Garrettstown House Holiday Park** 10km southwest

of Kinsale, beyond Ballinspittle ☎021 477 8156, ⓦgarrettstownhouse.com. Campsite on the extensive grounds of the ruined eighteenth-century *Garrettstown* *House*, 1km from the beach, with a shop, laundry snooker lounge for adults, and lots of activities for children such as a playground and tennis. Closed mid-Sept to April. €20

## EATING
SEE MAP PAGE 244

There's a great **farmers' market** on Wednesday (9am–2.30pm) on Market Quay (Short Quay), with cheeses, olives, salads, breads, crafts and live acoustic music.

★ **Bastion** Cnr of Market and Main St ☎021 470 9696, ⓦbastionkinsale.com. This outstanding Michelin-starred bistro stands apart even in foodie Kinsale. Only the best local seafood and land-based produce makes it onto the tasting menu (€80), such as Skeaghanore duck with plum, fennel and truffle. The prix-fixe early bird menu (5–6pm) is €45. Wed–Sun 5pm–late.

**Bulman** Summercove, 2km out towards Charles Fort on the east side of the harbour ☎021 477 2131, ⓦthe bulman.ie. The attractive downstairs bar, adorned with nauticalia and warmed by open fires, dishes up good food such as pan-seared fillet of local hake (€24.50), while the upstairs restaurant, *Toddies*, which enjoys great views of the harbour, serves more sophisticated fare. Bar daily noon–9pm; restaurant Tues–Sat 6.30–9pm, Sun 12.30–5pm.

**Dino's** Pier Rd ☎021 477 4561. Waterfront chippy of good repute, whose menu stretches to chowder, fish cakes, wine and craft beers, with plenty of comfy tables inside and a few outside if you want to sit down and eat; fish and chips with tartare sauce is €10.95 to eat in, much cheaper to take away. Daily 1–10pm.

★ **Fishy Fishy** Crowleys Quay, Pier Rd ☎021 470 0415, ⓦfishyfishy.ie. Superb seafood restaurant with very attractive tables on a quiet, leafy terrace in the summer, dishing up excellent daily specials such as scallops and Rosscarbery black pudding (€25.95), as well as the trusty "Fishy Fish Pie" (€23.95). Three-course set menu €45. Reservations for dinner only. Daily noon–9pm; shorter, changeable hours in winter.

**Max's** 48 Main St ☎021 477 2443, ⓦmaxs.ie. Cosy, upmarket, "Irish-French" spot with a small conservatory, specializing in seafood in summer, game in winter on a constantly changing menu that's posted on their website. Good-value early-bird two-course menu for €26 (until 7.15pm, Sat 7pm). Feb to mid-Dec daily 6–9.30pm; hours may be shorter in the shoulder season.

## DRINKING AND NIGHTLIFE
SEE MAP PAGE 244

The town boasts a wide array of genial **pubs**, many of which also serve good food. Pick up a copy of the free *Kinsale Advertiser* (ⓦkinsalenews.com) at the tourist office, or go to their website to check out what's on around town each week.

**The Greyhound** 6 Market Square ☎021 477 2889. Popular, cosy, seventeenth-century pub with quaint wooden partitions and seats outside on the pedestrianized alley. Mon–Thurs roughly 1/2–11.30pm, Fri & Sat 1/2pm–12.30am, Sun 1/2–11pm.

★ **Jim Edward's** Market Quay ☎021 477 2541, ⓦjim edwardskinsale.com. Cosy, welcoming, central pub with an extensive choice of craft beers, wine by the glass and cocktails. There's a pleasant evening-time restaurant; the same menu of excellent, simple, fresh seafood, sourced from named local suppliers, is served in both. Daily noon–10pm.

**The Spaniard** 1km from the centre around the east side of the harbour, in the suburb of Scilly ☎021 477 2436, ⓦthespaniard.ie. Named after the plucky leader of the Spanish at the Battle of Kinsale, a cosy flagstoned pub that offers good food, either at the bar or in the restaurant, and regular traditional music, usually Wed. Mon–Thurs 10.30am–11.30pm, Fri & Sat 10.30am–12.30am, Sun 12.30–11.30pm.

**Tap Tavern** Guardwell ☎021 477 3231. Simple, sociable inn hung with bric-a-brac, good for a quiet pint most nights, with a nice beer garden. Mon–Thurs 5–11.30pm, Fri & Sat 5pm–12.30am, Sun 5–11pm.

**The White House** Pearse St ☎021 477 2125, ⓦwhite house-kinsale.ie. This family-friendly pub is smartly decorated and offers reasonably priced, good-quality bar food, plus frequent live music, usually traditional or ballads. Mon–Thurs 8am–11.30pm, Fri & Sat 8am–12.30am, Sun 8am–11pm; food served till 10pm.

# Clonakilty and around

**CLONAKILTY** is an appealing if undramatic service town, whose main draw is the **beach**, 4km to the south, on **Inchydoney Island**, which is now locked to the mainland by two causeway roads that enclose reclaimed pasturage. This gorgeous expanse of pristine white sand is split in two by Virgin Mary's Point, where the road ends, and flanked by headlands of rolling green fields. Clonakilty also offers plenty of traditional music in the pubs, but is most famous as the home of award-winning **black puddings** –

especially from Twomey's the butcher on the main street – and as the birthplace of Republican leader **Michael Collins**. In September, the **international guitar festival** (ⓦclonguitarfest.com) is hosted at varied venues across town, and includes workshops and live music on the streets.

## West Cork Model Railway Village

On the southeast edge of town off the Inchydoney road • **Railway Village** Daily: July & Aug 10am–6pm; Sept–June 11am–5pm • €9, children €5.50, family ticket €25 • **Road train** Usually June–Sept daily; Oct–May Sat & Sun • €13, children €8, family ticket €36, all including entry to model village • ☎ 023 883 3224, ⓦ modelvillage.ie

Both kids and adults will enjoy the **West Cork Model Railway Village**, which replicates the 1940s West Cork Railway and the towns it served in great detail at 1:24 scale. There's also a quirky cafeteria serving tea and cakes, housed in a full-size 1940s train carriage outside. Departing from here, a "road train" makes a tour of Clonakilty several times daily.

## West Cork Regional Museum

The west end of Clonakilty's main street (here Western Road) • Summer Tues–Sat 11am–4pm; staffed by volunteers, so hours liable to change • Donation requested • ☎ 023 883 3115

If poor weather rules out any outdoor exploration, you could do worse than holing up in the **West Cork Regional Museum**, which covers the area's contribution to the War of Independence and Clonakilty's once-prosperous linen industry, and displays a host of agricultural implements.

## Michael Collins Centre

5km northeast of Clonakilty, off the R600 towards Timoleague • Roughly mid-June to mid-Sept Mon–Fri 10.30am–5pm, Sat 11am–2pm • €5 donation requested • ☎ 023 884 6107, ⓦ michaelcollinscentre.com

The eclectic but highly recommended **Michael Collins Centre** offers engaging guided tours led by Tim Crowley, a distant relative of Michael Collins; features include photos, memorabilia and an audiovisual on Collins, and the Ambush Trail, a reconstruction of Collins' fatal ambush in 1921 at Beal na Bláth. If you want to explore further, you can book Mr Crowley for tours (usually in your own car) of nearby sites associated with Collins and the War of Independence, taking in the actual Beal na Bláth and what is left of Collins' birthplace, incinerated in 1921 by the Black and Tans.

## Drombeg

Accessible via the R597 Rosscarbery–Glandore road, signposted after 5km • No public transport

About 17km west of Clonakilty lies one of the area's few compelling historical sites, the Bronze Age **Drombeg stone circle**. Looking out over pretty cattle pastures with the Atlantic in the distance, these seventeen well-preserved stones are associated with the winter solstice, when the sun sets on the southwest horizon at a point aligned with the lowest, axial, stone (known as the "Druid's Altar") and the two tallest portal stones. Close by in the same field sits one of the best examples of a *fulacht fiadh*, a ritual cooking site (literally "deer roast"), in Ireland. It consists of a 1.5m-long stone-lined trough for water, into which red-hot stones from the adjacent hearth would have been rolled.

## Glandore

A popular yachting haven 20km west of Clonakilty, **GLANDORE** enjoys a particularly beautiful elevated position, overlooking the turquoise waters of a deep inlet and the village of Union Hall opposite, and surrounded by lush, tree-carpeted slopes.

## ARRIVAL AND INFORMATION

**By bus** Buses stop either on Pearse St – part of the town's long, one-way (westward) high street, which to the east becomes Ashe St and then Wolfe Tone St, to the west Western Rd – or on the short bypass, just south of Wolfe Tone St.

**Tourist information** The helpful tourist office at 25 Ashe

## CLONAKILTY AND AROUND

St (Tues–Sat 9/9.15am–1pm & 1.30/1.45–5pm; ☎ 023 883 3226, ⓦ clonakilty.ie) stocks a free *What's On* guide, which includes local road-bowling fixtures (see page 544).

**Surfing** Inchydoney Surf School (☎ 086 869 5396, ⓦ inchydoneysurfschool.com).

## ACCOMMODATION

### CLONAKILTY

**An Súgán** 41 Wolfe Tone St ☎ 023 883 3719, ⓦ ansugan.com. Guesthouse in a tasteful contemporary style with comfortable beds and great breakfasts that use local produce wherever possible, in a quiet Georgian town house behind the seafood bar and restaurant. Very good rates for singles. €110

**Bay View** Old Timoleague Rd ☎ 023 883 3539, ⓦ bayviewclonakilty.com. Flower-bedecked, brightly decorated and welcoming en-suite B&B on the east side of town, with good breakfasts, a lovely garden and fine views of Clonakilty Bay; rooms include a garden suite with private sun lounge. €80

**Desert House** On a dairy farm 500m from the centre of Clonakilty ☎ 023 883 3331, ⓦ deserthousecamping.ie. Campsite with campers' kitchen, laundry facilities and a playground, with great views of Clonakilty Bay; head east out of town, turn right at the roundabout and follow the signs. Closed Nov–April (unless by prior arrangement). €24

★ **Inchydoney Island Lodge and Spa** Mid-point of Inchydoney Beach ☎ 023 883 3143, ⓦ inchydoneyisland.com. Beautifully sited luxury retreat, decorated in plush but

cheery contemporary style, with extravagant touches such as espresso-makers in the rooms, which all have sea views and a balcony or terrace. Attached are a bistro-pub, a fine-dining restaurant and a well-equipped spa, offering a wide range of seawater and other treatments, as well as a large indoor heated seawater pool. €198

**O'Donovan's Hotel** Pearse St ☎ 023 883 3250, ⓦ odonovanshotel.com. Collins, Parnell and Marconi have all stayed at this lively traditional meeting place on the main street, and it's still run by the welcoming O'Donovan family, retaining much of its period charm. Very good rates for singles. €120

### GLANDORE

**Bay View** Centre of the village ☎ 028 33115, ⓦ bayviewglandore.ie. Your best bet for B&B accommodation, a bright and comfortable, all-en-suite, waterside house in the centre of the village with great views. €80

**Meadow** On the R597, about 1km east of Glandore ☎ 028 33280, ✉ meadowcamping@eircom.net. Trim and peaceful campsite, with a campers' kitchen and laundry facilities. Closed mid-Sept to Easter/May (unless by prior arrangement). €22

## EATING

**An Súgán** 41 Wolfe Tone St ☎ 023 883 3719, ⓦ ansugan.com. Good, fresh fish and shellfish, ranging from chowder and oysters to lobster and seafood pie (€17.95), in this plush, cosy bar-restaurant with a pretty courtyard. Food daily noon–9.30pm.

**Hart's** 8 Ashe St ☎ 023 883 5583, ⓦ hartscafeclonakilty. This small, attractive café, which can be found on the main street in the centre of town, serves tasty ciabattas, hot meals and all-day breakfasts like scrambled eggs, smoked salmon and toast (€6.95), as well as scrummy cakes and

good coffees. Mon–Sat 10am–5.30pm.

### GLANDORE

**Hayes Bar & Kitchen** Glandore ☎ 028 33214, ⓦ hayesrestaurant.ie. You can tuck into some chowder, smoked mackerel or mussels with home-made beer bread, sitting either on a sofa or armchair inside, or at one of the gorgeous tables outside, overlooking the village's beautiful community garden and harbour. Summer Mon–Thurs 11am–11.30pm, Fri & Sat 11am–12.30am, Sun noon–11pm.

## DRINKING AND NIGHTLIFE

**An Teach Beag** O'Donovan's Hotel, Pearse St ☎ 023 883 3250, ⓦ odonovanshotel.com. This storehouse, which has been reconstructed as a traditional cottage ("the little house") at the back of the hotel, hosts traditional sessions all summer (sometimes augmented by set dancing and storytelling), and there's more trad year-round on Tuesdays in the hotel itself. Mid-June to mid-Sept daily 9.30pm–midnight; mid-Sept to mid-June Sat only 9.30pm–

midnight, plus a song night the last Sun of the month from 9pm.

★ **De Barra's** 55 Pearse St ☎ 023 883 3381, ⓦ www.debarra.ie. The pick of Clon's old-time pubs, with great live music most evenings, including a popular traditional session on Mon and an acoustic session on Tues. Mon–Thurs roughly 10am–11.30pm, Fri & Sat 10am–12.30am, Sun noon–11.30pm.

**Shanley's Piano Bar** Connolly St, running south from Pearse St ☎ 023 883 3790. Plush, welcoming, well-tended bar with a pretty, flower-filled beer garden, hosting an acoustic session on Thurs, easy listening/jazz/American folk at weekends. Mon–Thurs roughly 3–11.30pm, Fri 3pm–12.30am, Sat noon/1.30pm–12.30am, Sun noon/1.30pm–11pm.

# Skibbereen

**SKIBBEREEN** (often shortened to "Skibb"), the lively administrative centre for this part of west Cork, is a good spot to take a break and recharge your batteries, with plenty of restaurants and accommodation options and an excellent heritage centre. To the south, it gives access to a rich coastal landscape where green pastures begin to alternate with the scrubby, rocky slopes so typical of more westerly parts. If you have your own wheels, you shouldn't miss the uniquely beautiful lagoon of **Lough Hyne**. Bypassed by the main N71 to the north, the town's **layout** is easy once you've got the hang of it, though sometimes clogged with traffic: beneath a slow bend in the Ilen River, the two narrow main streets form a V shape, North Street pointing to the northeast, and Main Street (which becomes Bridge Street) pointing northwestwards. The town's two big festivals are the **arts festival** at the end of July, featuring music, poetry, dance and drama (ⓦskibbereenartsfestival.com), and the ten-day **Taste of West Cork** food festival in September (ⓦatasteofwestcork.com), which is actually dispersed throughout the region.

## The Heritage Centre

Upper Bridge St • Mid-March to April & Oct Tues–Sat 10am–6pm; May to Sept Mon–Sat 10am–6pm; Nov to mid-March Thurs–Sat 10am–5pm; genealogy service by appointment • €6; Heritage Island • ☎ 028 40900, ⓦ skibbheritage.com

The first-rate **heritage centre**, set in an attractively restored gasworks, is the home of two contrasting exhibitions. Introduced by actor and local resident Jeremy Irons, *The Great Famine Commemorative Exhibition* film provides a sensitive and vivid commentary on the Famine of the 1840s. The Skibbereen area was especially badly hit, with nearly a third of its population of a hundred thousand losing their lives and a further eight thousand being forced to emigrate – even though the Famine's effects on the town were widely publicized by the famous stark drawings of James Mahony for the *Illustrated London News*. The one-hour-thirty-minute **Skibbereen Trail**, marked by bronze plaques and detailed in a leaflet available from the heritage centre, takes in some of the Famine sites, including **Abbeystrewery Cemetery** on the N71 on the western edge of town, where between eight and ten thousand victims were buried in pits.

---

### WHALE WATCHING AND KAYAKING AROUND SKIBBEREEN

The seas off Skibb, rich feeding grounds for herring and sprat, are earning a reputation as one of Europe's premier **whale-watching** sites, with minke (roughly from April), fin (from June or July), more rarely, humpback (from September) and occasional killer whales, as well as scores of dolphins and porpoises, coming remarkably close to shore; September to November is the peak time. For further information, consult the website of the Irish Whale and Dolphin Group, ⓦiwdg.ie. Two companies run daily four-hour boat trips, costing €55 per adult: Cork Whale Watch (☎086 327 3226, ⓦcorkwhalewatch.com) from Reen Pier, well to the southeast of Skibb on Castlehaven Harbour; and Whale Watch West Cork (☎086 120 0027, ⓦwhalewatchwestcork.com) from Baltimore. Along the coast here, there are also half-day **sea-kayaking** trips (€65) run by Atlantic Sea Kayaking based in Skibbereen (☎028 21058, ⓦatlanticseakayaking.com); they also offer starlight outings in Castlehaven Harbour or Lough Hyne, accompanied, at certain times of year, by an astonishing bioluminescence emitted by marine life.

The other exhibition introduces the amazing diversity of nearby **Lough Hyne**, with an audiovisual and abundant pictures of its flora and fauna.

## West Cork Arts Centre

The Uillinn, off Bridge St • Mon–Sat 10am–4.30pm • Free • ☎ 028 22090, ⓦ westcorkartscentre.com

The home of the lively **West Cork Arts Centre**, which hosts temporary exhibitions, especially of contemporary visual art, as well as drama, films and all sorts of other events including artist talks and discussions, is well worth a look. There's a lovely branch of *Kalbo's Café* on-site (see page 252).

## Lough Hyne

If you head out of Skibb on the Baltimore road and take a left turn after about 3km, you'll come upon **Lough Hyne** (Lough Ine) after a further 3km or so. Ireland's first marine nature reserve, this tidal lake is joined to the sea only by a narrow channel, known as the rapids, but reaches depths of 45m in places. A combination of warm waters from the Gulf Stream and diverse habitats – sea caves, whirlpools, shallow and deep areas – supports an astonishingly rich variety of saltwater species here, over a thousand in less than a square kilometre. Many are rare species that are generally only found in the deep ocean or the Mediterranean, such as the triggerfish and the red-mouthed goby. Sheltered by varied slopes of gorse, woods and bare rock, the placid waters are also popular among swimmers and kayakers (see page 250). To make the most of a visit, see the exhibit at the Skibbereen Heritage Centre first (see page 250), where you can also pick up a brochure for the **Knockomagh Wood Nature Trail**. Beginning where the road from Skibb meets Lough Hyne, at its northwestern corner, this 2km trail zigzags upwards and westwards past fine viewpoints of the lake, ancient sessile oaks and bluebell meadows, to the 197m summit of Knockomagh Hill, which affords a panorama of the coastline stretching from Galley Head in the east to Mount Gabriel above Schull.

7

### ARRIVAL AND INFORMATION | SKIBBEREEN

**By bus** Buses on the Cork–Schull route drop off and pick up from *Cahalane's* bar on Bridge St. Destinations Cork (7 daily; 1hr 50min); Schull (Mon–Sat 3 daily, Sun 1 daily; 40min).
**Tourist office** 39 North St (April & May, Thurs, Fri & Sat 10am–3pm; June to end Sept Mon–Sat 10am–4.30, plus Sun 11am–2pm in roughly July & Aug; ☎ 028 21766, ⓦ skibbereen.ie).
**Bike rental and tours** Cycle West Cork, 11 Market St (€20/day; ☎ 087 392 1894, ⓦ cyclewestcork.com).

### ACCOMMODATION

**Bridge House** 46 Bridge St ☎ 028 21273, ⓦ bridge houseskibbereen.com. Very centrally located on the busy main street, this is the standout among the town's handful of B&Bs, an eccentric, Victorian-styled place stuffed with antiques, swags and china dolls. **€70**
**Russagh Mill Hostel and Adventure Centre** 1km southeast on the R596 Castletownshend road (IHO) ☎ 028 22451, ⓦ russaghmillhostel.com. A fine hostel encompassing two kitchens, a BBQ area and several common rooms in a lovingly restored, 200-year-old mill; camping available. Simple breakfast included. Dorms **€17.50**, doubles **€50**
**West Cork Hotel** Ilen St ☎ 028 21277, ⓦ westcorkhotel. com. A traditional hotel and hub of local social life that makes the most of its riverside setting, including spacious, colourful and well-equipped bedrooms, and tables out on the old railway bridge over the Ilen. Eggs Benedict and other breakfasts served until noon. **€79**

### EATING AND DRINKING

There's a great **farmers' market** on Sat (9.30am–2pm) on Fair Field, behind Bridge St, where you'll also find crafts and antiques (ⓦ skibbereenmarket.com).
**Corner Bar** 37 Bridge St ☎ 028 21522, ⓦ thecorner barsibbereen.business.site. Sessions are held at this cosy pub on Sat throughout the year and on Mon in July and Aug, with a singers' club on the first Fri of the month. Mon–Thurs 3–11.30pm, Fri 1–11.30pm, Sat noon–

12.30am, Sun 1–11pm.

**Island Cottage** Heir Island ☎028 38102, ⓦisland cottage.com. For a meal with a touch of adventure thrown in, make a reservation at this excellent, charming island restaurant that uses local and organic or wild ingredients whenever possible; it's lunches only though (two-courses €20), which are served between mid-June and mid-September. To get here you'll need to drive or cycle west along the N71 towards Ballydehob for 5km, then follow the signs down the small peninsula for about another 5km to Cunnamore, from where a small boat will ferry you across to the island in 5min (€7 return, book in advance). Lunch set menu €20, dinner set menu €40. Mid-June to mid-Sept Fri–Sun noon–3pm.

**JC's Takeaway** Fields car park ☎028 23332. Tucked behind Main St, this family-owned business has four small tables. The open kitchen cooks up speciality burgers and freshly caught fish, with enormous portions of chips and sides of home-made coleslaw or tartare sauce. Hake and chips €9. Daily 1–10pm.

**Kalbo's** 26 North St ☎028 21515, ⓦkalbos.ie. Small, justifiably popular café that uses local, seasonal produce wherever possible, in dishes such as a delicious open Castletownbere crab mayonnaise sandwich (€5/€10) and the house chilli on rice (€5). They've got a second outlet at Uilliinn, the West Cork Arts Centre (Tues–Sat 10am–5pm). Tues–Sat 9am–4pm.

**Riverside** North St ☎028 40090, ⓦriversideskibbereen. ie. Airy, modern café-restaurant with a pretty riverside terrace and a menu that ranges from home-made fish cakes (€11.95) to West Cork lamb koftas (€12.95). Mon–Sat 10am–9pm.

# Baltimore

Though isolated at the end of a stubby peninsula to the southwest of Skibbereen, **BALTIMORE** comes as a lively surprise, bustling with fishing and pleasure boats, and ferries to Sherkin and Clear islands. In fine weather, there are few more pleasant spots in Cork than the small, sun-trap square above the harbour, filled with café and bar tables. Basking in the shelter of large inshore islands, the port is particularly busy during the **regatta** held in early August, but there's also a fiddle **festival** in mid-May (ⓦfiddlefair.com) and a combined food and sailing festival during the last weekend in May (ⓦbaltimorewoodenboatfestival.com).

## Baltimore Castle

The Square • March–Oct daily 11am–6pm • €5 • ☎028 20735, ⓦbaltimorecastle.ie

Overlooking the square stands **Baltimore Castle** (**Dún na Séad**), a thirteenth-century tower house that was the chief residence of the infamous pirates, the O'Driscolls, but fell into ruins from the end of the seventeenth century until its painstaking recent restoration as a private home. It's worth a visit in summer to see the imposing great hall on the first floor and to take in the commanding views of the harbour and Roaringwater Bay from the battlements.

## Sherkin Island

Ferries 5–12 daily; 10min • €12 return • ☎087 244 7828, ⓦsherkinisland.eu/ferry

Guarding the west side of Baltimore Harbour, **Sherkin** (Inis Arcáin, "Island of the Porpoise") is a tranquil, pretty island that shares the mixed scrub and pastoral landscape

---

**BALTIMORE: MESSING ABOUT IN BOATS**

In summer, **boat tours** from Baltimore include trips via Cape Clear to the famous hundred-year-old lighthouse out in the open sea on **Fastnet Rock** (ⓦfastnettour.com), known as "Ireland's Teardrop" because it was the last part of Ireland seen by thousands of emigrants to North America. In addition, Baltimore Sea Safari offers a variety of trips in a smaller, speedier RIB (☎028 20753, ⓦbaltimoreseasafari.ie). You can take a **diving** course or trip at Aquaventures (☎028 20511, ⓦaquaventures.ie), who also run half-day **snorkelling** trips.

of the mainland hereabouts. On a half-day stroll around the boot-shaped island, you could take in the highest point, Slievemore, to the southwest on the toe of the boot, and the best beaches, Trá Bawn, Trá Eoghan Mhór and Silver Strand, to the north of Slievemore. **Ferries** from Baltimore land at the easterly pier, behind which stands a plain fifteenth-century Franciscan **abbey**, with its 15m tower intact; you can still see the outline of its cloister and the walls of a curious seventeenth-century fish "palace", where pilchards were salted and barrelled for export to Spain.

## INFORMATION                                                    BALTIMORE

**Tourist information** As well as selling some beautiful pottery and knitwear made on Sherkin and Clear islands, Island Crafts, in a hut down by the quay, provides tourist information on Baltimore and the islands in summer (Easter–Sept daily 10am–6.30pm; ☎028 20022, ⊛islands crafts.com). In winter, call ☎028 20347.

## ACCOMMODATION AND EATING

The village specializes in hospitality all-rounders, where you can **sleep**, **eat** and **drink** under the same roof. Standards are generally very high, and you'll find a surprisingly diverse range of food for somewhere so small and remote. Booking accommodation in advance is highly recommended in July and August, over bank holiday weekends and during festivals.

**Baltimore Townhouse** New Rd, roughly halfway between Casey's and the harbour ☎028 20197, ⊛caseysofbaltimore.com. Owned by *Casey's Hotel*, this gleaming house encompasses four stylish and well-equipped suites. Breakfast is either continental, including freshly baked bread, or full Irish, taken at *Casey's*, which is also where you check in. **€140**

**Bushe's Bar** On the main square ☎028 20125, ⊛bushesbar.com. With the best view of the harbour from its seats outside on the main square, this popular pub serves excellent cheap chowder and seafood sandwiches and platters during the day. Upstairs are basic but comfortable bedrooms, with TVs and en-suite bathrooms; you'll pay €10 more for a harbour view. Self-service continental breakfast is taken in your room. Bar Mon–Thurs 9/10am–11.30pm, Fri & Sat 9/10am–12.30am, Sun 12.30–11pm. **€70**

★ **Casey's Hotel** On the main Skibbereen road, 1km from the harbour ☎028 20197, ⊛caseysofbaltimore. com. Charming, family-run hotel with large and very comfortable en-suite bedrooms, very good food in the bar and restaurant, and glorious views over the peaceful inlet to Ringarogy Island, especially from the beer garden. Traditional music Sat year-round, more frequently in high summer. All sorts of packages on offer, as well as self-catering apartments. **€140**

**Glebe Gardens and Café** On the main Skibbereen road, 1km from the harbour ☎028 20579, ⊛glebegardens. com. A sharp turn off before *Casey's Hotel*, Glebe Gardens houses a beautiful café and courtyard where fresh, seasonal produce is on the menu for breakfast and lunch – there's also a selection of freshly baked cakes for afternoon tea (cream tea €6). Easter–Sept Wed–Sun 10am–6pm; Oct–Easter Sat & Sun 10am–5pm.

★ **Rolf's** Left turn off the main road into the village, a 15min walk from the harbour ☎028 20289, ⊛rolfs countryhouse.com. Civilized, tranquil and friendly spot in beautiful subtropical gardens with fine sea views. The good-value pine-furnished rooms are bright and spruce, with a continental buffet breakfast included, and well-equipped self-catering cottages are also available. The relaxing restaurant uses as much home-grown, organic and local produce as possible in generously proportioned dishes such as grilled Irish salmon on spicy lentils (€19.50). Restaurant Wed–Sun 6–9pm, plus 12.30–2.30pm in summer. **€120**

**Waterfront Hotel** On the main square ☎028 20600, ⊛waterfrontbaltimore.ie. Bright, pleasant, spacious, en-suite rooms; the best are done out in nautical blue and cream in a new extension, and have either great views of the harbour or a patio-style garden. Good rates for singles. **€160**

# Clear Island (Oileán Chléire)

Ireland's most southerly inhabited point, **Clear Island** (Oileán Chléire, also known as **Cape Clear**; ⊛capeclearisland.ie) is an isolated outpost of the **Gaeltacht**, which welcomes teenagers from all over the country to learn Irish during the summer, and generally reaches out to visitors, with plenty of facilities and information available. The island also holds a traditional story-telling **festival**, with concerts, workshops, walks and music, over the first weekend of September (⊛capeclearstorytelling.com).

Clear describes a very rough figure-of-eight, just 6km square, with **North Harbour**, where ferries dock, and cliff-girt **South Harbour** almost meeting in the middle; the westerly part of the figure-of-eight is home to a fifteenth-century castle, **Dún an Óir** ("Fort of Gold"), a ruined O'Driscoll stronghold on an isolated rocky outcrop near North Harbour. The island's landscape of steep, rolling hills of heather and pasture is crossed by narrow, hedge-lined roads and paths, affording fine views of Roaringwater Bay and of Fastnet Rock to the west in the open sea, where whales, dolphins and sharks can sometimes be spotted. Clear Island is most famous as one of the best places to watch seabird migration in Europe, as well as supporting breeding colonies of black guillemots, choughs and rock doves; twitchers can take field courses and stay at the **bird observatory** at North Harbour (ⓦbirdwatchireland.ie).

Up the steep bank to the east of North Harbour, visitors are welcome at **Cleire Goat Farm** (ⓣ087 797 3056) which offers goat husbandry courses, starting from as little as two hours in duration, and produces ice cream, cheese and sausages.

## The Heritage Centre

To the east of North Harbour, a short walk further along the same road from the goat farm • June to early Sept daily roughly noon–4pm • €3 • ⓣ028 39119, ⓦcapeclearmuseum.ie

The tiny **heritage centre** in an old schoolhouse building hosts some detailed and interesting displays, especially on maritime history and archaeology. Exhibitions are rotated and often relate to anniversaries of events on the island.

## St Ciarán's Church

To the east of North Harbour, close to the heritage centre

The island is reputed to have been the sixth-century birthplace of **St Ciarán of Saighir** (not to be confused with Ciarán of Clonmacnois), who is (spuriously) claimed to have brought Christianity to Ireland thirty years before St Patrick. According to legend, he ended his days in Cornwall, where he was known as St Piran and credited with the discovery of tin. His twelfth-century church, graveyard and holy well lie a twenty-minute walk east from North Harbour.

### ARRIVAL AND INFORMATION                                    CLEAR ISLAND

**By ferry** The *Cailín Óir* sails from Baltimore (2–4 daily; 45min; €18 return; ⓣ028 41923, ⓦcailinoir.com), and there are summertime boats from Schull (see page 255); Baltimore–Clear return tickets are accepted on the Clear–Schull ferry. A minibus meets all ferries and charges €2/person to anywhere on the island.

**Tourist information** The crafts shop at North Harbour dispenses tourist information (June & Sept Mon–Sat 11.15am–12.30pm & 3.30–4.30pm, Sun 11.45am–1pm & 4–5/6pm; July & Aug daily 11am–1pm & 2–6pm; ⓣ028 39100). There's no ATM on the island – the nearest is in the supermarket in Baltimore.

### ACCOMMODATION AND EATING

As the island can get busy in high summer, it's best to book **accommodation** before you come.

**An Siopa Beag** North Harbour ⓣ028 39099, ⓦsiopa beag.ie. The island's grocery store at North Harbour offers internet access and wi-fi, as well as a café serving sandwiches, salads, seafood and, on Fri and Sat evenings in summer, handmade pizzas. Upstairs is the island's social club, *Club Cléire*, which hosts traditional music on summer weekends. Shop open year-round, hours depending on boat times; closed Sun in winter; Club Cléire no fixed hours.

**Ard na Gaoithe** Up behind the youth hostel along a steep lane above South Harbour ⓣ028 39160, ⓦcape clearbandb.ie. This welcoming en-suite B&B, in a renovated nineteenth-century house on a working farm, offers organic eggs and pancakes on a varied breakfast menu. **€80**

**Cape Clear Hostel** By the pebbly beach at South Harbour ⓣ028 41968, ⓦcapeclearhostel.ie. This basic hostel occupies the old coastguard station. As well as four-to ten-bed dorms, it offers a cosy lounge with an open fire, a large kitchen and dining room, laundry facilities and table tennis. Jan–April & Oct–Dec pre-booking only. Dorms **€20**, four-bed room **€78**

**Chléire Haven** South Harbour ⓣ086 197 1956, ⓦchleire-haven.com. The island campsite at South Harbour has expanded its horizons to offer yurts (sleeping up to six) with wooden beds, stoves, gas cookers and cool boxes, and teepees with self-inflating mattresses. Those bringing their own tents have to pre-book. Camping €20, yurts €135, teepees per person €20

**Ciaran Danny Mike's** On the road between the two harbours ☎028 39153, ⓦcapeclearisland.eu. This spacious pub with a pool table and outdoor seating is popular for lunch (until 5pm) and dinner (7–9pm) and often hosts traditional music. (It also has self-catering cottages and a guesthouse.) Open all year; check the blackboard at the gate for the latest opening times (pub usually closed Sun).

# The Mizen Head Peninsula

**Mizen Head** is a wild and beautiful peninsula, projecting southwestwards around the substantial mass of copper-rich **Mount Gabriel**. The whole of its empty northern coast presents sheer cliffs and stupendous views. The south coast is more populous, sheltering safe harbours, the large village and resort of **Schull** and the remote sandy beaches of **Barley Cove** and **Galley Cove**, while the only tourist attraction of any note is the signal station at the very tip, the **Mizen Head Visitor Centre**.

7

## Schull

The peninsula's main settlement, **SCHULL**, is a congenial harbour town that's not only popular with yachties but also has an artistic bent, with crafts shops, galleries and a weekly food and crafts market (Sun morning Easter–Sept; ⓦschullmarket. com). It shelters in the lee of 407m **Mount Gabriel**, to the north, topped by an aircraft-tracking station and blessed with fine views. The walk up there (about 8km round trip) is detailed, along with four other local walks, in a very useful booklet, *Discover Schull*, that's available around the town or online at ⓦschull.ie; since the mountain was actively mined for centuries, take care on the way that you avoid uncovered mine shafts.

Schull also boasts a **planetarium**, developed by a local German resident in the village's community college on Colla Road, which runs south off Main Street. It's generally open only in the summer (June to late Aug), with a detailed programme of star shows (€6, children €4; ☎028 28315, ⓦschullplanetarium.com). Schull's annual events include a five-day **short-film festival** in late May (ⓦfastnetfilmfestival.com) and **Calves Week** sailing regatta in early August (ⓦshsc.ie).

### INFORMATION AND ACTIVITIES                                    SCHULL

**Tourist information** The community office for information and the short film festival is on Main St near the start of the pier road (summer daily roughly 10am–6pm; winter hours variable, perhaps three days/week; ☎028 28600). The town's website is ⓦschull.ie.

**Activities** Fastnet Marine and Outdoor Education Centre offers sailing courses (☎028 28515, ⓦschullsailing.ie), while diving is organized by Divecology (☎086 837 2065, ⓦdivecology.com).

### GETTING AROUND

**By ferry** In summer, a ferry runs from Schull to Clear Island (June–Sept 1–6 days/week; 45min; €16 return; ☎087 389 9711, ⓦcapeclearferries.com); on the days when this is running, you could hook up with the Fastnet Rock tours from Baltimore (see page 252). Schull–Clear return tickets are accepted on the Clear–Baltimore ferry.

### ACCOMMODATION AND EATING

★ **Hackett's** Main St ☎028 28625. Great old bar with stone floors, bench seating and a vaguely alternative feel, helped along by a good soundtrack, regular live music and bottles of craft beer. Tasty bar lunches include beef in Guinness stew (€8.50). Bar Mon–Thurs noon–11.30pm, Fri & Sat noon–12.30am, Sun noon–11pm; bar food Mon–Sat noon–3.30pm, Sun 12.30–3.30pm.

**L'Escale** Harbourside ☎028 28599. Your best bet for dinner is this high-class chipper (fish and chips €9.80), which has lots of outdoor tables, some of them covered, for enjoying the harbour views. It also offers seafood platters, pancakes and wine. June–Aug daily 10am–10pm.

**Newman's West** Main St ☎028 27776. Wine bar and café serving tasty breakfasts (pancakes and bagels are popular), salads (from €7.90) and seafood (Bantry Bay mussels €8.50). Don't miss the upstairs art gallery. Daily 9/10am–11pm.

**Nickie's Kitchen** East End ☎028 00000, ⓦnickies kitchen.com. Bright, well-run country kitchen style café-

deli that's popular with locals. Open sandwiches (think crab and lemon dill mayo) around €10 and soup of the day €5, plus proper coffee, and tasty cakes. Daily 9.30am–5.30pm, plus Sat 7pm–late.

## Goleen, Crookhaven, Brow Head and Mizen Head

Infrequent buses run 15km southwest down the peninsula from Schull as far as the quiet village of **GOLEEN**. The southernmost tip of the Mizen Head Peninsula, **Brow Head**, which is also the southernmost point of mainland Ireland, rather surprisingly shelters a golden sandy beach in **Barley Cove**, punctured by a stream and backed by dunes, which are thought to have been thrown up by the tsunami that followed an earthquake off Portugal in 1755. A wild spit of land pushes east of here, past another beautiful sandy beach, **Galley Cove**, to the village of **CROOKHAVEN**, which would feel like the end of the world were it not for the pleasure boats anchored in the long, fjord-like inlet.

### Mizen Head Signal Station

Mid-March to May, Sept & Oct daily 10.30am–5pm; June daily 10am–6pm; June–Aug 10am–6pm; Nov to mid-March Sat & Sun 11am–4pm • €7.50; Heritage Island • ☎028 35115, ⓦmizenhead.ie

To the west of Barley Cove, the narrow road heads upwards and outwards to **Mizen Head** itself. The **visitor centre** here, which comprises a café and various maritime exhibits, isn't up to much, but be sure to pay the entrance fee to walk out to the head and the its hundred-year-old **signal station** (now automatic), accessed by a slender, arched bridge. Follow the narrow pathways to signposted viewpoints: with the 50m Fastnet lighthouse and the tip of the Beara Peninsula to either side and the whole of Ireland behind you, you're left to plot the folds of the jagged cliffs, the movements of the clouds and the churning contours of the ocean.

| ACCOMMODATION AND EATING | GOLEEN, CROOKHAVEN AND MIZEN HEAD |
|---|---|

**The Crookhaven Inn** Crookhaven ☎028 35309. Cosy pub-restaurant in the village itself, with an open stove and outside tables overlooking the inlet, serving excellent food including home-cured gravlax (€8.90 with warm potato salad). April to mid-Oct daily 12.30–8/9pm.

**Fortview House** 9km northeast of Goleen on the R591 towards Durrus ☎028 35324, ⓦfortviewhouse. ie. Lovely farmstay, where guests are welcome to walk the estate and help with the milking. Smart en-suite rooms

feature large brass and iron beds, and top-notch breakfasts include home-made pancakes, freshly laid eggs and local farmhouse cheeses. Self-catering cottages available year-round. Very good rates for singles. Closed Nov–March. **€100**

**Galley Cove** Just west of Crookhaven ☎028 35137, ⓦgalleycovehouse.com. Welcoming en-suite B&B, in a spruce, modern, pine-floored bungalow with fine views of the sea and Fastnet lighthouse. Good rates for singles. **€90**

# The Sheep's Head

The **Sheep's Head**, a precarious sliver of land between Dunmanus and Bantry bays, is the quietest and smallest of the major southwestern peninsulas. Gorse and heather sprout from its long granite spine, leaving room for narrow pockets of green pasture on its north and especially its south coast. With magnificent views of the larger peninsulas on either side, it can be best appreciated by pedalling the easy-to-follow 120km **Sheep's Head Cycle Route** from Ballylickey (6km north of Bantry), or by walking the 93km **Sheep's Head Way** (ⓦthesheepsheadway.ie) from Bantry; the latter is relatively easy walking, avoiding the round-peninsula road for most of the way, and is covered by OS Discovery Series map number 88. It can be done in four days, with two nights in Kilcrohane after two long days' walking and a night in Durrus; the last day is missable, so you might want to catch a bus back to Bantry from Durrus.

# Durrus

**DURRUS** is a relatively busy junction village between the Mizen Head and Sheep's Head peninsulas, supporting several local pubs and, just outside town, a fine restaurant. Sitting at the head of Dunmanus Bay, Durrus is a great place to base yourself if you're keen to go kayaking or fishing.

On a hillside just beyond the village, a farm produces the award-winning **Durrus Irish Cheese**; their shop is open Mon–Fri 9am–2pm, but contact them in advance if you'd like to view the cheesemaking (ⓦdurruscheese.com).

## ACCOMMODATION AND EATING                                    DURRUS

**Blairscove House & Restaurant** About 2km southwest down the R591 towards Crookhaven ☎027 61127, ⓦblairscove.ie. In beautiful grounds overlooking Dunmanus Bay, *Blairs Cove House* combines spacious luxury apartments with an excellent restaurant, renowned for its buffet-style starters and grilled meats and fish (set menu €65). Good rates for singles. Closed early Nov to mid-March.

Restaurant Tues–Sat 5.30–9.30pm. **€220**
**Sea Lodge** About 2km west of Durrus on the road to Kilcrohane ☎027 62830. On a remote country road that hugs the bay, the views from this B&B are stunning. Guest rooms and the shared lounge room are comfortable and simply furnished. Pack lunches can be arranged. Closed Oct–Easter. **€70**

## TOURS AND ACTIVITIES

**Darrens Kayaks** ☎027 615115, ⓦdarrenskayaks.com. This outfit rents kayaks (customised with motors or sails if required) and organises tuition, guided tours and fishing expeditions (rental from €25/3hr).

# Kilcrohane and beyond

**KILCROHANE**, 15km southwest of Durrus, is a traditional sleepy village strung along the main road, with a church, a couple of decent **bars** serving food and a combined shop, petrol station and post office. The Old Creamery on the road in from Durrus shelters the Sheep's Head Producers Shop (Mon–Fri 11am–5pm, Sun 11am–4pm), where local artisans sell everything from jams to jewellery (including Sheep's Head Way maps), plus there's a café and a bike rental shop.

From Kilcrohane, a road loops along the quieter north coast of the peninsula, reaching its highest point at a spectacular pass 2km north of the village; for even better views, it's possible to walk to the top of **Seefin**, Sheep's Head's highest hill (344m), in about twenty minutes from the pass.

West of Kilcrohane, the Sheep's Head is dotted with small lakes and becomes more jagged and hummocky as it narrows to a lighthouse at the tip. The tarmac runs out at the *Sheep's Head Café*, from where it's a thirty-minute walk down to the lighthouse.

## ACCOMMODATION AND EATING                        KILCROHANE AND BEYOND

**Bernie's Cúpan Tae** 11km west of Kilcrohane ☎086 877 8604, ⓔbernietobin7@eircom.net. In a wild, end-of-the-road setting, this cosy café nourishes travellers with hearty soups, sandwiches and home-made cakes and offers walking information. Mid-March to Oct daily 11.30am–6/7pm.
**Bridge View House** By the church ☎027 67086, ⓦbridgeviewhouse.com. This attractive house provides friendly en-suite B&B, a large garden and excellent home

cooking. Self-catering available. Good rates for singles. **€70**
**Seamount Farmhouse** Glenlough, 10km from Kilcrohane towards Bantry ☎027 61226, ⓦseamount farm.com. Outstanding B&B less than 1km off the Sheep's Head Way. The welcoming all-en-suite farmhouse provides magnificent views of Bantry Bay, fine home baking, walking tours and plenty of useful information about exploring the area. **€90**

# Bantry

**BANTRY** enjoys a glorious location, ringed first by lush wooded slopes and then by wild bare mountains, at the head of 35km-long **Bantry Bay**, one of the finest natural harbours in Ireland. The prime viewpoint is naturally occupied by **Bantry**

> **BANTRY FESTIVALS**
>
> Bantry hosts the prestigious nine-day **West Cork Chamber Music Festival**
> (ⓦwestcorkmusic.ie), generally at the beginning of July, followed immediately by the seven-
> day **West Cork Literary Festival** (ⓦwestcorkliteraryfestival.ie). August sees a five-day
> **traditional-music festival**, "Masters of Tradition" (ⓦwestcorkmusic.ie).

**House**, which with its sumptuous interior and garden is one of West Cork's few unmissable historic sites. At the junction of several important roads, Bantry is also a substantial market (Fridays 9.30am–5pm) and service town, with plenty of amenities for visitors.

## Wolfe Tone Square

Bantry gathers itself around the expansive, bayside **Wolfe Tone Square**, which features a statue of the eponymous United Irishman pointedly holding a telescope behind his back. In December 1796, Tone persuaded the French to send a fleet carrying some thirteen thousand seasoned soldiers to invade Ireland in support of a Republican Revolution. Contrary winds prevented them from landing in Bantry Bay – though they were "close enough to toss a biscuit on shore" according to Tone – and the fleet was forced to return to Brest. Had they landed, it's likely that they would have overwhelmed the inexperienced forces in Ireland at the time.

## Bantry House

1km west of the centre of Bantry, along the bay • Easter to end May, Sept & Oct Tues–Sun 10am–5pm; June–Aug daily 10am–5pm • House and garden €11, garden €6; guided tour €15 • ☏ 027 50047, ⓦ bantryhouse.com

On the southern approach to town, **Bantry House** is one of Ireland's most compelling country houses, both for its lavish artworks and for its magnificent setting, among formal gardens overlooking the bay. Built in the early eighteenth century and extended a hundred years later, it was spared destruction during the Irish Civil War, when it acted as a hospital for the wounded of both sides. Many of its beautiful furnishings were gathered by the Second Earl of Bantry on his nineteenth-century grand tour and boast name-dropping provenances, such as the gorgeous Aubusson tapestries made for Marie Antoinette on her marriage to the future Louis XVI. The highlight is the dining room, which resembles an extravagant stage set: rich Chartres-blue walls, a marble colonnade and vast seventeenth-century sideboards carved with cherubs and classical scenes. There's a very attractive **café**, with tables under the house's west balcony, which serves teas and simple lunches.

### ARRIVAL AND INFORMATION — BANTRY

**By bus** Buses from/to Cork (4–6 daily; 1hr 50min) and Castletownbere (Mon 2 daily, Tues, Fri & Sat 1 daily; 1hr 20min) stop on the central Wolfe Tone Square.
**Tourist office** At the east end of Wolfe Tone Square (April–Oct Mon–Sat 10am–6pm; Nov–March Fri 10am–2pm;

☏ 027 50229, ⓦ bantry.ie). Guided historical walks (June–Aug Tues & Thurs 11am; €2).
**Bike rental** O'Donovan Cycles on Market St (Tues–Sun 10am–1pm & 2–5pm; ☏ 086 128 0307).

### ACCOMMODATION

There's a decent range of **accommodation** in Bantry, with dozens of B&Bs lining the Glengarriff road on the north side of town, but it's advisable to book ahead in July and Aug, especially during the town's festivals.

★ **Bantry House** On the N71 at the southern entrance to town ☏ 027 50047, ⓦ bantryhouse.com. Luxurious digs with great views in one of the country's finest mansions, which is still the home of the White family, former Earls of Bantry. The huge, chandeliered library, with its coffered ceiling, and the billiards room are now guest lounges. Close Nov–Easter. €169

**Eagle Point Caravan and Camping Park** Ballylickey, 6km from Bantry along the Glengarriff road ☎027 50630, ⓦeaglepointcamping.com. This large, well-organized campsite has terraces that make the most of its Bantry Bay location; a laundry, a small playground, pebbly beaches for swimming and a slipway to launch kayaks.

Closed late Sept to Easter. Motorhomes €38, tents €26

**The Maritime** Just off Wolfe Tone Square on the main road to Skibbereen ☎027 54700, ⓦthemaritime.ie. This smart contemporary hotel is plush and thoughtfully equipped, with very helpful reception staff and a leisure centre that features a 19m pool, gym, Jacuzzi and sauna. €99

## EATING AND DRINKING

**The Anchor Tavern** New St, off the southeast corner of Wolfe Tone Square ☎027 50012. A popular haunt for visiting musicians, this sociable 150-year-old traditional pub is adorned with nautical memorabilia, plain stone floors and communal pews around the walls. Mon–Thurs roughly noon–11.30pm, Fri & Sat noon–12.30am, Sun 12.30–11pm.

**The Brick Oven** Wolfe Tone Square, southwest corner ☎027 52500, ⓦthebrickovenbantry.com. Accomplished all-rounder serving good baguettes and salads (spicy chicken €11.50), plus pizzas from a wood-burning oven and tasty bistro dishes. Daily noon–10pm.

★ **Ma Murphy's** 7 New St, off the southeast corner of Wolfe Tone Square ☎027 50242. Cosy bar-grocery with a cool soundtrack and a very pleasant cobbled back yard; quirky, old fashioned and plenty of whiskeys and bottles of craft beer. Open mic Thurs, live music at weekends. Mon–Thurs roughly noon–11.30pm, Fri & Sat noon–12.30am, Sun noon–11pm.

★ **O'Connor's** Wolfe Tone Square ☎027 55664, ⓦoconnorseafood.com. Elegant, top-quality restaurant specializing in seafood (including oysters from its own seawater tank) and local lamb, pork and steaks, in ample portions. Try the Bantry Bay scallops with pea, garlic, spinach and parmesan risotto (€26), and leave room for excellent desserts such as rhubarb crumble. Early bird €20 for two courses (until 6.30pm). Mon–Sat 9am–11pm, Sun 10am–9pm.

**Organico** 3 Glengarriff road, 100m off Wolfe Tone Square ☎027 55905, ⓦorganico.ie. Popular, easy-going vegetarian and organic café, bakery and health-food store, dishing up tasty hummus salads (€7.50), sandwiches and soups. Mon–Sat 9am–6pm.

**Stuffed Olive** 2a Bridge St, the continuation of New St, off the square's southeast corner ☎027 55883, ⓦthestuffed olive.wordpress.com. Excellent deli-café and bakery serving creative sandwiches and salads such as smoked duck (€5.50), cakes, good coffees and juices. Mon–Sat 8.30am–6pm.

# The Beara Peninsula

The largest and most remote of Cork's peninsulas, the **Beara** (ⓦbearatourism.com) careers southwestwards for 50km between Bantry Bay and the Kenmare River. Patterns in the landscape are hard to distinguish here, and contrasts are frequent. Indeed, the peninsula's most popular tourist spot, **Glengarriff**, has built an industry on the stunning contrast between its lush subtropical setting and the irregular barren rocks of the Caha Mountains behind. The mountainous spine is often augmented by ribs, and particularly in the awesome Slieve Miskish Mountains at the Beara's tip, the coast road is forced to climb through whatever passes can be found. Round on the north coast, half of which belongs to County Kerry (see page 286), the only settlements occupy occasional cups of green farmland beneath the stony ridges.

The diverse scenery can be explored by car following the **Ring of Beara** (ⓦringofbeara. com) around the peninsula; the 138km **Beara Way Cycle Route** mostly follows this quiet main road too. Away from the coastal route, and splicing the peninsula north–south, the outstanding **Healy Pass** is a lonely mountain road of hairpin bends and panoramic viewpoints that shouldn't be missed. For those on foot, take the **Beara Way**, a 200km waymarked walk (9–11 days) following mostly tracks and minor roads from Glengarriff west (via Adrigole, Castletownbere and a ferry to Bere Island, which can easily be missed out) to Dursey Island, then along the north coast of the peninsula (via Allihies, Eyeries, Ardgroom and Lauragh) to Kenmare and back to Glengarriff. Route guides are available locally, there's a downloadable map guide of the walking route at ⓦbearatourism.com, and the Ordnance Survey 1:50,000 Discovery map 84 covers nearly the whole peninsula.

# Glengarriff

The founders of **GLENGARRIFF** were perhaps having an off-day when they named it *An Gleann Garbh*, the "rugged glen" – or, to be charitable, maybe the climate has changed since then. It's true that above and behind stands the magnificent backdrop of the wild, bare Caha Mountains, but the village itself sits in a sheltered oasis of balmy greenery. This picturesque juxtaposition, warmed by the Atlantic Gulf Stream, has attracted tourists since the eighteenth century, when the *Eccles Hotel* was built. The village now straggles east–west for several kilometres from the *Eccles*, with most of its amenities towards the western end around the N71–R572 junction. Glengarriff's popularity means there's a decent range of places to stay and eat, making it a good base for exploring some of Cork's most beautiful countryside or for just hopping over to see the horticultural delights of **Garinish Island**. Over a weekend in June, Glengarriff hosts a vibrant **uilleann pipes festival**, with concerts, workshops and sessions of traditional music (⊛ jimdowlingfestival.ie).

## Bamboo Park

1km along the N71 Bantry Rd · Daily 9am–7pm · €7, kids free · ☎ 027 63007, ⊛ bamboo-park.com

Glengarriff's microclimate is mild enough to support the **Bamboo Park**, a beautiful thirteen-acre private garden with a tearoom towards the east end of the village, planted with thirty different species of bamboo, as well as various palms, ferns and eucalyptus. The maze of paths here are great for kids to have a very long game of hide-and-seek, while the seashore frontage, with private beach and picnic area, reveals idyllic views of tufted green islets in the bay.

## Glengarriff Woods Nature Reserve and around

1km along the N71 Kenmare Rd · Daily 24hr · Free · ⊛ glengarriffnaturereserve.ie

**Glengarriff Woods Nature Reserve** is a forest park of ancient sessile oaks, birch and holly, that shelters Mediterranean species such as strawberry trees. It's crossed by waymarked nature trails (about 3hr walking in total), including the short climb up to **Lady Bantry's Lookout**, which is rewarded with panoramic views of Glengarriff, Bantry Bay and the Sheep's Head.

Beyond the reserve you can veer west for 7km to reach **Barley Lake**, a beautiful armchair or corrie lake, or if you're keen for more rambles in nature, continue a few kilometres along the N71 to reach the **Ewe Experience** (daily 10am–6pm 6pm; €7.50; ⊛ theewe.com), a magical sculpture garden that opens only in the summer months.

## INFORMATION                                                    GLENGARRIFF

**Tourist information** There's not an official tourist office in Glengarriff, but a souvenir shop next to the Blue Pool ferry service and the bus stop has a few local brochures. The town's website is ⊛ glengarriff.ie. Note that there are no banks in Glengarriff, though the Spar supermarket and post office can change foreign cash.

## ACCOMMODATION AND EATING

**Casey's Hotel** Main St ☎ 027 63010, ⊛ caseyshotel glengarriff.ie. Friendly, family-run nineteenth-century hotel, with crisply refurbished rooms, a patio and garden. Very good food such as beef and Guinness pie, and plenty of seafood in the bar or smart evening restaurant. Good rates for singles. **€90**

**Glengarriff Caravan and Camping Park (Dowling's)** About 2km out on the R572 Castletownbere road ☎ 027 63154, ✉ glengarriffccp@gmail.com. You can camp in some comfort at this woodland site, which has laundry facilities, a playground and traditional music in its on-site bar. Closed Nov–March. **€25**

**Glengarriff Park Hotel** Main St ☎ 027 63000, ⊛ glengarriffpark.com. Tasteful, modern "standard" rooms, some with baths, plus slightly more expensive "luxury" rooms with more space, more elaborate decor and armchairs. Downstairs are a bistro and *MacCarthy's*, a pleasant, well-run bar serving tasty food. **€110**

**Jim's Coffee House** 1.5km east of Glengarriff on the N71 ☎ 027 63030. Close to the Bamboo Park, *Jim's* serves up full Irish breakfasts until midday and then light lunches and home-made cakes until close. There's a few tables outside that take in the beautiful bay view. April–Oct Tues–Sun 10am–4pm (limited hours in winter).

**The Maple Leaf** Main St ☏ 027 63021. Located among a tight concentration of pubs at the main junction, this friendly spot offers live music every night in summer, at weekends in winter. Mon–Thurs noon–11.30pm, Fri & Sat noon–12.30am, Sun noon–11pm.

# Garinish Island (Ilnacullin)

April, May, Sept & Oct daily 10am–5.30pm; June Mon–Fri & Sun 10am–5.30, Sat 10am–6pm; July & Aug Mon–Fri & Sun 9.30–5.30pm, Sat 9.30am–6pm • €5; Heritage Card • ⓦ garinishisland.com • Boat €12 return with Harbour Queen Ferries (every 30mins 9.45am–3.45pm; ☏ 027 63116, ⓦ harbourqueenferry.com) from opposite the *Eccles Hotel* at the east end of Glengarriff; or €10 either with Blue Pool Ferry (☏ 027 63333) in the centre of Glengarriff, or with the *Lady Ellen*, from Ellen's Rock, about 2km west of the village off the Castletownbere road (☏ 027 63110)

In 1910, the MP Annan Bryce bought **Garinish** (aka Ilnacullin) from the British War Office and, after shipping in all the topsoil, gradually turned the rocky inshore island into an exotic garden oasis. Having passed into public ownership in 1953, the island is now a delightful and accessible escape from the mainland, especially in summer, when colourful plants from around the world set the island alight against a backdrop of the sparse, jagged mountains just across the water. The island's centrepiece is a formal **Italianate garden**, surrounded by a walled garden and wilder areas, a Grecian temple with magnificent views of the Caha Mountains, and a Martello tower. There's a coffee shop and a self-guided trail around the gardens, and serious horticulturalists should pick up the Heritage Service's guidebook, which includes detailed plant lists. The ten-minute **boat trip** to the island takes you past the lush islets of Glengarriff Harbour, where you may see basking seals.

# Castletownbere and around

Over 100km west of Cork city at the end of the peninsula, the bustle of **CASTLETOWNBERE** (sometimes referred to as Castletown Berehaven or just Castletown) comes as quite a surprise. Benefiting from the country's second-largest natural harbour, it's Ireland's biggest white-fish port, and especially during strong winter gales, Atlantic trawlers of many nationalities put in here. Not surprisingly, there's a good range of amenities for visitors, with the fairly compact area around the main square offering cafés, restaurants, banks and some boisterous pubs.

## Dunboy Castle

Just off the R572 Dursey road • Open access

To the west of town, there's a pleasant 3km walk through the grounds of **Puxley Mansion**, the fenced-in skeleton of a neo-Gothic pile that's been left to moulder, to the overgrown seafront ruins of **Dunboy Castle** and its dramatic views back along the Beara Peninsula. Built in the fourteenth century, the castle was besieged by the English in 1602 after the Battle of Kinsale. Facing an army of four thousand, its garrison of 143

---

### THE LONG MARCH OF O'SULLIVAN BERE

Beara is the ancestral lands of the O'Sullivan's, but in the seventeenth century during the Nine Years War, their leader **Donal Cam O'Sullivan Bere** (1561–1618) allied with the Spanish. After the loss of Dunboy Castle and faced with death if he was captured by the English, O'Sullivan set out to reach friends in the north. He travelled with a thousand men, women and children, and set off with only one day's worth of provisions. Harassed by the English and the Irish, and overwhelmed by harsh winter conditions, he arrived two weeks later with just 35 followers left. The march is now commemorated by the **Beara-Breifne Way** (ⓦ bearabreifneway.ie), a 500km walking route from Dursey Island to Blacklion on the borders of Leitrim, Cavan and Fermanagh, where it links with the Ulster Way.

men held out for eleven days, but in the end were all slaughtered and the castle blown up. Their chieftain, **Donal Cam O'Sullivan Bere**, then embarked on his famous long **march** up to County Leitrim.

## ARRIVAL AND INFORMATION                                    CASTLETOWNBERE

**By bus** Buses stop on the main square, except Harrington's which pick up from the Supervalu supermarket just to the east.

Destinations Bus Éireann: Cork (4 weekly; 3hr); Kenmare, via Eyeries, Lauragh and the north side of the Beara (July & Aug Mon–Sat 2 daily; 1hr 20min).

Harrington's Buses (☎027 74003, ⌖harringtonsbus.com): Cork (Mulligan's Bar, opposite the bus station on Parnell Place; Mon–Wed, Fri & Sat 1 daily 8am, Sun 1 at 4.30pm; 2hr).

O'Donoghue's Buses (☎027 70007): Bantry (Mon 2 daily,

Tues, Fri & Sat 1 daily; 1hr 20min); Cork (Mulligan's Bar, opposite the bus station on Parnell Place; 1 on Thurs; 2hr 30min).

**Tourist office** Just west of the square along the main street (usually Mon–Fri 10.30am–3.30pm, but worth checking on ☎027 70054); they have details of short, signposted loop walks on the peninsula.

**Bike rental** Bike'n'Beara, Great Gas petrol station, 2km east of the centre on the Glengarriff road (Tues–Sat 10am–1pm, 2–5pm; ☎086 128 0307).

## ACCOMMODATION

**Berehaven Golf Club** 5km east on the Glengarriff road at Filane ☎027 70700, ⌖berehavengolf.com. You can camp on the shores of Bantry Bay at the golf club, shower in the clubhouse and drink in the daytime bar in the summer. Laundry room and reduced green fees for campers. Motorhome €25, tents €20

**Garranes Hostel** 8km west of town on the Dursey road ☎027 73032, ⌖dzogchenbeara.org. Segregated dorms and a family room open to all-comers at a Tibetan

Buddhist retreat centre in a traditional farmhouse cottage. It offers a fully equipped kitchen, a sitting room and plenty of tranquillity; there's a café on site too. Dorms €22, family room €65

**Rodeen Country House** 2km east of town ☎027 70838, ⌖rodeencountryhouse.com. Charming retreat set in beautiful subtropical gardens overlooking the bay, with stylish en-suite rooms, and home-baked scones for breakfast. Very good rates for singles. €80

## EATING AND DRINKING

**Breen's Lobster Bar** On the main square ☎027 70031. It's impossible to miss this bright pink building on the square; the interior is a little more subdued and offers a low-key menu of sandwiches (from €5.50), home-made burgers (€13.90) and seafood chowder (€6.80). Mon–Sat 12.30–8pm.

**Café at Dzogchen Beara** 8km west of town on the Dursey road ☎027 73032, ⌖dzogchenbeara.org. The small café and bookshop at this meditation retreat has unparalleled views of the Atlantic. The menu offers cakes and pastries, inexpensive vegetarian lunch specials and soups with with freshly baked soda bread; take a stroll around the meditation garden too. Daily 10am–5pm.

★ **MacCarthy's** On the main square ☎027 70014, ⌖maccarthysbar.com. This grocery-bar-coffee shop

does soups (from €3) and fresh crab and smoked salmon sandwiches (from €6) for lunch, and is the best place to drink, with tables on the street and regular traditional sessions. Mon–Thurs 9.30am–11.30pm, Fri & Sat 9.30am–12.30am, Sun 12.30–11pm.

**Murphy's** East of the square on the main street ☎027 70244. Unprepossessing restaurant, famous for its fresh, simple fish and seafood (lemon sole with chips and salad €10). Daily 9am–8.45pm.

**Twomey's** On the main street west of the square ☎027 70114. Spruce bar with a sunny yard running down to the harbour, which runs trad music on summer Fri and live music on Sat. Mon–Thurs noon–11.30pm, Fri & Sat noon–12.30am, Sun 2.30–11pm.

# Garnish Bay and Dursey Island

Cable car: Daily: May–Oct 9.30am–7.30pm (closed 1–1.30pm); Nov–April 9.30am–4.30pm (closed 1–1.30pm) ; note in peak months the island might exceed a max number of visitors, so depart early • €10 return • ⌖durseyisland.ie

Beyond Castletownbere, you can skirt round through a few tiny, remote but dramatically set villages to the north side of the peninsula and on towards Kerry. Three kilometres before the tip of the peninsula, the R572 passes beautiful, north-facing **Garnish Bay**, which boasts one of the Beara's few sandy beaches and crystal-clear water.

The Beara lays on a bit of excitement at its very end, in the form of Ireland's only **cable car**, which teeters across the roaring sound to the bird sanctuary of **Dursey Island** and sometimes attracts long queues in summer. There are no facilities on the island (wild camping is legal), but you can walk its circular 11km stretch of the Beara Way for seemingly endless views across the Atlantic, beyond Calf, Cow and Bull islands.

# Allihies

Looping round an especially harsh and rocky part of the peninsula on the R575, you'll come upon **ALLIHIES**, its brightly coloured houses dramatically huddled together against the leathery creases of Slieve Miskish's western flank and blessed with superb sunset views.

## Allihies Copper Mine Museum

100m south of the village centre • Daily: April–Oct 10.30am–5pm; Nov–March usually closed but may open if called in advance • €6 • ☎ 027 73218, ⓦ acmm.ie

In 1812, the Industrial Revolution descended on remote Allihies with a vengeance, bringing state-of-the-art engineering and Cornish mining techniques to work the copper ore in the mountains above the village. At any one time, up to 1500 people, including women and children, worked for the mines here in desperate conditions, until their closure in the 1880s, when many of the miners emigrated to the huge copper lode in Butte, Montana. The story is now engagingly told at the excellent **Allihies Copper Mine Museum**, set up by a group of dedicated local enthusiasts, in a renovated Methodist church that was built for the immigrant Cornish miners. Highlights of the thoughtful displays include video recollections of local men who worked in the mines when they briefly reopened in the 1950s, bits of ore that you can handle and a small-scale reconstruction of a steam pump. There's also a very attractive **café** and an upstairs exhibition area for local artists. In addition, a network of **signposted loop trails** has been laid out in the surrounding countryside, allowing you to take in ruined mine buildings and spectacular views.

## Ballydonegan Strand

One of the trails from the copper mine museum leads down to **Ballydonegan Strand** and its simple campsite (☎027 73002), 1km to the southwest. This sandy beach is actually composed of crushed quartz produced in the copper extraction process, but you'll need to beware the currents when swimming.

---

**ACCOMMODATION AND EATING**                                          **ALLIHIES**

---

**The Copper Café** Allihies Copper Mine Museum ☎027 73218, ⓦacmm.ie. The café in the copper mine museum near the southern entrance to town serves good coffee, home-made cakes, chowder and lunch dishes such as West Cork mussels. April–Oct daily 10.30am–4.30pm.

**O'Neill's Bar** Main St ☎027 73008, ⓦoneillsbeara.ie. Boasting an unmissable crimson facade, this pub serves inexpensive bar food such as toasties and fish and chips, and is also your best bet for traditional music (weekends year-round,

more often in summer). Choose between tables out front on the street with great views, or the log fire inside, depending on the weather. Daily noon–9pm (later in summer).

**Sea View** On the main street in the village centre ☎027 73004, ⓦallihiesseaview.com. In a two-storey terrace house, *Sea View* offers ten comfortable en-suite bedrooms in pastel and earth tones and good breakfasts, as well as self-catering accommodation. **€80**

# Kerry

GREAT BLASKET

# Kerry

Kerry has been making visitors' romantic dreams of Ireland come true since the eighteenth century, when the grandeur of the lakes and mountains around Killarney first came to widespread attention. Encompassing the highest range in the country, Macgillycuddy's Reeks, the landscape here is, of course, still magnificent today, and the Killarney area shelters some fine, underrated architectural sights too. The town itself has plenty of amenities and entertainment, but hordes of tourists mean it can often feel a little crowded. Indeed, the launch of the Wild Atlantic Way driving route (see page 26) has brought a new wave of visitors to Kerry, many of them drawn to the county's three big peninsulas, seductively billed by marketing gurus as "the southern peninsulas with an edge-of-the-world feel".

Of these, the most visited is the **Iveragh peninsula**, southwest of Killarney. Measuring around sixty by thirty kilometres, it's bordered by a highly popular scenic road known as the **Ring of Kerry**, and there are plenty of tracks across its vast, rugged hinterland and coastal branch roads such as the **Ring of Skellig**, which you can explore by car, bike or on foot, and avoid the crowds. The small-scale but intriguing attractions of **Valentia Island** and **Caherdaniel**, perched on a hillside above a great beach, should be enough to tempt you off the Ring of Kerry to spend at least a night out here. Off the end of the peninsula, the island of **Skellig Michael**, one of the most remarkable hermitages in the world and now a UNESCO World Heritage Site, remains the ultimate place to get away from it all. Its profile has recently been raised since it featured in the latest *Star Wars* films, *The Force Awakens* and *The Last Jedi*, introducing the island to a new generation. At the southeastern corner of the peninsula, **Kenmare** contrasts well with Killarney, providing excellent accommodation, restaurants and nightlife in a trim setting, as well as access to further scenic delights on Kerry's part of the **Beara Peninsula**.

Kerry's other peninsula, **Dingle**, experienced its own minor visitor boom on the release of David Lean's film, *Ryan's Daughter*, in 1970, which pumped as much as £3 million into the local economy during a long and troubled location shoot here (including the near-drowning of star Robert Mitchum off Dunquin and the building of an entirely new village, Kirrary, on the remote slopes above). It's still nothing like as touristy as the Ring, and offers a jagged landscape of stark mountains and spectacular beaches, an especially rich heritage of early Christian sites, and a fine, all-round base in the main settlement, **Dingle town**.

Despite the centuries of tourist traffic, Kerry has maintained a strong sense of independence, though perhaps doesn't shout about it as much as its neighbour, Cork. It's one of the least urbanized counties in Ireland, with a sweet, country lilt to the accent. Distinctive H-shaped goalposts are everywhere, not just on village GAA fields but also on most farms, evidence of the county's obsession with **Gaelic football**. The self-styled "Brazil" of the sport, the county team has won the All-Ireland Championship far more than anyone else – 37 times and counting – and produced the finest team ever between 1975 and 1986, winning the championship eight times in those eleven years. The Dingle Peninsula, one of Ireland's strongest Gaeltacht areas, has nurtured not only great footballers, but also a fine community of musicians and the extraordinary **writers** of the wild **Blasket Islands**, who put their rich oral tradition of Irish-language storytelling to paper in the early twentieth century. The county's other most obvious concentration of literary talent has been in the flatlands of **North Kerry**, as celebrated in the genial market town of **Listowel**.

# Highlights

**① Killarney National Park** Beautiful landscape of mountains and lakes, which can be explored by boat, bike and on foot. See page 269

**② The Puck Fair** Bacchanalian festival in August, when Killorglin comes under the reign of a wild goat. See page 275

**③ The Kerry Way** A 213km walking route through the wild, awe-inspiring scenery of the Iveragh Peninsula. See page 277

**④ The Skelligs** Spectacular, inhospitable islands, haunt of seabirds and the ghosts of early medieval hermits. See page 281

**⑤ Kenmare** An agreeable base with a great selection of places to eat, sleep and drink. See page 284

**⑥ Dingle town** Traditional music, great pubs and seafood – what more could you want? See page 289

**⑦ The Blaskets** Lonely islands off the scenic Dingle Peninsula, with an astonishing literary heritage that's imaginatively documented in the visitor centre. See page 293

**⑧ Gallarus Oratory** A unique, early Christian remnant and a graceful, evocative piece of architecture. See page 294

**⑨ Skywalk Rope Bridge** Take a dizzying walk across Ireland's longest rope bridge for spectacular views of the Ring of Kerry. See page 278

**HIGHLIGHTS ARE MARKED ON THE MAP ON PAGE 268**

## GETTING AROUND

**By bus** In this deeply rural county, public buses are few and often far between. Bus Éireann is augmented by Kerry Community Transport (Ⓦ localinkerry.ie), whose minibus network may be of use to visitors, though its complex weekly timetable is mostly designed to get people from rural areas into the big towns for the day.

# Killarney and around

**KILLARNEY** was developed as a resort on the doorstep of Ireland's finest lakeland scenery in the eighteenth and nineteenth centuries, and has steadily grown as a tourist town since. Today it's busy, lively and easily accessible, with hundreds of places to stay across all price ranges. Backpackers are particularly well catered for, with an appealing selection of hostels

## KERRY

**HIGHLIGHTS**

1. Killarney National Park
2. The Puck Fair
3. The Kerry Way
4. The Skelligs
5. Kenmare
6. Dingle town
7. The Blaskets
8. Gallarus Oratory
9. Skywalk Rope Bridge

and all manner of land- and water-borne tours available for those without their own transport. The town's kiss-me-quick hedonism and souvenir shops are not to everyone's taste, but its big draw is still the same as three hundred years ago: beginning in the very heart of town, **Killarney National Park** encompasses three beautiful lakes, beyond which rise the splendid **Macgillycuddy's Reeks**, the country's highest mountain range, known in Irish as Na Cruacha Dubha, the "Black Stacks". The only building of architectural interest in the town is Pugin's elegant **cathedral**, but the national park shelters three diverse and very well-preserved monuments, **Ross Castle**, **Muckross Friary** and **Muckross House**.

## St Mary's Cathedral

On the west side of the town centre • Hours variable • Free

Seat of the Bishop of Kerry, **St Mary's Cathedral** is Ireland's finest neo-Gothic church, built in stages between 1842 and 1912 to a design by Augustus Pugin. Set in spacious gardens by the entrance to the national park, its exterior, with a lofty steeple over the transept, is strikingly elegant. Inside, the rough grey stonework is colourfully lit by dozens of stained-glass windows, which depict in their upper range the life of Christ, in the lower the lives of the Irish saints, notably Patrick and Brendan the Navigator, patron saint of the diocese. The huge redwood tree outside the west door marks a mass children's grave from the time of the Famine: work on the church was suspended in the late 1840s, when the partly roofed building was used as a hospital and shelter.

## Killarney National Park

**Visitor centre** Muckross House, Dromyrourk, 6km south of Killarney town centre • Daily: July & Aug 8.30am–7.30pm; Sept–June 9.30am–4.30pm • **Information point** Killarney House gate lodge, Muckross Rd, Killarney town centre • June to mid-Sept daily 9.30am–5.30pm • ☎ 066 663 1440, ⊚ killarneynationalpark.ie

**Killarney National Park** now protects the glaciated limestone valleys around the three lakes, Leane (or Lower), Muckross (or Middle) and Upper. The lakeshores are covered with virgin forest that features oak, yew and such Mediterranean plants as the arbutus, or strawberry tree – so termed because of its red, but inedible, fruit. Among the park's notable mammals are Ireland's only wild herd of red deer, otter, pine marten, red squirrels and Irish hare, while its 140 bird species include the white-tailed sea eagle (reintroduced from Norway in 2007), the peregrine falcon and the hen harrier. Running roughly parallel to, but just outside, the park's western border is the dramatic glacial breach known as the Gap of Dunloe (see page 273). The **National Park Visitor Centre** at Muckross House provides information about all aspects of the park, including a twenty-minute audiovisual on the landscape, flora and fauna. A useful free **map** of the park is available both here and at the **National Park Information Point** in the centre of town, while the Ordnance Survey of Ireland produces a more detailed (1:25,000) map.

There's all manner of tours and transport available (many of which can be booked at the tourist office), including boats at Ross Castle and Muckross House (see page 271), and rented bikes (see page 275).

## Ross Castle

Ross Island, 2km from Killarney, off the N71 Kenmare Rd • Guided tours (40min) early-March to late Oct daily 9.30am–5.45pm, last admission 5pm; maximum 15 people per tour, so you may have a wait at busy times • €5; Heritage Card • ☎ 064 663 5851, ⊚ heritageireland.ie

The gates of Knockreer Estate opposite the cathedral and the "Golden Gates" by the National Park Information Point on Muckross Road give immediate access from the town centre to the national park. Paths through the grounds, which blaze in spring with rhododendrons, azaleas and magnolias, lead south after less than half an hour to **Ross Castle**.

**ACCOMMODATION**

| | |
|---|---|
| The Brehon | 10 |
| The Copper Kettle | 3 |
| Fairview | 4 |
| Fleming's White Bridge | 6 |
| Great Southern Hotel | 7 |
| Killarney International Hostel | 2 |
| Loch Lein Country House Hotel | 1 |
| Muckross Park Hotel | 11 |
| Neptune's Hostel | 5 |
| Old Weir Lodge | 9 |
| The Ross Hotel | 8 |

**EATING**

| | |
|---|---|
| The Bricín | 2 |
| Cellar One | 7 |
| Gaby's Seafood Restaurant | 1 |
| Jam | 3 |
| Milano | 6 |
| Murphy's | 5 |
| Quinlan's Seafood Bar | 4 |

**DRINKING & NIGHTLIFE**

| | |
|---|---|
| Buckley's | 2 |
| Courtney's | 3 |
| Jimmy O'Brien's | 1 |
| The Killarney Grand (aka Sheehan's) | 4 |

Engaging and informative **tours** focus on the history, architecture and day-to-day life of the castle. It's an impressive example of a medieval tower house, probably built in the late fifteenth century by one of the O'Donoghue Ross chieftains, who had undisputed hold over the Killarney area at the time. They clearly had something to fear, however: the austere stronghold features murder holes and stumble steps – of irregular dimensions, designed to trip unwary attackers – while the cross-planked and spiked oak doors are further protected by raised thresholds and pointed arches. The flagstoned rooms, which include a Great Hall with its own pantry and minstrels' gallery and a tiny cubbyhole for around fifteen servants to sleep in, have been decked out with authentic furniture and tapestries.

## Lough Leane

Rowing boats for rent at Ross Castle (€5/hr); boat trips to Inisfallen (€10/person) are best booked through the Killarney Discover Ireland Centre (☎ 064 663 1633)

The largest of Killarney's three lakes, **Lough Leane** sits in a serene mountain-ringed valley and is dotted with uninhabited islands and a restored castle. Catch the right day and you'll be enchanted by the light – though the lake also takes on a special beauty in the drizzle. From Ross Castle you can rent a rowing boat to row out to one of the lake's wooded islands, **Inisfallen**, about 1.6km offshore, where romantic ruins date from the sixth or seventh century. It was here, between AD 950 and 1350, that the *Annals of Inisfallen* – a chronicle of world and Irish history – were written by monks; today the book survives in the Bodleian Library in Oxford. Although the original churches have disappeared, you can still see on Inisfallen the weathered ruins of a thirteenth-century **oratory** and an **Augustinian priory**.

## Muckross Estate

The huge section of the national park known as **Muckross Estate** begins about 3km south of Killarney off the N71, where a gate and a gaggle of jaunting cars signal the short walk through the woods to **Muckross Friary** (free access). Founded in the fifteenth century, this strict Franciscan friary originally enshrined a miraculous statue of the Virgin Mary. It's in a remarkable state of preservation, with an intact two-storey cloister shaded by a gnarled yew tree at its centre.

### Muckross House

**House** Guided tours daily: July & Aug 9am–7pm; April–June & Sept–Oct 9am–6pm; Nov–March 9am–5pm; last tour 1hr 20mins before closing; closed one week at Christmas • €9.25; Heritage Card • **Farms** March & Oct Sat, Sun & public hols 1–6pm; April, May & Sept daily 1–6pm; June–Aug daily 10am–6pm • €9, joint ticket including the house €15; Heritage Card not accepted • ☎ 064 667 0144, Ⓦ muckross-house.ie

From Muckross Friary, you can continue through the estate on foot or by bike, but car drivers will have to continue down the main road for 1km to **Muckross House**. Guided tours lead visitors around the rich Victorian interiors of this fine nineteenth-century neo-Elizabethan stately home. On the other side of the car park are three traditional **working farms** where you can chat to actors playing out the roles of farmers and their wives. In fine weather, you can sit outside at the splendid **café-restaurant**

---

### KILLARNEY FESTIVALS AND EVENTS

Killarney lays on a long menu of seasonal **festivals and events**, with music and sport featuring strongly. There's a five-day festival of traditional music in late February (Ⓦ inec.ie), while Spraoí Chiarraí is a series of free concerts of traditional music, dancing and storytelling in the summer.

In May, July and August, Killarney's **racecourse** (Ⓦ killarneyraces.ie), in a scenic spot on Ross Road, hosts boisterous, well-supported racing. The first weekend in May, when the Rally of the Lakes (Ⓦ rallyofthelakes.com) pulls crowds of motoring fans to the area, is not a good time to experience the serenity of the mountains.

Killarney is a good place to sample the Kerry fervour for **Gaelic football**: major matches are held at Fitzgerald Park on Lewis Road (Ⓦ kerrygaa.ie), which is named after Dick Fitzgerald, greatest player of the early twentieth century and author of the first training manual on the game, and enjoys a magnificent mountain backdrop from its north terraces. The local side, Dr Croke's, All-Ireland club champions in 1992, have their stadium across the road.

---

## KILLARNEY NATIONAL PARK TOURS AND ACTIVITIES

### GUIDED WALKS

Two-hour **guided walks** through the park set off from opposite St Mary's Cathedral every morning at 11am (Nov–April advance booking required; €12; ☎087 639 4362, ⓦkillarneyguidedwalks.com).

### PONY TRAPS

**Jaunting cars** (pony traps) tout for business at several locations, including Kenmare Place in town, Muckross House and *Kate Kearney's Cottage* (see page 273) for the Gap of Dunloe. On the east side of the Kenmare Place roundabout, a sign in front of the Celtic cross war memorial and the *Killarney Avenue Hotel* gives a map of their routes and a detailed price list, though you might still have to haggle with the "jarveys" – as the drivers are known. A one-hour trip, for example, through the national park and along the lakeside to Ross Castle should cost €45 for up to three passengers (add €12 for each extra passenger). Reputable jarveys include Paul and Michael Tangney, usually to be found at Kenmare Place (☎064 663 3358, ⓦkillarneyjauntingcars.com).

### HORSERIDING

Killarney Riding Stables, 1km west of town on the Killorglin road (☎064 663 1686, ⓦkillarney-riding-stables.com), offer **horseriding** in the national park on day-trips, as well as on the two- or five-day Reeks Trail.

### KAYAKING

**Kayaking** on the lakes is offered by Outdoors Ireland (☎086 860 4563, ⓦoutdoorsireland.com) and Cappanalea Outdoor Education Centre (☎066 976 9244, ⓦcappanalea.ie).

### ORGANIZED TOURS OF THE PARK

Several tour operators, including O'Donoghue Brothers, based at *Old Weir Lodge*, Muckross Rd

---

in the crafts centre, overlooking the pretty **gardens**, which are noted for their rhododendrons and azaleas.

### Muckross Lake

Boat trips can be organized at the nearby Dundag Boathouse (☎087 278 9335 or ☎087 120 0420)

Starting from Muckross House (where you can pick up a walks leaflet), there's a delightful 10km **trail** around **Muckross Lake**, mostly on paved paths, but with a short section on the main Kenmare road. Passing through gnarled, mossy, ancient woods with a thick undergrowth of heather and ferns, you'll reach Brickeen Bridge where lakes Muckross and Leane meet, and shortly after the Meeting of the Waters, where the outflow from the Upper Lake runs into Muckross Lake. Just above this second meeting, towards the end of the walk, is an irresistibly photogenic, tree-shaded pool with the arches of the ruined Old Weir Bridge as a backdrop is a delightful tea room, **Dinis Cottage**, older than Muckross House itself – you can arrive on foot, by bike or by boat as the cottage has its own pier. Originally built as a hunting lodge in the 1700s, Dinis has been used as a tea room since the early 1800s. Some of its window etchings date from 1816. The cottage's fascinating pedigree and the area's history are displayed on walls, alongside old visitor books. Light refreshments are served all day and include sandwiches, quiches and scones. On your way back, you can take in 20m **Torc Waterfall** on a short detour, or take on the steep climb up to the summit of **Torc Mountain** (535m) for magnificent views of the lakes and the Reeks.

### The Upper Lake

Further down the main N71, 16km from Killarney, is **Ladies' View**, which apparently was chosen by the ladies-in-waiting of Queen Victoria on her visit in 1861 as the finest

(☎064 663 1068, ⓦkillarneydaytour.com), and Gap of Dunloe Tours, with a base at *O'Connors Pub*, 7 High St, in the summer (☎064 663 0200, ⓦgapofdunloetours.com), offer full-day **combination tours**, which take you by bus to the starting point of Kate Kearney's Cottage, from where you walk or ride a jaunting car or pony through the Gap; then after a lunch stop at Lord Brandon's Cottage you take a boat ride through the three lakes to Ross Castle, and finally a bus brings you back into town (€30/person, €50 with jaunting car, €60 with pony-trekking). Simpler **bike-on-boat tours** (you cycle through the Gap of Dunloe and sling your bike on a boat between Lord Brandon's Cottage and Ross Castle) can be arranged through the hostels, or O'Donoghue Brothers (as above) or Gap of Dunloe Tours. Or you can put this together yourself: from roughly early March to late October, the boats leave Ross Castle at 11am, returning from Lord Brandon's at 2pm (€15), and bikes can be rented from O'Sullivan's (see page 275).

### ORGANIZED TOURS OF LOUGH LEANE

From the pier at Ross Castle, **tours of Lough Leane** are operated by two large waterbuses, which in summer each run up to five one-hour trips a day (€10): the *Lily of Killarney* (contact O'Donoghue Brothers, as above); and the *Pride of the Lakes* (☎064 663 2638, ⓦkillarneylaketours. ie), which offers a connecting shuttle bus from town.

### HOP-ON HOP-OFF BUSES

Killarney currently supports two **hop-on hop-off bus** services (all €15/day). The Big Red Killarney Bus Tour (☎087 250 8122, ⓦkillarneytour.com), is an open-top double-decker which runs south to Ross Castle, Muckross House and Torc Waterfall three times a day and which reduces its service to once daily in winter. Killarney Shuttle Bus (☎087 138 4384, ⓦkillarneyshuttlebus.com) starts at the tourist office, offers single tickets (from €5) as well as day passes, and covers three routes: west to the Gap of Dunloe (2 daily) and south to Muckross House and Torc Waterfall (5 daily), and Ladies' View (1 daily).

**8**

view in the land – with some justification. From the car park here, you look directly down on the **Upper Lake**, with its many channels running down to lakes Muckross and Leane on one side, and the Carrauntoohil massif rising on the other. Just before reaching Ladies' View on the main road, there's a signposted path, part of the Kerry Way, through Derrycunihy Woods to Lord Brandon's Cottage; beyond Ladies' View, spectacular vistas continue at least as far as **Moll's Gap**, where the Avoca craft shop and its good café mark the parting of the Kenmare road and the R568 to Sneem.

## The Gap of Dunloe

West of Muckross Lake, the **Gap of Dunloe**, a glacial defile which cuts off Tomies and Purple mountains from Macgillycuddy Reeks, is justifiably one of the area's most popular attractions. Try, if you can, to come here late in the day, when the light is at its best and the road at its quietest.

The usual approach is from the north, where **Kate Kearney's Cottage**, a pub and restaurant 4km from Beaufort, stands at the foot of the Gap. Beyond here the narrow road is not designed to handle motor traffic at busy times, and should be left free for walkers, cyclists, pony trekkers and jaunting cars; at quiet times, you should be OK to drive it if you need to. It's a starkly beautiful 7km climb to the **Head of the Gap**, walled in by a steep patchwork of grass and bare purple rock, with tumbling waterfalls after rain, past reedy lakes and one or two sheep. Then from the Head, you can make a glorious descent into the broad **Black Valley**, hemmed in by 784m Broaghnabinnia at its western end and so named because all its inhabitants died during the Famine. It now supports a few sheep farms, a primary school and a basic An Óige hostel, on the Kerry Way 3km

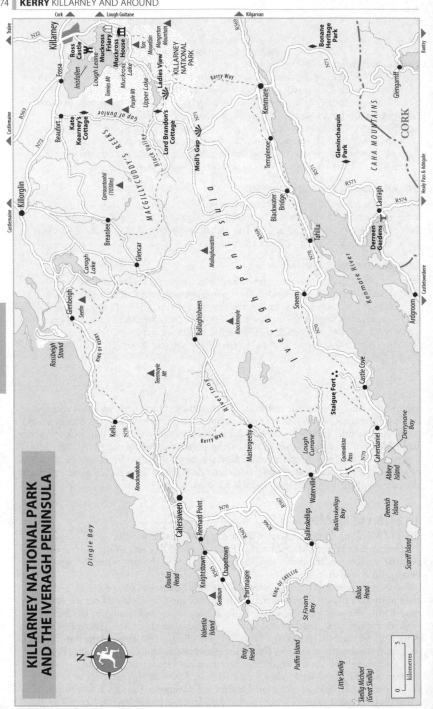

**KILLARNEY NATIONAL PARK AND THE IVERAGH PENINSULA**

## THE PUCK FAIR

For three mad days in the middle of August, the **Puck Fair** (⦿ puckfair.ie) draws in crowds of up to thirty thousand to the small, otherwise missable town of **Killorglin**, 19km west of Killarney. Granted its charter by James I in 1613, the fair begins when a wild goat is stalked in the mountains, then caged and crowned as king of the town, which raises the curtain on a Dionysian festival of wine and song, accompanied by a traditional horse fair. The event has pagan roots in the Celtic harvest festival of Lughnasa, though these particular ceremonies are meant to commemorate the herd of goats that ran down into Killorglin, to warn the townsfolk that Cromwell's army was on its way. For further information, contact Killorglin's Mid-Kerry Tourism office (☎ 066 976 1451, ⊚ gokerry.ie).

from the Head of the Gap. About 2km further down the road, in a delightful spot at the head of the Upper Lake, is **Lord Brandon's Cottage**, a nineteenth-century hunting lodge, now summertime café, where the boats from Ross Castle terminate (see page 269).

## ARRIVAL AND DEPARTURE

### KILLARNEY AND AROUND

**By plane** Kerry's airport (☎ 066 976 4644, ⊚ kerryairport. ie) is 15km from Killarney on the N23, 2km northeast of the village of Farranfore, which is on the Tralee–Killarney train line. Buses between Limerick and Killarney (plus a few Tralee–Killarney services) call at the airport roughly every 2hr; a taxi into town costs about €25 (a list of taxi drivers is listed on the airport website).

**By train** Killarney's train station is very centrally placed, off East Avenue Rd.

Destinations Cork (6–9 daily, often with a change at Mallow; 1hr 30min–2hr); Dublin (6–9 daily, most with a change at Mallow; 3hr–3hr 30min); Farranfore (7–8 daily; 20min); Tralee (7–8 daily; 40min).

**By bus** The Bus Éireann station is on Park Rd, while Citylink

buses use East Avenue Rd.

Destinations Bus Éireann: Caherdaniel (July & Aug 1 daily; 2hr 15min); Cahersiveen (July & Aug 1–3 daily, rest of year Mon–Sat 2 daily; 1hr 30min); Cork (hourly; 1hr 30min); Dingle, changing at Tralee (2–5 daily; 2–3hr); Dingle, via Inch and Anascaul (July & Aug Mon–Sat 2 daily; 1hr 20min); Kenmare (via Kilgarvan; July & Aug 2–3 daily, rest of year Mon–Fri 2 daily; 50min); Kerry Airport (Farranfore; 6–7 daily; 20min); Killorglin (4–6 daily; 30min); Limerick (5–6 daily; 2hr); Ring of Kerry (July & Aug 1 daily; 5hr 15min, with a break in Sneem); Tralee (10–16 daily; 40min); Waterford (hourly; 4hr 10min); Waterville (July & Aug 1–2 daily, rest of year Mon–Sat 1 daily; 1hr 55min).

Citylink (⊚ citylink.ie): Galway (2 daily; 2hr 45min).

## GETTING AROUND AND INFORMATION

**Bike rental** O'Sullivan's, Beech Rd opposite the tourist office (☎ 064 663 1282, ⊚ killarneyrentabike.com), as well as from several of the hostels.

**Car rental** Budget (⊚ budget.ie) has a car-rental outlet at the airport (☎ 066 976 3199).

**Taxis** There's a taxi rank on College St or call, for example, Euro Taxis (☎ 064 663 7676).

**Tourist office** The tourist office is on Beech Rd (June–Sept Mon–Sat 9am–6pm, Sun 9am–1pm; Oct–May Mon–Sat 9am–5pm; ☎ 064 663 1633, ⊚ killarney.ie).

## ACCOMMODATION

### SEE MAP PAGE 270

It's worth booking **accommodation** in Killarney in advance, but there are scores of B&Bs, upmarket guesthouses and hotels in town – if none of the listings below can fit you in, the friendly tourist office should be able to help.

**The Brehon** 1km south of town on the N71 Muckross Rd ☎ 064 663 0700, ⊚ thebrehon.com. Imposing and stylish contemporary hotel with 125 spacious and well-equipped rooms, a fine restaurant, *Danú*, and an excellent spa. All guests have free access to the spa's vitality suite, and to the comprehensive leisure centre at the adjacent *Gleneagles Hotel*. €169

**The Copper Kettle** 5 York Terrace, Lewis Rd ☎ 064 663 4164. Pleasant B&B on the north side of the town centre

with a variety of tasteful en-suite rooms, all with cable TV, some with Jacuzzis and king-size beds. €90

**Fairview** College St ☎ 064 663 4164, ⊚ killarney fairview.com. Attractive and welcoming central hotel with good-sized, well-appointed rooms (some with Jacuzzi) as well as an accomplished restaurant and lounge bar. €110

**Great Southern Hotel** East Avenue ☎ 064 663 8000, ⊚ greatsouthernkillarney.com. This ivy-clad Victorian railway hotel comes with chandeliers and marble floors in the huge lobby, an ornate gilded ceiling in the breakfast room, and attractive guest rooms, especially in the original building. Also has extensive gardens with two tennis courts plus a spa and swimming pool. €250

8

**Loch Lein Country House Hotel** Fossa, 5km west of town off the N72 ☎ 064 663 1260, ⓦ lochlein.com. A good-value choice if you'd prefer to stay away from the town's bustle, this peaceful, welcoming and well-run small hotel has views of Lough Leane and the mountains, spacious, tastefully decorated rooms and a restaurant that specializes in local produce. €160

**Muckross Park Hotel** N71, about 5km south of town ☎ 064 662 3400, ⓦ muckrosspark.com. Dating from 1795, and much extended since, this opulent hotel is right opposite the entrance to Muckross Friary, giving immediate access to the national park trails (bicycles available free of charge). Some rooms have four-posters and views of the Blue Pool River, and there are eighteen two-bedroom apartments. There's a fine spa and good restaurant. A complimentary shuttle bus operates between the hotel and town. €200

**Old Weir Lodge** Muckross Rd, a 10min walk from the centre ☎ 064 663 5593, ⓦ oldweirlodge.com. Thirty-room, mock-Tudor guesthouse that feels like a hotel, with spacious, well-equipped and comfortable rooms. It retains a personal touch, with a warm welcome and plenty of local information. €130

**The Ross Hotel** East Avenue Rd ☎ 064 663 1855, ⓦ the ross.ie. Luxurious boutique hotel right at the heart of the action, with bright bedrooms and excellent service. Guests are free to use the 20m indoor swimming pool, gym, sauna, Jacuzzi and outdoor hot tub at sister hotel, *The Park*, across the road. €190

## HOSTELS

**Killarney International Hostel** 5km west of town just off the Killorglin road ☎ 064 663 1240, ⓦ anoige. ie. Well-run, eco-conscious hostel in a renovated eighteenth-century country house in spacious grounds, with an open fire in the large common rooms and over 130 beds, including single and double/twin rooms (both standard and "deluxe"; no en suites) and four- to ten-bed dorms. Laundry facilities available. Catch the Bus Éireann service towards Killorglin to Fossa Cross, then it's a 5min walk up the Dingle road. Closed Nov–Feb. Dorms €17, doubles €50 ("deluxe" rooms €60)

★ **Neptune's Hostel** Bishop's Lane, off New St (IHH) ☎ 064 663 5255, ⓦ neptuneshostel.com. Ecofriendly central hostel, huge but welcoming, with plenty of local information on offer. There's a superb choice of three- to eight-bed dorms, twins, doubles and singles, some en-suite; laundry facilities and free luggage storage. Simple breakfast included. Dorms €16, doubles €50

## CAMPSITE

**Fleming's White Bridge** 1km east of town, signposted off the N22 Cork road ☎ 064 663 1590, ⓦ killarney camping.com. Among several campsites around Killarney, this quiet spot on the banks of the River Flesk has a summertime shop, two laundries, a campers' kitchen, games room, TV lounge and bike rental. Closed Nov to mid-March. €31

## EATING

SEE MAP PAGE 270

**The Bricín** 26 High St ☎ 064 663 4902, ⓦ bricin.ie. Homely restaurant that serves traditional Irish food, notably filled boxties (potato pancakes), as well as more eclectic dishes such as Thai red chicken curry with jasmine rice in a coconut milk sauce. Early-bird (€23 for two courses before 6.45pm) and set three-course menus (from €38) available. Tues–Sat 6–9pm.

**Cellar One** The Ross Hotel, East Avenue Rd ☎ 064 663 1855, ⓦ theross.ie. Cool cellar restaurant where the wine store has become part of the decor, enhanced by a dramatic curving glass staircase. Seasonal produce from local suppliers is used wherever possible in dishes such as tequila prawns with chilli and garlic butter and coriander scented basmati rice; leave room for the bread and butter pudding with ice cream for dessert. €34 for two courses, €42 for three. Daily 6–9pm; closed Mon–Thurs in winter.

**Gaby's Seafood Restaurant** 27 High St ☎ 064 663 2519. Killarney's finest and most expensive seafood restaurant, formal but not at all stuffy, serving platters of seafood (€30) and lobster from the tanks in the front window. Non-seafood lovers are catered for with rack of

lamb, beef sirloin or fillet steak. Mon–Sat 6–10pm.

**Jam** Old Market Lane, off Main St ☎ 064 663 7716. Branch of Kenmare's thoroughly modern bakery-café, serving an array of beguiling pastries, cakes, scones, sandwiches, quiches (€9 with two salads) and soups. Mon–Sat 8am–5.30pm, Sun 10am–5.30pm.

**Milano** 16 Main St ☎ 064 662 0620, ⓦ milano.ie. Typically fresh, contemporary setting for the Irish version of Britain's *Pizza Express*, offering a huge range of top-notch pizzas (from €11) plus salads and simple pastas. Mon–Thurs & Sun noon–10pm, Fri & Sat noon–11pm.

**Murphy's** 37 Main St ☎ 087 052 3145, ⓦ murphysice cream.ie. Branch of Dingle's excellent ice-cream shop (eat in or take away) with deckchairs out on the street in summer. Also serves cakes and coffees. Daily noon–10pm.

**Quinlan's Seafood Bar** 77 High St ☎ 064 662 0666, ⓦ seafoodbar.ie. Branch of Tralee's superior fish'n'chip shop – take away or tuck into dishes such as lemon sole, crab, scallops or deep water Atlantic prawns (€13.95) in the informal seafood restaurant. Daily noon–9pm.

## DRINKING AND NIGHTLIFE

SEE MAP PAGE 270

**Buckley's** Arbutus Hotel, College St ☎ 064 663 1037, ⓦ arbutuskillarney.com. Smartly refurbished traditional

bar with long, sociable bench seats and Irish music sessions Fri & Sat, plus Sun lunch time and evening. Mon–Sat

10.30am–2.30am, Sun 12.30pm–2.30am.

**Courtney's** 24 Plunkett St ☎ 064 663 2689, ⓦ courtneys bar.com. Appealingly plain, bare-wood and stone-floored pub, popular among a 20-something crowd, with a great range of whiskeys and beers. In the summer, it hosts traditional music Wed and Thurs, live bands on Fri and DJ sessions on Sat. Mon–Thurs 2–11.30pm, Fri & Sat 2pm–12.30am, Sun 2–11pm.

**Jimmy O'Brien's** Fair Hill ☎ 087 961 3482. The yellow and green facade gives the game away – this traditional lounge bar is a veritable museum of Kerry Gaelic football,

hung with dozens of photos (plus material on the notably lively dance music and *sean-nós* singing of Sliabh Lucra, the mountains to the east of Killarney). Decent pint of Guinness, too. Mon–Thurs 1–11.30pm, Fri 1pm–12.30am, Sat noon–12.30am, Sun noon–11pm.

**The Killarney Grand (aka Sheehan's)** Main St ☎ 064 663 1159, ⓦ killarneygrand.com. A large but often crowded bar with nightly live entertainment: ballads or traditional music 9–11pm, with a cover charge for bands and a club after 11pm (after 10pm on Sat), and for set dancing on Wed evenings (9pm). Mon–Sat 7.30pm–2.30am, Sun 7.30pm–1.30am.

# The Iveragh Peninsula: the Ring of Kerry

The **Ring of Kerry** is often used as a substitute name for the **Iveragh Peninsula**, but more properly it refers to the 175km road that encircles this vast, scenic leg of land. Tourists have been coming to the peninsula in ever-increasing numbers over the past century, but most of them do the Ring by bus or car in a day from Killarney. If you stay in one of the Iveragh's few small towns or venture off the main route, for example onto the **Ring of Skellig** at the very tip, you'll have to yourself this giant's landscape of mountains, lakes and long ocean views, which is at its most spectacular when illuminated by a sudden shaft of light through the clouds like a flash bulb.

**GETTING AROUND**                                        **THE IVERAGH PENINSULA: THE RING OF KERRY**

**By bus** Bus Éireann circles the whole Ring only in July and Aug (I daily; 1hr 15 min, with a break In Sneem), at other times venturing out of Killarney only as far as Waterville (1hr 55 min) via the north coast.

**On foot** You can walk around the peninsula on the Kerry Way (see page 278).

**By bike** Cycling, often up steep gradients and against strong winds, is a shorter option than walking (three days at the least), but perhaps just as physically demanding. The waymarked 215km Ring of Kerry Cycle Route (map guide available from local tourist offices) of necessity follows the main road for around a third of its journey, but includes

---

## THE KERRY WAY AND CARRAUNTOOHIL

The 213km-long **Kerry Way** is a spectacular, circular, waymarked footpath that starts in Killarney, takes in the Muckross Estate, Torc Waterfall, the Upper Lake and the Black Valley before crossing to Glencar, then goes right around the Iveragh Peninsula anticlockwise, with short offshoots to Glenbeigh, Cahersiveen, Waterville and Caherdaniel, finally passing through Sneem and Kenmare. Mostly following a network of green roads, many of which are old "butter roads", the route provides magnificent views both of the Iveragh's mountains and of the neighbouring peninsulas, Dingle and Beara. OS 1:50,000 **map** numbers 78 and 83 are essential, and Cork Kerry Tourism produces a useful *Kerry Way Map Guide*. The whole thing can be done in nine or ten days, or, with careful study of bus timetables, you could do day-walks along the Way beyond Glenbeigh in summer, or on the section between Glenbeigh and Waterville in winter.

An excellent **website**, ⓦ kerryway.com, provides trail descriptions, maps and full details of hostels and other walker-friendly accommodation, offering services such as luggage transfer, evening meals and packed lunches, along the route.

Experienced walkers may well be tempted off the Kerry Way to tackle Ireland's highest peak, **Carrauntoohil** (1038m). Two of the finest approaches are described in *Best Irish Walks* by Josh Lynam: the Coomloughra Horseshoe, a seven-hour, occasionally vertiginous circuit, starting from the bridge at Breanlee on the Beaufort–Glencar road, which also takes in the second- and third-highest peaks, Beenkeragh and Caher; and a tough, nine-hour Macgillicuddy Reeks ridge walk, beginning at *Kate Kearney's Cottage*, bagging six peaks and ending at the Breanlee bridge.

a long, scenic loop through Ballinskelligs, Portmagee and Valentia Island, and covers the north coast of the peninsula and the area around Killarney almost entirely on minor roads. Coach tours from Killarney, which ply the Ring of Kerry in flotillas in summer, are required to travel anticlockwise: you can weigh up the disadvantages of getting stuck in a convoy against meeting the buses on the many blind corners. We've covered the Ring anticlockwise.

## Cahersiveen

CAHERSIVEEN (sometimes spelt Caherciveen or Cahirsiveen, but always pronounced with the stress on the last syllable) is the main service town for the west end of the peninsula. Functional rather than attractive, its one long, narrow street is at various points named East End, Church Street, Main Street and New Street. Cahersiveen holds a lively **music and arts festival** (ⓦcelticmusicfestival.com) over the bank holiday weekend at the beginning of August, which has attracted big names such as Sinead O'Connor and the Hothouse Flowers. By the side of the N70 as it enters the town from the east is a striking local landmark, Éamonn O'Doherty's *To the Skelligs*. Installed in 1995, the sculpture depicts Brendan the Navigator (see page 316) and fellow monks making their way to the islands.

### O'Connell Memorial Church

Main St • Hours variable • Free

The town's most famous son was Daniel O'Connell (see page 574), to whom the **O'Connell Memorial Church** on the main street was dedicated – a remarkable tribute for a politician. Built between 1888 and 1902, largely with money from the US and Australia, it's a huge, lumbering edifice made of concrete, faced with Irish granite.

### The Old Barracks

Bridge St • April–Oct Mon–Sat 10am–5pm; Nov–March Mon–Fri 10am–4pm • €4 • ☎ 066 401 0430, ⓦtheoldbarrackscahersiveen.com

The heritage centre in the fearsome castle-like **Barracks**, has been renovated with new exhibits on local history but still retains its external appearance of an atmospheric ruin. The interpretation includes the story of the Fenian Rising of 1867 and the Easter Rising of 1916. Stories about the life and times of Daniel O'Connell with touch screens are spread over two floors. There's also a café, craft shop and tourist information. The construction of these heavily fortified quarters for the Royal Irish Constabulary was prompted by the 1867 rising when local Republicans tried to cut the transatlantic cable at Valentia.

---

**ARRIVAL AND INFORMATION**  CAHERSIVEEN

**By bus** Buses from/to Killarney (2 daily; 1hr 30min) stop at the Market House petrol station/supermarket on Glenbeigh Rd.

**Tourist office** Old Barracks, Quay St (June–Sept Mon–Sat 9.30am–1pm & 2–5pm; Oct–May Mon–Fri 9am–1pm & 2–5pm; ☎066 947 1300, ⓦcahersiveen.ie). Pick up details of the Beentee (8km) and Laharn (12km) loop walks and of attractive spots on the nearby Bolus Head peninsula that are accessible on foot or by bike, including a ruined fifteenth-century tower house, a couple of well-preserved ring forts and the sandy beach of White Strand.

**Bike rental** Casey's, New St (€16/day; ☎066 947 2474, ⓦbikehirekerry.com).

---

### SKYWALK ROPE BRIDGE

Thrill-seekers will love Ireland's longest rope bridge, the **Skywalk** (Feb–Dec daily 9am till dusk; €8; ☎066 947 7975, ⓦkellsbay.ie). Known as a Burmese Rope Bridge and with a span of 34m, it is positioned 11m above the Delligeenagh River in **Kells Bay House & Gardens**, halfway between Glenbeigh and Cahersiveen on the Ring of Kerry, just south of Kells Bay beach. Spectacular views from the bridge look across to the **gardens**, which were planted more than 160 years ago and include rare flowers and ferns from the Himalayas. The admission ticket includes access to both the rope bridge and the gardens – while you're here, be sure to seek out Ireland's largest **palm tree**, found in the Succulent Garden at the front of the house: a staggering eleven-tonne specimen with a 7.5m trunk imported from Chile.

## ACCOMMODATION

**The Final Furlong** 1.5km from the town on the road to Killorglin ☎ 066 947 3300, ⊛ thefinalfurlong.com. Pleasant, seafront, en-suite B&B accommodation on a working farm. Discounts for longer stays. April & Oct open by prior arrangement only; closed Nov–March. **€70**

**Mannix Point Camping and Caravan Park** West side of town ☎ 066 947 2806, ⊛ campinginkerry.com. Welcoming and very well equipped waterfront campsite which features evening impromptu music sessions in the evening. Closed mid-Sept to Easter. **€26**

★ **Quinlan & Cooke** 3 Main St ☎ 066 947 2244, ⊛ qc.ie. Beautifully designed, wood-panelled rooms in a boutique townhouse with a separate street door behind the restaurant (*QC's*); large and bright with comfy beds, iPod docks, espresso machines and power showers. There's also a spacious sitting room, a sun deck and a gym. Continental breakfasts are taken in your room. **€149**

**Sive Townhouse** 15 New Market St ☎ 087 275 4561, ⊛ sivetownhouse.com. Friendly, family-run budget hotel with simple but colourful rooms – singles, doubles, triples and family – plus a sitting room and laundry facilities. Substantial breakfast included. **€65**

## EATING

**An Bonnán Buí (McCarthy's)** 11A West Main St, a few doors west of QC's ☎ 066 948 1731. Good, varied pub grub such as chicken, burgers, or fish with prices from €13 can be had at this welcoming place, which has a beer garden and is a likely spot for traditional music in summer. Mon–Thurs noon–11.30pm, Fri & Sat noon–12.30am, Sun noon–11pm.

**Petit Delice** 11 Main St, a few doors east of QC's ☎ 087 990 3572. Small but authentic French patisserie and café, serving quiches, filled baguettes, croissants and artisan breads, and loved by the Cahersiveen caffeine cognoscenti. Don't leave without sampling a drool-worthy mille-feuille vanilla slice (€4). Mon–Sat 8am–6pm.

**O'Neills The Point** 5km west at Reenard Point ☎ 066 947 2165, ⊛ oneillsthepoint.ie. Located at the terminus of the Valentia Island ferry (see page 280), this pub-restaurant is very popular for its high-quality seafood (lobster, monkfish, crab claws and so on). Mon–Thurs 12.30–11.30pm, Fri & Sat 12.30pm–12.30am, Sun 12.30–11pm; closed for two (variable) months in winter, then open only on weekend evenings in the shoulder season.

★ **Quinlan & Cooke** 3 Main St ☎ 066 947 2244, ⊛ qc. ie. One of the best places to eat on the Ring of Kerry, a nautical-themed bar-restaurant with a lovely, covered back patio. As the owners' family have their own boats and fish-processing factory, seafood is, unsurprisingly, the speciality, in dishes such as hake fillet on a broth of smoked haddock, Atlantic prawns, and sizzling Valentia crab claws (€16.50). Also has a cheaper lunch menu and a keenly priced early bird until 6.45pm (€21 for two courses). Easter–Sept Mon–Sat noon–9.30pm, Sun 5.30–9.30pm; Oct–Easter Thurs & Sun 5.30–9.30pm, Fri & Sat noon–3pm & 5.30–9.30pm, with longer hours during holidays.

**8**

# Portmagee

The attractive harbour village of **PORTMAGEE** is the jumping-off point by road for Valentia, situated beside the long bridge to the island.

## The Skellig Experience

**Visitor centre** Daily: March & Nov 10am–5pm; April–June, Sept & Oct 10am–6pm; July & Aug 10am–7pm; last admission 45min before closing • €5 • **Cruises** Standard cruises 2hr (subject to demand – contact the centre in the morning); in worse weather, 45min mini-cruises around Valentia channel occasionally laid on • Standard ticket €40, including admission to the visitor centre; mini-cruise €28, including admission to the visitor centre • ☎ 066 947 6306, ⊛ skelligexperience.com

Portmagee's **Skellig Experience**, which is actually just across the bridge from the village, gives some fascinating background on seabirds and other marine life, lighthouses and early monastic life, with an impressive short film about Skellig Michael. The centre also has a café with fine views of Portmagee, and runs **cruises** around, but not on to, Skellig Michael, which are useful for those who can't manage the 650 steps to the island's summit.

## ACCOMMODATION AND EATING　　　　　　　　　　　　　PORTMAGEE

★ **The Moorings** 7 Harbour View ☎ 066 947 7108, ⊛ moorings.ie. Tastefully decorated and well-equipped accommodation is available – it's worth paying extra for a room overlooking the harbour – at this well-run, eco-conscious inn, which offers various half-board deals and activities packages. Sumptuous hot and cold seafood platters are served here and there's traditional music on Fri (with set dancing) and most Sun nights; music and storytelling on Tues in July and Aug, and a festival of music and dancing over the May bank holiday weekend. Bar/restaurant Mon–Thurs & Sun 8.30am–11.30pm, Fri & Sat 8.30am–1am. **€130**

## Valentia Island

Separated from the mainland by a long, narrow channel that's now bridged, **VALENTIA** barely feels like an island. For such a small, remote spot, it boasts a surprising number of claims to fame: as well as being known from the radio shipping forecasts and for Valentia slate, which was used for the Houses of Parliament in London and the Paris Opera House, it was from here that the first transatlantic telegraph cable was laid in 1866. To add to the island's repute, the oldest fossilized footprints in the northern hemisphere, the so-called Tetrapod Trackway, were discovered here in 1992 by a Swiss geology student. Most of the island's amenities are in or around **Knightstown** at the northeastern tip, which provides dramatic views of the Iveragh Mountains, as well as a seasonal **ferry** link to the mainland.

At the western edge of the village, the **Valentia Heritage Centre** (April–Sept daily 10.30am–5.30pm; €3.50; ☎066 947 6411) houses a display on the island's history in the old primary school.

### Glanleam House

In the northern part of the island, 2km west of Knighstown • Gardens daily: 10am–7pm April–Oct; 10am–4pm Nov–March • €6 • ☎066 947 6176, �🌐glanleam.com

Walking up School House Road from the heritage centre, then forking right, will bring you after about 1km to **Glanleam House**, which was formerly the seat of the Knight of Kerry. Developed in the 1850s, the beautiful subtropical **gardens** here encompass lily-of-the-valley trees, ferns and other exotic specimens from South America, Australasia and China, which thrive in this mild, sheltered location. For children, there's a pirate trail and a fairy garden.

### Tetrapod Trackway

About 5km from Knightstown near the island's northernmost tip, it's possible to see for yourself the **Tetrapod Trackway**, though you might have to show some perseverance as it's not very well signposted (basically, head up School House Road from the heritage centre and take the second right). From a car park by the island's radio station, a short path leads down to a precarious shelf of black rock by the Atlantic, on which the small foot- and tail-prints of the creature – a metre-long, crocodile-like amphibian with a large, paddle-shaped tail, that lived some 385 million years ago – are quite clearly visible. What can feel like the end of the world on a stormy day is a suitably awesome location to come toe-to-toe with our first landborne ancestors.

### Valentia Island Farmhouse Dairy

1km southwest of Knightstown on the main island road, the R565 • May–Oct daily 11am–6pm (July & Aug til 7pm) • ☎087 349 7385, �🌐valentiaicecream.ie

This traditional **dairy farm** makes its own delicious ice cream, which it sells at its farm and craft shop. It also offers sightseeing tours of the area around Knightstown in a horse-and-carriage (€9/person; booking recommended).

### Geokaun Mountain and Bray Head

Geokaun Mountain car parking €6; pedestrians and cyclists €3 • �🌐geokaun.com

Near the middle of the north coast, the spectacular **Fogher Cliffs** and **Geokaun Mountain**, the island's highest point, have been turned into a viewing area, with the installation of fifty information panels and a 1500m loop walk. Further exciting views are provided by the ruined lookout tower on **Bray Head**, at the southwestern end of the island.

---

**ARRIVAL AND INFORMATION**　　　　　　　　　　　　　**VALENTIA ISLAND**

**By ferry** From Reenard Point, 5km west of Cahersiveen (see page 278), a ferry operates a continuous shuttle service across to Knightstown on Valentia Island (April–Oct Mon–Sat 7.45am–9.30pm, Sun 9am–9.30pm (July & Aug last ferry 10pm); cars €10 return; cyclists €3 return; ☎087 241 8973).

**Tourist office** 2 Watchhouse Cottages, Knightstown, almost opposite the clock tower (May–Sept Tues–Sun

10am–5pm, Oct–April Mon–Fri 10am–5pm; ☎066 947 6985, ⓦvalentiaisland.ie). In front of the office, kayaking, sailing and other watersports are available in summer (☎086 871 7846).

## ACCOMMODATION

**Atlantic Villa** Behind the Y-junction at the church in Knightstown ☎087 212 6798, ⓦatlanticvilla.ie. Overlooking the sea in the nineteenth-century former cable-master's house, this B&B offers five pleasant en-suite bedrooms, fresh produce from their organic garden for breakfast, open fires and a sauna. Two self-catering cottages also available. **€80**

★ **Glanleam House** About 2km west of Knightstown ☎066 947 6176, ⓦglanleam.com. This elegant eighteenth- and nineteenth-century house set in subtropical gardens offers delightful accommodation in spacious rooms, with especially attractive bathrooms and views of Valentia Harbour. Dinner available if booked the previous day. Good rates for singles; self-catering cottages available. Closed early Nov to mid-March. **€165**

## EATING

**Pod** By the church in Knightstown ☎066 947 6995. Cheery pancake café and gift shop with outdoor tables, serving imaginative savoury galettes (€12 for local crab), sweet crêpes and espresso coffees. Summer daily 10/10.30am–8pm.

**The Royal Pier** Knightstown ☎066 947 6144, ⓦroyal valentia.ie. The town's landmark 200-year-old inn enjoys glorious views of the harbour and the mainland mountains from its seafront lawn, serves delectable dishes such as chowder, or fish and chips (€17.50) for lunch and dinner (not Jan & Feb) and hosts traditional music on Wed and Sun nights. Mon–Thurs 10.30am–11.30pm, Fri & Sat 10.30am–12.30am, Sun noon–11pm.

# The Skellig Islands

8

*An incredible, impossible, mad place…I tell you the thing does not belong to any world that you and I have lived and worked in: it is part of our dream world…*

George Bernard Shaw

A voyage to the **Skelligs** (Na Scealga, "the crags"), islands of durable Old Red Sandstone that rise sharply from the sea 12km off the tip of the Iveragh Peninsula, is one of the most exciting and inspiring trips you can make in Ireland. On top of the larger of these two inhospitable, shark's-tooth islands, **Skellig Michael** (or Great Skellig), a monastery was somehow constructed in the late seventh or early eighth century, in imitation of the desert communities of the early Church fathers, and dedicated to St Michael, the patron saint of high places. The exposed, often choppy boat-ride out, followed by seabirds from Puffin Island, a nature reserve at the edge of St Finan's Bay, only adds to the sense of wild isolation. **Little Skellig** is a nature reserve too, crawling with over fifty thousand gannets; landing is forbidden, but the boatmen will come in close so you can watch the gannets diving for fish and hear their awesome din.

The Skelligs have been thrust into the international spotlight in recent years with the filming of scenes of the latest Star Wars films (*The Force Awakens* and *The Last Jedi*) in 2014 and 2015. The main island was occupied for several weeks by camera crews when Luke Skywalker took up residence. Not everyone, though, was pleased about the Irish government's decision to permit filming and allow helicopter traffic. It was criticised by heritage and ecological experts, as well as Birdwatch Ireland, who expressed concerns about the welfare of the colonies of puffin, Manx shearwaters, kittiwakes, and storm petrels that breed here.

## Skellig Michael

If you come in spring or early summer, you'll have thousands of cute breeding puffins to keep you company on the 200m ascent from Skellig Michael's quay. The compact, remarkably well-preserved **monastery** in the lee of the summit is a miracle of ingenuity and devotion. It was built entirely on artificial terraces, facing south–southeast for maximum sunlight, with sturdy outer walls to deflect the winds and to protect the vegetable patch made of bird droppings; channels crisscross the settlement to funnel rainwater into cisterns. You can walk into the **dry-stone beehive huts**, **chapels** and **refectory**, which would have sheltered a total of twelve to fifteen monks at any one time and have withstood the worst the Atlantic can throw at them for 1300 years. The high cross beside the large oratory probably marks the burial of the founder, reputed to have been St Fionán, or an early saint.

At least three Viking raids in the ninth century were not enough to dislodge the monks, but during the climatic change of the twelfth and thirteenth centuries, the seas became rougher and more inhospitable. Around the same time, pressure was brought to bear on the old independent monasteries to conform, and the monks adopted the Augustinian rule and moved to Ballinskelligs on the mainland. Pilgrimages to Skellig Michael, however, continued until the eighteenth century, even after the Dissolution of the Monasteries.

A **visit to the island** is only for those with good mobility, as there's a vertical ladder up on to the quay, and then 640 steep, uneven steps with unprotected edges – slippery when wet – to the windy summit (the alternative is a cruise around the islands). Bring walking shoes, warm waterproof clothes, water and food (but take all litter away with you), as there are no facilities on Skellig Michael (toilets are on the boats).

### ARRIVAL AND INFORMATION                                      THE SKELLIG ISLANDS

**BY BOAT**
Only a dozen operators are allowed to land on Skellig Michael (May–Sept, sometimes with extra departures April & Oct, dependent on the weather); they need to be booked the day before your trip at the latest. However, there's sometimes a delay of several days before the boats will sail, due to bad weather – the captains make a decision on the weather early each morning. The boats operate mostly from Portmagee (departing 10–11am; 45min–1hr to reach Skellig Michael; allow at least 2hr on the island; from €50/person).

**Operators** John O'Shea departs from Caherdaniel (€100/person for a 6hr 30min trip; ☏ 087 689 8431, ⓦ skelligtours.com). A complete list of operators is available from local tourist offices and on ⓦ valentiaisland.ie. Most accommodation owners in the area will offer to do the booking for you, which is the easiest way to arrange your trip.

**Cruises** Cruises around the islands are offered by the Skellig Heritage Centre (see page 279) and Skellig Michael Cruises (☏ 087 617 8114; ⓦ skelligmichaelcruises.com); both charge €40 for a 2hr 30min cruise around the islands from Portmagee harbour.

## The Ring of Skellig

To the south of Portmagee runs the **Ring of Skellig**, a scenic though often very steep route around the most westerly promontory of the Iveragh Peninsula, via wild and exposed **St Finan's Bay** – which is the unlikely home of the high-quality **Skelligs Chocolate Factory** (visitors welcome to taste and buy: Feb–Easter & mid-Sept to mid-Dec Mon–Fri 10am–4.30pm; Easter to mid-Sept Mon–Fri 10am–5pm, Sat & Sun 11am/noon–5/5.15pm; ☏ 066 947 9119, ⓦ skelligschocolate.com) and its seasonal coffee shop (Easter to mid-Sept). From the highest point of the road between Portmagee and St Finan's Bay, you can climb the hill on the seaward side of the saddle in twenty minutes or so for magnificent views out to the Skellig Islands, across to the Dingle Peninsula and the Blaskets, and inland to the Iveragh Mountains.

### Ballinskelligs (Baile an Sceilg)

On the far shore of the promontory lies the village of **BALLINSKELLIGS** (Baile an Sceilg; ⓦ visitballinskelligs.ie), set behind a lovely, curving, sheltered beach with great views of Waterville and the mountains, where Skelligs Watersports (☏ 087 917 8808, ⓦ skelligsurf.com) offers **surfing**, **wind-surfing**, **kayaking** and **stand-up paddleboarding**. The monks of Skellig Michael retreated here in the twelfth century, constructing a new **abbey** which in turn was largely rebuilt in the fifteenth century. By walking south along the shoreline for five minutes, beyond a ruined tower house, you can still see its delicate purple-grey sandstone church and traces of its cloister. The small but sprawling village of Ballinskelligs is part of a Gaeltacht (Irish-speaking) enclave, Uíbh Ráthach, and draws hosts of teenagers to Irish college in the summer.

The striking thatched roundhouse at the north end of the village is the **Cill Rialaig Art Centre** (mid-May to Aug daily 11am–5pm; Oct to mid-May by appointment Thurs– Sun 11am–5pm; ☎066 947 9277, ⓦcillrialaigartscentre.com) and café-restaurant (Wed–Sun noon–8pm). Attached to the Cill Rialaig retreat for artists, writers and composers, it hosts art workshops for children and adults in July and August.

## EATING                                                    BALLINSKELLIGS

**Caife Cois Tra** 6–10 Sunny Beach Holiday Homes ☎087 296 5874, ⓦfacebook.com/cafecoistra. In a beachside wooden chalet with plenty of outside tables on the grass, this café serves soup, sandwiches and home-baked cakes. It also houses a craft shop specializing in historical photographs. On Sun (11am–4pm) from June to Aug, there's a country market with live music. March–Oct daily 10am–6pm.

# Waterville

On the east side of Ballinskelligs Bay, **WATERVILLE** (An Coireán, "the little whirlpool") is an incongruously genteel resort in this distant wilderness. Its exposed, pebbly beach is backed by a long, grassy promenade – now sporting a statue of Charlie Chaplin, who spent several holidays here – and large, neat houses with well-tended lawns, many of them built for workers on the transatlantic telegraph cable, which was extended from Valentia to Waterville in the 1880s. August sees a five-day **festival of classic and contemporary films**, with attendant street entertainment and music (ⓦchaplinfilmfestival.com). There's no bank in Waterville but the post office behind the prominent *Butler Arms Hotel* on the seafront changes money.

**8**

## ACCOMMODATION AND EATING                                  WATERVILLE

**Butler Arms Hotel** Seafront ☎066 947 4144, ⓦbutler arms.com. Steeped in history, the *Butler Arms* has been welcoming guests to this part of Kerry since 1884, among them Charlie Chaplin, Walt Disney and the Queen of Tonga. There's a choice of dining, and in the sociable *Charlie's Restaurant*, overlooking Ballinskelligs Bay, you can enjoy fresh oysters, lobster and mussels, Thai-style monkfish curry, or rack of Kerry lamb (€26.95). Stylishly furnished standard and executive rooms come with an Atlantic view while six on the ground floor have garden views. €140

**Old Cable House** 9–10 Iveagh Terrace ☎066 947 4233, ⓦoldcablehouse.com. Set back from the seafront in part of the nineteenth-century cable station, this attractive and congenial establishment set in a pleasant garden offers good-value, en-suite accommodation. €99

**Smugglers' Inn** 1km north of the centre on the beach ☎066 947 4330, ⓦthe-smugglers-inn.com. Comfortable upmarket rooms are provided by this well-run inn, a restored nineteenth-century farmhouse, which has the best views of Ballinskelligs Bay. Noted for its seafood such as prawn kataifi for starters and black sole for mains, it's your best bet for eating in Waterville, whether in the bar, the conservatory restaurant or the beer garden. Closed late Oct to early April. Food served daily noon–3pm & 6–8.30/9.30pm. €110

# Derrynane Bay and around

Beyond Waterville, the Ring of Kerry climbs steeply to the **Coomakista Pass**, where a viewing point affords glorious views of Deenish and Scariff islands in the foreground at the mouth of the Kenmare River, and Bull, Cow and tiny Calf islands off the end of the Beara Peninsula.

Hidden away beneath, at the southernmost point of the Iveragh Peninsula about 10km south of Waterville, is **Derrynane Bay** (pronounced "Derrynaan", meaning the "oak wood of St Fionán"). From the wide, sandy beach with 3km of dunes and good swimming, you can stroll across to atmospheric Abbey Island, which shelters a graveyard and ruined abbey, founded by St Fionán in around 700. At the inlet on the western side of the island causeway, Derrynane Sea Sports (☎087 908 1208, ⓦderrynaneseasports.com) offers canoeing, sailing, windsurfing and other **waterborne activities** in the summer. From here you can pick your way west for over 1km along a beautiful Mass Path – which formerly led worshippers to the secret Mass Rock at Derrynane House – to Béaltrá Pier; follow the lane uphill from the pier and turn onto the Kerry Way heading east back towards Derrynane House for a satisfying circular **walk** of a couple of hours or so. Above the bay, attractively sited on its steep eastern flank, the sprawling village of **Caherdaniel** is one of the most attractive bases on the Ring of Kerry.

### Derrynane House

Derrynane More, Caherdaniel • April–Nov 10.30am–5.30pm; entry half past the hour from 10.30 am to 4.30pm,• €5; Heritage Card • ☎ 066 947 5113, ⓦ derrynanehose.ie

On the north side of the bay, **Derrynane House** was once the home of, and is now a shrine to, **Daniel O'Connell**, the hugely popular, nonviolent campaigner who in 1829 achieved partial Catholic emancipation (see page 574). The plain, elegant house, which was largely rebuilt by the "Liberator" himself when he inherited it in 1825, contains all manner of memorabilia, as well as a tea room and a lively, 25-minute audiovisual that's well worth catching. The most striking relic is a chariot presented by Dubliners to O'Connell on his release from prison in 1844: modelled on a Roman triumphal car, with gold and purple silk, mouldings and armchairs, it carried him at the head of a crowd of 200,000 to his home in Merrion Square, Dublin.

The pretty **gardens** and wooded parklands around the house, accessible on signposted trails, have been declared a national historic park, and give onto the beach in Derrynane Bay.

### Staigue Fort and around

Around 7km east of Caherdaniel on the N70 a sign points left to **Staigue Fort**, near the village of Castlecove; there's a small visitor centre (summer daily 10am–9pm; €2.50) near the junction, attached to a café and friendly bar with outdoor tables. After 4km up a narrow road, you'll come to a sophisticated ring fort, at least 2000 years old, with 5m-high dry-stone walls surrounded by a bank and ditch; it's in an excellent state of preservation. Beyond Castlecove at Sneem, there's a fork in the main road eastward: a mountain road (the R568) heads up to **Moll's Gap** (see page 273) and from there to Killarney, while the less scenic N70 continues along the seashore to Kenmare.

---

**ACCOMMODATION AND EATING**  **DERRYNANE BAY AND AROUND**

**The Blind Piper** Caherdaniel ☎ 066 947 5126, ⓦ blindpiperpub.ie. Lovely old stone-built pub decorated with colourful flowers, with outdoor tables on a large lawn by the stream. You can eat well in either the bar or, in the summer, the restaurant, and you can often catch live music (Thurs & Sat in summer). Mon–Thurs 11am–11.30pm, Fri & Sat 11am–12.30am, Sun 12.30–11pm.

**Derryclare** Down the lane by the Scarriff Inn, 4km west of Caherdaniel on the N70 ☎ 066 947 5119, ⓦ iskeroon.

com. Set in a peaceful location in extensive, semi-tropical gardens running down to the sea. this delightful self-catering cottage sleeps six in two doubles and two singles. **€200**

**Traveller's Rest** On the main road in the centre of Caherdaniel ☎ 066 947 5175. Very good hostel in an attractive cottage, with small dorms (up to five beds) plus a well-equipped kitchen and a dining area with open fire. Closed Nov to mid-Feb. Dorms €18.50, doubles €43

# Kenmare

Sitting at the head of the Kenmare River – actually a narrow, 40km-long sea inlet – **KENMARE** is an excellent base for exploring not only the Ring of Kerry but also the **Beara Peninsula**, part of which, including the contrasting scenic beauties of **Gleninchaquin** valley and **Derreen Gardens**, lies in County Kerry. The cosmopolitan town is neat, with an array of restaurants and accommodation and a lively, sociable nightlife. Kenmare's major streets are Henry St (one-way, south–north) and Main St (one-way, north–south), which meet at Fair Green and are linked at their southern ends by Shelbourne St. Apart from its heritage centre, Kenmare's only sight as such is a Bronze Age **stone circle** on the riverbank, a five-minute walk from the Green (signposted). Around 17m in diameter, it's the largest of its kind in Kerry and may be orientated on the setting sun. At its centre stands a burial dolmen, three standing stones supporting a large capstone. Otherwise, there are some nice local **walks**, including 3km of trails in lovely **Reenagross Woodland Park**, which lies between the *Park Hotel* and the river; you can pick up a leaflet at the tourist office.

## Brief history

Kenmare was established after the 1652 Act of Settlement, which followed Cromwell's brutal campaign in Ireland and forced Irish landowners to give up their estates to English settlers. Sir William Petty, who mapped and allocated these forfeited lands, managed to get hold of a quarter of Kerry for himself, and in 1670 established **Nedeen** (or An Neidín, "the little nest") here, a colony of English and Welsh Protestants to work in his lead mines, pilchard fisheries and ironworks. His descendant, the first Marquis of Lansdowne, rebuilt the town on its current X-shape in 1775, with the pretty, tree-shaded **Fair Green** (which still belongs to the Lansdownes) at its fulcrum, and rechristened it **Kenmare** – mistranslating *Neidín* as "nest of thieves", he adapted an earlier Irish name, *Ceann Mara* ("head of the sea inlet"), with which he was also able to honour his good friend, Lord Kenmare. The town's colourful history is carefully detailed in the **heritage centre** at the back of the tourist office (same hours; free).

---

### ARRIVAL AND INFORMATION

**By bus** Buses stop at the top of Main St.
Destinations Castletownbere via Lauragh and Eyeries (July & Aug Mon–Sat 2 daily; 1hr 20min); Cork (via Glengarriff, Bantry, Skibbereen, Clonakilty, Kinsale and Cork Airport; July & Aug 1 daily; 4hr); Killarney (via Kilgarvan; July & Aug 2–3 daily, rest of year Mon–Fri 2 daily; 50min).

**Tourist information** Kenmare Heritage Centre, Henry St (Easter–June, Sept & Oct Mon–Fri 9.30am–5.15pm, July & Aug daily 9.30am–5.30pm; 064 664 1233, kenmare. ie).

**Bike rental** Finnegan's, at the top of Henry St (064 664 1083, finneganscycles.com).

### TOURS AND ACTIVITIES

**Tours** In summer Finnegan's (064 664 1491, kenmare coachandcab.com) runs scheduled minibus tours of the Ring of Kerry (Mon, Wed & Fri), Beara Peninsula (Tues) and Glengarriff and Garinish Island (Thurs); book at the tourist office or the Kenmare Lace Centre upstairs, or by phone.
**Cruises** Seafari run cruises (roughly April–Oct; 2–3hr; €25; 064 664 2059, seafariireland.com) from the pier, taking in the islands of the Kenmare River, a colony of a hundred seals and prolific birdlife.

**Activities** Based at Dauros, 6km away on the north shore of the Beara, Star Sailing and Adventure Centre (064 664 1222, staroutdoors.ie) lays on a range of activities including sailing and kayaking, as well as boat trips on the Kenmare River (1hr; €20). Diving trips and courses are on offer either from further along the Beara, at Kilmakilloge Harbour near Lauragh, or from Sneem (087 699 3793, kenmarebaydiving.com).

### ACCOMMODATION

**Fáilte** Corner of Shelbourne and Henry streets, near the post office (087 711 6092, kenmarehostel.com (IHH & IHO). Spacious, well-kept hostel in the town centre, with spick-and-span dorms and en-suite and standard private rooms, a cosy sitting room and a well-equipped kitchen. Closed mid-Oct to mid-May. Dorms €18, doubles €44
★ **Hawthorn House** Shelbourne St 064 664 1035, hawthornhousekenmare.com. Highly recommended spot in the centre of town: great hospitality, attractive, well-appointed, en-suite rooms, plenty of local information and fine breakfasts. Self-catering apartments also available. €100

**O'Donnabhain's** Henry St 064 664 2106, odonnabhain-kenmare.com. The large, bright, modern rooms, decorated in earth tones, at this friendly B&B are spread over several floors of a long, zigzagging building, so all are well away from the pub downstairs. Self-catering also available. Closed mid-Dec to mid-Jan. €115
★ **Park Hotel** Shelbourne St 064 664 1200, park kenmare.com. Dating from the late nineteenth century, this elegant luxury hotel stands in splendid grounds above the Kenmare River. Service is charming, and a stunning modern spa has been carefully blended into its leafy setting. There's an excellent restaurant with a tasting menu and a cheaper

casual brasserie, plus plenty of free activities such as guided walks and croquet. Closed early Dec to mid-Feb. **€410**

**Sallyport House** Off Shelbourne St, by the river ☎ 064 664 2066, ⓦ sallyporthouse.com. Spacious, upmarket guesthouse on the shore of the Kenmare River. Rooms are furnished with antiques and boast large bathrooms and fine views of the gardens or the harbour. Closed Nov–April. **€145**

**Silver Trees** Killowen Rd ☎ 064 664 1008, ⓦ silvertrees kenmare.com. A friendly, efficient and rather plush B&B, a 5min walk from the centre, opposite the golf course on the road towards Kilgarvan, with spacious, comfortable en-suite rooms. Good rates for singles. Closed Nov–Feb. **€70**

### EATING AND DRINKING

Kenmare has a good reputation for **eating out**, and now claims to be the only town in Ireland with more restaurants than pubs. Henry St and Main St shelter about a dozen **pubs**, so finding somewhere congenial to drink is straightforward, and many of them host traditional music once or twice a week.

**Crowley's** 26 Henry St ☎ 064 664 1472. Atmospheric old-time bar with a snug and communal seating around the walls, and traditional sessions on Mon, Tues & Wed in summer, Sun in winter. Mon–Thurs roughly 5.30–11.30pm, Fri & Sat 4pm–12.30am, Sun 4–11pm.

**Florry Batt's** Henry St. A traditional old-style Kerry bar with an open fire and regular music sessions. Worth a visit to sample a pint and soak up the local atmosphere. Mon–Thurs noon–11.30pm, Fri & Sat noon–12.30am, Sun noon–11pm.

**McCarthy's** Main St ☎ 064 664 1516, ⓦ pfskenmare. com. Lively, sociable spot that pulls in the 30-somethings with a popular food menu and early traditional sessions on Fri & Sun. Mon–Thurs noon–11.30pm, Fri & Sat noon–12.30am, Sun noon–11pm.

★ **Mulcahy's** 16 Main St ☎ 064 664 2383, ⓦ mulcahys kenmare.com. Crisp, modern decor and pricey but excellent creative cuisine with global influences, such as halibut with a mussel, bacon and clam cream sauce (€26). Summer Mon & Wed–Sun 5–10pm, shorter hours in winter.

**The Purple Heather** Henry St ☎ 064 664 1016, ⓦ the purpleheatherkenmare.com. A relaxing daytime bistro-bar, serving light meals such as home-made chicken-liver pâté with Cumberland sauce (€10.20). Mon–Sat 10.30am–6.30pm.

# South of Kenmare: the Beara Peninsula

To the south of Kenmare lies the **Beara Peninsula**, most of which is in County Cork (see page 259). At first the countryside here is green and thickly wooded, but head west on the R571 towards the end of the peninsula (served by buses from Kenmare in July and August), or uphill on the scenic N71 towards Glengarriff (also served by Kenmare buses in July and August), and the terrain soon becomes more windswept and lonely. The other main route across the peninsula is the R574, which heads south from Lauragh towards Adrigole, climbing to the county border at the narrow and dramatic **Healy Pass** and providing magnificent views.

## Bonane Heritage Park

Signposted off the N71, 8km from Kenmare • Open access but €5 entry fee • ☎ 083 106 0894, ⓦ bonaneheritagepark.com

Heading south from Kenmare, it's worth taking a short detour off the N71 to **Bonane Heritage Park**, where a large, grassed-over ringfort, a stone circle, and other ancient remains have been linked by a circular 2km gravel trail. There are fine views of the lush Sheen valley and the bare, wrinkly Caha Mountains behind.

## Gleninchaquin

Around 13km from Kenmare along the R571, it's well worth turning onto the dramatic minor road up **Gleninchaquin**, a narrow coomb valley which bowls out at its head around the eponymous lake. After 3km, you'll come upon **Uragh Stone Circle** in a truly magical setting: hemmed in by glaciated hills, on a slender rise between lakes Inchaquin and Uragh, with views down the valley and across to the Macgillycuddy Reeks.

### Gleninchaquin Park

Gleninchaquin • Daily 10am–5pm • €6 • ☎ 087 712 8553, ⓦ gleninchaquin.com

Five kilometres further up the valley road from Uragh Stone Circle, you'll reach **Gleninchaquin Park**, where easy-to-follow **walks** have been laid out around the head of the beautiful valley. It's not the wild, man-against-nature experience of the Beara Way, but it seems to be a neat solution to the problems between walkers and farmers that have been occurring in some parts of the country – and it's hard to get lost. The main two-hour **circular trail** takes you up via a corrie lake to the top of the waterfall. If you fancy an easier outing, there's a river and water garden walk (30min), a farm walk (1hr) and a heritage trail (90min).

## Derreen Gardens

Lauragh • Daily 10am–6pm • €8 • ☎ 087 430 8001, ⓦ derreengarden.com

On the northwest side of **Lauragh**, 25km southwest of Kenmare, the extensive, subtropical **Derreen Gardens** run down to the sea. Still owned by the descendants of Sir William Petty, they're planted with mature exotic species such as giant Australian ferns, Chilean myrtles, acacias, bamboo and mighty eucalyptus trees and are known especially for their rhododendrons. There are plenty of marked **trails** to keep you going for anything from thirty minutes to two hours, including paths along Kilmakilloge Harbour where a belvedere affords fine views across to the Iveragh Peninsula. Further opportunities for walking, and for cycling, are provided by the nearby *Pedals and Boots* café.

### ACCOMMODATION AND EATING            THE BEARA PENINSULA

**Pedals and Boots** At the post office on the R571 in Lauragh (west of the turn-off for Derreen Gardens) ☎ 064 668 3101, ⓦ pedalsandboots.ie. This café rustles up home-baked cakes, scones and biscuits, soups and sandwiches, and can provide info and maps for cycling and walking in the vicinity. June–Aug daily 10am–6pm; Sept–May Fri & Sat 11am–4pm.

# The Dingle Peninsula

*One wonders, in this place, why anyone is left in Dublin, or London, or Paris, when it would be better one would think, to live in a tent, or a hut, with this magnificent sea and sky, and to breathe this wonderful air, which is like wine in one's teeth.*

*J.M. Synge, In West Kerry*

The last of southwestern Ireland's five peninsulas, **Dingle** is perhaps the most distinctive of them all. Arrowing westwards for over 50km, its heavily glaciated topography is especially irregular, with an L-shaped ridge of mountains that peaks at its north end at **Mount Brandon**, the highest summit in Ireland outside of the Macgillycuddy Reeks. Five-hundred-metre **Mount Eagle** at the very tip of the peninsula sets up a spectacular drive, cycle or walk around **Slea Head.** On the coasts, the long, exposed sandbars at **Castlegregory** and **Inch** draw surfers and wind-surfers, while the deeply recessed sandy beaches at **Ventry** and **Smerwick Harbour** encourage gentle swimming.

Dingle has an unusually rich heritage, including over five hundred Celtic *clocháns* (corbelled, dry-stone beehive huts) and the early Christian **Gallarus Oratory**, with its stunningly simple dry-stone construction. The peninsula is also one of the strongest **Irish-speaking** districts in the country, known as **Corca Dhuibhne** (meaning "the followers of Davinia", a Celtic goddess). As the main settlement at the heart of this thriving Gaeltacht (which officially begins just west of Anascaul and Castlegregory), **Dingle town** (An Daingean) feels like a capital. It supports some top-notch restaurants and places to stay, complemented by a vibrant traditional music scene, and is perfectly located for varied day-trips. One of the best of these is the boat trip to the abandoned

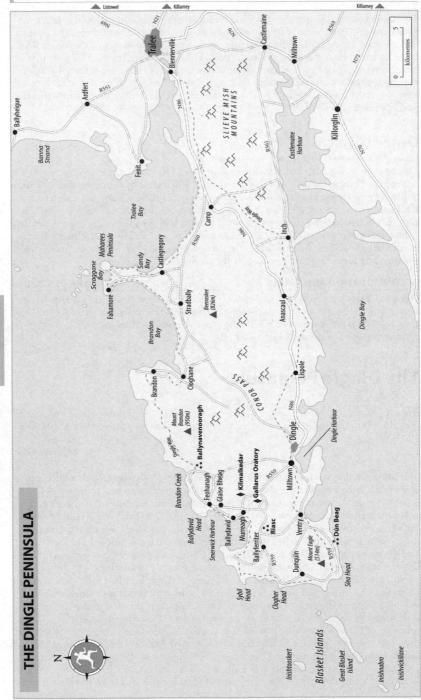

## THE DINGLE PENINSULA

**Blasket Islands** just off Slea Head, which were responsible for an astonishing body of Irish-language writing in the early twentieth century.

## The south coast

If you're heading towards Dingle town from Killarney or the Ring of Kerry, a direct, often narrow road, served by summertime buses from Killarney, will bring you along the peninsula's south coast, with fine views of Dingle Bay and the Iveragh Peninsula. At **Inch**, a dune-covered sandbar with a beautiful 5km-long beach on its western side thrusts out into the bay, mirrored by Rossbeigh Strand over on the Iveragh. In the summer, Kingdom Waves offer **surfing** lessons, board and wetsuit rental (☎087 744 7958, ⍟kingdomwaves.com).

**EATING AND DRINKING**  **THE SOUTH COAST**

★ **The South Pole Inn** Anascaul, 7km west of Inch ☎066 915 7388, ⍟southpoleinn.com. Founded in 1927 by local man, Tom Crean, unsung hero of Shackleton's and Scott's Antarctic expeditions, this pub is an atmospheric and very congenial spot in a pretty riverside location. Hung with polar memorabilia and photos, it offers traditional music most Saturdays (plus Sundays in summer) and food. Mon–Thurs noon–11.30pm, Fri & Sat noon–12.30am, Sun noon–11pm.

## Dingle town (An Daingean)

Sheltered from the ravages of the Atlantic by its impressive natural harbour, **DINGLE** is an excellent base, not only for exploring the western end of the peninsula ("back west" as it's known locally), but also for a variety of water-borne activities. Even if the weather gets the better of you, there are plenty of welcoming cafés, restaurants

**8**

| ■ ACCOMMODATION | | ● EATING | | | | ■ DRINKING & NIGHTLIFE | |
|---|---|---|---|---|---|---|---|
| Ashe's | 5 | An Café Liteártha | 6 | Murphy's Ice Cream | 3 | Adam's | 4 |
| Benners Hotel | 3 | Ashe's | 5 | Novecento | 7 | An Droichead Beag | 6 |
| Captain's House | 6 | Bean in Dingle | 2 | Out of the Blue | 1 | The Blue Zone | 1 |
| Castlewood House | 1 | The Chart House | 8 | Wren's Nest | 4 | Dick Mack's | 2 |
| Hideout Hostel | 4 | Half Door | 9 | | | John Benny's | 3 |
| Pax House | 7 | | | | | O'Flaherty's | 5 |
| Rainbow Hostel | 2 | | | | | O'Sullivan's Courthouse | 7 |

● **SHOPPING**
The Dingle Record Shop 1
Lisbeth Mulcahy 2

and pubs to retreat to. Tourism is far from the only industry here: in medieval times, Dingle was Kerry's leading port, protected by town walls, and it's still a major fishing harbour. From the extensive quays, narrow streets of stone houses, colourfully painted and appealingly substantial, run up the slope to the bustling main street. It's worth noting that in summer the town's population swells from two thousand to nearly nine thousand, which means it's essential to book early for accommodation. Until 2020, most visitors to Dingle came to catch a glimpse of its most famous resident, **Fungie**, a playful 300kg bottlenose dolphin who had made the harbour his home since 1983. However, Fungie's sudden disappearance in 2020 left not only the town's residents heartbroken, but also the town without a valuable source of income.

## Dingle Oceanworld

Farrannakilla, on the edge of town, on the road to Ventry • Daily: July & Aug 10am–7pm; Sept–June 10am–5pm; last admission 1hr before closing • €16, child €11, family from €50 • ☎ 066 915 2111, ⓦ dingle-oceanworld.ie

If nautical pursuits have whetted your curiosity, head for **Dingle Oceanworld** (Mara Beo). As well as a centre for marine conservation, Oceanworld is a richly detailed aquarium, where you can stick your hands in the touch pool, observe sharks, stingrays, piranhas, turtles and penguins (feeding at 1pm & 4pm) at close quarters, and walk underneath a variety of fish from around the Irish coast in the tunnel tank.

## Díseart

Green St • May–Sept Mon–Fri 9am–5pm, Sat 10am–4pm • €3 • ⓦ diseart.ie

At **Díseart Institute of Irish Culture and Spirituality**, a former convent of the enclosed order of Presentation Sisters on Green Street, you can admire twelve **stained-glass windows** by Harry Clarke, one of the foremost artists in the medium in the last century; commissioned in 1922, they depict scenes from the life of Christ in opulent detail.

### ARRIVAL AND INFORMATION                                    DINGLE TOWN

**By car** If you're driving, you'll need to get used to Dingle's fierce, roughly anticlockwise one-way system. Holy Ground and its continuation, Dykegate Lane, are up only (south–north), Main St is up only (east–west), while Green St, which leads back down towards the harbour, is down only. There's a useful free car park on Green St near Díseart.
**By bus** Buses stop in the car park behind the Supervalu store, down near the harbour.

**Destinations** Ballyferriter (Mon & Thurs 2 daily; 20min); Dunquin (Mon & Thurs 2 daily; 30min); Gallarus (Tues & Fri 1 daily; 10min); Killarney, via Inch (July & Aug Mon–Sat 2 daily; 1hr 20min); Tralee (via the N86; 3–5 daily; 1hr 20min).
**Tourist office** Strand St by the harbour (Mon–Sat 9am–5pm; ☎ 066 915 1188, ⓦ dingle-peninsula.ie).

### TOURS AND ACTIVITIES

**Archeological tours** Fascinating archeological tours of the peninsula by minibus are run in the summer by Sciúird Tours, Avondale St (daily at 10am; 3hr; €30/person; ☎ 066

915 1606, ⓦ ancientdingle.com).
**Boat trips** There's a choice of boat trips to Great Blasket (see page 293).

---

### DINGLE FESTIVALS

The principal events on Dingle's busy calendar are a four-day **Animation Dingle Festival** in March (ⓦ animationdingle.com); **Feile na Bealtaine** (ⓦ feilenabealtaine.ie), a week-long multidisciplinary festival of arts and politics in late April/early May; a well-received series of **folk and traditional concerts** in summer (roughly May–Oct) at the pretty St James's Church in Main St (☎ 087 284 9656); the riotous **Dingle Races** at Ballintaggart Racecourse on the east side of town over three days in early August (ⓦ dingleraces.ie); the **Dingle Regatta** for traditional *currachs* later in the month; a four-day **festival of traditional music** in September; a diverse **food festival** over a weekend in early October (ⓦ dinglefood.com); and **Other Voices**, a music festival in December (ⓦ othervoices.ie).

**Bike rental** Paddy's, Dykegate Lane (€15/day; ☎066 915 2311, ⓦpaddysbikeshop.com).

**Kayaking and mountain biking** Irish Adventures, off Strand St, behind *Out of the Blue* restaurant (kayaking €45/3hr; ☎087 419 0318, ⓦirishadventures.net).

**Sailing** Dingle Sailing Centre at the marina (☎087 718 7557, ⓦdinglesailingclub.com) offers sailing courses in July and Aug.

**Surfing and paddleboarding** Dingle Surf, Green St (☎066 915 0833, ⓦdinglesurf.com), for equipment rental and lessons in stand-up paddle boarding.

## ACCOMMODATION SEE MAP PAGE 289

**Ashe's** Main St ☎066 915 0989, ⓦashesbar.ie. Attractive, bright and central rooms with smart, en-suite bathrooms, in a whitewashed nineteenth-century building above a pub. Breakfast not served. **€80**

**Benners Hotel** 12 Main St ☎066 915 1638, ⓦdingle benners.com. Characterful and welcoming town house hotel and social hub that's been skilfully refurbished: bedrooms are brightly furnished with pine and floral prints, while the dark-wood lobby and bar are warm and cosy. **€239**

**Captain's House** The Mall ☎066 915 1531, ⓦcaptains housedingle.com. Hospitable, central, en-suite B&B, quirkily furnished with items collected on the eponymous captain's voyages. Great breakfasts, including home-made bread, scones and jam, are served in the bedrooms. Closed Dec–March. **€110**

★ **Castlewood House** 1km from the tourist office along the continuation of Strand St ☎066 915 2788, ⓦcastlewooddingle.com. Quiet, welcoming guesthouse with large and very thoughtfully and lavishly designed rooms, which stretch to DVD players and whirlpool baths; nearly all have fine views of the bay. Excellent, varied breakfasts and plenty of local information. **€150**

**Hideout Hostel** Dykegate Lane ☎066 915 0559. Friendly, laidback and all en-suite hostel in a modern terrace house, with a well-equipped kitchen, a sitting room with an open fire and laundry facilities; light breakfast included. Dorms **€20**, doubles **€70**

**Pax House** Upper John St, 1km east of the town centre ☎066 915 1518, ⓦpax-house.com. Peaceful, upmarket B&B, tastefully decorated with colourful paintings in contemporary style, with spectacular views of the bay from rooms and the large patio, and great breakfasts and afternoon teas. **€140**

**Rainbow Hostel** 2km west of the centre in Milltown ☎066 915 1044, ⓦrainbowhosteldingle.com. Sociable, family-run hostel, with landscaped gardens, large kitchen, bike rental and laundry facilities. Free lifts from the bus stop in town. Camping available too (€12).Dorms **€17**, doubles **€44**

## EATING SEE MAP PAGE 289

Although it doesn't shout about being a foodie town, Dingle has several first-rate **restaurants**. Seafood, naturally, features strongly on their menus, while homely **cafés** are great for whiling away rainy afternoons. On Fri mornings, there's a farmers' market in the car park on Holy Ground. Dingle is a hotbed of **traditional music**, with some locally based, nationally known performers turning up in the town's **pubs**. *West Kerry Live* (ⓦwestkerrylive.ie), a free fortnightly magazine available from the tourist office, details sessions in town and across the peninsula.

**An Café Liteártha** Dykegate Lane ☎066 915 2204. Daytime bookshop-café – with an eclectic mix of Irish language and English books, many on the local area – that offers cheap, unpretentious food, including soup, scones, cakes, sandwiches and warm brie with raspberry jam, salad and bread (€5.50). Mon–Sat 10am–6pm, plus Sun in August.

**Ashe's** Main St ☎066 915 0989, ⓦashesbar.ie. Easygoing spot, more restaurant than pub, which specializes in seafood, but also offers some cheaper dishes such as three oysters and glass of Guinness for €9.50. Also offers an early-bird two course deal for €27.50 till 6pm. Daily noon–3pm & 5.30–9.30pm.

**Bean in Dingle** Green St ☎087 299 2831, ⓦbeanin dingle.com. Caffeine addicts will love the smooth and unctuous coffee full of complex flavours blended for this sleek café by the boutique roasters Badger & Dodo of Cork and served in biodegradable cups. Creamy porridge is on the morning menu and local treats such as cinnamon rolls can be enjoyed in the soothing grey and yellow decor. Mon–Sat 8.30am–5pm.

**The Chart House** By the roundabout at the bottom of The Mall ☎066 915 2255, ⓦthecharthousedingle.com. Relaxing restaurant in a stone cottage with posh-rustic decor, preparing dishes such as pan-fried fillet of hake cod (€28.00). There's a good-value early evening menu offering three courses for €37. May–Sept daily 6–9.30pm; Oct–April Wed–Sun 6–9.30pm.

★ **Half Door** John St ☎066 915 1600, ⓦthehalfdoor. ie. Relaxing, white-tablecloth restaurant with excellent cooking, mostly seafood such as shellfish platters, mussels, crab and lobster, a good wine list, desserts such as apple and pear crumble, and friendly, efficient service. It's pricey, but there are various set menus on offer (including €44 for a three-course dinner menu and a three-course early bird menu at €33.50). May–Sept Mon–Sat 12.30–2.30pm & 5–10pm; winter hours depend on trade, but at least weekends, though closed Jan & early Feb.

**Murphy's Ice Cream** Strand St ☎087 133 0610. Delicious ice cream, home-made from seawater collected to

8

harvest the salt. Choose from a large selection of flavours or sample some of their desserts. Daily: May–Sept 11am–9.30pm; Oct–April 11am–5/6pm.

**Novecento** Main St ☎ 066 915 0663, ⓦ novecento.ie. Great pizzas, either whole (starting at €10.50) or by the slice, to take away in the evenings. Mon–Thurs & Sun 4–10pm, Fri & Sat 4–11pm.

**Out of the Blue** Opposite the tourist office on Strand St ☎ 066 915 0811, ⓦ outoftheblue.ie. Unpretentious seafood restaurant, serving up the freshest and most succulent fish and shellfish, depending on what is available from the pier opposite, in excellent dishes such as Blasket Islands scallops with Calvados flambé (€29). March–Oct Mon–Sat 5/5.30–9.30pm, Sun 12.30–3pm & 5/5.30–9.30pm.

**Wren's Nest** Dykegate Lane ☎ 086 177 3119. Laidback café in a simple stone cottage with a lovely, secluded garden at the back. Tuck into tasty quiche and salad (€6.50), omelettes, baked potatoes, cakes and home-made blueberry ice cream. March–Nov daily 11am–5pm.

## DRINKING
SEE MAP PAGE 289

**Adam's** Main St ☎ 066 915 2133. This likeable pub offers reasonable and tasty home-made lunches – including lemon chicken and walnut salad (€8) and Irish stew – and traditional music at weekends. Mon–Thurs 10.30am–11.30pm, Fri & Sat 10.30am–12.30am, Sun 10.30am–11pm.

★ **An Droichead Beag** At the bottom of Main St ☎ 066 915 1723, ⓦ androicheadbeag.com. A cosy, popular spot, "The Small Bridge" has lively sessions just about every night at 9/9.30pm, usually followed by a DJ. Mon–Thurs 3pm–late, Fri–Sun noon–late.

**The Blue Zone** Above the Dingle Record Shop on Green St ☎ 066 915 0303. For something completely different, head for this late-night wine bar, which offers jazz (Thurs & Fri in winter, most nights, though not Sat, in summer) & pizzas. Daily 5.30pm–late.

**Dick Mack's** Green St ☎ 066 915 1787, ⓦ dickmackspub.com. Crusty former cobblers' shop, with attractive tables in a quiet courtyard at the back and stars on the pavement outside to commemorate such diverse former customers as Robert Mitchum and Julia Roberts. They sell Dick Mack's IPA from a microbrewery and stock a huge variety of whiskies and Dingle gin. Mon–Thurs 11am–11.30pm, Fri & Sat 11am–12.30am, Sun 11am–11pm.

**John Benny's** Strand St ☎ 066 915 1215, ⓦ john bennyspub.com. Cosy pub popular for its microbrewed beers and reasonably priced bar food, such as Irish stew (€15), bacon and cabbage, Glenbeigh oysters, salads and sandwiches, with vegetarian options. John and his wife are noted musicians who host traditional music every night in summer (and often enough in winter). Mon–Thurs 10.30am–11.30pm, Fri & Sat 10.30am–12.30am, Sun 12.30–11pm.

**O'Flaherty's** Bridge St, down by the roundabout ☎ 066 915 1983, ⓦ oflahertysdingle.com. Spartan but sociable pub, with a flagstone floor and an old stove, its walls hung with memorabilia. Owned by a family of musicians, it hosts sessions most nights. Mon–Thurs roughly 11.30am–11.30pm, Fri & Sat 11.30am–12.30am, Sun 11.30am–11pm.

**O'Sullivan's Courthouse** The Mall ☎ 066 915 2853, ⓦ osullivanscourthousepub.com. Another Dingle pub owned by a musician: "no TV, no juke box, no pool table", just bare wood, white paint and an old stove – with a cute beer garden – as the setting for great nightly sessions, washed down with craft beers. Mon–Fri 4–11.30pm, Sat & Sun 3–11pm.

## SHOPPING
SEE MAP PAGE 289

Dingle's shopping hub is **Green St**, where you'll find all manner of crafts shops, art galleries, delicatessens and bookshops. See ⓦ originalkerry.com for information about the county's craft makers, most of whom are in Dingle.

**The Dingle Record Shop** Green St ☎ 087 298 4550, ⓦ dinglerecordshop.com. This tiny shop with a big welcome has a great selection of traditional CDs, especially by local musicians, and is a good source of information about sessions, as well as selling tickets for the St James's Church concerts (see page 290). Mon–Sat 10am–6pm.

**Lisbeth Mulcahy** Green St ☎ 066 915 1688, ⓦ lisbeth mulcahy.com. Gorgeous scarves, jumpers and other wool items, as well as pottery by Lisbeth's husband, Louis (see page 294). May–Sept Mon–Fri 9.30am–7pm, Sat 10am–6pm, Sun noon–5pm; Oct–April Mon–Sat 10am–5pm.

# The Slea Head Loop

The vast, spectacular mountain- and seascapes which stretch out to the tip of the peninsula, **Slea Head**, are the undoubted highlights here, followed by the **Blasket Islands heritage centre** at Dunquin – or even a **boat trip to the islands** themselves – and the elegant, dry-stone **Gallarus Oratory**.

## Ventry (Ceann Trá)

**VENTRY**, the first bay to the west of Dingle, is an impressive sheltering crescent of fine, sandy, gently sloping beach and low dunes in the lee of 514m Mount Eagle. The strand here was the suitably epic location for the legendary single combat between Fionn Mac Cumhaill and Daire Donn, the King of the World, to save Ireland from invasion by Daire's armies.

## Celtic and Prehistoric Museum

West side of Ventry Bay • March–Nov daily 10am–5.30pm • €5 • ☎ 087 770 3280, ⓦ discoverireland.ie

It's well worth calling in to the small but fascinating **Celtic and Prehistoric Museum**, where you can gawp at a fossilized nest of dinosaur eggs, a baby dinosaur skeleton and the complete skull and tusks of a woolly mammoth, of the type that would have been roaming Ireland over twenty thousand years ago. When the engaging owner is around, he'll show you how the Stone Age jewellery, statuettes and tools were used.

## Dún Beag

Slea Hed Drive, Fahan, 7 km soutwest of Ventry • Entry fee includes a 10min audiovisual in the *Stonehouse* restaurant opposite • €3 • ☎ 066 915 9070

It's a fine drive or cycle out to **Slea Head** (Ceann Sléibhe), as the road narrows beyond Ventry and the slopes of Mount Eagle steepen towards the end of the peninsula. This landscape is dotted with several Iron Age dry-stone forts, known as the **Fahan Group**, of which the most interesting is the first, around 1km beyond the Celtic Museum. In a spectacular setting above the boiling sea overlooking the Iveragh Peninsula, **Dún Beag** has four lines of defensive banks and five corresponding ditches, traversed by a 16m souterrain, or underground escape route. Within the 3m-high walls stand the remains of beehive huts, or *clocháns*. Dún Beag used to be even more spectacular, but in January 2014 winter storms eroded the cliff and caused a large section of the site to fall into the Atlantic.

**8**

## The Blasket Islands (Na Blascaodaí) and Dunquin (Dún Chaoin)

Just off Slea Head lie the **Blaskets**, dramatic island mountains with steep, gashed sides. Despite their inhospitable appearance, the largest island, Great Blasket (An Blascaod Mór), was inhabited by up to two hundred people for at least three centuries until 1953, when, with no school, shop, priest or doctor, it was finally abandoned. Because of their isolation, however, the islanders maintained a rich oral tradition in the Irish language, which in the early twentieth century, encouraged by visiting scholars, evolved into a remarkable body of written **literature**. Works such as *An tOileánach* (*The Islandman*) by Tomás Ó Criomhthain, *Fiche Blian ag Fás* (*Twenty Years A-Growing*) by Muiris Ó Súilleabháin and *Peig* by Peig Sayers (an oral account written down by her son) give a vivid insight into the hardships of life.

---

### BOAT TRIPS TO THE BLASKETS

In the summer, **boats** to Great Blasket leave the pier on the south side of **Dunquin** in good weather every hour or so (15–30min; €30 return; ☎ 066 915 6422, ⓦ blasketisland.com). There are also other types of tour from **Ventry** (booking essential on ☎ 086 335 3805, ⓦ marinetours. ie): a guided cruise around the Blasket Islands in the afternoon (4hr; €60), taking in the spectacular Cathedral Rocks on Inishnabro, puffins (in spring and early summer, depending on the weather) and grey seals and red deer on Inishvickillane, and possibly basking sharks, whales and dolphins; and a seven-hour trip that combines the guided cruise with landing on Great Blasket (€75). In addition, from **Dingle town**, tours run ferries to Great Blasket once a day (50min, leaving you 3hr 30min on the island; €35 return), and guided cruises around the islands that include an hour on Great Blasket (6hr; €50).

The island's story is told with great imagination at the Great Blasket heritage centre, **Ionad an Bhlascaoid Mhóir** (April–Oct daily 10am–6pm; last admission 5.15pm; €5; Heritage Card; ☎066 915 6444, ⊛blasket.ie) on the mainland opposite, at the north end of Dunquin. Excerpts from the island writers, and a moving section on Great Blasket's abandonment in 1953 and the migration of many islanders to Springfield, Massachusetts – where they still receive the *Kerryman* newspaper from Tralee every week are highlights.

If you take a boat trip (see box) to **Great Blasket**, you can wander the white-sand beach, Trá Bán, at its eastern end and the grassy footpaths that cross its 6km length, passing the ghosts of the old village. Accompanied by seals, puffins, storm petrels and shearwaters, you can contemplate the 3000km that separates you, here on Europe's most westerly islands, from North America where most of the islanders ended up, and the treacherous 2km of Blasket Sound which made living on the island untenable.

## Ballyferriter (Baile an Fheirtearaigh) and around

**BALLYFERRITER**, 8km on from Dunquin, is a byword for remoteness in Ireland, but ticks a surprising number of boxes when it comes to amenities. There's a lovely beach, **Wine Strand**, just to the north on sheltered **Smerwick Harbour**, and pleasant walking to the northwest where the peaks of **Sybil Head** and the **Three Sisters** rise like a row of waves to meet the sea. In late February, the village hosts a five-day **traditional music school**, Scoil Cheoil an Earraigh (⊛scoilcheoil.com), featuring classes, concerts and lectures.

### Músaem Chorca Dhuibhne

Ballyferriter village centre • June to mid-Sept daily 10am–5pm; off-season by appointment • €2.50 • ☎066 915 6333, ⊛westkerrymuseum.com

The old village school has been converted into the **Músaem Chorca Dhuibhne**, which houses a display on the archaeology and history of the peninsula since Mesolithic times, its geology and more recent role as a location for movies such as *Ryan's Daughter*. There's a café that does home baking at the museum, where you can find out about looped walks around the village and about the wealth of ancient ruins in the area, such as Riasc, a sixth-century monastic site, and the ring fort at Ballynavenooragh.

### Louis Mulcahy Pottery

4km west of Ballyferriter on the R559 (about 4km from Dunquin) • Summer Mon–Fri 9am–7pm, Sat & Sun 10am–7pm; winter Mon–Fri 9am–5.30/6pm, Sat & Sun 10am–5.30/6pm • ☎066 915 6229, ⊛louismulcahy.com

One of Ireland's leading potters, Louis Mulcahy, has his **pottery**, shop and café near the tip of the Dingle Peninsula. You can watch a potter at work on the wheel and have a go at throwing a pot yourself (pre-booking recommended). For €9 you can make your own pot or splash out €19 and have your masterpiece fired and glazed with the help of an expert.

### Gallarus Oratory

5km east of Ballyferriter, off the R559 towards Ballydavid • Visitor Centre Easter–Oct 9am–5pm (site accessible year-round) • €3 • ☎066 915 5333, ⊛lheritageireland.ie

(An Mhuiríoch), the beautiful **Gallarus Oratory**, is the Dingle peninsula's most compelling historic monument, dating from somewhere between the seventh and twelfth centuries. Built of dry gritstone in the shape of an upturned boat, the building – thought to be an early Christian church – sits unadorned in a field like a Platonic ideal of architectural purity.

### Kilmalkedar

At the crossroads at Murreagh, the R559 turns right, passing after 2km **Kilmalkedar**, an attractive, mid-twelfth-century church in the Irish Romanesque style. Dedicated to local saint, Maolcéadair, who died in 636, it offers fine views west to the sea. Look out for a strange, carved animal head inside, above the doorway, and, in the surrounding graveyard, an early sundial, a high cross and an ogham stone, whose inscription is probably asking for a prayer for the soul of one Maile Inbir.

## GETTING AROUND

**By bike/car** You can make an immensely satisfying day-trip from Dingle by driving or cycling the R559 on its meandering, circular route, or by taking a tour (see page 290). Coaches are required to follow the narrow road in a clockwise direction and it's best to follow suit, rather than risk meeting them head-on.

**By bus** The bus schedules from Dingle (see page 290)

## THE SLEA HEAD LOOP

allow you half-day trips to Dunquin or Ballyferriter on Mon or Thurs and to Gallarus on Tues or Fri.

**On foot** An 18km waymarked path, Cosán na Naomh (The Saint's Road), crosses this area mostly on minor roads, from Ventry Strand via Gallarus and Kilmalkedar to the foot of Mount Brandon, with an associated map-guide (ⓦheritagecouncil.ie).

## ACCOMMODATION AND EATING

### VENTRY
**Páidí Ó Sé's** By the church ☎066 915 9765, ⓦpaidiose. com. An old-fashioned country pub with a sense of tradition. Menu staples include bacon and cabbage, seafood chowder, chicken curry, steaks, and mixed veg and rice in the €11–15 price range. At weekends musicians turn up for traditional and contemporary sessions; formerly owned by the eponymous late Kerry Gaelic star footballer and manager, it's hung with sporting memorabilia. Mon–Thurs 11am–11.30pm, Fri & Sat 11am–12.30am, Sun noon–11pm.

### DÚN BEAG
**The Stonehouse** Opposite the fort ☎066 915 9970. Built in a *clochán* style with stone walls and roof, this café-restaurant menu features main courses such as enticing crab salad (€16), Irish lamb stew, and Thai noodles, all of which you can enjoy at outdoor tables with stunning views of the Skelligs. Mid-Feb to Dec daily: high season 10.30am–9pm; low season 11am–5.30pm.

### DUNQUIN
**An Portán** In the middle of the village ☎066 915 6212, ⓦanportan.ie. En-suite B&B in a one-storey quadrangle of large, bright rooms around a lawn, with a dining room for guests and a daytime café. Closed Oct–March. €85
**Dún Chaoin Youth Hostel** Near the heritage centre ☎066 915 6121, ⓦanoige.ie. An Óige hostel on the Dingle Way, with great views over the Blaskets, four- to

ten-bed dorms, en-suite twins, a kitchen, laundry facilities and a drying room for walkers. Note that there are no shops for 8km (Ballyferriter), but the owner can supply dry food, breakfast and packed lunches as extras; linen is €2. Closed Nov–Feb. Dorms €17, doubles €44

### BALLYFERRITER AND AROUND
★ **Gorman's Clifftop House** Glaise Bheag, north of Murreagh towards Feohanagh (An Fheothanach) ☎066 915 5162, ⓦgormans-clifftophouse.com. The lovely, large, bright rooms at this welcoming and well-informed guesthouse are very comfortable and thoughtfully equipped, with great views of either the Three Sisters or Mount Brandon. Closed mid-Oct to mid-March. €140
**Tig Áine** Just west of Louis Mulcahy's pottery on the R559 ☎066 915 6214, ⓦtigaine.com. Boasting fine views of Sybil Head from its picture windows and outside terrace (with binoculars and telescopes for bird-spotting), *Tig Áine* encompasses an art gallery and a café-restaurant, rustling up dishes including omelettes (€13), salads, chowder (€7), and lamb cutlets. May–Sept daily noon–6pm.
**Tigh an tSaorsaigh (Sears)** On the R559 in the village ☎066 915 6344, ⓦsearspub.com. Pleasant, en-suite B&B is available at this genial 160-year-old flagstoned pub done out in striking green and red. With its piano and open stove, the bar offers simple pub grub. For €5 you can make a wish in their wishing well – alternatively put it towards hiring a bike and exploring the peninsula with the owner's brother, who runs tours. €70

# The Conor Pass and the north coast of the peninsula

To the northeast of Dingle town rises an L-shaped ridge of mountains, running south from the highest, **Mount Brandon** (Cnoc Bréanainn; 950m), and across to Beenoskee (826m). The steep and narrow **Conor Pass** road, which cuts across the ridge to the peninsula's north coast, ascends to a car park at over 500m giving spectacular views of stark uplands, corrie lakes and the huge sweep of **Brandon Bay** to the north, and back over Dingle harbour to the Iveragh Peninsula and the Skelligs.

## Cloghane

Signposted archaeological and walking trails, including the Dingle Way, crisscross the area around **CLOGHANE** (An Clochán), a hamlet fringed by lovely beaches on the eastern flank of Mount Brandon. Experienced walkers could take on the classic, six-hour there-and-back ascent of Mount Brandon, roughly marked by yellow painted arrows, from Faha, 2km northwest of Cloghane. Cloghane comes to life over the last weekend in July for the **Feile Lughnasa**, celebrating the Celtic harvest festival with guided walks, poetry and music.

### ACCOMMODATION
CLOGHANE

**Mount Brandon Hostel** Village centre ☎ 085 136 3454, ⓦ mountbrandonhostel.com. All en-suite, eco-conscious hostel with spruce wooden floors and furniture, a well-equipped kitchen, a cosy lounge and a patio overlooking the bay. Evenings of music, poetry and storytelling are held every Monday throughout the year and in July and Aug on a Thursday. Luggage transfer can be arranged for walkers. Light breakfast included. Dorms €25, doubles €58

## Castlegregory and the Maharees

Separating Brandon Bay from Tralee Bay, the **Maharees** is an exposed, beach-girt spit of land to the north of **CASTLEGREGORY**. What's reckoned to be some of the best **windsurfing** in the world is possible here – it's good in all wind directions, with a variety of west-, north- and east-facing spots suitable for all levels of ability; there's a good break for **surfers**, too. If all that sounds too energetic, just flop out on the nearest beach to Castlegregory, east-facing **Sandy Bay**.

### ACCOMMODATION AND EATING
CASTLEGREGORY AND THE MAHAREES

**Anchor** About 5km east of the village on the R560 ☎ 066 713 9157, ⓦ anchorcaravanpark.com. This well-signposted campsite gives on to kilometres of quiet, sandy beach, and has a campers' kitchen, a children's play area, laundry facilities and a rinsing area for wetsuits. Closed Oct–March. €28

**Fitzgerald's Euro-Hostel** Strand St ☎ 066 713 9951, ⓦ eurohostelireland.com. If you're not on a package with Waterworld (see Activities below), you might want to crash at this hostel back in town, which has basic dorms, single, twin and double rooms and a large kitchen above a shop, café and bar. Dorms €15, doubles €30

**Spillane's Bar and Restaurant** About halfway along the Maharees spit ☎ 066 713 9125, ⓦ spillanesbar.com. Your best bet for something to eat in the area, specializing in steaks (€22.50 for Irish sirloin) and seafood, with the day's catch – maybe local mussels, crab claws and prawns – listed on a blackboard. Self-catering accommodation available. March–June & Sept–Nov daily 5–9pm; July & Aug daily 1–9pm.

### ACTIVITIES

**Surfing, diving and other watersports** Jamie Knox (☎ 066 713 9411, ⓦ jamieknox.com) offers windsurfing and surfing tuition and rental, and stand-up paddleboard rental. Diving trips, courses and accommodation packages are run by Waterworld (☎ 066 713 9292, ⓦ waterworld. ie), a PADI five-star IDC Centre, from their base, Harbour House, at Scraggane Bay at the end of the Maharees; they also offer surf lessons and rentals, as well as canoeing and other watersports.

# North Kerry

**North Kerry**, flat, rich farmland that runs as far as the Shannon estuary, feels quite different from the rest of the county – and they've even been known to play hurling rather than Gaelic football up here. Instead of the remote, spectacularly set coastal villages of the peninsulas, you'll find – or avoid – the traditional kiss-me-quick resorts of Ballyheigue and Ballybunion, while the county town of **Tralee** seems quite anodyne if you've just come up from Dingle, for example. It is worth making time, however, for **Listowel**, an easy-going small town that's a hotbed of literary activity. North again from here, the useful **Shannon ferry** cuts down travelling time to County Clare from **Tarbert**.

## Tralee and around

Although **TRALEE** has a long history as a market town, originally built around an Anglo-Norman castle and priory, its attractions today are modern and rather functional. Among them, the County Museum, Wetlands Centre and Blennerville Windmill can be visited on a good-value combination ticket for €33 (which includes admission for up to two adults and three children).

### Kerry County Museum

Ashe Memorial Hall, Denny St • Tues–Sat 9.30am–5pm • €6 • ☎ 066 712 7777, ⓦ kerrymuseum.ie

Chief among Tralee's sights is the **Kerry County Museum** in the centre of town, which incorporates a comprehensive run-through of the history of Ireland and Kerry since the Stone Age, with plenty of activities for kids, as well as the Medieval Experience, a series of re-created scenes of mid-fifteenth-century Tralee complete with artificial smells.

### Tralee Bay Wetlands Centre

Ballyard Rd, on the southwest side of the centre, just off the Dingle road • Daily: July & Aug 10am–7pm; Sept–June 10am–5pm • €6 • ☎ 066 712 6700, ⓦ traleebaywetlands.org

Dug out from the marshland where three rivers meet Tralee Bay, this attraction offers fascinating, guided, nature-watching tours in silent electric boats around one of the largest beds of eelgrass in Europe. Gliding through the rustling reeds here, you're likely to see herons, warblers, curlews, frogs, dragonflies and, in winter, thousands of Brent geese and the rare Whooper swans. There are also hides, a short boardwalk and a 20m observation tower with views of Slieve Mish on the Dingle Peninsula, as well as a leisure lake with pedalos and rowing boats. The *Lakeside Café* here serves snacks and hot meals throughout the day.

### Blennerville Windmill

Windmill Lane, Ballyvelly, roughly 3km southwest of the centre on the Dingle road • April–Oct daily 9am–5pm • €8 • ⓦ blennerville-windmill.ie

The largest working windmill in Ireland and Britain, the **Blennerville Windmill**, dates from 1800. It has a visitor and crafts centre where the millers will give you a 25-minute guided tour of the flour-making process; there's also an exhibition on emigration on the first floor with a short video. A word of warning: it's a steep climb of 52 steps to the top.

## Ardfert Cathedral

Ardfert, 9km northwest of Tralee on the R551 • May–Sept daily 10am–6pm, last admission 5.15pm • €5; Heritage Card • ☎ 066 713 4711, Ⓦ heritageireland.ie • The bus schedules between Tralee and Ardfert only allow a return trip to the cathedral July & Aug afternoons

Probably the most interesting visit you can make in the Tralee area is to the ruined **cathedral** at **Ardfert**, on the site of a monastery that was established by St Brendan the Navigator in the sixth century near his birthplace. The slender tenth-to-thirteenth-century cathedral is the largest pre-Gothic church in Ireland and features fine lancet windows behind the altar. Look out especially for some beautiful Romanesque sandstone carving, in geometric and floral designs, on the west doorway and around the window of the small twelfth-century church nearby.

### ARRIVAL AND INFORMATION

### TRALEE AND AROUND

**By train** The train station, which has left-luggage facilities, is just a few mins' walk northeast of the centre of town.
Destinations Cork (6–8 daily, often with a change at Mallow; 2hr–2hr 30min); Dublin (6–8 daily, most with a change at Mallow; 4hr); Farranfore (7–8 daily; 20min); Killarney (7–8 daily; 40min).

**By bus** Buses stop at the train station.
Destinations Adare (6–7 daily; 1hr 40min); Ardfert (July & Aug 2 daily, rest of year Mon–Fri 1 daily; 15min); Castlegregory (2 on Fri; 40min); Cloghane (2 on Fri; 1hr 10min); Cork (hourly; 2hr 15min); Dingle (via the N86; 3–5

daily; 1hr 20min); Killarney (10–16 daily; 40min); Limerick (6–7 daily; 2hr 5min); Listowel (6–8 daily; 30min); Ring of Kerry (July & Aug 1 daily; 6hr 35min, with a break in Sneem).

**Tourist office** The friendly and helpful tourist office (Mon–Sat 9am–5pm, plus July & Aug Sun 10am–5pm; ☎ 066 712 1288), in the Ashe Memorial Hall underneath the Kerry County Museum, has maps of town and details of local traditional sessions.

**Bike rental** Tralee Gas Supplies, High St, on the west side of town (☎ 066 712 2018).

### ACCOMMODATION AND EATING

**The Grand** Denny St ☎ 066 712 1499, Ⓦ grandhotel tralee.com. Traditional county-town hotel with lots of dark wood panelling and leather banquettes in its bar and restaurant, though its rooms, most of which are set back from the busy street, have had a colourful, modern makeover. €120

**Quinlan's** The Mall ☎ 066 712 3998, Ⓦ kerryfish.com. Your best bet for somewhere to eat is this superior chipper and fishmonger, which serves beer-battered fish from their

own boats out of Valentia (from €10), seafood chowder and deep-fried squid with home-made sweet chilli jam. Eat in or take away to the nearby town park (down Denny St by the tourist office). Daily noon–10pm.

**Seán Og's** Bridge St ☎ 066 712 8822. Friendly, dimly lit and cosy pub just off The Mall, with open fires, bare stone walls and traditional music most nights. Mon–Thurs 11am–11.30pm, Fri & Sat 11am–12.30am, Sun noon–11pm.

### ENTERTAINMENT

**Siamsa Tíre (National Folk Theatre of Ireland)** Next to the tourist office ☎ 066 712 3055, Ⓦ siamsatire.com. Excellent Irish shows in the summer, as well as a varied

international programme of drama, music, dance and art and literary events during the rest of the year.

## Listowel

Up the N69, 27km northeast of Tralee, **LISTOWEL** is a congenial market town in a leafy setting on the north bank of the River Feale. It's best known for its literary associations (see The Kerry Writer's Museum below) – the town's most celebrated literary figure is probably the late **John B. Keane**, author of plays such as *The Field*, a dramatization of a shocking murder that took place in this region in the 1950s.

## Seanchaí – The Kerry Writers' Museum

24 The Square • Jan–May & Oct–Dec Mon–Fri 10am–4pm; June & Sept Mon–Fri 9.30am–5pm; July & Aug Mon–Fri 9.30am–pm, Sat & Sun 11am–3pm • €6 • ☎ 068 22212, ⓦ kerrywritersmuseum.com

In a Georgian house in the imposing town square stands **Seanchaí**, the **Kerry Writers' Museum**. As well as hosting literary workshops and readings and a good, cheap café, the museum provides tourist information about the area. Its rooms are devoted to local writers such as Keane, Bryan MacMahon and Brendan Kennelly, and have been imaginatively designed, with recorded extracts, to reflect the personality of each. Audiovisuals include Kerryman Eamon Kelly, Ireland's most famous storyteller (or *seanchaí*, pronounced "shanakee"), reading old stories about rural Ireland that have been handed down through the oral tradition.

## Listowel Castle

The Square • Guided tours late May to Aug Wed–Sun 9.30am–5.30pm; last tour 4.45pm • Free • ☎ 086 385 7201 • ⓦ heritageireland.ie

From Seanchaí's reception, informative and entertaining tours depart for formidable **Listowel Castle** next door. When the castle was built in the early or mid-fifteenth century for the Fitzmaurices, the Lords of Kerry, the adjacent River Feale would have been navigable and was probably forded at this point, but from the eighteenth century onwards, in more peaceful times, the building fell into disrepair and was quarried for stone. Nevertheless, two of the four original towers remain, rising to a height of 15m.

## The Lartigue Monorail and Museum

North side of town, off John B. Keane Rd • Early May to mid-Sept daily 1–4.30pm • €6 • ☎ 068 24393, ⓦ lartiguemonorail.com

Between 1888 and 1924 a low-cost railway system covered the 15km between Listowel and Ballybunion on the coast, attracting much interest and curiosity since it carried not only passengers but also animals and freight. A 500m section has been restored for ten-minute jaunts as part of the **Lartigue Monorail and Museum**, where you can see footage of the original steam-powered monorail alongside models and memorabilia.

---

**ACCOMMODATION AND EATING** · · · · · · · · · · · · · · · · · · · · · · · · · · · · · · · · · · · · **LISTOWEL**

★ **Allo's** 41 Church St ☎ 068 22880, ⓦ allosbarbistro-townhouse.com. The pick of Listowel's accommodation, off the northeast corner of the square, offering three rooms furnished with antiques, including one with a four-poster and a huge bathroom, above an appealing, antique-furnished bar and bistro. Here you can dine on dishes such as pork rack cutlet with sun-dried tomato tapenade (€23), or simpler, cheaper lunches. Breakfast not served. Bistro Tues & Wed noon–7pm, Thurs–Sat noon–9pm. **€70**

★ **The John B. Keane** William St ☎ 068 21127. At this cosy pub off the northeast corner of the town square, John B's son Billy keeps the literary flame burning, with poetry readings, history talks, music sessions and informal pub theatre. Mon 7–11.30pm, Tues–Thurs 1–11.30pm, Fri & Sat 1pm–12.30am, Sun 1–11pm.

**Listowel Arms** The Square ☎ 068 21500, ⓦ listowelarms.com. Charming traditional hotel in a creeper-covered, Georgian mansion, where some of the rooms, which are attractively furnished with antiques, have views of the river. Good-value three-night packages available. **€130**

# Limerick and Clare

QUIN ABBEY

**9**

# Limerick and Clare

Although Limerick lives somewhat in the shadow of its neighbours Kerry and Clare, the county is ideal for activities such as cycling, walking and golf. Some of Ireland's most impressive archaeological sites are to be found here too, alongside cathedrals, priories and abbeys. There is a distinctly pastoral feel to much of Limerick as it sweeps from the rolling farmland of the Golden Vale over to the Shannon estuary. Limerick city, meanwhile, has gone through a sea change in recent years, reinventing itself with a vibrant cultural life.

The superb **Hunt Museum** houses the Republic's richest art and antiquities collection outside Dublin, while outside the city, the enigmatic Neolithic sites of **Lough Gur** and the historic village of **Adare** are reasons to branch out. You'll need your own transport for the former but the city is well served by trains – from Galway and points east and south via Limerick Junction – and by buses from just about anywhere.

Across the broad River Shannon, **County Clare** has a wealth of scenic attractions and is renowned worldwide for its vibrant musical traditions. Its coastline all the way from **Kilkee** to **Fanore** is dotted with golden beaches. Near the village of **Doolin**, famed for its year-long, tourist-driven diet of traditional music, stand the awesome **Cliffs of Moher**, while the county's northern interior is characterized by the craggy, mysterious landscape of **the Burren**, home to numerous prehistoric sites. Its county town, **Ennis**, is an animated place with excellent music pubs and some atmospheric religious remains, further examples of which are dotted around the countryside, such as at **Quin Abbey**, **Dysert O'Dea** and the settlement on **Scattery Island**. The castles and tower houses of Clare's erstwhile dynasties, the O'Briens and MacNamaras, inform the landscape too, notably at **Bunratty** and **Leamaneh**. At Clare's eastern extremity lies the expansive **Lough Derg**, whose waters are best explored by renting your own boat or taking a cruise. Shannon International Airport, in Clare's southeast, lies within easy reach of Ennis, which itself is the county's transport hub. Clare is reasonably well covered by buses in summertime, though the county's north is best accessed from Galway.

## Limerick city and around

All manner of routes – road, rail and air – lead to **LIMERICK**, the Republic's third city and a place that has been revitalized in recent years. An imaginative urban improvement project alongside the river, the renovation of **King John's Castle** and the gloriously restored **Milk Market** in the **Market Quarter** – not to mention the newly designated **Fashion Quarter** and **Medieval Quarter** – have all contributed to a feel-good atmosphere. As well as substantial renovation of the Shannon **quays**, regeneration efforts have included the extensive campus at **Plassey**, 3km southeast, which is also the site of the **National Technological Park**. The three colleges here (the university, Institute of Technology and College of Education) certainly help to enliven the city's cultural pulse and nightlife. More than anything, though, Limerick is synonymous with sport – in particular with **rugby** – and the expansion of **Thomond Park Stadium** has helped boost the city's status.

### Brief history

The **Vikings** sailed up the Shannon in about 922 and established a settlement here on a river island, formed by a narrow branch off the main flow that is today called the Abbey River. This port at the lowest fording point of the river was coveted by the **Anglo-Normans** who, in 1197, seized and set about fortifying the town. This involved

# Highlights

**❶ Hunt Museum** This diverse, personal collection of beautiful art and antiquities is Limerick's finest attraction. See page 307

**❷ Lough Gur** Atmospheric rural lake surrounded by fine Neolithic remains. See page 312

**❸ Quin Abbey** Evocative monastic settlement in an idyllic setting. See page 316

**❹ Ennis** The county town offers numerous opportunities to experience Clare's lively traditional music scene. See page 316

**❺ Scattery Island** Deserted for more than thirty years, this tranquil island in the middle of the Shannon estuary was once a major ecclesiastical settlement. See page 321

**❻ The Cliffs of Moher** Massive sea-battered cliffs, providing exhilarating views of the Atlantic Ocean. See page 325

**❼ The Burren** A desolate rock-scape peppered with numerous Neolithic and Iron Age remains. See page 326

**HIGHLIGHTS ARE MARKED ON THE MAP ON PAGE 304**

**9**

building high city walls around what became Englishtown, to keep out the local Irish, who retreated to a ghetto to the southeast across the Abbey River – Irishtown.

### The seventeenth century

In the late seventeenth century, the final bloody scenes of the War of the Kings were played out here. After their defeat at the Boyne in 1690, the Jacobite forces in Limerick castle, under the Earl of Tyrconnell and local hero **Patrick Sarsfield**, refused to surrender.

**HIGHLIGHTS**

1. Hunt Museum
2. Lough Gur
3. Quin Abbey
4. Ennis
5. Scattery Island
6. The Cliffs of Moher
7. The Burren

Though beset by a vastly superior force, Sarsfield managed to raise the siege by creeping out at night with five hundred men and destroying the Williamite supply train. When William's army came back in 1691, however, the medieval walls of the castle were unable to withstand the artillery bombardment. Tyrconnell having died of a stroke, Sarsfield surrendered on October 3, 1691, on supposedly honourable terms, according to the **Treaty of Limerick**. The Jacobites – some twelve thousand in all, later known as the "Wild Geese" – were permitted to go to France, in whose cause Sarsfield fought and

**9**

later died. The treaty also promised Catholics the comparative religious toleration they had enjoyed under Charles II, but the English went back on the deal, and between 1692 and 1704 the Irish Parliament passed the harshly anti-Catholic penal laws.

### The eighteenth century onwards

The eighteenth century proved to be far more prosperous for Limerick, which in the 1750s received a grant of £17,000 from the Irish Parliament towards a major redevelopment. Completed in 1840 and named after the local MP, **Newtown Pery** comprised a grid of broad Georgian terraced streets, built well to the south of the cramped, fetid medieval city.

### THE LIMERICK

**Limericks** became common in Britain in the nineteenth century, popularized by Edward Lear, but their origin is shrouded in the mists of time. In Limerick city you'll find one on the walls of the city's oldest pub, the *White House* (see page 311):

*The limerick is furtive and mean;*
*You must keep her in close quarantine,*
*Or she sneaks up to the slums*
*And promptly becomes*
*Disorderly, drunk and obscene.*

In the early **twentieth century**, however, Limerick suffered greatly during the Nationalist struggles, which, in 1919, gave rise to a radical movement that's unique in Irish history: in protest against British military action during the War of Independence, the local Trades Council called a general strike and proclaimed the **Limerick Soviet**. With help from the IRA, they took over the city, controlling food distribution, setting up a citizens' police force and even printing their own money. It lasted only a few weeks, however, collapsing under pressure from the Catholic bishop. In 1921 both Limerick's mayor, George Clancy, and the former mayor, Mícheál O'Callaghan, were murdered by the Royal Irish Constabulary. One of the effects of the Troubles was that the rich were persuaded to move out of the city: many of their Georgian houses in Newtown Pery became tenements and some remain dilapidated to this day. The traditional distinctions between Englishtown – focused on the castle and now signposted as King's Island – Irishtown and Newtown Pery no longer matter very much, as there's little of the medieval city left in the first two areas, while Newtown Pery's grid is scattered with modern developments.

## The Hunt Museum

The Custom House, Rutland St • Mon–Sat 10am–5pm, Sun 2–5pm • €7.50 • ☎ 061 312833, ⓦ huntmuseum.com

The fascinating displays in the **Hunt Museum**, dating from the Stone Age to modern times, are the best place to start a tour of the city. Over the course of the twentieth century, John and Gertrude Hunt gathered together this diverse collection of art and antiquities, especially known for its religious works, and bequeathed it to the people of Ireland. You'll get the best idea of the spirit of the place in the **Epilogue Room**, which juxtaposes pieces of wildly different origins, such as an eighteenth-century Chinese porcelain cockerel and an English stone rabbit from the fifteenth century.

There are regular guided tours every day (phone for details) and a light-filled basement café. Particular pieces to look out for include the beautiful, early ninth-century **Antrim Cross**, one of the finest examples of early Christian metalwork from Ireland. Made of bronze decorated with enamel in geometric and animal designs, it was discovered by chance in the River Bann in the nineteenth century. Keep an eye out also for the **Beverley Crozier**, a piece of walrus ivory intricately carved with miracles of healing, dating from the eleventh century. Other highlights include works by Irish artists William Orpen, Jack B. Yeats and Roderic O'Connor.

## St Mary's Cathedral

Bridge St • Summer Mon–Sat 9am–4.30pm, except during services; winter Mon–Fri 9am–4.30pm, Sat 9am–1pm, except during services • Suggested donation €4 • ☎ 061 310 93, ⓦ saintmaryscathedral.ie

Just across the river from the Hunt Museum, the Church of Ireland **St Mary's Cathedral** boasts a fine, almost homely interior of rough stone walls, brightly coloured stained glass and beautiful barrel-vaulted ceilings. It was founded on the site of the Viking *thingmote* or meeting place in 1168 – from which time dates the Romanesque west doorway, carved with monstrous heads, stylized flowers and chevrons – but has gained so many accretions over the centuries that it's now as broad as it is long, with an intriguingly confused layout.

The cathedral's highlight is its set of dark-oak **misericords** in the Jebb Chapel, the only example left in Ireland. Dating from the late fifteenth century, they're ornately carved with symbols of good and evil, including a delicate, sinuous swan, cockatrices, griffins and all sorts of other mythical monsters. Look out also for the limestone **reredos** behind the main altar, which was carved in Celtic Revival style by Michael Pearse, father of the Irish patriot, Pádraig, and the nearby tomb of the cathedral's founder, King Donal Mór O'Brien of Munster, decorated with three heraldic lions and a Celtic cross. The cathedral stages lunch-time **music recitals** every Wednesday (1.15pm) during the summer.

## Limerick Museum

Old Franciscan Friary, 100 Henry St • Mon–Fri 10am–1pm & 2–5pm • Free • ☎ 061 557740, ⓦ www.limerick.ie/limerick-museum

Housed within the former Franciscan friary in the heart of the city, the **Limerick Museum** is an eclectic and varied collection dedicated to the memory of **Jim Kemmy**, a former mayor and proud Limerick man. The rooms are filled with prehistoric finds, examples of Limerick silver and lace, medieval coins, an old-fashioned diving suit, World War II gasmasks, a mummified cat and fragments of a meteorite which fell in Co. Limerick in 1813, the largest ever to fall in Ireland. If you want to see the infamous **treaty stone** on which the surrender terms of the 1691 siege were signed (see page 305), cross Thomond Bridge to the west bank, where the stone was put on a 2m-high pedestal facing the castle in 1865.

## King John's Castle

King's Island • Daily 10am–5pm; last admission 1hr before closing • €12.60; Heritage Island • ☎ 061 370500, ⓦ kingjohnscastle.com

The dramatically sited Anglo-Norman **King John's Castle** is the city's most eye-catching building – especially when viewed from the banks of the Shannon. An imposing five-sided fortification inaugurated by the king himself in 1210, it had no keep and no tower at its southeast corner facing Englishtown, until a rectangular artillery bastion was added at the beginning of the troubled seventeenth century. A shiny **visitor centre** has facilitated the castle's twenty-first-century rebirth, bringing fresh life into the building with dazzling new displays. Imaginative audiovisuals cover a range of subjects, including early Gaelic society; the Normans, whose arrival in 1169 made Limerick a Royal city; the change and conflict during the sixteenth-century Reformation; the three horrendous sieges the castle suffered in 1642, 1651 and 1690–91; and the history of the castle's excavation. The sights, smells and sounds of the times are graphically captured in the galleries.

---

### LIMERICK FESTIVALS

The city lays on a compelling menu of **festivals** throughout the year. One highlight is **EVA** (ⓦeva. ie), Ireland's pre-eminent biennial exhibition of contemporary art. From mid-March to late May, works by Irish and foreign artists, as selected by a leading international curator, are installed at galleries and around the city. In late May, the **Limerick International Music Festival** (☎061 202620, ⓦirishchamberorchestra.com) is a four-day showcase for the Irish Chamber Orchestra and prestigious guest artists. Also in May, **Riverfest** (ⓦriverfest.ie), is one of Ireland's biggest festivals, with fireworks, fashion shows and street performances. In June and early July, **Blas** (ⓦblas.ie), a highly regarded two-week summer school of traditional music and dance, takes place at the Irish World of Academy of Music and Dance, Limerick University, with associated concerts and sessions around the city. An international poetry festival, **Cuisle** (☎061 407421, ⓦlimerick.ie), encompassing readings, open-mike sessions and workshops, takes place in mid-October.

# Belltable Arts Centre

69 O'Connell St • Mon–Sat noon–5.30pm • ☎ 061 953400, Ⓦ limetreetheatre.ie

A multidisciplinary arts centre, the **Belltable** was rebranded in 2016 under the auspices of the Lime Tree Theatre and houses a cinema, theatre and gallery exhibition space. Every Monday night a film is shown, while in October the **Richard Harris International Film Festival** (Ⓦ richardharrisfilmfestival.com) is held here. The centre also stages a wide variety of concerts, drama, musicals and comedy shows.

**9**

# Terry Wogan Statue

Harvey's Quay

Since its erection in 2017, the controversial life-size bronze **statue** of the Limerick-born BBC broadcaster, **Terry Wogan** – who died in 2016 – has attracted criticism and ridicule for its questionable resemblance to the much-loved Sir Terry (who in 2017 was named "the greatest radio presenter of the last fifty years" in a BBC poll of broadcasting experts). Sculpted by artist Rory Breslin, it depicts a seated Wogan holding a microphone in one hand and book in the other. Perhaps inevitably, given the furore surrounding it, the statue has become a popular tourist attraction.

# Limerick City Gallery of Art

Carnegie Building, Pery Square • Mon–Sat 10am–5pm, Sun noon–5pm • Free • ☎ 061 310633, Ⓦ gallery.limerick.ie

By the entrance to the People's Park stands the **Limerick City Gallery of Art**. Remodelled with renovated galleries, the building is a hybrid of the old and new. Displayed on a rotating basis, the permanent collection of eighteenth- to twenty-first-century paintings and drawings by artists such as Sean Keating, Paul Henry and Jack Butler Yeats will appeal to aficionados of Irish art, but best of all is the gallery's exciting programme of **contemporary exhibitions** by Irish and international artists. A sculpture, *The Siege of Limerick*, by the renowned New York-based artist Brian O'Doherty, was installed to mark the reopening.

# Thomond Park Stadium and Museum

Old Cratloe Rd, 2km northwest of the city centre • Mon–Fri 10am–5pm • Stadium and museum tour €10 (advance booking essential; Sat or Sun tours minimum 6 people) • ☎ 061 421100, Ⓦ thomondpark.ie

Limerick's **Thomond Park Stadium** is home to the **Munster rugby team** – a huge presence in this part of the world – and also stages rock concerts following a redevelopment which doubled its capacity to 26,500. **Tours** offer an intimate account of the Munster players' experience on match day, taking in the dressing room, dugouts and the pitch itself. Also included is a short film recounting the team's history and a visit to the **museum**, which features club memorabilia as well as footage from the "match of all matches" when Munster beat the mighty All Blacks 12-0 in 1978.

## ARRIVAL AND DEPARTURE — LIMERICK CITY

**By plane** Limerick is the nearest city to Shannon International Airport (☎ 061 712000, Ⓦ shannonairport.ie), which serves direct flights from North America, the UK and several other European countries, as well as Irish internal services. The airport has good bus links with Limerick and Ennis, as well as with Cork, Dublin, Galway and Killarney. For timetables consult Bus Éireann (☎ 061 418855, Ⓦ buseireann.ie). A taxi to either Limerick or Ennis will cost around €40–45; there's a taxi desk (daily 6am–midnight; ☎ 061 471538) in the arrivals hall, and information desk (daily 6am–11pm; ☎ 061 712000),

a bureau de change (daily 6am–10pm), ATMs and car-rental.
**By train** The train station (☎ 061 418855) is on Parnell St. Destinations Athenry (4–5 daily; 1hr 40min); Cork (7–12 daily, with a change at Limerick Junction; 2hr); Dublin Heuston (hourly, often with a change at Limerick Junction; 2hr 20min–2hr 40min); Ennis (8–10 daily; 40min); Waterford (Mon–Sat 3 daily, with a change at Limerick Junction; 2hr 25min–3hr 10min).
**By bus** The bus station (☎ 061 418855) is on Parnell St, adjacent to the train station.

**9**

Destinations Adare (hourly; 20min); Athlone (2–4 daily; 2hr 10min); Birr (2–4 daily; 1hr 15min); Bunratty (hourly; 20min); Cliffs of Moher (2–3 daily; 1hr 50min); Cork (hourly; 1hr 50min); Doolin (2–3 daily; 2hr 15min); Dublin (hourly; 3hr 40min); Ennis (hourly; 1hr); Galway (hourly; 2hr 20min); Killaloe (Mon–Sat 4–5 daily; 40–55min); Killarney (6 daily; 2hr); Lisdoonvarna (2–3 daily; 2hr); Listowel (7–8 daily; 1hr 25min); Shannon Airport (Mon–Sat frequent service, Sun at least hourly; 30–55min); Tralee (8–9 daily; 2hr); Tulla (Wed 1 at 5.30pm; 55min); Waterford (6–8 daily; 2hr 30min).

## INFORMATION AND TOURS

**Tourist office** 20 O'Connell St (Mon–Sat 9am–5pm/ 5.30pm, plus July & Aug Sun noon–5pm; ☎061 317522, ⓦlimerick.ie). Dispenses a useful guide-map of the city and county.

**Bus tours** A hop-on-hop-off city bus tour with nine pick-up locations is run by Red Viking Tours (April–Oct 7 daily; €12; ☎061 220555, ⓦredvikingtours.ie), operating from Arthur's Quay Park. Barratt Tours (☎061 333100, ⓦbarrattstours.ie) runs coaches daily to the Burren and Cliffs of Moher (€27) as well as to further-flung destinations such as Cork and Blarney. **Rail tours** Railtours (☎01 856 0045, ⓦrailtoursireland.com) takes in the Cliffs of Moher and Bunratty Castle Mon–Sat.

**Carriage tours** Limerick Carriage Tours operate 1hr horse-drawn trips around the city (June–Aug daily; €25; ☎085 157 8356, ⓦlimerickcarriagetours.com).

**Walking tours** Limerick City Walking Tours (☎061 484 911, ⓦlimerickcitywalkingtours.com) offer a wide range of tours including a two hour walking tour of the city daily at 10am (€18); for a flavour of nature join Albert Nolan on a 1hr looped riverside walk from the city centre to Westfields nature reserve (☎089 423 0502).

**Kayaking trips** Limerick City Kayaking Tours offers kayaking trips on the Shannon (€35 for half day; ☎086 330 8236, ⓦnevsailwatersports.ie).

## ACCOMMODATION                              SEE MAP PAGE 306

**Clayton Hotel** Steamboat Quay ☎061 444100, ⓦclaytonhotellimerick.com. The tallest hotel in Ireland, the building is a distinctive landmark on the cityscape, and juts out over the river with spectacular views. Fantastically plush rooms are complemented by a health and leisure club with swimming pool overlooking the river. €120

**The George Hotel** O'Connell St ☎061 460400, ⓦgeorge limerick.com. Contemporary boutique hotel on the upper floors above the main street, offering well-equipped rooms in a dark wood and red or green contemporary style. Free overnight parking. €159

**Glen Eagles** 12 Vereker Gardens ☎061 455521, ✉glen eaglesbandb@eircom.net. The closest B&B to the city centre on a peaceful cul-de-sac off the N18 Ennis road. All rooms are en-suite with TVs. Closed Christmas and New Year. €70

**Limerick City Hotel** Lower Mallow St ☎061 207000, ⓦlimerickcityhotel.ie. No-frills hotel with over 141 comfortable rooms. Very handy for the centre, but right on one of Limerick's busiest junctions, so unless you're eager for a view of the river, ask for a room at the back. €76

**Mary Immaculate College** Courtbrack, Tarbert Rd. ☎061 302500, ⓦmic.ul.ie. During summer (May to mid-Aug), the university's Mary Immaculate College opens its student accommodation to visitors. A light breakfast is included in the room price. Singles €30, twins €52

★ **No 1 Pery Square** 1 Pery Square ☎061 402402, ⓦoneperysquare.com. Beautifully designed boutique hotel occupying a restored Georgian town house next to People's Park. Some rooms reflect the building's period origins, featuring sash windows and individually designed beds, while others have a spruce contemporary finesse. There's a spa too and a restaurant offering everything from brunch to gourmet tasting nights. €195

## EATING                                      SEE MAP PAGE 306

**Cornstore Restaurant** Thomas St ☎061 609000, ⓦcornstore.ie. Covering three floors and incorporating a wine and cocktail bar, the lively *Cornstore* specializes in seafood such as gourmet fish pie (€18) and dry-aged steaks including chateaubriand (€32). Lunch and dinner menus offer à la carte while Sunday brunch is €25 for two courses. Mon–Wed noon–4pm & 5–9.30pm, Thurs–Sat noon–4pm & 5–10pm, Sun noon–4pm & 5–9pm.

★ **Freddy's Bistro** Theatre Lane ☎061 418749, ⓦfreddysbistro.com. A cosy hideaway with a rustic feel, natural stone walls and a cosmopolitan menu, with dishes such as braised lamb shank, pork belly or fish tacos with tortilla wrap. The early evening menu (until 6.30pm) offers three courses for €40. Tues–Sat 5.30–11pm.

**French Table** 1 Steamboat Quay ☎061 609274, ⓦfrench table.ie. Scintillating French food featuring Languedoc- and Dordogne-style classics such as escargots garlic or Toulouse sausage with an imaginative Irish twist. Confit of duck leg, hake and marinated chicken are menu standards. Three-course dinner menu €28. Tues–Fri noon–4pm & 6–10pm, Sat & Sun 6–10pm.

**Hook and Ladder** 7 Sarsfield St ☎061 413778, ⓦhook andladder.ie. This family-run establishment, housed in a former bank, is open for breakfast, lunch and early evening meals (most mains around €11). Sandwiches, bagels and wraps as well as Mediterranean salads, chowder and chicken and bacon on a blaa (local bread) are all available. You can also indulge in home-baked cakes, pastries and breads, speciality teas, premium coffees and a wide wine selection. Mon–Wed & Sun 9am–5pm, Thurs–Sat 9am–9pm.

**House** Howley's Quay ☎ 061 513282, ⓦ houselimerick. ie. Watch the swans preening in the Shannon as you dine al fresco at this elegant quayside restaurant with a choice of snacks (€5.50), as well as small or large plates; prices are from €12.50 for baked Cooleeny camembert with plum jam and toast, with fish and steak dishes up to €27. Jazz enlivens weekend brunch (noon–4pm). Wed–Fri 4–11.30pm, Sat & Sun 10am–11.30pm.

**Marco Polo** 38 O'Connell St ☎ 061 412888, ⓦ marco polo.ie. This buzzy restaurant's two-course lunch is excellent value at €10 and runs until 5pm. A range of dinner choices are available: two courses are €18, three courses €22, and four €28, and include lamb shank, Atlantic cod, steak or vegetarian options. Mon–Wed & Sun 12.30–9pm, Thurs–Sat 12.30–10pm.

**Mortell's** 49 Roches St ☎ 061 415457, ⓦ mortell catering.com. Established in the 1950s, this appealing, family-run business – a combination of seafood restaurant and deli – is a Limerick institution. Irish fish fresh off the boats is cooked to order by your chosen method with main courses averaging €13. Mon–Sat 8.30am–4pm.

**Nelly's Corner Café** 46 Nicholas St ☎ 061 596333. Occupying a prime corner site beside St Mary's Cathedral, *Nelly's* is a gloriously bustling café that comes with a historic link stretching back 800 years – a line of the inner town wall from 1200 still stands at the back of the building. Their produce is fresh from the butcher's next door and for lunch substantial plates of bacon and cabbage, corn beef, or lamb stew are served on solid oak and pine tables (average price €8–10). Local history books are available for browsing. Mon–Sun 9.30am–6pm.

## DRINKING AND NIGHTLIFE
SEE MAP PAGE 306

**Dolan's** Dock Rd ☎ 061 314483, ⓦ dolans.ie. Top dog for live music, *Dolan's* features traditional tunes in the bar every night, and everything from jazz and singer-songwriters to indie and tribute bands – plus comedy nights – in its two gig venues, The Warehouse and Upstairs. Snow Patrol, Franz Ferdinand and Sharon Shannon have all performed here. Mon–Fri noon–11.30pm, Sat 9am–1.30am, Sun 10am–11pm.

**Locke Bar** 3 George's Quay ☎ 061 413733, ⓦ lockebar. com. Congenial gastropub offering traditional music every night. Tables out the front overlook the River Abbey – a great spot on a sunny day; sample the Hell's Gate lager from the Treaty City Brewery or choose from the wide choice of cocktails. Mon–Thurs 9am–11.30pm, Fri 9.30am–12.30am, Sat 10am–12.30am, Sun 10am–11pm.

**Michael Flannery's** 17 Upper Denmark St ☎ 061 436677, ⓦ flannerysbar.ie. Whiskey connoisseurs love this pub with a pedigree stretching back to 1898. It has a

hundred different types of Irish whiskey and once bottled its own Jameson: a "Whiskey Bible" complete with tasting notes lists them all, and you can sample three tipples in a whiskey tasting (€15). Mon–Wed 10am–11.30pm, Thurs–Sat 10am–1am, Sun noon–11.30pm.

**Nancy Blake's** 19 Upper Denmark St ☎ 061 416443. Time-burnished watering hole with bare wooden sawdust floors, home to traditional music Mon–Wed & Sun. Through the back, a large, covered and heated courtyard and modern bar hosts a DJ on Fri. Mon & Tues 10.30am–11.30pm, Wed–Sun 10.30am–2am.

★ **The White House** 52 O'Connell St ☎ 061 546825, ⓦ thewhitehousebar.ie. Established in 1812 and furnished in dark wood, this is Limerick's oldest pub, and despite modernisation, has managed to retain some of its old essence. Mon–Wed 10am–11.30pm, Thurs 10am–midnight, Fri 10am–12.30am, Sat noon–1am, Sun noon–11.30pm.

## ENTERTAINMENT

For details of all arts events, pick up a copy of the *Limerick Events Guide* (*LEG*), a free **monthly listings magazine** available at the tourist office and in cafés and bars. Although many poetry, music and comedy performances take place in **pubs**, Limerick has its share of quality theatre and concert venues.

**Lime Tree Theatre** Mary Immaculate College, Courtbrack Ave ☎ 061 953400, ⓦ limetreetheatre.ie. This 500-seater hosts drama, music and children's shows.

Two excellent theatrical touring companies – the Abbey from Dublin and the Druid from Galway – stage shows here. **University Concert Hall** Foundation Building, University of Limerick, Castletroy ☎ 061 331549, ⓦ uch. ie. Audiences have enjoyed large-scale operas including *Aida, Carmen* and *Madame Butterfly* at the UCH. Sir James Galway, Christy Moore and Billy Connolly have all performed here, and the Irish Chamber Orchestra holds an annual programme of events.

## SHOPPING
SEE MAP PAGE 306

Limerick's deep-rooted connections with the past are reflected in the many **traditional shop fronts** and you will stumble across victuallers, saddlers and barbers. Don't miss **Fox's Bow**, a funky alleyway of craft, jewellery and gift

shops between Thomas and William streets. For pharmacies, branches of **O'Sullivan's** are on O'Connell St (Mon–Fri 9am–6pm; ☎ 061 405509, ⓦ osullivanspharmacy.com) and round the corner on Sarsfield St (Mon–Fri 9am–11pm).

**9**

**Arthur's Quay Shopping Centre** Patrick St ☎061 412462, ⓦarthursquay.ie. A bright mall with plenty of Irish and British chain stores and designer names. Mon–Sat 8am–10pm, Sun 10am–8pm.

**The Celtic Bookshop** 2 Rutland St ☎061 401155, ⓦcelticbookshop-limerick.ie. A place to lose yourself for an hour or so on a quest for rare or out-of-print Irish classics. Mon–Sat 11am–4.30pm.

**Milk Market** Cornmarket Row ☎061 214782, ⓦmilk marketlimerick.ie. Saturday morning is the best time to enjoy this bustling food market, held in a stone building that was once a corn market and featuring fresh farm produce from all over Munster. Under its canopy you'll find a superb selection of stalls offering farmhouse cheeses, organic sausages, spelt breads, fruit and vegetables,

chutneys, jams and artisan chocolates. You can also snack on soup, crunchy salads, inventive sandwiches, wraps and crêpes, and freshly brewed tea and coffee. Fri 10am–3pm, Sat 8am–3pm, Sun 11am–3pm.

**O'Mahony's Booksellers** 120 O'Connell St ☎061 418155, ⓦomahonys.ie. Long-established independent bookshop, particularly strong on Irish fiction and non-fiction, plus local heritage and maps. Mon–Sat 9am–6pm, Sun 1–5.30pm.

**Silverwood Jewellery** 32 Cruises St ☎061 415973 ⓦsilverwoodjewellery.com. Artfully crafted bespoke jewellery, ranging from Celtic to abstract pieces, are on sale in this eye-catching store. Brooches, necklaces, pendants and rings sit alongside gold and silver, freshwater pearls and semi-precious stones. Downstairs is an Irish graft gallery and a Goldsmiths workshop. Mon–Sat 9.30am–5.30pm.

# Lough Gur

20km south of Limerick city on the R512 towards Kilmallock • Open access to site • ⓦ loughgur.com • The only bus from Limerick to Lough Gur is the 10.30am (Mon–Sat) Kilmallock service – ask for Holycross – with returns at 12.30pm and 4.50pm; a taxi from Limerick will cost €20 each way

Set in a serenely peaceful valley 20km south of Limerick city is one of Ireland's most astonishing and atmospheric places. A cluster of grassy limestone hills springs unexpectedly from the plain, sheltering in their midst **Lough Gur**, the site of dozens of largely **prehistoric monuments**. Their importance lies in the fact that many of them are not ceremonial sites but stone dwelling places, dating from around 3000 BC onwards, which have furnished archaeologists with most of their knowledge of the way of life in Neolithic Ireland. That's not to say that this curious landscape did not have a ritual aspect, as it was also revered as the territory of the sun goddess, Áine, and accrued a powerful mythical reputation, for example as the location of some of Fionn Mac Cumhaill's adventures in the *Ulster Cycle*. Before it was partly drained in the nineteenth century, the lake (now C-shaped) formed an approximate square, with a 9km shoreline around a large triangular island, **Knockadoon**. The drainage, which left a marsh on the eastern side of the island and lowered the lake's level by 3m, revealed hoards of prehistoric items, including gold and bronze spearheads, a bronze shield, swords and stone and bronze axes.

## Heritage Centre

March–Sept Mon–Fri 10am–5pm, Sat & Sun noon–6pm; Oct–Feb Mon–Fri 10am–4pm, Sat & Sun noon–5pm; last admission 30min before closing • €5 • Guided tours (2hr 30min; €50 for a minimum of two people, with admission to site included) must be booked one day in advance on ☎061 385386

The **Heritage Centre** features numerous exhibits and a multimedia exhibition that bring alive six thousand years of history through touch screens, listening posts and audiovisual presentations. The centre also provides a pamphlet detailing **trails** around Lough Gur (also downloadable from the website) – you can explore on your own or join a guided tour.

## The stone circle

The first site you'll come to, on the R512 to the west of the lake at Holycross, is the largest and finest **stone circle** in Ireland. Now set in a grassy glade surrounded by majestic trees, it consists of 113 large stones propped upright in sockets, around an artificial floor of gravelly earth 70cm above the original ground level. Built around 2100 BC, the circle is associated with **Crom Dubh**, the harvest god. The entrance to the northeast is aligned towards sunrise around May 21 before the summer solstice and, correspondingly, around July 22 as the sun travels southwards on the horizon after the summer solstice.

## Gallery grave

About 1km south of the stone circle, the access road to Lough Gur heads east off the R512 around the south shore. Just over 1km in, on the south side of the road, you'll see the so-called Giant's Grave, a wedge-shaped **gallery grave** dating from about 2600 BC, where the remains of eight adults and four children were discovered. It's yet another ancient Irish site where Diarmuid and Gráinne are meant to have lain together on their flight from Fionn Mac Cumhaill, though it has added significance as Gráinne is the alter ego of Áine, the sun goddess.

## Knockadoon

Causeways lead across from near the visitor centre and the Giant's Grave to the island of **Knockadoon**, which is fun to explore though parts are covered in dense woodland. Visible from the visitor centre at the northeast corner of the island is **Bourchier's Castle**, a privately owned, fifteenth-century tower house, while the overgrown remains of the thirteenth-century **Black Castle** face the Giant's Grave from the southern shore. Working west from here, you'll see traces of huts and ring forts on the grassy slopes, and around on the northwest-facing shore of the island, a limestone seat on a small, grassy mound known as the **Housekeeper's Chair**. This was held to be the birth-chair of Áine, from which she turned green corn to gold, for Crom Dubh to carry off at harvest time. A little further on, near the northernmost point of the island, is a **cave** said to be the entrance to Tír na nÓg, the land of eternal youth.

# Adare

With its broad main street lined with thatched cottages and colourful doors, **ADARE** has long been a much-admired stopping place for tourists and draws in coach parties from far afield. Its chocolate-box quaintness can be too sickly for some, however, and, sited some 15km southwest of Limerick on the N21 towards Kerry, it is also marred by its location on a major national road. As the **Heritage Centre** reveals, it was made picturesque by design: the earls of Dunraven, landlords of Adare Manor, beautified their estate village (according to the contemporary fashion for pastoral romanticism) with ornamental thatched cottages in the early nineteenth century, and with Arts and Crafts-style houses in the early twentieth century. Set beside a prim town **park** on the south bank of the River Maigue, Adare's appeal is enhanced by some impressive remnants, mostly ecclesiastical, of its medieval heyday.

## Heritage Centre and castle

Main St • Daily: April–Sept 9am–6pm; Oct–March 9am–5pm • Free; Heritage Island • Castle tours June–Sept daily; €10 • ☎ 061 396425, ⦿ adareheritagecentre.ie

The best place to start is the **Heritage Centre**, centrally located opposite the park on Main Street, which houses the tourist office and sells castle admission tickets. The centre also houses a free exhibition, and there's a restaurant with outdoor terrace seating. From June to September, the restored, early thirteenth-century **Desmond Castle**, on the north side of the Maigue River bridge, can be visited on hour-long guided tours which set off by bus from the Heritage Centre (departure times vary so check with the reception desk).

## The Trinitarian Abbey and Augustinian Friary

The Catholic parish church next door to the Heritage Centre, a trim, multi-aisled affair with an imposing, oak-beamed roof, was part of the **Trinitarian Abbey** until the mid-nineteenth century. Founded around 1230 with an attached hospital, it was the

**9**

only house of the Order of the Holy Trinity in Ireland. Down an alley to one side is a circular stone tower with a conical roof, where the monks kept pigeons – not as a hobby, but for the refectory table. Five minutes' walk away, on the south side of the Maigue bridge, stands the **Augustinian Friary**, which is now an Anglican parish church and school. Founded in 1315, it has an attractive, fifteenth-century cloister, carefully restored by the Dunravens in the nineteenth century then spoiled by the insertion of their brutal family mausoleum.

## ARRIVAL AND INFORMATION ADARE

**By bus** There are hourly buses from/to Limerick (20min).
**Tourist office** Heritage Centre, Main St (April–Sept daily 9am–6pm; Oct–March daily 10am–5pm; ☎ 061 396255, ⓦ adareheritagecentre.ie).

## ACCOMMODATION

**Adare Camping and Caravan Park** 4km south of Adare off the R519 Ballingarry road ☎ 061 395376, ⓦ adarecamping.com. This well-equipped site is handy for exploration of the village and countryside. Closed Oct–April. €22

**Adare Manor Hotel** Limerick Rd ☎ 061 605200, ⓦ adaremanor.com. This Gothic pile dating from 1832 and set in 840 acres, now has 104 luxurious rooms alongside a Michelin-starred restaurant, several bars, a swimming pool and spa, golf course, and pursuits such as falconry, archery and clay pigeon shooting. €595

**Berkeley Lodge** Station Rd ☎ 061 396857, ⓦ adare. org. There are dozens of B&Bs in and around Adare, including this neat and homely pick. It makes a comfy and quiet base, and after a high-quality breakfast you can stroll into the town centre. €85

★ **Fitzgerald's Woodlands House Hotel & Spa** 2km south of the centre, off the Limerick road ☎ 061 605100, ⓦ woodlands-hotel.ie. A gym, pool and spa are part of the deal at this welcoming family-owned hotel in a secluded setting. Many of the sizeable rooms are furnished with comfy settees, and the delightful bistro, *Timmy Macs*, features beef from the owners' very own cattle herd. Good-value midweek breaks are available. €125

## EATING AND DRINKING

**1826 Adare** Main St ☎ 061 396004 ⓦ 1826adare.ie. The focus of this chic restaurant, set in a delightful row of thatched cottages, is on keenly priced casual dining. Their signature dish is the free-range pork tasting plate of loin belly cheek and black pudding (€22.95), but you'll also find blackboard specials such as sole and braised meats. Wed–Sat 5–10pm, Sun 4–10pm.

**Aunty Lena's** Main St ☎ 061 396114, ⓦ auntylenas. com. The extensive bar menu offers salads, sandwiches, wraps and panini, plus bangers and mash and burgers (mains around €15). Traditional music several nights a week. Food served daily 9am–10pm; bar daily 9am–11.30pm.

**The Good Room Café** Main St ☎ 061 396218, ⓦ the goodroomadare.ie. A calming bistro café with outdoor seating, serving breakfast, brunches and lunches. Has a large selection of teas, including detox and caffeine-free varieties, plus juices, smoothies and healthy options.

Mon–Thurs 8.30am–4pm, Fri & Sat 8.30am–5pm, Sun 9.30am–5pm.

★ **The Mustard Seed** Ballingarry, 8km south of Adare on the R519 ☎ 069 68508, ⓦ mustardseed.ie. Set in *Echo Lodge*, a country residence (offering stylish B&B accommodation), this is one of the country's foremost restaurants, with an inspired modern Irish menu drawing from the produce of its organic garden. The four-course "classic" dinner is €67; main courses include rib-eye of beef, monkfish and guinea fowl. Dinner daily 7–9.30pm.

**Wild Geese Restaurant** Rose Cottage, Main St ☎ 061 396451, ⓦ thewild-geese.com. Delicious food served up for breakfast, lunch or dinner in a picture-postcard cottage. Evening cuisine might include pan-seared scallops with pork belly, roast Atlantic cod with crabmeat, or lamb and chicken dishes. Quality doesn't come cheap – the early bird menu (6–7pm) is €30 for two courses, €34 for three. Tues–Sat 6–9.30pm.

# Kilmallock

To escape the crowds and tour coaches of Adare, head south along the N20 and then east on the R515 to **KILMALLOCK**. On the face of it a workaday market town, Kilmallock's position at the centre of Ireland's political development for five centuries has made it something of a heritage hub. Wander around and you'll encounter vestiges of its medieval history, including the town walls, early church sites, a priory and castle standing foursquare, and the formidable **Blossom Gate**, the only one surviving of five sixteenth-century town gates. Kilmallock makes a superb base from which to explore the **Ballyhoura Mountains**, noted for mountain biking, cycle loops and walking trails, and you can also sample part of the **Ballyhoura Way**, a waymarked trail running through southeast Limerick and on to Tipperary.

### ARRIVAL AND INFORMATION KILMALLOCK

**By bus** Buses run from Limerick to Kilmallock (3 daily; 40min).
**Tourist office** County Council Office on Millmount off Lord Edward St (daily 9am–5pm; ☎063 91300, ⍟visit

ballyhoura.com). Pick up a town map which will take you on a self-guided tour of the main historic sites. Information is also available on mountain-biking trails and looped cycle routes of the area and the Ballyhoura Way.

### ACCOMMODATION AND EATING

**Deebert House Hotel** ☎063 31200, ⍟deeberthouse hotel.com. This delightful family-run hotel on the site of an historic mill at the edge of town makes a good base, with twenty spacious and comfortable en-suite rooms. Its restaurant is open daily for lunch and dinner, offering

locally sourced produce such as sausages, O'Sullivan's black pudding and cheese from Effin. There are traditional music nights on Tues in summer, and special packages for cyclists and walkers. €85

# Southeast Clare

Heading north from Limerick to Galway along the busy N18, it's easy to miss some of the attractions of the county's nether region. Consisting largely of flat farmland, its lanes, ideal for cycling, lead to several sites of historic interest. The most southerly is the impressive **Bunratty Castle**, while a short hop further north lies the imaginative **Craggaunowen Project**, with its re-creations of dwellings from bygone times, and the idyllically set monastic site of **Quin Abbey**.

## Bunratty Castle and folk park

Bunratty, 12km west of Limerick • Daily 9.30am–5.30/6pm; last admission to castle 4pm and to folk park 4.15pm • €16.55; Heritage Island • Banquets (€57.75) daily subject to demand 5.30pm & 8.45pm • ☎061 711200, ⍟bunrattycastle.ie • Served by buses from Ennis (hourly; 35min) and Limerick (hourly; 25min)

West of Limerick, bypassed by the main N18 Ennis road, lies the village of **Bunratty** whose **castle** and **folk park** form one of Ireland's most popular attractions. A castle was first built here in 1277 during the Anglo-Normans' brief occupation of southeast Clare, though the present version dates back to the mid-fifteenth century and was constructed for the MacNamaras, a branch of the O'Brien clan. Majestically restored in the 1950s, its keep contains an impressive array of artwork and furniture, mostly dating from the fifteenth and sixteenth centuries. In the evenings, **"medieval banquets"** are staged here, their entertainment consisting of a somewhat twee form of traditional dance, music and song. The expansive castle grounds host the **folk park**, a re-creation of a nineteenth-century village, replete with post office, shops, a church and a pub, all populated by actors in contemporary dress.

### ACCOMMODATION AND EATING BUNRATTY

**Bunratty Castle Hotel** ☎061 478700, ⍟bunratty castlehotel.com. In the village centre, this Georgian hotel has elegant accommodation in period-furnished rooms, as well as fine meals and a spa. Special package rates are available for two nights' accommodation and dinner at the "Bunratty Earl's Banquet" in the castle. €149
**Bunratty Villa** ☎061 369241, ⍟bunrattyvilla.com. A comfortable modern house a short stroll from the castle. The

buffet breakfasts of full Irish or pancakes with maple syrup will sustain you for most of the day. Closed Nov–Feb. €80
**Durty Nelly's** Low Rd ☎061 364861, ⍟durtynellys. ie. A choice of dining is available here at one of Ireland's best-known pubs. The relatively expensive *Loft* restaurant offers an evening menu which might include baked fillet of salmon, Nelly's surf 'n' turf or beef and vegetable stir fry (mains around €18–€27). Pub grub is cheaper (averaging

**9**

€14 for main dishes) and the bar's calendar of events
includes traditional sessions every night from March to

Oct. Mon–Thurs & Sun 10.30am–11.30pm, Fri & Sat
10.30am–12.30am.

## The Craggaunowen Project

14km north of Bunratty • April to early Sept daily 9.30am–5pm; last admission 4pm • €9.95; Heritage Island • ☎ 061 367178,
ⓦ craggaunowen.ie • By car, take the turning east off the R462 7km northeast of Bunratty, just past Sixmilebridge

The **Craggaunowen Project** features reconstructions of dwellings, hunting sites and other aspects of life during prehistoric and early Christian times. Hour-long self-guided tours begin with a sixteenth-century tower house whose displays of medieval art and artefacts include some notable European wood-carvings, before moving on to re-creations of a *crannóg*, ring fort and souterrain, as well as **The Togher**, a real Iron Age wooden roadway which was moved here from County Longford (see page 162). Proof that replicas can sometimes match the real McCoy comes in the form of **The Brendan**, a *curragh* whose hull consists of leather hides stretched over an ash frame, in which Tim Severin and his four-man crew crossed the Atlantic in 1976. A ninth-century manuscript describes how St Brendan the Navigator became the first European to reach the Americas in the sixth century in such a boat – and, though impossible to prove that Brendan did so, Severin certainly demonstrated that the technology described was sufficient for the task.

## Quin Abbey

7km northwest of Craggaunowen, and 10km southeast of Ennis, on the R469 • April–Oct Tues–Sun 10am–4.30pm, Sat & Sun
9.30am–3.30pm • Free

The ruined **Quin Abbey** occupies a glorious pastoral setting. Unusually, the original building incorporated parts of a castle, built by Thomas de Clare in the late thirteenth century, which was subsequently attacked by the Irish, leaving it "a hideous, blackened cave" according to one contemporary observer. In the 1430s the MacNamaras brought Franciscans to Quin to found the friary and used the ruins of the old castle as a base, constructing a remarkable edifice in the process.

# Ennis and around

With a population of around 25,000, **ENNIS** is far and away Clare's largest town. It began its life in the thirteenth century as a small settlement grouped around a long-disappeared O'Brien castle. Nowadays it's a buzzing town set on both sides of the River Fergus, and still largely based around its medieval street pattern and the central, often traffic-clogged O'Connell Street. Though there's little to see here apart from the ruins of a medieval **friary**, to the north of O'Connell Street, the town has decent restaurants, a joyous range of bookshops and independent boutiques and, above all, a thriving **traditional music** session scene. Glór, on Causeway Link (☎ 065 684 3103, ⓦ glor.ie), is a purpose-built **concert hall** with traditional music concerts and festival summer schools. A **farmers' market** takes place every Friday (8am–2pm) in the car park on Upper Market Street.

---

### ENNIS FESTIVALS AND TRADITIONAL MUSIC

Ennis is home to two major festivals: the **Fleadh Nua** (ⓦ fleadhnua.com), over the last week of May, and the **Ennis Traditional Music Festival** (ⓦ ennistradfest.com), which runs for five days in early November. The best source for information about the local traditional music scene, and a good place to pick up CDs by Clare musicians, is Custy's Music Shop on Cook's Lane, off O'Connell Street (Mon–Sat 9am–6pm; ☎ 065 682 1727, ⓦ custysmusic.com).

## The friary

Abbey St • April, May & mid-Sept to Oct Tues–Sun 10am–5pm; June to mid-Sept daily 10am–6pm • €5; Heritage Card • ☎ 065 682 9100, ⓦ monastic.ie/history/ennis-ofm-friary/

Ennis's only real building of note is its thirteenth-century Franciscan **friary**, founded by the O'Briens, and considered, at one time, to be one of Ireland's major educational institutions. While other such establishments did not survive the Reformation, this one did thanks to Murchadh O'Brien's acknowledgement of the rule of the Tudors – he became the first Earl of Thomond in the process, though the friars were finally expelled in the 1570s. Subsequently, the buildings were used as assizes and a jail, as well as providing rooms for visiting dignitaries. In the late seventeenth century the friary became a parish church of the Church of Ireland, before finally being abandoned in 1871. In a niche on one of the fifteenth-century tower's piers is a **carved relief** of St Francis, complete with a habit whose girdle bears the three characteristic knots of the Franciscans, representing chastity, poverty and obedience. In the chancel is the **Creagh Tomb**, which dates from 1843 and incorporates sculptured panels from an earlier fifteenth-century tomb, decorated with astonishingly detailed scenes of Christ's suffering.

## O'Connell Square and around

Away from the friary are several monuments devoted to Ennis's later political significance. O'Connell Square is dominated by a tall obelisk celebrating **Daniel O'Connell**, elected as Clare's MP in 1828. As a Catholic he could not take his seat, but his large majority was a factor in Westminster's subsequent implementation of the

**9**

Catholic Emancipation Act and he was able to attend the Commons when re-elected in 1830. The former Taoiseach **Éamon de Valera**, who represented East Clare (including Ennis) at the Dáil for more than thirty years, is commemorated by a monument outside the Courthouse on Gort Road.

For a fuller picture of Clare's history, the **Clare Museum**, which shares the same building and opening hours as the tourist office on Arthur's Row, covers everything from local archaeological finds to the West Clare Railway (see page 323), taking in a re-creation of a Viking longboat, sport, music and dance on the way. A permanent exhibition, "The Riches of Clare", tells the story of the people, places and treasures of the county.

## ARRIVAL AND DEPARTURE                    ENNIS AND AROUND

**By plane** Buses and taxis run into town from Shannon Airport (see page 309).

**By bus** The bus station on Station Rd is a 15min walk from the town centre.

Destinations Bunratty (hourly; 35min); Cliffs of Moher (2–3 daily; 50min); Cork (hourly; 3hr); Corofin (Mon–Sat 1 daily; 20min); Doolin (2–3 daily; 1hr 15min); Ennistymon (3 daily; 35–50min); Feakle (Thurs 1; 55min); Galway (hourly; 1hr 15min); Kilkee (3–4 daily; 1hr 10min); Kilrush (3–4 daily; 55min); Lahinch (3 daily; 40min–1hr); Limerick

(hourly; 1hr); Liscannor (2–3 daily; 45min); Lisdoonvarna (2–3 daily; 1hr 10min); Miltown Malbay (Mon–Sat 1 daily; 1hr 20min); Shannon Airport (hourly; 30min); Tulla (Thurs 1; 35min).

**By train** The train station (☎ 065 684 0444) is on Station Rd, adjacent to the bus station.

Destinations Athenry (4–5 daily; 1hr); Galway (4–5 daily; 1hr 20min); Gort (4–5 daily; 30min); Limerick (9–11 daily; 40min).

## INFORMATION AND TOURS

**Tourist office** Arthur's Row (July & Aug Mon–Sat 9.30am–5.30pm; Sept–June Tues–Sat 9.30am–5.30pm; ☎ 065 682 8366, ⓦ visitennis.com).

**Tours** Walking tours set off May–Oct from outside the tourist office (May–Oct Mon, Tues & Thurs–Sat 11am; 1hr

30min; €12; ☎ 087 648 3714, ⓦ enniswalkingtours.com). For a coach tour of Clare's major sites, Barratt Tours run summer trips (Mon–Thurs, Sat & Sun; €27; ☎ 061 348700, ⓦ 4tours.biz) to the Cliffs of Moher and the Burren.

## ACCOMMODATION                           SEE MAP PAGE 317

**Newpark House** Tulla Rd, around 2km east of town off the R352 Scarriff road ☎ 065 682 1233, ⓦ newpark house.com. Occupying a lovely woodland setting, this splendid house dates from 1750 and provides stylish period rooms, some including canopy beds. Closed Nov–March. **€110**

**Old Ground Hotel** O'Connell St ☎ 065 682 8127, ⓦ old groundhotelennis.com. The town's finest hotel is set in an ivy-clad, eighteenth-century building with its own relaxing gardens. The rooms are spacious, elegantly designed and furnished, and include a number of suites. There's a library too, plus a bar, bistro and restaurant. **€160**

★ **Rowan Tree Hostel** Harmony Row ☎ 065 686 8687, ⓦ rowantreehostel.ie. A former gentlemen's club is now home to one of Ireland's finest hostels, with rooms ranging from doubles to fourteen-bed dorms. Well-equipped and

thoughtfully furnished, accommodation is mostly en-suite, and there's a café-bar on site plus laundry, lounge and bike storage. **€18**, doubles **€48**

★ **Temple Gate Hotel** The Square ☎ 065 682 3300, ⓦ templegatehotel.com. A soothing blend of old and new, this hotel's swish design incorporates a nineteenth-century former convent that retains its exquisite stained glass. Rooms are modishly decorated, especially the classy suites with kingsize beds and tapestry wall coverings. An on-site pub and restaurant serve a wide choice of excellent meals. **€129**

**Treacy's West County Hotel** Limerick Rd, 1km south of town ☎ 065 682 3000, ⓦ treacyswestcounty.com. This modern hotel comes with a leisure centre featuring three swimming pools, a gym, a hot tub and sauna, and several classy dining options. **€110**

## EATING                                   SEE MAP PAGE 317

**Ennis Gourmet Store** Barrack St ☎ 065 684 3314. The place to pick up premium ingredients for a picnic, and also a source of terrific lunchtime sandwiches, salads, tapas and mini quiches – not to mention the town's finest coffee. Enjoy it – or perhaps a craft beer – out on the terrace or

indoors. Mon–Sat 10am–9pm, Sun noon–8pm.

**Mocha Coffee Company** Arthur's Row ☎ 065 689 1326. A dazzling range of coffees and teas (think everything from soya-milk lattes to wild-berry infusions) to wash down bagels, panini, Greek salads and low-carb wraps. Wine is also available, and you can choose from indoor and outdoor seating. Daily 9am–5.30pm.

**Peckish Vegan Café** Merchant's Sq ☎065 684 3503, ⓦ meanwell.life. Caesar butterbean salad with coconut bacon, falafel pitta or sourdough French toast (mains around €8) are a sample of the fare in this hip hangout with a lively vibe. You can enjoy a silky flat-white or filter fix too.

Mon–Sat 9am–6pm.

**★ Rowan Tree Café Bar** Harmony Row ☎065 686 8669, ⓦ rowantreecafebar.ie. Fine café at the eponymous hostel, offering a tasty blend of tapas, pizzas and pasta at reasonable prices. Vegetarians and vegans are well catered for. Daily 10.30am–9pm.

### DRINKING AND NIGHTLIFE
SEE MAP PAGE 317

**Brogan's Bar** 24 O'Connell St ☎065 684 4365, ⓦ brogansbarennis.com. Local musicians feature here every night in summer with exhilarating performances and a chance to join in a sing-along. Mon–Thurs 11am–11.30pm, Fri & Sat 11am–12.30am, Sun noon–11pm.

**Considines Bar** 15 Parnell St ☎087 908 2599. Known as *Faffa's*, this welcoming pub is highly regarded for its music and holds weekly sessions each Thurs evening, as well as

some other nights. Mon–Thurs 11.30am–11.30pm, Fri & Sat 11.30am–12.30pm, Sun noon–11pm.

**Cruises Bar** Abbey St ☎065 684 1800. Dating from 1658 and named after John Cruise, an English settler and an original merchant of Ennis, this building was one of the "houses of hospitality" attached to the abbey and converted to a pub in 1993. It is still renowned for its hospitality and for links to traditional Irish music. Wed–Sun 5–11pm.

## O'Dea Castle and Dysert O'Dea

Well signposted off the R476, 12km north of Ennis, **O'Dea Castle** (May–Sept daily 10am–6pm; €7; ☎065 683 7401, ⓦ dysertcastle.com) was the stronghold of the O'Dea branch of the O'Brien clan until 1691. Nowadays it houses an archaeological centre and is the best starting point for a history trail leading across fields to the **Dysert O'Dea** site, where St Tola founded a **monastery** in the eighth century. Several later religious remains can be found here, including a twelfth-century Romanesque **church**, extensively rebuilt in the seventeenth. This features a finely carved doorway and gargoyle-like carvings of human faces and animal heads. Nearby stands a **round tower**, badly damaged by Cromwell's guns, and the twelfth-century **White Cross of Tola**, which bears elaborate patterning and several impressive carvings.

## Corofin

On the R476, **COROFIN** is a sturdy, well-defined village that makes a fine base for visiting the Burren. It is noteworthy as the birthplace of one of Ireland's foremost traditional musicians, the accordionist Sharon Shannon. The displays at the **Clare Heritage Centre** on Church Street (May–Oct daily 10am–6pm; €4; ☎065 683 7955, ⓦ clareroots.com) provide a fascinating glimpse of bygone living conditions and focus on the Famine and emigration.

### ARRIVAL AND DEPARTURE
COROFIN

**By bus** Buses drop off/pick up outside the Centra Supermarket halfway along the main street.
Destinations Ennis (Mon–Sat 1 daily; 25min); Ennistymon

(Mon–Sat 1 daily; 35min); Lahinch (Mon–Sat 1 daily; 35min); Miltown Malbay (Mon–Sat 1 daily; 50min).

### ACCOMMODATION

**Corofin Camping & Hostel** Main St ☎065 683 7683, ⓦ corofincamping.com. Comfortable budget accommodation and camping is available at this family-run hostel. The Burren Way walking trail starts outside its door and the owners supply maps to help you find your way. Closed Oct–March. Camping €25, twins €50

**Corofin Country House** Station Rd ☎065 683 7791, ⓔ corofincountryhouse@eircom.net. Comfortable en-

suite rooms and a handy base for touring the southern Burren region and climbing Mullaghmore mountain, known as the Ayers Rock of Ireland. Closed Jan. €74

**Lakefield Lodge** Ennis Rd ☎065 683 7675, ⓦ lakefield lodgebandb.com. Pleasant accommodation on the edge of the Burren. The owners will set up a glorious breakfast and help you plan hiking, cycling or fishing trips. Closed Oct–March. €72

**9**

# East Clare

Less visited than other parts of the county, East Clare still has plenty of attractions, with most focused upon small towns and villages, of which **Killaloe**, sitting by the edge of **Lough Derg**, is the highlight. Offering numerous angling opportunities, the lake itself constitutes the county's eastern boundary and is popular with the more upmarket set, with its villages reminiscent of the English Cotswolds. Away from the lough, the countryside has a vastly different character from the remainder of Clare – it's a mass of hills and a warren of tiny lanes, with interest focused upon two of the county's greatest traditional music centres, **Tulla** and **Feakle**.

## Killaloe

Hillside **KILLALOE** commands a strategic position above the point where the Shannon leaves Lough Derg. It was here that Brian Ború, the eleventh-century High King of Tara and founder of the O'Brien clan, built his palace, Kincora, a massive fort that was the centre of power in Ireland until Brian's death at the Battle of Clontarf in 1014 (see page 571). This stood on the summit of the hill in the spot now occupied by the Catholic church, though no trace of the building remains. About 1km to the north of the town, off the Scarriff road, is the Bronze Age ring fort **Béal Ború**, perhaps occupied by Brian Ború before Kincora's construction.

The local **festival**, Féile Brian Ború, is held over the first weekend of July with street entertainment.

### St Flannan's Cathedral

Just down Royal Parade from the bridge • Open access 9.30am–5pm

Killaloe later became a religious centre, based around thirteenth-century **St Flannan's Cathedral**, featuring an impressive Romanesque doorway, taken from an earlier church that occupied the site, as well as a low, square bell tower. Just beside the doorway is the massive **Thorgrim Stone**, unusually bearing both runic and ogham inscription.

### ARRIVAL AND INFORMATION                    KILLALOE

**By bus** Killaloe is served by regular buses from/to Limerick (Mon–Sat 5 daily; 55min).

**Tourist information** There's a community-run office by the bridge (opening hours vary; ⓦ discoverkillaloe.ie).

**Boat tours** Lough cruises on *The Spirit of Killaloe* (May to mid-Sept daily 1pm; €15; ☎ 086 814 0559, ⓦ killaloeriver cruises.com) leave from across the bridge in Ballina.

### ACCOMMODATION AND EATING

The best options for accommodation and eating are over the bridge in **Ballina**, around 1.5km away.

**Gooser's** Limerick Rd, Ballina ☎ 061 376791, ⓦ goosers. ie. More restaurant than pub, *Gooser's* menu features a local favourite: bacon and cabbage (€12.95) or a choice of steaks, mixed bean and potato curry and vegetarian specials. Their White Gypsy Ruby beer ale is noted for its caramel sweetness and toffee-roast flavour. Mon–Sat noon–10pm, Sun 12.30–9.30pm.

**Kincora House B&B** Church St, Killaloe ☎ 061 376149, ⓦ kincorahouse.com. An attractive town house with four well-appointed rooms that come with crisp linen, good-quality beds and modern showers – in a building whose pedigree stretches back 350 years. €90

**Lakeside Hotel** Ballina ☎ 061 376122, ⓦ lakesidehotel. ie. This place boasts an unbeatable waterside location with its own private jetty. Some rooms overlook the river (for an extra €30) and there are fine views from the restaurant, too. Restaurant Mon–Sat noon–10pm, Sun 12.30–9pm. €110

# Southwest Clare

It's a relatively long haul from Ennis to Clare's southwest, but well worth the effort for the attractions offered by two popular holiday spots and the chance to explore the glorious

**MUSICAL TULLA AND FEAKLE**

The villages of **Tulla** and **Feakle** are renowned for their musical pedigree. The **Tulla Céilí Band** is famed throughout the land – although you're more likely to catch them at a festival somewhere else than in Tulla. Feakle, meanwhile, 20km east of Ennis, proudly hosts the week-long **International Traditional Music Festival** (Ⓦfeaklefestival.ie) in early August, featuring major singers and musicians. You'll hear some majestic performers such as the searing voice of Sean Tyrrell from the Burren, the trad superstar Martin Hayes and the celebrated accordion player Donal Murphy. If you're attending the festival, village **accommodation** consists of the lovely *Clare Ecolodge* (Ⓣ061 924200, Ⓦclareecolodge.ie; €50), and a friendly farmhouse B&B in *Laccaroe House* (Ⓣ061 924150, Ⓦlaccaroehouse.com; doubles €70). Impromptu sessions are often held in the two major **music pubs** in Feakle: *Shortt's* and *Pepper's*. Both villages have sporadic bus links with Ennis (see page 316) and each other (Thurs 1 daily; 20min), while a once-weekly bus also runs from Limerick to Tulla.

scenery of the **Loop Head peninsula**. Of the resorts, **Kilkee** is the livelier, with a sweeping beach and access to Loop Head; **Kilrush** is more stolid, but still attractive in its own way and is a base for dolphin watching and the ferry to **Scattery Island**, a major monastic site.

# Kilrush

Some 40km from Ennis, **KILRUSH** is a graceful planned town whose broad main drag, Frances Street, leads down to a bustling marina where you can catch a ferry to **Scattery Island**. At the town's core stands the **Maid of Éireann** statue, honouring the Manchester Martyrs, three Fenians who were executed in the English city in 1867 for a daring attempted rescue of some of their comrades arrested during a failed uprising.

## Vandeleur Walled Garden

800m east of town by the Killimer road (N67) • Daily 10am–5pm • Free • Ⓣ 065 905 1760, Ⓦ vandeleurwalledgarden.ie

In the early nineteenth century, wealthy landlord John Ormsby Vandeleur built Kilrush House, which once stood in a four-hundred-acre estate. The building was demolished in 1973, but the restored **Vandeleur Walled Garden** is an attractive spot featuring an abundance of subtropical plants.

## Scattery Island

June–Sept daily 9am–6pm • €25 payable at the ticket office at Kilrush marina, includes return ferry and Island Centre admission • Ⓣ 085 250 5512, Ⓦ scatteryislandtours.com.

In high season three or four daily ferries (depending on the tides) run from Kilrush's marina to **Scattery Island**, 2.5km offshore. A monastery was established here by St Senan in the sixth century, and the island retained ecclesiastical importance until its exposed position attracted Viking raiders in 870, who occupied it until defeated by Brian Ború in the late tenth century. Medieval church building is evident in the form of several ruins, and there's a reasonably well-preserved, 35m-high **round tower** which is most impressive when the sun seems to reflect off its yellowy, lichen-covered stone. Derelict since the last inhabitants left in 1978, Scattery has a timeless air. It's well worth making a trip to the island's southern point – where a **lighthouse** and gun battery remain from the time of the Napoleonic wars – for the sense of peaceful isolation and spectacular views. By the pier the **Scattery Island Centre** houses an exhibition on the island's history.

### ARRIVAL AND INFORMATION                                                          KILRUSH

**By bus** Kilrush is served by buses from/to Ennis (2–3 daily; 55min) and Kilkee (2–3 daily; 15min).

about the Loop Head peninsula's towns and villages.

**Tourist information** Ask at *Crotty's Pub* for information

**9**

## ACCOMMODATION AND EATING

★ **Crotty's Pub & B&B** Market Square ☎ 065 905 2470, ⓦ crottyspubkilrush.com. Occupying a prime corner position with charmingly furnished rooms and good-value bar food, this is the pick of places to stay. The bar retains its original Victorian mirrors, and shelves and walls are filled with historical memorabilia. Lunch and evening meals are available and there are traditional sessions in summer. €80

**The Haven Arms** Henry St ☎ 065 905 1267. Bar food is available during the day, with seafood a speciality, but you'll also find burgers and chicken curry on the menu along with other specials. Mon–Thurs 10.30am–11.30pm, Fri & Sat 10.30am–12.30am, Sun 12.30pm–11.30pm.

**Katie O'Connor's Hostel** Frances St ☎ 065 905 1133, ⓦ katieshostel.com. Close to the main town square, this is a well-run place with a fully equipped kitchen. Turf fires in the living room are a big attraction. Ten-, six- and four-bed dorms are available, as well as private rooms. Closed Nov to mid-March. Dorms €18, private rooms €25

**Kelly's Steak and Seafood House** 26 Henry St ☎ 065 905 1811. A variety of steaks and fish dishes such as baked salmon, crab cakes or squid make up the menu in this informal and relaxing restaurant, with main course prices starting at around €11. Daily 6–9.30pm.

# Kilkee and around

Thirteen kilometres northwest of Kilrush, **KILKEE** is a jaunty holiday resort, long popular with Limerick city folk, whose main attraction is a gorgeous, sandy, crescent-shaped **beach** that offers breathtaking cliff-top walks at both its ends. If the sun's hiding, alternative activities include the indoor 60m slide at **Waterworld** (June Sat & Sun 11am–5.45pm; July & Aug daily same hours; €8; ☎ 065 905 6855, ⓦ kilkeewaterworld.ie).

## Loop Head peninsula

A tapering, elongated stretch of land, the **Loop Head peninsula** reaches southwest from Kilkee for some 25km. Though mostly low-lying, there are some staggeringly beautiful **cliff-top walks**; alternatively, it's possible to encompass virtually the whole peninsula by taking the scenic signposted drive from Kilkee or from just west of Moyasta. From the harbour at the village of **Carrigaholt**, which also houses the ruins of a fifteenth-century castle, Dolphinwatch runs excellent summer trips (2hr; €35; ☎ 087 917 5984, ⓦ dolphinwatch.ie; advance booking essential) to see and hear (through a hydrophone) the Shannon **dolphins**. The village also holds an oyster and traditional music **festival** in early May. To the north are the so-called **Bridges of Ross** at Ross Bay – natural arches formed by the ocean's erosion of the cliffs – though in fact there's now only one of the original pair.

## ARRIVAL AND INFORMATION                    KILKEE AND AROUND

**By bus** There are buses to Kilkee from Ennis (2–3 daily; 1hr 10min) and Kilrush (2–3 daily; 15min).

**Tourist information** Ask at Any Occasion Gift Shop on

Circular Rd or Williams' hardware store next door, which also rents bicycles (Mon–Sat 11am–6pm; ☎ 065 905 56041).

## ACCOMMODATION

**Green Acres Campsite** Doonaha ☎ 065 905 7011, ⓦ greenacrescamping.ie. A well-equipped site near the sea and handy for an exploration of Loop Head. It's also in an ideal location for a cycle tour of a section of the Wild Atlantic Way. €20

**Kilkee Thalassotherapy Centre** Grattan St, Kilkee ☎ 065 905 6742, ⓦ kilkeethalasso.com. A family-run health spa which also provides thalassotherapy in the form of seaweed baths and other related relaxations. Five

en-suite rooms are available: one triple, one twin, two doubles and one single. €100

★ **Strand Guest House** Strand Line, Kilkee ☎ 065 905 6177, ⓦ thestrandkilkee.com. Enjoying panoramic views of the ocean, this guesthouse features modern, well-presented rooms, often with special offers available. The business also supports the *Strand Seafood Bistro* whose signature dish is oven-roasted fillet of hake; fresh fish is delivered six days a week straight off the fishing boats at Carrigaholt. €90

## EATING

**Kilbaha Gallery Café** Henry Blake Heritage Centre, Lighthouse Rd, Kilbaha, Loop Head ☎ 065 905 8843, ⓦ kilbahagallery.com. Delicious home-baked snacks and

lunches are one reason to visit this gallery-cum-café-cum-tourist information point where they will help you navigate your way around the peninsula; you can admire local artwork and crafts as well. March–Sept daily 10am–6pm; Oct–Feb Fri & Sat 11am–5pm.

★ **The Long Dock** Main St, Carrigaholt ☎ 065 905 8106, ⓦ thelongdock.com. The best place to eat in Loop Head, with an extensive menu highlighting fruits of the sea such as fish pie (€15.95) surf 'n' turf (€20.95), chowder and a range of shellfish. Outdoor tables make for a memorable dining experience. Mon–Thurs & Sun 12.30–11.30pm, Fri & Sat 11am–12.30am.

**Naughton's** O'Curry St, Kilkee ☎ 086 649 3307, ⓦ naughtonsbar.com. Fishy dishes such as sea bass, hake, sole, turbot and halibut along with the ever-popular fish and chips. Main courses from €13. Daily 6–9pm.

**O'Mara's** O'Curry St, Kilkee ☎ 065 906 0967. A decent old-fashioned bar where the music happens spontaneously most weekends when walk-in musicians arrive at short notice armed with their instruments. Daily 11am–midnight.

# West Clare

More than any other area of Clare, the county's west is associated with **traditional music** – there's many a vibrant session in village pubs all along the coast and **Miltown Malbay** hosts one of Ireland's major music festivals. There are also sandy **beaches**, notably at the attractive resort of **Lahinch**, while, further north, you'll come to the towering **Cliffs of Moher**, close to the traditional music magnet of **Doolin** and, inland, the old-fashioned town of **Ennistymon**. This part of the county has also benefitted immeasurably from the **Wild Atlantic Way** driving route (see page 26), which follows the spectacular coast northwards from Spanish Point up to Ballyvaughan.

## Miltown Malbay

Though set back some distance from the sea, **MILTOWN MALBAY**, 30km northeast of Kilkee, originated as a Victorian holiday resort. Today a thriving small town with an appealing mix of modern cafés, restaurants and pubs and traditional, family-run shops, it makes an excellent base for exploring sections of the Wild Atlantic Way or to soak up some traditional music. The town hosts the week-long **Willie Clancy Summer School** (ⓦ scoilsamhraidhwillieclancy.com), beginning on the first Saturday in July and named after the *uilleann* piper, singer and raconteur who died in 1973. More than a thousand people turn up for the music and dance classes, with seats at a premium.

### ARRIVAL AND ACCOMMODATION                    MILTOWN MALBAY

**By bus** There are infrequent bus connections (Mon–Sat 1 daily) with Ennis (40min–1hr 20min), Ennistymon (30min) and Lahinch (20min).

**An Gleann** Ennis Rd, 1km east of town ☎ 065 708 4281,

ⓦ angleann.net. A friendly two-storey house with four en-suite rooms. Powerhouse breakfasts are generous, and vegetarians are catered for. €80

---

### THE WEST CLARE RAILWAY

A few kilometres north of Kilrush at **Moyasta** is the only extant section of the **West Clare Railway** (May–Sept Mon–Sat 10am–5pm, Sun noon–5pm; €10; ☎ 086 805 2614, ⓦ westclarerailway.ie), which opened in August 1892 and linked Ennis – via a roundabout route through Corofin – to southwest Clare until its closure in 1961. Much of the track was then sold to a Kenyan railway company, but the Moyasta station house and a 2km stretch of the line have been restored and it's possible to take a trip back and forth. The railway was immortalized by the singer **Percy French** who, in 1902, along with his troupe of music-hall entertainers, was due to play an engagement in Kilkee. Unfortunately, the train broke down in Miltown Malbay and French arrived late to discover that most of his audience had already left. He sued the railroad for damages, winning the princely sum of £10, and wrote the song *Are Ye Right There Michael?* as an account of his experiences, the Michael in question being Michael Talty, who was the guard on the train when the incident occurred.

# Lahinch

The seaside resort of **LAHINCH**, 12km north of Miltown Malbay, is renowned for its glorious sandy strand. If the Atlantic is too cold then right by the beach is **Seaworld** (April–Sept Mon–Wed 7am–9.30pm, Thurs & Fri 9am–9pm, weekends 10am–8pm; €7; ☎065 708 1900, ⓦlahinchseaworld.com) with a 25m swimming pool, leisure centre and gym.

## ARRIVAL AND DEPARTURE         LAHINCH

**By bus** Bus Éireann's drop off and pick up point is at the Liscannor Rd bus shelter on the edge of town.
Destinations Cliffs of Moher (2–3 daily; 10min); Corofin (Mon–Sat 1 daily; 25min); Doolin (2–3 daily; 45min); Ennis (2–3 daily; 45min–1hr); Ennistymon (2–3 daily; 5–15min); Liscannor (2–3 daily; 5min); Lisdoonvarna (2–3 daily; 25min); Miltown Malbay (Mon–Sat 1 daily; 20min).

## ACCOMMODATION AND EATING

**Atlantic Hotel** Main St ☎065 708 1049, ⓦatlantichotel. ie. Flickering log fires greet guests at this intimate, family-run hotel. Its fine selection of en-suite rooms comes with crisp cotton duvets, and special offers include discounts for staying a second or third night. **€140**

★ **Barrtrá Seafood Restaurant** 5km south of Lahinch on the N67 ☎065 708 1280, ⓦbarrtra.com. For a sumptuous dinner, the owners of this conservatory restaurant provide a seafood "symphony" featuring the fresh fish of the day. They also have a surprise seafood menu for €50 which changes daily and is only revealed when your plate arrives. Meat and vegetarian (€45) options are all available. Wed–Sat 12.30–4.30pm & 5.30–9pm, Sun noon–7pm.

**Lahinch Surf Hostel** Church St ☎065 708 1040, ⓦlahinchhostel.ie. A well-appointed hostel with four-to ten-bed dorms, plus singles and doubles, which offers laundry facilities and can arrange group tours to the Cliffs of Moher and the Burren. **€17**, doubles **€45**

# Ennistymon

Straddling the River Cullenagh, the relaxed town of **ENNISTYMON**, 4km east of Lahinch, promotes itself as "the town of old shop fronts", to which its long main street bears ample testimony. The **Cascades Walk**, signposted on Main Street, leads along the riverbank past the falls, whose waters tumble over rocks by an old arched bridge. Ennistymon's most famous son was the poet **Brian Merriman**, born here in 1747, who wrote the epic and juicily salacious 1200-line poem, *The Midnight Court*. There aren't many ATMs in West Clare, but you'll find one on Parliament Street in Ennistymon.

## ACCOMMODATION AND EATING         ENNISTYMON

**Byrne's** Main St ☎065 707 1080, ⓦbyrnes-ennistymon. ie. Pleasant rooms – some looking out over the cascading Cullenagh River – in a nineteenth-century Edwardian town house. The high-ceilinged restaurant is noted for its pan-fried fresh fish. **€75**

**Falls Hotel** Lahinch Rd ☎065 707 1004, ⓦfallshotel.ie. A Georgian-style hotel set in woodlands by the water, with pleasant and spacious accommodation. Activities include an aqua and fitness centre. **€160**

# Doolin and around

In the 1960s the then tiny village of **DOOLIN**, 7km north of the Cliffs of Moher, developed a reputation for its **traditional music**, largely thanks to the reputation of a bachelor farmer Micho Russell, a singer, flute and whistle player who enjoyed an international touring career. Attracted by his music, a trickle of enthusiasts began to visit Doolin's pubs to hear the playing of Micho and his two brothers Packie and Gussie, all sadly departed. Today, Doolin is awash with visitors virtually throughout the year, with **pubs** such as *O'Connor's* (in Fisher Street on the way to the harbour), *Fitzpatrick's Bar* in the *Hotel Doolin* (see page 325) and *McGann's* and *McDermott's* at the northern end frequently packed with tourists. Unfortunately, most of the music churned out nightly is not the "pure drop", but either neatly adjusted to suit popular tastes or amplified garbage, and in truth there are many better places to hear Clare's often fabulous traditional music. Non-musical highlights include **Doolin Cave** (mid-Feb to mid-March & Nov Fri–Sun noon–5pm; mid-March to June daily 11am–5pm; July–Sept daily 10am–6pm; Oct daily noon–5pm; tours hourly from opening time; €17.50; ⓦdoolincave.ie), where a 7m silver-gleaming stalactite hangs from the ceiling of the dome-like central cavern; and **boat-trips** from Doolin pier to the Aran Islands (see page 350) and to view the Cliffs of Moher.

## The Cliffs of Moher

**Visitor centre** Daily: Nov–Feb 9am–5pm; March, April, Sept & Oct 8am–7pm; May–Aug 8am–9pm • €10, includes car parking; Heritage Island • ⓣ 065 708 6141, ⓦ cliffsofmoher.ie • **O'Brien's Tower** Open daily but hours vary so check with staff

Some 10km south of Doolin are the **Cliffs of Moher**, stretching downwards to the Atlantic for almost 200m. The cliffs take their name from an old promontory fort, Mothar, and extend some 8km from Hag's Head, west of Liscannor, to a little beyond **O'Brien's Tower**, which was constructed by a local altruist in 1835 at their highest point. Hidden within the hillside, the visitor centre is an impressive architectural feat with a first-floor **restaurant** that offers panoramic seascapes and a reasonable choice of meals. The centre houses the Atlantic Edge exhibition whose interactive touch screens, computer games and 3-D film do in part provide lucid explanations of the cliffs' evolution and wildlife, but overall form a ludicrous electronic counterpoint to the actual glories outside. The best bet is to head straight past the centre and to the steps that curve upwards towards the cliff-top. Then you can opt for turning south towards Hag's Head or in the opposite direction to O'Brien's Tower where a **viewing platform** offers the best sight of the wave-battered cliffs below, enhanced by the resonant roar of the Atlantic waves pummelling the rocks at shore level. Alternatively, you can gain a different perspective of their prodigious stature from one of the regular **boat-trips** that run from the pier at Doolin.

### ARRIVAL AND TOURS                                    DOOLIN AND AROUND

**By bus** All Bus Éireann services stop at the *Doolin Hostel* on Fisher St, where you can also buy tickets for journeys.
Destinations Ballyvaughan (1 daily; 40min–1hr); Cliffs of Moher (2–3 daily; 30min); Ennis (2–3 daily; 1hr 30min); Ennistymon (2–3 daily; 50min); Fanore (1 daily; 40min); Galway (Mon–Sat 2 daily, Sun 1; 1hr 35min–2hr 10min); Lahinch (2–3 daily; 45min); Limerick (2–3 daily; 2hr

15min); Lisdoonvarna (3–5 daily; 15min).
**By boat** Doolin2Aran Ferries (ⓣ 065 707 5949, ⓦ doolin2 aranferries.com) runs services to all three Aran Islands: Inisheer (30min), Inishmaan (45min) and Inishmore (1hr 15min), between March and October (2–4 sailings daily; single €20) They also run a Cliffs of Moher cruise (€20).

### ACCOMMODATION AND EATING

**Aille River Hostel** At the crossroads on the R479, 2km from Doolin Holiday Cottages (IHH) ⓣ 065 707 4260, ⓦ ailleriverhosteldoolin.ie. Centrally situated cottage-style hostel offering a variety of dorms, a big kitchen and wood-burning stove. Camping facilities are sheltered in a flat garden behind a stone wall. Dorms **€15.50**, camping **€20**
**Aran View Country House** Coast Rd ⓣ 086 379 4120, ⓦ aranview.com. Dramatically sited above the village, this is a fine country house hotel offering tremendous views from its attractive rooms. **€120**
★ **Cullinan's Guesthouse** On the R479, 2km from Doolin Holiday Cottages ⓣ 065 707 4183, ⓦ cullinans doolin.com. Excellent B&B run by welcoming hosts, adjacent to the T-junction in the village centre. Well-appointed en-suite rooms. Closed Dec & Jan. **€100**
**Hotel Doolin** On the R479, 2km from Doolin Holiday Cottages ⓣ 065 707 4111, ⓦ hoteldoolin.ie. Doolin's plushest hotel also features a restaurant, pizzeria (6–

11pm), café (11am–4pm) and *Fitz's Bar and Eatery*, where "The Trawler", a platter towering with fresh seafood, is best washed down with a glass of their own smooth red "Dooliner" ale. The annual Doolin craft beer festival is based here at the end of Aug each year. **€160**
**Rainbow Hostel** Roadford, Doolin (IHH) ⓣ 065 707 4415, ⓦ rainbowhostel.net. Unquestionably the cosiest Doolin hostel, by *McDermott's* pub in the north of the village; it is also well equipped, with three common areas, kitchen and dining room. Dorms **€17**, private rooms **€35**
**Roadford House Restaurant and B&B** Roadford, Doolin ⓣ 065 707 5050, ⓦ roadfordrestaurant.com. A "melody" of seafood (a combination of shellfish and white fish) is the signature offering at this delightful restaurant and guesthouse. As well as standard double rooms there's a family room plus a two-bedroom self-catering apartment (minimum three-night stay). Closed Nov–March. Restaurant Tues–Wed & Fri–Sun 6–8.30pm. **€95**

**9**

# The Burren

**The Burren**'s name derives from the Irish word *boireann*, meaning "stony place" – an apt description for this desolate plateau that occupies the county's northwest. Its northern and western edges hug the coast road from Doolin up to Ballyvaughan, while, to the south and east, the rocks gently slope towards lush green fields. Formed mainly of fissured limestone pavement, pitted by occasional valleys hidden beneath ominous-looking cliffs, the Burren is a thoroughly otherworldly place with barely a sign of life. The starkness of the landscape, crisp white in sunlight, deep grey-brown in rainfall, has a primeval allure and remains utterly fascinating. Few now live within its bounds, but many endured this harsh environment in the past, leaving relics of their habitation. Ancient burial practices are reflected in the abundance of **Stone Age monuments**, while later, Iron Age people built **ring forts** and **circular stone** dwellings, many of which remain well preserved. The area's coastal outskirts include attractive resorts such as lively **Ballyvaughan** and tiny **Fanore**, while inland lie the spa town of **Lisdoonvarna**, famous for its matchmaking festival, and the renowned traditional music village **Kilfenora**; all make fine bases.

## INFORMATION AND ACTIVITIES

THE BURREN

**Walking tours** Themed walks and treks are organized by Burren Hill Walks of Corkscrew Hill, Ballyvaughan (☎ 065 707 7168, ⊕ burrenhillwalks.ie); and Heart of Burren Walks, with the knowledgeable local author Tony Kirby (☎ 087 292 5487, ⊕ heartofburrenwalks.com).

**Horseriding** The Burren Riding Centre (☎ 065 707 6140,

⊕ jjq@eircom.net) in Fanore offers horseriding, including trails along the "green roads", trekking in the Burren and beach hacks.

**Surfing** The Aloha Surf School at Fanore beach (☎ 087 213 3996, ⊕ surfschool.ie) offers lessons and all necessary equipment.

## Lisdoonvarna

**LISDOONVARNA**, 8km east of Doolin, is a small town with a long street that developed in the nineteenth century around its old spa, whose sulphated waters were believed to have curative properties. Reinvigoration aside, Lisdoonvarna's calendar is focused upon its **matchmaking festival** (⊕ matchmakerireland.com), an annual September rally for the lovelorn, which runs for almost a month. The festival dates back to the times when dealers at street fairs acted as matchmakers, arranging marriages for bachelor farmers too land-tied to seek their own nuptial bliss.

### Burren Smokehouse

Just west of the central crossroads • May–Sept daily 9am–6pm; Oct–Dec, March & April Mon–Fri 9am–5pm, Sat & Sun 10am–4pm; Jan & Feb Mon–Fri 9am–5pm, Sat 10am–4pm • Free • Tours €8.50 • ☎ 065 707 4432, ⊕ burrensmokehouse.com

You may be tempted by the **Burren Smokehouse**, which specializes in smoked salmon and sells a tantalizing range of local artisan gourmet foods. The visitor centre includes a video about the smoking process.

## ARRIVAL AND DEPARTURE

LISDOONVARNA

**By bus** Buses drop off and pick up on the main square, beside Burke's garage.

Destinations Ballyvaughan (Mon–Sat 2 daily, Sun 1; 25–45min); Cliffs of Moher (2–3 daily; 15–25min); Doolin (2–3

daily; 10min); Ennis (2–3 daily; 1hr 10min); Ennistymon (2–3 daily; 30min); Galway (Mon–Sat 2 daily, Sun 1; 1hr 20min); Lahinch (2–3 daily; 25min); Limerick (2–3 daily; 2hr).

## ACCOMMODATION AND EATING

**Burren Sleepzone Hostel** Kincora Rd ☎ 065 707 4036, ⊕ sleepzone.ie. An excellently equipped An Óige-affiliated hostel set in the landscaped grounds of a former hotel; kitchen/dining room, TV and reading room. **€15**

★ **Rathbaun Hotel** Main St ☎ 065 707 4009,

⊕ rathbaunhotel.com. A well-maintained hotel with ten en-suite rooms. In the summer, music is guaranteed every night since the hotel has a pool of live-in musicians, ranging from banjo players to *uilleann* pipers who perform in the bar. Closed mid-Oct to Easter. **€85**

**Roadside Tavern** Kincora Rd ☎ 065 707 4084, ⓦ roadsidetavern.ie. Just how an Irish pub should be, with mighty craic, nightly food and weekend music. The owner, Peter Curtin, runs a microbrewery producing craft beers such as the Burren Black. He can also explain the link between J.R.R. Tolkien and the Burren. Mon–Thurs 10.30am–11.30pm, Fri & Sat till 12.30am, Sun noon–11pm.

**Royal Spa Hotel** Main St ☎ 065 707 4288, ⓦ royalspahotel.com. Dating from 1832, this hotel features tastefully decorated en-suite bedrooms – but ask to see a few as some are on the small side. Tasty pizzas are available in the bar (Tues–Sun 5.30–9.30pm). Daily 5.30–11.30pm. €90

★ **Sheedy's Hotel & Restaurant** ☎ 065 707 4026, ⓦ sheedys.com. The oldest building in the village, with rooms decorated in traditional country house style, with floral patterns and mahogany furniture. Local produce is used for everything from bread and jam to ice cream. In the restaurant (four-course menu €60), duck, scallops and risotto are among the dishes, while the rack of Burren lamb is highly recommended and evening bar meals are available. Closed Oct–Easter. €150

**Wild Honey Inn** Kincora Rd ☎ 065 707 4300, ⓦ wildhoneyinn.com. A stylish bistro that serves much-talked-about food and offers accommodation in fourteen amenable rooms, many with original features. All ground-floor rooms have doors that open onto the garden, each with its own terrace. The set dinner menu is from €40 and includes such dishes as wild turbot with courgettes and anchovy cream, farmed chicken and lamb. Closed Nov–Feb. €120

# Kilfenora

Nine kilometres southeast of Lisdoonvarna, the village of **KILFENORA** is one of Clare's most celebrated **traditional music** centres. Its fame is intrinsically linked to the **Kilfenora Ceili Band**, Ireland's oldest and most illustrious, and on Wednesday nights in summer some of its members play in *Linnane's* pub. *Vaughan's* pub, meanwhile, has set dancing in its barn (Sun) as well as a session in the pub itself (Tues & Thurs in high season).

## The Burren Centre

Main St • March–Oct daily 10am–5pm • €6; Heritage Island • ☎ 065 708 8030, ⓦ theburrencentre.ie

The **Burren Centre** provides an entertaining account of the area's history, with its "In a Walk through Time" exhibition featuring imaginative and interactive displays and models that explain its geology and antiquities. Don't miss the permanent exhibition on traditional music ("The Kilfenora Ceili, Band Parlour"), which traces the one-hundred-year history of Ireland's oldest and most illustrious ceili band, which sometimes performs live here.

---

### THE COAST TO BALLYVAUGHAN

One of the most dramatic routes around the Burren is the **R477** – now part of the **Wild Atlantic Way** driving route (see page 26) – which traces the shoreline from just northwest of Lisdoonvarna to **Ballyvaughan** (see page 328), via the tiny village of **Fanore**, (which offers a couple of peaceful accommodation options). Inland, and inaccessible by car, is a crisscross pattern of the old **"green roads"**, offering upland walking and majestic panoramic views. Just 5km northwest of Lisdoonvarna, near the junction with the R479 Doolin road, you'll spot **Ballinalacken Castle**, a fifteenth-century tower house, perched high above the road. The coast road north of Ballinalacken is dramatic and sometimes shrouded in the mornings by the haze of a sea fret. The road rounds Black Head, where you can climb up to **Caheerdoonfergus** ring fort and gaze across Galway Bay before heading on to Ballyvaughan.

#### ACCOMMODATION

★ **Ballinalacken Castle** R477, near the ruins of Ballinalacken Castle ☎ 086 361 3719, ⓦ ballinalackencastle.com. Converted Victorian mansion, now a hotel, where some of the bedrooms enjoy fantastic views of the Aran Islands. Its restaurant serves sumptuous dinners (closed Tues) using local produce such as scallops and lamb. Closed Nov to mid-April. €170

**Rocky View Farmhouse** Fanore ☎ 065 707 6103. Tremendous views, relaxing en-suite rooms and a great base for touring the coastline and the enigmatic Burren landscape. Closed Oct–Easter. €75

**9**

## Kilfenora Cathedral

Main St • Open access

Hard by the Burren Centre stands the ruined twelfth-century **Kilfenora Cathedral**, site of the county's largest concentration of high crosses. The twelfth-century Doorty Cross in the chancel is especially impressive; its faces depict various ecclesiasts and a scene from the Crucifixion.

### ARRIVAL AND ACCOMMODATION                                                KILFENORA

**By bus** June–Aug there's a daily Bus Éireann service from Galway to Kilfenora (check times ☎091 562000); there is no longer a direct service to the village during the rest of the year.

**Vaughan's** Main St ☎065 708 8004, ⓦvaughanspub.ie.

This sparkling guesthouse offers nine lovely rooms (mostly doubles), while the neighbouring pub is forever known as the "Father Ted Pub", since one episode of the Channel 4 comedy series featured scenes in the bar; the folk here also have their finger on the village's musical pulse. **€90**

# Ballyvaughan and around

Built in 1829 to assist the fishing industry, **BALLYVAUGHAN**'s harbour saw the village develop as a major trading centre and, not long afterwards, steamers began to ply between here and Galway, bringing visitors and establishing the tourist trade. It's an eye-catching village, especially when the sun gleams on its predominantly white and cream houses, and is an ideal base for exploring the Burren. Roads south from Ballyvaughan lead to a wealth of **ancient** and some **medieval sites**. The first of these, a kilometre or so down the R480 and off to the west, is **Newtown Castle** (May–Sept Mon–Fri 9am–2pm; free; ☎065 707 7200, ⓦnewtowncastle.com). This restored sixteenth-century tower house with walls almost 4m thick, complete with murder holes and gun loops, is now part of the grounds of the Burren College of Art.

## Aillwee Cave

Ballyallaban Rd • Daily 10am–5.30pm; July & Aug until 6.30pm; flying displays May–Aug daily noon, then hourly til 5pm • €18; Heritage Island • ☎065 707 7036, ⓦaillweecave.ie

A little way south of Newtown Castle, **Aillwee Cave** is reckoned to be two million years old. Guided tours visit caverns and bridged chasms, allowing you to marvel at weird rock formations, numerous stalagmites and stalactites, and the hibernation chambers of a long-extinct species of brown bear. The ticket price also includes entry to the **Burren Bird of Prey Centre** (same hours), which stages flying displays of various avian predators and offers the opportunity to "take a hawk for a walk".

## Gleninsheen Wedge Tomb and the Poulnabrone dolmen

About 3km south of Aillwee Cave, and just off the eastern side of the R480, is the **Gleninsheen Wedge Tomb**, the best preserved of its kind in the area. In 1930 a remarkable, finely worked gold collar was discovered here by a boy hunting rabbits and is now held by Dublin's National Museum. Just a kilometre south from here is the **Poulnabrone dolmen**, the best known and most photographed of the Burren's seventy or so megalithic tombs. When excavated in 1986, the remains of some thirty people were uncovered, along with tools, utensils and jewellery, providing evidence that the tomb dated from around 2500 BC.

## Caherconnell Stone Fort

1km south of the Poulnabrone dolmen • Daily March–Oct 10am–5.30pm; July & Aug until 6pm • €7 • ☎065 708 9999, ⓦcaherconnell.com

**Caherconnell Stone Fort** is the most substantial of the Burren's many ancient remains. Such circular homesteads, with their dry-stone walling, were built from around the fifth century onwards; this one is 40m in diameter with nearly 4m-thick walls. Displays recount how the daily life of its residents might have been spent, as well as describing the building's design and other Burren monuments.

## ARRIVAL AND DEPARTURE

**By bus** The Galway to Lisdoonvarna service stops outside the Spar Foodstore (also known as The Village Store) on Ballyvaughan's main street.

Destinations Cliffs of Moher (1 daily; 55min); Doolin (Mon–

Sat 2 daily, Sun 1; 40min); Galway (Mon–Sat 2 daily, Sun 1; 1hr 10min); Kinvara (Mon–Sat 2 daily, Sun 1; 30min); Lisdoonvarna (Mon–Sat 2 daily, Sun 1; 25min).

## ACCOMMODATION AND EATING

**An Fear Gorta** Pier Rd ☏ 065 707 7023, ⓦ tearooms ballyvaughan.com. A daytime café with a delightful conservatory for lunches and substantial snacks, noted for its delectable cakes and lip-smacking coffee. Steven Spielberg is a fan – he has visited the café on several occasions while passing through this part of the west. May–Sept daily 10am–6pm; Oct Thurs–Sun 11am–5pm; Nov & Dec Fri–Sun 11am–5pm.

**Dolmen Lodge** Tonarussa ☏ 065 707 7202, ⓦ dolmen lodge.com. A modern farmhouse 800m east of the village in a rural setting, perfect for immersing yourself in the mystery of the Burren. Closed mid-Sept to March. **€80**

★ **Gregans Castle Hotel** 5km south of Ballyvaughan on the N67 ☏ 065 707 7005, ⓦ gregans.ie. A luxurious eighteenth-century building with astonishing evening dining-room views of the ever-changing colours of the limestone landscape. The setting and food combine to create the perfect ambience. Closed Dec to mid-Feb. **€280**

**Larder Deli & Café** Ballyvaughan Enterprise Centre

☏ 086 733 3454. Local produce of Clare lamb, pork, beef and St Tola goat cheese dominates the menu along with soup and quiche for lunch, with main course prices around €7–12. Smooth, sweet and full-bodied blends of coffee from the Anam Roastery in Kilfenora will help kick-start your limestone pavement walk. June–Aug Wed–Sun 10.30am–4.30pm.

★ **Ó Loclainn's Bar** Pier Rd ☏ 065 707 7006. As good for local lore as it is for drinks – Margaret, who runs the bar with her husband, dispenses tourist information and drams from their dazzling array of whiskies in equal measure. Mon–Sat 8.30–11.30pm, plus Sun after Mass from around 2.30pm.

**The Wild Atlantic Lodge** Main St ☏ 065 707 7003, ⓦ thewildatlanticlodge.com. Top-class accommodation in this rebranded lodge with a bar and adjoining *Wildflower Restaurant* where the menu includes pork belly (€13.95) cod, steak, or smoky vegetable lasagne. March–Oct daily 1–9pm; Nov–Feb Wed–Sun 1– 9pm. **€95**

# Galway and Mayo

DIAMOND HILL

# Galway and Mayo

Sweeping strokes of geology have carved up the landscape of Galway and Mayo, forming a many-pronged block between Galway and Sligo that's almost cut off from the mainland by a string of lakes. In the south, the 40km stretch of Lough Corrib neatly bisects County Galway, the second-largest county in Ireland after Cork. On one side, the flat, gentle grasslands of east Galway stretch across to the Shannon, sheltering a fascinating diversity of historic castles, cathedrals, monasteries and country estates. Between the Corrib and the sea, however, stands the violent jumble of Connemara, a much-romanticized land with glittering islands, shimmering lakes, wild mountains and bog land. Both counties are on the Wild Atlantic Way driving route, where the ocean crashes fiercely against headlands and inlets filled with deserted beaches, wide skies and seascapes. It is, in short, a place of nature on a grand scale.

If you're looking for specific tourist attractions, there's a diverting cluster around the lakeside village of **Oughterard**. Connemara's main base, however, is **Clifden**, which boasts a fine range of facilities at the heart of the mountains. On the narrow neck of land between these eastern and western halves sits **Galway city**, an animated, historical town with an enjoyable social, musical and artistic life. The city gives a whiff of the Gaelic culture that's far more noticeable out on the **Arans**, starkly beautiful islands that used to form a barrier across the entrance to Galway Bay. As well as sheltering some breathtaking prehistoric and early Christian sites, the islands are part of the country's largest Irish-speaking area, which also comprises the eastern section of Connemara.

Though ranking just behind Galway in terms of size, **County Mayo** has only half its population and is less developed for tourism. An exception is the eighteenth- century planned town of **Westport**, a comfortable, elegant base from which to tackle the pilgrims' path to the top of **Croagh Patrick**, and to visit the diverse inhabited **islands** at the mouth of Clew Bay. In the north of the county, the intriguing Neolithic agricultural remains at **Céide Fields** provide a compelling focus, surrounded by kilometre after unexplored kilometre of desolate bogland.

# Galway city

Known for its festivals, music and bars, **GALWAY** (Gaillimh) is a culturally vibrant, fun-loving place and, though it has few sights to visit, many people end up staying longer than they'd intended. Conveniently, history and leisure combine here: the **pubs**, many of which retain their original, huge fireplaces and other Gothic features, are the best places to get a feel for the medieval city. As the **capital** of the Gaelic West – it's the only city in the country where you might possibly hear Irish spoken on the streets – Galway draws young people to study at the National University of Ireland, Galway and the Institute of Technology. In the summer holidays, however, its bohemian diversity becomes more overt, as hundreds of English-language students renew the city's traditional maritime links with the Continent, while dozens of buskers from all over the world sing for their supper.

This cosmopolitan atmosphere is reinforced by the setting: Galway is the only coastal city in Ireland that really seems to open up to the sea, and its **docks** sit cheek by jowl with the compact **city centre**, as you're constantly reminded by salty breezes and seagulls. Though small, the city divides into distinct areas: the **Latin Quarter**, the **West End**, **Woodquay** and the **East Village**, each with its own special ambience. The jewel in

INISHEER CEMETERY

# Highlights

❶ **Galway festivals and pubs** It's hard not to have a good time in the vibrant, youthful capital of the west. See pages 337 and 343

❷ **Islands** Choose between the wild beauty of the Arans, the grandiose scenery of accessible Achill, and Inishbofin's small-scale charms. See pages 350, 365 and 378

❸ **Dun Aengus, Inishmore** The most exciting of the many ancient forts on the Aran Islands, spectacularly sited on a 90m cliff face. See page 353

❹ **Walking in Connemara** The best way to appreciate the dramatic mountains, bogs and lakes. See page 360

❺ **Croagh Patrick** A tough climb, enriched by historical and religious associations, and outstanding views. See page 373

❻ **National Museum of Country Life, Castlebar** A fascinating peek at the realities of traditional life in rural Ireland, debunking the nostalgic myths. See page 377

❼ **Céide Fields** A 5000-year-old farming community preserved under the bog. See page 381

**HIGHLIGHTS ARE MARKED ON THE MAP ON PAGE 334**

# GALWAY & MAYO

0 ——————————— 25
kilometres

N

**HIGHLIGHTS**

1 Galway festivals and pubs
2 Islands
3 Dun Aengus, Inishmore
4 Walking in Connemara
5 Croagh Patrick
6 National Museum of Country Life, Castlebar
7 Céide Fields

**10**

# GALWAY CITY

**● EATING**

| | |
|---|---|
| Ard Bia at Nimmo's | 12 |
| Black Gate Café | 3 |
| Brasserie on the Corner | 2 |
| Corrib House Tearooms | 1 |
| The Dail Bar | 8 |
| Goya's | 5 |
| Kappa-ya | 7 |
| Martine's | 11 |
| McDonagh's Seafood Bar | 10 |
| Oscar's Seafood Bistro | 13 |
| Trattoria Magnetti | 9 |
| Tulsi | 6 |
| Upstairs @ McCambridge's | 4 |

**■ ACCOMMODATION**

| | |
|---|---|
| Adare | 18 |
| Ardawn | 2 |
| Cappa Veagh | 14 |
| Corrib Village | 9 |
| G Hotel | 1 |
| The Galmont | 3 |
| Galway Bay Hotel | 16 |
| Harbour Hotel | 8 |
| The Hardiman | 5 |
| Heron's Rest | 12 |
| The House Hotel | 11 |
| Kinlay Hostel | 6 |
| Marless House | 15 |
| St Jude's | 13 |
| Salmon Weir Hostel | 7 |
| Salthill Caravan Park | 17 |
| Sleepzone | 4 |
| Snoozles | 10 |

**■ DRINKING & NIGHTLIFE**

| | |
|---|---|
| Busker Browne's | 4 |
| The Crane Bar | 8 |
| The King's Head | 3 |
| Neachtains | 5 |
| O'Connell's | 1 |
| The Quays | 6 |
| Róisín Dubh | 7 |
| Tigh Coili | 2 |

**● SHOPPING**

| | |
|---|---|
| Charlie Byrne's Bookshop | 5 |
| Eason's Bookshop | 3 |
| McCambridge's Deli | 2 |
| Ó Máille | 4 |
| Sheridan's Cheesemongers | 6 |
| Treasure Chest | 1 |
| Weekend Market | 7 |

River Corrib Cruises

PROSPECT HILL

FORSTER STREET

Private Coach
Station

BÓTHAR NA MBAN

STATION ROAD

EYRE
SQUARE

Bus Éireann
& Train Station

VICTORIA PLACE

Town Hall
Theatre

EYRE STREET

ST VINCENT'S AVENUE

ST FRANCIS STREET

MARY STREET

EGLINTON STREET

WILLIAMS GATE

WILLIAM STREET

Eyre Square
Shopping Centre

QUEEN ST

SALMON WEIR
BRIDGE

UPPER ABBEYGATE ST

LOWER ABBEYGATE ST

MERCHANTS ROAD

DOCK RD

St Nicholas's
RC Cathedral

BOWLING GREEN

MARKET STREET

Lynch's
Castle

SHOP STREET

ST AUGUSTINE STREET

MIDDLE STREET

Earl's
Island

GAOL ROAD

Lynch's Window

CHURCH LANE

St Nicholas's
Church

LOMBARD STREET

CHURCHYARD STREET

MAINGUARD STREET

HIGH STREET

Dillon's
Jewellers

The Mick
Lally Theatre

River Corrib

CROSS STREET

KIRWAN'S
LANE

QUAY STREET

The Hall of the Red Earl

NEW DOCK STREET

BRIDGE STREET

FLOOD STREET

SPANISH PARADE

NUNS' ISLAND STREET

Spanish
Arch

LONG WALK

Galway
City Museum

MILL STREET

Police
Station

LOWER DOMINICK STREET

WOLFE TONE BRIDGE

Fishery
Tower

RAVEN TCE

UPPER DOMINICK STREET

FAIRHILL ROAD LOWER

FATHER GRIFFIN ROAD

NEW ST W

WILLIAM ST W

0    100
metres

13, 14, 15, 16, 17, 18, Salthill & Spiddal

**GALWAY'S FESTIVALS**

The city's biggest shindig is the two-week **Galway International Arts Festival** in July (@giaf. ie), a volatile mix of drama, music, poetry, dance and the visual arts. Hard on its heels, in late July or early August, comes the even headier brew of the **Galway Races** at Ballybrit, about 5km east of town (@galwayraces.com), when farmers and politicians rub shoulders to party and bet. The diverse festival calendar also includes part of the **Father Ted** jamboree (see page 38); **Cúirt**, an international festival of literature in late April (@cuirt.ie); the **Galway Early Music Festival** in late May (@galwayearlymusic.com); the **Galway Sessions** of Irish and Scottish music in June (@galwaysessions.com); and a prestigious, week-long cinema festival in early July, the **Film Fleadh** (@galwayfilmfleadh.com). There's a weekend **jazz festival** in mid-September (@galwayjazzfest.com), while at the end of September the riotous, four-day **Galway Oyster Festival** (@galwayoysterfest.com) includes the world oyster-shucking championships. Towards the end of the year, **Baboró** is an international arts festival for children in October (@baboro.ie), while November's **TULCA** is a festival of contemporary visual art (@tulca.ie).

**10**

the city's crown is the long, pedestrianized main drag of **William**, **Shop**, **High** and **Quay streets**, which becomes a boisterous, Mediterranean- style promenade during summer, lined with pub and restaurant tables. At its lower, western end, the street narrows to its original medieval dimensions, then flows into Galway Bay along with the thundering **River Corrib**, providing faraway views of the Burren hills of County Clare.

### Brief history

Strategically located in the narrow gap between Lough Corrib and the sea, Galway was little more than the site of a twelfth-century fort when it was captured from the Gaelic O'Flaherty clan in 1232 by the Anglo-Norman **Richard de Burgo**, who built a castle by the river. From the fifteenth century, the town was controlled by an oligarchy of mostly Anglo-Norman families, by the names of Athy, Blake, Bodkin, Browne, Darcy, Deane, Ffrench, Ffront, Joyce, Kirwan, Lynch, Martin, Morris and Skerrett. Cromwell later dubbed them the "**Tribes of Galway**", an epithet which they adopted as a badge of honour – to this day, Galwegians nickname themselves the Tribesmen. Under this oligarchy, Galway grew wealthy as a largely independent **city-state**, far removed from the centres of power in Dublin and London but trading extensively with Europe, especially Spain and France.

The town remained proudly loyal to the English Crown, but this only elicited harsh treatment when Cromwell's forces arrived in 1652. Thereafter, Galway went into decline, exacerbated by the **Williamite War** later in the century, and fluctuating with the development of adjacent Salthill as a seaside resort in the early nineteenth century, the arrival of the railways and the building of navigable waterways to Lough Corrib in the 1840s and 1850s, alongside the depredations of the Great Famine. Growth returned in the **late 1960s** with industrial and tourism development, and Galway is now the fourth-largest city in the Republic.

## Eyre Square

The natural place to begin an exploration of the city is **Eyre Square**. This former common land, jousting ground and market square outside the city walls was until recent times a municipal wasteland, but has been pleasingly renovated. Here you'll find a splendid **fountain**, erected in 1984 to mark the city's quincentenary, which evokes a hooker (the traditional sailing boat of Galway Bay) in rusted metal and rushing water; and the **Browne doorway**, a finely carved mercantile town house entrance forlornly set in a concrete wall. The square's fourteen fluttering **flags** each represent one of the Tribes of Galway. In the Eyre Square Shopping Centre, on the southwest side, stands an extensive, heavily restored section of the medieval **city wall** with a couple of towers, now built into the back wall of Dunnes Stores.

## Lynch's Castle

On the corner of Shop St and Abbeygate St

Strolling down William Street and Shop Street from Eyre Square, you'll come upon **Lynch's Castle**, home of the city's leading family of the fifteenth to seventeenth centuries, who provided no fewer than 84 mayors of Galway – it's now a branch of the Allied Irish Bank. Dating from the fourteenth and fifteenth centuries, it's probably the finest medieval town house in the country, with several elaborately sculptured slabs on the façade: among various Lynch coats of arms, you can make out the insignia of King Henry VII, featuring a dragon and greyhound, and, above the doorway, an image of an ape holding a child – legend has it that the animal saved one of the Lynch children from a fire. In the bank vestibule are display boards on the history of the house and the family, and an impressive fireplace.

## Collegiate Church of St Nicholas

Market St • Daily 9am–6pm • €2 suggested donation • Tunes in the Church June–Aug (except July 29–Aug 6) 8–9.45pm; €15 (ⓦ tunesinthechurch.com) • ☎ 091 564648, ⓦ stnicholas.ie

Founded around 1320 and dedicated to the fourth-century St Nicholas of Myra, patron saint of sailors and revered as Santa Claus, the **Collegiate Church of St Nicholas** is the largest functioning medieval church in Ireland – but only by virtue of several slate-grey extensions over the centuries which have given it a particularly disharmonious external appearance. The interior, however, is worth a quick look. There's a simple but beautifully carved font dating from around 1600 to the right of the entrance, while a banner in the north aisle shows the arms of the Tribes of Galway, many of whom endowed the church. Most of the interest lies in the south transept, built by the Lynches and containing many of their ornate **tombs** – including Mayor James Lynch Fitzstephens – and a curiously personal thirteenth- or fourteenth-century tomb of a Crusader, Adam Bure, promising that "whoever will pray for his soul will have twenty days' indulgence". In this same transept, from June to August each summer (apart from July 29–Aug 6), a traditional Irish music session, "**Tunes in the Church**" is held each night, when musicians play everything from the bodhrán to bouzouki, while sean-nós dancers perform on Lynch's tomb.

## Hall of the Red Earl

Druid Lane • Mon–Fri 9am–4.45pm, Sat 11am–3pm • Free • ☎ 091 564646

If you want to experience where justice was dispensed, taxes collected and banquets held in Galway's early days, make your way to the stunning **Hall of the Red Earl**. The

---

### A GALWAY LYNCHING

The most famous story of the **Lynch family** is embodied in the ornately carved **Lynch's Window**, around the corner from Lynch's Castle on Market Street, behind St Nicholas's Church. In the 1490s young Walter Lynch Fitzstephens, jealous of the attentions a Spanish guest was giving his lover, Ann Blake, stabbed the man and threw him into the sea. The boy was duly sentenced to death, but the town pleaded for mercy and the usual executioner refused to do his duty. It was left to the boy's father, James, the mayor, to hang him from this jail window, which is now carved with the image of a skull and crossbones. Galwegians claim this to be the origin of the term "**lynching**".

ruins, protected by glass panelling with a raised viewing walkway, were opened in 2010 and are the oldest surviving settlement within Galway's ancient walls. There are interpretive panels explaining the significance of the site, plus display cabinets holding clay pipes, a gold cuff link and a human skull. Free guided tours are available.

## Claddagh Museum

Quay Lane • Mon–Sat 9am–6pm, Sun 11am–6pm • Free • ☎ 091 566635, ⓦ claddaghring.ie

**10**

A small, informal museum at the back of Dillon's Jewellers traces the engaging cultural history of the **Claddagh ring**. Designed by a late seventeenth-century Galwegian who had been captured by pirates and enslaved to a Moorish goldsmith, this style of ring has been worn by the likes of Queen Victoria and John Wayne. It features a pair of hands, symbolizing friendship, a heart, for love, and a mitred crown, traditionally for loyalty, and is often given as a love token. The museum also displays old photos of **the Claddagh** (An Cladach; "a flat, stony shore"), a former fishing village on the south bank of the river.

## Galway City Museum

Spanish Parade • Tues–Sat 10am–5pm & Easter Sun to end of Sept noon–5pm • Free • ☎ 091 532460, ⓦ galwaycitymuseum.ie

Down by the river, near the sixteenth-century **Spanish Arch**, stands the glass-fronted **Galway city Museum**, which hosts some temporary exhibitions. Its permanent collection has relatively few artefacts, but traces the city's history in vivid fashion, dealing with the Claddagh, the medieval town and the present day on the ground floor. On the second floor, the **Wild Atlantic Sea Science Gallery** is filled with interactive displays and a mock-up of a model submarine. Other highlights are a 9m hooker boat, suspended in all its glory in the atrium, and a statue of Galway-born **Pádraic Ó Conaire** (see page 601), the first modernist fiction writer in Irish.

## Fishery Tower

Wolfe Tone Bridge • Mon–Sat 10am–3pm • Free • ☎ 091 564646

One of Galway's most delightful landmark buildings, the unique **Fishery Tower** was built in 1852 as a draught netting station. It was used as a lookout point to monitor fish stocks coming up the Corrib River and to spot any illegal fishing.

## Salthill and Silver Strand

About 1km southwest of Wolfe Tone Bridge begins the resort suburb of **Salthill**, Galway's summer playground. The long promenade is lined with high-rise apartment blocks, hotels and amusement arcades, as well as safe **beaches** with fine views across the bay to the Burren. It's a Sunday afternoon tradition to walk its length and kick the wall at the end by the diving platform (for good luck, of course) before turning back.

On the front, the National Aquarium of Ireland, **Galway Atlantaquaria** (Mon–Fri 10am–5pm, Sat & Sun 10am–6pm; Oct–Feb closed Mon and Tues; €11.50, children €7.50; ☎ 091 585100, ⓦ nationalaquarium.ie), is a big hit with kids, entertainingly showcasing Ireland's sea, river and canal life. Beyond Salthill and just 5km west of the centre, **Silver Strand** is the nicest beach in the vicinity of the city, a small, sandy affair with a Blue Flag and a gentle shelf, beneath a grassy headland. It's accessible on buses towards Spiddal.

---

**ARRIVAL AND DEPARTURE**                                         **GALWAY CITY**

**By train** Céannt Station (☎ 1800 366222) is on Station Rd, on the southeast side of Eyre Square.

Destinations Athenry (11–13 daily; 15min); Athlone (7–9 daily; 1hr); Dublin (6–8 daily; 2hr 30min–3hr); Ennis (4–5

**10**

daily; 1hr 20min); Gort (4–5 daily; 50min); Kildare (2–4 daily; 2hr); Limerick (4–5 daily; 2hr).

**By bus** The city's Bus Éireann station is beside the train station, while private companies mostly use the new coach station behind the tourist office on Forster St (☏091 662000). Of the latter, Citylink (☏091 564164, ⊛citylink.ie) and Gobus (☏091 564600, ⊛gobus.ie) each run frequent coaches between Galway city and Dublin city centre and airport, with some buses running via Loughrea and Athlone. Citylink also runs several coaches a day to Gort and Shannon Airport; to Gort, Limerick, Killarney, Cork city centre and Cork airport; and to Oughterard, Clifden, Cleggan and Letterfrack. Feda O'Donnell Coaches (☏091 761656, ⊛fedaodonnell. littleireland.ie) operates daily services between Galway city (departing from the Catholic cathedral) and Knock, Sligo, Bundoran, Donegal, Letterkenny and Gweedore.

Destinations by local bus Achill (Fri & Sun 1 daily; 3hr 20min–4hr); Athenry (Mon–Sat 3–4 daily; 35min); Athlone (hourly; 1hr 30min); Ballina (4–7 daily; 2hr 15min); Castlebar (5–6 daily; 1hr 45min); Clarenbridge

(hourly; 20min); Clifden (summer Mon–Sat 4–5 daily, Sun 2 daily; winter Mon–Sat 3 daily, Sun 1 daily; 1hr 45min–2hr 15min); Cliffs of Moher (summer 2–4 daily; winter 1 daily; 2hr); Cong (2–3 daily; 45min–1hr); Cork (hourly; 4hr 15min); Derry (3–5 daily; 5hr 15min); Doolin (summer 2–5 daily; winter 1–2 daily; 1hr 30min); Dublin (hourly; 3hr 45min); Ennis (hourly; 1hr 15min); Gort (hourly; 45min); Ireland West Airport (5–7 daily; 2hr); Kilcolgan (hourly; 30min); Kinvarra (1–6 daily; 30min–1hr); Kylemore (summer Mon–Sat 1 daily; winter 1 weekly; 1hr 45min–3hr); Leenane (summer Mon–Sat 1 daily; winter 1 weekly; 1hr 20min–3hr); Letterfrack (winter 1 weekly, summer Mon–Sat 1 daily; 1hr 50min–3hr); Letterkenny (3–5 daily; 4hr 40min); Limerick (hourly; 2hr 15min); Loughrea (hourly; 35min); Oranmore (at least hourly; 10min); Oughterard (Mon–Sat 4–7 daily, Sun 2–3; 40min); Rosmuc (Mon & Fri 1; 1hr 15min); Roundstone (winter 3 weekly, summer 1–2 daily; 1hr 30min); Shannon Airport (hourly; 1hr 45min); Sligo (5–6 daily; 2hr 30min); Spiddal (Mon–Sat 5–9 daily, Sun 2; 40min); Westport (3–4 daily; 2hr).

## GETTING AROUND

**By bus** Bus Éireann (☏091 562000) city and suburban services leave Eyre Square for many parts of the city including Salthill (#401; every 20min 9am–7pm; every 40min 7–11.40pm) and College Rd (#40; every 15min 9am–7pm) for B&Bs (see page 341). An all-day, unlimited pass costs €4.10 (€1.70 per single journey). A weekly pass costs €20.20.

**By taxi** Galway Taxis at 57 Lower Dominick St (☏091 561111). There are taxi ranks at Eyre Square.

**By car** Pay and display on the street; there's a car park next to the tourist office off Forster St and multistoreys on Dock Rd and Merchants Rd.

**By bike** West Ireland Cycling on Earls Island St (☏091 588830, ⊛westirelandcycling.com).

## INFORMATION

**Tourist office** Forster St (summer daily 9am–5.45pm; winter Mon–Sat 9am–5.45pm; ☏091 537700, ⊛discover ireland.ie).

**City listings** For local listings, pick up a copy of the *Connacht Tribune* at Eason's Bookshop (see page 344).

## TOURS AND ACTIVITIES

**Walking tours** In the summer themed walking tours of the city depart from either the tourist office or the City Museum (see page 339), generally lasting 1hr 30min–2hr (€10; book at the tourist office).

**Bus tours** Hop-on, hop-off, open-top bus tours of Galway and Salthill operate in the summer from the tourist office or Eyre Square (1hr; €12), where you can also sign up for longer-distance tours. Tours to Connemara, the Burren and the Cliffs of Moher run from the private coach station with the Galway Tour Company (€15; ☏091 566566, ⊛galwaytourcompany.com).

**River tours** In summer, 1hr 30min *Corrib Princess* cruises (May, June & Sept 2 daily; July & Aug 3 daily; €16; ☏091 592447, ⊛corribprincess.ie) depart from Woodquay

(beyond Salmon Weir Bridge and behind the Town Hall Theatre). Cruises head 8km up the river, passing a couple of ruined castles, before entering Lough Corrib. Buy tickets at the tourist office.

**Bike tours** West Ireland Cycling offer bike tours of the city and longer tours around Connemara and the Wild Atlantic Way, as well as bike rental at €20/day (☏087 176 8480, ⊛westirelandcycling.com).

**Watersports** Windsurfing rental and tuition, plus kayaking and SUP, is available at Rusheen Bay, at the west end of Salthill (☏087 260 5702, ⊛rusheenbay.com). Various kayaking trips are on offer with Kayakmór (☏087 756 5578, ⊛kayakmor.ie).

## ACCOMMODATION                                    SEE MAP PAGE 336

At festival time (see page 337), especially during the Galway Races, rooms are at a premium – often in both

senses of the word. The city centre boasts a high standard of **hotels**, while the scores of **B&Bs** are nearly all on the outskirts, including large clusters on College Rd (the continuation of Forster Street) and Dublin Rd, and in Salthill.

## HOTELS

**G Hotel** Wellpark, Dublin Rd, 2km from the centre on the N6 ☎091 865200, ⓦtheghotel.ie. Designed by local lad, the milliner Philip Treacy, this hotel is a bold fashion statement in an inauspicious location next to a shopping centre. The public rooms, featuring mirror-ball lamps, veer towards high camp, but the spacious bedrooms are beautifully designed and equipped, and there's an elegant, black-marble, Japanese-themed ESPA and fitness centre. **€170**

**The Galmont** Lough Atalia Rd ☎091 538300, ⓦthe galmont.com. A modern, Scandinavian-run luxury hotel overlooking Galway Bay from a fine position on the northeast side of the train station. The list of leisure facilities includes an extensive spa, swimming pool, gym, outdoor hot tub and sauna. Colour schemes in the bedrooms are dominated by purple and beige, set off with elegant furnishings and soft lighting. **€240**

★ **Galway Bay Hotel** The Promenade, Salthill ☎091 520520, ⓦgalwaybayhotel.net. Stylish hotel with attractive rooms and a terrace overlooking the bay. The pool and leisure centre offer added value and there's a range of special offers. **€180**

**Harbour Hotel** The Harbour ☎091 894800, ⓦharbour. ie. This crisp, modern hotel offers bright, well-equipped rooms, decorated in strong colours and blonde wood, as well as a gym. **€169**

★ **The Hardiman** Eyre Square ☎091 564041, ⓦthe hardiman.ie. This imposing Victorian railway hotel, formerly the *Great Southern*, has been renovated and brought into the same stable as the *G Hotel*. The bedrooms attractively mix traditional and modern decor, and there's a top-floor spa with outdoor hot tub and gym. Various offers available. **€199**

**The House Hotel** Lower Merchants Rd ☎091 538900, ⓦthehousehotel.ie. A luxurious boutique hotel converted from a warehouse, featuring well-equipped rooms with soundproofed windows and colourful, contemporary public rooms. **€209**

## B&BS

**Adare** 9 Father Griffin Place ☎091 582638, ⓦadare guesthouse.ie. Just a few mins' walk from Wolfe Tone Bridge, this B&B is a convenient base, with eleven bright bedrooms. The owner likes to sing from the kitchen as she prepares the full Irish breakfast or delicious pancakes with a large choice of organic teas. Look out for the polystyrene statue of the famed Galway writer Pádraic Ó Conaire in the garden. **€120**

**Ardawn** 31 College Rd ☎087 223 1960, ⓦardawnhouse. com. Welcoming, upmarket B&B a 10min walk from the centre in a redbrick, modern house. Smart, comfortable

rooms, plenty of local information, free wi-fi and lavish breakfasts. **€110**

**Cappa Veagh** 76 Dalysfort Rd, Salthill ☎091 526518, ⓦcappaveagh.com. This comfortable and clean, modern house with en-suite rooms is close to the seafront and on the #401 bus route, with knowledgeable hosts. Closed Dec–Feb. **€95**

**Corrib Village** Newcastle Rd, 3km north of the centre ☎091 527112, ⓦcampusaccommodation.ie. In summer (June–Aug), this large complex on the campus of Galway University offers a variety of standard and en-suite B&B accommodation or apartment rentals, all with wi-fi access. Sited on the banks of the River Corrib, the "village" includes a café and deli, tennis courts, laundry facilities and a complimentary shuttle bus to Eyre Square (noon–7pm). Guests also have reduced-rate access to the university's wide-ranging sports facilities. **€50**

★ **Heron's Rest** 16 Long Walk ☎091 539574, ⓦthe heronsrest.com. Hospitable B&B in a peerless location, steps from the city centre but overlooking the quiet river and Galway Bay. Attractive rooms come with extras such as bathrobes and binoculars. They also have a three-bed self-catering townhouse. Gourmet breakfasts include a sumptuous cheeseboard and home-baked breads. **€160**

**Marless House** 8 Threadneedle Rd, Salthill, 3km from the centre ☎091 523931, ⓦmarlesshouse.com. Comfortable, mock-Georgian modern home out by the beach, with kingsize beds and bright, colourful, en-suite rooms; there's free wi-fi and a varied breakfast menu. **€90**

**St Jude's** 110 Lower Salthill ☎091 521619, ⓦst-judes. com. Grand, manorial 1920s family home with elegant, en-suite bedrooms and good breakfasts, a 10min walk from the centre. Dinner, cookery courses and good single rates available. **€100**

## HOSTELS

**Kinlay Hostel** Merchants Rd (IHH) ☎091 565244, ⓦkinlaygalway.ie. Modern hostel that's friendly and well run, with laundry, a kitchen, free wi-fi, and some en-suite rooms. Prices include a simple continental breakfast. The mixed dorms have six to ten beds, and there are private rooms. Dorms **€25**, doubles **€70**

**Salmon Weir Hostel** St Vincent's Ave (IHO) ☎091 561133, ⓦsalmonweirhostel.com. Small and simple, with some en-suite rooms, this comfortable hostel has a kitchen, laundry facilities, wi-fi and friendly atmosphere. Breakfast not included. Dorms **€15**, doubles **€36**

**Sleepzone** Bóthar na mBan ☎091 566999, ⓦsleep zone.ie. Modern, well-maintained, 200-bed hostel affiliated to An Óige, a 5min walk north of Eyre Square. All rooms are en suite, with singles, twins and doubles available, as well as free internet and wi-fi, kitchen, laundry facilities and a bureau de change. Dorms **€25**, doubles **€79**

**Snoozles** 10 Quay St (IHH) ☎091 568644, ⓦbarnacles.

**10**

ie. Large and efficiently run hostel right in the hub of Galway's nightlife. All rooms are en suite, and a light breakfast is included. There are laundry and kitchen facilities, free internet and wi-fi. Dorms come in various sizes, from four to twelve beds, plus private twins and doubles. Dorms €18, doubles €58

## CAMPING

**Salthill Caravan Park** Knocknacarra ☎091 523972, ⓦsalthillcaravanpark.com. Beside the seashore with superb views of Galway Bay and access to an excellent beach. A new walkway from the park leads straight into Galway city centre. The campsite has room for thirty tents. Closed Sept to mid-May. €26

## 10

## EATING                                    SEE MAP PAGE 336

★ **Ard Bia at Nimmo's** Spanish Arch Long Walk ☎091 561114, ⓦardbia.com. Set in a stone-built medieval customs house by the river, with rustic-chic decor, and modern art on the walls. The perfectly paced modern Irish food focuses on expertly prepared local, seasonal ingredients, with a few Middle Eastern touches. Lunch includes power salad, potato hot pot or pulled pork with prices averaging €8. Main dinner courses start from around €20. Daily 10am–3.30pm & 6pm–midnight (kitchen closes 10pm).

**Black Gate Café** 14 Francis St ☎085 220 5049, ⓦblackgate.ie. A café-cum cultural centre set up by two young men from Inishbofin. Lunches from €10 include charcuterie and cheese board, sandwiches and wine. With comfy chairs and a library, this is a place to linger or catch an evening of music or poetry. Daily noon–11pm.

**Brasserie on the Corner** 25 Eglinton St ☎091 530333, ⓦbrasseriegalway.com. Galway is shellfish central and many come here to sample "Marty's Meaty Mussels", rope-cultivated specimens from Killary Harbour, served with zingy sauces. Delicious brown soda to mop up. Main courses are around €14–18. Daily noon–10pm.

★ **Corrib House Tearooms** 3 Waterside, Woodquay ☎091 446753, ⓦcorribhouse.com. This delightfully situated café in a Georgian-style mansion has a range of lunchtime dishes such as grilled chicken, quiches, salads and soups. Grab a window seat to look out on the salmon weir and the Corrib. Mains average €10. Mon–Fri 9.30am–5pm, Sat 10am–5pm.

**The Dail Bar** 42 Middle St ☎091 653777, ⓦthedailbar.com. An excellent choice for lunch or dinner, the *Dail* has raised the standard of pub grub, with its tasty light bites such as goat's cheese and sundried tomato, or southern fried chicken wings (€6.45) and heartier mains like bacon and cabbage, cajun chicken penne, or chilli prawn and monkfish linguine (average prices €12–16). Food served daily noon–2.30pm & 5.30–9pm; bar 11am–2am.

**Goya's** 2–3 Kirwan's Lane ☎091 567010, ⓦgoyas.ie. Elegant café with tables on the alley, serving home-baked cakes and pastries that are little short of perfection. Lunchtime goodies include soups, salads, quiches and pies (main dishes €7–10). Mon–Sat 9.30am–6pm.

**Kappa-ya** 4 Middle St ☎091 865930, ⓦkappayagalway.com. Small, relaxing café-restaurant serving carefully prepared and reasonably priced Celtic-Japanese food – the chicken teriyaki sushi rolls are especially good, and leave room for some wasabi and pistachio ice cream. On Sat evenings (by reservation), you can sample more elaborate dishes such as nigiri sushi. Prices for mains are around €11–17. Mon–Fri noon–9.30pm, Sat 1–10.30pm.

**Martine's** Quay St ☎091 565662, ⓦmartines.ie. Friendly, wood-panelled bistro with tables outside. The fairly conservative evening menu (think rack of lamb, chicken, duck or lasagne) is enlivened by a more adventurous list of daily specials, notably seafood. The €20 early-bird set menu is served all evening. Daily noon–4pm & 5–10pm.

**McDonagh's Seafood Bar** 22 Quay St ☎091 565001, ⓦmcdonaghs.net. This Galway institution features nautical paraphernalia and a menu that casts its net wide: pan-fried mackerel, baked monkfish, lemon sole, red gurnard, grilled ray, wild Clarinbridge oysters, and scallops are on offer. The two-course set menu with a glass of wine is €19.95, while battered cod or ray are popular from the takeaway section. Mon–Sat noon–11pm, Sun 2–9pm.

★ **Oscar's Seafood Bistro** Lower Dominick St ☎091 582180, ⓦoscarsseafoodbistro.com. Savvy locals like this plush bistro just a few mins' walk from the crowds of Quay St. And it's worth the short hike for some of the freshest local seafood, such as fillet of haddock, fishcakes or Galway rock oysters. The prix fixe menu at €19.50 for two courses is a steal and is served Mon–Fri evening till 6.30pm. Mon–Sat 6–10pm.

**Trattoria Magnetti** 12 Quay St ☎091 563910, ⓦmagnetti.ie. Cheery Italian place, dishing up reliable home-made pastas, risottos, huge pizzas and a few meat and fish mains with prices from €12. Good-value set menus. Daily noon–11pm.

**Tulsi** Buttermilk Walk, Middle St ☎091 564831, ⓦtulsi-galway.com. Galway's best Indian restaurant rustles up very good vegetarian and meaty food and even tries its hand at Indo-Galwegian fusion dishes such as tandoori mackerel for an appetizer. Main courses average €12. Early-bird offer Mon–Thurs till 7.30pm. Mon–Sat 5–11pm, Sun 1–10pm.

★ **Upstairs @ McCambridge's** Shop St ☎091 562259, ⓦmccambridges.com. A wonderful addition to the Galwegian culinary scene, above a deli that has been in business since 1925. Prepare to indulge yourself in the all-day menu featuring cold platters of cheese, meat or seafood, salads, frittatas, and hot dishes such as lamb kebabs or roasted prawns. Prices average €11–15. Mon–Sat 8am–5pm.

## THE GALWAY WHISKEY TRAIL

In the nineteenth century whiskey distilling was Galway's largest employer – Persse Galway Whiskey was marketed internationally, and with its slogan "favourite in the House of Commons", it sold particularly well in the English colonies. A newly established **whiskey trail** around the central streets of Galway reflects this colourful pedigree in a tour of ten bars and one off licence. Follow the trail's limestone plaques to find out about the twenty-first-century renaissance in Irish whiskey; en route, sample a dram or two and enjoy the fun of inhaling some full-bodied aromas in bars that reek of a rapturous combination of whiskey and history (ⓦ galwaywhiskeytrail.ie.).

**10**

## DRINKING AND NIGHTLIFE

SEE MAP PAGE 336

A slow crawl through the **pubs** of Shop, High and Quay streets is a must, soaking up the atmosphere of their historic interiors in winter, and the buzzy street life at their outdoor tables in summer. You're bound to find a traditional session here, although the best pub for music is *The Crane Bar*, just over the bridge (see page 343).

**Busker Browne's** Cross St ⓣ 091 563377, ⓦ busker brownes.com. This popular bar in a former Dominican convent offers medieval fireplaces, a lofty, Gothic hall, and floor upon floor of alcoves and armchairs in a complementary modern design. Food is served – try the seafood chowder – and there are DJs at weekends, plus jazz Sun lunchtimes. Daily 10.30am–1.30am.

★ **The Crane Bar** Sea Rd ⓣ 091 587419, ⓦ thecranebar. com. Atmospheric pub with an upstairs venue, this is the top spot for traditional music with sessions every night, which can involve up to twelve musicians, plus all manner of other folk music, blues and singer-songwriters. Occasional entry charge. Daily 3pm–midnight.

**The King's Head** High St ⓣ 091 566630, ⓦ the kingshead.ie. Busy three-storey pub in a medieval building with flagstone floors, stone walls and an early seventeenth-century marriage stone above the 1612 fireplace. The bar's name comes from the fact that the man who requisitioned this building, Colonel Peter Stubbers, was widely rumoured to have been Charles I's executioner. Includes a popular bistro and an extensive whiskey menu, plus their own K.H. Blood Red Ale from the Galway Hooker brewery. Traditional music on Wed plus DJs on Sat. Mon–Thurs & Sun 10.30am–11pm/ midnight, Fri & Sat till 2am.

★ **Neachtains** 17 Cross St ⓣ 091 568820, ⓦ tighneach tain.com. Galway's finest traditional pub, serving a wide choice of whiskies and craft beers such as Bogmen Irish

Ale or Cosmic Cow in what was once the town house of Humanity Dick (see page 363). In winter, the homely warren of small rooms, bars, bench seats and snugs draws a diverse crowd, who migrate to the plentiful tables on the busy corner of Cross and Quay streets in summer. The *Kasbah* wine bar next door (same owners) serves tapas, olives, silver darlings (aka pickled herrings) and a charcuterie board. Daily noon–11pm.

**O'Connell's** 8 Eyre Square ⓣ 091 563634. This 150-year-old pub has a traditional front bar with tiled floors and antique lighting, quirky parlour rooms behind, and a large beer garden with old shop fronts in the newly opened Gin Lane. Craft and international beers available on tap. Daily 11am–11.30pm, Fri & Sat till 2.30am.

**The Quays** 11 Quay St ⓣ 091 568347, ⓦ quaysgalway. ie. A regular two-storey facade conceals an eccentric, warren-like pub, decorated with mullioned and stained-glass windows, carved beams and Gothic wooden arches. Traditional sessions Mon, Tues (summer only) and early evening Sun, plus a balconied venue with a stage for live cover bands and DJs. Late bar every night. Mon–Sat 10.30am–2am, Sun 12.30pm–1am.

**Róisín Dubh** 9 Upper Dominick St ⓣ 091 586540, ⓦ roisindubh.net. This pub is Galway's best general live venue, hosting gigs of every style from rock and reggae to folk and funk, with a late bar every night and a pleasant terrace overlooking the river. Daily 11am–1am.

★ **Tigh Coili** Mainguard St ⓣ 091 561294. Welcoming, central and sociable family-run pub with daily sessions in old-fashioned surroundings (Mon–Sat around 6pm & 9.30pm, Sun 2pm & 8pm). Getting a seat in here on a busy night is difficult, but on a sunny evening you can enjoy your drink outside. Daily 10.30am–11.30pm, Fri & Sat to 12.30am.

## ENTERTAINMENT

**The Mick Lally Theatre** Druid Lane ⓣ 091 568660, ⓦ druid.ie/the-mick-lally-theatre. Local theatre company whose acclaimed productions have included the complete cycle of six plays by John Millington Synge. **Town Hall Theatre** Courthouse Square, Woodquay

ⓣ 091 569777, ⓦ tht.ie. Built in the 1820s, this theatre is the city's main performance venue, staging drama, dance, music and opera by visiting companies throughout the year.

★ **Charlie Byrne's Bookshop** Cornstore Mall Middle St ☎ 091 561 766, ⊛ charliebyrne.com. A much-cherished institution with a vast selection of new, secondhand and discounted books and an extensive Irish section – the ideal place to dip into some of Tim Robinson's magisterial trilogy on the topography of Connemara or to meet writers and artists, and pick up some Galwegian gossip. Mon–Sat 9am–5pm, Sun noon–5pm.

**Eason's Bookshop** 33 Shop St ☎ 091 562284, ⊛ easons. com. A large general bookshop that sells a wide variety of magazines and newspapers: everything from the *Connacht Tribune* (for local listings) to *Le Monde*. Mon–Wed & Sat 9am–6.15pm, Thurs & Fri 9am–9pm, Sun noon–6pm.

**McCambridge's Deli** Shop St ☎ 091 562259, ⊛ mccambridges.com. A dazzling array of chutneys, preserves, olives, herbs and spices alongside Butlers Irish chocolates, Skellig truffles, hand-cut shortbread, the unique Hadji Bey's Irish Turkish delight and Murphy's ice cream. On-site café too. Mon–Sat 8am–5pm.

**Ó Máille** 16 High St ☎ 091 562696, ⊛ omaille.com. If you're after woollen garments such as scarves, hats, throws, rugs or Aran sweaters, this is the best place. Their proud boast

is that the shop supplied many of the tailored costumes for *The Quiet Man* (see page 370), filmed in Galway and Mayo in 1951. Mon–Sat 10am–6pm, Sun noon–6pm.

★ **Sheridan's Cheesemongers** 14–16 Churchyard St ☎ 091 564829, ⊛ sheridancheesemongers.com. Outstanding Irish, Swiss and French cheeses and other speciality foods. A wine bar upstairs offers carefully sourced cheese, meat and smoked-fish plates. A mixed board is €12. Tues–Fri 1–11pm, Sat noon–midnight, Sun 4–midnight.

**Treasure Chest** 31–33 William St ☎ 091 563862, ⊛ treasurechest.ie. An elegant gift, craft and fashion shop on a large corner site showcasing many of Ireland's leading brand names. You'll find Waterford and Galway crystal, Belleek china, Claddagh rings, Irish linen and knitwear. Mon–Sat 9.30am–6pm, Sun 1–5pm.

**Weekend Market** Churchyard St ⊛ galwaymarket.com. The lively Saturday market transforms the area around St Nicholas's Church (there's a smaller version on Sunday) and hosts craftspeople, market gardeners and foodstalls. You could make up a picnic of cheese, bratwurst, home-made bread, smoked salmon, hummus, olives and doughnuts. Sat 8am–6pm, Sun (Fri in July & Aug) noon–6pm.

# East Galway

**East Galway** (⊛ galwayeast.com) is a vast tract of flat, fertile land bordered by the Shannon and its tributary the River Suck, the southern half of which shelters some compelling places to visit. The west's first designated "heritage town", **Athenry**, is a fascinating stop, while **Kinvarra** is a justly popular honeypot down on the shores of Galway Bay. Several historic attractions ring the town of **Gort** just inland, notably **Coole Park**, Lady Gregory's idyllic woodland estate, W.B. Yeats's tower house, Thoor Ballylee and the monastic ruins and round tower at **Kilmacduagh**. Out on a limb on the shores of Lough Derg, **Portumna** is an easy-going boating resort, with a fine castle and forest park, which gives access to **Clonfert Cathedral**, one of the country's finest Romanesque churches.

Southeast of Galway city, the N18 runs around the shores of **Galway Bay**, which are lined with native European Flat Oyster beds. The oysters are celebrated at the long-running **Clarenbridge Oyster Festival** (⊛ clarenbridge.com), held over three days in early September. This kicks off the season, which lasts until April. Beyond Kilcolgan, the N18 heads inland towards Gort, Ennis and Limerick, while the N67 towards the Burren hugs the coast via the village of Kinvarra following the route of the Wild Atlantic Way (see page 26).

## Kinvarra and around

Tucked away at the head of its own inlet in the southeastern corner of the bay, pretty **KINVARRA** is a popular getaway for Galwegians, with several attractive pubs and cafés. The village lays on a music **festival**, the *Fleadh na gCuach* (the Cuckoo Fleadh), over the bank holiday weekend at the start of May, and the *Cruinniú na mBád* (the Meeting of the Boats), over a weekend in August (depending on the tides). The latter features the racing of Galway Bay's traditional, wooden, red-sailed boats – known as **hookers** – which can often be seen docked in the harbour.

## Dunguaire Castle

Dungory East, 2km from Kinvarra • May–Oct daily 10am–5pm • €6.60 • ☎ 091 637108, ⓦ dunguairecastle.com

The name of **Dunguaire Castle**, an intact, four-storey tower house built in 1520, comes from Guaire – the seventh-century king of Connacht who was so renowned for his generosity that his right arm was said to have grown longer than his left – and *dún* (fort), which may refer to the ancient earthwork on the headland to the east.

## Doorus Peninsula

On the west side of Kinvarra Bay, the tranquil **Doorus Peninsula**, which was an island until the eighteenth century, shelters on its north shore the Blue Flag **Traught beach** (6km from Kinvarra), and provides ample opportunity for scenic walks or cycle rides.

**10**

### ARRIVAL AND INFORMATION

**KINVARRA AND AROUND**

**By bus** There's a limited seasonal bus service (June–Aug 2 daily) from Galway to Kinvarra (40min), which continues to Ballyvaughan, Doolin and the Cliffs of Moher.

**Tourist information** The town's website is ⓦ kinvara.ie.

### ACCOMMODATION

**Breacan Cottage** Parkmore Pier ☎ 091 638266, ⓦ breacan.com. Out near the northeastern corner of the Doorus peninsula, this rustic, tastefully designed B&B at the water's edge is named after a holy well in a nearby field. Excellent breakfasts, including fresh fruit salad, Greek yoghurt and cold meat platter, accompany stunning views across Galway Bay. **€90**

**Merriman** Main St, Kinvarra ☎ 091 638222, ⓦ merriman hotel.com. Most people visit Kinvarra for the day from Galway, but if you want to stay over the village has a good-value hotel named after the eighteenth-century satirical Irish-language poet (see page 594) from nearby Ennistymon in Clare. Boasting one of Ireland's largest thatched roofs, the hotel is tastefully decorated with well-appointed rooms. **€120**

### EATING AND DRINKING

**Connolly's** The Quay, Kinvarra ☎ 091 637131. This flower-bedecked pub with attractive outdoor tables has been here since 1898 and sells Kinvarra (made in Offaly) on draught. Traditional musicians flock here in the summer every night (except Thurs) and on Sun afternoon at 5pm. Daily noon–midnight.

**Greens** Main St, Kinvarra ☎ 091 637110, ⓦ greens ofkinvara.com. Part of the fabric of Kinvarra for many generations, this is an old-fashioned spot where the shelves heave with a variety of beers and whiskies. They hold frequent impromptu sessions, so it's best to call in advance if you want to hear some trad. Daily 5–11.30pm, Fri & Sat till 12.30am.

**Keogh's Bar and Restaurant** Main St, Kinvarra ☎ 091 638481. Reasonably priced snacks and full meals, including local smoked salmon and the signature dish scallop risotto

(€18). There's an open fire to keep things cosy, and music in the bar every Fri. Daily noon–10pm, Sat till 10.30pm.

**Moran's Oyster Cottage** The Weir, Kilcolgan ☎ 091 796113, ⓦ moransoystercottage.com. A bar and restaurant set by the bay and famed for native oysters (from their own beds) accompanied by brown bread and a creamy pint of stout. Seafood platters, crab claws, mussels or Aran Islands prawns are all available as well as vegetarian lasagne. Mains from €14.50. Tues–Thurs noon–11.30pm, Fri & Sat noon–midnight, Sun noon–11pm.

**Paddy Burke's** Main St, Clarenbridge ☎ 091 796226, ⓦ paddyburkesgalway.com. A renowned pub which has fed and watered royalty and celebrities for many years. Shellfish dominates but the menu also offers cod, trout and Sun lunchtime alternatives such as duck or beef. Main courses from around €14.50. Daily 10am–11.30pm.

# Gort and around

About 12km southeast of Kinvarra and 19km south of Kilcolgan, **GORT** is a traffic-laden workaday town of multicoloured houses on the busy N18 Galway–Limerick road, with some relief provided by the large, triangular market square in the centre. Kinvarra and Galway make be more congenial bases for exploring the surrounding **historic sites** (for which you'll need your own transport).

## Coole Park

3km north of Gort on the N18 • Visitor centre open daily: April & May 10am–5pm; June–Aug 10am–6pm; park open daily: summer 8.30am–7.30pm; winter 8am–6pm • Free • ☎ 091 631804, ⓦ coolepark.ie

**10**

**Coole Park** is the former estate of **Lady Augusta Gregory** (1852–1932), dramatist, folklorist and co-founder of the Abbey Theatre in Dublin (see page 79), the world's first national theatre. At the beginning of the last century, Coole was the centre of the **Irish Literary Revival**, visited by Synge, Shaw, O'Casey and, most of all, Yeats, who spent over twenty summers here or at Thoor Ballylee. After Lady Gregory's death, however, the estate passed into the hands of the Department of Agriculture and Lands, who left the house to fall into disrepair and demolished it in 1941. The demesne is now a beautiful **woodland park**, home to pine martens, red deer and red squirrels, and laid out with two signposted **nature trails** (6km in total), which will bring you down to a seasonal lake and its many swans. In the walled garden stands the **autograph tree**, a beautiful, swooping copper beech on which all the great writers and painters who stayed here carved graffiti.

The **visitor centre** features a highly engaging exhibition based on the memoirs of Lady Gregory's granddaughter, who was born and brought up at Coole, including computer re-creations of the house, and film footage and sound recordings of Yeats. There's also a thirty-minute presentation on Lady Gregory and the Literary Revival.

## Thoor Ballylee

5km west of Coole Park • Tower open April–June & Sept Mon–Fri 10am–4pm, Sat & Sun 11am–5pm; July & Aug 10am–6pm daily • €7 • ☎ 091 631436, ⊕ yeatsthoorballylee.org

Follow signposted narrow roads from Coole to **Thoor Ballylee**, a newly renovated fourteenth-century Hiberno-Norman tower where Yeats spent summers with his family and wrote some of his best poetry. It is now a cultural and educational centre run on a voluntary basis by the Yeats Thoor Ballylee Society and stages plays, poetry readings and other literary events. The tower houses an audiovisual presentation along with two permanent exhibitions: Yeats and the West of Ireland, and Yeats and His Muses, which considers the importance of women in the poet's life. Tours are self-guided, and include tea or coffee; after exploring the tower you can wander around the grounds, bridge and riverside.

## Kilmacduagh

5km southwest of Gort, off the R460 to Corofin • Open access • Free

The extensive monastic ruins of **Kilmacduagh** stand in an unspoilt setting with magnificent views of the Burren's limestone terraces to the west. The monastery was founded by Saint Colman Mac Duagh, a member of one of the local royal families, around 632, though the buildings you can see today date mostly from around five hundred years later. They're impressive by virtue of their scale and quantity – a **cathedral**, four churches, the "Glebe House" (possibly the abbot's house) and a 35m-high, leaning round tower – rather than any architectural finery, but look out for the grim-faced bishop carved over the cathedral's south doorway.

### ARRIVAL AND DEPARTURE                                    GORT AND AROUND

**By bus** On weekdays Bus Éireann services run hourly from Galway to Gort (Mon–Fri; 45min), dropping (and picking up) passengers outside the Allied Irish Bank in the Square.

**By train** Gort is a stop on the Galway–Limerick line (Mon–Sat 6 daily, Sun 4 daily; 54min to Galway, 1hr 5min to Limerick).

### EATING

**The Gallery Café** The Square ☎ 091 630630, ⊕ the gallerycafegort.com. Formerly a spinning house, and retaining its original whitewashed stone walls, this stylish café is a popular spot. Dishes on offer include meze, pizzas and hearty salads (some with St Tola goat cheese from nearby Inagh). Wash it down with Con's organic cider, apple juices or lemonades. Wed & Sat 11am–9pm, Thurs & Fri 11am–10pm, Sun 11am–7pm.

**O'Grady's Bar** The Square ☎ 091 631096, ⊕ ogradys gort.net. At lunchtime, expect buffet-style carvery roasts plus burgers and lasagne (around €8–12); dinner (from 4pm) includes grills and fish such as scampi or Corrib salmon (average price of main courses €16). Daily 11am–11.30pm.

# Portumna and around

**PORTUMNA**, 47km east of Gort through the pine-clad Slieve Aughty mountains, is a compact market town surrounded by forests and open land that run down to the meeting of the River Shannon with Lough Derg.

## Portumna Castle

Off Abbey St • April–Sept daily 9.30am–6pm; Oct Fri–Sun 9.30am–5pm; last admission 45min before closing • €5; Heritage Card • ☎ 090 974 1658, ⓦ heritageireland.ie

On the southwest side of the town centre stands the early seventeenth-century fortified mansion **Portumna Castle**, which was gutted by fire in 1826 and is currently being renovated. The ground floor is arrayed with display boards on the de Burgo family who lived here, the house and its conservation. In front of the house, the elegant, geometric Renaissance **garden**, one of the first in Ireland, has been re-created, as has the walled kitchen garden to one side, and there's a coffee shop in the courtyard.

## Portumna Friary and Forest Park

Off Abbey St, 400m south of Portumna Castle entrance • Open access

Beyond the castle gatehouse, about 400m down the road towards the lake, lie the extensive remains of **Portumna Friary** in a leafy setting. Originally a Cistercian chapel, it was rebuilt by the Dominicans in the early fifteenth century, with ornate traceried windows in the east wall and south transept of the church, and a small, pretty cloister, now heavily restored. Part of Portumna Castle's former estate – still home to a sizeable herd of fallow deer – constitutes the **Portumna Forest Park**, where you can stroll along marked trails through the woodland to the lakeshore.

## Irish Workhouse Centre

Northern end of St Brigid's Rd • Daily: April–Sept 9.30am–6pm; Feb, March & Oct 9.30am–5pm; last admission 1hr before closing • €7 • ☎ 090 975 9200

Buildings in the former Portumna Workhouse (a poorhouse for the destitute opened in 1852) have been converted into the **Irish Workhouse Centre**. You can visit the waiting hall, boardroom, schoolroom and women's quarters. Interpretive panels tell the history of the workhouse, which at one time was described as the most feared and hated institution ever established in Ireland.

## Clonfert Cathedral

25km northeast of Portumna • May–Oct daily 9.15am–6pm • Free

Infrequently used by the Church of Ireland, **Clonfert Cathedral** was founded in the sixth century by St Brendan, who was later buried here, and the present building has been in continuous service from around the tenth century. Regarded as the high point of Irish Romanesque, its rounded, golden-brown, sandstone **doorway**, topped by a triangular gable, may have been added for a synod held at Clonfert by St Laurence O'Toole, Archbishop of Dublin, in 1179. It's carved with a remarkable diversity of inventive motifs, some of which have been traced to Scandinavia and western France, including human and animal heads, interlace and other geometrical devices. Dating from around 1600, the adjacent **bishop's palace** later became home to the English fascist, Oswald Mosley, but has rapidly rotted since it was accidentally burned down in 1954.

---

**ARRIVAL AND INFORMATION**                           **PORTUMNA AND AROUND**

**By bus** Kearns Transport (☎ 057 912 0124, ⓦ kearns transport.com) runs daily services between Portumna and Dublin, via Birr, and at weekends between Birr and Galway city (Merchant's Rd) via Portumna and Loughrea.

**Tourist office** In the Irish Workhouse Centre (see page 347) on St Brigid's Rd (Feb–Nov daily 9.30am–5pm;

☎ 090 975 9200). Provides maps and brochures on East Galway. The town's website is ⓦ portumna.net.

**Boat hire** If you're so tempted by the water that you want to live on it for a week or two, contact Emerald Star (☎ 071 962 7633, ⓦ emeraldstar.ie), who rent out self-drive cruisers from the marina at the east end of town.

## ACCOMMODATION AND EATING

**The Beehive** St Patrick's St ☎ 090 974 1830. A basic café-restaurant serving salads, sandwiches, simple pastas and other main courses and cakes, plus tasty, popular pizzas in the evenings. Mains average €10. Tues–Sat 9am–5pm, Thurs–Sun 6–9pm.

**Horan's Pub** Brendan St ☎ 090 974 1007. One of the best spots for an impromptu session on any night and a good spot to meet the locals. Daily 6–11.30pm.

**Oak Lodge B&B** St Brendan's Rd ☎ 090 974 1549, ⓦ oak lodgeportumna.ie. A conveniently located guesthouse with four en-suite rooms. The common room is a focal point for visitors, featuring a wood-burning stove and local interest books. €80

# Loughrea and around

**LOUGHREA**, 32km northwest of Portumna, is a small market town on the lake of the same name. It's unlikely that you'll want to stay here, but it's well worth detouring off the N6 bypass to visit the late nineteenth-century **St Brendan's Cathedral**.

## St Brendan's Cathedral

Barrack St • Mon–Fri 10am–1pm & 2–5.30pm • ☎ 091 841212, ⓦ loughreacathedral.ie • 30min audio-tour available from adjacent presbytery at weekends

**St Brendan's Cathedral** is a shining product of the Arts and Crafts movement – which in its Irish manifestation is often referred to as the Celtic Revival. The interior is decorated with rich marble, playfully carved Irish-oak pews and Mediterranean-style column capitals in the nave telling the story of St Brendan. Its most notable feature, however, is the stained glass, which was mostly produced by **An Túr Gloine** ("The Shining Tower"), a cooperative Arts and Crafts studio based in Dublin from 1903 to 1944. Look out especially for the 1930s works by the Dublin-born artist **Michael Healy**, who was heavily influenced by the Renaissance art he'd studied in Florence. His *St Joseph* in the right-hand aisle is sombrely emotive, but in *The Queen of Heaven*, further down the same aisle, he deals only in brilliant colours and composition, to convey Mary's regal splendour. Healy's masterpieces, however, are *The Ascension* and *The Last Judgement* in the west transept, sparkling tapestries of colour inlaid with the dramatic heads of his characters.

## Clonfert Diocesan Museum

Adjoining the cathedral • Open on request Mon–Fri 10am–5.30pm • Donation requested • ☎ 091 841212

The **Clonfert Diocesan Museum** houses tapestries designed by Jack B. Yeats and made by the **Dun Emer Guild**, the weaving and printing arm of the Irish Arts and Crafts movement, founded in 1902 and named after the needleworking wife of the mythical hero, Cúchulainn. There's also a primitive, polychrome carving of the Virgin and Child dating from the late twelfth or early thirteenth century, the oldest surviving wooden statue in Ireland.

## EATING — LOUGHREA AND AROUND

**Maggie Mays** Bride St ☎ 091 847880, ⓦ maggiemays loughrea.com. A bustling bar and restaurant whose menu brims with locally sourced produce. Typical offerings might include glazed pork fillet, duck, duo of salmon and lemon sole, and vegetarian dishes. Main course prices average €16. Daily noon–11.30pm.

**Taste Matters** Millennium House, Westbridge St ☎ 091 880010. Among the town's best places to eat with a menu that might include haddock with risotto, grilled marinated chicken, or braised pork belly and pork schnitzel. Main courses from €11 for lunch, rising to an average €18 for dinner. Wed–Sun 1–9.30pm.

# Athenry

**ATHENRY**'s name in Irish, Baile Átha an Rí, "town of the ford of the king", reveals its ancient significance as a crossing point of the River Clarin, 20km due east of Galway city on what is still the main road-and-rail route to Dublin. Many of its historic sites

**THE FIELDS OF ATHENRY**

Athenry is probably most famous for the song **The Fields of Athenry**, penned by singer-songwriter Pete St John in the 1970s as an adaptation of a poignant 1880s ballad about the abominations of the Famine. It's an emotive, catchy number, popular in pubs and at football and rugby matches, and you may well find yourself joining in, at least with the chorus:

**10**

*Low lie the fields of Athenry
Where once we watched the small, free birds fly
Our love was on the wing
We had dreams and songs to sing,
It's so lonely round the fields of Athenry*

are well preserved, including nearly all its fourteenth-century town **walls**, plus the North Gate, five towers, and castle. In the market square stands the only **market cross** *in situ* in the country, though it's a badly damaged stump; dating from the fifteenth century, it's carved with scenes of the Crucifixion and the Virgin and Child. East from here, just across the river, the extensive remains of the thirteenth- to fifteenth-century Dominican **Priory of SS Peter and Paul** (open access) include a fine collection of carved grave slabs from medieval times onwards.

## Athenry Castle

Gorteenacra, 2km off the M6 exit, on the southwest outskirts of town • Easter–Sept daily 9.30am–6pm; Oct Mon–Thurs 10am–6pm; last admission 5.15pm • €5; Heritage Card • ☎ 091 844797, ⓦ heritageireland.ie

Standing at the northeast corner of the town walls, guarding the ford, the **castle** dates back to the thirteenth century. It is a forbidding, almost windowless, three-storey hall with a keep that features some fine Romano-Gothic floral carvings.

## Athenry Heritage Centre

Opposite the castle • Mon–Fri 10am–4.30pm • €5 (45min guided tour included in price); Medieval Experience €8 • ☎ 091 844661, ⓦ athenryheritagecentre.com

The lively **Athenry Heritage Centre** occupies a nineteenth-century church built within the ruins of a medieval predecessor. The big attraction for kids is the "Medieval Experience", which comes complete with stocks, a re-created dungeon, summertime archery and lots of objects to handle – and everyone, big or small, gets to wear a medieval costume.

### ARRIVAL AND DEPARTURE                                              ATHENRY

**By train** The station is on Church St.
**Destinations** Athlone (10 daily; 1hr); Galway (18 daily;

45min); Limerick (5 daily; 1hr 45min).

### ACCOMMODATION AND EATING

★ **Caheroyan House** Monivea Rd ☎ 091 844858, ⓦ caheroyanhouseathenry.com. Athenry's outstanding B&B choice is a 5min walk from the North Gate. Set in a pretty garden, this tastefully refurbished eighteenth-century manor house offers spacious bedrooms and fine breakfasts that feature home-grown grapes and home-made jam. Guests are free to explore the organic farmland and woodland. Two self-catering three-bedroom cottages also available. **€100**

**The Old Barracks** Cross St ☎ 091 877406, ⓦ oldbarracks.ie. Set in a former RIC police barracks, the place combines pantry, bakery and a restaurant offering lunch and dinner. Mains (averaging €13) include steak, burgers, chicken and vegetable fajitas; be sure to finish off with the delicious Linnalla artisan ice cream made in the Burren. Mon–Thurs 8.30am–6pm, Fri & Sat 8.30am–9pm, Sun 9am–6pm.

# The Aran Islands

Once part of a land barrier across the south side of Galway Bay, the **Aran Islands** (Oileáin Árann) – **Inishmore**, **Inishmaan** and **Inisheer** – have proved alluring to travellers for centuries. Until recently, their isolation allowed the continuation of an ancient Gaelic culture, traces of which remain, while Irish is still the main language of the islands. Fishing and farming are to this day the principal activities on Inishmaan, with tourism the major earner on Inishmore and Inisheer.

As well as the islands' heritage, their dramatic landscapes, continuing the limestone pavement of the Burren in County Clare into the sea, are a major draw. This bleak geology manages to sustain over four hundred varieties of wild flower, including the rare Alpine Spring gentian, as well as a healthy population of butterflies and endangered bird species such as the chough and the little tern. Here too is one of the richest concentrations of pre-Christian and early Christian archaeological sites in Europe, including seven massive **stone forts**, some of which are survivals from the Bronze Age (1100 BC). The pick of these is **Dun Aengus**, a spectacular prehistoric ring fort on the edge of Inishmore's sea cliffs.

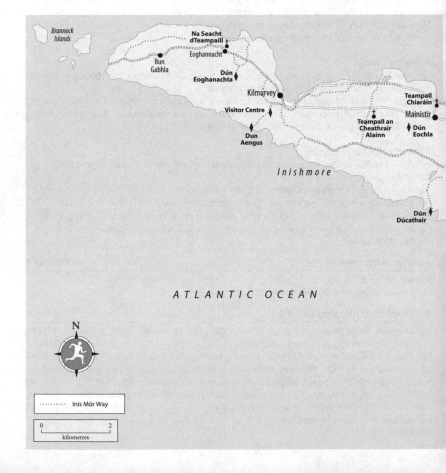

## Brief history

From the fifth or sixth century onwards, the islands were a centre of **monastic learning**, their wildness and remoteness drawing students from far and wide. St Enda's monastery on Inishmore, the first of Ireland's dozens of island monasteries, was also one of the most influential of the age, training monks who went on to found important houses of their own, such as Brendan of Clonfert, Ciarán of Clonmacnois and Colmcille of Iona.

The monasteries of the Arans had gone into decline by the early thirteenth century, at which time Galway city began to take off as a trading port under the Anglo-Normans. For controlling piracy – and their own piratical instincts – in Galway Bay, the Gaelic lords of Aran, the **O'Briens** of County Clare, received an annual payment from the city. In the sixteenth century, however, the O'Briens fell into dispute with the O'Flahertys of west Galway over the islands – to their mutual detriment. The argument was eventually resolved by Queen Elizabeth I who, seeing the Arans as strategically important against the Spanish and French, annexed the islands to the Crown. In 1588, the Arans were sold to the **Lynch** family of Galway, who were required to keep a garrison of soldiers there. The family, however, remained loyal to the king during the English Civil War of the 1640s, and the victorious Cromwell declared Sir Robert Lynch a traitor and his lands forfeit.

**10**

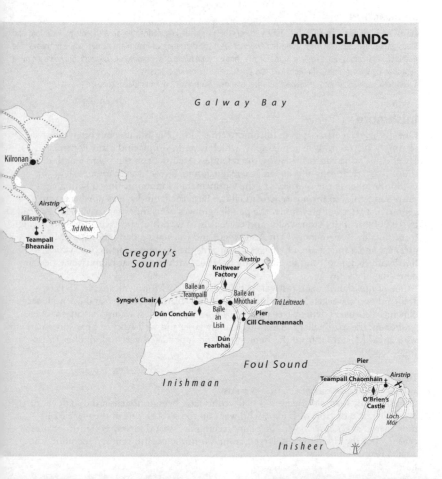

**10**

Thereafter, the islands passed through a succession of landowners, whose main interest was the income from ever-increasing rents. The islands escaped the worst effects of the Famine of the 1840s, as the availability of **food from the sea** and the shore helped to compensate for the failure of the potato crop. It wasn't until 1922 that the absentee landlords sold their interests and the islands' farmers finally came to own their land.

## ARRIVAL AND DEPARTURE                                          THE ARAN ISLANDS

There are coach connections (€4–5) from Galway to Rossaveel (25min) and Inverin airport (45min from Galway city) for most flights and boat departures.

**By boat** Ferries sail from Rossaveel (Rós an Mhíl) and from Doolin in County Clare (see page 324) to the Aran Islands. Aran Island Ferries has branches on Forster St and on Merchants Rd in Galway city (☎ 091 568903, evenings ☎ 091 572273, ⓦ aranislandferries.com). All destinations cost €30 return or €17 single; packages are available with the *Kilronan* hostel (see page 355) and cost €37 for one

night's B&B and return ferry.

Destinations Inishmore (2–3 daily with extra sailings in summer; 35min); Inisheer (2 daily; 1hr); the Inisheer boat calls at Inishmaan (50min from Rossaveel) on both outward and return journeys.

**By plane** Flights operate from Connemara Regional Airport at Inverin (Indreabhán), around 30km west of Galway city. Aer Árann Inverin (☎ 091 593034, ⓦ aerarannislands. ie) flies to all three islands (up to 4 daily). Flights cost €30 single, €55 return, and must be booked in advance.

## INFORMATION

**Maps and guides** The Ordnance Survey cover the Arans on a single 1:25,000 map, while *The Aran Islands: A World of Stone* is an excellent introductory book, published by O'Brien Press. Tim Robinson has produced a comprehensive map and guidebook of the islands,

which is knowledgeable on archaeology, local lore and the derivation of Irish place names, while his books, *The Aran Islands: Pilgrimage* and *Labyrinth*, provide even more fascinating analysis.

**Website** ⓦ visitaranislands.com.

# Inishmore

One of the great attractions of **Inishmore** (Inis Mór, "Big Island", but often referred to simply as Árainn) is its topography, which is stark, simple and easily appreciated. Sheer cliffs, lashed at their base by the relentless Atlantic, run the 14km length of its south coast, their tops offering an ethereal panorama, from the echoing wall of the Cliffs of Moher in the southeast to the Connemara Mountains, tinged with green, purple and gold, to the north across Galway Bay. The land declines northwards in a geometric pattern of grey stone, the parallel grooves of its limestone pavement overlaid by 10,000km of **dry-stone walls**, and there's also a wealth of spectacular dry-stone ring forts, notably **Dun Aengus** (Dún Aonghasa), and fascinating **early churches**. More greenery and a smattering of villages lie towards the sheltered north coast, which is lined with rock pools and several sandy **beaches**, with the one at Kilmurvey especially deserving of a visit.

One of the island's main **festivals** is Féile Patrún Inis Mór, dedicated to SS Peter and Paul over a weekend in late June or early July, featuring *currach* and open-air set dancing. February's Tedfest (see page 354) is a somewhat less traditional alternative.

**Kilronan**, the main village, has a surprisingly large and well-stocked Spar supermarket, with an ATM, not far from the Bank of Ireland (open Wed year-round, plus Thurs June–Sept).

## Teampall Chiaráin
About 1.5km northwest of Kilronan on the coast road • Open access

The church of **Teampall Chiaráin** is believed to have been founded in the sixth century by St Ciarán, a disciple of Enda's, who went on to establish one of the great Irish monasteries at Clonmacnois. The plain, rectangular west doorway is eighth- or ninth-century, but the church was enlarged around it in the twelfth century, including the arched Romanesque east window.

## Dún Eochla and around
3km from Kilronan off the middle road • Open access

Standing near the island's highest point, **Dún Eochla** ("Fort of the Yew Wood") is an oval hill fort – heavily reconstructed in the nineteenth century – consisting of two massive, roughly concentric walls, with great views across Galway Bay. A couple of kilometres further along the middle road lies the fifteenth-century **Teampall an Cheathrair Alainn** (Church of the Four Beauties), named after four saints who are said to have lived and been buried here. This ruined chapel is reached along a rough, signposted path through grassy fields and over stone walls; water from the well on its south side, hung with crosses and other votive offerings, is believed to cure eye complaints.

**10**

## Dun Aengus (Dún Aonghasa)
Signposted to the south of Kilmurvey • Daily: April–Oct 9am–6pm; Nov–March 10am–4pm • €5; Heritage Card • ☎ 099 61008, ⓦ heritageireland.ie • Access to the site is via a visitor centre and café, from where it's an uphill walk of nearly 1km to the fort

By far the Aran Islands' most compelling ancient site, **Dun Aengus** is a semicircular fort of three concentric enclosures, hard up against the edge of sheer, 90m-high cliffs. From here, on a clear day, you can see Kerry Head, northwest of Tralee, and occasionally Mount Brandon on the Dingle Peninsula – if you're truly blessed, you might spot the island of Hy Brasil to the west. The fort is named after Aengus of the **Fir Bolg**, a legendary ancient race, said to have been of Greek origin and to have ruled Ireland for 37 years, before being conquered by the equally mythical Tuatha Dé Danann.

The **inner citadel** comprises a wall, 6m high and 4m wide, of massive blocks of limestone that were quarried on site and put together without mortar. In the site's heyday, the inhabitants would have lived here and in the middle enclosure, with livestock in the outermost enclosure. Some time after 500 BC, Dun Aengus contracted, and a still-imposing *cheval de frise* was constructed between the middle and outer walls, a 10m-wide field planted with razor-sharp standing stones up to 1.8m high, designed to slow down attackers.

## Dún Eoghanachta
Just under 2km northwest of Kilmurvey

Look out for signposts pointing south along a dwindling trail for the twenty-minute walk up to the impressive **Dún Eoghanachta**. Probably built between 650 and 800 AD, it's the smallest of the Aran forts, a perfect circle of rectilinear, almost brick-like, light-grey, limestone blocks.

## The Seven Churches
To the north of Eoghanacht village

The monastic complex of **Na Seacht dTeampaill**, or the **Seven Churches**, actually consists of the substantial ruins of two churches and five domestic buildings. It was founded by St Brecan, who arrived on the island in the fifth or early sixth century, succeeded Enda as the abbot of the main monastery at Killeany, and was famous for his

---

### HY BRASIL

From Dun Aengus, you might be lucky enough to see the famous **mirage** known as **Hy Brasil** (after which the South American country was supposedly named), which appears in the sea to the west as a mountainous island. Local folklore represents this mythical land variously as the island of the blessed, the Garden of Eden, Tír na nóg (the land of eternal youth), the Isle of Truth, of Joy, of Fair Women and of Apples. In the early twentieth century, islanders believed it appeared once every seven years, but up until the mid-nineteenth century it was actually shown on some sea charts of the Atlantic. On the unforgiving, sea-battered Arans, it's easy to understand how this fantasy of a prosperous paradise grew up.

piety and severity. Occupying land with some of the deepest soil on the island, the site is still used as a graveyard. The older of the churches, Teampall Bhreacáin, dates from the eighth century but was gradually enlarged with some fine arches.

### Dún Dúchathair (Black Fort)
To the south of Kilronan

Enjoying a spectacular location on a promontory, **Dún Dúchathair** ("Black Fort") is guarded by cliffs on three sides, and a *cheval de frise* on the fourth. The fort consists of a single massive wall, 60m long, that slices across the neck of the headland. Once through the narrow entrance at the eastern end (the main gate here collapsed into the sea in the early nineteenth century) you'll find the remains of four oval *clocháns*.

### Teampall Bheanáin
Just south of and above the village of Killeany

The eleventh-century **Teampall Bheanáin** stands in a magnificent hilltop location that's especially enchanting at sunset. Built of huge stone slabs, it's notable for its north–south alignment, its unusually steep gables and its size – at just 5m long, some claim it to be the smallest church in Europe. It was probably part of St Enda's early monastic site (*Cill Einne*, "Church of Enda"), formed around 490, which was torn down by Cromwell's soldiers to strengthen Arkin Castle in the village in 1652.

---

**ARRIVAL AND DEPARTURE**                                   **INISHMORE**

**By boat** Ferries (see page 352) dock at the main village Kilronan (Cill Rónáin) from either Rossaveel in Connemara or Doolin in Clare, usually arriving around 11am.

**By plane** Flights from Inverin on the nine-seat Islander planes arrive during the day into the airstrip at An Trá Mhór. A minibus will pick you up and drop you at your accommodation or chosen destination.

**GETTING AROUND**

**By minibus** Minibuses operate all over Inishmore with a basic shared journey costing €10 per person. Drivers also offer set tours that take up to 3hr, including 1hr 30min at Dun Aengus and 15min at the Seven Churches.

**By bike** Aran Bicycle Hire by the pier in Kilronan (☎099 61132, ⓦaranislandsbikehire.com). It's easier if you follow a circuit going out on the coast road and coming back by the hillier middle road, with the prevailing west wind at your back.

**On foot** The most scenic way to get around is to follow looped walks of 3–5hr; route leaflets are available at the tourist office. Make sure you have stout walking boots. For more information, go to ⓦdiscoverireland.ie/walking.

**By pony buggy** Tours of the island cost €40–60 for a group of up to four adults, with a choice of three set routes.

**INFORMATION**

**Tourist office** The office opposite the pier (daily: Nov–June 10am–5pm; July–Sept 10am–6pm; ☎099 20862) has maps and walking route leaflets for all of the islands, information on accommodation and details of sailing and flight timings.

---

### TEDFEST

On the last weekend in February, a friendly invasion of visitors – amounting to nearly half the island's population – arrives en masse for a madcap festival on Inishmore. Since 2006 they have been coming in their hundreds to celebrate cult classic **Father Ted**, the TV comedy whose setting, the fictitious Craggy Island, was inspired by the Arans. Based in Kilronan in *Tí Joe Watty's* bar (see page 355), the weekend is a party place for "Ted Heads". Entertainment includes comedy shows, sketches, a "lovely girls" competition and a raft of other shenanigans. Musical parameters are wide, stretching from traditional Irish, country and folk to bluegrass and rock 'n roll, featuring up to twenty bands from Ireland and the UK. Tickets are limited to 420 so book early and organize your accommodation well in advance. It all kicks off at noon on the Thursday, continuing unabated until the small hours of Monday morning. Go to ⓦtedfest.org for information and tickets.

## THE ARAN ISLANDS AND THE GAELIC REVIVAL

In the late nineteenth century, the Arans became a living museum for anthropologists, antiquarians and linguists, seeking out the unbroken heritage of Irish language, beliefs and customs here, which in turn provided fuel for the **Gaelic Revival** and the Nationalist movement. Written and spoken Irish was a particular focus of interest, as even by this time the islands were one of the few areas of the country where the native language was in daily use. Patrick Pearse came specifically to learn Irish on Inishmaan, which was also visited by writers Yeats, Lady Gregory and, most notably, J.M. Synge – George Russell later joked that Synge's knack was to discover that if you translated Irish literally into English, you achieved poetry.

The Arans themselves have nurtured several excellent writers, notably **Liam O'Flaherty** (see page 599) and poet **Máirtín Ó Direáin** (see page 601), both from Inishmore. In 1934 the documentary-maker **Robert Flaherty** released his classic *Man of Aran* in which he sought to record the islands' vanishing way of life – some of it had already disappeared, but he wasn't averse to re-creating scenes that were no longer witnessed. A few of the traditions captured in the film still exist – you'll still see people collecting seaweed for fertilizer, building dry-stone walls and fishing from **currachs** (traditional pointed skiffs), though these are no longer covered with animal skins. In more recent years, *The Cripple of Inishmaan*, Martin McDonagh's black comedy starring Daniel Radcliffe, has been performed to packed houses on stages in Broadway and the West End, and has captured the imagination of the critics. The storyline – about a crippled teenager who tries to get a role in the *Man of Aran* – focuses on a Hollywood director visiting the island.

### ACCOMMODATION

**Aran Islands Hotel** Lower Kilronan ☎099 61104, ⓦaranislandshotel.com. Smart, modern hotel, tastefully fitted with pine floors and bare stone walls; the best rooms have kingsize beds and panoramic balconies. From the hotel's restaurant (try the seafood pasta) there are spectacular views of Kileaney Bay. €120

**Kilmurvey House** Kilmurvey ☎099 61218. Near the Dun Aengus visitor centre, but quiet at night, this B&B occupies an impressive and welcoming eighteenth-century country house with a ruined church in its extensive garden. Closed mid-Oct to March. €95

**Kilronan Hostel** Kilronan (IHO) ☎099 61255, ⓦkilronanhostel.com. Beside *Tigh Jo Mac*'s pub, this hostel has small (four- to six-bed) en-suite dorms, with a kitchen and TV room. Breakfast included. Dorms €18, doubles €30

**Pier House** Kilronan ☎099 61417, ⓦpierhousearan.com. Richly decorated guesthouse with attractive, pine-furnished rooms, occupying a peerless spot by the jetty with panoramic views. Self-catering apartments available. €90

**Seacrest** Kilronan ☎099 61292, ⓦaranaccommodations.com. Out of ten or so B&Bs in and around the main village, this bungalow is a good bet in the centre, with smart, en-suite rooms, a spacious living room and hearty breakfasts. They also run 3hr horse-and-carriage tours of the island (€25). €80

### EATING AND DRINKING

**The Bar** Kilronan Pier ☎099 61130, ⓦinismorbar.com. Convenient waterfront bar serving sandwiches, soup, fish and chips, as well as gluten-free and vegetarian meals from lunchtime till 9pm. They also hold traditional music sessions most nights in summer. Daily noon–11.30pm.

**Man of Aran Café** Main St Klronan ☎085 710 5254. This is the place to come to watch the *Man of Aran* film, which they show daily for €5. The café also sells crafts, guidebooks and maps, and offers a left luggage facility, charging €2 per bag. March–Oct daily 10am–5pm.

**The Pier House** Waterfront, Kilronan ☎099 61811. This is the ideal spot for food on a sunny day overlooking the waterfront. Lunches might be grilled potato fish cakes, smoked chicken salad or Aran seafood platter. For dinner, expect brill, lobster or oysters. Main courses from €15. Daily noon–11.30pm.

**Ti Joe Watty's** Cottage Rd, Kilronan ☎099 20892, ⓦjoewattys.com A tree-shaded beer garden at a crossroads with all sorts of live music (nightly in summer; weekends only from Oct). It's popular for varied lunches and dinners such as crab claws, steamed mussels, fish and chips or Irish stew. Daily noon–11.30pm.

### INISHMAAN AND J.M. SYNGE

Inishmaan's most famous visitor was **J.M. Synge**, who, on the advice of W.B. Yeats, spent long periods of time on the island between 1898 and 1902, living on mackerel and eggs. He found artistic liberation here, as well as plenty of plot ideas in the stories told him by the islanders, writing his first play, *When the Moon has Set*, in 1901. His book *The Aran Islands* is a moving account of the way of life he encountered.

**10**

# Inishmaan

Approaching from the west or east, **Inishmaan** (Inis Meáin, "Middle Island") looks like a rising wave about to break over Galway Bay to the north. From the grey limestone pavement at its northern end, tiny pastures, separated by a maze of dry-stone walls, rise to the main east–west ridge, along which lies a ribbon of villages. The so-called "back of the island" slopes off more gradually to the south. This is the most unspoilt of the Arans, and the most thoroughly Irish-speaking (though English is understood), where people are still largely engaged in farming and fishing, with wild salmon caught from black, pointed *currachs*. The island's historic sites are on a smaller scale than Inishmore's – though the imposing ring fort of **Dún Conchúir** is worth singling out – and there are far fewer amenities, but for some people this tranquil, low-key place will be the perfect getaway.

The **Bank of Ireland** operates on the second Tuesday of every month, while Baile an Mhothair, the Inis Meáin Knitting Company (☎099 73009, ⊕inismeain.ie), on the north side of the island, produces beautiful **knitwear** based on traditional Aran patterns, usually for exclusive export markets, but available here at discounted prices.

## Cill Cheanannach and around
East side of the island, immediately southwest of the pier

A tiny, roofless church with steeply pitched gables, **Cill Cheanannach** was built some time before 1200. Just to the north, in the graveyard, lies a curious, roughly triangular slab of limestone: the end-stone of a tomb-shrine, it is pierced with a hole through which pilgrims could touch the bones of the saint inside (possibly the shadowy Cheanainn). On the slope above the church perches the overgrown **Dún Fearbhaí**, a small, rectilinear ring fort, probably dating from the ninth century AD or later.

## Baile an Teampaill

From the pier, the island – and the main road – rises in rough steps through the adjoining hamlets of Baile an Mhothair and Baile an Lisín to **Baile an Teampaill** at its midpoint. It's well worth calling in to the village **church** here to see the gorgeous stained-glass windows executed by Harry Clarke in 1939. Made up of glass pieces of varying thicknesses, the richly coloured images swim before your eyes – look out especially for Cavan (Caomhán), the patron saint of Inisheer, with a man rowing a *currach* behind his feet.

### Teach Synge
On the road a few hundred metres before Fort Dún Conchúir • June–Sept noon–2pm & 2.30–4.30pm; by appointment at other times • €3 • ☎099 73036

Further along from the church stands **Teach Synge**, a former post office where Synge stayed, as well as Lady Gregory, W.B. Yeats and Patrick Pearse before him. It's a charming 300-year-old cottage, thatched and whitewashed, with typically small windows (rents on the islands were often calculated on the basis of the size and number of windows). A dresser, a butter churn and most of the other furniture from Synge's time are still inside, as well as fascinating photos taken by the playwright, on the first camera to be brought to the island.

## Dún Conchúir

Signposted up a lane from Teach Synge

Near Inishmaan's highest point, **Dún Conchúir** is one of the Arans' most imposing forts, with fine views of Connemara and down Ireland's west coast. Its ramparted, dry-stone walls are 5m thick and 6m high, with a walled gateway defending the main entrance at the northeastern corner. According to legend, Conchúir was the younger brother of Aengus, who is commemorated with his own fort on Inishmore, backing up the theory that there was a prehistoric confederation of the islands, with its capital at Dun Aengus. The last inhabitant of the fort was a nineteenth-century Connemara man called Malley, who, having accidentally killed his father, hid out here for several months, before escaping to America – a tale used as inspiration by Synge for the plot of *Playboy of the Western World*.

10

## Synge's Chair

About 20min walk west of Baile an Teampaill

The playwright's favourite contemplative spot, **Synge's Chair**, is a semicircle of stones he gathered himself, on the site of an old lookout facing Gregory's Sound. From here, you can take a two- to three-hour west-coast hike along towering cliffs to the blowholes at the southwest corner, before cutting up the middle of the island to the village.

### ARRIVAL AND DEPARTURE INISHMAAN

**By plane** Flights operate from Connemara Regional Airport at Inverin (Indreabhán). Aer Árann (☎091 593034, 🖥aerarannislands.ie; €30 single, €55 return; book in advance) flies three times daily to Inishmaan and Inisheer.

**By boat** Ferries to Inishmaan and Inisheer sail twice daily from Rossaveel (☎091 568 903, 🖥aranislandferries. com) and from Doolin in County Clare (☎065 707 4455, 🖥doolinferries.com).

### ACCOMMODATION AND EATING

**An Dún** Dún Conchúir ☎099 73047, 🖥inismeain accommodation.ie. An attractive, well-designed guesthouse with five en-suite rooms and a sauna. The restaurant menu (7–9pm) showcases home-grown organic vegetables, including the delectable Inishmaan floury potatoes that are fertilized in seaweed; in summer there's a daytime café. Closed Dec–Feb. **€103**

**Ard Alainn** ☎087 285 6778, ✉ardalainn_inismeain@ eircom.net. A hospitable guesthouse in a lofty position between Dún Conchúir and Synge's Chair, offering a fine panorama of Galway Bay. Modern standard and en-suite rooms and self-catering also available. Phone for free pick-up from the pier. **€80**

**Inis Meáin Suites & Restaurant** North side of island ☎086 826 6026, 🖥inismeain.com. The family that owns the knitwear factory (see page 356) also runs this place as a luxury nature lodge, whose contemporary style blends in beautifully with the landscape. Each suite has a huge picture window to make the most of the views of Galway Bay. Expect breakfasts of free range eggs, fresh fish and treacle bread, while shellfish, lobster and scallops dominate the dinner menu (dinner available to residents Mon–Sat and to non-residents Wed–Sat by advance booking; four-course menu €80). Prices include breakfast, a hotpot lunch and bicycle use. Closed Oct to mid-March. **€350**

# Inisheer

Lying just 10km off the Clare coast, **Inisheer** (Inis Oírr, "East Island") is the smallest and least dramatic Aran. Its historic sites aren't quite as appealing as Inishmaan's, and it's much more of a lively pleasure ground, attracting crowds of teenagers from the local Irish college and day-trippers from Doolin in summer. There's a lovely, partly sheltered, sandy **beach** east of the pier on the north coast, along which nearly all of the habitation on this 3km-wide island spreads. The 10km, waymarked **Inis Oírr Way** traces a circular route round the northern half of the island, taking in O'Brien's Castle and Teampall Chaomháin, and you could easily branch off between the latter and Loch Mór to add on a walk down the road to the **lighthouse** at the southeastern tip of the island, which affords fantastic views of the Cliffs of Moher.

---

**INISHEER FESTIVALS**

Musicians flock here at the end of June when the island hosts a five-day **bodhrán festival** (Ⓦcraiceann.com), while mid-September sees enthusiasts of **stone walls** (and there are more than you'd think) arrive for a weekend of events and activities that include tuition on the art of stone wall building and carving.

---

**10**

There are no ATMs on the island, but the Bank of Ireland visits on the fourth Tuesday of the month.

## O'Brien's Castle

Above and behind the beach, **O'Brien's Castle** (Caisleán Uí Bhriain) is attractively sited above low, ivy-covered cliffs, a short, green valley and a network of dry-stone walls. It's well worth walking up to the castle for views of the harbour and the north half of the island, if nothing else.

## Teampall Chaomháin

Climb the sand dune, topped with modern gravestones and wild flowers, on the southeast side of the beach and you're in for a surprise: sunk into the dune's summit lies **Teampall Chaomháin**, a roofless church dedicated to St Cavan (still a common boy's name on the island), who is thought to have been the brother of St Kevin of Glendalough. Retaining walls now help to protect the ruin from the shifting sand, but it still has to be shovelled out every year on June 14, the saint's feast day.

## Áras Éanna

A 15min walk south from the West village in the north of the island • ☎ 099 75150

A multipurpose arts centre, **Áras Éanna** has a gallery showing temporary art exhibitions, runs demonstrations of traditional basket-making and weaving in the summer and hosts music, films and plays in its theatre.

### GETTING AROUND AND INFORMATION                                    INISHEER

**Inisheer Island Co-operative** Situated beyond the east end of the beach, this business (☎099 75008, (Ⓦdiscover inisoirr.com) can provide tourist information as well as internet access.

**Bike rental** Bikes can be rented from the helpful office (☎099 75049) in front of the pier, where you can also charter a pony and trap for a tour of the island.

### ACCOMMODATION AND EATING

**Brú Radharc na Mara hostel** (IHH) ☎099 75024, Ⓦbruhostelaran.com. Sited hard by the pier, this hostel offers laundry facilities, a kitchen, dining room and common room with open fire, as well as smarter en-suite accommodation in the attached B&B. Closed Nov to mid-March. Dorms €18, doubles €60, B&B €70

**Island Co-operative Campsite** ☎099 75008. The only place to camp is this site by the beach, which has toilets and hot showers. Closed Nov–April. €10

**Radharc an Chláir** ☎099 75019, ✉bridpoil@eircom. net. A dormer bungalow near the castle, with a conservatory and fine views. Breakfasts cover the spectrum from the full Irish to porridge or kippers. Closed mid-Sept to Easter. €65

**South Aran House** ☎087 340 5687, Ⓦsoutharan.com. At the west end of the village, this place has bright, tasteful en-suite rooms with underfloor heating and free wi-fi. The attractive onsite restaurant rustles up crab linguini, fish pie and vegetarian dishes, with main course prices around €17 (reservations essential). Minimum stay two nights from Oct to March. Adults only. Restaurant daily 7.30–9.30pm. €85

**Tigh Ned's** West village ☎099 75004. A cosy pub by the Brú Radharc na Mara hostel with a pleasant garden overlooking the harbour, and food and traditional sessions in summer. Food served daily noon–4pm; bar noon–11.30pm.

### SHOPPING

**Inisheer Heritage House** This heritage house and craft shop near the main pier at the north end of the island is worth visiting to browse local sweaters, books and indigenous craftwork (☎099 75021).

# Connemara

Comprising all of Galway to the west of the city, **Connemara** is a ravishingly diverse tract of land. Cut off from the rest of the county by the sweep of **Lough Corrib**, the lie of the land at first looks simple, with two statuesque mountain ranges, the **Maam Turks** (Mám Tuirc, the "boar pass") and the **Twelve Bens** (or sometimes Twelve Pins; Na Beanna Beola, the "Peaks of Beola", a mythical giant), bordered by the deep fjord of **Killary Harbour** to the north. The coast, however, is full of jinks and tricks, a maze of little islands, winding roads, bogs and hills, where it can be hard to tell small loughs from sea inlets. All around the littoral are quiet white-sand **beaches** that are great for swimming. It's hard to miss out **Clifden** on your travels, the likeable and lively main town, poised dramatically between steep hills and the harbour. Other likely bases are the pretty fishing village of **Roundstone**, and **Oughterard**, an angler's delight, not far out of Galway city on the lush banks of Lough Corrib. Oughterard has a good selection of visitor attractions, but the only really compelling historic sight in west Connemara is **Kylemore Abbey and Gardens**. Just off shore near here, you can sample easy-going island life on **Inishbofin**.

**10**

**GETTING AROUND AND INFORMATION**                                              **CONNEMARA**

**By bus** Bus Éireann's main services from Galway run along the coast via Spiddal to Carraroe, and along the N59 via Oughterard to Clifden, sometimes branching off to Roundstone. A few of their services to Clifden branch off at Maam Cross and detour via Leenane, Kylemore and Letterfrack, and in summer they operate a daily (Mon–Sat) bus from Clifden to Westport, via Letterfrack, Kylemore and Leenane. Citylink buses (☎ 091 564164, ⓦ citylink.ie) from Galway serve Oughterard, Clifden, Cleggan and Letterfrack three or four times a day.

**By car** The major route through the area is the N59 from Galway, which cuts across to Clifden before skirting the Twelve Bens en route to Westport, but there are plenty of scenic side-roads through the mountains and around the frilly coastline.

**Tourist information** ⓦ connemara.ie.

## Oughterard and around

Around 28km from Galway on the N59, **OUGHTERARD** is a busy little town, at the start of the Western Way (see page 360), with plenty of varied attractions in the surrounding area to keep you occupied. Its main asset, however, is not immediately obvious from the long main street: behind the trees to the north of town lies the great expanse of **Lough Corrib**, a paradise for angling or for just messing about in boats, studded with hundreds of tree-clad islets (365 of them, one for each day of the year, if you believe the locals). May is the busiest time for fishing, when the mayflies hatch from the lake bed, while the annual agricultural and horticultural show at the end of August also attracts crowds (ⓦ oughterardshow.com).

### Inchagoill island

If taking a boat tour (see page 361), you'll likely stop off at **Inchagoill island**. Little is known of this uninhabited island's history beyond the meaning of its name, "Isle of the

**CONNEMARA AND THE IRISH LANGUAGE**

Connemara's harsh land has always been thinly populated and isolated, and this has ensured the persistence of rural traditions and of the **Irish language**. It contains the country's largest Gaeltacht, stretching as far west as Roundstone, with Raidió na Gaeltachta and TG4, the Irish-speaking radio and TV stations, both broadcast from here. Four-week **Irish-language courses** for adults, supplemented by cultural activities and singing and dancing classes, are held each summer by NUI Galway at Árus Mháirtín Uí Chadhain (ⓦ nuigalway.ie) in An Cheathrú Rua (Carraroe).

## WALKING IN CONNEMARA

Connemara offers a stunning variety of **walking**, including mountains over 700m – though be aware that the nearest rescue team is in Galway. A good **map** and guidebook for serious walkers is *The Mountains of Connemara*, available from local bookshops and tourist offices, with a 1:50,000-scale map derived from aerial photography and fieldwork by Tim Robinson, and an excellent guide to eighteen walks of varying length and difficulty by Joss Lynam. The Ordnance Survey has produced their own maps at 1:50,000.

A good introduction to the Maam Turks, with breathtaking views of the Twelve Bens across Lough Inagh, would be the ascent of **Cnoc na hUilleann** and **Binn Bhriocáin** from the **Inagh Valley** back road north of Recess, on a three- to four-hour circuit described in *The Mountains of Connemara*, which also covers the waymarked **Western Way**, which runs for 50km from Oughterard to Leenane. This varied, low-level trail starts as a pleasant, sometimes boggy, walk beside Lough Corrib, before crossing over from the village of Maam into the dramatic Inagh Valley, which runs between the Bens and the Turks. The walk can be done in two long days, with an overnight near Maam. You can also extend the walk into Co. Mayo. Walking trail map leaflets are available at tourist information offices.

Worthy **short walks** include the ascent of Errisbeg and other routes near Roundstone (see page 362), the sky road from Clifden (see page 363), a circuit of Inishbofin (see page 365), the excellent trails at Connemara National Park (see page 367) and the climb up Tully Hill (see page 368). **Walking tours** are organized from Clifden by Connemara Safari on the sky road (☎ 095 21071, ⓦ www.walkingconnemara.com), which runs five-day walking and island-hopping trips.

Foreigners". It was, however, the site of an early monastery, featuring the Romanesque Saints' Church, which was restored by Sir Benjamin Guinness in the nineteenth century and is most notable for its attractively carved west doorway.

### Aughnanure Castle

Signposted 3km from the centre of Oughterard, about 1.5km off the N59 • March–Nov daily 9.30am–6pm • €5; Heritage Card • ☎ 091 552214, ⓦ heritageireland.ie

Just east of Oughterard stands a particularly impressive and well-preserved early sixteenth-century tower house, **Aughnanure Castle**, which rises to six storeys and still retains its outer defensive walls; it occupies what is virtually a rocky island near the banks of Lough Corrib. The strongest bastion of the O'Flahertys, who were masters of Connemara from the thirteenth to the sixteenth century, Aughnanure boasts a frightening array of defensive features, including arrow slits aimed at the main staircase, secret prison chambers and a trap door in the hall above a subterranean river, through which were thrown guests who had outstayed their welcome.

### Brigit's Garden

Pollagh, Roscahill; look for signs pointing off the N59, 4km southeast of the turn-off for Aughnanure Castle • Daily 10am–5.30pm • €9, children €6, family ticket €26 (discounts off season) • ☎ 091 550905, ⓦ brigitsgarden.ie

The delightful **Brigit's Garden** is named after the saint (see page 126) whose feast day, February 1, and symbol, the snowdrop, mark the start of spring. This beautifully designed ten-acre garden includes an area devoted to the four Celtic seasons, featuring sculptures, standing stones, symbolic plantings and a thatched roundhouse. Beyond this, you'll find a stand of ancient woodland, a herb garden, wild-flower meadows, a small lake, a ring fort and Ireland's largest sundial, with nature discovery trails laid on for adults and kids. There's an excellent **garden café**, a gift shop and various talks and events.

## Glengowla Mine

3km west of Oughterard on the N59 • March–Oct daily 10am–6pm • €11 • ☎ 091 552360, ⓦ glengowlamines.ie

For a fascinating change from all the glorious scenery hereabouts, head underground into the restored **Glengowla Mine**. This silver and lead mine was worked between 1850 and 1865 and reluctantly yielded from the area's tough marble around three hundred tons of the ore galena. Entertaining guided tours (40min) bring to life the hardships of drilling by hand and blasting the rock by candlelight, often in deep pools of water.

10

### ARRIVAL AND INFORMATION

**OUGHTERARD AND AROUND**

**By bus** Bus Éireann services (Mon–Sat 5 daily; Sun 2 daily) from Galway to Clifden stop in Oughterard.

**Tourist office** Oughterard's tourist office is in Camp St café (daily 9am–5.30pm; ☎ 091 866066).

**Boat tours** From June to August you can take a day cruise (☎ 087 283 0799, ⓦ corribcruises.com) across to Cong in County Mayo from the pier 2km north of the main street along Pier Rd. The tour takes in Inchagoill Island and the gardens of Ashford Castle (see page 370), and costs €28.

### ACCOMMODATION AND EATING

**The Boat Inn** The Square ☎ 091 552196, ⓦ theboatinn. ie. A pleasant and affordable restaurant where wild mushroom ravioli, fillet of hake or Connemara mountain lamb are typical offerings on the dinner menu. Prices are around €14 for mains. Daily 12.30–9.30pm.

**Breathnachs Bar** Camp St ☎ 091 552818, ⓦ breathnachs. com. A family-run bar by the central junction offering breakfast, lunch and dinner – and music at weekends. You can choose from sandwiches, salads, chowder, shellfish tagliatelle, Irish stew or grilled Atlantic salmon. Main courses from €10. Daily 10am–11.30pm, Fri & Sat till 12.30am.

**Camillaun** Eighterard ☎ 091 552678, ⓦ camillaun.com. A tastefully decorated, modern guesthouse, with a tennis court, hot tub and snooker table, set in gardens on the banks of the Owenriff River (rowing and motor boats for rent). €90

★ **Currarevagh House** Glann Rd, 6km northwest of town ☎ 091 552312, ⓦ currarevagh.com. This charming traditional country house was built in the 1840s on the lakeshore. It has boats and ghillies, and there's walking on the wooded 100-acre estate and immaculate gardens with fine views of the lake. The unpretentious dinners are based on local produce and there's complimentary afternoon tea for residents. Closed mid-Nov to mid-Feb. €170

**Oughterard Hostel** Station Rd ☎ 087 248 8964, ⓦ oughterardhostel.com. Good hostel in a large, modern house with an extensive lawn, signposted off the west end of the main street, less than 1km from the tourist office. Rooms are en suite, and there's fishing tuition. Closed Nov–Jan. Dorms €17, doubles €48

# Spiddal (An Spidéal)

The R336 coast road arrows west out of Galway through a gently sloping landscape of shrubs, ferns and boulders, offering fine views of the slate-grey Burren across the water but marred by a monotonous ribbon development of white bungalows. Relief comes after 18km with the lofty trees and church of **SPIDDAL** (An Spidéal, "the hospital"), the effective capital of the Gaeltacht, which is known for its traditional-music sessions. The daytime draw here is the **Spiddal Craft Village** (Ceardlann an Spidéil; ☎ 091 897847, ⓦ spiddalcrafts.com), a group of studios – with an on-site bistro-café – making and selling pottery, weaving, jewellery, leather goods, sculpture and musical instruments. In open country 5km north of the central crossroads, **Cnoc Suain** ("restful hill"; ☎ 091 555703, ⓦ cnocsuain.com) is a "cultural hill-village" of restored thatched and slate-tiled stone cottages that hosts residential programmes in Irish music, language and natural history.

### ACCOMMODATION AND EATING

**SPIDDAL (AN SPIDÉAL)**

**An Crúiscín Lán** Main St ☎ 091 553148, ⓦ cruiscin.ie. An upmarket option with large, bright rooms – two with sea-view balconies – and a smart evening restaurant. Closed Jan. €130

★ **Builín Blasta** 16 An Ceardlan ☎ 091 558559, ⓦ builinblasta.ie. Tucked away at the back of the Craft Village is this top-notch café, whose name translates as "The Tasty Loaf". Lunch includes salads (€7.50), soup or chowder with breads (€6.50), as well as cakes, pastries and scones, all made in-house. Mon–Sat 10am–6pm.

**Cloch na Scíth** 2km east of town ☎091 553364, Ⓦthatchcottage.com. An en-suite B&B in a traditional thatched cottage, with pine furniture and brass beds, where your hostess demonstrates how to cook bread in a pot over the peat fire. €76

**Páirc Saoire an Spidéil** ☎087 760 7698, Ⓦspiddal mobilehomes.ie. Campers should head for this well-equipped site, 1.5km inland from the centre of the village. Closed Nov–Easter. €18

## Teach an Phiarsaigh

**10**

Near Rosmuc, at the end of a small peninsula off the R340 • Mid-March to Oct daily Mon 9.45am–6pm; Nov to mid-March 9.45am–4pm; last admission 45min before closing • €5, family €13; Heritage Card • ☎091 574292, Ⓦheritageireland.ie and Ⓦicpconamara.ie

A thatched and whitewashed traditional cottage, **Teach an Phiarsaigh** was the summer residence of the revolutionary and writer, Patrick Pearse (see page 578). Here Pearse ran summer schools for his pupils from St Enda's in Rathfarnham, Dublin, and wrote his famous eulogy for the nationalist Jeremiah O'Donovan Rossa on his death in 1915. Inside are mementos and an exhibition on Pearse, but the cottage is more noteworthy for its atmosphere and setting, with dramatic views of the sea and mountains. The **Connemara Cultural Centre**, with a café, exhibition space and audiovisual displays, is reached via a 400m scenic looped walk from the cottage across a newly constructed bog path with interpretation panels. The centre explains Pearse's historical and cultural legacy and looks at contemporary life in Connemara and how the Irish language is part of everyday life.

## Roundstone and around

On the R341 coast road, which eventually loops round into Clifden, **ROUNDSTONE** is a delightful fishing village set amid some of Connemara's finest scenery. The stone harbour looks out on the many islands of Bertraghboy Bay and across to the peaks of the Twelve Bens and the Maam Turks, while behind looms a lone mountain, the 300m-high Errisbeg. There are some beautiful woodland **walks** along the lakeshore and riverbank in the estate of **Ballynahinch Castle** (see page 363), which are described in a leaflet available from the hotel reception. Three kilometres southwest of the village, the beautiful sandy beaches of **Gurteen Bay** and **Dog's Bay** are separated by a narrow, dune-covered isthmus.

The village is well known for its **crafts shops**, including Malachy Kearns' famous *bodhrán* workshop in a former Franciscan monastery in Killeen Park at the south end of the village (☎095 35875, Ⓦbodhran.com). Here you can watch the drums being made, test them out in a sound room or have one painted in the Celtic motif of your choice while you wait. Ferron's Supermarket on the main street contains a post office and ATM.

The highlight of the year for many is the Roundstone Hooker Regatta, a **boating festival** held over the third weekend of July (Ⓦroundstoneregatta.com). It includes *currach* racing, hooker sailing events, maritime heritage walks and live music gigs.

### Erissbeg and the Roundstone bog

From the centre of the village, you can take a very satisfying **walk** to the summit of **Errisbeg** (approximately 1hr), which offers majestic views in all directions. Take the paved lane beside *O'Dowd's* bar (see page 363) and follow the rough track that it turns into; you'll have to pick your way over often boggy ground and boulders towards the top, which, despite appearances from below, turns out to be a ridge of three summits. On three sides runs a coastline of white-sand beaches, where peninsulas are barely distinguishable from islands; to the north, set against one of the finest prospects of the Bens and the Turks, lies huge, sparse **Roundstone Bog**, one of the finest blanket bogs in the country, covered with a glittering crazy-paving of tiny lakes and crossed by a single narrow road.

**ARRIVAL AND INFORMATION**

**By bus** Bus Éireann (☏ 091 562000) runs daily services to Roundstone from Clifden.

**ROUNDSTONE AND AROUND**

**Tourist information** ⓦ roundstonevillage.ie

### ACCOMMODATION AND EATING

★ **Angler's Return** Toombeola, 4km from Roundstone on the main road to Galway ☏ 095 31091, ⓦ anglers return.com. A no-children (under 14) policy leads to a deep sense of adult calm in this stylish 1820s sporting lodge set in semi-wild gardens, favoured not just by fisher folk but also cyclists and walkers. Home-made breads, jams and organic muesli adorn the breakfast table. Minimum stay three nights. **€110**

**Ballynahinch Castle** ☏ 095 31006, ⓦ ballynahinch-castle.com. Set on its own fishing river and lake towards the N59, this eighteenth-century castle was once the home of Richard Martin – aka Humanity Dick – the animal-rights campaigner and co-founder of the RSPCA in 1824, and later of cricketing maharaja, Ranjitsinhji. It's now a romantic luxury hotel in a gloriously peaceful setting, with an excellent restaurant decorated with twentieth–century Irish art and a wood-panelled fishermen's bar where food is available; activities include cycling, fly-fishing tutorials, and guided walks. **€320**

**Cashel House Hotel** ☏ 095 31001, ⓦ cashelhouse.ie. About a 20min drive east from Roundstone, this elegant country house is set in beautiful gardens. Rooms are well-appointed and the dinner choice includes early bird, à la carte or fixed menu options; bar meals are served during the day. Closed Jan. **€200**

**Gurteen Bay Caravan Site** ☏ 095 35882, ⓦ gurteen bay.ie. West of Roundstone, this idyllic site is right by the beach of the same name and offers self-catering apartments as well as camping pitches. **€20**

★ **O'Dowd's Seafood Bar & Restaurant** Main St ☏ 095 35809, ⓦ odowdsseafoodbar.com. The chowder at this sociable spot is still made daily to the same family recipe that has been in use for generations (it features stock made using brill or turbot to give it a rich kick). Daytime bar food includes a variety of shellfish as well as meat and chicken dishes (mains average €13). Attached to the pub is an evening restaurant, while *O'Dowd's Café* a few doors down offers coffee, salads and pizzas. Daily: bar noon–11.30pm; restaurant 5–10pm; café 9am–6pm (9pm in summer).

**St Joseph's** Main St ☏ 095 35865, ⓦ stjosephsrround stone.com. A welcoming place in the heart of the village with en-suite rooms and great breakfasts. Free off-street parking and wi-fi. **€75**

## Clifden and around

**CLIFDEN**, the English-speaking capital of Connemara, is a popular, animated service town, enhanced by a spectacular setting: it perches on a steep, grassy hillside, where the lofty grey spires of the Catholic and Anglican churches compete for attention, while on its western side the land plunges abruptly down to the deeply indented harbour. Several stately town houses sprinkle the three major streets – **Main Street**, the continuation of the Galway road culminating in Market Square, with **Bridge Street** and **Market Street** branching off it at either end and meeting to form a rough triangle. By basing yourself here, you'll be able to explore the varied attractions of coast and mountain hereabouts, and sample the lively nightlife.

There's not much to do on a rainy day in the town itself, although you may find some diversion at the **Station House Museum** near the tourist office on the Galway road (May–Oct Mon–Sat 10am–5pm; €2; ☏ 095 21494), which has displays on local history and on the history, breeding and racing of Connemara ponies. These rugged, passive workhorses have their day in mid-August, when they're judged at the **Connemara Pony Show** (ⓦ cpbs.ie). The other highlight of Clifden's calendar is the prestigious and lively **arts festival** (ⓦ clifdenartsfestival.ie) at the end of September.

### The sky road and bog road

A fine diversion is to walk or cycle the spectacular **sky road**, signposted from the west side of the town, which loops scenically round the narrow peninsula on the north side of Clifden Bay (13km in total). It ends up by the long, thin inlet of Streamstown Bay, passing a quarry for the streaky, green Connemara marble, before hitting the Westport road just north of Clifden.

10

Alternatively, you can complete an excellent, scenic bicycle ride from Clifden by turning left off the R341, 4km north of Roundstone, on to the **bog road**, which undulates westward across the stark peatland back to town.

About 5km off the R341, southwest of Ballyconneely at Bunowen Pier, you can watch the process of preparing smoked salmon and taste some of the finished product at the **Connemara Smokehouse** (Mon–Fri 9am–5pm; guided tours Wed 3pm, €5; booking advisable on ☎095 23739; ⊛smokehouse.ie).

**10**

## Dan O'Hara's Homestead and the Connemara Heritage and History Centre

Lettershea, 7km east of Clifden on the N59 • April–Oct daily 10am–6pm; last admission 5pm • €8.50; Heritage Island • ☎095 21246, ⊛connemaraheritage.com

The area's main set-piece tourist attraction is **Dan O'Hara's Homestead and the Connemara Heritage and History Centre**, which sounds rather kitsch but is quite engaging. Fascinating displays by local archaeologist Michael Gibbons and a short video introduce you to the history of Clifden and Connemara, and to Dan O'Hara himself. A tenant farmer whose house was famous for its ceilis, O'Hara was evicted in 1845 and eventually found his way to New York, where, having little English, he sold matches and inspired the famous eponymous song. Outside, you can view reconstructions of an oratory, a dolmen tomb, a wooden ring fort and a *crannóg*, a thatched dwelling set in a small lake. If there are enough people around, you can take a **guided tour** in a tractor-borne bus up to Dan O'Hara's refurbished cottage for great views south over the bogs and lakes to Roundstone and Errisbeg, and for demonstrations that might include sheep-shearing, thatching and turf-cutting. There's also a craft shop and daytime tea room for snacks such as soup and sandwiches.

### ARRIVAL AND DEPARTURE

**CLIFDEN AND AROUND**

**By bus** Bus Éireann services run from Galway to Clifden (Mon–Sat 3 daily, Sun 2 daily; 1hr). The drop-off/pick-up point is outside the library on Market St. Citylink also operates five daily services (1hr 30min) from Galway to Clifden. Other destinations include Westport via Letterfrack (Mon–Sat 2 daily).

### INFORMATION AND ACTIVITIES

**Tourist information** Galway Rd, near the Station House (mid-March to May & most of Sept Mon–Sat 10am–5pm; June–Aug until 5.45pm; ☎095 21163). Provides information on the town and Connemara.

**Bike rental** John Mannion's, Bridge St (☎095 21160). **Horseriding** Cleggan Beach Equestrian Centre (☎095 44746, ⊛clegganridingcentre.com), 10km to the northwest, offers horseriding, often on one of the area's fine beaches.

---

## THE BOG ROAD TO DERRIGIMLAGH

A newly-developed 5km signposted **looped walk** across flat blanket bog at **Derrigimlagh** tells the story across seven stop points of the local area's role in two remarkable events in early twentieth-century history. Leave your car about 4km south of Clifden at the signposted parking area on the R341, where the path begins, and you'll come to the site of a telegraph station where the Irish-Italian innovator **Guglielmo Marconi** sent the **first commercial wireless transmission** across the Atlantic in 1907. A series of shelters with photoscope, panoramoscope and historioscope, as well as a parabolic mirror, create the impression of how the site might have looked in Marconi's time. The fascinating link to John Alcock and Arthur Brown, who landed here on the **first transatlantic flight** in June 1919, is also recounted. After circling Clifden twice in celebration they nosedived into the bog, wrecking their plans to continue their triumphant flight to London. Nearby, on the Errislannan peninsula, an aeroplane wing-shaped memorial, stands as a tribute to the two intrepid aviators. Depending on how long you spend at the shelters, the return walk should take approximately one and a quarter hours.

## ACCOMMODATION

**Ardagh** 2km south of town on the Ballyconneely road ☎095 21384, ⓦardaghhotel.com. Relaxing and comfortable family-run hotel with views of the bay, pleasant staff, wi-fi and an excellent restaurant offering ten percent discount for residents. Various special offers available online. Sea-view rooms €15 extra per night. Closed Nov–Easter. **€160**

**Ben Lettery Hostel** (An Óige) 13km east of Clifden on the N59 ☎086 849 3712, ⓦanoige.ie. Right at the foot of Ben Lettery, one of the Twelve Bens, with fine views, this is a cosy and welcoming forty-bed hostel, geared towards walking in the mountains (it has drying rooms, for instance). Closed Oct–May. Dorms **€20**, doubles **€36**

**Ben View House** Bridge St ☎095 21256, ⓦbenview house.com. Very central, flower-bedecked nineteenth-century house, offering friendly and comfortable B&B accommodation. Plenty of local information available from the owners on cultural activities in the area. **€85**

**Buttermilk Lodge** 400m out on the Westport road ☎095 21951, ⓦbuttermilklodge.com. A well-appointed modern guesthouse set in a large garden, with spacious en-suite bedrooms, wi-fi and internet access. **€90**

**Clifden Town Hostel** Market St (IHH) ☎095 21076, ⓦclifdentownhostel.com. Attractive hostel in a central, terraced house, with family rooms, two well-equipped kitchens and a comfy sitting room. Closed Dec & Jan. Dorms **€16**, doubles **€50**

**Dolphin Beach Country House** 5km west on Lower Sky Rd ☎095 21204, ⓦdolphinbeachhouse.com. Skilfully converted farmhouse by the seashore with its own sandy cove and spectacular views. Thirteen elegantly simple bedrooms, spacious, open-fired sitting rooms and local meat, baked salmon, and organic veg for dinner (7–9pm with advance booking; not open to non-residents). **€100**

★**The Quay House** ☎095 21369, ⓦthequayhouse. com. Down at the harbour and set in an early nineteenth-century harbourmaster's house, which later became a convent, this is an outstanding guesthouse with a sociable, house party atmosphere. Rooms are elegantly decorated with antiques and paintings; most overlook the water, and some have working fireplaces, four-posters or balconies. Breakfasts are served in the large conservatory. Closed early Nov to mid-March. **€150**

**Sea Mist House** Near Market Square ☎095 21441, ⓦseamisthouse.com. Relaxing and central, this 200-year-old stone cottage in a lush garden offers four stylish en-suite rooms, wi-fi, great breakfasts and plentiful local knowledge. **€95**

**Shan Shanaheever Campsite** 2km out of town off the Westport road ☎095 22150, ⓦclifdencamping.com. A quiet and efficiently run site in peaceful surroundings. Handy for the town but also a wonderful place to drink in the ever-changing light of the Twelve Bens. Closed Oct–April. **€22**

**10**

## EATING AND DRINKING

**Cullen's Café** Market St ☎095 21983. Basic, economical and easy-going place serving unpretentious dishes for lunch and dinner such as poached Connemara salmon, BLTs, and rhubarb crumble dessert. Main courses from €12. Daily 10.30am–9pm.

**Guy's Bar & Restaurant** Main St ☎095 21130. There's a tremendous range of seafood on the menu here, including tempura prawns, crab salad and calamari, plus Thai red chicken curry. Main courses for lunch and dinner range from €15 to €19. Daily 10.30am–11.30pm.

**Mannion's pub** Market St ☎095 21780. One of the best spots for pub grub, serving soup, sandwiches, fish cakes, and Irish stew with local lamb, all in hearty portions; prices

around €16 for main dishes. Traditional music sessions take place twice daily in summer at 6.30pm and 8.30pm. Daily noon–11pm.

**Mitchell's Seafood Restaurant** Market St ☎095 21867. Clifden's best restaurant, providing well-judged and beautifully presented cuisine, heavily weighted towards fresh fish and seafood platters. Cheaper, simpler dishes are available at lunchtime. Mid-March to Oct daily 12.30–3pm & 5.30–10pm.

**Walsh's Bakery & Coffee Shop** Market St ☎095 21283. Traditional daytime café serving delicious cakes, a varied menu of sandwiches and hot and cold plates at lunchtime. Daily 8am–6.30pm.

# Inishbofin

With just two hundred inhabitants, **INISHBOFIN** continues the diversity of the Connemara landscape into the sea, though in a gentler, miniature format. A mere 5km wide, the island – which rises to just 90m at its highest point, **Cnoc Mór** – encompasses cliffs and the rocky outcrops known as **the Stags** on its western side; tranquil, reedy **Lough Boffin**, the haunt of swans, at its centre; and several sandy beaches – the one in the southeast corner provides the best swimming, while beautiful **Trá Ghael**, beneath Cnoc Mór in the west, is also worth visiting, though its currents are too dangerous for a dip. A combined **heritage museum** and gift shop (☎087 969 6732) opens during

**10**

the summer months a short way east of the pier, and over a weekend in May – or sometimes early September (check with the tourist office) – there's a lively, three-day **arts festival**. Year round you're assured plenty of traditional music, featuring the island's own renowned ceili band. Note that the only shop (and post office) near the pier is pricey, so bring as much stuff over with you as you can.

The first historical reference to Inishbofin comes from the seventh century: after the Irish and Roman Churches fell out at the Synod of Whitby in 664, St Colman left Lindisfarne and journeyed here via Iona. Though the monastery he established was destroyed in 1334, you can still see the atmospheric shell of a fourteenth-century **chapel** on the site, to the east of the pier, beyond a small, lily-strewn lake. In the island cemetery surrounding the chapel, two stone crosses and a couple of **holy wells** are said to date from Colman's foundation. The island's other historic site is visible on the right as you enter the excellent natural harbour, a forbidding, mottled-black **castle**, built in the sixteenth century and strengthened by Cromwell, which is accessible at low tide.

### ARRIVAL AND DEPARTURE — INISHBOFIN

**By bus and ferry** The MV *Island Discovery* (☎095 45819 or 44878, ⓦinishbofinislanddiscovery.com; €20 return) crosses the 11km to Inishbofin from Cleggan, 10km northwest of Clifden, with sailings year round (30min; Easter–Aug 3 daily; 2–3 daily for the rest of the year). Citylink buses run from Galway, via Clifden, to Cleggan (3 daily).

### INFORMATION

**Tourist information** You can get information at the island community centre above the pier (Mon–Fri 9.30am–11pm; ☎095 45895). Maps of the island are available on the boat or at the tourist office/community centre. For online information, see ⓦinishbofin.com.

**Bike rental** If there's no sign of Paddy Joe King and his bikes, head to his house 700m east of the pier near the hostel or call ☎095 45833.

### ACCOMMODATION AND EATING

**Dolphin Hotel** 700m east of the pier ☎095 45991, ⓦdolphinhotel.ie. This small hotel offers large, bright, well-equipped en-suite rooms, some with outdoor terraces. Its restaurant menu includes the likes of rump of roast lamb, mackerel, pollock and shellfish. Closed Nov to mid-March. **€110**

**Inishbofin House Hotel** Just east of the pier ☎095 45809, ⓦinishbofinhouse.com. The pick of the accommodation on Inishbofin, this chic, modern hotel offers rooms that mostly have balconies overlooking the harbour. There's also a spa and an evening restaurant, plus cheaper bar food. **€150**

★ **Inishbofin Island Hostel** 700m east of the pier (IHH & IHO) ☎095 45855, ⓦinishbofin-hostel.ie. Well-maintained hostel in a converted farmhouse with a conservatory and garden, laundry facilities and camping space. They'll pick up your luggage at the pier, and offer reduced prices if you stay a second night in private rooms. Closed Nov–March. Camping **€12**, dorms **€16**, doubles **€45**

## Letterfrack and around

The tiny, nineteenth-century Quaker village of **LETTERFRACK**, around 15km northeast of Clifden, is the unlikely site of the Galway Mayo Institute of Technology, and plays host to two notable, longstanding festivals (ⓦceecc.org), both featuring plenty of traditional music: **Bog Week**, celebrating the landscape with walking events at the end of May; and **Sea Week**, with a conference on marine heritage in late October.

### Connemara National Park and Visitor Centre

Entrance on the west side of Letterfrack • March–Oct 9am–5.30pm; grounds open all year round • Free • ☎ 095 41054, ⓦ connemaranationalpark.ie

The **Connemara National Park** covers a thin slice of the northwest sector of the Twelve Bens, stretching east as far as Benbrack, Bencullagh, Muckanaght and Benbaun. It includes an excellent walkway to the top of **Diamond Hill** (445m; about 2hr 30min return), which affords fantastic views of the mountains, bays and islands all around. There are three shorter **nature trails** across the lower slopes, through some natural woodland and over bogland, with free guided walks on Wednesday and Friday mornings in July and August. The park's **visitor centre** contains a fascinating exhibition on the wildlife and geology of Connemara and a café. There's also a children's playground. A trail map is available to download from the website.

**10**

### ARRIVAL AND DEPARTURE
### LETTERFRACK AND AROUND

**By bus** Letterfrack is served by Bus Éireann services from Clifden (Mon–Sat 1–2 daily).

### ACCOMMODATION AND EATING

**Cloverfox** By the central junction ☎ 095 41042, ⓦ cloverfox.ie. This pub offers en-suite hostel rooms and lays on a wide variety of food including chicken and lamb stew. Main courses average €10–13. Food served noon–9pm; €50

**Letterfrack Lodge and Walking Centre** North side of central junction (IHH) ☎ 095 41222, ⓦ letterfracklodge.com. This partly en-suite hostel in a modern, stone-clad and pine-floored house offers local information, laundry facilities and three kitchens. Lunch and dinner are available in summer with the lamb burger (€15) the hot favourite. Closed mid-Sept to late May. Dorms €20, doubles €70

★ **Rosleague Manor** 1.5km west of village ☎ 095 41101, ⓦ rosleague.com. An elegant, early nineteenth-century hotel with a relaxed country-house atmosphere. The sitting rooms are charming, and extensive gardens and woodlands stretch down to the sea. The restaurant (open 7.30–9pm) offers lamb, steak and fresh seafood. Half-board and other packages are available. Closed Nov to mid-March. €190

## Kylemore Abbey

5km east of Letterfrack on the N59 • Easter–Oct 9am–6pm; Nov–March 10am–4.30pm; 20min history talk daily at 11.30am, 1pm and 3pm; 30min garden tour Tues 2.30pm June–August; shuttle bus from the abbey to the walled garden every 15min • €13; Heritage Island • ☎ 095 52001, ⓦ kylemoreabbey.com.

Grey, castellated **Kylemore Abbey** sits behind a glassy lake against the rugged green backdrop of Dúchruach hill. Built with Manchester cotton money in the 1860s, it's now a small Benedictine convent, but you can visit three of the reception rooms and the main hall, and learn about the place's history from the display boards and audiovisual presentation. There's an extensive crafts shop and restaurant too, and **fishing** on the lake and Kylemore River can be arranged. Also on the lakeshore is a beautiful neo-Gothic **church**, which incorporates elements copied from the great English cathedrals of the late twelfth and early thirteenth centuries.

From the abbey, you can walk (20min) or catch a shuttle bus to the restored **walled garden**. Laid out in the 1860s with no fewer than 21 glasshouses, the huge garden deteriorated after the estate was sold in 1903, but an ambitious project has returned it more or less to its former state, using only original Victorian plant specimens. Beyond the beautifully tended ornamental flower garden lie stream and fern walks and beds of herbs and vegetables, with everything from dill to parsnips (all labelled), divided by a long herbaceous border. The head gardener's house and his workers' far more basic bothy have been refurbished, but the most striking remnants are the very fine, original cabbage trees.

## Renvyle Peninsula

North of Letterfrack, it's well worth exploring the minor roads that crisscross the **Renvyle Peninsula**, eventually looping around by the gentle waters of Lough Fee to

**10**

meet the N59 near Killary Harbour. On the south side of the peninsula, 3km from Letterfrack overlooking Ballynakill Harbour, you'll come to the **Ocean and Country Visitor Centre** (March–Nov daily 10am–6pm; ☎095 43473 or ☎086 199 1988; €5, €20 with a cruise), which features exhibits of sea life and local maritime history, lots of children's activities and hour-long wildlife cruises in a glass-bottomed boat four times a day until the end of October (if there are enough takers), to view deserted islands and, hopefully, seals and dolphins. From the museum quay, a walk up **Tully Hill** is highly recommended (about 3hr return), whose 355m summit affords a matchless panorama, with the towering mountains of Connemara arrayed to the east.

In summer, the **Renvyle Teach Ceoil** centre (☎095 41047), whose name means "music cottage", hosts a weekly show of Irish music, song, dance and storytelling (Tues 8.30–11pm). The peninsula's main settlements are the adjacent hamlets of **Tully Cross** and **Tully**, 4km north of Letterfrack.

### ACCOMMODATION AND EATING · RENVYLE PENINSULA

**Connemara Campsite** 5km east of Tullycross ☎095 43406. This popular campsite is situated near Lettergesh Beach, a concave stretch of fine sand with views of the offshore islands. **€21**

**Paddy Coyne's** Tullycross ☎095 43499, ⓦpaddy coynespub.com. A 200-year-old pub noted for its food and traditional music. The menus showcase fresh mussels, wild salmon and grilled hake; the signature dish of Renvyle scallops with black pudding costs €18. In the summer, there's music on Mon. Daily noon–3pm & 5–9pm; closed Jan.

**Renvyle Beach** 2km west of Tully Cross towards end of peninsula ☎095 43462, ⓦrenvylebeachcaravanpark

.com. Upgraded in 2016 with new facilities, this campsite has direct access to a fine beach and is ideally placed for exploring the villages and countryside. Closed Oct–March. **€22**

**Renvyle House** Renvyle ☎095 43511, ⓦrenvyle.com. In a dreamy location, seemingly on the edge of the world, this relaxing luxury hotel occupies the former home of the surgeon, writer and wit Oliver St John Gogarty (see page 89). It is set amid pretty gardens, woodland and a lake, and comes with a long menu of facilities such as golf, tennis, boating, and a heated outdoor swimming pool. The perfect place to de-stress. Closed for part of Jan. **€220**

### ACTIVITIES

**Diving** Scuba Dive West in Glassillaun (☎095 43922, ⓦscubadivewest.com) is a PADI 5-star resort offering courses and diving off the coast and nearby islands.

## Killary Harbour

**Killary Harbour** is one of Ireland's very few fjords, a truly dramatic oddity with Connacht's highest mountain, Mweelrea (817m), plunging sheer into the dark water on its north bank. This glacial gouge runs for 16km between the uplands of Galway and Mayo, and with a typical depth of 15m is perfect for salmon and mussel farms, and for enjoying a relaxing boat cruise or indulging in some adventure sports. The only waterside settlement, **Leenane** (ⓦleenanevillage.com), enjoys a snug, scenic location near the head of the fjord.

### Sheep and Wool Centre

Leenane · Mid-March to Oct daily 9.30am–6pm · €5, €3 children, €13 family ticket · ☎095 42323, ⓦsheepandwoolcentre.com

The **Sheep and Wool Centre** may not sound too promising, but makes for a fascinating visit. Accompanied by an enthusiastic guide, you'll get to see demonstrations of spinning and weaving; the centre also has a good, inexpensive café-restaurant.

### ARRIVAL AND DEPARTURE · KILLARY HARBOUR

**By bus** A Bus Éireann service (Mon–Sat 1–2 daily) runs from Clifden.

### TOURS AND ACTIVITIES

**Boat tours** Killary Fjord Boat Tours (☎091 566736, ⓦkillaryfjord.com), based at Nancy's Point, 2km west of Leenane, offers 1hr 30min fjord cruises (April–Oct daily 10.30am, 2 & 4pm; €22.50, under-10s free).

**Activities** Killary Adventure Centre (☎095 43411, ⓦ killary adventure.com) about 5km west of Leenane on the N59, offers all manner of activities and courses, from rock climbing and kayaking to giant swing and paintballing.

## ACCOMMODATION AND EATING

**Blackberry Café** Letterfrack Rd, Leenane ☎095 42240. An attractive, welcoming café-restaurant, offering reasonably priced dishes (mains around €13–15), such as wild salmon with dill sauce, hake, duck and steak. Easter–Sept noon–9pm.

**Connemara Hostel** Leenane (IHO) ☎095 42929, ⓦ sleep zone.ie. A superb variety of en-suite hostel accommodation, plus free wi-fi, outdoor barbecue facilities and camping. Daily bus service in summer from Westport to Galway. Reductions for online bookings. Dorms €18, doubles €49

**Leenane Hotel** Leenane ☎095 42249, ⓦ leenanehotel. com. A traditional coaching inn with a delightful garden and fountain right on the water's edge. An ideal location from which to launch yourself into a hike over the Maumturk Mountains. Also has a restaurant (daily 6.30–9pm). €109

**Portfinn Lodge** Leenane ☎095 42265, ⓦ portfinn. com. Bright, attractive en-suite rooms with free wi-fi and an evening restaurant, in a large modern bungalow. It's a magical location offering stunning views of the fjord and the mountains. €90

**10**

# County Mayo

Far from pulling up at the county border, the wonderful mountain scenery found in Connemara marches on into the south of **County Mayo** (Maigh Eo), in the substantial shape of Mweelrea, the Sheefry Hills and the Partry Mountains. These ranges culminate in the conical peak of Ireland's holy mountain, **Croagh Patrick**, beyond which change is announced by the trough of **Clew Bay**, the extension of a geological fault that runs all the way to the Scottish Highlands. Unless you're beetling direct to Westport on the N59, two possible routes out of Connemara into south Mayo present themselves. You can detour east to the abbey town of **Cong**, right on the county border and sharing many similarities with Oughterard, to which it is linked by boat trips across Lough Corrib. Or you can forge through the heart of the mountains from Leenane to **Louisburgh**, which gives access to the islands of **Inishturk** and **Clare** at the mouth of Clew Bay. Either way, you're almost certain to end up in **Westport**, a refined, lively, Georgian base, terminus of the railway line from Dublin and hub for local buses. The county's other main tourist centre is **Achill** at the northwest corner of Clew Bay, Ireland's largest island and a popular resort. Beyond this, there's kilometre after kilometre of wild, dramatic landscape, all now part of the **Wild Atlantic Way** driving route. Attractions include the remains of a Neolithic farm system at **Céide Fields**, which alone justify a journey to the north coast; the impressive **National Museum of Country Life** at Castlebar, and the **Great Western Greenway**, an off-road walking and cycle track along a former railway line from Achill Island to Westport.

## ARRIVAL AND GETTING AROUND

COUNTY MAYO

**By plane** Some 40km east of Castlebar and 8km south of Charlestown, Ireland West Airport (☎094 936 8100, ⓦ irelandwestairport.com) provides a useful, often cheap, way into the county. It is still generally known by its former name of Knock Airport. The airport is served by the Bus

Éireann Galway–Derry express service and a local service to Westport (see page 374). Car rental is available at the airport from Avis (☎094 936 7707, ⓦ avis.ie) and Casey's (☎094 906 0500), among others.

## Cong

The pretty village of **CONG** sits right on the county border, between the green plains of south Mayo and Galway's Connemara Mountains, on the neck of land separating loughs Corrib and Mask. Its main claim to fame these days is that the film *The Quiet Man*, a famed if sentimental emigrants' portrayal of Ireland that starred John Wayne and Maureen O'Hara (who was herself born in Dublin), was filmed here in 1951.

## Quiet Man Museum

April–Oct daily 10am–5pm; closed 30min for lunch • €5 • ☏ 094 954 6089, ⓦ quietman-cong.com/cong-museum

If you're happy to get into the kitschiness of it all, head for the **Quiet Man Museum** just around the corner from the tourist office, a painstaking replica of the cottage built for the making of the film; the only "real" thing in it is a horse's harness used in the film.

## Cong Abbey and the Cross of Cong

**10**

The village does boast a site of genuine historical interest, **Cong Abbey**, which was originally founded in the seventh century and rebuilt in the twelfth and thirteenth centuries by Turlough, Rory and Cathal O'Connor, kings of Connacht and the last high kings of Ireland. The ruined Augustinian abbey's sculpture-work suggests links with western France, particularly the very fine geometrical and foliate carvings on the doorways to the chapterhouse from the cloister. Inside, the elaborate **Cross of Cong**, which was created for Turlough O'Connor in 1123, reflects the place's former wealth.

At one time the abbey housed a population of three thousand, and the logistics of feeding such a crowd are hinted at in the **fishing house** over the River Cong, whence a line ran to a bell in the refectory to let cook know when fish had been caught. From the **bridge** over the river by the abbey, you can stroll through the woods to Lough Corrib, passing through *Ashford Castle Hotel*'s grounds, though in summer be aware that it charges €5 for the privilege.

### ARRIVAL AND INFORMATION

**CONG**

**By bus** Bus Éireann run a Galway–Ballina service (Mon–Fri 2 daily) that stops at Cong each weekday, and a summer service via Lennana to Clifden.

**Tourist information** Abbey St (March–Oct Mon–Thurs & Sun daily 9.15am–5.15pm, closes 1–1.45pm for lunch; ☏ 094 954 6542). Has plenty of detailed literature about the area's sights.

**Boat tours** Corrib Cruises (☏ 087 994 6380, ⓦ corribcruises. com) operates a number of boat trips around and across Lough Corrib. A history cruise (daily 11am; 1hr; €20) runs from Lisloughrey pier (near the hostel) and there's also a cruise from here to Inchagoill Island (June–Sept daily 3pm; 2hr 15min; €20), which includes 40min on the island (see page 359).

### ACCOMMODATION

**Ashford Castle Hotel** ☏ 094 954 6003, ⓦ ashfordcastle. com. Standing at the point where the River Cong runs into Lough Corrib, this lavish – and eye-wateringly expensive – hotel was built by Sir Arthur Guinness in the nineteenth century. Its grounds are far larger than the adjoining village – expect fine views and a long list of amenities that includes a health spa, horseriding and falconry. **€624**

**Lakeland House** 2km from the centre of the village off the Headford road in Lisloughry (Án Oige, IHH & IHO) ☏ 094 954 6089, ⓦ quietman-cong.com. This well-run,

comfortable hostel screens *The Quiet Man* every night, rents out fishing rods and rowing boats, and has a campsite, a playground and a bureau de change. Camping **€25**, dorms **€17**, doubles **€42**

★ **Michaeleen's Manor** ☏ 094 954 6089, ⓦ quietman-cong.com. A smart, en-suite, *Quiet Man*-themed B&B (named after the film's drunken matchmaker), with each room bearing the name of a character in the film. There's a tennis court, a DVD player in every room, tourist information and discount vouchers for local cafés, restaurant and bike rental. **€70**

### EATING

★ **Cullen's at the Cottage** ☏ 094 954 5332, ⓦ ashfordcastle.com. Housed in a traditional thatched cottage with outdoor seating in the grounds of *Ashford Castle Hotel*, this seasonal bistro serves everything from chowder, salads and sandwiches to fresh lobster from the tank and the signature dish of fish curry. Average dinner mains cost €25. April & May Wed–Sun 12.30–9.30pm; June–Sept daily 12.30–9.30pm.

**Danagher's** Abbey St ☏ 094 954 6028. Reasonably

priced bar meals, such as the ever-popular bacon and cabbage or Irish stew, plus salads and sandwiches. Dinner menu main courses from around €15. Daily noon–4pm & 6–9.30pm.

**Hungry Monk Café** Abbey St ☏ 094 954 5842. A smart little café near the tourist office which rustles up wholesome meals (around €10 for mains), snacks, salads and sandwiches, as well as great coffee. March–Oct Tues–Sun 10am–5pm.

# Delphi

The obvious road north from Connemara into Mayo is the N59 from Leenane to Westport, but the seemingly impenetrable mountains on the north side of Killary Harbour conceal a far more scenic route. Winding between the Mweelrea massif and the Sheefry Hills, the R335 brings you first to the noted fishing lake at **DELPHI**, so named by the second Marquis of Sligo in the early nineteenth century: after swimming the Hellespont with Byron, the Marquis arrived at Delphi in the mountains of central Greece, where he was overcome with homesickness as it reminded him so much of his fishery back here in Mayo.

**10**

## The Famine Memorial

Beyond Delphi, the road skirts the black water of Doo Lough, past an interesting memorial. In March 1849, hundreds of men, women and children marched the 16km from the small crossroads town of Louisburgh through this bleak, exposed valley to Delphi Lodge, where the Famine Commissioners were staying. When they arrived, the commissioners were eating a hearty lunch and would not be disturbed, then refused any help, leaving the starving people to struggle back through the snow to Louisburgh, a journey on which many of them died. Every year towards the end of May, a Famine Walk commemorates the event, as well as more recent famines.

---

**ACCOMMODATION**                                                        **DELPHI**

**Delphi Lodge** ☏ 095 42222, ⓦ delphiadventureresort. com. In a glorious setting by the lake facing the lower slopes of Mweelrea, this luxury hotel offers half-board packages and five self-catering cottages. Imaginative dinners are taken communally around one large table, with the angler who has caught the biggest fish that day at the head. The menu might feature leg of Connemara lamb, poached salmon, or other locally sourced dishes. Open for B&B and dinner March–Nov; self-catering all year. **€230**

**Delphi Mountain Resort & Spa** ☏ 095 42208, ⓦ delphi adventure.com. A spa and adventure resort running activities and courses in surfing, canoeing, mountaineering and more, for both adults and children. You can choose from seven different types of accommodation, ranging from luxury suites to simple doubles – all come with stunning views. Closed Jan. **€98**

---

# Louisburgh and around

With a range of cafés and accommodation choices, little **LOUISBURGH** makes an excellent base for exploring the area. The **Granuaile Centre** in the library (June–Sept Mon–Fri 10am–5pm; rest of the year Mon–Fri 11am–4pm; ☏ 098 66341; €5) focuses on seafaring in Ireland in the sixteenth century, in particular **Grace O'Malley** (Gráinne Ní Mháille, often corrupted to Granuaile; c. 1530–1603), the formidable sea captain and pirate queen of Clare Island, who ruled the sea from Galway Bay to Donegal Bay. Over the bank holiday weekend at the start of May, Louisburgh hosts a lively **festival** of traditional music, Féile Chois Cuain (ⓦ feilechoiscuain.com), featuring concerts, classes and plenty of impromptu sessions.

The sparsely inhabited coastline southwest of Louisburgh is lined with sandy **beaches**, notably **White Strand**, a long, west-facing stretch around the mouth of a stream about 15km away, and **Silver Strand**, a great desert of a beach at the mouth of Clew Bay, a couple of kilometres on from the end of the road to the north of the town, that is flanked by rocks and low dunes in the shadow of bulky Mweelrea. About 4km west of town at Carrownisky Strand, Surf Mayo (☏ 087 621 2508, ⓦ surfmayo.com) offers **surfing** instruction and equipment hire all year round.

---

**ARRIVAL AND DEPARTURE**                                   **LOUISBURGH AND AROUND**

**By bus** Bus Éireann runs services to Louisburgh from   Westport (Mon–Sat 3–4 daily; 30 min).

> ### CLARE ISLAND ACTIVITIES
>
> A leaflet available on the boats details five **walks** on the island, including a complete circuit which takes about six hours, while **scuba diving** is available May to October with Islands West (☎087 222 7098), and a variety of activities, including snorkelling, orienteering, rock-climbing and abseiling, is offered by **Clare Island Adventures** (☎087 346 7713, ⓦclareislandadventures.ie). Ballytoughey Loom & Craft Shop (Mon–Sat 11am–5pm, Sun noon–4pm; ☎098 25800, ⓦclareislandhandweaver.com) offers courses in **weaving** and **spinning** (May–Sept) and has wool, linen and silk for sale.

## Clare Island

Measuring just 8km by 5km, **Clare Island** features two hills – Knockmore (462m) and its little brother Knocknaveen (223m) to the east – behind which the mighty sea cliffs along the northwest shore are home to important breeding colonies of **seabirds**, notably fulmars. Other rare birds include peregrines, choughs and barnacle geese, while petalwort, a species of liverwort, figures among the notable plants. The harbour, which shelters a Blue Flag **beach** with fine views of the mainland mountains, is guarded by a well-preserved sixteenth-century **tower house** ruin, which was the stronghold of Grace O'Malley (see page 371). The main island **festivity** is a currach and yawl regatta in July.

### The abbey

In the middle of the island's south shore, a mid-thirteenth-century Cistercian **abbey** (ask for the key at the nearby O'Malley's foodstore and post office) bears an ornate Gothic tomb in which Grace O'Malley – or more likely a relative of hers – is said to be buried. More notable from an artistic point of view are the **frescoes** in the chancel, among the finest extant medieval paintings in Ireland.

### ARRIVAL AND DEPARTURE                                    CLARE ISLAND

**By boat** Ferries run from Roonagh Quay at Clew Bay, 6km west of Louisburgh (May–Sept 4 boats a day; €17 return). Contact O'Malley's (☎098 25045, ⓦomalleyferries.com) or Clare Island Ferry (☎098 23737, ⓦclareislandferry.com), which operates up to six a day in summer and two in winter.

### GETTING AROUND AND INFORMATION

**By bike and taxi** You can rent bikes or hire a minibus taxi from the pier (☎098 25640).

**Tourist information** Online information is available at ⓦclareisland.info.

### ACCOMMODATION

**Macalla Farm & Yoga Retreat Centre** Ballytoughey, in the north of the island ☎087 250 4845, ⓦmacallafarm. ie. This centre offers courses in yoga, meditation, mindfulness, natural horsemanship and vegetarian cooking. Residential courses and occasional self-catering are also available. Accommodation is in refurbished traditional cottages which use natural materials such as wood, hemp and terracotta. €80 **Seabreeze** Capnagower, above the harbour ☎098 26746. This pleasant guesthouse, with both en-suite and standard accommodation, is an ideal base from which to roam around the island. Evening meals are available if requested in advance. €80

## Inishturk

To the south of Clare Island lies the even smaller and less developed island of **Inishturk**, a tranquil, 200m-high lump of rock and grass that survives on farming and lobster fishing. From the tiny harbour, the island's paved road branches north and south: to the north, there's a particularly fine **walk**, veering west off the road around a small lake, before climbing to a ruined watchtower in around 45 minutes. The south road rises to the **community centre** after about fifteen minutes, opposite which a narrow gate points down through the fields to the island's finest sandy **beach**, a sheltered strand with clear blue water and views of the mainland.

## ARRIVAL AND INFORMATION INISHTURK

**By boat** The Naomh Ciaran (☏ 098 25045, ⓦ omalleyferries. com) runs boats over from Roonagh Quay (May–Sept 2 daily Mon–Sun; Oct–April 1–2 daily; 50min; €20 return) though may be affected by weather.

**Tourist information** ⓦ inishturkisland.com.

## ACCOMMODATION

**Tránaun Beach House** ☏ 098 45641, ⓦ tranaunhouse. com. A 5min walk up the south road at the post office, with en-suite rooms, pick-ups from the harbour and day-trips to other islands organized by the owners. You get complimentary tea and fresh scones on arrival, and lovely grilled mackerel at breakfast. The community centre next door doubles as the island pub in the evenings, with regular music sessions and ceilis, and serves evening meals such as fresh pollock and crab claws. €75

**10**

# Croagh Patrick

Rising to 764m to the east of Louisburgh, the cone of **Croagh** (pronounced "croak") **Patrick** dominates Clew Bay and the Westport area. It was the pagan home of the mother goddess, now converted into the holiest mountain in Christian Ireland, and on a fine day offers an awesome panorama, stretching from the Twelve Bens in the south to Slieve League in the north. During his long missionary tour of the island, **St Patrick** is supposed to have passed the forty days of Lent in 441 alone on the mountain, finding time to hurl all of Ireland's snakes to their deaths over the precipice of Lugnanarrib just to the south of the summit. This association with the saint has made Croagh Patrick the focus of major **pilgrimages**, which take place three times a year, on March 17 (St Patrick's Day), August 15 (Assumption Day) and – the main event – on the last Sunday in July, Reek Day (which coincides with the pagan harvest festival of Lughnasa). On this day, tens of thousands of pilgrims still make the climb to attend Mass on the summit, some fasting and barefoot.

The starting point for the ascent of Croagh Patrick is the excellent **visitor centre** (daily: mid-March to Oct 10am–5pm; July & Aug 9am–6pm; ☏ 098 64114, ⓦ croagh-patrick.com) on the R335 on the north side of the peak, about halfway between Westport and Louisburgh. Here you'll find lockers, showers, advice about the climb and the weather, an excellent **café** and a DVD on the **history** of the mountain. The **climb** itself, taking on average three and a half hours return, is easy to follow, though steep in places – you'll need good walking shoes and a stick, available from the visitor centre. At the summit you'll find a small **chapel** that took twelve men six months to construct in 1905.

## The Famine Monument

In a small park opposite the visitor centre stands the national **monument** to *an nGórta Mór* (the Great Famine), commissioned in 1997 for the 150th anniversary. The bronze sculpture of a coffin ship, with skeletons floating around its masts and prow, looks more eerie and shocking now that it's been weathered green by the rain.

## Murrisk Abbey

On the shoreline behind the Famine Monument, well-preserved **Murrisk Abbey**, which features some unusual battlements on the south wall of the church, was established by the O'Malley family in 1457. An Augustinian foundation dedicated to St Patrick, in former times it housed famous relics such as the Shrine of St Patrick's Tooth and his Black Bell, both now in Dublin's National Museum. From the abbey there are fine views of the islands of **Clew Bay**, which are actually half-submerged drumlins (see page 614); there are said to be enough of them for a year and a day – 366.

**10**

## ARRIVAL AND DEPARTURE

CROAGH PATRICK

**By bus** If you're relying on public transport for a day-trip to Croagh Patrick, the best day to attempt the climb is Thurs (the main shopping day in Westport), with three or four buses in each direction between the town and Louisburgh; Tues and Sat are also possible.

## ACCOMMODATION AND EATING

**Croagh Patrick Hostel** Murrisk ☎ 098 64756, ⓦ tcroagh patrickhostel.ie. In a stunning location right beside Croagh Patrick, this sparklingly bright hostel, which opened in 2015, is an ideal base, not only for climbing the mountain, but also exploring the Wild Atlantic Way or cycling the Greenway. As well as a double room, it has a selection of dorms (4–12 beds), all en-suite. Fully equipped with bike rack, drying room and a laundry service (wash, dry and fold: small bag €8, large bag €11.) They also offer self-catering accommodation in stylish cottages. Continental breakfasts included. Dorms €25, doubles €55

**The Tavern Bar & Restaurant** Murrisk ☎ 098 64060, ⓦ tavernmurrisk.com. With Clew Bay on its doorstep it's no surprise local lobster (served with sea lettuce) and Achill sea trout are menu staples. You can choose from pub grub (mains average €14) or dine in the evening restaurant where prices rise to around €20. There's also a beer garden and outdoor tables. Daily 12.30–11.30pm.

# Westport

Set on the shores of Clew Bay, **WESTPORT** is an agreeable, easy-going town that matches its location with some fine architecture. Its main visitor attraction is **Westport House**, a graceful Georgian mansion now surrounded by a country park of rides and amusements, which separates the town centre from Westport Harbour. The centre itself was laid out in classical style in 1780 for the Browne family of Westport House by James Wyatt, who built a striking octagonal square and canalized the Carrowbeg River, flanking it with the tree-lined Mall. More recently, the town has developed an artsy, cosmopolitan feel, attracting many visitors and residents from other parts of Ireland and Europe. During the summer, the place is abuzz, especially for the prestigious ten-day **Arts Festival** in early October (ⓦwestportartsfestival.com). Another big attraction is the newly established **Great Western Greenway** (ⓦgreenway.ie), a 42km cycling and walking route on traffic-free roads along a former railway track running from Westport to Achill Island.

## Westport House

Entered from Westport Harbour • **House and gardens** April–Sept daily 10am–6pm; March & Oct Sat & Sun 10am–6pm • €13, children €6.50 • **Attractions** Easter week & June–Aug daily, May Sun plus bank holiday Mon • All attractions, plus house and gardens €21, children €16.50, one-day family ticket €60; check the website for cheaper deals; Heritage Island • ☎ 098 27766, ⓦ westporthouse.ie

Not one for the historical purists, **Westport House** has wholeheartedly embraced the concept of a former stately home as a modern pleasure ground. On the estate is a host of **attractions and rides**, such as a miniature railway, a log flume ride and swan pedaloes – and its new owners plan to develop these further. Meanwhile, the **gardens** are still well worth a stroll, and the creeper-clad Georgian **house** overlooking the lake is beautiful. It was built in 1730 by Richard Castle, with alterations later in the century by James Wyatt, and was owned until 2017 by the Browne family, descendants of the pirate queen, Grace O'Malley. Inside, highlights include the hall, with its fine barrel ceiling and ornate marble mantelpiece designed by Castle, the cantilevered marble staircase, executed by Italian craftsmen brought over specially for the purpose, and a delicate portrait by Sir Joshua Reynolds of Denis Browne, a member of Grattan's Parliament, in the Long Gallery. The large dining room is one of the finest examples of Wyatt's work, sporting boldly carved mahogany doors and relief medallions in Wedgwood style on playful classical themes. Upstairs look out for the playwright J.M. Synge's violin in one of the corridors.

## Clew Bay Heritage Centre

April, May & Oct Mon–Fri 10.30am–2pm; June–Sept Mon–Fri 10am–5pm; July & Aug also Sun 3–5pm • €3 • ☎ 098 26852,
ⓦ westportheritage.com • Walking tours July & Aug Wed 11am (€5)

Ten minutes' walk west around the harbour, **Clew Bay Heritage Centre** traces the history of Westport and the Clew Bay area through photographs, documents and other artefacts; it has a genealogical service and runs guided **walking tours** of the town, starting from the clock tower at the top of Bridge Street.

**10**

### ■ ACCOMMODATION
| | |
|---|---|
| Ardmore Country House Hotel | 9 |
| Carrabaun House B&B | 6 |
| Castlecourt Hotel | 2 |
| Mill Times Hotel | 7 |
| Mulranny Park Hotel | 1 |
| Old Mill Hostel | 4 |
| Parklands Caravan and Camping Park | 8 |
| Westport Plaza Hotel | 3 |
| Wyatt Hotel | 5 |

### ● EATING
| | |
|---|---|
| An Port Mór | 4 |
| Idle Wall Cottage | 8 |
| Il Vulcano | 7 |
| McCormack's | 3 |
| Sage | 6 |
| Sol Rio | 2 |
| The West Bar | 1 |
| Willow Café | 5 |

### ● SHOPPING
| | |
|---|---|
| Harvest Breeze | 3 |
| Liberties | 5 |
| Marlene's Chocolate Haven | 1 |
| O'Reilly Turpin | 4 |
| Westport Country Market | 2 |

### ■ DRINKING & NIGHTLIFE
| | |
|---|---|
| Matt Molloy's | 1 |
| McGing's | 3 |
| Walsh's | 2 |

## ARRIVAL AND DEPARTURE

WESTPORT

**By bus** Buses stop on Mill St.

Destinations Achill Island (1 daily; 1hr 10min–2hr); Athlone (2–3 daily; 2hr 50min); Ballina (2–5 daily; 55min–1hr 25min); Castlebar (8–14 daily; 20min); Cong (Tues & Thurs 1 daily; 1hr); Dublin (3 daily; 4–5hr 40min); Galway (2–4 daily; 2hr); Ireland West Airport (Mon–Sat 2 daily; 1hr 15min); Louisburgh (Mon–Sat 2–4 daily; 35min); Sligo (2–3 daily; 2–3hr).

**By train** The station is on the Ballinrobe road.

Destinations Athlone (3–4 daily; 2hr); Castlebar (3–4 daily; 15min); Dublin (3–4 daily; 3hr 35min–4hr).

**10**

## INFORMATION AND ACTIVITIES

**Tourist office** Bridge St (May–Oct Mon–Sat 9am–5.45pm; Nov–April Mon–Fri 9am–4.45pm, Sat 10am–1pm; ☎ 098 25711). Dispenses maps of the town and leaflets on the Clew Bay Trail linking 21 archaeological sites between Westport and Clare Island (ⓦ clewbaytrailride.com), looped walks and the Great Western Greenway. Ask for a brochure on the Gourmet Greenway, which details local artisan food suppliers along the route. The town's website is (ⓦ westporttourism.com).

**Bike rental** Clew Bay Bike Hire, Distillery Rd (☎ 085 703 0177, ⓦ clewbaybikehire.ie); Westport Bike Shop, Newport Rd (☎ 098 24966, ⓦ westportbikeshop.ie).

**Guided walks** Croagh Patrick Walking Holidays (☎ 098 26090, ⓦ walkingguideireland.com) organizes guided walks in the area lasting from a day to a week from April to Oct.

**Horseriding** Drummindoo Equestrian Centre (☎ 098 25616, ⓦ drumindoo.com), Knockranny, 1km from the centre of town (closed Oct–March).

**Sea-kayaking** Saoirse na Mara, Caraholly (☎ 086 173 3610, ⓦ irelandwestseakayaking.com).

## ACCOMMODATION

SEE MAP PAGE 375

**Ardmore Country House Hotel** The Quay ☎ 098 25994, ⓦ ardmorecountryhouse.com. Overlooking Clew Bay, this small, fashionable hotel has rooms decorated and equipped in stunning style, and a superb breakfast menu that includes eggs Benedict and Achill kippers. Closed Nov to mid-March. **€140**

**Carrabaun House B&B** On the road to Leenane ☎ 098 26196. Highly recommended B&B, with a wide range of breakfast options and fine views, in a spacious, en-suite, period-style modern house with tastefully decorated rooms. **€90**

**Castlecourt Hotel** Castlebar St ☎ 098 55088, ⓦ castlecourthotel.ie. Together with the adjacent, co-owned *Westport Plaza*, this family-orientated hotel offers a swimming pool, gym, a wide choice of restaurants, a kids' club in school holidays, and all manner of themed breaks, half-board offers and other packages. **€110**

★ **Mill Times Hotel** Mill St ☎ 098 29200, ⓦ milltimeshotel.ie. A conveniently located hotel with an informal and friendly atmosphere just a few minutes' walk to the town centre. Traditional rooms range from superior suites to doubles with queen-size beds. Good midweek deals available off season. **€98**

**Mulranny Park Hotel** Mulranny ☎ 098 36000, ⓦ mulrannyparkhotel.ie. In a stunning location looking out over Clew Bay, this contemporary hotel, with a hot tub and pool, is ideally sited to explore the area, particularly as the Greenway trail runs behind it. Rooms are stylish and comfy; if you want extra space, opt for the seaview apartments. **€190**

**Old Mill Hostel** Barrack Yard, James St (IHH & IHO) ☎ 098 27045, ⓦ oldmillhostel.com. Accessed through an archway, this former mill and brewery is now a comfortable hostel, with a light breakfast and laundry facilities included in the price. Closed Nov–Jan. Dorms **€30**, doubles **€55**

**Parklands Caravan and Camping Park** ☎ 098 27766, ⓦ westporthouse.ie. Campers should head for this park in the delightful grounds of Westport House estate – a perfect location from which to explore the town and countryside. Closed mid-Sept to late March. **€31**

**Westport Plaza Hotel** Castlebar St ☎ 098 51166, ⓦ westportplazahotel.ie. Welcoming, elegant, chic and contemporary hotel, offering spacious and well-equipped rooms with kingsize beds, Italian marble bathrooms and hot tubs. Shares facilities with *Castlecourt Hotel*. **€130**

**Wyatt Hotel** The Octagon ☎ 098 25027, ⓦ wyatthotel.com. Twelve new rooms were added in 2016 to this congenial hotel decorated in bare wood and bold colours, in an unbeatable central location. Check the website for various special deals. **€150**

## EATING

SEE MAP PAGE 375

**An Port Mór** Brewery Place, Bridge St ☎ 098 26730, ⓦ anportmor.com. Broad mix of modern Irish cuisine, especially fish and shellfish, artfully cooked and tastefully presented; expect to pay around €34 for three courses. Daily 5–9.30pm.

★ **Idle Wall Cottage** The Harbour ☎ 098 50692, ⓦ the idlewall.ie. Step through the door of this atmospheric stone cottage – its name comes from a nearby wall on which dockers used to sit waiting for employment – and you are immediately at ease. The early-bird menu (two courses

€22.50; 5.30–6.30pm) showcases Dexter beef pie and haddock mornay, while more expensive main dinner choices conjure up a delightful culinary combination of lamb and clams, rare breed pork belly or baked leek gratin. July & Aug daily 5.30–9.30pm; rest of year Wed–Sat same hours.

**Il Vulcano** High St ☏ 098 24888. Bustling, authentic Italian restaurant with an open kitchen, just up from the clock tower, which provides pasta, risotto, pizza, and some meat and seafood main courses. Daily 5.30–10pm.

**McCormack's** Bridge St ☏ 098 25619. Brightly painted, inviting café and art gallery above a butcher's, which serves coffee, salads, home-made soup and fine sandwiches. Mon, Tues & Thurs–Sat 9am–5pm.

**Sage** High St ☏ 098 56700, ⓦ sagewestport.ie. Italian-influenced restaurant, serving delicious pasta dishes and a wide range of tasty meat and fish specials, with plenty of vegetarian options. Expect to pay around €32 for a three-course dinner or €21.50 for the early bird, two-course option. July & Aug daily 5.30–10pm; rest of year closed Wed.

**Sol Rio** Bridge St ☏ 098 28944, ⓦ solrio.ie. Colourful and informal, if somewhat pricey, upstairs restaurant, with a Portuguese influence, that efficiently covers all the bases: salads, pasta, pizza and more expensive fish and meat dishes, augmented by sandwiches at lunchtime. Mon & Wed–Sun noon–3pm & 6–10pm.

**The West Bar** Bridge St ☏ 098 25886, ⓦ thewest.ie. A gastropub that is noted for its award-winning chowder. The bar menu includes platters of fish, cold meat and cheese, as well as surf 'n' turf, pasta, pork belly, chicken and burgers. Main courses from €13. Good range of cocktails too. Food served daily noon–9pm; bar 11am–11.30pm.

★ **Willow Café** High St ☏ 087 707 4500, ⓦ thewillow cafe.com. An elegant tea room with outdoor tables beside the clock tower, strategically sited to view the bustling town centre. They offer an exquisite selection of organic and herbal leaf teas as well as Chinese flowering teas, home-made cupcakes, scones and gluten-free food at lunch time. Daily 10am–6pm.

## DRINKING AND NIGHTLIFE SEE MAP PAGE 375

★ **Matt Molloy's** Bridge St ☏ 098 26655, ⓦ matt molloy.com. The town's most famous pub, owned by the eponymous Chieftains' flute player, is an affable place that fills up for its nightly traditional music sessions. A wide selection of craft beers is available. Daily 12.30–11.30pm.

**McGing's** High St ☏ 098 29742. Congenial bar that boasts the cheapest (and many claim best) craft beer in Ireland: Paddy's Pilgrims Porter (3P for short), a traditional porter

with deep roasted malty flavours made by the West Mayo microbrewery at Islandeady. The bright blue-and-yellow exterior means you'll have no trouble spotting it. Daily 4–11.30pm.

**Walsh's** James St. Also known as *Blouser's*, this is a popular spot with a 30-something crowd, who come for the weekend DJ nights, and the live music during the week. Daily 11am–11.30pm.

## SHOPPING SEE MAP PAGE 375

**Harvest Breeze** Bridge St ☏ 098 56339. A celebration of lavender products and a sensory experience as you browse the shelves and tables. Mon–Sat 10am–6pm, also Sun 11am–5pm in summer.

**Liberties** The Quay ☏ 098 50273, ⓦ liberties.ie. Large selection of fashion brands, accessories, gifts, art, jewellery, furnishings and homeware. Mon–Sat 10.30am–5.30pm, Sun noon–5pm.

**Marlene's Chocolate Haven** Limecourt James St ☏ 098 24564. A mouthwatering selection of home-made chocolates

(including some sugarless ones), ranging from truffles and nut pralines to luscious ganaches. Daily 10am–6pm.

**O'Reilly Turpin** Bridge St ☏ 098 28151, ⓦ oreillyturpin. ie. Long-established gift shop selling Irish silver and gold handcrafted jewellery, art and prints as well as ceramic, wood, glass and metal products. Mon–Sat 10am–6pm.

**Westport Country Market** James St car park ☏ 098 25645. An appetizing array of local farm produce and home baking sold from stalls that draw crowds of both locals and visitors. Thurs 8.30am–1pm.

# Castlebar and around

**CASTLEBAR**, the county town of Mayo, has a lot less going for it than Westport, just 18km away to the west. It's a busy workaday town with many long-established, family-run businesses. The oldest building, **Christ Church**, on the corner of the Mall, dates from 1769 and has survived rebellions, risings and the threat of demolition, but the main attraction hereabouts is the **National Museum of Country Life** at nearby **Turlough**.

## National Museum of Country Life

Turlough Park, 8km east of Castlebar off the N5 • Tues–Sat 10am–5pm, Sun 2–5pm • Free • ☏ 094 903 1755, ⓦ museum.ie/countrylife • A bus serves Turlough from Westport (Mon–Sat 9.55am, returning at 12.05pm); taxis are available in Castlebar on ☏ 094 903 4700, ⓦ museum.ie/Country-Life

10

The sleek, modern **National Museum of Country Life** digs beneath the dewy-eyed nostalgia that besets popular images of rural Ireland to reveal the harsh realities of country life from 1850 to 1950. The museum is spread over three levels, with **Level C** housing the main exhibition area, chronicling the unremitting work of farming and fishing, of housewives, craftsmen and tradesmen – exhibits include a recording of a poignant letter home from an emigrant to America, and footage of men making a coracle on the River Boyne. The most interesting section here deals with the seasons and festivals: churning butter on May Day to ward off evil, leaving food and drink out for dead relatives on Halloween, and grainy footage of **Wren Boys**, who would knock on doors on St Stephen's Day (December 26) with the corpse of a wren, asking for money to bury it while singing songs and telling jokes – the money, of course, would be spent on a party. You can also look inside the adjacent "Big House" of the landowners, the nineteenth-century Gothic Revival **Turlough Park House**, designed by Thomas Newenham Deane, architect of the National Museum in Dublin.

### ARRIVAL AND DEPARTURE                                                      CASTLEBAR

**By bus** Castlebar is served by buses from/to Ballina (Mon–    4hr 50min) and Westport (9–13 daily; 20min).
Sat 6–8 daily, Sun 2 daily; 30min–1hr), Dublin (3–5 daily;

## Achill Island

The grandeur of **ACHILL ISLAND**'s scenery, with its towering sea-cliffs and bare mountains that rise above 650m, can seem forbidding in poor weather, but on a sunny day the Atlantic glitters as though stolen from the Aegean Sea. It's the largest of the Irish islands and, connected to the mainland by a road bridge, among the most developed, with plenty of accommodation and a ribbon of white-painted holiday homes on the south coast. Drawn by sweeping **sandy beaches** (five of which

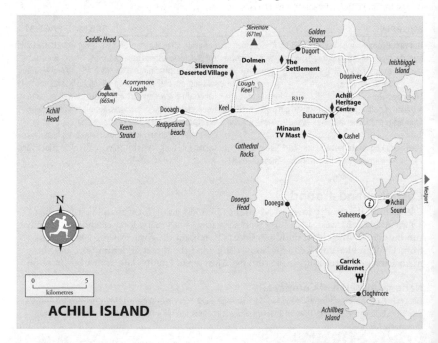

ACHILL ISLAND

## AN AMATEURISH SET FOR A GHOST FILM

A couple of kilometres north of Keel, at **Slievemore**, lies a settlement of almost a hundred crumbling stone dwellings – but what led to its **abandonment** is still unknown. Its most recent period of habitation ended in the early twentieth century, when locals used it as a **booley**: during the summer, they would occupy the cottages while grazing their cattle on the mountainside, returning to their homes in Dooagh for the winter months. This is one of the last places in Europe to have practised *booley*-ing, or transhumance, and the village is being excavated by the Achill Field School every summer, in the hope that it will give up its secrets. German novelist Heinrich Böll described the deserted village as looking like "an amateurish set for a ghost film."

10

have earned a Blue Flag) and fairground rides, fun-seekers descend in droves on August weekends, when the place can get a bit rowdy. Germans are also attracted to Achill by associations with novelist and Nobel Laureate **Heinrich Böll**, who lived at Dugort in the 1950s. One of the best times to come is during **Scoil Acla** (⊛scoilacla. com), a week of cultural programmes with plenty of traditional music at the end of July. There's also a walking festival over the St Patrick's bank holiday weekend in March, the Heinrich Böll literary festival in May and a seafood festival in mid-July, Féile Na Mara, which includes seaweed tasting, yawl racing and boat trips.

The road bridge crosses the narrow, winding strait to the island at **ACHILL SOUND** (Gob an Choire), is not the best base for exploration though it has some useful facilities. On the island side of the bridge, there's an ATM at the side of *Sweeney's* restaurant and supermarket. The lively village of **KEEL** is the nerve centre for much of the island, boasting a lovely 3km Blue Flag sandy **beach**, backed by a large lake.

### The south end of the island

The "Atlantic Drive", now part of the Wild Atlantic Way (see page 26), around the south end of the island from Achill Sound brings you after 6km to the ruined eighteenth-century **church** and holy well of Damhnait (Davnet or Dympna), a seventh-century saint who sought refuge and built a church (*cill*) here. Just beyond, its pink stone set attractively on the shoreline, rises the redoubtable outline of **Carrick Kildavnet**, an almost perfectly preserved, fifteenth-century, O'Malley tower house. Fantastic views of the Atlantic open up as you round the nearby headland, continuing as far as the village and Blue Flag beach of **Dooega**. Above the settlement looms **Minaun**, Achill's third-highest mountain; a left turn will bring you up to the TV mast near its summit for one of the island's most spectacular panoramas.

### Dooagh and the west of the island

West along the road from Keel is the small village of **DOOAGH**, overlooking its own sandy beach as well as a newly returned beach. At its base here, the enterprising **Achill Field School** (☎098 43564, ⊛achill-fieldschool.com) lays on a raft of activities, including weekly lectures from June to August. The field school also runs one- to eight-week archaeology courses, featuring the dig and summer open days at the **Deserted Village**.

Beyond Dooagh, the main road rises and descends very steeply to Blue Flag **Keem Bay**, a gorgeous strip of white sand hemmed in by steep, green slopes – on a sunny day, you'll feel as if you're looking down on a Mediterranean cove, with basking sharks often visible in the limpid waters. A turning off the up-slope towards Keem Bay will bring you to **Acorrymore Lough**, a black corrie lake, now reservoir, cradled by grassy scree slopes. From here you can set out on the steep ascent of **Croghaun**, the island's second-highest mountain (665m), which boasts spectacularly high cliffs on its seaward side

**10**

> ## THE BEACH THAT REAPPEARED
>
> Did you hear the one about the beach that reappeared? It's not an old Irish joke but a fact. One of Achill's best-known strands, near Dooagh, was washed away by storms in 1984, leaving only rocks. But 33 years later, in 2017, after a freak tide it astonishingly **reappeared** to local, national and international excitement. The 300m stretch of golden sand restored to its rightful topographic place has captured the attention of many and brought an influx of new tourists to enjoy the island's delights. Meanwhile it has become a firm favourite again with dog-walkers, strollers, joggers and courting couples.

## The north end

Heading north from Keel, a side road runs along the west side of Lough Keel, then skirts east around **Slievemore**, Achill's highest mountain at 671m, before looping around the north end of the island. About 2km from Keel, you'll come to the strange sight of the **Deserted Village** (see page 379) over to the left, before a further 2km east on Slievemore's southern flank brings you to the start of a signposted ten-minute walk up from the road to a keyhole-shaped **dolmen** with fine views of Keel Bay. Less than a kilometre beyond **The Settlement** lies **Dugort Beach**, a gently curving, Blue Flag stretch of sand in the shadow of Slievemore, overlooked to the east by Dugort.

### The Settlement

A kilometre or so to the north of the start of the dolmen walk is the site of **the Settlement**, the first Protestant mission in Ireland to minister in the Irish language. It was founded in 1834 by a Church of Ireland vicar, Edward Nangle, and at first proved successful, with stone cottages, schools, a small hospital and a printing press churning out regular publications. During the 1840s Famine, the Settlement came under fire for encouraging converts, known as "soupers" or "jumpers", with offers of soup and grain. The Catholic Church, which had previously been indifferent to the islanders' education, fought back by opening a National School in 1852, and the Settlement, further rocked by emigration and financial difficulties, eventually closed in 1886. Approached by an avenue of trees on the east side of the road, the mission's **church** of 1855 is still standing, containing a prominent memorial to Nangle.

### ARRIVAL AND INFORMATION ACHILL ISLAND

**By bus** Bus Éireann runs services twice daily from Westport to Achill Sound (1hr) and Dooagh (1hr 20min).

**Tourist office** Achill Sound (Mon–Fri 9am–6pm, plus Sat 10am–5pm in summer; ☏098 20400, ⓦ achilltourism. com). Sells detailed maps of the island and a guide to circular walks.

**Achill Heritage Centre** Bunacurry (Mon–Fri noon–5pm; ☏086 340 6396, ⓦ achillheritagecentre.com). Traces two hundred years of Achill's history; also offers genealogy service and free walking tours.

### ACCOMMODATION

#### ACHILL SOUND

**Óstán Oileán Acla** ☏098 45138, ⓦ achillislandhotel. com. Immediately before you cross the bridge at Achill Sound stands this comfortable hotel with fine views of the island. It's a local social hub too, with food served all day till 8.30pm in the summer (8pm rest of year); burgers, fish 'n' chips, chicken and steak are all available. **€100**

**Railway Hostel** (IHO) ☏098 45187, ⓦ railwayhostel.ie/ achill. By the bridge beside Blacksod Bay and based in an old station, this hostel is handy for bus pick-ups and drop-offs. Big log fires create a welcoming atmosphere, some of the rooms are en suite and camping is possible. Camping **€10**, dorms **€17**, doubles **€36**

#### DOOAGH

**Teach Cruachan** ☏098 43301, ⓔ teachcruachan@ eircom.net. On the west side of Dooagh, this comfy guesthouse has en-suite rooms and good breakfasts, as well as laying on guided tours of the island. **€75**

**West Coast House** School Rd ☏098 43317, ⓦ achill westcoasthousebandb.com. Set on an elevated site in the shadow of the majestic Croaghaun mountain, this well-run bungalow offers superb sea views. €70

## DUGORT

★ **Lavelle's Campsite** ☎ 086 231 4596, ⓦ lavelles caravanpark.com. Beside the pristine Blue Flag Golden Strand beach with good facilities, this site boasts an idyllic and serene location. Closed Nov–March. €18

**Valley House Hostel** ☎ 098 47204, ⓦ valley-house. com. A fine, mid-nineteenth-century house, formerly the Earl of Cavan's hunting lodge, with a sociable courtyard bar and camping. Dorms (four to twelve beds) are basic but functional – it's the house that steals the show. Dorms €19, doubles €25

## KEEL

★ **Achill Cliff House** ☎ 098 43400, ⓦ achillcliff.com. One of the island's best places to stay, this hotel in the centre of the village offers bright and spacious rooms, sea views, a sauna and a seafood restaurant for residents. €100

★ **Bervie Guest House** ☎ 098 43114, ⓦ bervieachill. com. In a former coastguard station right by the beach, this place enjoys a dream location and is unquestionably Achill's best accommodation. Summery ground-floor rooms lead out to a pretty garden which brings you, via a small gate, right out on to the beach. Dinner is served each evening 7–8.30pm. Closed Dec–March. €140

**Ferndale** Crumpaun ☎ 098 43908, ⓦ fernddale-achill. com. Hidden away 200m up the lane by the *Annexe* pub, this place has six lavishly furnished rooms. Its fabulous range of breakfasts includes eggs benedict, Barbary duck breast, Mexican omelette or a Mediterranean breakfast full of surprises. €90

**Joyce's Marian Villa** ☎ 098 43134, ⓦ joycesachill. com. First-class accommodation in a large seaside villa with fifteen bedrooms. The sunroom looks out to the beach and the cliffs of Minaun. Breakfasts include local jams and preserves, as well as Achill smoked salmon and seasonal fruit. €90

**Keel Sandybanks Caravan & Camping Park** ☎ 098 43211, ⓦ achillcamping.com. A swanky caravan park beside the beach, handy for the shops and cafés. Closed early Sept to March. €15

### EATING AND DRINKING

The island's best eating is in Keel, not least at *Ferndale's* restaurant. *Óstán Oileán Acla* at Achill Sound (see page 380) is also worth a look.

**Amethyst Bar** ☎ 098 43737. Reviving the name of one of Achill's oldest hotels, which had long been closed, the *Amethyst* opened in summer 2017 in a newly built two-storey property on the same site. The large, modern bar and grill room, featuring exposed brickwork and wooden beams, serves the likes of turkey and ham, seafood chowder or pasta with spinach and mushroom (mains from €13.50) all day, while a more formal dinner is served upstairs in the spacious dining room. Daily noon–9pm.

**Bayside Bistro** Keel ☎ 098 43798. Classic bistro-style cooking with dishes such as almond-crusted salmon, swordfish and handcut chips. Main courses from €12. Daily noon–10pm.

★ **The Beehive** Keel ☎ 098 43134. An informal daytime self-service café-restaurant and craft shop with outdoor tables on a terrace overlooking Keel beach. The menu promotes wholesome local produce, such as organic Clare Island salmon and Clew Bay mussels or smoked mackerel. Main-course lunches from €10. Feb–Nov daily 9.30am–6pm.

★ **Gielty's** Dooagh ☎ 098 43119, ⓦ gieltys.com. Large pub, restaurant and café at the west end of Dooagh village that claims to be Ireland's most westerly pub. Lunches and dinners served. Outdoor tables and live music, including regular weekend traditional sessions. Daily 10am–9pm.

# Céide Fields and around

8km west of Ballycastle • Early April to Oct daily 10am–5pm (till 6pm June–Sept) • €5; Heritage Card • ☎ 096 43325, ⓦ heritageireland.ie

Isolated on Mayo's dramatic, cliff-girt north coast, the prehistoric site of **Céide** (pronounced "cage-a") **Fields** is difficult to get to, but repays the effort. Here, archaeologists have discovered a unique, 5000-year-old agricultural landscape, miraculously preserved under a thick layer of peat and undisturbed by later farming. A highly organized system of **dry-stone field** dotted with individual houses and gardens in what were apparently peaceful times, covers an area of thirteen square kilometres, making Céide Fields the largest Stone Age monument in the world. Rough contemporaries of the tomb-builders of Newgrange (see page 139), these farmers cleared the area's forest to make field **walls** – said to be world's oldest – for their cattle, sheep, wheat and barley, and built **wooden houses**, of which trenches and postholes are now the only traces. However, after only five hundred years, the climate deteriorated, causing the bog gradually to rise up over their farms. What's remarkable about the site is its very ordinariness and similarity to much of the Irish countryside today, as Seamus Heaney noted in *Belderg*:

*A landscape fossilized, its stone wall patternings*
*Repeated before our eyes in the stone walls of Mayo.*

There's an impressive, well-designed **visitor centre**, which features exhibitions and audiovisuals on the history and geology of the area and the formation of the bog, as well as a viewing platform and a fine café. Regular fifty-minute guided tours take visitors outside to see excavated walls, animal and house enclosures and to learn about the ecology of the bog that swallowed them up. From the adjacent cliff-top viewpoint, you can see Donegal's Slieve League on a clear day, and in the near distance the sea stack of Downpatrick Head, neatly layered and tufted with grass: according to legend, this is the severed head of the last snake that St Patrick chased from Ireland.

## Ballycastle

The nearest town to Céide Fields is **BALLYCASTLE**, which comes as a pleasant surprise among the barren, grossly proportioned mountains of North Mayo. Set in the broad Ballinglen valley, it's surrounded by green fields, trees and cattle, with a fine sandy beach at the river mouth. Changing exhibitions of works by internationally known artists attached to the local **Ballinglen Arts Foundation** are held at the gallery opposite *Polke's* pub. For further exploration of the coast, the **North Mayo Sculpture Trail** (@mayoireland.ie/tirsaile.htm), marked by brown *Tír Sáile* ("Land of the Salty Wind") signposts, is a striking series of modern outdoor sculptures, celebrating the wild beauty and cultural heritage of the area. It starts just west of the town.

### ARRIVAL AND INFORMATION                                                    BALLYCASTLE

**By bus** There's no public transport to Céide Fields but Ballycastle is linked by bus to Ballina, 28km to the southeast, which in turn has regular services to and from Galway (see page 332), Westport (see page 374) and Castlebar (see page 377).

**Tourist information** Information on the local attractions and the Wild Atlantic Way is available at the Ballycastle Resource Centre (Mon–Fri 10am–5pm; @096 43407) on Main St, which also houses a craft shop and displays the work of local artists. The town's website is @ballycastle.ie.

### ACCOMMODATION AND EATING

**Keadyville B&B** Carrowcubic @096 43288, @keady villehouse.com. A modern and friendly four-room guesthouse, convenient for a tour of North Mayo with views of Bunatrahir Bay. If you don't have transport the owners will take you out to the Céide Fields or Downpatrick Head. €70
**Mary's Cottage Kitchen** Main St @096 43361. Breakfasts and simple lunches (sandwiches, soups and wraps) are served at this welcoming café and bakery; be sure to sample their moist soda loaf, made with buttermilk. A sloping ceiling divides two rooms with flagstone floors

while a turf fire burns all year round, giving it a homely feel. Easter–Oct Mon–Thurs 10am–6pm.
**Stella Maris Hotel** @096 43322, @stellamarisireland. com. Positioned on the Wild Atlantic Way, this elegantly refurbished former coastguard station and convent offers fine ocean views. The 11 luxurious rooms are individually furnished with their own antiques, and you can immerse yourself in the beauty of the Mayo landscape from the large conservatory. Dinner is served 7–8.30pm, with lamb's kidneys the most popular choice. Closed Nov–Easter. €150

### DRINKING AND NIGHTLIFE

**Healy's Bar** Main St @096 43019. A family-run bar where occasional music sessions are held on Fridays. The beer garden and decking area is popular with party-goers and, during the August bank holiday (first weekend in Aug)

they hold the Healy Fest, which attracts musicians from all over Ireland and further afield. Daily 4–11.30pm, Sun from noon.

10

# Sligo, Leitrim and Roscommon

STATUE OF W.B. YEATS IN SLIGO TOWN

# Sligo, Leitrim and Roscommon

Sligo, Leitrim and Roscommon are blessed with majestic scenery, mighty castles and a countryside littered with antiquities. The area is also renowned for the flamboyance of its traditional music: known as the North Connacht style, it is characterized by flutes and fiddles. The principal hub, lively Sligo town, has the best facilities for visitors, and makes a good base for day-trips along the Wild Atlantic Way. This new driving route has been a boon to seaside resorts such as Mullaghmore and Rosses Point, while Strandhill has reinvented itself as a busy playground for watersports. Inland from here, you can visit the remarkable prehistoric graveyard of Carrowmore Megalithic Cemetery, at the foot of Knocknarea Mountain, whose summit is marked by Medb's Cairn, said to be the burial site of the ancient Queen Medb.

**11**

**Lough Gill**, its celebrated island **Innisfree** and a number of other sites in the north of Sligo are inextricably linked with W. B. Yeats, an appreciation of whose writing is enhanced by a visit to **Drumcliffe**, the place of his burial, set below Benbulben Mountain. The cultural highlight of Sligo, however, is the stunning **Lissadell House**, which has been extensively renovated and showcases some of Ireland's most precious treasures. Yeats's brother, the painter Jack B., was also inspired by the county's dramatic land- and seascapes, which continue to its northern tip with fine beaches such as at **Mullaghmore**.

Ireland's least populated county by some stretch, **Leitrim** crams a dizzying diversity into its landscape, though lacks any really notable sights. Bordering no fewer than six counties, Leitrim extends some 80km from its southeastern border with Longford to a narrow strip of Atlantic shoreline in the northwest, with the expansive **Lough Allen** at its core. Two of its most attractive assets – **loughs Gill and Glencar** – lie to the west, spanning the border with Sligo. In the south, the River Shannon is the principal feature, not least in the attractive boating town, **Carrick-on-Shannon**, while rolling countryside to the river's east, especially between **Keshcarrigan** and **Ballinamore**, is sprinkled with tiny lakes and drumlins.

**County Roscommon** may not feature prominently on tourists' itineraries but, in its far north, the **Arigna Mountains** provide a wild and vivid contrast to the flat landscape that defines most of Roscommon, and can be explored from the historic town of **Boyle**. Further south, sites around **Tulsk**, including the rebranded **Rathcroghan Centre**, are intrinsically associated with major events in Celtic mythology. The planned town of **Strokestown** features a memorable Georgian mansion with an impressive museum devoted to the Great Famine.

# Sligo town

Bustling **SLIGO** town rose to prominence following the Anglo-Norman invasion of Connacht in 1235, its strategic importance linked to its location at the point where the River Garavogue enters the sea. A Dominican friary was founded here in 1252, but the town's shape was largely developed following the building of a castle by Richard de Burgo in 1310. This edifice lasted but five years, however, before it was destroyed by the O'Donnell clan which retained control of the burgeoning settlement over the next few centuries. After the terrible times of the Great Famine of the 1840s, Sligo re-emerged as a busy port and mercantile centre in the late nineteenth century.

LISSADELL HOUSE AND GARDENS

# Highlights

**❶ The Model** Sligo town's excellent art gallery is renowned for its exhibitions of experimental art and its Jack B. Yeats collection. See page 390

**❷ Lough Gill** This utterly tranquil and unspoilt lake was the inspiration, along with its island, Innisfree, for much of the poetry of Yeats. See page 395

**❸ Lissadell House** The ancestral home of the Gore-Booth family was the holiday retreat of W. B. Yeats and is a treasure trove of eclectic delights. See page 397

**❹ Carrowkeel Cemetery** The remains of a Bronze Age village, offering a stunning panorama of County Sligo from its hilltop position. See page 400

**❺ Arigna Mining Experience** Devoted to the vicissitudes of life for the miners who once literally scraped a living in the mountains here – completely gripping. See page 408

**❻ Strokestown Park House** Arguably the most eye-catching Plantation mansion in all of Ireland, whose former stables house the enthralling National Irish Famine Museum. See page 409

**HIGHLIGHTS ARE MARKED ON THE MAP ON PAGE 388**

# SLIGO, LEITRIM & ROSCOMMON

HIGHLIGHTS

1 The Model
2 Lough Gill
3 Lissadell House
4 Carrowkeel Cemetery
5 Arigna Mining Experience
6 Strokestown Park House

The town has long been renowned for its **traditional music**, but is also firmly on the tourist trail thanks to its numerous associations with the poet **W. B. Yeats**, along with a lively arts scene, which spawns several **festivals**, and its convenient location within striking distance of many of the county's attractions.

West of the **friary**, at the bottom of Market Street, the **Lady of Erin** statue commemorates the 1798 uprisings. The statue presides over the newly designated **Erin Quarter**, comprising long-established family businesses along Grattan, Market and Castle streets and set up to provide friendly rivalry with the Italian Quarter, a riverside area of Italian restaurants and cafés.

## Yeats Memorial Building

Douglas Hyde Bridge • Tues–Sat 10am–5pm • €3 • ☎ 071 914 2693, ⓦ yeatssociety.com

The attractions of Sligo town can easily be enjoyed in a day and a good place to start is the **Yeats Memorial Building** on Douglas Hyde Bridge. This houses the Yeats Society, serves as the venue for the International Summer School commemorating the poet each August, and includes displays on his life and works with photographs and copies of drafts of poems.

## Sligo County Museum

Stephen St • Tues–Sat 9.30am–12.30pm, also May–Sept 2–4.45pm • Free • ☎ 071 911 1850, ⓦ sligoarts.ie

Beside the library, **Sligo County Museum** holds drawings by Jack B. Yeats (as well as a portrait of him by Estella Solomons) and a fiddle once owned by Michael Coleman (see page 401). You will also find the apron worn by Countess Markiewicz (see page 397) while imprisoned in England, and a remarkable painting by Kathleen Fox of her arrest in 1916 outside the College of Surgeons in Dublin. West of the museum on Holborn Street, a **plaque** on the wall of no. 5 commemorates the house where Leo Milligan, the father of Spike, the late comedian and writer, was born – references to the town are included in Spike's comic masterpiece **Puckoon**.

## The Model

The Mall • Tues–Sat 10am–5.30pm, Thurs till 8pm, Sun 10.30am–3.30pm • Free; guided tours Sat 3pm €3 • ☎ 071 914 1405, ⓦ themodel.ie

A couple of hundred metres east of the museum stands one of Ireland's finest contemporary art galleries, **The Model**. Behind a drab Victorian facade, the spacious and airy modern extension houses a range of temporary, experimental exhibitions, as well as selections from the **Niland Collection**, including works by Jack B. Yeats and

---

### SLIGO FESTIVALS

**Sligo Sea Shanty Festival** Rosses Point ☎ 085 1204 781, ⓦ wildatlanticshanty.ie. A rip-roaring line-up share their sea-dog songs in village bars and hotels in mid-June.

**So Sligo Food & Culture Festival** ⓦ sligofoodtrail.ie. Held annually in mid-June.

**Tread Softly** Sligo town ☎ 071 917 1905, ⓦ treadsoftly.ie. Held in August, this festival is dedicated to the legacy of the Yeats brothers.

**Yeats International Summer School** Hyde Bridge ☎ 071 914 2693, ⓦ yeatssociety.com. Runs from mid-June to early August, attracting literary luminaries.

**Sligo Festival of Baroque Music** ⓦ sligobaroquefestival.com. Concerts, ensembles, masterclasses and workshops, in late September/early October.

**Sligo Live Music Festival** ⓦ sligolive.ie. An October festival of traditional music sessions, as well as a variety of major acts.

N15 Rosses Point, Drumcliffe & Bundoran

**SLIGO**

Paul Henry. In 2015, the actress Joanna Lumley opened the **Yeats Secret Garden**, an enclosed wildflower area behind the gallery, intended to represent Yeats' vision of a secret hideaway on Lough Gill (as evoked in his poem *The Lake of Innisfree*), complete with a makeshift mud cabin.

## The Abbey

Abbey St • April to mid-Oct daily 10am–6pm • €5; Heritage Card • ☎ 071 914 6406

The Dominican friary, more commonly known as **the Abbey**, was founded around 1252 by Maurice Fitzgerald. Accidentally burnt down in 1412, it was rebuilt shortly afterwards and, unusually, continued to be occupied after the Reformation on condition that the friars became secular clergy. Damaged during a siege of the nearby castle (of which no trace remains) in 1595, the friary, along with most of the town, was sacked in 1641 by Sir Frederick Hamilton and his Puritan army, and its friars massacred. However, the friary's remains are in remarkably good condition and include a delicately decorated **high altar**, gracefully carved tombs and sculptures, and well-preserved **cloisters**. Seek out the love knot found in the Cloister East Ambulatory, said to represent the bond between earthly and spiritual love and, according to local custom, a wishing stone.

**11**

## ARRIVAL AND DEPARTURE

## SLIGO TOWN

**By bus** The bus station (☎071 916 0066) is on Lord Edward St.

Destinations Ballymote (Mon–Wed 1 daily, Sat 2; 35–45min); Ballyshannon (8–9 daily; 40min–1hr); Boyle (5–6 daily; 40min); Bundoran (8–11 daily; 35–55mins); Carrick-on-Shannon (5–7 daily; 1hr); Derry (6–8 daily; 2hr 30min); Donegal town (6–8 daily; 1hr 5min); Drumcliffe (9am–12 daily; 15min); Dublin (5–7 daily; 3hr 15min–3hr 50min); Easkey (Mon–Sat 3–5 daily, Sun 1; 55min); Enniscrone (Mon–Sat 3–5 daily, Sun 1; 1hr 15min); Enniskillen (2–3 daily; 1hr 25min); Galway (5–7 daily; 2hr 45min); Gurteen (Sat 2; 1hr); Keadue (Fri 1; 50min); Lissadell (1 Mon–Fri during school terms, Sat 2 all year; 20min); Riverstown (Thurs & Fri 1 daily; 40min); Rosses Point (4–7 daily; 20min); Skreen (Mon–Sat 2–3 daily, Sun 1; 30min); Strandhill (3–7 daily;

20min); Strokestown (Mon–Sat 1 daily; 1hr); Tubbercurry (6–7 daily; 35min); Westport (2–3 daily; 1hr 55min).

**By private bus.** The arrival point for Feda O'Donnell (ⓦfedaodonnell.littleireland.ie) buses is opposite the Ulster Bank on Stephen St while the departure point is *Connolly's* pub on Markievicz Rd.

Destinations Donegal (Mon–Thurs & Sat 2 daily, Fri 4; 50min); Galway (Mon–Thurs & Sat 2 daily, Fri & Sun 3 daily; 2hr 10min).

**By train** The train station (☎071 916 9888), just off the Inner Relief Route, is close to the town centre. All services operate Mon–Sat 7–8 times daily, Sun 6.

Destinations Ballymote (20min); Boyle (35min); Carrick-on-Shannon (45min); Dublin (3hr 5min); Mullingar (1hr 55min).

## INFORMATION

**Tourist office** Old Bank Building, O'Connell St (May–Oct Mon–Sat 9am–5pm; Nov–April Mon–Fri 9am–5pm; ☎071 916 1201; ⓦwildatlanticway.com). For info on events check one of the two weekly newspapers, *The Sligo*

*Champion* or *Sligo Weekender*.

**Bike rental** Chain Driven Cycles ☎071 912 9008, ⓦchain drivencycles.com) on High St.

## ACCOMMODATION

## SEE MAP PAGE 391

There are numerous **hotel** options dotted around, plus plenty of **B&B**s along the main roads leading out of the town. For **camping**, your best bets are in Strandhill and Rosses Point (see pages 394 and 396).

**Clayton Hotel** Clarion Rd, Ballinode ☎071 911 9000, ⓦclaytonhotelsligo.com. Swish and modern establishment, 1km out of town off the N16 Enniskillen road, with sparklingly clean rooms and fresh fruit on the table; there's also a pool and gym, plus loads of activities for kids. **€129**

★ **The Glasshouse** Swan Point ☎071 919 4300, ⓦthe glasshouse.ie. This literally dazzling (when the sun shines) place by Hyde Bridge is a dramatic glassy counterpoint to the adjacent waters of the Garavogue. Its chic rooms offer floor-to-ceiling windows and a high degree of comfort. **€159**

**Railway Hostel** 1 Union Place (IHO) ☎071 914 4530, ⓦtherailway.ie. Small, welcoming, family-run hostel handy

for the train and bus stations. Most beds are singles, not bunks; all bathrooms are shared. Dorms **€18**, doubles **€50**

**Sligo City Hotel** Quay St ☎071 914 4000, ⓦsligocity hotel.com. Plush hotel providing efficient service and good deals, all just a 5min walk from the bus or train stations. **€160**

**Tree Tops** Cleveragh Rd ☎071 916 2301, ⓦsligobandb. com. A comfortable and well-appointed guesthouse with a pleasant garden, just off Pearse Rd. The best thing about staying here is the breakfast: choose from a dazzling buffet of cereals, fruit and yoghurt as well as pancakes, waffles, croissants, rice or cakes and brown bread. **€75**

**White House Hostel** Markievicz Rd (IHH) ☎085 172 3667, ⓦthewhitehousehostel.com. Handily placed in the town centre, this small and convivial if somewhat basic hostel provides mostly dorm accommodation with one family room. Good location also for bus connections to Galway and Donegal. Closed Nov–March. **€15**

## EATING

## SEE MAP PAGE 391

★ **Bistro Bianconi** Tobergal Lane ☎071 914 1744, ⓦbistrobianconi.ie. Lively Italian restaurant in the flourishing Italian Quarter serving excellent pasta and pizza. Early bird (5–7pm) pizzas from €10. Daily 5–10pm.

**Coach Lane** 1–2 Lord Edward St ☎071 916 2417, ⓦcoachlanesligo.com. The upstairs restaurant offers a diverse menu, with highlights including gnocchi Sorrentino (potato dumplings) (€19), Connemara lamb's liver (€21) or wild Atlantic cod (€25). Eat downstairs for cheaper bar meals such as fish pie and Italian meatballs served at red-check tablecloths. Restaurant Wed–Sun 5.30–10pm, bar

daily 2.30–10pm.

**Eala Bhán** 5 Rockwood Parade ☎071 914 5823, ⓦeala bhan.ie. Modern Irish food with a French twist. The three-course early bird (daily 5–6.15pm) is great value at €26.95. Tues–Sat noon–3pm, plus Mon & Sun 5–9.30pm.

**Fabbrica** Rockwood Parade ☎071 914 8987. This Italian brasserie serves up lunchtime standards of sandwiches, BLTs and salads and then reimagines its menu for a dinner of Toulouse sausage, glazed pork ribs, or parmigiana di melanzane (average main €18). There's also an extensive cocktail list. Daily noon–10pm.

★ **Kate's Kitchen** Castle St ☎ 071 914 3022, ⊛ kateskitchen.ie. Call in for a coffee and sample some of the gourmet artisan products on the heaving shelves: handcrafted farmhouse cheese, elderflower cordial, Aine's handmade chocolates and home-made tea brack are a selection of the offerings. Soup and sandwiches from €8. Tues–Sat 8.30am–4.30pm.

**Knox Café** 32 O'Connell St ☎ 071 914 1575, ⊛ knoxsligo. ie. Breakfasts (9–11.30am) of porridge, granola, eggs Benedict or Florentine (€8.50) will help you on your way at this all-day eatery that also serves lunch and dinner.

Lunches might be chicken quesadilla, falafels and pulled ham hock, or Thai green curry (€13) while the evening tapas menu (Thurs–Sat 6–10pm) bursts with Mediterranean flavours. Tues–Sat 10am–10pm, Sun 10am–4pm.

**Lyons Café** Quay St ☎ 071 914 2969, ⊛ lyonscafe.com. Upstairs in one of Sligo's old family-run clothing stores, this time-burnished café (breakfasts, soups, cakes) has been a popular meeting place since it opened in 1923 – some of the original lights, tables and chairs are still in place. Lunches from €10. Mon–Sat 8.30am–6pm.

## DRINKING AND NIGHTLIFE

SEE MAP PAGE 391

**Earley's** Bridge St ☎ 071 914 2171. This cosy old bar features a great Thurs night session and other music on Sat and Sun. Beamish is one of the top-selling beers and much cheaper than some of their dark rivals. Mon–Thurs 10.30am–11.30pm, Fri & Sat till 12.30am, Sun 12.30–11pm.

**Foley's** Castle St ☎ 071 916 8900. Traditional bar with a superb range of whiskeys, and sessions year-round on Thurs & Sat, plus Wed from June to Sept. Mon–Thurs & Sun 11.30am–11.30pm, Fri & Sat till 12.30am.

★ **Hargadon Bros** O'Connell St ☎ 071 915 3709, ⊛ hargadons.com. No visit to Sligo is complete without enjoying a drink or light meal in this early nineteenth-century

pub with snugs, snob screens and marble-top counter to boot. For lunch (noon–3.30pm) small plates of oysters, mackerel timbale, or whiskey and oak cold smoked salmon are on the menu; dinner (4–9pm) features moules frites, broiled seabass, burgers or steak. Jazz on Thurs from 9.30pm, live music on Fri from 10.30pm. Tues–Sat 1pm–late.

**Shoot the Crows** Grattan St. A long, narrow, slightly dishevelled bar across from the Lady of Erin statue, and a lively place to meet the locals. It has retained its original features including the timber wainscoting. Musicians frequently occupy a corner in the small bar at the front. Mon–Thurs 11.30am–11.30pm, Fri & Sat till 12.30am, Sun 11.30am–11.30pm.

## ENTERTAINMENT

**The Factory Theatre** Lower Quay St ☎ 071 917 0431, ⊛ blueraincoat.com. Hosts the innovative Blue Raincoat Theatre Company.

**Hawk's Well Theatre** Temple St ☎ 071 916 1518, ⊛ hawkswell.com. Presents a range of dramatic productions

and musical events.

**Omniplex Cinema** Wine St ☎ 071 910 4051, ⊛ omniplex.ie. A modern ten-screen cinema with a Kids' Club at 2pm at weekends.

## SPORT

**Football** Sligo Rovers FC play at The Showgrounds on Knappagh Rd (☎ 071 917 1212, ⊛ sligorovers.com).

**Horse racing** If you fancy a flutter, head for the Sligo Races

at Cleveragh Rd (☎ 071 918 3342, ⊛ countysligoraces.com) from May to Oct.

# Around Sligo town

West of Sligo town lies the famous surfing beach at **Strandhill**, a grand base for exhilarating coastal walks, while inland is one of Europe's most significant collections of passage graves at **Carrowmore Megalithic Cemetery**. Both the resort and the graveyard are overlooked by the numinous Knocknarea Mountain, on whose summit sits the mystical **Medb's Cairn**.

## Strandhill

Eight kilometres west of Sligo town and set against the backdrop of Knocknarea Mountain, seaside **STRANDHILL** boasts a gorgeous situation. It's just the way a seaside resort should be, too: traditional cafés and tea rooms, amusements, ice-cream parlours, beach stores and stunning sunsets. With its new tagline "The Thrill of Strandhill", it has upped its game with a selection of trendy restaurants and bars, while the creative community has come together to hold a funky **Peoples' Market** on Sunday mornings, selling local crafts, artisan foods, fresh fruit and vegetables.

## Dolly's Cottage

49 Dorrin's Strand (beside the rugby club) • June Sat & Sun 2–6pm; July & Aug daily 2–6pm • Free

On the way into the village look out for **Dolly's Cottage**, a tiny thatched dwelling named after its last occupant, Dolly Higgins, who died in 1970. Maintained as it was, with a turf fire and a pouch bed, the cottage sells handicrafts as well as home-made jams and preserves.

## The beach

Strandhill's renowned **beach** is a wild stretch pounded by huge Atlantic breakers. Because of rip currents it is absolutely unsafe for swimming but is massively popular with **surfers** and regularly witnesses the Sligo Open Championship over the first weekend in August. Right by the beach, the Perfect Day Surf School (☎087 2029 399, ⊛perfectdaysurfing.ie) offers a range of classes. Adjacent on the front you can luxuriate in the curative and pleasantly soporific waters of the **Voya Spa Seaweed Baths** (daily 10am–8pm; €30 single, two adults sharing €60; ⊛voyaseaweedbaths.com).

## Killaspugbrone Church

The beach offers bracing walks, especially a few kilometres north towards **Killaspugbrone Church**, whose ruins largely date from the twelfth and thirteenth centuries, though its tower is a later addition. Visiting the church some centuries earlier, St Patrick somehow contrived to stumble and dislodge a tooth in the process, which he promptly donated to the sacristan, Bishop Bronus. This relic was kept and passed down, and, in the fourteenth century, an exquisite **casket**, the Fiacal Pádraig, was created to house it – the tooth subsequently disappeared, but its container is on view in the National Museum in Dublin (see page 65).

### ARRIVAL AND TOURS
### STRANDHILL

**By bus** There are regular buses from/to Sligo (4–7 daily; 20min).

**Tours** Seatrails (☎087 240 5071, ⊛seatrails.ie) offers first-rate guided tours of Strandhill and the surrounding coastal areas, run by maritime archaeologist Auriel Robinson. The Streedagh beach tour gives intriguing insights into the Spanish Armada landings of 1588. Prices from €25.

### ACCOMMODATION

**Ocean Wave Lodge** Top Rd ☎071 916 8115, ⊛oceanwavelodge.com. An attractive guesthouse located on what is known locally as the "top road" in Strandhill, a 10min stroll from the seafront. The twelve rooms range from twins or doubles to family rooms, and there's also a reading room and well-equipped kitchen. **€70**

**Strandhill Caravan and Camping Park** Strandhill beach ☎071 916 8111, ⊛sligocaravanandcamping.ie. Campers can choose from a large area of grass with a sandy base which is mud-free even on wet days. Ideally placed for exploration, and for activities ranging from swimming and surfing to horseriding and golf. Closed Oct–March. **€23**

★ **Strandhill Lodge and Suites** Top Rd ☎071 912 2122, ⊛strandhilllodgeandsuites.ie. A sleekly designed boutique hotel overlooking Strandhill Bay. The modern bedrooms, in calming cream and beige decor, are finished to a high standard; some come with a patio opening on to a courtyard. **€129**

**Surf n Stay Lodge Hostel and Surf School** Shore Rd ☎071 916 8313, ⊛surfnstay.ie. A good-value, well-equipped hostel near the beach, with small but well-presented dorms and tastefully furnished private rooms in the adjoining lodge. Handy for the bus connection to Sligo – the stop is just 100m away. Dorms **€20**, doubles **€50**

### EATING AND DRINKING

**Mammy Johnston's Ice Cream Parlour** Shore Rd ☎087 288 6915, ⊛mammyjohnstons.org. Catch the right evening and *MJ's* is the best place from which to view the western sunset and Atlantic breakers while you agonize over a delectable choice of ice creams and crêpes. They've been making ice cream since 1938, and the walls, adorned with pictures of old Strandhill, reflect the historic link. April–Sept daily 10am–6pm.

★ **Shells Café** Shore Rd ☎ 071 912 2938, ⓦ shellscafe. com. This delightful combination of fish restaurant and bakery is a west of Ireland gem, with mismatched wooden chairs and an innovative menu that includes everything from buttermilk pancakes with bacon (€6.95), veggie burgers,

battered haddock and sardines on toast, to berries and wild garlic foraged from the beach. Daily 8.30am–5pm.

**Strand Bar** Shore Rd ☎ 071 916 8140, ⓦ thestrandbar. ie. At the bottom of Shore Rd with a turf fire, cosy snugs and wholesome pub meals (average price €10), this is a place where surfers meet the locals. Mon–Sat 10.30am–11.30pm, Sun 12.30–11pm.

## Carrowmore Megalithic Cemetery

4km west of Sligo town • April to mid-Oct daily 10am–6pm; last admission 5pm • €5; Heritage Card • ☎ 071 916 1534, ⓦ heritageireland.ie

**Carrowmore Megalithic Cemetery** presents a remarkable array of some thirty megalithic passage tombs – easily the biggest prehistoric graveyard in Europe. The oval-shaped cluster of monuments spreads out within a 1km-by-600m field and ranges from the most basic, a small circle of stones surrounding a central roofed chamber, through to the largest, known as **Listoghill**, covered by an impressive rounded cairn. Excavations have uncovered cremated human remains as well as jewellery carved from bones and antlers.

## Medb's Cairn

To get here from Carrowmore head west for 1km, take a right turn at the junction with the R292, then left at the first crossroads – after another 1km a lane leads right towards the car park at the base of the mountain, from where it's a steep 4km hike to the summit

Carrowmore is made all the more atmospheric for being set below one of Ireland's most significant burial places, the massive **Medb's Cairn** on the summit of **Knocknarea Mountain** – 55m wide and 10m high, and surrounded by a 3m-high earthen bank. Whether Medb, the legendary queen of Connacht and one of the protagonists of the **Táin Bó Cúailnge**, is actually buried here is unknown, since the site has not been excavated, but it's well worth making the trek, not only for views of the cairn itself, but for spectacular outlooks north to Donegal and west to Mayo. It takes around an hour to get to the top, following the 2.4km **Queen Medb Trail**; on your way up, pick up a stone and leave it on the cairn, making a wish as you do so and, as local legend has it, the force of Queen Medb may be with you.

## Lough Gill

To the east of Sligo town lies one of Ireland's most entrancing lakes, **Lough Gill**, set beneath wooded slopes which provide the backdrop to almost all its 40km shoreline. The best route around the lough, and one easily navigable in less than a day's cycling, is to follow the shore clockwise by following the R286 from Sligo town, and taking in the plantation **Parke's Castle**, just inside County Leitrim, from where you can board a cruise boat and catch a sight of idyllic **Innisfree**.

### Parke's Castle

Eastern end of Lough Gill • April–Sept daily 10am–6pm • €5; Heritage Card; free on first Wed of every month • ☎ 071 916 4149

Some 11km northeast of Sligo, towards the lake's eastern extremity, **Parke's Castle** is a plantation fort erected by Captain Robert Parke in the 1620s and elegantly restored in the late twentieth century by the Office of Public Works. A moated tower house once stood here, home of the Irish chieftain Brian O'Rourke, who in 1588 was charged with high treason after sheltering Francesco de Cuellar, one of the few survivors of the Armada ships wrecked off the Sligo coast. Wander around the battlements, admire expansive views of the lough and take in an **exhibition** on the remodelling of the castle with displays on other notable vernacular buildings.

**11**

## Innisfree

Waterbus Easter–Oct daily 12.30 & 3.30pm; €15; call ☎ 087 259 8869 to check sailings, ☜ roseofinnisfree.com

From the pier beside Parke's Castle, the "Rose of Innisfree" **waterbus** operates a tour of Lough Gill, taking in views of Yeats's beloved isle of **Innisfree**, and featuring recitals of the poet's works by the skipper, almost certainly including the poet's **Lake Isle of Innisfree**:

*I will arise and go now, and go to Innisfree,*
*And a small cabin build there, of clay and wattles made:*
*Nine bean-rows will I have there, a hive for the honey-bee,*
*And live alone in the bee-loud glade.*

Alternatively, head a few kilometres southwards through Dromahair and pick up the R287. About 4km along this road a signposted lane leads down to the water where there's a fabulous view of the lough and Innisfree in all its serene beauty. If you fancy exploring the area on two wheels then the **Lough Gill cycle loop** is a 40km flat route that takes you through peaceful scenery and along quiet roads – bike rental is available in Sligo town (see page 392). Note that there's no access to the island itself.

# North Sligo

The majority of **North Sligo**'s attractions are easily accessible from the county town. Much of the landscape is irrevocably associated with W. B. Yeats, particularly **Benbulben Mountain**, under whose green-tinged slopes and surmounting tableland the poet is buried at **Drumcliffe**. To the mountain's south lie the magical waters of **Glencar Lake** with its exhilarating waterfall, while to its west is **Lissadell House**, home to Yeats's friends Eva Gore-Booth and Constance Markiewicz, and a place filled with paintings, books and the lore of Irish cultural history. The coastline is less stimulating, though it includes a fine beach at **Mullaghmore**, a harbour village not far from one of Ireland's major funerary monuments, **Creevykeel Court Tomb**.

## Rosses Point

Eight kilometres northwest of Sligo town, off the N15, **ROSSES POINT** is a seaside resort which has not moved with the times and is all the better for its lapse. There's a grand **beach**, ideal for swimming, and splendid views across the bay, both of which provided inspiration for Jack B. Yeats, the poet's artist brother. From here, fine, often blustery, walks lead around the headland.

**ARRIVAL AND DEPARTURE**                                                   ROSSES POINT

**By bus** Regular buses run from/to Sligo town (Mon–Fri 7   daily, Sat 5; 20min).

**ACCOMMODATION AND EATING**

**Austie's Bar & Restaurant** ☎ 071 917 7111, ☜ austies. ie. A convivial bar where retired sea captains hold court alongside local musicians. The wooden snugs and table which the musicians gather round on weekend nights are made from shipwrecked timber, and maritime memorabilia lines the walls. For food, main courses average €14. Food served Mon–Sat 4–9pm, Sun 12.30–9pm; bar Mon–Thurs to 11.30pm, Fri & Sat till 12.30am.

**Greenlands Caravan and Camping Park** ☎ 071 917

7113, ☜ sligocaravanandcamping.ie. An efficiently run site close to two sandy beaches with good swimming and sailing facilities. Closed mid-Sept to March. **€21**

**Yeats Country Hotel & Spa Leisure Club** ☎ 071 911 7100, ☜ yeatscountryhotel.com. A sleekly designed boutique hotel looking out over Strandhill Bay, with bedrooms spread over three floors. The rooms come in beige and terra-cotta colour schemes, in keeping with the restful atmosphere of the hotel. Murder mystery weekends are a big hit. **€149**

# Drumcliffe

Eight kilometres north of Sligo along the N15, the tiny seaside village of
**DRUMCLIFFE** is the site of a **monastery** established in 574 by St Colmcille, though
only a round tower and an eleventh-century high cross, set on opposite sides of
the main road, remain today. The graveyard of the adjacent and somewhat stark
nineteenth-century **church** (which has a good café and craft shop next to it) is where
the poet **W. B. Yeats** is buried and, as a consequence, is very much on the tourist
trail. Yeats died in 1939 in Roquebrune, France, but before doing so requested
that his body be interred locally for "a year or so" before being returned to Sligo.
His wishes were granted in 1948 when his remains were transferred from France
to Drumcliffe, where his great-grandfather had been rector, and buried, as one of
his last poems stated, "Under bare Ben Bulben's head". His headstone, which also
marks the resting place of his wife George, bears the last three lines of that poem,
*Under Ben Bulben*:

Cast a cold Eye
On Life, on Death.
Horseman, pass by!

11

**ARRIVAL AND DEPARTURE**                                               **DRUMCLIFFE**

**By bus** Buses drop off/pick up on the main street in     and Sligo town (7–11 daily; 15min)
Drumcliffe, serving Ballyshannon (8–10 daily; 35–50min)

# Glencar Lake

Heading east from Drumcliffe along minor roads, you'll come to **Glencar Lake** after
some 8km, gorgeously set amid tree-lined slopes. Near the eastern extremity of its
northern shore a signposted footpath leads up to an impressive 15m-high **waterfall**,
cascading down into a deep pool from the rocky mountainside above, which provided
the inspiration for part of Yeats's poem *The Stolen Child*:

Where the wandering water gushes
From the hills above Glencar,
In pools above the rushes that
Scarce could bathe a star.

# Lissadell House

5km north of Sligo town • March to mid-Oct daily 10am–6pm • €14 • ☎ 071 916 3150, ⓦ lissadellhouse.com • Coming by car, turn off the
main N15 Sligo–Donegal road, take a left turn at Drumcliffe and follow the road northwest for 6km

**Lissadell House**, the lavishly restored ancestral home of the Gore-Booth family,
whose members Eva and Constance were close friends of W. B. Yeats, is a must-see
attraction. The house – an austere but classical residence built in 1834 – was the
holiday retreat of **W. B. Yeats** and the childhood home of Constance Gore-Booth,
who later became **Countess Markievicz** and fought in the 1916 Easter Rising in
Dublin. She was the first woman to be elected to the House of Commons (although
she did not take her seat) and later became the first female member of the Dáil, the
Irish Parliament. The building is a storehouse of **family archives** and other cultural
treasures: one room is crammed with the exhibits of Henry Gore-Booth's expedition
to the Arctic in search of a friend. The admission price includes a tour of the house,
entry to the exhibitions, and access to the **Alpine and Victorian gardens**, which make
for a pleasant stroll, as do the extensive woodland walks.

## Creevykeel Court Tomb

Cliffony, 22km north of Sligo town • Open access

Just north of the village of Cliffony, **Creevykeel Court Tomb** is probably the best example of its kind in Ireland. A cairn-covered, trapeze-shaped barrow constructed between 3500 and 3000 BC, though now lacking many of its stones, the tomb features two central burial chambers, faced by an oval-shaped court in which rituals were conducted. Excavations in 1935 uncovered cremated remains, alongside Neolithic pottery, axes and artefacts, all now held by Dublin's National Museum (see page 65).

## Mullaghmore

Just before Creevykeel a lane leads northwards for 4km to **MULLAGHMORE**, an enticing village set around a secluded, walled harbour with a glorious expanse of sandy beach, offering fabulous views north to the mountains of Donegal and back towards Benbulben.

**11**

### ACCOMMODATION AND EATING                                                        MULLAGHMORE

**Beach Hotel** The Harbour ☎085 251 2262, ⓦbeach hotelmullaghmore.com. Ideally situated at the waterfront with leisure facilities and activity breaks. The 28 rooms are decorated in tranquil pastels, and many have sea views and window boxes. Weekends only Nov–mid-March. **€110**

**Eithna's By the Sea** The Harbour ☎071 916 6407, ⓦeithnasrestaurant.com. Serves deliciously fresh fish and seafood: for starters, think mackerel fillets with beetroot seaweed chutney and goat's cheese or crispy fresh squid, while mains (average €20) take in lobster, prawns and Dover sole (with plenty of meat options too). On sunny summer evenings, tables are placed outside for alfresco dining. Wed–Sun 11am–3.30pm & 5–9.30pm.

**Seacrest B&B** The Harbour ☎071 916 6468, ⓦseacrest guesthouse.com. A beautifully appointed guesthouse set in a stunning location beside the beach. The rooms look out over Benbulben Mountain and across Donegal Bay. **€80**

# West Sligo

The shoreline of **West Sligo**, stretching from near Sligo town almost as far as Mayo's Ballina, is probably the least visited in the county. Yet set against the looming southern backdrop of the Ox Mountains, it offers plenty of diversions including bracing seascapes at **Aughris**, exhilarating surfing at **Easkey** and a dazzling beach at **Enniscrone**. A little way inland, the memorable funerary sepulchres at **Skreen** are well worth a detour en route.

## Skreen and Aughris

Twenty-five kilometres west of Sligo town along the N59, the tiny village of **SKREEN** is worth visiting for the astonishing collection of 23 **box tombs** situated in its Church of Ireland's graveyard and created by a local family of stonemasons, the Diamonds, between 1774 and 1886. Named after one Andrew Black, who had the tomb erected in memory of his father in 1825, the most remarkable of these is the Black Monument, which carries an ornate carving of a ploughman, atypically dressed Fred Astaire-style in top hat and tails.

Back on the N59 and just west of the village, a signpost points towards the secluded hamlet of **AUGHRIS**. From the pier here you can follow a 5km cliff walk, which takes in splendid views, sights of numerous seabirds and, from June to August, basking dolphins.

## Easkey

The village of **EASKEY**, 15km west of Aughris, began life as a monastic community, much later becoming the base for the MacDonnells, originally gallowglasses who served the ruling O'Dowd clan and built seaside **Roslee Castle** (now ruined) in the fifteenth century. Thanks to the constancy of its waves, Easkey is a popular **surfing** centre and houses the headquarters of the Irish Surfing Association (☎096 49428, ⓦirishsurfing.ie).

## Enniscrone

Some 14km southwest along the coast from Easkey, **ENNISCRONE** is blessed with a gorgeous 5km arc of golden **strand**. Its other main draw is **Kilcullen's Bath House** (June–Sept daily 10am–9pm; Oct–May Mon–Fri noon–8pm, Sat & Sun 10am–8pm; bath and steam €25, or €40 for two sharing; ⓦkilcullenseaweedbaths.net) where you can wallow in a bath full of seaweed – the iodine-rich water is not only sheer relaxation but is also reckoned to offer relief for rheumatism and arthritis – before enjoying a hot steam in a cedarwood cabinet.

### ARRIVAL AND DEPARTURE
WEST SLIGO

**By bus** Buses (Mon–Sat 3–5 daily, Sun 1) run from Sligo town to Easkey (50min) and on to Enniscrone (1hr 15min). Buses also run between Easkey and Enniscrone (Mon–Sat 3–4 daily, Sun 1; 20min).

### ACCOMMODATION AND EATING

**Atlantic and Riverside** On the R297, Easkey ☎096 49837, ⓦeaskeybandb.com. Beside the River Easkey with comfortable en-suite rooms, convenient to shops and pubs, and an ideal stopover while touring the coastline. €80

**Atlantic Caravan Park** Enniscrone ☎096 36132, ⓦatlanticcaravanpark.com. Camp by the golf course beside natural sand dunes in a pleasant park looking across Killala Bay. Closed Oct–Feb. €21

★ **The Beach Bar** Aughris ☎071 917 6465, ⓦthe beachbarsligo.com. A thatched pub serving such delights as creamy seafood chowder, freshly steamed mussels or Irish stew. It also provides amenable en-suite B&B in the adjacent bungalow. Food served daily 1–8pm; bar noon–11.30pm. €60

# South Sligo

South Sligo's attractions are spread over a wide area, ranging from the glorious **Lough Arrow** in the east, via megalithic sites, such as **Heapstown Cairn** and the atmospheric **Carrowkeel Cemetery**, set in the Bricklieve Mountains, to creeper-clad castles and **Lough Talt** in the west. Above all, however, the area is renowned for its **traditional music**, especially within the triangle of **Ballymote**, **Gurteen** and **Tubbercurry**.

## Riverstown and Sligo Folk Park

Folk Park Mon–Fri 10am–4pm (also May–Sept Sun noon–5pm) • €6 • ☎071 916 5001, ⓦsligofolkpark.com • Buses (Thurs & Fri 1 daily) run from Riverstown to Boyle (35min) and Sligo (40min)

The tranquil village of **RIVERSTOWN**, some 20km southeast of Sligo, is home to the **Sligo Folk Park**, a well-designed collection of buildings that includes a museum devoted to rural history and farm implements, re-created craft workshops with occasional craft demonstrations, a nature trail along the banks of the Unshin, plus a crafts shop and café.

During the August bank holiday weekend Riverstown is taken over by the **James Morrison Traditional Music Festival** (ⓦjamesmorrisonfestival.com), celebrating the music of the famous fiddler born in nearby Drumfin in 1893. He emigrated to the US in 1915 and became famous playing with his bands in the dancehalls of New York.

## Heapstown Cairn and Lough Arrow

Five kilometres south of Riverstown, by the road to Ballindoon, stands the impressive **Heapstown Cairn**, which, at 60m in diameter, is Ireland's largest megalithic passage tomb outside the Boyne Valley. From the cairn it's a short jaunt to the eastern shore of **Lough Arrow**, whose limpid waters are peppered with tiny islands.

## Castlebaldwin and Carrowkeel Cemetery

At **CASTLEBALDWIN**, 6km south of Riverstown on the N4, minor roads of diminishing width and reliability lead towards the Bronze Age **Carrowkeel Cemetery**. The last kilometre or so has to be negotiated on foot, but your efforts will be rewarded by a spellbinding panoramic view of the surrounding countryside. Here on the uplands of the Bricklieve Mountains is a remarkable collection of fourteen cairns, plus an assortment of other stonework. Excavation in 1911 produced a wealth of jewellery and relics, and several of the cairns, consisting of roofed, cruciform **passage graves**, can be entered. The most striking is **cairn K**, which, in complete contrast to County Meath's Newgrange (see page 139), is illuminated by the sun's rays during the summer solstice (June 21).

## Ballymote and around

The largest place in southern Sligo is **BALLYMOTE**, 20km from the county town. Richard de Burgo built a **castle** here in 1300 which, switching ownership numerous times during its history, proved to be a veritable straw in the wind of Irish politics. In 1317 it fell to the O'Connors and remained in Irish hands until captured by Bingham, the governor of Connacht, in 1584. It was soon afterwards reclaimed by the McDonaghs who then sold it to Red Hugh O'Donnell (see page 441) for £400 and three hundred cows – he marched from here to catastrophic defeat at Kinsale in 1601. Later taken by Cromwell's army, it fell yet again to the O'Connors in 1690, before they in turn surrendered the castle to Williamite troops who determined to put an end to the whole farrago by tearing down much of the building and filling in the moat. The **ruins** lie just west of the town centre, and the stripped **interior** can be visited by acquiring a key from the Enterprise Centre (Mon–Fri 9am–5pm) on Emmet Street. Towards the end of the fourteenth century, the **Book of Ballymote** was assembled here, significant not just for the vast deal of information on Irish lore and history it contains, but also because it unlocks the secrets of the carved ogham letters that appear on numerous Neolithic standing stones. The book is held by the Royal Irish Academy in Dublin.

The **Paddy Killoran Traditional Music Festival** is held in Ballymote on the third weekend in June.

### ARRIVAL AND DEPARTURE

### BALLYMOTE AND AROUND

**By bus** Buses stop outside the Church of Ireland parish church on Main St.
Destinations Boyle (Mon–Wed & Sat 1 daily; 30min); Gurteen (Sat 1; 20min); Sligo (Mon–Wed 1 daily, Sat 2; 40min); Tubbercurry (Wed 2; 30min).

**By train** Ballymote is on the Sligo–Dublin route (Mon–Sat 7 daily, Sun 6); the train station is opposite the castle ruins, off the Tubbercurry road.
Destinations Boyle (17min); Dublin (2hr 40min); Sligo (18min).

### ACCOMMODATION AND EATING

**Hayden's** Lord Edward St ☎071 918 3188. An old-style welcoming bar that boasts 350 years of history and was the former home of the Sheriff of Sligo. Irish traditional music is played on Sun nights in the summer months. Mon–Thurs 3–11.30pm, Fri & Sat till 12.30am, Sun 12.30–11.30pm.
**Millhouse** Keenaghan, on the southern outskirts of Ballymote ☎071 918 3449, ⓦsligo-accommodation. com. An agreeable, modern guesthouse with comfortable if slightly small bedrooms (singles, doubles, twins and triples) and delicious breakfasts. €84

**Stonepark** Teeling St. A central restaurant and café offering reasonably priced meals with main courses running €9–14. The menu features burgers, chicken, pork, steak and fish. Daily 9am–9pm.
★ **Temple House** 5km northwest of town ☎087 997 6045, ⓦtemplehouse.ie. The area's most exclusive accommodation, offered in a lakeside setting. Dating originally from the late seventeenth century, this majestic country house offers six of its hundred rooms as recently refurbished en-suite guest accommodation. Closed Dec–March. €150

## MICHAEL COLEMAN

Arguably the greatest of Irish fiddlers, **Michael Coleman** was born in 1891 in Killavil, north of Gurteen, and grew up in a household noted for its strong musical tradition. Taking up the fiddle in childhood, he developed rapidly under the tuition of his elder brother James and acquired a phenomenally extensive repertoire. Coleman moved to **New York** in 1914, making a living playing first on the vaudeville circuit and in the city's Irish dancehalls and bars. With a ready-made Irish market for the nascent US recording industry, Coleman made his first 78s in 1921 and over the next fifteen years released numerous others on a variety of labels, while frequently broadcasting on the radio. He made his last commercial recording in 1936.

The impact of these recordings, the embodiment of the fluid **Sligo style** of music – characterized by its sweet tone and sometimes flamboyant ornamentation – was enormous, not just in the US but also back home, and the approach taken by Coleman and his fellow Sligo émigrés, Paddy Killoran and James Morrison (see page 399), came to dominate Ireland's traditional music. Coleman died in 1945, but you'll still encounter many a traditional session throughout Ireland where the sequence of tunes exactly replicates one of his 78rpm recordings.

**11**

# Gurteen

South of Ballymote the R293 runs parallel to the Dublin railway line before drifting away through fertile farmland and reaching the crossroads village of **GURTEEN** after 11km. Gurteen sits at the heart of South Sligo's **traditional music** scene, and its greatest son was the fiddler Michael Coleman (see box). Gurteen hosts the **Coleman Traditional Festival** over the last weekend in August.

### Coleman Irish Music Centre

By the crossroads • Mon–Sat 10am–5.30pm; shows (€10) July & Aug Wed & Sat 9pm; exhibition €4 • ☎ 071 918 2599, ⓦ colemanirishmusic.com

The **Coleman Irish Music Centre** stages traditional music and dance shows, has an interactive exhibition area and a shop selling a range of books and CDs, including several collections of recordings from its own archives.

| **ARRIVAL AND ACCOMMODATION** | **GURTEEN** |
|---|---|
| **By bus** Gurteen is served by buses from/to Ballymote (Sat 1; 20min); Boyle (Thurs 2; 25min); Sligo (Sat 2; 55min–1hr 5min); and Tubbercurry (Sat 1; 25min). **Church View B&B** Main St ☎071 918 2935, ⓦthe | churchview.com. A modern town house, centrally placed, with attractive en-suite rooms. Each room is decorated in a different colour scheme and comes with tea- and coffee-making facilities. **€75** |

# Tubbercurry and around

Some 30km southwest of Sligo, **TUBBERCURRY** is a rather docile small town but traditional music thrives here, focused on the week-long **South Sligo Summer School** (ⓦsssschool.org) in mid-July, with classes, pub sessions and concerts. Tubbercurry's origins date back to the late fourteenth century, but it remained a sleepy little settlement until becoming a stop on one of Bianconi's coaching routes in 1853. The burgeoning town was all but destroyed by fire during a zealous Black and Tan reprisal in 1920, and little remains from earlier times.

Some 15km to Tubbercurry's west, along a lonely road that passes through flat land before rising into the Ox Mountains, lies **Lough Talt**. Trout-rich, the lake attracts plenty of anglers as well as walkers keen to enjoy the 6.5km path circumnavigating its waters.

| **ARRIVAL AND DEPARTURE** | **TUBBERCURRY AND AROUND** |
|---|---|
| **By bus** There are bus connections with Ballymote (Wed 2; 30min); Galway (6–8 daily; 1hr 55min); Gurteen (Sat 1; | 25min); Sligo (6–8 daily; 35min); and Westport (1–2 daily; 1hr 20min). |

**ACCOMMODATION AND EATING**

**Cawley's** Emmet St ☎071 918 5025, ⓦcawleysguest house.ie. A comfortable guesthouse with fourteen rooms. The restaurant is open to non-residents and serves a mix of French-inspired and Irish cuisine. €79

**Killoran's** Teeling St ☎071 918 5679. A traditional restaurant supplying filling breakfasts and lunches with

an adjacent bar. Main courses might include steak, chicken, haddock or oysters, and average €10. Daily 9am–9pm.

**Murphy's Hotel** Teeling St ☎071 918 5598, ⓦmurphys hotel.ie. Well-equipped en-suite rooms and a range of meals in both its restaurant and bar. Music sessions are held in the bar most weekends. €80

# Carrick-on-Shannon and around

**CARRICK-ON-SHANNON**, Leitrim's county town, grew up around a strategic crossing point on the River Shannon, the importance of which was recognized by the English who began building a planned settlement that was incorporated as a borough in 1613. Modern Carrick developed after the 1840s when the Shannon navigation scheme reached the town; its stone bridge and quays date from this period.

At the tourist office you can pick up a booklet, *A Walk through Carrick-on-Shannon* (€2), detailing a signposted **trail** of the historic buildings. But Carrick's main draw is its proximity to the river, its busy **marina** often jam-packed with barges and cruisers – and a top-class selection of restaurants.

## The Dock Arts Centre and Leitrim Design House

St George's Terrace • Mon–Sat 10am–5.30pm • ☎071 965 0828, ⓦthedock.ie

Just above the river, off the top of Bridge Street, stands the former courthouse, built in 1821 and known as **The Dock**. The arts centre within includes a performance space staging theatre, comedy and music events, as well as a café. The building houses the **Leitrim Design House**, showcasing contemporary works by local artists and craft workers, and hosts regular exhibitions.

## St George's Heritage Centre

St Mary's Close • Mon–Sat 10am–5pm • €7 (includes admission to Workhouse) • ☎071 962 1757, ⓦcarrickheritage.com

The **Heritage Centre**, adjacent to St George's Church (1827), tells the story of Leitrim, its landscape and people through an engaging audiovisual presentation. The church is also worth visiting to see the magnificent altarpiece, *The Adoration of the Shepherds*, restored and hanging in a gilt frame.

## Carrick Workhouse

Gallows Hill • Daily 11am–4.30pm • €7 (includes admission to St George's Heritage Centre) • ☎042 966 4540, ⓦcarrickmacrossworkhouse.com

**Carrick Workhouse** opened in 1842 to accommodate eight hundred people but it was besieged during the Great Famine of 1845–47. With its long rectangular rooms, bare floorboards and whitewashed walls, it looks much as it did in the 1840s and is an

---

**GETTING OUT ON THE WATER IN CARRICK-ON-SHANNON**

Moon River (☎071 962 1777, ⓦmoonriver.ie) runs €15 **river trips** with commentary, departing from the bridge. If you want to go it alone, Emerald Star (☎071 962 7621, ⓦemeraldstar.ie) offers Shannon **cruisers** for weekly rental; expect to pay around €750–3000, depending on the size of the boat and season. Carrick Craft (☎01 278 1666, ⓦcruise-ireland.com) rents two to twelve-berth cruisers. Inland Waterways Association of Ireland (ⓦiwai.ie) supplies more **information** on the Shannon–Erne waterway and sells guides and navigation charts.

---

**CARRICK-ON-SHANNON FESTIVALS AND EVENTS**

**Water Music Festival** ⊕ carrickwatermusicfestival.com. Held over the second weekend in July, featuring concerts ranging from traditional to classical music.

**Carrick Rowing Club Regatta** ⊕ carrickrowingclub.com. At the beginning of August a lively regatta, run by the oldest rowing club in Ireland, is the high point of the boating season and attracts large crowds.

**Coarse Fishing Festival** ☎ 071 962 0313. In mid-September anglers come from many countries for a week-long festival devoted to coarse fishing.

---

atmospheric place to linger. The significance of the Workhouse has been interpreted by the Wexford artist Alanna O'Kelly through a permanent multimedia installation, *No Colouring Can Deepen the Darkness of Truth*.

## Costello Memorial Chapel

Bridge St • Daily 11am– 4pm, or contact the tourist office for a key • Free

The restored **Costello Memorial Chapel** – one of the smallest churches in Ireland – was erected in 1879 by Carrick businessman Edward Costello in memory of his wife, Mary Josephine. The interior is lined with yellow Bath stone and its tiny dimensions measure a mere 5m long, 4m wide and 6m high.

## James Gralton wall plaque

As you walk along Carrick's main street admiring the handsome shop fronts, you come to the site of the **Allied Irish Bank**, formerly a shop where **James Gralton** (1888–1945) worked in the early 1900s. Gralton was a left-wing political activist who joined the Revolutionary Workers Group, but following a political witch-hunt he became the only Irishman ever to be deported from his native land. His fascinating story is told in a 2014 Ken Loach film *Jimmy's Hall*. In 2013 a bilingual **memorial plaque**, in Irish and English, was erected in his honour on the outside wall of the bank as part of the Carrick-on-Shannon historic town trail.

### ARRIVAL AND INFORMATION

### CARRICK-ON-SHANNON

**By bus** Buses drop and collect near *Coffey's Pastry Case*, by the Shannon bridge (☎ 071 916 0066).

Destinations Boyle (5–7 daily; 15min); Drumshanbo (Sat 1; 25min); Dublin (5–7 daily; 2hr 30min–3hr); Sligo (5–7 daily; 1hr).

**By train** The train station (☎ 071 962 0036) is a short distance off the Elphin road on the southern side of the river. All services operate Mon–Sat 7–8 times daily, with 6 on Sun.

Destinations Boyle (15min); Dublin (2hr 20min); Mullingar (1hr 10min); Sligo (45min).

**Tourist office** In the Old Barrel Store, under the bridge (mid-May to mid-Sept Mon–Sat 9.30am–5pm; ☎ 071 962 0170, ⊕ leitrimtourism.com).

### ACCOMMODATION

**Bush Hotel** Main St ☎ 071 967 1000, ⊕ bushhotel. com. The rooms at this traditional-style hotel range in size, though they are all well equipped and comfortable. A fascinating mini-museum of local photographic history lines the walls of the main corridor. **€149**

★ **The Landmark Hotel** Dublin Rd ☎ 071 962 2222, ⊕ thelandmarkhotel.com. A modern hotel with sprucely furnished rooms and views of the Shannon. Great cocktail bar and *Boardwalk* café too, for views of the riverfront with free newspapers. **€129**

### EATING

**Café Lounge** Mercantile Plaza ⊕ cafelounge.ie. Connoisseurs love this relaxing place where you can order your coffee black, milk-based, with syrup, or as a cocktail. Peruse papers and books while enjoying the barista's choice or the lounge blend along with a slice of decadent cake. Mon–Sat 9.30am–5pm.

11

**Coffey's Pastry Case** Bridge St ☎ 071 962 0929. A buzzy daytime café in a central location for coffee, muffins, scones, vegetarian pizza, salads and light bites; the seating upstairs is ideal for river gazing. Daily 8am–7pm.

**The Cottage Restaurant** Jamestown, 4km southeast of Carrick ☎ 071 962 5933, ⊛ cottagerestaurant.ie. Nicely located beside the river, this is one of the classiest restaurants in the area. The two-course midweek set menu (Wed & Thurs is €25; otherwise mains, which might include duck breast, loin of lamb or glazed chicken, average €21. Thurs–Sun 6–10pm, Sun noon–4pm.

★ **The Oarsman** Bridge St ☎ 071 962 1733, ⊛ the oarsman.com. Imaginative, modern Irish cuisine such as farmhouse pork or sea trout for half the price you'd pay in Dublin (around €40 for three courses plus wine). Try some of their local craft beers including Sunburnt Red, Howling Gale Ale or Knock me down Porter. Mon–Thurs 11.30am– 11.30pm, Fri & Sat till 12.30am.

### DRINKING

**Anderson's Thatched Pub** 5km south of Carrick on the R368 Elphin road ☎ 087 228 3288, ⊛ andersonspub. com. An inviting bar with a pedigree stretching back to 1734. Sessions are held most nights from June to Aug (rest of the year Wed & Sat). Mon–Thurs & Sun 8–11.30pm, Fri & Sat 8pm–12.30am.

**The Barrel Store** Bridge St ☎ 071 962 6252, ⊛ thebarrel store.ie. Styling itself as a craft beer haven, cocktail den and wine haunt, this spacious bar stocks Carraig pale ales such as Grand Soft Day and Shepherd's Delight, as well as the famed Gunpowder gin from Drumshanbo. Meanwhile bar bites such as cured meat platters, mixed cheeses, or pizzas can be ordered from the Italian restaurant across the road so you don't have to leave your seat. Live music at the weekend. Mon–Thurs 4–11.30pm, Fri & Sat noon–12.30am, Sun 12.30–11pm.

# Drumshanbo and Lough Allen

Some 12km north of Carrick, **DRUMSHANBO** is a lively village with a strong musical tradition at the tip of **Lough Allen**'s southern shore. In the third week of July, the seven-day Joe Mooney Summer School (⊛ joemooneysummerschool.com) is held here, offering **traditional music** classes and concerts. At the beginning of June the village also hosts the **An Tostal Festival** (⊛ antostalfestival.ie) with a variety of music.

From Drumshanbo roads lead north along both eastern and western shores of **Lough Allen**. The western route crosses into Roscommon and skirts the Arigna Mountains (see page 407) while its alternative to the east heads up through bleak flatlands below Slieve Anierin. The waymarked 48km **Leitrim Way** (map available from local tourist offices) follows Lough Allen's shoreline before taking in higher ground on its way to the remote village of **Dowra**, the starting point for the **Cavan Way** (see page 159).

### Sliabh an Iarainn Visitor Centre

Acres Lake on the Carrick-on-Shannon road, on the outskirts of Drumshanbo but within the limits of the town • May to Oct Mon–Fri 9am–5pm • ⊛ leitrimtourism.com

The **Sliabh an Iarainn Visitors Centre** is an excellent introduction to the area. Exhibitions feature topography and geology as well as musical heritage and scenic attractions. Audiovisuals take you on a local history journey, focusing on transport and industry. A **Musicians' Corner** showcases the flautist John McKenna and other renowned Leitrim musicians; you can listen to tracks featuring the different styles of the area's music.

### ARRIVAL AND GETTING AROUND DRUMSHANBO

**By bus** Buses pick up and drop off opposite the library in the main street.

Destinations Ballinamore (Fri & Sat 1 daily; 25min); Carrick-on-Shannon (Sat 1; 25min); Dowra (Sat 1; 25min); Keadue (Fri 1; 15min); Sligo (Fri 1, Sat 2; 1hr 15min–1hr 40min).

**By bike** Bike rental is available at Moran's on Convent Avenue (⊛ moransbikeshop.ie).

### ACTIVITIES

**Lough Allen Adventure Centre** Ballinaglera, 13km north of Drumshanbo ⊛ loughallenadventure.ie. Offers a variety of activities, such as wind-surfing, kayaking and hill-walking.

## ACCOMMODATION AND EATING

**Fraoch Ban** 1km up the Dowra road ☎071 964 1260. This comfortable modern bungalow surveying the lake makes an ideal location for walking, cycling or driving around the serene north Leitrim countryside Closed Nov– March. €80

**Henry's Haven** Convent Ave ☎071 964 1805. The best place in the area for good-value bar meals starting from around €10.50 for main courses. Food served daily to

9pm; bar Mon–Thurs 10.30am–11.30pm, Fri & Sat till 12.30am, Sun noon–11.30pm.

**Lough Allen Hotel & Spa** ☎071 964 0100, ⓦlough allenhotel.com. Don't be put off by the approach road; the setting is a stunning location beside Lough Allen. Elegantly furnished bedrooms and spectacular suites await you, as well as a spa, fitness centre and pool. €159

## East from Drumshanbo

**KESHCARRIGAN**, about 8km east of Drumshanbo on the Shannon–Erne Waterway, is worth a brief stop for its amiable bars. **FENAGH**, 6km east, was once an important ecclesiastical centre, founded by St Caillin in the sixth century. The area's history is recounted in the **Heritage Centre** (Mon–Fri 10am–5.30pm; free; ☎071 964 5590, ⓦfenagh.com), which also has a café. **BALLINAMORE**, 5km northeast of Fenagh, is a focus for **cruising** on the Shannon–Erne Waterway, with barges available from Riversdale Holidays (☎071 964 4122, ⓦriversdaleholidays.com; €650–1540 per week).

11

## ACCOMMODATION AND EATING                                  EAST FROM DRUMSHANBO

**The Canal Stop** Main St, Keshcarrigan ☎071 964 2252. Beside Ballyconnell canal and known locally as *Gerties*, this is an ideal place to tuck into hearty meals at reasonable prices. The menu includes steak, chicken and lasagne; main courses from €12. Food served Fri & Sat 6–9pm, Sun 1–8pm; bar Mon–Thurs 11am–11.30pm, Fri & Sat till 12.30am, Sun noon–11pm.

**The Commercial and Tourist Hotel** High St, Ballinamore ☎071 964 4675, ⓦhotelcommerical.

com. A good base to explore the Erne–Shannon Waterway and surrounding countryside, with spacious, comfortable rooms. €85

★ **The Old Rectory** Fenagh Glebe, Ballinamore ☎071 964 4089, ⓦtheoldrectoryireland.com. A child-friendly Georgian house (dating from 1827) on a working farm with well-kept en-suite period rooms (and some self-catering apartments), brilliant breakfasts, canoes and bikes for rent, and views of Fenagh Lough from the grounds. €110

# Boyle and around

Rising gently above its own namesake river, engaging **BOYLE** is a relaxed town with congenial bars, a couple of sites of noteworthy historical interest and a lively arts festival. It also makes an ideal base for exploring not only Roscommon's northern attractions, such as **Lough Key Forest Park**, but neighbouring Leitrim and South Sligo too. The town hosts several summer **festivals**, of which the biggest is the Boyle Arts Festival (ⓦboylearts.com) at the end of July with a broad-ranging programme of drama, concerts, exhibitions and lectures. Some 3km north of Boyle, overlooking the N4 Sligo–Dublin road where it skirts the Curlew Mountains, stands an intriguing metal **sculpture** representing Gaelic chieftain Red Hugh O'Donnell. Known locally as "the ass in the pass", artist Maurice Harron's work marks the site of the Battle of the Curleius between Irish and English forces in 1599.

### Brief history

Boyle's origins lie in the establishment of a **Cistercian monastery** in 1161, but as it was situated on an important trading route, the abbey became embroiled in numerous internecine and Irish–English skirmishes and was sacked on a number of occasions. It lingered on for several decades after the Dissolution – its last abbot was executed in 1584 for refusing to disavow allegiance to Rome – and from 1599 until the end of the eighteenth century it was used as a barracks by the English and known as Boyle Castle. In 1603 the building passed into the hands of Sir John King and remained in the family's possession until 1892. It was Staffordshire-born King who transformed Boyle, constructing a grand **mansion** to the west of the abbey and an avenue (now the town's main street) leading up to it. At the same time he began to amass thousands of acres of land, which would eventually become the largest estate in County Roscommon, **Rockingham**.

## Boyle Abbey

Less than 1km off the N4 Dublin–Sligo Rd • April–Sept daily 10am–5pm • €5; Heritage Card • ☎ 071 966 4817, ⓦ heritageireland.ie

It's easy to find your way around Boyle, and the town's two major attractions are well signposted from the centre. The first of these is **Boyle Abbey**, consecrated in 1218, whose alluring remains abut the river on the eastern side of town. Despite various onslaughts during the course of its history, it remains perhaps the finest surviving Cistercian church in Ireland and its sixty-year building process bears traces of both the Romanesque and the then newly arrived Gothic styles of architecture. The abbey's ruins are entered via its gatehouse, which contains an **exhibition** on the foundation's history and a model of how it once might have looked. Inside the nave the transition from Romanesque to Gothic is neatly contrasted by windows and arches, circular facing pointed. Some of the capitals bear intriguing secular decorations – one features little figures standing between trees and clutching the branches somewhat stiffly – while high on the western wall is a carving of a **Sheila-na-Gig** (see page 616).

## King House

Military Rd • April–Sept Mon–Sat 11am–5pm, plus July & Aug Sun 11–4pm • €5; Heritage Island • ☎ 071 916 3242, ⓦ visitkinghouse.ie • 1hr weekday guided tours available

The original seat of the King family was destroyed by fire, but its replacement, **King House**, is well worth visiting. This impressive stone mansion was built around 1730 and sold to the War Office when the Kings moved to Rockingham, becoming the barracks for the Connaught Rangers from 1788 until 1922. The Irish Army then occupied the building until the 1940s, after which it passed into private hands, before falling into dereliction. Thoroughly restored, its ground floor now houses Boyle's **Civic Art Gallery**, largely displaying works by local painters, while upper storeys employ interactive high-tech gadgetry to retell the story of the house and the family who built it, with child-oriented exhibits. The story of Henry's son Edward, who built Rockingham, is wittily recounted in one exhibit, "How to become an earl in six easy stages", describing how he rose to become Earl of Kingston in 1768. One section of the house is devoted to the Connaught Rangers and recalls their role in various military campaigns.

## Lough Key Forest and Activity Park

Just off the N4, 3km east of Boyle • **Lough Key Experience** March–May, Sept & Oct daily 10am–6pm; July & Aug daily 10am–7pm; Nov–Feb Fri–Sun 10am–6pm; last admission 1hr before closing • €8; parking €4 (parking free if spending €20 or more on activities or in the restaurant); Heritage Island • ☎ 071 967 3122, ⓦ loughkey.ie • **Boat trips** (June–Aug) €15, rowing boat hire €30/hr (☎ 086 084 6849, ⓦ loughkeyboats.com)

Occupying what was once the focal area of the Kings' Rockingham estate (the demesne was abandoned by the family in 1957 after their mansion was destroyed by fire), **Lough Key Forest and Activity Park** offers a number of signposted **walking trails** – ranging from easy to strenuous – around the estate, and you can take a **boat trip** out on the lake, or rent a rowing boat during the summer months. Though almost all the park's woodland and trails remain unsullied, a massive commercial revamp has restricted access to certain areas, focal to which is the **Visitor Centre** at the end of a driveway 2km from the park's Gothic gateway on the N4. It's here that you can buy tickets to the **Lough Key Experience** and pick up the headset that provides a guided commentary to a walking trail around a segment of the park. The route takes you through two subterranean **servants' tunnels** that survived the mansion's fire, as well as to the top of the five-storey **Moylurg viewing tower**. From here, there are splendid vistas of the lake and its numerous islands, including **Trinity Island**, which was once the site of a Cistercian foundation and a medieval castle. The trail concludes with the 300m-long **Tree Canopy Walk** whose timber-and-steel construction rises steadily to a 9m-high view of the park from the treetops.

### Adventure Play Kingdom, Boda Borg and other activities

**Adventure Play Kingdom** Last admission 1hr before closing • €5 • **Boda Borg** Last admission 2hr before closing; minimum of three participants • €18

Near the visitor centre there's the children's outdoor **Adventure Play Kingdom** and **Boda Borg**, a Swedish-designed two-storey puzzle-house which relies upon teamwork to solve various, instruction-less problems. Other attractions include a zipwire, electric bike trails and woodland segways.

**11**

### ARRIVAL AND INFORMATION

### BOYLE

**By train** Boyle's train station (☎ 071 966 2027) is 200m south of the centre, just off Elphin St. All services operate Mon–Sat 7 times daily, Sun 6.

Destinations Ballymote (15min); Carrick-on-Shannon (15min); Dublin (2hr 35min); Mullingar (1hr 25min); Sligo (35min).

**By bus** Buses set down on Carrick Rd.

Destinations Ballymote (Mon, Wed & Sat 1 daily; 30min);

Carrick-on-Shannon (5–6 daily; 15min); Dublin (5–6 daily; 3hr); Gurteen (Thurs 2; 25min); Riverstown (Thurs & Fri 1 daily; 35min); Sligo (5–7 daily; 40min); Strokestown (Mon–Sat 1 daily; 40min).

**Tourist office** The Una Bhán tourist office (daily 9am–6pm; ☎ 071 966 3033, ⓦ unabhan.ie) is just by the entrance to King House and stocks maps and other information on the area.

### ACCOMMODATION AND EATING

**Abbey House** ☎ 071 966 2385, ⓦ abbeyhouse.net. In the abbey's shadow is this delightful Victorian structure, with five spacious and well-furnished en-suite rooms. Visitors are greeted on arrival with tea or coffee and home-baked cakes, and the mature gardens are pleasant for a stroll. Closed Nov–Feb. **€70**

**King House Tea Rooms** ☎ 087 643 0326, ⓦ kingshouse tearooms.ie. Set within the grounds of King House, this café serves wholesome lunches (prices average €9.50). Poached eggs and bacon is the signature dish, but you'll also find salads and vegetarian options such as spinach and goat's cheese tart. Mon–Sat 8.30am–5pm, Sun 10am–4pm.

**Kate Lavin's** Patrick St. All dark oak panelling and wooden benches, this old-style bar is a great place to meet the locals. Its strength is its simplicity: no television or pool table, but a glow from the turf fire and friendly welcome from the owners. The Guinness has a "short run" because it comes from underneath the stairs. Fri, Sat & Sun 6–11.30pm.

★ **Lough Key House** 5km from Boyle ☎ 071 966 2161, ⓦ loughkeyhouse.com. An exquisite Georgian house set in beautiful grounds adjacent to the main entrance to Lough Key Forest Park (see page 406). Sumptuous breakfasts are served by the affable owners and bedrooms have period features and four-posters. **€98**

# The Arigna Mountains

The far north of County Roscommon stretches up to Lough Allen where gentle farmland ascends to the moors and lakes of the **Arigna Mountains**. Albeit small-scale, this was once one of the few areas of Ireland to play a role in the Industrial Revolution, based first on **iron** extraction for a fifty-year period after 1788 – the local ironworks forged pikes in preparation for the 1798 Rebellion – and, subsequently, **coal**, which was worked here until 1990. The **Arigna Miners Way** is a waymarked 120km walking trail through the area, linking up with both the Leitrim Way and a historical trail taking in Boyle and parts of Sligo.

## Keadue

**KEADUE**, 12km northeast of Boyle, is an attractive village of traditional cottages, stone walls and well-kept gardens. It is associated with the blind harper Turlough O'Carolan (see page 588), whose grave lies by the ruins of Kilronan Abbey, just out on the Sligo road. The musician is commemorated at the **O'Carolan Heritage Park**, a well-kept public park in the heart of the village with, as its centrepiece, a bronze replica of one of his harps. Keadue also hosts a harp and traditional music festival (Ⓦocarolanharpfestival. ie).

### ARRIVAL AND ACCOMMODATION            KEADUE

**By bus** Keadue is served by a weekly bus service on Friday from/to Drumshanbo (20min) and Sligo (50min).

**Harp & Shamrock B&B** Main St ⊕071 964 7288, Ⓦharpandshamrock.net. A delightful combination of bar, beer garden, grocery shop and accommodation all rolled into one friendly service. None of the seven rooms is en-suite but there are three separate bathrooms along the corridor. €60

**Kilronan Castle Hotel** 2km down the Ballyfarnon road ⊕071 961 8000, Ⓦkilronancastle.ie. This luxury hotel set in a tranquil parkland estate features a fine spa and the *Douglas Hyde* restaurant, where mains might include fillet of dry-aged beef, rack of Irish lamb or roast monkfish. €189

## Arigna Mining Experience

Arigna Hall, 2 km north of Arigna • Daily 10am–6pm (last tour 5pm) • €13; Heritage Island • Ⓦarignaminingexperience.ie

From the dusty village of **Arigna** itself, a little further north, a winding lane leads a couple of kilometres upwards, past a smokeless fuel plant, to the **Arigna Mining Experience**. Perched high on a hilltop and commanding stunning views of Lough Allen, this brilliantly designed and enthralling museum is based around one of the last working pits in the area. The history of local coal mining is documented in the reception area, but, once equipped with a hard hat, it's the forty-minute **tours** of the mine that are most informative and thought-provoking. Led by ex-miners, these are rich in anecdote and thoroughly explore both the nature of the industry and the atrocious and exploitative working conditions the miners endured – the tunnels are dark and foreboding, and the sound of dripping water and footsteps is amplified by the acoustics.

# Strokestown and around

The impressively planned settlement of **STROKESTOWN**, with its wide, tree-lined mall, embodies Ireland's troubled history in microcosm. It is the ideal base from which to delve into the historic riches of this part of south Roscommon, an area of rolling agricultural land. At the western end of Strokestown's mall sits an octagonal church, now housing the **County Roscommon Heritage and Genealogy Company** (Mon–Fri 2.30–4.30pm; ⊕071 963 3380, Ⓦroscommonroots.com), which conducts research for anyone seeking to trace their Roscommon roots; the eastern end of the mall terminates in a three-arched gateway, marking the entrance to Mahon's massive estate.

### Brief history

The land on which Strokestown lies, and the surrounding area, known as **Corca Achlann**, belonged for more than a thousand years to the MacBranan clan, underlords of the powerful O'Connor kings who ruled Connacht, until dispossessed by Cromwell in the 1650s. Subsequently, part of their territory was granted by Charles II to Nicholas Mahon, whose kin later amassed more than thirty thousand acres for their huge estate, second only in size to Rockingham (see page 406) in Roscommon, becoming one of the great landed families of Ireland in the process. In the early nineteenth century, his descendant Lieutenant-General Thomas Mahon, Second Lord Hartland, requiring a grandiose symbol reflecting the extent of his property, determined to have constructed a **central avenue** wider than Vienna's Ringstrasse.

# Strokestown Park House

Bottom of Bawn St, 150m east of the crossroads in Strokestown • Mid-March to Oct daily 10.30am–5.30pm; house tours April–Oct daily at noon, 2.30pm & 4pm, Nov–March at 2.30pm only • House, Famine museum and gardens €9 each, €13.50 for all three; Heritage Island • 📞 071 963 3013, 🌐 strokestownpark.ie

The magnificent Georgian **Strokestown Park House** was the seat of the Mahon family from its completion in 1696 for almost three hundred years. This huge Palladian mansion originally consisted of a two-storey central block and basement until the 1740s when Thomas Mahon, MP for Roscommon, hired the architect Richard Castle to construct a third storey and two extra wings. Mahon's son, Maurice (who became the First Lord Hartland in 1800), made subsequent additions including the library and many decorative features, such as cornices and chimneypieces, while the Second Lord Hartland added the porch and its huge pilasters. The house remained in Mahon ownership until 1979 when it was sold, along with its contents, to a local garage owner who undertook restoration work and opened it to the public in 1987.

Few Irish "big houses" retain their original owners' property (in this case ranging from furniture to children's toys), which is a vital factor in making the **guided tours** so entertaining. The main hall features early eighteenth-century wood panelling, while the spacious dining room, decorated in rich rose-pink damask wallpaper, is equipped with furniture from the early 1800s and a mammoth turf-bucket. The library was originally a ballroom – hence the bowed space at one end, which housed musicians – and has glorious Chippendale bookcases, while the smoking room was converted into a laboratory and photographic darkroom by Henry Pakenham-Mahon in the 1890s. The north wing includes a superb kitchen, replete with spits and ovens, and a balustraded gallery, the only surviving example in Ireland of a kind favoured by Castle, from which the housekeeper could keep an eagle eye on business down below and, according to Strokestown legend, drop menus for the week's meals down to the cook.

## National Irish Famine Museum

Among the property passed on by the Mahons were numerous documents and letters relating to the family's role in relation to the Great Famine of 1845–51. The house's former stables – marvellously vaulted buildings in their own right – house an often chilling and stimulating **museum** detailing the Famine's effects upon the Mahons' tenants and its wider impact across Ireland. The intricate, informative displays and films focus on the concatenation of factors in Ireland – the growth of the rural population, the conacre system of agricultural tenancy, the reliance on the potato crop and the spread of the potato blight – that combined with Britain's economic policy of non-interference to have such a devastating effect on human life. Exhibits also highlight the role in local events of **Major Denis Mahon**, who had inherited the Strokestown estate after the death of the third and last Lord Hartland in 1845. The malevolent major not only evicted the majority of his tenants, but contracted dangerously unseaworthy vessels (the infamous coffin ships) to transport some of them in atrocious conditions to North America. The displays document contemporary newspaper reports condemning his actions and, in 1847, his assassination by vengeful ex-tenants.

**ARRIVAL AND DEPARTURE**                                                   **STROKESTOWN**

**By bus** The bus stop is 10m from the *Percy French Hotel* in Bridge St. | Destinations Boyle (1 daily; 40min); Dublin (6 daily; 2hr 25min); Frenchpark (7–8 daily; 25min); Sligo (Mon–Sat 1

> ## DOUGLAS HYDE
>
> Born in Castlerea, 13km south of Frenchpark, to Anglo-Irish Ascendancy stock, **Douglas Hyde** (1860–1949) learnt Irish at an early age and developed a lifelong interest in the nation's rich vernacular tradition and folklore. After attending Trinity College, he became professor of **Modern Irish Language and Literature** at the National University of Ireland and produced numerous articles, essays and reviews in Irish, as well as collaborating on a number of Irish-language plays with Lady Gregory (see page 346). Hyde travelled the country widely, gathering material, much of which was transcribed in collections such as the highly influential *Love Songs of Connaught*. In 1893, he was a co-founder of the **Gaelic League**, which aimed to enhance Irish culture via a revival of musical and linguistic traditions, though Hyde later became concerned by the League's increasing links with the Independence movement and resigned as its president in 1915. Elected to the Irish Senate in 1925, he retired from public life in 1932 until he was appointed the country's first **president** in 1938.

11

daily; 1hr); Tulsk (6–7 daily; 15min).

### ACCOMMODATION AND EATING

**Hanly's** Bridge St ☎071 963 3073. This venerable institution is a great place to soak up some stories from the locals. It hosts traditional music sessions on the first Thursday of each month. Daily 6–11.30pm.

**Percy French Hotel** Bridge St ☎071 963 3300,

ⓦ thepercyfrenchhotel.com. Lively social hub with eighteen pleasant en-suite rooms and a decent bar. Meals are available in the bar – carvery roasts are popular – throughout the day up to 9pm. €105

## Douglas Hyde Interpretive Centre

Frenchpark, 26km northwest of Strokestown • Open by appointment May–Sept • Free • ☎087 782 3751

A forty-minute drive from Strokestown lies the village of **Frenchpark**, where the former Church of Ireland parish church is home to the **Douglas Hyde Interpretive Centre**. The centre recounts the life of **Douglas Hyde** (see box), one of the key figures in the Irish cultural revival, with informative displays and an entertaining video. Note that it is essential to phone in advance to gain admission to the centre.

## Tulsk

Located around the village of **TULSK**, 15km southeast of Frenchpark, is **Rathcroghan**, a rich array of earthworks, ring forts, standing stones and caves betokening one of Ireland's major mythological areas. According to *The Annals of the Four Masters* (see page 421) it was here that Medb, the warrior queen and earth goddess who features heavily in the *Táin Bó Cúailnge* (see page 152), sited her palace Cruachan, the location of the epic's opening and gory conclusion.

### Rathcroghan Visitor Centre

Just west of the crossroads in Tulsk • Mon–Sat 9am–5pm; tours Mon–Fri at noon (plus May–Aug 2pm) • €12 combined tour price • ☎071 963 9268, ⓦ rathcroghan.ie

Before visiting the monuments, it's wise to head for the **Rathcroghan Visitor Centre**, where audiovisuals bring the history of the site to life: you'll see a reconstruction of the **Oweynagat** ("the cave of the cats"), which supposedly provided the entrance to the otherworld. A highlight is the collection of ten black-and-white facsimile illustrations of the *Táin*, drawn by the Irish artist Louis le Brocquy, who died in 2012.

11

# Donegal

SLIEVE LEAGUE

# Donegal

Second in size only to County Cork, County Donegal has unquestionably the richest scenery in the whole of Ireland, featuring a spectacular 300km coastline – an intoxicating run of headlands, promontories and peninsulas rising to the highest sea-cliffs in Europe. Perhaps the most satisfying landscape is that of northern Donegal, not least the Rosguill and Inishowen peninsulas, while the interior region around Errigal Mountain, Lough Beagh and Lough Gartan merits an extended visit. Elsewhere, Donegal manifests a wonderful, and often wonderfully bleak, terrain of glens, rivers and bogland hills.

Donegal's original name was *Tír Chonaill*, which translates as "the land of Conal"; Chonaill was one of the twelve sons of Niall of the Nine Hostages, reputed to have ruled Ireland in the fifth century. After the Flight of the Earls in 1607 (see page 572), the English changed the name to that of their main garrison *Dún na nGall* ("fort of the foreigners"), which has a certain irony, because Donegal always eluded the grip of English power thanks to its wild and infertile terrain. Donegal is the most northerly part of Ireland, which confuses some into believing that it is part of Northern Ireland. It never actually has been, since in 1922, at the time of Partition, the Unionists believed that Donegal's Catholic population would threaten the stability of the new statelet by voting the county and the whole of the North back into the Republic.

Aside from the aforementioned places, Donegal's best-known destinations are the **Glencolmcille Peninsula** and around **Ardara** and **Glenties** in the southern part of the county, while other noteworthy areas are **the Rosses** and **Gweedore**, which are reminiscent of the more barren stretches of Connemara and make up the strongest Irish-speaking districts (*gaeltacht*) in the county.

## GETTING AROUND  DONEGAL

**By bus** The county has an extensive network of public and private bus services, with the sporadically interesting towns of Letterkenny and Donegal serving as its major transport hubs. However, there are limited services to some areas, especially outside high season.

**By car** You'll need your own transport to reach some outlying attractions, such as Glenveagh and parts of the Rosguill, Fanad and Inishowen peninsulas.

### THE DONEGAL CYCLE ROUTE

A 200km scenic cycle route which snakes around the Donegal coastline, the **DCR** is the best way to explore the area by bike. Taking in some of the county's most spectacular landscapes, it has been broken down into fourteen manageable stages. Although it officially starts in Newtowncunningham, it's more straightforward to start in **Letterkenny** and finish in **Donegal town**. The route is well signposted throughout, but as this is Donegal, expect some steep climbs and narrow roads where extra care should be taken. For downloadable **maps** and route-planning, visit ⓦ donegalcycleroute.com.

### BIKE RENTALS AND REPAIRS

**The Bike Stop** Bundoran ⓣ 085 248 8317, ⓦ the bikestop.ie.
**Cycle Inishowen** Carndonagh ⓣ 087 9722 532, ⓦ cycleinishowen.com.
**Don Byrne Bikes** Ardara ⓣ 074 9541 658, ⓦ don

byrnebikes.com.
**Ireland by Bike** Carrick ⓣ 087 2118 638, ⓦ ireland bybike.com.
**LK Bikes** Letterkenny ⓣ 074 9126 728, ⓦ lkbikes. com.

BUNBEG

# Highlights

**❶ Slieve League** No visit to Donegal would be complete without a walk along the top of this mountain's awesome sea-cliffs. See page 426

**❷ Teach Húdaí Beag's pub** Unquestionably one of the best traditional music sessions in Ireland takes place here in the small village of Bunbeg on Monday nights. See page 433

**❸ Tory Island** Bleak, barren, wet and windy – why would anyone choose to live here? Take a trip and discover a thriving local culture and a world quite different from the mainland. See page 433

**❹ Glebe House** Home of the late artist Derek Hill, Glebe House contains some of the most remarkable modern art in Ireland. See page 437

**❺ The Grianán Ailigh** This restored, circular stone fort commands unbeatable panoramic views of Donegal from its hilltop setting. See page 446

**❻ Malin Head** Ireland's most northerly point offers dramatic seascapes and, thanks to a lack of visitors, wonderfully unspoilt landscapes too. See page 449

**HIGHLIGHTS ARE MARKED ON THE MAP ON PAGE 416**

# DONEGAL

**ATLANTIC OCEAN**

N

Tory Island
West Town  East Town  **3**

Tory Sound

Horn Head

Inishbofin

Sheep haven Ba

Marble Hill Strand

Dunfanaghy

Bloody Foreland

Magheroarty  Falcarragh

Gortahork  Creeslough

Gola Island  Derrybeg

Muckish Mountain

Donegal Airport  Bunbeg  **2**

**GWEEDORE**

N56

Rosses Bay  Rannafast  Errigal Mountain (752m)

Meenaleck  Crolly  R251  Lough Beagh

Torneady Point  Lough Nacung  **Glenveagh Castle**

Arranmore Island  Upper Rosses  Annagry  Money Beg  Poisoned Glen  **Glebe House**

Leabgarrow  Burtonport  **DERRYVEAGH MOUNTAINS**  Lough Gartan  Ch

Lower Rosses

Rutland Island  Slieve Snaght (683m)  R250

Inishfree Upper  Dungloe

Crohy Head  N56  Doocharry  Ulster Way

R254  **DONEGAL**

Gweebarra Bay  Fintown  Lough Finn

Portnoo  Narin  Lettermacaward

Dawros Head  Kilclooney  R253

Rosbeg  **Kilclooney Dolmen**

Glenties  **BLUE STACK MOUNTAINS**

Maghera  **Assarancagh Waterfall**  Atdara  N56

Port  R263  N1

Glen Head  Glengesh Pass  Lough Eske

Glen Bay  Glencolmcille

Malin Bay  Malinmore

Malinbeg  **SLIEVE LEAGUE**  **1**  Carrick

**Bunglass Cliffs**  Teelin  Kilcar  Killybegs  Dunkineely  Donegal

Carrigan Head  Inver Bay  Lough Derg

Muckros Head

St. John's Point

Rossnowlagh

**Donegal Bay**

Creevy

Ballyshannon

Bundoran  Belleek

Mullaghmore Head  N15  N15

0  20
kilometres

Malin Head
6

Trá na Rossan
Bay

Fanad Head

Dunaff
Head

Pollan
Bay

Doagh
Isle

Culdaff
Bay

Malin

Culdaff

Rosguill
Peninsula

Downings

Portsalon

Dunree
Head

Clonmany

Ballyliffin

Carndonagh

R238

Kinnagoe
Bay

Inishowen
Head

Carrigart

Mamore
Gap

R244

Inishowen

Greencastle

Magilligan
Point

Glen

Kilmacrennan

Rock of
Doon

N56

Rathmullan

Ramelton

R245

R247

Dunree
Head

Lough Swilly

Ferry

Inch
Island

Buncrana

Fahan

Slieve Snaght
(615m)

Gráinne's
Gap

Moville

R238

Ferry

Lough
Foyle

Burnfoot

Burt

A2

Letterkenny

N13

N13

Grianán
Ailigh
(Stone Fort)
5

Derry

A6

N14

Raphoe

Cavanacor
House

A5

N56

Beltany
Stone
Circle

Lifford

Strabane

R52

N15

A505

on
d

Pettigo

Lower
Lough
Erne

A35

Omagh

A5

A32

**HIGHLIGHTS**
1 Slieve League
2 Teach Húdaí Beag's pub
3 Tory Island
4 Glebe House
5 The Grianán Ailigh
6 Malin Head

# South Donegal

Entered via the N15 from Sligo (which now largely bypasses the most scenic spots), **south Donegal** might lack the wildness characteristic of much of Donegal's coastline, but the area still has some marvellous beaches, especially at **Bundoran** and **Rossnowlagh**, both popular surfing spots, while **Ballyshannon** is an attractive hillside town situated at the mouth of the River Erne. Further north, **Donegal town** has a pleasant bayside setting and remains of a notable castle, while to its north and southeast respectively lie graceful **Lough Eske** and **Lough Derg**, a major site for Catholic pilgrimage.

## Bundoran

Once described by an Irish newspaper as like "the back streets of Las Vegas only with cheaper hookers", **BUNDORAN** isn't quite that bad, but it's hard to avoid disappointment if the town is your first sight of Donegal. Lying at the county's southern extreme, this popular, though intermittently tacky, seaside resort offers little indication of the pleasures that lie beyond. Its 5km of Blue Flag **beaches, however,** are among the finest in the country, and are a real pull for surfers of all abilities.

The tiny River Doran separates the more genteel **West End** from the **East End**, with its down-at-heel Main Street and a headland dominated by a **golf course**. Bundoran's chief attraction is the lovely golden-sanded **Tullan Strand**, a bracing stroll along the coastal promenade from the northern end of the town beach. The walk takes in rock formations known as the **Fairy Bridge** and the **Puffing Hole**, with the Atlantic thundering below and appetizing views across to the much more rewarding Glencolmcille Peninsula.

### ARRIVAL AND DEPARTURE BUNDORAN

**By bus** Buses stop at various points along Main St. Destinations Ballyshannon (Mon–Sat 10 daily; 10min); Donegal town (6–7 daily; 30min); Sligo (Mon–Sat 10 daily; 35–50min).

### INFORMATION AND ACTIVITIES

**Tourist office** The tourist office is by the bridge on Main St (Mon–Fri 9.30am–5pm, Sat & Sun 11am–5pm; ☎071 984 1350, ⓦdiscoverbundoran.com).
**Surfing** Tullan Strand and Rossnowlagh beach are exciting surfing spots, and tuition is available from Bundoran Surf Co., Main St (☎071 984 1968, ⓦbundoransurfco.com), Surfworld, Main St (☎071 984 1223, ⓦsurfworld.ie), and Donegal Adventure Centre, Bayview Ave (☎071 984 2418, ⓦdonegaladventurecentre.net); the latter also offers kayaking and canoeing.

### ACCOMMODATION AND EATING

**Great Northern Hotel** On the headland east of town ☎071 984 1204, ⓦgreatnorthernhotel.com. Prominently sited, this huge hotel adjoining the fabulous Bundoran golf course has glorious views from just about every room; facilities include a spa and gym. €120
**Maddens Bridge Bar** West End, near the Protestant Church ☎071 984 2050, ⓦmaddensbridgebar.com. Wonderful, woody bar cluttered with hanging pots, jars, boots and suchlike. Heading upstairs to the restaurant, grab a window seat and soak up the sparkling ocean views while tucking into meaty dishes like Lough Erne lamb shank (€14.95) and beef and Guinness casserole (€11.75). Mon–Fri 8am–11.30pm, Sat 10.30am–midnight, Sun 11am–11.30pm.

## Ballyshannon

The lively town of **BALLYSHANNON**, 6km north of Bundoran, was the site of a major battle in 1591 when Hugh Roe O'Donnell saw off the besieging English army, but nowadays its hilly streets become most animated during several upbeat festivals (see box).

---

**BALLYSHANNON FESTIVALS**

The town's main event is the **Folk Festival** (ⓦballyshannonfolkfestival.com) over the first weekend in August, featuring major Irish and international musicians. Sticking with the musical theme, the **Rory Gallagher International Festival** (ⓦrorygallagherfestival.com) at the beginning of June pays homage to the local guitar legend, with concerts on several stages throughout town. Lastly, in November, the **Allingham Festival** (ⓦallinghamfestival.com) brings to life the works of the native poet, through storytelling, screenings and workshops.

---

## St Anne's Church

Upper Main St • ☎ 074 9734025

Ballyshannon's main arteries form a wishbone leading up the town's steep northern slope, and signposted near the top of the left-hand branch is **St Anne's Church** and graveyard, built on the site of the ancient palace of Mullaghanshee. A simple marble slab, inscribed with the word "poet", lies left of the church, marking the burial place of locally born **William Allingham** (1824–89). His first volume, *Poems* (1850), includes his best-known work, *The Fairies* ("Up the airy mountain/Down the rushy glen/We daren't go a-hunting/For fear of little men…"). Such verse attracted him to the Pre-Raphaelites – another work, *Day and Night Songs*, was illustrated by Rossetti and Millais – before Allingham moved on to the more serious poetic subject of his homeland. His posthumously published *Diary* recounts his friendships with literary contemporaries, most notably Tennyson.

## Ballyshannon Museum

Slevins Department Store, Market Yard • Mon–Sat 10am–6pm • Free • ☎ 087 193 7166

To gain further insight into the history of the town – it lays claim to being Ireland's oldest – pop your head into the **Ballyshannon Museum**, peculiarly located on the top floor of the local department store (past the beds). In truth, it's a curiously mixed bag, with exhibits ranging from a cannonball from the Battle of Ballyshannon and wreckage retrieved from one of the three ships from the Spanish Armada sunk in the waters hereabouts, to some personal effects belonging to local notables William Allingham (first editions, writing box and ink well) and rock star Rory Gallagher, who died in 1995 (see box).

**12**

### ARRIVAL AND DEPARTURE                                    BALLYSHANNON

**By bus** Buses drop off on, and depart from, the bottom of Main St, near the bridge.
Destinations Belleek (9 daily; 10min); Bundoran (Mon–Sat 10 daily; 10min); Donegal town (6–7 daily; 25min); Sligo (Mon–Sat 10 daily; 45min–1hr).

### ACCOMMODATION AND EATING

**Dorrian's Imperial Hotel** Main St ☎071 985 1147, ⓦdorriansimperialhotel.com. Handsome eighteenth-century building with warm and comfortable, if agreeably old-fashioned, rooms and public spaces, plus a decent bar and restaurant; it's fairly pricey, mind. **€130**

**Elmbrook** East Port ☎071 985 2615, ⓔelmbrook bandb@eircom.net. Across the river and over the round-about, this friendly B&B offers four tidily furnished en-suite rooms, and a comfy lounge for guests to enjoy, and you'll get a home-baked treat or two as well. Closed Nov–Feb. **€70**

**Lakeside Caravan and Camping** Off the R230 Belleek Rd ☎071 985 2822, ⓦlakesidecaravanandcamping. com. Superb lakeside campsite with a full complement of facilities including modern shower blocks, laundry, games room plus a kids' playground. Canoe rental available too. Closed Nov to early March. **€20**

**Nirvana** The Mall ☎071 982 2369. Sharp-looking restaurant-cum-wine-bar, serving comfort-food lunches and more extravagant evening meals like pan-fried duck breast with figs and a Cointreau reduction (€22.50). Mon–Sat 5.30–9.30pm, Sun 12.30–9pm.

★**The Thatch** Bishop St ☎071 985 1147. An old fisherman's haunt, this diminutive little pub manifests a sweet cottage-kitchen interior with white-painted walls and red-painted doors – it's known for its legendary traditional music sessions, which could be any night the pub happens to be open. Wed, Fri & Sat 7pm–late.

## ENTERTAINMENT

**The Abbey Centre** Market St ☎ 071 985 2928, ⓦ abbey centre.ie. Dynamic arts centre hosting a range of musical, cinematic and theatrical events, plus a regular, rotating programme of exhibitions. It's also one of the main venues for the town's several festivals.

## Donegal town and around

**DONEGAL** town is not the most exciting of places, but it's a pleasant enough spot to pass a few hours, rating one or two attractions and a fair sprinkling of hotels and restaurants clustered around its triangular and central **Diamond**, the old market place.

Many tourists head for the town in the mistaken belief that they'll find themselves in the midst of the county's famously wild terrain, and then discover its rather more sedate setting. However, southeast of the town, the landscape is replete with little lakes well stocked for fishing; the largest of these, and a place of pilgrimage, is **Lough Derg**. Less than 8km upriver from Donegal town is another spot of gentle natural beauty, **Lough Eske**, from where you can walk into the wilds of the **Blue Stack Mountains**, which rise to the north.

### Donegal Castle

Tirconnell St • Easter to mid-Sept daily 10am–6pm; mid-Sept to Easter Thurs–Mon 9.30am–4.30pm • €5; Heritage Card • ☎ 074 972 2405

Donegal's original "fort of the foreigners" was thought to have been built on the banks of the River Eske by invading Vikings. Later, the first Red Hugh O'Donnell, king of Tír Chonaill, had a Norman-style tower house, known as **O'Donnell's Castle**, constructed on its site in the fifteenth century. When the English defeated the second Red Hugh in 1603, Sir Basil Brooke was given command of the town and it was he who rebuilt and extended the old castle, retaining the lower parts of the original tower, which had been razed to the ground by Red Hugh to prevent its capture. This well-restored example of Jacobean architecture is a fine marriage of strong defence and domestic grace, featuring mullioned windows, arches, ten gables and no fewer than fourteen fireplaces, over the grandest of which are carved the escutcheons of Brooke and his wife's family, the Leicesters. Brooke topped the tower with a Barbizon turret and added the mansion on the left, with the kitchens and bakery on the ground floor and living quarters on the floor above. Brooke was highly prolific in Donegal and was responsible for the overall design of the town.

**DONEGAL TOWN**

0 — 100
metres

N

Donegal Railway Heritage Centre

TIRCONNELL STREET
NEW ROW
NEW ROW
CASTLE STREET
MEETING HOUSE STREET
KILLYBEGS ROAD
BRIDGE STREET
Donegal Castle
MAIN STREET
WATER STREET
UPPER MAIN STREET
Harvey's Point (7.5km) & Letterkenny
Lough Eske / Blue Stack & 2
Obelisk
THE BANK WALK
QUAY STREET
River Eske
ⓘ
QUAY BRAE
Donegal Waterbus
Friary
Donegal Bay
BALLYSHANNON ROAD

■ **DRINKING & NIGHTLIFE**
The Reel Inn ............................ 1

■ **ACCOMMODATION**
Atlantic Guest House ............ 4
The Central Hotel ................... 5
Donegal Town
   Independent Hostel ......... 2
Harvey's Point Country
   Hotel ................................. 3
Lough Eske Castle ................ 1

● **EATING**
Aroma ...................................... 5
The Blueberry Tearooms ...... 2
Chandpur ................................ 3
The Harbour ........................... 4
La Bella Donna ...................... 1

▼ ⑤ , Ballyshannon, Sligo & Donegal Craft Village

12

## THE ANNALS OF THE FOUR MASTERS

In Donegal town's Diamond stands an obelisk commemorating the compilers of the famed **Annals of the Four Masters**. The Annals were begun in the town's **Franciscan friary**, whose ruined remains stand on the left bank of the River Eske, and were a systematic attempt to collect all known Irish documents into a history of the land beginning in 2958 BC, including mythical invasions by Firbolgs and Milesians, and ending in 1616 AD. The friary itself was built in 1474 by the first Red Hugh and his wife Nuala O'Brien of Munster. It was occupied by the English in 1601 and seriously damaged by the besieging O'Donnell army, being finally abandoned after the Flight of the Earls (see page 572). The Annals were completed by friars who had moved to a site by the River Drowse, near Kinlough, Country Leitrim. Manuscript copies of the Annals are occasionally on display at **Trinity College library** in Dublin.

### Donegal Railway Heritage Centre

Tirconnell St • Mon–Fri 10am–5pm (April–Sept Sat & Sun noon–4pm) • €5 • ☎ 074 972 2655, ⓦ donegalrailway.com

Railway fans will enjoy a visit to the **Donegal Railway Heritage Centre**, which occupies the Old Station House, standing just as it did when the County Donegal Railway, which ran from Derry to Ballyshannon, closed in 1959. Inside you'll find a model of the old railway alongside nostalgic memorabilia and some of the original station signs. Outside, you can enter a restored nineteenth-century coach and railcar, and while there's nothing inside, save for a DVD on the history of the railway, you may be lucky enough to catch one of the model railway exhibitions that are often held here.

### Donegal Craft Village

Just outside town, down the Sligo road • Easter–Sept Mon–Fri 10am–5pm; Sept–Easter Tues–Fir 10am–5pm • ☎ 074 972 5928, ⓦ donegalcraftvillage.com

The **Donegal Craft Village** comprises half a dozen or so workshops showcasing a range of local crafts, including glassware, textiles, painting and ceramics, jewellery and wood sculpture. Many of the items are available to buy, and there's a fabulous little café here too (see page 422).

### Lough Eske and the Blue Stacks

The soft beauty of **Lough Eske** is easily accessible from Donegal town. To get here take the minor road that runs north of the river, signposted "Lough Eske Drive", 500m out on the Killybegs road. This leads to a forgotten forested estate, once belonging to the Brooke family but now owned by the Forestry Commission. The lough is no longer a particularly great fishing spot, though it is known as a place to catch char, a tasty 20cm-long species of the salmon family, which lurk in the depths at the centre of the lake, moving out to the shallower edges around late October, where they can easily be fished using worms. The sandy banks of the River Eske are also known for freshwater oysters – some of which are reputed to contain pearls – but they're a protected species so it's illegal to take them. The ruins of an **O'Donnell tower**, once a prison, stand on one of the small islands on the lake.

Carrying on along the western shore of Lough Eske, you'll reach the spot where the river flows in at the lough's northern tip. A dirt road here runs off to the left into the Blue Stack Mountains. At the top of the pathway that leads on from the track there are superb views over the lough. From here you can join the waymarked **Bluestack Way**, which passes Lough Belshade, guarded in legend by a huge black cat. If you're intending to tramp around the mountain range, it's best to keep to the skirts of the hills as there are many marshy patches on lower ground – and be prepared for misty pockets during bad weather.

**12**

## Lough Derg and Station Island

25km east of Donegal town • Retreats May to end Sept (€40–70) • ☎ 071 986 1518, ⓦ loughderg.org • Buses from Ballyshannon or Enniskillen drop you in Pettigo village (9km south), though some continue to Lough Derg in the summer

In the middle of **Lough Derg** is a rocky islet known as **Station Island** or, more popularly, **St Patrick's Purgatory**, a retreat for Catholics needing rigour and solitude to recharge their faith. A national shrine of pilgrimage since the fifth century, it was described by Girardus Cambrensis in *Topography of Ireland* (1186) as "an island, one part of which is frequented by good spirits, the other by evil spirits". Contemporary scholars have argued that, as St Patrick never referred to Lough Derg in his writings, he probably never visited the island, but nevertheless it still thrives today as a strong centre for **pilgrimage**.

Some retreat programmes are more challenging than others, with the one-day activities offering a shorter retreat experience where shoes remain on and lunch is served. The **Three Day Pilgrimage**, as written about down the centuries, is a powerful experience that requires endurance (24hr Vigil, walking barefoot in prayer and fasting with one simple meal of dry toast or bread, oatcakes and black tea or coffee) and an openness to enter deeply into the spirit of the pilgrimage. *Station Island*, a collection by Seamus Heaney, contains a number of poems dealing with the mystique surrounding this ritual, while the late Pete McCarthy graphically recounted his experience of a retreat in *McCarthy's Bar* (see page 610). The island is approached via the R233 from the village of **Pettigo**, 9km south.

### ARRIVAL AND DEPARTURE

**By bus** Buses stop outside the *Abbey Hotel* on The Diamond. Destinations Ardara (Mon–Fri 3 daily, Sat & Sun 1 daily; 45min–1hr 10min); Ballyshannon (every 1hr–1hr 30min; 20–30min); Bundoran (7–9 daily; 30min); Derry (6–7 daily; 1hr 25min); Dungloe (Mon–Sat 3 daily, Sun 1; 1hr 30min);

### DONEGAL TOWN AND AROUND

Enniskillen (8 daily; 1hr 10min); Glencolmcille (2–4 daily; 1hr 15min–1hr 30min); Glenties (Mon–Sat 3 daily, Sun 1; 35min–1hr 20min); Killybegs (Mon–Sat 8 daily, Sun 1; 30–45min); Letterkenny (7–9 daily; 50min); Sligo (7–8 daily; 1hr 5min).

### INFORMATION AND ACTIVITIES

**Tourist office** The tourist office is located in a waterside building in The Quay car park (Mon–Sat 9am–5.30pm, Sun 10am–4pm; ☎ 074 972 1148).

**Boat tours** Down at the quay, a Waterbus offers trips around Donegal Bay (€20; ☎ 074 972 3666, ⓦ donegalbay waterbus.com; 1hr 15min).

### ACCOMMODATION

SEE MAP PAGE 420

**Atlantic Guest House** Main St ☎ 074 972 1187, ⓦ atlanticguesthouse.ie. The best-value, and certainly the most hospitable, place in town, offering brightly coloured, if modestly sized, rooms, most with bathrooms but some just with sinks. €85

**The Central Hotel** The Diamond ☎ 074 972 1027, ⓦ centralhoteldonegal.com. Prominently positioned on the main town square, this refined hotel has bright and airy rooms (some overlooking the bay), and its own leisure centre with pool; although it's not cheap, they do offer some good deals. €135

**Donegal Town Independent Hostel** 800m out on the Killybegs road ☎ 074 972 2805, ⓦ donegaltownhostel. com. One of the county's best hostels, this welcoming and efficiently run place has two- to five-bed rooms (some with bathrooms), self-catering kitchen and lounge areas.

Dorms €22, doubles €50

★ **Harvey's Point Country Hotel** Towards the southern end of Lough Eske ☎ 074 972 2208, ⓦ harveys point.com. The rooms – essentially mini-suites – here offer nothing less than unbridled luxury, from the magnificently upholstered furnishings to the sumptuous, marble-tiled bathrooms and imperious lake views. The restaurant, with its theatrical open kitchen, is no less impressive (€59 for a four-course dinner). €200

**Lough Eske Castle** South of the Lough (and best approached from Donegal town via the N15 Lifford road) ☎ 074 972 5100, ⓦ lougheskecastlehotel.com This glorious five-star hotel and spa is set within a renovated Victorian castle in perfectly maintained grounds. Accommodation here ranges from swish doubles to lavish suites. Here too are all manner of dining possibilities and a fancy spa. €275

### EATING

SEE MAP PAGE 420

**Aroma** Donegal Craft Village, just outside town, down the Sligo road ☎ 074 972 5928, ⓦ donegalcraftvillage. com. Exceptionally good coffee shop and home bakery serving a range of salads and savouries, including some spicy Mexican specials, plus lush cakes fresh from the oven. Mon–Sat 9.30am–5.30pm.

**The Blueberry Tearooms** Castle St ☎ 074 972 2933. A friendly place with a pretty, fairy-lit interior, serving excellent soups (€4.50), sandwiches and daily specials such as corn-fed chicken with sage and apple stuffing (€11.95). For a real treat, try one of the desserts, perhaps the steamed chocolate pudding or a slice of home-made blueberry pie. Mon–Sat 9am–7pm.

**Chandpur** Main St ☎ 0749725452, ⓦ chandpurdonegal. com. Serving some of the best Indian food in the country, this multi-award-winning restaurant always lives up to the hype. With plush decor, friendly staff and a cracking atmosphere, it's the food that steals the show. Try the Shami

Kebab (€6.95), followed by the Monkfish Curry (€19.95). Mon–Sat 4.30–11.30pm, Sun 1–10pm.

**The Harbour** Quay St ☎ 074 972 1702, ⓦ harbour donegal.ie. Long-standing, local institution offering a wide-ranging, if slightly curious, mix of menus comprising seafood and steaks alongside stone-baked pizzas and a handful of Mexican dishes. Mon–Thurs 5–9pm, Fri & Sat 5–9.30pm, Sun 1–9pm.

**La Bella Donna** Bridge St ☎ 074 972 5789, ⓦ labella donnarestaurant.com. This sleek Italian establishment just about shades it as the pick of the town's restaurants, offering up some interesting variations on traditional dishes, such as Italian sausage and wild mushroom tagliatelle (€14.95). Mon–Sat 10.30am–1am, Sun 10.30am–midnight.

### DRINKING
SEE MAP PAGE 420

**The Reel Inn** Bridge St ☎ 087 11 9994. The place to come in town for traditional music – it's no exaggeration to say that there's something on here every night of the week, every day of the year. Music aside, this is a real boozer's pub with oodles of character, and characters. Mon–Thurs 10.30am–11.30pm, Fri & Sat 10.30am–12.30am, Sun noon–11pm.

# Southwest Donegal

The most appealing route out of Donegal town heads west along the shore of Donegal Bay all the way to Glencolmcille, some 50km away. Highlights along this coast include the tapering peninsula leading to **St John's Point** and extraordinarily dramatic coastal scenery, which reaches an apogee in the mammoth sea-cliffs of **Slieve League**. The **Glencolmcille Peninsula** is a Gaeltacht (Irish-speaking area) and its attractive villages are rich in traditional folklore and music.

**12**

## St John's Point

Just west of the single-street village of **Dunkineely**, 17km west of Donegal town, a deviation left from the main road brings you down to *Castle Murray House Hotel*. In the small car park opposite stands a sandstone rock **memorial** to some forty fishermen (it may have been more) who lost their lives in Bruckless Bay during a great storm on February 11, 1813; what is undisputed is that more than two hundred curraghs (wooden-framed boats covered in animal hides) were lost at sea that night. Though little documented, it constitutes one of Ireland's worst ever fishing tragedies.

From here, continue down a long, narrow promontory to **St John's Point**, where a crumbling castle stands at the tip and there are great **views** over Donegal Bay, especially back towards the narrow entry of Killybegs Bay, with **Rotten Island** at its mouth. This is one of the finest spots in all of Europe for scuba diving.

### ACCOMMODATION AND EATING
ST JOHN'S POINT

**Castle Murray House Hotel** St John's Point ☎ 074 973 7022, ⓦ castlemurray.com. A high-end B&B with ten individually decorated boutique bedrooms, some with incredible views of the bay. Breakfast is very impressive, with in-house smoked fish, home-made preserves and granola, and local farm-to-fork full Irish. €140

## Killybegs

Sticking to the coast road west of Bruckless, you'll round Killybegs Bay and arrive in what was once the most successful fishing port in Ireland: **KILLYBEGS**, the halfway point between Donegal town and Glencolmcille.

After years of decline, this atmospheric little town appears to be on the up again, partly due to the ongoing development of the marina, though no less important has been the introduction of Killybegs as a destination for major cruise liners, this being one of very few deep sea ports in the country. Moreover, there are some excellent places to stay and eat at in and around town.

Around 8km west of town, en route to Kilcar, the road divides: for the scenic route, take the left-hand fork, a narrow switchback ride along the coastline with stupendous views over the ocean, especially from **Muckross Head**, and the looming presence of the hills and mountains to your right.

## Killybegs International Carpet Making & Fishing Centre

Fintra Rd • Mon–Fri 9.30am–5pm • €5 • ☎ 074 974 1944, ⓦ visitkillybegs.com

Ever since Alexander Morton began producing hand-knotted carpets here in Donegal in 1898, the county has been one of the world's foremost carpet manufacturers, producing bespoke pieces for Buckingham Palace, the White House and the Vatican, among others. At the **Killybegs International Carpet Making & Fishing Centre**, housed within the magnificent stone-and-timber framed barn that is the Killybegs carpet factory, you can witness first hand some of these beautiful pieces, many of which were produced on the factory's colossal 13m-long loom, the largest of its kind in the world. In its heyday, there were thirty looms rattling away here, but today there are just six, operated by a similar number of women. As well as watching a demonstration of the weaving process, visitors are encouraged to have a go themselves.

The second part of the centre focuses on the local fishing and maritime industry, with various displays, though the obvious attraction here is the Bridge Simulator, whereby you can attempt to navigate a vessel safely into dock.

### ARRIVAL AND INFORMATION

KILLYBEGS

**By bus** Buses generally stop off and pick up in front of the *Tara Hotel*.

Destinations Ardara (Mon–Sat 4 daily, Sun 2; 20min); Carrick (2–4 daily; 30min); Donegal town (Mon–Sat 4 daily, Sun 2; 30–45min); Glencolmcille (2–4 daily; 45min); Glenties (Mon–Sat 4 daily, Sun 2; 45min); Kilcar (2–4 daily; 20min).

**Tourist office** The tourist office is located in a cabin on Shore Rd (Mon–Fri 9.30am–5.30pm, Fri 9.30am–5pm, plus June–Aug Sat 11am–4pm; ☎ 074 973 2346, ⓦ killybegs.ie); they can book accommodation here, and there are a couple of terminals for internet access. Note that there are no ATMs beyond Killybegs in the direction of Slieve.

### ACCOMMODATION AND EATING

★ **Bay View Hotel** Main St ☎ 074 973 1950, ⓦ bay viewhotel.ie. Handsome harbour-facing building which mixes classic and contemporary styles to dazzling effect, from the cool, crisp all-white rooms to the glittering elegance of the restaurant, which is where breakfast is taken. Pool and sauna too. **€109**

**Kitty Kelly's** Largy, on a bend in the road some 5km west of Killybegs ☎ 074 973 1925. This sensitively restored farmhouse looks terrific and the food is divine; seafood is king here, so expect the likes of pan-roasted hake with crab hollandaise sauce and a cardamom and peach chutney (€22). They even offer a shuttle service from Killybegs for €2.50 per person. June–Sept daily 1–4.30pm & 5–9.30pm.

**Mrs B's** Main St ☎ 074 973 2656, ⓦ mrsbscoffeehouse.

com. Perky, cheerily staffed coffee shop knocking up freshly prepared seafood chowder, sandwiches and quiches – including gluten-free options – but best of all, an enticing selection of home-made treats; takeaway coffee too. Mon–Sat 9am–5pm.

**The Ritz** Fintra Rd, parallel to Main St ☎ 074 973 1309, ⓦ theritz-killybegs.com. As the name suggests, this was a former cinema, but it now operates as a stylish little guesthouse with single, double and family rooms; the self-catering facilities plus lounge and dining areas give it a real home-from-home feel. **€70**

**Tara Hotel** Main St ☎ 074 974 1700, ⓦ tarahotel.ie. A few paces from the *Bay View Hotel*, the *Tara* is a little more discreet, with sunny, if unspectacular, rooms facing either the harbour, or less attractively, the street behind. **€129**

# Kilcar

The roads meet again at **KILCAR**, a pleasant village and a centre for the Donegal **tweed industry**: there are a couple of small factories open to visitors; try Studio Donegal (☎074 973 8194, ⊛studiodonegal.ie) at the Glebe Mill in the centre of the village, where you can watch the spinners and weavers at work. The village hosts a three-day folk, blues and bluegrass **festival** on the May bank holiday weekend, plus a raucous street festival over the first weekend in August and a week-long traditional music festival during the same month. There are traditional music **concerts** in the Community Hall on Saturday evenings in summer.

## ARRIVAL AND ACCOMMODATION KILCAR

**By bus** Buses drop off and depart from the main street. Destinations Carrick (2–4 daily; 10min); Donegal town (1–3 daily; 50min–1hr 5min); Glencolmcille (2–4 daily; 25min); Killybegs (1–3 daily; 20min).

**Derrylahan Hostel** 3km west on the coast road towards Carrick ☎074 973 8079. This place, set on a working farm, must be one of the friendliest hostels in the country, with a mix of small dorms, a kitchen, common room with turf fire, and laundry. Camping is also available, with its own washing and kitchen facilities. Camping €8, dorms €18, doubles €50

**Ocean Spray** On the road towards Muckross Head ☎074 973 8438. A welcoming seaside B&B with three pine-heavy en-suite rooms, though only one has ocean views. €60

# Carrick and Teelin

*Derrylahan Hostel* is an ideal base for exploring the beautiful countryside around **CARRICK**, especially Teelin Bay and the awesome **Slieve League** cliffs to the west (see box). The southern road from Carrick to **TEELIN** follows the west bank of the River Owenee, whose rapids and pools are good for **fishing**. The village is Irish-speaking and rich in storytelling, with many stories having been recorded by the late Seán Ó'hEochaidh, Donegal's great folklorist.

**12**

## ARRIVAL AND INFORMATION CARRICK AND TEELIN

**By bus** Buses drop off on, and depart from, Main St. Destinations Donegal town (1–3 daily; 1hr–1hr 15min); Glencolmcille (2–4 daily; 15min); Kilcar (1–3 daily; 10min); Killybegs (1–3 daily; 30min).

**Fishing and boat trips** Licences are available from Teelin Sea Angling Club (☎074 973 9079). Sea-angling and sightseeing boat trips to the Slieve League cliffs are provided by Paddy Byrne, based down at the pier in Teelin (€25; ☎074 973 9365, ⊛sliabhleagueboattrips.com). They also run bird, whale and dolphin watching tours, as well as trips to some idyllic swimming spots.

## ACCOMMODATION AND EATING

**The Rusty Mackerel** Teelin, 2.5km south of Carrick ☎074 973 9101, ⊛therustymackerel.com. Teelin has a long musical tradition, and the best place to hear some local sounds is this cosy village pub, which has a dynamic Saturday session, plus occasional music on other evenings too. Mon–Thurs 5–11.30pm, Fri & Sat 1pm–12.30am, Sun 1–11pm.

**Slieve League Lodge** Carrick, in the centre of the village ☎074 973 9973, ⊛slieveleaguelodge.com. This jolly pub keeps twelve hostel-type rooms, all en suite and sleeping between two and four, plus a self-catering kitchen. The pub itself is Carrick's social hub, and has traditional music sessions most weekends. Set to one side of the pub is *Kelly's Kitchen*, where you can pick up light lunches, cakes and coffee. Pub and café daily 11am–11pm. €50

# Glencolmcille and around

As the road from Carrick approaches **GLENCOLMCILLE**, it traverses desolate moorland that's dominated by oily-black turf banks amid patches of heather and grass. After this, the rich beauty of the Glen, as it's known, comes as a welcome surprise. Settlement in the area dates back to the Stone Age, as testified by the enormous number of **megalithic remains** scattered around the countryside, especially court cairns and standing stones. There's evidence, too, of the Celtic era, in the form of earthworks and stone works. According to tradition, **St Columba** founded a monastery here in the sixth century,

**WALKS AROUND SLIEVE LEAGUE**

There are two routes up to the ridge of **Slieve League**. The less-used back one, known as Old Man's Track, follows the signpost pointing to the mountain just before **Teelin** and looks up continually to the ridge, while the frontal approach follows the signs out of Teelin to **Bunglass**, swinging you spectacularly round sharp bends and up incredibly steep inclines to one of the most thrilling cliff scenes in the world, the **Amharc Mór**. The sea moves so far below their peak that the waves appear silent, and the 600m face glows with mineral deposits in tones of amber, white and red. They say that on a clear day it is possible to see one-third of the whole of Ireland from the summit. **Sightseeing tours** of the cliffs from the waters below are organized from Teelin, weather permitting (see page 425).

If you want to make a full day of it, you can climb up to the cliffs from the Bunglass car park and follow the path along the top of the ridge, which eventually meets Old Man's Track. From here One Man's Pass, a narrow path with steep slopes on each side, leads up to the **summit** of Slieve League. Bear in mind that the route can often be muddy and very windy – it is certainly not advisable in misty weather or if you suffer from vertigo. From the top of Slieve League, you can either retrace your steps to Teelin or continue west over the crest of the mountain and down the heather-tufted western slope towards the headland village of **Malinbeg**, where there's a sublime, crescent-shaped golden strand enclosed by a tight rocky inlet. Malinbeg itself is a village of white bungalows, with the land around ordered into long narrow strips. On the cliff edge a ruined Martello tower faces **Rathlin O'Beirne Island**, 5km offshore, a place with many folklore associations. There are occasional boats across (enquire in Teelin), but nothing to see aside from some early Christian stone relics and a ruined coastguard station.

Beyond Malinbeg, it's relatively easy to extend your walk through **Malinmore** and on to Glencolmcille. The whole distance from Teelin to Malinmore can be comfortably completed in six hours.

**ACCOMMODATION**

**The Malinbeg Hostel** Malinbeg ☎074 973 0006, ⊛malinbeghostel.com. Just a 5min walk from the beach, this well-equipped hostel offers exhilarating views from most of its rooms. Dorms €15, doubles €38

and some of the **standing stones**, known as the Turas Cholmcille, were adapted for Christian usage by the inscription of a cross. Every Columba's Day (June 9) at midnight, the locals commence a barefoot circuit of the fifteen Turas, including Columba's Chapel, chair, bed, wishing stone and Holy Well, finishing up with Mass at 3am in the village church. (Columba and Columbcille/Colmcille are the same person – the latter is the name by which he was known after his conversion, and means "the dove of the church".)

Widespread emigration post-Famine and in the early twentieth century left the Glencolmcille area a typical example of rural decay. In 1951, however, a new and energetic curate, Father James McDyer, instigated efforts to revitalize the community, while retaining and strengthening its culture. Electricity arrived and road improvements reduced its isolation and allowed new collective enterprises in knitting and agriculture to thrive, and encouraged the development of local tourism.

### Folk Village Museum and Heritage Centre

Doonalt, less than 1km west of Glencolmcille on the R263 • Daily: Easter–Sept 10am–6pm; 10am–4.30pm • €6.50 • ☎074 973 0017, ⊛glenfolkvillage.com

Just a stone throw's from the beach stands the wonderful **Folk Village Museum and Heritage Centre**, a cluster of replica thatched cottages, each equipped with the furniture and artefacts of the era it represents. Founded in 1967, the museum was the initiative of Father James McDyer, whose life is celebrated in the first of the six buildings as you enter. The older cottages are notable for their bog oak and straw roofs and uneven flooring, in marked contrast with those from the mid-nineteenth century, which manifest smoother, neater lines.

One building introduces you to the area's history and cultural heritage, including a door from a cupboard reputedly used by Charles Stuart (Bonnie Prince Charlie), who sought refuge here following the Battle of Culloden in 1746. The **Dooey School House** replica has a display of informative photographs and research projects, and a section on the American painter Rockwell Kent, who painted marvellous treatments of the area's landscapes during his time here in 1926. Close by is a wonderful example of an old-style **Pub-Grocers**, few of which exist today, but sweetest of all is the tiny **Fisherman's cottage**, which relays the history of the local fishing industry.

### Glen Head, Port and Glenlough

From behind *Dooey Hostel*, **cliff walks** steer off around the south side of the bay above a series of jagged drops. Rising from the opposite side of the valley mouth, the promontory of **Glen Head** is surmounted by a Martello tower. On the way out you pass the ruins of **St Colmcille's Church**, with its "resting slab" where St Columba would have lain down exhausted from prayer. North across this headland you can climb and then descend to the forgotten little cove of **Port** a few kilometres away, a village deserted since the 1940s. Absolutely nothing happens here – although Dylan Thomas once stayed in the next valley at **Glenlough**, renting a cottage for several weeks in a doomed attempt to "dry out" in an area replete with poteen stills.

### The Glengesh Pass and Maghera

Heading northeast from Glencolmcille, the minor road to Ardara runs through the heart of the peninsula, travelling via the dramatic **Glengesh Pass** before spiralling down into wild but fertile valley land. Just before reaching Ardara, a road to the left runs along the southern edge of **Loughros Beg Bay** for 9km to **MAGHERA**, passing the transfixing **Assarancagh Waterfall**, from where you can embark on a hardy 10km waymarked walk uphill to the Glengesh Pass.

Maghera itself is an enchantingly remote place, dwarfed by the backdrop of hills and glens and fronted by an expansive and deserted strand that extends westwards to a rocky promontory riddled with **caves**. One of the largest is said to have concealed a hundred people fleeing Cromwell's troops; their light was spotted from across the strand and all were massacred except a lucky individual who hid on a high shelf. Most of the caves are accessible only at low tide and a torch is essential. Beware of the **tides**, however, as even experienced divers have been swept away by the powerful currents. Behind the village, a tiny road, unsuitable for large vehicles, runs up to the **Granny Pass**, an alternative and very scenic route to Glencolmcille.

**12**

### ARRIVAL AND DEPARTURE

### GLENCOLMCILLE AND AROUND

**By bus** Buses stop in the centre of the village. Services to the Glencolmcille peninsula are much reduced outside July and Aug.

Destinations Carrick (1–3 daily; 15min); Donegal town (1–3 daily; 1hr 15min–1hr 30min); Kilcar (1–3 daily; 25min); Killybegs (1–3 daily; 45min).

### ACCOMMODATION AND EATING

**Dooey Hostel** Glencolmcille ✆074 973 0130, ⓦ glencolmcille.ie/dooey.htm. On the Wild Atlantic Way, positioned high above the fine shingle strand at the mouth of the valley, this offbeat hostel offers sensational views from each of its eight-bed rooms, as well as the communal areas, which means you'll hardly ever want to leave. To get here on foot, keep on the village road as far as the Folk Village, and then take a path up to the left; in wet weather the longer route by road may be easier (fork left 800m

before the Folk Village). Dorms €17, camping €10

**Folk Village Tearoom** Folk Village Museum, Glencolmcille ✆074 973 0017. After visiting the Folk Village Museum (and even if you don't), the teahouse at the Folk Village makes for a welcome pit stop with its warming comfort food like minestrone soup and fresh brown bread, and apple pie with cream, all of which is freshly made/baked on the premises. Easter–Sept Mon–Sat 10am–6pm, Sun 11am–6pm; Oct Mon–Sat 11am–4.30pm, Sun noon–4.30pm.

# Central Donegal

The area around the bustling town of **Ardara** contains some of the most contrasting landscapes in Donegal. Rugged mountains lie to the southwest, traversed by the steeply sinuous **Glengesh Pass** and fringed by the unspoiled expanse of **Maghera** strand. Inland to the northeast sits the stately village of **Glenties**, while to the north the coastline forms peninsulas punctuated by the **Gweebarra** River, which, in turn, leads inland to the tranquil villages of Doocharry and Fintown, virtually surrounded by mountain scenery of an almost lunar quality.

## Ardara

Sixteen kilometres north of Killybegs on the N56 lies lively **ARDARA**. Traditionally a weaving and knitwear centre, this is an excellent place to buy cheap **Aran sweaters**. Molloy's, 1km south of town, is the biggest outlet, but Kennedy's, uphill from The Diamond, the main square, is handier (its owner is also a mine of local tourist information); both stores are well stocked with hand-loomed knitwear and tweeds.

The Catholic **church** west of Ardara's Diamond has a striking stained-glass window, *Christ among the Doctors*, by the Modernist-inspired **Evie Hone**, one of the most influential Irish artists of the twentieth century. The authors of the Gospels are depicted symbolically with the infant Christ at the centre and David and Moses above and below. Traditional music is big business in this part of Donegal, and Ardara stages a plethora of festivals, the best of which are the **Cup of Tae** traditional music festival (ⓦcupoftaefestival.com) over the first weekend of May and the **Johnny Doherty** Music and Dancing Festival (ⓦjohnnydohertyfestival.com) at the end of September.

### ARRIVAL AND INFORMATION
ARDARA

**By bus** Buses drop off on, and depart from, The Diamond. Destinations Donegal town (2 daily; 30min–1hr 30min); Dungloe (Mon–Sat 3 daily; 40min); Glenties (Mon–Fri 3 daily, Sat & Sun 1 daily; 10–20min); Killybegs (Mon–Sat 1–2 daily; 20min).

**Tourist office** Inside the Heritage Centre on The Diamond (June–Aug Mon–Fri 10am–6pm, Sat 11am–4pm; Sept–May Mon–Fri 10am–6pm; ⓣ074 954 1704, ⓦardara.ie).

### ACCOMMODATION AND EATING

**Brae House** Front St ⓣ074 954 1296, ⓔbraehouse@ eircom.net. Spruce, mint-coloured townhouse with five pleasing rooms spread over two floors, generally painted in gentle mauve and magenta tones – and a super-friendly welcome is guaranteed too. €90

★ **Nancy's** Front St ⓣ074 954 1187, ⓦnancys barardara.com. Run by the same family throughout its 200-year-old history, the warren of small, cosy rooms spreading out from a central front bar are utterly delightful. The food is first-rate too, with mussels in white wine and garlic (€12) typical of a largely seafood-oriented menu. They also serve some great craft beers on tap. Mon–Thurs noon–11.30pm, Fri & Sat noon–12.30am, Sun 12.30–11pm.

**Nesbitt Arms Hotel** The Diamond ⓣ074 954 1103, ⓦnesbittarms.com. Named after George Nesbitt, a prominent eighteenth-century landowner in these parts, this similarly aged hotel is a decent, if somewhat pricey, option. €109

**Woodhill House** 1km east of town ⓣ074 954 1112, ⓦwoodhillhouse.com. This stylish seventeenth-century manor house is set in its own extensive grounds with rooms in both the main house and converted outbuildings. Its restaurant offers classic Irish cuisine (think slow-cooked Irish lamb with parsnip crisps) and is well worth the €42.50 per head for the three-course dinner. Restaurant daily 6.30–10pm. €130

## Glenties

Set at the foot of two glens 10km east of Ardara, **GLENTIES** is a tidy village, with a beautiful modern **church**, at the Ardara end of town, designed by the Derry architect Liam McCormack; its vast sloping roof reaches down to 2m from the ground, and rainwater drips off the thousand or so tiles into picturesque pools of water. In October, the town is overrun, thanks to the enormously popular **Fiddlers Festival**, when the town's pubs heave with fiddlers from across the world.

## St Conall's Museum and Tea Room

Opposite the church • May–Oct Mon–Sat 10am–1pm & 2–4.30pm • €2.50 • ☎ 087 292 1016

The **St Conall's Museum and Tea Room** is charming little museum with an extensive collection of Patrick MacGill and Brian Friel literature, as well as items relating to the famine, the Donegal Railway and local history curios. The town's most famous son is author **Patrick MacGill**, whose semi-autobiographical *Children of the Dead End* brilliantly recounts the wayward lives of migrant navvies. A summer school is held in his honour in late July, attracting hundreds of people to its exhibitions, seminars and literary debates (⬤ macgillsummerschool.com).

| ARRIVAL AND DEPARTURE | GLENTIES |
|---|---|
| **By bus** Buses drop off on, and depart from, Main St. Destinations Ardara (2–3 daily; 10–20min); Donegal town | (2–3 daily; 45min–1hr 30min); Dungloe (Mon–Sat 2–3 daily; 30min). |

## ACCOMMODATION AND EATING

**Highlands Hotel** Main St ☎ 074 955 1111, ⬤ highlands hotel.ie. Longstanding village hotel with comfortable, if occasionally dated, rooms. A plaque commemorates the room where actress Meryl Streep stayed for the local premiere of *Dancing at Lughnasa*. The Sunday night music sessions here are worth looking in for. €110

**Kennedy's** Main St ☎ 074 955 1050, ⬤ kennedysbar andrestaurant.com. Modern gastro-pub set over two floors serving big portions of steaming comfort food like beer-battered fish and chips (€15.50), though it's just as much fun to take a stool at the long bar and kick back with a pint. Tues–Sat 5pm–midnight, Sun 1pm–midnight.

**Lisnadar B&B** Mill Rd ☎ 074 955 1800. Just a 5min walk from the centre of the village, this is by far the most appealing of Glenties' several guesthouses. Set within extensive gardens, the house has four big rooms, with a guest lounge and breakfast conservatory attached – the hospitality is second to none. €85

# The Dawros Head Peninsula and around

To the immediate north of Ardara, the **Dawros Head Peninsula** is much tamer than Glencolmcille, with many tiny lakes dotting a quilt of low hills. The terrain of purple heather, fields, streams and short glens makes a varied package for the enthusiastic walker. The first turning off the R261 Narin road leads to **ROSBEG**, an isolated village, straggling beside a series of rock-strewn coves, which nevertheless has a campsite (see page 430).

If you're heading directly from Ardara towards Narin and Portnoo, in **Kilclooney** look out for the **Kilclooney dolmen**, just before the pastel-shaded church on the right. These are probably the best-preserved portal stones in the country, with the capstone measuring over 4m long and the structure reckoned to date from around 3500 BC.

## Doon Fort

Turn left at the "Rosbeg/Tramore Beach" signpost 1km or so before Narin, then head right up the lane just after a school; a few hundred metres later you'll see a sign for boat rental leading down to a farmhouse, where you can rent a rowing boat inexpensively to take you across to the island

Continuing onwards towards Narin, the most worthwhile sight on the peninsula is **Doon Fort**, which occupies an entire oval-shaped islet in the middle of **Lough Doon**. The idyllic setting, rarely disturbed by visitors, makes the hassle of getting there worth it: although its walls are crumbling, the fort has been untouched for over two thousand years. The walls stand 5m high and 4m thick; their inner passages were used in the 1950s for storing poteen.

## Narin and Iniskeel Island

In **NARIN** the spearheaded, 4km-long **strand** is a wonderful beach, safe for bathing. At low tide you can walk out to **Iniskeel Island**, where St Conal founded a monastery in the sixth century. This has long since disappeared, but there are the ruins of two twelfth-century churches with some cross-inscribed slabs.

## Doocharry

East of Narin the N56 hugs the shoreline, twisting and turning until it crosses the Gweebarra and enters Lettermacaward. From here a minor road follows the river 8km inland to tiny **DOOCHARRY**, with just a pub and a grocery, which acts as the gateway to some of the most dramatic scenery in the county. From here, you can head further upstream northeast along a narrow and tortuous lane past **Slieve Snaght**, through the **Glendowan Mountains** and skirting the southern edge of the **Glenveagh National Park** to **Lough Gartan** (see page 436). The desolate though beautiful countryside bears little sign of human impact and you'll be lucky to see any life beyond the odd sheep or fluttering bird.

## Fintown

A more major road heads 9km southeast from Doocharry through rugged, rock-strewn moorland to **FINTOWN**, a simple roadside village set at the foot of towering mountains in the Finn Valley where the river broadens to form an elongated strip of lake.

### Narrow-gauge railway

Village centre, just south of the main road • 40min journeys on the hour: June–Sept Mon–Sat 11am–4pm, Sun 1–5pm • €8 • ☏ 074 954 6280

You can take a waterside trip along a restored section of the old County Donegal **narrow-gauge railway**. In its late nineteenth- and early twentieth-century heyday, the railway extended for some 200km, before the gradual increase in the use of road traffic to shift freight forced the line's closure in 1959.

### ACCOMMODATION AND EATING

**Lake House Hotel** Clooney, 1.5km east of Narin ☏ 074 954 5123, ⓦ lakehousehotel.ie. This lovely country residence dates from 1847 and provides high-quality accommodation, including self-catering cottages with open-hearth fires, and a fine restaurant with an eclectic menu. Restaurant Mon–Sat 6–9pm, Sun 1–9pm. **€100**

### DAWROS HEAD PENINSULA AND AROUND

**Tramore Beach** Rosebeg ☏ 074 955 1491, ⓔ camp bella@eircom.net. Wonderful little camping spot among the dunes, with some two dozen pitches and decent facilities including shower/toilet block and shop. Closed Oct–April. **€16**

# The Rosses

The **Rosses**, a vast expanse of rock-strewn land and stony soil, is a strong Gaeltacht area. Dotted with over 120 tiny lakes, the crumpled terrain stretches from **Dungloe** in the south to **Crolly** in the north, but the forbidding nature of much of the landscape

### JOHN DOHERTY

Fintown's cemetery is the resting place of Donegal's **greatest traditional fiddler**, **John Doherty** (c.1895–1980), whose dynamic yet intricate style remains a major influence on the region's fiddle players, over thirty years after his death. Many of the tunes you'll hear played in Donegal today owe their origins to his repertoire and that of his brothers, Mickey and Simon, and several excellent CDs of his work are still available.

## PADDY "THE COPE" GALLAGHER

Dungloe is synonymous with the rejuvenating work of **Paddy "the Cope" Gallagher** (1871–1966), who envisaged the salvation of the Rosses' then poor communities through cooperative ventures, in particular by reducing their dependency on moneylenders. Oddly enough, the enterprise's practical origins lay in Paddy's discovery that the price of manure was reduced when purchased by societies. As a result, he founded the Templecrone Co-operative Agricultural Society (the "Cope") in 1906, and its central branch still stands proudly on Dungloe's main street, with others elsewhere in the Rosses.

meant most settlements could only survive near the sea, so following the shoreline route around the Rosses is far more rewarding than the more direct road north.

## Dungloe

**An Clochán Liath** is the name you'll see on signposts approaching **DUNGLOE**, referring to the grey-coloured stepping stones that were once used to cross the river here. The modern Anglicized version comes from Dún gCloiche, the name of a stone fort situated on a rock a few kilometres offshore. When the fair that was held at the fort moved in the eighteenth century to the village of An Clochán Liath, which had grown up around the stepping stones, the fort's name stuck, though Irish-speakers still refer to the town by its original name. For fans of Daniel O'Donnell aside, there's little to detain you here, but at the end of July, the **Mary From Dungloe festival** (📳maryfromdungloe.ie), centred around a rather wholesome beauty pageant, provides a good pretext for general festivities, plenty of music and street entertainment. There's no antiquity behind the festival's origins or name – it dates from 1968 and the title comes from an Irish hit single by the Emmet Spiceland band.

12

### ARRIVAL AND INFORMATION                                                    DUNGLOE

**By bus** Buses drop off on, and depart from, Main St.
Destinations Ardara (2 daily; 45min); Donegal town (2 daily; 1hr 15min–1hr 30min); Glenties (2 daily; 30min).
**Tourist office** The tourist office is on Chapel Rd, in the

old church just off the top of Main St (June & Sept Mon–Fri 10am–1pm & 2–5.30pm; July & Aug Mon–Fri 10am–1pm & 2–5.30pm, Sat 10.30am–1pm & 2–4pm; ☎074 952 1297).

### ACCOMMODATION AND EATING

**Doherty's** 16 Main St ☎074 952 1654. A no-fuss all-rounder serving breakfasts, lunches and dinners, plus takeaways. Coffees and pastries too. Mon–Thurs 9am–8.30pm, Fri & Sat 9am–9.30pm, Sun 11am–8pm.
**Patrick Johnny Sally's Bar** Main St ☎074 952 1479. At the top of the street, this chunky grey-stone building is a genuine old-timers' pub, with a terrace offering fabulous views of the ocean. No TVs or music, just a good old-

fashioned drinking den. Mon–Sat 10.30am–11.30pm, Sun noon–11pm.
**Radharc an Oileain** Quay Rd ☎074 952 1093, 📳dungloebedandbreakfast.com. Located a few mins' walk from Main St, this modern, family-run bungalow has three terrific en-suite rooms, with wet rooms, all of which overlook the bay. €75

## Burtonport

Seven kilometres northeast of Dungloe, **BURTONPORT** is the embarkation point for **Arranmore Island** and, if you can find a boatman at the harbour to take you out, for other smaller islands. In the late eighteenth century, the village's founder, William Burton, attempted to establish **Rutland Island**, just offshore, as a major trading centre, and consequently this area became the first English-speaking district in the whole of Donegal. During the 1798 Rebellion **James Napper Tandy** landed on the island with French troops, but became somewhat inebriated on hearing of Wolfe Tone's capture and was carried back on board (see page 574). Apart from busy activity at the harbour, Burtonport has little to say for itself.

## Arranmore Island

**Arranmore**'s permanent population of around eight hundred people is almost entirely concentrated along the eastern and southern coastlines – the island's main village, **LEABGARROW**, is on the eastern side. The high centre-ground of bogland and lakes reaches a greater altitude than anywhere else in the Rosses, and it's well worth hiking a few hundred metres upland for great views back across the water to Burtonport.

A circuit of the whole island, with cliff-top views of the Atlantic, takes around six hours, and the terrain isn't especially taxing, though it can be blustery. Many ships have foundered in the choppy seas hereabouts, but in 1983 the lone American yachtsman Wayne Dickenson landed on the island's west coast after 142 days at sea in the smallest boat ever to cross the Atlantic. In the cliffs below St Crone's Church on the southern shore is **Uaimh an Áir** (the "cave of slaughter"), where seventy hiding islanders were massacred in the seventeenth century by a certain Captain Conyngham, in an action that lay somewhat outside his remit from Charles I to rid the Rosses of "rogues and rapparees". Two islanders later took revenge by killing the captain in Dunfanaghy. Uninhabited **Green Island**, at the southwestern tip, is now a **bird sanctuary** and rare species have been spotted hereabouts, including the snowy owl in 1993. The most dramatic of the several **beaches** is at the northwestern end of the island, on the way to the lighthouse and approached by a set of steps down the side of a perpetually crumbling cliff.

Note that **facilities** on the island are limited, but there are a number of places to sleep, and several pubs – none particularly stands out, but they suffice for a pint and some local banter.

**12**

### ARRIVAL AND ACCOMMODATION ARRANMORE ISLAND

**By boat** Arranmore Ferry runs a car ferry (6–9 sailings daily; 15min; €15 return, €30 with car; ☎074 954 2233, ⓦarranmoreferry.com), as does the almost identically titled The Arranmore Ferry (5–7 sailings daily; 15min; €15 return, €30 with car; ☎087 317 1810, ⓦthearranmoreferry.com). **Glen Hotel** Leabgarrow ☎074 952 0505, ⓦtheglen

hotel.weebly.com. Nineteenth-century hotel in pleasant grounds just a 5min walk from the ferry pier; the rooms won't set the pulse racing, but they're clean and decently priced. The restaurant here is the best place to eat on the island. Restaurant daily 12.30–8pm. **€80**

# Gweedore and Tory Island

Like its southern neighbour, the Rosses, the interior of the **Gweedore** district is largely desolate and forbidding country, and settlements again cling to the shoreline. To the southwest lie the villages of **Bunbeg** and **Derrybeg**, their cottages sprinkled across a blanket of gorse and mountain grasses. The ruggedness intensifies as it continues up the coast and round the Bloody Foreland to Gortahork in the Cloghaneely district, yet surprisingly, there has been significant house-building here and the area is quite densely populated. Some distance offshore lies Ireland's most literally isolated community, Irish-speaking **Tory Island**, a place rich in folkloric and musical traditions.

## Bunbeg

The main appeal of the roadside village of **BUNBEG** is its gorgeous little harbour, 1.5km from the village along an enchanting rollicking road. Packed with smallish trawlers, it's also the departure point for year-round **ferries** to Tory Island (see page 433), as well as boat trips to uninhabited **Gola Island** in summer (€10; ☎087 660 7003).

**ACCOMMODATION AND EATING** BUNBEG

**Bunbeg House** By the harbour ☎ 074 953 1305, ⓦ bunbeghouse.com. Pleasant B&B in a fantastic spot, with sparky little rooms offering waterside views. It's almost worth staying here just to enjoy breakfast on the outdoor terrace. Closed Nov–Feb. €90

★ **Leo's Tavern** Meenaleck, 5km south of Bunbeg ☎ 074 954 8143, ⓦ leostavern.com. This famous pub is run by a member of the Brennan family. Parents, Leo and Baba, were both well known on the dance band circuit in the 1950s and 1960s, though other family members have achieved greater fame. Three of their children (Máire, Pól and Ciarán) were members of the group Clannad, and another is the celebrated singer/musician Enya – the pub's walls are decorated with a variety of awards and mementos. As you might expect, the music sessions, including open-mic nights, are superb. Mon–Fri 4pm–midnight, Sat 1pm–midnight, Sun 1–11.30pm.

★ **Teach Húdaí Beag** By the harbour crossroads ☎ 074 953 1016. Fantastic pub, which hosts a famous Mon night traditional session, sometimes involving as many as twenty musicians, as well as a smaller Fri night one too. Best of all, though, is the riotous Cabaret Craiceáilte on the last Sat of the month, where all manner of genres (roots, reggae, contemporary) are performed in Gaelic. Like Leo's, it pulls in some stellar names. Opening times often at whim of owner, but typically daily 4pm–midnight.

## Glassagh

At **GLASSAGH**, about 7km north of Derrybeg, the road climbs abruptly to Knockfola, loosely translated as the **Bloody Foreland**, a grim, stony, almost barren zone, crisscrossed by stone walls, and so-called because of the red hue acquired by its heather from the light of the setting sun. From Knockfola, the road turns eastwards hugging the side of the mountain, with the bogland and its hard-worked turf banks stretching below towards the Atlantic. You should be able to spot the distinctive shape of **Tory Island** far out to sea and, at **Magheroarty**, 8km east of Derrybeg, a road runs down to the pier, where you can pick up a ferry to the island (see page 434) and possibly arrange a trip to largely deserted **Inishbofin**, just offshore.

**12**

**ACCOMMODATION** GLASSAGH

**Teac Jack** Glasslagh ☎ 074 953 1173, ⓦ teacjack. com. If you fancy lingering a while, the best place to stay is this prominent roadside hotel, with 26 en-suite rooms. The hotel's enormous horseshoe-shaped bar, meanwhile, is a great venue for the regular programme of music and dancing, typically Tues, Thurs and Sat nights. €70

## Tory Island

With its ruggedly indented shores pounded by the ocean, **TORY ISLAND**, though only 12km north of the mainland, is notoriously inaccessible. Only 4km long and less than 1.5km wide, its vulnerability to the elements means little can grow here. Yet despite the island's barren landscape and the ferocity of the elements, the Tory islanders are thriving, a situation no one could have predicted thirty years ago. Back then, conditions on the island were very poor, lacking essential amenities such as a water supply, proper sanitation, reliable electricity and a ferry service. The arrival of a new priest, **Father Diarmuid Ó Péicín**, in the early 1980s stimulated a transformation. Rallying the islanders, the pastor began to lobby every possible target, securing backing from such disparate characters as the US senator Tip O'Neill (who had Donegal ancestry) and the late Ian Paisley. The campaign attracted media attention and conditions gradually began to improve. Nowadays, around 160 people live permanently on the island.

### Brief history

According to local mythology, Tory was the stronghold of the **Fomorians**, who raided the mainland from their island base and whose most notable figure was the cyclops **Balor of the Evil Eye**, the Celtic god of darkness. Intriguingly, the local legend places his eye at the back of his head. There's also said to be a crater in the very heart of the island that none of the locals will approach after dark, for fear of incurring the god's

---

**THE TORY ISLAND ARTISTS**

Tory islanders are famed for their **painting**, a development that originated in a chance encounter between the English painter Derek Hill and one of the island's fishermen, **James Dixon**, in 1968, both now deceased. Dixon had never lifted a brush before the day he told Hill that he could do a better job of painting the Tory scenery, but he went on to become the most renowned of the island's school of **primitive painters** – Glebe House has a remarkable painting by him (see page 437). You can view the islanders' work and, more than likely, meet the artists, at the **James Dixon Gallery**, the originator's former home, a little way to the east of the harbour.

---

wrath. In the sixth century, **St Colmcille** landed on Tory with the help of a member of the Duggan family. In return, the saint made him king of the island; the line has been unbroken ever since, and you're more than likely to meet the present king, **Patsy Dan Rodgers**, who regularly greets arrivals at the harbour.

### Around the island

Some monastic relics from St Columba's time remain on Tory, the most unusual of which – now the island's emblem – is the **Tau Cross**. Its T-shape is of Egyptian origin, and is one of only two such monuments in the whole of Ireland. It has now been relocated and set in concrete on Camusmore Pier in West Town, one of the island's two villages. There are other mutilated stone crosses and some carved stones lying around, several by the remains of the **round tower** in West Town, which is thought to date from the tenth century and is uniquely constructed from round beach stones. A local superstition focuses on the **wishing stone** in the centre of the island, three circuits of which will supposedly lead to your desires being granted.

**12**

**ARRIVAL AND ACCOMMODATION** | **TORY ISLAND**

**By boat** Turasmara (☎087 199 3710, ⌨toryferry.com) operates a year-round, passenger-only service from Magheroarty, with 2–3 sailings daily (times vary depending on the season; services are often affected by the tides and the weather, so always call ahead to check at 8.30am or 9am, 11.30am; €25 return).

**Tory Island Harbour View** By the landing stage ☎074 913 5920, ⌨hoteltory.com. Translating as the "Harbour View", this place provides comfortable accommodation in twelve rooms, plus one of only two bars on the island, and a fine seafood restaurant. The owners also organize a range of summer events, including traditional music and song, painting and birdwatching weekends, as well as running the Dive Tory centre for aquatic fans. **€110**

# The Derryveagh Mountains and Glenveagh

Inland from Gweedore lies some of the most dramatic scenery in Donegal, an area dominated by mountains such as **Errigal** and **Slieve Snaght**, and loughs of startling beauty. This is popular hill-walking country, especially along the **Poisoned Glen,** part of the much-visited **Glenveagh National Park**. Further on, towards Letterkenny, the countryside becomes gentler and increasingly verdant, especially in the environs of **Lough Gartan**, an area rich in associations with St Columba.

## The loughs and Mount Errigal

Heading east on the N56 from Gweedore, the imposing and starkly beautiful mass of **Mount Errigal** becomes increasingly prominent. From a distance the mountain appears to be snow-covered, but skirting the northern shore of **Lough Nacung**, it becomes apparent that the white coloration has geological, rather than meteorological, causes.

Quite often the area around Errigal is shrouded in mist, but on a clear day the beauty of the mountain is unsurpassable, its silvery slopes resembling the Japanese artist Hokusai's images of Mount Fuji. The hour-long hike up to the **summit** is a must, and there's a waymarked trail from the road, 2km past the Poisoned Glen turn-off, up the southeast ridge. You'll be rewarded with stupendous **views**: virtually all of Donegal, and most of Northern Ireland, is visible, and you could easily spend several hours just sitting and absorbing the contrasts provided by coastline, loughs and mountains.

## Dunlewey Lakeside Centre

Lakeshire, Dunlewey Lough • Daily 10.30am–5pm • Tour of cottage, farm and outbuildings €6.50; boat trip €5.95; combined tour and boat ticket €11; pony rides €5; treks €20–25 • ☎ 074 953 1699, ⓦ dunleweycentre.com

Back down in Money Beg, a lane runs south to the narrow strip of land which divides Lough Nacung from Dunlewey Lough. On the way there's the **Dunlewey Lakeside Centre**, an impressive visitor centre by the shore. The key attractions here are a tour around the cottage of the notable local weaver, Manus Ferry, where you'll get to see demonstrations of spinning and weaving, and a **boat trip** around Dunlewey Lough, which is a lovely thirty-minute excursion. This extremely child-friendly centre extends to a small farmyard "zoo", adventure playground (included in tour price) and pony rides; the trekking centre here also offers a range of cross-country treks. And once you're done with that little lot, there's an excellent **restaurant** and a crafts shop.

Dunlewey is also an important centre for traditional music and there are concerts (€8) in the centre every Sunday from 1.30–3.30pm.

**12**

### ACCOMMODATION                                    THE LOUGHS AND MOUNT ERRIGAL

**An Chúirt Hotel** On the N56, 5km east of Bunbeg ☎ 074 953 2900, ⓦ gweedorecourthotel.com. You can stay very comfortably at the rather grand "*Gweedore Court*" *Hotel*, which, although largely catering to wedding parties, makes for a good base if spending some time in the loughs. **€130**

**Errigal Hostel** Dunlewey ☎ 074 953 1180, ⓦ anoige.ie.

Situated in the shadow of Mount Errigal, this is a stunning purpose-built place, entirely in keeping with the area. It features private en-suite doubles, plus four-bed rooms and innovative split-level six-bed dorms, internet room, laundry and self-catering kitchen, plus bike rental (€20/day). Closed Nov–Feb. Dorms **€20**, doubles **€53**

# Glenveagh National Park

According to legend, the **Poisoned Glen** – east of Dunlewey Lough, and one of the most popular spots of the **Glenveagh National Park** – is where the cyclops Balor of the Evil Eye (see page 433) was slain by Lugh, poisoning the ground on which his single eyeball fell. There are many other explanations for the origins of its name, from the darkly conspiratorial (the glen's waters were polluted to kill English soldiers) to the purely botanical (poisonous Irish spurge used to grow here).

## National Park Visitor Centre

Northernmost end of Lough Veagh • Daily: March–Oct 9am–5.15pm; Nov–Feb 9am–4.45pm; restaurant Easter–Sept 10.30am–5pm • Free • ⓦ glenveaghnationalpark.ie

The **Glenveagh National Park Visitor Centre** has detailed and interactive displays on the area's ecology and geology. More interesting is the exhibition on the park's wildlife, and in particular its eagles, whose population died out here in the early 1900s; in 2000, a programme to reintroduce golden eagles was established, and it is estimated that there are currently seven pairs in this corner of County Donegal. There's also a reasonably priced restaurant here, though it's not as enjoyable as the Castle tearooms.

## Glenveagh Castle

Visits by guided tour daily 10am–5pm; tea rooms Easter–Sept 10.30am–5pm • €7 • Minibuses (€3 return) from visitor centre (no cars beyond here), otherwise a 40min walk

From the visitor centre, minibuses shuttle back and forth to **Glenveagh Castle**, built on a small promontory for wealthy landowner George Adair between 1870 and 1873. Adair was the creator of the estate that now forms much of the park, but while you might admire the end product, it's impossible to condone the means by which it was achieved. Though some land was obtained through purchase, during what is now known as the **Derryveagh Evictions**, Adair evicted 244 tenants during the bitterly cold April of 1861, forcing many into the workhouse and others to emigrate to Australia. The rhododendron-filled gardens surrounding the castle were very much the work of Adair's wife, Cornelia, who also introduced herds of red deer to the estate. The steep ascent to the viewpoint behind the gardens is more than worthwhile for the wonderful views down to the castle and along the lough deep into the glen. From here it's easy to imagine why the castle was so popular during the Golden Age of Hollywood, with Greta Garbo, Marilyn Monroe and Clark Gable all spending time here. Guided tours of the castle focus on the furniture and artwork collected by the millionaire Irish–American, Henry McIlhenny, the last owner of Glenveagh, who in 1983 bequeathed the castle and its contents to the nation.

## Lough Gartan and around

The environs of **Lough Gartan** are one of the supreme beauties of Ireland. **St Colmcille** was born into a royal family here in 521; his father was from the house of Niall of the Nine Hostages and his mother belonged to the House of Leinster. If you walk over from Glenveagh you'll pass Colmcille's **birthplace** – take the first road right at the first house you see at the end of the mountain track, and you'll come to a colossal **cross** marking the spot; the site is also signposted from the road running along the lough's southern shore. Close by is a slab known as the **Flagstone of Loneliness**, on which Colmcille used to sleep, thereby endowing the stone with the miraculous power to cure the sorrows of those who also lie upon it, though nowadays it's bestrewn with coins. During times of mass emigration, people used to come here on the eve of departure in the hope of ridding themselves of homesickness. Archaeologically, it's actually part of a Bronze Age gallery tomb and has over fifty cup marks cut into its surface.

---

### WALKING IN GLENVEAGH

To reach the **Poisoned Glen**, head a little way further east of Money Beg on the R251 and take the signposted lane leading downhill to the right. Just below the ruined church at the eastern end of Lough Nacung turn off to the left and follow the track over the old bridge. The path dwindles away and you should follow the left bank of the river deep into the gorge until it turns sharply left. Walk through the water here, usually just a trickle in summer, to the opposite bank and climb up towards a granite crest. From here, walk beside the small stream through a gully and finally you'll emerge on a ridge. It's not an easy tramp, for a lot of the ground is marshy, but the views are fantastic, with the River Glenveagh flowing into Lough Beagh down below.

You're now in the **Glenveagh National Park** and may well see deer hereabouts. If you don't want to retrace your tracks and are prepared for a longer hike, you have a number of options. However, it's vital to follow all the basic rules of hill-walking and essential to keep to the designated roads and paths during the winter deer-culling season (Sept–Feb), or you run the risk of being **shot**. Experienced hill-walkers will probably be tempted by the sight of **Slieve Snaght**, the highest point in the park, off to the southwest. Alternatively, if you head downhill to the southeast, the Glendowan road at the bottom leads eastwards to **Lough Gartan** and westwards to **Doocharry** (see page 430). If you take the road east towards Gartan for a short distance, an old disused vehicle track to the left will lead you down the barrel of the glen alongside the river to Lough Glenveagh.

Going back to the track leading downhill will bring you to the lakeside road, where a left turn leads to the remains of a church known as the **Little Oratory of St Colmcille**. It's an enchanting ruin, no larger than a modern living room, with a floor of old stone slabs with grass growing up through the cracks. A holy well is here too and nearby the Natal Stone, where the baby Colmcille first opened his eyes; to this day pregnant women visit the slab to pray for a safe delivery.

## Glebe House

Northwest shore of Lough Gartan • Visits by guided tour Easter week daily 11am–6.30pm; June & Sept Sat–Thurs 11am–6.30pm; July & Aug daily 11am–6.30pm • €5 • ☎ 074 913 7071, ⓦ glebegallery.ie

**Glebe House** is a gorgeous Regency building set in beautiful gardens on the northwest shore of Lough Gartan. Richly decorated both inside and out, it owes its fame to the time of its tenure by the English artist Derek Hill (1916–2000), though it's now run as a **gallery** by the Heritage Service. The converted stables are used for visiting exhibitions, while the rooms of the house itself display a rich collection of paintings, sketches and numerous other items once owned by Hill, including works by Kokoschka, Yeats, Renoir and Picasso. The study is decked out in original William Morris wallpaper and there are Chinese tapestries in the morning room. The kitchen has various paintings by the Tory Island group of primitive painters (see page 434), most remarkably James Dixon's impression of Tory from the sea.

## Colmcille Heritage Centre

Northeast shore of Lough Gartan, opposite Glebe House • Easter week & May–Sept Mon–Sat 10.30am–5pm, Sun 1.30–5pm • €3 • ☎ 074 913 7306, ⓦ colmcilleheritagecentre.ie

Moving on round the northeast of the lake, in the direction of Church Hill, a right turn immediately after crossing the bridge will take you down to the modern **Colmcille Heritage Centre**, on the opposite shore from Glebe House. The exhibition space is devoted to St Colmcille's life and the spread of the Celtic Church throughout Europe. If you have no interest in ecclesiastical history, there are other intriguing items, including very beautiful stained-glass windows of biblical scenes by Ciarán O'Conner and Ditty Kummer, and a step-by-step illustration of vellum illumination and calligraphy.

**12**

# Doon

Lying a few kilometres northeast of Lough Gartan, **the Rock of Doon** and **Doon Well** are signposted off the R255 shortly after the village of **Termon** on the way to Kilmacrennan. Following the directions leads to a rural cul-de-sac right next to the well. A path from here ascends to a large bushy outcrop that is the Rock of Doon. From 1200 to 1603 this was the spot where the O'Donnell kings were crowned, standing above a huge gathering of their followers. The inauguration stone on the summit is said to bear the imprint of the first Tír Chonaill king, a mark into which every successor had to place his foot as his final confirmation. Doon, an ancient pagan healing **well**, is still a place of pilgrimage, marked out by a bush weighed down with personal effects left behind by the sick, hoping for a cure.

# Kilmacrennan

**KILMACRENNAN** is a crossroads village 10km north of Letterkenny on the N56. Four hundred metres towards Ramelton is yet another site with Colmcille connections, **Cill Mhic n-Eanain**, where Columba was fostered and educated by Cruithnechan in around 528. A monastery stood here from the sixth century to 1129, and it was also the site of the O'Donnells' religious inauguration following the rites at Doon. The ruins on the left are of a sixteenth-century Franciscan **friary**, while the Church of Ireland building to the right dates from 1622 and fell into disuse around 1845.

# The north Donegal coast

Running from the Cloghaneely district, which adjoins Gweedore, the **north Donegal coast** holds some of the most spectacular scenery in the whole country, where the battle between the elements is often startlingly apparent. Overshadowed at first by the bleak beauty of **Muckish Mountain** to the south, the main road from **Gortahork** to Milford passes through verdant countryside as it meanders around the deep bays and inlets and alongside the glorious and often deserted beaches which punctuate the shoreline. On the way, the Plantation town of **Dunfanaghy** provides a good base for exploring one of the coastline's two breathtaking peninsulas: **Horn Head**, with its rugged, sea-battered cliffs; and, further to the east, **Rosguill**, almost circumscribed by the marvellous Atlantic Drive.

## Gortahork to Falcarragh

The first place you'll encounter in **Cloghaneely**, east of the Bloody Foreland, is **GORTAHORK**, an Irish-speaking village with a strong cultural history, albeit with little in the way of sights.

Three kilometres east of Gortahork, **FALCARRAGH** is livelier and better supplied with shops. A short distance east of the central crossroads is **An tSean Bhearic** (Falcarragh Visitor Centre; Mon–Fri 10am–4pm, Sat 11am–4pm; free; ☏074 918 0655, ⓦfalcarraghvisitorcentre.com), housed in the old police barracks. This has a craft shop and café, as well as displays on the town and its policing history, and regularly hosts temporary exhibitions and cultural events. Falcarragh **beach** is reached by heading north at the village crossroads and turning right about 1.5km further on, then continuing east for 3km. This is one of the more beautiful strands on this northwest coast, but a strong undercurrent makes it **unsafe for swimming**.

### Muckish Mountain

The road south from Falcarragh to Glenveagh passes through **Muckish Gap**. The slate-grey mass of **Muckish Mountain** dominates the view, its sides pitted with old workings where quartzite sand was extracted for the manufacture of optical glass. It's a relatively easy climb from the roadside shrine at the Gap up a grassy ridge to the **summit** and, on a clear day, the entire coastline from the Bloody Foreland to Malin Head is splendidly visible from here.

## Dunfanaghy

The small Plantation town of **DUNFANAGHY**, 10km east of Falcarragh, is the gateway to the **Horn Head Peninsula**, and while there's little to get excited about in the town itself, it is a good little base, and there are a couple of fabulous places to eat.

### Workhouse Heritage Centre

Figart, Dunfanaghy, just off the N56 • April Mon–Sat 9.30am–5pm; May, June, Sept & Oct daily 9.30am–5pm; July & Aug, Halloween & Easter daily 9.30am–5.30pm; rest of year Mon–Wed 9.30am–4.30am • €5 • ☏074 913 6540, ⓦdunfanaghy.info

On Dunfanaghy's western outskirts you'll find the **Workhouse Heritage Centre**, sympathetically restored as a local history and community resource. Built in 1845 on the eve of the Great Famine, at first it had only five inmates, but by 1847, as the Famine intensified, over six hundred people were crowded inside. The Famine story is recounted upstairs through the tale of one local inmate, Hannah Herrity, who lived until 1926 – though the narrative method (a distinctly dull and disappointing series of tableaux) undermines the power of her story. The centre also displays work by local artists, and it has a coffee shop, and, somewhat surprisingly, a screen for film viewings, which usually take place on the last weekend of each month.

**12**

**Arnold's** Main St ☏ 074 913 6208, ⓦ arnoldshotel.com. The rooms here are nothing beyond the ordinary, but as it's the town's sole hotel, the prices are rather inflated; much better is the food, served in both its bar and restaurant. They also have riding stables and organize a variety of activities (including writing, photography and cycling). Nov–March weekends only. €140

**The Mill** By the lake on the western edge of town ☏ 074 913 6985, ⓦ themillrestaurant.com. This family-run restaurant serves scrumptious evening meals (€45); its seafood is especially well regarded, for example spiced Greencastle Monkfish and grilled Killybegs turbot. It also has superbly furnished en-suite rooms (available March–Nov), four of which have lake views. Restaurant May–Sept Wed–Sun 7–8.30pm; Oct Thurs–Sun same hours. €110

**Muck'n'Muffins** The Square ☏ 074 913 6780, ⓦ mucknmuffins.com. This once derelict grey-stone building is now a super little pottery studio and café; watch the ceramicists at work downstairs before heading upstairs to the warm café for coffee and a pastry. Summer Mon–Sat 9.30am–6pm, Sun 10am–6pm; winter Mon–Sat 9.30am–5pm, Sun 10.30am–5pm.

# Horn Head

**Horn Head** is magnificent, an almost 200m rock face scored by ledges on which perch countless guillemots and gulls, and small numbers of puffins. The best view of the cliffs, sea stacks and caves is from the water, but the cliff road is vertiginous enough in places to give you a good look down the sheer sides.

To get here, take the slip road at the western end of Dunfanaghy village; it descends to skirt the side of a beautiful inlet before rising steeply to go round the east side of the head. A spectacular vista of headlands opens up to the east – Rosguill, Fanad and Inishowen – but none can match the drama of Horn Head's **cliffs**, their tops clad in a thin cover of purplish heather. Alternatively, you can walk from Horn Head Bridge, 800m from Dunfanaghy on the Horn Head road, and head west across the dunes to **Tramore Beach**. Then follow the sheep track north, passing two small blowholes called the **Two Pistols** and then a much larger one, **McSwyney's Gun**, so-called because of the power of the sonic boom produced by the explosion of compressed air from the cavern. Erosion has occurred over the years, however, and you'll be lucky to hear anything these days. Continuing onwards, you'll come to **Pollaguill Bay** and beach. The next wondrous site is the more than 20m-high **Marble Arch**, cut by the sea through the base of Trawbreaga Head. Horn Head itself soon becomes visible as you ascend the next headland.

The **walk** as far as here takes around two hours from Dunfanaghy, and you can either complete the whole circuit of the peninsula (allow for a further 1–2hr) or head back by road.

# Marble Hill and Ards Forest Park

East of Dunfanaghy, the road follows the edge of **Sheephaven Bay**, and, shortly after passing through Portnablagh, a signposted turn-off leads to **Marble Hill Strand**, a vast, glorious sweep of sand. Overlooking the strand, Marble Hill House was once owned by **Hugh Law**, MP for Donegal from 1902 to 1918 and TD for the county from 1927 to 1932, who entertained all manner of celebrities here, including W.B. and Jack Yeats. Nearby, **Ards Forest Park** (daily: April–Sept 8am–8pm; Oct–March 8am–5pm; free, cars €5) occupies the former demesne of the Capuchin friary of Ard Mhuire; a 1.5km-long avenue alongside Lough Lilly takes you into its centre, where there are fine walks through the woodland as well as along the shore of Sheephaven Bay.

# Creeslough and around

The sleepy village of **CREESLOUGH** occupies a slope commanding gorgeous views across the head of Sheephaven Bay. Partway down its main street is a **church** designed by Liam McCormack, its whitewashed whorl and back-sloping table roof reflecting the thickly set Muckish Mountain nearby. **Lackagh Bridge**, about 6km east of Creeslough,

**12**

offers a tremendous viewpoint of Sheephaven Bay, the curving silted shoreline lying downstream and a ginger-brown picture of rushes and heather reaching deep into the hills. Immediately after the bridge there's a turn-off running for 3km to **Glen**, well worth taking for the opportunity to drop in at the *Olde Glen* **bar**. A minor road south from Glen leads up through gorgeously lonely landscapes and past a tremendous viewpoint overlooking Lough Salt before descending to Termon (see page 437).

**EATING AND DRINKING**          **CREESLOUGH AND AROUND**

**Olde Glen** Glen ☎083 158 5777, ⓦoldeglen.ie. Great-looking red-and-white-painted pub with an atmospheric, low-ceilinged interior and wonky stone flooring. People come from miles around to try the crab linguine or roasted duckling (€19.50) in the modern restaurant, but it's equally fab just for a pint of ale and some chatter in the front bar. Tues–Sun 11am–11pm.

# The Rosguill Peninsula

The route onto the extremely beautiful and very manageable **Rosguill Peninsula** starts by the side of the church in **Carrigart**, 13km northeast of Creeslough, and passes rabbit-infested dunes at the back of a tremendous and usually deserted **beach**. At the top of the strand is **DOWNINGS**, a sprightly holiday centre patronized mainly by Northern Irish tourists, with caravan sites hogging the rear end of the beach and holiday chalets creeping up the hillside behind the village.

Downings' main street heads northwards to become the panoramic **Atlantic Drive**, which runs around the headland and also makes for a stupendous 13km walk. The range of views encompasses the essence of Donegal – rugged landscapes in constant tussle with the Atlantic Ocean – though, sadly, this is becoming increasingly blighted by large numbers of new-build houses and caravan sites. About halfway along, a turning leads to **Melmore Head**, where you'll find the rather fine **Trá na Rosann** beach. A quicker way to get here is to take the right-hand fork on the way into Downings from Carrigart.

**ACCOMMODATION AND EATING**        **THE ROSGUILL PENINSULA**

**Harbour Bar** Uphill at the far end of Downings ☎074 915 5920. This is one of the most enjoyable pubs along this stretch of coast; along with glorious views of the bay, there's a toasty fire, lots of *craic* and music at weekends. Daily 10.30am–midnight.

**Rosapenna Hotel** Downings ☎074 915 5301, ⓦrosapenna.ie. Two of the north coast's finest golf courses straddle this upmarket hotel whose rooms are as plush as you might expect and, naturally, have stunning ocean views. Closed Nov–March. **€190**

**Trá na Rosann Hostel** Downings ☎074 915 5374. Designed by Edwin Lutyens, this erstwhile hunting lodge – a listed building – is now a superb alpine-style hostel with a mix of dorms and a self-catering kitchen. Closed early Sept to May. **€18**

**The Singing Pub** 5min drive from Downings ☎087 917 1950. The perfect pit stop on the Wild Atlantic Way, this welcoming pub has a traditional thatched roof, warm open fires and plenty of character. The menu changes weekly, with freshly caught seafood a regular feature. Daily 11am–11pm.

**SHOPPING**

**McNutt of Donegal** The Pier, Downings ☎074 915 5662, ⓦmcnuttofdonegal.com. For over sixty years the McNutt family have been making some of the world's finest weaves, from Donegal tweed to Irish linen, at their mill in Downings. The shop contains a wealth of crafts and gifts, with a tour of the factory also available (€5). March–Oct Mon–Sat 10.30am–5.30pm.

# The Fanad Peninsula

The least tempting of Donegal's peninsulas is **Fanad**, circumnavigated by the well-signposted **Fanad Drive**. The western shoreline has little to offer scenically, and the whole peninsula is best approached from Kilmacrennan through the pleasant towns of **Ramelton** and **Rathmullan**, the latter with some very swish accommodation, before heading on to **Fanad Head** itself.

## Rathmullan and around

Heading east out of Kilmacrennan, it's worth a quick stroll through **Ramelton**, a quaint and sedate little town sitting attractively on the eastern bank of the broad black flow of the salmon-rich River Leannan. Beyond here, **RATHMULLAN** is no less pretty, with its long row of multicoloured houses facing **Lough Swilly**; like Ramelton, though, the town has suffered badly in recent years, and many places have closed down, as has the ferry across to Buncrana in Inishowen. In 1587 the rebellious **Red Hugh O'Donnell** was lured onto a British merchant ship here on the pretext of a merry drink, and ended up in Dublin gaol for six years; and in 1607 Rathmullan was a departure point for the **Flight of the Earls**, the event that marked the end of the Gaelic nation. In October 1798 the French frigate *Hoche*, with Wolfe Tone on board, was intercepted in the lough nearby and Tone was captured and taken to Dublin for trial.

### ACCOMMODATION AND EATING                    RATHMULLAN AND AROUND

★ **Rathmullan House** By Lough Swilly ☏ 074 915 8188, ⓦ rathmullanhouse.com. Gracious country house set amid lush landscaped gardens. Most of the magnificent, classically furnished rooms have water views, while some have their own patio. Meanwhile, log fires burn away in sumptuously furnished lounges, but if you fancy more vigorous activity, you can avail yourself of the stunning indoor pool. **€190**

**The Taproom** Rathmullan House, by Lough Swilly ☏ 074 915 8874. The original kitchens in *Rathmullan House* have been converted into this brilliant cellar bar, offering a simple but cracking combination of wood-fired pizzas and craft beers, the latter from the neighbouring Kinnegar Brewery. Opening hours are seasonal and change regularly; check website.

## Portsalon

North of Rathmullan the R247 climbs to give great views across to **Dunree Head** and the **Urris** range of mountains on the Inishowen Peninsula to the east. Taking the first right turn will lead you along a minor road hugging the coastline, as it twists and turns up to the cliff-top approach to **Saldanha Head**. Here you'll witness the most spectacular views on the entire peninsula, looking across to Inishowen and down onto the 5km stretch of golden sand at Ballymastocker Bay.

### ACCOMMODATION AND EATING                                PORTSALON

★ **Portsalon Luxury Camping** Cashelpreaghan, Portsalonough ☏ 074 915 9957, ⓦ donegalglamping. com. With stunning views of Lough Swilly, the five luxury yurts in the grounds of this beautifully restored traditional farmhouse have kingsize beds, sofas and wood-burning stoves. About as romantic as it gets. Self-service, so no breakfast included. Minimum two night stay in July and Aug. **€100**

## Fanad Head

Most of the 8km route north from Portsalon to **Fanad Head** is through humpy and barren land, with clusters of granite pushing through marshy ground. Before reaching the Head, there is one curiosity worth taking in, just 2km north of Portsalon: the rock formation known as the **Seven Arches**, created by the constant erosive battering of the waters. To get here, follow the signpost on the right of the road, then take the path down to the new house, and finally cross the fields to the rocky strand. From here the main road leads straight on to **Fanad Head**, where it reaches a dramatically placed cliff-edge **lighthouse**.

# Letterkenny

Whatever your means of transport, if you're travelling through northern Donegal, you're almost certain to pass through **LETTERKENNY**, the county's largest town. There's

**LETTERKENNY**

EATING
| | |
|---|---|
| The Lemon Tree | 3 |
| Mulberry | 4 |
| The Quiet Moment | 1 |
| The Yellow Pepper | 2 |

DRINKING & NIGHTLIFE
| | |
|---|---|
| The Brewery | 1 |
| McGinley's | 3 |
| Voodoo Lounge | 2 |

ACCOMMODATION
| | |
|---|---|
| Apple Hostel | 3 |
| Castle Grove Country House | 1 |
| Dillons Hotel | 4 |
| Oaklands | 2 |
| Radisson Blu Hotel | 5 |
| Station House Hotel | 6 |

0          200
metres

very little by way of actuals sights in the town itself, which has undergone massive redevelopment in recent years, though it does retain a lively arts scene and some thriving nightlife. Its most notable visual element is the huge nineteenth-century **Cathedral of Saints Eunan and Columba** at the top of Church lane, with its intricate stone-roped ceiling, flying buttresses and Gaelicized Stations of the Cross.

## Donegal County Museum

High Rd • Mon–Fri 10am–12.30pm & 1–4.30pm, Sat 1–4.30pm • Free • ☎ 074 912 4613

The main point of interest in town is the **Donegal County Museum**, housed in part of the old Letterkenny workhouse. Temporary exhibitions occupy the downstairs area while the display in the first-floor gallery highlights the history of Donegal from the prehistoric period to the twentieth century using artefacts, archives and images. Visitors can also view both the Northwest Film Archive and Islands Archive which contain over a hundred hours of documentaries, news and drama.

## Tropical World

Alcorns Garden Centre, Loughnagin, 3km north of town on the R245 to Ramelton • April–Sept Mon–Fri 10am–5.30pm, Sun 1–5.30pm • €9 • ☎ 074 912 1541, ⓦ tropicalworld.ie

The Alcorns garden centre north of town is the unlikely setting for the sweet little **Tropical World**, which comprises a **mini-zoo**, housing sections on mammals (including lemurs, raccoons and otters), reptiles (snakes, geckos and lizards), creepy crawlies and birds. Here, too, is a wonderful **Butterfly House**, with a fabulous array of colourful specimens from around the world. Afterwards, parents can partake in some refreshment in the tea room while the little ones fool around in the excellent monkey swing indoor play area.

## ARRIVAL AND INFORMATION           LETTERKENNY

**By bus** The bus station is at the bottom of Port Rd. Destinations Ballyliffin (Mon–Fri 4 daily, Sat 1; 1hr 10min); Buncrana (Mon–Fri 4 daily, Sat 1; 45min); Derry (7–9 daily; 35min); Donegal town (7–9 daily; 50min); Lifford (hourly; 25–50min); Moville (Mon–Fri 3 daily, Sat 1; 1hr 30min); Raphoe (Mon–Sat 7 daily; 20–35min); Sligo (6 daily; 2hr).

**Tourist office** The tourist office is on Neil T. Blaney Road, by the roundabout 800m out of town towards Derry (June–Aug Mon–Fri 9am–5.30pm, Sat 10am–4pm; Sept–May Mon–Fri 9.15am–5pm; ☎ 074 912 1160, ⓦ letterkennytourism.ie).

## ACCOMMODATION           SEE MAP PAGE 442

**Apple Hostel** Covehill House, Port Rd ☎ 074 911 3291, ⓦ letterkennyhostel.com. Smart hostel located in secluded grounds up behind the cultural centre, with a mix of private and dormitory accommodation in two adjacent buildings; there's also a large kitchen, lounge with pool table, and laundry facilities. Camping is possible in the grounds and campers are free to use the hostel's facilities. Dorms €20, doubles €40, camping €8

**Castle Grove Country House** Ballymaleel, 3km out on the Ramelton road ☎ 074 915 1118, ⓦ castlegrove.com. This elegant seventeenth-century house, pitched among stately grounds overlooking Lough Swilly, offers splendidly furnished, Georgian-era rooms. €130

**Dillons Hotel** 29–45 Main St ☎ 074 912 2977, ⓦ dillons-hotel.ie. This most central of hotels offers impeccably turned out rooms, alongside a classy bistro and bar. €89

**Oaklands** 8 Oaklands Park, Gortlee Rd ☎ 074 912 5529, ⓦ letterkennybandb.com. A 10min walk from the centre, this tidy B&B is a little tricky to find – it's at the end of a residential cul-de-sac – but the six rooms are immaculately kept and the hospitality is genuinely warm. €70

★ **Radisson Blu Hotel** The Loop Road ☎ 074 919 4444, ⓦ radissonhotels.com. The location, on a main road opposite a retail park, is rather dull, but this discreet high-rise is as plush as you'd expect from this hotel chain; the rooms are supremely comfortable, the service is impeccable, and there are a couple of superb eating areas. €109

**Station House Hotel** Lower Main St ☎ 074 912 3100, ⓦ stationhouseletterkenny.com. You wouldn't think so to look at it, but this is the old station house building, hence the name and the occasional nod to the old railway that used to run through these parts; bright, light-filled corridors lead to perky rooms with gleaming glass-panelled bathrooms. €109

**12**

## EATING           SEE MAP PAGE 442

**The Lemon Tree** Lower Main St ☎ 074 912 5788, ⓦ the lemontreerestaurant.com. Delicious modern Irish cuisine with a discernible French influence, manifest in dishes like baked duck breast with caramelized pear soy and honey sauce (€21); the restaurant, with its subtle pastel colours and candle-topped tables, looks fantastic. Mon–Sat 5–9.30pm, Sun 1–2.30pm & 5–9pm.

**Mulberry** Radisson Blu Hotel ☎ 074 919 4444. Tip-top dining in the *Radisson's* dazzling restaurant, featuring a great (if meat-heavy) menu, with exceptional steaks (€23–34), as well as seafood and gourmet burgers. Daily noon–9.30pm.

**The Quiet Moment** Upper Main St ☎ 074 912 8382, ⓦ quietmoment.ie. Letterkenny's most enticing café

captures the ambience of Dublin's *Bewley's* (see page 98) with some success, thanks to its thick, oak-panelled walls and deep green leather armchairs; great coffee, snacks, lunches and breakfasts. Mon–Sat 8am–6pm, Sun 10am–4pm.

★ **The Yellow Pepper** 36 Lower Main St ☎ 074 912 4133, ⓦ yellowpepperrestaurant.com. The cast-iron pillars and thick stone walls are reminders of what was once an old shirt factory; these days, however, this is a cheery, family-run restaurant where you can tuck into dry-aged sirloin and seafood platters along with one of the many bottles of wine stacked up high behind the bar. Exemplary service too. Daily noon–10pm.

## DRINKING AND NIGHTLIFE SEE MAP PAGE 442

**The Brewery** Market Square ☎074 912 7330, ⓦthe brewerybar.com. Popular bar-restaurant with a striking all wood and brass interior. An exciting line-up of more than twenty craft beers complements fine menus in both the bar and restaurant. Live music Tues–Sat. Mon–Thurs 10.30am–11.30pm, Fri & Sat 10.30am–12.30am, Sun noon–11pm.

**McGinley's** Lower Main St ☎086 784 0783. Of all this street's many hostelries, *McGinley's* is by far the most agreeable – and most frequented – thanks to its dark yet cosy bar, and pretty much nightly music sessions, the most popular of which takes place on Wed. Daily 10.30am–midnight.

**Voodoo Lounge** 36 Lower Main St ☎074 910 9815. Good-time, state-of-the-art multi-roomed club with top-name DJs at weekends and occasional live bands; they also offer food. Opening times vary.

## ENTERTAINMENT

**An Grianán** Port Rd ☎074 912 0777, ⓦangrianan.com. Top-notch local theatre offering an impressive drama programme. It's also one of Ireland's best music venues, from traditional to classical. There's a super little café here too. Café Mon–Fri 9.30am–3pm.

**Regional Cultural Centre** 46 Port Rd ☎074 912 9186, ⓦregionalculturalcentre.com. Just behind An Grianán, the regional cultural centre mounts a variety of exhibitions and a regular programme of concerts, covering jazz to traditional music. It's also the principal venue for the two-week Earagail Arts Festival in mid-July (ⓦeaf.ie). Tues–Fri 9.30am–5pm, Sat 11am–5pm.

# Raphoe

Thirteen kilometres southeast of Letterkenny, **RAPHOE** is set trimly around one of the largest Diamonds in the county. Once a see in its own right, its ecclesiastical importance is still indicated today by its inclusion in the Church of Ireland bishopric of Derry and Raphoe. The town's **cathedral**, dedicated to St Eunan (the biographer of St Columba), was founded in the ninth century, but the present plain Gothic-cathedral version dates merely from 1702. Transfixed in the inner wall is a stone block with some peculiar, indecipherable carvings, and there's a very impressive and resonant wooden baptismal chapel.

## Beltany Stone Circle

Three kilometres south of Raphoe is the **Beltany Stone Circle**, one of the best-preserved circles in the country. Consisting of approximately sixty stones, varying in height between 30cm and over 1m, it provides an atmospheric vantage point for a marvellous panoramic view of the local valleys and distant mountains. To get here, follow the signs from the south of The Diamond in Raphoe and you'll arrive at the entrance to a farm. The circle is 400m up the bridle path to the right, over a stile and across a field full of sheep.

## ARRIVAL AND DEPARTURE RAPHOE

**By bus** Buses serving Letterkenny (Mon–Sat 6 daily; 20–35min) and Lifford (Mon–Sat 3 daily; 15min) stop in the centre of the village.

# Lifford and around

Six kilometres southeast of Raphoe, **LIFFORD** was formerly Donegal's legal centre and the County Council is still based here. The graceful **Old Courthouse**, dating from 1746, houses a **visitor centre** on The Diamond (Mon–Sat 10am–5pm, Sun 1–5pm; €6; ☎074 914 1733, ⓦliffordoldcourthouse.com) which tells the story of the O'Donnell clan and Napper Tandy (see page 431), as well as notable events in Donegal's history. In the basement cells there's a pretty gruesome re-creation of the prison conditions and you can have your mugshot taken behind the bars (€3).

Standing 3km northwest of Lifford, off the N14, **Cavanacor House** (Wed–Sat 2–6pm; free; ☎085 164 2525, ⓦcavanacorgallery.ie) is a fine seventeenth-century mansion where **James II** dined in 1689, and which was also the ancestral home of **James Knox Polk**, US president from 1845 to 1849. The real treat is its **art gallery**, displaying a changing array of work by contemporary Irish and international painters and sculptors.

**By bus** Lifford is served by buses from/to Letterkenny   (hourly; 25–45min) and Raphoe (Mon–Sat 5 daily; 15min).

# The Inishowen Peninsula

The **Inishowen Peninsula** in the northeast of County Donegal is perhaps the great overlooked treasure of the Irish landscape (and certainly has the longest signposted scenic drive – the "Inishowen 100"), offering a diverse and visually exciting terrain, where the views usually encompass the waters of the loughs or the Atlantic waves. Virtually every aspect of the landscape is superb – the **beaches** (especially Kinnego Bay, Culdaff, Tullagh and Pollan), the towering headland bluffs (Malin, Inishowen, Dunaff and Dunree) and the central mountain range, with towering **Slieve Snaght** at the middle of it all.

The peninsula derives its name from **Eoghán**, who was made First Lord of the island by his father Niall, High King of Ireland. Phases of the peninsula's history before and after Eoghán have left a legacy of fine antiquities, from the **Grianán Ailigh** fort to a host of beautiful early **Christian crosses** (Cloncha, Mura, Carrowmore and Cooley).

## GETTING AROUND                                                THE INISHOWEN PENINSULA

**By bus** Services on the peninsula are extremely limited and, though you can reach places such as Buncrana and Ballyliffin fairly easily, you'll certainly need your own transport to explore Malin Head.

## Burt Church

Near Bridgend on the N13 Letterkenny–Derry road • ☎ 074 936 0151, ⊚ dunleweycentre.com

The approach to the most stimulating of all Inishowen's sights, the ancient fort known as the Grianán Ailigh, passes the Liam McCormack-designed **Burt Church**, the most beautiful twentieth-century church in all Ireland – like other McCormack designs in Donegal (see pages 428 and 439), its structure is evocative of the mystical landmark nearby. The seating is set concentrically, under a whitewashed ceiling that sweeps up into a vortex to allow sunlight to beam down directly upon the altar; the allusions in every detail to Neolithic sepulchral architecture, especially Newgrange (see page 139), are fascinating and very atmospheric. In a survey of Irish architects the church was voted Ireland's building of the twentieth century.

To learn more about the church and its legends, head to the *An Grianan Hotel*, just down the road in the village of **Burt**, which incorporates the somewhat confusingly named **Old Church Visitor Centre** (daily 11am–5.30pm; €3; ☎074 936 8900, ⊚oldchurchvisitorcentre. com), which concentrates on both Burt Church and the area's myths and legends.

## Grianán Ailigh

3km up the hill from Burt Church • Open access

The origins of the **Grianán Ailigh** date from 1700 BC, and it's thought to be linked to the Tuátha Dé Danann, pre-Celtic invaders. It was sufficiently significant to be included by Ptolemy, the Alexandrian geographer, in his second-century AD map of the world, and was the base of various northern Irish chieftains. Here, in 450, St Patrick is said to have baptized Eoghán, the founder of the O'Neill clan that ruled the kingdom of Ailigh for more than five hundred years. In the twelfth century, the fort was sacked by Murtagh O'Brian, King of Thomond, in retribution for a raid on Clare, and a large amount of its stone was carried away. Today's impressive building was largely reconstructed in the 1870s by Walter Bernard from Derry and is the only remaining terraced fort in Ireland.

## Fahan and Buncrana

**FAHAN**, 6km north of **Burnfoot**, a main entry-point to Inishowen, boasts impressive monastic ruins. The first abbot here was St Mura, and surviving from his time is a seventh-century **cross slab**, a spellbinding example of early Christian stone decoration. Long-stemmed Latin crosses are carved on both faces with typical Celtic interlacing.

Five kilometres north of Fahan, **BUNCRANA** is the largest town on Inishowen and bills itself as a resort, though, frankly, the town's only attractions are its Lough Swilly setting some distance west of the centre. That said, Inishowen's sole tourist office is located here, and there are some enticing possibilities for sleeping and eating.

## ARRIVAL AND INFORMATION                                      FAHAN AND BUNCRANA

**By bus** In Buncrana buses set down on Market Square in the centre of town, and on Corkhill Rd, the main road heading north. In Fahan they stop on the main road by the old rectory, at the south end of the village.

---

### DRIVING DONEGAL'S WILD ATLANTIC WAY

Arguably the most spectacular portion of the **Wild Atlantic Way**, the Donegal route hugs the coastline right up to Ireland's most northerly point. Taking in major sites such as Glenveagh National Park, Malin Head, Tory Island and Slieve League, it's the constant and breathtaking scenery that makes it so special. Although it's best to explore the area at a leisurely pace, if your time is limited you could follow the handy one- or two-day itinerary suggested below.

**Day 1** consists of a looping 154km trip which begins and ends in Buncrana. Traveling along the R238 there are stops in Grianán Áileach, Greencastle and Malin Head, with plenty to see in between. The total drive time should be about three hours. **Day 2** again begins in Buncrana, this time taking the N13 to Rathmullan. From there it's a forty-minute drive along the R268 to **Fanad Head**, home of the Wild Atlantic Way's iconic lighthouses. From there it's on to **Glenveagh National Park** with a stop in The Singing Pub on the way. The time spent driving should be around two hours forty-five minutes.

---

**Destinations** Ballyliffin (Mon–Fri 4 daily, Sat 1; 25min); Derry (Mon–Sat hourly, Sun 2; 35min); Letterkenny (Mon–Fri 4 daily, Sat 1; 45min); Malin (Mon–Sat 1 daily; 40min); Moville (Mon–Fri 3 daily, Sat 1; 1hr).

**Tourist office** The Inishowen tourist office is on Railway Rd, the main road leading into Buncrana (June–Sept Mon–Sat 9am–5pm; Oct–March Mon–Fri 9am–5pm; ☎ 074 936 2602, ⌨ govisitinishowen.com). Its friendly staff can supply you with information on the whole peninsula.

### ACCOMMODATION AND EATING

★ **Beach House** The Pier, Swill Rd, Buncrana ☎ 074 936 1050. Not only the best restaurant in Buncrana, but one of the finest on the peninsula; the glorious views aside, the food here is exceptional, with a main dinner menu featuring the likes of Silverhill duck breast with salt baked celariac (€21.95), and a lighter lunch-time café menu, which might include a Lough Swilly seafood chowder. Mon, Thurs & Fri 4–10pm, Sat & Sun 12.30–4pm & 5–10pm.

**Inishowen Gateway Hotel** Railway Rd, Buncrana ☎ 074 936 1144, ⌨ inishowengateway.com. The most prominent accommodation in town is this large roadside hotel, with spruce rooms, its own leisure centre and pool, spa and wellness centre. €114

**Tullyvaran Mill Off** Drumree Rd, 2km north of Buncrana ☎ 074 936 1613, ⌨ tullyarvanmill.com. This renovated corn mill, picturesquely set on the banks of the Crana River, has spotless en-suite dormitory, family and private accommodation, and a self-catering kitchen. Dorms €17, doubles €50

## Fort Dunree

Dunree Head, 10km north of Buncrana • Mon–Fri 10.30am–4.30pm, Sat & Sun 10.30am–6pm • €7, family ticket €15 • ☎ 074 936 1817, ⌨ dunree.pro.ie

Perched on a headland overlooking the mouth of Lough Swilly, just past the village from which it takes its name, **Fort Dunree** began life as a Martello tower and stands near the spot where Wolfe Tone was brought ashore in 1798. The tower was subsequently enlarged into a fortress to guard against the possible return of the French and was further developed in the late nineteenth century. It now has a **museum** of predictable military memorabilia, with interactive displays providing an insight into the fort's former use; more interesting is a Siemens searchlight dating from 1899, which is still put to use on special occasions. The fort's upper reaches, meanwhile, keep two impressive breach-loading guns dating from 1911. It also houses a Wildlife Discovery room, and a coffee shop with wonderful views.

## Mamore Gap

North out of Dunree village the road climbs steeply past a scattering of weather-beaten thatched cottages before crossing a small bridge close to the **MAMORE GAP,** which seems like a chunk bitten out of the Urris Hills. From the top of the Gap the road spirals

**12**

steeply downwards, each bend providing an ever wider and more spectacular view of the flat foreground to **Dunaff Head**. The gorgeous, 1.5km-long **Tullagh Strand** to the east of Dunaff Head is a safe bathing beach.

## Ballyliffin

From Tullagh Strand, the route insinuates itself inland between the mountains to **Clonmany**, a neat village of predominantly cream-coloured houses, quiet for most of the year but hyperactive during its week-long **festival** in early August (⊛clonmanyfestival.com). Two kilometres beyond is the more upmarket **BALLYLIFFIN**, home to the Ballyliffin **golf** club – comprising two championship links courses. Golfing aside, there is some excellent accommodation here, plus one or two enjoyable places to eat and drink.

### ARRIVAL AND DEPARTURE BALLYLIFFIN

**By bus** Buses stop in the centre of the village.
Destinations Buncrana (Mon–Fri 4 daily, Sat 1; 25min); Letterkenny (Mon–Fri 4 daily, Sat 1; 1hr 15min); Moville (Mon–Fri 3 daily, Sat 1; 35min).

### ACCOMMODATION AND EATING

**Ballyliffin Hotel** Main St ☎ 074 937 6106, ⊛ballyliffin hotel.com. It's a toss-up between the four hotels in the village, but the Ballyliffin is as accomplished as any of them; warm, maroon-coloured rooms and a very creditable restaurant. Good midweek deals available. **€110**

**Nancy's Barn** Main St ☎ 086 843 28977, ⊛nancysbarn. ie. Handsome stone barn with a warming cottagey interior, serving great coffee, delicious home-baked treats and desserts, and more substantial fare like warming soups and toasted sandwiches. Mon–Fri 11am–4pm, Sat & Sun 9.30am–5.30pm.

**The Rusty Nail** Crossconnell, Clonmany ☎ 074 937 6116. Cheery roadside pub offering good-value bar food, but better known for its gut-busting Sunday lunches, plus there's live music at weekends. Wed–Fri 3–11.30pm, Sat 3pm–12.30am, Sun 2–11pm.

## Carrickabraghy Castle and Doagh Isle

North of Ballyliffin is the entrancing **Pollan Strand**, at whose furthest tip stands the ruin of **Carrickabraghy Castle**, a sixteenth-century O'Doherty fortification. Much weathered by spray and sea salt, the castle's stones are streaked with colours ranging from the darkest hues to golden yellows. The strand itself has wonderfully wild breakers, which unfortunately make swimming dangerous. The castle sits on the western side of **DOAGH ISLE**, now linked to the mainland through centuries of silt accumulation, on whose eastern edge lies **Trawbreaga Bay**, an exquisite piece of coastline. The mouth of the bay is bewitching: strolling onto the beach here you'll discover rocks fashioned into extraordinary shapes and colours by the sea.

### Doagh Famine Village

Lagacurry, 6km north of Ballyliffin • Mid-March to Oct daily 10am–5pm • €10 • ☎ 086 846 4749, ⊛ doaghfaminevillage.com

One sight not to be missed in this part of the peninsula is the outdoor **Doagh Famine Village**, which, for the most part, recalls the struggles of those who lived through the Famine of the 1840s. That aside, the museum manifests an enlightening, if slightly peculiar, coterie of attractions, including a Wake House, a Republican Safe House and an eviction scene. Visitors are free to nosey around by themselves, but you'll get much more out of the visit if you partake in one of the hugely entertaining **guided tours** (included in the price) – and once you're done, you'll be invited inside the teahouse for a cup of tea and some wheaten bread with jam, which is also included.

## Culdaff

**CULDAFF** is a cosy village whose nearby **beach** forms a stunning natural crescent. There's a major **sea-angling festival** here at the end of July and, in early October, a cultural weekend commemorates the eighteenth-century actor, **Charles Macklin**. Otherwise, its main point of interest is the superb village hotel/pub.

### ARRIVAL AND DEPARTURE
CULDAFF

**By bus** Buses drop off on, and depart from, Main St. Destinations Ballyliffin (Mon–Fri 2 daily, Sat 1; 25min); Buncrana (Mon–Fri 2 daily, Sat 1; 55min); Letterkenny (Mon–Fri 2 daily, Sat 1; 1hr 40min); Malin town (Mon–Fri 2 daily, Sat 1; 5min).

### ACCOMMODATION AND EATING

**McGrory's** Main St ☎074 937 9104, ⓦmcgrorys.ie. This fabulous all-rounder offers classy rooms, many having retained their original exposed brickwork, and an equally fine bar, offering cracking meals including locally caught shellfish. Entertainment-wise, its *Backroom* is one of the best venues in Ireland for live music, regularly pulling in some big names, while the Front Bar hosts traditional sessions, typically on Tues and Fri. The three-course menu (€19.95) is a bargain. Bar daily 11.30am–midnight. €118

## Malin and Malin Head

Seven kilometres west of Culdaff is the planter settlement of **MALIN**, tucked picturesquely into the side of Trawbreaga Bay, with a charming grassy Diamond at its centre. A little way north of Malin, a signpost points to **Five Fingers Strand**, across the bay from Doagh Isle – it's worth the diversion to experience the ferocity of the breakers on the beach and the long walks on its sands, though the strand has undergone recent severe coastal erosion.

Sixteen kilometres north of Malin village, **Malin Head**, the northernmost extremity of Ireland, might not be as stupendous as other Donegal headlands but is nevertheless excellent for blustery, winding coastal walks – and for ornithologists: choughs, with their glossy black plumage, red legs and bill, inhabit the cliffs, and the rasping cry of the rare corncrake can be heard in the fields. The tip of the headland is marked by **Bamba's Crown**, a ruined Napoleonic signal tower, and the western path from here heads out to **Hell's Hole**, a 75m chasm in the cliffs, which roars with the onrushing tide.

**12**

### ARRIVAL AND DEPARTURE
MALIN AND MALIN HEAD

**By bus** Buses drop off on and depart from the Diamond. Destinations Buncrana (Mon–Fri 2 daily, Sat 1; 40min); Culdaff (Mon–Sat 1 daily; 5min); Derry (Mon–Sat 2 daily; 1hr).

### ACCOMMODATION AND EATING

**Sandrock Holiday Hostel** Port Ronan Pier ☎074 937 0289, ⓦsandrockhostel.com. In a fantastic location just above the beach, this bungalow-like building has two simple dorms, each sleeping ten, and both with wonderful sea views. Self-catering kitchen, lounge with library, and bikes for rent (€10/day). It stays open for most of the year, but does close occasionally so it's worth checking online ahead of time. Dorms €13.50

**Seaview Tavern** Malin Head ☎074 937 0117, ⓦseaviewtavern.ie. Attached to a tiny bar, this rather ordinary-looking restaurant is actually very good, though you'll not want to venture far from the ocean-facing terrace in warmer weather. Its speciality is fish straight off the boat, including unbeatable Atlantic wild lobster. The guesthouse has some very comfortable rooms at decent prices. Free camping available. Restaurant daily 11am–9.30pm. €85

★ **Whitestrand B&B** Malin Head ☎074 937 0335, ⓦwhitestrand.net. Delightful three-room guesthouse just a short stroll from the beach, whose proprietor couldn't be more welcoming – you'll get home-baked goodies upon arrival and a sumptuous breakfast to see you on your way. €80

## Greencastle

The harbour village of **GREENCASTLE** on the eastern side of Inishowen has a pleasant view across to Magilligan Strand on the opposite side of Lough Foyle, and there's a **ferry** from here to Magilligan Point in Derry. By the road to Stroove are the ruins of the fourteenth-century Anglo-Norman **castle** from which the village gets its name, built on a rocky knoll to guard the narrowest part of the lough.

## Maritime Museum and Planetarium

Greencastle harbour • Easter–Sept Mon–Sat 9.30am–5.30pm, Sun noon–5.30pm; Oct–Easter Mon–Fri 9.15am–5.30pm • Museum €5, museum and planetarium €10 • ☎ 074 938 1363, ⊛ inishowenmaritime.com

By the harbour, in the old coastguard station, is the **Maritime Museum and Planetarium**, which recalls maritime travel from bygone times through a range of Irish boats from 2m to 20m in length. Among the maritime memorabilia, pride of place goes to a nineteenth-century rocket cart used to fire flares to aid survivors of wrecked ships. The state-of-the-art planetarium takes you on exhilarating trips through the universe, while regular laser light shows feature a traditional-music soundtrack; there are also custom shows (minimum ten people) where you can choose your own musical backing.

### ARRIVAL AND DEPARTURE

GREENCASTLE

**By bus** Buses from/to Derry (3 daily; 1hr 10min) and Moville (3 daily; 25min) stop on Main St.

**By boat** Magilligan Point (daily on the hour: March–June, Sept & Oct 9am–7pm; July & Aug 9am–8.15pm; Nov–Feb 9am–5pm; pedestrians €2.50 single, €3.50 return; cars €12 single, €16 return; ☎ 074 938 1901, ⊛ loughfoyleferry.com).

### EATING AND DRINKING

★ **Kealy's** The Harbour ☎ 074 938 1010, ⊛ kealys seafoodbar.ie. Unsurprisingly, Greencastle is a great spot for seafood, but the one place to aim for is *Kealy's* seafood bar, reckoned to be one of the best in Donegal, and here's why: lobster thermidor, pan-fried medallions of monkfish, whole Dover sole on the bone with capers, plus loads more. The early-bird menu is incredible value, with three courses for €26. Thurs–Sun 12.30–3pm & 5–9.30pm.

**12**

12

# Belfast

TITANIC BELFAST

# 5 Belfast

Bustling and vibrant Belfast is a city reborn. Not only has Northern Ireland's capital successfully shaken off the "war-torn" label it earned during the Troubles – it's fair to say the city has undergone a full-blown renaissance. In the aftermath of the peace process, instigated by the 1998 Good Friday Agreement, investment has poured in, resulting in a thriving restaurant scene and a buzzing café culture, while new hotels – running the gamut from five-star glitz to funky and boutique – have sprung up in response to dramatically increasing tourist numbers. In keeping with its long tradition of supplying a stream of musicians, poets, artists and writers to the world stage, Belfast has also welcomed several new arts and music festivals: the Belfast International Arts Festival at Queens still takes place every autumn, but Tennents Vital, Belsonic, Festival of Fools, Cinemagic and the Cathedral Quarter Arts Festival (CQAF) are also established fixtures in the city's calendar.

At first glance, Belfast has much in common with the large industrial ports found elsewhere in the UK, with its docklands and business districts. But then you encounter the people, a set of inhabitants whose pride and sense of humour remained undimmed even as the world's media camped on their doorstep, broadcasting their woes and turmoil around the globe. It is they, together with the near-miraculous revival in their city's fortunes over the past decade, that really set the place apart. You can easily – and richly – fill at least a few days here, although the geography of the North makes Belfast a good base for exploring virtually anywhere else in the province.

Though the **city centre** is still characterized by numerous elegant Victorian buildings, there's been an enormous transformation, not least in the greater prosperity of the shopping streets. Big brands that once shunned Belfast because of its escalating insurance costs now occupy large units in the main commercial drags leading off from **Donegall Square North** (home to the iconic City Hall with its distinctive copper dome) and in the newly developed upmarket shopping complex, Victoria Square.

The rejuvenated area of refurbished warehouses and shop fronts from Ann Street to Donegall Street is now known as the **Cathedral Quarter** and plays host to a lively arts scene and a fantastic choice of bars and restaurants. A short walk northeast across the River Lagan brings you to the newly developed **Titanic Quarter**, where the multi-million pound **Titanic Belfast** visitor attraction charts the design, build, launch and sinking of the world's most famous ocean liner, RMS *Titanic*. This area is fast becoming the city's media hub with the recent opening of new film studios and broadcast facilities – the globally successful HBO fantasy series, *Games of Thrones*, is already filmed here in the Paint Hall Studios. To the south of the city centre proper lie **Queen's University** and the extensive collections of the refurbished **Ulster Museum**, set in the grounds of the **Botanic Gardens**.

Further out, around 3km to the north, a climb up **Cave Hill** rewards with marvellous views of the city, spread out around the curve of its natural harbour, **Belfast Lough**. The city's once-formidable security presence and fortifications are now virtually invisible, but the iron blockade known as the **Peace Line** still bisects the Catholic and Protestant communities of **West Belfast**, a grim physical reminder of sectarian divisions. A short bus ride to the east of the city delivers visitors to the **Stormont Estate**, home to the Northern Ireland Assembly. On a sunny day, the grounds surrounding the instantly recognizable "white house on the hill", as locals refer to it, provide the ideal picnic spot with woodland walks.

BELFAST CITY HALL

# Highlights

**❶ The Titanic Quarter** The city's redeveloped docklands are home to the multimillion-pound interactive visitor centre, Titanic Belfast, which tells the story of the ill-fated RMS *Titanic*. See page 461

**❷ Ulster Museum** A multitude of fascinating exhibits dating back to prehistoric times, as well as one of Ireland's major art collections and a superb children's zone. See page 464

**❸ Stormont** The seat of government in Northern Ireland is set in glorious parkland to the east of the city. See page 466

**❹ Cave Hill** The best spot for a panoramic view of the city, with Belfast Lough spread out below. See page 467

**❺ West Belfast** An essential part of any visit to the city: the murals, Peace Line, cemeteries and fortified bars put everyday life into stark political context. See page 467

**❻ The Cathedral Quarter** Belfast's cultural hub, with a plethora of great restaurants, cafés, pubs, arts centres, music venues and its very own Cathedral Quarter Arts Festival (CQAF). See page 459

**HIGHLIGHTS ARE MARKED ON THE MAPS ON PAGES 457 AND 463**

**5**

### Brief history

Belfast began life as a cluster of forts built to guard a ford across the **River Farset**, which nowadays runs underground beneath the High Street. An **Anglo-Norman castle** was built here in 1177, but its influence was limited, and within a hundred years or so control over the Lagan Valley had reverted firmly to the Irish, under the O'Neills of Clandeboye. In 1604, **Sir Arthur Chichester**, whose son was to be the First Earl of Donegall, was "planted" in the area by James I, and shortly afterwards the tiny settlement was granted a charter creating a corporate borough. It was not until the end of the seventeenth century, though, that Belfast began to grow significantly, when French Huguenots fleeing persecution brought skills which rapidly improved the fortunes of the local **linen industry** – which, in turn, attracted new workers and wealth.

#### The eighteenth and nineteenth centuries

Through the eighteenth century, the cloth trade and **shipbuilding** expanded tremendously, and the population increased tenfold in a hundred years. With economic prosperity, Belfast became a city noted for its **liberalism**: in 1791, three Presbyterian Ulstermen formed the **Society of United Irishmen**, a gathering embracing Catholics and Protestants on the basis of common Irish nationality, from which sprang the **1798 Rebellion**. However, the rebellion in the North was quickly and ruthlessly stamped out by the English, and within two generations most Protestants had abandoned the Nationalist cause. Presbyterian ministers began openly to attack the Catholic Church, resulting in a **sectarian divide** that as time drew on became wider and increasingly violent. At the same time, the nineteenth century saw vigorous commercial and industrial expansion, and by the time Queen Victoria granted Belfast **city status** in 1888, its population had risen to 208,000, soon exceeding that of Dublin.

#### The twentieth century to the present day

With **Partition** came the creation of Northern Ireland with Belfast as its capital and Stormont as its seat of government. Inevitably, this boosted the city's status but also ensured that it would ultimately become the focus for much of the Troubles. The economic status of the Catholic population was deliberately maintained at a low level by a **Stormont government** that largely consisted of Protestant landowners and businessmen and saw no reason to challenge existing sectarian employment, housing and policing policies – all fuel to the fire which was to follow.

For 25 years from 1969, Belfast witnessed the worst of the **Troubles** (see pages 468 and 581), and by the time the IRA declared a **ceasefire** in 1994, much of the city resembled a battle site. There then followed a sea change in the city's fortunes as Britain and the EU funded a **revitalization** programme costing billions of pounds. Major shopping centres were built, swish hotels, bars and restaurants seemed to spring up almost overnight, and buildings such as the Waterfront Hall and Odyssey complex fundamentally altered the city's skyline. In the past decade, a crop of new entrepreneurs returned home, many having cut their teeth in businesses, restaurants and bars overseas, and set about effecting a new round of changes. Derelict buildings have been successfully restored and reopened in various guises, serving as everything from restaurants to accommodation options for all budgets. At times, sectarianism still raises its ugly head – but on the whole, vibrant new areas such as the Cathedral and Titanic Quarters keep Belfast looking to the future.

## The city centre

The core of Belfast is stately **Donegall Square**, home to the copper-domed City Hall and its pristine gardens, where locals and visitors congregate for lunchtime picnics in fine weather. Buses and taxis depart for every part of the city from the sides of the

## CENTRAL BELFAST

### HIGHLIGHTS

1. The Titanic Quarter
2. Stormont
3. Cave Hill
4. West Belfast
5. The Cathedral Quarter

### ◼ DRINKING & NIGHTLIFE

**DRINKING**

| | |
|---|---|
| The Crown Liquor Saloon | 15 |
| The Duke of York | 6 |
| The Harp Bar | 7 |
| The John Hewitt | 5 |
| Kelly's Cellars | 13 |
| The Morning Star | 12 |
| Muriel's Café Bar | 10 |
| Sunflower | 4 |
| White's Tavern | 11 |

**NIGHTLIFE**

| | |
|---|---|
| The Dirty Onion | 8 |
| Love & Death Inc | 14 |
| Ollie's | 9 |
| LGBTQ | |
| Kremlin | 1 |
| Maverick | 3 |
| Union Street Bar | 2 |

### ● EATING

| | |
|---|---|
| Boojum | 11 |
| Bubbacue | 9 |
| Coppi | 13 |
| Cyprus Avenue | 15 |
| Deanes | 16 |
| Established Coffee | 3 |
| General Merchants | 14 |
| Grapevine | 5 |
| Hadskis | 4 |
| Holohan's at the Barge | 8 |
| Home Restaurant | 12 |
| House of Zen | 2 |
| Howard Street | 15 |
| James St | 17 |
| Kaffe O | 10 |
| Mourne Seafood Bar | 7 |
| OX | 6 |

### ● SHOPPING

| | |
|---|---|
| Fresh Garbage | 2 |
| Sawers | 3 |
| Sick Records | 1 |

### ◼ ACCOMMODATION

| | |
|---|---|
| Bullit | 5 |
| Europa Hotel | 9 |
| The Fitzwilliam Hotel | 8 |
| George Best Hotel | 7 |
| Malmaison | 4 |
| The Merchant | 2 |
| Premier Inn | 3 |
| Ramada by Wyndham | 1 |
| Ten Square | 6 |

0  200 metres

5

**5**

square, ensuring that it's always busy with both pedestrians and traffic. The city's main shopping area once lay a stone's throw to the north until upstaged by the Victoria Square complex, with its raft of upmarket retailers, just to the east. Entertainment and accommodation options proliferate immediately south and north of the square, although the rejuvenation of St Anne's Square has helped to establish the **Cathedral Quarter** as Belfast's coolest night-time hub. Most of the grand old Victorian buildings that characterize the city are to the north and east, towards the river, including St Malachy's church.

The **River Lagan** flows towards Belfast Lough along the eastern side of the city centre, offering excellent riverside walks. It is also home to the first of the city's radical new developments in peace times, the **Laganside**, focused on the Waterfront Hall and the Odyssey Complex across the water. Beyond the Odyssey, in the heart of the **Titanic Quarter**, stands the city's latest success story, **Titanic Belfast**, a fully interactive museum built at a cost of £77 million to commemorate the centenary of the ill-fated RMS *Titanic*.

## City Hall

Donegall Square North (access for tours is via the main entrance, though on Sat it's the back door on the south side of the square) • Ground floor exhibitions Mon–Wed & Fri 9.30am–5pm, Thurs 9.30am–8pm, Sat 10am–5pm; tours (45min) Mon–Fri 11am, 2pm & 3pm, Sat & Sun 2pm & 3pm, with additional tours June–Sept Mon–Fri 10am & 4pm, Sat & Sun noon & 4pm • Free (audio-tour £3.50) • ☎ 02890 320202, ⓦ belfastcity.gov.uk/cityhall

The vast Neoclassical bulk of **City Hall** dominates Donegall Square and the entire centre of Belfast. Completed in 1906 and made of bright white Portland stone, its turrets, saucer domes, scrolls and pinnacle pots are all representative of styles absorbed by the British Empire. In front stands an imposing statue of Queen Victoria, the apotheosis of imperialism, while at her feet, sculpted in bronze, proud figures show the city fathers' world-view: a young scholar; his mother with spinning spool; and his father with mallet and boat, the three representing "learning, linen and liners", the alliterative bedrock of Belfast's heritage.

Inside, arching almost 50m above you, is the **main dome** with its (inaccessible) whispering gallery; modelled on St Paul's Cathedral in London, it is adorned around its rim with zodiac signs, both painted and in stained glass. The palatial marbled **entrance hall** features staircase pillars, colonnades and bronze and marble statues, while the principal landing is graced by a **mural** executed in 1951 by John Luke, celebrating Belfast's now mostly defunct traditional industries – rope-making, shipbuilding, weaving and spinning. The building's highlight is the oak-decorated **council chamber**, with its hand-carved wainscoting and councillors' pews as well as a visitors' gallery. Regular free guided **tours** show visitors around the building – or there's free access to the **ground floor visitor areas**, where an exhibition in the east wing charts the city's history and development via six themed zones over sixteen rooms (hire an audio-tour for £3.50 to get the most out of this).

## Linen Hall Library

17 Donegall Square North (entrance at 52 Fountain St) • Mon–Fri 9.30am–5.30pm, Sat 9.30am–4pm; closed public hols; tours (£5) Mon–Fri 10.30am • ☎ 02890 321707, ⓦ linenhall.com

At the northwest corner of Donegall Square stands Belfast's oldest library, the substantially revamped **Linen Hall Library**, established in 1788. Its main feature is the **Political Collection**, a unique accumulation of over 100,000 publications reflecting every aspect of Northern Irish political life since 1966; also here are prison letters smuggled out of the Long Kesh detention centre which, in its more widely used name of the Maze, was the scene of the 1981 hunger strike (see page 582). The library also boasts excellent facilities for tracing family trees, a café, and stocks all the daily newspapers. Regular literary events take place throughout the year, including specialist workshops.

# The Entries and around

A little way northeast of Donegall Square, a handful of narrow alleyways known as the **Entries** links Ann Street and the High Street. You'll stumble across some great old saloon bars down here, such as *The Morning Star* in Pottinger's Entry, with its large frosted windows and Parisian-café-like counter (see page 475), and *White's Tavern* in Winecellar Entry, which dates from the seventeenth century (see page 475). Crown Entry was where the Society of United Irishmen (see page 574) was born, led by the Protestant triumvirate of Wolfe Tone, Henry Joy McCracken and Samuel Nielson. Nielson also printed his own newspaper in this area, the *Northern Star*, heavily influenced by the French revolutionary ideals of liberty, equality and fraternity, the newspaper's inflammatory material led to his being hounded out of town.

Just to the north, no. 2 Waring Street was originally built as a market house in 1769, but is more renowned as the venue for the **1792 Belfast Harp Festival**: by the end of the eighteenth century, the old Gaelic harping tradition had reached almost terminal decline and the convention was a deliberate attempt by its organizers, the United Irish Society, to record some of the harpers' airs for posterity. The transcriber, Edmund Bunting, was stimulated to tour Ireland collecting further airs, 77 of which were published in his illustrious collection of 1809.

# The Cathedral Quarter

The area north of Waring Street has experienced more than two decades of regeneration, a process kick-started when chef Nick Price gambled on the then mainly derelict area by opening his *Nick's Warehouse* restaurant in 1989. With Price's retirement, that Hill Street venue, which proved a huge success, is now *The Harp Bar* (see page 475). His punt, meanwhile, is looking a sure thing, with an ever-increasing number of restaurants and bars and a fresh title, the **Cathedral Quarter** (ⓦ thecathedralquarter.com), for this once-scruffy patch. Testament to the changes is that the city's much heralded five-star hotel, *The Merchant* (see page 472) – whose owner, Bill Wolsey, has converted building after building in the Quarter – is located here.

The University of Ulster's Belfast Campus sits across from the Metropolitan Arts Centre – better known as the **MAC** (see page 477) – on the edge of **St Anne's Square**, a foodie honeypot with some of Belfast's finest restaurants in residence around its fringes, *Coppi* (see page 474) and *House of Zen* (see page 474) among them. Arts and music venues such as the *Black Box* (see page 477) and *Oh Yeah Music Centre* (see page 477) and live music pubs throng the cobbled streets, while the Quarter's cultural hub status is cemented by its hosting of a number of Belfast's more bohemian **events**, including the Cathedral Quarter Arts Festival (see page 476) and the quirky Out to Lunch Festival.

### Belfast Cathedral (formerly St Anne's)

Donegall St • Mon–Sat 9am–5pm, Sun 1–3pm; between services only • £5 (includes guidebook or audio-tour) • ☎ 02890 328332, ⓦ belfastcathedral.org

A couple of hundred metres up Donegall Street from where it meets Waring Street you'll find the most monolithic of all the city's grand buildings: the Protestant **Belfast Cathedral**, a neo-Romanesque basilica started in 1899, but not fully completed until 1981. Entrance is via the huge west door, immediately to the right of which is the baptistery, with an intricately designed representation of the Creation on its ceiling consisting of 150,000 tiny pieces of glass. Most significant, however, is the cathedral's only tomb, marked by a simple slab on the floor of the south aisle, which contains the body of **Lord Edward Henry Carson** (see box). The symbol of Partition, he's seen either as the province's saviour or as the villain who sabotaged Ireland's independence as a 32-county state. The cathedral attracts a lot of media attention in the run-up to Christmas each year as the incumbent Dean undertakes a "sit-out" on Donegall Street to collect donations for the poor and

**5**

## LORD EDWARD CARSON

**Lord Edward Carson** is a name that Northern Ireland has never forgotten. A Dubliner of Scots-Presbyterian background, he took the decision in 1910 to accept the leadership of the opposition to Home Rule, which in effect inextricably allied him to the **Ulster Unionist** resistance movement. Yet, though this association is about the only thing for which he is remembered, his personality and integrity went far deeper than this. He abhorred religious intolerance, and behind the exterior of a zealous crusader was a man who sincerely believed that Ireland couldn't prosper without Britain and only wished that a federalist answer could have involved a united Ireland. Nonetheless, this was the same man who, as a brilliant orator at the bar, and in the role he loved the most, brought about the humiliating destruction of Oscar Wilde at the writer's trial in 1895.

charitable causes, a tradition started by Dean Sammy Crooks in 1976. Dressed in the black Anglican clerical cloak, he is referred to as "Black Santa".

## Great Victoria Street

The strip of Belfast running south along **Great Victoria Street** to Shaftesbury Square and thence to the university area and beyond was once known as the "Golden Mile". It's rarely called that these days, but Great Victoria Street itself is worth checking out, not least for the grandiose Victorian **Grand Opera House** (see page 477), which sits at its northern end. Although locals complained about the modern extension added to the theatre in 2006, it is now accepted as part and parcel of the city skyline. A few paces south lies the **Europa Hotel**; once renowned for being Europe's most bombed, it now stands as one of Belfast's finest. Almost opposite the *Europa* stands one of the greatest of Victorian gin palaces, the **Crown Liquor Saloon** (see page 474), now owned by the National Trust. The saloon has a glittering tiled exterior resembling a spa baths more than a serious drinking institution, while inside, the scrolled ceiling, patterned floor and the golden-yellow and rosy-red hues led John Betjeman to describe it as his "many-coloured cavern".

## The Laganside

The beginning of the **Laganside** area is marked at the High Street's eastern end by the **Prince Albert Memorial Clock Tower**. Built in 1867–69 and tilting slightly off the perpendicular as a result of its construction upon gradually sinking wooden piles, it's a strange memorial – especially as Prince Albert never had anything to do with Belfast – but it's a handy landmark.

North of the Albert Clock, along Dunbar Link, you'll come across a series of grand buildings, chief among which is the restored **Custom House** on Donegall Quay – a Corinthian-style, E-shaped edifice designed between 1854 and 1857. Unfortunately, it's not open to the public, leaving you unable to verify rumours of fantastic art masterpieces stored in its basements – though it's known that Anthony Trollope, the nineteenth-century novelist (and inventor of the pillar box), once worked here as a surveyor's clerk.

Just beyond the Custom House on Donegall Quay is the ambitious **Laganside** development project, the first component of which to be completed was the **Lagan Weir**, designed to protect the city against flooding. Millions of pounds have been pumped into dredging the river to maintain water levels and revive the much depleted fish population – successfully it seems: there was salmon fishing on the weir's inauguration day in 1994. Look across the river to the **Harland & Wolff shipyard** (see page 461) and you'll spot its landmark yellow cranes ("Samson" and "Goliath").

Further south along Oxford Street, on Lanyon Place, stands a 20m-high metal **statue** depicting a girl holding aloft a ring of thanksgiving (for the peace process). Erected in 2007, *Beacon of Hope* (or "Nuala with the Hula", as locals affectionately call her) has fast become a city icon. Nearby sits the glittering 2000-seater **Belfast Waterfront** concert hall and conference centre.

## The Titanic Quarter

Located across the river from the city centre on Queen's Quay, a 10min walk from Donegall Square (alternatively take Metro bus #26 from Donegall Square West or the train from Belfast Central or Great Victoria St, disembarking at the Titanic Quarter stop)

Across the river on Queen's Quay, the massive **Odyssey** leisure complex marks the beginning of the **Titanic Quarter** (ⓦ titanicquarter.com), an area of the city that has seen huge financial investment in recent years. Luxury apartments now line the water's edge, overlooking the area's eye-catching figurehead, **Titanic Belfast**, an immersive visitor attraction dedicated to the world's most famous ocean liner. Alongside it, the **SS Nomadic Belfast** was the *Titanic*'s tender ship and is the last remaining White Star Line ship in the world – it's now permanently moored in Hamilton Dock, and visitors can step on board to explore a century of maritime history. The Quarter is gaining a reputation as a media hub, with Paint Hall studios the setting for several big-budget Hollywood movies and the HBO series, *Game of Thrones*, and the sprawling Belfast Harbour Studio. To the rear of the Odyssey building is the **Whowhatwherewhenwhy** scientific discovery centre (ⓦ w5online.co.uk), known as **W5**, with more than 150 interactive exhibits, aimed primarily at children. For more grown-up insights, it's worth taking a tour of the area (see page 472).

### Titanic Belfast

1 Olympic Way, Queens Rd • April–May Mon & Thurs–Sun 9am–6pm; June Mon & Thurs–Sun 9am–7pm; July & Aug daily 9am–7pm; Sept daily 9am–6pm; Oct–March Mon & Thurs–Sun 10am–5pm • £19.50 (children 5–15 £8.75, under 5 free) • ☎ 02890 766399, ⓦ titanicbelfast.com

The city's newest landmark, the £77 million **Titanic Belfast**, opened its doors on the ship's centenary in April 2012 to great aplomb, with a concert staged on the slipway where the ill-fated liner was first launched. The prow-like structure is the same height as the ship's hull (38m) and glistens in the sunlight courtesy of some three thousand silver-anodized aluminium shards.

---

#### THE DOCKS AND THE RMS TITANIC

Much of Belfast's waterside heritage is associated with English engineer Edward James Harland (1831–95) who, together with his German-born assistant Gustav Wilhelm Wolff (1834–1913), founded the **Harland & Wolff** shipbuilding company here in 1861. Starting from a small shipyard on Queen's Island, the company grew rapidly and over the following decades had gained a reputation for innovations such as iron (rather than wooden) decks and flatter, squarer hulls designed to maximize capacity. The firm continued to flourish after Harland's death and Wolff's retirement, most notably when it constructed three steamships for the **White Star Line** – the *Olympic*, the *Britannic* and, most famously, the **Titanic**. Completed in 1912, the RMS *Titanic*, then the world's largest passenger-carrying steamship, sank on April 14 of the same year, just four days into her maiden voyage from Southampton to New York, having collided with an iceberg in the North Atlantic. More than 1500 of the 2200-plus passengers and crew drowned, a tragedy that continues to hold a macabre fascination today. Belfast is still proud of its role in creating the world's most famous ship ("She was fine when she left here" goes the saying, along with "Built by Irishmen, driven by an Englishman"), and the centenary of her launch was marked by numerous events focused upon the Laganside and the new Titanic Quarter.

**5**

Inside, a fully immersive journey awaits, propelling visitors back to the last century to join virtual residents on the streets of Victorian Belfast. Nine galleries provide a multi-media experience from the ship's conception and build through to the discovery of its decaying remains as they rest today on the Atlantic seabed. A highlight is the shipyard experience **ride** that sees passengers travel through the sights and sounds of Harland & Wolff as they circumnavigate a replica of the ship's rudder during construction.

### HMS Caroline
Alexandra Dock, Queens Rd • Daily: 10am–5pm • £9.50, children 5–15 £4, under 5 free • ⓦ nmrn.org.uk

After an extensive restoration project to halt the deterioration of the World War One light cruiser, **HMS Caroline** is finally welcoming back visitors on board. The last floating survivor of the Battle of Jutland now houses state-of-the-art interactive exhibitions allowing visitors to experience "Signal School" and "Torpedo School" while investigating the events leading up to the Battle of Jutland from the point of view of both the German and British Naval Forces.

# South Belfast

Towards the old Golden Mile's southern extremity lies the **university area**, the focal point for South Belfast's attractions (ⓦ southbelfast.org), with plenty of eating places, pubs and a range of budget accommodation options. Near Queen's University are the lush **Botanic Gardens**, within which sits the vast **Ulster Museum**, displaying everything from dinosaur bones and an Egyptian mummy to contemporary art and a 77m hand-embroidered *Game of Thrones* tapestry. Heading south from here along Stranmillis Road it's a relatively short step east to the river-skirting **Lagan Towpath**, which runs several kilometres southwest to Lisburn, while a detour along the way leads to the Neolithic earthwork known as the **Giant's Ring**.

## The University Quarter

Just south of Shaftesbury Square stand three churches – Moravian, Crescent and Methodist – whose distinctive steeples frame the entrance to the **University Quarter**. From here, leading up to the university buildings, the roads are lined with early Victorian terraces that represent the final flowering of Georgian architecture in Belfast. The **Upper Crescent** is a magnificent curved Neoclassical terrace, built around 1845 but sadly neglected since; it is now used mainly for office space. The **Lower Crescent**, perversely, is straight.

### Queen's University
University Rd • Visitor centre Mon–Fri 8.30am–5pm • Free • ☎ 02890 245133, ⓦ qub.ac.uk/home/welcome-centre

**Queen's University** is the architectural centrepiece of the area, flanked by the most satisfying example of a Georgian terrace in Belfast, **University Square**, where the red brickwork mostly remains intact, with the exception of a few bay windows added in the Victorian era. The university building itself was constructed in 1849 as a mock-Tudor remodelling of Magdalen College, Oxford, to a design by Charles Lanyon, and houses a **visitor centre** which provides information about the university and runs guided tours.

The Italianate **Union Theological College**, nearby on College Park, also by Lanyon, was temporarily the site of the Northern Ireland Parliament until 1932 when Stormont was built.

# The Botanic Gardens

College Park, Botanic Ave • Daily 7.30am–sunset; Palm House April–Sept 10am–5pm, Oct–March 10am–4pm; Tropical Ravine Tues–Sun 10am–5pm • Free • Buses #8A, #8B and #8C from Donegall Square East

Just below the university are the popular **Botanic Gardens**, first opened in 1827 and well protected by trees from the noise of the surrounding traffic. Within the gardens is the **Palm House**, a hothouse predating the famous one at Kew Gardens in London, but very similar in style, with a white-painted framework of curvilinear ironwork and glass. It was the first of its kind in the world, another success for Lanyon, who worked in tandem on this project with the Dublin iron-founder Richard Turner. The nearby **Tropical Ravine** is a classic example of Victorian light entertainment – a hundred-year-

**ACCOMMODATION**

| Belfast International Hostel | 2 |
| Camera House | 5 |
| Dukes at Queens | 4 |
| Hotel Etap | 1 |
| Malone Lodge Hotel & Apartments | 6 |
| The Old Rectory | 7 |
| Vagabonds | 3 |

**EATING**

| General Merchants | 2 |
| Kaffe O | 1 |

**SHOPPING**

| No Alibi Bookstore | 1 |

**HIGHLIGHT**

2 Ulster Museum

**DRINKING & NIGHTLIFE**

DRINKING

| The Five Points Whiskey & Alehouse | 3 |

NIGHTLIFE

| Cuckoo | 8 |
| The Empire Bar & Music Hall | 5 |
| Filthy McNasty's | 2 |
| Lavery's Gin Palace | 4 |
| The Limelight Complex | 1 |
| The Pavilion Bar | 7 |
| Shine | 6 |

**UNIVERSITY AREA (QUEEN'S QUARTER)**

**5**

old sunken glen chock-full of "vegetable wonders" extracted from far-flung jungles and replanted for the delight of the visiting Belfast public.

## Ulster Museum

Tues–Sun and bank holiday Mondays 10am–5pm • Free • ☎ 02890 440000, ⓦ nmni.com

The Botanic Gardens also house the **Ulster Museum**, whose clever design sheds light both literally and figuratively on subjects ranging from the North's troubled history to Ireland's geological past. The grand, open-plan **ground floor** includes everything from an impressive dinosaur skeleton to contemporary haute couture. From here, the curators recommend heading up to the **third floor** to explore the art exhibits, where the **modern art collection** is home to Francis Bacon's macabre *Head II*, Bridget Riley's unnerving *Cataract IV* and Stanley Spencer's thought-provoking *The Betrayal*. You'll also find some stunning landscapes and rural scenes up here, by painters such as Belfast's Sir John Lavery, plus Turner's highly symbolic *Dawn of Christianity*.

The **second floor** features the "**Nature Zone**", depicting the Earth's origins and Ireland's development up to the Ice Age. Far more engrossing are the **first floor**'s **history** galleries, which begin with Neolithic remains and Bronze Age finds (including a remarkable decorated shield), before taking a detailed look at the **medieval** period – two exhibits to look out for here are the somewhat skewwhiff stone inauguration chair of the O'Neills of Clandeboye and the silver gilt arm-reliquary supposedly created to house St Patrick's hand. **The Armada gallery** includes plenty of relics from the ill-fated *Girona*, which sank off the Antrim coast in 1588, while the Ascendancy section includes a remarkable rag-bound tally-stick, used to record the number of prayers said during the then illegal outdoor Catholic service, as well as highlighting the effects of the Great Famine. From here the exhibits quicken up a pace, especially when focusing upon the **War of Independence** and the North's resistance to Dublin rule, before looking at Belfast during World War II and concluding with a space devoted to the **Troubles**. A very popular addition to the museum is a 77m-long hand-embroidered tapestry depicting the story of the **Game of Thrones** (the HBO series filmed on location in Northern Ireland) in its entirety.

## The Lagan Towpath and Giant's Ring

Beyond the university area lie the glades of middle-class suburbia. A gate at the southern tip of the Botanic Gardens leads to the river and the **Lagan Towpath**. This tarmacked trail can be tramped for about 13km south to Lisburn, passing old locks and lock houses, woodland and marshes on the way. The waterway became fully navigable in the late 1790s, ready to carry the newly discovered coal from Lough Neagh, but its utility declined with the advent of the railway in 1839. Today, it's been harnessed as part of the Ulster Way, for rambling and canoeing enthusiasts.

### Giant's Ring

Off Ballynahatty Rd, Lisburn, 1.5km south of Shaw's Bridge • Free access dawn to dusk

If you leave the towpath at Shaw's Bridge (the ring-road crossing), it's a 1.5km signposted walk along country lanes to the **Giant's Ring**, a colossal, 183m-wide earthwork thought to have served as a burial ground or meeting place. You wouldn't be far wrong in thinking that its inwardly sloping wall would make an excellent speed-track circuit, for in the eighteenth century it was used for horse racing: six circuits made a two-mile race, with the punters jostling for position on the top of the rampart. Most captivating of all is the huge **dolmen** at the central hub of this cartwheel structure. As a single megalithic remain, it's immediately more impressive than even the great structures of the Irish High Kings at Tara, though here there's little information concerning its origins and usage. The setting chosen for the site, high above the surrounding lowlands (probably once marshy lake), is impressive – there's a powerful feeling that the great dramas and decision-making of the ancient northeast must have been played out here.

# East Belfast

From Donegall Square West, the Metro bus #4A runs every 8min to East Belfast; alternatively, from Belfast Central train station, it's a 25min walk straight down the Alberbridge Rd to the Holywood Arches

**East Belfast**'s skyline is dominated by the cranes – named "Samson" and "Goliath" – which tower above the **Harland & Wolff shipyard** (see page 461). The shipyard is the city's proudest international asset – though the company's work is nowadays centred on offshore wind farm installations – and is said to possess the largest dry dock in the world: over 600m long and 90m wide. The surrounding area is now home to one of Europe's biggest redevelopment projects, the Titanic Quarter (see page 461), and increased financial investment is being channelled towards housing developments and retail outlets as well as community and cultural projects.

The area's pride in the famous figures it has given to the literary, sporting and music worlds remains undimmed; the theologian and author of the Chronicles of Narnia, **C.S. Lewis**, was born in Dundela Villas, and there's a plaque commemorating him at Dundela Flats. Fans of the Chronicles should also pay a visit to the Holywood Arches railway bridge, where a magnificent **bronze statue** depicts one of the Narnia characters, Digory Kirke, peering into the famous wardrobe. Next door is **C.S. Lewis Square**, a public place costing £2.5million with seven sculptures celebrating the acclaimed writer's most famous characters. Another plaque on Burren Way in the Cregagh Estate marks the childhood home of the late footballer **George Best** (see box),

## GEORGE BEST

*Maradona good, Pele better, George Best*

popular Belfast sporting adage

Born in East Belfast in 1946, **George Best** became (and remains to this day) Northern Ireland's most celebrated footballer, signed by Manchester United after being rejected by local clubs. Making his debut aged 17, Best starred in the 1964–65 and 1966–67 league-winning teams, cementing his reputation as a dazzling, jinking and goal-scoring winger. His good looks, long hair, gift of the gab and love of the high life also led to his acquisition of the sobriquet "the fifth Beatle". Further fame was assured when United beat Benfica 4–1 in the 1968 European Cup Final, Best scoring one of the goals and running the Portuguese team's defence so ragged before a vast televised audience that his award of **European Footballer of the Year** was a foregone conclusion.

The latter half of the 1960s saw Best's celebrity lifestyle (by then he owned nightclubs and boutiques and had dated at least one Miss World) consumed by gambling, **alcoholism** and chasing women. He walked out of United in 1974, and after that his footballing career declined rapidly, taking in spells in the US and Australia. Alcohol addiction led to a stint in prison in 1984, after which Best was found guilty of drunk driving and assaulting a police officer. By 2002 his health was so poor that he underwent a liver transplant, but continued to drink after its success and eventually succumbed to multiple organ failure in November 2005.

Some 100,000 mourners lined the streets of Belfast as Best's coffin travelled to his **funeral** service at Stormont. Belfast City Airport was subsequently renamed in his honour and, in 2006, the Ulster Bank issued one million £5 notes bearing his picture – the entire issue was rapidly snapped up for keepsakes. The great sadness of Best's football career was that, despite 37 caps for Northern Ireland, he never appeared in a major international competition such as the World Cup, but he inspired a host of young footballers and, indeed, numerous jokes, not least his own oft-quoted remark: "I spent a lot of my money on booze, birds and fast cars. The rest I just squandered." Avid fans can now book to stay overnight in the Best family home on the Cregagh Estate (see page 473).

**5**

whom many herald as being the greatest footballer of all time. Fans of **Van Morrison** (see box), meanwhile, might want to seek out his birthplace, a private house (with no public access) at 125 Hyndford Street, off Beersbridge Road, and the many streets that feature in his songs (Cyprus Avenue, Castlereagh Road and others). The Connswater Community Greenway group has developed a series of **trails** (available to download on ⓦconnswatergreenway.co.uk/trails) for all three East Belfast sons, each leading you through the streets where the men grew up and the places that influenced and inspired them.

## Stormont

6.5km east of the centre, off the Newtownards Rd • Mon–Fri 9am–4pm; guided tours 11am & 2pm, except during summer recess when tours leave on the hour 11am–3pm • Free • ☎ 02890 521802, ⓦ parliamentbuildings.org • Buses #20A and #23 from Donegall Square West

The home of the Northern Ireland Parliament until the introduction of direct rule in 1972, **Stormont** now houses the Assembly created by the 1998 Good Friday Agreement. It's a magnificent sight, a great, white Neoclassical mansion crowning a rise in the middle of a park at the end of a long, straight drive. You can wander freely in the grounds, and free public tours have recently been introduced. There's also a wonderful children's playground, named in honour of the late Mo Mowlam, previous Northern Ireland Secretary of State. Also here, though not open to the public, is **Stormont Castle**, the office of the British Secretary of State for Northern Ireland.

# North Belfast

**North Belfast** boasts baronial **Belfast Castle**, the impressive wildlife collection of **Belfast Zoo** and superb panoramic city views from **Cave Hill**. The castle and the city's zoo, both out on the Antrim Road, sit conveniently alongside one another on the slopes of Cave Hill, served by bus #1 from Donegall Square West.

## Belfast Castle

Antrim Rd • Mon 9.30am–4pm, Tues–Thurs 9.30am–7pm, Fri & Sat 9.30am–9pm, Sun 9am–4.30pm • Free • ☎ 02890 776925,
Ⓦ belfastcastle.co.uk

Built in 1870 to the designs of Lanyon and surrounded by a wooded estate, the sandstone **Belfast Castle**'s exterior is in Scottish Baronial style, inspired in part by the reconstruction of Balmoral Castle in Aberdeenshire in 1853. It features a six-storey tower, a series of crow-stepped gables and conically peak-capped turrets, but the most striking feature of all is the serpentine Italianate stairway that leads down from the principal reception room to the garden terrace below. Restored and refurbished in 1990, the interior is, however, virtually empty of Victorian period accoutrements. Upstairs, the **visitor centre** traces the locality's history from prehistoric cave-dwellers to the castle's construction. It also houses a restaurant and pub, and there's a children's adventure playground in the grounds of the estate.

## Belfast Zoo

Antrim Rd • Daily: April–Sept 10am–7pm; Oct–March 10am–4pm • £13.50 (children 4–16 £6.75, under 4s free, family £38) • ☎ 02890
776277, Ⓦ belfastzoo.co.uk

Adjoining the castle is the well-landscaped parkland of **Belfast Zoo**, which stretches up towards Cave Hill. Within its impressive layout, you'll find primates and big cats, elephants, penguins and sea lions, and a free-flight aviary, where rare species have room to breed. There's also an impressive annual programme of family-friendly events.

## Cave Hill

Castle and zoo aside, it's **Cave Hill** itself that should be your main port of call in North Belfast. Several paths lead up from the castle estate to the hill's summit – a rocky outcrop known as "Napoleon's Nose" (believed to have been an inspiration for Jonathan Swift's novel, *Gulliver's Travels*) – which affords an unsurpassable overview of the whole city and lough. From here you can't help but appreciate the accuracy of the poet Craig Raine's aerial description of the city in his *Flying to Belfast* as "a radio set with its back ripped off". Cave Hill was once awash with Iron Age forts, for there was flint (for weapon making) in the chalk under the basalt hill-coverings. In 1795, Wolfe Tone, Henry Joy McCracken and other leaders of the United Irishmen stood on the top of Cave Hill and pledged "never to desist in our efforts until we have subverted the authority of England over our country and asserted our Independence".

# West Belfast

Metro bus #11A/B/C/D runs down the Fall from Chichester St; for the Shankill, take Metro bus #10A/B/C/D/E/F/G/H from Queen St

Though the nexus of the Troubles for 25 years, today **West Belfast** (Ⓦ visitwestbelfast. com) is as safe as anywhere else in the city to visit. There is, however, little of architectural note among the mainly residential streets, and most of the "sights" are associated with the area's troubled past. Much of the old terraced housing has been replaced in recent years by rows of modern estates, but it's impossible to miss examples of the partisan **mural paintings** that decorate walls and gable ends in both Catholic and Protestant areas (see page 469). Tourist information about the area is available from the West Belfast Tourist Information Point located inside the Cultúrlann Arts & Culture Centre (see page 477). You might also consider taking a Black Taxi Tour (Ⓦ niblacktaxitours.com) covering both sides of the Peace Line – a divide longer than the Berlin Wall.

**5**

## THE TROUBLES IN WEST BELFAST

The **Troubles in West Belfast** have their origins in the nineteenth century, when the city's population expanded dramatically as people flocked from the countryside to work in the booming new flax and linen industries. Many of these migrants were crammed into jerry-built housing in the grids of streets which still today define this part of the city. Conditions were deplorable and did nothing to ease tensions between Catholic and Protestant residents. There were numerous **sectarian riots** – the worst was in 1886, during the reading of the Home Rule Bill, when 32 people died and over 370 were injured – leading to the almost inevitable definition of two separate neighbourhoods, as Protestant and Catholic families alike began to migrate to more secure surroundings.

In 1968 and 1969, this division was pushed to its limit when, across the city, sectarian mobs and gunmen evicted over eight thousand families from their homes, mainly in Catholic West Belfast. The Royal Ulster Constabulary, or **RUC**, called for government assistance, and **British troops** arrived on the streets on August 15, 1969. A month later the makeshift barrier dividing the **Catholic Falls** from the **Protestant Shankill** had become a full-scale reinforced "peace line". British intervention may have averted a civil war, but it failed to prevent an escalation in sectarian conflict. Indeed, the army soon came to be viewed as an occupying force and a legitimate target for a reviving IRA, though local sympathies for its aims were much diminished by the 1972 Bloody Friday bombings (see page 582). In return, Loyalist paramilitaries sought to avenge Republican violence, often through indiscriminate killings. A cycle of tit-for-tat attacks ensued, finally reaching its nadir with the **Shankill Road bombing**, a botched attempt to blow up Loyalist paramilitary leaders supposedly meeting above a fish shop on the Shankill Road in 1993, which instead killed customers and the shop's owner.

## The Falls Road

From the city centre, Divis Street, a westward continuation of Castle Street, leads to the **Falls Road**, which heads on for a further 3km west past Milltown Cemetery and into Andersonstown. The first part of the Falls Road is known as the **Lower Falls** where, these days, most of the land to the left (south) consists of modern red-brick terraced housing. The right-hand side of the road features some of the main local landmarks, including the bright blue and pink leisure centre and the last remaining of the three Carnegie Libraries built in Belfast, this one dating from 1908. Turn right off the Falls Road at the leisure centre on to North Howard Street and Cupar Way and you'll encounter the infamous **Peace Line** – a wall of concrete and iron separating the area from the Protestant working-class district of Shankill.

### Conway Mill

5–7 Conway St • Mon–Fri 9am–5pm • Tues–Sat 10am–2pm • ☎ 02890 240504, ⓦ conwaymill.org

Down Conway Street stands the old **Conway Mill**, revitalized by a concerted community effort. Inside you can investigate the wares of the numerous small businesses and local artists who operate from here, as well as an art gallery and a small exhibition depicting the mill's linen history. The Eileen Hickey Irish Republican History Museum is also housed in the former mill, boasting a vast collection of prison artefacts.

### Cultúrlann MacAdam Ó Fiaich

216 Falls Rd • Mon–Thurs 9am–9pm, Fri & Sat 9am–6pm, Sun 11am–4pm • ☎ 02890 964180, ⓦ culturlann.ie

Housed in a disused Presbyterian church, the **Cultúrlann MacAdam Ó Fiaich** is a cultural centre for Irish-speakers, housing an extensive bookshop (that also sells traditional music CDs), an excellent café and a thriving theatre, often host to musical events. Although you're unlikely to hear it spoken on the streets or in most pubs, the Irish language is flourishing in Catholic areas of Belfast and throughout the North.

# The Shankill Road and around

The Protestant population of West Belfast lives in the area abutting the Falls to the north, between the **Shankill Road** and the Crumlin Road, with a Peace Line running along Alliance Avenue. As an interface between the Protestant and Catholic communities, the Crumlin Road area was the scene of many violent sectarian incidents during the Troubles – and despite regeneration and new housing developments it remains a potential flashpoint, particularly during the July marching season. As with the Falls, the main draw for visitors to the area is the **murals**.

## Crumlin Road Gaol

53–55 Crumlin Rd • Daily: first tour 11am, last tour 3pm (1hr 15min) • £12 • ⓦ crumlinroadgaol.com

### BELFAST'S MURALS

The politically inspired **murals** of Northern Ireland are among the most startling sights not just in Belfast, but in the whole country. This ephemeral art form, which recycles the images and slogans of the **Troubles**, characterizes the violent struggles of the last few decades. Though many have been in place now for over a decade, some of the slogans and murals mentioned here may have vanished by the time you visit: new murals are painted over old ones or the houses they adorn are demolished. One of the consequences in the immediate aftermath of the Good Friday Agreement (see page 583) was that many of the sectarian Loyalist murals were replaced by murals celebrating sporting heroes and local history, including the *Titanic* – yet when trouble flares or discontent rises, the old-style murals frequently reappear. A detailed **archive** of Northern Ireland's murals is maintained by the University of Ulster at ⓦ cain.ulst.ac.uk/mccormick.

### LOYALIST MURALS

For most of the twentieth century, mural painting in Northern Ireland was a predominantly **Loyalist** activity. The first mural appeared in East Belfast in 1908 and, like many of its successors, celebrated William of Orange's (King Billy) victory at the **Battle of the Boyne**. Loyalist murals have tended to use imagery symbolic of power, such as the clenched scarlet fist, known as the **Red Hand of Ulster**, or flags, shields and other heraldic icons. However, the Loyalist response to the Troubles translated into what is now the most common form of painting, the militaristic mural. The greatest concentration of Loyalist murals is to be found on and around the **Shankill Road**, especially the Shankill Estate, to the north, and Dover Place, off Dover Street, to the south. Other areas are Sandy Row and Donegall Pass in South Belfast, and Newtownards Road, Martin Street and Severn Street in East Belfast.

### REPUBLICAN MURALS

**Republican** murals were at first limited to simple sloganeering or demarcation of territory, the best-known example being the long-standing "You are now entering Free Derry" in that city's Bogside district (see page 505). As with much else in Republican politics, however, the 1981 hunger strikes had a significant influence. Murals in support of the ten hunger strikers abounded and the (usually smiling) face of **Bobby Sands** – the IRA commander in the Maze prison who led the strike – remains an enduring image. Murals soon became a fundamental part of the Republican propaganda campaign: prominent **themes** have been resistance to British rule, the call for the withdrawal of troops and questioning the validity of the police. More recently, however, Republican muralists have turned increasingly to Irish legends and history as their sources of inspiration, and the only militaristic murals tend to be found in flashpoints such as the Ardoyne area of North Belfast. Equally, artists have paid tribute to other international liberation movements, as in a striking series of murals on Divis Street just before the beginning of the Falls Road. Further Republican murals can be found nearby on Beechmount Avenue, further west on Lenadoon Avenue in Andersonstown, and on New Lodge Road in North Belfast.

**5**

From the Westlink you'll pass between the **courthouse** and the notorious **Crumlin Road Gaol**, the two connected by an underground tunnel; former inmates include Éamon de Valera, Gerry Adams and Ian Paisley before it closed in 1996. The gaol has now been successfully refurbished and offers fascinating and entertaining guided tours as well as occasional cultural events. There's an excellent on-site café.

## ARRIVAL AND DEPARTURE                          BELFAST

Belfast's two **airports** are well connected to the city centre by public transport, while a limited Metro bus service operates between the city centre and the **ferry terminals** Mon–Fri. The city also has an efficient bus network. Visit the excellent journey planner at ⓦ translink.co.uk (or get the associated app) to fine-tune your rail and bus journey to and from Belfast.

### BY PLANE
**Belfast International Airport** ☎02894 484848, ⓦ belfastairport.com. The larger of the city's two airports is located 30km west of the city in Aldergrove; from here, the 24hr Airport Express 300 bus drops passengers at the city's Europa Buscentre (30–40min; £8 single, £11.50 return). A metered taxi to the city centre costs around £35 (for a meet-and-greet service try ☎02894 484353, ⓦ belfastairporttaxis.com). The airport's arrivals hall has an ATM, a bureau de change, car rental outlets and a tourist information desk (Mon–Fri 7.30am–7pm, Sat 7.30am–5pm, Sun 8am–11am).

**George Best Belfast City Airport** ☎02890 939093, ⓦ belfastcityairport.com. Many domestic flights from Britain use this airport, just 5km northeast of the centre, from which the Airport Express 600 bus runs to the Europa Buscentre (Mon–Fri every 20–35min 6am–10.05pm, Sat every 20–40min 6am–9.50pm, Sun every 40–50min 7.30am–9.45pm; £2.60 single, £4 return). Alternatively, take the free shuttle bus to Sydenham train station and hop on a train to Belfast Central or Great Victoria Street stations (Mon–Fri every 20–30min 6.20am–10.50pm, Sat every 30min 6.35am–10.50pm, Sun hourly 9.20am–10.20pm; £1.90). A taxi from City Airport to the city centre costs around £10 (☎02890 809080, ⓦ valuecabs.co.uk). The terminal's ground floor has ATMs, a bureau de change, car rental outlets and a tourist information desk (Mon–Fri 7.30am–7pm, Sat 7.30am–4.30pm, Sun 11am–6pm).

### BY BOAT
**Larne** P&O ferries (☎0871 664 4999, ⓦ poferries.com) from Cairnryan in Scotland dock at the town of Larne, 32km to the north, which is connected by Ulsterbus to the Europa Buscentre and by train to Great Victoria Street and Central stations.

**West Bank Road terminals** Stena ferries (☎0844 770 7070, ⓦ stenaline.co.uk) from Cairnryan and Liverpool dock here, a 30min walk from Donegall Square. A metered taxi costs around £9 (☎02890 333333, ⓦ fonacab.com).

Metro Bus 96 runs daily to Belfast High St (limited weekend service; £2).

### BY TRAIN
Most trains call at the central Great Victoria Street Station, except trains from Dublin and some from Larne, which terminate at Central Station near the Waterfront Hall on East Bridge Street, a little way east of the centre.

**Getting into town** Various Metro buses stop outside Central Station en route to Donegall Square – travel is free to holders of railway tickets. From Central Station you can also hop on a connecting train for the 10min journey to the Great Victoria Street Station, which stops en route at Botanic and City Hospital stations, both of which are useful if you're staying in the University Quarter. Alternatively, a 10min journey in the opposite direction will take passengers to the Titanic Quarter.

Destinations from Belfast (Central) Bangor (Mon–Sat every 15–30min, Sun hourly; 20–30min); Carrickfergus (Mon–Sat every 30min, Sun 9; 25min); Cultra for the Ulster Folk and Transport Museum (Mon–Sat every 20–30min, Sun hourly; 15min); Derry (Mon–Sat 8–9 daily, Sun 5; 2hr); Drogheda (5–7 daily; 1hr 35min); Dublin (5–8 daily; 2hr–2hr 15min); Larne harbour (Mon–Sat hourly, Sun 10; 55min); Larne town (Mon–Sat hourly, Sun 10; 50min); Newry (5–7 daily; 55min).

Destinations from Belfast (Great Victoria St) Bangor (Mon–Sat every 15–30min, Sun hourly; 25–40min); Cultra for the Ulster Folk and Transport Museum (Mon–Sat every 20–30min, Sun hourly; 20min); Derry (Mon–Sat 8–9 daily, Sun 5; 2hr 15min); Larne harbour (Mon–Sat hourly, Sun 10; 1hr 5min); Larne town (Mon–Sat hourly, Sun 10; 1hr).

### BY BUS
Express buses arrive at one of Belfast's two stations. The Europa Buscentre, accessed via the Great Northern shopping mall on Great Victoria St, handles services to the Republic and the airports. It also serves all parts of Northern Ireland except North Down and the Ards Peninsula, which utilize the Laganside Buscentre in Queen's Square (near the Albert Clock), though even on weekday evenings and Sundays even these use the Europa. Aircoach (ⓦ aircoach.ie) services from Dublin Airport arrive at Glengall St.

Destinations from Belfast (Europa) Armagh (Mon–Fri 13–14 daily, Sat 6, Sun 4; 1hr 5min–1hr 25min); Cavan (Mon–Sat 1 daily; 2hr 45min); Derry (Mon–Fri every 30min, Sat 20, Sun 11; 1hr 40min); Downpatrick (Mon–Sat 15–18 daily, Sun 6;

50min–1hr); Drogheda (14 daily; 1hr 40min–1hr 55min); Dublin (24 daily; 2hr 40min–2hr 55min); Dublin Airport (24 daily; 2hr 10min–2hr 35min); Dungiven (Mon–Fri every 30min, Sat 20, Sun 11; 1hr 5min); Enniskillen (Mon–Fri hourly, Sat 7, Sun 2; 1hr 50min–2hr 15min); Hillsborough (Mon–Sat hourly, Sun 8; 25min); Larne (Mon–Fri 19 daily, Sat 9, Sun 2; 55min–1hr 15min); Magherafelt (Mon–Fri & Sun 2 daily, Sat 5; 1hr 10min); Moneymore (Mon–Fri & Sun 2 daily, Sat 5; 1hr 25min); Newcastle (Mon–Sat 18–20 daily, Sun 8; 1hr 10min); Newry (Mon–Fri every 30min, Sat hourly, Sun 8; 1hr 10min); Omagh (Mon–Fri hourly, Sat 11, Sun 6; 1hr 30min–1hr 50min).

Destinations from Belfast (Laganside) Bangor (Mon–Sat every 30min, Sun 8 daily; 45min); Cultra for the Ulster Folk and Transport Museum (Mon–Sat every 30min, Sun 8 daily; 30min); Newtownards (Mon–Sat very frequent, Sun 10 daily; 35min); Portaferry (Mon–Fri 10 daily, Sat 9, Sun 2; 1hr 15min–1hr 45min).

## GETTING AROUND

Although you can easily **walk** around the city centre, distances to some of the outlying attractions are considerable, and a number of **places to stay** are also a little way out.

### BY BUS

**Network and times** The excellent Metro service provides frequent buses to almost every conceivable destination within the city, while the blue-and-white, long-distance services of Ulsterbus (which principally covers the rest of the North beyond Belfast's boundaries) connect to some of the sights on the city's fringes, such as the Giant's Ring. Almost all Metro buses set off from Donegall Square or the streets immediately around it, while Ulsterbus uses the Europa Buscentre on Great Victoria St. You can pick up a network map from the Visit Belfast Welcome Centre or the Metro kiosk in Donegall Square West (Mon–Fri 8am–6pm, Sat 8.30am–5.30pm; bus information on ☎ 02890 666630, ⓦ translink.co.uk). In general buses operate 6am–11pm from Monday to Saturday, and 9am–11pm on Sunday.

**Tickets and fares** Metro fares are determined by a zonal system within twelve geographical corridors. An unlimited Metro Day Travel ticket that is valid network-wide costs £3.50 (5 days £15, 10 days £30). Alternatively, there's a Belfast Visitor Pass available for unlimited bus and rail travel over one (£6), two (£11) or three (£14.50) consecutive days (it also provides discounts to many visitor attractions, tours, shops and restaurants). Cards can be purchased from the Metro kiosk on Donegall Square West, the two central bus stations and any Smartlink agent (including many newsagents).

### BY TAXI

Metered black taxis, based at the main rank in Donegall Square East and other points throughout the city, charge a minimum of £3, which rapidly starts to increase if you're going any distance. Alternatively, you can phone a minicab (try Citi Cabs ☎ 02890 665566, fonaCAB ☎ 02890 333333 or Value Cabs ☎ 02890 809080); these too are metered, charge similar rates to the black cabs and are a good idea late at night as passing taxis are hard to grab.

### BY BIKE

The Belfast Bikes public rental scheme (ⓦ belfastbikes. co.uk) has three hundred unisex bicycles and nearly fifty docking stations located throughout the city. Users can choose to register online for either a 3-Day Account or an Annual Fee (£5 or £20). Usage is free for the first 30min and thereafter 50p for up to an hour, £1.50 up to 2hr, £2.50 up to 3hr and £3.50 up to 4hr.

## INFORMATION

**Tourist information** The Visit Belfast Welcome Centre is at 9 Donegall Square North, opposite the City Hall (Mon–Sat 9am–5pm, Sun 11am–4pm; ☎ 028 9024 6609, ⓦ visit belfast.com). It stocks a vast range of information on the city and the rest of the North, provides an accommodation booking service (Northern Ireland), has interactive tourist information touch-screen terminals and sells tickets for tours and events. It also has free customer wi-fi, a bureau de change and the only left-luggage facilities in the city (£4 per item for up to 4hr, £6 for the day, no overnight facility). The West Belfast Tourist Information Point is in the Culturlaan arts centre (see page 477).

**Listings** Consult the monthly listings freesheet *The Big List* (ⓦ thebiglist.co.uk), the free official guide, Visit Belfast's Belfast City Guide (ⓦ visitbelfast.com/whats-on) or *Belfast in Your Pocket* (ⓦ inyourpocket.com), all available at the Welcome Centre and from pubs, clubs and record shops. There's also *Love Belfast* (ⓦ lovebelfast.co.uk), providing listings and blogs on local events for visitors to the city. Families should check out *ni4kids*, a free monthly paper and online resource that focuses on family-friendly activities and events in Belfast and beyond (ⓦ ni4kids.com). The *Belfast Telegraph* newspaper (ⓦ belfasttelegraph.co.uk) also has daily listings.

## TOURS

Many of the tours listed below can be booked at the **Visit Belfast Welcome Centre**, which also publishes a visitor map with information on Belfast tours.

### WALKING TOURS

**Political tours** The "A History of Terror in Belfast" tour (☎ 07716 949460, ⓦ deadcentretours.com; £18 plus

**5**

booking fee), led by a conflict resolution specialist, lasts 2hr 30mins and covers over 3km of the city, visiting places significant to the Troubles. There are also various political walking tours of West Belfast, delivered by former political prisoners (£12; ☎ 02890 200770, ⍟ coiste.ie), which depart from the Divis Tower at the city end of the Falls Road; advance booking is essential.

**Other tours** The "Hidden Belfast Walking Tour" (£12; ☎ 07971 895746, ⍟ belfasthiddentours.com) lasts 1hr 30min and aims to uncover the city's less well-known gems, both historical and recent. There are also walking tours (⍟ titanicwalk.com) around the docks, taking in the Titanic's Docks and Pump House, and a pub crawl that hits the city's finest watering holes (Fri & Sat 8pm, meeting at the Albert Clock; £12; book ahead ☎ 07731 977774, ⍟ belfastcrawl.com). There's also the "Belfast Food Tour", providing a 4hr guided tour sampling some of the city's most memorable food and drink spots – options include the Belfast Gin Jaunt and the Belfast Whiskey Walk (online booking essential; from £58; ⍟ tasteandtour.co.uk).

**BUS TOURS**

Several companies operate hop-on, hop-off open-top bus tours, with most taking in the Laganside, city centre, Titanic, Cathedral and University quarters and West Belfast, including City Sightseeing (daily 10am–4.30pm; ☎ 02890 321321, ⍟ belfastcitysightseeing.com; £15/one day, £17.50/two days), running from Chichester St and City Tours Belfast (daily 10am–4pm; ☎ 02890 321912, ⍟ citytoursbelfast.com; £15/one day, £17.50/two days) running from High St.

**TAXI TOURS**

West Belfast is one of the features of several guided taxi tours, including the recommended Paddy Campbell's "Famous Black Cab Tours" (☎ 07990 955227, ⍟ belfastblackcabtours.co.uk), World Famous Belfast Black Taxi Tours (☎ 02890 642264, ⍟ belfasttours.com) and Belfast Taxi Tours (☎ 02890 315777, ⍟ taxitrax.com). Each tour lasts around 1hr 30min, exploring the Falls and Shankill roads (including the murals and the Peace Line), plus Milltown Cemetery, the docks and the university. Tours operate daily, must be pre-booked and usually cost a minimum of £30.

**BOAT AND BIKE TOURS**

The Titanic Quarter and docklands can be enjoyed via a boat tour (⍟ laganboatcompany.com), which relates Belfast's rich maritime history. Visit ⍟ belfastcitybiketours.com for information on guided cycling tours.

## ACCOMMODATION SEE MAP PAGES 457 AND 463

Belfast has a broad range of **accommodation**, especially at the top end of the market, while the recent tourist boom has seen a number of well-known **budget hotels** open up across the city. The main concentration of hotels can be found on Great Victoria Street, around the University area and in the Cathedral Quarter.

### CITY CENTRE

**Bullitt** 40a Church Lane ☎ 02895 900600, ⍟ bullitthotel.com. By far the coolest addition to the city's hotel scene for a long time, *Bullitt* offers uber-stylish "Dinky", "Comfy" and "Roomy" rooms, plus free "Grub to Go" bags with granola, fruit and orange juice when setting off to explore. Arrive back to a top-notch meal at the *Taylor & Clay* restaurant and a nightcap in one of the hotel's three bars. £130

★ **Europa Hotel** Great Victoria St ☎ 02890 271066, ⍟ hastingshotels.com. Belfast's Grand Old Dame, looking resplendent after a multimillion-pound refurbishment, offers views across the city with modern, spacious and luxurious bedrooms and suites. £190

**The Fitzwilliam Hotel** 1–3 Great Victoria St ☎ 02890 442080, ⍟ fitzwilliamhotelbelfast.com. One of the latest additions at the city's luxury end of the market features astonishingly well-equipped and thoughtfully accoutred rooms, with kingsize beds sheeted in Egyptian cotton, mini hi-fi systems and flatscreen TVs. £160

**Ten Square** 10 Donegall Square South ☎ 02890 241001, ⍟ tensquare.co.uk. A gem of a hotel in a much-refurbished former linen house bang opposite City Hall, featuring bespoke rooms, with an utterly opulent feel that draws its influences from colonial Shanghai. The hotel also houses several bars as well as the excellent *Josper's Steakhouse*. £148

### CATHEDRAL QUARTER

★ **Malmaison** 34–38 Victoria St ☎ 02896 001405, ⍟ malmaison.com. Installed in an elegantly converted warehouse on the periphery of the city's cultural hub, *Malmaison* features chic doubles, sumptuous suites named after the Samson and Goliath cranes (see page 460), and an attractive bar and restaurant. £125

**The Merchant** 16 Skipper St ☎ 02890 234888, ⍟ themerchanthotel.com. Once the HQ of the Ulster Bank, this Victorian sandstone edifice has been converted into a wonderful hotel, complete with many of the original Italianate fittings and its own art gallery and spa. Rooms are spacious and luxuriously furnished in either Victorian or Art Deco style and its suites are impeccably elegant. £240

**Premier Inn** 2–6 Waring St ☎ 08715 278070, ⍟ premierinn.com. A more affordable option for the budget conscious, situated right in the heart of the Cathedral Quarter. Rooms are basic but modern and clean. £79

**Ramada by Wyndham** 20 Talbot St ☎ 02890 261800, ⍟ wyndhamhotels.com. Sitting on the edge of St Anne's Square and surrounded by some of the area's finest restaurants, the reasonable room rates here mean more money for eating out. The 165 rooms are bright and contemporary, all with en-suite wet rooms. **£95**

## UNIVERSITY AREA (QUEEN'S QUARTER) AND AROUND

**Belfast International Hostel** 22–32 Donegall Rd ☎02890 315435, ⓦhini.org.uk. Large HINI hostel with twins and a couple of en-suite doubles, but mainly four- and six-bed dorms. There's also a café, self-catering kitchen and laundry, and tours of Belfast and to the Giant's Causeway are offered. **£14**

**Camera House** 44 Wellington Park ☎02890 660026, ⓦcamera-guesthouse.co.uk. An elegantly decorated town house offering en-suite and standard accommodation, complete with open fire and library. The guesthouse is family run with top notch cooked Irish breakfasts. **£60**

**Dukes at Queens** 65–67 University St ☎02890 236666, ⓦdukesatqueens.com. Smart, modern, four-star redevelopment of a fine Victorian building, a few minutes' walk from the university, featuring luxurious bedrooms and a fashionable bar. **£82**

**Hotel Etap** 35 Dublin Rd ☎02890 328126, ⓦall.accor. com. Modern, minimalist, clean and budget pretty much sums this place up. Ideal if you're not bothered about the absence of frills. **£83**

**Malone Lodge Hotel & Apartments** 60 Eglantine Ave ☎02890 388000, ⓦmalonelodgehotelbelfast.com. Welcoming and well-equipped hotel near Queen's, with off-street parking, pleasantly decorated rooms and a notable restaurant, *The Gallery*. **£109**

**The Old Rectory** 148 Malone Rd ☎02890 667882, ⓦanoldrectory.co.uk. This beautifully converted former clergyman's house (Church of Ireland), around 1.5km south of the university, offers both standard and en-suite rooms, and high-quality breakfasts. **£98**

★ **Vagabonds** 9 University Rd ☎02890 209600, ⓦvagabondsbelfast.com. A modern and funky hostel in the Queen's Quarter, designed and run by seasoned travellers, Tara and Curt. Close to bars, restaurants, Botanic Gardens and the Ulster Museum. Dorms **£15**, doubles **£50**

## EAST BELFAST

**George Best House** 16 Burren Way, Cregagh Estate ☎02890 451900, ⓦgeorgebesthouse.com. An opportunity to spend the night in George Best's old bedroom in his family home. Landmark East purchased the house in 2011 and have lovingly restored it to the way it would have looked before George left to join Man Utd in 1963. It's jam-packed with memorabilia and there are three bedrooms to choose from. Self-catering only. **£70**

## EATING
SEE MAP PAGES 457 AND 463

There are plenty of options for food during the day in the city centre and around the university area, ranging from **cafés**, many of which in the city centre stay open until 8.30pm on Thursday nights, to award-winning **restaurants** and **traditional pubs**. Most of the city's well-established **restaurants** are around Donegall Square, although the Cathedral Quarter has fast become a dining-out hub. Restaurants are often fully booked on Friday and Saturday evenings, so **reserving** is essential unless you're prepared to eat early. There's a great range of cuisine, from modern Irish and European, with French and Italian especially popular, to a smattering of Indian and East Asian restaurants and some new chicken and barbecue joints.

### CAFÉS

★ **Established Coffee** 54 Hill St ☎02890 319416, ⓦestablished.coffee. Award-winning barista Mark and his partner Bridget offer arguably the city's finest coffee (though *Kaffe O* fans might disagree) here in the Cathedral Quarter, using filter, Chemex and Aeropress. Expect simple industrial decor (and beards) and a warm and welcoming atmosphere. Mon–Fri 7am–6pm, Sat 8am–6pm, Sun 9am–6pm.

**General Merchants** 361 Ormeau Rd and 481 Upper Newtownards Rd ☎02890 652708, ⓦgeneralmerchants. co.uk. Australian inspired all-day breakfasts that are hearty and tasty yet packed with superfoods for a healthy, nutritious

kick. The Brisbane Breakfast comes Aussie style, complete with guacamole and Vegemite (£8.50). Both branches Mon & Tues 8am–6pm, Wed–Sat 8am–11pm, Sun 9am–6pm (Upper Newtownards branch from 8am on Sun).

★ **Grapevine** 5 Pottingers Entry ☎07794 653259, ⓦgrapevinebelfast.com. Tucked away but worth seeking out for soul-warming soups, stews and gumbo plus home-made sandwiches that cost under £5 (gluten-free options too). Mon–Fri 8am–4pm, Sat 10am–3.30pm.

**Kaffe O** 411 Ormeau Rd and 73 Botanic Ave ☎02890 642434, ⓦkaffeo.coffee. For coffee aficionados, either branch of this Nordic-inspired café is well worth visiting. Simple vegetarian, often vegan, soup, stews and salads occupy the menu alongside locally smoked salmon and smoked meats. Lunch and a sublime coffee experience for around £10. Mon–Sat 8am–5pm, Sun 9am–5pm.

### RESTAURANTS

**Boojum** 19–27 Chichester St ☎02890 230600, ⓦboojummex.com. Minimalist interior with a canteen feel but serving the best burritos in Belfast for less than £7. Long midweek lunch queues attest to its popularity, and there are now three additional branches on Botanic Ave, Great Victoria St and in Victoria Square. Daily 11.30am–10pm.

**Bubbacue** 12 Callender St ☎02890 278220, ⓦbubbacue.com. Deep South barbecue cooked to perfection for twelve hours in a traditional smoker. Pulled

**5**

pork and beef brisket are the house specialities with a choice of home-made barbecue sauces. A beef sandwich and a side of mac cheese will cost you £6.95. Mon–Sat 11.30am–8pm, Sun 1–6pm.

**Coppi** St Anne's Square ☎ 02890 311959, ⓦ coppi.co.uk. Contemporary Italian cooking, serving up a range of *cichetti*, mains and tempting desserts. Expect to pay £17.50 for a selection of five *cichetti*. Mon–Thurs & Sun noon–10pm, Fri & Sat noon–11pm.

**Cyprus Avenue** 228 Upper Newtownards Rd ☎ 02890 656755, ⓦ cyprusavenue.co.uk. Named after the nearby leafy street that Van Morrison made famous over fifty ago, this new addition to Belfast's restaurant scene hits the mark with cooked breakfasts, delicious fish dishes and mouthwatering steaks. Breakfasts start at £8 with the 28-day salt-aged ribeye costing £22. Daily 9am–late.

**Deanes** 28–40 Howard St ☎ 02890 331134, ⓦ michael deane.co.uk. An elegant venue for stunning modern Irish cuisine with a strong French influence. Standing shoulder to shoulder are a dedicated fish restaurant *Loves Fish*, the so-called "Meat Locker" and the intriguing, *EIPIC* (serving five-, six- and seven-course set menus and awarded a coveted Michelin Star). The Friday three-course lunch menu at EIPIC is a decadent way to finish the week at £30. Loves Fish and Meat Locker Mon–Sat noon–10pm; EIPIC Wed–Thurs & Sat 5.30–9pm, Fri noon–1.30pm.

**Hadskis** 33 Donegal St ☎ 02890 325444, ⓦ jamesstand co.com. Now firmly established in the über-cool Cathedral Quarter, offering game, seafood and pasta dishes made with locally sourced produce, often served with a twist. The 1kg T-Bone for two at £58 is the stuff of legends. Mon–Wed noon–9.30pm, Thurs & Fri noon–10pm, Sat 11am–10pm, Sun 11am-9.30pm.

★ **Holohan's at the Barge** 1 Lanyon Quay ☎ 02890 235973, ⓦ holohansatthebarge.co.uk. The *Belfast Barge*, moored on the River Lagan next to the Waterfront Hall, is a fine setting for *Holohan's* hearty dishes of traditional Irish cuisine with a heavy dose of charm, some based on the chef's own family recipes. The boxty (£15) alone is worth a special visit, created using seasonal ingredients. Tues–Thurs 1–11pm, Fri & Sat 1pm–midnight, Sun 1–7pm.

**Home Restaurant** 22 Wellington Place ☎ 02890 234946, ⓦ homebelfast.co.uk. Originally a pop-up restaurant, *Home*'s simple, hearty offerings proved to be such a success that it's now moved to permanent premises and continues to be a huge hit with local foodies and critics, picking up a Michelin Bib Gourmand in 2017. Now serving breakfasts with gluten-free, "Skinny" and children's menus available for lunch and dinner. The fillet of hake with saffron gnocchi comes highly recommended at £16.50. Mon–Thurs 8am–11.45am, 12–4pm & 5–9pm, Fri & Sat 12–4pm & 5–10pm, Sun 1–4pm & 5–9pm.

**House of Zen** 3 St Anne's Square ☎ 02890 278688, ⓦ houseofzenbelfast.co.uk. Fine Asian cuisine (four-course set meal costs £29.95) served in the beautiful setting of St Anne's Square. Mon–Fri noon–3pm & 5–11.30pm, Sat 1–11.30pm, Sun 1.30–10.30pm.

**Howard Street** 56 Howard St ☎ 02890 248362, ⓦ howardstbelfast.com. This has fast become one of the city's finest restaurants, offering wholesome dishes ranging from beer-battered fish to dry-aged steaks and an excellent range of vegetarian options. Located near to the Grand Opera House, its three-course pre-theatre menu at £28 is a firm favourite with theatre-goers. Tues–Sat noon–2.30pm & 5–9.30pm.

**James St** 21 James St South ☎ 02895 600700, ⓦ jamesst andco.com. Chargrilled steaks, fresh fish dishes and heavenly Sunday roasts earned the restaurant a Michelin Bib Gourmand in 2017. For special occasions, push the boat out with the Co. Antrim dry-aged fillet for £34.50. Daily noon–late.

**Mourne Seafood Bar** 34–36 Bank St ☎ 02890 248544, ⓦ mourneseafood.com. Cracking place for all piscivores, serving everything from shellfish and oysters to exotic dishes incorporating hake or monkfish. Reasonably priced too, and there's even an on-site fishmonger's if you fancy cooking your own. £10 will buy you a plate of baked oysters topped with bacon crumb and garlic cream spinach. Mon–Thurs noon–9.30pm, Fri & Sat noon–10pm, Sun 1–9pm.

★ **OX** 1 Oxford St ☎ 02890 314121, ⓦ oxbelfast.com. Attracting culinary praise from foodies far and wider for its creative use of local produce, *OX* is worth a visit if you're keen to sample the city's finest dining, with seasonal dishes that showcase Northern Ireland's local produce. Booking essential. To sample the restaurant's very best, opt for the six-course tasting menu at £60/person. Tues–Fri noon–2.30pm & 6–9.30pm, Sat 1–2.30pm & 6–9.30pm.

## DRINKING

SEE MAP PAGES 457 AND 463

Whether you're after raucous dancing, **traditional music** or simply a quiet pint of the black stuff, you're going to be spoilt for choice. First-time visitors tend to be drawn to the older pubs on **Great Victoria Street**, while the city's trendier residents and students frequent the **University Quarter** and the **Lisburn Road**. For a more eclectic mix of pubs in a smaller area (making for a great pub crawl), head to the **Cathedral Quarter**. A good resource for pub reviews is ⓦ belfastbar.co.uk.

★ **The Crown Liquor Saloon** 46 Great Victoria St ☎ 02890 243187, ⓦ nicholsonspubs.co.uk/thecrown liquorsaloonbelfast. Owned by the National Trust, Belfast's most famous and spectacular pub is an old Victorian gin palace with an ornate ceiling, painted mirrors and frieze-decorated oak panelling. Once armed with drinks, try to grab one of the snugs, where you press a button to receive service. If the snugs are busy, it's still a great experience to linger at the bar, with its carved-timber dividing screens.

There's a good repertoire of Northern Ireland food on offer too, along with pints of Strangford oysters, when Oyster season descends in Sept. Mon–Wed 10am–11.30pm, Thurs–Sat 10am–midnight, Sun 10am–11pm.

★ **The Duke of York** 11 Commercial Court, off Donegall St ☎ 02890 241062, ⓦ dukeofyorkbelfast.com. Nestled on a cobbled alleyway in the Half Bap area in the heart of the Cathedral Quarter. The decor takes you back to bygone times, its walls strewn with memorabilia and antiquities. Regular traditional music sessions and outdoor benches for balmy summer evenings. Mon 11.30am–11pm, Tues–Sat 11am–1am, Sun 3–8pm.

**The Five Points Whiskey & Alehouse** 44 Dublin Rd ☎ 02890 994124, ⓦ thepointsbelfast.com. Named after a notorious area in New York City where Irish Immigrants ruled the streets, this terrific addition to Belfast's pub scene serves up an impressive range of whiskies and craft beers to a live soundtrack of traditional Irish music. Mon–Thurs 1pm–1am, Fri & Sat 1pm–2am, Sun 1pm–midnight.

**The Harp Bar** 35 Hill St ☎ 02890 329923, ⓦ dukeofyork belfast.com. The more refined big brother of the *Duke of York*, housed in the former head office of the Old Bushmills whiskey distillery. Plush, red-velvet fabrics and antique furnishings recall Victorian Belfast, and there's an impressive range of whiskies and independent draught beers. Regular music nights upstairs. Daily noon–12.30am.

**The John Hewitt** 53 Donegall St ☎ 02890 233768, ⓦ thejohnhewitt.com. Light and airy pub run by the Belfast Unemployed Resource Centre, with newspapers, paintings by local artists on sale, plus an excellent traditional session (Sat 6pm), traditional jazz on Fri (8.30pm), singer-songwriters on Mon (9pm) and various other events during the week. Also serves healthy, reasonably priced meals. A great place to while away a few hours sampling local craft beers and ciders. Mon–Fri 11.30am–1am, Sat noon–1am, Sun 7pm–midnight.

**Kelly's Cellars** 30 Bank St ☎ 02890 246058, ⓦ kellys cellars.co.uk. Belfast's oldest-surviving continuously run pub was opened in the sixteenth century. According to legend, it was a frequent meeting place for the United Irishmen behind the doomed 1798 Rebellion (Henry Joy McCracken is said to have hidden under the bar counter from British soldiers). Good lunches, including thumping portions of home-made Irish stew and steak pie, a turf fire and traditional music several nights a week. Mon–Sat 11.30am–1am, Sun 1pm–midnight.

**The Morning Star** 17 Pottingers Entry ☎ 02890 235986, ⓦ themorningstarbar.co.uk. This fine old-fashioned bar is something of a living museum, retaining many of its original fittings and fixtures including the original mahogany counter. It tends to be busy by day and quiet at night, and serves a wonderful lunch menu. Mon–Sat 11.30am–11pm.

**Muriel's Café Bar** 12–14 Church Lane ☎ 02890 332445. Named after a Belfast Madam who, rumour has it, sold hats by day and ran a brothel by night, the ground floor here is themed on a 1920s millinery shop while the upstairs lounge area is all "Parisian boudoir", with its opulent furnishings and candlelight. The food is top-notch, with a full bistro menu and deli-style platters on offer. Mon–Fri 11.30am–1am, Sat 10am–1am, Sun 10am–midnight.

★ **Sunflower** 65 Union St ☎ 02890 232474, ⓦ sun flowerbelfast.com. This former working man's drinking den has had a revamp, turning it into quite a cool pub, with an interior that offers more than a passing nod to the Seventies and Eighties. Regular live music upstairs and impromptu traditional sessions downstairs make it a popular haunt for the city's music lovers. Also holds comedy nights. Mon–Thurs noon–midnight, Fri & Sat noon–1am, Sun 5pm–midnight.

**White's Tavern** 2–4 Winecellar Entry, High St ☎ 02890 312582, ⓦ whitestavernbelfast.com. Founded in 1630, *White's* is an atmospheric old Entries bar, with stone floors and an open fire, serving excellent lunches and hosting traditional sessions downstairs. Upstairs is *Vandal*, a dedicated "geek and movie bar" serving pizzas with a licensed cinema. They also offer seasonal outdoor retro screenings in the courtyard. Mon–Tues noon–8pm, Wed noon–10pm, Thurs noon–11pm, Fri & Sat noon–2am, Sun noon–midnight.

## NIGHTLIFE

SEE MAP PAGES 457 AND 463

As in most UK cities, Belfast's "superclubs" have long gone, replaced with numerous smaller **clubs**, usually housed in an upstairs room above a popular city bar and catering for all tastes. **Admission** may be free early in the week (and at some places all week) and as low as £2 or £3 up to Thurs, while weekend prices are usually around £5 to £15. For the latest **listings**, the monthly listings freesheet *The Big List* is essential (online version at ⓦ thebiglist.co.uk), or check out the Clubs section of ⓦ viewbelfast.co.uk. As well as the traditional **music** on offer in pubs (see Drinking), Belfast also benefits from a thriving, grass-roots indie and rock scene, while the number of visiting international performers has increased dramatically since the arrival of the Waterfront Hall and Odyssey Complex with its SSE Arena (see page 477).

### CLUBS AND VENUES

**Cuckoo** 149 Lisburn Rd ☎ 02890 667776, ⓦ cuckoo-belfast.com. The trendy folk of the Lisburn Rd flock to Cuckoo for craft beers, ping pong and dancing. Club nights vary but there's dancing, live music or a DJ set on Fri & Sat nights from 9pm till late. Cool rooftop beer garden too.

**Lavery's Gin Palace** 12–18 Bradbury Place ☎ 02890 871106, ⓦ laverysbelfast.com. A Belfast institution, particularly popular with students, with "Retro Disco" and "Rip It Up" (soul, funk and indie) nights currently alternating

**5**

## FESTIVALS IN BELFAST

Belfast has numerous festivals: below is a selection of the highlights; visit ⓦvisit-belfast. com/whats-on/festivals for a full calendar. Note that although **Open House Festival** (ⓦopenhousefestival.com) has officially relocated to nearby Bangor, there are still Open House events held around the Cathedral Quarter at various dates throughout the year.

### FEBRUARY, MARCH & APRIL

**Belfast Nashville Songwriters Festival** ⓦbelfastnashville.com. The North's love of country is reflected by this citywide weeklong event in late February, featuring local talent and major US names (Nanci Griffith is a favourite headliner).

**St Patrick's Day** ⓦbelfastcity.gov.uk/stpatricks. Carnival parade on March 17, followed by a major open-air concert in Custom House Square.

**Belfast Film Festival** ☎02890 246609, ⓦbelfastfilmfestival.org. The second half of April sees a host of left-field films and related events with screenings in cinemas, pubs, clubs and other venues.

### MAY & JUNE

**Festival of Fools** ⓦfoolsfestival.com. Five-day international street-theatre festival, held over the first weekend in May, with events around the city centre.

**Belsonic** ⓦbelsonic.com. The month of June sees A-list music acts giving open-air performances in the heart of the city. Previous headliners include Green Day, Arctic Fire, Biffy Clyro, Chemical Brothers and Rudimental.

**Belfast City Blues Festival**. Three days of 12-bar honky-tonk and foot-stomping riffs at the end of June.

### JULY & AUGUST

**Orangefest** Orange Order Lodges throughout Belfast commemorate the Battle of the Boyne with parades on July 12.

**Belfast Pride** ⓦbelfastpride.com. At the end of July into early August, over a hundred LGBTQ events take place across the city over a ten day period, culminating in the Belfast Pride Parade.

**Féile An Phobail** ⓦfeilebelfast.com. Week-long music and dance festival at the beginning of August, based in West Belfast.

**Woodstock Rhythm & Blues Festival**. East Belfast's grassroots music festival continues to grow year on year, now providing a long weekend of live music events in mid-August, showcasing new local talent alongside perennial favourites.

**Belfast Mela** ⓦartsekta.org.uk/festivals. The region's largest multicultural festival, celebrating South Asian culture through live music, dance, food, arts and crafts in the city's Botanic Gardens (see page 463) at the end of August.

### SEPTEMBER & OCTOBER

**Cathedral Quarter Arts Festival** (ⓦcqaf.com) Lively arts festival, featuring Irish and international acts (music, comedy, film and theatre) spread over ten days in early September.

**Culture Night Belfast** ⓦculturenightbelfast.com. For one Friday night in September, buildings across Belfast open their doors to host free live performances by musicians, dancers and entertainers: expect everything from carnival parades to BMX displays.

**Cinemagic Festival** ⓦcinemagic.org.uk. The month of October sees an impressive programme of film screenings and workshops take place across Belfast, aimed at a youth audience with bespoke family events. Expect some Hollywood A-listers to be in town to lend their support.

**Belfast International Arts Festival** ⓦbelfastinternationalartsfestival.com. Fortnight-long event held in late October which claims to be Britain's second-biggest arts festival after Edinburgh.

on Sat in the Back Bar, and "Beat Connection" (funk, soul, hip-hop and house) in the Ballroom. On Sun night in the Ballroom it's DJ request night, with punters racking up their next game of pool to a soundtrack of favourites. Mon–Thurs 5pm–midnight, Fri & Sat 1pm–1am, Sun 2–11pm.

**Love & Death Inc** 10a Ann St ☎ 02890 247222, ⓦ love anddeathcocktails.co.uk. A popular Sat haunt for its regular "Love Party" night, featuring house, disco and 80s and 90s dance anthems. Cover £5–7. Sat 10pm–3am.

**Ollie's** 16 Skipper St ☎ 02890 267964, ⓦ olliesbelfast. com. Part of the five-star *Merchant* hotel, *Ollie's* delivers all that you might expect that to entail, with a decadent, velvet-and-mahogany bedecked club area alongside a private members' bar. Regular club nights take place on Mon (£5), Thurs (£5), Fri (£7) and Sat (£10). Mon, Thurs, Fri & Sat 8pm till late.

**Shine** Queen's University Student Union ☎ 02890 243418, ⓦ shine.net. *Shine* has a UK-wide reputation, spanning almost twenty years, for attracting the biggest DJs to Northern Irish shores, from Felix Da Housecat and David Guetta to Deadmau5 and Dave Clarke. Keep an eye out on the website for what's coming up.

### LIVE MUSIC

**The Dirty Onion** 3 Hill St ☎ 02890 243712, ⓦ thedirty onion.com. This live music pub, a clever conversion of one of the city's oldest buildings, offers something different every night – from *bodhrán* lessons to bluegrass sessions. On-site chicken rotisserie restaurant too. Mon–Sat noon–1am, Sun noon–midnight.

**The Empire Bar & Music Hall** 42 Botanic Ave ☎ 02890 249276, ⓦ thebelfastempire.com. Cellar bar in a former church just up from the station, with a boisterous beer-hall atmosphere. Good-value food and bands most nights of the week with DJs and bigger name bands upstairs. Mon–Sat 11.30am–1am, Sun 12.30pm–midnight.

**Filthy McNasty's** 45 Dublin Rd ☎ 02890 246823, ⓦ thefilthyquarter.com. With a secret garden, a club room (the "gypsy lounge") and a backdrop of quirky furnishings, local Belfast musicians can be heard doing their thing from 10pm most nights, with an open mic session on Sun. Daily 1pm–1am.

★ **The Limelight Complex** 17 Ormeau Ave ☎ 02890 327007, ⓦ limelightbelfast.com. This Belfast institution – one of the North's leading live music venues – is home to two music venues, a bar and the open-air "Rock Garden". Expect an eclectic mix of singers and bands, plus DJs and club nights. Daily noon–2am.

**The Pavilion Bar** 296 Ormeau Rd ☎ 02890 283283, ⓦ pavilionbelfast.com. Possibly *the* place to catch up-and-coming young indie bands as they take to the stage to pedal their tunes. Mon–Sat 11.30am–1am, Sun 12.30pm–midnight.

## ENTERTAINMENT

### CONCERT VENUES AND THEATRES

**Belfast Waterfront** Lanyon Place, Laganside ☎ 02890 334455, ⓦ waterfront.co.uk. Hosts classical music and ballet, comedy, mainstream jazz and occasional big names from the world of middle-of-the-road pop and rock.

**Grand Opera House** Great Victoria St ☎ 02890 241919, ⓦ goh.co.uk. Belfast's most prestigious venue, featuring regular operatic performances as well as many of London's West End productions.

**Lyric Theatre** 55 Ridgeway St, off Stranmillis Rd ☎ 02890 381081, ⓦ lyrictheatre.co.uk. The Lyric's stages serious contemporary drama along with family performances.

**Oh Yeah Music Centre** 15–21 Gordon St ☎ 02890 310845, ⓦ ohyeahbelfast.com. A music venue in the heart of the Cathedral Quarter that aims to showcase local music and educate the ears of the good people of Belfast. A hidden gem worth seeking out for live gigs and DJ sets.

**SSE Arena** 2 Queen's Quay ☎ 02890 739074, ⓦ ssearena belfast.com. Where the biggest rock and pop singers and bands perform when they come to town.

**Ulster Hall** Bedford St ☎ 02890 334455, ⓦ ulsterhall. co.uk. Most of the city's classical music performances are given by the Ulster Orchestra (ⓦ ulsterorchestra.com); the hall is also used for big rock and pop concerts.

**Whitla Hall** Queen's University ☎ 02890 245133. Stages some professional and amateur classical concerts.

### ARTS CENTRES AND CINEMA

**Black Box** 18–22 Hill St ☎ 02890 244400, ⓦ black boxbelfast.com. An arts and performance space in the Cathedral Quarter with an eclectic programme of live events and exhibitions including art, dance and music.

**Crescent Arts Centre** 2–4 University Rd ☎ 02890 242338, ⓦ crescentarts.org. A focus for much of Belfast's left-field arts and performance activities.

**Culturlaan** 216 Falls Rd ☎ 02890 964180, ⓦ culturlann. ie. An arts centre with an exciting and vibrant programme that promotes the Irish language and culture. Also houses the West Belfast Tourist Information Point.

**The MAC** Saint Anne's Square ☎ 02890 235053, ⓦ the maclive.com. The Metropolitan Arts Centre (MAC) occupies a modern six-storey building in the Cathedral Quarter with a programme that focuses on experimental and fringe productions, while also hosting major art exhibitions.

**Queen's Film Theatre (QFT)** 20 University Square ☎ 02890 971097, ⓦ queensfilmtheatre.com. Two-screen independent cinema, showing art-house movies at exceptionally good prices.

**5**

## LGBTQ BELFAST

The number of LGBTQ **bars** and **venues** in Belfast has increased substantially over the last few years and the majority are geared towards men. The area around **Union St** is affectionately known as "Queer Quarter" or the "Gay Village" by the city's LGBTQ community. **Pride** (ⓦ belfast pride.com) week begins on the last Sat in July.

### RESOURCES

The main resource for Belfast's LGBTQ scene is Queerspace at 23–31 Waring St. It's part of Cara-Friend, a collective that aims to serve the needs and raise the profile of the LGBTQ community of Belfast and Northern Ireland. It holds collective meetings on the afternoons of the first and third Sat of the month (2.30pm), followed by drop-in sessions at their *InSpace Coffee Lounge* (3.30pm). Helpline service provided by Cara-Friend (ⓣ 0808 8000390; Mon–Fri 1–4pm, Wed 6–9pm ⓦ cara-friend.org.uk).

**VENUES; SEE MAP PAGE 457**

**Kremlin** 96 Donegall St ⓣ 02890 316060, ⓦ kremlin-belfast.com. Ireland's biggest LGBTQ venue, featuring three bars and various themed nights of music, fun and games, including the hugely popular "Revolution" on Sat. Tues, Thurs & Sun 10pm–2.30am, Fri–Sat 9pm–3am.

**Maverick** 1 Union St ⓣ 02890 246925, ⓦ themaverick belfast.com. The newest LGBTQ bar in town bills itself as a "Den, Lounge & Disco". It offers plenty of kitsch decor and an eclectic mix of theme nights. Mon–Sat 5pm–1am, Sun 5pm–midnight.

**Union Street Bar** 8-14 Union St ⓣ 02890 316060, ⓦ unionstreetbar.com. This trendy daytime gastropub has been a firm favourite in Belfast's LGBTQ scene since first opening its doors in 2003, offering a variety of themed nights for men seven days a week, ranging from karaoke to bingo, via deck-thumping DJs. Mon–Sat noon–1.30am, Sun 2pm–1.30am.

## SPORT

The Northern Irish are very passionate about their sport, with a reputation for producing excellent **individual players**, such as George Best (football), Mary Peters (athletics), Dennis Taylor and Alex Higgins (snooker), Joey Dunlop (motorcycling) and Rory McIlroy (golf).

**Football (soccer)** Northern Ireland's team enjoyed little success on the international stage over the last twenty years until the Euros 2016, when the Green and White Army (GAWA), as sports fans refer to the Northern Irish supporters, travelled to France in their droves. Although the national team narrowly missed out on a quarter final place, the GAWA endeared themselves to other supporters and the world's media for their enthusiasm and passion. Back home, international games attract a loyal following at Windsor Park (the home ground of the Linfield club) near the Lisburn Rd. If there are no international matches being played during your visit, you may still be able to get tickets for an Irish League Premiership game with four teams – Cliftonville, Glentoran, Linfield and Crusaders – all based in Belfast.

**Gaelic football (GAA) and hurling** Although both are immensely popular nationwide, neither sport has a huge following in Belfast city. However, you can still see both sports being played most weekends at Roger Casement Park, on Andersonstown Rd.

**Rugby Union** The provincial team, Ulster Rugby, has an ever-growing fan base that has resulted in a significant extension at the club's Kingspan Stadium (85 Ravenhill Park). It can now hold over 18,000 spectators, yet many home games are sold out. Cup and league successes have seen the team go from strength to strength in recent years, regularly supplying the national squad (Ireland) with players, along with the British & Irish Lions.

**Ice hockey** The Belfast Giants – most recently champions of the UK's Elite Ice Hockey League in 2018/19 – regularly play at the SSE Arena in front of over four thousand fans. The SSE Arena also plays host to the annual Friendship Four Ice Hockey Tournament every Thanksgiving, showcasing talent from four of America's top universities.

## SHOPPING

**SEE MAP PAGES 457 AND 463**

With post-ceasefire insurance premiums more affordable, **shopping** in Belfast has vastly improved in recent years with the arrival of many high street names. The **Victoria Square** shopping centre (ⓦ victoriasquare.com) is home to over fifty different stores, including a multi-floored House of Fraser, while the top two floors feature a multiscreen Odeon cinema and a number of well-known restaurants that had previously ignored Belfast, such as *Wagamama* and *Prezzo*. The mall is open daily, with late-night shopping until 9pm from Wednesday to Friday. Take the lift to the **Viewing Dome** for spectacular vistas across the city and beyond.

**Fresh Garbage** 24 Rosemary St ⓣ 02890 242350,

ⓦ freshgarbage.co.uk. This Belfast institution first opened in 1969 and is awash with band memorabilia, tour T-shirts, jewellery and funky accessories. Locals often refer to it simply as "Fresh". Mon–Wed & Sat 10am–5.30pm, Thurs 10am–9pm, Sun 1–5pm.

**No Alibi Bookstore** 83 Botanic Ave ⓣ 02890 319601, ⓦ noalibis.com. A specialist crime fiction store immortalized in local author Colin Bateman's *Mystery Man* series. The staff are friendly and passionate about the genre, and there's a coffee and reading area. Regularly readings and literary events too. Mon–Sat 9am–5.30pm, Sun 1–5pm.

**Sawers** Fountain Centre, College St ⓣ 02890 322021,

**5**

## ST GEORGE'S MARKET

Belfast is immensely proud of **St George's Market** (East Bridge St), which oozes Victorian charm and is home to speciality markets (Fri 6am–2pm, Sat 9am–3pm, Sun 10am–4pm). It first opened as a covered market in the 1890s and underwent a £4.5 million facelift in 1999. The Friday food and variety market is by far the most popular, with about two hundred traders taking part, while Saturday focuses on organic produce and gardens. The Sunday market operates at a more leisurely pace, with live music and takeaway food on offer. It was voted the Nation's Favourite Heritage Project in the 2014 National Lottery Awards.

ⓦsawersbelfast.com. This Aladdin's cave of tasty local delicacies and exotic delights from far-flung shores was first established in 1897 and once had outlets in Glasgow, Birmingham and Dublin; the Belfast store is the only one that remains. Mon–Sat 9am–5.30pm.

**Sick Records** 78 North St. An independent record shop with friendly and knowledgeable staff, stocking new vinyl releases alongside retro titles.

## DIRECTORY

**Hospital** Royal Victoria Hospital, Grosvenor Rd ☎02890 240503.

**Internet access** Visit Belfast Welcome Centre, 9 Donegall Square North; Belfast Central Library, Royal Ave; *Browsers Café*, 77 Dublin Rd.

**Laundry** Globe, 39 Botanic Ave (Mon–Fri 8am–9pm, Sat 8am–6pm, Sun noon–6pm; ☎02890 243956).

**Left luggage** Visit Belfast Welcome Centre (see page 471), 9 Donegall Square North.

**Lost property** Musgrave St police station, off Ann St ☎02890 650222.

**Pharmacy** Boots, 35–47 Donegall Place (Mon–Sat 8am–7pm, Thurs 8am–9pm, Sun 1–6pm).

**Police** In an emergency, call ☎999 or ☎112. The main city centre police station is in North Queen St.

**Post offices** 16 Howard St; 1–5 Botanic Ave; and 12–16 Bridge St (Mon–Sat 9am–5.30pm).

# Antrim and Derry

DARK HEDGES

# Antrim and Derry

Much of the coastline of County Antrim is as spectacular as anything you'll find across the whole of Ireland – consequently, unlike other parts of the North, it has always attracted an abundance of tourists. Beyond the fabulous Gobbins cliff path, the A2 coast road takes in attractive villages and small towns, such as Carnlough, Cushendall and the port of Ballycastle, all set against or within the verdant Antrim Glens. A short boat trip from Ballycastle, meanwhile, is rugged Rathlin Island, while further along the coast to the west, blustery cliff-top walks lead to the strange basalt formations of the Giant's Causeway. With an attractive backdrop, Portrush and, just over the county border in Derry, Portstewart are popular seaside holiday resorts.

**14**

County Derry's coastline is also blessed with wonderful strands, though most visitors make an immediate beeline for **Derry city** itself; set on the banks of the Foyle, with its hilltop core enclosed by some of the best-preserved city walls in Europe, Derry was at the forefront of the Troubles, and the city's past struggles are documented in a couple of superb museums. The county's hinterland is more dramatic than Antrim's, especially where it skirts the Sperrin Mountains. The flatter territory towards Lough Neagh features some noteworthy Plantation settlements at **Magherafelt** and **Moneymore**, though the most noteworthy destination hereabouts is **Bellaghy**, home to the superb Seamus Heaney HomePlace.

## GETTING AROUND                                                    ANTRIM AND DERRY

**By train** From Belfast, trains run to Larne via Carrickfergus but go no further up the Antrim coast; otherwise, the other main line through Antrim heads south to Lisburn before looping up towards Ballymena and Coleraine, where it branches off, with one line going to Portrush and another to Derry.

**By bus** Both Antrim and Derry are well served by buses, with most services operated by Translink (ⓦ translink.co.uk). The hop-on, hop-off Causeway Rambler (#172/#402) runs daily (June–Sept every 30min–1hr; £9) from Coleraine to Ballycastle via Bushmills, the Giant's Causeway, Dunseverick

Castle, Ballintoy and Carrick-a-rede; weather permitting, some of these are open-top buses. Between June and September, the Antrim Coaster (#252) runs Mon–Fri from Larne via the Glens to Ballycastle, with a further connecting service from Ballycastle to the Giant's Causeway, Bushmills and Coleraine. Departures from Larne are at 10.20am and 3.20pm, with the returns from Ballycastle at 12.05pm and 5.05pm. Buses from Belfast's Europa Buscentre will take you to Larne.

**By ferry** P&O ferries (ⓣ 0800 130 0030, ⓦ poferries.com) operate between four and six crossings daily (2hr) from Larne, 35km north of Belfast, to Cairnryan in Dumfries, Scotland.

# North from Belfast

The coastal strip heading **north from Belfast** to Larne is largely uninspiring farmland, although there are a few spots to detain you as you head towards the more enticing Antrim Glens further north, notably the spectacular Gobbins cliff path.

## Carrickfergus Castle

Marine Highway • Daily: April–Sept 10am–6pm; Oct–March 10am–4pm • £5 • ⓣ 028 9355 1273, ⓦ discovernorthernireland.com • Can be reached from Belfast by train (every 30min–1hr; 25min) or bus (every 20–30min; 40min)

Heading out of Belfast's northern suburbs, the A2 skirts the edge of Belfast Lough before reaching the unremarkable town of **CARRICKFERGUS**, whose seafront is dominated by the well-preserved **Carrickfergus Castle**. One of the earliest and largest

# Highlights

**❶ The Gobbins** Dramatic and ingenious in equal measure, this 3km-long cliff-face path is utterly enthralling. See page 486

**❷ Causeway Coast Road** The route from Larne to Portrush, skirting the Glens of Antrim, is one of Ireland's most scenic, with magical seascapes, staggering cliff-top walks and some of the North's prettiest villages. See page 486

**❸ Rathlin Island** Northern Ireland's only inhabited offshore island, Rathlin offers exhilarating walks and views, top-class birdwatching opportunities and insights into a thriving local culture. See page 491

**❹ The Giant's Causeway** Get there early to beat the crowds and marvel at one of the strangest geological formations in Europe. See page 493

**❺ Portstewart Strand** The north coast's top beach where you can swim, surf, sunbathe or walk the dunes before ending your visit with dinner at the rustic *Harry's Shack*. See page 498

**❻ Walls of Derry** A circuit of these seventeenth-century defences is an essential part of any visit to the "Maiden City". See page 502

**❼ Seamus Heaney HomePlace** Immerse yourself in the life and works of one of Ireland's foremost poets, and Nobel Laureate. See page 511

**HIGHLIGHTS ARE MARKED ON THE MAP ON PAGE 484**

# ANTRIM & DERRY

## HIGHLIGHTS

1 The Gobbins
2 Causeway Coast Road
3 Rathlin Island
4 The Giant's Causeway
5 Portstewart Strand
6 Walls of Derry
7 Seamus Heaney HomePlace

Greencastle
Magilligan Point
Lough Foyle Ferry
Ramore Head
Portballint
Portrush
Dunluce Castle
Mussenden Temple
Castlerock
5 Portstewart
Downhill
Hezlett House
Coleraine
Bellarena
Mount Binevenagh
A2
B201
A29
A54

Lough Foyle

DONEGAL

Letterkenny
N13

Derry
6

A2

Limavady
Roe Valley Country Park
A37

A29

DERRY

A6
Dungiven
Banagher Old Church
A6
Maghera

River Foyle

Strabane

SPERRIN  MOUNTAINS

Draperstown
Magherafelt
A29
A31

Slieve Gallion

TYRONE

Moneymore
Springh

A5

A505

Cookstown

Omagh

A29

A5

Dungannon

A4

0          15
kilometres

Irish castles, built on a rocky promontory above the harbour around 1180 by the Anglo-Norman invader John de Courcy (and garrisoned until 1928), the castle reflects the defensive history of this entire region. In 1315, the castle endured a year's siege before falling to the combined forces of Robert and Edward Bruce, after which the English retook it. It's great fun exploring the castle's warren of dank passages and staircases, and there's also an informative exhibition on its history.

## 14  The Gobbins

68 Middle Rd, Islandmagee • Visitor Centre daily 9.30am–4.30pm; tours (must be pre-booked) May–Sept every 30min • £20 • ☎ 028 9337 2318, ⊛ thegobbinscliffpath.com

Dramatically cut into the rock face on the eastern flank of the long, crooked-finger-like peninsula of Islandmagee is the **Gobbins cliff path**. The path was originally constructed in 1902 by railway engineer Berkley Dean Wise as part of his grander vision to expand tourism in the area – indeed it was quite the tourist attraction back in the day. Numerous factors contributed to its eventual decline and the path closed in the early 1960s, thereafter falling into a state of disrepair.

Following a safety briefing, and kitted out with hardhat and appropriate footwear (boots can be supplied if yours aren't sturdy enough), visitors are bussed down to the start of the path. First off, you head up to a **viewing point** affording tremendous views of the sea-bitten coastline and, in the distance, the distinctive hump of Ailsa Craig just off the Ayrshire coast. Passing through **Wise's Eye** – the original, and surprisingly small, hole in the rock face – the new path roughly tracks Wise's original, albeit now almost totally eroded, version; the 3km path runs through a series of dramatic **tunnels**, **staircases** and **suspension bridges**, including a replica of Wise's iconic tubular bridge. Aside from birdlife, you may also get to see dolphins, porpoises and seals along the way. Note, though, that the path is not always open in its entirety (variously due to inclement weather, path maintenance or breeding birds), and while the walk – which takes around two and a half hours – is not especially demanding, a reasonable degree of fitness is required.

Before heading out, allow yourself a little time to peruse the illuminating **exhibition** inside the visitor centre, which relays the history of the path courtesy of some captivating black and white photos and informative wall panels; there's also one of the pillars from a section of the original railing. You can also enjoy some refreshments in the café.

# The Glens of Antrim

The Causeway coast road surges north in quite spectacular fashion along the nine **Glens of Antrim**, a curious landscape in which pretty seaside villages – notably **Glenarm**, **Cushendall** and **Cushendun** – contrast vividly with the rough moorland above, which itself affords some memorable walking. The Glens' largest town is **Ballycastle**, a sprightly little spot on the northern tip, which is also the departure point for the ferry to rugged **Rathlin**.

## Glenarm

The southernmost of the Glens, **Glenarm**, is headed by a village of the same name, which grew up around a hunting lodge built by Randal MacDonnell after Dunluce Castle, further up the coast, was abandoned (see page 496). Set around a graceful sandy bay and run through with handsome Georgian buildings, Glenarm is a delightful spot to linger in, and makes a great base for local walks. The village is also the location for the prestigious **Festival of Voice** (⊛ niopera.com), a three-day series of recitals and events in mid-August.

### Glenarm Castle and the Walled Garden

2 Castle Lane • Walled Garden Easter–Sept Daily 9am–5pm • £6 • ☎ 028 2884 1203, ⓦ glenarmcastle.com

Dominating the village, **Glenarm Castle** was built in 1636, becoming the major seat of the Earls of Antrim, though it was razed just a few years later – its current incarnation dates from 1756. Today the castle is a private residence, hence is off-limits (save for a handful of days when special events are on – check the website), but the stunning **walled garden** is open to the public and certainly worth an hour or so of your time. Highlights here include the circular yew hedge, a zesty-smelling herb garden (unusual for its four capitols), kitchen garden and glasshouse, which backs onto a row of whitewashed bothies – formerly gardeners' residences but which now accommodate various craft shops. Bring a picnic and make the most of the setting, or failing that, retire to the posh little tearoom for a cuppa and a slice of cake.

**14**

### ARRIVAL AND INFORMATION

**GLENARM**

**By bus** Glenarm is served by buses from/to Carnlough (Mon–Fri 4 daily, Sat 2; 10min) and Larne (Mon–Sat 6–7 daily; 25min).

**Tourist information** Glenarm Visitor Centre is opposite the harbour at 17 New Rd (March–Sept Mon–Fri 9.30am–2.30pm, Sat 9.30am–1.30pm; ☎ 028 2884 1087, ⓦ glenarm tourism.org); the super-helpful staff here can assist on any aspect of visiting the Glens and the Causeway coast, including organising local walks.

### ACCOMMODATION

★ **Water's Edge** 11–13 The Cloney ☎ 028 2884 1117, ⓦ watersedgeglenarm.com. Occupying Glenarm's erstwhile police station, on the coastal road heading towards Carnlough, this fabulous five-star bed and breakfast has three sweet rooms (one with a wet room), each with unencumbered sea views. Coffee and freshly baked treats await upon arrival, while hosts Jenny and Peter are a font of local knowledge. **£80**

## Carnlough

Rounding the next bay from Glenarm, you'll arrive at **CARNLOUGH**, standing at the head of **Glencloy**. Until the 1960s, Carnlough's way of life was linked to its limestone quarries, and the village's most striking feature today remains its sturdy limestone buildings, dating mainly from the mid-nineteenth century. Right in the village centre, running over the main road, there's a solid **stone bridge** that once carried a railway bringing material down to the **harbour**, which itself has an impressive breakwater, clock tower and limestone courthouse. The harbour has also served as the setting for several *Game of Thrones* scenes, and is the departure point for half-hour boat trips out to Black Rock.

---

### GAME OF THRONES

Winterfell, House Stark, Vaes Dothrak, Renly's Camp, and the Wildling Pit – all of these names will be familiar to fans of the fantasy drama, **Game of Thrones**, which has principally been filmed in Northern Ireland, since series one aired in 2011; the eighth (and last) series hit the screen in 2019. Legions of fans make the trip here to seek out **filming locations** like Ballintoy and Carnlough harbours, Castle Ward, Cushendun Caves, Inch Abbey and Tollymore Forest. The most iconic, however, is the **Dark Hedges**, near Armoy some 13km southwest of Ballycastle; a remarkable, haunting avenue of enormous beech trees planted by the Stuart family in the eighteenth century, they have become one of the most visited sites in the country. In 2016 storms brought down a number of these trees, the result being that the wood was salvaged and transformed into a set of ten **doors**, each one intricately carved with a scene from series six; these are now *in situ* at ten pubs, or inns, across the country, for example *Fiddler's Green* in Portaferry (see page 526), *Mary McBride's* in Cushendun (see page 489), and *Blakes of the Hollow* in Enniskillen (see page 561).

**14**

**By bus** Carnlough has bus services from/to Cushendall (Mon–Fri 2 daily; 25min); Glenarm (Mon–Fri 4 daily, Sat 2; 10min); and Larne (Mon–Sat 6–7 daily; 35min).

**Boat trips** Carnlough Bay Boat Tours (☎07720 464044 ⓦ carnloughboattours.weebly.com) offers 30min tours out to Black Rock (£6), as well as longer tours.

**ACCOMMODATION AND EATING**

★ **Londonderry Arms Hotel** 20 Harbour Rd ☎028 2888 5255, ⓦ londonderryarmshotel.com. A former coaching inn once briefly owned by Winston Churchill, the *Londonderry* oozes character. The building comprises a warren of agreeably old-fashioned rooms variously conferred with carved oak and antique furnishings, while the *Coach House Bar and Grill* is a convivial spot to chow down on the likes of Cajun chicken fillet (£12.95). Once done there, sidle next door to the *Arkle* bar, whose collection of mementos celebrates the legendary 1960s champion steeplechaser. **£70**

# Cushendall and around

**CUSHENDALL**, which lies at the head of three of the nine Glens, is a delightfully understated village, its charming colour-washed buildings grouped together on a spectacular shore. The red-sandstone **tower** at the central crossroads was built in 1817 by Francis Turnley, an official of the East India Company, as "a place of confinement for idlers and rioters", and the village makes a fine base for exploring the countryside and catching a traditional music session. If possible, time your visit to coincide with the **Heart of the Glens** festival in early August, one of the area's oldest events, replete with music, sporting events and much merriment, culminating in a huge street ceili on the Sunday.

**By bus** There are buses from/to Carnlough (Mon–Fri 2 daily; 25min) and Cushendun (Mon–Fri 6 daily, Sat 3; 15min).
**Tourist information** The tourist office is a few paces west of the central crossroads at 25 Mill St (June–Sept Mon–Fri 10am–5pm, Sat 10am–4pm; Oct–March Tues–Sat 10am–1pm; April & May Tues–Sat 10am–1pm; ☎028 2177 1180, ⓦ visitcausewaycoastandglens.com).

**ACCOMMODATION**

**Cushendall Caravan Park** 62 Coast Rd ☎028 2177 1699, ⓦ glenscoastcaravanparks.com. Hovering right over the water's edge at the entrance to the village (from Carnlough), this small but well equipped campsite also has four wooden camping pods, with artificial turfed roofs and bench-like beds. Closed Nov–March. Tent pitches **£10**, pods **£20**
**The Meadows** 81 Coast Rd ☎028 2177 2020, ⓦ the meadowscushendall.com. A quiet but friendly B&B located at the entrance to the village (just beyond the caravan park) with six spacious rooms, each with a double and single bed. Also offers disabled access. **£60**

**Sundial House** 11 High St ☎028 2177 1340, ⓦ sundial house.weebly.com. Super-friendly hostel-cum-guesthouse located on the steep hill just north of the tower offering a double (en suite), and three triple-bedrooms; self-catering kitchen plus lounge with log fire too. Triples **£25**/bed, doubles **£55**
**The Village B&B** Mill St ☎028 2177 2366, ⓦ thevillage bandb.com. Welcoming, central option with nine generously sized en-suite rooms, including singles doubles and family rooms. The owner dispenses maps, logistical and practical walking information, and will enrich your stay with local cultural history. Closed Nov–Feb. **£70**

**EATING AND DRINKING**

**Harry's** 10 Mill St ☎028 2177 2022, ⓦ harryscushendall. co.uk. This hugely popular two-floored bistro won't win any prizes for culinary flair, but it serves good-value, big portion meals, such as freshly battered scampi with chunky chips and tobacco onions (£12.95). Daily noon–9pm.
★ **Johnny Joe's** 23 Mill St ☎028 2177 1992, ⓦ johnny joes.co.uk. A convivial, cottage-style pub which hosts traditional music sessions on Fridays, in addition to music on Tues, Sat and Sun in high season. Tues–Thurs 8–11.30pm,

Fri–Sun from 4pm.
**Upstairs at Joe's** 23 Mill St ☎028 2177 2849. The first-floor rooms above *Johnny Joe's* pub serve as one of the area's better restaurants, thanks to a menu of imaginatively designed dishes like sautéed scallops with spinach gnocchi and crispy dulse (seaweed), and pea and mint risotto beetroot and goat's cheese crumble (£14.50). March–June & Sept daily 5.30–9pm, July & Aug noon–9pm; Oct–Feb Thurs–Sun 5.30–9pm.

## Cushendun and around

The once-fashionable resort of **CUSHENDUN**, some 8km northwest of Cushendall, is an architectural oddity almost entirely designed by Clough Williams-Ellis, the innovative architect of Portmeirion in Wales, and constructed between 1912 and 1925. Built to a commission from Ronald McNeill, the first (and last) Baron Cushendun, and his Cornish wife, Maud, Cushendun's houses are of rugged, rough-cast whitewash with slate roofs – a Cornish style that clearly weathers the sea storms as efficiently here as in Cornwall. Much of Cushendun is National Trust property, and it shows: it's a tiny and well-tended place.

The main road from Cushendun northwest to Ballycastle runs inland, traversing some impressively rough moorland, and passes **Loughareema**, the "vanishing lake", so termed because of its tendency to drain away completely in hot weather. The narrow, winding **coastal road** is a better bet, however; edged with fuchsia and honeysuckle, it switches back violently above the sea to **Torr Head**, the closest point on the Irish mainland to the Mull of Kintyre in Scotland.

**14**

### ARRIVAL AND DEPARTURE
### CUSHENDUN AND AROUND

**By bus** Cushendun is served by buses from/to Cushendall (Mon–Fri 6 daily, Sat 3; 15min).

### ACCOMMODATION AND EATING

**Mary McBride's** 2 Main St ☎ 028 2176 1511. Wonderful, warming pub that's as popular these days for its *Game of Thrones* door (see page 487) as its fabulous Saturday evening and Sunday afternoon music sessions; good pub grub too (beef and guinness pie; £9.95). Upstairs you'll find the *Little Black Door*, the pub's superbly accomplished seafood bistro (spiced cod with babagnash and prawn croquettes; £15.50). Pub daily 11am–11pm; restaurant Thurs–Sun 6–9.30pm.

**Sleepy Hollow** 107 Knocknacarry Rd ☎ 028 2176 1513, ⓦ sleepyhollowcushendun.com. 1.5km or so back down the road from Cushendun, this small but perfectly formed B&B comes with kingsize beds and sweeping views of the countryside; an ideal location for exploration of the coast and glens. £60

## Murlough Bay and Fair Head

**Murlough Bay** is the most spectacular of all the bays along the northern coast. From the rugged cliff-tops, the hillside curves down to the sea in a series of wildflower meadows that soften an otherwise harsh landscape. The last headland before Ballycastle is **Fair Head**, whose massive 200m cliffs offer stunning views across the North Channel to Scotland – the Mull of Kintyre and further to Islay and the Paps of Jura – a proximity that sheds light on the confusion of land ownership between Ireland and Scotland. A prime example is Rathlin Island (see page 491), which was hotly contested up until the seventeenth century. **Lough na Cranagh**, one of three lakes in the hinterland behind the cliffs, houses a *crannóg*, encircled by a parapet wall. A walk from the Fair Head car park to Murlough Bay takes 45 minutes, but muddy paths and changeable weather make walking boots and waterproofs essential.

## Ballycastle

The lively market town and port of **BALLYCASTLE** sits at the mouth of the two northernmost Antrim Glens, **Glenshesk** and **Glentaisie**, and makes a pleasant base for exploring the Causeway Coast or the Glens themselves. The best time to visit Ballycastle is for the **Ould Lammas Fair**, Ireland's oldest fair, dating from 1606. Held on the last Monday and Tuesday in August, it features sheep and pony sales, while stallholders do a roaring trade in dulse, an edible seaweed, and yellowman, a tooth-breaking yellow toffee that's so hard it needs a hammer to break it up. These delicacies feature in a sentimental song that originates locally:

**14**

*Did you treat your Mary Ann*
*To dulse and yellowman*
*At the Ould Lammas Fair in Ballycastle–O?*

Ballycastle has a prosperous feel about it that derived originally from the efforts of an enlightened mid-eighteenth-century landowner, Colonel Hugh Boyd, who developed the town as an industrial centre, providing coal and iron ore mines, a tannery, a brewery and soap, bleach, salt and glass works, all now defunct. It was from its **coal mines** particularly that the town garnered most of its wealth; lignite was mined at Ballintoy on the coast a few kilometres further west, an enterprise which came to an abrupt end when the entire deposit caught fire and burned for several years.

At the seafront there's a memorial to **Guglielmo Marconi**, the inventor of wireless telegraphy, who in 1898 made his first successful radio transmission between Ballycastle and Rathlin. From here, Quay Road leads gradually uphill past houses and shops to **The Diamond**, the town's focus, and thence up the steeper Castle Street.

## Ballycastle museum

59 Castle St • April–June & Sept Fri & Sat 10am–6pm, Sun noon–4pm; July & Aug daily 10am–6pm • Free • ☎ 028 2076 2225

The tiny but highly engaging **Ballycastle museum** occupies the old eighteenth-century courthouse, whose former cells now hold a collection of artefacts produced by the pre-World War I Irish Home Industries Shop – mostly exquisite wood-carved furnishings. Elsewhere, there are Stone Age tools from Rathlin Island and a replica of Marconi's oscillator (one of just ten in existence), though pride of place goes to the Glentaisie banner for the first *Feis na nGleann* ("festival of the Glens") in 1904.

## Bonamargy Friary

1.5km south of town on the Cushendall Rd • Open access

Just out of town lie the ruins of **Bonamargy Friary**, founded by the dominant MacQuillan family around 1500. One family member, Julia, insisted on being buried in the main walkway, so that she might be humbled for eternity by the stepping feet of others. A number of the rival MacDonnell family are also buried here, including the hero of Dunluce Castle, Sorley Boy MacDonnell, and his son Randal, first Earl of Antrim (see page 496). An indication of the erstwhile strength of the Irish language in these parts is that the tomb of the second earl, who died in 1682, is inscribed in Irish as well as the usual English and Latin; the Irish translation reads, "Every seventh year a calamity befalls the Irish" and "Now that the Marquis has departed, it will occur every year". The **River Margy**, on which the Friary stands, is associated with one of the tragic stories of Irish legend, that of the Children of Lir, whose jealous stepmother turned them into swans and forced them to spend three hundred years on the Sea of Moyle (the narrow channel between Ireland and the Scottish coast).

### ARRIVAL AND INFORMATION                    BALLYCASTLE

**By bus** Ballycastle is well served by local buses.
Destinations Ballintoy (every 30min; 15min); Bushmills (every 30min; 35min); Cushendall (July & Aug Mon–Fri 2 daily; 50min); Cushendun (July & Aug Mon–Fri 2 daily; 30min); Giant's Causeway (every 30min; 25min); Glenarm (July & Aug Mon–Fri 2 daily; 1hr 15min).

**Tourist information** Opposite the marina in Portnagree House, 14 Bayview Rd (July & Aug Mon–Fri 9.30am–7pm, Sat 10am–5pm, Sun 1–5pm; Sept–June Mon–Fri 9.30am–5pm, Sat 10am–4pm; ☎ 028 2076 2024, ⊛ visitcausewaycoastand glens.com), the welcoming visitor centre has stacks of info on the region as well as an accommodation booking service.

### ACCOMMODATION, EATING AND DRINKING

**Cellar** 11b The Diamond ☎ 028 2076 3037, ⊛ cellar ballycastle.com. A distinctive tangerine-and-green-painted frontage conceals an atmospheric little cellar restaurant with layered slate walls and cosy,

compartmentalized seating areas with low-hanging lights; the menu invariably includes whole lobster, dover sole or tiger prawns from the cold Atlantic waters, with mains from around £14; there's a good-value early bird menu

(Mon–Sat 4–6pm) with two courses for £9.95. Mon–Sat noon–11pm, Sun 4–11pm.

**Central Wine Bar** 12 Ann St ☎028 2076 3877. A hostelry of sorts since 1861, and distinguished by its three thatched "eyes" above the entrance, this lively barn of a bar/restaurant is the most spirited place in town. The food is terrific, for example seafood cassoulet (£19.95) or the three-course Sunday lunch (£15.95), while the nightly music sessions pull in the punters by the shedload. Mon–Thurs 11am–11pm, Fri & Sat till 1am, Sun noon–11pm.

**The House of McDonnell** 71 Castle St ☎028 2076 2975. Also known as *Tom's*, this bar has been in the same family for an astonishing fourteen generations, stretching back to 1766, and is just the place to channel the "spirit" of an older age via Irish, American or Scotch whiskies galore. Friday is music night, attracting visitors and youngish locals. Fri & Sat 2.30–11.30pm.

**Marine Hotel** 1–3 North St ☎028 2076 2222, ⓦmarine hotelballycastle.com. This prominent and well-run hotel with 34 comfortable bedrooms is handy for the ferries to Rathlin Island (or simply gazing across to it), though it's slightly overpriced for what it is; the corner coffee bar is worth venturing to if waiting for a ferry. **£115**

★ **Ursa Minor** 45 Ann St ☎07955 192389, ⓦursa minorbakehouse.com. A gorgeous waft of freshly baked bread hits you smack in the face as soon as you enter the "Little Bear" bakehouse, part of a local Économusée project designed to showcase local crafts and artisan producers; you can even venture downstairs to see the breads being prepared. Back upstairs in the lovely, sparingly furnished café, scrumptious offerings include fried eggs on sourdough with cherry tomatoes and salsa verde (£7.95), while the coffee, which comes with notes of origin, isn't half bad either. Tues–Sat 9am–4pm.

**14**

# Rathlin Island

Shaped like a truncated figure seven, **Rathlin Island**, 8km north of Ballycastle and just 21km west of the Mull of Kintyre in Scotland, is an impressive, craggy place, with a coastline consisting almost entirely of cliffs, and a lighthouse at each tip. The sea dominates the landscape and its salty winds discourage the growth of vegetation – wind turbines harness this energy source for electricity generation. A great time to be here is the end of May for the **Rathlin Sound Maritime Festival** (ⓦrathlinsoundmaritimefestival. com), a week-long programme of events, the highlight of which is the opening, and quite spectacular, Blessing of the Boats ceremony.

### Brief history

In 795 AD Rathlin was the first place in Ireland to be raided by the **Vikings**. Later raids saw two bloody massacres, first by the English and then by the Scots. In 1575, the mainland MacDonnells sent their women, children and old people to Rathlin for safety from the English, but that didn't stop the invading fleet, under the Earl of Essex (whose soldiers included Sir Francis Drake), from slaughtering the entire population. In 1642, a later generation of MacDonnells was then butchered by their Scottish enemies, the Campbells, causing Rathlin to be deserted for many years afterwards.

### Church Bay and around

The presence of dry-stone walls and numerous ruined cottages points to a time when the population was far larger than the 150 or so current inhabitants concentrated

---

### BIRDS AND WILDFLOWERS ON RATHLIN ISLAND

The island's cliffs are superb for **birdwatching**, particularly Bull Point, on the western tip, part of a large RSPB nature reserve. The **West Light Seabird Centre** (April to mid-Sept daily 10am–5pm; £5; free to RSPB members), inside the western lighthouse, provides wonderful views of Northern Ireland's largest colony of seabirds that includes puffins, guillemots and razorbills. If you are here in the spring you may also see a rare **wildflower**, the sky-blue pyramidal bugle, which is widespread from near the West Lighthouse to the north of Church Bay – the only recorded sighting of it in Northern Ireland. During summer, a minibus (£5) plies between the seabird centre and Church Bay in summer.

**14**

around the shallow arc of **Church Bay**. Halfway towards the western lighthouse is the site of a **Stone Age** axe-making site, and, to its north, earthworks known as **Doonmore**. In the early Christian period, the island was a haven for monks, who left evidence of their presence in the form of a sweathouse (a kind of primitive sauna) at **Knockans**, back towards Church Bay. You can discover more about the island's history and culture in the **Boathouse Visitor Centre**, at the southern end of the harbour; here, too, are photos of Richard Branson after his hot-air balloon infamously crash-landed just off the island's west coast in 1987. From the Boathouse, there's a fine 5km walk down to **Roonivoolin** ("Point of the Gulls") on the island's southern tip; along the way, you've got a good chance of spotting seals as well as oystercatchers and ringed plovers.

### Bruce's Cave

On the northeast point of the island, below the lighthouse, is **Bruce's Cave**, a cavern carved in the black basalt where, in 1306, so the story goes, the despondent Robert the Bruce retreated after being defeated by the English at Perth. Seeing a spider determinedly trying to spin a web gave him the resolve to "try, try and try again", so he returned to Scotland and defeated the English at Bannockburn.

**ARRIVAL AND INFORMATION**                                        **RATHLIN ISLAND**

**By ferry** Two ferries (☎028 2076 9299, ⓦrathlinbally castleferry.com) make the trip from Ballycastle harbour to Rathlin: the *Spirit of Rathlin* vehicle ferry (mid-April to mid-Sept 4 daily; 45min) – though note that vehicles can only be taken across if you're staying on the island for five nights or more – and the *Rathlin Express* passenger-only ferry (mid-April to mid-Sept 5–7 daily; 25min); services are much reduced during the winter. A return ticket costs £12, bikes £3.30.

**Tourist information** Housed inside the old boathouse, the visitor centre is a 5min walk south of the ferry slip (April–Sept daily 10am–5pm; ☎028 2076 2024).

**ACCOMMODATION AND EATING**

**Manor House** Church Bay ☎028 2076 0046, ⓦmanor houserathlin.com. A few paces from the ferry port, this beautifully restored late Georgian home dates from around 1760 on the site of weavers' cottages and is now run by the National Trust. The eleven stylish rooms are painted in a fetching green-blue colour and fitted with low sash windows through which you can savour the splendid sea views. Closed Nov–Easter. £95

**McCuaig's Bar** Church Bay ☎028 2076 0011. The island's social hub combines a plain but convivial bar/ restaurant offering lunches and early evening meals such as apple and pork burger with fries (£7.50), sandwiches and paninis; there's occasional music and other events too. Daily 11am–8pm.

**Soerneog View Hostel** ☎028 2076 3954, ⓦrathlin-island.co.uk. Overlooking Mill Bay, a 10min walk to the south from Church Bay, this tiny hostel has just three rooms all sleeping two (one with a double and two with a bunk). They also rent out bikes. Closed Oct–March. Per person £20

**Water Shed Café** Rathlin Island Harbour ☎07517 354990. Right next to the ferry slip, this colourful, cosy little bolthole is the perfect spot in which to refuel before catching the ferry back to the mainland; grab a coffee and a slice of cake, or something more substantial. April–Sept Tues–Sat 9.30am–5pm; Oct–March Thurs–Sat 10am–4pm.

# The north Antrim coast

The north coast of County Antrim, west of Ballycastle, is dominated, from a tourist perspective, by Northern Ireland's most famous tourist attraction, the bizarre formation of basalt columns at the **Giant's Causeway**, a UNESCO World Heritage site. On the way, near the town of **Ballintoy**, there are several pleasant diversions, not least the precarious rope bridge to **Carrick-a-rede Island**. West of the Causeway, you can sample some whiskey at **Bushmills** and visit the imposing and well-preserved remains of **Dunluce Castle**, the stronghold of the local MacDonnell clan. The coastline west of Dunluce is another major holiday spot, with **Portrush** filled with tourists in summer and students the rest of the year.

## Carrick-a-rede Island

**Rope bridge** Daily, weather permitting: Feb 9.30am–5pm; March–June, Sept & Oct 9.30am–6pm; July & Aug 9.30am–7pm; Nov–Jan 9.30am–3.30pm • £7 • ☎ 028 2076 9839, ⓦ nationaltrust.org.uk/carrick-a-rede

As you draw level with **Carrick-a-rede Island**, not far before Ballintoy on the coast road west from Ballycastle, you'll see the island's **rope bridge**, first erected some 350 years ago. Strung almost 30m above the sea, the rope-connected planks lead to a commercial salmon fishery on the southeast side of Carrick-a-rede (the name means "rock in the road": the island stands in the path of migrating salmon) – but its main function seems to be to scare tourists, something it does very successfully. Like the Giant's Causeway, it gets murderously busy, so you'd do well to visit as early in the day as you can.

**14**

## Ballintoy and around

Around 1.5km beyond the village of **BALLINTOY**, a road snakes down to a dramatic **harbour**, without doubt one of the most picturesque spots anywhere along the Causeway coast. Lively with boats in the summer, but bleak and exposed in winter, it's much loved by artists, with a dark, rock-strewn strand contrasting oddly with the neat, pale-stone breakwater. At the top of the harbour road stands a little white **church**, which replaced an earlier one in which local Protestants took refuge from Catholics in 1641 before being rescued by the Earl of Antrim.

### Portbraddan and Dunseverick Castle

The coastal path from Ballintoy leads west to **PORTBRADDAN**, a tiny hamlet of multicoloured houses, where St Gobban's, a slate-roofed little church, just 3.5m by a little under 2m, is supposedly the smallest church in Ireland. Needless to say, there are other contenders: the ruins of an even smaller one, St Lasseragh's, stand on the cliff above.

From Portbraddan the coast path leads round a headland, through a spectacular hole in the rock and then, by degrees, up to the cliffs of **Benbane Head**. The road and path almost converge at the ruins of a sixteenth-century gatehouse, all that's left of **Dunseverick Castle**. This was once the capital of the old kingdom of Dalriada, which spread over north Antrim and Scotland, and the terminus of one of the five great roads that led from Tara, the ancient capital of Ireland.

| ARRIVAL AND DEPARTURE | BALLINTOY AND AROUND |
|---|---|

**By bus** Ballintoy is served by buses from/to Ballycastle (every 30min; 15min); Bushmills (every 30min; 20min); and Giant's Causeway (every 30min; 15min).

### ACCOMMODATION AND EATING

**Fullerton Arms** 22 Main St ☎ 028 2076 9613, ⓦ fullerton-arms.com. A comfortable, family-run guest-house with twelve rooms, all of which have been recently renovated. The restaurant, entered via another *Game of Thrones* door (see page 487), offers tasty, traditional staples like steak and guinness pie (£11), and fish and chips. £105

**Red Door Tea Room** 14A Harbour Rd ☎ 07813 903199. On the road down to Ballintoy harbour, this warming, cottagey café-cum-bistro rustles up comforting dishes like Irish stew with wheaten bread (£7), and fish chowder alongside a delectable selection of cakes. March–May & Sept–Oct Sat & Sun 9am–5pm; June–Aug daily 9am–5pm.

**Whitepark Bay Hostel** 157 Whitepark Rd, 3km west of Ballintoy ☎ 028 2073 1745, ⓦ hini.org.uk. With glorious views over Whitepark Bay, this seasonal hostel offers four- and six-bed dorms, as well as twins; all rooms are en suite while the twin rooms have TVs and tea/coffee making facilities. Closed mid-Oct to mid-March. £42

## The Giant's Causeway

Ever since 1693, when the Royal Society first publicized it as one of the great wonders of the natural world, the **Giant's Causeway** has been a major tourist attraction. The highly romanticized pictures of the polygonal basalt rock formations by the Dubliner

14

Susanna Drury, which circulated throughout Europe in the eighteenth century, did much to popularize the Causeway; two of them are on show in the Ulster Museum in Belfast (see page 464). Not everyone was impressed, though. A disappointed William Thackeray commented, "I've travelled a hundred and fifty miles to see *that*?", and especially disliked the tourist promotion of the Causeway, claiming in 1842 that "The traveller no sooner issues from the inn by a back door which he is informed will lead him straight to the causeway, than the guides pounce upon him." Although the tourist hype is today less overtly mercenary, the Causeway (now managed by the National Trust) still attracts hundreds of thousands of visitors annually; indeed, the site can get crushingly busy, which can really put a dampener on the visit, so you'd do well to visit as early (or as late) in the day as you can. It's worth pointing out that you only have to **pay** if you're parking at the site or accessing the stones via the Visitor Experience – otherwise follow the signposted path to the stones that starts near (but bypasses) the Visitor Experience.

For sheer otherworldliness, the Causeway can't be beaten. Made up of an estimated 37,000 **black basalt columns**, each a polygon (hexagons are by far the most common, with pentagons second, though sometimes the columns have as many as ten sides), the sight is the result of a subterranean explosion, some sixty million years ago, that stretched from the Causeway to Rathlin and beyond to Islay, Staffa (where it was responsible for the formation of Fingal's Cave) and Mull in Scotland. A huge mass of molten basalt was spewed out on to the surface, which, on cooling, solidified into what are, essentially, crystals.

### Giant's Causeway Visitor Experience

60 Causeway Rd • March–June, Sept & Oct 9am–6pm; July & Aug 9am–7pm; Nov–Feb 9am–5pm; last admission to centre 1hr before closing • £13; price includes parking and an audio-guide for visiting the stones • ☎ 028 2073 1855, ⓦ nationaltrust.org.uk/giantscauseway and ⓦ giantscausewaytickets.com

Sunken into the ground and made from locally quarried basalt, the **Giant's Causeway Visitor Experience** blends into the landscape with indigenous grasses on the roof providing a habitat for wildlife. Inside, a rather haphazard set-up features exhibition panels and 3-D displays providing detail on the geological and scientific nature of the area, while you get to meet the various characters that have shaped the landscape hereabouts – most of it, though, just seems to be taken up by the enormous National Trust shop.

### The stones

From the visitor centre, it's a fifteen-minute walk down to the stones, though there is also a minibus that shuttles back and forth (£1 one way; free to NT members). The first of the distinctive stone columns once you reach the pavement are the 12m-high **Organ Pipes**. Many of the other formations have names ("the Camel", "the Wishing Chair" and "the Granny") invented for them by the guides who so plagued Thackeray

---

### FIONN MAC CUMHAILL: THE GIANT OF THE CAUSEWAY

According to mythology, the Giant of the Causeway was Ulster warrior **Fionn Mac Cumhaill** (also known as Finn McCool), and two legends of Fionn's exploits provide an entertaining alternative to geologists' explanations of the Causeway's origins. In one, Fionn became besotted with a woman giant who resided on the Scottish island of Staffa (where the Causeway's fault-line resurfaces) and constructed a **highway across the sea** by which he could travel to woo her. An alternative version of the story suggests that Fionn built the Causeway in order to head over to Scotland to give another giant a good kicking, but, when confronted by his enemy's superior size, fled back to Ireland and hid in an extra-large cot which he'd persuaded his wife to construct. When the pursuing Scots giant arrived, he took just a glance at the sheer size of Fionn's supposed "baby" and fled back to Scotland.

and his contemporaries. At least one, **Chimney Point**, further north, has an appearance so bizarre that in September 1588 it persuaded the crew of the *Girona*, a ship of the Spanish Armada, to think it was Dunluce Castle (see page 496), where they thought they might get help from the MacDonnells. Instead, their vessel was wrecked on the rocky shore at Port-na-Spánaigh, just before Chimney Point. Its treasure was recovered by divers in 1968, and some of the items are on show in the Ulster Museum in Belfast (see page 464) and in Derry's Tower Museum (see page 502). Guided tours (hourly from 10am, every 30min in July & Aug) of the stones depart from the visitor centre and are included in the admission charge.

**14**

### ARRIVAL AND INFORMATION                          THE GIANT'S CAUSEWAY

**By bus** The Causeway is served by a number of buses, including the Causeway Rambler and the Antrim Coaster (see page 482).

**By car** The roads around the Causeway are congested, particularly on weekends, so it's best to use the park-and-ride bus in Bushmills (March–Oct) and buy a Green Travel Admission Ticket, thereby saving £1.50 on the standard adult admission price to the Visitor Experience. Visitors arriving by bike or on foot also receive a £1.50 discount.

**By train** A restored narrow-gauge railway runs between the Causeway and Bushmills (June, Sept & Oct Sat & Sun; July & Aug daily; 6 trains daily on the hour 11am–5pm (except 1pm), returning 30min later from Bushmills; ☎028 2073 2844, ⊚giantscausewayrailway.webs.com; £6 one-way).

**Tourist information** The tourist office (☎028 2073 1855) is located inside the Giant's Causeway Visitor Experience (same opening times).

## Bushmills

**Distillery** 2 Distillery Rd • Tours March–Oct Mon–Sat 9.15am–4.45pm, Sun noon–4.45pm; Nov–Feb Mon–Sat 9.30am–4.45pm, Sun noon–4.45pm; last tours 4pm • £9 • ☎028 2073 3218, ⊚bushmills.com

The foremost attraction in **BUSHMILLS** is the **Old Bushmills Distillery** on the outskirts of town, where whiskey has been distilled here legally since 1608, making it the oldest licit distillery in the world. Bushmills whiskey – of which there are five core products – is distilled three times, once more than Scotch, but perhaps the biggest surprise is just how little subtlety is involved in the industrial manufacture of alcohol, despite all the lore that surrounds it. You can enjoy learning about the process on a guided **tour,** which takes in the mash house, the malt barn (though malting is not done on site), the vast warehouse, and the equally impressive bottling plant; the tour ends with a complimentary tasting.

### ARRIVAL AND INFORMATION                                           BUSHMILLS

**By bus** Buses drop off and pick up at the War Memorial on Main St, from where it's a 10min walk to the distillery.
Destinations Ballintoy (every 30min; 20min); Ballycastle (every 30min; 35min); Coleraine (every 30min; 40min); Portrush (every 30min; 25min).

**Tourist office** 44 Main St (March, April & Oct Sat & Sun 10am–4pm; May, June & Sept daily 10am–5pm; July & Aug till 6pm; ☎028 2073 0390, ⊚visitcausewaycoastand glens.com).

### ACCOMMODATION AND EATING

★ **Bushmills Inn** 9 Dunluce Rd ☎028 2073 3000, ⊚bushmillsinn.com. This former coaching inn has a pleasantly rambling, cottage-style interior replete with inglenook turf fires, hayloft snugs and the like. Rooms come in several categories, though all are impeccably turned out, while the smart restaurant, located in the old stables building, features traditional dishes such as the Botchan (local soup) or Dalriada cullen skink (smoked haddock fillet; £14.50). Better still is the atmospheric, gas-lit *Gas Bar* where, every Saturday night, local band Scad the Beggars strike up. **£120**

**Bushmills Youth Hostel** 49 Main St ☎028 2073 1222, ⊚hini.org.uk. Rather clinical, but modern, clean and very convenient hostel with three-, four and six-bed dorms, plus, twins, all of which are en suite; facilities include a large self-catering kitchen. Dorms **£16**, twins **£40**

**The French Rooms** 45 Main St ☎028 2073 0033, ⊚thefrenchrooms.com. The fragrant smell of lavender draws you into this elegant restaurant, café and gift shop all rolled into one. Whether you fancy an egg, ham and cheese *galette* (£6) for breakfast, or some Cajun French sea bass (£14.85) for lunch or dinner, this is top-drawer food. Thurs & Sun 11am–4pm, Fri & Sat 11.30am–11pm.

**14**

# Dunluce Castle

8km southwest of Giant's Causeway • Daily: March–Oct 9.30am–5pm; Nov–Feb 9.30am–4pm • £5 • ☎ 028 2073 1938, ⓦ discovernorthernireland.com

The most impressive ruin of this entire coastline is the dramatically sited sixteenth-century **Dunluce Castle**. Perched on a fine headland, high above a cave, it looks as if it only needs a roof to be perfectly habitable once again. Its history is inextricably linked to that of its original owner, **Sorley Boy MacDonnell**, whose clan, the so-called "Lords of the Isles", ruled northeastern Ulster from this base. English incursions into the area culminated in 1584 with Sir John Perrott laying siege to Dunluce, forcing Sorley Boy ("Yellow Charles" in Irish) to leave the castle. But as soon as Perrott departed, leaving a garrison in charge, Sorley Boy hauled his men up the cliff in baskets and recaptured the castle, later repairing the damage with the proceeds of the salvaged wreckage of the *Girona* (see page 495) and arming the fort with three of its cannons. Having made his point, Sorley Boy agreed a peace with the English, and his son, Randal, was created Viscount Dunluce and Earl of Antrim by James I. In 1639, Dunluce Castle paid the penalty for its precarious, if impregnable, position when the kitchen fell off the cliff during a storm, complete with cooks and dinner. Shortly afterwards, the MacDonnells moved to more comfortable lodgings at Glenarm, and Dunluce was left empty.

The castle remains an extraordinary place. The MacDonnells' Scottish connections – Randal continued to own land in Kintyre – are evident in the **gatehouse**'s turrets and crow-step gables, and in the tapering chimneys of the seventeenth-century **Great Hall**. There's a strange touch of luxury in the **loggia**, though it oddly faces away from the sun. A steep path takes you down to the **cave** below the castle that pierces right through the promontory, with an opening directly under the gatehouse.

# Portrush

The town of **PORTRUSH** has everything you'd expect from a seaside resort: sandy **beaches** backed by dunes, which run both east and west, a raft of waterborne activities, along with amusement arcades and funfairs galore. Moreover, the huge popularity of the local dance scene draws clubbers from all over the North, meaning the town can have a distinctly raucous feel at weekends. The long, sandy **beach** towards Dunluce ends at the **White Rocks**, where the weather has carved the soft limestone cliffs into strange shapes, most famously the so-called **"Cathedral Cave"**, nearly 60m from end to end. This is **surfing** country par excellence and there is rewarding surfing off the West Strand and White Rocks, as well as good **paddleboarding**.

Much of the townscape changed dramatically for the 2019 Open Golf championship (one of golf's four majors), which was quite some coup for Portrush given that Northern Ireland hadn't staged the tournament since 1951. Otherwise, Portrush is certainly not short on annual events, with the perennially popular **North West 200 motorbike race** (ⓦ northwest200.org) held over four days in mid-May; the **Portrush Raft Race** (ⓦ portrushraftrace.co.uk) at the end of May, which sees participants race each other across the harbour on all manner of wacky home-made rafts; and the spectacular two-day **Northern Ireland Air Show** (ⓦ airwavesportrush.co.uk) at the beginning of September, based around the East Strand – though this has only been held intermittently in the last few years.

## ARRIVAL AND DEPARTURE                                        PORTRUSH

**By train** The train station is a short hop south of the town centre on Eglinton St.
Destinations Coleraine (hourly; 15min) for connections to Belfast (hourly; 1hr 20min) and Derry (Mon–Sat hourly, Sun

6; 40min).
**By bus** The bus station is near the train station on Dunluce Ave. There are regular services from/to Portstewart (Mon–Sat every 30min, Sun 5; 15min).

## INFORMATION AND ACTIVITIES

**Tourist office** Town Hall, 2 Kerr St (April–Sept Mon–Fri 9.30am–5pm, Sun 11am–4pm; ☎ 028 7082 3333, ✆ visit causewaycoastandglens.com).

**Surfing and paddleboarding** Surfing and SUP lessons (£20/2hr), as well as board hire (£10/hr) and gear, are offered at the Portrush Surf School (☎ 07894 854791, ✆ portrushsurfschool.com), located at the Yacht Club in the harbour, and the Alive Adventures on the West Strand beach

(☎ 07935 952532, ✆ aliveadventures.co.uk).

**Golf** Royal Venue for the 2019 Open Championship, Portrush Golf Club (☎ 028 7082 2311, ✆ royalportrushgolfclub.com) is the North's premier club, boasting two eighteen-hole courses; the championship Dunluce course (£240/18 holes) and the Valley course (£60/18 holes). Demand is high in the summer but in any case you'll need to book ahead; note that green fees are much reduced in winter.

## ACCOMMODATION

**Adelphi Portrush** 67–71 Main St ☎ 028 7082 5544, ✆ adelphiportrush.com. The wide selection of rooms in this centrally located hotel feature contemporary elegant design, some with sea views. Good off-season special deals are available Oct–March; the rate includes access to the hotel's spa facilities. **£90**

**Beulah Guesthouse** 16 Causeway St ☎ 028 7082

2413, ✆ beulahguesthouse.com. A super-friendly welcome and nine well-presented rooms await guests at this convenient B&B near the East Strand beach. There's a lovely guest lounge with antique piano, and splendid breakfasts covering everything from the full fry-up to gluten-free and vegetarian dishes; adults only. Closed Nov–Feb. **£90**

## EATING AND DRINKING

★ **Arcadia Café** West Strand Ave ☎ 07525 496968. Once known as the Ladies' Bathing Place, this landmark building perched on the water's edge was a popular ballroom venue in the 1950s and 1960s. Today, it's a popular spot for breakfasts (such as French toast with cinnamon and maple syrup) and lunches (wraps, melts), with coffee, cake and ice cream adding to the seaside vibe. Dine outside, where there's a little splash pool for kids, and gaze across to the Skerries or watch the waves break on the beach. The upstairs art gallery rounds things off beautifully. Easter–Sept daily 9am–6pm.

**Kiwi's Brew Bar** 47 Main St ☎ 028 7082 9500, ✆ kiwis brewbar.com. This banging little bar is one of the best places on the coast to sample Ireland's terrific craft beers – including those from breweries in Cork, Armagh and Donegal as well as the local Lacada brewery. On Wednesdays there's an acoustic session at 9pm, on Fridays live music and guest beers, and at 4.30pm on Sundays, it's the superb "Brews and

Blues" session. Mon–Thurs 3pm–late, Fri–Sun 1pm–late.

**Neptune & Prawn** 54 Kerr St ☎ 028 7082 2448, ✆ ramore restaurant.com/neptuneandprawn. The best of the bunch of restaurants clustered around the harbour, this is arguably more style than substance (and children are not allowed) – lots of white wood panelling and bare brick walls, and picture windows showing off the harbour – but the largely Asian-tinged food is worth a punt – try the Portrush lobster with special fried rice and coconut sauce (£15.95). The upstairs cocktail bar, meanwhile, is frequented by an altogether glitzier crowd. Restaurant Mon–Fri 5–9.30pm, Sat 5–10.30pm, Sun 4–9.30pm; cocktail bar daily 5pm–1am.

**Springhill Bar** 17 Causeway St ☎ 028 7082 3361, ✆ the springhillbar.com. Lively locals' bar located just off the main strip, with a traditional session every Thursday from 9.30pm, plus open mike sessions on Wednesdays. Mon–Sat 11.30pm–1am, Sun 12.30pm–midnight.

# Northern County Derry

West of Portrush the A2 continues to hug the coastline as it traverses the northern part of County Derry, taking in marvellous beaches all the way from **Portstewart**, near which it crosses the River Bann, to **Magilligan Point**. On the way there are impressive seascapes visible from the cliff-top **Mussenden Temple** and stunning views from the land around **Mount Binevenagh**.

## Portstewart

Derry's largest coastal resort, **PORTSTEWART**, like its near neighbour Portrush, is full of Victorian boarding houses. Of the two, Portstewart is decidedly more sedate and has always had more airs and graces: the train station is said to have been built away from the town centre to stop hoi polloi from coming. In terms of sheer location, though, Portstewart wins hands down.

**14**

## Portstewart Strand

Cars March–June & Sept £4.50, July & Aug £7.50, free to NT members

Just west of the town is the National Trust-owned **Portstewart Strand**, a glorious, 3km stretch of sand firm enough to drive on – which the locals delight in doing – with some of the best **surfing** in the country. It's a grand place, too, if you hit fine weather and feel like getting out your bucket and spade. The best way to take the sea air is the bracing **cliff-side walk**, which runs between the beach and the town, passing battlements and an imposing Gothic mansion, now a Dominican college.

### ARRIVAL AND DEPARTURE
PORTSTEWART

**By bus** There are regular buses between Portstewart and Portrush (Mon–Sat every 30min, Sun 5; 15min).

**Surfing, kayaking and SUP** Operating out of a van at the entrance to the car park, Ocean Warriors (☎ 07921 164134, ⓦ oceanwarriors.co.uk) rents out surfboards, paddleboards and kayaks, and associated gear.

### ACCOMMODATION

**Cul-Erg House** 9 Hillside ☎ 028 7083 6610, ⓦ culerg. co.uk. Just a couple of minutes from the strand, this large Victorian guesthouse offers eleven en-suite rooms – some with sea views – and a private kitchen for guests. **£90**

**Juniper Hill Caravan Park** 70 Ballyreagh Rd ☎ 028 7083 2023. Space for caravans and camping about 1.5km down the A2 towards Portrush. Closed Nov–March. **£20**

**Rick's Causeway Coast** 4 Victoria Terrace (IHH) ☎ 028 7083 3789, ⓔ rick@causewaycoasthostel.fsnet.co.uk. Well-run hostel with rooms sleeping between two and six (some en suite) that's also handy for the many cafés, bars and restaurants on the nearby seafront. Price includes breakfast. Dorms **£15**, doubles **£40**

### EATING AND DRINKING

**Amici Ristorante** Portmore Rd ☎ 028 7083 4444, ⓦ amiciportstewart.com. Transformed from an old golf clubhouse, this is one of the most scenically sited of all the north-coast restaurants. You can keep it simple, with authentic Neapolitan pizzas (£10) made from home-made dough, or plump for more sophisticated dishes such as roast salmon fillet with grilled artichokes and chilli oil (£14). Mon–Sat noon–2.30pm & 5–9.30pm, Sun noon–9pm.

★ **Harry's Shack** The Strand ☎ 028 7083 1783. Boasting an unbeatable beachside location, a beautifully styled interior – raw wood tables and big bay windows – and exquisite food, *Harry's* ticks all the boxes. Starters might be smoked mackerel fish cakes or shoreline mussels in cider with sourdough (£7), while main course favourites include hake or plaice (£15) fresh from Greencastle in Donegal; alternatively, make for the canopied terrace where cheery staff dispense coffees and ice creams from a little wooden cabin. Mon–Fri noon–3pm & 5–9pm, Sat & Sun 10am–3pm & 5–9pm; closed Mon in winter.

**Warke's Deli** 1 Carrig na cule ☎ 028 7083 3388, ⓦ warkesdeli.com. Tucked away at the northern end of the promenade away from the general hubbub, this super little deli quietly goes about its business offering the likes of pancakes with bacon and maple syrup for breakfast and warm goat's cheese salad (£6.50) for lunch. Daily 9am–5.30pm.

## Hezlett House

Mussenden Rd • April to mid-Sept daily 10am–5pm; mid-Sept to March Sat & Sun 11am–5pm • £5, includes Mussenden Temple (see page 499) • ⓦ nationaltrust.org.uk

Lying 11km west of Coleraine along the A2, at the Castlerock crossroads, is **Hezlett House**, built in 1690. The house is a fine example of cruck-truss construction, an early method of prefabricated building using wooden frames filled with clay and rubble that was common in England but is enough of a rarity here to warrant preservation by the National Trust. The last owner of the house is buried in the graveyard at Downhill, where his gravestone quaintly bears both his own version of the spelling of his name and that of his father, a Mr Hazlett.

## Downhill Palace

Mussenden Rd, Castlerock • Daily dawn–dusk • Free

Ornate gates alongside the A2 mark the main entrance to the ruins of **Downhill Palace**, built in the 1780s by **Frederick Augustus Hervey**, Anglican Bishop of Derry and fourth Earl of Bristol. Hervey was an enthusiastic grand traveller (all the many Hotel Bristols throughout Europe are named after him), and was also an art collector and sportsman, once organizing a preprandial race between Anglican and Presbyterian clergy along the local strand. His palace, accessed through pleasant **gardens**, was last occupied by US troops, billeted here during World War II, and was dismantled on their departure.

**14**

## Mussenden Temple

Mussenden Rd, Castlerock • Call ☎ 028 7084 8728 for opening times • £5, includes admission to Hezlett House • ⓦ nationaltrust.org.uk

Across fields at the back of Downhill Palace is the diminutive **Mussenden Temple**, which clings precariously to the eroding cliff-edge and offers stunning sea views. Its classic domed **rotunda** was apparently modelled on the Temple of Vesta in Rome and was built by Hervey in honour of his cousin Mrs Frideswide Mussenden, who died aged 22 before it was completed, after which it was used as a summer library. Later, with characteristic generosity and a fairly startling lack of prejudice, Hervey allowed a weekly Mass to be celebrated in the temple, as there was no local Catholic church. The inscription on the temple **frieze** translates rather smugly as: "It is agreeable to watch, from land, someone else involved in a great struggle while winds whip up the waves out at sea." Overlooked by Mussenden Temple on the cliff-edge above is the enormously long **Downhill beach**, which is accessible by car. From Downhill Palace it's possible to take the Bishop's Road (constructed at Hervey's bidding) southwards to reach **Mount Binevenagh** and its fabulous viewpoints.

## Limavady and around

**LIMAVADY** was once a major settlement, its old site lying 3km further south down the valley of the River Roe. The town was refounded as Newtown Limavady in the early seventeenth century by Thomas Phillips, speaker of the Irish House of Commons. It still possesses a few features of its illustrious past: the six-arch **bridge** spanning the river was built in 1700, and Main Street, which runs down from it, is still recognizably Georgian. In mid-August, Limavady hosts the two-day **Stendhal Festival** (ⓦ stendhalfestival.com), one of Ireland's finest small music festivals, while in late October, there's the lively **Roe Valley Folk Festival** (ⓦ roevalleyarts.com). June, meanwhile, sees the town host the annual **Danny Boy Jazz and Blues Festival** (see box).

### Roe Valley Country Park

41 Dogleap Rd, 3km south of Limavady • **Visitor centre** April–Sept daily 9am–6pm; Oct–March Sun noon–4pm • **Free** • **Museum** April, May & Sept Sat & Sun 1–4.45pm; June–Aug daily 1–4.45pm • **Free** • ☎ 028 7772 2074

---

#### DANNY BOY

The lyrics for the quintessential "Oirish" ballad **Danny Boy** were actually composed by an English lawyer, Fred E. Weatherley, in 1912 and, a year later, fitted to *The Londonderry Air*, a tune collected by Jane Ross, a resident of 51 Main St, Limavady, from a travelling fiddler in 1851. The song achieved renown in Ireland when recorded in the 1930s by Margaret Burke-Sheridan and has since seen many other tear-jerking renditions (Sinéad O'Connor recorded an idiosyncratically spine-tingling version); it still remains endearingly popular with dewy-eyed expats and Irish-Americans. Limavady holds the annual **Danny Boy Jazz and Blues festival** in June, featuring a variety of music.

The **Roe Valley Country Park** preserves Northern Ireland's first hydroelectric power station, opened in 1896, with much of the original equipment intact and viewable, as well as a **visitor centre** and the **Green Lane Museum**. This focuses on the area's history, including its erstwhile importance in linen production, and features craft displays on Saturdays (2–4pm).

**14**

## ARRIVAL AND INFORMATION

**By bus** Limavady Buscentre is northeast of town, just off Main St.

Destinations Castlerock (Mon–Sat 6–10 daily; 45min); Derry (Mon–Sat 8–14 daily, Sun 4; 40–55min); Dungiven

## LIMAVADY AND AROUND

(Mon–Fri 5 daily; 35min).

**Tourist information** Roe Valley Arts Centre, 24 Main St (Mon–Fri 9.30am–5pm; ☎ 028 7776 0650, ✆ roevalleyarts. com).

# Derry

**DERRY**, which lies at the foot of Lough Foyle, is a crossroads city in more ways than one: roads from all cardinal points arrive here, but it was also a major point of emigration from the eighteenth century onwards, an exodus that reached tumultuous proportions during the Great Famine. Derry is the fourth-largest city in Ireland and the second biggest in the North, but it has a markedly different atmosphere from Belfast, being two-thirds **Catholic**. While roads into the city are signposted in Irish welcoming visitors to Derry, the city still appears as "**Londonderry**" on many road maps and signs, a preference adhered to by the British government, Unionists and television news bulletins. It is referred to by the press and broadcast media as "Derry-Londonderry", a tactful placating of both Nationalist and Unionist.

Approached from the east in winter twilight or under a strong summer sun, the city presents a beguiling picture, with the vista of the **River Foyle** and the rise of the city's two hillsides, terraced with pastel-shaded houses and topped by the hueless stone spires of the ever-present religious denominations. With its rich history, Derry has a clutch of worthwhile attractions, mostly enclosed within the seventeenth-century **walls**, themselves the most significant reminder of the city's past.

## Brief history

Though **St Columba** established a monastery here in 546 AD, the development of Derry (originally called Doire Calgaigh, "oakwood of Calgach", after a legendary warrior) only really began in medieval times, when in the fourteenth century it was granted to the Anglo-Norman de Burgos. By 1500, the power of the O'Dohertys had spread from Inishowen and they constructed a tower house, which was later absorbed into the seventeenth-century walls.

Towards the end of the sixteenth century the uprising of Hugh O'Neill, Earl of Tyrone, provoked an English invasion. Doire's strategic position on the River Foyle was quickly appreciated, though it took some years for it finally to be captured. In 1600, the English commander **Sir Henry Docwra** began fortifying the remains of the medieval town as a base for incursions against the Irish, but in 1608 Sir Cahir O'Doherty rebelled against Docwra's successor, Pawlett, and burnt Doire, by now anglicized as Derry, to the ground. This destruction made the city ripe for the plantation of English and Scottish settlers, and the financial assistance of the wealthy businessmen of the City of London was obtained to achieve this. A new walled city was constructed and renamed **Londonderry** in 1613 in honour of its backers, the Twelve Companies of the Corporation of London.

The seventeenth century was the most dramatic phase of Derry's evolution, culminating in the **siege** of 1688–89 (see page 505). Following this, many Derry people emigrated to America to avoid harsh English laws, and some of their descendants, such as the pioneer frontiersman Daniel Boone, achieved fame there. Derry's heyday as a **seaport** came in the nineteenth century, a period when industries such as shirt-making began to flourish – by the beginning of the twentieth century the city was the largest shirt-manufacturer in the UK. However, after **Partition**, the North–South dividing line lay just over 3km from Derry's back door, and the consequent tariffs reduced much of its traditional trade. The shirt industry began its long decline, finally being phased out in the face of much cheaper imports from Asia.

Though Derry remained relatively peaceful after Partition, its politics were among the North's most blatantly discriminatory, with the substantial Catholic majority denied its civil rights by gerrymandering geared towards ensuring the Protestant minority's control of local institutions. In October 1968 Derry witnessed a two-thousand-strong **civil rights march**. Confronted by the batons of the Protestant police force and the notorious B Specials, rioting spilled over into the Catholic

**14**

Bogside district and over eighty people were injured. The clash is seen by many as the catalyst for the modern phase of the Troubles: faith in the impartiality of the Royal Ulster Constabulary was destroyed once and for all, and the IRA was reborn a year or so later. The following year's Protestant **Apprentice Boys' march** (see page 505) was another significant step, and, on January 30, 1972, came **Bloody Sunday** (see page 507).

These days Derry is a quite different place. Its stint as the UK's City of Culture in 2013 was the catalyst for a major facelift, which included the renovation and repackaging of much of the city's built heritage. Meanwhile, one of the legacies of the peace process has led to the opening of the spectacular **Peace Bridge**.

## Peace Bridge and Ebrington Square

Forming a graceful arc across the River Foyle, the **Peace Bridge**, which opened in 2011, represents a symbolic, curvilinear-shaped handshake between the city's largely Protestant east bank and the overwhelmingly Catholic west bank – a new landmark that has helped rebalance the communities, meaning that the Foyle is no longer seen as a religious divide. Popular with walkers, joggers and cyclists, the bridge links the city centre with **Ebrington Square**, a redeveloped military parade ground that is now a fast-developing cultural hub, venue for open-air concerts and a growing number of restaurants and bars.

## The Guildhall

Guildhall Square • Daily 11am–4pm • Free • ☎ 028 7137 6510, ⊛ derrystrabane.com

Just outside the city walls stands the neo-Gothic **Guildhall**, whose largely ecclesiastical appearance belies its function as the place where the political parties hold their monthly meetings. Inside, you can nose around the main hall, with its elaborate ceilings, baronial wood panelling and magnificent organ (there are free, weekly recitals throughout August), while the city's history is depicted in a series of beautifully restored stained-glass windows. On the ground floor, a permanent **exhibition** tells with flair and imagination the story of the Plantation of Ulster and the building of the walls; here, too, on the ground floor is a Carrara marble statue of Queen Victoria, minus her hands, which were blown off when the Guildhall was bombed by the IRA in 1972. The terrace at the very agreeable *Guild Café* offers fine views of the Peace Bridge.

## The medieval walls and within

Derry's centre, focused on its **medieval walls**, is remarkably compact, and it's easy to combine all the main attractions in one circuit. The walls are one of the best-preserved defences in Europe. Spanning 1.6km in length and as high as a two-storey house in places, they are reinforced by bulwarks and bastions and a parapeted earth rampart as wide as any thoroughfare. Within their circuit, the original medieval street-pattern has remained, with four **gateways** surviving from the original construction, albeit in slightly revised form.

### The Tower Museum

Union Hall Place • Daily 10am–5pm • £5 • ☎ 028 7137 2411, ⊛ derrystrabane.com/towermuseum

A reconstruction of the medieval O'Doherty Tower houses the **Tower Museum**, whose two permanent exhibitions are very worthwhile. The first of these recounts the **history of Derry** in easy to follow chronological fashion, from the Plantation period and the Siege (including the original effigy template of Robert Lundy), through to the Troubles, which is, inevitably, the section in which most visitors linger longest – on

14

# DERRY CITY WALLS

River Foyle

GUILDHALL
SQUARE
ROUNDABOUT

FOYLE EMBANKMENT

WATERLOO
PLACE

Coward's
Bastion

Magazine
Gate

Guildhall

Bus Station

GUILDHALL
SQUARE

Shipquay
Gate

Water
Bastion

WATER ST

UNION HALL STREET

Hangman's
Bastion

Tower
Museum

Craft Village

SHIPQUAY STREET

BANK PLACE

FOYLE STREET

Foyleside
Shopping
Centre

THE BOGSIDE

HIGH ST

Castle
Gate

MAGAZINE ST

CASTLE STREET

Nerve
Centre

NEWMARKET ST

Millennium
Forum

ORCHARD STREET

WATERLOO ST

Gunner's
Bastion

Richmond
Shopping
Centre

LINEN HALL ST

Newgate
Bastion

MARKET ST

FAHAN STREET

Butcher's
Gate

BUTCHER ST

THE
DIAMOND

FERRYQUAY STREET

BRIDGE STREET

MAGAZINE STREET

Apprentice Boys'
Memorial Hall

Siege Museum

PUMP STREET

The Playhouse

Ferryquay
Gate

CARLISLE RD

Ferry
Bastion

ARTILLERY ST

FOUNTAIN ST

Royal
Bastion

St Augustine's
Church

PALACE STREET

SOCIETY STREET

BISHOP STREET WITHIN

LONDON STREET

New Gate

HAWKIN STREET

Verbal Arts
Centre

Courthouse

St Columb's
Cathedral

GRAND PARADE

Double
Bastion

Bishop's Gate

BISHOP STREET WITHOUT

THE
FOUNTAIN

Church
Bastion

THE FOUNTAIN

| 0 | | metres | 50 |

---

**DRINKING & NIGHTLIFE**
| Peadar O'Donnell's | 1 |
| Sandino's Café Bar | 3 |
| Taphouse | 2 |

**ACCOMMODATION**
| Bishop's Gate Hotel | 2 |
| Shipquay Hotel | 1 |

**SHOPPING**
| Bedlam Market | 3 |
| Craft Village | 2 |
| Yellow Yard | 1 |

display are uniforms of the British army and the Royal Ulster Constabulary, as well as IRA combat jackets and balaclavas, canisters and bullet casings, and a piece of stained glass window from the Guildhall, when it was bombed in 1972.

The second exhibition focuses on the *La Trinidad Valencera*, from the **Spanish Armada**, which sank in Kinnegoe Bay (off Inishowen) in 1588, but was only discovered in 1971. Among the extraordinary, and extraordinarily well preserved, treasures brought to the surface were fragments of clothing, pewter dishes, a pair of exquisite salt cellars, and some finely worked jewellery; most impressive of all, however, is the ship's cannon.

### St Columb's Cathedral

17 London St • Mon–Sat 9am–5pm • £2 suggested donation • ☎ 028 7126 7313, ⓦ stcolumbscathedral.org

Occupying the southwestern corner of the walled city, the Church of Ireland **St Columb's Cathedral** was built in 1633 in a style later called Planters' Gothic and was the first post-Reformation cathedral in the British Isles. Displayed in the entrance porch is a cannon shell catapulted into the church during the 1688–89 blockade by the besieging army – their terms of surrender were attached. The cathedral was used as a battery during the siege, its **tower** serving as a lookout post; today it provides the best view of the old city. The present **spire** dates from the late Georgian period, its lead-covered wooden predecessor having been stripped to fashion bullets and cannon shot during the siege.

Inside, an open-timbered **roof** rests on sixteen stone corbels carved with figures of past bishops. Other things to look out for are the finely sculpted stone reredos behind the altar, the eighteenth-century bishop's throne and the window panels showing scenes as diverse as the relief of the city on August 12, 1689, and St Columba's mission to Britain. In the **chapterhouse museum** are more relics of the siege, including the padlocks and keys used to lock the city gates, plus the grand kidney-shaped desk of the eighteenth-century philosopher George Berkeley, erstwhile dean of the cathedral (who only visited Derry once), and mementos of Cecil Frances (1818–95), wife of Bishop Alexander and composer of the famous hymns *Once in Royal David's City* and *There is a Green Hill Far Away*.

### The Courthouse and The Fountain

Close to Bishop's Gate stands the **courthouse**, built of white sandstone from Dungiven in crude Greek-Revival style. The gate itself was remodelled for the first centenary of the siege and reopened in 1789. Immediately outside the walls here is **The Fountain** area, named after the freshwater source that once supplied the city, though few remnants of any antiquity remain apart from a tower of the old Derry jail, jammed up against the grim modern houses. The Fountain is a tiny enclave, the only remaining Protestant area on the west bank, and is of interest solely for its Union Jack kerb paintings and huge **murals**, which read as direct responses to the more famous Catholic "Free Derry" mural in the next valley.

### The Double Bastion and Verbal Arts Centre

North from Bishop's Gate, you reach the **Double Bastion**, where the "Roaring Meg" cannon sits. During the siege, it was said that "the noise of the discharge was more terrifying than were the contents of the charge dangerous to the enemy". Just by here is the **Verbal Arts Centre** (Mon–Thurs 9am–5.30pm, Fri 9am–4pm; ☎ 028 7126 6946, ⓦ theverbal.co), a unique project aimed at sustaining and promoting forms of communication and entertainment once central to Irish culture: legend, folklore, *sean-nós* – an unaccompanied narrative form of singing (see page 592) – and storytelling performed by a *seanachie* (storyteller). The centre, incorporating designs by Louis le Brocquy, commissions works from writers, and hosts poetry readings and storytelling events; the centre's lovely *Café on the Walls* serves scones, soups and stews.

## The Siege Museum

13 Society St • Mon–Sat 10am–5pm • £5 • ☎ 028 7125 1219, 🖥 thesiegemuseum.org

As its title implies, the enlightening **Siege Museum** recalls the events behind the Siege of Londonderry, in particular focusing on the contributions of its principal personalities, such as one Colonel Adam Murray, whose sword and sheath – which he carried throughout the duration of the siege – is on display here. Here, too, are the remains of the statue of George Walker blown up by the IRA in 1973. The floor above is given over to the history of the Apprentice Boys, which comprises eight parent clubs (all based within the city), with a further 240 or so branch clubs dispersed throughout the UK, Ireland and Canada.

**14**

## The Royal Bastion

Constructed between 1826 and 1828, the **Royal Bastion** used to be topped by a 3m-high statue of Reverend George Walker, the defender of Derry "against an arbitrary and bigoted monarch" (to quote the still-legible inscription); the statue was blown up by the IRA in 1973. The Bastion and surrounding area remains the focal point for the annual Relief of Londonderry parade every August 12 when the Apprentice Boys march in their predecessors', and Walker's, memory. The view from here across the Bogside district is expansive.

# The Bogside

In the valley below the northern city walls is the Catholic **Bogside** district where, at the start of the Troubles, ferocious rioting took place following the Apprentice Boys' march, with the army and police responding to bricks and petrol bombs with tear gas, rubber bullets and careering Saracen armoured cars. The area at the foot of the escarpment used to be full of streets of compact terraced housing, but was redeveloped in the 1960s in the form of a dual carriageway, an estate of tenement flats and empty concrete precincts. Clinging to the opposite hillside, and in stark contrast, are early twentieth-century terraces of stucco façades, blue tile roofs and red chimney stacks.

---

### THE SIEGE OF DERRY

Derry's walls underwent – and withstood – siege on a number of occasions during the seventeenth century. The last of these, in **1688–89**, played a key part in the Williamite army's victory over the Catholic James II at the **Battle of the Boyne** (see page 573), when the Derrymen's obduracy crucially delayed the plans of James and his ally Louis XIV to maintain Catholic ascendancy over the kingdom.

The suffering and heroism of the fifteen-week siege, the longest in British history, still have the immediacy of recent history in the minds of Derry Protestants. James's accession in 1685 had seen the introduction of a policy of replacing Protestants with Catholics in leading positions in the Irish administration and army. In December 1688, a new garrison attempted to enter the city, but was prevented when a group of young apprentices seized the keys and locked the city's gates. Eventually, after negotiation, an **all-Protestant garrison** under Governor Robert Lundy was admitted. Over the following few months the city's resident population of two thousand swelled to thirty thousand as people from the surrounding area took refuge from Jacobite forces advancing into Ulster. Fearing that resistance against the Jacobite army was futile, Lundy departed; his effigy is still burnt each December by Protestants. Around seven thousand Protestants died during the siege that followed, the survivors being reduced to eating dogs, cats and rats. Today, the siege is commemorated with a skeleton on the city **coat of arms**, and the lyrical tag "maiden city", a somewhat sexist reference to the city's unbreached walls.

**14**

## BOGSIDE MURALS

Spanning much of the length of Rossville Street is an eye-catching panorama of twelve **murals** – collectively entitled the **People's Gallery** – painted between 1994 and 2006 by Bogside artists Kevin Hasson, Tom Kelly and William Kelly. One, a gable-end mural, shows the former Independent Republican MP and one of the organizers of the People's Democracy movement, Bernadette Devlin, megaphone in hand, in front of the old "You are now entering Free Derry" mural. Nearby, and perhaps the most affecting mural, is the "**Death of Innocence**", which commemorates a 14-year-old girl, Annette McGavigan, who died in 1971, caught in crossfire between the British Army and IRA. Just around the corner, on Westland Street, another mural depicts those killed on Bloody Sunday. There are also striking murals featuring a gas-mask-clad petrol bomber and a British soldier smashing down a door with a sledgehammer during Operation Motorman (see page 507).

### The Museum of Free Derry

55 Glenfada Park, off Rossville St • Mon–Fri 9.30am–4.30pm, Sat 11am–4pm, plus July–Sept Sun 11am– 4pm • £7 • ☎ 028 7136 0880, ⓦ museumoffreederry.org

Brilliantly conceived from an old block of flats that had long gone to rack and ruin is the superb **Museum of Free Derry**. Inside, bare concrete walls provide a suitably chilly backdrop to the history of the Bogside. Following coverage of Ireland's civil rights heritage, the focus turns to the Battle of the Bogside of August 1969, with a selection of items, including flags, rubber bullets and canisters, and (now colourfully decorated) metal bin lids that were used to signal an impending army raid.

The greater part of the museum is given over to events surrounding Bloody Sunday (see page 507). With live British Army radio commentary playing in the background, the exhibits on show are truly sobering, and include the banner carried on the anti-internment march that day, blood-soaked and bullet-pierced items of clothing of some of the victims (for example the jacket belonging to Michael McDaid, bullet hole clearly visible in the back – above this is a photo of him just moments before being shot), and the blood-soaked handkerchief waved by priest Edward Daly, as recalled in the iconic piece of television footage (and photograph) of him escorting a group carrying the mortally-wounded Jackie Duddy. Back outside, and to the rear of the museum, is a glass-encased section of bullet-riddled wall.

### ARRIVAL AND DEPARTURE                                                    DERRY CITY

**By plane** The tiny City of Derry Airport (☎ 028 7181 0784, ⓦ cityofderryairport.com) is 11km northeast of town on the A2 road. It's connected by Ulsterbus services #44, #143 and #234 to the train station and Foyle St bus station. A taxi from the airport to the city centre costs around £15.

**By train** Derry's train station (☎ 028 7134 2228) is in the Waterside district on the east bank, from where it's a 15min walk to the town centre across the Craigavon Bridge, or there's a free shuttle bus service (Mon–Sat) which drops you in Foyle St.

Destinations Belfast (Mon–Sat hourly, Sun 6; 2hr); Coleraine (Mon–Sat hourly, Sun 6; 35min).

**By bus** The central bus station on Foyle St is served by Ulsterbus (☎ 028 7126 2261) for all the main Northern Ireland destinations and Bus Éireann (information from Ulsterbus), which operates buses to Dublin, Donegal town,

Galway and Sligo. In addition, North West Busways (☎ 074 938 2619) run services across the border into Donegal, with buses departing from Patrick St, while McGonagle Bus and Coach Hire operates a service between Derry (Guildhall) and Buncrana (Main St).

Destinations Belfast (every 30min; 1hr 50min); Buncrana (McGonagle: Mon–Sat hourly; 35min); Carndonagh (North West Busways: Mon–Sat 3–4 daily; 45min); Culdaff (North West Busways: Mon–Fri 2 daily, Sat 1; 55min); Donegal town (Bus Éireann: 6–8 daily; 1hr 25min); Dublin (Bus Éireann: 11 daily; 4hr); Greencastle (North West Busways: Mon–Sat 4 daily; 1hr); Letterkenny (Bus Éireann: every 1–2hr; 40min); Monaghan (Bus Éireann: 11 daily; 1hr 50min); Moville (North West Busways: Mon–Sat 5 daily; 40min); Omagh (Mon–Sat hourly, Sun 7; 1hr 5min); Sligo (Bus Éireann: 5–7 daily; 2hr 40min).

## GETTING AROUND AND INFORMATION

**By taxi** Taxis wait on Foyle St and William St, or call Delta Cabs (☏ 028 7127 9999) or the Derry Taxi Association (☏ 028 7126 0247).

**By bike** Bike hire is available from the tourist office, costing £5/2hr, £8/4hr and £12/day.

**Tourist office** 1–3 Waterloo Place (April & Oct Mon–Fri 9.30am–5pm, Sat & Sun 10am–5pm; May & Sept Mon– Sat 9am–6pm, Sun 10am–5pm; June–Aug Mon–Fri 9am–7pm, Sat 9am–6pm, Sun 10am–5pm; Nov–March Mon–Fri 9.30am–5pm, Sat 10am–4pm; ☏ 028 7126 7284, ⓦ visitderry.com). Books accommodation, has a bureau de change, bike hire, and provides a mass of information about both the North and the Republic.

## TOURS

**Walking tours** The well-established and hugely popular Martin McCrossan city walking tours take in a full circuit of the city walls, leaving from the tourist office (10am, noon, 2pm & 4pm; £4; ☏ 028 7127 1996, ⓦ derrycitytours.com). Departing from the Guildhall, Bogside History Tours (daily 11am & 1pm; £10; ☏ 07731 450088, ⓦ bogsidehistorytours.

com) take in the Bogside, politics and murals.

**Bus tours** Open-top bus tours (April–Sept daily & hourly 10am–5pm; Oct–March call for times; £12.50; ☏ 028 7137 0067, ⓦ city-sightseeing.com) depart from near the tourist office and stop at a further six points, including the Guildhall, the Bogside and Waterside on the east bank.

## ACCOMMODATION                          SEE MAPS PAGES 501 AND 503

Although Derry has plenty of upper-end **accommodation**, finding a more economically priced room in the centre can be difficult, especially in high season and at weekends.

★ **Beech Hill Hotel** 32 Ardmore Rd, 4km southeast of the city centre ☏ 028 7134 9279, ⓦ beech-hill.com. In a wonderfully tranquil setting away from the centre, *Beech Hill* is a graceful eighteenth-century country house that has hosted many of the world's top politicians, actors and musicians in its time. Rooms are impeccable, as is the service, while the hotel's fascinating museum room documents the exploits of the United States Marine corps who were stationed here during World War II. **£125**

★ **Bishop's Gate Hotel** 24 Bishop St ☏ 028 7114 0300, ⓦ bishopsgatehotelderry.com. From the original revolving wooden doors and the magnificent sweeping staircase above reception, it's pretty obvious that this Edwardian hotel – an erstwhile gentleman's club – is something special. The thirty rooms don't disappoint either, coloured dove grey and orange, sage green, and plum, with oak writing desks and antique phones, and beautifully tiled-bathrooms with enormous rain showers; once settled in, pop down to the gorgeous *Wig & Gown* champagne bar for a drink or two. The cooked-to-order breakfast is nigh on perfect. **£149**

## BLOODY SUNDAY

For the first two years of the Troubles, the part of the Catholic Bogside area beyond the original "Free Derry" mural was a notorious no-go area, the undisputed preserve of the IRA, its boundary marked by a gravestone-like monument declaring: "You are now entering free Derry". This autonomy lasted until 1972, when the British army launched **Operation Motorman**; the IRA men who had been in the area were tipped off, though, and got across the border before the invasion took place.

To the right of the "Bernadette Devlin" mural in the Bogside stands a **memorial pillar** to the thirteen Catholic civilians killed by British paratroopers (a fourteenth died later of his wounds) on "**Bloody Sunday**", January 30, 1972, in the aftermath of a civil-rights demonstration. The soldiers immediately claimed they had been fired upon, an assertion later disproved, though some witnesses came forward to report seeing IRA men there with their guns. The bitter memory of the subsequent Widgery Commission's failure to declare anyone responsible for the deaths festered in Catholic Derry, and pressure was maintained on successive governments to reopen investigations. In 1999, after years of mounting demands for a full examination, the British government established the **Saville Inquiry**, which conducted its proceedings in Derry's Guildhall until moving to Westminster in 2002. It finally reported in June 2010, concluding that the British Army's actions were "unjustified and unjustifiable", that all those killed or wounded were innocent victims and that some soldiers had committed perjury in giving their evidence. However, no single member of the British Army has ever been prosecuted.

**14**

**The City Hotel** 14–18 Queens Quay ☎ 028 7136 5800, ⊕ cityhotelderry.com. A prominent building overlooking the Foyle, this fashionable hotel offers spacious rooms furnished in a warm, contemporary style, and all the leisure facilities imaginable. __£112__

**Ramada Da Vinci's Hotel** 15 Culmore Rd ☎ 028 7127 9111, ⊕ davincishotel.com. This impressively modish hotel offers a wide range of crisply furnished rooms, while its small coterie of lively bars means that you can forego the rather dull traipse into town. __£70__

**The Saddler's House** 36 Great James St ☎ 028 7126 9691, ⊕ thesaddlershouse.com. Stylish, period-furnished Victorian town house B&B with seven tidy rooms, either double or twins, in a fairly peaceful spot very near the city centre. Guests are encouraged to avail themselves of the lounge, while breakfast is taken around a large, communal table. Closed Jan & Feb. __£75__

**Shipquay Hotel** 15–17 Shipquay St ☎ 028 7126 7266, ⊕ shipquayhotel.com. After the Bishop's Gate, this is the city's classiest outfit, a superbly renovated former bank building with 21 modestly sized but exquisitely appointed rooms, some adorned with prints by Irish artist Terry Bradley. Superior rooms, which cost around £40 more, have river views. __£99__

## EATING
SEE MAP PAGE 501

Derry's eating options are vastly improved these days, with a core selection of accomplished establishments to choose from; for more high-end stuff, head for the smarter hotel restaurants. And if you're here on the first Saturday of each month, make for the **Walled City Market** in Guildhall Square, where you can partake in some fabulous local produce and delicious street food.

**Browns in Town** 23 Strand Rd ☎ 028 7136 2889, ⊕ brownsintown.com. A sleek candlelit city-centre restaurant that showcases the likes of Greencastle seabass and squid, as well as Donegal crab, turf smoked beef, lamb and duck. The three-course early bird (5–6.30pm) is excellent value at £21.95. Daily noon–3pm & 5–9pm.

★ **The Coffee Tree** 49 Strand Rd ☎ 07472 466414. Despite its rather anonymous location, this good-looking, cheerfully staffed café is one heck of a popular place, and rightly so. Plonk yourself down on one of the deep leather sofas and enjoy a steaming bowl of yellow split pea soup with sweet potato and a hunk of doughy bread, or a gooey chocolate brownie with a cup of coffee. Tues–Fri 9.30am–5pm, Sat 10.30am–5pm.

**Saffron** 2 Clarendon St ☎ 028 7126 0532, ⊕ saffron derry.co.uk. The city's longest-established Indian restaurant is still the best, offering a well-priced menu (two courses for £15.85) with tandoori dishes and Punjabi cuisine a speciality. Tues –Sun 4.30–10pm.

**La Sosta** 45a Carlisle Rd ☎ 028 7137 4817, ⊕ lasosta derry.com. Secreted away in a rather unprepossessing location, this longstanding, family-run establishment is deservedly a locals' favourite. The Italian-inspired food is as authentic as you could wish for, with the likes of fillet of rabbit stuffed with apples, pancetta and calvados (£19), and pea and lemon zest risotto with mint and mascarpone; the wine card is of a similarly high order. Tues–Sat 6–10pm.

**Spaghetti Junction** 46 William St ☎ 028 7141 4242, ⊕ spaghettijunctionderry.co.uk. The clue's in the name, though there's far more to this fun, wildly colourful *trattoria* than mere spaghetti: how about monkfish risotto or black penne with squid and pistachio cream sauce (£15), washed down, naturally, with a bottle of Peroni? Thurs–Sun 5–9.30pm.

## DRINKING AND NIGHTLIFE
SEE MAPS PAGES 501 AND 503

**Peadar O'Donnell's** 59 Waterloo St ☎ 028 7126 7295. In the same family since 1847, *Peadar's* and the attached *Gweedore Bar* are at the social and musical centre of the city – there's traditional music every night in the former while its neighbour is more DJ-centric with music on Fridays and Saturdays. Peadar O' Donnell's Mon–Sat 11.30am–1.30am, Sun 12.30pm–12.30am; Gweedore Bar Mon–Fri 6.30pm–1.30am, Sat & Sun noon–1.30am.

**Sandino's Café Bar** Water St ☎ 028 7130 9297, ⊕ sandinoscafebar.com. Despite its somewhat dishevelled exterior, this is Derry's hippest hangout, featuring a variety of live music in its back bar and club room. Mon–Sat 12.30pm–1am, Sun 1pm–midnight.

**Taphouse** 5 Guildhall St ☎ 028 7136 4888. Cool, contemporary bar with a darkened interior sprinkled with fairy lights and a long bar stocking some of the best ales

in town, including Brewdog from Scotland and a selection from the Derry-based Dopey Dick brewery; soak it all up with a house steak sandwich. Tuesday is games night while Wednesdays are reserved for trad music. Daily noon–1am, food served noon–6pm.

**Tinney's** 3–4 Patrick St ☎ 028 7136 2091. One of the best places for traditional music with a regular Tues night session. You can also get the lowdown here on "the bars", which is how local news and gossip is referred to in Derry. Mon–Thurs 11.30am–12.30am, Fri & Sat 11.30am–1am, Sun 12.30pm–11.30pm.

★ **Walled City Brewery** 70 Ebrington Square ☎ 028 7134 3336, ⊕ walledcitybrewery.com. Adding a welcome dollop of colour to the city's east side, this erstwhile medical centre in the centre of the old barracks quarter has been superbly repurposed as a craft brewery, the first in Derry for more than a century. Beers are brewed

## DERRY'S FESTIVALS

Derry is awash with great festivals. In early March, a week-long **drama festival** is held at the Waterside Theatre while early May sees the **Jazz and Big Band Festival** (Ⓦcityofderryjazzfestival.com) come to town, the biggest and most prestigious jazz festival outside of Cork. In late June, the **Celtronic Dance Music Festival** (Ⓦceltronicfestival.com) takes over various venues across the city, while the second week of August witnesses the **Maiden City Festival** – a four-day programme of dance, theatre and music organized by the Apprentice Boys of Derry, culminating in the Relief of Londonderry parade (see page 505). The **Big Tickle Comedy Festival** occupies eleven days in early September, followed by the **Foyle Film Festival** in November (Ⓦfoylefilmfestival.org). Finally, there's the mammoth **Halloween Carnival**, five days of mayhem culminating in a massive costume parade and spectacular fireworks display on October 31.

**14**

on site and there are typically ten or so on the go at any one time, which you can enjoy with *pinxtos* (Basque-style tapas), such as gazpacho or smoked mackerel, or more substantial fillers (house smoked braised beer pork; £14). Mon–Thurs 5–9pm, Fri & Sat 1–4pm & 5pm–late, Sun 1–4pm & 5pm–late.

### ENTERTAINMENT

**Cultúrlann Uí Chanáin** 37 Great James St Ⓣ028 7131 4132, Ⓦculturlann.org. Dedicated to the promotion of the Irish language, arts and culture and hosts occasional events, such as traditional music concerts.

**Millennium Forum** Newmarket St Ⓣ028 7126 4455, Ⓦmillenniumforum.co.uk. This huge theatre offers a broad if somewhat middle-of-the-road programme, including well-known ballets and opera.

**Nerve Centre** 7–8 Magazine St Ⓣ028 7126 0562, Ⓦnervecentre.org. The main focus of Derry's dynamic cultural world, the Nerve Centre contains sound, film and video studios and editing suites, an art-house cinema, two music venues, a bar and café; it stages regular screenings of left-field films.

**The Playhouse** Artillery St Ⓣ028 7126 8027, Ⓦderry playhouse.co.uk. A more innovative range of theatre, dance and comedy is on the bill at The Playhouse.

**Waterside Theatre** Glendermott Rd Ⓣ028 7131 4000, Ⓦwatersidetheatre.com. Across the river and dishing up a mixed bag of a programme, ranging from classic drama to local versions of TV game shows.

### SHOPPING

SEE MAPS PAGES 501 AND 503

**Bedlam Market** 20 Bishop St Ⓣ028 7136 4613. Up to fifteen traders operate in an eclectic maze of rooms brimful of vintage clothes, holistic treatments, antiques and everything retro imaginable. Mon–Sat 10am–5.30pm.

**Craft Village** Shipquay St Ⓣ028 7136 8276, Ⓦderry craftvillage.com. A wonderful array of craft and artisan producers come together in this collective that has re-created life between the sixteenth and nineteenth centuries. You'll find tweeds and knitwear, exquisite jewellery and glass, soaps and candles and secondhand books. Mon–Sat 9am–9pm.

**Faller The Jeweller** 12 Strand Rd Ⓣ028 7136 2710, Ⓦfaller.com. Look out for the golden teapot that hangs outside the shop and discharges a plume of environmentally friendly smoke from its spout. Inside you can buy a selection of brooches and charms from their "Drop of Derry" range, which reflects the city's culture. Mon–Sat 9.30am–5pm.

★ **Yellow Yard** 2 Palace St. Housed within an old shirt factory, Yellow Yard is a quartet of local enterprises, namely a bookstore, record shop, gift shop and café, the latter making for a relaxing pit stop after a lengthy browse around the shops. Look out for the occasional Sunday flea market held in the yard outside. Daily 10am–5.30pm.

### DIRECTORY

**Hospital** Accident and emergency department, Altnagelvin Hospital, Glenshane Rd (Ⓣ028 7134 5171); call this number also for dental emergencies after working hours or at weekends.

**Police** The main police station is located on Strand Rd (Ⓣ028 7136 7337).

**Post Office** 3 Custom House St (Mon & Wed–Fri 9am–5.30pm, Tues 9.30am–5.30pm, Sat 9am–12.30pm).

# Southern County Derry

The Derry–Antrim A6 road follows a river valley through fertile farmland then ascends to the Glenshane Pass on the northeastern fringe of the **Sperrin Mountains**. Southeast from here are Magherafelt and Moneymore, two attractive and entirely **planned towns**, the latter adjacent to the grand Plantation manor house of **Springhill**. The huge expanse of Ireland's biggest lake, **Lough Neagh**, laps against the county's southeastern corner, which is where you'll also find the village of **Bellaghy**, a place of pilgrimage for fans of Seamus Heaney.

## The plantation towns and around

Southeast of Dungiven and over the Glenshane Pass on the way to the northern tip of Lough Neagh, it is worth making a detour to see some examples of town planning – the **plantation towns** of the London companies, most of them characteristically focused around a central Diamond. One example is **Magherafelt**, granted to the Salters' Company by James I, which has a wide, sloping main street and makes a reasonable base for exploring the lough and the Bellaghy area. **Moneymore**, about 8km further south, was originally constructed by the Drapers in the early seventeenth century (and restored by them in 1817), and was the first town in the North to have piped water – amazingly enough, as early as 1615.

### Springhill

20 Springhill Rd, around 1.5km outside Moneymore off the B18 • **House** April, Sept & Oct Sat & Sun noon–5pm; May Fri–Sun noon–5pm; June Thurs–Sun noon–5pm; July & Aug daily noon–5pm • **Grounds** Daily 10am–5pm • £5.45 • ☎ 028 8674 8210, ⓦ nationaltrust.org.uk/springhill

**Springhill** is a grand Plantation manor house built between 1680 and 1700 by William "Good Will" Conyngham in order to fulfil a marriage contract with the father of his bride-to-be, Anne Upton. Elegant both without and within, its sober whitewashed architecture houses fine rooms, equipped with original period furniture and paintings belonging to William and his descendants, who occupied the house until 1959. Upstairs, the **Blue Room** is said to be haunted by the ghost of Olivia Lenox-Conyngham, whose husband George was found shot here in 1816. Outside, the stables house a **costume collection**, which adopts a specific theme each year, drawing upon three thousand items collected from the mid-seventeenth century to the 1970s. There are delightful **gardens**, a tower dating from the 1730s, which was probably originally part of a windmill, and a pleasant walk through beech and yew trees.

### ARRIVAL AND INFORMATION — THE PLANTATION TOWNS AND AROUND

**By bus** Buses run from Magherafelt to Bellaghy (Mon–Sat 5–8 daily; 15min) and Moneymore (Mon–Fri 10 daily, Sat 3; 15min). From Moneymore, buses run to Magherafelt (Mon– Sat 6 daily; 15min).

**Tourist information** The Bridewell, 6 Church St (Mon– Sat 9.30am–5.30pm; ☎ 028 7963 1510).

### ACCOMMODATION AND EATING

**Church Street Restaurant** 23 Church St, Magherafelt ☎ 028 7932 8083, ⓦ churchstreetrestaurant.co.uk. Church-style furnishings (pointy, high-backed chairs) and crisply laid tables await at this classy establishment just across the road from *Laurel Villa*. The menu runs the gamut from smoked trout and crab with apple and cucumber (£7.50) to roast pork fillet with black pudding mash (£15), all of it beautifully executed, and there's a very creditable wine menu too. Wed–Sat 5–9pm, Sun noon–8pm.

**Laurel Villa** 60 Church St, Magherafelt ☎ 028 7930 1459, ⓦ laurel-villa.com. A graceful Victorian town house with four elegantly furnished, personality-packed rooms, each named after a poet, namely Kavanagh, Longley, MacNeice and, of course, Heaney, whose gorgeous little attic room features framed versions of his best-known work. Indeed, as an expert in all things Heaney, the owner organizes tours of Heaney country as well as an annual festival in Sept (see page 512). __£95__

# Lough Neagh

East of Magherafelt and Moneymore are the fish-filled waters of the biggest lake in Ireland, **Lough Neagh**. Tributaries flow from every point of the compass: the Lower Bann, which drains the lake and runs north to **Lough Beg** (finally reaching the sea north of Coleraine), contains some huge trout, including the dollaghan, unique to these waters. Similar to salmon (which are also common), dollaghan grow by three pounds every year and can be caught by spinning, worming and fly-fishing: the Ballinderry Black and the Bann Olive are famous flies derived from this region. The best fishing is from mid-July to October, but you will need a Fisheries Conservation Board Rod **licence**, available from tourist offices; they can also prove information on day-tickets for fishing and specialist boat-trips, which are issued and run by the Lough Neagh Angling Association.

**14**

# Bellaghy

Like many of the plantation settlements in the area, **BELLAGHY**, just west of Lough Beg, has a history that reflects the divisions between communities. Indeed, two of the ten 1981 hunger strikers (see page 582) – cousins Francis Hughes and Thomas McElwee – came from the village, and Orange parades have been a regular flashpoint.

### Bellaghy Bawn

20 Castle St • Easter–Sept Sun noon–4pm • Free • ☎ 028 9082 3207

Bellaghy is neatly laid out around a T-junction, and wandering south past the whitewashed terraces on Castle Street leads to one of the best surviving examples of a Plantation castle, **Bellaghy Bawn**, built in 1618 by the Vintners' Company. Most of its fortifications were lost in 1641, but it still retains a striking circular flanker tower which has been well restored. Inside you'll find fascinating interpretive **displays** explaining the 7000-year-old history of the settlements in this area, the construction of the village – today's houses still occupy the same original allocated plots of land – and the diverse ecology of the Lough Beg wetland area. It was here that Seamus Heaney's father rented grazing rights on the strand at Lough Beg; in his poem *Ancestral Photograph*, Heaney recalls helping to herd the cattle that grazed there down Castle Street on their way to market.

### Lough Beg and Church Island

You can see the shimmering Lough Beg from the windows of the Bawn's flanker tower, and a stroll down to the lake is well worthwhile. In summer, its waters recede and **Church Island** becomes accessible from the shore. Besides a walled graveyard, you'll find the ruins of a medieval church here, said to have been founded centuries before by the ubiquitous St Patrick, with a tower and spire added in 1788 by the eccentric Frederick Augustus Hervey (see page 499) to improve his view from Ballyscullion House on the mainland nearby. He commissioned Charles Lanyon to build a huge replacement for the original house which stood here with, apparently, 365 windows, but died abroad before ever moving in, and the building subsequently fell into ruin.

### Seamus Heaney HomePlace

45 Main St • Mon–Sat 10am–5pm, Sun 1–5pm • £7 • ☎ 028 7938 7444, ⓦ seamusheaneyhome.com

Whether you're a fan of Seamus Heaney or not, the **Seamus Heaney HomePlace** is well worth an hour of your time, reflecting as it does on the extraordinary life and works of one of the world's greatest contemporary poets. Housed within the village's old police station, now sporting a handsome stone and wood clad exterior, the exhibition is split into two parts: on the ground floor, "People and Place" documents the poet's prodigious output, with Heaney himself reciting many of his poems; this section is

**14**

## SEAMUS HEANEY (1939–2013)

It's impossible to conceive of a contemporary poet, Irish or otherwise, whose works are more evocative of time and place than **Seamus Heaney** who, at the time of his death aged 74 on August 30, 2013, was arguably the best-known poet in the world. Heaney was born, the eldest of nine children, on the family farm of Mossbawn (itself the title of two poems in his fourth collection, *North*), in the townland of Tamniarn, near Castledawson, on April 13, 1939. Heaney's family background, his Catholic upbringing and his study of Irish at school imbued him with a strong sense of being Irish in a state that considered itself British, a paradox that would form a major motif in his work during the 1970s. While at Queen's University, Belfast, he was further influenced by the literature he discovered in Belfast's **Linen Hall library** (see page 458), especially the works of John Hewitt, the Antrim-born "Poet of the Glens", and the English "naturalist" poet Ted Hughes, in whose work he found an "association of sounds in print that connected with the world below".

Heaney's first poem, *Tractors*, was published in the *Belfast Evening Telegraph* in 1962. His first significant collection, *Death of a Naturalist*, followed in 1966 and was immediately recognized for its earthiness and command of diverse metrical forms. In the 1960s, while lecturing at Queen's, Heaney's career expanded into journalism and television and he became increasingly involved in the **civil rights movement**. His response to the Troubles saw him seeking for "images and symbols adequate to our predicament" and he began to see poetry as a mode of resistance. Eventually, though, the violence so disturbed him that he moved with his family to County Wicklow, prompting Ian Paisley's *Protestant Telegraph* to bid farewell to "the well-known papist propagandist" on his departure to his "spiritual home in the popish republic". While his 1970s collections *North* and *Field Work* had mixed receptions – some saw the strong influence of Robert Lowell on the former – Heaney found himself turning increasingly to his **Irish heritage** as a source of inspiration, particularly the long medieval poem *Buile Suibhne* (*The Madness of Sweeney*), and published his own *Sweeney Astray* collection in 1983. The following year's *Station Island* drew on his experiences as a participant in St Patrick's Purgatory (see page 422).

The hunger strikes of the early 1980s brought a new urgency to Northern politics and a revival of Heaney's polemicism. Prompted by the staging in Derry in 1980 of Brian Friel's play *Translations*, which showed English surveyors travelling through eighteenth-century Ireland anglicizing all the place names, Heaney co-founded the **Field Day Theatre Company** with Friel, his old friend and fellow academic Séamus Deane, the actor Stephen Rea and others. While the group's theatrical activities were themselves controversial, it was their publications that engendered the most antipathy. Their pamphlets were criticized as attempts to over-intellectualize the Troubles, and the 1991 *Field Day Anthology of Irish Writing* was decried for its under-representation of work by women writers, though a subsequent volume entirely devoted to them has since been published.

In 1995, Heaney's body of work was more widely recognized by the award of the **Nobel Prize for Literature**. His later works included a translation of the Anglo-Saxon epic poem *Beowulf*, his dramatic retelling of this tale of monster- and dragon-slaying managing to breathe new life into a work that was long considered too dense and metaphorical for a modern readership; his collection, *District and Circle*, which won the prestigious T.S. Eliot Prize for Poetry in 2006; and his twelfth and final collection, *Human Chain* (2010), which is overshadowed by ageing and mortality.

The **annual festival** celebrating Heaney's life and work, "On Home Ground" (ⓦ onhomegroundfestival.com) is held in mid-September and reflects the inspiration and influence of the area on his Derry childhood.

augmented by a handful of personal belongings, like his school bag and a duffel coat, as well as some beautiful, mostly family-oriented, photographs. Upstairs, "Imagination and Inspiration" dwells on some of the many objects that fired Heaney's imagination, for example a fireman's helmet from Boston (*Helmet*), an anvil (*The Forge*), and a turf spade (*Digging: Death of a Naturalist*). Here, too, is a mock up of his Dublin attic study, with a collection of his books and manuscripts, and footage of him receiving the Nobel Peace Prize in 1995.

From the HomePlace, it's a ten-minute walk through the village to St Mary's church and Heaney's **grave**, tucked away in one corner of the graveyard and whose plain, grey headstone simply reads "Walk on air against your better judgement", a line from his poem *The Gravel Walks*.

**14**

### ARRIVAL AND DEPARTURE                                        BELLAGHY

**By bus** Magherafelt (Mon–Sat 5–9 daily; 15min).

# Down and Armagh

THE MOURNE MOUNTAINS

# Down and Armagh

Counties Down and Armagh occupy the southeastern corner of Northern Ireland, between Belfast and the border, and contain some of the region's most attractive countryside, especially around the coast. You're also never far away from places associated with St Patrick, who sailed into Strangford Lough to make his final Irish landfall in County Down, founded his first bishopric at Armagh and is buried at either Downpatrick or Armagh, depending on whose claim you prefer.

Heading south from Belfast, the glowering **Mourne Mountains** increasingly dominate the panorama, and it's in this direction that most of the attractions lie. If you simply take the main roads in and out of Belfast – the A1 for Newry and the border, or the M1 motorway west – you'll come across very little to stop for: it's in the rural areas, the mountains and coast, that the charm of this region lies. One of the best options is to head east from Belfast around the Down shore – past the **Ulster Folk and Transport Museum**, one of the best in the North, and the blowsy suburban resort of **Bangor** into the **Ards Peninsula** or along the banks of **Strangford Lough**. Near the Lough's southern tip, **Downpatrick** is closely associated with the arrival of St Patrick. There are plenty of little beaches, early Christian sites, defensive tower houses and fine mansions to visit on the way towards **Newcastle**, the best base for excursions on foot into the Mourne Mountains. Beyond the Mournes a fine coast road curves around to **Carlingford Lough** and the border. Inland, **Hillsborough**, resembling an English Cotswolds-style village, is closely linked to the political development of the North.

Below **Lough Neagh**, **Armagh city** is well worth visiting for its ancient associations, cathedrals and fine Georgian streets, while the nearby village of **Loughgall** is a popular stop off for those wishing to explore the region's strong Protestant links; moreover, **The Argory**, a fine stately home, lies close by. The villages of **South Armagh** – a predominantly Catholic area – were the heartland of violent Republicanism, and often referred to as "Bandit Country" or "The Killing Fields", even by locals. However, the region possesses some startlingly attractive country, especially around the peak of **Slieve Gullion**, a short way south of **Newry**.

# Hillsborough

Around 20km southwest of Belfast, the historic village of **HILLSBOROUGH** merits a quick detour, courtesy of its stately castle and chintzy ambience, which is reinforced by a sprinkling of tea rooms and antique shops lining the main street. You get the best of Hillsborough by following a route that starts from the **war memorial** and heads up the magnificent approach to the eighteenth-century Gothic **parish church**. Bear right here for the main entrance to Hillsborough's elegant but ruined **fort** (April–Sept Mon–Sat 10am–6pm, Sun 11am–6pm; Oct–March Mon–Sat 10am– 4pm, Sun 11am–4pm; free), constructed by Colonel Arthur Hill (after whom the village is named) in 1650 and remodelled in the eighteenth century as a venue for family feasts and entertainment. Beyond this, a deciduous **forest** (dawn–dusk; free) opens up, curving around a **lake** stocked with brown and rainbow trout. Footpaths meander through the trees in all directions – a circuit of the lake takes around thirty minutes.

ST PATRICK'S CHURCH OF IRELAND CATHEDRAL

# Highlights

**❶ The Ulster Folk and Transport Museum**
Possibly the best museum in Northern Ireland – it
consummately encapsulates much of the North's
cultural and industrial history. See page 521

**❷ Portaferry** A superb waterside location,
tremendous sunsets and the best base for
exploring Strangford Lough and the Ards
Peninsula. See page 525

**❸ The Mourne Mountains** Brooding and
dominating South Down, the Mournes offer
magnificent walking, intoxicating views and
a total escape from the contemporary world.
See page 535

**❹ Slieve Gullion** Drive or hike to the top of
this mountain and enjoy the panorama of the
unmissable South Armagh countryside laid out
below. See page 539

**❺ Armagh city** Probably the most graceful
city in the North, with two cathedrals and a
captivating Mall. See page 540

**❻ The Argory** A magnificent nineteenth-
century mansion, set in gorgeous grounds and
featuring one of the most illuminating guided
tours in Ireland. See page 547

**HIGHLIGHTS ARE MARKED ON THE MAP ON PAGE 518**

## Hillsborough Castle

The Square • Castle tours hourly: April–June & Sept Sat & Sun 11am–4pm; July & Aug daily 11am–4pm; gardens 10am–sunset • Castle and gardens £8, gardens only £3.50 • ☎ 028 9268 1300, ⓦ hrp.org.uk/hillsborough

Dominating the town is **Hillsborough Castle**, built in 1770 by Wills Hill, the first Marquis of Downshire; indeed, the Hills were, at one stage, the largest landowners in Ireland. From 1925, it was the residence of the governor of Northern Ireland, but since 1973 – following the imposition of direct rule from London – it has been the official residence of the British secretary of state for Northern Ireland. Hillsborough has also played an important role in the peace process, for it was here that the **Anglo-Irish Agreement** was signed in 1985, while informal negotiations leading up to the Good Friday Agreement were also held here.

Guided **tours** take you through half a dozen or so rooms, including the State Drawing and Dining Rooms, replete with Georgian furniture and silver from HMS *Nelson*. Most rooms, too, have a smattering of important paintings from the Royal Galleries collection, including ones of Charles II, William of Orange and James II, while there are photos galore of notable politicians, alongside snaps of visiting royalty. The **gardens**, meanwhile, are lovely, particularly in May and June when the many roses and Europe's largest rhododendron bush are in bloom. There are several marked-out walks around the gardens, which take in numerous monuments, including the Quaker Burial Ground, Ice House and Cromlyn Ruin, a late eighteenth-century sham ruin of standing stone and lintel. Note that the castle is undergoing a major **renovation** project until at least 2022, and while it's still open to the public, this will eventually see a new entrance located on the opposite side of the estate alongside the addition of a new visitor centre and café, among other facilities.

### ARRIVAL AND INFORMATION
HILLSBOROUGH

**By bus** Buses from/to Belfast (Mon–Sat every 30min, Sun 10; 25min) pull in at the War Memorial towards the bottom of Main St.

**Tourist office** The tourist office is housed in the elegant Georgian courthouse on The Square at the top of Main Street (Mon–Sat 9.30am–5.30pm, plus April–Sept Sun 11am–4pm; ☎ 028 9244 7640, ⓦ visitlisburncastlereagh.com).

### ACCOMMODATION AND EATING

**Dunhill Cottage** 47b Carnreagh ☎ 07887 678792, ⓦ dunhillcottage.co.uk. A 10min walk from Hillsborough on the A1 Lisburn road, this ecofriendly guesthouse has six modern rooms in two buildings, all tidily furnished with marble tiling and walk-in showers. **£80**

**Out of Habit** 21 Lisburn St ☎ 07803 795587. Easily recognizable by its sunflower-yellow stable door, this sweet little two-floored café-cum-art gallery serves up good, strong coffee, sandwiches, and a delectable array of tray bakes. Mon–Sat 8.30am–4pm.

**The Plough Inn** 3 The Square ☎ 028 9268 2985, ⓦ ploughgroup.com. Centuries-old coaching inn comprising a great-looking bistro and the retro-vibed *Vintage Rooms*, the former serving dishes such as pork belly with blue cheese sauce and truffle polenta chips (£14.50), alongside posh burgers, the latter offering everything from breakfasts and tapas to tea trays for two. Bar daily 11.30am–11pm, Fri & Sat till 1am; kitchen Mon–Sat noon–3pm & 5–9.30pm, Sun noon–8pm.

# East of Belfast

Heading east into County Down from Belfast, you've a choice of two routes: the A20, which heads due east past Stormont (see page 466) to **Newtownards**, at the head of Strangford Lough; or the A2, which heads northeast past the excellent **Ulster Folk and Transport Museum** to **Bangor**.

## Scrabo Tower

16km east of Belfast on the A20 · Easter week, April–June & Sept daily 1–5pm; July & Aug daily 10am–5pm; Oct Sun noon–4pm · Free

Following the A20, the single interesting sight as you near Newtownards is **Scrabo Tower**, whose looming presence dominates the surrounding area. The tower protrudes from the top of a rocky, gorse-strewn hump of a hill (a long-extinct volcano) – follow the signs to **Scrabo Country Park** and you'll arrive in the car park just below. The hill itself is pitted with quarries used to extract Scrabo stone, employed for all manner of local buildings. Built in 1857 as a memorial to the third Marquess of Londonderry, in recognition of his efforts for his tenants during the Great Famine, the tower looks like a monstrous rocket in its launcher, hewn out of rough black volcanic rock. The spot was originally a Bronze Age burial cairn, probably the resting place of one of the grand chieftains of the area, and there's evidence of a huge hill fort here, too. It's well worth ascending the 122 steps to the tower's top for the wonderful **views** across Strangford Lough and the healthy, blustery weather that often curls around the side of the hill.

# The Ulster Folk and Transport Museum

11km east of Belfast on the A2 • March–Sept Thurs–Sun 10am–5pm; Oct–Feb Thurs & Fri 10am–4pm, Sat & Sun 11am–4pm • Museums £9 each, combined ticket £11 • ☎ 028 9042 8428, ⓦ nmni.com • Train from Belfast Central to Cultra or bus #1 or #2 from Belfast's Laganside Buscentre (every 30min–1hr; 30min)

One of the most fascinating museums in all of Ireland, the **Ulster Folk and Transport Museum** comprises two distinct, and very large, sites straddling the A2: on one side of the road is the Folk Museum, and on the other, the Transport Museum – indeed, you'd do well to take a lengthy pause in between visiting each one.

## Folk Museum

The **folk museum** is an open-air **village** where about thirty typical buildings from all over the North, some dating from the eighteenth century, have been taken from their original sites and rebuilt here, complete with authentic furnishings. Furthermore, many of them are "inhabited" by a member of staff, garbed in period costume and keen to offer information about the buildings and their origins.

Just beyond the entrance you enter **Ballycultra Town**, whose focal point is the Diamond, framed by an assortment of community buildings, such as the late eighteenth-century **Kilmore church** (moved here in 1976), a mid-nineteenth century courthouse from Cushendall, and the delightful **Gilford Picturehouse** from County Down, a silent cinema dating from the 1850s that functioned until 1929. Just beyond here is the old **rectory**, a thatched, two-storey dwelling where you can sample some soda bread baked on the open fire. More widely dispersed is **Discovery Farm,** a vast rural area of a dozen or so traditional farm dwellings, and other buildings used in light manufacture, with assorted livestock roaming between them. Farms range from the fairly luxurious – for example the handsomely furnished **Drumnahunshin Farm** from County Armagh – to the basic (but cosy), like the **Duncrun Cottier's House**. Don't miss the **Coalisland Spade Mill**, complete with a fine cast-iron wheel; inside, an illuminating exhibition reveals that during the nineteenth century there were more than sixty spade mills in Ulster, with more types of spade produced here than in any other European country – a fact possibly explained by the fact that a sixth of Ireland's land surface is bog, from where turf (peat) is dug.

15

## Transport Museum

The superb **transport museum** packs in every conceivable form of transport, from horse-drawn carts to lifeboats and even a vertical take-off plane. First up is the **rail gallery**, featuring a stellar cast of locomotives arranged around an original turntable, the pick of which is **Old Maeve**, the largest loco ever built in Ireland. Highlights from the remarkable **road transport gallery** include a Belfast Telegraph van from 1952 and, from the late nineteenth century, a wonderfully old-fashioned ice-cream van and a Giant's Causeway tram, the first tram system in the world to be operated by hydro-electricity. Below here, in the voluminous **car gallery**, is a Model T Ford, a Sunbeam that won the 1924 Spanish Grand Prix, and a DeLorean sports car (of *Back to the Future* fame) from the infamously defunct factory.

As a fascinating aside, the **Titanica** exhibition documents the origin and fate of the *Titanic* as well as of her sister ships, *Olympic* and *Britannic*, built by the Harland and Wolff shipyard and collectively known as *Olympic*-class (see page 461). Inevitably the focus is on the *Titanic* itself, with a stack of artefacts salvaged from the wreck, including part of a porthole, a soup tureen and a launch ticket among other poignant items. Also on this site is a miniature railway that runs on summer Saturdays. You'd be wise to bring a picnic, but if you haven't, there are **tea rooms** on both sites.

## Crawfordsburn Country Park

Bridge Road South, Helen's Bay • Daily: March–May & Sept–Oct 9am–7pm; June–Aug 9am–9pm; Nov–Feb 9am–4.30pm; Visitor Centre daily 10am–4pm • Free • ☎ 028 9185 3621, ⓦ discovernorthernireland.com

The short stretch of coast east from Helen's Bay is part of the **Crawfordsburn Country Park**, an estate handed down from the Scottish Presbyterian Crawford family, then acquired by Lord Dufferin (whose mother Helen gave her name to the bay) and which is now in public hands. Its glens and dells are replete with beeches, cypresses, exotic conifers, cedars, the usual burst of rhododendrons and also a Californian giant redwood, but the park's best features are the wild-flower meadow and the woodland planted with native species. From the visitor centre, there are three delightful **trails**: the Glen trail (45min), the Meadow trail (1hr 15min) – part of which skirts **Crawfordsburn beach** – and the Coastal trail (2hr), which heads down to **Helen's Bay beach** and then onto Grey Point Fort.

## 15 Grey Point Fort

The Fort, Bangor • April to mid-Sept daily 10am–5pm; mid-Sept to March Sat & Sun 10am–4pm • Free • ☎ 028 9082 3207

From Crawfordsburn Country Park, the path to **Grey Point Fort** leads through the best of the woodland, under a fine nineteenth-century railway viaduct and up to a waterfall at the head of the glen and thence to the bay. Positioned to command the mouth of Belfast Lough, along with its sister fort at Kilroot on the other side, Grey Point has an impressive battery of gun emplacements, ready to challenge the shipping that entered the lough during the two world wars. In the event, the two six-inch breech-loading guns were never fired except in practice (local residents had to be warned to open their windows and doors to prevent blast damage), apart from one occasion in World War II, when a merchant ship failed to respond to the signal "heave to or be sunk" and received a warning shot across its bows. The guns were sold for scrap in 1957 when the Coast Artillery was disbanded. After the fort was opened to the public in 1987, an identical six-inch gun was relocated here from the prison on Spike Island in Cork harbour. There's also a selection of photos showing the original guns and their positions; but it's really as a **viewpoint** that the fort is worth a visit for nowadays.

## Bangorand around

With a curving bay set between a pair of symmetrical headlands, **BANGOR**'s sheltered position made it ideal for exploitation as a holiday resort. The town has been hugely popular with Belfast people since the railway came in the 1860s, but today it's as much a suburb of Belfast as a holiday spot. Still, it's well worth a visit for its renovated waterfront, while inland, the superb little museum and walled garden – inside the old castle grounds – make for a most enjoyable hour or two. If you're here in August it's well worth seeking out what's on as part of the **Open House Festival** (ⓦ openhousefestival.com), an inspired, month-long programme of music, art and culinary happenings taking place in locations all over town, and the suburbs.

### North Down Museum

Town Hall, Castle Park Ave • Tues–Sat 10am–4.30pm, Sun noon–4.30pm, plus July & Aug Mon • Free • ☎ 028 9127 1200, ⓦ andculture.org.uk

Bangor's period of greatest historical significance was almost entirely associated with its **abbey**, which was founded by St Comgall in 586 AD, and from which missionaries set forth to convert pagan Europe. Though the abbey remained powerful for eight hundred years, there's not a trace of the building left. The only vestige of its fame is the *Antiphonarium Benchorense*, one of the oldest-known ecclesiastical manuscripts, consisting of collects, anthems and some religious poems; the original now lies in the Ambrosian Library in Milan, but you can view a facsimile of it in the **North Down Museum**, tucked away in the old stables of Bangor Castle. Other displays trace the rise of the Ward family (see page 531), who were largely responsible for the town's development and who built the castle.

Best of all are the archaeological discoveries, notably the Ballycroghan swords, three superb bronze weapons dating from 500 AD, and the ninth-century Bangor Bell, a splendid one-piece casting which was retrieved from a local graveyard in 1780. On a more recent note, there's a lovely little exhibition on the history of local cinematography and, more specifically, the once beautiful Art Deco Toni cinema, which stood on Hamilton Road; once the hub of Bangor's social scene – it also functioned as a ballroom – the cinema's last screening was in 1983 before it burnt down in 1992.

## Bangor Castle Walled Garden

Castle Park • April, May, Sept & Oct daily 10am–6pm; June–Aug Mon–Thurs 10.30am–8pm, Fri–Sun 10am–6pm • Free • ☎ 028 9127 1200

**15**

A short walk from the North Down Museum, through the tree-laden Ward Park, you'll come to the delightful **Bangor Castle Walled Garden**. Originally the site of a Victorian walled garden, which supplied the castle kitchen with vegetable, fruits and herbs, the garden fell into disrepair after World War I, before its quite spectacular renovation just a few years ago. Hidden beyond a 4m-high redbrick wall, the garden is divided into quadrants, namely, the flower garden, the herb and topiary garden, kitchen garden and damp garden; separating these are neatly gravelled avenues with fragrant, rose-covered arches, while a beautifully sculpted fountain stands as the garden's central feature. On a warm summer's day, it's a wonderful spot to rest up, and there's a café on-site too.

## Somme Museum

233 Bangor Rd, 8km south of Bangor on the A21 • Visits by guided tour hourly April–June & Sept–Nov Mon–Thurs 10am–4pm, Sat 11am–4pm; July & Aug Mon–Sat 10am–5pm; Dec–March Mon–Thurs 10am–4pm & first Sat of each month 11am–4pm • £8.50 • ☎ 028 9182 3202, ⓦ sommeasscoiation.com

The **Somme Museum** features re-created front-line trenches staffed by guides in battledress who provide a sobering and moving account of the role of the Irish and Ulster divisions in the futile World War I battle that took place in July 1916 – 5500 men of the 36th (Ulster) Division alone were reported dead, wounded or missing in only the first two days. The Battle of the Somme itself is brought to life courtesy of an unusually informative audiovisual presentation.

### ARRIVAL AND DEPARTURE
### BANGOR AND AROUND

**By train** The train station is at the top of Main St, which itself leads down to the waterfront.
Destinations Belfast (Mon–Sat every 15–30min, Sun hourly; 30–40min).

**By bus** The bus station is adjacent to the train station.
Destinations Belfast (Mon–Sat every 20–30min, Sun 5; 50min); Newtownards (Mon–Sat every 30min, Sun 7; 20min).

### INFORMATION AND ACTIVITIES

**Tourist office** Down by the marina in the Tower House at 34 Quay St (Mon, Tues, Thurs & Fri 9.15am–5pm, Wed 10am–5pm, Sat 10am–4pm, plus May–Aug Sun 1–5pm; ☎ 028 9127 0069, ⓦ visitardsandnorthdown.com).
**Fishing and boat trips** Bangor Boats (☎ 07510 006

000) runs family-friendly, deep-sea fishing trips from the harbour (July & Aug daily 9.15am & 6.30pm; June, Sept & Oct call for times; £17), and short boat trips (July & Aug 2pm; £5) around the bay from the Pickie Fun Park.

### ACCOMMODATION

★ **Cairn Bay Lodge** 278 Seacliff Rd ☎ 028 9146 7636, ⓦ cairnbaylodge.com. Charming, family-run guesthouse with eight beautifully finished rooms, all quite distinct from one another, and some of which have stunning bay views. The gourmet breakfast is reason alone to pitch up here: smoked salmon omelette with rocket and lemon crème fraiche, or crab with scrambled eggs and chilli jam are just two of the possibilities. **£90**

**Old Inn** Main St, Crawfordsburn, 4km west of Bangor ☎028 9185 3255, ⓦtheoldinn.com. This rambling, centuries-old inn is where CS Lewis honeymooned with his wife, Joy Gresham, in 1958. Little has changed since that time, it would seem, though that's no bad thing; the individually designed rooms, variously sporting oak beamed ceilings, wood-panelled walls and sumptuous fabrics, are run through with character. **£105**

**Salty Dog** 10–12 Seacliff Rd ☎028 9127 0696, ⓦsalty dogbangor.com. By far the most attractive of an otherwise unappealing cluster of hotels down by the marina, this smallish hotel has a range of differently configured rooms decked out in fetching cream and mauve; try and bag a sea-facing room if you can, though these do cost more. **£85**

### EATING AND DRINKING

**Blu BBQ** 52 High St ☎028 9147 0698, ⓦblubbq.co.uk. Authentic wood-smoked barbecued meats from the grill, including beef ribs (£15.95) and peppered burger with sautéed mushrooms (£9.95), make this a tempting possibility for dinner; the decor is muted and the atmosphere pleasingly informal. Wed–Fri 5–9pm, Sat 12.30–9.30pm, Sun 12.30–8pm.

**The Boat House** 1A Seacliff Rd ☎028 9146 9253, ⓦboat housebangor.com. The cool, brick-vaulted cellar of the old Harbour Master's Office – an inconspicuous grey stone building by the marina – is now home to a distinguished restaurant whose wonderfully original dishes, like Ballinteer quail with Alsace bacon popcorn and girolles, and mackerel with pickled watermelon and lemon sherbert, will leave you purring. Three-course evening menu £30, plus five- and seven-course tasting menus (£45–60). Wed–Sat noon–2.30pm & 5.30–9pm, Sun 1–9pm.

**Jamaica Inn** 188 Seacliff Rd ☎028 9147 1610, ⓦthe jamaicainn.co.uk. In a fantastic location overlooking the bay, this warm and lively inn is by far the best spot in Bangor for a good night out, with live music (folk, rock, bluegrass) several nights a week and a rollickingly good pub quiz on Tues. Daily 11.30am–midnight.

**The Starfish** 278 Seacliff Rd ☎028 9146 7636, ⓦcairnbay lodge.com. As warm and welcoming as the guesthouse it's housed in, the super daytime café – park yourself outside on the summery terrace – offers up a wicked section of breakfast and brunches (chilli eggs, steak burger), though most punters make a trip here to inspect the awesome crabs benedict (£8.50). Tues–Sat 9am–4pm (food served until 2.30pm).

# Strangford Lough

Ancient annals record that **Strangford Lough** was formed around 1650 BC by the sea sweeping in over the lands of Brena. This created a beautiful, calm inlet, the archipelago-like pieces of land along its inner arm fringed with brown and yellow bladderwrack and tangleweed, and tenanted by a rich gathering of bird life during the warmer months and vast flocks of geese and waders in the winter.

Travelling the scenic **western shore** is enjoyable in itself, but there are a couple of spots worth making for, the first of which is **Castle Espie Wildfowl and Wetland Centre**, from where narrow roads wind down to **Mahee Island**. From here, back on the road along the lough, follow the signs to Ardmillan, Killinchy and then Whiterock to reach **Sketrick Island**. The tiny coves and inlets at the feet of little drumlins continue as far as Killyleagh, almost any of them worth exploring. The **eastern edge** of Strangford Lough is not as indented as its opposite shore but betters it in having a major road (the continuation of the A20) that runs close to the water virtually all the way down. Also, the scenery is delightful, and there's the engrossing **Mount Stewart** house and gardens to stop off en route to **Portaferry**.

## Mount Stewart House and Garden

8km southeast of Newtonwards • Gardens daily: March–Oct 10am–5pm; Nov–Feb 10am–4pm; house April–Oct daily 11am–5pm; Nov–March Sat & Sun 11am–3pm • £10 • ☎028 4278 8387, ⓦnationaltrust.org.uk/mount-stewart • Bus #9 and #10 (Mon–Sat 9 daily, Sun 2) from Belfast's Laganside Buscentre

Pressed up hard against the shore road is **Mount Stewart House and Gardens**, the ancestral home of the Londonderry family. Leading protagonists of the Protestant

Ascendancy, its members included Lord Castlereagh, who was Foreign Secretary under Pitt the Younger and is best remembered for guiding the Act of Union into operation.

### The gardens

The undoubted highlight of the estate is the 98 acres of **gardens**, laid out by Edith, Lady Londonderry, wife of the seventh marquess, in the 1920s – and a thorough job she made of it: among others, there are **Spanish** and **Italian** gardens, a **Sunk Garden**, and the **Shamrock Garden** (with a topiary harp and an appropriately leaved Red Hand of Ulster). The trees and shrubs here are no more than seventy to eighty years old, but they've grown at such a remarkable rate that they look twice that. The principal reason for this is the unusually warm and humid microclimate: the gardens catch the east-coast sun, causing a heavy overnight dew, and the Gulf Stream washes the shores only a stone's throw away. Despite the northerly latitude, conditions here rival those of Cornwall and Devon. Amid all this lush greenery, look out for the **Dodo terrace** which flaunts various bits of giant statuary, including the eponymous bird alongside lizards, griffins and the like. There are numerous marked **trails**, too, ranging from just under 1km to 3km.

**15**

### The house

The **house** itself is certainly worth viewing, with guided tours (every 15min) in the morning, and a free-flow system in place from 1pm. Among the splendid (and occasionally eccentric) furniture inside is a set of 22 Empire chairs used by the delegates to the Congress of Vienna in 1815, who included the Duke of Wellington and Talleyrand; the chairs were a gift to Castlereagh's brother Lord Stewart, another high-ranking diplomat of the time. The Continental connection is flaunted further in bedrooms named after various historically important cities: Rome, St Petersburg, Madrid, Moscow and Sebastopol (from the time of the Crimean War). The house contains a number of **paintings**, particularly portraits of Castlereagh's political contemporaries, but the most notable and largest is **Rubbing Down** (1799) by George Stubbs, showing the celebrated thoroughbred, *Hambletonian*, being rubbed down after a victory at Newmarket. Continuing the horsey theme, in the dazzling silver collection, look out for a pair of hooves (which have been fashioned into inkwells) that belonged to Fighting Charlie, winner of the 1965 Ascot Gold Cup and ridden by the great Lester Piggott.

## Portaferry

**Portaferry**, at the mouth of the lough, is a pretty spot from which to admire the marvellous **sunset** looking across the "Narrows" to Strangford, a view enhanced by a ten-minute climb to the stump of the old windmill just behind the town. It's quite likely that you'll wind up here, as it's the departure point for ferries across to Strangford and the Lescale Peninsula.

### Exploris Aquarium

Castle St • Daily 10am–5pm (last admission 4pm) • £9.50 • ☎ 028 4272 8062, ⦿ explorisni.com

Portaferry's principal attraction is the **Exploris** aquarium, featuring the North's only **seal sanctuary**, where they've been rescuing and rehabilitating common and grey seal pups for nearly thirty years. Much better than your average aquarium, it has bright, well-kept tanks containing native and tropical fish, alongside menacing black-tip and white-tip reef sharks, an otter enclosure and a reptile room. The aquarium also has a "touch tank" for lots of hands-on fun, plus daily feeding sessions for otters and seals, and various talks.

**15**

**By bus** Buses depart from the main square.
Destinations Belfast (Mon–Sat 3 daily; 1hr 25min); Newtownards (Mon–Sat every 30min–1hr, Sun 4; 50min–1hr 10min).
**By ferry** Regular ferries make the 5min ride across the lips

of the lough to Strangford (every 30min, Mon–Fri 7.45am–10.45pm, Sat 8.15am–11.15pm, Sun 9.45am–10.45pm; ☎028 4488 1637; £1 single, £2 return; car £5.80 single, £10 return).

**ACCOMMODATION AND EATING**

**Fiddlers Green** 10 Church St ☎028 4272 8393, ⓦfiddlersgreenportaferry.com. You can't miss the turquoise-green painted exterior of this erstwhile grocery store – or one of the *Game of Thrones'* doors (see page 487) – now a convivial hostelry, with sing-along folk sessions and traditional music on Fri and Sat, plus quiz night on Thurs. Mon–Thurs 11.30am–11pm, Fri & Sat 11.30am–1am, Sun 12.30pm–midnight.

**Portaferry Hotel** 10 The Strand ☎028 4272 8231, ⓦportaferryhotel.com. This distinctive all-white building right by the ferry harbours fourteen decent, high-ceilinged rooms with antique furnishings and smart sash windows; there's a £20 supplement for lough-facing rooms. At the hotel's restaurant or bar (they serve the same menu), you can feast on the likes of Strangford Lough mussels in garlic, or smoked haddock chowder (£11.50). **£90**

# Ballyquintin Point and Kearney

The coast road south of Portaferry leads to **Ballyquintin Point** and, on the way, passes the entrance lane to **St Cowey's Wells**, where the faithful optimist is spoilt for choice: there's a drinking well, a wishing well and a well for bathing sore eyes. Look out for the rock nearby – the indentations are supposed to mark the places where the saint's hands and feet rested as he prayed. Northeast from here **KEARNEY** is a charming seaside village, consisting almost entirely of whitewashed cottages and now mostly owned by the National Trust. You can walk from here to **Kearney Point**, an often blustery ten-minute stroll with panoramic views across the Irish Sea.

# Castle Espie Wildfowl and Wetland Centre

78 Ballydrain Rd · Daily 10am–5pm · £9.40 · ☎028 9187 4146, ⓦwwt.org.uk/wetland-centres/castle-espie

At the **Castle Espie Wildfowl and Wetland Centre**, admission earnings are ploughed back into conserving the wetlands area for the seven thousand birds that visit it as well as the resident population of waterfowl, including the largest gathering of ducks, geese and swans in Ireland; the outdoor duckery is not to be missed, particularly in summer when the new hatchlings arrive. Part of the wetlands site was formerly a brick and lime works, and the old kiln here has been superbly converted into the **Limekiln Observatory**, now the centre's principal birdwatching spot. The centre also has a coffee shop and art gallery and hosts numerous events throughout the year, related both to ornithology and arts and crafts, as well as plenty of activities for children, including a climbing wall in the Limestone Pavilion nearby.

# Mahee Island

Visitor Centre Easter–Sept daily 10am–6pm; Oct–Easter Sun noon–4pm · Free · ☎028 9182 6846

**Mahee Island**, named after St Mochaoi, supposedly the first abbot of the island, is reached via a twisting lane and several causeways. Heading past the crumbling remains of sixteenth-century Mahee Castle at the entrance to the island, and over the final causeway, you come to the Celtic **Nendrum Monastic Site**, a few hundred yards further on. It's a marvellously isolated spot, surrounded on three sides by water. Annals and excavations indicate that a sizeable community lived here from the seventh century onwards, but the remaining ruins probably date from the twelfth century at the very earliest. It was clearly a substantial establishment, with church, round tower, school and living quarters all housed in a cashel of three concentric wards. Today, the inner wall shelters the ruined church, and a reconstructed sundial uses some of the original remnants. There's an illuminating reconstruction map at the site and a helpful visitor centre.

# The Lecale region

Jutting into the southern reach of Strangford Lough, the **Lecale Peninsula** is above all **St Patrick** country. Ireland's patron saint was a Roman Briton, first carried off as a youth from somewhere near Carlisle in northern England by Irish raiders. He spent six years in slavery in Ireland before escaping home again and, at the age of 30, decided to return to Ireland as a bishop, to spread Christianity. Christianity had already reached Ireland a while earlier, probably through traders and other slaves, and, indeed, St Patrick was not in fact the first bishop of Ireland, but he remains easily the most famous. He arrived in Ireland this second time, according to his biographer Muirchú (also his erstwhile captor, converted), on the shores of the Lecale region, and his first Irish sermon was preached at **Saul** in 432. Today the region commemorates the association with sites at Struell Wells and Saul, as well as at **Downpatrick**.

A great way to see the region is to tackle the **Lecale Way**, a 75km waymarked walking tour of the peninsula starting in Downpatrick and running to Strangford and thence around the coast to Killough and onwards to Newcastle – maps are available from the Downpatrick tourist office (see page 530).

## Downpatrick

**DOWNPATRICK**, 37km south of Belfast, is a pleasant enough place of little more than ten thousand people, and its compact size and the proximity of some rich and well-preserved historical sites make for an easy and worthwhile day's visit.

The **Hill of Down**, at the north of the town, was once a rise of great strategic worth, fought over long before the arrival of St Patrick made it famous. A **Celtic fort** of mammoth proportions was built here and was called first Arús Cealtchair, then later Dún Cealtchair. Celtchar was one of the Red Branch Knights, a friend of the then King of Ulster, Conor MacNessa, and, according to the *Book of the Dun Cow*, "an angry terrific hideous man with a long nose, huge ears, apple eyes, and coarse dark-grey hair". The Dún part of the fort's name went on to become the name of the county, as well as the town.

By the time the Norman knight **John de Courcy** made his mark here in the late twelfth century, a settlement was well established. Pushing north out of Leinster, and defeating Rory MacDonlevy, King of Ulster, de Courcy dispossessed the Augustinian canons who occupied the Hill of Down to establish his own **Benedictine abbey**. He flaunted as much pomp as he could to mark the occasion, and one of his festive tricks was to import what were supposedly the disinterred bodies of St Brigid and St Columba to join St Patrick, who was (allegedly) buried here. One of the earliest accounts of Patrick's life asserts that he's buried in a church near the sea; and since a later account admits that "where his bones are, no man knows", Downpatrick's claim seems as good as any.

### St Patrick Centre

St Patrick's Square • Mon–Sat 9am–5pm • £5.75 • ⓣ 028 4461 9000, ⓦ saintpatrickcentre.com

Just off the main drag, Market Street, the large glass-and-brick-built **St Patrick Centre** aims to recount the life of the saint and his influence in extensive detail. Its hagiographic, multimedia approach is pretty arid, however, and by the time you've been round its maze of interactive displays and sat through the five-screen 180-degree virtual helicopter ride through Christian history, you might even wish you'd never heard of him.

15

**15**

## ON THE TRAIL OF ST PATRICK

About 6.5km west of Inch Abbey (take the B2 to Annacloy and then the first turning on the left), **Loughinisland** is probably the most worthwhile of all the sites in the area associated with St Patrick, and indeed one of the most idyllic spots in County Down. It comprises a reed-fringed lake contained by ten or so little drumlin hills, one of which forms an island in the lake. Here, across a short causeway, are the ruins of three small churches, set next door to each other. The smallest one, **MacCartan's Chapel** (1636), has an entrance door little taller than a metre high. The larger northern church was used by both Catholics and Protestants until they quarrelled on a wet Sunday around 1720 over which camp should remain outside during the service. The Protestants left and built their church at Seaforde instead.

The next St Patrick landmark is at **Saul**, around 3km northeast of Downpatrick off the Strangford road. St Patrick is said to have landed nearby, sailing up the tiny River Slaney, and it was here that he first preached, immediately converting Dichu, the lord of this territory. Dichu gave Patrick a barn as his first base and the saint frequently returned here to rest from his travelling missions – legend has it that he died here in 461. Today a **memorial chapel** and round tower in the Celtic Revival style, built of pristine silver-grey granite in 1932 to commemorate the 1500th anniversary of the saint's arrival, is open to visitors (daily 9am–5pm; free). Two cross-carved stones from between the eighth and twelfth centuries still stand in the graveyard, though there's not a trace of the medieval monastery built here by St Malachy in the twelfth century.

A short distance further south, between Saul and Raholp, **St Patrick's Shrine** sits atop Slieve Patrick, a tract of hillside much like a slalom ski-slope, with the Stations of the Cross marking a pathway up. This huge Mourne-granite statue, clad at the base with bronze panels depicting Patrick's life, was erected in the same year as Saul church. The summit is no more than a twenty-minute climb and offers a commanding view of the county, a vista of the endless little bumps of this drumlin-filled territory.

At **Raholp** is the ruined church of **St Tassach**, named after the bishop from whom the dying Patrick received the sacrament. Patrick gave Raholp to Tassach as a reward for crafting a case for Christ's crozier, the Bachall Isú, one of Ireland's chief relics until its destruction in 1538. The ruins here were mainly restored in 1915 from the rubble that lay around, but their material is thought to date from the eleventh century. If you're eager for the complete St Patrick experience, it's 1.5km from the car park of the *Slaney Inn* in Raholp to the spot on the lough shore where he is believed to have first landed: head towards Strangford, then left down Myra Road; cross the main Strangford road and turn left at the first fork; at the bottom of the hill, take the track on the right to the shore.

The easiest way to find the last St Patrick site, **Struell Wells**, is to return to Downpatrick. Take the Ardglass road southeast, turn left just past the hospital, then right down a narrow track into a secluded rock-faced valley and you'll come to the wells. The waters here, believed to be the wells referred to in early accounts of Patrick's mission, have been attributed with healing powers for centuries. In 1744 Walter Harris described the scene: "Vast throngs of rich and poor resort on Midsummer Eve and the Friday before Lammas, some in the hopes of obtaining health, and others to perform penance." The site contains a couple of wells, one for drinking and another known as the eye well whose waters are supposed to have curative powers, and men's and women's bathhouses. Mass is still said here on midsummer night, and people bring containers to carry the water home with them.

## Down Cathedral

36 English St • Mon–Sat 9.30am–4pm, Sun 1–4pm • Free • ☎ 028 4461 4922, ⓦ downcathedral.org

Uphill from the St Patrick Centre, you'll reach the elegant, spacious Mall, at the end of which stands **Down Cathedral**. Built by John de Courcy, the cathedral was destroyed in 1316 during Edward Bruce's invasion, and a new abbey erected in the early sixteenth century was even more short-lived. Today's cathedral dates basically from the early

1800s, though it incorporates many aspects of earlier incarnations. Its unique feature is the private box-pews, characteristic of the Regency period and the only ones remaining in use in Ireland.

In the adjacent graveyard, you'll find the site of Patrick's supposed **grave**, marked today by a rough granite boulder put there around 1900 by Francis Joseph Biggar to cover a huge hole created by earlier pilgrims searching for the saints' bones.

### Down County Museum

The Mall • Mon–Fri 10am–4.30pm, Sat & Sun 1.30–5pm • Free • ☎ 028 4461 5218, ⟨W⟩ downcountymuseum.com

Where the Mall segues into English Street, both streets crowded with handsome Georgian buildings, you come to the eighteenth-century jail, now home to the **Down County Museum**. The three-storey Georgian **Governor's House** in the centre of the walled courtyard houses a local history gallery entitled "Down through Time"; the displays are both varied and enlightening, ranging from some superb artefacts – notably Bronze Age tools and Norman grave covers – to photos of local worthies, including the town's most famous musical export, the indie band, Ash. Not to be missed, either, are a couple of beautifully embroidered **quilts**: the Ballybranagh Quilt, dating from 1849, depicts biblical scenes, as well as important events that have taken place in Down, while the Killyleagh Quilt is a dazzling velvet and silk patchwork made by local girl Martha Geddis in 1894.

The **cell block** at the back of the enclosure once held the United Irishman Thomas Russell, who had already survived the 1798 Rebellion but was found guilty of complicity in Robert Emmet's uprising and was duly hanged in 1803 from a sill outside the main gate of the jail; the restored cells remain, while an exhibition in the neighbouring room displays one of the original, graffiti-strewn doors. Here, too, you can view the last speech of William Gaddis before his execution for the murder of one Adam Heslip during a robbery in 1818, and a selection of hideous contraptions, notably a "Scold's Bridal", an iron muzzle designed to stop women gossiping.

To the rear, a specially constructed extension houses the 1100-year old **Downpatrick High Cross**. Ornamented with biblical scenes, this Mourne granite cross had, from 1897 to 2014, stood outside the east end of the cathedral, before it was dismantled, cleaned up and reassembled; a replica now stands in its place outside the cathedral. Film footage recalls the various stages of the project, but otherwise this illuminating little exhibition includes stone architectural fragments and some exquisite metalwork.

### Mound of Down

Between the jail and the barricaded courthouse and inauspiciously tucked behind a secondary school, you'll find the **Mound of Down**, a smaller prominence than the Hill of Down and half-submerged in undergrowth. It's in fact 18m high and inside its outer ditch is a horseshoe-shaped central mound of rich grass. Once a rath, or round hill fort, it was considerably altered and enlarged to create a Norman motte-and-bailey fortification, with a **bretasche** (a wooden archery tower) at the centre. Its view of the Hill of Down clearly displays the attractions the hill had for its earliest settlers; it's believed by some to be the site of the palace of the kings of Ulster.

### Downpatrick and County Down Railway

Market St • Mid-June to mid-Sept Sat & Sun 1–4pm, plus bank holidays and special event days • £8 return • ☎ 028 4461 5779, ⟨W⟩ downrail.co.uk

At the rear of the market car park is the enthusiast-run **Downpatrick and County Down Railway**, which operates short steam-train trips along a restored section of the Belfast–Newcastle main line to Inch Abbey. The station has a small photographic exhibition (free) on railways in County Down, as well as several steam and diesel locomotives on show.

15

**By bus** The bus station (☎ 028 4461 2384) is on Market St, 100m or so south of the St Patrick Centre.
Destinations Ardglass (Mon–Fri 11 daily, Sat 7, Sun 2; 25min); Belfast (Mon–Fri every 30min, Sat hourly, Sun 8; 1hr); Castlewellan (Mon–Fri 10 daily, Sat 4, Sun 3; 30min); Killough (Mon–Fri 9 daily, Sat 6, Sun 2; 20min); Newcastle (Mon–Sat every 30min–1hr, Sun 6; 20–35min); Newry (4–6 daily; 1hr 15min); Strangford (Mon–Fri 9 daily, Sat 5; 30min).

**Tourist office** Inside the St Patrick Centre (Mon–Fri 9am–5pm, Sat 9am–5.30pm; plus Sun 1–5pm July & Aug; ☎ 028 4461 2233); offers an accommodation booking service.

## ACCOMMODATION

**Denvir's** 16 English St ☎ 028 4461 2012, ⓦ denvirs.com. One of Ireland's oldest coaching inns, with six en-suite rooms that are surprisingly simple, furnished throughout in dark, heavy wood, but cosy all the same. **£70**
**Dunleath House** 33 St Patrick's Drive ☎ 028 4461 3221, ⓦ dunleathhousebb.com. Tucked away in a residential area very close to the centre of town, this welcoming family home has four good-sized, ground-floor rooms with French doors leading off to a patio area; cracking breakfast as well. **£80**
**The Mill** Drumcullen Rd, Ballydugan ☎ 028 4661 3654, ⓦ ballyduganmill.com. This converted flour mill, dating from 1792, retains eleven rustically styled rooms on the building's upper two floors, each with exposed beams and rough-hewn stone walls and variously sleeping one- to four-people. The Mill also has its own café and restaurant. **£90**

## EATING AND DRINKING

**The Daily Grind** 20a St Patrick's Ave ☎ 028 4461 7173. The permanently packed tables will tell you how popular this place is; pop in for late morning coffee or one of the utterly scrumptious fruit salads, perhaps topped with a honey mustard vinaigrette (£5.50). Mon–Sat 10am–4pm.
**Denvir's** 16 English St ☎ 028 4461 2012, ⓦ denvirs.com. Chunky oak beams, flagstoned floors and a fine inglenook fireplace comprise the restaurant, lounge and snug bars of this hotel, and provide the setting for a very creditable all-day menu (the three course lunch is top value at £15), featuring, for example, Irish pork and leek sausages with champ mash and caramelised onion jus, in addition to some rather lovely Sunday roasts. Daily noon–11pm.

## ENTERTAINMENT

**Down Arts Centre** 2–6 Irish St ☎ 028 4461 0747, ⓦ www.downartscentre.com. The excellent Down Arts Centre has an extensive programme of events, and you'll find all genres of art and performance here, from poetry and painting to music and comedy.

# Inch Abbey

Around 1.5km northwest of Downpatrick • Open access

Lying on the other side of the Quoile Marsh from Downpatrick are the remains of the Cistercian **Inch Abbey**. The exquisite setting is visible from the town, but the river's intervention means that the only access is 1.5km out along the Belfast road, taking the left turn down Inch Abbey Road just before the defunct *Abbey Lodge Hotel*, followed by another signposted left turn shortly afterwards – alternatively, you can take a train ride from Downpatrick (see page 529). The site was once an island, and an earlier nearby foundation was destroyed by John de Courcy in 1177 because it was fortified against him. In atonement he built a replacement here and, in 1180, invited Cistercian monks from Furness Abbey in Lancashire over to populate the building, with the intention of establishing a strong centre of English influence. Little of it is now left standing – it was burnt in 1404 and monastic life was completely over by the mid-sixteenth century. Still, its setting, among small glacial drumlins and woodland, is picturesque, and strolling up the valley sides is a pleasant way to pass half an hour or so.

# Strangford

If you're following the A2 round the coast of the Ards Peninsula, your arrival on Lecale will be at tiny **STRANGFORD** village, directly opposite Portaferry and linked by a regular ferry service. The earlier name of this inlet was Lough Cuan (*cuan* being Irish for "harbour" or "haven"), but it was renamed Strangford by the Vikings over a thousand years ago because of the strong eight-knot current in the narrows. The centre of the village is a neatly manicured green framed by pastel-coloured stone tenements, while its small harbour makes a pleasant setting for watching the to and fro of the ferry boats. Good (if busy) times to be here are at the beginning of July for the **Strangford Sailing Regatta**, and the end of August for the **Strangford Festival**, when the quayside and village green burst into life with all manner of activities, including traditional music, food and craft fairs, and raft races.

## ARRIVAL AND DEPARTURE                                                    STRANGFORD

**By bus** Buses from/to Downpatrick (Mon–Fri 10 daily, Sat 5; 30min) stop by the main square just up from the ferry landing stage.

**By ferry** Regular ferries make the 5min trip across to Portaferry (every 30min, Mon–Fri 7.30am–10.30pm, Sat 8am–11pm, Sun 9.30am–10.30pm; ☎ 028 4488 1637; £1 single, £2 return; car £5.80 single, £10 return).

## ACCOMMODATION AND EATING

★ **The Artisan Cookhouse** 4 Kildare St ☎ 028 4488 1654, ⓦ artisancookhouse.com. A short distance up from the village green on the Downpatrick road, this sparkling little bistro is highly rated in these parts with a stylish menu covering all bases: crispy Cajun squid with mango salsa (£11), wild rainbow trout with lumpfish roe and champagne, and seared fillet of pork with apple bon bons and pancetta (£17). Wed, Thurs & Sun 10am–8pm, Fri & Sat 10am–9pm.

**The Cuan** Village green ☎ 028 4488 1222, ⓦ thecuan. com. This long-established inn offers nine elegantly furnished, fragrant-smelling rooms with splashes of artwork. In addition, there's a splendid restaurant with plenty of fish dishes on offer; and if you fancy a quiet pint, make for the sociable bar, which had the honour of receiving the first *Game of Thrones* door (see page 487). **£90**

**Lobster Pot** 9–11 The Square ☎ 028 4488 1288, ⓦ the lobsterpotstrangford.com. If fresh lobster straight off the boat takes your fancy, then look no further than this smart but easy-going, restaurant; lobster, prawn and mussel tagliatelle (£16.95), and hot smoked mackerel with Jersey Royals, are typically mouthwatering dishes. Daily noon–9.30pm.

15

# Castle Ward

1.5km west of Strangford on the A25 • House daily mid-March to Oct noon–5pm; grounds daily: April–Sept 10am–8pm; Oct–March 10am–4pm • £10 • ☎ 028 4488 1204, ⓦ nationaltrust.org.uk/castle-ward

The most worthwhile place in the immediate surrounds of Strangford is **Castle Ward**, the eighteenth-century residence of Bernard and Anne Ward, later Lord and Lady Bangor, but now owned by the National Trust. It's a thoroughly eccentric building, thanks to the opposing tastes of its creators (they later split up): Bernard's half is in the Classical Palladian style, Anne's neo-Gothic, a split carried through into the design and decor of the rooms inside. This is manifest in Anne's Arabesque boudoir, all flowing, fancy curves and pointy bits, a stark counterpoint to the neat straight lines of Bernard's drawing room. There are some entertainingly oddball exhibits too, not least a display of stuffed squirrels posing as boxers, believe it or not.

Having absorbed all that the house has to offer, there's plenty to explore within the extensive **grounds**, including a sixteenth-century tower house (Old Castle Ward) and the fifteenth-century **Audley's Castle** just outside on the lough shore, with a superb view across the lake. Castle Ward has also featured prominently in *Game of Thrones*, so fans might like to pick up a filming locations map at reception.

# Cloghy Rocks

A signposted turning 1.5km south of Strangford directs you to the **Cloghy Rocks** observation point. The rocks themselves are 20m or so out in the lough and for most of the day look decidedly inconsequential, but this is the best place to spot basking **seals**, both common and grey seals. They're well camouflaged against the seaweed, so a pair of binoculars would be handy. Here, too, you can see herons, redshank and oystercatchers, and you may even be lucky enough to spot an otter or two.

## St Patrick's Well

1.5km south of Ballyhornan

**St Patrick's Well** is set on a wonderful rocky shore between Ballyhornan and Chapeltown. You can get to within a few hundred metres of the well by road, but the best approach is to start from Ballyhornan – where you'll see a narrow strip of water separating the village from Guns Island, accessible at low tide and still used for grazing – and follow the foreshore path for about a 1.5km. The well is easily spotted: it looks rather like a sheep dip with concrete walls, but with a crucifix at its head. Its holy water has turned into something closer to stagnant consommé than an ever-youthful source of new life.

## 15 Ardglass

**ARDGLASS** is set on the side of a lovely natural inlet. Its domestic buildings, rising steeply from the harbour, are interspersed with seven fortified mansions, towers and turrets, dating from a vigorous English revival in the sixteenth century, when a trading company first arrived to found a colony here. In the nineteenth century, Ardglass was the most thriving **fishing** port in the North; and even today, aside from the prawns, herrings and whitefish brought in by the fishing fleet, there's very good rod-fishing to be had off the end of the pier for codling, pollack and coalfish. It's often sometimes possible to buy direct from fishing boats or from the cannery on the quay.

### The castles

The best preserved of the fortifications, though it's no longer open to the public, is **Jordan's Castle**, next door to the *Anchor* pub on the Low Road, the most elegant and highly developed of all the Down tower houses. The tall, crenellated building with white-plaster trimming up on the hill was once **King's Castle**; its nineteenth-century renovation is obvious, as is modern work to turn it into a nursing home. The lone ornamental-looking turret on the hilltop is **Isabella's Tower**, a nineteenth-century folly created by Aubrey de Vere Beauclerc as a gazebo for his disabled daughter.

### ARRIVAL AND DEPARTURE                                                         ARDGLASS

**By bus** Buses stop on the main road just above the harbour.

**Destinations** Downpatrick (Mon–Fri 12 daily, Sat 7, Sun 2; 20–30min); Killough (Mon–Fri 9 daily, Sat 6, Sun 2; 5min).

### ACCOMMODATION AND EATING

**Aldo's** 7 Castle Place ☎ 028 4484 1315, ⓦ aldosardglass. com. Well-regarded restaurant that's been in the hands of the same Italian family for more than forty years, though (the house lasagne aside), there's little actually Italian on the menu; instead, you've got the likes of wok-fried monkfish with pea risotto, and Irish lamb rump with carrot jam and goats cheese mousse (£16.95). Thurs–Sat 5–9pm, Sun noon–3.30pm & 5–10pm.

★ **Margaret's Cottage** 9 Castle Place ☎ 028 4484 3328, ⓦ margarets-cottage.co.uk. Named after the adjoining fifteenth-century tower house, this home-from-home guesthouse, directly opposite the golf course, offers three pretty rooms, two of which offer fantastic sea views. Guests are positively encouraged to avail themselves of the warming lounge – with papers galore, a roaring log fire and selection of lush, home-baked goodies rustled up by Ciara, *Margaret's* charming host. She also does a tremendous afternoon tea for £17.50. **£90**

## Killough

**KILLOUGH**, a few kilometres west of Ardglass, is a tranquil village stretching around a harbour that is much larger than its neighbour's but is now silted up. Killough's main street is a fine French-style avenue of sycamores with a string of picturesque cottage terraces at its southern end, making an unlikely major thoroughfare. The Wards, of Castle Ward, built the harbour in the eighteenth century, and there's still a road running inland, virtually in a straight line, from Killough to their castle. Untouched by tourism, there is no accommodation in the village and only bar meals in a couple of pubs.

## St John's Point

From the southern end of Killough you can head out to **St John's Point** – much favoured by birdwatchers – on which lie the ruins of one of the North's best examples of a **pre-Romanesque church**; it's an enjoyable 4km walk. The tiny west door of the tenth-century church has the distinctive sloping sides, narrowing as the doorway rises, that were a common feature of these early churches. Also still apparent are the **antae**, enclosures created by the extension of the west and east walls to give extra support to the roof. Excavations in 1977 showed up graves that extended under these walls, indicating that an even earlier church existed in the early Christian period, probably made of wood.

**15**

### ARRIVAL AND DEPARTURE                                              KILLOUGH

**By bus** Buses stop in the centre of the village.
**Destinations** Ardglass (Mon–Fri 9 daily, Sat 6, Sun 2; 5min);
Downpatrick (Mon–Fri 9 daily, Sat 6, Sun 2; 15min).

# Newcastle

**NEWCASTLE**, with its lovely stretch of sandy beach, is the biggest seaside resort in County Down – packed with trippers from Belfast on bank holidays and summer weekends. Although the resort isn't exactly exciting – there's next to nothing by way of sights, and the main strip is interspersed with tacky amusement arcades and souvenir shops – it does have some superb dining possibilities, and, with Slieve Donard rising behind the town, it's by far the best base if you want to do any serious walking or climbing in the nearby **Mourne Mountains**.

The town has a few literary connections too: **Seamus Heaney** was a waiter in the 1950s at the long-gone *Savoy Café*; Brook Cottage, on Bryansford Road, was home to the dramatist and dialect-poet Richard Valentine Williams, better known as Richard Rowley; and a fountain on The Promenade commemorates the popular Irish songwriter Percy French, composer of *The Mountains of Mourne* and numerous comic songs.

### ARRIVAL AND INFORMATION                                           NEWCASTLE

**By bus** The bus station (☎ 028 4372 2296) is on Railway St at the eastern end of Main St. The Mourne Rambler (service #405; May–Aug Tues–Sun 5 daily, 8.30am–4.30pm; all-day ticket £6.50) is a circular service starting in Newcastle with numerous stops including Tollymore and the Silent Valley. **Destinations** Belfast (Mon–Sat every 30min–1hr, Sun 9; 1hr 10min–1hr 30min); Castlewellan (Mon–Sat every 30min–1hr, Sun 6; 10min); Downpatrick (Mon–Sat every 30min–1hr, Sun 7; 25–35min); Newry (4–6 daily; 55min).

**Tourist office** The tourist office is at 10–14 Central Promenade (April–June & Sept–Oct Mon–Fri 9.30am–5pm, Sat 10am–5pm, Sun 2–6pm; July & Aug Mon–Sat 9.30am–7pm, Sun 1–7pm; ☎ 028 4372 2222, ⓦ visit mournemountains.co.uk).

### ACCOMMODATION

**Beach House** 22 Downs Rd ☎ 028 4372 2345, ❸ beach house22@tiscali.co.uk. The chief appeal of this refurbished Victorian dwelling is the sea view from each of the three, mostly all-white, rooms (two twins and a double). Closed Nov–Jan. **£90**

**Hutt Hostel** 30 Downs Rd ☎ 028 4372 2133, ⓦ hutt hostel.com. Occupying a fine seafront town house, this buzzy, well-appointed hostel has a variety of three- to eight-bed dorms, plus "The Padd", an apartment-like annexe sleeping six (£25/person). There's also a cool lounge with woodburner, a games room, and a large self-catering kitchen for use, though breakfast is included. **£22**

**Slieve Donard** Downs Rd ☎ 028 4372 1066, ⓦ hastings hotels.com. This ostentatious redbrick pile, positioned on

**15**

## WALKS IN THE MOURNES

While there's little to see in Newcastle itself, the **Mourne Mountains** offer some beautiful walks close to town, as well as plenty of more serious hiking routes, including the **Newcastle Way**, a two-day, 45km-long waymarked hike, split into six sections, starting and finishing in the town; see ⓦwalkni.com for more details. There's also an annual **walking festival** (ⓦmournewalking. co.uk) over three days at the end of June, featuring a variety of lowland and mountain walks, rambles and hikes.

### SLIEVE DONARD

The climb up **Slieve Donard** (850m), just south of Newcastle, is the obvious first choice. Although it's the highest peak in Northern Ireland, there are two relatively easy **ascents** from town: one on a well-marked trail that starts around 5km south of town on the Annalong road at Bloody Bridge (see page 536), and another (slightly shorter) trail from the Donard Park car park – both end at the massive hermit cell on the summit, from where there are stupendous views.

For gentler local walking, there are several pleasant parks created from the estates of old houses in the vicinity. The nearest is **Donard Park** (free access) on the slopes of Slieve Donard. There's a good meander along the River Glen from Newcastle town centre to the park, and if you keep following this path uphill you'll emerge on the other side and eventually come to the Saddle, a col between the two mountains of Slieve Donard and Slieve Commedagh. If you want to carry on further into the mountains from here, a good route is via **Trassey Burn** towards the **Hare's Gap**, where minerals have seeped through the rock to form precious and semiprecious stones – topaz, beryl, smoky quartz and emerald – in the cavities of the **Diamond rocks** (hidden behind an obvious boulder stone on the mountainside).

### TOLLYMORE FOREST PARK

Around 3km inland from Newcastle, along the Bryansford road, **Tollymore Forest Park** (daily 10am–dusk; cars £5; ⓦnidirect.gov.uk) is considerably bigger and better equipped than Donard, and has a **campsite**. The park creeps up the northern side of the Mournes, and its four picturesque **trails** (ranging from less than 1km to 8km in length) wind through woodland and beside the river. You enter the park by one of two ornate Gothic folly gates, and there's an information kiosk in the car park.

### CASTLEWELLAN FOREST PARK

**Castlewellan Forest Park** (same hours and prices as Tollymore) is also inland, about 8km further north, outside the elegant market town of Castlewellan. The estate lies in the foothills

the beachfront and next to the Royal County Down golf course, is Newcastle's premier hotel, a mega-luxurious establishment with grand rooms in all manner of category – most with a sea view – and its own spa. **£120**

## EATING AND DRINKING

**Anchor Bar** 9 Bryansford Ave ☏028 4372 3344, ⓦanchorbar.co.uk. A fun, funky pub fitted out with nautical and railway paraphernalia that's popular with ramblers and climbers; there's decent bar food, plus pool tables and live music at weekends. Daily noon–midnight.

**Railway St** 2 Railway St ☏07507 625933. There are dozens of cafés around town, but this great-looking coffee house opposite the *Slieve Donard* resort is the best by a country mile, serving up Aussie-inspired brekkies and lunches (fried chicken and smoked tomato aioli on toasted sourdough; £6.50) and the freshest, tastiest coffee in town.

Unusually for a coffee bar, it's open evenings too. Mon–Fri & Sun 8.30am–11pm, Sat 8.30am–6pm.

**Sea Salt Bistro** 51 Central Promenade ☏028 4321 8091, ⓦseasaltnewcastle.com. Bright'n'breezy café-cum-bistro which serves breakfast, brunch and lunch (the sea salt burrito really hits the spot) and – on Fridays and Saturdays – superb dinners, for example seafood and white bean *cassoulet* served with a herb and parmesan crust (£17). You'll need to bring your own wine, which is no bad thing (corkage £2.50). Mon–Thurs & Sun 9am–5pm, Fri & Sat 9am–4pm & 5pm–late.

of the Mournes, and a 4km trail from the entrance leads to the highest point in the forest, **Slievenaslat**, providing panoramic views. A wonderful **arboretum** is the forest park's outstanding feature: the sheltered south-facing slopes of its hills, between the Mournes and the Slieve Croob range, allow exotic species to flourish. There's trout **fishing** in its main lake and coarse fishing in the smaller lakes (enquire at the Newcastle tourist office for details).

There's a pleasant **campsite** in the park here, too, as well as the Life One Great Adventure centre (☏028 4377 0714, ⓦonegreatadventure.com), which offers various activities, including **canoeing** and **kayaking** (rental for both £25/3hr), and trail **biking** (rental £27/3hr, £37/6hr). Nearby **riding schools** offering trekking through the forest parks include Mount Pleasant Riding and Trekking Centre, 15 Bannanstown Rd, Castlewellan (☏028 4377 8651, ⓦmountpleasantcentre.com) and Mourne Trail Riding Centre, 96 Castlewellan Rd, around 3km out of Newcastle on the A50 (☏028 4372 4351, ⓦmournetrailridingcentre.co.uk); expect to pay around £25 for an hour's ride.

### LONGER HIKES

If you're planning on more serious hiking in the Mournes, heights worth chasing include **Slieve Binnian** (747m), beyond the Hare's Gap, reached through the Brandy Pad passes by the Blue Lough and Lough Binnian; **Slieve Commedagh** (767m), with its Inca-like pillars of granite; and **Slieve Bearnagh** (739m), up to the right of the Hare's Gap. Also, try and cross the ridge from **Slieve Meelmore** (681m) to **Slieve Muck**, the "pig mountain", descending to the shores of Lough Shannagh, where there's a **beach** at either end – useful for a dip, though the water's freezing. In the panorama beyond the Hare's Gap, the places not to miss are the eastern slopes of the **Cove Mountain** and **Slieve Lamagan** (704m). If you're sticking to the roads, all you can really do is circle the outside of the range, though there is one road through the middle, from Hilltown to Kilkeel.

**15**

### ACCOMMODATION IN THE MOURNE MOUNTAINS

**Castlewellan Camping** Castlewellan Forest Park (signposted) ☏028 4377 8664. This pleasant campsite offers showers, fresh water, and dishwashing station and electric hook-ups, but only operates from end Apr to early Nov. **£19.50**

**Meelmore Lodge** 52 Trassey Rd, Bryansford ☏028 4372 5949, ⓦmeelmorelodge.co.uk. Superbly positioned complex some 10km west of Newcastle, just beyond Tollymore Forest Park, offering hostel accommodation (dorms and private en-suites), a field for camping and two basic pods (sleeping up to four). Also has a smashing little café (Sat & Sun 8.30am–6pm; daily during school hols). Dorms **£20**, doubles **£50**, pods **£45**, camping **£20**

**Tollymore Caravan and Camping** Tollymore Forest Park (signposted) ☏028 4372 2428. Year-round site with decent facilities including showers, compost loos and electric hook-ups. **£19.50**

# The Mourne Mountains

The **Mourne Mountains** are a relatively youthful set of granite mountains, which explains why their comparatively unweathered peaks and flanks are so rugged, forming steep sides, moraines and occasional sheer cliffs. Closer up, these give sharp, jagged outlines; but from a distance they appear much gentler, like a sleeping herd of buffalo. The wilder topography lies mostly in the east, below Newcastle, although the fine cliff of **Eagle Mountain** (636m), to the southwest, is wonderful if you can afford the time and effort to get there, and the tamer land above Rostrevor has views down into **Carlingford Lough** that rival any in Ireland.

In summer at least (winters can be surprisingly harsh), there are plenty of straightforward hikes in the Mournes that require no special equipment, with obvious tracks to many of the more scenic parts. There are also more serious climbs and **climbing courses** in the Mournes run by the Tollymore National Outdoor Centre in Bryansford (ⓦtollymore.com), but they must be booked well in advance.

## The Legananny dolmen

The **Legananny dolmen** is worth a considerable detour, which it will be, wherever you are, due to its remoteness; it's signposted at the village of Leitrim, 5km north of Castlewellan. Approaching the site, you'll find yourself on narrow humped lanes, gradually ascending the southern edge of the Slieve Croob range, and feeling increasingly distant from modern realities. You may also experience a sense of *déjà vu* when you arrive at the site, for the dolmen is a popular choice of guidebook and tourist-board photographers. There's no doubting the impressiveness of the structure, looking for all the world like a giant stone tripod.

## Silent Valley

Valley and visitor centre daily: May–Sept 10am–6.30pm; Oct–April 10am–4pm; café daily: April–Sept 10am–5pm; Oct–March 10am–4pm • Pedestrians £1.60, car £5 • Sandy Lough shuttle bus May, June & Sept Sat & Sun; July & Aug daily (£1.50 return) • ☎ 03457 440088, ⓦ niwater.com/silent-valley

The A2 south along the coast from Newcastle is a beautiful road, trailing the shore around the edge of the mountains. It takes you past the chasm known as **Maggie's Leap**, after a local woman who jumped to avoid the attentions of an unwanted suitor, and over the **Bloody Bridge**, reputedly so-called because of a nearby massacre during the 1641 Rebellion. Inland, 1.5km or so from the fishing village of Annalong (11km south of Newcastle) and serviced by the summer-only Mourne Rambler bus (see page 533), signposts point to the aptly named **Silent Valley**, where you'll find Belfast and County Down's **reservoir**, a huge thirty-year engineering project that was completed in 1933. There's a car park by the lower reservoir, bounded by the Mourne Wall, a sturdy 35km-long granite boundary to the catchment area that links the summits of fifteen mountains along its route. The views out to Slieve Binnian and Ben Crom, behind it to the west, are worth the effort of the 5km circular **Viewpoint Walk** (starts at the car park). Less energetic, but still superb, is the less than 1km Sally Lough stroll up to the dam at Ben Crom; again the views are spectacular. Halfway between the car park and the dam there's a small café and a **visitor centre** exhibiting displays on the reservoir's development.

## Rostrevor

On the western edge of the Mournes, 24km further on from Annalong along the A2, a signpost points to the **Kilfeaghan dolmen**, 500m inland then a short walk through a couple of fields and kissing gates. Its capstone is enormous and could only have arrived here during the retreat of the glacial drift.

Further up the lough, the village of **ROSTREVOR** lies at the point where the bay waters dramatically begin to narrow towards Newry – and where the population and political climate turn more in favour of the Nationalist communities of County Armagh and those across the ever-nearing border. Rostrevor is a charming and sleepy village of Victorian terraces and friendly pubs, meandering up the lower slopes of **Slieve Martin**. A good time to be here is the last week of July for the Fiddler's Green Festival (ⓦ fiddlersgreenfestival.eu), a major event attracting folk and traditional musicians from across Europe.

### ARRIVAL AND DEPARTURE ROSTREVOR

**By bus** Buses drop off on, and depart from, Warrenpoint Rd, the main through road.

Destinations Newry (Mon–Sat every 30min–1hr, Sun 7; 25min); Warrenpoint (Mon–Sat every 30min–1hr, Sun 7; 10min).

**By ferry** The Carlingford car ferry (☎ 086 415 0585, ⓦ carlingfordferry.com) makes the 15min journey across Carlingford Lough from Greencastle, 14km south of Rostrevor, to Greenore, near Carlingford in County Louth; from Greencastle ferries depart on the hour (Mon–Sat 7am–8pm, Sun 9am–8pm) and from Greenore on the half hour (Mon–Sat 7.30am–8.30pm, Sun 9.30am–8.30pm; passengers €2.25, cars €11).

## ACCOMMODATION AND EATING

**Kilbroney Caravan Park** Shore Rd ☎028 4173 8134. Camping is available at this park where you can hike up the hill to the thirty-ton Cloughmore ("big stone") for views across the lough to the Cooley Mountains over the border. Closed Oct–March. £20

**The Old School House** 39 Church St ☎028 4173 8211, ⓦoldschoolhouserostrevor.com. The erstwhile school house might look quite ordinary, but the food here is anything but; beyond light lunches, you can sit down to more substantial, and sophisticated, evening fare later in the week with the likes of tandoori monkfish with roast peppers and garlic potatoes (£18.95). Mon–Thurs 9am–5pm, Fri & Sat 9am–9pm, Sun 9am–9pm.

**The Sands** 4 Victoria Square ☎028 4173 8151, ⓦthe sandsbandbrostrevor.co.uk. Fabulously located B&B on a spruce Victorian square out on the road towards Newcastle, offering one double and one twin room, each with a clear sea view. £85

# Warrenpoint

**Warrenpoint** is as picturesque as Rostrevor, with a colourful esplanade of seafront housing and a spacious central square. It's a much more traditional seaside resort than its neighbour and has been attracting visitors since the early nineteenth century, when an enterprising local man advertised warm baths for the "gentry, nobility and public". The town really only comes alive, however, during the four-day Blues on the Bay **music festival** in late May (ⓦbluesonthebay.com), and for the **Maiden of the Mournes festival** (ⓦmaidenofthemournes.com), which takes place over the first week of August, a local version of the Rose of Tralee (see page 297).

**15**

## ARRIVAL AND INFORMATION                                    WARRENPOINT

**By bus** Buses drop-off on, and depart from, Church St. Destinations Newry (Mon–Sat every 30min–1hr, Sun 11; 15min); Rostrevor (Mon–Sat every 30min–1hr, Sun 7; 10min).

**Tourist office** Easy to miss, the tourist office is in the town hall on Church St (Mon–Fri 9am–1pm & 2–5pm; ☎028 4175 2256).

## ACCOMMODATION AND EATING

**Whistledown Hotel** 6 Seaview ☎028 4175 4174, ⓦthewhistledownhotel.com. Tidy boutique hotel with coloured furnishings, stripey carpets and regulation mod cons. Grab a posh pizza from the garishly decorated *Finn's Bar*, or treat yourself to more refined fare in the bistro. Bar daily noon–11pm (food till 9pm), bistro noon–2.30pm

& 5.30–9.30pm. £90

**Ye Old Ship Inn** 14 The Square ☎028 4175 3125. A venerable old pub with a distinct nautical theme, from the wood-panelled bar to the sweet little table lamps; top-notch beer – try the local Mourne Mist – and live music Thurs–Sat. Daily 11.30am–midnight, Fri & Sat till 1am.

# Newry

Although **NEWRY**, astride the border of Down and Armagh, is this region's most important commercial centre and bustles with an urban vibrancy, it's worth little more than a short visit. However, its key position means that you're highly likely to pass through here, and it does make a possible base for exploring Slieve Gullion and the south Armagh district.

Newry was founded by Cistercian monks in 1144, but for most of its history has been a **garrison**, guarding the borders of Northern Ireland at the narrow point between hills on either side known as the Gap of the North. There's no trace at all of the bitterly contested early fortresses; what you see dates mostly from the eighteenth and nineteenth centuries, when a canal to Lough Neagh (cut in 1742, the first in the British Isles) brought the produce of the inland towns to the markets here; indeed, **market days** (Thurs & Sat) remain integral to the town.

## Catholic Cathedral

Hill St · Daily 8.30am–5pm · Free · ☎028 3026 2586

One of the most interesting buildings in town is the **Catholic Cathedral**, constructed in 1829 and the first such building to be opened following Catholic Emancipation. Despite an unpromising granite exterior, the rich mosaic pattern along its interior walls gives a Byzantine feel, and there's also a striking vaulted ceiling of decorative sweeping plaster arcs and vivid stained-glass windows. Nearby, there's a strange bronze totem pole by sculptor Paddy McElroy, which depicts, in tortured relief, scenes from Newry's past.

## Bagenal's Castle

Castle St • Museum Mon–Sat 10am–4.30pm, Sun 1.30–5pm • Free • ☎ 028 3031 3182, ⓦ bagenalscastle.com

A short walk from the centre of town, **Bagenal's Castle** is a superb example of a fortified house. Located within the environs of a Cistercian abbey, the castle was confiscated during the Reformation of 1548, and the premises were leased to a certain Nicholas Bagenal, who had apparently earlier fled his native Staffordshire to escape indictment for murder. After acting as a secret agent infiltrating the O'Neill clan, he was granted a pardon and subsequently became marshal of the English army in Ireland and established a garrison in Newry. While Bagenal was largely successful in defending the area against the O'Neills, his daughter Mary eloped and married Hugh O'Neill, a story that became the subject of Brian Friel's play *Making History*. The castle functioned as McGann's bakery for more than a century, until its closure in 1996.

### Newry and Mourne Museum

The castle is now home to the nicely presented **Newry and Mourne Museum**, where you can inspect some of the building's original elements, most notably a cross section of its sixteenth-century cellar, which contains the original bread oven. Upstairs, in the impressively authentic Great Chamber, you can't miss the crater-like holes along the walls where the joists were removed years ago. There's a fascinating local history exhibition too, with an emphasis on the area's strong folk traditions. There's coverage, too, of life here during the Troubles, when Newry – the so-called capital of "Bandit Country" – was at the bloody forefront of the struggles; exhibits include British coins overstamped with IRA insignia, and an order of service for the ten men gunned down in the infamous Kingsmill massacre of January 1976.

### ARRIVAL AND INFORMATION

NEWRY

**By train** The train station (☎ 028 025 6446) is 500m west of town on Millvale Rd and connected to the centre by local bus #41H (free with valid rail ticket).

Destinations Belfast (Mon–Sat 8 daily, Sun 5; 55min–1hr 5min); Drogheda (Mon–Sat 8 daily, Sun 5; 40min); Dublin (Mon–Sat 8 daily, Sun 5; 1hr 10min–1hr 30min).

**By bus** Newry's bus station (☎ 028 3026 3531) is on The Mall alongside the canal.

Destinations Armagh (Mon–Fri hourly, Sat 7; 50min); Belfast (Mon–Fri every 30min, Sat hourly, Sun 9; 1hr 10min); Carlingford (*Bus Éireann*: Mon–Sat 3 daily; 20min); Crossmaglen (Mon–Sat 5–6 daily; 55min); Downpatrick (Mon–Fri 6–7 daily; 1hr 15min); Dublin (hourly; 1hr 30min); Newcastle (4–6 daily; 55min); Rostrevor (Mon–Sat every 30min–1hr, Sun 6; 25min); Warrenpoint (Mon–Sat every 30min–1hr, Sun 6; 15min).

**Tourist office** In Bagenal's Castle on Castle St (Jan–June & Sept–Dec Mon–Fri 9am–5pm, Sat 10am–4pm; July & Aug Mon–Fri 9am–6pm, Sat 10am–4pm, Sun 1–5pm; ☎ 028 3031 3170, ⓦ visitmournemountains.co.uk).

### ACCOMMODATION AND EATING

**Canal Court Hotel** Merchants Quay ☎ 028 3025 1234, ⓦ canalcourthotel.com. On the opposite side of the canal from the bus station, this vast hotel is run through with class, from the opulent reception area to the extravagantly decorated rooms; it's also equipped with a gym and sauna. £80

**Grounded** 25 Merchants Quay ☎ 028 3083 3868. There aren't many places in Newry where you can grab a hearty lunch or a decent cup of coffee, but you can do just that at *Grounded*, an easy-going café a few paces along from the *Canal Court Hotel*; moreover, the squishy leather sofas and floor-to-ceiling windows are perfect for people-watching. Daily 8am–11pm.

# South Armagh

Overshadowed by Slieve Gullion, the **South Armagh** countryside is among the most attractive in the North. Proximity to the border and a predominantly Catholic population resulted in this once being a nucleus of resistance to British rule. There's much evidence of prehistoric settlement here, important ecclesiastical remains and plenty of traditional music.

## The Ring of Gullion

Most of South Armagh's attractions are concentrated in and around the area known as the **Ring of Gullion**, a naturally formed ring-dyke of low-lying hills that encircles (and predates) the mountain at its core. People have lived here for more than six thousand years, and there's a rich heritage of remains and monuments. On the ring's western fringe is the **Dorsey Enclosure**, two huge earthen banks and ditch ramparts dating from the Iron Age, running for 500m either side of the old route to Navan Fort. Elsewhere are numerous dolmens and cairns, Christian relics and monuments from the Plantation era.

**15**

Slieve Gullion, which dominates the southeastern corner of County Armagh, is one of the most mysteriously beautiful mountains in the country. A store of romantic legends is attached to it, especially concerning **Cúchulainn**, the hero of the **Táin Bó Cúailnge** (see page 152), who took his name here after slaying the hound (Cú) of the blacksmith Culainn. Due south at Glendhu is where Cúchulainn single-handedly halted the army of Queen Medb of Connaught, who was intent on capturing the great bull of Cooley. **Fionn Mac Cumhaill**, who founded the **Fianna**, a mythical national militia whose adventures are told in the *Fenian Cycle*, also appears in stories here.

## Bessbrook and Killeavy

A scenic way to **approach Slieve Gullion** is from the north, passing the turning to **BESSBROOK**, a nineteenth-century model village developed by a Quaker linen entrepreneur; the Cadbury family's Bourneville estate in Birmingham, England, followed a very similar layout. After **Camlough** turn off the main road to go down by the eastern slopes of Camlough Mountain and you'll see the beautiful **lake**, set like a jewel within its green banks. A little further on, between Camlough Mountain and Slieve Gullion, are the ruined **Killeavy churches**. Two churches of different periods share the same gable wall: the west church is pre-Romanesque and one of the most important survivors of its kind in the country; the other, larger, church dates from the thirteenth century. A granite slab marks the **grave of St Monenna**, the founder of a fifth-century nunnery sited here – there's a holy well dedicated to her a little further up the slopes of Slieve Gullion, which pilgrims visit on her feast day (the Sunday nearest to July 6).

The official, tarmacked, **entrance** up into Slieve Gullion is on the mountain's forested southern face, after you've passed through the village of **KILLEAVY**. You'll find a small **forest park** (daily 10am–dusk; free), fronted by the **Courtyard Centre**, where there's a small exhibition on the area, craft workshops and a café. From the centre it's a 13km winding drive up to the summit (or you can follow a walking trail), where there's a couple of megalithic **cairns**. Fionn Mac Cumhaill was legendarily bewitched here by Miluchra, and local superstition holds that bathing in the small summit **lake** will turn your hair white; another tale states that under certain conditions a visitor to the site will be given the power to foresee everything that will happen that day. Various vertiginous spots offer spectacular **views** over the Ring of Gullion and the surrounding countryside.

## Crossmaglen and around

In the far southwestern corner of Armagh just inside the border, **CROSSMAGLEN** has reputedly the largest market square in Ireland, the scene of a fortnightly Friday **market**. During the Troubles the town's reputation for armed struggle against the British was fearsome, and, in truth, it has been a cauldron of activity ever since Partition. Indeed, had the 1924 Boundary Commission's proposals been fully implemented, the town and surrounding countryside would have been transferred to Dublin rule rather than staying inside the North. All this said, on arrival you'll find the pubs much friendlier than you might have expected.

Around 3km east of Crossmaglen on the B30 Newry road, **CREGGAN** has a **Poets' Graveyard**, so named because three eighteenth-century Gaelic poets are buried here: Art Mac Cooey, Patrick Mac Aliondain and Séamus Mór Mac Murphy (who was also an outlaw of some notoriety). The inscription on Mac Cooey's stone is taken from his most famous poem, *Úr-Chill an Chreagáin* – "That with the fragrant Gaels of Creggan I will be put in clay under the sod".

Crossmaglen is at the forefront of the local revival of interest in Gaelic games, and the town's **Gaelic football** team, Crossmaglen Rangers, is consistently strong, though the last of their six All-Ireland championship victories came in 2012. If you fancy watching a game, their ground is St Oliver Plunkett Park.

---

### ARRIVAL AND INFORMATION

CROSSMAGLEN AND AROUND

**By bus** Buses from/to Newry (Mon–Fri 6 daily, Sat 4; 55min) drop off on, and depart from, Ó Fiaich Square.

**Tourist office** The tourist office is in Ó Fiaich House on The Square (July & Aug daily 9am–6pm, Sept–June Mon–Fri 9am–5pm; ☎ 028 3086 8900, ⓦ visitmournemountains. co.uk).

### ACCOMMODATION AND EATING

**Cross Square Hotel** 4–5 Ó Fiaich Square ☎ 028 3086 0505. Very amenable accommodation in the centre of town, and though the rooms are slightly on the old-fashioned side, they're immaculately kept, and the staff couldn't be friendlier. The hotel's restaurant, meanwhile, is noted for its superb steaks. £80

**Keenans Bar** Ó Fiaich Square ☎ 028 3025 2767. The most agreeable of the town's pubs, this place has been around for the best part of eighty years, and hosts a notable traditional music session on Thurs. Mon–Sat 11am– midnight, Sun 4pm–midnight.

---

# Armagh city and around

**ARMAGH** is one of the most attractive places in the North, and the rich history of the city and its surroundings has plenty to keep you occupied for a day or two. The city offers **cathedrals** and **museums** set in handsome Georgian streets, and 3km west is the ancient site of once-grand **Navan Fort**. Armagh has been the site of the **Catholic** primacy of All Ireland since St Patrick established his church here, and has rather ambitiously adopted the title of the "Irish Rome" for itself – like Rome, it's positioned among seven small hills. Paradoxically, the city is also the seat of the **Protestant** Church of Ireland's archbishop of Armagh.

## St Patrick's Roman Catholic Cathedral

Cathedral Rd • Daily: April–Oct 10am–5pm; Nov–March 10am–4pm • Free • ☎ 028 3752 2045, ⓦ armagharchdiocese.org

The best way to get your bearings is to walk up the steps of **St Patrick's Roman Catholic Cathedral**, built on a hillside just northwest of the Shambles Market. The view of the town from here is impressive, and you should be able to identify most of the key sites spread out below. The cathedral's foundation stone was laid in 1840, but completion was delayed by the Famine and a subsequent lack of funding. While the pope and local nobility chipped in, money was also raised by public collections and raffles – one prize of a grandfather clock has still not been claimed. On the outside, the cathedral first appears little different from many of its nineteenth-century Gothic-Revival contemporaries, but it is impressively large and airy. Inside, as befits the seat of the cardinal archbishop, every inch of wall glistens with **mosaics**, in colours ranging from marine- and sky-blue to terracotta pinks and oranges. Other striking pieces include the white-granite "pincer-claw" **tabernacle holder**, reflected in a highly polished marble floor, and a **statue** of the Crucifixion, which suggests (deliberately or otherwise) the old city's division into **Trians**.

## St Patrick's Church of Ireland Cathedral

Cathedral Close • Daily: April–Oct 9am–5pm; Nov–March 9am–4pm • £3 • ☎ 028 3752 3142, ⊕ stpatricks-cathedral.org

**St Patrick's Church of Ireland Cathedral** lays claim to the summit of the principal hillock, Drum Saileach, where St Patrick founded his first church in 445 AD. It commands a distinctive Armagh view across to the other hills and down over the clutter of gable walls and pitched roofing on its own slopes. A series of churches occupied the site after 445, and, although the core of the present one is medieval, a nineteenth-century restoration has coated the thirteenth-century outer walls in a sandstone plaster of which Thackeray remarked, "It is as neat and trim as a lady's dressing room." Many of the ancient decorations were removed, leaving the spartan interior you see today. Just as you enter from the highly distinctive timber porch, you'll see a few remnants of an eleventh-century **Celtic cross** and a startling **statue** of Thomas Molyneux. Inside, high up, you should be able to sight the medieval carved heads of men, women and monsters. One other unusual feature is the tilt of the chancel, a medieval building practice meant to represent the slumping head of the dying Christ. The **chapterhouse** has a small collection of stone statues (mostly gathered from elsewhere), the most noticeable of

**15**

---

**ARMAGH FESTIVALS**

Armagh has a tremendous roster of annual events, and, as you'd expect, the local **St Patrick's Day Parade** (March 17) is one of the largest in the country. Armagh is particularly well known for its **choral music**, and this manifests itself in the annual week-long **Charles Wood Festival of Music and Summer School** in mid-August (ⓦcharleswoodsummerschool. org), featuring a daily series of recitals in the city's cathedrals and churches. In September, the **Armagh Food and Cider Festival** (ⓦvisitarmagh.com/foodandcider) celebrates the region's cuisine, with tours, tastings and suppers at various venues around town; while November sees the staging of the prestigious **John O'Connor Literary Arts Festival**, and the five-day **William Kennedy Piping Festival** (ⓦarmaghpipers.org/wkpf), one of Ireland's major *uilleann* piping events (see page 590).

---

which are the Stone Age **Tandragee Idol** and a Sheila-na-Gig (see page 616) with an ass's ears. Outside the north transept a plaque on the west wall commemorates the burial of **Brian Ború**. There's also a plaque dedicated to composer Charles Wood, who was born just across the way on Vicars' Hill and who was himself a chorister in the cathedral.

## Armagh Robinson Library

43 Abbey St • Mon–Fri 10am–1pm & 2–4pm; guided tours on request • Free, donations welcomed; tours £2 • ☎ 028 3752 3142, ⓦ armaghrobinsonlibrary.co.uk

The wonderful **Armagh Robinson Library** is Ireland's oldest, founded in 1771 by Archbishop Richard Robinson (1708–94), who was described as converting Armagh "from mud to stone" and who is responsible for almost all the older buildings in the city – the nearby infirmary was one of his, too, though it's now occupied by the university. The core of the collection is Robinson's own library, mostly seventeenth-and eighteenth-century books on theology, philosophy, politics and the sciences, though there is also a superb collection of medieval manuscripts and incunabula. Among the many rare tomes is a first edition of **Gulliver's Travels** annotated by Swift himself, and an early copy of Handel's **Messiah**, plus material belonging to Charles Wood (born just a few doors away).

## The Mall

**The Mall** is an elegant tree-lined promenade fringed to the east by two terraces of handsome Georgian houses designed by the Armagh-born architect Francis Johnston at the behest of Archbishop Robinson. Johnston was responsible for many of Dublin's best Georgian buildings, including its GPO (see page 78), and you'll encounter more examples of his work around town, including the classical **courthouse** at The Mall's northern end; the former **jail** occupies the southern end. The Mall owes its largely oval shape to the fact that it was once a racecourse in the late eighteenth century; nowadays, there's nothing more athletic than the occasional jogger and Saturday cricket matches.

Dotted throughout the park are three **memorials**; at the northern end, you'll find two monuments to those who fell during the Boer War and World War I, while at the southern end is the Railway Disaster Memorial, which remembers the 89 people who were killed in the crash in 1889; a simple yet affecting piece, it portrays a young girl holding a bucket and spade.

## Armagh County Museum

The Mall East • Mon–Fri 10am–5pm, Sat 10am–1pm & 2–5pm • Free • ☎ 028 3752 3070

A former schoolhouse on the east side of The Mall houses the **County Museum**, a charmingly old-fashioned space with all the usual local miscellany on display, including an alarmingly vivid collection of stuffed wildlife. One display devoted to railway history recounts the story of Ireland's worst **railway disaster**, when two passenger trains collided outside Armagh in 1889, killing 89 people, many of whom are buried in nearby St Mark's churchyard. Along with photos of the wreckage, there's a rather poignant letter, written in 1958, from one of the survivors, in which he recalls the events of that day.

Rotating art exhibitions complete the museum's ensemble, though one picture on permanent show is local artist J.B. Vallely's *The Red Fiddle*, a superb oil showing five musicians enjoying a session; the theme of traditional music figures in more than three thousand of Vallely's canvases (some of which are occasionally on display here), and, with his wife Eithne, he currently runs the town's Armagh Pipers' Club.

## The Royal Irish Fusiliers Museum

The Mall • Mon–Fri 10am–12.30pm & 1.30–4pm • Free • ☎ 028 3752 2911, ⓦ royal-irish.com

Occupying Sovereigns House, the leftovers of the courthouse, is the **Royal Irish Fusiliers Museum**. It's pretty much as you'd expect: tons of weaponry, uniforms, medallions and silverware from the regiment formed in 1793 in response to the Napoleonic crisis and subsequently known as the Faughs, from their battle cry *Faugh a Ballagh!* ("Clear the way!"). The Fusiliers subsequently fought in the Crimean and Boer wars (where they relieved the Siege of Ladysmith) and in both world wars before amalgamating with the Inniskilling Fusiliers (see page 560) and Ulster Rifles in 1968 to form the Royal Irish Rangers; in 1992, they joined with the Ulster Defence Regiment to form the present-day Royal Irish Regiment.

## Armagh Planetarium

College Hill • Mon–Sat 10am–5pm, plus Sun in July & Aug; shows 30–40min each • Adults £8.50 per show, children 6–15 £6.25 (pre-booking required); exhibition hall £2; Astropark free • ☎ 028 3752 3689, ⓦ armagh.space

The **Armagh Planetarium** boasts "the world's most advanced digital production projection system, Digistar 3", with full animation of the planetarium's dome (and reclining seats to enjoy the full effects), as well as an extraordinarily good sound setup. Various shows are on offer, including the child-oriented "Secret of the Cardboard Rocket" which explores the solar system; "Pole Position", touring the constellations; and "Violent Universe", a crash-and-burn account of comets and meteors. Inside there's also an exhibition hall featuring a range of high-tech interactive displays of the cosmos, as well as images of deep space and an assortment of meteorite chunks from the Moon and Mars. Outside there's the landscaped Astropark, a series of trails depicting the extent of the solar system in comparison to the known universe – a stroll up the Hill of Infinity leads to its very edge and also offers a glorious view of the city.

## Armagh Friary and Demesne Palace

The ruins of **Armagh Friary** (open access), founded by the Franciscans in 1263, lie within easy walking distance south of the city centre on Friary Road, though they are marred somewhat by the continuous roar of traffic. Nearby is the entrance to the grounds of the Archbishop's Palace, otherwise known as the **Demesne Palace**; it now houses the District Council offices, hence is off-limits to the public, but you can wander around the adjacent **Palace Stables** – which is home to a superb restaurant – along with a well-preserved **ice house**, a curious **tunnel** by which servants accessed the basement kitchens, and a stimulating **sensory garden**.

**ARRIVAL AND INFORMATION**                                              **ARMAGH CITY**

**BY bus** The Ulsterbus station (☎ 028 3752 2266) is on Lonsdale Rd, just north of the centre.     Destinations Belfast (Mon–Fri hourly, Sat 8, Sun 5; 1hr 15–25min); Loughgall (Mon–Fri 7 daily; 15min); Monaghan

## ROAD BOWLS

The sport of **road bowls** is popular in Holland and Germany and was once played throughout Ireland, but is now limited mainly to Cork and Armagh, where it's also known as "road bullets".

The principle of the game is simple: a pair of rival contestants each propels an 800g (28oz) solid-iron ball along a course of country roads (usually about 4km long), the winner being the player who reaches the finishing line with the **fewest number of throws**. In practice, it's a complicated business. The Armagh roads twist and turn, up and down, and bowlers are assisted by a team of camp followers, including managers and road guides who advise on the most advantageous spots to aim for and the force of the throw.

Roads around Armagh where you're likely to catch sight of the game – usually on Sunday afternoons – include Cathedral Road, Knappagh Road, Blackwater Town, Rock, Tassagh, Newtownhamilton and Madden roads. The most reliable information on forthcoming games is probably to be had in local pubs. The **Ulster Finals** are held in the city over two weekends in late June or early July, with the **All-Ireland Road Bowls Final** in early August.

(Mon–Fri 10 daily, Sat 4, Sun 2; 40min); Newry (Mon–Fri hourly, Sat 8; 50min).

**Tourist office** In the Old Bank Building at 40 English St (April–Sept Mon–Sat 9am–5.30pm, Sun 1–5.30pm; Oct–March Mon–Sat 9am–5pm; ☎ 028 3752 1800, ⦿ visit armagh.com); walking tours of the city operate from here during the summer (mid-June to mid-Sept Wed–Sat 11am & 1pm; 1hr; £4).

### ACCOMMODATION
SEE MAP PAGE 541

**Armagh City Hostel** 39 Abbey St ☎ 028 3751 1800, ⦿ hini.org.uk/hostels/armagh-city-hostel. Modern, excellently equipped HINI hostel, superbly situated near the Church of Ireland Cathedral, with small dorms, plus twins and doubles, all en-suite. Lots of good-sized communal areas including a self-catering kitchen, plus laundry and bike storage. Groups only Nov–March. Dorms £18, doubles £42

**Armagh City Hotel** 2 Friary Rd ☎ 028 3751 8888, ⦿ armaghcityhotel.com. Behind the facade of its somewhat bland exterior, there's a great buzz about this large, modern hotel, which offers plush accommodation in a range of room categories; note, though, that its main business is conferences and weddings, so you'll need to book well in advance. £80

**Charlemont Arms Hotel** 57–65 English St ☎ 028 3752 2028, ⦿ charlemontarmshotel.com. It doesn't look particularly exciting from the outside, but this long-established, family-run establishment offers polished rooms, a congenial welcome and is in a terrific location just a few paces from the city centre. £79

**Fairylands Country House** 25 Navan Fort Rd, 1.5km from the centre ☎ 028 3751 0315, ⦿ fairylands.ie. In a quiet rural setting, this very agreeable modern house offers simply furnished en-suite rooms, a warming guest lounge, and a cracking breakfast to see you on your way. Good value. £75

### EATING
SEE MAP PAGE 541

**The Craic'd Pot** 25 Upper English St ☎ 028 3778 9657. Justifiably a local favourite, this cracking espresso café offers a delicious array of caffeine fixes, brewed various ways, for example Aeropress, Chemex and French Press; if you fancy something truly heart-stopping, ask for a *hammerhead* (filter with double espresso); the pastries aren't half bad either. Mon–Fri 8am–10pm, Sat 9am–6pm, Sun noon–8pm.

**Uluru Bar & Grill** 3–5 Market St ☎ 028 3751 8051, ⦿ ulurubarandgrill.com. Ostensibly an Australian restaurant (to be fair, there is kangaroo loin on the menu), the real draw here is the josper charcoal grill, where you can tuck into any number of juicy burgers (£13) and steaks (from £17), served, perhaps, with tobacco onions and a green peppercorn sauce. Daily 10am–10pm.

### DRINKING
SEE MAP PAGE 541

**Hole in the Wall Bar** 9 Market St ☎ 028 3752 3515. Dating from the early seventeenth century, this dark, low-beamed inn was the former holding centre for the town's prison. It's the most inviting hostelry around, with great beer, interesting characters and a resident parrot if you're stuck for conversation. Daily 11.30am–11pm.

# Navan Fort

81 Killylea Rd, 4km west of Armagh • **Fort** Open access • Free • **Navan Centre** Daily: April–Sept 10am–6.30pm; Oct–March 10am–4pm • April–Sept £8, Oct–March £6.50 • ☎ 028 3752 9644, ⓦ visitarmagh.com • Bus #73 from Armagh (Mon–Fri 6 daily; 10min)

For nearly seven hundred years **Navan Fort** was the great seat of northern power, rivalling Tara in the south. It was here that the kings of Northern Ireland ruled and Queen Macha built her palace on the earthwork's summit. It's a site of deeply mystical significance, but also one of enormous archaeological interest. The court of the **Knights of the Red Branch**, Ireland's most prestigious order of chivalry, was based here too. The knights, like those of the Round Table, are historical figures entirely subsumed into legend, their greatest champion being the legendary defender of Northern Ireland, **Cúchulainn** (see pages 152 and 539). The stories of these warriors' deeds are recited and sung in what's now known as the **Ulster Cycle**. Their dynasty was finally vanquished in 332 AD, when three brothers (the Collas), in a conquest known as the Black Pig's Dyke, destroyed Navan Fort, razing it to the ground and leaving only the earthen mounds visible today. The defeated Red Branch Knights were driven eastwards into Down and Antrim, and were little heard of again.

Before visiting the site, you may wish to pop into the **Navan Centre**, which features an exhibition on the fort, courtesy of various archaeological bits and bobs excavated from the site, and a multimedia show on the Ulster Cycle – in itself though, it's not really worth the entrance fee. Skirting the centre, you'll discover that the site area is defined by a massive bank with a defensive **ditch**. When you reach the fort, you'll find an **earthen mound**, which gives a commanding view but no hint of its past. Excavation of the mound took place over a ten-year period (1961–71) and revealed a peculiar structure, apparently unique in the Celtic world. Archaeologists reckon that around 100 BC the buildings that had existed since the Neolithic period were cleared, and a huge structure 33m diameter was constructed. An outer wall of timber surrounded five concentric rings of large posts, 275 in all, with a massive post at the very centre. This was then filled with limestone boulders and **set on fire**, creating a mountain of ash that was then covered with sods of clay to make a high mound. It is anybody's guess what the purpose of the structure was – possibly a temple, or maybe a monumental funeral pyre.

It's worth heading over to "Living History" (April–Sept only; included in Navan Centre ticket price), where, in a reconstructed Iron Age dwelling, costumed characters regale visitors with ancient stories, demonstrate various crafts and prepare food on an open fire. Adults will find it just as entertaining as kids. There's a very agreeable café in the centre too.

**15**

# Loughgall and around

**LOUGHGALL**, a tranquil and pretty estate village about 8km north of Armagh, lies in the middle of apple-orchard country, beautiful in the spring, and is worth visiting mainly for its historical connections. Like many of its neighbours in Armagh's rural north, Loughgall is strongly **Protestant**; indeed it was at Diamond Hill, a few kilometres away, that the Battle of the Diamond took place in 1795, which led to the foundation of the first Protestant **Orange Order** (see page 546).

## Museum of Orange Heritage

86 Main St • Tues–Sat 10am–4pm • £3 • ☎ 028 3889 2048, ⓦ orangeheritage.co.uk

The history of the Orange Order is comprehensively relayed in the **Museum of Orange Heritage**, which occupies Sloan's House – the house owned by James Sloan, one of the Order's three founders, the others being James Wilson and Daniel Winter (see page 546). The parlour in which the Order came into being still has the original table and gavel (ceremonial mallet) used by Sloan while chairing the meeting; it was here, too, that the first warrants were signed for the Order's various lodges. Elsewhere, there's stacks of memorabilia from Orders around the world: documents, sashes and other regalia accessories, plus a few pieces of weaponry used in the Battle of the Diamond, though you may have to ask to view these as they're usually locked away.

To the rear of the building, the **Garden of Remembrance** has 68 plaques listing the names of all those Orangemen killed in the county during the Troubles. Having perused the exhibition, pop into the most agreeable *Sloan's* coffee shop, on the ground floor of the building.

### Dan Winter's Cottage

9 Derryloughan Rd, 5km northeast of Loughall • Mon–Sat 10.30am–5.30pm, Sun 2–5.30pm • Voluntary donation • ☎ 028 885 1344, ⓦ danwinterscottage.com

Positioned directly across from the site of the Battle of the Diamond, **Dan Winter's Cottage** is where the initial discussions regarding the formation of the Orange Order took place, though in the event the order was officially formed at Sloan's House. The cottage itself – whose roof still contains original lead shot from the battle – dates from 1703, and has been the ancestral home ever since Dan Winter lived here. Inside,

**15**

---

### THE ORANGE ORDER AND THE MARCHING TRADITION

Ireland's oldest political grouping, **The Grand Orange Lodge of Ireland**, was founded in September 1795 following the so-called **Battle of the Diamond**, which took place in or near **Dan Winter's farm** near Loughgall. The skirmish involved the Peep O'Day boys (Protestants) and the Defenders (Catholics) and was the culmination of a long-running dispute about control of the local linen trade. The Defenders attacked an inn, unaware that, inside, the Peep O'Day boys were armed and waiting. A dozen Defenders were killed, and in the glow of victory their opponents formed the **Orange Order**.

The first Orange Lodge march in celebration of the 1690 **Battle of the Boyne** (see page 573) took place in 1796, and they've been happening ever since. The Boyne is the Loyalist totem, even though the actual battle at Aughter that ended Jacobite rule did not take place until the following year. **William of Orange** is their icon, despite the fact that his campaign was supported by the pope and most of the Catholic rulers of Europe, and that William himself had a noted reputation for religious tolerance. For Protestant Northern Irish, the Boyne came to represent a victory that enshrined Protestant supremacy and liberties, and the Orange Order became the bedrock of Protestant hegemony. Between 1921 and 1969, for example, 51 of the 54 ministers appointed to the Stormont government were members of the Orange Order; at its peak, so were two-thirds of the Protestant male population of the North.

The **Loyalist** "marching season" begins in March and culminates in celebration of the Battle of the Boyne on July 12, followed by the **Apprentice Boys'** traditional march around the walls of Derry on August 12. Most Loyalist marches are uncontentious – small church parades, or commemorations of the Somme – but it can't be denied that some of them are something other than a vibrant expression of cultural identity. Marching can be a means by which one community asserts its dominance over the other – Loyalists selecting routes that deliberately pass through Nationalist areas, for instance, or their "Kick the Pope" fife-and-drum bands deliberately playing sectarian tunes and making provocative gestures such as the raising of five fingers on Belfast's **Lower Ormeau Road** (where five Catholics were shot dead in 1992). Though Loyalist marches have tended to be the flashpoints for major disturbances in recent years, not least in the late 1990s at **Drumcree** near Portadown, it shouldn't be forgotten that the marching tradition is common to both communities. Around three thousand marches take place throughout Northern Ireland each year and, although the vast majority are Loyalist parades, a significant number are **Nationalist**. The latter include the St Patrick's Day (March 17) marches of the Ancient Order of Hibernians and the Irish National Foresters, and commemorative parades and wreath-laying ceremonies by Sinn Féin and other Republican bodies on Easter Monday and various anniversaries.

you can see maps and relics from the battle, family photos, and a hoard of banners and sashes. There's some notable seventeenth-century furniture here too, including a remarkable French chair believed to have been here during Winter's time.

## The Argory

144 Derrycaw Rd, Dungannon • Visits by guided tour (hourly): Easter week, July & Aug daily noon–5pm; mid-March to May, Sept & Oct Sat & Sun noon–4pm; June Wed–Sun noon–5pm • £5.45, including grounds • Ⓦ nationaltrust.org.uk/the-argory

Set in 350 acres by the River Blackwater, 9km north of Loughgall, **The Argory** is a fine Neoclassical building dating from 1824. The splendid **grounds** include very pleasant gardens, but it's the **house** that's the real attraction. Built of Caledon stone, its entrance hall features a fine cantilevered staircase, and the rooms contain Victorian and Edwardian furniture among many other period items, including a fabulous cabinet barrel organ. The house is still lit by an original 1906 acetylene gas plant in the stable yard, and during the summer it stages musical events and organized garden walks. Tours provide entertaining anecdotes about the house's erstwhile owners, the McGeough-Bonds.

15

# Tyrone and Fermanagh

SUNSET OVER LOUGH NEAGH

# Tyrone and Fermanagh

Much of inland Northern Ireland is formed by neighbouring Tyrone and Fermanagh, predominantly rural counties whose few sizeable towns, with the exception of Omagh, lie at the eastern and western fringes of the region. Stretching from the shores of the vast Lough Neagh in the east to the Donegal border in the west, Tyrone is primarily a farming country with little evidence of industrialization apart from the neat planters' villages that grew up with the linen industry and a smattering of heavier industries in the towns near Lough Neagh.

The county's chief scenic attractions can be found in the wild and desolate **Sperrin Mountains** in the north, where the village of **Gortin**, on the Ulster Way footpath, makes a good base. The region's towns hold little of interest, though the largest, **Omagh**, is near the **Ulster American Folk Park**, which explores the connections between the Northern Ireland province and the US.

In contrast to Tyrone, **Fermanagh** attracts plenty of visitors – chiefly for its watersports, boating and fishing. Justly famous for the intense beauty of its lakes, much of the landscape is dominated by their waters, which, along with numerous rivers, constitute more than a third of the county's area. At its core is **Lough Erne**, a huge lake complex dotted with islands and surrounded by richly beautiful countryside. Lower Lough Erne, in the northwest, draws the most visitors, but the Upper Lough in the southeast also has its attractions, its hills wooded with oak, ash and beech. There are plenty of opportunities for watersports, while the less energetic can get onto the lough by renting a boat or taking a cruise. Walkers will find mostly gentle hills and woods which rise to small mountains in the south and west of the county, made accessible by the **Ulster Way**. For cyclists, there are well-surfaced, empty roads, though routes around the Upper Lough are harder to negotiate, with little lanes often leading to the reed-filled shore – an atmospheric spot for a picnic.

At the point where the Upper and Lower loughs meet, the county town of **Enniskillen** has long been a strategic bridging point: today, with more amenities than the rest of Fermanagh put together, it makes an ideal base for touring the area and getting out on the water. With your own transport you can easily access Fermanagh's impressive series of **planters' castles**, along with two of the country's finest stately houses in **Florence Court** and **Castle Coole**.

**16**

## GETTING AROUND · TYRONE AND FERMANAGH

In both Tyrone and Fermanagh, the sights of interest are dispersed, and buses can be very infrequent away from the main routes – you're likely to see little of the most interesting parts of the region without a car or a bike. In the Sperrins, hiking is the best way to get around, although sporadic buses also serve the area.

# Omagh and around

The name of Tyrone's largest town, **OMAGH**, is synonymous with the worst single atrocity in the history of the Troubles when, on the afternoon of Saturday August 15, 1998, a five-hundred-pound **car bomb**, planted by the dissident Republican group the Real IRA, exploded on Market Street. Twenty-nine people, and two unborn twins, died and more than two hundred were injured. Much of the eastern part of Omagh's main street was devastated by the bombing, though has since undergone major reconstruction. Two sites that recall that day form part of the **Town Trail**,

DEVENISH ISLAND

# Highlights

❶ **Ulster American Folk Park** Plot your way around this wonderful assemblage of vernacular buildings, which recall the history of Irish emigration to America. See page 553

❷ **The Sperrin Mountains** Ruggedly picturesque, the Sperrins offer a splendid variety of hikes and trails. See page 554

❸ **Beaghmore Stone Circles** Seven Bronze Age stone circles and numerous other relics set in a lonely spot with tremendous views. See page 555

❹ **Lough Neagh** Ireland's largest lake – and indeed the biggest in the British Isles – is best viewed from the churchyard at Ardboe. See page 556

❺ **Castle Coole** Perhaps the most magnificent building of its kind in Northern Ireland, this gorgeous eighteenth-century mansion is richly decorated inside and set in wonderful grounds. See page 560

❻ **Devenish Island** Getting out on the water is an essential part of any trip to Fermanagh, and there's no better place to do it than at this former monastic settlement in Lower Lough Erne. See page 562

❼ **Marble Arch Caves** Take a boat trip along a subterranean river to view these caves filled with stalactites and other marvellous rock formations. See page 566

**HIGHLIGHTS ARE MARKED ON THE MAP ON PAGE 552**

which is well worth an hour or so of your time; a copy of the trail can be picked up at the tourist office.

The area uphill to the west contains two adjacent buildings that would grace any town – the fine classical **courthouse**, adorned with a splendid Tuscan columned portico; and the irregular twin spires of the Catholic **Sacred Heart Church** – inside, take a look at the Rose Window above the high altar. Though there's little else to see in the town itself, it's a useful place to base yourself for exploring the area.

## The Glass Pillar and Memorial Garden

At the bottom of Market Street, a 4m-high cenotaph-like **Glass Pillar** – with a three-dimensional heart inside – stands at the point where the bomb exploded, next to a plaque on the wall. From here, head across the Strule Bridge to the **Memorial Garden**, a beautifully landscaped park with thirty-one pole-mounted mirrors strategically placed so that when the sun shines, they direct light on to the glass pillar, a rather ingenious feat of engineering. Engraved on a semicircular granite wall are the names of all those who died, which included six children – despite the traffic rushing by, it's a deeply affecting place.

## ARRIVAL AND INFORMATION

**By bus** The bus station (☎ 028 8224 2711) is just across the river from the town centre in Mountjoy Rd.

Destinations Belfast (Mon–Sat hourly, Sun 5; 1hr 50min); Derry (Mon–Sat hourly, Sun 6; 1hr 10min); Dublin (Bus Éireann; 7 daily; 2hr); Enniskillen (Mon–Fri 8 daily, Sat 5, Sun 1; 1hr); Gortin (Mon–Fri 8 daily; 25min); Letterkenny (Bus Éireann; 7 daily; 1hr 5min); Monaghan (Bus Éireann; 10 daily; 45min); Ulster American Folk Park (Mon–Sat hourly, Sun 5; 15min).

**Tourist office** On the ground floor of the riverside Strule Arts Centre on Townhall Square, just west of the bus station (Mon–Sat 10am–5.30pm; ☎ 028 8224 7841, ⊕ visitomagh.co.uk).

## ACCOMMODATION AND EATING

★ **Mullaghmore** 94 Old Mountfield Rd ☎ 028 8224 2314, ⊕ mullaghmorehouse.com. A couple of kilometres down the Cookstown road, this listed Georgian house – birthplace of actor Sam Neill (of *Jurassic Park* fame) is packed with extraordinary features, from a marble steam room to an Adams fireplace, not to mention some priceless antiques like Meissen porcelain. You can also make use of the library, orangery and games room, complete with full-size snooker table. **£80**

**Number 19** 19 High St ☎ 028 8225 7772. In a town with limited dining possibilities, this popular place is as good a spot as any for a bite to eat (snacks and hot lunches) or a coffee. Its sunny floral interior comes with leather couches and big bay windows looking out onto the street. Mon–Sat 8.30am–5pm.

**The Riverfront Café** 38 Market St ☎ 028 8225 0011. Directly opposite the glass pillar memorial, this is a cosy hideaway for a quiet mug of coffee and slice of cake, or perhaps a warming lunch; super home-made ice cream too. Mon–Sat 8.30am–5pm.

**Silverbirch Hotel** 5 Gortin Rd ☎ 028 8224 2520, ⊕ silverbirchhotel.com. Although aimed largely at the business end of things, this rather ungainly low-rise, out on the Gortin road, is the only hotel in town and the rooms offer a high level of comfort. Some good deals available too. **£75**

## ENTERTAINMENT

**Dún Úladh Cultural Heritage Centre** Drumnakilly Rd, 3km east of town off the B4 ☎ 028 8224 2777, ⊕ dun uladh.ie. Fabulously vibrant regional centre that promotes traditional Irish music and culture, with some big names; there's also a traditional session on Saturday nights.

**Strule Arts Centre** Townhall Square ☎ 028 8224 7831, ⊕ struleartscentre.co.uk. Stages a lively programme of music, drama and other events, and has a regular roster of excellent touring companies.

**16**

# Ulster American Folk Park

Mellon Rd, Castletown • March–June, Sept & Oct Thurs–Sun 10am–5pm; July & Aug daily 10am–5pm; Nov–Feb Thurs & Fri 10am–4pm, Sat & Sun 11am–4pm; last admission 1hr 30min before closing • £9 • ☎ 028 8224 3292, ⊕ nmni.com • Bus #273 Belfast to Derry from Omagh

The most successful of Northern Ireland's American-heritage projects is the wonderful **Ulster American Folk Park**. The first significant emigration from Ireland to North America was that of Northern Irish folk in the early eighteenth century, many of whom were of Scottish Protestant origin. Of all the immigrant communities in the United States, it was the Irish who most quickly – and profoundly – made their mark; the three first-generation US presidents of Irish origin were all of Ulster stock, and thirteen overall could trace their roots to here. Throughout the eighteenth and nineteenth centuries, thousands of people left to establish new lives in North America, a steady flow of emigrants that became a torrent during the Famine years.

Before heading out to the park itself, have a nose around the indoor **Emigrants Exhibition**, just beyond the reception desk, which documents the causes and patterns of migration, though, regrettably, little attention is paid to the Native Americans dispossessed by the Northern Ireland settlers.

## The Park

You enter the park in the **Old World**, where original buildings have been transplanted or replicas constructed to provide a sense of Northern Irish life in the past. Throughout, costumed guides and craftworkers cheerfully answer questions and explain their activities, augmenting the folk park's attention to authenticity.

The disparity in living conditions in nineteenth-century Ireland is illustrated by the juxtaposition of a typical pre-Famine **single-room cabin,** from the Sperrins, with the **Mellon Homestead**, a significantly more substantial dwelling and the only structure in the park in its original location; it was in this house that Thomas Mellon – founder of the Mellon Bank in 1869 in Pennsylvania, which now trades as The Bank of New York Mellon – was born in 1813, before the family emigrated five years later. Fittingly, the park was opened by descendants of Mellon in 1976. Even more impressive is the thatched, double-storey **Campbell House**, the ancestral home of Hugh Campbell, who also emigrated and became a successful Philadelphia merchant.

Look out, too, for the **Hughes House**, the one-time home of John Hughes, another successful émigré who became the first Catholic Archbishop of New York in 1842, though if his nickname, "Dagger John", was anything to go by, not a particularly popular one; one peculiar feature of this house is the "jamb" wall, a single brick wall between front door and hearth which prevented draughts, as well as offering a degree of privacy. A few paces away is the Victorian **schoolhouse**, which functioned from 1845 to 1950; it's furnished with its original, graffiti-strewn desks and is overseen by a suitably stern mistress quick to admonish anyone that steps out of line. A re-created Ulster **street**, including the impressively authentic O'Doherty's Spirit Grocers, whose shelves are packed with appropriate period stock, leads to the *Union*, a full-sized **brig**, reconstructed to demonstrate the gruelling conditions endured during the voyage across the Atlantic; with a thirty percent mortality rate, it's little wonder that they were coined "coffin ships".

Upon disembarking, you enter the **Old World**, starting with an American street featuring, among other concerns, a reconstruction of the first Mellon Bank. From here, leafy lanes wind down to edifices constructed by the Pennsylvanian settlers, notably a massive six-roomed log **farmhouse** and a Tennessee plantation house. One event of note here is the annual **Bluegrass Festival** held over the first weekend in September.

# The Sperrin Mountains

The impressive, undulating **Sperrin Mountains** form the northeastern limits of County Tyrone. Wild, empty and beautiful, they reach 680m at their highest point, yet the smooth and gradually curving slopes give them a deceptively low appearance. The covering of bog and heather only adds to this effect, suggesting nothing more than high, open moorland. For all this, views from the summits are panoramic, and the evenness of texture can make the mountains sumptuous when bathed in evening light. It's impossible not to catch sight of **wildlife**, too. Sparrowhawks and kestrels fly above, and you might see buzzards or the rare hen harrier, attracted by a rich range of prey in a landscape mostly undisturbed by development: the Sperrins teem with assorted mammals, including even the rare Irish hare. Over the years there's been many a tale about the discovery of "gold in them there hills", and you might encounter the occasional panner testing the story's veracity.

Much depopulated over the years, the local sheep-farming community is now sparsely scattered across the region; there are few **facilities** such as shops or pubs and little accommodation, except in Gortin, so planning ahead is essential if you're intending to walk in the mountains.

## Gortin

The best base for exploring the Sperrins is the one-street village of **GORTIN**, 16km north of Omagh. Around 5km south of the village is the **Gortin Glen Forest Park** (daily 10am–dusk; cars £3.50), with a 8km **forest drive** and various **trails** leading to viewpoints of the area. For mountain bikers, there are three variously graded trails in the park's

**WALKING THE SPERRINS**

The 64km-wide range of the Sperrin Mountains offers good long-distance **walking**, without necessarily involving steep inclines. You can ramble wherever you like, but remember that – despite appearances – these are high mountains, and changeable weather makes them potentially dangerous. A map and compass are essential for serious excursions.

The **Central Sperrins Way** (map available from most tourist offices) is a 40km waymarked trail, which begins and ends at Barnes Gap, halfway between Plumbridge and Cranagh. The two-day walk takes in a variety of countryside with spectacular views of the mountains, moorland and Glenelly Valley. The exposed moorland can often be very wet and boggy underfoot and, as there is no accommodation en route, taking a tent is essential.

For those not equipped for the high ground, the **Glenelly and Owenkillen** river valleys run through the heart of this fine countryside from Plumbridge and Gortin respectively and are particularly enjoyable by cyclists; you can pick up a copy of the Sperrins cycling guide from tourist offices. The **Sperrins and Killeter Walking Festival** (ⓦ sperrinskilleterwalking.com) is held in mid-September and involves various guided walks, graded according to difficulty.

northern reaches, above the Glenpark Road. The park's most popular attraction, however, is its herd of **Sika deer**, which are particularly fun to watch in rutting season, typically from the end of September through to November. Gortin Glen is accessible on any bus between Omagh and Gortin (see page 556).

**16**

# Beaghmore Stone Circles

Tyrone is peppered with **archeological remains**: there are more than a thousand standing stones in the Sperrins alone, and the county as a whole boasts numerous chambered graves. The most impressive relics are the Bronze Age **Beaghmore Stone Circles**, in the southeast of the Sperrins. From Gortin, take the B46 east onto the A505, from where they're well signposted up a track just over 5km north off the road. Although most of the stones on this lonely site are no more than a metre high, the complexity of the ritual they suggest is impressive: there are seven stone circles, ten stone rows and a dozen round cairns (burial mounds, some containing cremated human remains). All of the circles stand in pairs, except for one, which is filled with over eight hundred upright stones, known as the **Dragon's Teeth**. The alignments correlate to movements of the sun, moon and stars; two of the rows point to sunrise at the summer solstice.

# An Creagán Visitor Centre

24km east of Omagh on the A505 • Daily: April–Sept 11am–5pm; Oct–March 11am–4pm • Free; bike rental £10/day • ☎ 028 8076 1112, ⓦ ancreagan.com

Modelled on the many surrounding cairns, the **An Creagán Visitor Centre** explores the rare, raised bog terrain all around with interpretive **displays** and signposted **walking and cycling routes** over the countryside; the longest of the three trails is the circular, 5km-long Forest Walk. The farmers driven to these bogs in the eighteenth century made huge efforts to reclaim the soil: there are limekilns from which they treated the reclaimed land, and you can still see their **potato ridges** – these grassed-over Copney spade ridges point back to the devastating Famine of 1845–51 and illustrate the farmers' desperate attempts to survive.

An Creagán is, however, more of a **cultural centre** than a museum, with locals coming along to occasional traditional music concerts, dancing, storytelling and singing events; there's also a restaurant here.

**16**

## ARRIVAL AND DEPARTURE
## THE SPERRIN MOUNTAINS

**By bus** The Central Sperrins are tricky to reach without your own transport, but there is the useful Sperrin Rambler bus (£9), which runs from Omagh throughout the year (currently Mon–Fri 9.15am & 1.15pm) via Gortin through the Sperrins to Cranagh and on to Magherafelt in Co. Derry

(the return service from Magherafelt operates Mon–Fri 9.10am & 1.10pm).

Destinations An Creagán Centre to Omagh (Mon–Fri 2 daily, Sat 1; 50min); Gortin to Omagh (Mon–Fri 8 daily; 25min).

## ACCOMMODATION AND EATING

**An Clachan Cottages** An Creagán ☎ 028 8076 1112, ⓦ ancreagan.com. Eight self-catering cottages (with one to three bedrooms) are available in the traditional *clochán* settlements; the open turf fires are supplemented, fortunately, by central heating. Two-night minimum stay. **£180**

**Foothills** 16 Main St, Gortin ☎ 028 8164 8157. You can eat really well at this snug restaurant/bar, where there's contemporary Irish cooking of the highest order; try the

steak with whiskey and blue cheese sauce (£18).Daily noon–10pm.

**Gortin Accommodation Suite** 62 Main St, Gortin ☎ 028 8164 8346, ⓦ gortincentre.com. A friendly, multi-functional venue offering a range of self-catering units, six- and eight-bed dorms and family rooms sleeping up to four. A range of on- and off-site activities are available, including canoeing and cycling. Dorms **£15**, self-catering **£75**

# Eastern Tyrone

The dominant feature in the east of County Tyrone is the western shore of **Lough Neagh**, while there are a number of relics of both the region's historical heritage, such as the high cross at **Ardboe**, and its more recent industrial past at the **Wellbrook Beetling Mill**, close to Cookstown. The village of **Benburb**, to the south, is one of the most attractively situated in the North.

## Lough Neagh

According to legend, **Lough Neagh** (pronounced "nay") owes its origins to the mythical giant Fionn Mac Cumhaill, who was so unimpressed by east Tyrone's low-lying terrain that he took a massive lump of land from Ulster and hurled it across the Irish Sea. It landed midway and became the Isle of Man, and the hole it left behind became the lough. Its shores provide excellent fishing and plenty of bird life, though both the surrounding land and lake itself are almost featureless. Small settlements house eel fishermen, whose catches go to the Toome Eel Fishery at **Toome** at the northern tip of the lake.

### Ardboe high cross

Slight relief from the featurelessness is to be found at lakeside **Ardboe**, halfway along the lough's western shore, where there's a tenth-century **high cross**. The elements have eroded the various biblical scenes carved onto the sandstone almost beyond recognition, but its exceptional size – almost 6m high – is impressive. The cross stands in the grounds of an early monastery associated with St Colman, but the ruined church nearby dates from the seventeenth century and is of little interest. On a humid day in early summer, you'll also not fail to be impressed by the swarms of black Lough Neagh mayflies.

## Wellbrook Beetling Mill

20 Wellbrook Rd, 10km west of Cookstown • Mid-March to Sept Sat, Sun & public hols 2–5pm • £5 • ☎ 028 8674 8210, ⓦ nationaltrust.org.uk /wellbrook-beetling-mill

Positioned on a pretty stretch of the Ballinderry River, the eighteenth-century **Wellbrook Beetling Mill** is the last functioning water-powered linen mill in the country. "Beetling" was the final stage of production whereby linen was given a sheen and smoothness by hammering with heavy wooden "beetles". Harnessing the waters from the river is the superb almost-5m waterwheel, and although the mill ceased operation in 1961, it is extremely well preserved, and all the engines still work. The guides here are extremely enthusiastic and knowledgeable, and will give you a demonstration; it's also possible to have a go yourself.

## Benburb

Lying 11km northwest of Armagh (see page 540), the picturesque village of **BENBURB** merits a detour. Main Street's tiny cottages were once apple-peeling sheds, and the parish **church**, dating from 1618, is one of the oldest still in regular use in Ireland. It stands next to the gates of a **Servite priory** – the monastic order of Servants of the Virgin, which, though founded in Florence in 1233, did not establish itself in Ireland until 1948. The priory grounds offer a pleasant stroll, but far better are the walks along the Blackwater River in **Benburb Valley Park** (daily 9am–dusk; free), where, perched on a rock 30m or so above the water, are the substantial remains of a **castle** built by Viscount Powerscourt in 1615, which offer commanding views of the Blackwater valley.

# Enniskillen and around

A pleasant, conservative little town, **ENNISKILLEN** sits on an island like an ornamental buckle, the two narrow ribbons of water that pass each side connecting the Lower and Upper lough complexes – hence it can lay claim to being Ireland's only island town. The strategic strength of this position has long been recognized – indeed, the town takes its name from Innis Ceithleann, "the island of Kathleen", wife of Balor, who sought refuge here after a defeat in battle. Later the island became a Maguire stronghold before William Cole, a planter from Cornwall, was appointed governor in 1607. The town played a major role in the 1641 Rebellion and the later Williamite Wars, the latter leading to the formation of its two famous regiments, the **Inniskilling Dragoons** and the **Royal Inniskilling Fusiliers**, which played a significant role in the victory at the Battle of the Boyne. Much of Enniskillen's character comes from wealth derived from the care of a colonial presence, and evidence of British influence is widespread, not least in the stately **Portora Royal School**, which serves as a reminder of the continued elitism in the social order. Founded by Charles I in 1626, old boys include **Oscar Wilde** – the pride of the school, until his trial for homosexuality – and **Samuel Beckett**, after whom the town's most prestigious festival is named (see page 561).

However, the name Enniskillen is still often associated with one of the most devastating atrocities of the Troubles: on Remembrance Day 1987, an IRA **bomb** killed eleven and injured 61 people as they gathered to commemorate the dead of the two world wars. The resulting widespread outrage was instrumental in directing parts of the Republican movement towards seeking a political solution to the Troubles. Today, Enniskillen is worthy of a day's visit in its own right, with its **castle** and proximity to the elegant **Castle Coole**, plus a town centre relatively unspoilt by shopping developments. It's also ideally situated as a base for exploring Lough Erne and touring the attractive local countryside.

## The main street

The centre invites strolling: the main street undulates gently, lined with sturdy Victorian and Edwardian town houses, thriving shops and smart pub fronts, and, clustered together, three fine **church** buildings – Church of Ireland, Catholic and Methodist. This street changes its name six times between the bridges at either end, running from Ann Street to East Bridge Street; to either side, lanes drop down towards the water. On Down Street, just off the High Street, pop your head into the

**16**

16

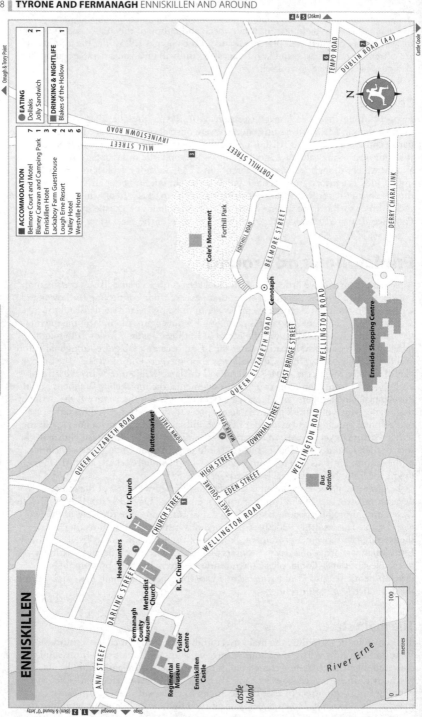

# ENNISKILLEN

**ACCOMMODATION**

| | |
|---|---|
| Belmore Court and Motel | 7 |
| Blaney Caravan and Camping Park | 1 |
| Enniskillen Hotel | 3 |
| Lackaboy Farm Guesthouse | 4 |
| Lough Erne Resort | 2 |
| Valley Hotel | 5 |
| Westville Hotel | 6 |

**● EATING**

| | |
|---|---|
| Dollakis | 2 |
| Jolly Sandwich | 1 |

**■ DRINKING & NIGHTLIFE**

| | |
|---|---|
| Blakes of the Hollow | 1 |

Forthill Park

Cole's Monument

Cenotaph

Buttermarket

C. of I. Church

Headhunters

Fermanagh County Museum

Methodist Church

R. C. Church

Regimental Museum

Visitor Centre

Enniskillen Castle

Castle Island

River Erne

Bus Station

Ernside Shopping Centre

Castle Coole

ANN STREET
DARLING STREET
QUEEN ELIZABETH ROAD
CHURCH STREET
DOWN STREET
HIGH STREET
WATER STREET
PAGET SQUARE
EDEN STREET
WELLINGTON ROAD
TOWNHALL STREET
EAST BRIDGE STREET
QUEEN ELIZABETH ROAD
BELMORE STREET
FORTHILL ROAD
FORTHILL STREET
MILL STREET
IRVINESTOWN ROAD
WELLINGTON ROAD
DERRY CHARA LINK
TEMPO ROAD
DUBLIN ROAD (A4)

N

Omagh & Trory Point
Sligo
Donegal (8km)
Round "O" Jetty
1 & 2

4 & 5 (26km)
6
7

metres
0 — 100

**Buttermarket** (Mon–Sat 10am–5.30pm), a superbly renovated dairy-market dating from 1835 that's now a craft and design centre where a range of artisans – potters, jewellers, woodturners and the like – happily ply their trade.

At the far end of East Bridge Street is the **cenotaph**, scene of the 1987 bombing; inscribed on a plaque are the names of those killed, along with eleven bronze doves, though plans are afoot for a dedicated memorial to stand close by.

## Headhunters

5 Darling St • Tues–Sat 9am–5.30pm • Free • ☎ 028 6632 7488, ⓦ headhuntersmuseum.com

"The Barber Shop with a difference" is how **Headhunters** styles itself – and indeed, this barber shop-cum-railway museum is quite unique. Entering the shop up on the first floor, you'll immediately be struck by the rather surreal sight of customers having a haircut amid a wonderful clutter of **railway memorabilia**, including locomotive nameplates, station signs and photos. Beyond the shop itself, several rooms offer up a voluminous array of exhibits – signalling equipment, lamps, timetables, tickets and so on – that recall the heyday of the long-defunct Great Northern Railway, which closed in 1958; ask, too, to see the fabulous model railway up on the second floor. And if you fancy a trim afterwards…

## Coles Monument

5 Forthill Park • May–Sept Sat & Sun, plus Mon July & Aug 1–3pm • Free • ☎ 028 6632 3110

Hidden away in a small park just beyond the cenotaph is one of Ennikillen's less visited sights. Completed in 1857, **Coles Monument** honours the distinguished general and parliamentarian Sir Galbraith Lowry Cole, a statue of whom tops the graceful, 30m-high doric-like column. Climbing the 108 stone steps brings you out onto a shallow, balconied platform affording a superlative panorama of the Fermanagh countryside – better still, you're likely to have the view all to yourself.

16

# Enniskillen Castle

Waterways loop their way around the core of Enniskillen, their glassy surfaces imbuing the town with a pervasive sense of calm and in places reflecting the mini-turrets of seventeenth-century **Enniskillen Castle**, which stands next to the island's westerly bridges. The castle was rebuilt by William Cole on the site of an old Maguire fort damaged by siege in 1594, and Cole's additions show obvious Scottish characteristics in the turrets corbelled out from the angles of the main wall. Today the castle grounds hold the town's two principal museums, which are accessed via a sparkling new visitor centre (see page 560).

## Fermanagh County Museum

Mon–Fri 10am–5pm, Sat 11am–5pm, plus June–Sept Sun 11am–5pm • £5 • ☎ 028 6632 5000, ⓦ enniskillencastle.co.uk

The old barracks now house the intermittently stimulating **Fermanagh County Museum**, which covers in some depth the region's history, mainly through archaeological displays. The most interesting of these concerns the Drumclay crannog, which was excavated in 2012 and is believed to have been inhabited between the

---

### THE KINGFISHER CYCLING TRAIL

Enniskillen is a good starting point for the 480-odd-km **Kingfisher Cycling Trail** (ⓦ kingfishercycletrail.com), whose circular route skirts Lower Lough Erne to Belleck and then south to Blacklion before running through the Leitrim lakelands to Carrick-on-Shannon (see page 402), then east to Belturbet in County Cavan (see page 158), and back, via Clones in County Monaghan (see page 155), around the Upper Lough to Enniskillen. The route passes through a wonderful variety of countryside, and though some of the hills are pretty steep, they are rarely too arduous to deter cyclists; the website has a list of places to stay along the route.

seventh and eighteenth centuries. Among the many superb finds on show here are bone combs, medieval dress pins and a pair of iron sheers; at one point there were nearly 140 crannogs (artificial island settlements) in Fermanagh alone. Other eye-catching exhibits include the River Erne Horn, ringed by nine bands of bronze, an immaculate bronze bell from Devenish Island, and a series of stone heads – look out for the suggestive male exhibitionist figure. The history of Enniskillen itself is covered downstairs, though disappointingly there's nothing on the town's recent past. The exhibition continues in a smaller building just beyond the visitor centre, though its displays pertaining to rural life in Fermanagh are eminently missable.

### Regimental Museum of the Royal Inniskilling Fusiliers

Same hours and ticket as Fermanagh County Museum

Occupying the adjacent keep is the **Regimental Museum of the Royal Inniskilling Fusiliers**, a proud and polished display of the uniforms, flags and paraphernalia of the town's historic regiment; formed in 1881 as an Irish infantry regiment of the British Army, the Fusiliers amalgamated with the Royal Ulster Rifles and the Royal Irish Fusiliers to form the Royal Irish Rangers in 1968, before their latest reincarnation, in 1992, as part of the Royal Irish Regiment.

## Castle Coole

1.5km southeast of Enniskillen • House mid-March to May & Sept Sat & Sun 11am–5pm; Easter week & June–Aug daily 11am–5pm; guided tours hourly, last tour starts 1hr before closing • Grounds open daily: March–Oct 10am–7pm; Nov–Feb 10am–4pm • House and grounds £5.45; grounds only £3.50 per car • ☎ 028 6632 2690, ⓦ nationaltrust.org.uk/castle-coole • The house can be approached either from the Dublin road (signposted just opposite the Ardhowen Theatre) or across the golf course from the Castlecoole road

Evidence of how the richest of the Enniskillen colonists lived can be found just outside town at **Castle Coole**, designed by James Wyatt and completed in 1797 as the lakeside home of the Earls of Belmore; the eighth earl and his family still live on site. A perfect Palladian-fronted building of silver Portland stone, the mansion is part of a huge seven-hundred-acre estate, whose beautiful landscaped **grounds** feature an impressive avenue of stately oak trees and a wealth of woodland walks.

Inside, the lavishly furnished **house** – indeed Wyatt indebted himself such was his extravagance – features scagliola (imitation marble) columns, exquisite plasterwork, Carrerra marble fireplaces, Cuban mahogany and an elegant library boasting Regency furnishings. A cantilevered staircase leads up to a dramatic and unusual lobby space and oval skylight, beyond which is a state bedroom decorated for George IV (who didn't actually come – in fact, the room was only ever used once, by the Bishop of Armagh in 1896). The tour ends in the labyrinthine basement, with its magnificent brick-vaulted cellar and capacious kitchen.

### ARRIVAL AND INFORMATION

### ENNISKILLEN AND AROUND

**By bus** Enniskillen's bus station is a 5min walk from the town centre on Wellington Rd (☎ 028 6632 2633).

Destinations Ballyshannon (Bus Éireann; 7 daily; 45min); Belcoo (Mon–Sat 3 daily; 25min); Belfast (Mon–Fri hourly, Sat 8, Sun 5; 2hr 15min); Belleek (Bus Éireann; 7 daily; 35min); Belturbet (Bus Éireann; 8 daily; 30min); Cavan (Bus Éireann; 8 daily; 50min); Clones (Mon–Sat 4 daily; 55min); Donegal town (Bus Éireann; 8 daily; 1hr 10min); Lisnarick (Mon–Sat 3–5 daily; 20–35min); Lisnaskea (Mon–Fri

8 daily, Sat 5; 30min); Omagh (Mon–Fri 7 daily, Sat 3, Sun 1; 1hr); Sligo (Bus Éireann; Mon–Sat 4 daily, Sun 2; 1hr 25min).

**Tourist office** The tourist office is inside the castle's visitor centre on Wellington Rd (Mon–Fri 10am–5pm, Sat 11am–5pm, plus June–Sept Sun 11am–5pm; ☎ 028 6632 3110, ⓦ fermanaghlakelands.com); this is also the place to come for information on all aspects of visiting Lough Erne, including fishing licences and permits.

### ACCOMMODATION

### SEE MAP PAGE 558

★ **Belmore Court and Motel** Tempo Rd ☎ 028 6632 6633, ⓦ motel.co.uk. There's a decent choice of different

accommodation here in this super-friendly hotel/motel; the motel, which is actually a large row of townhouse

## ENNISKILLEN FESTIVALS

Although no longer as big as it was, the town's chief annual event remains the Samuel Beckett-inspired **Happy Days Festival** (ⓦartsoverborders.com) at the end of August, which celebrates the eponymous novelist and playwright with a fantastic multi-arts programme of theatre, music, talks and readings in venues as diverse as the Buttermarket (see page 559) and the Marble Arch Caves (see page 566). **Fermanagh Live** (ⓦflive.org.uk), at the beginning of October, is a vibrant five-day festival of high-class music, drama and visual arts. Otherwise, there's the **Enniskillen Drama festival** (ⓦenniskillendramafestival.org) in March, hosted by the Ardhowen Theatre, while you should check with the tourist office for dates of the county **Fleadh**, the competitive traditional-music festival, in June (though it sometimes takes place in Derrygonnelly).

conversions, offers doubles, twins and family rooms, all with kitchenettes for self-catering, while the hotel itself has coolly furnished rooms with all mod cons. Breakfast is included but if staying in the motel costs £7. Hotel £85, motel £70

**Blaney Caravan and Camping Park** 21km northwest of Enniskillen, off the A46 directly behind the Blaney service station ☎028 6864 1634, ⓦblaneycaravanpark. com. A beautifully situated and well-equipped campsite that's ideal for families. Closed Nov to mid-March. £22

**Enniskillen Hotel** 72 Forthill St ☎028 6632 1177, ⓦenniskillenhotel.com. The building exterior is unremittingly dull, but the rooms looks fabulous in their various shades of grey, from the carpets and upholstery right down to the light switches; the only exception to the grey is the individually painted wall mural in each room. £85

**Lackaboy Farm Guesthouse** 51 Old Tempo Rd ☎028 6632 2488, ⓦlackaboyhouse.com. Good-quality B&B in a rural setting 1.5km northeast of town, whose six florally patterned, en-suite rooms promise a restful stay. There's a guest lounge with large flatscreen TV and open fire, plus lovely little extras like home-made tray bakes upon arrival.

£60

**Lough Erne Resort** Belleek Rd, 8km northwest of Enniskillen ☎028 6632 3230, ⓦlougherneresort.com. Spectacularly sited amid two lakeshore golf courses, *Lough Erne* offers large and supremely comfortable rooms – many with lake views – in its main building, alongside striking, turreted lodges sleeping up to six. Rooms, £110, lodges £220

**Valley Hotel** 60 Main St, Fivemiletown, 26km east of Enniskillen ☎028 8952 1505, ⓦthevalleyhotel.com. This smart, family-run hotel is a good choice if you're wanting to stay in the heart of the Tyrone countryside and also serves as a useful gateway to the Fermanagh countryside; good-sized, well turned out rooms are complemented by a very creditable restaurant/bar that functions as the lively hub of the local community. £80

**Westville Hotel** 14–20 Tempo Rd ☎028 6632 0033, ⓦwestvillehotel.co.uk. The location is distinctly underwhelming and the grey, rough-hewn exterior is far from enticing, but this is actually a sparkling little boutique hotel offering tastefully designed rooms in warming chocolate brown and beige, or turquoise, colours. £80

### EATING
SEE MAP PAGE 558

**Dollakis** 2b Cross St ☎028 6634 2616, ⓦdollakis. com. Three separate menus comprise this authentic Greek restaurant's offering: a lunch menu (noon–3pm) followed, between 5 and 7pm, by a meze menu, after which the à la carte menu is wheeled out; expect beautifully prepared dishes like feta cheese and honey filo pastry, or yoghurt-marinated chicken with chorizo souvlaki (£17), then round it off with a glass of Metaxa or frozen ouzo. Tues–Sat noon–3pm & 5–11pm.

**Jolly Sandwich** 3 Darling St ☎028 6632 2277. Jolly by name, jolly by nature, this busy, buzzy daytime café/deli, laid out with dinky tables and bar stools, serves all-day breakfasts (£7), hot wraps, salads and an eye-popping selection of cakes and scones. Mon–Sat 8am–4.30pm.

### DRINKING
SEE MAP PAGE 558

**Blakes of the Hollow** 6 Church St ☎028 6632 2143. With a *Game of Thrones* door in situ (see page 487), this agreeably careworn Victorian establishment should be your first port of call for a pint (the Guinness is reckoned to be the best in town), its dark wooden snugs perfect for cosying up in. Live music on Fridays and Saturdays, which could be either rock and pop or traditional. Daily 11.30am–midnight.

### ENTERTAINMENT

**Ardhowen Theatre** Dublin Rd ☎028 6632 5440, ⓦardhowen.com. The hub of Enniskillen's arts scene has a year-round programme of top-quality drama, film and ballet, and hosts a great range of music events as well as productions by local community groups.

16

# Lough Erne

**Lough Erne** has a profoundly important place in the history of Fermanagh. The earliest people to settle in the region lived on and around the two lakes, and many of the islands here are in fact *crannógs*. The lough's myriad connecting waterways were impenetrable to outsiders, protecting the settlers from invaders and creating an enduring cultural isolation. Evidence from stone carvings suggests that Christianity was accepted far more slowly here than elsewhere: several **pagan idols** have been found on Christian sites, and the early Christian remains to be found on the islands show the strong influence of pagan culture. Here, Christian carving has something of the stark symmetry, as well as a certain vacancy of facial expression, found in pagan statues. Particularly suggestive of earlier cults is the persistence of the human-head motif in stone carving – in pagan times a symbol of divinity and the most important of religious symbols.

**Devenish Island** and **White Island**, the most popular of the Erne's ancient sites, are on the Lower Lough, as is **Boa Island** in its far north, which is linked to the mainland by a bridge at each end. The **Upper Lough** is less rewarding, but has interesting spots that repay a leisurely dawdle. Aside from **cruising** the waterways (see page 563) and visiting the islands, there are a number of minor attractions around the loughs that are worth dropping into during your stay. Perhaps the most impressive are the early seventeenth-century planters' **castles** scattered around the shoreline.

## 16 Devenish Island

Heading around the eastern shores of Lower Lough Erne, **Devenish Island** is the easiest place to visit from Enniskillen without your own transport. A monastic settlement was founded on Devenish by St Molaise in the sixth century and became so important during the early Christian period that it had 1500 novices attached. Though plundered by Vikings in the ninth and twelfth centuries, it continued to be a major religious centre up until the early 1600s. It's a delightful setting, not far from the lough shore, and the **ruins** are considerable, spanning the entire medieval period. Most impressive are the sturdy oratory and perfect round tower, both from the twelfth century; St Molaise's church, a century older; and the ruined Augustinian priory, a fifteenth-century reconstruction of an earlier abbey with a fine Gothic sacristy door decorated with birds and vines. To the south is a superb **high cross**, with highly complex, delicate carving. Other treasures found here – such as an early eleventh-century book shrine, the Soiscel Molaise – are now kept in the National Museum in Dublin (see page 65).

### ARRIVAL AND DEPARTURE                                    DEVENISH ISLAND

**By ferry** Erne Water Taxis (☎07719 770588, ⌨erne watertaxi.com) operates ferries to the island from Trory Point, around 6.5km north of Enniskillen off the A32 Irvinestown road (July & Aug daily hourly 10am–5pm; June & Sept Mon, Thurs, Fri, Sat & Sun hourly 11am–3pm; Oct Sat & Sun hourly 11am–3pm; £5 return), though it's wise to check times before setting out, as poor weather can sometimes delay or cancel departures. To get to Trory Point from Enniskillen, take the Omagh bus to the Kesh turn-off.

## Castle Archdale Country Park

Near Lisnarick, about 6km north of Enniskillen, off the B82 Kesh road • Daily 9am–5pm; visitor centre Sun noon–4pm • Free • ☎028 6862 1333, ⌨castlearchdale.com

To immerse yourself thoroughly in the beauty of the lough scenery, it's well worth making a trip to **Castle Archdale Country Park**. The eighteenth-century manor house, on which the estate is centred, houses tea rooms and a small **visitor centre**, whose exhibits focus on local wildlife and Castle Archdale's role during World War II when flying boats were based here. The park is also perfectly placed for getting out on the lough, with bike and boat rental available, as well as a campsite. You can also take a ferry from the nearby marina to White Island.

## ARRIVAL AND GETTING AROUND

**By bus** The only public transport here is the Pettigo bus to Lisnarick, 3km away.

**Bike and boat rental** Between Easter and September, you can rent bikes (£10/half-day), canoes (£40/2hr), kayaks

### CASTLE ARCHDALE COUNTRY PARK

(£20/2hr), and boats holding up to six people (half-day £70, full day £100) from Castle Archdale Boat Hire (☎ 028 6862 1156, ⍵ castlearchdaleboathire.com).

## ACCOMMODATION

**Castle Archdale Caravan Park** ☎ 028 6862 1333, ⍵ castlearchdale.com. In the grounds of Castle Archdale Country Park, by the shore of the lough, this campsite has

a small supermarket and a café in high season. Closed Nov–March. **£25**

# White Island

Castle Archdale Boat Hire operates a ferry from Castle Archdale Country Park marina to White Island: July & Aug daily 10.30am, 11.30am, 2.30pm, 3.30pm, 4.30pm; call in advance for travel on the ferry outside these months • £4

Mounted on the wall of a **ruined abbey**, the seven early Christian carvings of **White Island** look eerily pagan. Discovered early in the nineteenth century, they are thought to be caryatids – columns in human form – from a monastic church of the ninth to eleventh centuries. The most disconcerting statue is the lewd female figure known as a **Sheila-na-Gig** (see page 616), one of the best preserved in Ireland. Less equivocal figures continue left to right: a seated Christ holding the Gospels on his knees; a hooded ecclesiast with bell and crozier; David carrying a shepherd's staff, his hand towards his mouth showing his role as author and singer; Christ the Warrior holding two griffins by the scruff of their necks; and another Christ figure with a fringe of curly hair wearing a brooch on his left shoulder and carrying a sword and shield – here he is the King of Glory at his Second Coming. There is an unfinished seventh stone and, on the far right, a carved head with a downturned mouth, which is probably of later origin than the other statues. The **church** of White Island also contains eleventh-century gravestones; the large earthworks round the outside date from an earlier monastery.

**16**

## LOUGH ERNE CRUISES, RENTALS AND ACTIVITIES

The MV *Kestrel*, run by Erne Tours (May & Sept Tues, Sat & Sun 2.15pm; June daily 2.15pm & 4.15pm; July & Aug daily 10.30am, 12.15pm, 2.15pm & 4.15pm; 1hr 45min; ☎ 028 6632 2882, ⍵ ernetours.com; £10), sails from the **Round "O" Jetty** in Enniskillen around the Lower Lough, calling at Devenish Island. They also run an evening **dinner cruise** to the *Killyhevlin Hotel* on the Upper Lough shore (May–Sept Sat 6.30pm, return at 10pm; £32, booking essential). The *Inishcruiser* sails around the Upper Lough from the **Share Discovery Village** at Smith's Strand (Easter–Sept Sun & public hols 10.30am; 1hr 30min–2hr; ☎ 028 6772 2122; £10).

A number of companies offer possibilities to **rent your own boat**, with or without outboard motor. A good bet is Erne Boat Hire (☎ 07523 423232, ⍵ erneboathireltd.com), based at the Regal Pass Jetty near the Erneside Shopping Centre in Enniskillen, whose boats take up to six people (£60/4hr, £90/day). Unless you're going out on a small lake, you should always let the boat owner know where you're heading and ask to borrow navigation charts – Lough Erne can be dangerous, especially outside the summer months. Share Discovery Village also offers a host of water-based activities, including **windsurfing** (£15/2hr) and **stand-up paddleboarding** (£8/hr) taster sessions, as well as **canoe** and **kayak** hire (£10–12/hr).

## Boa Island

10km west of Kesh at the northern end of the Lower Lough

One of Lough Erne's most evocative carvings is on **Boa Island** (barely an island at all these days, as it's connected to the mainland by bridges), which takes its name from Badhbh, a Celtic war-goddess. The landmark to look out for is **Caldragh cemetery**, signposted off the A47 about 1.5km west of Lusty Beg Island. Follow the signs down a lane and the graveyard is through a gate to your left. Here in this ancient Christian burial ground of broken, moss-covered tombstones, encircled and shaded by low hazel trees, you'll find a double-faced **Janus figure**. An idol of yellow stone with very bold, symmetrical features, it has the phallus on one side and a belt and crossed limbs on the other. The figure was probably an invocation of fertility and a depiction of a god-hero, the belt being a reference to the bearing of weapons. Alongside it stands the smaller "**Lusty Man**", so called since it was moved here from nearby Lustymore Island. This idol has only one eye fully carved, maybe to indicate blindness – Cúchulainn (see page 539) had a number of encounters with war-goddesses, divine hags described as blind in the left eye.

### ACCOMMODATION AND EATING
BOA ISLAND

**Lusty Beg Island** ☎ 028 6863 3300, ⓦ lustybegisland.com. Set amid beautiful woodland just off Boa Island, this popular weekend retreat (accessible via a free car ferry; 5min) offers a host of accommodation, including B&B in its *Courtyard* guesthouse, lakeside cabins (each with a double bed), and self-catering chalets and luxury lodges (sleeping 4–6). First-rate spa facilities, a cracking restaurant (daily 12.30–9pm) and canoe add to its appeal. B&B £129, cabins £140 (including breakfast), chalets £260 (for a two-night minimum stay), lodges £390 (for a two-night minimum stay)

**16**

## Forest of Castle Caldwell

Over towards the western extremity of Lower Lough Erne, the **forest of Castle Caldwell** is formed by two narrow promontories, which make it a natural breeding site for waterfowl and a habitat of rarities such as the hen harrier, peregrine falcon and pine marten. Its seventeenth-century **castle** has long been dilapidated, and the surrounding estate is now a commercial, state-owned forest of spruce, pine and larch. At the castle's entrance, look out for the giant stone fiddle in front of the gate lodge, the sobering memorial to Denis McCabe, a local musician who in 1770 tumbled from the Caldwells' barge while inebriated and drowned. Its inscription "DDD" supposedly stands for "Denis died drunk!".

## Belleek Pottery

3 Main St • Jan–Feb Mon–Fri 9am–5.30pm; March–June & Oct–Dec Mon–Fri 9am–5.30pm, Sat 10am–5.30pm, Sun 2–5.30pm; July–Sept Mon–Fri 9am–6pm, Sat 10am–6pm, Sun noon–5.30pm; tours (£6) every 30min 9.30am, 12.15pm & 1.45–4pm • ☎ 028 6865 9300, ⓦ belleekpottery.ie

**BELLEEK** owes its fame to the local **Belleek Pottery**, Ireland's oldest, which was established in 1857. The enlightening 45-minute **tour** takes in the various stages of production, from mould-making and casting through to fettling – the process of sharpening or delineation of the pattern on the pottery – and dipping, where the glaze is added. As informative as the tour is, you'll be far more distracted by watching the craftsmen and women at work, especially the basket-makers – the level of skill required is quite something; indeed, a typical apprenticeship is anywhere between three and five years. The **museum** exhibits numerous pieces, from early hunting bowls and domestic sanitary ware to more recent decorative items, while the **shop** offers up the chance to buy its extraordinary array of products. There's a lovely tea room here too, where you can sit down to a substantial lunch or a cup of tea and one of their home-baked scones – all served, naturally, in the finest Belleek tableware.

**Fiddlestone** Main St, Belleek ☎ 028 6865 8008. Although it's unlikely you'll need to stop over, the village's main pub does have half a dozen solidly old-fashioned rooms, in addition to a little guest lounge. Otherwise, drop in for a pint or a bit to eat. Food served daily 11am–11pm. **£60**

**Thatch Café** Main St, Belleek ☎ 028 6865 8181. Sweet little thatched cottage with an inviting, warm interior complete with a thick-set stone fireplace and wood-burning stove – perfect for coffee, or something from the lunch menu like a baked potato with smoked salmon followed by a slice of home-baked blueberry pie. Mon–Sat 9am–5pm.

## Monea Castle to Lough Navar Forest

In a beautiful setting at the end of a beech-lined lane, **Monea Castle** (free access), 11km northwest of Enniskillen off the B81, is a particularly fine ruin of a planters' castle. Built around 1618, it bears the signs of Scottish influence in its design, with similar features to the reworked Maguire Castle in Enniskillen (see page 559). It was seriously damaged first by fire in the Great Rebellion of 1641 and later by Jacobite armies in 1689, and was eventually abandoned in 1750 after another fire. Lying 8km further north, beyond Derrygonnelly, are the fortified house and *bawn* of restored **Tully Castle** (June–Sept daily 10am–5pm; Oct–May Sun noon–4pm; free), itself burned by the Maguires in 1641, down by the lough shore. Further to the west, there are tremendous views of the lough and surrounds from **Lough Navar Forest** (daily 10am–dusk; £3.20 per car).

## Upper Lough Erne

16

**Upper Lough Erne** possesses neither the historic sites nor the scenic splendour of the Lower Lough, but it does have the best preserved of the planters' castles nearby in the **Crom Estate**. There's little to see in the region's main town, **Lisnaskea**, save for the ruins of **Castle Balfour** (free access), which was built for Sir James Balfour, a Scottish planter, in the early seventeenth century; it manifests strong Scottish characteristics in its turrets and parapets, high-pitched gables and tall chimneys.

### Crom Estate

5km west of Newtownbutler • Estate daily March–Oct 10am–6pm; June–Aug till 7pm, visitor centre daily March–Oct 11am–5pm • £6 • ☎ 028 6773 8118, ⓦ nationaltrust.org.uk/crom

On the eastern shore of the lough, the National Trust's **Crom Estate** has the largest surviving area of **oak woodland** in Northern Ireland, home to rare species such as the purple hairstreak and wood white butterflies. Unfortunately, the modern Crom Castle is privately occupied and not open to the public, though you can visit the ruins of the **old castle**. There is also a café and interpretive centre here, and you can rent **outboard engine boats** (£30/4hr), **rowing boats** (£7.50/hr) and **Canadian canoes** (£15/4hr) too. The estate has an interesting range of accommodation available too.

**Tourist office** The Upper Lough Erne region's visitor centre is in Lisnaskea, 8km north of Crom Castle, at 113 Main St (Mon–Fri 9am–5pm, plus June–Aug Sat 10am–4pm; ☎ 028 6772 3590).

### ACCOMMODATION AND EATING

**The Kissin Crust** 152 Main St, Lisnaskea ☎ 028 6772 2678. Prettily decorated café with chatty staff and a cracking little menu, including a steaming seafood chowder and a mouthwatering selection of home-baked treats like lemon cheesecake. The afternoon tea (3–4.30pm; £12) is great fun, but does need to be pre-booked. Mon–Sat 8.30am–5pm.

**Mullynascarthy Caravan Park** Gola Rd, 3km north of Lisnaskea ☎ 028 6772 1040, ⓦ mullynascarthy holidaypark.com. Picturesquely located on the banks of the Colebrook River, this clean and pleasant site has around ten pitches; facilities include showers, laundry and a play area for kids. Closed Nov–March. **£12**

# Western Fermanagh

The stretch of countryside on the western edge of the county offers some good **walking** opportunities, particularly in the hills to the south. The **Ulster Way** (see page 567), which runs northwest from the Upper Lough and east towards Tyrone, makes the riches of the terrain easily accessible.

This region also has two attractions that are well worth seeking out. The magnificent eighteenth-century **Florence Court** is the most assured achievement of the colonists, built 150 years after the initial defensive planters' castles. If you have your own transport, a visit to the house can be combined with an hour or so at the **Marble Arch Caves**, the finest cave system in Northern Ireland. Walkers can reach both along the Ulster Way, accessible from the A4 near **Belcoo**; the path runs 6.5km south past **Lower Lough Macnean** to the Marble Arch Caves and then a further 8km east to Florence Court.

## Florence Court

13km southwest of Enniskillen, just off the A32 • Gardens and park daily: March–Oct 10am–7pm; Nov–Feb till 4pm; house mid-March to April & Oct Sat & Sun 11am–5pm; May & Sept daily except Fri 11am–5pm; June–Aug daily 11am–5pm • £8, house tour £6.50 • ☎ 028 6634 8249, ⊛ nationaltrust.org.uk/florence-court

The magnificent three-storey mansion of the National Trust-owned **Florence Court** was commissioned by John Cole and named after his wife. The house, completed around 1775, is notable for its restored rococo plasterwork and rare Irish furnishings, though overall the rooms are surprisingly modest in size. The **dining room** is especially lavish, its ceiling hosting a cloud of puffing cherubs with Jupiter disguised as an eagle in the centre, all flying out of a duck-egg-blue sky. There are some notable exhibits too, not least a chunky travel chest belonging to William of Orange. In 1955, a fire destroyed the top floor of the house, which has never been renovated internally.

Beyond the house lie the **pleasure gardens**, a lovely expanse of park and woodland, where you'll also find an ice-house, sawmill, and a pretty thatched summer house, now restored after having burnt down in 2014 and offering marvellous views across to Benaughlin mountain. On the opposite side of the estate, a glorious walled **garden** comprises rows of neatly tended flowerbeds, vegetable plots and an apple orchard. If you want to go the whole hog, there are some 15km of **trails** to enjoy, after which you can repair to the fabulous Stables **tea room**.

## Marble Arch Caves

8km west of Florence Court in Legnabrocky • Daily: mid-March to June & Sept 10am–4.30pm; July & Aug 10am–5pm; Oct 10.30am–3pm; tours roughly every 20min • £10 • ☎ 028 6634 8855, ⊛ marblearchcaves.co.uk

Fermanagh is renowned for its cave systems, the most spectacular of which is the **Marble Arch Caves**. The caves are one of seven geoparks in the UK (run under the umbrella of UNESCO), although the Marble Arch Caves Global Geopark – to give it its full title – also incorporates Cavan across the border (see page 159), thus making it the first cross-border geopark in the world. The caves were first discovered in 1895 by Frenchman Edouard Martel and Dublin zoologist, Lyster Jameson, with more extensive explorations undertaken in the 1930s by the Yorkshire Rambler's Club; they were finally opened to the public in 1985.

Following a pleasant little walk down through the reserve, the **tour** (which lasts around an hour and a quarter) begins with an atmospheric five-minute boat journey along the subterranean **Cladagh river**, before continuing through a succession of atmospherically lit chambers and passages. Throughout there are clusters of weirdly shaped stalactites and stalagmites, as well as other impressive formations, such as flowstones and scallops (sculpted indentations caused by water flow). Following a heavy Irish downpour, the caves are prone to flooding, so do check before you visit.

16

## THE ULSTER WAY

From Marble Arch Caves the southwestern section of the **Ulster Way** heads past Lower and Upper Lough Macnean before traversing the bog and granite heights of the Cuilcagh Mountains to **Ballintempo Forest** with its fabulous views over the loughs. The Way then continues north, through the **Lough Navar Forest**, a well-groomed conifer plantation with tarmacked roads and shorter trails. Although a great deal of fir-plantation walking is dark and frustrating, this forest does, at points, provide some of the most spectacular views in Fermanagh, looking over Lower Lough Erne and the mountains of surrounding counties. The Lough Navar Forest also sustains a small herd of red deer, as well as wild goat, fox, badger, hare and red squirrel. See ⓦ walkni.com/ulsterway for more details.

### ACCOMMODATION AND EATING

Finding somewhere to stay and eat along this section of the Ulster Way is fairly tricky, though there are several possibilities near **Belcoo**, 4km west from the trail's ascent to the Ballintempo Forest, plus one or two options in neighbouring Blacklion (see page 159), over the border in County Cavan.

**Bella Vista** Cottage Drive, Belcoo ⓣ 028 6638 6469. Perched right on the edge of Lough MacNean a few minutes' walk away from *Customs House*, this pretty little guesthouse has just two rooms, both with water views. **£70**

**Customs House Country Inn** 25–27 Main St, Belcoo ⓣ 028 6638 6285, ⓦ customshouseinn.com. The nine rooms in this rambling country house are beautifully designed, with all mod cons and luxury features such as Italian marble and handmade pewter tiling. The inn's *Fiddlesticks* restaurant is not half bad either, with very

reasonably priced dishes such as salmon with spring onion mash and sauvignon sauce (£11.95). *Restaurant* daily 12.30–3.30pm & 5–9.30pm. **£90**

**Lough Melvin Holiday Centre** ⓣ 028 6865 8142, ⓦ melvinholidaycentre.com. A bit further away from the route of the Way, west near the border at Garrison (take the minor road from Derrygonnelly), this place offers hostel-style accommodation and camping alongside numerous activities, including archery, caving, canoeing and wind-surfing. **£18**

**Rushin House Caravan Park** Holywell ⓣ 028 6638 6519, ⓦ rushinhouse.com. 1.5km up the road from Belcoo, this smart caravan park, attractively sited on the shores of Lough MacNean, has comprehensive facilities including barbecue, picnic and play areas, and a service block with kitchen and laundry. Closed Nov–Feb. **£22**

**16**

From whichever direction you approach the caves, you'll travel along the **Marlbank Scenic Loop**, with tremendous views of Lower Lough Macnean, and on either side you'll see limestone-flagged fields, much like those of the Burren in County Clare. It was fifty thousand years of gentle water seepage through the limestone that deposited the calcite for the amazing stalactite growths in the caves below.

## Legnabrocky Trail and Cuilcagh Mountain

Almost opposite the entrance to the Marble Arch Caves is the start of the 7.5km-long **Legnabrocky Trail**, which runs through rugged limestone scenery and peatland to the shale-covered slopes of **Cuilcagh Mountain** (666m), Fermanagh's highest peak. This forms part of an environmental conservation area and offers a wonderful, if strenuous, six- or seven-hour walk to the mountain's summit and back (be prepared to turn back if the weather turns sour) – on a clear day it's possible to see the Mourne Mountains. A part of the Marble Arch Caves centre is now devoted to an exhibition describing the restoration of the mountain park's damaged peatland and bogland habitats.

MUIREDACH'S HIGH CROSS

# Contexts

# History

Ireland's history is as rich and colourful as that of any European nation, and comprehending its troubled past is vital to an understanding of its current situation. Though the following pages can merely summarize key events, our book list (see page 606) provides sources of further enlightenment.

## Prehistory

Originally connected to mainland Europe, and at times completely glaciated, Ireland's geographical form has developed over the last two million years as a result of global climate change. The end of the last major **Ice Age** saw sea levels rise and the gradual separation of both Britain and Ireland from the European landmass, leaving just a few connections between the two regions. The first plant life is reckoned to have appeared around 12,000 BC, and the first mammals, such as reindeer, arrived a millennium or so later. A subsequent period of glaciation resulted in their extinction in Ireland, though warming again occurred around 9000 BC, at which point the country began its long process of forestation and various animals crossed the last remaining land-bridges.

The **first human settlements** are thought to date from around 8000–7000 BC. These Mesolithic hunter-gatherers, who made various implements and artefacts from flint, lived largely around coastal areas, such as Belfast Lough and the Shannon estuary. Developments

---

### IRELAND'S PREHISTORIC TOMBS

Ireland is sprinkled with an extraordinary number of megalithic tombs, of which more than 1500 examples have been identified, and many are in remarkably fine condition. The oldest tomb-form, dating from around 4000 BC, is the **passage grave**, consisting of a rounded mound or cairn with a stone-lined passage leading from the perimeter to a central chamber. Of the three hundred-plus surviving examples, mostly found in Ireland's north and east, **Newgrange** (see page 139) is the most renowned, remarkable not just because of its intricate construction – and the site's sheer scale – but also for its implicit associations with magic and ritual.

Dating from before 3000 BC, **court tombs** feature an open area beside the entrance, probably used for religious ceremonies. The majority are found in the country's north, **Creevykeel** in County Sligo being the best known (see page 398).

**Portal tombs** (known as **dolmens**), from around 2500–2000 BC, are the most easily recognizable form, consisting of three or more sturdy upright boulders, dragged into position, on which an often bigger capstone was placed. This tripod-like structure would then have a gallery tomb excavated beneath. Found in the north, west and southeast, a particularly fine example is at **Kilclooney** in County Donegal (see page 429).

Lastly, **wedge tombs** date from the early Bronze Age (around 2000–1500 BC), and are so termed because their burial chamber narrows and decreases in height as one moves inwards. More than a quarter of the recorded four hundred examples are located in **the Burren** in County Clare (see page 326).

---

| c. 11,000 BC | c. 8000–7000 BC | c. 4000 BC | c. 2000 BC |
|---|---|---|---|
| The first mammals arrive in Ireland | The first human settlements: Mesolithic hunter-gatherers | The first passage graves appear | The arrival of bronze casting |

elsewhere were slow to reach Ireland and it was not until the **Neolithic** period, around 3500 BC, that people skilled in farming settled here – equipped with stone axes (numerous examples have been found across the country), they were capable of clearing forests for their crops and animals. Subscribing to ritual and magic, notably in their burial ceremonies, they left numerous megalithic monuments across Ireland, including graves and stone circles (see box) similar to those found throughout Western Europe's coastal areas, indicating their place in a much broader network. Archaeological discoveries reveal the increasing subtlety of the products of this culture, first in the form of pottery and later, after the arrival of bronze casting techniques around 2000 BC, jewellery.

## The Iron Age

Ireland is usually considered a **Celtic** country, one colonized by the Indo-European people who spread rapidly across continental Europe from the East from around 1000 BC onwards. However, while they certainly reached the French coast, recent evidence suggests that far from being Celtic themselves, the peoples of Britain and Ireland gradually became Celticized through contact with traders. As a result, iron reached Ireland around 700 BC and, over the course of the next few centuries, the island's inhabitants adopted the Celtic ritual-based culture and language, though this would diversify significantly over the next millennium.

Other innovations followed, including the development of stone-built ring forts, a response to the need for protection brought about by Celtic systems of land ownership and fealty, which increasingly provoked intertribal warfare. A hierarchical system was gradually established, with individual **kingdoms** forming parts of larger fiefdoms based on the five provinces of Connacht, Leinster, Meath, Munster and Ulster. These fiefdoms in turn supposedly paid homage to a High King (*Ard Rí*) based at Tara, though in fact no such regal figure gained sway over the whole of Ireland until Brian Boru. However, like its Norse contemporary, this was also a myth-making culture, based on the cult of the hero. One of these, Cúchulainn, stars in the Irish epic nonpareil, the *Táin Bó Cúailnge*, a bloodthirsty tale of war and revenge whose characters are ever prey to the whims of their gods.

## Early Christianity

If the myths are to be believed, Ireland subsequently embraced **Christianity** with remarkable rapidity thanks to the efforts of its patron saint, **St Patrick** (who also eradicated the snakes that had never inhabited the island). Truth be told, the process was far more gradual and never entirely included the abandonment of Celtic pagan beliefs, as proven by the presence of Sheila-na-Gigs (see page 616) in medieval church-building. Missionaries began to arrive from the fourth century AD onwards, though the establishment of monastic settlements did not really begin for another two hundred years. By the eighth and ninth centuries monasteries such as Clonmacnois in County Offaly and Lismore in County Waterford had risen to become major seats of learning in an increasingly church-focused Europe. Extant evidence of such prowess exists in the form of **illuminated manuscripts**, such as the *Book of Durrow* and the renowned *Book of Kells*, on show in the Library of Trinity College, Dublin.

| **c. 700 BC** | **Fourth century AD** | **c. 800** |
| --- | --- | --- |
| Iron reaches Ireland | Christian missionaries begin to arrive | Production of the magnificent illuminated manuscript, the *Book of Kells* |

# The Vikings and the Normans

The **Vikings** reached Ireland towards the end of the eighth century and conducted sporadic raids on coastal areas, usually on monasteries – the defensive round tower dates from this period – before embarking on a more coordinated assault in 914. The upshot was the formation of fortified settlements at places such as Dublin, Cork and Waterford, though one hundred years later the Norsemen were vanquished at the Battle of Clontarf by the *Ard Rí*, Brian Boru.

One branch of the Norsemen, in the shape of the **Normans**, did finally conquer England in 1066, but it was more than a century before a successful Anglo-Norman incursion was made into Ireland, when Irish infighting resulted in Dermot MacMurrough, the dethroned king of Leinster, seeking the support of Henry II to regain his throne. The English king agreed to allow one of his knights, Richard FitzGilbert de Clare ("Strongbow"), to take a contingent of troops across the Irish Sea, but soon became concerned by the extent of Strongbow's success and arrived shortly afterwards to claim sovereignty over Ireland and establish a court in Dublin.

Norman rule over Ireland was largely restricted to the former Viking townships, and attempts to introduce feudalism foundered against the resistance of the Irish chieftains. In reality, the process of assimilation, which saw many of the victors becoming "more Irish than the Irish", resulted in the conquest becoming limited to a small area surrounding Dublin. This became known as the "English Pale" (from the word for an enclosure), and those who lived beyond its bounds were demeaningly described as **"beyond the pale"**, a term which subsequently became synonymous with barbarism.

Attempts to coerce the Irish into submission by force were abandoned, and those Norman settlers who had established themselves gradually became integrated into a society, now usually described as Gaelic, founded on the domains of Irish chieftains. The outcome was a flowering of **Gaelic culture**, with its emphasis on the place of the bard (a court musician-cum-poet) in storytelling and music-making. However, this did not prevent certain Anglo-Norman dynasties from broadening their own power bases, not least the de Burgo family in Ulster and Connacht, and the Fitzgeralds of Kildare.

# Tudor and Stuart incursions

The succeeding centuries saw various English interlopers attempting to establish themselves in Ireland, but it was not until **Henry VIII** broke with Rome that a concerted effort to demolish the hegemony of the Irish overlords began, linked to the dissolution of the powerful Irish monasteries with their wealth up for the grabs of any supporter of the Tudor regime. An abortive insurrection in 1534 offered Henry the excuse to send troops to Ireland, quash the revolt and establish himself as both sovereign ruler and ecclesiastical head of his domain.

His daughter **Elizabeth I** continued the process, but adopted much more stringent and far-reaching tactics, geared towards undermining Gaelic authority and its allegiance to Catholicism while simultaneously reinforcing Ireland's position as an English colony. Taking up her elder sister Mary's policy of **plantation**, which had seen parts of Laois and Offaly sequestered from their Irish owners, Elizabeth unsuccessfully attempted to "plant" colonists from Scotland in the area around Belfast Lough during the 1570s.

| 795 | 1169 | 1534 |
|---|---|---|
| The Vikings begin their century-long plunder of Irish monasteries, before building fortified settlements | Henry II of England's barons land at Wexford, kicking off the 750-year colonization of southern Ireland | Henry VIII sends the troops in to establish his hegemony |

The threat of further infiltration provoked Irish offensive reaction, of which the most crucial was the revolt led by **Hugh O'Neill** of Northern Ireland. This chieftain had been deliberately targeted by the Tudors as a potential convert to the Protestant plantation process, but, realizing he had been duped, he took up arms against the Crown. At first successful, his armies were crucially defeated at Kinsale in 1601 and, finally forced into submission by a siege at Mellifont in County Louth in 1603, he signed a treaty granting all his land and that of his underlords to the English, which was leased back to them under an oath of fealty. This opened the door for a flood of "planters", mainly ex-soldiers from England and the Scottish Lowlands who were encouraged to establish themselves in the newly gained territories. Though the Irish chiefs were still ostensibly in control of their land, their power was fatally diminished and a significant number decided to leave their country en masse in 1607, embarking from Rathmullen, County Donegal, in what was later described as the **Flight of the Earls**, heading variously for Flanders and Italy. The power of the old Gaelic kingships was at an end, and the plantation broadened its scale as **James I** urged more Lowland Scots to cross over to Northern Ireland and take over the Earls' impounded lands. This established a significant division between the Protestant planters and the evicted Catholic Irish, the ramifications of which endure to this day.

## The 1641 Rebellion and Oliver Cromwell

Concerns about the apparently pro-Catholic religious policies of James I's successor, **Charles I**, resulted in a Scottish rebellion in 1640. Having failed to persuade parliament to vote for taxes to raise new troops to quell the Scots, Charles negotiated a deal with Irish Catholics whereby their troops would be provided to suppress the rising in return for concessions regarding land ownership and religious tolerance. Alarmed that the king might be about to impose Catholicism across his dominion, a Scottish–Parliamentarian alliance proposed invading Ireland to subdue the population. A small group of Irish landowners planned their own rebellion in turn, conspiring to take Dublin Castle, Derry and other northern towns in October 1641. Their assault on Dublin was foiled by an informer, but their Northern Ireland campaign, led by Phelim O'Neill, was initially successful. Charles himself sent an army to put down the rising (and the Scots sent their own to protect Ulster Protestants, four thousand of whom had died in the fighting and a further eight thousand succumbed to the harsh winter conditions after being expelled from their homes by O'Neill's army), but the outbreak of the English Civil War delayed the resolution of the Irish question.

An Irish alliance called the **Catholic Confederation** was created to coordinate attacks on English and Scottish troops in Ireland, though **Oliver Cromwell**'s victory in the Civil War saw the overthrow of the monarchy and a determination to conquer all of Ireland. Cromwell arrived in Dublin with a large contingent of his New Model Army in August 1649 and embarked on a merciless and bitterly fought crusade to establish his authority. His prime targets were those towns occupied by Royalist garrisons, first taking Drogheda, where he massacred the troops and numerous citizens, before sweeping down through the southeast of Ireland and on to Cork and Kinsale. By 1652 all of Ireland was under Cromwell's control, his bloodthirsty troops slaughtering a quarter of the Catholic population in the process and dispatching many others into slavery in the Caribbean. The subsequent **Act of Settlement** saw widespread sequestration of Catholic-held land

| 1601 | 1607 | 1649 |
|---|---|---|
| The Irish chieftains are decisively defeated by Elizabeth I at the Battle of Kinsale | Many of them flee to Europe – the "Flight of the Earls" – opening the way for mass plantation of Ulster | Oliver Cromwell descends on Ireland with legendary cruelty |

and all the evictees were instructed to move west of the Shannon River by the beginning of May 1654 or face death – in Cromwell's cold terms, "to Hell or to Connacht". Many more died on the journey to places such as Connemara and the boglands of Mayo, while Cromwell's troops were rewarded with their confiscated land. Unsurprisingly, Cromwell's name remains reviled across much of Ireland.

## The Williamite War and the penal laws

Though the monarchy was restored in 1660, Charles II remained in thrall to his Protestant Parliament and it was not until he was succeeded by his brother, the Catholic **James II** in 1685, that Irish hopes were revitalized. However, anti-Catholic concerns, particularly about James's close relationship with Louis XIV of France, led the English Parliament to offer the throne to the Dutch **Prince William of Orange**. James fled to Ireland and enlisted an army to try and overthrow what had become known as the "Glorious Revolution". Though initially successful, the city of **Derry** presented a major stumbling block (see page 505), allowing William's forces the time to arrive in Ireland. James was finally defeated at Limerick, though the most celebrated encounter in William's campaign took place earlier, on July 12, 1690, when he was victorious at the **Battle of the Boyne**, an event commemorated as the highpoint of the Loyalist marching season (see page 546).

Subsequently, under William, the English Parliament consolidated the legal process (begun under Charles II) of furthering control over Ireland by diminishing the rights of the native Catholic population in terms of land ownership, marriage, religion and enfranchisement. A series of Acts passed between 1695 and 1728, which later became known as the **penal laws**, aimed at safeguarding the Protestant planters while suppressing Irish Catholic identity and culture and dragging the population into penury. Catholics were barred from purchasing land and on a landowner's death his property was split equally between all of his sons, thus incrementally diminishing familial wealth by each generation (an essential factor in the Great Famine of the nineteenth century – see page 575), though any son who converted to Protestantism became entitled to his brothers' inheritance. Catholic priests were banned from practising unless they paid two £50 bonds for registration, and even then were not allowed to say Mass; alternatively, conversion to the Church of Ireland attracted a £20 stipend, levied on their former congregations. Targeting cultural transmission, Catholics were barred from teaching, though some operated surreptitious "hedge schools" in the countryside, using the Irish language as a medium. Despite these exigencies, native Irish culture somehow survived.

## Revolution and rebellion

Towards the end of the eighteenth century, revolution was in the air throughout much of bourgeois Europe. Its initial catalyst was the **American War of Independence**, which saw British troops diverted across the Atlantic from Ireland. The series of laws establishing the primacy of the Anglican Church had not only affected Irish Catholics, but Presbyterian Northern Ireland planters, too, many of whom had emigrated to the Americas (see page 553), bringing about some sympathy among Ireland's burgeoning Protestant mercantile class for Washington's campaign demand of "no taxation without representation". Though

| **1690** | **1695–1728** | **1795** |
|---|---|---|
| Protestant William of Orange decisively defeats Catholic James II and the French at the Battle of the Boyne | Passage of the penal laws, suppressing Irish Catholics, their culture and identity | Northern Protestants found the Orange Society (later Orange Order) to oppose Catholic emancipation |

not directly taxed by the English Parliament, Ireland was the subject of numerous trade levies and the American war led **Henry Grattan**, leader of the Patriot Party, not only to make increasing demands for proper representation at Westminster and some form of constitutional independence, but to recruit troops to replace the departing English militia in order to defend Ireland against the threat of a French invasion.

More crucially, segments of the Irish middle class saw the **French Revolution** of 1789, with its underlying concepts of liberty, equality and fraternity, reinforced by the publication of Thomas Paine's *Rights of Man* (1792), and the consequent possibility of an invasion from France, as the potential means of securing independence. Formed by Belfast Protestants in 1791, the **Society of United Irishmen** promulgated Nationalist views regarding democratic reform and Catholic emancipation never likely to be taken up by the Grattan Parliament. After the English declaration of war against France in 1793, the Society was forced underground, and adopted agitational policies aimed at severing the link with Britain, linking with militant Catholic agrarian groups in the process. France became the means of breaking the connection with England, and one of the Society's leaders, Theobald **Wolfe Tone**, a Dublin Protestant barrister, was sent there to secure French support for an insurrection. Realizing the possibility of gaining a back-door victory over England, a French army set sail to invade Ireland, but was prevented from landing in Bantry Bay in 1796 by bad weather and indecision (see page 257).

Plans revised, the **Rebellion** took place in 1798 (see page 196), but met brutal English resistance, supported, especially in the North, by Protestant yeomanry, many of whom belonged to the Orange Society (later Orange Order), established in 1795 to oppose Catholic Emancipation (see page 546). The French, under General Humbert, finally landed at Killala, Mayo, in late August, by which time much of the uprising had been quelled. Drawing local support, they marched towards Dublin, until defeated at Ballinamuck in Longford. Subsequently, a larger Gallic force, with Tone on board, tried to land in County Donegal, but was intercepted by the British navy. Tone was taken to Dublin and sentenced to death, but slit his own throat before the execution.

As a result, the British enacted the 1801 **Act of Union**, dissolving Dublin's Parliament and ensuring total legislative control over Ireland, which now became part of the United Kingdom. The act did not deter one further Irish revolutionary, **Robert Emmet**, whose wholly ill-planned attempted coup failed ignominiously in 1803.

## Catholic Emancipation

The cause of Catholic enfranchisement became the major focus for agitation. Its catalyst was the lawyer **Daniel O'Connell**, who founded the Catholic Association in 1823 to build on successful British popular campaigns to expand the franchise beyond its previously limited bounds, and was returned to the British Parliament as MP for Clare in 1828. Though legislation prevented him from taking up his seat, his victory played no small part in the subsequent passage of the Catholic Emancipation Act, which, though only enfranchising a tiny number of middle-class voters, had enormous repercussions by making Catholics eligible for a number of previously excluded public offices.

O'Connell was elected as Dublin's first Catholic Lord Mayor in 1841 and subsequently embarked on a campaign to repeal the Union with Britain. Adopting populist

| **1798** | **1801** | **1829** |
| --- | --- | --- |
| The '98 Rebellion, led by the United Irishmen, is brutally defeated | The Act of Union dissolves the Parliament of Ireland, which becomes part of the United Kingdom | The Catholic Emancipation Act gives limited rights to Catholics |

techniques acquired from the Chartists, he called a series of "**monster meetings**" across all of Ireland except Ulster, attended on each occasion by as many as 100,000 people. Alarmed, the British government outlawed his October 1843 assembly at Clontarf and jailed him for sedition. More radical supporters of independence, the Young Ireland Movement, attempted their own uprising in 1848, but such was its lack of support that it became known as "The Battle of Widow McCormack's Cabbage Patch".

## The Great Famine

The **Great Famine** of 1845 to 1851, during which Ireland's population declined by 1.5 million – almost twenty percent – was one of the most devastating tragedies in human history. In the early 1840s a potato blight spread across Western Europe, and, while resolved reasonably well elsewhere, struck at the core of an Irish peasantry excessively dependent on their potato yields. Britain's laissez-faire economic policy throughout the Famine years allowed continued export from Ireland of other agricultural products, which might have alleviated the situation. By the worst year of the Famine, Black '47, hundreds of thousands faced starvation, a situation exacerbated by mass evictions across Ireland as landlords removed tenants unable to pay their dues. Workhouses were crammed to overcapacity and, while some were fed by soup kitchens or received support from individual landlords, the majority faced death or emigration.

Though Dublin, Belfast and much of the Northern Ireland province remained relatively unscathed, at least a million people died during the Famine and hundreds of thousands migrated to Britain or risked death by travelling on one of the infamous "coffin ships" to North America or Australasia, which, often crammed beyond capacity, were not fit to sail and floundered en route.

Nationalist action had been fuelled by British policy during the Famine years. The **Irish Republican Brotherhood** (sometimes termed Fenians and funded in part from the US) carried out an abortive uprising in 1867 and incurred a massive backlash, though this failed to destroy the organization. Agrarian groups focused particularly on

### THE IRISH DIASPORA

Even when Ireland's Great Famine was finally quelled, a pattern had been set, with **emigration** becoming regarded as the only means of escaping poverty. Sixty years after the Famine, Ireland's population had sunk to just over half its 1841 level of 8.2 million, and further waves of emigration occurred during the twentieth century. This **diaspora** established large Irish communities in other countries, especially Britain (where ten percent of the population are now thought to have an Irish grandparent) and the USA, where **Irish-Americans** played a major role in supporting moves towards independence and still remain a powerful lobbying group. The list of US presidents with Irish roots now runs into the low twenties (including Ulysses S. Grant, John F. Kennedy, Ronald Reagan, Bill Clinton and perhaps more tenuously Barack Obama), and over forty million Americans, one fifth of the white population, claim Irish descent. Other countries with significant populations of Irish descent include Australia, Canada, South Africa and, perhaps more surprisingly, Mexico and Argentina, the latter explaining how the great Latin American revolutionary Che Guevara came to have an Irish grandmother.

| 1841 | 1845–51 | 1848 |
| --- | --- | --- |
| Daniel O'Connell is elected as the first Catholic Lord Mayor of Dublin | Around a million people die and hundreds of thousands emigrate in the Great Famine | Unsuccessful uprising in favour of independence by the Young Ireland Movement |

**absentee English landlords** and those who continued to evict tenants unable to pay their rent – one of the most notorious wide-scale evictions took place at Derryveagh in Donegal (see page 436).

## The Home Rule Movement

Over the remaining decades of the nineteenth century the struggles over land and tenants' rights retained pivotal importance and were accelerated by **Michael Davitt**'s formation of the **Land League** in 1879. Its aims, however, became increasingly linked to a concerted campaign to secure independence via parliamentary democracy. The movement's guiding light was **Charles Stewart Parnell** (1846–91), who won County Meath for the **Home Rule Party** in the 1875 election and became its leader two years later. Parnell gained huge popularity in Ireland for his support of the ideal of an Irish Parliament, his use of obstructive tactics in the House of Commons and his full-blooded backing for agrarian action against recalcitrant landlords and their agents, using the tactic of social excommunication. One of the first victims, in 1880, of this device was a Mayo estate factor, Captain Charles Boycott – the action introduced his eponym into the English language.

**William Gladstone**'s government put Parnell, Davitt and other leaders of the Land League on trial for seditious conspiracy in 1881 and, though the jury failed to agree a verdict, Davitt was shortly afterwards re-arrested for breaching his "ticket of leave". A new Land Act, based on the principles of fair rent, fixed tenure and freedom of sale, became law later that year, but was rejected by the Land League which embarked on a new campaign of violence against landowners and thus was declared illegal. On the very day of Davitt's release from prison the following year, the British viceroy Lord Frederick Cavendish and his Under Secretary T.H. Burke were assassinated in Phoenix Park by a Fenian group calling itself "The Invincibles". Parnell denounced the murder in the Commons, but attitudes hardened against the Irish.

Though Gladstone had been persuaded by Parnell's arguments, his first Home Rule Bill failed in 1886 (as did his second in 1893), while Parnell's political career was terminated when his long-term affair with Kitty O'Shea saw him named as co-respondent in a divorce trial launched by her husband.

## Towards identity

From the late nineteenth century onwards Nationalist ideas became increasingly intertwined with the concept of cultural revival, especially via the establishment of two new opinion-forming organizations. Founded in 1884, the **Gaelic Athletic Association**'s fundamental aim was to preserve and nurture Irish sports such as Gaelic football and hurling. Avowedly Nationalist, its members were banned from playing foreign games and Crown forces were excluded from membership. The **Gaelic League** was formed in 1893. While aiming to preserve and maintain the Irish language and native culture, it too became increasingly nationalistic, viewing its goals as central to the "de-Anglicization" of Ireland. At the same time, a group of writers, centred on W.B. Yeats and Lady Gregory, set about establishing a **cultural revival**, based on the creation of distinctly Irish works written in English.

| 1867 | 1877 | 1884 |
|---|---|---|
| Abortive uprising by the Irish Republican Brotherhood | Charles Stewart Parnell, the "uncrowned king of Ireland", becomes leader of the Home Rule Party | Foundation of the Gaelic Athletic Association to nurture Irish sports |

Almost simultaneously, and in response to Parnell's failure to achieve Home Rule via parliamentary means, a current of opinion was developed and promulgated by a Dublin printer, **Arthur Griffith**, in his newspaper *The United Irishman* (established 1898). Initially, this espoused self-determination, involving the withdrawal of Irish MPs from Westminster and the formation of an independent Irish Parliament in Dublin as the only means to achieve economic and political freedom. Supporters of this view coalesced to form the political party **Sinn Féin** in 1905, an organization increasingly influenced by the views expounded by Scotsman **James Connolly**'s Irish Socialist Republican Party, which sought to establish a workers' republic in Ireland. A significant further factor was the rise of the trade-union movement in Ireland, especially the role of the militant workers' leader **James Larkin**, who formed the Irish Transport and General Workers' Union in 1909. Its philosophy was encapsulated in Larkin's slogan, "The land of Ireland for the people of Ireland".

## Resistance ...

The General Election of 1910 resulted in the slimmest of majorities for Asquith's Liberal Party, leaving it utterly reliant on the Irish Nationalist Party to enact legislation. Seizing the moment, the Nationalists pressed for a new Home Rule Bill, which the Commons passed in 1912. This aroused a bitterly intransigent response from Northern Protestants who united under the direction of **Sir Edward Carson**, a Dublin barrister, Tory MP and leader of the Irish Unionists. In September 1911 he and James Craig initiated a campaign to resist Home Rule and any threat of the imposition of Catholicism on Protestant Ulster. More than 200,000 signed up to a covenant pledging to defeat Home Rule by "all means necessary". In readiness for such action, Protestants formed their own militia, the **Ulster Volunteers**, which was armed by munitions from Germany. Indeed, Carson went so far as to lunch with the Kaiser in 1913 to discuss German aid for the resistance strategy.

Unsurprisingly, Nationalists and the British responded vigorously. The former founded its own armed force, the **Irish Volunteers**, the second Nationalist militia to form after James Connolly's Irish Citizen Army. The British responded by banning the use of armed weapons in Ireland and went so far as to plan a raid on the Ulster Volunteers, though this was abandoned when troops stationed in Northern Ireland refused to take action against the militia. Lloyd George devised a compromise whereby the province of Northern Ireland would be excluded from the introduction of Home Rule for six years, but the whole issue was deferred when war broke out between Britain and Germany late in the summer of 1914.

## ... and revolt

While Carson and the Irish Nationalist leader **John Redmond** pledged the support of both the Ulster and Irish Volunteers in guarding Ireland from German invasion (and, indeed, more than 230,000 Irishmen enlisted in the British Army), others saw the war as a fruitful opportunity ripe for the picking. In particular, leaders of the **Irish Republican Brotherhood** (IRB) made preparations for a rising, using the strength of the Irish Volunteers, to be instigated if the Germans entered Ireland or if the British tried to implement conscription. When army and police embarked on a series of raids

| 1893 | 1905 | 1912 |
|------|------|------|
| Foundation of the Gaelic League to nurture Irish language and culture | Formation of the Sinn Féin ("We Ourselves") political party | Home Rule Bill passed by the House of Commons – but deferred with the outbreak of World War I in 1914 |

against Irish Nationalist and revolutionary newspapers in late 1914, plans were made for a rising in September 1915, but were deferred when the Irish Volunteers' leaders declared themselves unready. The IRB sent an envoy to Germany, the former British diplomat **Sir Roger Casement**, who successfully secured German support for the rising.

When it finally occurred on Monday April 24, 1916, the **Easter Rising**, as it became known (see page 78) was a drastically limited affair. The British had already captured the German ship bringing arms and had arrested Casement when he landed from a German submarine in Cork four days earlier. Tipped off by informers, the British had also made plans to arrest all the leaders of the various organizations involved on that Easter Monday (though such action was then largely deferred until the rebels' surrender), and the leader of the Irish Volunteers, Eoin MacNeill, ordered his men not to take part in the rebellion. In the regions, action was limited to the north of County Dublin, Enniscorthy in Wexford and parts of County Galway, while the focus for the rebels' action became the Dublin General Post Office with simultaneous assaults on key targets across the city. Patrick Pearse, a poet and political activist, delivered the **Proclamation of the Irish Republic** from the steps of the GPO, but the rebels were powerless to resist the heavy British bombardment that ensued. After five days of fighting, the leaders surrendered, though it was two more days before combat ended. Over the course of the week, more than 1350 people were killed or wounded and numerous buildings in central Dublin destroyed.

Dubliners were initially aghast at their city's devastation, but public anger turned to outcry when all of the Rising's leaders and numerous other insurgents, with the exception of **Éamon de Valera** who had US citizenship, were executed by the British at Kilmainham Gaol in Dublin after a secret court martial. Connolly himself was so ill from infected wounds that he wouldn't have survived long enough for the planned execution and was shot while tied to a chair. As a consequence of the resulting public revulsion, all other death sentences were commuted, with the exception of Casement, who was hanged in London in August.

## The War for Independence

Far from losing support, as the British had hoped, the rebels' ideals were embraced by the next wave of leaders. Key figures were **Michael Collins**, working within the Irish Volunteers, and de Valera, who was elected MP for East Clare in 1916. The Volunteers grew in strength and Sinn Féin achieved a crushing success in the 1918 General Election, though none of its elected members took their seats, instead convening as the Dáil Éireann ("Ireland's Parliament") and issuing a declaration of independence. With de Valera as its leader and Collins as Minister of Finance, the Dáil reorganized the Volunteers and Citizen Army under the new name of the **Irish Republican Army (IRA)**. The British poured troops into Ireland and war effectively began in September 1919, when a soldier was killed in Fermoy, County Cork, and the British subsequently sacked the town.

In consequence, a campaign of guerrilla warfare broke out across most of Ireland which the Royal Irish Constabulary proved powerless to restrain. Irish sentiment was much heightened by the arrival of the **Black and Tans**, British soldiers re-recruited after World War I (and so called because of the colour of their uniforms), whose reprisals

| 1912 | 1913 | 1916 |
|---|---|---|
| Formation of the Ulster Volunteers to oppose home rule | Formation of the Irish Volunteers to oppose the Ulster Volunteers | The Easter Rising wins widespread sympathy only after the brutal execution of its leaders |

were merciless. However, even they were unable to prevent the situation of virtual stalemate, which dragged on until a truce was called in July 1921.

Meanwhile, in 1920 Westminster passed the **Government of Ireland Act**, establishing separate new parliaments for the six counties of "Northern Ireland" and the residual 26 of "Southern Ireland". Elections the following year resulted in a simple reinforcement of the Nationalist majority in the latter, which promptly reconstituted itself as Dáil Éireann, led by de Valera, and demanded independence as a 32-county state. Since Ulster's Protestants clearly held sway in the North and the armed independent struggle had reached deadlock, de Valera sent a delegation to London to negotiate an agreement with Lloyd George (thus absolving himself of any role in the process). In the face of the British prime minister's intransigence regarding the Unionist stand-off, the representatives, who included Michael Collins, agreed to the partition of Ireland as defined by the 1920 legislation, with the South gaining independence as the Irish Free State but retaining allegiance to the Crown through membership of the Commonwealth.

## The Irish Civil War

A provisional government was established in the South shortly after the signing of the **Anglo-Irish Treaty** in December 1921, which granted independence at the cost of partition. However, while Collins had signed the treaty on the basis that it was a major leap towards independence and a halfway step towards gaining control of all 32 counties, de Valera rejected the proposals as a diminution of Republicanism and refused to truck with their enactment. By July 1922, pro- and anti-Treaty forces had become embroiled in a bitter **civil war** which would have a lasting impact on Ireland's politics and economy. Though most of the population of the 26 counties supported the "Free Staters", opinion was seriously divided owing to the scale of the fighting and the reprisals taken by the provisional government, not least the execution of the prominent Republican Erskine Childers (who had run guns into the country in 1914) after his arrest for possessing a revolver given him by Collins, and the counter-reprisals that ensued. Eventually, the much weaker Republican forces were restricted to control parts of the southwest and west and were forced to surrender in May 1923. Collins himself died in 1922 in an ambush in County Cork.

## The Free State

Since one of the main candidates, Arthur Griffith, had also died (of a brain haemorrhage) during the civil war, leadership of the new government passed on to **William T. Cosgrave**, whose regime set about establishing a new infrastructure for the country's development, including the formation of a civil service and police force. Republicans boycotted the Dáil until 1926 when de Valera formed a new political party, **Fianna Fáil**, drawing members largely from the anti-Treaty element within Sinn Féin. Cosgrave remained in power until 1932, overseeing the initiation of the Shannon hydroelectric scheme and the foundation of the Electricity Supply Board, but his Cumann na nGaedheal party lost the election that year to Fianna Fáil ushering in de Valera's subsequent sixteen-year reign as Taoiseach. Cumann na nGaedheal

| 1918 | 1919–21 | 1921 |
|---|---|---|
| The first Dail Éireann ("Ireland's parliament") issues a declaration of independence and forms the Irish Republican Army | The War of Independence | Anglo-Irish Treaty signed, setting up the Irish Free State in 26 of Ireland's 32 counties |

itself merged with the National Centre Party and the right-wing Army Comrades Association (known as the "Blueshirts") the following year to form **Fine Gael**.

Throughout this period, the economic situation remained austere, exacerbated first by the Depression after 1929 and then by high British trade-levies on imports from Ireland, a result of de Valera's refusal to repay land annuities to Britain, which forced his government into frugality and self-sufficiency. These stern policies were reflected in Ireland's social and cultural life, and ties with the Catholic Church were reinforced at the time. However, de Valera's government also saw the establishment of state boards for road, rail and air transport (Aer Lingus) and peat production.

De Valera's determination to sever links with Britain resulted in a new **constitution** in 1938 whose central premise was the renunciation of Crown sovereignty and a new system of government for the state henceforth known as **Éire**. The model adopted was bicameral with the Dáil retained, but with a new upper chamber, the Seanad (or Senate), added, and the role of president (Uachtarán) created – the first holder of the office was the Protestant Douglas Hyde (see page 410).

## Northern Ireland's first decades

Following the enactment of the Anglo-Irish Treaty, Northern Ireland's new-found status as a largely self-governing entity had begun in June 1921 with the establishment of its parliament under James Craig, whose **Ulster Unionist Party (UUP)** would run the mini-state until 1972. Rather than including all nine counties of the Ulster province, leaders of the majority Protestant community had negotiated a settlement for their separation from the Free State on the basis of just six, thus ensuring the retention of a secure mandate which might have been threatened by the inclusion of the largely Catholic counties of Donegal and Cavan. Though a significant and gradually increasing Catholic minority remained, it was largely concentrated on agricultural areas west of the River Bann, plus the city of Derry, while the economically thriving linen and shipbuilding industries east of the river remained almost entirely in Protestant hands.

Britain needed Belfast's industrial strength as much as the UUP wanted Britain's economic and financial support and Unionists quickly set about reinforcing their domination. As well as establishing a largely Protestant police force, the **Royal Ulster Constabulary (RUC)**, and a military adjunct, the B Specials, the new parliament (originally based in Belfast, but moved to Stormont in 1932) strengthened its position by favouring the Protestant population with economic support, housing allocations and gerrymandering (for example, Derry's electoral boundaries were changed to ensure a Protestant council remained in power for decades despite the city's two-thirds Catholic majority).

## World War II

As part of the United Kingdom, Northern Ireland was heavily involved in the war effort, particularly Belfast, whose shipyards proved a major target for German bombing raids. In contrast, Éire adopted a position of neutrality throughout and negotiated its security with Germany, though it did make certain concessions to the UK regarding flights over its airspace. It also remained utterly dependent on imports from the UK and suffered drastically when British ships carrying goods such as coal and cattle feed

| 1922–23 | 1926 | 1932 | 1933 |
|---|---|---|---|
| Civil War between pro- (led by Michael Collins) and anti-treaty (led by Éamon de Valera) forces | De Valera forms a new political party, Fianna Fáil ("Soldiers of Destiny") | De Valera wins the general election, at the start of a sixteen-year reign as prime minister | Formation of the Fine Gael ("Tribe of the Irish") political party out of pro-treaty elements in Sinn Féin |

were attacked by U-boats. In recent years the Irish Republic's neutral role in World War II has been re-examined to some extent. New estimates suggest that despite the position adopted by de Valera's government during "The Emergency", as it termed World War II, around fifty thousand Irishmen from south of the border volunteered to fight for the British army, roughly the same as those from the north.

## The postwar Republic

De Valera lost the 1948 election to a wide-ranging coalition of opposition parties, led by John A. Costello's Fine Gael, which set about the removal of any surviving legislative links with Britain by establishing Éire as the **Republic of Ireland** in 1949. However, the new Republic's economic position remained dire and the early 1950s were characterized by fresh waves of rural depopulation and migration both to Dublin and abroad. De Valera was returned as Taoiseach twice during the decade (in 1951 and 1957), but it was not until his long-serving deputy Seán Lemass took office in 1959 that the policies needed to boost Ireland's stagnant economy began to be enacted. Lemass directed Ireland away from protectionism and firmly towards free trade, drawing foreign investment in the process, and sowed the seeds for membership of the **European Economic Community** in January 1973 – though by this time Jack Lynch's government was fully embroiled in developments in the North.

While the Republic, not least its farmers, initially prospered from EEC membership, the country suffered badly during the recession of the early 1980s, leading to a new wave of emigration. Its remaining population seemed to become increasingly conservative, rejecting referenda to allow abortion and divorce in 1983 and 1986 respectively.

## The Troubles and the peace process

Though Northern Ireland had benefited hugely from the social policies begun by the post-World War II Labour government, not least in terms of health and social care, its Catholic population continued to suffer levels of social deprivation far worse than anywhere else in the UK. In 1967 the **Civil Rights Movement**, a nonsectarian coalition demanding equal rights, was formed, promoting its campaign via protest marches. One of these, through Derry in 1968, saw demonstrators attacked by a police baton charge and television pictures of the West Belfast MP Gerry Fitt with blood streaming down his face from a wound – transmitted around the world, these provoked international condemnation of the RUC's tactics. Severe rioting the next year following the Apprentice Boys' August parade led to the barricading of the Bogside area of Derry and Irish Taoiseach Jack Lynch's movement of Irish troops to the border to await developments.

British troops arrived shortly afterwards, ostensibly to keep the peace in Derry and Belfast, where Protestant assaults on West Belfast's Catholics had taken place. Though initially welcomed by Catholics, the army soon shifted its approach in line with the laissez-faire and often repressive tactics of the RUC. After years in the wilderness, and bolstered by new recruits, the IRA took up the gauntlet as defenders of the Catholic turf, though its own internal disputes led to the formation of the **Provisional IRA**, which broke away from the Dublin-led Official IRA and began an armed campaign against the army, RUC and Loyalists. As a result, the British introduced **internment without**

| 1938 | 1939–45 | 1949 | 1959 |
| --- | --- | --- | --- |
| Promulgation of a new constitution for the State, henceforth to be known as Éire | Éire remains neutral in World War II, which is known as "The Emergency" | Éire becomes the Republic of Ireland and severs all remaining ties to Britain | Sean Lemass succeeds de Valera and begins to stimulate the economy |

## THE MAZE HUNGER STRIKES

In the late 1970s IRA inmates at Long Kesh prison (also known as **The Maze**) began a series of protests against the abolition of the Special Category Status they had been granted, which gave them the right to be treated as political prisoners. This began as a "**blanket protest**" in which prisoners refused to wear prison clothes, instead opting to remain naked under a blanket draped over their shoulders, and later moved on to the infamous "**dirty protest**" where the inmates smeared their cell walls with excrement rather than emptying their chamber pots. Despite a 1978 European Court of Human Rights verdict finding the British Government guilty of "inhuman and degrading treatment", the British position remained intransigent, both under the outgoing Labour Government and even more so when a new regime under Conservative leader Margaret Thatcher was elected in 1979. The H-blocks of The Maze had become a hotbed for Republican education and action and, in the early 1980s, a new tactic was employed – the **hunger strike**. The first of these ended ignominiously in 1980, but the second, led by **Bobby Sands**, commander of the Provisional IRA within the prison, who was elected MP for Fermanagh and South Tyrone in the course of the fast, had more effect. The hunger strike resulted in ten deaths, including Sands' own, but Thatcher remained obdurate despite worldwide condemnation of Britain's position.

**trial**, indiscriminately rounding up any Catholic thought to be linked to the violence. On January 30, 1972, British paratroopers shot and killed thirteen unarmed civil-rights demonstrators in Derry in an incident known ever afterwards as **Bloody Sunday** (see page 507). Three days later, the British Embassy in Dublin was burnt down and shortly afterwards Westminster's direct rule was reinstated over Northern Ireland. On **Bloody Friday**, July 21, 1972, the IRA exploded twenty car bombs in Belfast's city centre, killing nine people and injuring 130.

### Sunningdale and the mainland bombing campaign

The 1970s were marked by increasing violence and diplomatic attempts to produce a political solution. A first attempt at power-sharing, established by the 1973 **Sunningdale conference**, proved impossible to implement in the face of a massive campaign of disruption led by the **Reverend Ian Paisley** and the strike called by the Ulster Workers Council in May 1974, which paralyzed much of Northern Ireland. During the strike the Loyalist UDA (Ulster Defence Association) detonated three car bombs in central Dublin, killing 33 people. The power-sharing executive was disbanded and direct rule reinstated once again, which continued until 1999.

Meanwhile, the IRA had transferred its bombing campaign to mainland Britain in an attempt to force the reunification of Ireland, and in 1974 set off massive **explosions** in pubs in Birmingham, Woolwich and Guildford, killing 28 people. It declared a ceasefire later that year – subsequently discovered to be a consequence of clandestine negotiations with the British Government – but the failure to secure a lasting agreement led to the resumption of the campaign the following year. In retaliation, Harold Wilson introduced the **Prevention of Terrorism Act**, allowing extended detention without charge. In two major trials, those found guilty of the Guildford and Birmingham bombings were sentenced to life imprisonment, but increasing concerns

| 1967 | 1972 | 1973 | 1973 |
|------|------|------|------|
| Formation of the Civil Rights Movement to demand equal rights in the north | Bloody Sunday: British paratroopers kill thirteen unarmed civil rights protestors in Derry | The Sunningdale Agreement, an unsuccessful attempt at power-sharing | The Republic joins the European Economic Community |

about the reliability of the forensic evidence and their confessions led to the release of the Guildford Four in 1989 and the Birmingham Six in 1991.

Though refusing to respond to the Hunger Strikes (see box) by IRA inmates, Margaret Thatcher's government did attempt another power-sharing initiative with the formation of the **Northern Ireland Assembly** in 1982, but this was shunned by both Nationalists and Republicans. In 1984 the IRA notoriously bombed the Brighton hotel hosting the Tory party conference, in an unsuccessful attempt to kill Thatcher. However, parallel political developments saw a sea change in the form of the Republicans' tactical decision to employ the democratic process alongside the armed campaign. Instrumental in this strategy were two Republican leaders who would become pivotal figures in the peace process: former Maze internee **Gerry Adams**, from 1983 Sinn Féin's party leader and MP for West Belfast, and **Martin McGuinness**, a former member of the Provisional IRA and Sinn Féin's vice president from 1983.

## Towards the Good Friday Agreement and the Assembly

The IRA kept up its bombing campaign during the 1990s, beginning with a brazen mortar attack on 10 Downing Street in February 1991 targeting a cabinet meeting chaired by the new British leader, John Major. Loyalist sectarian attacks on Catholics also continued relentlessly, matching the numbers killed by Republicans. Undeterred, Major concluded an agreement with the Irish Prime Minister Albert Reynolds in December 1993, the **Downing Street Declaration**, largely shaped by the diplomacy of the SDLP's leader, **John Hume**, which sought to bring peace to Northern Ireland by democratic means.

The IRA launched another audacious mortar attack, this time on Heathrow Airport, in March 1994, but after focused lobbying by Dublin and the US vice president Al Gore, announced a ceasefire at the end of August, followed two months later by a similar Loyalist move. The following year witnessed intense negotiations involving the London and Dublin governments and the Republicans, which floundered in the face of the IRA's refusal to decommission its weaponry. Its bombing of Canary Wharf in London's financial centre in February 1996 re-emphasized its determination to continue the armed struggle, but lobbying for all-party talks on a resolution of the settlement intensified further. The key players were John Hume, who repeatedly met Gerry Adams with the intention of restoring the IRA's ceasefire, and the US president **Bill Clinton**, whose involvement and support for change went way beyond any intention to bolster his Irish-American electoral support.

The most significant broker, however, became British Prime Minister **Tony Blair**, the Labour leader elected with a vast majority in 1997, alongside his Northern Ireland Secretary, **Mo Mowlam**. They targeted a solution by diplomatic discussions with Bertie Ahern's government and the securement of the commitment of the **David Trimble**-led Ulster Unionists and Gerry Adams to all-party talks on Northern Ireland's future. The IRA's resumption of a ceasefire in July 1997 eased the process, but continuing violence throughout the following months, including the assassination of the LVF leader, Billy Wright, inside The Maze, provided further stumbling blocks.

Blair's commitment to a democratic solution culminated on April 9, 1998. After anxious negotiations late into the night, an accord was somehow agreed, and the **Good Friday Agreement** was signed the following morning. The Agreement committed its signatories "to exclusively democratic and peaceful means of resolving differences on political issues".

| 1981 | 1983 | 1991 | 1993 |
|------|------|------|------|
| Bobby Sands and nine other Republican prisoners die on hunger strike; Margaret Thatcher is unmoved | Gerry Adams and Martin McGuinness take control of Sinn Féin and Adams becomes MP for West Belfast | Mary Robinson becomes Ireland's first woman president | The Downing Street Declaration by the Irish and British prime ministers |

More vitally, the agreement laid down the principle that any subsequent changes in the government of Northern Ireland – whether it remained part of the UK or opted to amalgamate with the Republic – relied entirely on the consent of the majority of both the Catholic and Protestant communities. An **Assembly** would be elected, based on proportional representation, with an executive of ministers drawn equally from both camps operating departments previously run by the British. Political prisoners would be rapidly released and an independent commission appointed to determine the future of Northern Ireland's policing.

The agreement was ratified by the North's population in May, and elections in June 1998 saw the UUP's David Trimble returned as First Minister and the SDLP's **Séamus Mallon** as his deputy.

### Impasse …

Almost as soon as the agreement was signed, however, the new administration, opposed by **Ian Paisley**'s DUP and numerous other Loyalists, became embroiled in debate regarding the right of the Orange Order to march from a Church of Ireland in Drumcree, prior to celebrations of the Battle of the Boyne (see page 573), through Catholic areas of Portadown. Drumcree became a significant annual flashpoint over the next few years and the marching issue remains a significant element in the sectarian divide to this day.

It was not just Loyalist unrest that threatened to derail the peace process, though. A breakaway Republican grouping, the self-styled **Real IRA**, soon perpetrated the most murderous act of the whole history of the Troubles. As part of a campaign of town-centre assaults, it exploded a car bomb in the centre of **Omagh**, County Tyrone, on Saturday August 15, 1998, killing 29 people and injuring hundreds more. In the face of uniform condemnation, the group declared a ceasefire two weeks later.

David Trimble and John Hume were jointly awarded the **1998 Nobel Peace Prize**. However, while general optimism remained in place, the ramifications of parts of the Good Friday Agreement soon became apparent, as the UUP became concerned at the reduction of army numbers. Their worries were exacerbated by the report of the **Patten Commission** into the future of the **Royal Ulster Constabulary**, which proposed the force's abolition and replacement by a new body – with a new name – whose members were to be recruited equally from Catholic and Loyalist communities. The loss of the words "Royal" and "Ulster" from the new organization's title were impossible for Unionists to accept, and the new secretary of state, **Peter Mandelson** (who had replaced Mo Mowlam), bowed to pressure by rejecting many of the Commission's findings, despite strong Nationalist and Republican protest. The new **Police Service of Northern Ireland** (**PSNI**), however, came into existence in November 2001, but has not yet managed to recruit equally from the two communities.

However, the two key issues, interrelated in the eyes of many Unionists, were the release of political prisoners and the **decommissioning of weaponry**. While the release of prisoners passed relatively smoothly, the operation of the Assembly was thoroughly bedevilled by the decommissioning issue from the day it opened for business on December 1, 1999, and over the next six years its powers were regularly suspended by a succession of different British Northern Ireland Secretaries.

On May 6, 2000, an unexpected and hugely significant **statement from the IRA's leadership** declared that, while they remained committed to a united Ireland, they

| 1994 | 1998 | 1999 | 2000 | 2001 |
|---|---|---|---|---|
| Short-lived Republican and Loyalist ceasefires | The Good Friday Agreement commits all parties to democratic and peaceful solutions | The new Assembly convenes but is bedevilled by the issue of arms decommissioning | The IRA announces that it will initiate a process to put its arms beyond use | The Royal Ulster Constabulary becomes the Police Service of Northern Ireland |

would "initiate a process that will completely and verifiably put IRA arms beyond use". Neither the UUP nor the DUP, which despite its complete abhorrence of the Good Friday Agreement had taken its seats in the Assembly, would accept that the IRA really meant business, despite the reports of the independent arms inspectorate led by the Canadian General John de Chastelain. In response, Sinn Féin's leadership of Gerry Adams and Martin McGuinness argued that, as a political party, it had no powers over decommissioning. Many now worried for the future of devolution, fearing that this apparent stalemate would see many IRA members defecting to the reactivated Real IRA (which indeed subsequently began a bombing campaign in London), based on the belief that the Adams–McGuinness strategy for political progress had been a mistake. If Gerry Adams could not persuade the IRA to decommission, they reasoned, then nobody could.

As the impasse continued, conventional crime seemed to hoover up the activities of Loyalist and Republican paramilitaries. The former were involved in a violent feud over the illegal drugs trade, while in December 2004, a staggering £26.5 million **bank raid** of Belfast's Northern Bank had fingers immediately pointing towards the IRA (though only a financial adviser has been convicted of money laundering).

### … and resolution

Local and national **elections** in May 2005 witnessed a sea change in public opinion. The SDLP suffered badly at the hands of Sinn Féin, while the UUP was virtually wiped off the political map by the DUP, leading to Trimble's resignation as minister. The centre ground had now completely disappeared, leaving hardline Republicans and Loyalists as the arbiters of the peace process's continuation. In September 2005, the IRA announced that it was putting all of its weaponry beyond use, thus effectively declaring the end of its armed struggle for unification and against British rule (the UVF would follow suit in 2007).

**Assembly elections** in early 2007 ratified the DUP's and Sinn Féin's positions as the North's two leading parties. Subsequently, following the ending of a suspension which had begun in late 2005, Ian Paisley and Martin McGuinness took up their positions as, respectively, leader and deputy leader of the Assembly. The DUP's **Peter Robinson** succeeded Paisley (who passed away in 2014) as both DUP leader and the Assembly's First Minister in 2008. Robinson and McGuinness continued their roles after the 2011 Assembly elections, which again returned the DUP and Sinn Féin as the largest parties.

### … and a new stalemate

Early in 2016 Robinson resigned from politics to be replaced as DUP leader and First Minister by **Arlene Foster**. This led to yet another change in the political temperature, plunging the power-sharing Assembly at Stormont into its worst crisis in a decade. An added dimension was created with the **death of Martin McGuinness** in February 2017. Obituaries characterized McGuinness as a former IRA chief of staff who had his finger on the pulse – and the trigger – of terrorism, but who matured into an advocate of peace, becoming a lynchpin of the process that led to the Good Friday Agreement.

**Michelle O'Neil**, replaced McGuinness as deputy leader of the Assembly and leader of Sinn Féin, but relations between her and Foster became strained and the Assembly was **suspended**, pending negotiations. The disputed issues were over legal recognition

| 2005 | 2007 | 2008 | 2010 |
| --- | --- | --- | --- |
| The more extreme DUP and Sinn Féin succeed the UUP and SDLP as the north's major parties | Ian Paisley (succeeded by Peter Robinson) and Martin McGuinness become leader and deputy leader of the Assembly | Fianna Fail's Bertie Ahern resigns after eleven scandal-hit years as prime minister | Ireland accepts an €85 billion bailout to survive the international economic crisis |

## THE RISE AND FALL OF THE CELTIC TIGER

The 1990s witnessed a remarkable economic boom in the Republic, leading to the country's acquisition of the soubriquet **Celtic Tiger**. Ireland's emergence resulted from a combination of huge European Union subsidies (especially to farmers) and massive tax concessions to multinational companies, encouraging them to site operations in Dublin and elsewhere. For the first time in decades, Irish people actually returned home from abroad to seek work, reinvigorating an economy already bolstered by an increase in the number of graduates emerging from the country's universities. The most visible changes were apparent in the Dublin skyline, where new edifices seemed to emerge almost daily, and in the wave of "mansion" building reflecting the increasing affluence of Ireland's nouveaux riches. Additionally, sparked partly by the redevelopment of Dublin's Temple Bar, the vigorous local music scene (epitomized by the worldwide success of the band U2 and the singer Sinéad O'Connor) and the liberal tax concessions given to artists, writers and musicians, Ireland became for the first time a hip place to visit.

However, as it later emerged, the economy's growth was largely that of a boomtown built on silt, with vast wealth created for a relatively small number of investors in high-tech industries, bankers and property developers, but little legislation to tackle the social deprivation facing those way down the pecking order.

for the Irish language, a new settlement for unsolved Troubles cases, legalizing same-sex marriage (the DUP was strongly opposed to it) and the underlying tensions of Brexit, the United Kingdom's exit from the European Union. The DUP also came in for criticism in June 2017 when they entered into an agreement with the minority Conservative government led by Theresa May after the party suffered a shock election loss. To retain her position as British Prime Minister, May struck a deal to secure the DUP's support, and in exchange the party received £1bn for investment in infrastructure projects in Northern Ireland.

Twenty years on from the IRA ceasefire of 1997, the North has made immeasurable progress, although some problems remain intractable. The electoral successes of the DUP and Sinn Féin – at the expense of the Ulster Unionists and SDLP – have resulted in a hardening of attitudes, a refusal to compromise, and stalemate. But whatever the political bickering, a newly rich Northern Ireland is enjoying the greatest prosperity and longest period of peace in its history; it is a small country in transformation and an infinitely better place than the dark days of the Troubles.

## Meanwhile in the Republic

While events in the North had been completely dominated by the peace process and the continuing wrangling at Stormont, the story of the Republic in the 1990s and 2000s was one of **rapid economic development** (see box) and a series of political scandals. The first major event of the new decade was the election of **Mary Robinson** as Ireland's first woman president in 1991. This heralded a more liberal outlook for the country, but her time as head of state was overshadowed by the resignation of two of Ireland's Taoiseachs. **Charles Haughey** was the first to go in 1992, his administration smeared by long-lasting

| 2011 | 2014 | 2015 | 2016 |
|------|------|------|------|
| Enda Kenny of Fine Gael becomes prime minister | President Michael D. Higgins makes the first official visit by an Irish head of state to Britain | In a historic referendum, the Republic of Ireland votes overwhelmingly to legalize same-sex marriage | The DUP's Arlene Foster becomes new First Minister of the Stormont Assembly, which is suspended over political bickering with Sinn Féin |

and later substantiated allegations of corruption, and brought down by the revelation that journalists' private telephone calls had been tapped by the Republic's police. In 1994 his successor, **Albert Reynolds**, was also forced to resign after revelations that his government had covered up allegations of paedophilia made against a Catholic priest.

Following a brief interlude of a Fine Gael coalition under **John Bruton**, the Republic was run for fourteen years by a series of Fianna Fáil–headed alliances. The Taoiseach from 1997 until 2008 was **Bertie Ahern**, whose ministries were dogged by further revelations of financial corruption involving key members of his party, resulting in the establishment of the **Flood Commission**'s long-standing investigations into innumerable transactions, as well as major enquiries into the operation of Ireland's police force, centred on various nefarious goings-on in County Donegal.

Ahern's government somehow stumbled on until May 2008, when he resigned following the **Mahon Tribunal**'s investigation into corrupt payments to politicians. He was succeeded by **Brian Cowen**, whose 2007 budget while Minister of Finance was widely regarded as the biggest spending spree in Irish political history. However, the international monetary crisis of 2008–2009 saw all of Ireland's boom-and-bust economic chickens come home to roost in alarming numbers. Cowen's government (forced to enact three budgets within a calendar year) struggled to maintain control of a situation verging upon national insolvency, and enforced austerity measures which cut the salaries of public servants and lowered welfare benefits, while simultaneously attempting to safeguard the Irish banking system. Added to this was the 2009 **Murphy Report** which resulted from investigations into sexual abuse by priests and others within the Catholic archdiocese of Dublin which exposed widespread exploitation of children, numerous cover-ups and a widespread failure to prosecute the perpetrators.

In 2010, the government was forced to turn to the EU and the IMF for an €85 billion **bailout** to save the banks, which has put the country in hock for generations to come. Some optimism returned with the success of Fine Gael, led by Mayoman Enda Kenny and in coalition with Labour, in the 2011 election. By 2014, the unemployment rate had fallen to 11 percent and the country recorded a year-on-year economic growth rate of 7.7 percent, the highest in the Eurozone. Seasoned observers of Ireland's boom-and-bust economy, however, could only wince as newspapers coined the term "The Celtic Phoenix".

Since then the Republic has continued to prosper economically (albeit in a patchy manner outside the major cities): for four successive years, from 2014 to 2017 it was Europe's fastest-growing economy with GDP growth of 4.8 percent. At the same time, it has slowly been transformed into a more liberal and multicultural country. In a historic 2015 referendum, Ireland voted overwhelmingly in favour of legalizing **same-sex marriage**. The following year, the 2016 Census showed a population of 4.7m, and while it remains a predominantly Catholic country, the numbers identifying as such fell sharply from 84.2 per cent to 78.3 per cent, evidence that it is no longer in thrall to the Catholic Church. But the most astonishing political move came in the summer of 2017 with the election as Taoiseach of **Leo Varadkar**, the openly gay son of an Indian immigrant. He took over from Enda Kenny who led Fine Gael for fifteen years and was Taoiseach for six of them. Varadkar's appointment, which made headlines around the world, is being seen by commentators as a sign of a generational shift in Irish politics and may well signify a transition from conservative traditionalism to liberal modernity.

| 2017 | 2020 | 2021 |
| --- | --- | --- |
| Ireland elects Leo Varadkar, leader of Fine Gael, as its first openly gay prime minister | Ireland forms a coalition government between Fine Gael, Fianna Fáil and the Green Party | Rankings state that Ireland has handled the Covid-19 pandemic better than any other country |

# Traditional music

Ireland and music are as inseparable as fish and chips. Though the country has developed a thriving rock music scene over the last forty years and artists such as U2, Sinéad O'Connor and Van Morrison have achieved massive international success, it's Ireland's traditional music that in many ways continues to hold centre stage.

The country's musical traditions remain essentially based on the age-old practice of passing down tunes and songs by oral transmission, from generation to generation and from friend to friend. Its core has become the **pub session**, where the richness of the musical tradition can be experienced at first hand, and the *craic* (or crack) – that idiosyncratically Irish, heady combination of drink-fuelled chat, banter and fun – simply takes over.

The best sessions are always the ones you never expected to find, spontaneous and uproarious affairs, and the areas where you'll most likely find them are in the counties along the western and southern seaboards, especially Donegal, Sligo, Galway, Clare, Kerry and Cork, though there are excellent session scenes in Belfast and Dublin. Otherwise, the places to visit are festivals, and we've listed the best of both these and the session pubs throughout the Guide. For more information on the music itself and its instruments, see page 590.

## Irish music rediscovered

While the musical traditions of other Western European countries were dissipated by the process of industrialization and political change, Ireland's indigenous music remained at the centre of its people's social life until well into the twentieth century, when its survival became threatened by emigration and governmental controls aimed at curbing dance forms regarded as immoral. It needed two major shots in the arm in the 1960s – the **folk song boom**, which originated in the USA, and the pioneering work of **Seán Ó Riada** in establishing ensemble playing as the new norm – to reinvigorate its existence.

Ireland's greatest musical ambassadors, **The Chieftains**, emerged from Ó Riada's initiative in the 1960s, and the following decade saw the formation of the country's two most influential groups, **Planxty** and **The Bothy Band**. Their performances and recordings effectively laid out the ground for others to tread, not least **De Dannan**, the Donegal-based **Altan**, and, in more recent times, **Lúnasa**, **Danú** and the US-based **Solas**.

## The tunes

Almost all of Ireland's traditional music tunes are based on imported **dance** forms. The only exceptions to this rule are slow airs which largely owe their origins to the song tradition (see page 590), a few special pieces belonging to the *uilleann* piping tradition (such as *The Fox Chase*, in which the instrument mimics the sound of fox, hunters and hounds), and a body of more than two hundred tunes composed by the blind itinerant harper **Turlough O'Carolan** (1680–1738), which carry some influence by Italian classical composers of that era.

There are several thousand reels, jigs (in various formats), hornpipes, barndances, strathspeys, waltzes and numerous other dance tunes, though many are only rarely played. At most sessions it is reels and jigs that predominate. Particular tune forms are favoured in different parts of the country – the polka for example is especially popular in Cork and Kerry. The authors of the vast majority of tunes are unknown, though some do bear their composer's name, such as *Martin Wynne's No. 1*, and many more are added to the canon each year in the form of new compositions. Apart from such eponymous works, tune titles should not be taken as anything more than a labelling device (and some have particularly arcane titles – witness *Wallop the Spot* or *The Cat That Kittled in Jamie's Wig*).

This depth of the tradition owes much to fears at certain times in Ireland's history that it was on the wane, spurring collectors to amass as much information as possible from musicians. The most notable collector was **Captain Francis O'Neill**, erstwhile Chicago police chief, who in the early twentieth century gathered tunes together in publications such as *The Dance Music of Ireland*. Later collectors of note include **Séamus Ennis**, who assiduously accumulated material for Radio Éireann and the BBC, and **Breandán Breathnach**, who published several volumes of material under the title *Ceol Rince na hÉireann* ("Dance Music of Ireland"). Today Dublin's Irish Traditional Music Archive continues the process of storing and cataloguing newly found material.

While these tunes were originally played at house or "crossroads" dances (held in a suitable open space – frequently a road junction), and often at weddings or wakes, they form merely a staging post for skilled traditional musicians, who embellish their renditions with all manner of musical ornamentation, though rarely straying from the essential rhythms of the dance. Nowadays, most dance tunes are played as part of a set, usually consisting of two or three of the same form, each played through a couple of times (or sometimes more) before segueing into the next one.

## Sessions

The pub session as we know it today is in fact another import, having emerged in pubs in London and elsewhere where there were plenty of Irish émigrés in the years following World War II. During the folk and ballad boom of the 1960s, led by **The Clancy Brothers and Tommy Makem** and their more raucous contemporaries **The Dubliners**, Ireland's pub landlords began to welcome traditional musicians and the practice continues to this day. The session has become the focal point for the tradition and usually consists of a regular and informal gathering of local musicians on a particular evening, one of whom is usually paid to ensure that it takes place.

The majority of sessions (except some in extremely popular tourist areas) are relatively informal affairs where the musicians play the tunes of their choice, breaking off whenever they feel like doing so for a chat or an outdoor fag-break. Sessions can be found throughout the year in cities such as Belfast, Cork, Dublin and Galway, but in smaller towns and rural areas the months between June and September are usually the best time. Most begin at around 9.30pm, though on the west coast in high summer you'll find plenty not starting until 10.30pm and sometimes later. The lure for the pub's punters is the chance to hear top-class musicianship for the price of a pint or two, as well as participating in the associated *craic*.

Bear in mind that the musicians' seats are sacrosanct, so don't plonk yourself down next to a fiddler to enjoy the music from a closer aspect – the vacant seat you've just occupied was reserved for a musician who might or might not appear later.

You'll only rarely come across dancing at a session (and you'll probably be in Kerry or Clare if you do), thus the best bet, if you want to twirl the light fantastic, is to look out for a **ceili dance**. Plenty of these take place during local festivals, but there are also a number of renowned venues along the west coast that feature regular nights of set dancing to the accompaniment of a ceili band. These bands normally feature just the usual main traditional instruments, though some also include oddities such as the saxophone and accompaniment via piano and/or snare drum.

## INSTRUMENTS AND PLAYERS

We've mentioned some of the best instrumentalists on the Irish music scene in this roundup of traditional instruments. If you get the chance to see any of them at the festivals, don't miss it.

### UILLEANN PIPES

The English folk singer Martin Carthy once aptly described seeing the renowned **Séamus Ennis** playing the *uilleann* pipes as like "watching a man wrestling an octopus". The world's most complex set of bagpipes (variously pronounced "illun" or "illyun") is an extraordinarily temperamental creature and notoriously hard to master. The instrument has several components, consisting of a nine-holed chanter capable of producing a double-octave range, powered by air squeezed from a bag positioned under the left arm, itself driven by bellows pressed against the player's torso by his or her right elbow. The pipes also come equipped with three drones and a set of three regulators that can be flipped on and off to provide chordal accompaniment. No other instrument in the Irish canon is as capable of replicating the vocal ornamentations of *sean-nós* singers via the playing of slow airs.

Since the late nineteenth century two distinct styles of playing have evolved: one more gentle and ornamentally delicate, exemplified by Séamus Ennis and **Leo Rowsome**; and the other (often termed "open" or "legato") much more intricate, crisp, showy and rhythmically driven, and associated with members of the Traveller community who earned a living playing at country fairs – key protagonists of this style were the late brothers **Johnny and Felix Doran**, and, more recently, **Davy Spillane**.

Pipers have long held a special place in Ireland's musical heritage and among today's virtuosos are **Liam O'Flynn**, famed for his solo recordings, work with the classical composer Shaun Davey and poet Seamus Heaney, and membership of Planxty. **Paddy Keenan**, memorably once described as "the Jimi Hendrix of the *uilleann* pipes", rose to fame via The Bothy Band and continues to produce performances of astonishing majesty. Other pipers of note include **Neillidh Mulligan**, one of the best exponents of slow airs, **Ronan Browne** (also adept on flute and whistles), the Belfast-born **John McSherry** and the phenomenally talented young Dubliner **Seán McKeon**.

### FLUTES AND WHISTLES

The flute preferred by Irish musicians is the simple wooden version with fingers used to cover the holes rather than keys as in its classical cousin, though some players do employ semi-keyed instruments. The long-standing hotbed of Irish flute music is North Connacht, famed for its seeming production-line of players incorporating a mellifluous, sometimes flamboyant style, in their music. The best known of these is **Matt Molloy** of The Bothy Band and The Chieftains, but **Séamus Tansey** has also been hugely influential. Belfast too has produced some fine flute players, often influenced by the North Connacht style or that of neighbouring Fermanagh (from which **Cathal McConnell** is a major figure), including **Desi Wilkinson** and **Harry Bradley**, while Dublin's **Paul McGrattan** has drawn much from the Donegal fiddle tradition.

The essential learning instrument of Irish music is the tin whistle, and one is still carried around by many players of other instruments keen to learn new tunes quickly – if you're tempted to buy one, make sure it's a D-whistle, as many tunes are played in this key. In the hands of a skilled operator – such as **Mary Bergin**, **Gavin Whelan** or **Bríd O'Donohue** – the whistle utterly surmounts its apparent technical limitations.

### FIDDLES

The fiddle is Ireland's most popular traditional instrument and perhaps the best exemplar of regional musical styles (although these have been undermined as players learn their tunes and adaptations from the radio, CDs and MP3s rather than their neighbours). Donegal is famed for its captivating rhythmic style, often referred to as "driving" and best heard in the recordings of **John Doherty**

## The song tradition

Sadly, unaccompanied songs play little part in today's sessions, despite Ireland's (see page 430) and **Tommy Peoples**. The Sligo style, encapsulated in the recordings of **Michael Coleman** (see page 401) and **James Morrison**, is generally regarded as more ornamented and flashy, but continues to be a major influence. The eastern parts of Galway and Clare are noted for their more lonesome style, produced by a tendency to play in flattened key signatures and exemplified by the playing of **Martin Hayes**, who uses his native tradition as an extraordinary springboard for musical exploration. To the south, in Kerry and Cork, the polka remains the most popular dance tune and much of the most atmospheric playing dates back to the fiddle-master **Pádraig O'Keeffe**, though his enduring influence can be heard in the playing of **Matt Cranitch** and the late **Séamus Creagh**.

## MELODEONS, ACCORDIONS AND CONCERTINAS

Squeeze-boxes come in a variety of shapes and sizes in traditional music. The simplest is the one-row button accordion, usually known as a melodeon in Ireland. One of its true masters is the Connemara box-player **Johnny Connolly**, generally regarded as the acme of accompanists for dancing. The far more popular two-row button accordion comes in a range of tunings, usually either B/C (favoured by the highly influential **Joe Burke**), which produces a more rolling and frilly style of play, or the C sharp/D variety (whose well-known exponents include **Dermot Byrne** and **Séamus Begley**). Also well worth seeking out are **Jackie Daly** and **Máirtín O Connor**, both of whom play boxes in a variety of tunings, while the music of Clare's **Sharon Shannon** continues to attract a global audience. The piano accordion is less well favoured, though there are some cracking musicians using it, including **Alan Kelly**, **Mirella Murray** and **Martin Tourish**.

The smaller concertina was once thought of as primarily a women's instrument and was especially popular in County Clare (for too many reasons to list here). Again, it's ideal for accompanying dancers. Probably the best-known exponents are **Mary Mac Namara**, **Noel Hill**, **Chris Droney** and **Micheál Ó Raghallaigh**.

## THE BOUZOUKI AND OTHER STRINGED INSTRUMENTS

The Greek *bouzouki* was first introduced to Ireland by **Johnny Moynihan** of the band Sweeney's Men in the late 1960s and made popular by **Dónal Lunny** of Planxty and The Bothy Band, and **Alec Finn** of De Dannan. Along with the guitar, it's the most common form of stringed accompaniment found at sessions, though, thanks to its open tuning and flat back, it's nowadays more akin to the mandolin than its Greek forebear. As a relatively quiet instrument, the mandolin itself, as played by **Paul Kelly**, is rarely seen at sessions, though you may see a larger version known as the mandola, whose well-known protagonists include **Andy Irvine**. Lastly, there's the banjo, an instrument reviled by many for its "plunker-plunker" sound, but which does have some exceptional exponents, including **Gerry O'Connor** and **Darren Maloney**.

## THE BODHRÁN

This goatskin frame drum (pronounced "bore-run" or "bough-ron"), resembling a tambourine without jingles and played with the hand or a wooden beater, divides opinion among Irish sessioneers more than any other instrument. Some musicians appreciate the driving rhythm provided by a good percussionist (such as **John Joe Kelly**), but others regard it as the devil's detritus and sounding, in one fiddler's memorable words, "like a sack of spuds tipped down the stairs". Originally associated with the "wren boys" who went out revelling ("hunting the wren") and playing music on St Stephen's Day (Dec 26), it was adopted for ensemble playing by **Seán Ó Riada** in the 1960s. Many music or souvenir shops sell the drum and, if you're tempted to buy one, do listen to recordings of the best players (**Johnny McDonagh** and **Colm Murphy** with De Dannan or **Donnchadh Gough** with Danú) before even considering whether your own formative skills might be welcome at a session.

remarkable vocal tradition. Essentially, this falls into two categories: songs in the Irish language and songs in English. Many Irish-language songs are of great antiquity and together they form part of what has become known as **sean-nós**, which literally means "old style". The tradition is strongest in the Irish-speaking areas of the west coast, particularly in West Kerry (Dingle), Connemara and Donegal, and incorporates an unaccompanied singing style of great emotional intensity when applied to the "big songs" of the tradition – tales of love, loss and longing – or sprightly frivolity when handling more light-hearted matters. Singers essentially construct a soundscape in which their use of vocal ornamentation and changes in tempo and tone lead the listener through the lyrics' twists and turns. Though knowledge of the Irish language is essential to a full understanding of their abilities, even without this it's still possible to appreciate singing that can be very beautiful. Some of the best contemporary members of the tradition, not least **Iarla Ó Lionáird** (from West Cork), well known through his work with the Afro Celts fusion band, and **Lasairfhíona Ní Chonaola** (from the Aran Islands), have produced albums of extraordinary splendour.

Simultaneously, Ireland possesses a vast wealth of traditional songs in English, including many derived from the broadsheet ballad-sellers of the nineteenth and earlier twentieth centuries and others shared with the heritage of England and Scotland, and there are traditional singing clubs in several of Ireland's towns and cities. The country's foremost interpreter of these and many other contemporary songs is unquestionably **Christy Moore**.

## DISCOGRAPHY

The following selection of albums provides a solid foundation for investigation of Ireland's musical traditions. They can be purchased at Claddagh Records in Dublin (see page 106), Custy's in Ennis (see page 316), other record stores and online.

**Seamus Begley** *The Bold Kerryman* (IRL Independent Records). Tender-voice west Kerry singer, accordionist and storyteller.

**Mary Bergin** *Feadóga Stáin* (Gael Linn). Marvellously adept whistle-playing.

**The Bothy Band** *The Bothy Band 1975* (Jasmine). Short-lived but still incredibly influential, this band set the template for so many others to follow.

**Cran** *Lover's Ghost* (Black Rose Records). A gripping melange of songs and flute/*uilleann* pipes interplay.

**Séamus Creagh and Jackie Daly** *Same* (Gael Linn). Polkas from the mountains of Sliabh Luachra on the Kerry–Cork–Limerick border and much more on this exhilarating fiddle/accordion album.

**Martin Hayes and Dennis Cahill** *Live in Seattle* (Green Linnet). Ireland's most soulful and imaginative fiddler, in cahoots with long-time guitarist buddy, produces one of the most invigorating live performances you'll ever hear.

**Joe Heaney** *The Road from Connemara* (Topic). A double-CD which encapsulates the singing of perhaps Ireland's finest exponent of the *sean-nós* style.

**Noel Hill and Tony Linnane** *Same* (Tara). Tremendous concertina/fiddle duets from the Clare duo, recorded when both were in their late teens.

**Cathal Lynch** *The Jolly Roving Tar* (Claddagh). The renowned traditional Tyrone singer has made a name touring extensively.

**Seán Maguire** *The Master's Touch* (Áinm Records). The multi-talented Belfast fiddle player died in 2005 but his music has been digitally remastered with classics such as The Blackbird, The Humours of Bandon and *Madame Bonaparte*.

**Christy Moore** *At the Point Live* (Columbia). Captures the singer in his heyday when he was justifiably regarded as a national treasure.

**Maighread and Tríona Ní Dhomhnaill** *Idir an Dá Sholas* (Gael Linn/Hummingbird). Glorious singing in both Irish and English.

**Gerry O'Connor** *Journeyman* (Lughnasa Music). One of the finest fiddle albums of recent years.

**Máirtín O Connor** *The Road West* (Sun Street Studios). Button accordionist O Connor teams up with some of Ireland's best musicians including Cathal Hayden, Nollaig Casey and Garry O Briain that will have you heading for the Wild Atlantic Way.

**Planxty** *Same* (Shanachie). AKA "The Black Album" and featuring a dazzling array of songs and tunes from Christy Moore, Andy Irvine, Liam Ó Flynn and Dónal Lunny, this magical release redefined Ireland's musical landscape.

**Sharon Shannon, Frankie Gavin, Michael McGoldrick and Jim Murray** *Tunes* (The Daisy Label). A splendid constellation of accordion, fiddle, flute and guitar.

**Solas** *Reunion* (Compass Records). A fabulous live recording (including film footage on DVD) of a concert reuniting the Irish-US band's former and present members.

**Séamus Tansey** *King of the Concert Flute* (Sound Records). Outstanding flute-playing from the Sligo master.

**Various** *The Rough Guide to Irish Folk* and *The Rough Guide to Irish Music* (both World Music Network). Two excellent compilations providing an overview, respectively, of the song and instrumental traditions.

# Literature

For an island of fewer than six million people, Ireland has an astonishingly rich literary tradition, the oldest in Europe outside of Italy and Greece. While most of this literature up to the seventeenth century was written in Gaelic (usually called Irish in Ireland today), and to a lesser extent Latin, English would become pre-eminent from the eighteenth century onwards and is today the first language not just of most Irish writing but also of the vast majority of Irish people. Ireland's literary tradition has developed over two thousand years from the first markings on rocks around the time of Christ, to the acclaimed poetry, prose and theatre of writers such as W.B. Yeats, James Joyce and Samuel Beckett, producing startling works of originality and influence.

## Beginnings

The oldest writing in Ireland was ogham script, a system of parallel notches that survives on standing stones from the fourth century AD, but was likely in existence for several hundred years previous. However, it was the arrival of Christianity in the fifth century that would have the most significant early influence on the emergence of literature in Ireland. With the growth of the monasteries between the seventh and tenth centuries, a rich culture of Latin manuscripts developed, the finest surviving example of which is the *Book of Kells* in Trinity College, Dublin (see page 63).

During the same period, a thriving literary culture in the vernacular of Irish life, Gaelic, began to emerge and develop, too. While the oldest surviving manuscripts in this language date from around the twelfth century, much of the material was copied and recopied for many hundreds of years before that. The oldest datable work of Gaelic literature is **Amra Choluim Chille** (Elegy of St Columba), a poem attributed to the poet Dallán Forgaill and written soon after the death in 597 of one of Ireland's most famous early saints, Colmcille, regarded as the patron saint of Irish poets. The Gaelic manuscripts also incorporated ancient, often fantastic and supernatural tales which had been preserved in a primarily oral culture. One such classic Irish story is the **Táin Bó Cúailnge** (The Cattle Raid of Cooley), which features the legendary figures of Cúchulainn, the larger-than-life Ulster warrior, and Queen Medb of Connaught.

While the manuscript tradition preserved tales concerning Cúchulainn, found in a larger narrative called the Ulster Cycle, a further popular hero in Gaelic oral culture was **Fionn Mac Cumhaill**, the leader of a band of warriors defending Ireland called the Fianna. The stories of Fionn and his men are commonly referred to as the *Fiannaíocht* tales and include the classic *Tóraíocht Dhiarmada agus Gráinne* (The Pursuit of Diarmuid and Gráinne), in which Fionn's intended, Gráinne, seduces one of his handsome warriors, Diarmuid, and elopes across Ireland, chased by Fionn and his men. Another famous early Gaelic tale is **Buile Shuibhne** (The Frenzy of Sweeney), the story of Suibhne Geilt, a king who, after being cursed by a local cleric, is transformed into a bird, banished and condemned to wander through Ireland's most desolate landscapes enduring great hardship and loneliness. These Gaelic legends have provided recurring inspiration for Irish writers, including W.B. Yeats, Synge, Joyce, Beckett, Flann O'Brien and Seamus Heaney.

The arrival of the Anglo-Normans in Ireland in the twelfth century brought another influence to bear on the Irish language and literature, and some of the finest poets of the Middle Ages would descend from Anglo-Norman stock, including in the fourteenth century Gearóid Iarla Fitzgerald, the Third Earl of Desmond. The thirteenth-century version of what is today known as Middle Irish was preserved as a literary language through the **bardic schools** that emerged in this period and continued in Ireland down to the mid-seventeenth century. These provided structured training for the *filí*, or poets, who were both feared and highly respected in a very hierarchical society. One significant aspect of poetry in this period was its close association with music, an association that would continue throughout the history of Irish literature. Surviving records suggest that bardic poetry was always performed with the accompaniment of the harp, the instrument that remains the national emblem of Ireland today. The esteem in which these poets were held is evident from the fact that many examples of this richly ornate and highly sophisticated bardic poetry survive, despite the tumultuous events that would lead to the decline of Gaelic Ireland.

### Irish-language works of the seventeenth and eighteenth centuries

With the undermining of the Gaelic order following the Battle of Kinsale in 1601, the structures that had supported indigenous poetic and musical production went into decline. Furthermore, as the power of musicians and poets had been feared by the British establishment throughout the sixteenth century, efforts were made to persecute them and generally limit their influence. Previously exalted *filí* were now often reduced to **sráid-éigse** or "street poetry". The result was to bring the formerly independent professions of musician and poet together in the one performer whose compositions, particularly by the eighteenth century, gradually became more and more associated with the folk tradition of song. The passing on of Irish poetry through song ensured its survival and some songs from the eighteenth century, including *Dónal Óg* and *Úna Bhán*, continue to be sung today in the *sean-nós* or old-style tradition.

The eighteenth century would also witness, inspired by the Jacobite insurrections in Scotland of 1715 and 1745, the emergence of an indigenous, politically engaged poetry, as poets such as Piaras Mac Gearailt, Seán Ó Tuama, Seán Clárach Mac Domhnaill and Eoghan Rua Ó Súilleabháin produced work confident of the return of the Catholic Stuart kings to power and the revival of the Gaelic aristocracy. One of the most popular genres to evolve in this period was the **aisling**, its finest exponent **Aogán Ó Rathaille** in works such as *Mac an Cheannaí* (The Merchant's Son) and *Gile na Gile* (Brightness Most Bright). These "vision poems" feature the poet, on falling asleep, imagining he is visited by a beautiful woman who reveals herself as Ireland and laments her oppression. Such was the popularity of the *aisling* that one of the finest Gaelic poems of the eighteenth century is actually a parody of the genre, **Brian Merriman**'s *Cúirt An Mheán Oíche* (The Midnight Court). Here the poet encounters no beautiful maiden but rather an old hag, who summons him to a court where he witnesses an attack by Queen Aoibheal on the young men of Ireland for their refusal to marry and lack of virility. A ribald and satiric piece, regarded as the greatest comic poem in the language, it was banned in English when translated by Frank O'Connor in 1945, though the Irish-language version remained on the shelves.

Another highly accomplished Gaelic work of the eighteenth century is the *Caoineadh Airt Uí Laoghaire* (Lament for Art Ó Laoghaire), a long, traditional *caoineadh* or lament composed *ex tempore* by **Eibhlín Dhubh Ní Chonaill**, the aunt of Daniel O'Connell. It is a haunting piece lamenting the killing of Eibhlín's husband by the local sheriff, Abraham Morris, for refusing to sell his horse to him for £5, at a time when no Catholic was allowed under the hated penal laws to own a horse worth more than that figure.

## The emergence of Irish literature in English

While Irish-language literature took a downturn from the seventeenth century onwards, Irish literature in English began to come to the fore, most importantly in

the angry little shape of the poet, essayist and satirist **Jonathan Swift** (see page 75).
Other notable writers in English from the eighteenth century include **Laurence Sterne**,
the Tipperary-born clergyman and author of the innovative and highly influential satire
on the biographical novel, *The Life and Opinions of Tristram Shandy, Gentleman*; the
Longford doctor, **Oliver Goldsmith**, best known for his elegy *The Deserted Village*, novel
*The Vicar of Wakefield* and play *She Stoops to Conquer*; and **Richard Brinsley Sheridan**,
author of *The Rivals* and *The School for Scandal*, one of the first in a long tradition of
leading Irish playwrights in the English language.

Despite the decline of Irish language and culture, the late eighteenth and early
nineteenth centuries were nonetheless important for the rejuvenation of Irish
nationalism, Irish music and the emergence of a distinctive Irish poetry in English.
The efforts of primarily Anglo-Irish antiquarians, concerned to promote the
distinctiveness of the adopted country of their ancestors, would help to preserve
some of the native literature and music. In 1789, the first translations of Gaelic
poetry and songs, *Reliques of Irish Poetry*, were published by **Charlotte Brooke**, a
pioneering mediator between the Anglo-Irish Ascendancy and the local tradition. Her
work would inspire subsequent antiquarians such as **Sir Samuel Ferguson**, the most
important collector and translator of Gaelic poetry and mythology in the nineteenth
century and a crucial influence on the writers who emerged in the Literary Revival at
the end of the century, including W.B. Yeats.

## Thomas Moore and the Young Ireland Poets

In the early nineteenth century, "the darling of the London drawing rooms" was
**Thomas Moore**, born of a Catholic family in Dublin, whose romantic and nostalgic
nationalist compositions – such as the still-popular songs *The Minstrel Boy* and *The
Last Rose of Summer* – were included in *Irish Melodies*, published in ten volumes
between 1808 and 1834. These poems were set to traditional Irish tunes from Edward
Bunting's *General Collection of Ancient Music of Ireland* (1796), a compilation of the
airs of some of the few remaining Irish harpists who performed at the Belfast Harpers'
Festival of July 1792. Moore's *Melodies* has been called "the secular hymn-book of
Irish nationalism" in the nineteenth century and he was regarded by many during his
lifetime as Ireland's national poet. He represents the beginnings of the articulation of
Irish identity and culture, on a national scale, in the English language.

While Moore had found in Irish music a means of access to what he believed to be
the national spirit, the **Young Ireland Poets** associated with the nationalist newspaper,
*The Nation* (which began publication in 1842), would find similar sustenance in the
ballad. Among the most influential contributors to *The Nation* were **Thomas Davis**
and **James Clarence Mangan**, both of whom would be alluded to in the work of W.B.
Yeats and Joyce. While Davis's *A Nation Once Again* is still sung and was given serious
consideration as the national anthem of Ireland, his emphasis on the importance of
literature for national identity would have a vital influence on the Literary Revival.
Mangan's free translation of the Gaelic song *Róisín Dubh* (Dark Rosaleen) has been
described as the "most widely known nationalist poem" of the nineteenth century, but
his overall ambivalence towards the nationalist project would find resonance in the
work of Joyce, who wrote an essay on the poet.

## Irish playwrights of the nineteenth century

Born in Dublin of Huguenot stock, **Dion Boucicault** found inspiration in Irish history
and legend for plays such as *The Colleen Bawn* (1860), *The Shaughran* (1875) and
*Robert Emmet* (1884). His work was renowned for its humour and enjoyed considerable
popular success in Ireland, Britain and the US during his life, but subsequent Irish
writers and commentators would accuse him of perpetuating the figure of the drunken

and pugnacious "stage Irishman", a popular stereotype that had gained currency in the early eighteenth century in the work of Irish playwright George Farquhar.

Better known to her readers by her pseudonym **Speranza**, Jane Francesca Wilde was an Anglo-Irish author and literary hostess who contributed nationalist poems and anti-British writings to *The Nation*. While her work was of limited artistic value, her son **Oscar Wilde** would become one of the most famous (and eventually infamous) dramatists of the British stage in the late nineteenth century. Oscar did not share his mother's engagement with Irish politics and left the country for England shortly after graduating from Trinity College, where he was an outstanding student of classics, in 1874. He was awarded a scholarship to Magdalen College, Oxford, where he joined the Aesthetic Movement, a society dedicated to making an art out of life. Although Wilde published prose – his novel *The Picture of Dorian Gray* provoked a storm of protests in Victorian society because of its implied homoerotic theme – and poetry, his dazzling plays, including *Lady Windermere's Fan* and *The Importance of Being Earnest*, enjoyed the most success during his lifetime and continue to be performed today. Wilde managed to satirize the pretensions of the English upper and middle classes with humour and insight in a way that only someone coming from outside this society could. He was respected on both sides of the Atlantic for his work and enthralling lectures, and admired in polite society for his ability as a raconteur – as he said himself, to W.B. Yeats, "we Irish have done nothing, but we are the greatest talkers since the Greeks". However, a homosexual relationship with Lord Alfred Douglas, son of the Marquis of Queensbury, would eventually lead to his demise following a conviction and imprisonment for gross indecency. He was sentenced to two years' hard labour, an experience, given chilling insight by one of his finest works *The Ballad of Reading Gaol*, that would break him both physically and psychologically. Wilde died in Paris on November 30, 1900, a broken man who could never ignite his fires of creativity after prison. He left not just great literature but also some of the most memorable aphorisms in the English language, some of which too sadly described his own fate: "The secret of life is to appreciate the pleasure of being terribly, terribly deceived."

The other major playwright to emerge in England in the late nineteenth century was also Irish, the Dublin-born, life-long socialist, **George Bernard Shaw** (see page 68), whose career and influence extended well into the twentieth century. Shaw's work for the theatre was ground-breaking in bringing his own economic, moral and political concerns to the fore, but like Wilde he was also a legendary wit, combining acerbic humour with potent insights into human nature: "Gambling promises the poor what property performs for the rich – something for nothing." Nothing short of prolific, Shaw wrote over sixty plays, including *Arms and the Man*, *John Bull's Other Island* and *Pygmalion*, as well as five less successful novels and an impressive array of literary criticism and political commentary, before his death at the age of 94 in November 1950.

## The emergence of the Irish novel

A relatively new form that was to play an increasingly central part in cultural life in the nineteenth century, the novel in Ireland generally traces its beginnings to *Castle Rackrent* (1800), written by **Maria Edgeworth**. Although from an Anglo-Irish Ascendancy family, who gave their name to Edgeworthstown in County Longford, Edgeworth reveals the inequitable and sometimes abusive treatment estate tenants endured at the hands of their landlords. *Castle Rackrent* began one of the most popular genres in Irish literature, the "Big House" novel, concerning the experiences of the landholding class on an Anglo-Irish estate.

Though dominated by writers from the Ascendancy class in Ireland, the nineteenth century was also important for the emergence of female writers such as Edgeworth. Others include **Lady Morgan** (Sidney Owenson), whose *The Wild Irish Girl* (1806) is regarded as an important early feminist text, and the co-authors Edith Somerville and her cousin Violet Martin, known for works such as *The Irish R.M* written under their pseudonyms **Somerville and Ross**.

Other important writers of fiction to emerge in the nineteenth century include **William Carleton**, whose *Traits and Stories of the Irish Peasantry* would be a very influential text for writers such as Yeats; the brothers **John and Michael Banim**, whose major work is the 24 volumes of *The Tales of the O'Hara Family*; and Limerick-born novelist **Gerald Griffin**, whose *The Collegians* was based on events surrounding a trial in which Daniel O'Connell acted as attorney for the defence. The most popular novel in Ireland of the nineteenth century, however, was *Knocknagown; or The Homes of Tipperary* (1879), a convoluted and sentimental account of Tipperary rural life and critique of landlordism, written by the patriot and Young Irelander, **Charles Kickham**.

The Gothic genre was given much of its shape by Irish writers in this period, including **Charles Robert Maturin**, particularly in his dark tale of a man who sells his soul to the devil, *Melmoth the Wanderer* (1820); and **Joseph Sheridan Le Fanu**, the leading ghost story writer of the nineteenth century, best known for his novel *Uncle Silas* (1864) and collection of short stories *In a Glass Darkly* (1872). But they pale in comparison to **Bram Stoker**, whose *Dracula* (1897) is still one of the most popular and adapted works of fiction today. Born in Dublin and educated at Trinity College, Stoker spent most of his life in London as manager to the famous Shakespearean actor, Henry Irving.

# The Literary Revival

While Oscar Wilde and George Bernard Shaw were dominating the stage in Britain at the end of the nineteenth century, Irish cultural nationalism was on the rise back home. This period is collectively referred to as the **Irish Literary Revival**, though there were at least two revivals apparent: the Anglo-Irish, concerned with the promotion of Hiberno-English, the English language as sculpted by the particularities of Irish accent and the structures of Gaelic; and the Gaelic Revival, focused on the Irish language, which by now had been devastated by famine, emigration, poverty, lack of support and, indeed, outright discouragement in education. During the Literary Revival, literature in both languages would become a central focus for the revitalization of Irish culture, though attempts were also made through organizations such as Conradh na Gaeilge (the Gaelic League), founded in 1893, to preserve and encourage indigenous musical practices. The League's first president, **Douglas Hyde**, who later became Ireland's first president, would do much to popularize the Gaelic poetic tradition through his translations in *Abhráin Grádh Chúige Connacht* (The Love Songs of Connacht; 1893) and *Abhráin Diadha Chúige Connacht* (The Religious Songs of Connacht; 1905). These collections were an important inspiration for both Irish- and English-language writers, contributing to the idealization of the rural peasantry of the west, particularly in Yeats's work, as the well-spring from which, it was thought, a new, invigorated Irish literature and identity would emerge.

## W.B. Yeats

Though **William Butler Yeats** was born in Dublin in 1865 into an aristocratic Protestant family, it was Sligo in the west of Ireland, where he spent a considerable part of his formative years, that would fire his creative imagination. The most important writer of the Revival period, Yeats was in many ways the father of modern Irish literature. One of his major roles was in bringing material in Irish – including elements from the *Táin* and *Fiannaíocht* tales – into mainstream English-language literature through collections such as *The Wanderings of Oisin* (1889). But, more importantly, as a dramatist, essayist and, above all, poet, Yeats brought Irish culture onto a world stage, winning the Nobel Prize for Literature in 1923 and producing some of the finest poetry in any language of that era. While influenced by and commenting on the turbulent years in Ireland of the early twentieth century, his work resonated internationally in a time of calamity and change during and after World War I, with the lines of *The Second Coming*, published in 1921 as the Irish war of independence was coming to an end, still among the most quoted in modern literature:

*Things fall apart; the centre cannot hold;*
*Mere anarchy is loosed upon the world,*
*The blood-dimmed tide is loosed, and everywhere*
*The ceremony of innocence is drowned;*
*The best lack all conviction, while the worst*
*Are full of passionate intensity.*

From his Late Romantic beginnings, Yeats's work developed through the trauma of lost love – Maude Gonne, a recurring presence throughout his work – and the disappointment of the Ireland he saw emerging, more mercantile than artistic, to produce a harder, more realist and direct poetry. Among the best examples of this work are *September 1913*, *Easter 1916* – his elegy for the executed leaders of the Republican Rising of that year – and *The Fisherman*. But it was in Yeats's last decade that the challenges of ageing and declining health inspired some of the finest moments in modern poetry, including *Among School Children* and *Sailing to Byzantium*. Yeats died in January 1939 in France, with his body returning to Ireland after the war in 1948 to be reburied in Drumcliffe churchyard in County Sligo.

### The Abbey and Synge

One of the major ambitions of Yeats, Lady Gregory and other leaders of the Literary Revival was the development of an Irish national theatre, realized with the opening of the **Abbey Theatre** in 1904. The Abbey would define a distinct form of Irish theatre, combining a concern with the English language as spoken in Ireland with an attempt to revive belief in the value of Irish culture. In its early years, its greatest playwright was **John Millington Synge**, whose work would provide some of the most memorable characters and narratives of this period, particularly in his masterpiece *The Playboy of the Western World*, first performed in 1907. This dark and yet at times very humorous play, featuring Christy Mahon who achieves fame in a rural Mayo community by claiming that he killed his father, was more than the nationalist audience of its day could accept and resulted in a riot during its first performance. Synge was not afraid to reveal the full gamut of the rural peasant's language, inflected with the Irish language, in both its vulgarity and wit, and an audience that had been conditioned to view the peasant as the very paragon of pure Irishness could not tolerate such a blasphemy. Synge died all too young at the age of 37 in 1909, but helped to inspire later dramatists to create realistic depictions of Irish life.

## Joyce

**James Joyce** was born in Dublin in 1882 into a middle-class Catholic family, which by his early teens had declined into poverty, due largely to his father's carelessness with money. Joyce's challenging experiences, however, provided considerable material for characters and narratives, giving rise to one of the most innovative and imaginative voices in English literature. Although Joyce began writing when the Literary Revival was at its height, he would become one of its strongest critics: as Stephen Dedalus, the protagonist of his semi-autobiographical *A Portrait of the Artist as a Young Man* (1916), remarks to his nationalist school-friend Davin, "You talk to me of nationality, language, religion. I shall try to fly by those nets." For Joyce, each of these elements placed constraints on the writer that could only limit his creativity and expression, something he could not countenance. In the end, he found Ireland too oppressive socially and culturally for his art and headed for the continent, rarely returning to the country of his birth after 1904, and visiting for the last time in 1912. However, while much of his writing was done in Trieste, Paris and Zürich – the city in which he died in 1941 – Ireland, and particularly Dublin, remained the central locale of his work. Indeed, arguably no other writer in twentieth-century literature mapped a city so effectively, epitomized in his finest work, *Ulysses* (1922), which recounts the happenings of a single day in the life of Dublin. Joyce's partner, and eventual wife, during his years on the continent was Nora Barnacle, and the day on which they first met in Dublin, June 16, 1904, has become immortalized as "Bloomsday" (see page 81), the day on which all the events of the novel, concerning the life and ruminations of a Jewish advertising canvasser, Leopold Bloom, take place.

## Irish fiction after Joyce

The short story, a form pioneered in Ireland by George Moore in *The Untilled Field* (1903) and developed by Joyce in *Dubliners* (1914), has been an important genre for Irish writers ever since. **Liam O'Flaherty**, born in 1896 on the Irish-speaking Aran Islands off Galway, wrote several acclaimed novels, including *The Informer* (1925), a salty tale of an ex-IRA man who betrays an associate to the police and is hunted down by his former colleagues. However, it is his short stories, in both English and his native Irish, including "Going into Exile", "The Shilling" and his Irish-language collection, *Dúil* (1953), that constitute his best work. Two other notable exponents of the short-story form were **Seán Ó Faoláin** and **Frank O'Connor**. Among Ó Faoláin's finest collections are *Midsummer Night Madness and Other Stories* (1932) and *The Man Who Invented Sin* (1948), while his story "Lovers of the Lake" remains a classic in modern Irish writing. Ó Faoláin was also an editor of the seminal literary journal of the 1940s and 1950s, *The Bell*, and an outspoken critic of the anti-intellectualism that characterized Irish society during his life, under the considerable influence of the Catholic Church. O'Connor is best remembered for the short stories "The First Confession" and "The Luceys", and the collection *Guests of the Nation* (1931).

One of the most experimental writers of the twentieth century was **Flann O'Brien**, born Brian Ó Núalláin in 1911. While O'Brien's finest work is arguably found in the novel *At Swim-Two-Birds* (1939), his wonderfully surreal and funny *The Third Policeman* (1967) enjoyed renewed popularity after its brief appearance in the TV serial *Lost*. O'Brien's first language growing up in Tyrone and later Dublin was Irish, and he also wrote some of the most satirically humorous work in this language, including *An Béal Bocht* (The Poor Mouth; 1941), published under the pseudonym Myles na gCopaleen ("Myles of the little horses"). A parody of the celebrated Blasket Island autobiographies of writers such as Tomás Ó Criomhthain and Peig Sayers, *An Béal Bocht* is an unrestrained attack on the pretensions of the Irish-Ireland movement.

## Irish poetry after Yeats

The generation of poets that followed Yeats could not escape the long shadow cast by the Nobel Laureate, but were also concerned to critique the legacies of the Literary Revival, especially its reliance on the idealization of the peasant. While **Austin Clarke** charted the urban experience, Patrick Kavanagh's work provided one of the first authentic catalogues of rural life in twentieth-century poetry. Clarke began writing verse in the 1910s much influenced by early Yeats and concerned with similar goals of bringing Gaelic literature into the English language; for example in his free translations of stories about Fionn Mac Cumhaill in *The Vengeance of Fionn*. As his work matured, he became one of the most consistent and acerbic commentators on Irish life and particularly the suffocating influence of the Church, apparent in one of his finest poems *Martha Blake at 51*, and his short lyric *Penal Law*:

> *Burn Ovid with the rest. Lovers will find*
> *A hedge-school for themselves and learn by heart*
> *All that the clergy banish from the mind,*
> *When hands are joined and head bows in the dark.*

Clarke's legacy has been particularly influential in the work of **Thomas Kinsella**, who continues Clarke's mapping of the urban geography of Dublin. Kinsella has also turned to Gaelic literature and Irish mythology for themes and motifs in his work and, influenced by Jungian psychology, as part of his exploration of his own unconscious, in collections such as *Notes from the Land of the Dead* (1973) and *Fifteen Dead* (1979). Kinsella has also been one of the most important translators of Gaelic literature into English, in works such as *The Táin, An Duanaire 1600–1900: Poems of the Dispossessed* and *The New Oxford Book of Irish Verse*.

The poetry of **Patrick Kavanagh**, who was born in 1904 and raised on a small farm near Inniskeen, County Monaghan, revealed the challenges of rural life in a manner that included an implicit, and sometimes explicit, critique of the Revival's pretensions. Though his work also includes striking lyrics recognizing the power and beauty of the natural world – "the spirit-shocking wonder of a black slanting Ulster hill" – for Kavanagh rural life was often characterized by deprivation, both physical and psychological, as demonstrated in *The Great Hunger* and the pounding rhythms of *Stony Grey Soil*:

> *O stony grey soil of Monaghan*
> *The laugh from my love you thieved;*
> *You took the gay child of my passion*
> *And gave me your clod-conceived.*

Kavanagh, who died in 1967, was arguably the most influential Irish poet after Yeats for poets such as Seamus Heaney and **John Montague**. Raised in Tyrone, Montague inherited Kavanagh's rural concerns, but added to them a political consciousness focused on the Troubles in Northern Ireland, apparent in the volume *The Rough Field* (1972).

As Montague's work, and that of other Northern poets suggests, the setting-up of Northern Ireland in 1920 created distinct historical and political processes within that region. Issues such as culture, language, history and identity became all the more important to writers attempting to articulate distinctive voices in a contested space, coming to a head with the outbreak of the Troubles in the late 1960s. However, these themes were already apparent in the work of the major writers from Northern Ireland in the early and mid-twentieth century: **John Hewitt** and **Louis MacNeice**. In the work of MacNeice, who is often associated with the British poetry movement of the 1930s that included Cecil Day Lewis, Stephen Spender and W. H. Auden, one finds an ambiguous relationship with the country of his birth, though his focus on the west of Ireland in particular, in poems such as *Galway* and *Western Landscape*, anticipates the concern with this part of the island in the work of the next generation of Protestant poets, Michael Longley and Derek Mahon. Meanwhile Hewitt promoted his belief in cultural regionalism, in writing from and for the community in the North from which he emerged:

> *I write for my own kind*
> *I do not pitch my voice*
> *that every phrase be heard*
> *by those that have no choice:*
> *their quality of mind*
> *must be withdrawn and still,*
> *as moth that answers moth*
> *across a roaring hill.*

## Irish-language literature in the twentieth century

The Revival was important for the emergence of prose writers in Irish in the twentieth century, most notably Galway-born **Pádraic Ó Conaire**, the author of over four hundred short stories, several plays, numerous essays and the ground-breaking novel *Deoraíocht* (Exile; 1910), still one of the most remarkable Irish works of fiction and regarded as the first modern novel in the Irish language. Set in London at the beginning of the twentieth century, the narrative concerns an Irish emigrant, who after losing an arm and a leg and being seriously disfigured in an accident shortly after arriving from Galway, ends up working in a travelling circus as a sideshow freak.

Autobiography emerged as an important form in Irish-language literature in the early twentieth century. This was most apparent in the work of writers from the now-uninhabited **Blasket Islands** (see page 293) off the coast of Kerry, including Peig Sayers, Muiris Ó Súilleabháin and Tomás Ó Criomhthain, whose *An tOileánach* (The Islandman; 1929) is probably the most accomplished of all these texts.

The dwindling audience for Irish-language literature would be a matter of concern for writers throughout the twentieth century. As **Máirtín Ó Cadhain**, author of the century's most innovative novel in Irish, *Cré na Cille* (Graveyard Clay; 1948, translated as *The Dirty Dust* and republished in 2015), remarked, "[i]t is hard for a man to give of his best in a language which seems likely to die before himself, if he lives a few years more". Despite the decline in the number of native speakers, however, writers such as Eoghan Ó Tuairisc, Bréandán Ó hEithir, Pádraig Standún, Mícheál Ó Siadhail and Pádraig Ó Cíobháin have all produced substantial fiction in Irish, while Pádraic Breathnach, Alan Titley and Micheál Ó Conghaile continue to produce critically acclaimed collections of short stories.

In poetry, the major Irish-language writers to emerge in the mid-twentieth century were **Máirtín Ó Direáin**, **Máire Mhac an tSaoi** and **Seán Ó Ríordáin**. For Ó Direáin, from his first self-published collection, *Coinnle Geala* (1942), the speech of the Aran Islands where he grew up was an important source, but he would turn, particularly from the collection *Ó Mórna agus Dánta Eile*, to forms apparent in the work of earlier Gaelic poets. Mhac an tSaoi would bring a thorough knowledge of the Gaelic literary tradition to her work, reflected in her use of both bardic and *amhrán*, or Gaelic song, metres in poems such as *Caoineadh* and *Ceathrúintí Mháire Ní Ógáin*. For collections such as *Brosna* (1964), Ó Ríordáin is regarded as the great modernist of Gaelic poetry, whose conscious rearranging of language would produce an original and, for many, controversial, poetics in Irish.

Other accomplished Irish-language poets over the past forty years have included Michael Hartnett – who was also a major poet in English – Michael Davitt, Gabriel Rosenstock, Liam Ó Muirthile, Nuala Ní Dhomhnaill, Cathal Ó Searcaigh, Gréagóir Ó Dúill, Micheal Ó Siadhail, Áine Ní Ghlinn, Biddy Jenkinson, Colm Breathnach and Louis de Paor.

## Irish theatre after Synge

Whereas Synge had focused on rural Ireland, the Abbey's next great dramatist, **Sean O'Casey**, would bring the lives and challenges of the urban poor onto the stage, in some of the theatre's most famous and controversial productions, including *The Shadow of a Gunman* (1923) and *Juno and the Paycock* (1924). As with Synge's *Playboy of the Western World*, O'Casey's next, and arguably finest play, *The Plough and the Stars*, resulted in a riot in the theatre when first staged in 1926. Depicting the events of the 1916 Rising from the perspective of ordinary tenement-dwellers in Dublin, O'Casey cast a critical eye over events considered sacred in Irish nationalist history, regarding the leaders as more concerned with their own egos than with the welfare of the populace. O'Casey, however, felt suffocated as many Irish writers before and after by the oppressive forces of religion and orthodoxy in Ireland. After his subsequent play, the experimental *The*

*Silver Tassie*, dealing with World War I, was rejected by the Abbey, he left Ireland in 1928, spending the remainder of his life in Devon, England.

Among those who assisted James Joyce in his work during his years in Paris was a young writer who had similarly left Ireland in his early twenties, and would himself go on to achieve worldwide fame as a modernist writer: **Samuel Beckett**. While creating some of the century's most memorable dramatic works – including *Waiting for Godot* (1952), *Endgame* (1958) and *Krapp's Last Tape* (1959) – Beckett developed a minimalist and sometimes severe theatre of the absurd, if one relieved by occasional moments of insight and humour. He brought to his writing the attention to detail characteristic of one writing in an acquired tongue (many of his greatest works were written in French) and was awarded the Nobel Prize for Literature in 1968.

**Brendan Behan** is today unfortunately remembered almost as much for his effusive personality and drunken interviews as for his important literary work, which included the autobiographical *Borstal Boy* (1958) and the plays *The Quare Fellow* (1954) and *The Hostage* (1958; originally produced in Irish as *An Giall*), a piece that in many respects anticipated the narrative of Neil Jordan's Oscar-winning 1992 film, *The Crying Game*. Behan's weakness for alcohol was a major factor in both his small, if accomplished, output as a writer and his early death at the age of 41.

## Contemporary theatre

Among the recurring themes of Irish theatre since the middle of the twentieth century has been the legacy of colonialism, including the Troubles in Northern Ireland. Reflecting the nationalist standpoint, **Brian Friel**'s *Translations* (1980) and *Dancing at Lughnasa* (1992) remain modern classics of the Irish stage. One of the most important studies of Unionist identity is found in the Donegal-born **Frank McGuinness**'s *Observe the Sons of Ulster Marching Towards the Somme* (1985). Similar critical acclaim has attended **Thomas Kilroy** (*The Death and Resurrection of Mr Roche*, 1968; *The O'Neill*, 1969; *Sex and Shakespeare*, 1976) and **Tom Murphy** (*Famine*, 1968; *Conversations on a Homecoming*, 1985; *Bailegangaire*, 2001), while **Hugh Leonard** and **John B. Keane** have written some of the most popular dramatic works since the 1960s, several of which have been adapted for film, including Leonard's *Da* (originally produced in 1977) and Keane's *The Field* (1965).

A significant development over the past forty years has been the emergence of new theatre companies to challenge the dominance of the Abbey, including **Field Day**, founded in 1980 in Derry by Seamus Heaney, Brian Friel and Thomas Kilroy, among others. Galway's **Druid Theatre** has produced some of the most important contemporary works on the Irish stage, including the plays of **Martin McDonagh**, born in London of Irish descent. McDonagh, who won an Academy Award for best short film in 2006 and a BAFTA for 2008's *In Bruges*, has garnered widespread critical acclaim for his provocative and violent work, notably *The Beauty Queen of Leenane* (1996) and *The Cripple of Inishmaan*, a dark comedy which had successful runs in the West End and off-Broadway. A feature of younger playwrights such as **Conor McPherson**, **Enda Walsh** and **Mark O'Rowe** has been a willingness to bring the vernacular and popular culture onto the stage. Each of these writers has moved between theatre and film, with Walsh's *Disco Pigs* (1996) being adapted for the screen by Kirsten Sheridan in 2001, O'Rowe providing the script for one of the most successful independent Irish films in recent years, *Intermission* (2003), and McPherson going on to direct his own films, including *Saltwater* (2000) and *The Actors* (2003) starring Michael Caine. One of the most significant new voices to have emerged from the North is **Gary Mitchell**, whose plays such as *As the Beast Sleeps* (1998), *The Force of Change* (2000) and *State of Failure* (2006) draw strikingly on his own Belfast working-class Loyalist experience. However, following first threats then full-scale intimidation by the paramilitaries (angered by TV adaptations of his work), Mitchell and his family were forced to flee Belfast in 2005 and live in hiding for five years. Other playwrights of note to emerge in recent years include Paul Mercier, Marina Carr, Christian O'Reilly and **Sebastian Barry**, who has also achieved recognition for his fiction, including *A Long Long Way* (2005) and *The Secret Scripture* (2008), which were both shortlisted for the Man Booker Prize. In 2016 his novel, *Days Without End*, set partly during the American Civil War, won the Costa Book Award.

## Contemporary Irish poetry

Undoubtedly the leading light of the contemporary poetry scene has been the late Nobel Prize-winner **Seamus Heaney** (see page 512), who built on the legacy of Patrick Kavanagh to produce lyrical verse relating the experiences of rural life. Heaney unearthed empowering metaphors in the Irish, and Danish, landscape, particularly bogs, for the Troubles, finding parallels for contemporary violence in ancient ritualistic killings, in poems such as *Bogland*, *Punishment* and *Tollund Man*:

*Out here in Jutland*
*In the old man-killing parishes*
*I will feel lost,*
*Unhappy and at home.*

**Michael Longley**, born in Belfast in 1939, the same year as Heaney, has written some of the most evocative poems of the Troubles, including *Wounds* and *Ceasefire*, which draws on Book XXIV of the *Iliad* and was printed on the front page of the *Irish Times* on the eve of the IRA ceasefire on August 31, 1994. Indeed, Northern Ireland has been a particularly fertile ground for poetry since the 1960s. Other poets of note from the region include **Padraic Fiacc**, **Derek Mahon**, **Paul Muldoon**, the Armagh-born but American-based poet whose collection *Moy Sand and Gravel* won the 2003 Pulitzer Prize for poetry, and **Ciaran Carson**, one of the most distinctive and innovative voices to emerge since the 1970s and a fiction writer of considerable talent, in novels such as *The Star Factory*, *Fishing for Amber* and *Shamrock Tea*.

Significant women's voices in Irish poetry have emerged, including **Eavan Boland**, **Eiléan Ní Chuilleanáin**, **Medbh McGuckian**, **Paula Meehan**, **Rita Ann Higgins**, **Mary O'Malley** and **Sinead Morrissey**, each of whom has brought the female experience to the fore, while critiquing previous representations of women in a primarily male-dominated canon. Another important development in recent years has been the growing number of literary festivals – including the Cúirt Festival in Galway, Listowel Writers' Week and the Dublin Writers' Festival – and the increasing engagement of contemporary poets in the performance of their work. Audiences have had many more opportunities to encounter new writers, and poets such as **Paul Durcan**, **Brendan Kennelly** and **Gearóid Mac Lochlainn** have established considerable reputations through performing.

## Contemporary Irish prose

Much as in poetry, the North of Ireland has produced some of the most popular prose writers. One of the most admired since World War II is **Bernard MacLaverty**, whose most famous novels are *Lamb* and *Cal*, both of which he adapted for the screen, and his most recent *Midwinter Break* (2017) which has been critically acclaimed. **Eoin McNamee**'s *Resurrection Man* (1994) is a disturbing fictionalized account of the notorious Loyalist paramilitaries, the Shankill Butchers, while **Glenn Patterson** has turned to moments before the Troubles to explore other possibilities that might have emerged, in *Burning Your Own* (1988), *The International* (1999) and *The Mill for Grinding Old People Young* (2012). One of the North's most innovative voices has been **Robert McLiam Wilson**, notably in his 1996 novel *Eureka Street*, focusing on the relationship between a Catholic and a Protestant before and after the IRA ceasefire in 1994. Meanwhile, Derry-born **Sean O'Reilly** has been compared to Isabel Allende, producing experimental and magical realist prose in works such as the short-story collection *Curfew and Other Stories* (2000) and novel *Watermark* (2005).

The death in 2006 of **John McGahern** robbed contemporary readers of one of the finest Irish writers since Joyce. McGahern had an almost uncanny insight into human nature and rural Irish society – he was born and lived for most of his life in County Leitrim – and rarely has a writer managed to realize as effectively the details of his life experience in literature. From his first novel *The Barracks* (1963) to his final autobiographical work *Memoir* (2005), McGahern's work evinced a deceptively accessible plain technique, which disguised a unique stylistic meticulousness and inner order.

While Wicklow-born **Claire Keegan**'s work – including her acclaimed 2007 short-story collection *Walk the Blue Fields* – has been indebted in style and theme to McGahern, **Colm Tóibín** has also been regarded as the heir to the Leitrim writer in his focus on aspects of the rural Irish experience. Tóibín's childhood town of Enniscorthy provides the setting for some of his most accomplished work, including *The Heather Blazing* (1992), *The Blackwater Lightship* (1999), a novel that explores the theme of homosexuality in contemporary Ireland, and 2014's *Nora Webster*. Fellow Wexford-born novelist **John Banville** has, like many of his contemporaries, moved outside the Irish context, with subjects ranging from eminent European scientists (*Dr Copernicus*, *Kepler* and *The Newton Letter: An Interlude*) to reflections on a European city (*Prague Pictures: Portrait of a City*). He remains the most critically acclaimed of modern Irish authors, winning the Man Booker Prize in 2005 for his novel, *The Sea*.

**Colum McCann** has also moved outside his Irish roots for inspiration and subject matter, in novels such as *The Dancer* (2003), concerning the Russian ballet legend Rudolf Nureyev, and *Zoli* (2007), focused on the gypsies of Eastern Europe. A key influence on McCann's work was the novelist and short-story writer **Desmond Hogan**, who along with Neil Jordan founded the influential **Irish Writers' Cooperative** in 1974. Hogan focuses repeatedly on the marginalized, isolated and unconventional, in settings that include rural County Galway where he grew up (*The Ikon Maker*) and 1950s Dublin (*The Leaves on Grey*). While **Neil Jordan** is better known today for his Oscar-winning film work, he continues to produce well-crafted and, indeed, powerfully visual literature, including his 2004 gothic tale *Shade*, entirely narrated by a murder victim.

Other members of the Writers' Cooperative include **Ronan Sheehan**, author of *The Tennis Players* and *Foley's Asia*, and **Dermot Bolger**. A poet and dramatist as well as novelist, Bolger has charted Dublin life, especially the Northside, since his first novel *Night Shift* (1985), including reimagining in the context of contemporary working-class Dublin *Caoineadh Airt Uí Laoghaire* (see page 594) as the play *The Lament for Arthur Cleary* (1989). Bolger also founded Raven Arts Press in 1979, one of several Irish publishers, including Dolmen, Gallery, Brandon, Salmon and Arlen House, that have emerged since the 1960s to provide a vital outlet for the work of Irish writers.

Clones-born **Patrick McCabe** has written some of the most provocative and sometimes deeply unsettling fiction of the past twenty years, including *The Butcher Boy* and *Breakfast on Pluto*. Meanwhile, few have managed as successfully to chart the urban experience in contemporary Ireland as **Roddy Doyle**, notably in the Barrytown trilogy (*The Commitments*, *The Snapper* and *The Van*) and the 1993 Booker Prize-winning *Paddy Clarke Ha Ha Ha*, an absorbing portrayal of a child's experience growing up in Dublin in the 1960s. His 2007 collection of short stories, *The Deportees*, is just one of a growing number of texts focusing on multicultural Ireland.

**Edna O'Brien** has remained in the vanguard of Irish novelists since her pioneering work charting the female experience in 1960s Ireland, including the Country Girls trilogy: *The Country Girls, Girl with Green Eyes* and *Girls in Their Married Bliss*. Her 23rd book (and first for ten years) *The Little Red Chairs*, about a war criminal who reinvents himself in an Irish village, was published to acclaim in 2015 when she was 85 and described by critics as "a chilling masterpiece." Meanwhile, the award of the 2007 Man Booker Prize to **Anne Enright** for her fourth novel *The Gathering*, a powerful study of the trauma of suicide for those family members left behind, confirmed her position as one of the leading novelists of her generation. Described by John Banville as "one of the subtlest and most penetrating of the latest generation of Irish writers", **Mary Morrissey** has followed Banville in focusing on non-Irish themes, in particular in *The Pretender* (2000), the story of a Polish factory worker who claims to be the daughter of the last tsar of Russia. **Eilis Ní Dhuibne**, who writes in both Irish and English, has also attracted increasing attention for her work internationally, including her 1999 novel *The Dancers Dancing*. One of the most innovative voices to emerge from Northern Ireland in the 1990s was **Antonia Logue**, notably in *Shadow Box*, while **Anne Haverty's** *The Free and Easy* (2006) marked a movement among contemporary novelists to finally explore twenty-first-century Ireland in their work.

In similar vein, Cork-born poet, short-story writer and novelist **William Wall** wrote in 2005 a pointed critique of the Celtic Tiger, *This is the Country*, featuring a man trying to leave a life of drug abuse behind in an increasingly corrupt and uncaring Ireland. **Mike McCormack** also cast a critical eye on the new Ireland, though in a futuristic context, in *Notes from a Coma* (2005), an account of a penal experiment in which five volunteers, including the former Romanian orphan J.J. O'Malley, are kept in a coma for three months aboard a prison ship in Killary Harbour. His novel *Solar Bones* was shortlisted for the Man Booker Prize in 2017. The academic **Seamus Deane** emerged as one of the most accomplished contemporary writers with the 1996 publication of his semi-autobiographical *Reading in the Dark*. While Deane focused on his formative experiences in the North, one of the most popular recent works of autobiography was **Frank McCourt**'s Pulitzer Prize-winning *Angela's Ashes* (1996), an evocative, and at times deeply moving, account of growing up in poverty in 1930s Limerick which in 2017 was turned into a smash hit musical. While **Joseph O'Connor** began his career as a journalist and writer of popular nonfiction – including the satirical and insightful *The Secret World of the Irish Male* (1994) – he has turned in recent years to fiction, often informed by a meticulous study of history. His 2002 bestselling novel *Star of the Sea* explored the experiences of travellers on a famine ship sailing to the United States in 1847.

The remarkable boom in Irish writing since 2012 has led to critics referring to a new **Irish Literary Renaissance**. The leaders of this youthful charge include Donal Ryan (*The Spinning Heart*, 2012, and *All We Shall Know*, 2016), Eimear McBride, author of the prize-winning *A Girl is a Half-formed Thing* (2013), and Kevin Barry whose novel *City of Bohane* won the 2013 International IMPAC Dublin Literary Award; Barry's other titles include *There are Little Kingdoms* (2007) and *Beatlebone* (2015), which won the Goldsmiths Prize. In her writing, Lisa McInerney, famous for her Arse End of Ireland blog, combines the tradition of Irish crime writing with a foul-mouthed wit. Her novel, *The Glorious Heresies*, featured a cast of low-life Cork city types for which she won the Baileys women's prize for fiction in 2016. Her sequel, *The Blood Miracles*, is a story of drugs and descent in the Cork criminal underworld.

Seán Crosson, with additional contributions by Paul Clements

# Books

Most of the books listed below should be available around the English-speaking world, though you may need to visit one of Ireland's many good bookshops to track down one or two.

## CLASSIC FICTION

★ **J.P. Donleavy** *The Ginger Man*. Riotous and roguish, this is a semi-autobiographical tale of a Trinity College student, full of energy and humour, which unsurprisingly fell foul of the Irish censor in the 1950s. Reprinted in 2015 for its sixtieth anniversary.

★ **Myles na gCopaleen** *The Best of Myles*. Funny, quirky collection of *Irish Times* columns, under Flann O'Brien's other pseudonym.

**Oliver Goldsmith** *The Vicar of Wakefield*. Goldsmith used his experiences as the son of a clergyman to write his most successful novel, a masterpiece of gentle irony.

★ **James Joyce** *Portrait of the Artist as a Young Man*; *Ulysses*. A largely autobiographical tale of a claustrophobic religious education and social oppression, *Portrait* is Joyce's most accessible novel, while *Ulysses* is one of the greatest modernist works, a stylistically brilliant parody of Homer's *Odyssey* that roams over Dublin in a single day.

**Brian Moore** *The Lonely Passion of Judith Hearne*. Set in Moore's native Belfast, a moving tale of a lonely Catholic woman's descent into alcoholism and mental breakdown.

★ **Flann O'Brien** *At Swim-Two-Birds*. Hilariously subversive reworking of *Buile Shuibhne*, the medieval saga of the mad King Sweeney, in which the characters try to take control of the story from their "author". *The Third Policeman* is a darkly absurdist vision of Purgatory. See also Myles na gCopaleen.

★ **Laurence Sterne** *The Life and Opinions of Tristram Shandy, Gentleman*. An eighteenth-century comic masterpiece, described as "the greatest shaggy-dog story in the English language".

**Bram Stoker** *Dracula*. Stoker penned his most famous novel as a psychological thriller, though it's taken on a life of its own since then.

★ **Jonathan Swift** *Gulliver's Travels*; *The Tale of a Tub and Other Stories*. Glorious satires by the Dean of St Patrick's Cathedral, Dublin (see page 75).

★ **Oscar Wilde** *The Picture of Dorian Gray*. Wilde developed similar Gothic themes to his acquaintance Bram Stoker's in this novel, an allusive exploration of "the enemy within".

## MODERN FICTION

★ **John Banville** *The Sea*. One of Ireland's most innovative stylists, the former literary editor of the *Irish Times* won the 2005 Booker Prize for this tale of a widower returning to the seaside village where he spent a formative childhood summer. Look out also for his superior crime fiction, written under the pen name Benjamin Black.

**Kevin Barry** *City of Bohane*. High-energy, muscular gangland thriller, set somewhere between Cork and Limerick in the not-too-distant future.

**Sebastian Barry** *The Secret Scripture*. Perhaps Barry's finest work, this engrossing tale of a woman's mental breakdown and subsequent committal is firmly set within the last century's social and political changes. Beautifully written and observed, it packs a powerful finale.

**Dermot Bolger** *The Valparaiso Voyage*. A tale of a violent homecoming, dealing with themes of political corruption and alienation in contemporary Ireland. *The Family on Paradise Pier* is a vivid account of an eccentric Protestant Big House family as their world collapses after 1915.

★ **Ciaran Carson** *Fishing for Amber*. A "long story" by one of Ireland's most original writers that pulls together Irish fairy tales, Ovid's *Metamorphoses* and the history of the Dutch Golden Age into the form of a magic alphabet.

*Shamrock Tea* is a wildly imaginative fantasy based on a herbal remedy that can cleanse the windows of perception infiltrating a Belfast reservoir.

**Emma Donoghue** *The Wonder*. Dublin-born Emma Donoghue shot to international fame with her 2010 novel *Room*, shortlisted for the Man Booker and Orange prize, about a 5-year-old boy and his mother, held in captivity. Her most recent novel, *The Wonder*, tells a story of a "fasting girl" in an Irish midlands village in the 1850s.

**Roddy Doyle** *Barrytown Trilogy* (*The Commitments*, *The Snapper* and *The Van*). The former Dublin teacher made his name with these humorous tales of the ups and downs of working-class Dublin life, and later won the 1993 Booker Prize for *Paddy Clarke Ha Ha Ha*, which shifted the focus, still laced with comedy, to family breakdown. In 2014, he ghost-wrote a memoir of footballer and manager Roy Keane, *The Second Half*.

**Anne Enright** *The Pleasure of Eliza Lynch*. Historical novel, based on the true story of the nineteenth-century Irish courtesan, who became the richest woman in the world, and her adventures in Paraguay. In 2007, Enright's *The Gathering*, a bleak, compelling tale of family dysfunction, won the Man Booker Prize. *The Green Road*, a moving family drama set in the west of Ireland, was published in 2015.

**Dermot Healy** *Sudden Times*. A rich tale of paranoia, innocence and the tragedy of the working-class Irish in England. Healy has also published some fine poetry collections, including *A Fool's Errand*, which charts the annual migrations of barnacle geese between their breeding grounds in Greenland and their winter quarters in Sligo, where he lived until his death in 2014.

**Patrick McCabe** *The Butcher Boy*. Darkly humorous – and at times disturbing – tale of rural Ireland that was nominated for the Booker Prize.

**Colum McCann** *Thirteen Ways of Looking*. This lyrical novella and three short stories includes the remarkable story of a mother and son adrift on the west coast of Ireland. McCann has also written *Let the Great World Spin* (2009), which won the National Book Award in the US, and *This Side of Brightness* (1998), regarded as his breakthrough novel.

**John McGahern** *The Leavetaking*. Semi-autobiographical tale, in which a teacher at a Clontarf national school reviews his life on the day he expects to be sacked for marrying an American divorcée. One of McGahern's finest works is *Amongst Women*, which details the final years and recollections of a disillusioned former IRA soldier, who dominates the women of his family on a small farm in the west of Ireland. *That They May Face the Rising Sun*, McGahern's last novel, is a dark and elegiac narrative set in rural County Leitrim (published as *By the Lake* in the US).

**Bernard MacLaverty** *Cal*. The Belfast-born writer's best-known book, which tells of the tragic relationship between a young IRA man and his victim's wife. In 2017, *Midwinter Break*, his first novel for sixteen years, features a married couple who go off to Amsterdam to take stock of their lives.

**Eoin McNamee** *The Ultras*. Set in 1970s Northern Ireland, this dark, claustrophobic tale centres on the disappearance of a captain in the British Army Special Forces, employing the film noir and postmodern stylistics found in McNamee's earlier works, *Resurrection Man*, about the Shankill Butchers, and *The Blue Tango*, about a real-life murder.

**Deirdre Madden** *Authenticity*. Evocative and ambitious novel, both a love story and a reflection on being an artist in contemporary society.

★ **Christopher Nolan** *Under the Eye of the Clock*. Powerful, largely autobiographical story of a boy with severe disabilities and joys.

**Joseph O'Connor** *Star of the Sea*. Rich, tragic historical thriller set on a refugee ship bound for New York in 1847. *Ghost Light* is a work of historical fiction set in the Dublin of the 1950s.

**Seán O'Reilly** *Love and Sleep*. A bleak, distinctive novel set in Derry, blending hard-edged realism with vivid, dream-like qualities.

**Keith Ridgway** *The Long Falling*. Ridgway's often harrowing debut novel is both a love story and murder story, set in a Dublin that is dangerous and alienating. He followed it up with *The Parts*, a compelling and stylistically inventive mystery, also set in Dublin.

★ **Colm Tóibín** *Brooklyn* Tóibín's best-known novel, *Brooklyn*, is a keenly observed, humane story of 1950s emigration and return, set partly in the author's home town of Enniscorthy – which is also the setting of his exquisitely written follow-up novel, *Nora Webster*.

**William Trevor** *The Story of Lucy Gault*. Nominated for the Booker Prize, this powerful tale beginning in rural Cork – where Trevor was born – during the troubles of 1921 tells the story of the disasters that ensued for one family. Regarded as one of the greatest writers in contemporary fiction, Trevor died in November 2016 leaving a string of elegiac novels such as *Love and Summer*, *The Children of Dynmouth*, *The Silence in the Garden*, *Reading Turgenev*, and a two-volume *Collected Stories*. He once said that his work involved making Irish provincialism universal.

## POETRY

**Samuel Beckett** *Poems 1930–1989*. The most complete collection of Beckett's poetry, in both English and French (with his own translations), and including translations of major twentieth-century French poets such as Rimbaud and Eluard.

**Eavan Boland** *Collected Poems*. Ireland's leading female poet, also a central voice in American poetic circles, explores the boundaries of women's experiences.

★ **Paul Durcan** *Greetings to Our Friends in Brazil*. A good starting point for this accessible Dublin-born poet. Many of the poems centre on a priest who, far from being repressive and hypocritical as in his earlier works, is honourable and truly spiritual.

**Michael Hartnett** *Collected Poems*. A richly lyrical and rhythmical collection covering Hartnett's forty-year career.

★ **Seamus Heaney** *Opened Ground: Poems 1966–96* is a huge selection of Heaney's work (see page 512), while *New Selected Poems 1988-2013* features his later work up to the time of his death. *Finders Keepers* is an anthology of his energetic prose, consisting of essays and lectures written between 1971 and 2001.

★ **Patrick Kavanagh** *Collected Poems*. Ireland's best-loved poet is perhaps most famous for *The Great Hunger*, in which he attacked sexual repression in 1940s Ireland.

**Thomas Kinsella** *Collected Poems: 1956–2001*. The full variety of Kinsella's work is on display here, employing modernist and traditional elements, on subjects ranging from love to political satire, social commentary and metaphysical speculation.

**Michael Longley** *Gorse Fires*; *The Ghost Orchid*; *The Weather in Japan*. Three fine collections, which show Longley as a highly skilled poet with a strong moral voice.

**Nuala Ní Dhomhnaill** *The Astrakhan Cloak*; *The Water*

*Horse*. Good introductions to her work, in Irish and English, with translations in the former by Paul Muldoon, in the latter by Medbh McGuckian and Eileán Ní Chuilleanáin.
**Derek Mahon** *New Collected Poems*. A comprehensive fifty-year retrospective of this prodigious poet's far-ranging oeuvre that includes the much-loved "Disused Shed in Co. Wexford."
**John Montague** *Collected Poems; The Rough Field*. The first holder of the Ireland Chair of Poetry in 1998, Montague was much-garlanded, highly influential, and author of numerous slim volumes. Although he died in December 2016, his work continues to resonate as a master of *dinnseanchas* or "place wisdom".
★ **William Butler Yeats** *Collected Poems*. Love, anger, meditation and disillusionment from W.B., one of the greatest figures of twentieth-century literature.

## GAELIC LITERATURE AND FOLKLORE

**Ciaran Carson** *The Midnight Court*. Vibrant rendering of Brian Merriman's bawdy, eighteenth-century Gaelic poem, *Cúirt an Mheán Oíche*.
**Seamus Heaney** *Sweeney Astray*. The late Nobel laureate's version of *Buile Shuibhne*, the twelfth- or thirteenth-century tale of Sweeney's mad wanderings and healing.
**Thomas Kinsella** *The Táin*. The best translation of the *Táin Bó Cúailnge* (The Cattle Raid of Cooley), the heroic centrepiece of the Ulster Cycle.
**Tomás Ó Criomhthain** (aka Thomas O'Crohan) *An tOileánach* (The Islandman). Vivid insights into the cruelties of life on the Blasket Islands.
★ **Maurice O'Sullivan** *Twenty Years A-Growing*. The story of O'Sullivan's youth and the traditional way of life on the Blasket Islands in the early twentieth century, in a style derived from folk tales.

## HISTORY AND POLITICS

**Jonathan Bardon** *A History of Ulster*. A comprehensive account from early settlements to the Troubles.
**Michael Barry** *Courage Boys: We are Winning, Illustrated History of the 1916 Rising*. The 100th anniversary of the Easter Rising in 2016 prompted a surge of new books and this one, moving from the panoramic to the particular, is brought alive with over five hundred stunning images telling the story in a clear but nuanced manner.
**Angela Bourke** *The Burning of Bridget Cleary*. Impeccably researched account of nefarious goings-on in Tipperary in the 1890s, describing the sensational case of a young woman supposedly taken by the fairies, tortured and murdered, and the subsequent trial of her husband, father, aunt and four cousins.
**John Bowman (ed.)** *Ireland: The Autobiography*. Engaging anthology of a hundred years' worth of storytelling, essays and journalism ranging from Patrick Pearse's letter to his mother to Fintan O'Toole's account of the Irish referendum in 2015 which legalized same-sex marriage.
**Garrett Carr** *The Rule of The Land: Walking Ireland's Border*. Variously travelling by foot and by boat, this is a compelling account of the author's jaunt along the border between North and South, in which he reflects upon the people, places and events that have shaped this often troubled landscape – it's an account that's more pertinent than ever following Brexit.
★ **Tim Pat Coogan** *Ireland in the Twentieth Century*. An engrossing account of political and social developments, both North and South, by the former editor of the *Irish Press*, who has written many readable histories, notably *The IRA*, *1916: The Easter Rising* and biographies of Michael Collins and Éamon de Valera.
**Richard English** *Irish Freedom: A History of Nationalism in Ireland*. Lucid and fascinating scholarly dissection of Irish nationalism over the last three centuries.
**Diarmaid Ferriter** *The Transformation of Ireland 1900–2000*. Extensive and insightful account of the making of modern Ireland, combining politics, economics and social history.
**Garret FitzGerald** *Reflections on the Irish State*. The former Taoiseach offers perceptive insights and challenging theories on the big issues of Irish public life.
★ **R.F. Foster** *Modern Ireland 1600–1972*. The best history of the period, authoritative and comprehensive, though heavy going at times for the lay reader. In contrast, *Luck and the Irish* gambols entertainingly through the period from 1970 to 2000, while *The Irish Story: Telling Tales and Making It Up in Ireland* is a provocative, witty deconstruction of myth-making and clichés in Ireland's telling of its own history.
**Tom Garvin** *Preventing the Future: Why Was Ireland So Poor for So Long?* Perhaps the most important socio-historical analysis of postwar Ireland, not least in terms of the "lost" decades of the 1950s and 1960s. Garvin offers not only an acute analysis of the rotten core of Irish social policy but a persuasive and often witty account of its impact upon future generations.
★ **Robert Kee** *The Green Flag*. Lucid and incisive account of nationalism from the Elizabethan Plantations to "ourselves alone" after Independence.
**Conan Kennedy** *Ancient Ireland: The User's Guide*. Extremely useful descriptions of Ireland's various types of megalithic field monuments, plus a fascinating account of the place of magic, ritual and mythology.
★ **Declan Kiberd** *Inventing Ireland*. Witty and thought-provoking re-reading of the literature of the modern nation.
**Christine Kinealy** *This Great Calamity: The Irish Famine*. Unravels fact from fiction through systematic analysis of

primary source material related to the Great Famine.

**Susan McKay** *Northern Protestants: An Unsettled People.* Utterly grim but absolutely essential account of the North's Protestant community and its disparate views, based on numerous interviews, simultaneously offering hope for the future and showing sheer desperation.

**David McKittrick and David McVea** *Making Sense of the Troubles.* Clear, dispassionate and authoritative crash-course on the conflict.

**Ed Moloney** *A Secret History of the IRA.* Authoritative account, with Gerry Adams as its sinisterly intriguing central character, of the struggle within the Republican movement over the last forty years.

**George Morrison** *The Irish Civil War.* A powerful collection of photographic images of the Civil War, accompanied by commentary by Tim Pat Coogan.

**Henry Patterson** *Ireland Since 1939: The Persistence of Conflict.* At times iconoclastic, Patterson's account of an Ireland divided not only by boundaries, but by ideologies and class-related interests, breaks new ground and provides utterly stimulating reading.

★ **Colm Tóibín and Diarmaid Ferriter** *The Irish Famine: A Documentary.* Highly readable analysis of the Great Famine, which takes an incisive look at both the complex issues surrounding the failure of the potato crop, and the inadequacy of previous historical accounts of the crisis.

## BIOGRAPHY AND MEMOIRS

**Christy Brown** *My Left Foot.* Born with cerebral palsy, Brown painstakingly typed out this unsentimental autobiography, published in 1954 when he was 22, focusing on his upbringing in a huge Dublin family, dominated by the remarkable character and endurance of his mother.

**Ruth Dudley Edwards** *James Connolly.* A short biography of the socialist leader, which gathers pace around the time of his relations with Larkin, the 1913 Lock-Out in Dublin and the 1916 Rising.

★ **Richard Ellmann** *James Joyce; Oscar Wilde.* Ellmann's wonderful biography of Joyce is a literary masterpiece in its own right. His work on Wilde was, unfortunately, unfinished when he died, but is still an excellent insight into the work of this often misunderstood writer.

**Christopher Fitz-Simon** *The Boys.* Frank and conscientious biography of the founders of Dublin's Gate Theatre, Micheál Mac Liammóir and his equally mysterious lifelong lover, Hilton Edwards.

★ **R.F. Foster** *W.B. Yeats: A Life – Volume I, The Apprentice Mage; Volume II, The Arch-poet.* A magisterial work, the first fully authorized biography, incisive, exhaustive and compellingly readable.

**Michael Harding** *Staring at Lakes.* An absorbing memoir of love and magical thinking by a playwright and author who chronicles his ordinary life in the Irish midlands in a popular weekly column in *The Irish Times.*

**James Knowlson** *Damned to Fame: The Life of Samuel Beckett.* Excellent biography by one of the world's pre-eminent Beckett experts.

**Hugh Leonard** *Home before Night; Out after Dark.* Beautifully written evocations by the noted playwright of, respectively, his childhood and his adolescence in south Dublin around the 1940s. At times moving, often hilarious.

**Kevin Myers** *Watching the Door; A Single Headstrong Heart.* Controversial journalist and author who has pioneered the study of WWI in Ireland. Funny and moving, his memoir *A Single Headstrong Heart* is a prequel to *Watching the Door* about his early career in journalism.

**Antoinette Quinn** *Patrick Kavanagh: A Biography.* Astute and often gently paced account of the life and poetry of County Monaghan's favourite son.

## MUSIC

★ **Helen Brennan** *The Story of Irish Dance.* Not just a fascinating history of the development of traditional dancing in Ireland, but a (literally) step-by-step guide to some of the most popular set-dances.

**Victoria Mary Clarke and Shane MacGowan** *A Drink with Shane MacGowan.* MacGowan's wife takes the singer and songwriter through his personal history and several large martinis on the way.

**Gerard Hanberry** *On Raglan Road.* The story of the women who inspired Irish love songs such as "Galway Girl", "Nancy Spain", and "Down by the Salley Gardens".

**Colin Harper and Trevor Hodgett** *Irish Folk, Trad & Blues: A Secret History.* Fascinating accounts of key figures in Ireland's recent musical history, from Van the Man to Altan.

**Colin Irwin** *In Search of the Craic.* Wittily written account of a quest to hear some of the best of Ireland's traditional music.

★ **Christy Moore** *One Voice.* Not just a scintillating account of Moore's own life through song, but a hard-hitting analysis of Ireland over the last thirty years.

**Pádraigín Ní Uallacháin** *A Hidden Ulster.* Mammoth and utterly engrossing account of the Irish song tradition, centred on the area known as Oriel (containing parts of Armagh, Monaghan and Louth).

**Tommy Sands** *The Songman.* Illuminating, droll and incisive autobiographical account by the singer and broadcaster of growing up in 1950s rural Down, being enticed by and rejecting the idea of the priesthood, and moving on to a musical career whose increasingly sharp-edged political tone saw him play a pivotal role in the peace process.

★ **Fintan Vallely** (ed) *The Companion to Irish Traditional Music.* Provides constant delight in its copious accounts of the music's form, style and qualities, and brief biographies of many key participants; required reading.

**Fintan Vallely and Charlie Piggott** *Blooming Meadows: The World of Irish Traditional Musicians*. The fascinating biographical snapshots of a broad range of singers and musicians are enhanced by evocative photographs of their subjects.

**Geoff Wallis and Sue Wilson** *The Rough Guide to Irish Music*. A quintessential account of the roots and current state of traditional music in Ireland, containing a comprehensive directory of more than four hundred singers, musicians and groups, and details of the best places to see them in action.

## MISCELLANEOUS

★ **Aalen, Stout and Whelan** (eds) *Atlas of the Irish Rural Landscape*. Fascinating, lucid exploration of the geography of the Irish landscape, illustrated with photographs and maps. *Newgrange and the Bend of the Boyne*, by Geraldine Stout, is an offshoot of the atlas.

**Paul Clements** *Wandering Ireland's Wild Atlantic Way*. Detours and diversions on a lively meander along the 2500km route of the Wild Atlantic Way. The author has also written *The Height of Nonsense*, a humorous account of his journey to the highest point of every county in Ireland, described by the *Irish Independent* as "gloriously daft yet irresistible".

**Gordon D'Arcy** *The Breathing Burren*. A personal tour and fascinating exploration of the remarkable area of limestone pavement in the Burren, Co. Clare. The author has also written a book on the Burren walls.

**Deirdre and Laurence Flanagan** *Irish Place Names*. Exhaustive guide to the names of over three thousand towns, villages and physical features and their derivations.

**Alannah Hopkin** *Eating Scenery*. The serenely beautiful "Independent Republic of West Cork" as it is sometimes known, is brought alive through interviews and reflection, quirky detail and laugh-out-loud snapshots. The author's collection of stories, *The Dogs of Inishere* is also worth looking out for.

★ **Pete McCarthy** *McCarthy's Bar*. Runaway bestseller by the late, former travel-show presenter and stand-up comedian. An extended crawl around the *McCarthy's* bars of Ireland provides occasion for insight and humour.

★ **Tim Robinson** *Connemara: Listening to the Wind*. Fascinating story of the Roundstone area around the author's home, ranging over everything from geology to folklore, written in a deceptively plain, easy style. *Connemara: The Last Pool of Darkness* gives similar treatment to the coast from Killary Harbour to Ballyconneely.

## GUIDES

★ **Mairead Carew** *Tara: The Guidebook*. Quick-reference guide to one of Ireland's mythical sites, the Hill of Tara in Co. Meath, presented succinctly and with clarity.

**Zoe Devlin** The Wildflowers of Ireland. Lavishly illustrated with more than five hundred wildflowers and the author's photographs, this is an essential vade mecum. For a more specific book on flora, Charles Nelson's The Wild Plants of the Burren and the Aran Islands is recommended.

**Paddy Dillon** *The Mournes Walks* and *The Complete Ulster Way Walks*. A series of detailed, easy-to-follow guides covering mostly circular day-walks, with information about the wildlife and landscape.

**Felicity Hayes-McCoy** Dingle and its Hinterland. Dingle is a mecca for tourists but the western part of the peninsula is not so well known. This book offers both practical information and cultural insights into the area.

**Neil Jackman** Ireland's Ancient East. Historic treasures and the built heritage are showcased as part of the newly established Ancient East driving route from Co. Cork to Co. Louth.

★ **Joss Lynam** (ed) *Best Irish Walks*. Authoritative guide to over 75 hill walks all around Ireland. Lynam's *Easy Walks near Dublin* and the more recent *Leisure Walks near Dublin* each cover around forty mostly circular walks of between half an hour and three hours on the city's doorstep, mainly the Wicklow Mountains.

**Dan MacCarthy** *Cycling Munster*. Explore on two wheels the byways of the counties of Munster, including the thigh-burning Ring of Kerry, with this first-class guide complete with maps and gradient graphs. It is published by the Collins Press, which has produced numerous other excellent cycling and walking guides to different parts of Ireland.

**Frank McNally** *111 Places in Dublin That You Shouldn't Miss*. Filled with the strange and the incongruous, McNally – who writes the Irishman's Diary in *The Irish Times* – knows Dublin intimately and includes less obvious places in his ramblings.

# The Irish language

You're most likely to hear the distinctive sounds of spoken Irish if you travel in the Gaeltacht regions, designated areas of Irish-speakers (*Gaeilgeoirí*), the largest of which are in Kerry, Galway and Donegal. Here in summer, you'll come on crowds of teenagers from all over Ireland who are passing through the annual ritual of Irish college, learning the language by immersion.

If you're interested in having a go yourself, courses are run by the well-respected Gael Linn, 35 Dame St, Dublin (☎01 675 1200, ⊕gael-linn.ie), whether in Dublin usually over six weeks or in summer staying for a week in the Donegal Gaeltacht; by the excellent Oideas Gael in Glencolmcille, Donegal; and in Connemara, Galway (see page 359). Among language-learning materials, Gael Linn produces *Gaeilge agus Fáilte*, an easy-to-follow combination of book and two CDs aimed at adult beginners.

### Some history

Irish is one of the Celtic languages, along with Welsh and Breton, and belongs in particular to the **Gaelic** branch, sometimes known as **Goidelic**, which also includes Scottish Gaelic. Celtic language and culture had become dominant in Ireland by around 300 BC, but **Primitive Irish**, the earliest form known to us, is found only in **ogham** inscriptions on stone monuments, dating from the fifth to seventh centuries AD. This highly unusual script consists of tally-like notches cut along the edge of standing stones, rather than conventional letters. In the next linguistic phase, **Old Irish** (seventh to ninth centuries), the language changed quickly, as Christian monks, now writing in Latin script, adopted a more colloquial form of Irish; from this period comes a fine body of lyric poetry and the earliest version of the *Táin Bó Cúailnge* ("The Cattle Raid of Cooley"), the central saga of the Ulster Cycle. **Middle Irish** (eleventh to thirteenth centuries) was a phase of linguistic confusion and new grammatical forms, with the language going into a decline after the twelfth-century Anglo-Norman conquest. By the fourteenth century it had recovered, entering the period known as **Early Modern** or **Classical Modern Irish**. The use of the language was now governed by the **filí**, a class of professional scholars and poets, among whom the most respected might have the status of a bishop or minor king. Meanwhile, the Anglo-Norman settlers had mostly integrated with the native population, adopting Irish language and customs.

In the seventeenth and eighteenth centuries, however, with the Flight of the Earls, Cromwell's Act of Settlement and the penal laws, the structures of traditional society were comprehensively destroyed. At the beginning of the nineteenth century, just under half the population was purely Irish-speaking, mostly in poor rural areas. These were the very areas, however, that were decimated by the Great Famine of the 1840s and the mass emigration that followed. As early as 1851, the proportion of Irish speakers had declined to a quarter of the population, and by the end of the century it was down to one percent.

Despite the decline of Irish in the nineteenth century, several organizations dedicated to reviving its use sprang up, most notably the **Gaelic League** (Conradh na Gaeilge), founded in 1893 by Douglas Hyde and others. The League ensured that, after Independence in 1921, Irish was constitutionally recognized as the first official language, and was compulsory in the school system and for entry to the Civil Service. Today, around fifteen percent of the Republic's population have a good competence in Irish, 92,000 of whom live in the **Gaeltacht** areas, in counties Donegal, Mayo,

Galway, Kerry, Cork, Waterford and Meath. A recent decline in the actual use of Irish in the *Gaeltachtaí* can be detected, however: a 1980s survey of schoolchildren there, for example, showed that nearly half of them spoke only English at home, while just twenty percent of them spoke only Irish.

Outside of the *Gaeltachtaí*, however, there's been a remarkable recent growth throughout the island, both North and South, in the number of **Gaelscoileanna**, schools in which every subject is taught in Irish and which are known for their high general standards of education. From just sixteen such schools in 1974, the figure has now risen to over two hundred. In **the North**, where the British government is committed to supporting Irish-medium education, the use of Irish has naturally been more politicized. However, about ten percent of the North's population can now speak Irish, and since the Good Friday Agreement of 1998 there's been an all-Ireland body to promote the language, Foras na Gaeilge (ⓦgaeilge.ie).

Set up in 1972, the **Irish-language radio station**, Raidió na Gaeltachta, known especially for its support for traditional music, has been broadcasting all over the country from its base in Connemara; it's now 24-hour, with studios in Donegal, Kerry, Mayo and Dublin. In 1996, it was joined in Connemara by a **national television station**, TG4 (Teilifís na Gaeilge Cathair), which, through its often progressive and upbeat programming, has tried hard to reinvigorate the language.

But despite the renewed interest, and the fact that the language as a communicative subject appears to be thriving, the harsh reality is that the number of everyday Irish speakers is **declining**. On the three Aran Islands, for example, the percentage of active daily Irish speakers fell from 63 percent of the population in 2011 to 57 percent in 2016. And in the Gaeltacht heartland of Connemara, the numbers have dropped alarmingly to less than four thousand , compared to 25,000 in the 1980s. Many feel the political will is simply not strong enough to promote the language, as well as other aspects of the culture such as traditional singing and dancing.

## Basic pronunciation of Irish

Irish **pronunciation** is notoriously difficult for outsiders, bearing little resemblance to English pronunciation. A few basic, simplified pointers are given below. To complicate things further, Ulster, Connacht and Munster have distinct dialects, with different pronunciations and, to a lesser extent, grammars.

### Vowels

Note the acute accent, a *fada*, which is used to lengthen vowels.

| | |
|---|---|
| **a** as in "bat", or like the "o" in "slot" | **í** as in "machine" |
| **á** as in "paw" | **o** as in "ton" |
| **e** as in "bet" | **ó** as in "bone" |
| **é** as in "prey" | **u** as in "book" |
| **i** as in "bit" | **ú** as in "rule" |

### Consonants

Irish distinguishes between slender consonants – when beside an "e" or "i" – and broad consonants – when beside an "a", "o" or "u". For many consonants the slender pronunciation is different from the broad one.

| | |
|---|---|
| **bh** broad, **mh** broad – "w" or "v" | **dh** slender, **gh** slender – "y" as in yes |
| **bh** slender, **mh** slender – "v" | **fh** is silent |
| **c** – always hard, as in "cot" | **g** – always hard, as in "gift" |
| **ch** – like Scottish "loch" | **ph** – as in "phone" |
| **d** broad – "th" as in "**th**is" | **s** broad – "s" as in "some" |
| **d** slender – sharp "d", almost a "j" as in "jelly" | **s** slender – "sh" as in "sugar" |
| **dh** broad, **gh** broad – "gh", like a voiced version of "ch" in "Bach" | **sh, th** – "h" as in "hat" |
| | **t** broad – aspirated, with the tongue against the upper |

teeth, somewhere between the "t" in "toad" and the "th" in "**thin**"

**t** slender – as the "t" in "**tin**"

## A FEW SIMPLE PHRASES

**Hello (lit. "God be with you")** Dia duit
**Hello (in reply, lit. "God and Mary be with you")** Dia is Muire duit
**Welcome (lit. "a hundred thousand welcomes")** Ceád míle fáilte
**What is your name?** Cad is ainm duit?
**My name is...** ... is ainm dom
**How are you?** Conas atá tú?

**Well** Go maith
**Please** Más é do thoil é
**Thank you (very much)** Go raibh (míle) maith agat
**I don't understand** Ní thuigim
**Goodbye (to the person staying)** Slán leat
**Goodbye (to the person leaving)** Slán agat
**Bye (more informal)** Slán

## SIGNS AND PLACE NAMES: SOME COMMON IRISH TERMS

**an lár** city centre
**árd** height
**áth** ford
**baile** town – often anglicized as "bally"
**beag** small – "beg"
**bóthar** road
**bun** base
**caiseal** stone ring fort – "cashel"
**caisleán** castle
**carn** cairn
**carraig** rock – "carrick"
**cathair** fort – "caher"
**ceann** head, headland – "can" or "ken"
**cill** church – "kill" or "keel"
**cnoc** hill – "knock"
**doire** oak wood – "derry" or "derreen"
**dún** fort
**eaglais** church
**fir** men
**geill slí** give way
**glean** valley – "glen"
**go mall** slow down

**gort** field
**inis** island – "inish"
**leithreas** toilet
**leitir** hillside – "letter"
**lios** ring fort – "lis"
**loch** lake – "lough"
**mná** women
**mór** big – "more"
**mullach** summit – "mullagh"
**oileán** island – "illaun"
**páirc** field – "park"
**ráth** ring fort
**rinn** point – "reen"
**ros** headland – "ross"
**sliabh** mountain – "slieve"
**sráid** street
**teach, tí** house, cottage
**teampall** church
**tír** country – "tyr"
**tobar** well
**trá** beach

# Glossary

**Ascendancy** The Protestant aristocracy, whether descended from Anglo-Normans granted land in Ireland or plutocrat planters subsequently installed in the country from the late sixteenth century onwards. Often prefixed by the term "Anglo-Irish".

**banjaxed** Anything that is broken or beyond repair, ranging from the Government to a bicycle.

**bawn** Fortification around a castle enclosure or cattlefold.

**big house** Mansion built by the Ascendancy.

**bodhrán** (pronounced "bore-run" or "bough-ron" depending on the region of Ireland). A shallow, hand-held goatskin-frame drum, played either with a wooden beater or the hand.

**bohreen** (pronounced "bor-een") Resonant Irish term for a laneway.

**B Specials** Auxiliary Northern Irish police force formed after Partition and disbanded in 1971.

**cashel** A stone ring fort.

**ceilidh/ceili** An evening of Irish traditional dancing usually accompanied by a band.

**clochán** An early Christian beehive-shaped hut constructed of stones fitted tightly together without the use of mortar.

**craic/crack** General term for a good time, usually accompanying drinking. "What's the crack?" means "What's going on?"

**crannóg** A Bronze Age artificial island in a lough, constructed to camouflage an otherwise vulnerable dwelling.

**Continuity IRA** Irish Republican paramilitary group which claims to be the legitimate continuation of the IRA. Opposed to the Northern Ireland peace process.

**culchie** Pejorative term used by city-dwellers to describe their country cousins. May have originated from the Co. Mayo town Kiltimagh, or "Coillte Mach", with "culchie" emerging from the Irish word "coillte", meaning woods.

**cute hoor** From "cute" as in sly, and "hoor", as in whore, aimed at those in politics, business or any other profession where deals are cut; normally interpreted as an insulting term but can also be flattering.

**Dáil** Literally means "meeting", but has come to stand for the lower house of the Republic's parliament.

**Diamond** A central area in a planned Irish town, sometimes actually diamond-shaped, but often triangular, with streets surrounding an open space where usually some form of memorial is erected.

**dolmen** Dating from around 2500–2000 BC, a burial chamber set below an often-triangular placement of standing stones, surmounted by an impressively weighty capstone. Also called a portal tomb.

**drumlin** A small oval hummock resulting from Ice Age glacial retreat, found especially in County Monaghan.

**DUP** The Democratic Unionist Party. A staunchly traditional right-wing and often controversial Loyalist party, co-founded by Ian Paisley in 1971, opposed to any attempts at loosening Northern Ireland's ties with the United Kingdom. The party shot to prominence in 2017 when they entered into an agreement with the Conservative government led by Theresa May after the party suffered a shock election loss. To retain her position as British Prime Minister, May struck a deal to secure the DUP's support and in exchange the party received £1bn pounds for investment in the infrastructure of Northern Ireland.

**Éire** The Irish name for the island of Ireland; often used to mean the Republic of Ireland.

**esker/eskar** A ridge of gravel and sand formed by a retreating glacier.

**famine wall/famine road** An enterprise of local landowners during the Great Famine of 1845–51 whereby starving tenants would be rewarded for work given them to build a wall or road rather than aid through hunger-relieving largesse.

**Fenian** A member of the nineteenth-century revolutionary organization that fought for an independent Ireland; often used as an anti-Catholic term of abuse by Northern Irish Loyalists.

**Fianna Fáil** Irish Republic political party that emerged from the Civil War, opposing the partitioning treaty, to become a major force under its long-time leader Éamon de Valera. Still largely conservative in aspect, it has retained governmental control for most of the last eighty years, despite being embroiled in a farrago of financial and political scandals in recent decades.

**First Minister and Deputy First Minister.** The Office of First Minister and Deputy First Minister (known as OFMDFM) of the Northern Ireland Assembly based at Stormont.

**Fine Gael** The Republic's long-term and long-suffering (usually) opposition party, whose origins go back to Michael Collins' support for the Independence Treaty (see page 578). Little distinguishes it from Fianna Fáil, though its social policies seem a little more liberal, and its membership is largely drawn from agricultural areas.

**Fleadh** Literally meaning a "festival", the term has become associated with the Irish traditional-music organization Comhaltas Ceoltóirí Éireann's music competitions in which musicians and singers compete at county and provincial levels before going on to the annual Fleadh Cheoil na Éireann ("Ireland's music festival"). This also includes the winners of the UK and US *fleadhanna* (the plural of "fleadh").

**Gaeltacht** Regions of Ireland where the Irish language is the predominant vernacular tongue, mainly in the country's west.

**gallivanting** Gadding about. A much-used phrase in Ireland although it comes from early nineteenth-century English as a term for flirting with women.

**galloglass** An armed mercenary in medieval times (from the Irish for "foreign soldier").

**Garda Siochána** The police force of the Republic of Ireland.

**High cross** A tall stone cross in which normally the cross itself is surrounded by a circle. The earliest known Irish examples date from the seventh century and are often richly ornamented with biblical scenes.

**IRA** Irish Republican Army. Longstanding upholders of the Republican drive to restore a united 32-county Ireland. Particularly from the late 1960s onwards, it embarked on an armed struggle to force the British to withdraw from Ireland, with major bombing campaigns in the UK and Northern Ireland. The IRA unreservedly renounced its military initiatives in late 2005.

**lash** Give it a lash means to attempt something, while to go on the lash is drinking to excess.

**lough** A commonly used term for lake; also a narrow coastal bay.

**Loyalist** Hardline Northern Irish Protestant loyal to the British Crown, sometimes linked to paramilitary activity, largely existing only as a criminal group.

**LVF** Loyalist Volunteer Force. Paramilitary group based around Portadown and founded by Billy Wright.

**Martello tower** Circular coastal tower built for defence during the Napoleonic Wars.

**MLA** Member of the (Northern Ireland) Local Assembly.

**motte** An early medieval fortification, much used by the Normans, consisting of a circular earthwork mound, flattened on top, on which would be sited a primitive form of castle.

**Nationalists** Those wishing to achieve a united Ireland, usually by peaceful means.

**The North** Politically neutral euphemism for Northern Ireland.

**ogham** Ancient twenty-letter alphabet used in both Celtic and Pictish inscriptions on standing stones, comprising parallel carved lines or notches.

**Oireachtas** The Republic's parliament.

**Orange Hall** A local building where members of the Orange Order meet.

**Orange Order** Loyalist Protestant organization founded in 1795. Subdivided into local lodges, it derives its name from William of Orange (see page 546) and annually celebrates his victory over Catholic James II at the 1690 Battle of the Boyne on July 12 with

parades across Northern Ireland. The majority of Unionist politicians and many Presbyterian clergymen belong to the Order.

**Palladian** A style of architecture derived from the designs of the Italian Andrea Palladio (1508–80), whose work incorporated a rigid adherence to mathematical proportions, first promulgated by the Roman architect Vitruvius. Among the most stunning examples of Palladian architecture in Ireland are Castletown (see page 129), Russborough House (see page 125) and Florence Court (see page 566).

**partition** The division of Ireland into the 26 counties of the Republic and six of the North created by the 1921 Government of Ireland Act.

**passage grave** The oldest form of megalithic tomb, dating from around 4000 BC, consisting of a rounded mound or cairn with a stone-lined passage leading from the perimeter to a central chamber.

**pishogue** A charm, spell, superstitious practice or tall tale.

**plámás** Flattery or empty praise.

**plantation** The process of colonization of Ireland by the English Crown by which land was confiscated from the indigenous people and given to English and Scottish Protestant settlers.

**poitín** (pronounced "pot-cheen") Illicit home-made spirits, once distilled from potatoes in a little pot – hence the name.

**portal tomb** see "dolmen".

**PSNI** The Police Service of Northern Ireland (see also "RUC").

**rath or ring fort** The most common form of ancient monument found in Ireland, dating from between the late Neolithic period and early medieval times. Consists of a circular (sometimes oval or D-shaped) enclosure surrounded by an earthen bank rising from a defensive ditch. A roofed dwelling, of stone or timber, would be constructed within the enclosure.

**The Real IRA** Breakaway political faction which rejects the Northern Ireland political process and maintains the armed struggle. Calls itself simply "the Irish Republican Army" or "IRA"; the media sometimes calls it the "New IRA" after its 2012 merger with Republican Action Against Drugs.

**Republicans** Supporters of the ideals incorporated in the 1916 Proclamation of the Republic, the overthrow of British rule in Ireland and the promotion of Irish language and culture.

**ring fort** see "rath".

**round tower** Usually part of a monastic settlement, these lofty and slenderly tapering, circular stone towers range in height from around 20–35m and were often capped with a conical roof. The earliest examples of this uniquely Irish construction date from around the ninth century. The building would have had a variety of purposes, serving as a belfry, a lookout post and a place for storage of goods and valuables. The entrance was often set some 3–5m above ground level, allowing the means of access, a ladder, to be withdrawn inside the building in case of a Viking raid, some claim.

**RUC** Royal Ulster Constabulary. The Northern Ireland police force from 1921 until 2001, when it was replaced by the Police Service of Northern Ireland.

**SDLP** Social Democratic and Labour Party. A left-of-centre Northern Irish Nationalist party that has lost considerable political clout to Sinn Féin and won no seats in the UK 2017 General Election.

**session** Normally refers to a traditional Irish music session, the "sesh", or used in relation to party-going and drinking.

**shebeen** An old term for an unlicensed house selling drink.

**Sheila-na-gig** A carved stone representation of a squatting woman, often displaying an over-large vulva; believed to avert death and prevent evil, they are similar to the carvings of Yoni found on Hindu temples. Many Irish churches once bore these carvings, particularly above doors or windows, but they were often removed during the Victorian era. Well-preserved examples are visible on White Island, Co. Fermanagh, in Boyle Abbey and on the ruined church at Kilnaboy, Co. Clare.

**Sinn Féin** ("We, Ourselves"). Republican political party opposed to the 1921 political treaty that played a major role in the subsequent civil war. From the late 1970s onwards, and, allegedly, closely linked to the IRA, it rose to electoral prominence among the North's Catholics and achieved significant success in the Republic. Since 1983 its leader has been Gerry Adams, one of the key figures in the gradual move towards peace in Northern Ireland. It is now the leading Nationalist political party in the North.

**The Six Counties** Nationalist/Republican euphemism for Northern Ireland.

**snug** Small area of bar where women used to drink discreetly, now open to all-comers.

**soft day** Misty rain with hazy cloud to the point of invisibility with drizzle lingering in suspended animation.

**souterrain** Prehistoric underground passage which offered sanctuary for those fleeing their enemies; in some mythical locations, seen as an entry to the otherworld.

**stone circle** A ring of spaced standing stones with a ritualistic purpose.

**sweathouse** A small stone-constructed, low-roofed building in which a turf fire was lit. Once sufficient heat had been generated, those suffering from aches and pains or a fever would enter and would stay long enough to generate a sufficient sweat before emerging to take a dip in the nearest cold stream. In other words, an early Irish version of the sauna.

**Taoiseach** Prime minister of the Republic of Ireland.

**TD** Teachta Dála. Member of the lower house of the Republic's parliament (see "Dáil").

**townland** An area of land, similar to a parish, but not necessarily a village, which could have ten fields in it or more than a hundred.

**thon** An Ulster-Scots word meaning "that", mostly heard in the North.

**Troubles** Euphemism for the vicious cycle of violence in Northern Ireland from the late 1960s to the announcement of the Good Friday Agreement in 1998.

**trumpadóir** Literal meaning is a "trumpeter", but can also mean an obnoxious loudmouth.

**turlough** A lake with a limestone base that causes water to drain away during drier months of the year.

**Twenty-six counties** Somewhat begrudging Republican description of the Republic of Ireland.

**UDA** (Ulster Defence Association)/**UFF** (Ulster Freedom Fighters) and **UVF** (Ulster Volunteer Force). Northern Irish Loyalist paramilitary organizations, which now seem more concerned about controlling the Northern Ireland drugs trade.

**Ulster** One of Ireland's four provinces, comprising Northern Irish counties Antrim, Armagh, Derry, Down, Fermanagh and Tyrone, plus Cavan, Donegal and Monaghan in the Republic. Often erroneously used by Unionists and journalists as a synonym for Northern Ireland.

**Unionists** A term describing those (mainly Protestant) who wish to maintain Northern Ireland's union with the rest of the UK.

**UUP** Ulster Unionist Party. The dominant party in Northern Ireland from 1921 to 1972, retaining control of its government for the period's entirety. Though initially retaining ascendancy under David Trimble following the enactment of the Good Friday Agreement in 1998, its support subsequently dwindled and it won no seats in the UK 2017 General Election.

# Small print and index

**A ROUGH GUIDE TO ROUGH GUIDES**

Published in 1982, the first Rough Guide – to Greece – was a student scheme that became a publishing phenomenon. Mark Ellingham, a recent graduate in English from Bristol University, had been travelling in Greece the previous summer and couldn't find the right guidebook. With a small group of friends he wrote his own guide, combining a contemporary, journalistic style with a thoroughly practical approach to travellers' needs.

The immediate success of the book spawned a series that rapidly covered dozens of destinations. And, in addition to impecunious backpackers, Rough Guides soon acquired a much broader readership that relished the guides' wit and inquisitiveness as much as their enthusiastic, critical approach and value-for-money ethos. These days, Rough Guides include recommendations from budget to luxury and cover more than 120 destinations around the globe, from Amsterdam to Zanzibar, all regularly updated by our team of roaming writers.

Browse all our latest guides, read inspirational features and book your trip at **roughguides.com**.

## Rough Guide credits

**Editors:** Zara Sekhavati, Kate Drynan
**Cartography:** Carte
**Picture editor:** Tom Smyth

**Head of DTP and Pre-Press:** Rebeka Davies
**Head of Publishing:** Sarah Clark

## Publishing information

Thirteenth edition 2021

**Distribution**
*UK, Ireland and Europe*
Apa Publications (UK) Ltd; sales@roughguides.com
*United States and Canada*
Ingram Publisher Services; ips@ingramcontent.com
*Australia and New Zealand*
Booktopia; retailer@ booktopia.com.au
*Worldwide*
Apa Publications (UK) Ltd; sales@roughguides.com

**Special Sales, Content Licensing and CoPublishing**
Rough Guides can be purchased in bulk quantities
at discounted prices. We can create special editions,
personalised jackets and corporate imprints tailored to
your needs. sales@roughguides.com.
roughguides.com

Printed in Poland

## Help us update

We've gone to a lot of effort to ensure that this edition
of **The Rough Guide to Ireland** is accurate and up-to-
date. However, things change – places get "discovered",
opening hours are notoriously fickle, restaurants and
rooms raise prices or lower standards. If you feel we've
got it wrong or left something out, we'd like to know,
and if you can remember the address, the price, the
hours, the phone number, so much the better.

Please send your comments with the subject line
"**Rough Guide Ireland Update**" to mail@uk.roughguides.
com. We'll credit all contributions and send a copy of the
next edition (or any other Rough Guide if you prefer) for
the very best emails.

## ABOUT THE AUTHORS

**Paul Clements** is a journalist, broadcaster and writer based in Belfast. A regular contributor to
*The Irish Times*, he is the author of four discursive travel books about Ireland, as well as works of
literary criticism. His biography of the Irish travel writer, Richard Hayward, was adapted for BBC
television. He has also written and edited two books about the travel writer Jan Morris.

**Darragh Geraghty** is a writer and researcher who has worked on numerous travel books,
including *The Rough Guide to Europe on a Budget*. He lives in Dublin.

**Norm Longley** has spent most of his working life in central/eastern Europe – he is the author
of the Rough Guides to Slovenia, Romania and Budapest – but more recently has turned
his hand to home shores, contributing to the Scotland, Wales and Ireland guides. He lives in
Somerset and can occasionally be seen erecting marquees on The Rec in Bath. Norm is the
updater of this thirteenth edition of *The Rough Guide to Ireland*.

**Rachel Mills** is a freelance writer and editor based by the sea in Kent. She is a co-author
for Rough Guides to New Zealand, India, Canada and Great Britain; a regular contributor to
Telegraph Travel and loveEXPLORING.com; and an expert in sustainable, responsible tourism.
Follow her @rachmillstravel.

**Ally Thompson** lives beside the sea in Bangor, County Down with her husband Stuart and
three young children, Libby, Isaac and Molly. She's an ex-BBC Producer turned guidebook
author and travel writer. Ally regularly contributes far-flung family travel features to a number
of national publications but is never happier than when tootling round Ireland and the UK in
her 1972 VW Campervan, Beryl, alongside her brood.

## Photo credits
(Key: T-top; C-centre; B-bottom; L-left; R-right)

**Alamy** 10
**Bernie Brown/Tourism Ireland** 13T
**Chris Hill Photographic** 483, 514/515
**Chris Hill/Tourism Ireland** 16B, 16C, 18B, 18T, 142/143, 264/265, 267
**Clare County Council** 300/301
**Corrie Wingate/Apa Publications** 28
**Courtesy of Tourism Northern Ireland** 9, 15TR, 452/453, 455, 480/481, 517, 548/549
**Failte Ireland** 13B, 15C, 15B, 16T, 17T, 19T, 22B, 50/51, 53, 108/109, 111, 160/161, 178/179, 181, 202/203, 205, 227, 303, 387, 412/413, 415
**Gareth McCormack/Failte Ireland** 22TR, 23B
**iStock** 23T, 224/225, 333
**Mícheál Howard/Failte Ireland** 145
**Shutterstock** 1, 2, 4, 5, 11, 14, 15TL, 19BR, 19BL, 20B, 20T, 21C, 21B, 22TL, 24, 330/331, 568
**Sligo Tourism** 384/385
**Stefan Schnebelt/Tourism Ireland** 21T
**Tourism Ireland** 551
**Valerie O'Sullivanf/Fáilte Ireland** 17B

**Cover:** Crohy Head Sea Arch on the west coast of Donegal **shawnwil23 (shawnwilliams.co.uk)/Shutterstock**

# Index

# Map symbols

The symbols below are used on maps throughout the book

| | | | |
|---|---|---|---|
| International boundary | International airport | Mountain peak | Zoo |
| County boundary | Airstrip | Cave | Gate |
| Chapter boundary | Transport stop | Waterfall | Statue |
| Motorway | Place of interest | Gardens | Lighthouse |
| Dual carriageway | Post office | Ruin/archeological site | Church (regional map) |
| Main road | Internet access | Windmill | Church (town map) |
| Minor road | Hospital | Castle | Market |
| Pedestrianized road | Information centre | Tower | Building |
| Steps | Parking | Fort | Stadium |
| Railway | Viewpoint | Stately home | Park |
| Path | Wildfowl reserve | Abbey | Cemetery |
| Wall | Mountain range | Museum | Beach |
| Ferry | | | |

## Listings key

Accommodation

Eating

Drinking/nightlife

Shopping

# YOUR TAILOR-MADE TRIP
## STARTS HERE

**Tailor-made trips and unique adventures crafted by local experts**

Rough Guides has been inspiring travellers with lively and thought-provoking guidebooks for more than 35 years. Now we're linking you up with selected local experts to craft your dream trip. They will put together your perfect itinerary and book it at local rates.

Don't follow the crowd – find your own path.

## HOW ROUGHGUIDES.COM/TRIPS WORKS

**STEP 1**

Pick your dream destination, tell us what you want and submit an enquiry.

**STEP 2**

Fill in a short form to tell your local expert about your dream trip and preferences.

**STEP 3**

Our local expert will craft your tailor-made itinerary. You'll be able to tweak and refine it until you're completely satisfied.

**STEP 4**

Book online with ease, pack your bags and enjoy the trip! Our local expert will be on hand 24/7 while you're on the road.

# BENEFITS OF PLANNING AND BOOKING AT ROUGHGUIDES.COM/TRIPS

### PLAN YOUR ADVENTURE WITH LOCAL EXPERTS

Rough Guides' English-speaking local experts are hand-picked, based on their experience in the travel industry and their impeccable standards of customer service.

### SAVE TIME AND GET ACCESS TO LOCAL KNOWLEDGE

When a local expert plans your trip, you save time and money when you book, even during high season. You won't be charged for using a credit card either.

### MAKE TRAVEL A BREEZE: BOOK WITH PEACE OF MIND

Enjoy stress-free travel when you use Rough Guides' secure online booking platform. All bookings come with a money-back guarantee.

## WHAT DO OTHER TRAVELLERS THINK ABOUT ROUGH GUIDES TRIPS?

## PLAN AND BOOK YOUR TRIP AT ROUGHGUIDES.COM/TRIPS